# The
# Garland
# CLASSICS OF
# FILM LITERATURE

REPRINTED IN PHOTO-FACSIMILE
IN 32 VOLUMES

# BEST FILM PLAYS
# 1945

## John Gassner
## and
## Dudley Nichols

GARLAND PUBLISHING, INC. ● NEW YORK & LONDON ● 1977

This edition reprinted by arrangement
with Crown Publishers, Inc.

Main entry under title:
Best film plays, 1945
     (The Garland classics of film literature ; 12)
     Reprint of the 1946 ed.  published by Crown,
New York.
     1.  Moving-picture plays.  I. Gassner, John,
1903-1967.   II.   Nichols, Dudley 1895-
II.  Series.
PN1997.A1B372    1977          822'.03      76-52103
ISBN   0-8240-2876-7

Printed in the United States of America

# BEST FILM PLAYS - 1945

# BEST FILM PLAYS
# - 1945

*Edited by*

JOHN GASSNER

*and*

DUDLEY NICHOLS

CROWN PUBLISHERS

NEW YORK

# ACKNOWLEDGMENTS

I am again indebted to the friends of the project among studio executives, critics, authors and publishers who have continued their encouragement and help. If I do not list all their names for the third time, it is for fear that repetition will dull the edge of an already ineffectual gratitude.

This volume owes three of its screenplays to the heads of Paramount Pictures Corporation, and four to the heads of Columbia Pictures Corporation, Metro-Goldwyn-Mayer, R.K.O. Radio Pictures Corporation, Twentieth Century-Fox Corporation, and Sidney Buchman. For three other inclusions I am indebted to Messrs. Lester Cowan, David L. Loew, and David O. Selznick. To all three, moreover, I am further obliged for enabling me to assemble scripts that can do some justice to their pictures.

In the case of *Spellbound,* Mr. Robert H. Dann expedited procedure; Mr. Ben Hecht, assisted by Miss Bobbie McKeon, did me the kindness of preparing a complete script, and Miss McKeon read the proofs. In the case of *The Southerner,* Miss Blanche A. Sproule, of Mr. David L. Loew's office, was generously helpful. In the case of the *Story of G.I. Joe,* Mr. Paige Cavanaugh went to much trouble in assembling a final shooting script.

Arrangements were completed and legal creases were ironed out by Sidney Barton (RKO), Robert H. Dann (Vanguard Films), Sidney Justin and Miss Harriet Nystuen (Paramount), B. B. Kahane (Columbia), Floyd Hendrickson (MGM), and George Wasson (Twentieth Century-Fox). Stills were supplied by the cooperative Eastern publicity departments of the picture producers and Mr. Tom Waller of United Artists.

I am also very grateful to Miss Betty Smith, John Steinbeck, Charles Jackson, James M. Cain, Farrar & Rinehart, Jack L. Wagner, Alfred A. Knopf, Bennett Cerf, Little, Brown & Company, Viking Press, Harper & Brothers, Henry Holt & Company, Macmillan Company, Liberty, Collier's, Curtis Brown Ltd., Annie Laurie Williams, and Brandt & Brandt for permission on the original matter in the screenplays.

In conclusion, the William Morris Agency—especially Miss Margaret Lyon of the Coast office, who was saddled with most of the details of the inter-regional communication, and Albert Taylor—is again entitled to credit for making the volume possible.

v

On the editorial side, Miss Bertha Krantz of Crown Publishers deserves special commendation. Mollie Gassner proved more than ever an invaluable adjutant, though I fear the term does her scant justice, as she was in effect a co-editor. And, of course, the continued collaboration of Dudley Nichols has been the *sine qua non* of this enterprise.

J. G.

# CONTENTS

NOTE: Credits to screenwriters, authors of original material, producers and directors are in accordance with instructions from the motion picture studios. In no case have the editors departed from this rule, as the granting of credits does not lie within their province.

# A SECOND ANNUAL

## By JOHN GASSNER

The present volume is the second in the annual series of film plays, and the third in the possibly quixotic attempt to distill the literature of the screen —or some notable part of it. If beginnings are proverbially difficult, continuations often bring their own difficulties. It would be comforting if the world were so ordered that everything proceeded in a constantly ascending scale of progression. It would be well—to particularize—if each successive year's harvest of screenplays could prove better or more significant than that which came before. We should then be confident that each new book was going to show American films becoming better and better; confident, too, that the public was breathlessly waiting to receive a second, third or fourth film annual.

Although the inclination to play Dr. Coué to oneself and the public is indeed great, it can be resisted. We shall not pretend that the present harvest is richer than last year's, or even as ample. And, for all we know, the season after this may be a year of the locust by comparison. We can leave "progress in a straight line" exactly where it will be found—in the fond heart, and in the gentle liberal's pipe-dream. For the sake of a veracious inventory of American motion pictures, we also refrain from enriching the book with such imported pieces as *Colonel Blimp*, *Mr. Emanuel*, *Love on the Dole*, *Blithe Spirit*, *The Silver Fleet* and the Swiss *Marie-Louise*.

Nevertheless, if hope can be a liar, despair can be even a worse deceiver. The absence of direct progress, even evidence of retrogression in some particular year as we proceed with our American film annuals, should not lead us to negativism. This can only immobilize those who endeavor to make better use of the medium while critical of its present state. Because the commissar has not brought about the millenium is no reason for succumbing to the yogi.

A perspective undistorted by our hopes and consequent despairs will reveal that the wavering course of Hollywood is inevitable. It responds, in the first instance, to the climate of opinion, to the public attitudes to which it tries to be sensitive, and to the level of its audience as reflected by box-office receipts. It derives much of its material from novels, plays, and stories which

ix

also reflect the temper of the times. And, finally, Hollywood's writers, producers, and directors are also subject to the *Zeitgeist;* they rise, at least a little, when the time-spirit lifts them up, and they subside when the time-spirit moves from crest to trough.

In some instances, fortunately, men of talent and resolution, can transcend the bonds of the immediate present; and they do this in motion pictures, too, except that it is especially difficult to throw off shackles forged in so large and complicated an industry. It is perhaps significant that three in our collection of ten pictures—*Story of G.I. Joe, Spellbound,* and *The Southerner* —were made by independent producers. There must also be a moral in the fact that Billy Wilder and Charles Brackett were able to violate convention in the making of *The Lost Weekend* within the confines of so large a business as Paramount, and that enlightened leadership within that studio itself should have turned out such genuine work as *A Medal for Benny.* Even venturesome spirits, however, cannot be exempt from requirements of business, the spirit of the age, and the quality of the large audiences they must reach.

*Best Film Plays of 1943–44,* our last chronicle, which ended in July 1944, represented a peak. We may say with some poetic license that in such pictures as *Wilson, Watch on the Rhine, Dragon Seed, The Purple Heart,* as well as in a number of superb documentaries, the American film was responding to an heroic age, and was heroic itself. "High-hearted" and "high-minded" are adjectives not to be lightly tossed around; but they can be used circumspectly, with due note of all that was pinchbeck, to describe a considerable number of pictures. After that came the gradual retreat.

The present compilation represents the last half of 1944 and the year 1945. Victory was drawing near, then victory was achieved—and it seemed almost too easy. It was anticlimactic to find that the monsters we were fighting had weak knees and that they crumbled like phantoms. The commonplaces began to replace the elegiac and the heroic moods. The light of common day displaced the sunset, the night, and the effulgent dawn.

The screenplays in the present book represent this transition. Many of them still carry the impress of the earlier period of war-time inspiration, and it is appropriate to give *Thirty Seconds Over Tokyo* and *Story of G.I. Joe* a place in our collection not only for their historical interest but because they are meaningful even now that the smoke of battle has lifted. *Thirty Seconds* stands not merely for the eventful first blow which carried the war to Tokyo, but for the awareness of an ally in the East whose part in the common struggle was vividly described in the picture. And to this interest must be added the vitality of the final sequence, which anticipated the brief vogue of the rehabilitation-of-the-veteran theme; entire films have been de-

voted to the same post-war problem with far less conviction. The one note-worthy exception, Warner Brothers' rehabilitation picture, *The Pride of the Marines,* also belonged to the "heroic age" by virtue of its largeness of spirit. But we found it impossible to include Albert Maltz's noteworthy screenplay based on the Al Schmidt story, and must content ourselves with a mere salute to its merits.

Fortunately, *Story of G.I. Joe,* the best of American war films, also falls within the boundaries of this annual. It is a distillation of the war documentaries, from the early reports to the latter-day achievements such as *San Pietro* and *The True Glory.* Like these, *G.I. Joe,* based on the reports of the infantry's Homer, Ernie Pyle, managed to convey the reality of battle without the all-too-frequent pseudo-reality and conventional romanticism of Hollywood-made drama. Hollywood-made in the sense that the screenplay was composed by the civilian writers Leopold Atlas, Guy Endore, and Philip Stevenson, and that the film was shot in Hollywood, *G.I. Joe* recalled at once the notable first World War spectacles of the silent films, the American and British documentaries made on the scene of battle in the recent period, and the Russian films that threatened for a time to preempt film realism for the efforts of a single ally. But realism and the absence of sticky sentimentality do not adequately describe the Ernie Pyle document, especially if literalism intrudes itself into our definition of realism. *G.I. Joe* was an extraordinary job of film shooting, and of film cutting in the broad sense; it is uniquely an achievement by its able director William Wellman. Its quick transitions created an effect of reality stronger and more insistent than any single story, no matter how true.

It was war itself, as experienced by the infantryman, that transpired on the screen. It was not the beautifully planned and executed war of newspaper reports, editorials, and military analysts' columns; not the war that the distant non-combatant takes for reality, but the real slogging warfare which possesses a large element of hypnotic repetitiousness and drugged unreality. In this sultry poem, different campaigns became one interminable campaign; romance wore a death-mask; a soldier's effort to hear his son's voice on a record was compounded of the pathetically inane and the violently insane; a marriage on the front, without the customary hearts and flowers, looked for a few moments like something transpiring in the second circle of hell.

The picture's real power lay in its expressiveness, and this was strengthened by the device of making the story Ernie Pyle's narrative. Present in the picture, but never obtrusive, his commentary pared to the bone, Pyle was not so much the narrator as the "reactor." He was the human being through whom the events were being refracted. His commentary said some things

that needed to be said. But, altogether removed from overt lecturing, *G.I. Joe* brought home to the spectator, in a manner elusive of words but not of any sensory impression, that modern war is more abnormal and has more of madness in it than speeches or preachment can possibly convey; that war is insanity barely surmounted by the flesh and spirit, and that it means people brought to the verge of the unendurably subhuman; that heroism is less the physical risk than the great effort to hold on to human reason and decency in the midst of the infernal.

There was almost a touch of greatness in *Story of G.I. Joe,* a probably unpremeditated, accidental greatness, which a single sitting before the picture might not disclose. Perhaps the screenplay can help us locate it although it is impossible to estimate how much the printed word can convey to the reader, and we may frankly confess ourselves defeated by the problem of transmission in a case like this. It may happen, however, that the screenplay will not only reinvoke but revivify the film; it may even shape our impressions more meaningfully. The speed of film impressions can be arrested in print to some advantage.

Additional gratification may be found in recalling other war pictures on a generally smaller scale of achievement. *Counterattack,* for example, possessed exceptional drive and considerable psychological force. Although its visual effect was limited by the confined setting in a cellar, and the film was released too late to capitalize on interest in Russia's counter-offensive, special merit adheres to the unity and the suspensive and human character of the picture. Others will have varying degrees of favorable opinion on *Destination Tokyo, Objective Burma,* and *Back to Bataan.*

One thought may be expressed with reasonable assurance. Although the war can continue to provide a notable picture now and then, although the greatest of all American-made war pictures may yet make their appearance, film-making has been deprived of a major stimulus by the cessation of hostilities. Hollywood will be hard put to it to discover another ferment as potent as the lately concluded struggle of nations and ideologies. That leavening substance for Hollywood's product in peacetime is present, that it is in fact right at hand, makes no difference. The studios are unlikely at this time to be galvanized into making heroic exertions by the challenge of the post-war problems. These are too complex and cut across too many strands of vested interest. So long as the fire does not start blazing in our own backyard, the temptation to fiddle will be great again. Should this prophecy seem too dark, this much is certain: unless American films quickly find new stimuli, the next few years will write pages of anticlimax in motion picture history.

The situation will not be desperate perhaps so long as the studios have universal masterpieces of drama and fiction which still remain to be screened. (As this preface is being written the Laurence Olivier *Henry V* is delighting a select public, the Theatre Guild and RKO are announcing a filming of O'Neill's *Mourning Becomes Electra* by Dudley Nichols, and David O. Selznick is registering several Shakespeare titles for future picturization.) The situation may also be alleviated by the rapid growth of independent producing in Hollywood, provided the independents are independent in creativeness. Yet optimism on this score can be tempered by the reflection that they, too, are subject to economic pressure. In stage production the equivalent of Hollywood's "independents" are the long-heralded little theatres; yet the latter, in trying to pay their way, have tended only to ape Broadway instead of surpassing it.

War-time comedy is, of course, a bird with a different wing-spread, and could not be reasonably expected to make the highest flights. It must be noted with regret, however, that humor and satire in the 1944-45 transition did not attain the altitudes of the previous volume's *Miracle of Morgan's Creek* and *Hail the Conquering Hero.* Quantity was supplied by a species of war comedies well represented by *What Next, Corporal Hargrove,* the sequel to *See Here, Private Hargrove.* Two comedies that could, nevertheless, completely invite an adult interest were Paramount's *A Medal for Benny* and Columbia's *Over 21,* both in this book.

In the former, Steinbeck's social sympathies and his eye for local color produced a work of wry humor mingled with pathos. Invading the cellophane-wrapped purlieus of the screen, Steinbeck's familiar *paisanos* of *A Medal for Benny* brought forth some sense of reality by which to measure the home front—and by which to know people in general. Some stinging satire on professional profiteering, when a mayor tries to exploit the grief of the Mexican father of an American soldier, also fell within the orbit of *A Medal for Benny,* and this was a welcome dash of bitters in the saccharine of romanticism that normally passed for war-inspired entertainment. By no means a major effort and somewhat too divided in subject matter, but spiced with flavorsome dialogue and colorful characterization, and transfigured by its feeling for the common man, this picture is nevertheless a meritorious addition to the scanty literature of recent American films.

Parenthetically, it may be said that we were treated to one honorable exception to routine war romance in *The Clock,* which had the customary charm of Robert Nathan's stories and was executed with a discreet balance between delicate humor and genuine pathos. The young people's frantic pursuit of a marriage license before the soldier's departure made a memorable sequence, which even a last minute concession to glamor in a hotel room could not lessen. Columbia's George Abbott production, *Kiss and Tell,* also made something acceptably fresh of a more adolescent love-match.

*A Medal for Benny* may be loosely denoted as folk comedy, a rarity except in "Westerns" which still lean, however, to melodrama. (*Along Came Jones* was a welcome spoof on the whole genre.) *Over 21* belongs to the more rarefied medium of high comedy. MGM's screen adaptation of Philip Barry's *Without Love,* an improvement over the Broadway play, was perhaps the only other noteworthy example. Sidney Buchman's screenplay for *Over 21* had the merit of a broader theme and more immediate relevance to the issues of war and peace. It could not convey the zany hilarity evoked by Ruth Gordon's performance in the Broadway production of her play. The film did not have the services of the inimitable comedienne who had tailored the play to her personality, and some of the stage humor was of that intimate variety which bubbles only in the three-dimensional theatre. There were, nevertheless, notable compensations in the screen treatment. The wisdom of a craftsman led Mr. Buchman to employ broader strokes for his particular medium, thereby assuring some solidity to a story that might otherwise have effervesced out of existence on the screen. A deeper wisdom also made him add solidity of theme and characterization to what was, in the main, stage improvisation. His heroine is no Dulcy, and editorials from her pen are far more credible than *Dulcy,* and editorials from the original scatterbrain. In Buchman's able hands *Over 21,* with its story of a liberal editor's encounters with the Army and with his indefatigable newspaper owner, proved meaningful and structurally sound.

In negotiating the shallows of liberal idealism with intelligence and light maneuvering, Buchman's screenplay set itself apart from the feeble exhibitions that so often make a pretense of mature sophistication. High comedy, especially when it includes comedy of ideas, remains an ungrateful assignment in motion pictures—at least in American motion pictures. Its spirit is easily dampened by the necessity of addressing a miscellaneous public. Film comedy cannot indulge without undue slowness in the verbal play that the theatre allows its practitioners, and yet verbal play seems indispensable when the comic characters' endowment is superior articulateness. Any achievement in this difficult art is therefore as welcome as it is rare. How we can make it prevail on the screen is an only partially revealed secret, and yet it is difficult to conceive a completely adult comic art without it. Pantomime, as employed by Chaplin at his best, and the witty utilization of objects, as in such a René Claire picture as *À Nous la Liberté,* is a partial

answer to the question, but obviously it cannot solve the whole problem for the talking picture.

Motion pictures are, naturally, not saddled with any such complicated problems of adjustment in the field of melodrama, in which action and reaction can be very suitably cinematic. Films have indeed virtually taken over the theatre's once ample stock of melodrama, and many a story that would seem feeble on the contemporary stage proves exciting enough on the screen. It is no wonder that Hollywood continued to acquit itself well in this department. *The Woman in the Window, And Then There Were None, Mildred Pierce, Hangover Square, Murder My Sweet, Laura, Double Indemnity,* and *Spellbound* may be cited for attention. Note may also be taken of *My Name is Julia Ross,* an exception in the so-called "Grade B doghouse," and *The House on 92nd Street* as a semi-documentary departure from ordinary spy melodrama, which naturally enjoyed a boom during the war. Like John Wexley's earlier superior *Confessions of a Nazi Spy,* Charles G. Booth's screenplay original evaded the traditional romantic fly-paper, and its air of factual reality compensated for the seemingly inevitable cloak and dagger effect.

Of the two melodramas chosen for this volume, *Double Indemnity* represents the pattern of crime and retribution that has long been a staple in Hollywood; *Spellbound,* the trend toward utilization of abnormal psychiatry, hitherto confined to novels and stage plays. Both pictures, however, had singular merit in their own right, and their matter, when well developed, not only exerts fascination and yields powerful screen drama but claims a place in the current scene.

*Double Indemnity* made some contribution to screen realism. In this respect, it is to be differentiated from extremist naturalism, which defeats itself by purposeless sensationalism or tastelessness. The realism of *Double Indemnity* was, in the first instance, sensitive and understanding. Its story of an insurance agent's crime and punishment dramatized error rather than conventional villainy. It approached tragedy in exhibiting a character writhing in the tentacles of evil, and therefore provided possibilities of purgation rare in crime films. Purgation is an inner experience, whereas Hollywood normally calls it a day and brushes off its busy hands the moment the criminal has been apprehended. Nothing can be more subversive of morality than the confusion of legal punishment with morality. The code which ordains that every crime is to be punished leads to some absurd prestidigitation in screenwriting, as well as to some rather ingenious skating over thin ice as in *Uncle Harry.* But, more importantly, the taboo has reduced morality to a routine. The hero's anguish in *Double Indemnity,* is of a different order, and is well punctuated by the confession into the dictaphone, which serves as the frame of the screenplay. Purgation is the essence of the picture; and so is morality, if one allows a term so reduced to pharisaical banality, since the story of the crime is refracted by the narrator's reawakened decency. Incidentally, crime detection is also treated with some originality; the hunter is tied to the hunted by sympathy rather than antipathy.

*Spellbound* is something of a *tour de force,* in which psychiatry and melodrama were successfully fused by Ben Hecht and Alfred Hitchcock. Their joint ingenuity provides exceptional suspense. But even more commendable, because less subject to formula, is the compassion of the work. Sensationalism, the thrill for the sake of the thrill, could easily have preempted the plot. The director and the author have turned out a civilized piece of work considerably beyond the melodrama and the merely clinical subject of amnesia, and the finished quality of the writing in Ben Hecht's screenplay reflects the spirit in which the film was conceived.

With *Laura, Double Indemnity* and *Spellbound* would make a very respectable trio in the genre of superior melodrama. Since we cannot have too much of the same thing in a collection, *Laura* has been excluded but without any intended slight to its merits. In this case, too, its humanity, here enhanced psychologically and sociologically, is the saving grace. At the other extreme, we had the intellectual or chess-game maneuvering of *And Then There Were None,* which can also become a positive quality in a macabre tale, as Poe was perhaps the first to discover. The more distance Hollywood can put between itself and the jejune thrillers, which are neither fish nor fowl, neither a human document nor an intellectual exercise, the better.

This brings us up to the remaining selections in the book, in which the *comédie humaine* predominates. Although there are no world-shaking themes in *A Tree Grows in Brooklyn, None but the Lonely Heart, The Southerner,* and even *The Lost Weekend,* each of these films recounts a human story against a well observed background of social reality. The screen treatment of Betty Smith's novel invites comparison with the original. Omissions and modifications can be noted with protest or defended on the grounds of expediency or necessity; and the difference between a book and a film has enforced other modifications. Whatever loss the novel may have sustained in the transformation, the effect is still rich and warm. The desires and aspirations of ordinary people are still present. A flavor of time and place is sustained without any objectionable quaintness or easy resort to period color. Humor spices the screenplay, as it does the novel, but it is true humor, and this is also a rare ingredient in American films, which are apt to substitute horseplay.

There will be more genuine humor in pictures in direct proportion to Hollywood's willingness to forego pseudo-cosmopolitanism. True cosmopolitanism would be productive of wit; the pinchbeck variety at best produces only a neutral sort of polite conversation among characters who are neuters regardless of how they pant with simulated passion. A touch of Dickens such as we find in *A Tree Grows in Brooklyn* makes the whole world kin, but the Dickensian spirit will be a stranger in the Los Angeles colony so long as film-makers try to extract humor out of characters who look and behave like magazine cover illustrations.

Hollywood has been somewhat successful with youngsters, as in *Janie, Snafu,* and *Kiss and Tell,* where the oddities of the characters are unlikely to challenge censorship since they run the gamut of acceptable cuteness. (Wedekinds have not yet invaded Hollywood's view of adolescence, and probably never will.) But an adult Dickens character is generally still relegated to a supporting role, though now and then delightfully, as in Charles Coburn's newspaper owner in *Over 21.* The day is not yet here when the character actor can become the core of Hollywood pictures with any consistency. Advances in this direction there have been—notably in *Going My Way,* and in a dozen or so other major screen dramas, spaced over a decade. The problem is to multiply the number of such instances until they cease to be singular, and also to infuse the humor that stems from them with greater sharpness. The ideal to be sought is, of course, proper stylization, the whittling of characters into shapes that are challenging in their self-revelation and can create awareness through their angularity or, even at times, their comic monstrousness, as is the case with Falstaff. We have tended, on the contrary, to round off the edges of this humor with sentimentality; the odd character in our films, unless he is a caricature like the intractable and great Groucho Marx, is generally a darling like Barry Fitzgerald in *Going My Way.* But enough of this divagation. . . .

Clifford Odets' *None but the Lonely Heart* screenplay shares many of the qualities that appear in *A Tree Grows in Brooklyn,* but it has, in addition, a distinctive style. It exhibits the brushwork we could expect from the author of such stage plays as *Awake and Sing* and *Golden Boy.* The marriage between Richard Llewellyn's cockney story and Odets' style and viewpoint has marked results, more apparent in the screenplay than in the film which received mixed notices and apparently missed popular support. Although unwieldy, repetitive, and somewhat chaotic, although hardly a "good film," it has a compelling quality.

A musical signature for this screenplay might well be "ostinato." The writing *insists* upon the seediness and confusion in the lower depths of poverty and crime; upon the questioning of life and the bewildered search for a path leading out of the bogs and miasmas; upon the theme of purposeless restlessness and the counterpointed music of purposive brotherhood. The results in *None but the Lonely Heart* may be haphazard, but they are nonetheless genuine. The story is a somewhat chaotic and bizarre evocation of a young man's blundering rebellion against underprivileged life in the East End. But his very blindness tugs at the heartstrings, and the vision long denied him, the vision of effectual revolt rather than anarchic individualistic effort, hovers over the horizon, making the tale provocative at least by implication.

In the shooting script, before the process of cutting tried to shape *None but the Lonely Heart* into a serviceable film, Odets was clearly struggling with his medium. But he was also making his work highly personal, giving it a distinctive character. If art is experience seen through a temperament, Odets was being faithful to art. This abused name must not be taken in vain. As a rule, it is a dangerous word to use in Hollywood, and it is rarely used without apologies in any other corner of America. But there is no use beating around the bush: you will not have art in the ultimate sense, you will merely have artisanship in films, unless the creator—the screenwriter, in the first instance—can filter his material, even the borrowed material from novels and stage plays, through a temperament; through something compounded of many things, of course, including his private hell, his idosyncratic crudities, and his personal faith, no matter how murky. The first results may be failure, but the final results are worth the risk.

Anything produced by other means, no matter how expert, is a surface manifestation. Only deep calls unto deep. Anything else is sheer tintinnabulation provided by competent office boys tinkling the bells and jingling their coins. The most important fact about *None but the Lonely Heart* is that a writer managed to put his personal sign—a broken sign perhaps—on the work. In no field, other than lyric poetry, is this frequent or easy. The stage is starved for lack of it, and most, although fortunately not all, contemporary fiction has little of it. But nowhere is it more infrequent and more difficult to achieve the personal effect than in the still young collective enterprise of film-making, especially for the writer.

To the urban realism of *A Tree Grows in Brooklyn* and *None but the Lonely Heart,* we may add the rural realism of David L. Loew's *The Southerner*. It doesn't stint on the realities of Southern agriculture, back-breaking labor, hunger and pellagra. It also evokes the high-heartedness of struggling against nature and, above all, resolutely fighting for independence. As a social document it is neither incisive nor challenging. It is a comparatively tame little human story, like MGM's milder, somewhat sentimental Wisconsin counterpart, *Our Vines Have Tender Grapes,* produced in the same year. These films do not belong to the depression decade of *The Grapes of Wrath,* and do not possess its stature. They are private tales, except that *The Southerner* casts the shadow of a larger story affecting a large area and many Americans. Misguided efforts were made to keep the picture out of Southern theatre circuits, and it is to Mr. Loew's credit that he refused to be intimidated.

*The Southerner* may be best described as a realistic idyl. The realism is supplied by the facts and the struggle; the idyllic quality, by the human warmth and the simplicity of elemental truth. It manages to combine reality and poetry, a story of common toil and suffering with the reminiscent charm of a dog-eared album. Possessing both strength and delicacy, it came as a finely carved miniature in the midst of pretentiously big pictures that promised much more and delivered much less substance.

Our remaining screenplay, *The Lost Weekend,* winner of virtually all motion picture awards, stands apart from the rest. That its subject—drunkenness, treated with intelligence and seriousness—should have seemed bold is a reflection on our curious standards. The *New York Times'* critic, Mr. Bosley Crowther, rightly remarked on the irony "that a film should be hailed as bold simply because it is candid in attacking a serious adult theme." He added that "whenever a film such as this one stands up to do that job, it is vaguely an insult to its caliber to label it 'daring.'" That the picture has violated an absurd taboo so successfully should prove a wholesome stimulus.

Good film-making would be enlarged if Hollywood were to turn to the fine literature that has been written on man's various obsessions. The visual possibilities can also be extended by such a policy. For a short while, expressionism opened channels for truly cinematic drama, as opposed to merely picturized story-telling, but these were promptly closed. Periodic tributes to an experiment like *The Cabinet of Dr. Caligari* by the estheticians have influenced no studio executives. If the bat-scene in *The Lost Weekend* has been hailed as so gripping, how shall we describe the effects latent in some other, as yet unfilmed, accounts of inner wrack and ruin. It is certainly too early to recommend De Quincey's *Confessions of an English Opium Eater* to the studios, but on the very day this preface was first drafted a producer announced his intention of filming *The, Turn of the Screw*—with what results we shall know later.

The mere fact that dipsomania was treated seriously, instead of being used for comic relief, was an advance, and if this leaves us open to the charge of gratitude for small favors the answer may well be that motion pictures still have a good deal to catch up with. Hollywood has studiously avoided the morbid realities taken for granted in other fields, and perhaps the best news in the case of *The Lost Weekend* is that for once Hollywood succeeded in shaking off its fear of morbidity, and with good results. Commonplaces in fiction or stage drama will not be commonplaces in pictures until they have been used often enough. Fiction and drama, after all, have had a three thousand year start. The same consideration must apply to the treatment of motivation in *The Lost Weekend,* which attributes the hero's alcoholism to his failure as a writer instead of uncovering the deeper psychological layers of his anxiety. The original story came up against a taboo that could not possibly be violated. Yet it is plain enough in the screenplay that the hero's behavior is compulsive and is conditioned by anxiety, and the sober view taken of his by no means singular failing gives *The Lost Weekend* a rare quality of understanding. The incompleteness of the clinical diagnosis may even be a less serious limitation than some of us imagine. Completeness could not necessarily have made this a better picture, or even a more convincing one for the public that was to be reached. Even slower-paced stage plays tend to make psychoanalytic portraiture seem schematized and only half-realized. I am not at all sure that there is wisdom in demanding of a stage or a screen play what the novel alone can provide by means of the novelist's step-by-step, detailed demonstration which leaves the actual visualization to the reader. The effect in dramatic form may prove lurid rather than convincing.

The most substantial limitation of *The Lost Weekend* is to be found rather in its form; in the moderate realistic pattern observed everywhere except in the single hallucination, which was intensified by the dipsomaniac's screaming and collapse rather than by uniquely created incidents. Billy Wilder's deliberate direction may have added a style to the realism, saving it from the commonplace, but the main effect is wedded to the generally level plane of story conception. Within these limits, nevertheless, this screen drama possesses an obsessive drive that engenders anguish and sympathy. It remains one of the more human exhibitions in the record of American film-making. Charles Brackett as author (with Billy Wilder) and Billy Wilder as director are entitled to the plaudits they have received.

In conclusion it should be noted that the efforts included in this volume and the classifications they represent do not of course exhaust the American screen's better exertions. A conscientious historian would have to reckon at least with the lusty comedy of Milton Holmes' original screenplay *Salty O'Rourke*, the pleasant comedy of *National Velvet*, and the barbed rough farce of *Practically Yours;* with Philip Yordan's tough-fibred *Dillinger*, voted the best original screenplay by the Screen Writers' Guild; with religious drama, to which Leo MacCarey's sequel to *Going My Way, The Bells of St. Mary's*, added some shrewd humor and non-mystical charm. The record would take note of the musical films ranging from charming, free-from-brashness Americana like *Meet Me in St. Louis* and *State Fair* to musical biography like *Rhapsody in Blue* and *A Song to Remember*, and including the spoof *Out of This World* and the musicals that took the war into their melodic stride, *Anchors Aweigh* and *Tonight and Every Night.* The keeper of the records would approve *The Corn is Green* and *A Bell for Adano*, for their idealism and portrayal of character; *Confidential Agent* for its dramatization of the beginnings of the war in the fascist *coup* in Spain; and *Tomorrow the World* for its democratic responsiveness to topical matter. A generous reviewer could tip his hat to competence in personal drama in the case of *Love Letters, The Valley of Decision*, and *The Enchanted Cottage*. Someone will find an occasion for compliment in Danny Kaye's *Wonder Man* and in other non-literary antics. Probably other films I have overlooked will be noted, and any injustice I have committed will be repaired by the judicious or the benign. And of course even a severe critic will not withhold tribute from the many war documentaries that cannot be successfully transcribed as screenplays, especially *The True Glory, The Fighting Lady, San Pietro*, and the post-war "short" *Hitler Lives.*

It is not our object, however, to provide a complete chronicle. Sufficient that this volume provides some samples of intelligent film plays that transcribe themselves on the printed page. And if the scripts do not unlock all the secrets of film making, if they merely cast the shadow of the form on the screen, the shadow, too, is something. It is also a test to some degree if the average non-documentary or non-musical motion picture betrays its worthlessness when it is observed in script, whereas superior films reveal qualities of meaning, organization, observation, and feeling. In script, the merely average film is comparable to a slick magazine novella; it has just as little life, except that it is not as well written. Since the picturized story is here to stay, American motion pictures will—in the main, and with the exceptions that obtain in the case of documentaries or musicals—improve to the degree to which their screenplays provide cinematic equivalents to superior drama and fiction. Ten such screenplays are presented here; perhaps another ten could be added to the roster, although I doubt that there would be that many. This may be little enough when we consider the hundreds of films that are made annually. Yet excellence is rare in any field; Broadway's average is certainly no greater. The nature of excellence in a particular medium, moreover, is often the best clue we have to the possibilities of progress within that medium. To explore this further is the responsibility of those who make motion pictures rather than of those who merely observe them or comment on them.

New York, June, 1946

# THE MACHINE FROM THE GOD

## By Dudley Nichols

Two times running, by way of preface to these annual selections of screen-plays, the writer has been guilty of looking only in one direction in discussing problems of film-writing. He has reviewed the potentialities of the modern film, examined theory and reflected on the film as an art-form; as if all that the gifted person who desires to work in film had to do were to initiate himself in fundamental principles, acquaint himself with the machinery, pick up his materials and set to work. Naturally this is an absurdly idealized view of things. The practical aspects of film-making in the United States—which means in Hollywood—present a different picture.

In film-making we are in the theatre, that is in a place where the poetic imagination should be expressed by techniques of acting. The dramatic and histrionic arts are fused. A third essential element is the audience in whose collective imagination the action really takes place. This latter fact is too seldom taken into account when discussing the theatre. It is as if there were two stages in every theatre, first the platform on which the actors move and speak and by so doing project the drama onto a second real and living stage within the minds and feelings of the watchers and listeners. An audience of one individual is ineffectual. There is an interaction between all the auditors, building up potentials of comic or tragic feeling, and between the collective audience and the primary stage where the actors move and speak.

That is why stage performances appear to vary. The variation is not only in the actors but in the audience, for the play partakes of three elements. The one fixed element is the work of the dramatist. How it is interpreted is another matter. It is no jest to say that "the play was a success but the audience was a failure." It can be bitter truth, just as the converse may occur.

Now you may imagine that these three elements are not equally inter-dependent in the motion picture theatre. Surely the dramatic and histrionic elements are fixed, recorded in final form, and each running of the film must be identical. This would be true if the drama or action really took place on the screen, which is the primary stage in the film theatre. But of course it is projected onto the secondary or main stage—into the imagination of the collective audience—and that is the variable element.

xxiii

It is impossible for one individual to get full enjoyment from the running of a film. This is evident at once in the case of comedies, less evident in the serious film. The same laws hold true as for the stage, the audience building up potentials among each other, and this collective potential of feeling interacting with the screen or the primary stage. The images of the actors of course are unaffected, but very strangely they *seem* affected. They seem not to be giving so good a performance when the audience does not react sympathetically.

This writer has seen films of quality absolutely destroyed by the vulgarity or bad taste or subnormal intelligence of an audience. Suddenly the film seems all wrong. Take it out to another preview and find a superior audience and suddenly the film will glow with life. I state these simple facts to point out that we cannot talk simply of raising the standards of motion pictures without also bearing in mind the standards of the masses who make up our modern civilization. Not all of the blame for bad films lies upon Hollywood. If newspapers for instance show contempt for the masses of people by stooping to anything that will increase mass circulation, playing up to vulgarity, to ignorance, to every worst prejudice, how can Hollywood raise the cultural level? If the radio is stupid how can films be wise? If book-publishing should show little cultural responsibility, pushing for large sales a worthless novel and putting no advertising behind the occasional novel of quality or merit, how can the motion picture be different? Or if films pander to ignorance and vulgarity and barbarous instincts, how can the publishers aim higher?

The simple truth is that culture and civilization and their instruments of propagation are all in one basket. The appalling truth is that American taste and American civilization, in spite of all scientific advances, are at their lowest ebb in history. In *spite* of all scientific advances, or *because* of?

Let us consider the theatre and not discriminate for the moment between stage and screen. Twenty-five hundred years ago in Athens there was a high civilization in which no mean part was played by the drama. The theatre has always been a potent tool of civilization, as the cinema is today whether we face it or not. But among the Greeks it was paramount. And the people participated, we know that, for audience participation is essential to the theatre. The great Theatre of Dionysus (the Theatron as it was called in Greece) would not have been built except for popular approval. And the dramas would not have gone on being written and produced for a hundred years. Of course the Attic civilization was infinitesimally small in numbers compared with the modern civilization we know, and every citizen could attend the drama festivals for a couple of obols, which would even be returned to him if he showed he lacked means. The idea of the great open-air Theatre (which became the Roman Colosseum) as a cultural cradle, as a place to give great pleasure to the people while enriching their lives, could only work in America for sports and football games, not for the drama.

But science, that very science we have just questioned, was to give us the tool in another form:

In the Greek tragedies whenever the poet was unable to resolve his climax by means of the drama (which means *action*) he introduced a god to settle things in short order. No catastrophe was beyond a god.

Being represented as a god he could not walk up the platform steps like an ordinary hero but must descend from the sky, and down from the sky he came, delivered by some sort of machine, the exact nature of which has thinned the hair and dimmed the eyes of many scholars. No doubt the pagan gods were full of human nature and susceptible of becoming stage-struck. At any rate, after waiting up in the wings for twenty-five centuries, during which time the Greek drama had been forgotten by all save writers and a few ambitious Thespians, the god from the machine grew tired of neglect and sent down to man the machine itself.

It was called the kinetoscope and like all gifts from the gods was at first regarded as a toy. Originally a movie was an object of childish curiosity. Here was a power to enrich culture and civilization, to bring infinite pleasure to mankind (for surely the purpose of art is to give pleasure) and yet the men of culture, the novelists at their desks, the playwrights who had gone into the theatre never to come out of it, the artists at their easels, never raised their heads from their work. The thinking hearts and feeling brains of artists were untroubled as they left the toy to the nickelodeons and the modern gods —the business men.

Yet here was, and here is, the Greek theatre of the people or the Colosseum adapted to our time. The 15,000 film theatres of the United States alone, where millions of people foregather by day and night to be entertained, are the modern Colosseum, beyond even the imagination of the Greeks and Romans.

The kinetoscope is really a gift from the gods. Yet the gods exact a stiff price for what they bestow. Or to put it more practically, man's discoveries demand a new responsibility of him and those responsibilities may not be shirked without hazard.

Our discoveries and technical advances change us, if only by changing our environment. And that is the paradox of the relentless march of the machines: unless each new responsibility is met, technical advances seem to be accompanied by cultural and moral regression. As newspaper presses have grown there has been less and less concern for what is printed by them. As the kinetoscope and its family of machines for the American Colosseum have been perfected there has been less and less concern for what the films contain. The same with the radio, with all our modern means of expression and communication. The people demand it! Give the people what they want! That is sufficient excuse for our greed, our cowardice, our indifference.

I am no fool to cry out against the machine. I believe the modern cinema to be the greatest instrument of culture the world has known. And who would set the clock back? There was war, pain, sorrow in the world ages before men pried out the secrets of the thunderbolt and the atom. The clocks of civilizations cannot be turned back. They need rewinding with responsibility or they will run down, the hands going always forward; though there may be a symbol in the fact that ordinary clocks go back to zero when they strike twelve.

But an instrument of culture such as the cinema can be no better than the civilization which uses it. The ancient men of Athens, possessed of one huge theatre, used it richly and heroically, giving infinite pleasure to the people of their time and echoes of that pleasure to all posterity. It was a temple of tears and laughter, where man and his fate were probed, where the chaos of life could be caught and momentarily given shining form, where the mystery and joy of being could be made intelligible and flicker forth in exalted feeling, where men could richly laugh at themselves and their fellows, where they could have vital imaginary experience beyond the range of their lives.

And after two thousand years of western civilization we have technically perfected our American Colosseum, the cinema, and in thousands of theatres spread over the country our people now find pleasure only in being terrified by werewolves and monsters of superstition sprung from mediaeval darkness; in finding out every hour-and-a-half who killed whom for virtually no reason whatever except that threadbare motive of insanity; in watching carbon-copy private detectives with the moral and intellectual equipment of a toad commit and have committed upon their persons endless violence which is devoid of any meaning or adult connotations; in finding out that every third person in our midst is a victim of amnesia; in watching corners of eternal triangles grow round with wear; in viewing machine-made lovers making machine-made love in machine-made love stories; laughing emptily at comedies which show contempt for all human beings by pretending that people are only funny when their behavior is lunatic, whereas it is obvious that to the humorous mind people are only funny when they behave quite seriously and that lunatics are a subject for compassion. There is no need to catalogue the contents of our modern Colosseum as there is no need for the present writer to deny complicity in this unthinking effort to contribute to the delinquency of the whole human race.

The fact is we have completely corrupted the meaning of the word entertainment in the modern theatre. And since the screen reaches millions to the stage's thousands, our corruption is the more grievous. Surely the aim of art, especially of the art of story-telling, is to give pleasure, which is to entertain. Entertainment means pleasure and not oblivion. Narcotics give oblivion, entertainment wakes us up, makes us richly alive. False users of the word entertainment, especially among film-makers, really mean oblivion and so cheat the people of real joy and pleasure. No man of sense would assert that the people of Athens who laughed with Aristophanes or wept with Aeschylus were not being entertained, were not experiencing pleasure. Nor can we deny, to take a comparison that lies prophetically at the opposite pole of the ideal, that the people of Nero's Rome were not being entertained in their Colosseum when they watched beasts devour human beings or gladiators in mortal combat. In entertainment the question is quality and degree. Man's nature is dual and we may invoke heaven or hell according to the way we use our cultural tools.

All this brings us round to the difficulties that beset the serious artist who wishes to work in film. It is such an exciting instrument that it attracts all manner of talented people. I sincerely believe that nowhere in the world will you find more people of talent aggregated than in Hollywood.

Suppose you are a dramatist or a writer of fiction and you wish to work in this medium which reaches millions of people with an impact that is beyond the power of the printed word. You needs must come to Hollywood. What then? First you will find that film-making is an industry, that it is organized much like any other industry in the modern world. I have written elsewhere that all popular arts inescapably become industries. There is no avoiding that fact, let us make the best of it. An industry is an organization of human workers on the strict pattern of a machine, with all its efficiency and inhumanity. We worship the efficiency of our machines and our admiration has got into all our thinking and shapes our collective efforts. Indeed there is no more collective thinker than the industrialist, who imagines he believes in the individual. He thinks of labor in terms of thousands of hands, as a machine "thinks" of its function in terms of thousands of parts, each performing its one function and nothing else.

We are no longer machine users, machine masters—we are machine thinkers. We will sacrifice all humanity, civilization itself, for the god of efficiency in production. Production for what? For the humanity that is sacrificed. If by technical improvements an industry employing a million men can get along with ten, it will quite logically keep the ten men and the devil take the dismissed. That is virtually an utilitarian law of Nature and man is part of Nature. The machine is a construction to produce a function by the application of power, man's personal power or the enormous power of Nature which he can release. This typewriter I am using converts finger-power into printed letters as its special function. If I am not careful my association with it will lead me into mechanical habits of writing, some of which may already be visible to the acute reader. Yes, the machine is a miraculous slave but a dangerous god.

Our whole lives, our modern civilization, are being patterned after the machine. The film industry is a machine for producing motion pictures in bulk. The steel industry and the publishing industry do the same thing. The modern branch-bank is a financial machine; the mail order house, a distributing machine. The corporation is an economic machine which uses legal principles instead of the wedge, the lever, the wheel and other mechanical principles. And all of these machines of our industrial, economic and political life have one aim, which is to eliminate human error by eliminating all human feeling and so attain perfect efficiency.

The consequence is that a corporation, for instance, has almost no personal or human responsibility. It has, as some wit has said, neither a body to be kicked nor a soul to be damned. Yet the thousands of people it has power over certainly have bodies to be kicked and souls to be damned. It is the triumph of the machine over humanity.

I know there is no going back and my purpose is not to point solutions. My purpose as a writer is only to observe life. But there must be ways and means, certainly in those industries which have power over our culture and our civilization, to reassert human responsibility for what is produced.

Now to return to the writer whom we have left knocking at the gates of the film industry. He has achievements to back his ability, so he is given an office in one of the film factories and is going to be inducted into the mysteries of making motion pictures. He is an individual, with thoughts and feelings and prejudices of his very own, or he could not be a writer of much consequence. He has created plays or stories by sitting at the wheel-and-throttle of his own imagination. But suddenly he discovers that he no longer has a wheel or throttle; they were checked outside when he entered the studio gates.

The control of production is in a mysterious place called the front office. It is in the hands of our modern demi-gods, the business men, who never have disciplined themselves for the sweat of writing, who have never created a character or a story, but who are very skillful at creating and running modern industrial organizations which we have seen are themselves machines of another order. Our writer discovers he has fallen plumb into the innards of a machine.

Do not think for a moment that these skillful men who run the film production-machines do not have their great abilities, their worries and perplexities. They have probably the most abominable task in modern industry: they must attempt to produce a standard product where the elements of production are human ideas and feelings and personalities, those most fluid, intangible, unstandard, inconstant things. They must envy the motor car manufacturers who can design ten standard models each year and then watch over the blueprints and the office records. Or the steel industrialists with their tangible goods. But the studio executives are themselves caught in the machine. They are part of the corporation which is part of the monopoly of loosely integrated corporations. If they do not achieve efficiency they will be discarded as quickly as a cracked spark plug. Our human machines, from the smallest to the Titans, demand maximum production with maximum efficiency, or they will discard.

So these Chief Engineers of the studio-machines rack their brains to produce a standard product. They must try to stabilize their industry as much as possible; that is, they must produce a constant and standard product; for the chains of theatres are another machine which must be fed at a steady rate as a real estate investment. They work zealously at this all along the line. They buy a backlog of stories already fabricated, stories that have been tested by a million readers or by large circulation magazines or by the New York theatre if possible. Ah, there is something standard about that. What next can be stabilized or standardized? Actors, names, personalities. Hence the film industry is the most publicized in the world. Every move of an actor must be emblazoned. Fan magazines are encouraged. Finally millions of people will crowd the box offices if only those magic names are put up on the marquees, without regard for what sort of film it is.

For this latter the film industries pay dearly. The actors, suddenly feeling their power of attraction, find they can demand a king's ransom for their services. And get it. Some mistake their manufactured publicity for a special personal gift, for unique talent, and are the hardest to handle. The wiser accept it with a sigh and search for good screenplays and competent directors, knowing that only a personal standard will endure.

Of course this selling of films by selling stars is not without hazard for the actor who wishes to improve himself in his profession and to build his career upon real ability. For the public demand that they see *the actor,* his own personality and little charming manners, and he is finally not permitted to exercise his art and find the joy of impersonating other characters. He is trapped in self and cannot escape from himself as other artists do in true creative endeavor. Being used by the machine he must obey the laws of the machine and draw upon no inner secrets of the imagination. A machine has no imagination, neither errors nor inspirations, and its soul is a slide-rule and a cash register.

The only other elements of the film industry that can be standardized by the unfortunate men who run studios are the technical elements. Here their happiness and relief know no bounds. The physical and technical departments of studios are models of machine organization. Each function is bottled off into a department, which is run like a small fortress by the employee in charge of it. The department head, once he gets seasoned and loses any creative enthusiasm he may once have had, organizes his department like a small machine which is obedient only to the big machine of the studio. All talent that is employed must be subject to his scrutiny and he prefers men who are inferior in talent to himself, for if the man is better and it gets around he may lose his high place on the studio battlements.

While our new writer sits and broods in his office, let us further examine what he is going to find out in the next few months. The god of the machine has two principles for the production of motion pictures in bulk with the utmost efficiency. They are standardization and specialization. These principles hold in every industry alike, only the film industry has a harder time to make them stick—because every now and then some rebel individual tries to upset the system. Specialization, which has been called knowing more and more about less and less, is hand-maiden to standardization. Keep any creative activity spread and carefully sectioned off among a hundred specialists, and the quality and character of your product need never change. Certainly it will not improve, except in technical proficiency. The industrial machine has a ready check on whether the product is pleasing the public: the box-office.

Yet how do they know the people would not want a better product if it were offered to them? Hollywood after several inept and unimaginative attempts decided the public did not want Shakespeare, yet *Henry V* has been made in England and it would be interesting to discover what the box-office barometer would indicate if the film were given the wide distribution and ballyhoo that a two-million-dollar standard Hollywood production receives. Naturally the film will not be given that test for it might be disturbing to find out, and the film industry has the means to avoid it by dominating, if not controlling, the three wheels of the machine—production, distribution and exhibition.

Perhaps our writer is growing restive in his office. He has just encountered a director and an actor and it is enthusiastically proposed that they go off the lot and make an independent film. Wonderful! This will be a revelation. At least it will not be production No. 527 from the studio mill. They call in a lawyer and are told the banks that put up the money must have script approval. The chief character in the writer's comedy is a banker. Very well, they will make him a lawyer. Their lawyer doesn't mind that if there is money in it. But one more thing the banks demand first—they must have a release. From whom? From the corporation machines of the industry from which our writer is trying to flee. The releasing corporation also asks script approval. . . . Very well, very well, our writer is back in his office waiting for that assignment. A benevolent tyranny is better than some things.

Or suppose the writer met instead a millionaire who was willing to put up his own money and take a chance on getting a release. Of course the millionaire not only wants script approval, he has the story also, about his father, or Aunt Susan, or a girl he cannot forget or some such subject. In the film world everyone wants to be a film-maker and the best thing our disillusioned writer can do for the moment is go back and lie down in his office.

He reflects. If only the medium of film were not so damned costly. Only a lunatic or a poet, which are much the same thing, throws a dollar around. Whoever heard of anyone throwing a million dollars around? You have got to prove your fitness by out-thinking or out-smarting others in respect to their material possessions before anyone will entrust you with his money. And artists are known to be notoriously careless with money, perhaps because they have had so little experience with it. Does a million dollars have conscience, does it have any sense of responsibility, does it have love or any human emotion, does it dream? Well, it has one recurrent dream: to marry another million and beget loads of little millions which will in turn generate the race of millions. But for the dreamers who have made everything that is wonderful and beautiful in this world, money and the machine are the flaming swords that bar the gates of Paradise.

Our writer recalls the first story he wrote. What mechanism of expression did he have? Not even a typewriter. A ten-cent pad of paper, a pencil, a furnished room—and himself. And that was what he put into it—himself. Of course the editor changed it a bit and he wasn't paid enough for it to cover his room-rent (he was up against the publishing industry there) but that story is still reprinted in anthologies, by Heaven! It was sold to the film industry—that's how he found his way to Hollywood. The situations were kept, the characters were followed after a fashion, but the film was standardized, streamlined and given the tempo of a bright little entertainment machine. And oh, it was successful. What matter if it did cause public taste to recede by as much as a grain of sand? The wheels of modern civilization can have a lot of sand thrown into them before they will grind to a stop. Everything was in that film except the author, except the idiosyncrasy of a human soul, the kind of individuality that differentiates O. Henry from O'Neill, or Shaw from Ibsen, or Chekhov from Dostoievsky, or Edgar Lee Masters from Edgar Guest. There is no place for idiosyncrasy in the scheme of standardization and the machine.

If only our writer had a million dollars of his own to make a movie. Unless it were standardized what chance would he have of getting it through the distribution and exhibition machines? He suddenly envies a bright young man named Howard Smith who possesses fifty million dollars and produces an occasional movie. Fortunate man. Then he goes to see Howard Smith's latest extravagance, *The Cretin,* and he realizes that Mr. Smith has no artistic dreams that yearn to be satisfied, no canons of taste to be conveyed, no thoughts about the problems of the poor human race, no passion to give pleasure and true entertainment. Mr. Smith is the product of the machines which gave him his fortune and is simply out to make another million dollars and an extra splash of publicity in this publicity-ridden world. . . . Our writer shakes his head. Well, perhaps . . . but God's Mercy, he is on salary! What moral right has he to waste the Machine's time mooning about like this? He realizes he doesn't fit this scheme of things: what the studio needs is a professional writer with the mind of a good ad man, the sort of mind that can wax enthusiastic about canned tomatoes or bottled soap, whichever account is the largest with the firm, and can write reams of inspirational stuff and then go out and kick the dog around to get even with the world that has made him so meaningless. It is the sort of work Sherwood Anderson ran away from to become a writer. . . Our man looks uneasily at the clock and then commences his script for Production No. 527. The story appeared in a two-million-circulation magazine last year and is about a returned soldier (from World War I) who is afflicted with amnesia and does not recognize his wife who is about to marry a second returned soldier who has aphasia and cannot protest. This time a little standardization will improve the story.

Do not get the idea that we are being flip. Our writer, being a man of some sense, has by this time become aware that there is a great deal to learn in the business of writing or making films beyond mere standardization. It is a complex and difficult craft. Within the industry are some fine craftsmen, directors mainly, men of genius who by pure force of personal character initiate films for themselves within the mechanism of studios and manage to put their personal stamp, their individual style, upon the finished product. That they are successful is not only glory for them but praise for the public which likes their films. I need name no names to point out these men: the public knows them as the public knows the names of the gifted producers.

But in general (and it is the main features of the film industry I touch on here) talented people are too busy adjusting themselves to the machine and to its rules of standardization to study the potentialities of film, to develop artistic techniques, to experiment and know more about their medium. And specialization will take care of that. Why worry about directing when there are plenty of directors to take care of that? Why learn film-cutting when there are good cutters around? Why investigate the wonderful cameras when cameramen are paid for doing just that? All you have to do is stick in your office and write . . . though of course you will never really know much about film-making that way or what the medium really is.

Although nobody wants to do all the hard work, everybody wants to be a film-maker. Not only everyone in Hollywood but in the United States, in the whole wide world. Already our writer receives every day illiterate letters from all sorts of people who have a great story to tell and are willing to write it with him if he will help them get to Hollywood.

Even the Chief Engineers in the front offices, the harassed men who run the giant machines of organization called studios—even these want to be film-makers. They buy the stories that make the stars that make the House that Jack (and lots of jack) built. Almost every executive is determined to be a creator, and if he lacks any creative ideas or ability, which is apt to be the case because an artist is too emotional to run a machine or even to be trusted near the wheel-and-throttle, then he will satisfy his creative urge by giving orders to men of creative capacity and so will create motion pictures by edict and sheer willpower.

It matters not that the will is almost invariably destructive and that desire alone can create: Hitler's Third Reich was a place where everything was run by will, and by banging his fist he could produce a film. We have seen some of the films.

But our own harassed studio heads, for which we must have much compassion, are really benevolent men. There is just no solution when the wonderful machine of the kinetoscope is operated within the complexity of machines which make up the modern world. These men for the most part have a sense of responsibility and would like to make better films. They too are trapped. They cannot depend upon individual artists going their own way and using extravagantly costly machinery to make films which perhaps the public will never want to see.

Let not the reader preen his moral feathers: you would almost certainly do the same in the place of these troubled men. It is an accepted fact that mass-taste is inferior to individual taste. Movies are made for the masses; the medium is too costly to make films for varied degrees of maturity as school-books are published for sixteen grades of development. Therefore, if the public has poor taste the only way of ensuring public favor and not having a failure on your hands is to gauge your product to that taste and never go a cut above it; so what happens is that you doubly-insure against failure by going two cuts below the mass level, following the example of the press and the radio, and the level keeps sinking instead of imperceptibly rising as it might if the agencies of mass-culture ventured to shade things on the plus side.

The cultivated individual is suspected of having tastes, interests and appreciations far above those of the people. This is a moot point, but not in the mind of Machine Authority. Indeed the artist is held to be a person never to be trusted to initiate a film; so the creative title in film-making is taken away from anyone suspected of being an artist and given to a man of more common taste who is called the producer. It is a nice generative word from a good Latin family and smacks of creative genius.

And the machine insists that this producer shall be the important man in the creation of films. Hence you will find every projected film announcing in bold type that the ensuing film was produced by a gentleman who very likely had a great deal to do with it if the film is pure standard product and perhaps very little to do, outside of making the business arrangements and hiring talent, if it ventures beyond the ordinary. Nothing is absolutely true; sometimes a producer is a creative person who has learned no technique of expression, who has no outlet for his energies except by exciting and stimulating men who know their craft, and so by working through other men of talent he can bring off an interesting film. But for every man of this type there are scores whose only function is to bring the product down to standard and wipe out all trace of individuality.

Now that writer we have left working in his office is a dogged fellow. By this time he has adapted three standard murder mysteries which were purchased by the front office. The studio has jumped his salary and though he realizes that in a curious way this is a bribe by which he agrees to submerge his individuality, his own personality, and go along with the machine for better or for worse, he finds that money has its uses and also his imagination has been captured by the infinite possibilities of film. He is not in the theatre of the stage, one theatre, but in the Colosseum of 15,000 theatres in the United States.and God-knows-how-many in the world. Being an American the magnitude of the thing alone fascinates him. Every time he writes *bang-bang* or *I love you,* which is about all he is allowed to write except witticisms which have a mean edge to them because that is the only way his frustrated soul can now ease itself, in little bites at others, he marvels that millions of people over the world will hear them spoken, people who are hungry for pleasure and the great emotional and comic experiences of art. (Or let us say "experiences of the theatre" for those who sneer at the word art.)

So he sticks around,for fifteen years. Let us, to keep this typewriter from running away with itself and its operator, lap-dissolve across the fifteen years. The lap-dissolve is a marvelous device for getting on, much better than the novelist's trick of taking a fresh page and writing *Chapter X.*

Our writer is not just one of the thousand members of the Screen Writers Guild. One thousand writers! Imagine it, when ten or twenty writers in a couple of millennia, without any machinery of expression except white paper and a bottle of ink, have given us the visions and dreams we live by. Our writer longs to be as free as possible within the machinery of industrial production and he has refused to be cribbed and cabined within the studio machine. He is a conspirator if the truth be told. He has jumped the fences of specialism and standardization. He has prowled within the fortresses of the departments. He has spent time in the cutting-rooms and on the recording stages and on the sets and among cameramen and directors and actors. And finally he has talked the benevolent head of the studio into letting him make a film himself. He believes that perhaps he can integrate all the specialized jobs and get people working together in enthusiasm, really working for the individual film instead of for the machine. Mind you, he has learned great respect for all these talented artists and technicians with whom he is going to work. And he has observed that egotism is the greatest enemy of the men who make films and he has determined to watch himself on that score, to work solely for the film and not for himself.

Very well. His script is approved by the man at the wheel-and-throttle. He gets his cast assembled. He wants his sets designed by an art director who he believes is right for the job. Bang! He has collided with the head of the art department who does not want an outside man coming in. After a fight he gets the art director he wants. He wants a certain cameraman. Bang! Why won't so-and-so do? He is stubborn within reason and finally gets his cameraman. He goes on the set and commences shooting. Bang! He is in conflict with the sound department. He is at great disadvantage because of his inexperience. But he knows what he wants at any rate. The sound men want technical perfection and by technical perfection they mean the smoothness and slickness of the efficient machine. It seems the range of the voice is 150 decibels, from audible sound to pain, whereas the sound camera will record a range of only thirty-five decibels. That is what they say but our now bemused writer doesn't believe it. What they are saying is that they will not give a true range to the human voice in our motion picture theatres. Even though a character must whisper a line to give it dramatic truth, there must be enough decibels to drown out the man eating popcorn two rows behind. Give up the popcorn concessions? Man, there's ten million a year in that!

Thus, as on every set, the skillful and competent sound men who are as interested in this film as the writer himself sit over dials and carefully iron out the spoken lines to a beautiful technical level, like a plateau of aluminum come from a magnificent planing mill. If an actor gets loud, down go the decibels. If he hushes, up come the dials. The machine has triumphed again over human feeling and expression.

But there is no need to proceed any further. The subject is boring and the reader can guess where it ends. It ends with a slick standard product. All of our films are slick and smooth and bright as steel nowadays—and most of them just as devoid of life. It ends with technical perfection. One begins to wonder foolishly if perhaps the death of every art is not technical perfection. The machine itself becomes more fascinating than the thing the machine was invented for. The gift of the god has been finally turned against the gods. It was so, as Jean Renoir has pointed out to me, with the art of making tapestries. In the very beginning, when there were no proper dyes for the threads and everything was laboriously done, masterpieces were made. Today with every technical perfection, with even machines to make the tapestries, the art is virtually dead.

It is so perhaps in every art and every industry. Certainly Hollywood is not unique. Everywhere in the world, by avoiding our responsibility as men, we have let the machine dominate our dreams and not used it to bring the promised land, which is the one dream it offered. We have let the inhuman ideal of the machine tyrannize over and shape our thinking, pattern our politics, our economy, our arts and industries. And by so doing we incessantly degrade our culture and taste and civilization instead of improving them. Our work gives less satisfaction to the worker. Our arts and entertainments give less pleasure, less entertainment. No one is responsible: all are. The industries that do not directly influence thinking and culture perhaps may be forgiven for their inexorable pursuit of the ideals of the machine; though there are other goals besides efficiency, human goals.

But the industries that deal in entertainment, in the expression of ideas and feelings and the portrayal of human behaviour, cannot get off lightly by assuming their products are meaningless entertainment. The printed word, the radio, the theatre are never meaningless. Nothing is unimportant that is experienced in a theatre. The theatre is one of the most potent instruments man knows. Always it shapes thought, even unconscious thought at low levels, it forms pictures and patterns of behaviour; it can deepen our understanding and so make life warm and rich, or it can corrupt us with vacuity and make life cruel and sentimental and heartless.

The men who deal in the word and the image must shoulder their responsibilities; and the shouldering need not conflict with profit; rather will it enhance it. Or, if we as individual men wish to surrender entirely to the machine instead of using it for what it is worth, we should cease the pretence of being half-men and straightaway build a hive. It would be the most wonderful hive ever constructed, of stainless steel and plexiglass with no connection with the earth; it would perpetuate the human race as certainly as a hive of bees perpetuates a hive of bees, though we should then take the prouder title of the inhuman race; every man's cell would be alike, we would wing forth each day to pollenize machines and the only music we would ever hear would be our own beautiful buzzing. Every day we would get the same newspaper, published by the Master Mechanic, standardized and perfect; and every night we would see a standardized perfected movie which would finally become the same movie, showing the hive-perfected love story ending in a double murder . . . But of course I am talking nonsense and I have, like a bad scenario writer, forgotten the main character of this story—our writer, who came to Hollywood seventeen-years-and-another-war ago.

After completing his thirty-third film he went to see *Henry V* and immediately flew to England, where he is now languishing in an office and waiting for a producer to send him a brand-new purchase, Story No. 999, which is about a returned soldier (from World War II) who is suffering from amnesia and . . . but this infernal typing-machine is running away with itself, for I have a vague feeling it has written something like that before. In any case our film-writer is biting his nails and gathering material to write a book about the frightful state of film-production in England and all of Europe. He will soon be back in Hollywood, either writing a script in which nine characters are sequentially killed by a maniac with amnesia or . . . he may with luck knock out a screenplay that will qualify for next year's volume of this series; for which volume the present writer, if he has not been lynched for outrageous heresy, promises to write a prefatory piece entitled *In Defense of Hollywood*.
Hollywood, June, 1946

# THE LOST WEEKEND

*(A Paramount Picture)*

*Screenplay by* CHARLES BRACKETT *and* BILLY WILDER

*From the Novel by* CHARLES JACKSON

*Produced by* CHARLES BRACKETT

*Directed by* BILLY WILDER

## The Cast

| | |
|---|---|
| DON BIRNAM | Ray Milland |
| HELEN ST. JAMES | Jane Wyman |
| WICK BIRNAM | Phillip Terry |
| NAT | Howard da Silva |
| GLORIA | Doris Dowling |
| BIM | Frank Faylen |
| MRS. DEVERIDGE | Mary Young |
| MRS. FOLEY | Anita Bolster |
| MRS. ST. JAMES | Lilian Fontaine |
| MR. ST. JAMES | Lewis L. Russell |
| ATTENDANT AT OPERA | Frank Orth |

*Film Editor*—DOANE HARRISON

# THE LOST WEEKEND

## PART ONE

The man-made mountain peaks of MANHATTAN fade in on a sunny day in October, 1938. The view moves across the distant ridge of midtown buildings, then slowly stops at the rear of a small apartment house on East 55th Street. It is a four-story affair of brick, housing some eight apartments, half of them giving on the garden or rather on the routine back yard with a sumac tree, a stone bench, and some mouldy flower boxes in which geraniums are dying. The moving view concentrates on the fourth-floor apartment, which boasts of three windows; two of them give on the living room and one on the bedroom of the brothers Birnam. Then the view narrows to the BEDROOM WINDOW. It is open, like a million other windows in New York that warm day. What gives it individuality is that from an awning cleat there dangles down the outside wall something which very few people hang from their windows: a bottle of whiskey.—Through the window we can see the brothers Birnam packing.

The BEDROOM: It is a smallish room with twin beds in opposite corners, both of them unmade. There are books on the night tables, two chests of drawers with some of the drawers open. The closet is open too. One door leads to the living room, another to the cramped entrance hall.

(Maybe this is the time to describe the apartment. You've seen that living room a hundred times if you know literate, artistically inclined people. On one wall are bookshelves surrounding a marble fireplace, on which stands a tiny plaster bust of Shakespeare. In the shelves, art books and serious works of fiction: Thomas Mann, F. Scott Fitzgerald, James Joyce and the like. There are Picasso, Van Gogh and Utrillo reproductions on the other walls. A comfortable, elderly armchair stands near one of the windows. There is a studio couch, a low, tiled table—oh, you know. Off the living room is the familiar kitchenette for the light housekeeping

of two bachelors—i.e. coffee and coffee. The bathroom, inconveniently enough, is off the entrance hall.)

To get back to the bedroom and the Birnam brothers: a small suitcase lies open on each bed. DON, the brother nearest the window, is bent over one, putting in socks, shirts, etc. He is thirty-three, an extremely attractive guy, but ten pounds underweight, and in his eye there is something rebellious, something sly. WICK, two years younger, is much sturdier; kindly, sympathetic, solid gold. He wears glasses and is smoking a cigarette. He is on his way from the closet to his suitcase with some stuff. He throws a sweater across to Don.

WICK. Better take this along, Don. It's going to be cold on the farm.

DON. Okay.

WICK. How many shirts are you taking?

DON. Three.

2

WICK. I'm taking five.

DON. Five?

WICK. I told them at the office I might not be back till Tuesday. We'll get there this afternoon. That'll give us all Friday, Saturday, Sunday, Monday. We'll make it a long weekend.

DON. Sounds long, all right.

WICK. It'll do you good, Don, after what you've been through.

Don has crossed to the chest of drawers and fished out more shirts and socks.

WICK. Trees and grass and sweet cider and buttermilk and water from that well that's colder than any other water.

DON. Wick, please, why this emphasis on liquids? Noble, upstanding, nauseating liquids.

WICK. Sorry, Don.

DON, his back toward Wick, is bent over the suitcase, packing. His eyes travel to the window.

DON. Think it would be a good idea if we took my typewriter?

WICK. What for?

DON (indignantly). To write. To write there. I'm going to get started on my novel.

WICK. You really feel up to writing?

DON. Why not?

WICK. I mean, after what you've been through.

DON. I haven't touched the stuff for ten days now.

WICK. I know you haven't. Where's the portable?

DON. In the living room closet, kind of toward the back.

Bent forward tensely, he watches Wick go into the living room. Left alone, he acts with lightning rapidity. He takes the sweater, goes over to the window, pulls up the whiskey bottle, wraps the sweater around it so that only the top with the string around it shows. He tries to loosen the noose but he's nervous and loses a precious second. From the living room has been coming the sound of Wick opening the closet door and ransacking. Now he calls out:

WICK'S VOICE. You sure it's in the closet? I can't find it.

DON (working desperately). Look by the big chair.

WICK'S VOICE (approaching fast). Isn't it under your bed?

Don sees he can't loosen the string in time. In the last fraction of a second before Wick enters, he manages to lower the bottle back down the wall. With what nonchalance he can muster he bends down and looks under the bed just as Wick enters, a sheaf of white paper in his hand.

DON. Of course. Here it is. (He pulls out a Remington portable, 1930 model).

WICK. Here's some paper. (He puts it in Don's suitcase.) We'll fix a table on the south porch. Nobody to disturb you—I'll see to it. Except maybe Saturday night we'll go over to the Country Club.

DON. I'm not going near that Country Club.

WICK. Why not?

DON. Because they're a bunch of hypocrites and I don't like to be whispered about: Look who's here from New York. The Birnam brothers— or rather the nurse and the invalid.

WICK. Stop that, Don. Nobody there knows about you.

DON. No? We get off the train and the alarm is sounded: The leper is back. Better hide your liquor.

Footsteps have been racing up the stairs outside the flat, and now there is a distinctive ring of the doorbell: short, short, long, short.

DON. Helen.

WICK. I'll take it.

He goes toward the door while the bell resumes short, short, long, short.— From the bedroom we can see him open the door. It's HELEN, all right. She is a clean-cut, good looking girl of twenty-six. Her face is brave, gay piquant. She's wearing a three-quarter-length leopard coat. The Indian Summer day is a good ten degrees too warm for the coat, but that doesn't stop Helen from wearing her beloved. In her hand are two books wrapped, and another small package. She enters breathlessly.

HELEN. Hello, Wick. Where's Don? (*Seeing him, she crosses to the bedroom.*) Glad I made it. I was afraid you might be gone. Presents. (*She puts the packages in the suitcase.*) The new Thurber book, with comical jokes and pictures, and a quiet little double murder by Agatha Christie. (*Putting in the second package*) Cigarettes and chewing gum.

DON. Thanks, Helen.

HELEN. Now have a good time, darling. And remember—lots of sleep, lots of milk—

DON. And sweet cider and some of that nice cold water from the well.

HELEN. Bend down.

It's a running gag between these two.

Don bends so that she can kiss him on the cheek.

HELEN. I'd better be going. I've missed ten minutes of the concert already.

DON. What concert?

HELEN. Carnegie Hall. Barbirolli conducting. They gave me two tickets at the office.

DON. Who are you going with?

HELEN. Nobody. (*At this, something flickers in Don's eye.*)

DON. What are they playing?

HELEN. Brahms' Second Symphony, something by Beethoven, something by Handel, and not one note of Grieg.

DON. Sounds wonderful.

HELEN. Goodbye, boys. See you Monday.

WICK. Tuesday.

DON (*holding Helen by the arm*). Just a minute. Wick— (*As Wick looks up*) I just had a crazy idea.

WICK. As for instance.

DON. Who says we have to take the three-fifteen train? We could go on the six-thirty.

WICK. What are you talking about?

DON. I just thought we could take a later train and Helen wouldn't have to go alone to the concert. She's got two tickets, hasn't she?

HELEN. No. I'm not upsetting any plans. You're going on the three-fifteen.

DON. But Helen, it's so silly! A whale of a concert and an empty seat next to you.

WICK. No, Don. Everything's all set.

They'll be at the station to meet us. Dinner'll be waiting.

DON. So what? We put in a call that we're taking the late train, have supper at nine o'clock, be in bed by ten.

WICK. Nothing doing. We're going.

HELEN. Wick's right. And don't worry about that empty seat. I'll find myself a very handsome South American millionaire.

DON. There. Did you hear her? And now we'd have to break our necks to catch the train anyway.

HELEN (*looking at her wrist watch*). Five to three.

DON. See?

WICK (*giving up*). All right. Go ahead.

DON. Wait a minute. *I'm* not going.

WICK. Then what are we talking about?

DON. I want you to go. You and Helen.

WICK. *Me* and Helen?

DON. Yes. That was the idea. Who likes Brahms, you or I?

WICK. Since when don't you like Brahms?

DON. I'll stay right here and finish packing. Take a little nap maybe.

WICK. Nonsense. If anybody goes . . . Helen's your girl.

There is an exchange of suspicious looks between Wick and Helen.

HELEN. There's something in that, Don.

WICK. What's more, I don't think you should be left alone.

DON. I shouldn't?

WICK. No.

HELEN. Really, Don.

DON. Why? I can't be trusted. Is that it?

WICK. What I meant to say—

HELEN. Wick—

WICK. After what Don's been through—

DON. After what I've been through, I couldn't go to a concert. I couldn't face the crowd. I couldn't sit through it with all those people around. I want to be alone for a couple of hours and kind of assemble myself. Is that such an extraordinary thing to want?

WICK. Don't act so outraged, would you mind?

DON. All right. Anything else?

HELEN. Please, boys.

Wick, who has been smoking a cigarette throughout the scene, throws it out the window. None of the three see, but we do, that it doesn't fall out the window but ricochets against the opened casement to the window sill, where it lies smouldering.

WICK. Come on, Helen.

HELEN. You'll stay right here, won't you?

DON. Where would I go?

HELEN. Then you'll be here when we come back?

DON. I told you I'm not leaving this apartment.

WICK. You've told us a good many things, Don.

Furious, Don takes a bunch of keys from his pocket.

DON. All right, if you don't believe me, why don't you take my key and lock me in like a dog.

HELEN (*to Wick*). We've got to trust Don. That's the only way.

WICK. Sorry, Don. (*To Helen*) Here we go.

HELEN. So long, Don.

DON. So long.

HELEN (*pulling him by the lapel*). Bend down.

His face is now close to hers. She kisses him. Wick turns away. His eyes fall on the cigarette still smouldering on the sill. He goes toward the window. Don, held by Helen, watches him tensely. Wick flips the cigarette into the garden and is about to turn back into the room when his eyes fall on the cleat and the string. He leans from the window. Don lets Helen go, staring at Wick, panic in his eyes. Helen, sensing something amiss, looks from one brother to the other.

WICK (*hauling up the bottle*). What's this, Don?

Helen and Wick watch Don. Don's face relaxes into an innocent grin.

DON. That? That's whiskey, isn't it?

WICK. How did it get there?

DON. I don't know.

WICK. I suppose it dropped from some cloud. Or someone was bouncing it against this wall and it got stuck.

DON. I must have put it there.

WICK. Yes, you must.

DON. Only I don't remember when. Probably during my last spell, or maybe the one before. (*His eyes meet Helen's. Hers are infinitely dis-*

*tressed.*) Don't look at me like that, Helen. Doesn't mean a thing. I didn't know it was there. And if I had, I wouldn't have touched it.

WICK (*twisting the string off the bottle*). Then you won't mind.

DON. Won't mind what?

Wick, the bottle in his hand, goes through the living room toward the kitchenette. Don looks after him, then follows him, a stubborn smile on his lips. Helen trails after them, acutely embarrassed.

In the KITCHENETTE: Wick has stepped to the sink. He opens the bottle, turns it upside down and lets the whiskey run out. Don and Helen come to the door from the living room and stand watching. Don has something of the feeling of a man watching the execution of a very good friend, but he senses Helen's eyes upon him and preserves his nonchalant expression. The bottle emptied, Wick puts it in the sink.

WICK. Now you trot along with Helen.

DON. Why? On account of that? (*Pointing at the bottle*) You think I wanted you out of the apartment because of that? I resent that like the devil, and if there's one more word of discussion, I don't leave on your blasted weekend.

HELEN. Let's go.

Wick shrugs and goes to the hall for his hat.

HELEN (*to Don*). Be good, won't you, Don, darling?

She turns to go, but Don holds her back.

DON. Of course, Helen. Just stop watching me all the time, you two.

Let me work it out my way. I'm trying, I'm trying.

HELEN. We're both trying, Don. You're trying not to drink, and I'm trying not to love you.

She kisses him on the mouth, a woman hopelessly in love. Then, so that he won't see her moist eyes, she turns and hurries into the entrance hall.

We see the little ENTRANCE HALL of the BIRNAM APARTMENT as Wick stands, hat in hand, holding the door open. Helen comes out quickly and, taking a handkerchief from her bag, hurries past Wick into the hall. Wick turns toward Don, who has followed Helen to the entrance hall.

WICK. You call the farm, Don. Tell them we're taking the six-thirty train.

DON. Sure.

WICK. So long.

He goes out, shutting the door behind him. Don steps quickly to the door, pressing his ear against it to hear what the two are saying outside.

The FOURTH FLOOR HALL and STAIRCASE of the APARTMENT HOUSE: It is narrow and simple. There is no elevator. A skylight, somewhat obscured by dirt and dust, lights the fourth floor back. Every so often down the stairs there is a light bracket, always burning. Helen stands at the top of the stairs, blowing her nose. Wick takes her arm quickly.

WICK. Come on, Helen.

HELEN. Oh, Wick, what are we going to do about him ever.

WICK. He'll be all right.

HELEN. What if he goes out and buys another bottle?

WICK. With what? He hasn't a

nickel. There isn't a store, there isn't a bar that'd give him five cents' worth of credit.

They descend a few steps.

HELEN. Are you sure he hasn't another bottle hidden somewhere?

WICK. Not any more, he hasn't. I went through the apartment with a fine-toothed comb. The places he can figure out! (*They go on down the stairs.*)

Back in the APARTMENT: Don stands at the door, panic in his face. Has his brother discovered the other two bottles? He puts the chain on the door to insure his privacy, then dashes into the bathroom.

The BATHROOM: It's old-fashioned, with a bathtub on claw feet, a shower curtain above it—all the plumbing on that scale. Don dashes in, takes a nail file, kneels beside the grille of a register in the side wall, pries it out with the file, looks inside, puts his hand in. The bottle is gone. He looks at the hole wide-eyed, pushes back the grille and runs out. Don runs into the living room, goes to the couch, pulls it away from the wall, throws himself on his belly on the couch and reaches under the side of it which was toward the wall. His hand explores among the springs. There is no bottle there. He sits up. His face is covered with sweat. He takes out his handkerchief and wipes his face. Just then, from the direction of the entrance door, there is the noise of a key being turned in the lock. Don freezes, his eyes turning toward the door, horrified.

We see the ENTRANCE DOOR to the apartment, from DON's angle: It opens as far as the chain will allow, then stops with a sharp bite of metal on wood. There is another try. Then the doorbell is rung.

DON has not stirred. He rises slowly from the couch, takes a few steps toward the entrance door.

> DON. Who is it? (*No answer—just the doorbell being rung again*) *Who is it?*

The CORRIDOR outside the apartment: At the door stands MRS. FOLEY, a middle-aged charwoman with a large utility bag over her arm. Her key is in the door, which is open as far as the chain will permit.

> MRS. FOLEY. Mrs. Foley. Come to clean up.

Following this we get close views of DON and MRS. FOLEY alternately.

> DON (*his nerves on edge*). Not today. Does it have to be today?

> MRS. FOLEY. I ought to change the sheets, and today's my day to vacuum.

> DON. You can't come in. I'm not dressed.

> MRS. FOLEY. Shall I wait, shall I come back, or what?

> DON'S VOICE. You come on Monday.

> MRS. FOLEY. All right, Mr. Birnam. Is your brother here?

> DON'S VOICE. No, he isn't.

> MRS. FOLEY. How about my money? Didn't he leave my money?

We see DON as he stands galvanized. The word "money" has sent an electric current through his mind.

> DON. What money?

> MRS. FOLEY. My five dollars. Didn't he leave it?

> DON (*stalking his prey*). Probably. Where would he leave it?

> MRS. FOLEY'S VOICE. In the kitchen.

> DON. Where in the kitchen?

> MRS. FOLEY'S VOICE. In the sugar bowl.

Don breathes like one who's found the combination to the safe with the crown jewels.

> DON. Just a minute. (*He goes to the kitchenette.*)

In the KITCHENETTE: On the counter under the cupboards stands the sugar bowl. Don lifts the lid. There's nothing but sugar in the bowl, but lining the lid is a folded five-dollar bill. Don takes it out, goes into the entrance hall and, even though Mrs. Foley can't see him, instinctively holds the five dollars behind his back.

> DON. Sorry, Mrs. Foley. It's not there. He must have forgotten.

We get a close view of MRS. FOLEY, who is disappointed.

> MRS. FOLEY. Oh, putt! I wanted to do some shopping.

> DON'S VOICE. You'll get it Monday all right.

> MRS. FOLEY. Goodbye, Mr. Birnam.

She closes the door, takes the key and starts down the stairs, following which we see DON as he brings the five dollars from behind his back. He looks at it, folds it neatly, pockets it, puts on his hat, then, with an after thought, goes into the living room. He pushes the couch back against the wall with his foot, then goes out.

We see the FOURTH FLOOR HALL and STAIRS as Don goes to the balustrade and looks down.—There is a steep shot of the STAIRS: Don's head is in the foreground. The coast is clear of Mrs. Foley. Like a convict escaping, Don slips down the stairs.

The scene slowly dissolves to BROPHY'S LIQUOR STORE: At first we get a close view of LIQUOR BOTTLES, a rackful of them filling the screen. (The camera is behind the rack of liquor in a store on Third Avenue. The camera moves slowly toward them so that only about eight bottles fill the screen and we can see, between them, the shop, its window on Third Avenue, its entrance door.) No one is visible in the shop. Through the glass door we see Don Birnam hurrying up. He gives a quick glance in each direction, to see that he's not observed. He peers into the shop to make sure there are no other customers, then quickly steps inside and stands breathing heavily. A salesman rises in the foreground, his back turned. Don points to two bottles in the foreground.

DON (*with all the nonchalance he can scrape together*). Two bottles of rye.

SALESMAN. I'm sorry, Mr. Birnam.

DON. What are you sorry about?

SALESMAN. Your brother was in here. He said he's not going to pay for you any more. That was the last time.

DON. He won't, huh?

He takes the five dollars from his pocket and unfurls it, like a card trickster.

DON. Two bottles of rye.

SALESMAN. What brand?

DON. You know what brand, Mr. Brophy. The cheapest.

SALESMAN. All right.

DON. None of that twelve-year-old, aged-in-the-wood chichi. Not for me. Liquor is all one, anyway.

The salesman has taken two bottles from the rack in the foreground and put them on the counter. Don gives him the money and picks up the bottles like a miser grabbing gold.

SALESMAN. Don't you want a bag?

DON. Yes, I want a bag.

The salesman hands him a bag and steps out of the scene toward the cash register. We hear the ping of its bell, the opening of its drawer. Meanwhile, Don thrusts the bottles in the bag. It is a little short and the necks of the bottles protrude. The salesman hands him his change. Don pockets it.

SALESMAN. You know, your brother asked me not to sell you anything even if you had money, but I can't stop nobody, can I, not unless you're a minor.

DON. I'm not a minor, Mr. Brophy, and just to quiet your conscience, I'm buying this as a refill for my cigarette lighter.

Another customer enters the shop. Don takes the package and walks past the newcomer toward the door, hiding it from him gracefully, like a football in a sneak play.

We get a view of THIRD AVENUE, outside BROPHY'S LIQUOR SHOP as Don comes out with the bottles in the paper bag. He wants to start down the street but about twenty-five feet away stand two middle-aged Hokinson ladies, one of them curbing her dog on a leash. They are chatting. Don stops. He'll have to pass them if he goes down the street and he doesn't want to, not with these bottles peeking out of that bag. He turns back and approaches the grocery store next door to Brophy's. In front of it is a fruit stand. Screening his gesture from the ladies with his back, he picks up three apples and puts them in the top of the bag, to camouflage the bottles. He puts down a coin, then walks down the street toward the ladies, flaunting a paper bag which is obviously full of apples. The lady with the dog sees him. Don removes his hat in a courtly bow, very much at ease with the apples.

DON. Good afternoon, Mrs. Deveridge.

MRS. DEVERIDGE. Hello, Mr. Birnam.

MRS. DEVERIDGE (*confidently, to her companion after Don has passed them*). That's that nice young man that drinks.

The other lady tsk-tsks. They both look after Don.

Don is about ten feet beyond them. Perhaps he has overheard the remark. In any case, he is looking back. His look meets theirs. Embarrassed, they turn. Mrs. Deveridge jerks on the leash.

MRS. DEVERIDGE. Come on, Sophie. Let's go. (*They walk down the street in the opposite direction from Don.*)

DON looks after them. He is just in front of NAT's BAR. He steps hurriedly into the bar.

INSIDE NAT's BAR: It is a typical dingy Third Avenue bar. The sun slants dustily into the walnut-brown room. There is a long bar with a mirror behind it, some marble-topped tables and bentwood chairs. The woodwork, the furniture, the plaster of the place have absorbed and give forth a sour breath of hard liquor, a stale smell of flat beer. As Don enters, there are three people in the bar: Nat, the bartender, a broad-shouldered, no-nonsense type of guy, squeezing lemons in preparation

for the evening trade; and, sitting at a table in the corner, a girl named GLORIA, with an out-of-towner who hasn't bothered to take off his hat. He's about fifty and the manager of a hardware store in Elizabeth, New Jersey. Gloria is a shopworn twenty-three. She's brunette, wears net stockings and a small patent leather hat, and is a little below the standards of the St. Moritz lobby trade.

DON (*going to the bar*). And how is my very good friend Nat today?

NAT (*on guard*). Yes, Mr. Birnam.

DON (*sitting on a bar stool, putting down the paper bag*). This being an especially fine afternoon, I have decided to ask for your hand in marriage.

NAT (*wiping his hands*). Look, Mr. Birnam—

DON. If that is your attitude, Nat, I shall have to drown my sorrows in a jigger of rye. Just one, that's all.

NAT. Can't be done, Mr. Birnam.

DON. Can't? Let me guess why. My brother was here, undermining my financial structure.

NAT. I didn't tell him nothing about the wrist watch you left here, or your cuff links.

DON. Thank you, Nat. Today, you'll be glad to know, we can barter on a cash basis.

He takes the bills and change from his pocket, and places them on the bar.

NAT (*reaching for the bottle and the jigger*). One straight rye.

DON. That was the idea.

Nat pours the drink, then returns to squeezing lemons. Don picks up the glass, is suddenly acutely aware of the people at the table, of Nat's eyes. The glass freezes halfway to his mouth. He puts it down and starts playing the nonchalant, casual drinker—the man who can take it or leave it. He fingers the glass, turning it round and round. He takes a pack of cigarettes from his pocket and shakes one out, lights it. As he puts the match in the ashtray, his eyes fall on that jigger of whiskey. It's hard to resist it any longer. He takes a handkerchief from his pocket, wipes his forehead, then his parched mouth. The time has come now. He puts the handkerchief back in his pocket, lifts the glass and drains it in one gulp. Actually, Don doesn't like the taste of liquor, actively hates it indeed, as a one-legged man might hate the sight of his crutches but needs them in order to walk. Now that he has the drink in him, a kind of relieved grin comes back to Don's face. He holds the empty jigger in his hand. Nat has come up with the bar towel to wipe off the wet ring left by the glass.

DON. Don't wipe it away, Nat. Let me have my little vicious circle. The circle is the perfect geometric figure. No end, no beginning . . . What time is it?

NAT. Quarter of four.

DON. Good. That gives us the whole afternoon together. (*He holds out his glass for another drink.*) Only tell me when it's a quarter of six. Very important. We're going to the country for a weekend, my brother and I.

From the table in the background comes Gloria, headed for the powder room. Passing Don, she runs her finger through the neckline of his hair.

GLORIA. Hello, Mr. Birnam. Glad to have you back with the organization.

DON. Hello, Gloria. (*She goes on, and Don turns back to Nat.*) Not just a Saturday-Sunday weekend. A very long weekend. I wish I could take you along, Nat. You— (*with a gesture toward the liquor shelves*) and all that goes with you. (*Without a change of expression, Nat pours the second drink.*) Not that I'm cutting myself off from civilization altogether.

He points at the bag with the apples showing. Nat looks, but doesn't get it. Like a magician, Don takes two apples out, revealing the necks of the bottles.

DON (*gulping down the whiskey*). Now of course there arises the problem of transportation into the country. How to smuggle these two time bombs past the royal guard. I shall tell you how, Nat, because I'm so fond of you. Only give me another drink. (*As Nat pours one.*) I'm going to roll one bottle in a copy of the Saturday Evening Post, so my brother can discover it like that. (*He snaps his fingers.*) And I want him to discover it, because that'll set his mind at rest. The other bottle —(*Confidentially to Nat*) Come here. (*As Nat leans over the bar toward him*) That one I'm tucking into my dear brother's suitcase. He'll transport it himself, without knowing it, of course. While he's greeting the caretaker, I'll slide it out and hide it in a hollow of the old apple tree.

NAT. Aw, Mr. Birnam, why don't you lay off the stuff for awhile.

DON. I may never touch it while I'm there. Not a drop. What you don't understand, all of you, is that I've got to know it's around. That I can have it if I need it. I can't be cut off completely. That's the devil. That's what drives you crazy.

NAT. Yeah. I know a lot of guys like that. They take a bottle and put it on the shelf. All they want is just to look at it. They won't even carry a corkscrew along, just to be sure. Only all of a sudden they grab the bottle and bite off the neck.

DON. Nat, one more reproving word and I shall consult our lawyer about a divorce. (*He points to the empty glass for Nat to fill it. Nat pours another jigger.*) Quarter of six. Don't forget. My brother must find me at home, ready and packed.

Gloria is back from the powder room. On her way to her gentleman friend at the table, she again runs her finger through the neckline of Don's hair. She is almost past him when he catches her hand and pulls her toward him.

DON. Shall we dance?

GLORIA. You're awfully pretty, Mr. Birnam.

DON. You say that to all the boys.

GLORIA. Why, natch. Only with you it's on the level.

DON. Is it? Whatever became of your manicurist job?

GLORIA. I've still got it. Only I find I can't work more than four hours a day, three days a week. It's too tough on your eyes, all those little hangnails.

DON. Sit down.

GLORIA. No thanks. Thanks a lot, but no thanks. There's somebody waiting.

DON (*as he looks off toward the table*). Him? I bet he wears arch supporters.

GLORIA. He's just an old friend of the folks. Lovely gentleman. Buys me dimpled Scotch.

DON. He should buy you Indian rubies, and a villa in Calcutta overlooking the Ganges.

GLORIA. Don't be ridic.

DON. Gloria, please, why imperil our friendship with these loathsome abbreviations.

GLORIA. I could make myself free for later on if you want.

DON. I'm leaving for the weekend, Gloria. Maybe another time.

GLORIA. *Any* time.

And as she leans over, she runs her forefinger again through the neckline of his hair.

GLORIA. Just crazy about the back of your hair. (*She returns to the table.*)

DON (*to Nat*). Nat, weave me another.

NAT. You'd better take it easy.

DON. Don't worry about me. Just let me know when it's a quarter of six.

NAT. Okay. (*He starts to pour.*)

DON. And have one yourself, Nat.

NAT. Not me, Mr. Birnam.

DON. I often wonder what the barman buys, one-half so precious as the stuff he sells.

Nat has poured the drink. Don points at it.

DON. Come on, Nat. One little jigger of dreams.

NAT. Nope.

DON. You don't approve of drinking?

NAT. Not the way *you* drink.

DON. It shrinks my liver, doesn't it, Nat? It pickles my kidneys. Yes. But what does it do to my mind? It tosses the sandbags overboard so the balloon can soar. Suddenly I'm above the ordinary. I'm competent, supremely competent. I'm walking a tightrope over Niagara Falls. I'm one of the great ones. I'm Michelangelo molding the beard of Moses. I'm Van Gogh, painting pure sunlight. I'm Horowitz playing the Emperor Concerto. I'm John Barrymore before the movies got him by the throat. I'm a holdup man—I'm Jesse James and his two brothers, all three of them. I'm W. Shakespeare. And out there it's not Third Avenue any longer. It's the Nile. The Nile, Nat, and down it moves the barge of Cleopatra. Listen:

Purple the sails, and so perfumed that
The winds were love-sick with them; the oars were silver,
Which to the tune of flutes kept stroke, and made
The water which they beat to follow faster,
As amorous of their strokes. For her own person,
It beggar'd all description.

During the last two lines he has picked up the jigger of rye. The camera is on the wet rings which the wet glass has left on the bar. Gradually the music swells under the Shakespearean quotation and drowns it out. In quick dissolves we see the *five* rings, then *six*, then *nine*. Over the last, the light has changed, and we see the BAR again. It is dusk. The electric lights are on. The place is about half filled—eight customers at the bar, five tables occupied. Gloria and her friend are still there. Don, an empty jigger in his hand, stands at the same spot, only now leaning with his back against the bar. He is doggedly quoting Shakespeare,

more to himself than to the others at the bar, who are ignoring him.

DON. The cloud-capp'd towers, the gorgeous palaces,
The solemn temples, the great globe itself—

Nat puts drinks before some other customers, then goes over to Don and taps him on the shoulder.

NAT. Mr. Birnam, you ought to go home. You're late.

DON. Yea, all which it inherit shall dissolve—

NAT *(leaning forward as tactfully as possible)*. You ought to be home, on account of your brother.

DON *(half turning to him)*. Who says so?

NAT. You said so yourself. On account of you're going away somewheres.

DON. Huh?

NAT. Don't you remember?

He pushes the bag with the bottles and the apples toward Don. Don looks at them. Suddenly it penetrates. He is seized with alarm.

DON. What time is it?

NAT. Ten past six.

DON. Why didn't you tell me?

NAT. What do you think I've been doing for half an hour?

Don snatches up the bag, the apples spilling out as he does so. He turns to go. Nat points at what's left of Don's money on the bar.

NAT. Take your change.

Don scoops up the money, and hurries out.

THIRD AVENUE, corner of 55th Street, comes into view as Don comes from Nat's bar, and runs around the corner to his house. It is evening now.—Next we see the APARTMENT HOUSE where the Birnams live as Don, clutching the bag with the bottles, runs into the house.

We see the FIRST FLOOR HALL of the apartment house as Don dashes in and starts upstairs. After a few steps he stops. What if his brother is up there already? He stands undecided, then sneaks down the steps and walks to the rear of the entrance hall, where there's a glass door leading into the shabby garden.

[We see the GARDEN in back of the apartment house. Don comes out into the darkness, and walks far enough to be able to look up at the back of the building. Are the lights on in their apartment on the fourth floor? There is a light on the second floor, nothing on the third, and on the fourth the lights are on in the living room and bedroom windows, all of which are open. Don stands looking up. What shall he do? Go up and face the music? Run away? Weakly he walks over to the stone bench and sits down, putting the bottles on the bench next to him. He takes out his handkerchief and mops his forehead. His eyes go up to the lighted windows again.

We see the LIGHTED WINDOWS, from down below. Someone has stepped to the bedroom window. It's Helen. He can recognize her, silhouetted against the light of the room.—This cuts to a view of DON, sitting on the bench: His eyes are fixed on the window above. Instinctively, he draws back into the shadow of the sumac tree, as though Helen could see him through the darkness. Then we see the BEDROOM WINDOW, from DON's point of view as Helen disappears from the window into the room.]

Inside the BEDROOM: Helen is moving away from the window. Wick stands before his suitcase, which is open and all packed save for slippers and bathrobe, which he is rolling together.

HELEN. Do you suppose he's at Morandi's, or Nat's bar, or that place on Forty-second Street?

WICK. What difference does it make?

HELEN. You're not really going, Wick.

WICK. I certainly am.

He puts the robe with the slippers inside it into the case.

HELEN. You can't leave him alone. Not for four days. (*Wick slams shut the suitcase, and snaps the lock.*) Wick, for heaven's sake, if he's left alone anything can happen! I'll be tied up at the office every minute. All Saturday. All Sunday. I can't look out for him. You know how he gets. He'll be run over by a car. He'll be arrested. He doesn't know what he's doing. A cigarette will fall out of his mouth and he'll burn in his bed—

WICK. Oh Helen, if it happens, it happens. And I hope it *does*. I've had six years of this. I've had my bellyful.

HELEN. You can't mean that.

WICK (*taking his suitcase, going into the living room*). Yes, I do. It's terrible, I know, but I mean it.

As Helen follows him, the scene cuts to the LIVING ROOM. Wick comes in, sets down the suitcase, and during the ensuing scene takes a topcoat from the closet.

HELEN. For heaven's sake, Wick—

WICK. Who are we fooling? We've

tried everything, haven't we? We've reasoned 'with him, we've babied him. We've watched him like a hawk. We've tried trusting him. How often have you cried? How often have I beaten him up? We scrape him out of the gutter and pump some kind of self-respect into him, and back he falls, back in, every time.

HELEN. He's a sick person. It's as though he had something wrong with his lungs or his heart. You wouldn't walk out on him because he had an attack. He needs our help.

WICK. He won't accept our help. Not Don. He hates us. He wants to be alone with that bottle of his. It's the only thing he gives a hang about.

Helen turns away from Wick and leans against the wall, hoping he won't see that she's crying. Wick leans into the bedroom and snaps off the light. He picks up the suitcase, puts the topcoat over his arm, and takes her very gently by the arm.

WICK. Come, Helen. (*He leads her toward the entrance door.*)

[We again see DON, on the bench in the dark garden, as he stares toward the windows, then the WINDOWS, from below, and this time the bedroom window is dark. In the next second the lights in the living room also go off.]

DON picks up the bottles, rises, walks across the garden toward the glass door to the hall, and peers through it cautiously.]—We see, from Don's point of view, the STAIRCASE and HALL of the first floor of the apartment house as Wick and Helen come down the stairs, Wick carrying the suitcase and topcoat. They go out the front door.—Then we see them outside the APARTMENT HOUSE, where Wick is hailing a taxi.

WICK. Taxi! Taxi! (*To Helen*) I'll give you a lift as far as Grand Central.

HELEN. No thanks, Wick. I'm going to wait here.

WICK. You're crazy.

HELEN. Because I won t give up? Maybe I am.

WICK (*as a taxi drives up*). Oh Helen, give yourself a chance. Let go of him.

HELEN. Goodbye, Wick.

As Wick opens the door of the taxi, the scene cuts to DON at the glass door to the garden. He stands with the bag of bottles in his hand, peering through the entrance hall out to the street. Next we see the STREET as Wick gets into the taxi, and it drives off. Helen paces up and down in front of the house.—Don opens the glass door and steps cautiously into the entrance hall.

The ENTRANCE HALL: Squeezing close to the staircase wall so that Helen won't see him, Don gets to the staircase, then leaps up the stairs as though pursued.

We see the APARTMENT HOUSE as Helen waits outside the house. A couple of kids chasing each other on roller skates almost run into her. She steps back and stands in the doorway, looking up and down the street.

The STAIRS between the third and fourth floors come into view as Don is hurrying up on tiptoe, two steps at a time. Suddenly the door of a third-floor apartment toward the street is opened. Don flattens himself against the wall, not to be seen by Mrs. Deveridge, who is coming out with her dog, Sophie, to give her her evening airing. Sophie gives one bark in the direction of Don, but Mrs. Deveridge pays no attention and descends the stairs. Don starts up the stairs again, as silently and as fast as he can.

We see the FOURTH-FLOOR LANDING as Don gets to his door, opens it cautiously and slips inside; then the little ENTRANCE HALL of the Birnam apartment: The only light is the light from outside, coming through the living room and bedroom. Don steps inside, closing the door. He doesn't turn on the light but very carefully adjusts the chain on the door, and puts his hat away.

The LIVING ROOM: It is dim but for the light outside. As Don enters, he slips the bottles from the paper bag and puts them on a table next to the armchair. He crumples the bag and throws it in the fireplace. He takes one bottle, starts toward a bookcase and is about to hide it behind the books when he changes his mind. He looks around the room. His eyes fall on the ceiling. He goes to the table next to the couch, pulls it into the middle of the room, brushes some magazines to the floor, takes a small chair, puts it on the table, climbs to the table, from the table to the chair. He is now directly below the ceiling lighting fixture, an inverted metal bowl about two and a half feet in diameter. Don reaches over the edge and deposits the bottle inside the bowl so it can't be seen from the room. He climbs down, readjusts the table, the chair, and puts the magazines back. Don picks up a glass which is over a carafe on the mantelpiece. He puts it next to the bottle by the wing chair. He opens the bottle, pours a glass about three quarters full, puts the glass down. He loosens his tie and lets himself fall into the easy chair. He looks through the open window on the lights of New York. His eyes slowly wander to the glass. He smiles. It's a smile of relief, of contentment at being alone with his vice. There's a little pain in his smile, too.

We see the GLASS of WHISKEY as the camera moves toward it until the glass isn't visible any more—just a smooth sea of alcohol, with a little light playing on it. The camera plunges deep into that sea, and the scene fades out.

# PART TWO

The STAIRCASE and fourth floor LANDING fade in. Through the skylight streams a dazzling shaft of sunlight, falling square on the door of the Birnams' apartment. On the threshold lies a copy of the *New York Times,* and beside it stands a quart of milk. Pinned to the door is a piece of paper from a notebook. From inside there is the sound of the chain being detached, and the door opens slowly. Don emerges. He is dressed exactly as he was the day before—same suit, same shirt, same tie. He has slept in them and they are wrinkled. He hasn't shaved. As he comes out and the sun hits his face, he squints in agony. As he carefully closes the door, his eyes fall on the note. He reads it.

Don dear:

I waited for you to come home. Please be careful. Get some sleep. Eat. And call me, call me, call me.

Helen

There's a sly expression on Don's face as he closes the door, leaving everything just where it is—note, milk bottle, paper. Peering down, he assures himself that the coast is clear, and slips down the stairs.

[This dissolves to the exterior of the APARTMENT ·HOUSE. The entrance door is half open and Dave, the janitor, an Italian-looking man about fifty-five, is sweeping the sidewalk in front of the house. Don comes to the doorway, waits until Dave's back is turned, then hurries out and slips down the street, the view following him. Two houses down, in a semi-basement, is MRS. WERTHEIM's HAND LAUNDRY. Don goes down the steps into it.

In MRS. WERTHEIM'S LAUNDRY: The outer room is a kind of office, with a counter and shelves of clean laundry in boxes and paper packages. Steam issues from the actual laundry at the rear. MRS. WERTHEIM, a gray-haired, stocky woman, is sorting laundry. The shop's bell rings as Don comes in. His nerves are on edge but he manages to work up a little nonchalance.

DON. *Guten Tag,* Mrs. Wertheim. How's business?

MRS. WERTHEIM. Business he is good, thank you. There isn't a fortune in it, but you know; small fish, good fish. And I keep young and healthy. Why shouldn't I, sitting in a Turkish bath all day for free? (*She has picked a package from the shelf, and now puts it on the counter.*) Three dollars and ninety.

DON. I wonder if you could do me a favor, *gnaedige Frau?*

MRS. WERTHEIM. Always glad, Mr. Birñam.

DON. My brother's gone away for the weekend and he took the checkbook along . . .

MRS. WERTHEIM. Oh, you want a blank check?

DON. It's not that. It's just that I'm a little short.

MRS. WERTHEIM (*sizing up his stature*). What do you mean, you're short?

DON. I wonder if you could let me have a little cash, *bitte schoen?*

MRS. WERTHEIM. A little cash?

DON. I thought about twenty dollars, maybe. Only till Monday, when my brother comes back.

MRS. WERTHEIM. You thought . . . No, Mr. Birnam. I cannot. Not that I don't want to, because I want to, but I cannot. And when I say not, I mean *absolutely* not.

Her eyes fall on his tortured face. It's too much for her. She rings open the cash register.

MRS. WERTHEIM. I'll let you have five dollars.

DON. That's all right. (*As she hands him the five dollars*) Danke schoen, Mrs. Wertheim.

He turns and leaves; doesn't even hear her calling after him.

MRS. WERTHEIM. Your laundry, Mr. Birnam! How about your laundry?

She looks after him but there's only the ringing of the shop bell as he leaves.] This dissolves to NAT's BAR. There is brilliant sunshine outside. No one is in the bar but Nat: he is cooking some ham and eggs for himself on an electric plate behind the bar. The floor has been mopped and is still shiny. The chairs are piled on the tables. Into the bar comes Don. He is walking rather slowly, but it's a tremendous effort not to race in and yell for what he needs so desperately.

NAT. Hi.

Don goes to the bar and sits down. He

takes 'the five dollars from his pocket and puts it on the bar.

NAT. Thought you were going away for the weekend.

Don does not answer him. He sits holding his head in his hands. The bar is silent except for the sizzling noise of the eggs and ham. Suddenly Don pounds the bar and explodes.

DON. For the love of Pete, what are doing, Nat. Give me a drink!

NAT. Right with you, Mr. Birnam. Just fixing my lunch.

DON. Well, stop it and come on and give me a drink, for heaven's sake. (*Banging the bar.*) Come on, *come on!*

NAT. Okay.

He stirs the food once more, takes the skillet off the stove, and snaps off the electricity with a slowness agonizing to Don.

DON (*quietly, though his nerves are cracking*). Can't you hurry it up a ·little, Nat?

NAT (*pouring a jiggerful*). Here you are, Mr. Birnam.

DON. Thank you, Nat.

Don chokes it down and holds out the jigger for another. Nat pours it.

NAT. That young lady stopped in last night, looking for you.

DON. What young lady?

NAT. The one with the leopard coat.

DON. Yeah?

NAT. She was acting like she just happened to drop in, but I know she was making the rounds after you.

DON (*panicky*). What did you say to her?

NAT. I said you hadn't been in for two weeks.

DON. Good. I can't let her see me. Not now while I'm "off" like this.

NAT. Then why in the name of— Why don't you cut it short?

DON. You're talking like a child. You can't cut it short! You're on that merry-go-round and you've got to ride it all the way, round and round, till the blasted music wears itself out and the thing dies down and clunks to a stop.

NAT (*bringing over the plate of ham and eggs*). How about you eating this?

DON. Take it away.

NAT. You got to eat something sometime.

DON. Give me another drink.

NAT. Look, Mr. Birnam, this is still morning. (*He pours another drink. Don downs it.*)

DON. That's when you need it most, in the morning. Haven't you learned that, Nat? At night this stuff's a drink. In the morning it's medicine.

NAT. Okay if *I* eat?

DON. Move it a little to one side.

Don taps with the jigger. Nat fills it, then sits down to his ham and eggs.

DON. Nat, are you ever scared when you wake up? So scared the sweat starts out of you? No, not you. With you it's simple. Your alarm clock goes off and you open your eyes and brush your teeth and read the *Daily Mirror.* That's all. Do you ever lie in your bed looking at the window? A little daylight's coming through, and you start wondering: is it getting lighter, is it getting darker? Is it dawn or dusk? That's a terrifying problem, Nat. You hold your breath and you pray that it's dusk, so you can go out and get yourself some more liquor. Because if it's dawn, you're dead. The bars are closed and the liquor stores don't open till nine. You can't last till nine. Or it might be Sunday. That's the worst. No liquor stores at all, and you guys wouldn't open a bar, not until one o'clock. Why? *Why,* Nat?

NAT. Because we got to go to church once in a while. That's why.

DON. Yes, when a guy needs it most. (*He drinks his jiggerful.*)

NAT. How about those two quarts? Did you polish them off last night?

DON. What two quarts?

NAT. The two bottles you had.

DON (*an electric current running through him*). That's right, I did have two bottles, didn't I? I hid one of them. I've still got it. I'm a capitalist, Nat! I've got untapped reserves. I'm *rich!* (*He taps the glass on the bar.*)

NAT (*pouring another drink*). Mr. Birnam, if you had enough money you'd kill yourself in a month.

Gloria enters from the street, wearing a shirtwaist and skirt, another foolish little hat, and high-heeled shoes with bows.

GLORIA. Say, Nat, was there a gentleman— (*She sees Don.*) Hello, Mr. Birman. Didn't you go away for the weekend?

DON. Apparently not, Gloria.

GLORIA (*back to Nat*). Was there a gentleman in here asking for me?

NAT. Not to my knowledge there

wasn't. (*He is drinking his coffee.*)

GLORIA. He was supposed to come around twelve o'clock. He's from Albany.

DON. Another friend of the folks?

GLORIA. More a friend of a friend of the folks type. A fellow telephoned me about him. Wants me to show him the town.

NAT. Like Grant's Tomb for instance?

GLORIA. But def.

NAT. Amazing, ain't it, how many guys run down from Albany just to see Grant's Tomb.

GLORIA (*to Don*). Sometimes I wish *you* came from Albany.

DON. Where would you take me?

GLORIA. Oh, lots of places. The Music Hall, and then the New Yorker Roof maybe.

DON. There is now being presented at a theatre on Fourty-fourth Street the uncut version of *Hamlet.* I see us as setting out for that. Do you know Hamlet?

GLORIA. I know Forty-fourth Street.

DON. I'd like to get your interpretation of Hamlet's character.

GLORIA. And I'd like to give it to you.

DON. Dinner afterwards, I think. Nothing before. Always see Shakespeare on an empty stomach.

GLORIA. Not even a pretzel? (*Don shakes his head.*)

[DON. But afterwards, dozens of bluepoints in the Rainbow Room. And a very light wine. Vouvray perhaps. Do you care for Vouvray?

GLORIA (*mystified*). Why, natch.

DON. We may blindfold the orchestra

so that I can dance with abandon.

GLORIA. Aren't you going to dance with me?

DON. Of course, little Gloria.]

A man has entered the bar, a round-faced, middle-aged man with pince-nez. There is a *Guide of New York* sticking from his pocket. He's the guy from Albany, all right.

ALBANY (*rather loud*). Could I have a glass of water?

NAT. Why, sure. And what shall it be for a chaser?

ALBANY (*confidentially*). Tell me: This is Nat's bar, isn't it?

NAT. That's what the man said.

ALBANY. I'm looking for a young lady name of Gloria.

With his thumb, Nat indicates Gloria.

ALBANY (*beaming*). Are you Miss Gloria?

GLORIA. Who, me? No, I'm not. I just live with Gloria. She's not here.

ALBANY. She isn't?

GLORIA. Ruptured appendix. Middle of last night. Went like that! (*She lets out her breath with an exploding noise.*) Scared the life out of me.

ALBANY. That's terrible.

GLORIA. Goodbye.

ALBANY. Goodbye. (*He takes a couple of steps toward the door, then turns.*) Could I have a word with *you?*

GLORIA. No thanks. Thanks a lot, but no thanks.

ALBANY. You're welcome, I'm sure. (*He walks out, bewildered.*)

DON. Wasn't that rather rude, Gloria,

to send that nice man all alone to Grant's Tomb?

GLORIA. When I have a chance to go out with you? Don't be ridic.

DON. Oh, is our engagement definite?

GLORIA. You meant it, didn't you?

DON. Surely, surely. (*He downs the jigger of rye.*)

GLORIA. I'm going to get a facial, a fingerwave, a manicure. The works. Right now. (*With a sudden thought*) You're going to call for me, aren't you? If you are, what time?

DON. What time do you suggest?

GLORIA. How about eight?

DON. Eight's fine.

GLORIA. I live right in the corner house. You know where the antique shop is, the one with the wooden Indian outside? They've got the Indian sign on me, I always say.

DON. I'll be there.

GLORIA. Second floor. Oh, Mr. Birnam, all I've got is a semi-formal. Will that be all right?

DON. That'll be fine.

GLORIA (*happily*). Goodbye, Nat. (*She starts for the door, and goes out.*)

DON. One last one, Nat. Pour it softly, pour it gently, and pour it to the brim.

NAT. Look, Mr. Birnam, there's a lot of bars on Third Avenue. Do me a favor—get out of here and buy it someplace else.

DON. What's the matter?

NAT. I don't like you much. What was the idea of pulling her leg? You know you're never going to take her out.

DON. Who says I'm not?

NAT. I say so. You're drunk and you're just making with your mouth.

DON. Give me a drink, Nat.

NAT. And that other dame—I mean the lady. I don't like what you're doing to her either.

DON. Shut up.

NAT. You should've seen her last night, coming in here looking for you, with her eyes all rainy and the mascara all washed away.

DON. Give me a drink!

NAT. That's an awful high-class young lady.

DON. You bet she is.

NAT. How the heck did she ever get mixed up with a guy that sops it up like you do?

DON. It's a problem, isn't it? That nice young man that drinks, and the high-class young lady, and how did she ever get mixed up with him, and why does he drink and why doesn't he stop. That's my novel, Nat. I wanted to start writing it out in the country. Morbid stuff. Nothing for the Book-of-the-Month Club. A horror story. The confessions of a booze addict, the log book of an alcoholic. (*Holding out the jigger*) Come on, Nat, break down. (*As Nat does break down and pours a drink*) Do you know what I'm going to call my novel? *The Bottle*—that's all. Very simply, *The Bottle*. I've got it all in my mind. Let me tell you the first chapter. It all starts one wet afternoon about three years ago. There was a matinee of *La Traviata* at the Metropolitan—

This slowly dissolves to the exterior of the METROPOLITAN OPERA HOUSE in a heavy rain on an autumn afternoon. The view shooting down, we look past the glass-and-iron marquee toward the entrance, beside which is a billboard announcing Verdi's LA TRAVIATA. A crowd of people is streaming into the building. They are wearing raincoats, carrying umbrellas.

The scene cuts to the VESTIBULE and CLOAKROOM WINDOW at the METROPOLITAN. It is doing a land-office business, checking dripping umbrellas and apparel. Among the crowd is Don Birnam. He is alone and wears a bowler and a straight raincoat. He takes off his hat and shakes the rain from it, then peels off his raincoat. In the side pocket of his suit is a pint of liquor. It bulges and the nose projects. For a second Don considers whether it'll pass muster, but it's a little too prominent. With a quick gesture he transfers the bottle to the pocket of the raincoat, rolls the raincoat up like swaddling clothes around a precious infant. Seeing an opening in the line at the cloak room counter, he steps into it. There is a great confusion of hands, coats, coat checks, customers and overworked attendants. Don hands his coat to an attendant. His eyes linger on its pocket with a certain tenderness, then he turns and starts toward the door of the auditorium.

The scene dissolves to a SECTION OF SEATS at the Metropolitan where Don sits about five seats from the aisle. He is under the pleasant spell of the overture of *La Traviata*. He sits between an elderly daughter and her age-old mother, and a middle-aged man and wife. He is glancing through the program as the curtain rises and the light changes. Don looks up, and we alternately see the STAGE and DON.

The STAGE: The set is a Louis XIVth salon, in the year 1700. It's Violetta's supper. The guests are singing "Libiamo, libiamo," which is a drinking song in waltz time.—Then we get a close view of DON. He loves music and especially Italian opera, but maybe he'd have come late if he'd remembered the content of the first scene.

On the STAGE: Powdered footmen are pouring wine into the glasses of the over-vivacious guests.—Then we get a close view of DON. Thirst in his eyes, he looks away from the stage and tries to concentrate on the ceiling of the Metropolitan. No go. His eyes wander back to:

The STAGE: Alfred and Violetta are batting the drinking song back and forth, as the chorus, glasses in hand, stands slowly swaying, echoing each couplet. —DON: That thirst is coming up again. The first drops of sweat are gathering on his forehead. As he looks at the stage, his imagination is working at top speed.

The STAGE: The swaying echelon of choristers slowly dissolves to a row of raincoats, exactly like the one Don wore. They hang from hangers and sway slowly to Verdi's rhythm.—DON's FACE: His eyes are glued to what he sees on the stage. He takes the handkerchief from his pocket and wipes his forehead.

The STAGE: The raincoats sway slowly. The camera approaches one of them. From the pocket projects a bottle of whiskey.—DON: He is wiping his parched mouth. He puts the handkerchief back. He fishes the coat check from his pocket, buries it in his fist, fighting the foolish impulse. It's a short struggle, which he loses. He rises and, to the irritation of his neighbors, leaves his seat amid some disapproving shushings from the row behind.

The scene dissolves to the CLOAK ROOM and VESTIBULE. It is completely empty save for the elderly attendant, who is dozing over his paper. From inside comes Verdi's music and Don Birnam. He puts the check on the counter. The attendant looks up from a newspaper.

ATTENDANT. Did you forget something?

DON. No. Going home, if it's all right with you.

The attendant takes the check and leaves. Don rolls his program and sticks it into the sand of the cuspidor. He is filled with a nervous anticipation of the drink which is on its way. The attendant returns.

ATTENDANT. Say, this isn't yours.

Don looks. The attendant holds a short leopard coat and a lady's small umbrella.

DON. No, it certainly isn't.

ATTENDANT (*comparing the check with the number on the hanger*). That's what it says though—417.

DON. I don't care what it says.

ATTENDANT. The checks must have got mixed up.

DON. Maybe they did. Find me my coat. It's a plain man's raincoat and a derby.

ATTENDANT. Are you kidding? Do

you know how many plain men's raincoats we have on a day like this? About a thousand.

DON. Let me get back there. I can find it.

ATTENDANT. That's ·against regulations, sir.

DON. I'm not going to wait till the end of the performance.

ATTENDANT. You can get your coat tomorrow.

Don's nervousness is mounting. He is searching his pockets.

DON. Look, man, there's something in the pocket of that coat I—It so happens I find myself without any money and I need that coat. And I need it *now*.

ATTENDANT. Listen, if everybody went in there digging through those coats . . . There's regulations. There's got to be regulations.

DON. What do you suggest?

ATTENDANT. You just wait till the other party comes and then you can swap.

DON. I want my coat.

ATTENDANT. As far as I'm concerned, that's your coat. (*He shoves the leopard coat and umbrella close to Don.*)

DON. You're a great help.

He is biting his lips, unable to find another argument. The attendant has returned to the other end of the counter and resumed his doze. Don gets out a cigarette. Without opening his eyes, the attendant calls out:

ATTENDANT. No smoking.

DON (*sourly*). I thought so. (*He puts the cigarette away and leans back on the counter, arms folded.*)

The scene dissolves to the VESTIBULE, near the CLOAK ROOM. It is empty, save for Don, who paces up and down nervously, carrying the leopard coat and the umbrella. He glances over the coat a little, at the initials inside, at the label. Over the scene comes a muted aria from the second act.

This dissolves to a STAIRCASE leading to the gallery. It is empty, save for Don, who sits on a step, the coat next to him. With the umbrella he is nervously tracing the pattern in the carpet. Inside, the music rises to a finale and the first people start streaming down from the gallery. Don grabs up the coat and hurries toward the cloak room.

The VESTIBULE and CLOAK ROOM: People are streaming up from all sides to get their belongings. Don comes into the scene, and, standing on his toes, tries to locate the claimant of his coat and hat.—Another dissolve indicates a lapse of time in the VESTIBULE and CLOAK ROOM. It is almost empty now, and Don still stands with the coat, looking. As the last few people leave, at the far end of the counter he sees Helen, his coat over her arm, his derby in her hand. She sees him with her coat and her umbrella and the two approach slowly.

DON (*trying to control his irritation*). That's my coat you've got.

HELEN. And that's mine, thank heaven. They mixed up the checks.

DON. They certainly did. I thought you'd never come.

He takes his coat rather brusquely, and thrusts the leopard coat at her.

HELEN. You can't have been waiting so long.

DON. Only since the first aria of the first act. That's all.

HELEN. Do you always just drop in for the overture?

Don takes the coat, feels it hurriedly to make sure the bottle is still there, and starts away.

DON. Goodbye. (*Helen is left with the leopard coat and his bowler.*)

HELEN (*waving the hat toward Don*). Hey, wait a minute!

Don comes back, takes the hat, and starts away again.

HELEN. My umbrella, if you don't mind.

His patience exhausted, Don stops again, takes the umbrella and tosses it in Helen's direction. Helen, who is getting into her coat, can't catch it. It falls right next to her.

HELEN. Thank you very much.

Don stands abashed. He goes back, picks up the umbrella.

DON. I'm terribly sorry.

HELEN. You're the rudest person I ever saw. What's the matter with you?

DON. Just rude, I guess.

HELEN. Really, somebody should talk to your mother.

DON. They tried, Miss St. John.

HELEN. My name is not St. John.

DON. St. Joseph, then.

HELEN. St. James.

DON. First name Hilda or Helen, or Harriet maybe?

HELEN. Helen.

DON. You come from Toledo, Ohio.

HELEN. How do you know?

DON. I've had three long acts to work you out from that coat of yours. Initials, label—Alfred Spitzer, Fine Furs, Toledo,·Ohio.

HELEN. Maybe I should have explored *your* coat.

DON. But you didn't.

HELEN. Didn't have time.

DON. Good. *My* name is Don Birnam.

As they go on talking, they walk from the cloak room, through the vestibule, to the street, Don carrying his coat over his arm.

DON. How do you like New York?

HELEN. Love it.

DON. How long are you going to stay?

HELEN. Oh, sixty years, perhaps. (*Don doesn't get it.*) I live here now. I've got a job.

DON. Doing what?

HELEN. I'm on *Time Magazine.*

DON. *Time Magazine?* In that case perhaps you could do something for me.

HELEN. Yes.

DON. Could you help me to become Man of the Year?

HELEN. Delighted. What do you do?

DON. Yes, what *do* I do? I'm a writer. I've just started a novel. I've started quite a few novels. I never seem to finish one.

HELEN. In that case, why not write short stories.

DON. I have some of those. The first

paragraph. Then there's one-half of the opening scene of a play. It all takes place in the leaning tower of Pisa and explains why it leans. And why all sensible buildings *should* lean.

HELEN. They'll love that in Toledo.

DON. Are you by any chance coming here to *Lohengrin* next week?

HELEN. I don't know.

DON. Because if you are, I'm not going to let this coat out of my hands.

HELEN. Don't worry.

DON. I do, though. To be really safe, maybe we should go together.

HELEN. We could.

DON. Are you in the telephone book?

HELEN. Yes, but I'm not home very much.

DON. Then I'll call you at the office.

HELEN. Editorial Research. If Henry Luce answers the phone, hang up.

They have reached the curb outside the Metropolitan. It is dark and the rain has settled to a drizzle.

DON. Taxi?

HELEN. No, thank you. I'm taking the subway.

DON. Very sensible.

HELEN. As a matter of fact, I'm going to an extremely crazy party on Washington Square. If you want, I'll take you along.

There is a split second of indecision but it is ended by Don's awareness of the bottle in his raincoat.

DON. Thank you very much, Miss St.

James, but I have to see a friend uptown.

HELEN. Goodbye, Mr. Birnam.

DON. Goodbye.

He is unfurling his raincoat in order to put it on before he steps from under the marquee. Helen is about a step and a half away when there is a crash. She stops and looks down, as does Don. On the sidewalk lies the pint of whiskey, broken.

HELEN. Who threw that?

DON (*casually*). It fell out of my pocket.

HELEN. Do you always carry those things?

DON. You see . . . that friend, the one uptown, he has a cold. I thought I'd take this along and make him a hot toddy.

HELEN. Now he gets hot lemonade and some aspirin.

DON. I shall.

HELEN. Goodbye.

She goes. Don looks at the broken bottle, then after Helen. With sudden decision he calls after her.

DON. Miss St. James!

HELEN (*turning*). Yes?

DON. What kind of a party was that you asked me to?

HELEN. A cocktail party.

DON. Invitation still stand?

HELEN. Of course. Come on.

He joins her, takes the umbrella out of her hand and holds it over them both as they go down the street.

This dissolves to NAT'S BAR as we have left it, empty save for Nat and Don. Sunlight can be seen outside. Nat is now taking the chairs from the tables and arranging the bar for the afternoon and evening trade, while Don leans back against the bar, the jigger of whiskey in his hand, and goes on talking.

DON. How's that for a first meeting, Nat? Cute, full of laughs. A charming girl, an extra special girl. Her coat-check might just as well have been mixed up with the coat-check of a solid citizen, the son of the chairman of some insurance company, highly eligible, no vices except that sometimes he plays the cello. But oh no, that would have made everything too simple. It had to be that young man with the bottle.

NAT. Listen, once that bottle smashes, doesn't she catch on?

DON. No, she doesn't.

NAT. Okay. So they go to that cocktail party and he gets stinko and falls flat on his face.

DON. He doesn't. He's crazy about that girl by then. He drinks tomato juice. Doesn't touch liquor for that whole week—for two weeks, for six weeks.

NAT. He's in love, huh?

DON. That's what's going to be hard to write. Love's the hardest thing in the world to write about. So simple. You've got to catch it through details, like the early morning sunlight hitting the gray tin of the ashcans in front of her house. A ringing telephone that sounds like Beethoven's *Pastoral*. A letter scribbled on her office stationery that you carry in your pocket because it smells of all the lilacs in Ohio.

NAT. And no drinking?

DON. He thinks he's cured. If he can get a job now, they can be married and that's that. Only it's not, Nat. Not quite. Because one day, one terrible day— (*He taps the jigger.*) Pour it, Nat.

NAT (*pouring the drink*). Yeah? (*Don drinks.*) Well, go on.

DON. You see, that girl's been writing to her family in Toledo. They want to meet this young man. So they come to New York. They stay at the Hotel Manhattan. Their very first day, she's to introduce him to her parents. One o'clock. Lobby of the hotel . . .

The scene slowly dissolves to the LOBBY of the MANHATTAN HOTEL. It is filled with the routine activity of a big commercial hotel on a hot summer day. Don Birnam, in a light summer suit, paces up and down the lobby. Under his arm is a florist's box. He keeps eyeing the doors to the elevators. He walks toward one of those circular plush settees common to hotels, sits down, puts the flower box next to him and adjusts the knot of his tie, his eye still on the elevator doors. On the other side of the settee are a middle-aged couple. Don can't see them, they can't see him, as he overhears their conversation, and it takes him a little time to realize that they are Helen's parents. MR. ST. JAMES is wearing a linen suit and a good but yellowing panama hat, the brim turned up. MRS. ST. JAMES is a cheerful little woman with glasses pinned to her dress, the kind that pull. Mr. St. James is fuming a little.

DON: I can't be trusted. Is that it?

NAT: Why don't you lay off the stuff for a while.

MAN: They're closed . . . we've got an agreement.

. . . There whirs past him a strange winged thing.

MR. ST. JAMES. Just walked in for a simple haircut. No, that wasn't enough, not for New York. They gave me a shampoo, a scalp massage, a manicure. Thought they'd tear my shoes off and paint my toenails.

MRS. ST. JAMES (*laughing comfortably*). I had a lovely morning. Just did a little window shopping. I didn't want to get all tired out.

MR. ST. JAMES. On account of meeting that young man? Now, Mother.

MRS. ST. JAMES. Who did you get a haircut for?

MR. ST. JAMES. Wonder what's keeping Helen.

MRS. ST. JAMES. She'll be here.

MR. ST. JAMES. This Birnam fellow went to Cornell, didn't he?

MRS. ST. JAMES. I believe so, but Helen says he never graduated.

MR. ST. JAMES. I wonder why. How old is he?

MRS. ST. JAMES. Thirty-three.

MR. ST. JAMES. He has no job. As far as I can find out, he never had one. I wish Helen wasn't so vague.

By now Don knows only too well that he is the subject of their discussion. He leans his head against the back of the settee, acutely uncomfortable.

MRS. ST. JAMES. Maybe he has a little money. Some people do, you know, Father.

MR. ST. JAMES. He ought to have a job anyway.

MRS. ST. JAMES. He's a writer.

MR. ST. JAMES. A writer? What does he write? I never heard of his name.

MRS. ST. JAMES. Now Father, relax. You always expect the worst. I've made up my mind he's a well-brought-up young man who wipes his feet before he enters a house and doesn't even smoke.

MR. ST. JAMES. I hope he realizes Helen's our only daughter and we ought to know a few things about him.

MRS. ST. JAMES. Those'll all come out —his background, his prospects, his church affiliations.

Don can't take any more of this. He picks up the florist's box, rises and moves away from the settee. When he has reached the security of some potted palms, he looks back. Through one of the revolving doors comes Helen, in a new spring suit. She looks around, sees her parents, and goes up to them. There is a greeting, some conversation apparently about Don and the fact that he'll get there any minute. She sits on the settee between her parents, all three of them waiting for Don.

Don stands undecided, then looks around, locates the public telephone booths and steps into one of them.

Inside the TELEPHONE BOOTH: Don deposits a nickel and dials the number of the Hotel Manhattan, which is above the mouthpiece of the phone.

DON. Manhattan Hotel? . . . Will you page Miss St. James? She must be in the lobby.

He holds the phone and looks through the glass door of the telephone booth. —We then see the LOBBY, from Don's point of view, as a bell-hop crosses the lobby, paging Miss St. James. Helen rises and follows him over to the line of house phones on a shelf. She picks up the phone and speaks.

DON (*at the phone*). Helen? . . .
Don. I'm terribly sorry but I can't
get there for a while. Please go ahead
with your lunch and apologize to
your parents . . . No, nothing serious. I'll be there. Goodbye. (*He
hangs up.*)

The LOBBY, from Don's angle, as seen
through the glass of Don's phone booth:
Helen has hung up too. She goes toward
her parents, her face a little crestfallen.
As she joins them she evidently starts
to explain.

Outside the TELEPHONE BOOTH: Don
emerges with the florist's box, careful
not to be seen. He leaves through one
of the side doors.

This dissolves to the LIVING ROOM at
the BIRNAM BROTHERS' APARTMENT at
twilight. In the dim foreground stands
a small table, beyond it the vague contours of Don lying on the couch. On
the floor beside him there is an empty
bottle, in his hand a half-filled glass.
There are footsteps from the stairs. A
key is turned in the lock, and Wick
enters. He wears a hat and carries a
brief case. He switches on the light in
the little entrance hall, flips his hat
jauntily to a hook on the coat-rack and
comes into the living room. As he
crosses the threshold he becomes aware
of Don's presence.

WICK. Don?

He snaps on the light, sees Don on the
couch, drunk. Don doesn't move an
inch, only his eyes close.

DON. Turn off that light.

WICK. For heaven's sake, Don.

DON. *Turn it off!*

Wick snaps off the light. From now on

there is no light save for the shaft of
light from the entrance hall. Wick
throws the brief case into a chair.

WICK. I thought you were with Helen
and her father and mother. (*Receiving no answer*) What happened?

Still no answer. Wick sits down beside
Don taking the glass from his hand.

WICK (*gently*). Come on, Don.

DON. I couldn't face it.

WICK. You couldn't face what?
Didn't you go to see them?

DON. Certainly I went. One o'clock
sharp. And I saw them, all right.
Only they didn't see me.

WICK. How was that?

DON. Such nice, respectable people.
I couldn't face them, Wick, and all
the questions they'd ask me. I couldn't
face them. Not cold. I had to have
a drink first. Just one. Only the one
didn't do anything to me.

WICK. So you had another and another. You poor idiot, Don. Won't
you ever learn, with you it's like
stepping off a roof and expecting
to fall just one floor?

DON (*putting his arm over his face*).
You're right, you're right. There's
nothing I can say. (*There is a long
second of silence, Wick looking at
Don.*) Go ahead. Bawl me out, Wick,
let me have it. Why don't you take
that bottle and smash it over my face.

There is another pause. Wick speaks
very quietly.

WICK. It's a quarter of eight. I suppose they're still in that hotel, waiting for you.

DON. Call her up, Wick, will you?

Tell her something. Tell her I'm sick. Tell her I'm dead. (*Wick has bent over Don and loosened his tie.*) Will you call her?

WICK. Yes, I'll call her.

DON. She must have written them a lot of nice things about me. What a gentleman I am. A prince.

WICK. Which hotel is it?

DON. The Manhattan. Mr. and Mrs. Charles St. James from Toledo, Ohio.

Paying no attention to the sound of steps which has been coming from the staircase, Wick rises, puts the glass of whiskey on the table and is about to cross toward the telephone when the doorbell rings—short, short, long, short. Wick freezes. Don sits up on the couch. They know that ring. There is a helpless look in Don's eyes.

WICK (*whispering*). Get up, Don.

Don, clinging to Wick's arm, pulls himself up. Wick pushes him through the doorway to the dark bedroom, closing the door after him. The bell rings again, that same ring.

WICK. Just a minute, Helen.

He snaps on the lights in the living room, rolls the empty bottle under the couch, takes the glass of whiskey, puts it behind the pile of records. As he is starting toward the door, the bottle rolls from under the couch. Wick stops and rolls it back again, then goes into the hall and opens the door. Helen, in a great hurry, stands outside, nervous.

HELEN. Hello, Wick. Is Don here?

WICK. Don? No.

HELEN (*coming into the living room*). Any idea where he could be?

WICK. Wasn't he meeting you?

DON, in the dark bedroom, stands leaning against the wall, breathing heavily. His eyes gleam with anxiety. Coming from the living room, stabbing him deep, is:

HELEN'S VOICE. He was supposed to meet us for lunch, then he telephoned he'd be late. Mother's beginning to think I just made him up.

In the LIVING ROOM:

HELEN. Do you suppose something's happened to him?

WICK. Nonsense.

HELEN. But surely he'd have called back if he were all right.

WICK. Where did he call you from?

HELEN. I don't know.

WICK. I think I've got an idea. He called from out of town.

HELEN. Out of town? Where?

WICK. Philadelphia.

HELEN. What's he doing in Philadelphia?

WICK. There's an opening on the *Philadelphia Inquirer*. The Book Section. Don wrote them. He wired. I think this morning early he just took a train.

HELEN. He never told me a word about it.

WICK. I'm not supposed to tell you either. He wanted it to be a surprise.

HELEN. He did!

DON, in the dark bedroom: He suffers like a dog as he hears what's being said in the living room.

WICK'S VOICE. He probably couldn't

get to the right people right away, missed a train. You know how it is.

HELEN'S VOICE. Oh, it would be just wonderful if he got the job and started working. Or would it, Wick, with him in Philadelphia and me in New York?

In the LIVING ROOM, we again see WICK and HELEN.

HELEN. Don't ever tell him I said that though, will you?

WICK. Of course not.

Suddenly his eyes are transfixed. The bottle has rolled out from under the couch. As Helen speaks, he tries to get near it without her noticing.

HELEN. I could never understand why somebody like Don, a person with so much talent, such flashes of real brilliance . . . Maybe I'm a little prejudiced.

Suddenly she sees Wick trying to kick the bottle back under the couch.

HELEN. What are you doing, Wick?

WICK. Nothing, Helen.

HELEN. Where'd that bottle come from?

WICK. It just rolled out.

HELEN. From under the couch?

WICK. Yes, Helen. (*With an attempt at casualness*) It's my guess that Don caught an early train.

HELEN (*guessing wildly*). Is that Don's bottle?

WICK. What makes you think that?

HELEN. There was a bottle the first time we met.

WICK. There was?

HELEN. It fell out of Don's pocket.

WICK. It was for me, Helen.

We again see DON in the DARK BEDROOM. He is standing with his head against the door post, listening, harassed.

WICK'S VOICE. This one is mine, too. You might as well hear the family scandal. I drink.

WICK and HELEN in the LIVING ROOM:

WICK. Don thinks I drink too much.

(*He walks over to the records and picks up the glass.*) I had to promise I'd go on the wagon. That's why I hid the bottle, so he wouldn't see it.

(*He takes a drink.*)

HELEN. I'm so sorry, Wick. I shouldn't have started asking questions. It was none of my business.

WICK. Forget it.

DON, in the DARK BEDROOM: His brother's gesture has shaken him.

HELEN'S VOICE. I'd better be getting back to the hotel. Don may be there already. And don't worry, Wick, I won't mention this to him.

WICK'S VOICE. Thank you, Helen.

HELEN'S VOICE. Goodbye, Wick.

WICK'S VOICE. Goodbye.

She goes toward the front door. With sudden decision Don opens the door to the living room and walks slowly out.

DON. Helen!

The LIVING ROOM and ENTRANCE HALL: Almost at the door to the entrance hall, Helen turns back. Wick stands, the glass of whiskey in his hand, startled taut at the sight of Don who comes in, not too steady on his feet.

DON. I'm sorry, Helen. I can't let you go. Not like that.

HELEN. Don!

WICK. Shut your mouth, Don. (*To Helen*) I'll take you downstairs.

DON. Thank you very much for your Philadelphia story, Wick. Nice try.

Helen comes back into the room, staring at Don. She is beginning to realize that he's drunk. Don looks at the glass in Wick's hand.

DON. That looks so silly on you.

He takes the glass out of Wick's hand.

WICK (*to Helen*). Don't listen to him.

DON. You don't have to. Just look at the two of us.

HELEN. Yes. What's all this covering up?

WICK. All that happened is that Don was nervous at the idea of meeting your parents and so he took a couple of drinks.

DON. Come on, Wick, she'd have found out sooner or later.

HELEN. Stop it, both of you. Don's a little tight. Most people drink a little. A lot of them get tight once in a while.

DON. Sure. The lucky ones who can take it or leave it. But then there are the ones who can't take it, but can't leave it either. What I'm trying to say is I'm not a drinker. I'm a drunk. They had to put me away once.

WICK. He went to a cure.

DON. Which didn't take. That first day we met, you see, the dirty trick

was I should have had the decency to get drunk, just for your sake.

HELEN. For *my* sake? We're talking about you. (*Turning to Wick*) Is it really that bad, Wick?

DON. Yes, it is.

WICK. Can't we go over this tomorrow, Don, when you're feeling more like yourself?

DON. Helen's heard the facts. That's all there is to it.

HELEN. I've heard them and they're not very pleasant. But they could be worse. After all, you're not an embezzler or a murderer. You drink too much. That's not fatal. One cure didn't take. There are others.

WICK. Of course there are.

DON. This has a familiar ring.

HELEN. There must be a reason why you drink. The right doctor can find it.

DON. I'm way ahead of the right doctor. I know the reason. The reason is me. What I am. Or, rather, what I'm not.

HELEN. What aren't you that you want to be, Don?

DON. A writer. Silly, isn't it? You see, in college I passed for a genius. They couldn't get out the college magazine without one of my stories. Boy, was I hot! Hemingway stuff. I reached my peak when I was nineteen. Sold a piece to the *Atlantic Monthly*. It was reprinted in the *Reader's Digest*. Who wants to stay in college when he's Hemingway? My mother bought me a brand new typewriter, and I moved right in on New York. Well, the first thing I wrote, that didn't quite come off. And the second I dropped. The public wasn't ready for that one. I started a third, a fourth, only about then somebody began to look over my shoulder and whisper, in a thin, clear voice like the E-string on a violin. Don Birnam, he'd whisper, it's not good enough. Not that way. How about a couple of drinks just to put it on its feet? So I had a couple. Oh, that was a great idea. That made all the difference. Suddenly I could see the whole thing—the tragic sweep of the great novel, beautifully proportioned. But before I could really grab it and throw it down on paper, the drink would wear off and everything be gone like a mirage. Then there was despair, and a drink to counterbalance despair, and one to counterbalance the counterbalance. I'd be sitting in front of that typewriter, trying to squeeze out a page that was halfway decent, and that guy would pop up again.

HELEN. What guy? Who are you talking about?

DON. The other Don Birnam. There are two of us, you know: Don the drunk and Don the writer. And the drunk will say to the writer, "Come on, you idiot. Let's get some good out of that portable. Let's hock it. We'll take it to that pawn shop over on Third Avenue. Always good for ten dollars, for another drink, another binge, another bender, another spree." Such humorous words. I tried to break away from that guy a lot of ways. No good. Once I even bought myself a gun and some bullets. (*He goes to the desk.*) I meant to do it on my thirtieth birthday.

He opens the drawer, takes out two bullets and holds them in the palm of his hand.

DON. Here are the bullets. The gun went for three quarts of whiskey. That other Don wanted us to have a drink first. He always wants us to have a drink first. The flop suicide of a flop writer.

WICK. All right, maybe you're not a writer. Why don't you do something else?

DON. Yes, take a nice job. Public accountant, real estate salesman. I haven't the guts, Helen. Most men lead lives of quiet desperation. I can't take quiet desperation.

HELEN. But you are a writer. You have every quality for it. Imagination, wit, pity—

DON. Come on, let's face reality. I'm thirty-three and I'm living on the charity of my brother. Room and board free, and fifty cents a week for cigarettes. An occasional ticket for a concert or a show, out of the bigness of his heart. And it is a big heart, a patient heart.

WICK. Now, Don, I'm just carrying you along for the time being.

DON. Shut up, Wick. I've never done anything, I'm not doing anything, I never will do anything. Zero, zero, zero.

HELEN. Now *you* shut up. We'll straighten it out.

DON. Look. Wick has the misfortune to be my brother. You just walked in on this, and if you know what's good for you, you'll turn around and walk out again. Walk fast and don't turn back.

Helen looks at him for a second, then takes off her hat and throws it into a near-by chair.

HELEN (*to Wick*). Why don't you make some coffee, Wick? Strong. Three cups. (*Wick goes into the kitchenette.*)

DON. Do yourself a favor, Helen. Go on, clear out.

HELEN. Because I've got a rival? Because you're in love with this? (*She points at the bottle.*) You don't know me, Don. I'm going to fight and fight and fight. Bend down. (*He doesn't bend. She raises herself to her tiptoes and kisses him warmly.*)

This dissolves back to NAT'S BAR, later in the day. Nat and Don are alone. Nat is behind the bar, putting toothpicks into olives which he takes from a bowl and arranges in a row on a plate. Don, about ten wet rings in front of him and what's left of Mrs. Wertheim's five dollars, is playing with a full jigger of rye.

DON. That was three years ago, Nat. That's a long time to keep fighting, to keep believing. They'd try a health farm, a psychiatrist, a sanatorium in New Jersey. No go. She'd be patient. She'd be gay. She'd encourage him. She'd buy a new ribbon for his typewriter—a two-color job, black and red. Just write, Don. Keep writing. That first paragraph came off so well . . . There was no second paragraph. There were drinks. Drinks sneaked in secret. In the bathroom, here, in Harlem. Promises again, lies again. But she holds on. She knows she's clutching a razor blade but she won't let go. Three years of it.

NAT. And what? How does it come out?

DON. I don't know. Haven't figured that far.

NAT. Want me to tell you? One day your guy gets wise to himself and gets back that gun. Or, if he's only got a dollar ten, he goes up to the Empire State Building, way up on top, and then— (*He snaps his fingers.*) Or he can do it for a nickel, in a subway under a train.

DON. Think so, Nat? What if Helen is right, after all, and he sits down and turns out something good—but good—and that pulls him up and snaps him out of it?

NAT. This guy? Not from where I sit.

DON (*jumping up*). Shut up, Nat. I'm going to do it. I'm going to do it now. It's all there. You heard it.

NAT. Yes, Mr. Birnam.

DON. That's why I didn't go on that weekend, see, so I can be alone up there and sit down at my typewriter. This time I'm going to do it, Nat. I'm going to do it.

NAT. By gosh, maybe you will.

DON. Thank you, Nat. (*He's up on his feet.*) Am I all paid up?

NAT. Yes, Mr. Birnam.

DON. Goodbye, Nat. I'm going home. This time I've got it. I'm going to write.

NAT. Good luck, Mr. Birnam.

This dissolves to the BIRNAM APARTMENT. Don enters, the fire of real purpose in his eye. He hangs his hat on the hatrack, goes to the bedroom, picks up the typewriter, grabs the sheaf of typewriter paper Wick has laid on top of his suitcase and carries them into the living room. He puts the typewriter on the desk. Sitting down, he inserts a sheet of paper in the roller and begins to type: "THE BOTTLE A Novel by

Don Birnam." He pauses, then types underneath: "For Helen—With All My Love."

He rolls the sheet of paper up, studies what he has typed as though it were a painting. Then he begins to try and formulate that first sentence of his book. To do so is absolute agony for him. He gets up, puts a cigarette in his mouth, takes a match from a folder, lights the cigarette, throws the folder on the small table next to the big chair. As he does so his eyes fall on the empty bottle and glass. He looks at them for a minute, then goes over to the bookcase, puts his arm in back of the books and runs his hand along the rear of the shelf, looking for that bottle. It's not there.

He runs into the bedroom, hurries to his bed, where his suitcase lies packed but not closed. He wipes the suitcase from the bed, the contents spilling over the floor. He pulls up one end of the mattress, looks under it. Nothing.

He goes back into the living room, pulls the couch from the wall and, lying on his stomach, probes among the springs. Nothing there. He lies on the couch, breathing heavily.

> DON. You had another bottle, you know you did. Where did you put it? You're not crazy. *Where did you put it?*

He jumps up, runs back to the bookcase, starts pulling out books, row by row. He goes to the closet, opens it wide, pulls out all its contents, throwing them on the floor. Nothing there.

He goes back to the big chair, throws himself down, exhausted. His eyes fall again on the empty bottle and the empty glass. Behind the glass lies the folder of matches. Something is written

on it but it is distorted by the glass. However, it attracts Don's attention enough to make him push the glass to one side. The folder reads: HARRY'S & JOE'S Where Good Liquor Flows 13 W. 52nd St.

This dissolves to HARRY'S & JOE'S on 52nd St.—You know how those places look: the lower floor of a brownstone house, narrow, intimate, smoky. One side is a bar. Along the other wall there is a long, built-in bench with individual tables in front of it. At a miniature piano a guy is playing and singing "It Was So Beautiful."

Don Birnam sits on the bench at one of the small tables. In front of him is an empty cocktail glass. It is about his fourth. At the next table on the bench sits a couple—a show girl type, about twenty-four, and a man about thirty-five. They are nuts about each other and are holding hands as they listen to the hoarse pianist. However, to Don the music means little. He is very much the man of the world, holding his alcohol superbly, smoking a cigarette. He snaps his fingers at a waiter, who is passing with a tray of drinks. The waiter stops.

> DON. Where is my check?

> WAITER. Right here, sir.

The waiter takes the check which is thrust between his vest and his stiff shirt and puts it face down in front of Don, then hurries on with the tray of drinks. Don turns the check over. It's for four dollars. Suddenly his financial situation dawns on him. He puts his hand in his pocket and pulls out what cash he has. He does it very cautiously, under the table, so that no one else can see it. He hasn't enough—only two one-dollar bills and some small change. Panic seizes him. At that moment the waiter returns, expecting to be paid.

WAITER. Yes, sir.

DON (*a little stiffly*). One more gin vermouth.

WAITER. Yes, sir.

Taking the check, the waiter leaves. Don has gained a little time, but what shall he do with it? He considers the situation. The door is some thirty feet away, and the check-room girl stands in front of it. Don looks around. Nobody in the bar he knows. Next to him the couple is cooing away like Spring, —but on the bench between him and the girl lies her bag. It's a handsome leather bag with gold initials, M.M. It's about a foot and a half away from him, but it seems like a mile and a half to Don. There must be some money in that bag. Don looks around the room, his plan forming. No one is looking at him. As though inadvertently, he drops his hand on the bench beside the bag.

The man is whispering something into the girl's ear. She is shaking her head. Don pulls the purse imperceptibly closer to himself. Guests and waiters are passing by. Very calmly Don smokes his cigarette, a great gentleman. The bag moves very close to his coat. Now, switching his cigarette, Don crosses his other arm so he can pull the bag up under his coat. He pulls it to his armpit and holds it there, tucked close to his ribs. Nothing in his face betrays him.

The lovers are still at it. The waiter comes back with the drink.

DON (*stiffly, haughtily*). Thank you. Where is your wash room?

WAITER. Over there, sir.

He points to a door at the other end of the room. On its panel is the stylized profile of a gentleman with a top hat. Don starts to rise. The waiter pulls the table away for him. Don carries the bag under his open coat by the pressure of his upper arm. Between his fingers is a cigarette, so that the whole thing looks fairly natural. There is a tiny puzzled look from the waiter as Don walks slowly toward the wash room.

Inside the WASHROOM: It's a two-wash-basin affair, with a colored attendant who, as Don enters, is brushing a customer.

ATTENDANT. How's about a carnation, sir?

CUSTOMER. What for?

ATTENDANT (*chuckling*). For your buttonhole, sir.

CUSTOMER. Okay.

On the shelf above the washstand between talcum powder, nail files and brushes, there stands a tumbler with carnations. The attendant takes one, puts it into the customer's lapel. The customer tips him and walks out.—Don is left alone with the attendant, who points to the other bowl, runs fresh water in it.

ATTENDANT. Right here, sir.

Don steps to the wash bowl. His brain is functioning perfectly.

DON. Wipe my shoes, will you?

ATTENDANT. Yes, sir.

As Don picks up the cake of soap, he watches the attendant get a polishing rag and bend down to dust off his shoes.

Now Don doesn't lose a split second. He plays his cards like a master. He puts down the cake of soap, pulls out the bag, opens it. There, between a compact, lipstick and keys, are some bills. He fishes out a ten-dollar bill, thrusts it in his pocket and is about to close the purse when he sees the carnations. He can't help smiling at the idea which flashes into his mind. He takes one of the carnations, puts it into the purse, closes the purse and thrusts it back under his coat. Just as the attendant straightens up, Don puts both hands into the water. The attendant holds out a towel and Don wipes his hands.

ATTENDANT. How's about a carnation?

DON. I took one.

ATTENDANT. You did, sir? (*He looks at Don's lapel, mystified.*)

DON. Yes, for a very kind lady.

Don tips the attendant with a fifty-cent piece. The attendant doesn't get the joke but chuckles automatically and opens the door into the bar.

The BAR: The piano isn't being played and the place is strangely quiet. Don walks from the wash room, slowly toward his. table. Suddenly he stops. The space where the lovers sat is *empty now.* That's the storm signal. Don looks around. Near the little piano stands Don's waiter, the head waiter, the piano player and the lovers. They're staring at Don. In fact, he's suddenly aware that he is the focus of every eye in the room. In the next second the storm breaks.

WAITER. That's him. That's the man.

HEADWAITER. You were sitting here, sir?

DON. I beg your pardon.

He doesn't play it very well now. M.M.'s escort is right at him, grabbing him by the coat.

M.M.'S ESCORT. You took this lady's bag, didn'tcha? Come on, give it back.

DON (*with very little hesitation and a wan smile*). Of course.

He takes the bag out from under his coat and hands it to the lady.

M.M.'S ESCORT. Somebody call a cop.

M.M. No, George, no. It doesn't matter as long as I have the bag.

M.M.'S ESCORT. Well, look in it. Maybe he's taken something.

DON. Ten dollars, to be exact.

Don holds out the bill. M.M.'s escort snatches it from his hand.

M.M.'S ESCORT. I ought to kick your teeth in.

M.M. George, George! He's drunk.

HEADWAITER (*grabbing Don*). Get out of here.

WAITER. How about the check?

DON. Exactly. That's why I had to borrow from the lady. I didn't have enough.

He fishes what money he has left from his pocket. The waiter snaps it up.

DON. I'll come back and pay the rest.

HEADWAITER. Don't you show your face here again—ever. (*Shouting toward the entrance door*) Mike! Mike! (*To the waiter*) Come on, Charlie.

He and the waiter grab Don and start him toward the door. From the street comes Mike, the huge doorman-bouncer. He helps with the ejection.

DON (*to the entire bar*). I assure you I'm not a thief. I'm not a thief!

As they drag him toward the entrance door, the pianist, in an excess of delicate humor, begins to pound the piano and sing "Somebody stole my purse, Somebody stole my purse."

By this time they've got Don to the door. The headwaiter gets Don's hat from the checkroom girl's hand. He puts it on Don's head; the bouncer pulls him through the door.

FIFTY-SECOND STREET at night: There is a line of waiting taxis along the brilliantly lighted night club street. The bouncer, dragging Don from Harry's and Joe's, gives him one last shove down the street.—

Don comes to a stop and leans heavily against an iron railing, wiping his face with his hand. He straightens his hat and looks back. The doorman and the taxi drivers are staring after him. Don turns, straightens himself as best he can and starts for home, shame weighing down every limb.

This dissolves to the STAIRCASE and FOURTH FLOOR LANDING of the Birnam apartment house at night. It is meanly lighted by the wall brackets. The newspaper, the bottle of milk, Helen's note

—are all as they were.—Don drags himself up the last few steps, unlocks the door and goes in, leaving paper, bottle and note untouched.

The BIRNAM APARTMENT: Don has entered. Automatically he switches on the light in the corridor. In a stupor of shame and misery he stumbles over to the living room couch, flings himself down on it and lies covering his face with his arms. After a time he brushes the tears from his eyes with his sleeve and as he does so, catches sight of something which rivets his attention and brings a half-crazed smile to his lips.—On the ceiling is the shadow of the bottle which he hid in the light fixture.

With new strength Don gets to his feet, nervous laughter shaking him. He pulls the coffee table under the light fixture, puts the chair on it, climbs up and retrieves his bottle. He climbs down again, opening the bottle fiercely. He goes to the table where his empty glass stands and pours it half full. Over his face as he looks at the glass of whiskey comes the uplifted peace of a worshipper at the high altar. There the glass stands, gleaming in the light from above. Again the camera slowly moves toward it, and immerses in its depths. Oblivion again.—The scene fades out.

# PART THREE

The LIVING ROOM of the BIRNAM APARTMENT fades in. It's about 9:30 the next morning. The living room is in the same wild disorder—books on the floor, a chair on the table under the ceiling fixture, the couch moved from the wall, clothes and shoes spilled from the closet. Two empty bottles and a sticky glass stand about, and the portable, with its almost virgin sheet of white paper is in the roller. It's a nasty sight, and its nastiness is emphasized by the sunlight streaming in and mixing with the yellow pallor of the electric light, forgotten and burning on. Don is not in sight. Only the telephone, which stands on the desk next the open portable, is alive. It is ringing at the top of its bell.

The BEDROOM: The same confusion reigns here: the suitcase flung on the floor, the window shade flapping, and on the unmade bed, not in it, fully dressed—shoes, suit, tie—lies Don, the comforter and bedspread pulled up over him.

The telephone rings remorselessly. Don opens his eyes slowly. The brightness of the day stabs them, he shuts them. Again the telephone.—Don gets up. He is weaker than he thought. Steadying himself on the bedpost and holding the door frame, he slowly moves out of the bedroom.

The LIVING ROOM: Don enters. He seems to be going straight to the ringing telephone—but he doesn't. He passes it and goes to the open window. He puts his arm against the window frame, presses his forehead against it, stands there, every vibration of the telephone bell shaking his nerves.

DON. Stop it, Helen, stop it, stop it. I'm all right. I just can't talk. Stop it.

There is another ring and another, then the phone stops. Don's eyes fall on the bottle and the glass by the big chair. He moves slowly toward it, picks up the bottle and holds it upside down over the glass. One slow drop is all it yields. Don puts down the bottle, goes to the other bottle on the mantel shelf, picks it up and goes to the kitchen.

The KITCHEN: In the sink is the bottle Wick emptied that first afternoon. Don picks it up and goes back into the living room. Then back in the LIVING ROOM, Don goes to the glass and holds the two bottles upside down over it. Two more meagre drops emerge, like thick syrup. They barely stain the bottom of the glass.—Don puts down the

two bottles, picks up the glass, empties the pitiable three drops into the parched desert of his throat. For a second it seems that he has found some relief. That's not true. His need for alcohol has been multiplied tenfold by that mockery of a drink. He's got to get another bottle, another drink.—What are his finances? Quickly he goes through his pockets. In the palm of his hand there are exactly two cents. He looks around the apartment. There on the desk stands the typewriter. Don walks toward it, rips the sheet of paper from the roller, slams the lid of the cover shut and picks up the typewriter. It is heavy, terribly heavy. He drags it to the little hall, picks up his hat and puts it on. At the door, weakness overcomes him. Dragging his hand with it, the typewriter sinks to the floor.

DON. You'll never make it. You'll never make that hock shop. It's a block and a half away.

He is crouched helplessly against the door. At that moment the telephone shrills again. Once more Don straightens himself, opens the door and leaves.

We see the OUTER DOOR: the note from Helen is still pinned to it. There are now two newspapers, two bottles of milk. Don steps over them carefully, closes the door and starts down the stairs.—This dissolves to the exterior of the BIRNAM APARTMENT HOUSE.

Mrs. Deveridge and her dog Sophie are outside the house. Mrs. Deveridge is talking to Dave, the janitor, who leans on his broom. It is a sunny morning.

Don comes from the house with the typewriter. He stops to make sure the two are absorbed in conversation, then steps quickly past them down the street toward Third Avenue. Looking back to see whether they have seen him, he turns into Third Avenue and starts uptown.

THIRD AVENUE: This is to be Don's *Via Dolorosa*, this black, roaring, perilous street up which he drags the hellish weight of that portable—that portable which grows heavier with every step —in quest of a pawn shop which will give him a few dollars for it. A few dollars which will mean drink, drink which he needs to live.—Setting his jaw and whipping on his will, he reaches the first hock shop. A steel gate is drawn across its entrance. Don stares at the obstruction, completely mystified. There is a woman standing near by, wheeling a baby in a baby carriage. Don turns to her.

DON. This isn't Sunday, is it, lady?

WOMAN. Huh?

DON. I asked is this Sunday.

WOMAN. No, Sattaday. Why?

DON. Because it's closed. (*Looking around*) Nothing else is closed.

WOMAN. Well, somebody passed away, most likely.

Don stands helpless for a moment, then, feeling the woman's intrusive stare, straightens up. In the next block, miles and miles away for the way he feels, is another pawn shop. He starts for it. —Again every step is agony. Overhead the elevated thunders excruciatingly. Sweat pours from his forehead. He changes the typewriter from one hand to another. At last he makes the second pawn shop. It too is closed. He peers through the iron gate into the dark shop, and turns around.—Across the street, in the same block, is the third pawn shop. He must make it, but to get there he must cross the raging tor-

rent of Third Avenue.—He makes a pillar of the El, leans against it, shaking. When a trolley car gets out of his way, he continues to cross the street. That pawn shop is closed too. Don takes a bar and shakes it.

DON. What's going on? What is it? Did you all go to a funeral, all of you? Maybe it's you that died, Don Birnam. Maybe it's your funeral.

He pulls himself away and recrosses the street. Reason has entirely deserted him, but blind instinct drives him on.

Sixty-first Street, Seventy-first Street. Four more pawn shops, all of them closed. Seventy-ninth Street. He's almost struck by a car. The typewriter falls from his hand. A truck runs over it but straddles it. Don gets it again. Up the street, up the street, up the street. One pawn shop closed afer another. His feet are burning, as if the sidewalk were hot lava. His ears are bursting.

Eighty-ninth Street, Ninety-fifth Street. Past bars, funeral parlors, children on roller skates, and always the recurrent torture of the elevated overhead. On and on, unable to stop.

Finally, half dead, he reaches a pawn shop on 120th St., and finds the answer to his crucifixion. Two men in dark suits with black bowlers and prayer books under their arms watch him as he rattles the closed gate of the pawn shop, almost out of his mind.

FIRST MAN. What's the matter with you?

DON. Why are they all closed? They're all closed, every one of them.

FIRST MAN. Sure they are. It's Yom Kippur.

DON. It's what?

FIRST MAN. It's Yom Kippur, a Jewish holiday.

DON. It is? (*That makes sense to him. Or does it?*) What are you talking about? How about Kelly's? How about Gallagher's?

FIRST MAN. They're closed too. We've got an agreement. They keep closed on Yom Kippur and we don't open on St. Patrick's. (*The two men stand grinning.*)

DON (*almost weeping*). That's a good joke. That's funny, that's very funny.

He picks up the typewriter, turns and starts walking back. The view moves slowly up to a sidewalk clock with a diadem of three balls, which stands outside the hock shop. The time is twenty minutes of one.

This dissolves very slowly to the CLOCK in NAT'S BAR: it says five minutes of four. The view moves down. Nat is at the bar. He and two or three customers are listening to race results on a little radio. Don drags himself in, drenched in sweat, his breath as short and agonized as that of a dying man. He goes to the end of the bar closest the door, hoists the typewriter on it with a final awful effort and leans his head on it.

DON. Nat—

NAT (*going to him*). What's the matter, Mr. Birnam?

DON. Let me have one, Nat. I'm dying. Just one.

NAT. I thought you were home writing that book.

DON. They're playing a trick on me. A dirty trick. Give me one, Nat. I'll pay you when I can. Just don't let me die here.

NAT. No credit, and you know it.

DON. All right, so it's charity. I'm begging you for one. Give me one.

NAT. Yeah, one. (*Pouring a drink*) One's too many and a hundred's not enough. (*He shoves the drink at Don.*)

Don is shaking so that he can't pick up the glass. He bends down, sucks half of it, then lifts the glass and drains the rest. He holds out the empty glass to Nat, his eyes imploring.

NAT. That's all.

DON. Come on, Nat, come on. I'll let you have my typewriter.

NAT. I'm no writer. You're the writer. Now go. Go away.

DON. Nat—

NAT. I mean it. Get out.

Don takes the typewriter and drags himself out of Nat's place. Then we see THIRD AVENUE, outside NAT's as Don emerges, and starts dragging himself up the street toward home. As he passes the antique shop, he suddenly stops. There stands the wooden Indian that Gloria spoke about, pointing up. That's where Gloria lives. Second floor, this same house. Don walks into the house.

This dissolves to the STAIRS and HALL-WAY outside Gloria's door. This is a really crummy Third Avenue house— dark woodwork, paint peeling from the walls. Beside the door at the head of the stairs there are about three bells, for the several occupants of the apartment within. Don drags himself up the stairs, puts down the typewriter and inspects the name tags by the bells. One of them says: GLORIA DE VRIES. Don rings the bell beside it. From inside comes:

GLORIA'S VOICE. Who is it? (*As Don rings again*) Who is it?

DON. It's me.

The door is opened by Gloria. She is wearing a dressing gown and bedroom slippers. Her hair is the ruined elaborate hairdress of yesterday, and her eyes are blazing with anger.

GLORIA. Why, Mr. Birnam, as I live and breathe! Only if you're coming for our date, you're a little late, aren't you, Mr. Birnam? And if you're coming to apologize—no thanks. Thanks a lot, but no thanks.

DON. Gloria—

GLORIA. Save your saliva. I've had enough of you. Def, but def. What do you think I am? I break a business date. I buy an evening purse, a facial, a new hair-do. Well, maybe you can do that to your ritzy friends. You can't to me, understand?

DON. Gloria.

GLORIA. Okay, what do you want, Mr. Don Birnam Esquire?

DON. I need some money.

GLORIA. You what?

DON. Could you let me have some money?

GLORIA. Say, you out of your mind? Don't be ridic. Get out of here. Make with those stairs. Go on!

She starts back into the apartment, but Don gets her by the hand, pulls her toward him and kisses her. At first she resists, then her hand creeps up to the back of his neck and clutches it hungrily.

GLORIA. I was waiting half the night, like it was the first date I ever had. And the other half I was crying. (*She*

*looks at him.*) How much money?

DON. Could you let me have ten or five, or something?

GLORIA. I'll see.

She slips into the apartment, leaving the door about three inches ajar. Don leans against the door jamb, breathing heavily.—After a couple of seconds Gloria reappears with a wallet. She takes five dollars out and gives it to him. Don takes it with a shaking hand.

GLORIA (*noticing this*). You look awful sick, honey. You got a fever or something? (*She brushes his forehead with the back of her hand.*)

DON. I'm all right now.

He takes her hand and kisses it. Gloria looks at him, then at her hand.

GLORIA. Thank you a lot. You do really like me a little, don't you, honey?

DON. Why, natch, Gloria. Natch.

He bends, picks up the typewriter and starts downstairs. Gloria looks after him. From inside the apartment comes a nagging feminine voice.

WOMAN'S VOICE. Gloria, where are you?

GLORIA. Coming. (*She reenters the apartment, closing the door.*)

The STAIRCASE of GLORIA'S HOUSE: Don is coming down, holding the banister with his left hand, the typewriter in his right. Up the staircase comes a little girl about seven, running a stick along the spindles of the banister and singing the *Hut Sut Song*. The sound makes Don wince, and as the child gives no sign of yielding precedence to him, he switches the typewriter to his other hand and leans against the stair wall.—The child passes him. As Don goes on, he slips, starts falling, clutches a light bracket trying to check his fall. It pulls from the wall under his weight and he falls, clutching the typewriter, down the long flight of stairs—a terrible, back-breaking fall. His hat has fallen off. He struck his head. He is in wild pain.—

The little girl stands horrified, then starts crying and runs up the stairs. Don lies sprawled out on his back as the scene fades out.

# PART FOUR

A WIRE BASKET with FOUR MILK BOTTLES in it fades in. Gradually we see that it is in the hand of a milkman ascending the stairs of the Birnam apartment house. He leaves a bottle at the door of the rear apartment on the third floor, one in front of Mrs. Deveridge's, then starts up to the fourth floor.—As he gets halfway up, he stops momentarily in surprise. In the embrasure of the banister at the top of the stairs, wrapped in her leopard coat, is Helen St. James, dozing wearily. Beyond her is the door to the Birnam apartment, her note still pinned to the panel, two milk bottles and the newspapers of the last two days on the threshold.— The milkman resumes his walk, careful not to wake up the young lady. He deposits a milk bottle beside the others and descends carefully. As he reaches the third floor, Mrs. Deveridge, in a kimono, has just opened her door and is taking in her milk bottle.

MRS. DEVERIDGE (*briskly*). Good morning.

The milkman motions to her not to speak so loudly, then makes a mysterious gesture of the thumb indicating the upper hall. Mrs. Deveridge looks up. The milkman proceeds down the stairs. Mrs. Deveridge sets down the milk bottle and goes up the stairs. As she goes, she calls sharply.

MRS. DEVERIDGE. Anything wrong up there? Anything wrong?

Helen wakens at the first syllable, orientates herself as to where she is, and gets up.

MRS. DEVERIDGE. Are you all right?

HELEN. I'm fine, thank you.

MRS. DEVERIDGE. Have you been here all night?

HELEN. I've been waiting for Mr. Birnam.

MRS. DEVERIDGE. Mr. Don Birnam?

HELEN. Yes. I suppose he must have stayed overnight with—some friends. He has some friends on Long Island.

MRS. DEVERIDGE. Now, now, what kind of story is that?

HELEN. I beg your pardon?

MRS. DEVERIDGE. Look, I'm his land-lady. I know what goes on in this house. I know Mr. Don Birnam. I knew all about him the first week they moved here, three years ago. Heard those bottles rattle in their garbage can. I know all about you. You're Don Birnam's girl. I also know he's not staying with any friends in Long Island. He's off on another toot and you know I'm darned right. Now come on down and I'll make you some breakfast.

HELEN. I don't care for any breakfast, nor do I care for that kind of talk, even supposing you were right.

MRS. DEVERIDGE. Which I am. Now you're going to have some coffee.

They start downstairs, Mrs. Deveridge talking as they descend.

MRS. DEVERIDGE. I could have kicked him out fifty times. The last when two taxi drivers dumped him into the entrance hall, out cold on the floor, with all my tenants going in and out, and children leaving for school.

HELEN. Oh please, please!

MRS. DEVERIDGE. Well, I *didn't* put him out, not as long as his brother could pay the rent. You couldn't help liking him anyway. He was so good-looking; he had such nice manners. He always had a little joke.

HELEN. Stop talking about him as if he were dead.

MRS. DEVERIDGE. Did I? I didn't mean to. Hope it wasn't bad luck.

An ALCOHOLIC WARD fades in. We start on Don Birnam's face. He is lying on a cot, his eyes closed. He has a three-day growth of beard. His face has the pallor and immobility of death.—Over the scene come curious sounds of moaning, of incoherent mumbling, of slippered feet shuffling along a concrete floor, of a mysterious metallic chattering.—Don isn't dead. The sounds reach his ears at last. His eyes open for a second. Then his gaze is directed emptily upward.

We see the bile-colored CEILING of a LARGE ROOM. We still hear the same strange noises. Don's eyes (i.e., the camera) slowly descend the bile-covered walls, broken by opaque leaded-glass windows and the large glass swinging door leading to an outer room. At last the nature of the room itself is revealed. It is filled with rows of strangely low cots, about thirty of them, standing on dwarf legs. Eight of them are occupied by men whose ages range from twenty to sixty. Six of them are white, two of them, colored. All are unshaven and dressed in shabby flannel hospital pajamas.

Don's dull eyes don't quite comprehend. His head aches furiously. In the cot next him is a man about fifty, burrowing into the mattress in drunken sleep, his mouth fallen open. In the cot opposite him, a very thin young fellow lies shaking and sweating profusely. His entire frame, all of it, trembles as if a fine motor operated somewhere beneath the mattress itself.

On the other side of Don's cot, a huge Negro lies babbling incoherently. No words are audible, save now and then a number. His voice has the sound of infinite worry.

Against the wall, not far from Don, stands a man about thirty, in a faded terry-cloth bathrobe. He has an incredibly sensitive face. One ear is bandaged. He looks as though he wanted to crawl into the wall from shame. The rest of the men in the cots are sleeping lumps.—Don addresses the man standing against the wall.

DON. What's this place? (*The man looks at Don but doesn't answer.*) Hey, you, what's this place? (*The man stands staring at him, terrified.*) I'm talking to you.

The man drifts away eerily. Then from the opposite direction comes BIM a male nurse. He is a robust guy with a sarcastic mouth, who is constantly joking, mostly at the listener's expense.

BIM. Good morning, merry sunshine. How's your head?

DON. Where am I? What is this?

BIM. This? This is the Hangover Plaza.

DON. What hospital is this?

BIM. Alcoholic Ward. How's the head?

DON. It aches.

BIM. We thought you'd fractured her till we seen the X-rays. All in one piece. Just a concussion.

DON. Why did they put me in the Alcoholic Ward?

BIM. Are you kidding? We took a peek at your blood. Straight apple-jack. Ninety-six proof.

DON. What day is this?

BIM. Sunday. (*He holds out the key-ring.*) These yours? They fell out of somebody's pocket. You and the colored fellow was being undressed at the same time.

DON. They're mine. (*Bim throws them at him.*) Are you a doctor?

BIM. Nope. I'm a nurse. Name of Dolan. They call me Bim. You can call me Bim. (*He gets a pad and pencil from his pocket.*) What's your name?

DON. Birnam.

BIM. What kind of Birnam?

DON. Don Birnam.

BIM. Where do you live?

DON. Two hundred and nine East Fif— Say, what do you need that for?

BIM. For the post card.

DON. What post card?

BIM. To your folks, so's they'll know

where honey-boy is and where they can pick him up when he's feeling better.

DON. No address.

BIM. Okay. We'll get it out of the telephone book, or the directory, or maybe you've got it in your wallet.

DON (*on his feet*). No post card. Understand? Nobody's going to pick me up.

BIM. The management insists. If we let you guys go home alone a lot of you don't go home. You hit the nearest bar and bounce right back. What we call the Quick Ricochet.

DON. Listen, I'm as well as you are. I can leave right now.

BIM. You think so?

DON. Where are my clothes?

BIM. Downstairs.

DON. How do I get out of this place?

BIM (*pointing to the glass doors*). Right through here.

Don has risen. He is wearing flannel pajamas like all the rest of the patients. There are canvas slippers on his feet. He is not quite as steady on his pins as he thought. However he manages to make the swinging glass door.—Bim stands quietly watching him, a great big grin on his face.

The ANTE-ROOM: It is L-shaped, about fourteen feet wide. Along the walls are benches and a collection of wheelchairs. Sitting on them and milling aimlessly around, are some thirty alcoholics. They wear terry-cloth bathrobes over their pajamas, canvas slippers on their feet. They are well on their way to normalcy, but they are still not a pretty sight—unshaven, bunged-up, shame-faced.—In the listless, burned-out collection, Don is the only person who moves with purpose. He scarcely notices the men as he passes them, intent on finding the door. He goes around the bend of the ell and there is the door, a heavy wooden one with a grated peep-hole and beside it a uniformed guard. Don goes to the door, tries to open it.

GUARD. Where do you think you're going?

DON. To get my clothes.

GUARD. You got your discharge?

DON. My what?

GUARD. Your release?

DON. I'm all right. Let me out.

At this moment the door is opened by another male nurse, carrying a pile of clean sheets and pillow cases. Don tries to take advantage of the opening of the door to get out, but the guard pulls him by the arm, while the entering nurse locks the door with his own key.

GUARD. Go on, get back.

DON. Keep your hands off me.

Over the scene comes:

BIM'S VOICE. Birnam!

Don turns. At the bend of the corridor stands Bim, with a tumbler of medicine in his hand.

BIM. Come here, Birnam.

DON (*approaching him slowly*). Is this a jail?

BIM. Well, this department—it's kind of halfway hospital, halfway jail, but we run it more like a flophouse.

He guides Don back toward the ward.

DON. Listen, Bim, in my clothes there's five dollars. That's for you if only you won't send that post card.

BIM. Nothing doing.

DON. I don't want anybody to know.

BIM. Listen, your folks might as well get used to our little post cards.

DON. What are you talking about?

BIM. There'll be more of them. You'll be back.

DON. Shut your face.

BIM. Listen, I can pick an alky with one eye shut. You're one and you'll come back. They all do. (*He points at a man in a wheel-chair.*) Him, for instance. He turns up every month, just as sure as the gas bill. (*He points at another man.*) And him there. That's another repeater. This is his forty-fifth time. Big executive in the advertising business. A lovely fellow. Been coming here ever since 1927. Good old prohibition days. You should have seen the place then. Say, this is nothing. Back then we really had a turnover. Standing room only. Prohibition! That's what started half these guys off. Whoopee! (*They have reached the ward by now.*)

The WARD: Bim seats Don on his bed.

BIM. Now lie down like a good boy and drink this.

DON. What is it?

BIM. Doctor's orders. It'll calm you down.

DON. I don't want it.

BIM. You better take it. Comes the night there's apt to be a little floor show around here. Might get on your nerves.

DON. Floor show?

BIM. Didn't you ever have the D.T.'s?

DON. No.

BIM. You will, brother.

DON. Not me.

BIM. Want to make a small bet? You're just a freshman. Wait till you're a sophomore. That's when you start seeing the little animals. (*He holds out the drink.*) Drink it.

DON. I don't want it.

BIM. That stuff about pink elephants, that's the bunk. It's little animals. Little tiny turkeys in straw hats. Midget monkeys that come through the key-holes. See that guy in the corner? (*He points to the man with the sensitive face who stands against the wall.*) With him it's beetles. Comes the night, he sees beetles crawling all over him. Has to be dark, though. It's like the doctor was saying to me, "Delirium is a disease of the night." Well, good night.

And on the grinning face of Bim, the scene dissolves to the WARD at night. It is lighted by a faint blue light, but the lights are on in the ante-room and some light comes through the glass doors. There are the sounds of a ward full of drunken men—sighs, heavy breathing, snoring, babbling, moaning. On his cot lies Don, his eyes wide open. Suddenly there comes a sharper sound—a violent slapping of a bed. Don pivots in the direction of the sound.

On a cot in the corner is the man with the sensitive face and the addiction to beetles. He is slapping wildly at his bed, moaning. He rises and begins to slap the wall and scream.—Don stares at him through the dimness.

Through the glass doors come two male nurses with flashlights. They run to the cot of the D.T. victim. There is

a wild scrabble as he fights them off. One of the nurses races back to the door and calls:

NURSE. Straitjacket! And the doctor!

By now, from several other beds in the ward comes demented screaming. A third nurse races in, throws a straitjacket to the first nurse, then hurries to one of the other beds.

Seen through the glass doors, a doctor comes running down the ante-room, followed by another male nurse with a cart on which are hypodermic syringes, etc. The doctor must have been in another building, because over his shoulders is flung a dark blue overcoat. He enters the ward and dashes in the direction of the beetle patient. As he goes, he tosses the overcoat on the empty cot next to Don.

Don looks after the doctor, then is fascinated by the coat lying beside him. In the corner the three nurses and the doctor are working over the beetle patient, the doctor giving him a hypo, the nurses getting him into the straitjacket. The ward is now really going off like a bunch of firecrackers.

DOCTOR (*to the nurses*). Get him up to the violent ward.

From the cot on the other side of the ward, the third male nurse calls:

THIRD MALE NURSE. Help me with this one, will you, Doc?

The doctor goes to him while the nurses drag the beetle patient through the swing door into the ante-room.

Don slips from his bed and, crouching on the floor, pulls the doctor's coat from the cot and, holding it tight, crawls to the swinging glass doors and slides through them.

The LIGHTED ANTE-ROOM: It is empty save for the two nurses, who are leading the beetle patient around the bend of the ell. In a crouching position, Don makes his way down the ante-room, holding the coat close. At the bend he looks around. The two nurses with the beetle patient have reached the outer door, beside which stands a night guard.

FIRST NURSE. Violent ward. Get the elevator.

The guard opens the door and leads the way. The nurses drag the patient out.— Don makes his way to the door, glances through the peep-hole, then sneaks out.

The CORRIDOR outside the WARD: The guard, the two nurses and the patient are at the elevator. Don sneaks behind them, through the door to the fire stairs. We see the FIRE STAIRS as Don runs cautiously down, putting the coat on as he goes. He feels something in the pocket, takes out a package of cigarettes, matches, a couple of nickels. He hurries down the stairs.—Then we see the GROUND FLOOR CORRIDOR. A guard stands at the steps leading from the main entrance to the psychiatric hospital. He is talking with three female nurses. Don slides behind them and out the entrance, which is by now gray with the cold dawn.

We see the ENTRANCE to the PSYCHIATRIC WARD as Don comes out, orientates himself quickly and runs through the gate. —A STREET in the 20's: It is deserted except for a water wagon. Don runs up toward the entrance of the elevated. Then we see the STAIRS of the ELEVATED as Don runs up just as a train rattles in. The scene moves with the train as it leaves for uptown.

This dissolves to DON inside the train as he sits watching the first rays of sunlight strike the tall buildings in the East 40's. The train comes to a stop and Don gets up.

This dissolves to 43RD STREET—about 6:30 in the morning. Don comes from the elevated and hurries down the street. The scene moves with him. Don stops in front of a shop. On its window is painted LIQUOR AND WINES, and a couple of bottles are in the foreground. It is closed. Don crosses the street and stations himself in front of the building opposite, leaning against an iron railing. Some elderly people pass him and go up some steps. Slowly Don becomes aware that he is standing in front of a church and the people are going to morning mass. Now the view moves up the church to the cross on its gable, then swings across to the Chrysler Building opposite, now bathed in bright sunlight.

As the view moves across the clear sky, the scene dissolves; and now the one-story building which houses the liquor shop comes into view. It is 9 o'clock by now and the owner, a middle-aged man in hat, coat and muffler, is just unlocking the door.—Don, tormented by the long wait, sees him open it and starts to cross the street.

Inside the LIQUOR STORE: The proprietor enters, hangs up his hat, takes off his muffler and is about to take off his coat when Don comes in. The scene between the two is played very quietly.

DON. I want a quart of rye. Quick.

PROPRIETOR. All right if I take my coat off first?

DON. No.

The proprietor senses that there is something wrong. He looks at Don. As his gaze reaches Don's pajama trousers and canvas slippers, Don speaks.

DON. No cracks, no questions. Just a quart of rye.

The proprietor grasps that this is no joking matter. He picks up a bottle.

PROPRIETOR. That'll be two fifteen.

DON. Give it to me.

PROPRIETOR. Two fifteen.

DON. Come on. I need that liquor, I want it, I'm going to get it. I'm going to walk out of here with that quart of rye, understand. One way or another.

There is murder in his eyes. The proprietor is completely under the spell of that terrible glance. He hands over the bottle. Don takes it and walks out. The proprietor takes a few steps toward the door as if he were about to summon help and catch Don, then he thinks better of it. With a what-the-hell gesture, he starts taking off his coat.

[The scene dissolves to the BIRNAM APARTMENT HOUSE as Don, holding the bottle under his blue coat, slips quietly past Mrs. Wertheim's laundry and into the entranceway. He looks inside to be sure he is not observed, then fishes the keys from his pajama pocket, where Bim dropped them, and opens his mail box. The post card is there. He takes it out, crumples it and, putting it in the pocket of his overcoat, goes inside the house.]

This dissolves to the BIRNAM APARTMENT. Don enters, looks around the apartment, which is still in utter disorder. The electric lights, burning on heedlessly, offend him and he snaps off the light switch. Automatically he takes the chain to hook it into its socket, but misses it. The chain slips down and dangles. Don, not noticing, walks to his big chair. On the small table next to it stand the three empty bottles. He sweeps them to the floor. He takes the new bottle from his pocket and, sinking into the big chair, starts opening it. On the desk behind him, the telephone starts ringing. He doesn't seem to hear it. Without winking an eyelash, he pours his glass half full, lifts it so that glass and hand obscure his face.

The scene dissolves to the APARTMENT at night. Don, passed out, sits in the dark. The bottle next to him is four-fifths empty. He opens his eyes, still in a half-stupor, staring straight before him. Out of the corner of one eye he sees something and slowly and with difficulty he turns his head.—In the wall above the couch, close to the door, there is a hole in the plaster, as if left by a large nail carelessly withdrawn so that some of the plaster went with it. Out of the hole peers a small mouse. —At first Don draws back, repelled, but the mouse is such a friendly, harmless creature that after a moment his face relaxes and he half smiles at it.— Just as he does so, from the direction of the window there whirs past him a strange winged thing. It is a bat, swooping in slow loops around the room. Don crouches into the back of his chair, staring in wild distaste. The top of the bat's hooked wing nicks his forehead as it speeds in swift but fluttering flight straight at the mouse.— Don stiffens against the back of his chair. The bat has made another swoop and spread its wings over the mouse. Beneath those black wings some hideous pygmy struggle is going on. Apparently the bat has seized the mouse in its claws.—Don gives a cry of horror. Now from behind the struggling wings comes a spurt of blood.—Don cries out so hard his throat seems to burst apart, and he buries his horrified eyes in the back of his chair.—From downstairs comes the barking of Mrs. Deveridge's dog.

We see the STAIRCASE between the FOURTH FLOOR and THIRD FLOOR LANDING as Mrs. Deveridge stands about four steps up, looking at the door to the Birnam apartment. She must have been listening since Don's first scream. Sophie, standing beside her, is barking wildly. Beyond her, the door to her apartment is open.

MRS. DEVERIDGE. ·Shut up, Sophie! Shut up!

Dragging Sophie after her, she hurries into her apartment, and we see the ENTRANCE HALL of MRS. DEVERIDGE'S APARTMENT. The telephone is on the table by the door, a memorandum pad beside it. Mrs. Deveridge picks up the phone and, glancing at the pad, dials a number.

MRS. DEVERIDGE (*into the phone*). Miss St. James? . . . He's back. He's upstairs . . . This is Mrs. Deveridge. He's back! In the apartment. I heard him yelling. He's just got to remember that there are other tenants . . . Miss St. James? Miss St. James? (*Helen has obviously hung up. Mrs. Deveridge, a little indignant, does the same.*)

This dissolves to the BIRNAM APARTMENT. Don still cowers in his chair, his face hidden in his arms, his breathing heavy with terror. From outside comes the sound of footsteps racing upstairs toward his door, then the doorbell: short, short, long, short.—Don's eyes turn slowly toward the door. His brain is still functioning, for there is new terror in those eyes.

At the DOOR of the BIRNAM APARTMENT:

Helen stands outside, ringing the bell. There is no answer.

HELEN. Don, open the door. Open it, please.

Still no answer; and she raps on the door.—DON, inside the APARTMENT, sits staring at the door, holding his breath not to betray his presence.

HELEN'S VOICE. Don, won't you let me in? I know you're there. Please open the door.

Don doesn't move, doesn't answer.— HELEN is seen again at the DOOR.

HELEN. Don, don't you hear me? I want to help you.

She bangs on the door, rattling the doorknob helplessly.—DON is seen staring at the door, listening.

HELEN'S VOICE. I won't go away, Don. Do I have to get the janitor with the pass key to let me in?

Don sits bathed in sweat, tears of terror in his eyes.—HELEN, at the DOOR, turns and runs down the stairs. Mrs. Deveridge stands in her door, peering up. She hurries to the stairwell and calls down.

MRS. DEVERIDGE. Dave! Dave!

DAVE'S VOICE. Yes, Mrs. Deveridge?

MRS. DEVERIDGE. Come on up with the pass key.

DON, inside the APARTMENT: his eyes are on the door. Now they focus *on the door chain.* It is not hooked in place but hangs limply. Don realizes he's forgotten to put it up, but it's not too late, is it? With a desperate effort he flings himself to the floor and starts inching his way to the door.

We again see the STAIRS leading to the FOURTH FLOOR as Dave, holding a ring with labelled keys on it in his hand, leads Helen and Mrs. Deveridge up the stairs.—Inside the BIRNAM APARTMENT: Don is almost at the door. There is the sound of ascending footsteps. With his last strength Don raises himself against the door, stretches out his hand, gets the door chain, tries to slip it in its notch, but misses. The footsteps have stopped by now. There is the noise of a key being pushed into the key-hole. Don tries again, but by this time the door is open. Don throws all his weight against the door but it is no use.

Outside the DOOR: Dave has opened the door and holds it open as far as he can. Helen slips into Dave's place in the doorway. From behind the door comes the sound of Don's agonized breathing.

HELEN (*holding the doorknob*). Thank you very much.

MRS. DEVERIDGE. You'd better let us come too. You can't go in there alone.

HELEN. I'll be fine, thank you.

She stands waiting until Dave and Mrs. Deveridge start downstairs.—Inside the APARTMENT: Don crouches behind the door. A shaft of light comes from the corridor. Helen enters, closing the door behind her. She kneels down beside Don.

HELEN. Don, darling—

DON. Go away, Helen.

HELEN. I'm here to help you, Don.

DON. No, no.

HELEN. Look at you. How long is it since you've had anything to eat? (*As Don doesn't answer*) You want to get up, Don. Put your hand on my shoulder. (*Don blindly does as she says.*) You'll have a bath. I'll help you shave. You'll eat and sleep, and when Wick comes back everything will be all right.

They are beside the light switch. Helen snaps it on.

DON. No, Helen, no!

HELEN. What's the matter, Don?

DON. The wall. Don't look.

HELEN. What wall?

Don gestures toward the spot where the bat and the mouse were.

DON. The mouse and the bat.

HELEN. What mouse? What bat?

DON. That hole in the wall—

HELEN. There isn't any hole in the wall. Look.

She leads Don toward it. He stares at the smooth, unstained wall.

HELEN. See? (*Don runs his hand over the wall.*) You had some kind of a nightmare. (*She leads him into the bedroom, talking as they go.*) Stop shaking, Don. Everything will be all right. I'll stay right with you.

She seats him on the bed. Don is panting hard, completely oblivious of the fact that Helen is in the room.

DON. Little animals. It's always little animals. That's what Bim said.

HELEN. You're not making much sense. (*She turns on the bed lamp.*)

DON. And do you know what Nat said about the ending? Like this. (*He snaps his fingers vertically.*) Or like that. (*He snaps them horizontally.*)

He goes on repeating the gesture, growing despair in his eyes as the scene fades out.

# PART FIVE

A window in the Birnam Apartment on Tuesday morning fades in.
It is raining outside and from the eaves comes a steady drip in the exact rhythm
in which Don snapped his fingers—"like this, or like that, like this or like that."—
The scene widens to include the whole living room. Helen lies asleep on the
couch, using the pillow and comforter from Wick's bed. She is wearing Wick's
foulard dressing gown. The room is all tidy now. On the armchair near the
kitchen door lies Helen's leopard coat. In the door to the bedroom stands Don.
Now that he is shaved, we can see how pale his face is. He wears the dark suit
(the one he wore to the opera) and as his eyes shift from Helen to the coat, he
is just tying his tie. He has not yet buttoned the buttons on the points of his soft
collar. Very cautiously he begins to tiptoe toward the chair. He picks up the
leopard coat and starts toward the entrance door. He opens it carefully but it
does creak a little. Just as he is slipping out, he hears:

HELEN'S VOICE. Don! Don!

Don shuts the door behind him. In the next second Helen hurries into the scene. She is barefooted, just wearing the foulard dressing gown. She flings open the door and runs out.

The FOURTH FLOOR LANDING and STAIRS: Helen runs to the banister and looks down. Don has already reached the second floor and is hurrying down the stairs, the fur coat over his arm, not paying any attention to Helen.

HELEN. Where are you going, Don?

This dissolves to the exterior of a PAWN SHOP on THIRD AVENUE. Don is just coming down the street in the drizzle about ten steps when Helen comes up to him. She wears the dress she wore last night. No hat, no coat.

HELEN. All right, Don. Give me the pawn ticket.

Don disregards her and tries to go on. Helen overtakes him and blocks his way.

DON. No scene, please.

HELEN. No scene. Just give me the pawn ticket.

DON. I don't want you to go in there now claiming it. It would look queer.

HELEN. You're ashamed of what the pawn broker may think, is that it? It doesn't matter what *I* think.

DON. Wick'll get you back your coat.

HELEN. You couldn't have taken my bracelet or my pay check? It had to be that coat?

DON. You mean the one that brought us together? Stop being sentimental.

HELEN. I have, Don, I assure you. It's finished. It's dead. For three years they couldn't talk me out of you. I was the only one who really understood you. I knew there was a core of something . . . And there was a core, and now I know what it is. A sponge. And to soak it full you'll do anything ruthless, selfish, dishonest.

DON. I asked you not to make a scene.

HELEN. Then give me the ticket.

DON. No, Helen, not now I told you. Cut it out.

HELEN. I don't want the money. You can get as drunk as you like for all I care.

DON. Thank you.

He goes on. Helen stands looking after him for a moment, then turns angrily and proceeds toward the pawn shop.— This cuts to the interior of the PAWN SHOP, where the pawn broker has put Helen's coat on a hanger and is brushing it. Helen enters, very matter-of-fact.

HELEN. A gentleman was here a while ago. How much did you give him for that coat?

PAWN BROKER. Huh?

HELEN. I want it back. It's my coat.

PAWN BROKER. It's your coat?

HELEN. It's all right. He had my permission. How much did you give him?

PAWN BROKER. He didn't want any money. He wanted to swap it.

HELEN. For what?

PAWN BROKER. Something he hocked here a long while back.

HELEN. What?

PAWN BROKER. A gun. Now if you want that coat I can—

But Helen is already out of the shop and running down the rainy street.

The scene dissolves to DON'S DESK. On it lies a revolver and the second page of a letter on which Don is writing:

". . . . But amid all the grimness can we share one little joke, dear Wick: I did finish something, didn't I? Goodbye.

Don"

We now see the BIRNAM APARTMENT: Don is seated at the desk. As he has been out in the rain, his hair is still a little damp. He puts down the pen, gets up, stands the letter conspicuously on the desk, picks up the revolver, gets the cartridges from the drawer and loads the gun. With a last look at the room, he walks into the bathroom.— Don stands and looks at himself in the mirror, the gun in his hand. He notices the unbuttoned points of his collar and with a rueful smile at the funny timing of his urge for tidiness, buttons one. As he is buttoning the second, there is a sound from outside. Startled, Don puts the gun into the empty wash bowl.—The door is being opened. Dave, the janitor, is letting Helen in. She looks around wildly. She is breathing hard from her race to get there. There is rain on her hair and her face, and her dress is wet.—Don comes from the bathroom. Helen stands staring at him, wiping the rain from her face, and maybe some tears too.

DON. What is it, Helen?

HELEN (to the janitor). Thank you very much.

DAVE. That's all right, Miss.

He leaves, closing the door. Don and Helen are alone. During the following scene, Helen's eyes are constantly on the lookout for the gun.

DON. What's the matter? Come on.

HELEN. Nothing's the matter, except the rain's worse and I can't get a taxi. Perhaps you can lend me a coat under the circumstances.

DON. Sure. How about my raincoat? (He takes it from the hook.)

HELEN. Funny, after all these years we should wind up just as we met— I with your raincoat—

DON. And I with your leopard coat. I always got the best of the bargain. Goodbye, Helen.

HELEN. Goodbye. (*She stands looking about.*)

DON. What are you looking for?

HELEN. I just thought if you had anything for my hair—

DON. Would you care to wear my black derby?

HELEN. Some old scarf or something.

DON. All right.

He steps to the chest of drawers in the bedroom.—Helen, looking around desperately, sees something reflected in the shaving mirror: *the gun in the wash bowl.*—Before she can step toward it, Don is back with the scarf.

DON. Here you are.

HELEN. Thanks.

DON. Well, goodbye.

HELEN. Oh, Don, there was still some whiskey left in the bottle when I cleaned up last night.

DON. Was there?

HELEN. Wouldn't you like to know where I put it?

DON. No.

HELEN. Don't you want a drink, Don?

DON. No.

Helen goes to the umbrella stand. She takes out the bottle.

HELEN. Just one. Look, it's right here.

She puts down the raincoat and the scarf and goes to the kitchen for a glass.

DON. What are you up to?

HELEN. Nothing. I'm just ashamed of the way I talked to you, like a narrow-minded, insensitive, dried-up small-town teetotaller.

DON. I don't feel like a drink. Not now, I told you.

HELEN. Come on, Don. Just one. I'll have one with you. I'm in no hurry. This is my easy day at the office.

DON. Helen, there are a few things I want to put in order before Wick comes.

HELEN. Let me stay.

DON. No. (*He picks up the raincoat and the scarf.*) I'm sorry. You'll have to run along. (*He bends down for a kiss. Helen stands looking at him.*) Don't let me bend for nothing.

HELEN (*holding out the glass*). You need this, Don. Drink it. I want you to drink it. I'll get you some more. I'll get you all you want.

DON. What kind of talk is that?

HELEN. It's just that I'd rather have you drunk than dead.

DON. Who wants to be dead?

HELEN. Stop lying to me.

She turns and runs into the bathroom and picks up the gun. Don follows her.

DON. Give it to me. (*Helen holds it behind her.*) Helen!

Helen turns toward the window, lifting her arm to throw the gun out. Don catches her arm and twists it.

DON. Let go! (*Helen drops the gun, and Don picks it up.*) All right! Go on now.

He half pushes, half leads her into the entrance hall.

DON. And no fuss, please. And don't

call in the neighbors. It won't do any good, I promise you.

HELEN. I won't. You've made up your mind. But could you tell me why? Why?

DON. Because it's best all around, for everybody. For you, for Wick, for me.

HELEN. But that's not true. We love you, Wick and I.

DON. All right then—for me. Selfish again.

HELEN. That's a sad final word, Don.

DON. Look at it this way, Helen. This business is just a formality. Don Birnam is dead already. He died over this weekend.

HELEN. Did he? What did he die of?

DON. Of a lot of things. Of alcohol, of moral anemia, of fear, of shame, of D.T.'s.

HELEN. Oh, that Don Birnam! And now you want to kill the other one.

DON. What other?

HELEN. There were two Dons. You told me so yourself. Don the drunk, and Don the writer.

DON. Let's not go back to a fancy figure of speech. There's only one Don.

His eyes close and he starts to sag weakly. He slumps against the door and she steadies him.

DON. He's through!

HELEN. Don . . .

DON (*pushing her away and straightening up*). I'm all right. I still have enough strength left.

HELEN. I know you have. I can see it.

But don't waste it by pulling a trigger, Don.

DON. Oh, let me get it over with. Or do you want me to give you another one of my promises that I never keep?

HELEN. I don't want you to give me your promise. I don't want you to give your promise to anybody but Don Birnam.

DON (*seen closely*). It's too late! I wouldn't know how to start!

HELEN (*also seen closely*). The only way to start is to stop. There is no cure besides just stopping.

DON. Can't be done.

HELEN. Other people have stopped.

DON. People with a purpose—with something to do!

HELEN. You've got talent and ambition.

DON. Talent! Ambition! That's dead long ago. That's drowned. That's drifting around with a bloated belly on a lake of alcohol.

HELEN (*intensely*). No, it isn't. You still have it.

DON. Quit trying to stall me, Helen. It's too late. There's no more writing in me. It's gone. What do you expect —a miracle?

HELEN. Yes, yes, yes. If I could just make you— (*The doorbell rings.*)

DON. Who is it?

NAT'S VOICE. It's me, Mr. Birnam.

DON. What is it, Nat?

NAT. I got something for you.

Don goes to the door and opens it. Nat

stands outside holding something under his wet raincoat.

NAT. You know when you had your accident? Well, afterwards I found this floating around on the Nile. (*He pulls out Don's typewriter.*)

DON. Thank you, Nat.

NAT. She writes real good. I oiled her up a little. And I didn't oil her up so you can hock her.

HELEN. I'll take it, Nat.

NAT. Hello, Miss.

Helen takes the typewriter and carries it toward the desk.

NAT. Goodbye, everybody. (*Discreetly, to Don*) How's all them lilacs in Ohio?

Don goes into the living room. Helen sits at the desk, opening the typewriter.

HELEN. Well, Don, here it is. What do you say now?

DON. Say about what?

HELEN. This. Someone, somewhere, sent this typewriter back. Why? Because you're to stay alive—because he wants you to write! I didn't ask for a big miracle.

Don sits down on the arm of the chair, holding out his shaking hands.

DON. Write—with these hands, and a brain out of focus?

HELEN. It will clear up again. You'll be well.

DON. And I'll be sitting there, staring at that white sheet, scared!

HELEN. No, you won't. You've forgotten what it feels like to be well.

DON. What am I going to write about? What?!

HELEN. What you always wanted to write. Where's that page I found? (*She picks it up.*) "The Bottle. A Novel by Don Birnam." What was that to be?

DON. About a messed-up life, about a man and a woman and a bottle, and about nightmares, horrors, humiliations. All the things I want to forget.

HELEN. Put it all down on paper. Get rid of it. Tell it to all whom it may concern—and it concerns many people, Don.

DON. Yeah.

HELEN. I'll fix us some breakfast.

DON. We have a supply of milk.

We then see Helen in the KITCHEN starting to make coffee.

DON'S VOICE. You'll notice I didn't even find a first line.

HELEN. Of course you couldn't write the beginning because you didn't know the ending. Only now—

She turns and looks into the living room and breaks off, reacting as she sees: DON go across the room to the table and picking up a glass of whiskey. We see HELEN in the kitchen watching anxiously.

The scene cuts back to the LIVING ROOM and we see DON staring down into the whiskey glass. He takes a puff on his cigarette—and drops it into the whiskey glass with a gesture of finality.

The scene cuts to the KITCHEN and we see HELEN smiling with relief and happiness.

HELEN. Only now you know the ending.

The LIVING ROOM: Don is sitting down on the end of the studio couch.

DON. I'm going to send one copy to Bim, one to the doctor who loaned me his coat, and one to Nat. Imagine Wick standing in front of a bookstore—a great pyramid of my books. "A Novel by Don Birnam."—"That's my brother, you know."

Helen has entered the room; she goes over to him and sits down beside him.

HELEN. That's by my fellow. Didn't I always tell you?

DON. I'm going to put this whole weekend down, minute by minute.

HELEN. Why not?

DON. The way I stood there, packing my suitcase. Only my mind wasn't on the suitcase and it wasn't on the weekend, nor was it on the shirts I was putting in the suitcase, either.

The scene slowly dissolves to the APARTMENT WINDOW with Don in the bedroom packing. He looks out. The view then moves down to the bottle suspended on a cord outside the window and moves away from it along the wall of the building.

DON'S VOICE (*synchronized with the scene*). My mind was hanging outside the window. It was suspended just eighteen inches below. And out there in that great big concrete jungle . . .

This dissolves to the ROOF, to the first scene of the picture, the splendid panorama of the skyscrapers of New York.

DON'S VOICE (*continuing*). I wonder how many others there are like me. Poor bedeviled guys on fire with thirst. Such comical figures to the rest of the world, as they stagger blindly toward another binge—another bender—another spree.

And with these words, the scene fades out.

ALFRED HITCHCOCK'S

# SPELLBOUND

*(A Selznick International Picture)*

Screenplay by BEN HECHT

Suggested by FRANCIS BEEDING'S *Novel*,

THE HOUSE OF DR. EDWARDES

*Adaptation by* ANGUS MACPHAIL

*Produced by* DAVID O. SELZNICK

*Directed by* ALFRED HITCHCOCK

## The Cast

| | |
|---|---|
| DR. CONSTANCE PETERSEN . . | Ingrid Bergman |
| "J.B." . . . . . . . . . . . . | Gregory Peck |
| DR. ALEX BRULOV . . . . . . | Michael Chekhov |
| DR. MURCHISON . . . . . . . | Leo G. Carroll |
| DR. FLEUROT . . . . . . . . | John Emery |
| MISS CARMICHAEL . . . . . . | Rhonda Fleming |
| DR. GRAFF . . . . . . . . . | Steven Geray |
| DR. HANISH . . . . . . . . . | Paul Harvey |
| DR. GALT . . . . . . . . . . | Erskine Sanford |
| HARRY . . . . . . . . . . . | Donald Curtis |
| MR. GARMES . . . . . . . . | Norman Lloyd |
| THE STRANGER . . . . . . . | Wallace Ford |
| THE HOUSE DETECTIVE . . . | Bill Goodwin |
| SERGEANT GILLESPIE . . . . | Regis Toomey |
| LIEUTENANT COOLEY . . . . | Art Baker |
| DR. EDWARDES . . . . . . . | Edward Fielding |

and others

*Released by* UNITED ARTISTS

*Supervising Film Editor*—HAL C. KERN

*Associate Film Editor*—WILLIAM H. ZIEGLER

*Dream Sequence based on Designs by* SALVADOR DALI

*Psychiatric Advisor*—MAY E. ROMM, M.D.

# SPELLBOUND

## PART ONE

Over a distant view of the exterior of Green Manors, a fairly conventional large country house in Vermont, the following title is superimposed:

THE FAULT IS NOT IN OUR STARS, BUT IN OURSELVES. . . .
—SHAKESPEARE

The title continues (after a lap dissolve), superimposed over a close view of the entrance doors to Green Manors:

> OUR STORY DEALS WITH PSYCHOANALYSIS, THE
> METHOD BY WHICH MODERN SCIENCE TREATS THE
> EMOTIONAL PROBLEMS OF THE SANE.

> THE ANALYST SEEKS ONLY TO INDUCE THE PATIENT
> TO TALK ABOUT HIS HIDDEN PROBLEMS, TO OPEN
> THE LOCKED DOORS OF HIS MIND.

> ONCE THE COMPLEXES THAT HAVE BEEN DISTURBING THE
> PATIENT ARE UNCOVERED AND INTERPRETED, THE
> ILLNESS AND CONFUSION DISAPPEAR . . . AND THE
> DEVILS OF UNREASON ARE DRIVEN FROM THE HUMAN
> SOUL.

The title dissolves out and the view stays for a moment on the doors.

This dissolves to a DRAWING ROOM: a very comfortable lounge, more or less like one in a hotel. A dozen or more patients sit around. They are playing cards, listening to the radio, sewing. Several of them sit in katatonic postures, staring. There is a nurse at each end of the room. We open on a group of women who are playing cards. They look up. One of them, a woman of thirty, is more attentive than the rest. She is thin, thyroidic, and aristocratic looking.

NURSE'S VOICE. Miss Carmichael, please. Dr. Petersen is ready for you.

Miss Carmichael rises. She speaks to her Rummy partner:

MISS CARMICHAEL (*in a very "social" voice*). Awf'ly sorry, I have to go. Had a perfect hand. Would have beaten the pants off you.

She crosses the room toward the nurse who is standing with a good-looking, white-shirted attendant, Harry.

The nurse and the attendant are then seen in a semi-closeup; their eyes are on Miss Carmichael. The view moves (camera pulls back and pans right)

EDWARDES: I remember, now . . .

FLEUROT: A woman like you could never become involved emotionally
with any man, sane or insane.

J.B: Darling, I have a confession to make.

BRULOV: I am calling the police!

to Harry and Nurse as Carmichael goes to the door in the background.

NURSE. Harry will take you, Miss Carmichael.

MISS CARMICHAEL. Oh, thank you.

NURSE (*quietly to the attendant*). Watch her carefully. Don't take your eyes off her.

Harry nods and walks to Miss Carmichael at the door and the scene dissolves to the CORRIDOR as they come out on the other side of the door. Miss Carmichael looks up at Harry.

MISS CARMICHAEL (*softly; flirtatiously*). How are you today, Harry?

HARRY. Fine.

MISS CARMICHAEL. You look a little bilious.

HARRY (*blandly—he is used to everything*). It's the light.

MISS CARMICHAEL (*softly*). I worry about you, dear.

HARRY. I'll be all right.

They have arrived outside a door marked "Dr. Petersen."

MISS CARMICHAEL. Must we dash into Dr. Petersen's office? Can't we go sit down somewhere in private and talk? Just you and I.

HARRY (*brusquely*). Love it. If I had time.

MISS CARMICHAEL (*clinging to him suddenly*). Would you?

Harry melts a little, whereupon Miss Carmichael looks very pleased and takes his hand.

THEIR TWO HANDS are then seen as Miss Carmichael viciously draws her sharp fingernails across the back of Harry's hand, leaving deep scratches.

HARRY and CARMICHAEL: Harry glares at her both from pain and indignation at being taken in. Miss Carmichael laughs in satisfaction. Harry rings the buzzer beside the door.

In DR. PETERSEN's OFFICE: DR. CONSTANCE PETERSEN sits behind a desk before a window at the far side of the room. She is a woman just under thirty, slightly austere and a bit arrogant looking. She takes off her glasses as she looks up on hearing the buzzer. She has a professional voice.

CONSTANCE. Come in.

Miss Carmichael enters as Harry stands behind her, holding the door. She becomes suddenly haughty.

MISS CARMICHAEL. You ruined a very interesting card game, Dr. Petersen.

CONSTANCE at the desk shows no emotion at Miss Carmichael's complaint.

CONSTANCE. You may go now, Harry.

Harry closes the door, while Miss Carmichael remains standing.

HARRY. I'll be outside.

Constance Petersen rises and puts a cigarette in a long holder. She lights it as she moves around the desk. Then (the camera pulling back) we see the two women.

CONSTANCE. I hope you feel better today, Mary.

Constance seats herself on a chair at the head of the couch.

MISS CARMICHAEL (*with a sneer*). Well, I don't.

CONSTANCE (*smiling*). You will.

MISS CARMICHAEL. I think this whole thing is ridiculous.

CONSTANCE (*quietly*). What whole thing, Mary?

MISS CARMICHAEL. Psychoanalysis. It bores the pants off me. Lying on a couch like some dreary nit-wit, telling all! (*She glares at Constance and speaks with highty-tighty sarcasm.*) You don't really expect to get anywhere listening to me babble about my idiotic childhood! Really!

CONSTANCE (*calmly*). My patients invariably regard me as a wretched nuisance—during our first talks.

MISS CARMICHAEL (*sarcastic still*). I see. It's my subconscious putting up a fight! It doesn't want me cured! (*She lies down on the couch.*)

CONSTANCE. Exactly. It wants to continue enjoying your disease. Our job is to make you understand why. When you know *why* you are doing something that is bad for you—and *when* you first started doing it—then you can begin curing yourself.

MISS CARMICHAEL (*sitting up on the couch*). You mean I've been telling you lies.

CONSTANCE. The usual proportion.

We get a closeup of Miss Carmichael as she lies back again. (The camera moves in to a BIG HEAD.)

MISS CARMICHAEL (*suddenly—as she stares at the ceiling*). You're right. I've been lying like mad. I hate men. I loathe them. When one of them so much as touches me, I want to sink my teeth into his hand and bite it off. In fact, I did that once. Would you care to hear about it?

She looks across to Constance, and we see the latter from Miss Carmichael's viewpoint.

CONSTANCE. Tell me anything you remember.

Miss Carmichael, seen in a closeup, continues thoughtfully:

MISS CARMICHAEL. We were dancing. He kept asking me to marry him—panting in my ear. And I suddenly pretended I was going to kiss him—and sank my teeth into his mustache. I bit it—clear off.

At this the view expands (the camera whips back) to include the two women as Miss Carmichael suddenly sits up and turns on Constance in a voice filled with rage.

MISS CARMICHAEL. You're laughing at me! That smug, frozen face of yours doesn't take me in!

Constance moves over to her desk to press a button as Miss Carmichael rants on.

MISS CARMICHAEL. You just want me to tell you all this so you can feel superior to me! You and your drooling science! I detest you!

She picks up a book and flings it at Constance. It strikes her shoulder and falls to the desk. Constance pulls her glasses out of the way to prevent the book falling on them.

MISS CARMICHAEL. I never want to see that nasty face of yours again!

There is a pause as Constance stands facing Miss Carmichael. Her manner is calm. She looks at the raging patient aloofly—and makes no attempt to interrupt her. Miss Carmichael begins to sob hysterically.

MISS CARMICHAEL. What do you know about anything? I can't bear you! You and your nickel's worth of nothing!

There is the sound of a door opening.

Constance looks up as Miss Carmichael turns.

The door has opened and Harry, the attendant, enters and moves into the room. The figure of a newcomer, Doctor Fleurot, a man of forty, remains in the doorway.

Harry enters the scene as Constance gestures to Miss Carmichael with her long holder. He takes Miss Carmichael's arm.

HARRY (*softly*). Come on, Miss Carmichael.

The scene moves with them (camera pans them) to the door as she goes with him, her sobs lessening.

MISS CARMICHAEL. The silly fool! Letting a creature like that worry me! Miss Frozen-puss! (*As she sees Fleurot*) Oh—Dr. Fleurot! I want to talk to you—alone—I can't stand that woman!

FLEUROT. I'll see you later, Mary.

HARRY. Come, Miss Carmichael.

Harry escorts her through the door, closing it after him. Doctor Fleurot comes into the room. He crosses to where Constance remains calm but intent. He seats himself on the edge of the desk, facing her. Then we get a semi-closeup of the two.

FLEUROT (*smiling at her*). Murchison must be really out of his mind to assign Carmichael to you.

CONSTANCE (*stiffly*). You may report your findings to the new head when he arrives.

FLEUROT. You can't treat a love veteran like Carmichael without some inside information.

CONSTANCE. I have done a great deal

of research on emotional problems and love difficulties.

FLEUROT. Research, my eye! If you read your head off for fifty years—you'll still be a scientist up a tree.

CONSTANCE. I see. You have some other course of instruction to suggest.

FLEUROT. Most definitely! I've been watching your work for six months. It's brilliant—but lifeless. There's no intuition in it. You approach all your problems with an ice pack on your head.

CONSTANCE. Are you making love to me?

FLEUROT. I will in a moment. I'm just clearing the ground first. I'm trying to convince you that your lack of human and emotional experience is bad for you—as a doctor. And fatal for you as a woman.

CONSTANCE. I've heard that argument from a number of amorous psychiatrists—who all wanted to make a better doctor of me.

He moves from his position on the edge of the desk and seats himself beside her on the arm of her chair.

FLEUROT. Ah, but I've got a much better argument. I'm terribly fond of you.

CONSTANCE (*coolly*). Why?

FLEUROT (*putting his arm around her*). It's very much like embracing a text book.

CONSTANCE. But why do you do it?

FLEUROT. Because you're not a text book. You're a sweet, pulsing, adorable woman—underneath. I sense it every time I come near to you.

CONSTANCE. You sense only your own

desires and pulsations. I assure you —mine in no way resemble them.

The camera moves in as he bends his head toward her.

FLEUROT (*his face close to her— softly*). Stop it. (*He holds her more tightly.*) I'm mad about you.

She stares at him. He kisses her intensely. He holds it for a few seconds and then draws away. Constance remains quite unperturbed. He looks at her with a frown.

FLEUROT. I'm afraid I'm boring you.

The camera recedes as the tension relaxes.

CONSTANCE (*coolly*). No. Your attitudes are very interesting.

FLEUROT. I feel exactly like Miss Carmichael. I'd like to throw a book at you—but I won't. (*He stares at her —then picks up a book.*) May I borrow this?

CONSTANCE. Certainly.

FLEUROT. Oh. And—forgive me for my criticism. I think you'd better stick to books. And another thing—

Both look up at a slight sound, whereupon we see a slim middle-aged man standing in the doorway.

Fleurot rises from the arm of Constance's chair as she looks up at the newcomer.

MURCHISON (*smiling*). Pardon me for marching in. But I'm spreading the tidings. My successor will be due any moment.

FLEUROT (*rising*). Well, Dr. Murchison—it's been a pleasure working under you.

MURCHISON. Thank you very much.

FLEUROT. Coming, Dr. Petersen?

CONSTANCE. Oh. I'm in no mad hurry to welcome Dr. Edwardes.

Fleurot goes out, and we get a semicloseup of CONSTANCE and MURCHISON.

CONSTANCE. It's hard to imagine this place without you, Dr. Murchison.

MURCHISON. Yes, I sort of go with the fixtures.

CONSTANCE. More than that—you are Green Manors. It seems unfair.

MURCHISON. You are very young in the profession. You haven't learned the basic secret of science. The old must make way for the new. Particularly when the old is suspected of a touch of senility.

CONSTANCE. But that's ridiculous. I should think the Board of Directors would realize you're feeling much better. You've been like a new man since your vacation.

MURCHISON. The Board's as fair and all knowing as a hospital board can be. Oh, I agree with you that I'm as able and brilliant as ever. But having crumbled once, I might crumble again.

CONSTANCE. You were overworked.

MURCHISON. A charming diagnosis for a broken-down horse.

CONSTANCE. I shall always remember your cheerfulness today—as a lesson in how to accept reality, Dr. Murchison.

The camera pulls back as Murchison rises.

MURCHISON. Don't be too taken in by my happy air, Constance. It's the least difficult way of saying goodbye to twenty years.

CONSTANCE. Yes, I know—

Both look up toward the door, as they hear the buzzer.

CONSTANCE. Come in.

The door is then seen opening and the attendant, Harry, enters.

HARRY. Your mail, Dr. Petersen. And Mr. Garmes.

Mr. Garmes is a plump, well-groomed, honest-looking gentleman.

CONSTANCE and MURCHISON are again seen in a semi-closeup.

CONSTANCE. Come in, Mr. Garmes. (*To Murchison*) You're not leaving —today? I'll see you again?

MURCHISON. I shall hover around for a while—like an old mother hen—at least until Dr. Edwardes is firmly on the nest.

Constance looks after him as he goes out, her eyes full of thought.

Harry crosses the scene in front of her to put the mail on her desk, and the view expands to include Mr. Garmes who comes toward her. As Harry leaves, Constance talks to her patient who comes up to the desk with her.

CONSTANCE. How do you feel today, Mr. Garmes?

GARMES (*politely*). Somewhat better, Doctor. The thing seems a little less troublesome.

Constance starts to open her mail. She is using a rather wicked-looking knife-like letter opener. Garmes comes forward and eyes the knife.

GARMES. May—I do that for you, Doctor?

Constance smiles at him and moves the knife out of his reach.

CONSTANCE. Thank you, no. I can do it myself—very well. Please sit down. I'll be with you in a moment.

As he seats himself, the camera moves in and we get a semi-closeup of GARMES. His face bears an expression of great interest as we hear the sound of tearing paper caused by Constance's inserting the knife into the envelopes.

The scene dissolves to MURCHISON'S OF-FICE. Assembled here are a group of doctors, Fleurot among them. They are gathered around a window looking down. Then over the shoulders of the three, we can see through the window to the ground below. Two men are seen. One has just alighted from a car which is driving away. A manservant is gathering up a suitcase.

FLEUROT (*at the window*). So that's the mighty Anthony Edwardes.

DR. GRAFF. He looks a little younger than I expected.

HANISH. He has only brought one suitcase. Perhaps he doesn't intend to remain very long.

FLEUROT. Leave those day-dreams to Dr. Murchison.

The group begins to turn away from the window as the two figures disappear below. (The camera pulls back with them.) Then the door opens, and Dr. Galt ushers in Dr. Edwardes. Edwardes is a vivid, healthy-looking man in his thirties. (The camera moves in slightly as Galt begins to introduce the newcomer.)

GALT. Gentlemen—our new chief— Dr. Anthony Edwardes. Dr. Fleurot.

EDWARDES. How do you do? (*He smiles.*)

FLEUROT. How do you do?

DR. GRAFF. I am Dr. Graff.

EDWARDES. How do you do?

GALT. And Dr. Hanish. There are still some staff members missing, Dr. Edwardes. These are your quarters.

EDWARDES. They're very festive—for an institution.

They all turn at the sound of the door opening, and we then see Murchison appearing in the doorway. The view moves with him to the group. Galt makes a quick introduction.

GALT. Dr. Edwardes—Dr. Murchison.

The camera moves in until the two men are in profile.

EDWARDES. How do you do, Dr. Murchison. I've heard a great deal about you, sir.

MURCHISON (*amiably*). And I, naturally, about you. You're younger than I thought you would be.

EDWARDES. My age hasn't caught up with me yet.

MURCHISON (*smiling*). Mine has—it seems. And I am pleased to hand over the reins to steadier hands. I am leaving you my library which contains among other items of interest, your latest volume—*The Labyrinth of the Guilt Complex*. An excellent work. I hope Green Manors will inspire others as fine.

EDWARDES. I am very grateful—

MURCHISON. I don't know the formal words for an abdication, Doctor Edwardes. May I say merely that these quarters which I have occupied for twenty years—are now yours. Will you excuse me?

(The camera pulls back so that we see him leave the room with the rest of the doctors remaining in tableau, their heads all turned in his direction.)

The scene dissolves to a LARGE PUBLIC DINING ROOM at night. First there is a closeup of Murchison at a table. Then the view expands disclosing the entire scene. (During the first speech the camera pulls back to reveal a full view of the staff table. Seated around it we find Doctors Graff, Fleurot, Galt, Petersen, as well as Murchison. There are two empty chairs between Constance and Fleurot. The latter two are conversing across the two chairs.)

FLEUROT. I spent a half hour with Dr. Edwardes and I must say I was most favorably impressed.

CONSTANCE. I intend to learn a great deal from Dr. Edwardes. I think we all can from a man of such obvious talents.

MURCHISON. You are familiar with his work?

CONSTANCE. Oh, yes. I have read all his books. A very keen and unorthodox mind, I think. It would be dreadful if Dr. Murchison's successor were—unworthy of him.

We get a semi-closeup of the group at the table, as Galt suddenly announces quietly:

GALT. He's joining us.

Then, from their viewpoint across the dining room, we see the approaching figure of Edwardes. The scene moves with him to include the rest of the people at the table.

MURCHISON (*rising*). I think you know every one here, Dr. Edwardes.

EDWARDES (*looking at Constance*). No. Not yet.

MURCHISON. Oh, this is Dr. Petersen.

EDWARDES (*holding out his hand*). How do you do?

CONSTANCE (*raising her hand to his*). Dr. Edwardes.

The camera moves in as Edwardes sits down in the empty chair next to Constance.

EDWARDES. Dr. Hanish has been showing me the grounds. A remarkable institution, Dr. Murchison. It must be quite beautiful in the summer.

HANISH. I pointed out to Dr. Edwardes—our various open air diversions for the patients.

CONSTANCE. Doctor Murchison always argued that we did not do enough in that direction. And I agree with him.

FLEUROT (*smiling at Edwardes*). Let me warn you that Doctor Petersen is a frustrated gymnast.

CONSTANCE. Well, Doctor Fleurot considers anything beyond sitting and standing—gymnastics.

EDWARDES. I imagine you're very fond of sports.

CONSTANCE. Yes—I am. And I miss them—particularly winter sports. . . . (*Smiling*) Did you show Doctor Edwardes the elm grove?

HANISH. Yes—yes, indeed.

CONSTANCE. That's where we hope to have our new swimming pool.

EDWARDES (*to Constance*). Oh, I'm a great believer in swimming pools.

CONSTANCE (*eagerly*). There's a perfect spot for it—among the elms. Not an oblong one, but an irregular pool something—something like this —you know—

Constance starts to draw a design on the tablecloth with the prongs of a fork.

—A closeup shows Constance's fork pressing fairly defined lines on the tablecloth.

CONSTANCE. The bath houses will be at . . .

A closeup shows Edwardes staring down at the table. We see his expression changing. He is no longer amiable. Suddenly he speaks sharply:

EDWARDES. I take it that the supply of linen at this institution is inexhaustible.

We get a semi-closeup of the group looking up at him.

EDWARDES (*catching himself and trying to make his voice smooth*). Forgive me.

SEMI-CLOSEUP: During this, Constance looks at him intently for a moment and then looks around at the others.— SEMI-CLOSEUP: The rest of the doctors are all smiling oddly at Edwardes. There is an awkward pause.—SEMI-CLOSEUP: The group. Constance speaks quickly, as if protecting him instinctively against their derision.

CONSTANCE. That reminds me of my professor in psychiatry, Dr. Brulov. He could never stand a sauce bottle on the table—or even a salt shaker. They took his appetite away. I remember once at a banquet in his honor, he refused to sit at the speakers' table because he was completely surrounded by—by catsup.

They all laugh, including Edwardes, who is smoothing out the marks on the tablecloth with his knife.

A closeup shows Constance looking down, the laughter dying from her face as she sees what Edwardes is doing. Another closeup shows the knife smoothing the marks out from the tablecloth. Then the scene fades out.

# PART TWO

CONSTANCE'S OFFICE fades in. Bright sunlight strikes across Constance, who is sitting at her desk in her office living room. She is busy writing up one of her case histories. Fleurot is sitting on the couch talking across to her.

FLEUROT (*grinning*). Last night at dinner, a dimple appeared in your cheek—that was never there before. And I detected the outcroppings of a mother instinct toward Dr. Edwardes.

CONSTANCE. Oh, I detest that sort of high school talk.

FLEUROT. Your reactions have upset one of my pet theories about you— to wit: that you were immune to psychoanalysts. And would end up in the arms of some Boob McNutt with spiked hair.

CONSTANCE (*coldly*). If I were looking for that type, Dr. Fleurot, I would long ago have adored you. (*Both look up, at a knock on the door.*) Come in.

The door opens and Harry, the attendant, appears and goes to Constance.

HARRY. I—oh, excuse me. It's from Dr. Edwardes.

He hands her a sealed envelope. She opens it. Fleurot rises and speaks as she reads.

FLEUROT. Ah—love notes, already! The French school of science.

We see the NOTE held in Constance's hand. It reads:

"Your patient Mr. Garmes is here. Please come immediately.
                    Anthony Edwardes"

The scene dissolves to DR. EDWARDES'

OFFICE, with Edwardes seated at his desk. Mr. Garmes, a patient, is seated on the couch. Garmes is talking in a low and intense voice.

GARMES (*seen in a semi-closeup as he addresses Edwardes*). I didn't want to come to this institution, but my brother insisted. I can see no sense in it, myself. You see, I am convinced I am not suffering from any hallucination, but that my guilt is very real. I know, Dr. Edwardes, that I killed my father—and I am willing to pay the penalty for . . . (*He breaks off.*)

EDWARDES (*hearing a knock on the door*). Come in. (*The door opens and Constance enters.*) Oh—thank you for coming so soon. I've been listening to Mr. Garmes, and thought you might help me out.

CONSTANCE. Mr. Garmes, you shouldn't have disturbed Dr. Edwardes.

EDWARDES (*slowly*). It's all right. I'm very interested in Mr. Garmes' case.

CONSTANCE. I knew you would be. He fits perfectly into your chapters on the guilt complex.

GARMES. Would you mind telling me what you are talking about?

CONSTANCE (*turning to Garmes*). You are here to see if we can cure your guilt complex by psychoanalysis, Mr. Garmes.

A closeup shows Garmes beginning to shake. He wipes his fingers down the side of his face.

GARMES. But I have no guilt complex. I know—what I know. I killed my father—and—

SEMI-CLOSEUP: Constance watches him and then moves across to sit down beside him.

CONSTANCE (*quietly, as she sits down beside him*). No—you didn't kill your father. That's a misconception that has taken hold of you. (*She turns to Edwardes.*) Oh—I'm sorry, Doctor —you were talking to him.

EDWARDES. No, no—go on.

CONSTANCE (*to Garmes*). People often feel guilty over something they never did. It usually goes back to their childhood. A child often wishes something terrible would happen to someone. And if something does happen to that person the child believes he has caused it. And he grows up with a guilt complex—over a sin that was only a child's bad dream.

GARMES (*slowly*). What I am thinking isn't true, then?

CONSTANCE. No. And in the course of analyzing yourself, you will see that. Would you care to go back to your room, Mr. Garmes?

Garmes rises. (The camera pulls back.) Constance moves across to the door and opens it, calling "Harry!" She looks back compassionately toward Garmes while waiting for Harry to appear. The attendant presents himself, crosses and takes Garmes by his arm and leads him out. Constance closes the door and goes to Edwardes.

CONSTANCE. I think we'd better put him under drugs for a few days. He looks agitated.

EDWARDES (*quietly*). His conviction —is curious.

CONSTANCE. But you've encountered such cases very often, Dr. Edwardes. You described them perfectly in your book.

EDWARDES (*softly*). Yes—yes—so I did. (*Rising and frowning*) Would you mind doing me a favor?

CONSTANCE (*smiling*). Not at all, Doctor.

EDWARDES. I've a headache. I'd like to take the afternoon off—with you. I understand you're not on duty till after dinner.

CONSTANCE. I—I intended typing up my notes.

EDWARDES (*coming to her side*). Please. I need a little fresh air, and you look as though it might do you a bit of good.

CONSTANCE. I was going to lunch with Dr. Hanish. He has an interesting new patient—a kleptomaniac who—

EDWARDES (*interrupting*). Kleptomaniacs for lunch! They'll steal the food out of your mouth. (*The phone rings.*) Excuse me. (*Edwardes picks up the phone and speaks into it.*) Hello. . . . Yes, Dr. Edwardes. . . . What? . . . Yes, Anthony Edwardes . . . Who? . . . Sorry, I don't get your name. . . . Norma Cramer. . . . (*He listens and then answers sharply:*) Please, Miss Cramer, I'm very busy and I don't know you. (*He hangs up and smiles nervously at Constance.*) Some girl claiming to be— (*He breaks off.*) I hate practical jokes, don't you? (*He smiles at her.*) People calling you up and chirping, "guess who I am!"

CONSTANCE. It sounds like some ex-patient of yours. They're always full of coy little tricks.

EDWARDES. Very likely . . . Come on. Let's go. We'll look at 'some sane trees, normal grass, and clouds without complexes.

As he leads Constance out of the office, Edwardes looks back over his shoulder at the telephone, vaguely disturbed. Then the scene dissolves to a beautiful view of the VERMONT COUNTRYSIDE and we see the figures of Edwardes and Constance climbing, in the distance, toward the top of a hill. It is late afternoon.—This dissolves to a nearer view of Constance and Edwardes showing that they are each carrying a sandwich package and a bottle of pop. The day is brisk, and a wind is blowing. Constance is talking as we come upon them.

CONSTANCE. I think the greatest harm done the human race has been done by the poets.

EDWARDES. Poets are dull boys, most of them—but not especially fiendish.

CONSTANCE (*firmly*). They keep filling people's heads with delusions about—about love. Writing about it as if it were a symphony orchestra and a flight of angels.

EDWARDES (*smiling, as they come to a field rail fence*). Which it isn't—eh?

Constance starts to stick her leg through the fence and duck under the rail. Edwardes helps her by lifting the half-rotted upper rail. Her stocking is torn on the lower rail as she pushes through.

CONSTANCE (*struggling thus to get through the fence*). Of course it isn't! People fall in love—as they put it—because they respond to certain hair coloring, or vocal tones, or mannerisms that remind them of their parents.

EDWARDES (*helping her out*). Sometimes for no reason at all.

CONSTANCE. But that's not the point. The point is that people read about love as one thing—and experience it as another. They expect kisses to be like lyrical poems and—and embraces to be like Shakespearean dramas.

EDWARDES. And when they find out differently—then they get sick and have to be analyzed, eh?

CONSTANCE. Yes—very often.

EDWARDES. Professor, you are suffering from mogo on the gogo.

CONSTANCE (*startled*). I beg your pardon.

They have come to another fence. This one is reinforced with old barbed wire. She starts to crawl through the wire by lifting one of the strands.

EDWARDES. Hey—you can't get through there like that.

CONSTANCE (*looking up at him*). Of course I can. Now really, I've crawled through here many times.

Edwardes tries to assist Constance, but she leaps out of his embrace and falls on the other side in some disarray.

CONSTANCE (*exasperated*). Oh! (*He vaults over and joins her.*)

EDWARDES (*bending over her*). Whoops—hurt?

CONSTANCE (*starting to get up*). No, not at all.

EDWARDES (*holding out his hands to help her*). Here.

CONSTANCE. No. No—I'm perfectly all right.

She takes his hands and he pulls her to her feet.

CONSTANCE (*as they resume walking uphill*). Well, I've usually gone on picnics here—alone.

EDWARDES. Well, that doesn't sound like much fun.

CONSTANCE. I haven't gone in for fun —as you call it. (*Looking around at the scenery*) Isn't this beautiful?

Her eyes are on the landscape below. Her voice is soft and happy as she speaks—and Edwardes watches her, held by her radiance.

EDWARDES. Perfect.

We get a semi-closeup of the two as Edwardes undoes the sandwiches.

EDWARDES. Oh, lunch—lunch, what'll you have—ham or liverwurst?

CONSTANCE (*her voice still full of mood*). Liverwurst.

She takes the sandwich and stares at the scenery; and as he eats and looks at her, the scene dissolves out.

The DINING ROOM dissolves in, at night. Present at the staff table are Murchison, Fleurot, Graff, Hanish and Galt. All heads are turned toward Murchison. Two empty chairs are conspicuous in the foreground.

GRAFF. Has anybody seen our new chief today?

FLEUROT (*smiling*). He has been— tied up.

MURCHISON. Yes—he frisked off with Doctor Petersen at noon.

HANISH. It's odd spending his first day running after Doctor Petersen like a drooling college boy.

FLEUROT. It'll do Constance good to be drooled over. The poor girl is withering away with science. I was telling her, only recently, that some-

thing vital was missing from her life.

They look around suddenly, and we see from their viewpoint that Constance is crossing the room. She looks a little flushed, with her hair slightly disarranged. Constance comes up to the table as the doctors rise.

CONSTANCE. Oh, please don't get up. I just came in because I learned Mr. Garmes became agitated again this afternoon.

GALT. Yes. I gave him a sedative.

CONSTANCE. I'm very sorry I wasn't here.

FLEUROT. Nonsense. You look as if you have had an instructive time.

Constance, seen in a semi-closeup, stares at him.

CONSTANCE. Instructive?

Then we again see the men at the table.

FLEUROT. Gentlemen, notice her stockings. The lady has been climbing trees. (*He points to a tear in her hose.*)

Constance, seen in a semi-closeup, looks down at her legs unconsciously, while over this we hear the voice of Galt.

GALT'S VOICE. Or lolling in a briar patch.

FLEUROT (*as the group comes into view again*). No, it's trees. There are two leaves in her hair. Allow me, Doctor Petersen. (*He removes a bit of greenery from her coiffure.*)

CONSTANCE (*coldly*). You are surpassing yourself as a charmer, Doctor Fleurot.

DR. GRAFF. Don't run away. Do have some coffee.

FLEUROT. Doctor Petersen has already eaten. As one can tell by the mustard on her right forefinger. I would say hot dogs on the State Highway.

CONSTANCE. Would you, really? Your diagnosis is, as usual, wrong, Doctor Fleurot. Not hot dogs. Liverwurst. (*She turns to go.*) I am very sorry I have to leave this nursery. I must see Mr. Garmes. (*She walks out.*)

AT THE TABLE, with the group looking after Constance:

FLEUROT. It looks like we have Casanova, himself, at the head of Green Manors. Did you notice her blushing every time we said his name?

The scene dissolves to a view of GREEN MANORS. It is a windy night. Then we get a closeup of Constance lying in bed, her eyes open. Almost reluctantly she looks upwards, her mind obviously on Edwardes. She hesitates for a moment or two, then sits up in bed. The scene expands (the camera pulls back) disclosing her BEDROOM, as she half gets out and sits on the side of the bed, with her feet on the floor. She puts them into a pair of slippers and picks up a negligee from a chair. It is a white tailored negligee made from a material that has a pattern of straight lines woven into it. The view moves with her as she moves across to the door and out of the room.

This cuts to the HALLWAY as Constance emerges into the hall and looks around her, slightly furtively. She mounts the stairs. There is an anxious, hopeful expression on her face. Then the view, leaving Constance, moves up the stairs, turns, and as soon as it leaves the upper floor level, we see the light is still burning under Edwardes' door.

A closeup shows that Constance's face has a slightly disturbed expression. Then we see her hurrying past Edwardes' door and going to the door of the library.

Constance enters the LIBRARY and switches on the light. At first a dim light shows, then she turns on two more switches so that the room is fully and brightly lit. She goes to some shelves, where we see three books, reading from left to right: *Amnesia*—Golden; *Recent Advances in Neuroses*—Wright; *The Labyrinth of the Guilt Complex*—Edwardes.—She takes down the last book. The camera moves in until the book fills the screen.

As she opens it, the first end leaf reads: "This special edition of *The Labyrinth of the Guilt Complex* is limited to seven hundred and fifty copies, each signed by the author."

Below the printed lines is the signature, "Anthony Edwardes." The book closes, and the camera pulls back as Constance moves across the room to the door. She switches off the lights and goes into the hallway.

Next we see Constance walking across the HALLWAY, but she stops short as she sees, from her viewpoint, the light showing under Edwardes' door.—In a semi-closeup we then see Constance's overpowering desire to go in and talk to Edwardes. But she passes his door and starts down the stairs. Then she hesitates, turns back, and quickly crosses to his door. She taps quietly. There is no answer. She gives a quick glance around, and then tries the doorknob. The door opens, allowing a flood of light into the half-lit hall.

In EDWARDES' OFFICE: She comes into the brightly lighted room and looks about her. It is empty. She looks into the bedroom beyond. The door is half opened. Sitting in an armchair, with a robe over his shirt and trousers, is Dr. Edwardes. He is dozing.

A semi-closeup shows that CONSTANCE doesn't know whether to attract his attention or not, and another semi-closeup, that EDWARDES opens his eyes and stares at her intently. Then, from his viewpoint, we see Constance standing in the outer room. She stands awkwardly; her manner is that of a school girl of fifteen. Her tones are apologetic and abstracted.

CONSTANCE. It's very late.

EDWARDES smiles and nods.—Constance advances slowly toward the camera and into the door frame between the two rooms.

CONSTANCE. I was going to read your new book. I would like to discuss it —I've never discussed an author's work with him. Of course, at school we had several literary professors. But that was quite different. (*Her embarrassment runs her down and she stands frowning at him.*) I sound rather nervous, don't I?

EDWARDES (*in a closeup, softly*). Not at all.

CONSTANCE (*seen with Edwardes*). I thought I wanted to discuss your book with you. I am amazed at the subterfuge. (*She stares at him a moment.*) I don't want to discuss it at all.

EDWARDES (*softly*). I understand.

CONSTANCE (*staring at him*). It's quite remarkable to discover that one isn't what one thought—one was. I mean, I have always been entirely aware of what was in my mind.

EDWARDES. And you're not, now?

CONSTANCE (*almost angrily*). This is quite ridiculous. It was stupid of me to come in here—like a distracted child.

EDWARDES. You're very lovely.

CONSTANCE (*frowning*). Please—don't talk that way. You'll think I came in to hear that— (*She breaks off.*)

EDWARDES. I know why you came in.

CONSTANCE (*softly*). Why?

EDWARDES. Because something has happened to us. (*He comes toward her.*)

CONSTANCE. But it doesn't happen like that—in a day—

EDWARDES (*softly*). It happens in a moment—sometimes. I felt it this afternoon. It was like lightning striking. It strikes rarely—

He advances toward the camera until his face fills the screen. He inclines his head slightly. His mouth goes out of the picture. Constance's eyes fill the screen. They begin to close slowly.— Edwardes' nose and eyes begin to blur and fade away. Their place is taken by a large door which opens by an unseen hand; beyond this is another door which swings open, and then another, until we see a whole succession of doors opening, one after another, as though down a long corridor. Then as the picture clears, we see the two profiles emerging from the kiss. Next the camera pulls back slightly, showing Constance still clinging to him.

CONSTANCE (*faintly*). I don't understand—how it happened.

A closeup shows Edwardes looking down at her neck, and in another closeup, from his viewpoint, we see the lines woven into the material of her negligee. Somehow they seem accentuated.

There is a closeup as Edwardes' stare increases. His face fills with the same curious look of fear that came to it when he looked at the fork lines drawn

on the tablecloth. He struggles to remove his eyes from her shoulder, but
his gaze is held. His alarm and tension
increase. He pushes her away.

Constance looks up and sees the expression of terror in his face. Confusion
overcomes her as she almost staggers
back from him.

CONSTANCE (*gasping*). What is it?

EDWARDES (*hoarsely*). It's not you. It's
something about your robe.

CONSTANCE (*staring*). My robe! I
don't understand.

EDWARDES (*recovering himself partly*).
Forgive me. Something struck me.
I've been having a—rather bad time
with my nerves lately. Your robe—
I mean, the dark lines—

The telephone rings from the other
room.

CONSTANCE (*tenderly*). You're ill.

EDWARDES (*as the phone continues
ringing*). No. I'll be all right.

He goes to the telephone and speaks
into it automatically.

EDWARDES. Hello. Yes—Dr. Edwardes
. . . Yes . . . Yes . . what! Where
is he? . . . . I'll be there right away.
(*He hangs up and crosses to Constance.*) Mr. Garmes has run amuck.
He tried to murder Fleurot and then
cut his own throat.

He slips his bathrobe off and picks up
his coat to put on.

CONSTANCE (*her voice suddenly calm
and professional*). Is it bad?

They both move out of the room as
Edwardes answers:

EDWARDES. I think so. He's in surgery.

CONSTANCE. I'll be right along.

The scene dissolves to the OPERATING
ROOM, and the camera moves in to take
a closer view of what is happening.
We see that Garmes is lying on the
surgical table. A blood transfusion apparatus is beside it. A transfusion is in
progress. Present are Drs. Murchison,
Fleurot and Graff, with two of the
night nurses. The room is lighted like
a surgery. As the camera gets nearer
we are able to see that Garmes' throat
is heavily bandaged and he is unconscious. Fleurot's face has been cut. His
cheek is taped and bandaged.—The
doctors and nurses are conversing in
low whispers.

GRAFF. He's lost a lot of blood—but
I think he will pull through. What is
the pulse?

NURSE (*holding Garmes' wrist*). One
hundred and forty.

GRAFF. Going down. (*He looks up toward the door.*)

From Graff's viewpoint, we see Edwardes and Constance hurriedly enter,
slipping into white surgical aprons as
they come in. They go to the surgical
table and join the others leaning over
Garmes.

Starting on the backs of Constance and
Edwardes, the camera, gradually moving in closer and tilting up slightly,
follows the unbroken circle of backs
around the table. It stops across the table
from Edwardes as he straightens up.
A closeup of Edwardes shows that a
wild expression is growing on his face.
He speaks now in a hoarsened voice.

EDWARDES. Why are the lights out in
the corridor?

We get a semi-closeup of the group as
Graff looks up from his work.

GRAFF. What do you mean?

Edwardes' voice is quiet, his words
tipped with slight hysteria.

EDWARDES. It's dark. That's why he did it. Because the lights are out. Put them on! And the doors! Unlock them! You can't keep people in cells. (*He is panting now as he talks.*)

The others are staring at him with growing alarm. Constance comes toward him.

CONSTANCE (*sharply*). Dr. Edwardes.

EDWARDES (*moving away from her*). You fools! Babbling about guilt complexes! What do you know about them! He did it. He told me. He killed his father. Put on the lights—quick. It's dark. It's dark.

Whispering these words hoarsely, Dr. Edwardes sways on his feet. Fleurot prevents him from falling.

GRAFF. He's in collapse.

CONSTANCE. Yes—he's ill.

FLEUROT. Here—help me.

Constance helps support the limp figure of Edwardes. They lower him onto a chair. Graff comes from the table to look at him. Constance takes his pulse.

We get a semi-closeup of GRAFF, Murchison looking on expressionlessly. We hear the voices of Graff and Fleurot.

GRAFF. Curious. Didn't look like a heart case.

FLEUROT (*shaking his head*). Not heart. Shock of some sort. Probably brought on by exhaustion.

CONSTANCE. Take him up to his room. I'll take care of him.

And now the scene dissolves to EDWARDES' BEDROOM. Constance is seated by Edwardes' bed. He is lying asleep. The camera moves in deliberately and slowly until it comes to rest on Edwardes' book which lies in her lap.

Sticking out between the pages is a slip of paper.

A closeup shows Constance looking from the sleeping Edwardes down to her lap. Next, she opens the book, and we are able to read what is on the slip of paper which is held between the pages. It reads: "Your patient, Mr. Garmes, is here. Will you please drop in?" Her hands turn the pages of the book until she reaches the front sheet, with Edwardes' signature.

A closeup shows her hands holding the note with the signature as close as possible to the signature in the book. The handwritings are startlingly different.

Constance looks from the book across to Edwardes and we then see, from her viewpoint, Edwardes opening his eyes and looking up at her.

EDWARDES (*in a semi-closeup*). I'm sorry. I suppose I made—quite an exhibition—of myself. Who brought me down here—you? (*He stares at her.*) It's rather a mess—going to pieces—in surgery.

Constance, seen in a closeup, draws in her breath before she speaks, then asks, quietly:

CONSTANCE. Who are you?

The camera moves slowly up to a big closeup of Edwardes' face, and holds there. Edwardes is silent. There is a long pause as we see terror and doubt sweep over him.—A closeup shows CONSTANCE looking at him tensely, following which we get a closeup of Edwardes. His eyes remain on hers for a long moment; then, a look of desperation on his face, his voice resumes quietly:

EDWARDES. I remember, now. Edwardes is dead. I killed him and took his place. I'm—someone else—I don't know who—I killed—him—Edwardes—

Constance sits rigidly, looking at him. For a moment her shock holds her motionless. Then her hand moves toward him, and she strokes his head tenderly as he lies muttering into the pillow.

The scene dissolves to EDWARDES' BEDROOM. Constance is still sitting. Edwardes is now out of bed, in pajamas, slippers and dressing robe. He's pacing slowly. She watches him. He crosses to the curtained window and looks out. A stream of light momentarily enters the room. Then, Edwardes, seen in a semi-closeup, lets the curtain drop and continues walking up and down.

EDWARDES (*quietly, as he walks*). I have no memory. It's like looking into a mirror—and seeing nothing but the mirror. Yet the image is there. I know it's there. (*He stands and stares ahead of him and speaks tensely.*) I exist! I'm there! (*He crosses to the bed and sits down on it, looking desperately at Constance.*) How can a man lose his name, his memory, and everything he has ever known—and still talk like this? As if he were quite sane. (*He takes her hands.*) Are you afraid of me?

We get a semi-closeup of Constance: her eyes are full but she speaks as if she were in a tête-à-tête with a fellow scientist.

CONSTANCE. No. You are ill. Loss of memory isn't a difficult problem.

EDWARDES. Yes, I know—amnesia . . . A trick of the mind for remaining sane. You remain sane—by forgetting something too horrible to remember. You put the horrible thing —behind a closed door.

Constance leans nearer to him, her eyes full of love and pity.

CONSTANCE. We have to open the door.

EDWARDES (*in a semi-closeup, his voice low*). I know what's behind the door. Murder.

We get a closeup of Constance. She shakes her head.

CONSTANCE (*softly*). No. No. That's a delusion you have acquired—out of illness. (*He closes his eyes as if in pain.*) Will you answer me truthfully —and trust me?

EDWARDES. I trust you but— (*looking at her desperately*) it's no use. I can't think. I don't know who I am. I don't know. I don't know.

CONSTANCE (*sharply*). Who telephoned you—yesterday?

EDWARDES (*vaguely*). Telephoned me?

CONSTANCE (*sharply*). Yes. There— in the office.

EDWARDES (*nodding — his voice fuzzy*). Oh, yes. I remember.

CONSTANCE (*sharply*). What did she say?

EDWARDES. She said that she was my office assistant—and was worried about me—hadn't heard—

CONSTANCE (*sharply*). You mean she was Dr. Edwardes' assistant. And hadn't heard from him. What else did she say?

EDWARDES. She didn't recognize my voice. That I wasn't Dr. Edwardes.

CONSTANCE (*sharply*). And you hung up—in anger?

EDWARDES (*painfully*). I was confused. My head ached.

CONSTANCE. Was that your first doubt?

EDWARDES (*dully*). My first doubt?

CONSTANCE (*intently*). Was that the first time you became confused—as Edwardes? Did anything else happen —before that?

EDWARDES (*rising and crossing to a suitcase*). Yes, when I was in the hotel room packing to come here. I found a cigarette case in my coat. It frightened me. I didn't know why it should. Here.

He opens the bag and produces a cigarette case which he brings back to her. He adds, painfully:

EDWARDES. The initials. J.B. See them? (*Constance nods.*) When I saw them—in the hotel room—they made by head ache.

He walks away toward a mirror. We hear Constance's voice.

CONSTANCE'S VOICE. They are probably your initials.

Edwardes stands looking into the mirror as he repeats:

EDWARDES. J.B.—J.B.

Through the mirror we can see Constance rising and coming toward him. She enters the picture and stands beside him.

CONSTANCE. You must sleep—I think when you wake up you'll be able to tell me more. If you trust me—

EDWARDES (*wearily*). I trust you. Sleep. You'd better get some sleep yourself. I'll be all right.

He returns to the bed. Constance follows him.

CONSTANCE. I'm sure there will be no police inquiry for a few days— We'll

talk about it—and straighten everything out before—anything happens. (*Edwardes sits on the bed and closes his eyes.*) I'll come in—in the morning, and report you too ill for service.

Constance, with a final look, tiptoes away from him, out the door, and the scene dissolves to J.B.'s hand writing a note. We see the note: "I cannot involve you in this for many reasons. One of them being that I love you. When the police step in, tell them I am at the Empire State Hotel in New York. I prefer to wait alone for the end. Goodbye.—J.B." His hands fold the note and put it into an envelope. He writes her name, "Dr. Petersen," on it in his bold, heavy script.

This dissolves to a CORRIDOR where we see a man's shadow and hand insert the envelope under the door to Constance's room.—

The envelope appears on the other side of the door, in CONSTANCE PETERSEN'S ROOM. The camera pans up and left from it, and we see through into the moonlit bedroom. We can just discern Constance pacing around, then sitting on the bed.

This dissolves to the RECEPTION ROOM at dawn. A group of figures is standing listening to a severe, middle-aged woman. Murchison, Fleurot, Graff, and Galt are present. They are in robes and slippers. Two local state policemen in uniform and the local sheriff are present. The severe looking woman is Norma Cramer.

NORMA. I have been in Dr. Edwardes' office for five years, and the man who spoke to me is not Dr. Edwardes. He let me have my vacation when he left on his. I was very worried when I didn't hear from him last week. Then I thought he might have just come here without reopening his office. That's why I telephoned.

We get a semi-closeup of the group as the sheriff turns to Norma.

SHERIFF. Show them the picture.

NORMA. Oh, yes. (*She takes it from her purse.*)

We see the photograph of a man ten years older than J.B. (as Edwardes will be called in the future) and in no way resembling him. (Voices come over the insert.)

FLEUROT'S VOICE. That's—a different man.

SHERIFF'S VOICE. He was taking a chance. Somebody might have known what Edwardes looked like.

We get a semi-closeup of Murchison. His face is composed, but his elation comes through in his tones.

SHERIFF'S VOICE. You never saw the real Edwardes?

MURCHISON. No. I never met him. (*After a pause*) But—I felt something wrong from the moment our man appeared. He didn't impress me as a scientist. And last night—when he collapsed—I became actually alarmed.

FLEUROT. What do you think made him break down last night?

MURCHISON. It's obvious now. Garmes. Our impostor is, I'm almost certain, an amnesia case. Garmes brought him back to reality for an instant— and being unable to face the truth of who he was, he collapsed.

SHERIFF. You think he may have killed Edwardes?

MURCHISON. There can be no question of it. He killed Dr. Edwardes and then took his place—in order to conceal his crime—by' pretending the victim was still alive. This sort of unrealistic act is typical of the short-sighted cunning that goes with paranoid behavior. (*He looks around triumphantly.*) But we are wasting time, gentlemen. His room is upstairs. (*He starts for the hall, and they all follow him down the corridor.*)

The scene dissolves to CONSTANCE'S BEDROOM at dawn. Constance is in bed asleep. The view moves from her to the white envelope under the door in the room beyond. The camera holds on the envelope a moment, then we hear a murmur of voices and the bell buzzer. —Next, Constance stirs in bed. The murmur of voices continues and knuckles begin to rap on the door beyond. Constance wakes, sits on the side of the bed, and putting her feet into slippers, slips on her robe and comes toward the door. The knocking continues over this. As she reaches the foreground she sees the note on the floor. She leans over to pick it up, but at the psychological moment the door opens and she is prevented from picking up the envelope.

In a closeup, we see Constance's eyes staring at the newcomers, and then her quick, furtive glance down. From her viewpoint we see the feet of the entering people walking over the envelope. —Then we see Constance backing away from the envelope as they come in.

MURCHISON. This is Dr. Petersen. These gentlemen are from the police.

CONSTANCE. The police! What has happened?

MURCHISON. Nothing to be alarmed about. Our Dr. Edwardes turns out to be a paranoid impostor—who is very likely guilty of having murdered the real Edwardes. He has disappeared—

CONSTANCE (*staring*). Oh—he is not in his room—

SHERIFF. You left him in his room, Miss?

CONSTANCE. Yes. About three o'clock.

SHERIFF. How'd you happen to leave him?

CONSTANCE. He was asleep.

SHERIFF. I understand he had a breakdown.

CONSTANCE. That's true. He was ill.

SHERIFF. He didn't say anything—about himself? About why he broke down?

CONSTANCE. No. He was—he was not himself—he was unable to speak coherently.

SHERIFF (*staring at Constance*). You don't seem very surprised to learn that this Dr. Edwardes is a fake—and maybe guilty of murder.

We get a semi-closeup of Constance, surreptitiously drawing her breath.

CONSTANCE. I—I am used to such surprises in my work.

Then we see the group in a semi-closeup.

SHERIFF (*quickly*). You suspected something, then?

CONSTANCE. No. I thought his collapse due to mental strain.

SHERIFF. That's a funny diagnosis for a fellow who's supposed to have just come from a vacation.

A semi-closeup shows Constance looking steadily.

CONSTANCE. I made no medical diagnosis. I was shocked to see him collapse, and I didn't think beyond that.

FLEUROT'S VOICE. We were all pretty shocked, Sheriff. The fellow took us all in—all except Dr. Murchison.

SHERIFF (*to Constance*). And he didn't say anything that might give you an idea—of where he went.

Constance tries hard not to look down at the envelope.

CONSTANCE. No.

SHERIFF. He may be hanging around. We'll have to go over the grounds first.

The camera pulls back as they move toward the door, and we get a semi-closeup of the feet of one of the detectives kicking the envelope from the floor nearly into the corridor again.

A semi-closeup shows Murchison lingering behind as the group leaves. He turns to Constance.

MURCHISON. I'm sorry this happened to you, Constance. I felt like warning you about him. But I wasn't certain. Don't worry—it's not your fault. And they're bound to find him—I'll keep you informed of—the police activities.

As soon as his back is turned to go through the door Constance looks down at the floor in alarm at the note not being there any longer.

In the CORRIDOR, next, a semi-closeup shows Murchison bending down to pick up the note. After glancing at the name on the envelope, he hands it to Constance in the doorway.—Constance takes it and goes into the room. As Murchison walks away, he is thoughtful and glances back toward the door of Constance's room. He turns and joins the group, who are waiting for him in the lobby.—In her OFFICE, CONSTANCE, seen in a semi-closeup, has her back to the door and is reading the note, which we see again. She glances apprehensively over her shoulder in the direction of Murchison as the scene dissolves.

The scene dissolves to the LIBRARY at night. It is after dinner. Seated in a group taking coffee around the fireplace are Murchison, Fleurot, Graff, and Constance. Graff is talking as we come onto the scene.

GRAFF. I say the fellow expected to get away with it—like any criminal.

FLEUROT. Nonsense. Obviously a case of amnesia. He hadn't the faintest notion of who he was or what he was doing. What do you say, Constance?

The camera is moving in slightly all the time, until Constance appears in a semi-closeup.

CONSTANCE (slowly). I—I don't know.

A semi-closeup shows Fleurot, looking steadily at Constance.

FLEUROT. You know, if you were anybody but Constance Petersen—the human glacier and the custodian of truth—I'd say— (He pauses.)

CONSTANCE (in a closeup). Yes—You'd say what?

FLEUROT (in a semi-closeup). My dear, forgive me my scurvy thoughts. You are telling the truth. I was going to say that you were holding something back. I'm a sentimental ass. A woman like you could never become involved emotionally with any man, sane or insane. (He laughs.)

A closeup shows Constance holding her breath during Fleurot's speech. She relaxes a little bit at the end of it.

MURCHISON (in a close shot, looking up from his paper). I suggest you change the subject, Dr. Fleurot.

GRAFF (as we get a semi-closeup of the group). I'll be very interested to ask him certain questions when they bring him back here—no matter what you think.

FLEUROT (quietly). You'll never ask our mystery man any questions.

GRAFF. And why not?

FLEUROT. For the very good reason that the police will never find him alive. An amnesic case of that sort—with the police after it—is an obvious suicide. The fellow will put an end to his pain and his nightmare fantasies either by blowing his brains out or by dropping himself out of a window.

Murchison has his eyes on Constance, and we see that Constance has risen. She stands by the mantleshelf and listens. Then the group appears again as Murchison interposes quietly:

MURCHISON. You are offending Dr. Petersen by your callousness. (He looks at her gently.) I am sorry, Constance, that our staff still retains the manners of medical students.

A semi-closeup shows Constance walking out.

CONSTANCE (as she leaves). I am not offended. I—I think Dr. Fleurot's ideas are quite accurate. But I'm rather tired. Good night.

This dissolves to CONSTANCE'S ROOM at night, starting with a closeup of the clock pointing to midnight; reflected in its convex face is Constance pacing the room. The camera then pulls back and we see that she is smoking and is fully dressed. She consults her wristwatch. The radio is playing a musical program.—Suddenly it is interrupted by an announcer's voice:

"The police have asked me to announce that our neighborhood roads are free of the dangerous madman who escaped from Green Manors. The search for the imposter has shifted to Manhattan. This is WQZK, Rutland, George Bell."

We see Constance recede from view and go into her bedroom. She opens a closet and takes out a suitcase. We see her packing as the scene fades out.

# PART THREE

A sign reading "empire state hotel" fades in and dissolves to the empire state hotel lobby. It is day, and the lobby of the hotel is filled with people moving in different directions. And now the camera booms down to a close shot of constance. She is looking around in slight bewilderment.

We see the elevator doors, with people passing out and fresh arrivals going up; then, Constance walking to a small settee near the elevator and sitting down.

A stranger comes over, and plunks himself down onto the sofa. It makes a tight squeeze and he is pleased with himself. Constance is too intent to notice him. The stranger essays a honeyed tone:

stranger (*a little high with liquor*). Sure feels good to take the weight off your feet. (*Constance sees him for the first time. He continues:*) I'm from Pittsburgh. There's a town for you. You really can meet people in Pittsburgh. Friendly. A fella could live and die in this town and couldn't meet nobody. (*He beams at her.*) How about you and me havin' a nice little drink, together—now that we're acquainted.

constance. No, thank you. I—

stranger. You don't have to be so snooty about it. (*He leans over her.*) I'll have you know, madam, that I know better people than you—in Pittsburgh.

constance (*being squeezed against the end of the settee*). I'm sure you're a great social success—given half a chance.

stranger (*eagerly*). Now you're talkin'.

constance. Do you mind—not sitting in my lap—in public—

A moon-faced, neatly dressed gentleman has come up to the sofa.

newcomer (*quietly*). That's enough of that.

They both look up.

newcomer (*coldly*). Beat it.

stranger (*glaring*). I'll have you know I'm a guest of this hotel. Who do you think you are?

newcomer (*taking his arm and lifting him up*). I'm the house detective. Get going.

The stranger sways on his feet; he is very bitter.

stranger. This town's gettin' worse and worse— (*He moves off toward the bar. The detective stands looking at Constance.*)

A semi-closeup shows that Constance's

face is full of apprehension. She starts to rise.

DETECTIVE (*soothingly*). Oh, that's all right, lady. You don't have to go. I'm sorry you were annoyed. I've been watching you for some time—and I figured something like this might happen. You see, the chief duty of a house detective is to spot trouble in advance. (*She looks at him with ill-concealed fear. He continues calmly:*) You're not registered, are you?

CONSTANCE (*with an effort*). No.

DETECTIVE. Well—I didn't think so—the way you were wandering around. (*He looks keenly at her.*) Looking for somebody, eh? (*Constance stares in front of her. The detective's voice grows kinder.*) Oh, now don't be afraid of me. I—I've got you spotted as a lady in trouble. And from out of town. School teacher or librarian, which is it? (*He lowers himself to her side.*)

Constance, seen in a closeup, hesitates for a moment, and then speaks nervously:

CONSTANCE. School teacher.

DETECTIVE (*in a semi-closeup; smugly*). I thought so. They always look—like they've just lost something. Maybe I can help you.

CONSTANCE (*seen in a semi-closeup of the two; slowly*). I don't think so—thank you.

DETECTIVE (*the thinker at work*). Looking for some man, I suppose. (*He halts her supposed answer and continues chummily:*) Ah—must be a relative. And from the worried look—I'd say a pretty close one. (*Archly*) A husband, f'rinstance.

CONSTANCE. I'm really amazed.

DETECTIVE. I hit it, eh?

CONSTANCE (*with feigned wonder*). But how could you tell?

DETECTIVE. Well—I'm kind of a psychologist. You know—you got to be in my line. (*He sneers.*) Now, would you mind filling in a few of the blank spaces for me?

CONSTANCE. Oh, no. It's just that we quarreled—

DETECTIVE. And then you got sorry and came running after him. That's the usual psychology. But now you're afraid to face him.

CONSTANCE (*eagerly—"telling all"*). Oh, no. No. It's—that I don't know what room he's in. He told a friend he was coming to this hotel—but under a different name, so I couldn't find him. But I must find him and apologize—and make him feel better.

DETECTIVE. When did he arrive here?

CONSTANCE. Yesterday morning.

DETECTIVE. Give me a description of him—

CONSTANCE (*eagerly*). He's very tall —and attractive—dark hair—a rather rugged face, and brown eyes—and one suitcase.

DETECTIVE. I'll go check on him. (*He pats her on the shoulder and rises.*)

A closeup shows Constance furtively watching him depart; next we see the detective moving toward the hotel desk; next Constance glancing off in another direction, and then from her viewpoint, we see the genial, coarse stranger once more emerging from the bar. He's probably had a couple of more drinks since we last saw him. His eye catches Constance again. He ambles over toward her.

He seats himself beside her once more. Constance is apprehensive of the fact that he does not speak to her this time. He looks at her with an almost aggressive expression. He puts a cigarette in his mouth and lights it with great, if unsteady, deliberation. As he shakes the match he looks up: The camera pulls back and once more our detective friend has returned. He is carrying a batch of cards in his hand. He looks down with a deadpan expression to the drunk, who gets up and mumbles as he again ambles off.

STRANGER (*as he goes off*). Flatfoot.

Constance rises, the camera moving in to a semi-closeup of the two.

CONSTANCE. Did you find—him?

DETECTIVE. Well, I think we got a line. About twenty-five guys answering your description registered here yesterday. These are their registration cards. I figured you might recognize the handwriting.

CONSTANCE. That's very clever—of you—

She looks through the handful of cards, and we get a closeup as her hands scan through them and we come upon the familiar writing of J.B. The name on the card is "John Brown."

CONSTANCE (*in a semi-closeup of the two.*) This is his handwriting.

DETECTIVE. John Brown, eh? Not much imagination for an alias. Room 3033.

CONSTANCE (*holding out her hand*). Thank you—very much. I was going to sit here all day—watching for him.

They then move over to the elevator. He guides her through the doors.

DETECTIVE. I knew you were. I'm glad to be of service. I'm a married man myself—and I know how it feels to have a wife come chasing after you —to apologize. (*He beams at her.*)

She enters the cage, and the scene dissolves to the HOTEL CORRIDOR as Constance walks toward the door. She stops and rings the bell. The door opens. The haggard J.B. puts his head out.

J.B. (*recognizing her—staring*). Constance!

She enters quickly, and the scene cuts to the HOTEL BEDROOM as she comes to the other side of the door.

J.B. (*looking past her; tensely*). What did you come for? You don't owe me anything—

CONSTANCE. I am going to do—what I want to do—take care of you, cure you, and remain with you till that happens.

J.B. (*angrily*). But you can't! You can't help hide a criminal. You're not going to jeopardize your standing as a doctor— You're just getting started. I won't let you be stupid about it.

CONSTANCE. I couldn't bear it—away from you. I went through yesterday holding my breath—as if I were being hunted. I couldn't eat or work. Or do anything but think of you. So I had to come—I'll rent a room on this floor. I'm here—as your doctor— only. It has nothing to do with love.

He takes her in his arms and kisses her.

CONSTANCE (*when the kiss is over*). Nothing at all.

The scene dissolves to the same room a few hours later, and as the camera pans around the room we see J.B. lying on a couch. Constance is sitting in a chair near his head.

CONSTANCE. Try remembering. Let your mind go back to your childhood

—was it happy? Whom did you know in your childhood?

J.B. (*talking with his eyes closed*). I'm haunted—but I can't see by what. It's no use.

CONSTANCE (*calmly*). You lived somewhere. You had a mother. You were loved. You had friends.

J.B. (*grimly*). Yes. Probably a wife.

A closeup shows Constance looking away for a moment.

CONSTANCE. Can you remember her?

J.B. (*in a semi-closeup of the two; irritably*). Oh—I didn't say I had one —I said I probably had. (*He looks at her and sighs.*) No, darling. Thank heaven I can't remember a wife.

CONSTANCE. I would like to ask you a medical question.

J.B. (*nervously*). Constance—do you mind not prodding me? It mixes me up and— (*He takes her hand.*) I can't remember anything—except that I love you.

CONSTANCE (*firmly*). How would you diagnose a pain in the right upper quadrant? A pain that is persistent.

J.B. Gall bladder—or possibly a heart case . . . or pneumonia. Depending on the patient's history.

CONSTANCE. It's obvious you're a doctor.

J.B. The eminent Doctor X. (*He smiles at her.*)

CONSTANCE. Your diagnosis just now. If we can unlock one tiny memory —it will give us a key to the others.

J.B. No. (*He sits up slowly.*) The only thing that comes to my mind —that I keep thinking of over and over—is the logic of the situation.

CONSTANCE (*quietly*). What logic?

J.B. (*grimly*). That it was I who was with Edwardes. (*He picks up the newspaper which lies on the couch beside him and reads:*) "Police believe the impostor who escaped from Green Manors to be the patient who visited the real Dr. Edwardes in the Cumberland Mountains the day that the noted psychiatrist disappeared. No trace of Dr. Edwardes has been found since he left the Cumberland resort in the company of his supposed patient."

CONSTANCE (*gently*). Do you remember that?

J.B. No.

CONSTANCE. Then why do you believe you were with him?

J.B. (*frowning*). Because wherever we went I came back with his indentity. I wouldn't have come back as Dr. Edwardes if I hadn't known that he was dead. And how would I have known that he was dead if I hadn't been with him when he died?

CONSTANCE. Were you?

J.B. (*frowning*). I—I don't remember. But—logically I know that I must have been, and logically I also know why the body hasn't been found. (*He pauses and stares at her, and then adds:*) Because it was hidden—by me.

CONSTANCE. Don't you see that you're imagining all this? You call yourself names. You insist without proof, that you're a murderer. (*She smiles at him.*) You know what that is, don't you? Whoever you are—it's a guilt complex that speaks for you— a guilt fantasy that goes way back to your childhood.

J.B. (*softly*). I think you're quite mad

—you're much crazier than I, to do all this for a creature without a name. To run off with a—a pair of initials.

CONSTANCE. The police haven't given your name or case history to the papers. (*As Constance is talking, J.B. reaches over and takes her hand.*) That must mean only one thing, that your name was not in Dr. Edwardes' files— (*Her eyes are on his hand; she speaks in a sudden, sharp, accusative voice.*) You were in an accident!

A closeup of J.B. shows that the sharpness of her voice startles him. He looks at her with sudden terror in his eyes. She continues in the same accusative tones:

CONSTANCE'S VOICE. Where was it? What happened to your hand? Your hand was burned. You've had an operation in the last six months. A skin graft. Third degree burns. Your hand was burned! Where!

While she speaks, the camera swings from his face down to his hand held by hers. It moves up her arm and comes to rest on her face. Then we get another closeup of J.B. as his face contorts.

J.B. It hurts.

CONSTANCE (*commandingly*). Try remembering.

J.B. My hand hurts!

CONSTANCE. Your hand is remembering. Open your mind and the pain will leave. Where did it happen?

J.B. (*sweat on his forehead*). I can't. It hurts!

CONSTANCE (*commandingly*). What happened?

J.B. (*in agony*). It's burning. My hand's burning!

CONSTANCE. Try to remember!

Constance, in a semi-closeup, watches him intently, almost desperately, her eyes holding him compellingly. She leans forward in alarm.—We see J.B., in a semi-closeup, falling back. Constance struggles to remain a doctor despite her pity and love, but at the sight of him inert and spent, her emotion overcomes her, and a closeup shows her leaning over him. There are tears in her eyes.

CONSTANCE (*whispering*). Oh, my dear—are you all right?

The camera pulls back slowly as J.B. answers her weakly:

J.B. I'm all right. (*He looks up at her.*) What happened?

CONSTANCE. You relived an accident you've been in. But the memory only touched the part of your mind that feels. But it's a beginning. It—really is. (*She smoothes his brow and her voice grows tender.*) You'll feel better—soon—

The doorbell rings. Constance looks around nervously and then, hesitating a moment, rises and goes toward the door.

J.B. Who could that be?

CONSTANCE. Oh, I know—I sent down for the later editions of the papers.

She opens the door. The bellboy is standing in the hall holding two newspapers.

BELLBOY. You ordered the afternoon papers, didn't you?

CONSTANCE. Yes.

BELLBOY. They just came in. I brought 'em right up.

CONSTANCE. Just a minute.

She goes into the room, and the camera moves in toward the bellboy who glances at the front page of the paper in his hand. A closeup shows a picture of Constance's face on the front page. The caption reads: "POLICE HUNT DR. CONSTANCE PETERSEN BELIEVED AIDING MADMAN WANTED IN EDWARDES' MYSTERY."

Then we see CONSTANCE again, in a semi-closeup, and the bellboy looks up as she speaks.

CONSTANCE. Here you are.

BELLBOY. Oh, thanks.

The bellboy looks quickly from her face back to the newspaper as he hands them over to her. He gives her another glance as he goes off.

The scene cuts to the CORRIDOR, and we see that, as the bellboy goes off down the passage, he turns and looks back twice.—CONSTANCE, in a closeup, is still watching him (the angle shooting through the open door from the hall), then she turns with an alarmed expression. She crosses quickly to J.B. She seizes his arm and says in a tense voice:

CONSTANCE. My picture's in the paper. He recognized me. We've got to go. Quick. We can't pack.

She closes the door, blotting the scene from the camera, and this dissolves to the CORRIDOR as Constance and J.B. emerge from the bedroom door and hurry away down the corridor. Next, we see Constance and J.B. emerge from the elevator and hurry through the crowds in the HOTEL LOBBY, then passing through the revolving doors to the street. The camera pans off and we see the bellboy hurrying to the house detective. We cannot hear what he is saying because of the general hubbub in the lobby. The camera creeps in all the time the boy is gesticulating and explaining

something to the moon-faced detective. As we get nearer to the detective's face we see its expression—at first unbelieving, now becoming more and more ferocious.

As he starts to move toward the reception desk in the lobby, the scene dissolves to a vast view of PENNSYLVANIA STATION with its swarming crowds crossing to and fro; this dissolves to a nearer view by the ticket windows, with a short queue of people as Constance and J.B. come toward the tail end of it; and this dissolves to a closeup of Constance and J.B. in line.

CONSTANCE (*quietly to him*). Listen, when you left the mountains, you must have passed through New York. Wherever you went, wherever you came from, you must have been in a railroad station. You must have heard Edwardes ask for tickets to somewhere. (*They move along again.*)

J.B. (*muttering*). I don't remember.

CONSTANCE. You will. When you come to the ticket window try to relive that other time with Edwardes. Try to repeat what was said then. Ask for the same tickets.

J.B. (*dully*). I'll try.

They move along and slightly away from the camera so that we see they are standing behind one last purchaser at the window. Then a closeup shows Constance whispering into his ear.

CONSTANCE. You went some place with Edwardes. Ask for tickets to that same place.

A semi-closeup shows that J.B., with Constance at his side, has arrived at the ticket window. He stands staring through the grille at the clerk. He makes no sound and doesn't move.

CLERK. What is it? (*As J.B. is silent, the clerk scowls.*) What do you want, sir? (*As J.B. still doesn't reply.*) Please step aside.

J.B. (*slowly*). I want two tickets— (*He breaks off.*)

CLERK. Where to?

We see the people in the queue behind J.B. and Constance beginning to lean their heads out impatiently. A policeman begins to stroll toward the scene.— A closeup shows that J.B. is almost sweating with desperation. His mouth moves as though he were suffering from a dreadful stammer. The clerk, seen in a closeup behind the counter, moves impatiently.—And now we see the policeman alongside Constance and J.B. looking curiously. Constance almost leads J.B. away in desperation; then slowly J.B. speaks.

J.B. Rome.

The clerk, in a semi-closeup, looks puzzled.

CLERK. To where?

We see the group as J.B. repeats:

J.B. Rome.

CLERK. What Rome?

CONSTANCE (*stepping beside J.B.*). He means Rome, Georgia.

The clerk busies himself with the ticket rack. J.B. almost mechanically puts a hundred-dollar bill down on the counter. The clerk busies himself with the tickets and change. The policeman comes alongside Constance, who is holding the swaying J.B.

POLICEMAN. Anything wrong?

CONSTANCE. My husband is ill. I'm taking him home.

CLERK. Here you are. Two tickets to Rome, Georgia.

CONSTANCE. He'll be all right in a minute. These dizzy spells go away —quickly.

POLICEMAN. He looks pretty sick. I'll call a doctor.

CONSTANCE. Oh, no. He'll be all right. (*She presses close to J.B.*) Do you feel better now, darling? (*His eyes turn to her and remain fastened. She repeats, tenderly but commandingly.*) Darling.

J.B. (*thickly*). Yes.

CONSTANCE (*close to his ear*). Pull yourself together! You're all right.

She collects the change from the counter while the policeman supports the swaying J.B. J.B. straightens up as she leans in and asks the clerk, who is busy with another passenger:

CONSTANCE. When does the train for Rome leave?

CLERK. Birmingham special leaves in ten minutes. Track Seventeen.

J.B. I feel better.

CONSTANCE (*to the policeman*). Thank you.

POLICEMAN. That's all right, lady. I'll take you to the train—in case anything happens.

CONSTANCE He's recovered now. You're very nice to offer help, but I can get along now. Thank you.

She moves off·out of the picture, leaving the policeman looking after them. One or two of the crowd watch them go. Then we get a long view of GATE 17 of the PENNSYLVANIA STATION, from the policeman's viewpoint, as they move to the gate. Constance turns and looks back over her shoulder.

A semi-closeup at the gate discloses Constance showing the tickets, and looking around casually as they enter the gate. Then we see them walking toward the train.

CONSTANCE (*softly, as they walk*). Act as if we're taking this train. We'll walk down a ways, and then turn back.

J.B. (*quizzically*). What's the matter with this train?

CONSTANCE. A policeman heard us buy the tickets.

J.B. Did he act suspicious?

CONSTANCE. No. He was very nice. (*She stops and looks back toward the entrance. She leads J.B. back the way they came.*) But when he goes to his police station tonight, he may find descriptions of us posted. And he'll remember us. And they'll telegraph Rome, Georgia, and have us picked up.

J.B. (*his head continuing to clear*). We can't go back to the hotel. They'll have a million police there—by this time.

CONSTANCE. We're not going back. (*Thinking fast*) We're going to Rochester. Come on—we're going to the Grand Central Station.

This dissolves to GRAND CENTRAL STATION; the same swarming crowd moves about the Grand Central Station as at the Pennsylvania. And this dissolves to a nearer view by one of the track entrances, with J.B. standing in the foreground. Constance approaches him. He is reading a newspaper. The camera moves up as Constance joins him and they start walking toward the barrier.

J.B. By the way, what are we going to Rochester for?

CONSTANCE. We're going to visit Dr. Brulov.

J.B. Oh. The fellow who doesn't like sauce bottles.

CONSTANCE. He was my analyst. He psychoanalyzed me.

J.B. Really! What—what was wrong with you?

CONSTANCE (*a little irritably*). All analysts have to be psychoanalyzed by other analysts before they start practicing.

J.B. (*owlishly*). Oh. That's to make sure they're not too crazy.

They are now walking toward the train gate.

CONSTANCE (*tartly*). Apparently the mind is never too ill to make jokes about psychoanalysis.

J.B. I'm sorry. (*He beams at her.*) I'm a pig.

CONSTANCE (*smiling*). No. I am. I keep forgetting you're a patient.

J.B. So do I. When I hold you like this I feel entirely well. Darling, will you love me as much—when I'm normal?

CONSTANCE. Oh—I'll be insane about you.

J.B. I am normal! At least there's nothing wrong with me that a nice long kiss wouldn't cure.

CONSTANCE (*softly*). I've never treated a guilt complex—that way—before.

They move away from the camera slightly. J.B. stops and looks about him. There are a number of couples kissing and saying goodbye. He takes her into his arms.

CONSTANCE (*as they kiss*). We don't want to attract attention.

J.B. (*still holding her*). Everybody's doing it.

They come out of the embrace and approach the gateman. Constance hands him the tickets. The gateman looks at her curiously.

GATEMAN. You both going?

CONSTANCE. Yes—yes.

The gateman punches their tickets and shakes his head as they pass through the gate. The camera moves in until the gateman is in a closeup. He looks after them and then turns back with a bewildered expression on his face.

The scene dissolves to a TRAIN COMPARTMENT as Constance and J.B. enter and, closing the door after them, become seated. Constance sits on the long seat while J.B. occupies the armchair. He opens a paper.

CONSTANCE. Don't read the papers. Let's pick up where we left off.

J.B. Pick up what?

We get a semi-closeup of the two as the train starts to move.

CONSTANCE. Try to recall the first moment you thought you were Edwardes.

J.B. (*leaning over and taking her hands*). Darling—I have a confession to make.

CONSTANCE. I'm listening.

The train emerges into the daylight from the tunnel of Grand Central Station. The compartment is flooded with light. We can see uptown New York streets through the window.

J.B. As a doctor you irritate me. I sit here swooning with love and then suddenly you ask me a question and I don't like you any more. (*Constance is smiling.*) Do you have to sit there smiling at me like some smug know-it-all school teacher?

CONSTANCE. I can't help smiling. That's what happens in analysis. As the doctor begins to uncover the truth in the patient, said patient develops a fine, hearty hatred—of said doctor. (*She smiles at him.*) You're going to hate me—a great deal—before we're through.

J.B. And you're going to like that?

CONSTANCE. As a scientist—yes.

J.B. (*softly*). If I should happen to biff you one, you'll consider it a sort of diploma?

CONSTANCE. Yes. But don't biff too hard.

He starts to embrace her, but Constance restrains him.

CONSTANCE. You know I think we should go on with our investigation. We have some new facts to work with now.

He returns to his seat and sits facing her again. A closeup shows J.B. staring, his manner subtly changing to resentment.

J.B. What facts?

CONSTANCE. You are a doctor. You were in an accident. Your hand and forearm were burned. And you were in Rome.

J.B. (*staring*). I was never in Rome in my life.

CONSTANCE (*seen in a semi-closeup*). You were either there, or going there. But you remembered something— no doubt connected with the burning of your hand. Rome—think of Rome —maybe Rome, Italy. (*She looks at him intently and then asks sharply:*)

When did you go to Rome? What did you do in Rome? Think!

A closeup shows J.B. looking out of the window and staring down, trying to remember.—We see, from his viewpoint, the railroad tracks and ties rushing by. Then we get a "big head" of J.B., breathing heavily from the strain of remembering.

J.B. (*tensely—as he looks out of the window*). Yes. I remember something. Fighter planes spotted us.

CONSTANCE (*in a closeup of the two; sharply*). You were flying.

J.B. Transport—medical corps. Over Rome. Heading north.

CONSTANCE (*sharply*). What happened?

J.B. (*in a sweat, as he struggles to hold the memory*). They hit us. Caught fire. Uniform burned. Bailed out.

CONSTANCE. What else!

J.B. (*staring dully at her*). I don't know. It blacks out.

CONSTANCE. You left the army.

J.B. (*angrily*). Yes. Probably deserted. I hated it. I hated killing. I can remember that much.

CONSTANCE (*firmly*). Your guilt fantasies were obviously inflamed by your duties as a soldier.

J.B. (*savagely*). Oh, stop it! Babbling like some phony King Solomon! You sit there full of half-witted double talk—that makes no sense. If there's anything I hate it's a smug woman.

A closeup shows Constance leaning forward and taking his hands. Then the camera moves in to take in their two "big heads."

CONSTANCE. Darling, we're just beginning. Don't biff too hard yet.

This dissolves to BRULOV'S HOUSE at night. Brulov's house is on a suburban street in Rochester. A cab is driving away as Constance and J.B. walk up the steps of the modest house.—We get a semi-closeup as they come up to the door.

CONSTANCE. I worked with Dr. Brulov as his assistant for a year. Immediately after my interneship. He got me the post at Green Manors. (*She rings the doorbell.*) You'll like Alex.

J.B. I doubt that. (*He grins at her.*) One psychoanalyst in my hair is enough. What are you going to tell him?

CONSTANCE (*smiling and holding his arm*). That we're on a honeymoon.

J.B. (*smiling at her*). Doctor, you think of the most wonderful prescriptions.

The door is opened by a middle-aged woman in a nondescript hat and coat. She is obviously a charwoman on her way home.

CONSTANCE. Good evening. Is Dr. Brulov in?

WOMAN. No. He went out right after dinner. He ought to be back soon. (*She picks up a bulging paper shopping bag from the floor and moves to go out.*) Would you mind telling him I've left his supper on the table? I'm sorry but I can't wait any longer. (*As an afterthought she indicates the living room.*) There are two gentlemen waiting for him in there. (*She goes out, closing the door behind her.*)

Constance and J.B. go toward the living room, and the scene cuts to BRULOV'S LIVING ROOM where two men half rise as Constance and J.B. enter. One is a tall, lean, sour-faced man; the other short and thickset. J.B. nods, and Constance mutters nervously:

CONSTANCE. How do you do?

GILLESPIE. How do you do?

J.B. How do you do?

Constance sits and J.B. takes a chair near her. The two men resume their seats on the opposite side of the room. The scene presents the appearance of a doctor's waiting room with four prospective patients.—There is an awkward pause, followed by a semi-closeup of the two men (*detectives*). The shorter one addresses the other.

GILLESPIE. How's your mother been lately?

COOLEY. Oh, she's still complaining about rheumatism. She figures I ought to get myself transferred down to Florida. I said, "Do you expect me to sacrifice all chance of promotion just because you've got rheumatism?"

GILLESPIE. Did you take the subject up with Hennessy?

COOLEY. Yes. He says a transfer could be arranged, but I'd probably have to start all over again as a sergeant. I said, "Personally, I think that's unfair, after all the work I did on that narcotics case."

GILLESPIE. What did Hennessy say to that?

COOLEY. Oh, a lot of things. He made some crack about me being a mama's boy.

Constance and J.B., seen in a semi-closeup, exchange looks. Constance quickly picks up a magazine, opens her purse and takes out her glasses which she puts on, preparatory to reading. Then, trying to hide her nervousness, she fits a cigarette into her holder and fumbles in her bag for a match. Seeing her, J.B. fumbles in his pockets, but can't find a match, either.—Constance's purse slides to the floor.

As J.B. picks up Constance's purse, Cooley jumps up and strikes a match for her cigarette. There is another awkward pause, broken by the ringing of the telephone on the desk. They all look at it. Constance starts to rise to answer it, but before she can reach it, Cooley turns to Gillespie.

COOLEY. Pardon me. That may be for me. I gave headquarters this number. (*Into the phone*) Hello. . . . (*A pause; then his voice changes slightly.*) Yes, this is Lieutenant Cooley . . . Any new developments? . . . Well. . . . When did you find out? . . . No. . . . Right . . . I'll be down later. Goodbye.

He hangs up and looks over at Constance and J.B. He purses his lips for a moment in thought and then rejoins Sergeant Gillespie. He sits down next to him; he leans over and whispers. There is smug satisfaction on Cooley's face and Gillespie listens in wonderment.

And now the camera moves in slowly until it includes CONSTANCE and J.B. alone. J.B. stares at her. Constance removes a compact from her purse and starts powdering the tip of her nose. We next hear the sound of a door opening off scene and Constance hearing it, rises quickly; J.B. stands up also. Then the camera pulls back to include the door and the two detectives. Dr. Brulov enters. He is a near-sighted fellow of seventy, full of Viennese amiability. He has a slight accent.

CONSTANCE (*going quickly to him*). Alex!

BRULOV (*peering through his thick-*

*lensed glasses*). Who is it, please? Ah, my old friend.

CONSTANCE (*interrupting before he can say her name, her manner gushing*). Alex! I just arrived. I didn't have time to let you know.

BRULOV. Imagine! I find you here! I would have come home quicker. I was giving a lecture at the army hospital. (*He notices the two policemen.*) Are these gentlemen with you?

CONSTANCE. No—I'm here with—

LT. COOLEY (*interrupting her and coming forward*). Dr. Brulov, I'm Lieutenant Cooley of the Central Station. This is Sergeant Gillespie.

BRULOV (*staring—irritation in his voice*). What for?

LT. COOLEY (*calmly*). We thought you might give us some data on Dr. Edwardes.

BRULOV. Data! What is this kind of persecution! I told the policeman yesterday, I know nothing about Edwardes.

LT. COOLEY (*quietly*). But yesterday you had some theory.

BRULOV (*angrily*). I explained to the policeman that if Edwardes took along with him on a vacation a paranoid patient, he was a bigger fool than I even knew he was. It is the same as playing with a loaded gun.

LT. COOLEY. Do you think this patient might have killed him?

BRULOV. I am not thinking anything. I am not a bloodhound.

LT. COOLEY. Was Dr. Edwardes a great friend of yours?

BRULOV. What are you talking about! The man was impossible!

LT. COOLEY. You had a quarrel with

him when you were back in New York, I understand.

BRULOV. Not New York. In Boston! At the psychiatry convention. What kind of an analyst is it who wants to cure psychoses by taking people skating or to a bowling alley!

LT. COOLEY. I understand you threatened to punch his nose.

BRULOV. All I did was get up and walk out and kick over a few chairs which nobody was sitting in. (*Turning to Cooley*) So you don't have to ask me any more questions. You have now the facts.

LT. COOLEY (*quietly*). Thank you very much. I'm sorry to have bothered you. If anything turns up we'll let you know. (*He turns to Constance.*) Goodbye, ma'am. (*To J.B.*) Goodnight, sir.

J.B. Goodnight.

The policemen go out, Brulov scowling after them.

BRULOV. What do you suppose they are snooping around me for? The next they will give me is the third degree. (*He smiles at Constance.*)

CONSTANCE. Alex—I'm so glad to see you. I was going to write you. But it happened so suddenly. I got married.

BRULOV. Who iss married?

CONSTANCE. Alex—my husband— John Brown.

Brulov stares out and then crosses in front of Constance, holding out his hand to J.B.

J.B. (*holding out his hand*). I'm glad to meet you—officially.

BRULOV (*shaking hands*). So you are married! There is nothing so nice as a new marriage. No psychoses yet. No aggressions. No guilt complexes. I congratulate you, and wish you have babies and not phobias. (*Turning to Constance*) How about we have a glass of beer—like in the old days?

CONSTANCE. The truth is—we have no hotel room. All the hotels were so crowded and—

BRULOV. What do you want with a hotel? That's for millionaires—not love-birds on a honeymoon. You will stay right here. Look—how I am living by myself—with a can-opener. My housekeeper is gone to war. My secretary is a WAC. And I got a cleaning woman who can't cook and who hates me. Cook me my coffee in the morning—and the house is yours.

CONSTANCE (*as they start into the kitchen*). That's wonderful of you, Alex.

The scene cuts to the KITCHEN as they enter; and as they talk, Constance goes to the ice box and takes out beer and cheese which she places on a table.

BRULOV. There's nothing wonderful about me. (*He takes her hand.*) It's nice to see my old assistant. (*To J.B.*) The youngest, but the best one I ever had. But who knows, now? As my old friend Zannebaum used to say, "Women make the best psychoanalysts till they fall in love. After that they make the best patients."

This dissolves to the HALLWAY as the three are walking up the stairs, nearing the top, Brulov leading.

BRULOV. Good night and happy dreams—which we will analyze at breakfast.

J.B. Good night, Dr. Brulov—and thanks for everything.

BRULOV. Any husband of Constance is a husband of mine—so to speak.

They are in the upper hall now, and stop at the door of one of the bedrooms.

CONSTANCE. Good night, Alex.

The scene cuts to the UPSTAIRS BEDROOM as Constance and J.B. enter the moonlit room and the latter turns on the light. We see that it is furnished in mid-Victorian style. It has a canopied bed, old Turkish-work couches and chairs. J. B. sits down in a chair in the foreground, very pleased with himself.

J.B. You were superb—with the police.

CONSTANCE (*turning and staring at him*). Was I?

J.B. (*grinning*). You carried it off like a grade A gun moll.

CONSTANCE. I felt terribly stupid for a few minutes. But it turned out—very well.

J.B. Providing the professor isn't wiser than he seems.

CONSTANCE. Alex? Oh, no.

She crosses and opens the bathroom door and peers in; her manner is half abstracted.

CONSTANCE. Things are a little different here. Someone's been here since my time. Oh, Alex didn't think anything. He's sweet.

J.B. He may be sweet—but he didn't even ask us where our bags were.

Constance comes out of the bathroom to the foreground, holding a brush.

CONSTANCE (*removing her hat*). Alex is always like that. He's usually in a complete dream state, socially. (*She begins brushing her hair. She looks around again.*) Do you know, this room does look changed. But it isn't.

It's I who am changed. (*She looks glowingly at J.B.*) It's called transfer of affects.

J.B. What is?

CONSTANCE. The fact that everything seems so wonderful in this room.

J.B. (*smiling*). Oh—that's what it's called, is it?

CONSTANCE (*looking at him, and asking in her professorial voice*). Did the police disturb you?

J.B. Oh, no—one ignores such trifles —on a honeymoon.

She stops her hair brushing and looks at him. He smiles at her.

J.B. (*tenderly*). I take it—this is your first honeymoon.

CONSTANCE. Yes. (*Nervously*) I mean, it would be—if it were.

J.B. rises and moves nearer to Constance, the camera going in closer. He embraces her gently and kisses her, while she stares at him.

J.B. For what it's worth—I can't remember ever having kissed any other woman before.

CONSTANCE. I have nothing to remember—of that nature—either.

J.B. (*softly*). You're very sweet.

CONSTANCE (*scowling*). Of course, I'm no child.

J.B. (*soothingly*). Far from it.

CONSTANCE. I'm well aware that—we are all bundles of inhibitions.

J.B. (*sagely*). Dynamite dumps.

She pulls away from him as he kisses her again.

CONSTANCE. No—No—Please—don't do that.

J.B. Why not?

CONSTANCE. It isn't—ethical. I'm here —as your doctor.

J.B. You may stop worrying, Doctor. I'm going to sleep on the couch.

CONSTANCE. No. That's—also unethical.

J.B. Now, this honeymoon is complicated enough—without your dragging medical ethics into it. I suppose the floor is out?

CONSTANCE. The patient always sleeps in the bed. The doctor occupies the couch—fully dressed.

J.B. Oh, I see—you know the ropes.

He turns away and approaches the bed. A closeup shows his eyes fastening on a white coverlet. Then we see, from his viewpoint, the old-fashioned coverlet with tufted trimming running down its length in straight lines.—A closeup shows him frowning at what he sees.— Constance, in a semi-closeup, turns and looks at him, and we see, from her viewpoint, J.B. staring at the bed cover.

CONSTANCE (*in a semi-closeup of the two*). You remember something?

J.B. No.

She crosses and stands behind him. Her voice becomes sharp and professional.

CONSTANCE. This room reminds you of something.

J.B. (*curtly*). No.

CONSTANCE (*sharply*). You are resisting a memory. What is in your mind?

J.B. (*turning angrily to her*). I don't know.

CONSTANCE (*sharply*). Yes, you do. You're resisting it.

J.B. (*with suppressed violence*). Don't start that again. Don't stand there with that wiseacre look! I'm sick of your double talk.

CONSTANCE. You were looking at the bed. What frightens you? White . . . . . lines. . . . . . (*She comes nearer to him; he is shaking.*)

She looks over his shoulder. We see J.B.'s face trembling and perspiring.

CONSTANCE. When I made fork marks on the tablecloth they agitated you. Then—that night you—you kissed me—you pushed me away. Because of my robe. It was white—it had dark lines on it. (*Her voice becomes tense and commanding.*) Try to think. Why does the color white frighten you? Why do lines frighten you? Think of white. White.

J.B. (*his eyes glaring at the coverlet; hoarsely*). Yes. It frightens me. I can't look. (*He wrenches his eyes away.*)

CONSTANCE (*intensely*). Don't run away. Stand still. Look at the white spread. Look at it! Remember!

He turns his face toward the bed again. His breathing becomes increased. Suddenly he covers his face with his hands and pitches onto the bed. Constance watches him anxiously and desperately. She moves toward him and bends over him. She stares at the white coverlet and then whispers to him:

CONSTANCE. Darling—darling—you mustn't be frightened. We are making progress. We have the word white—on our side.

She helps him to his feet and leads him to the sofa. He sits down. She begins to undo his collar and tie. We then get a closeup, with Constance's hands in the bottom of the picture, and as J.B. turns once more and looks furtively toward the bed, the scene dissolves out.

The BEDROOM dissolves in, and we see the first gray dawn light through the window of the room. Constance is now sleeping in the bed. The camera moves over and we see J.B. huddled on the sofa, a blanket over him. The camera moves in until J.B.'s sleeping face fills the screen. He opens his eyes and then stares at the window. He turns and looks in the direction of the bed. He rises from the couch slowly, the camera pulling back. He pauses beside the bed and looks at Constance, and from his viewpoint we see the white coverlet with dark vertical lines over the bed and Constance sleeping.—A closeup shows his eyes staring a little. He turns away (so that the scene becomes a medium shot). He crosses to a mirror and examines his unshaven face. He turns and paces the room a couple of times aimlessly, and then goes into the bathroom.

The scene then cuts to the BATHROOM as he comes in and switches on the light, and again examines his unshaven face in the mirror. He feels the stubble on his chin. He takes a drink of water, then in a gesture of sudden decision he takes up a brush from an old-fashioned shaving mug. He puts it down for a moment and takes an old-fashioned razor from a black case. He opens it and feels the edge. He puts it down and proceeds to lather his face from the mug.—We get a closeup of the WHITE SHAVING MUG AND BRUSH. Then we see J.B. putting the brush and mug down quickly. He looks at the white wash basin and is terrified.—We get a closeup of the WHITE WASH BASIN.

Next J.B. sees the white chair, and we get a closeup of the WHITE CHAIR.

J.B. looks and sees the white table, and we see a closeup of the WHITE TABLE.

J.B. looks at the white bathtub, and we get a closeup of the WHITE BATHTUB.

J.B. turns and starts to run out. He stops in the doorway, the razor still in his hand. He looks up, and we get a closeup of the WHITE BEDSPREAD in the bedroom, with its dark vertical lines. Then the camera pans up to the sleeping Constance. J.B. walks forward into a semi-closeup, staring, and a closeup shows CONSTANCE, asleep, strong moonlight across her and the white coverlet.

And now J.B., with razor in hand, comes to the bed. He stares down, clutching the razor. Then suddenly he turns, walks to the door, and goes out into the hallway.

This cuts to the HALLWAY as J.B. descends the stairs, and as he gets nearer and nearer the razor fills the screen and then passes on.

Then we see J.B. pulling up just short of the open door of the downstairs living room, through which a strong light is streaming. He moves forward stealthily. We hear Brulov's voice calling from inside.

BRULOV'S VOICE. Is that you, Mr. Brown?

J.B. stops in his tracks.—There is the sound of footsteps coming from the room. J.B. stands immobile.—Brulov appears in the doorway. He peers about him, unable to see clearly, then he sees J.B.

BRULOV (smiling, and "full of himself"). Ah, I thought it was you. I was unable to sleep a wink, so I came down to work. When you are old, you don't need to sleep so much. I am just having a glass of milk and some crackers. Join me, please. I'll get another glass.

The old man takes J.B. by the arm, and, full of chumminess, leads him into the room. Brulov babbles happily away.

BRULOV. I am glad to have company. Nobody likes to have crackers and milk by himself.

We then see the LIVING ROOM, with J.B. standing just inside the room, as the camera pans Brulov into the kitchen. We hear his voice coming from the open door.

BRULOV'S VOICE. When I was a young man I was always saying, Ah, if I could only get alone by myself—instead of wasting my time with people —I would be happy. (He emerges carrying two glasses of milk. He continues chatting.) Now I am saying always just the opposite. This is the secret of old age. Everything becomes just the opposite.

Brulov has turned his back on J.B. as he puts the things on the table.

A closeup shows J.B. staring at his back. Then the camera moves in until the back of Brulov's white coat fills the screen, following which a closeup shows J.B. beginning to breathe with difficulty. Brulov is still chattering on during this.

BRULOV. Do you know who makes the most trouble in the world—old people. They are always worrying what is going to be in the world tomorrow —after they are gone. That's why we have wars—because old people got nothing else they can get excited about.

A closeup shows J.B. still staring, then we see Brulov coming over to J.B. and handing him a glass of milk.

BRULOV. Well—we will drink to youth —to when we are young and know nothing except living.

J.B. raises his glass and drinks slowly, his eyes looking into the glass, and a closeup shows the milk in the glass; it fills the screen and turns the screen white.

This dissolves to the BEDROOM with Constance, fully dressed, sitting on the side of the bed hurriedly putting on her shoes. She glances nervously toward the open bathroom door. As soon as her shoes are on she commences to cross to the doorway, and then, hurriedly looking into a mirror, roughly straightens her mussed hair.

She comes out onto the LANDING and hurries down the stairs, to the open door of the living room. Suddenly, as the camera moves in, she stops, pulling up with a horror-stricken expression, and we next see what she sees: Slumped in a chair, his collar open, his head lolling lifelessly, is BRULOV.

We see Constance staring at the inert figure. Then her hand moves to her throat, and she goes over slowly to Brulov.

CONSTANCE. Alex! (*Forcing herself to calmness, she puts her hand under the lolling head and lifts it. The old man's eyes open slowly and look at her sightlessly for a moment.*) Alex —are you all right?

Brulov comes to. He yawns, and then smiles slowly at her.

BRULOV. Good morning. Yes. I am all right, thank you. (*He looks around.*) Oh—I fell asleep in the chair. (*He rubs his eyes.*) What time is it?

CONSTANCE (*tensely*). Seven o'clock.

BRULOV (*beaming*). I was dreaming, this morning I get some real coffee.

Constance, ignoring Brulov's last remark, speaks hesitantly, trying to conceal her fears.

CONSTANCE. My husband must have gone out very early this morning— You didn't happen . . .

Brulov nods, indicating the opposite side of the room.

BRULOV. He didn't go out—he's over there on the couch.

CONSTANCE turns and looks across the room in alarm; then we see, from her viewpoint, the figure of J.B. lying on a couch. Constance turns back to Brulov, inquiringly.

BRULOV. He is all right. He is sleeping fine. My dear child, do you think old Alex Brulov, one of the biggest brains who is in psychiatry, is unable to make two and two come out four?

CONSTANCE (*a little embarrassed*). I should have known!

BRULOV. The moment I see you with a husband whose pupils are enlarged, who has a tremor of the left hand, who is on a honeymoon with no baggage and whose name is John Brown —I know practically what is going on.

Constance crosses to the couch. She sits down beside the sleeping figure and looks at the closed eyes tenderly. She looks back to Brulov.

CONSTANCE. What happened?

We get a semi-close shot of BRULOV, from her viewpoint.

BRULOV (*smugly*). Only what I expected. There is no use taking chances with a possibly dangerous case. I sit here—waiting. If you scream, I am ready. So he comes downstairs. And he is dangerous. I can see by his face. So I keep talking while I put some bromide into a glass of milk—enough to knock out three horses. When he falls down, I run up to see you. You are sleeping like a baby. And I come back here—to watch out.

Constance moves her hand protectingly to the sleeping man's shoulder.

CONSTANCE. The struggle against his condition agitates him—at times. But there is no danger in him.

Brulov picks up an object from a nearby side table. He opens the razor.

BRULOV. This is what I found in his hand last night.

Brulov rises and crosses over to her, showing her the razor. We now have the two in a semi-closeup with the sleeping figure of J.B. beyond as Constance stares at the razor.

CONSTANCE. He didn't know he had that. (*Her voice grows anxious.*) Alex, you mustn't think that. He didn't try to do anything to you. He couldn't.

BRULOV (*gently*). My dear child, he is not responsible.

CONSTANCE (*straightening*). That's not correct!

BRULOV (*quietly*). I am just a little more experienced with this type than you.

CONSTANCE. I grant you, you know infinitely more than I do, but in this case—

BRULOV (*interrupting, his voice a little sharper*). Do not complete the sentence with the usual female contradictions. You grant me I know more than you, but on the other hand, you know more than me.

Women's talk! Bah! (*He starts to his desk.*)

CONSTANCE, in alarm, watches him cross the room.

CONSTANCE. Alex, what are you going to do?

BRULOV (*by the desk*). Something more for you than for me.

Constance rises and crosses to the desk beside him.

CONSTANCE. Alex—

BRULOV. I am calling the police.

CONSTANCE (*sharply*). No! No! Please.

BRULOV (*turning with surprise*). You are giving me orders! My own pupil!

CONSTANCE. You don't know this man! You know only science. You know his mind but you don't know his heart.

BRULOV. We are speaking of a schizophrenic and not a valentine.

CONSTANCE (*angrily*). We are speaking of a man.

BRULOV. Oh! (*He turns from the phone and starts filling a pipe. She is silent.*) Love! (*He looks up at her and smiles.*) Look at you. Dr. Petersen, the promising psychoanalyst is now all of a sudden a school girl in love with an actor. Nothing else!

CONSTANCE (*tensely*). Alex, let me tell you about him!

BRULOV. What is there for you to say? We both know that the mind of a woman in love is operating on the lowest level of the intellect. (*He lights his pipe, muttering:*) My doctor told me not to smoke in the morning, but I am too excited!

CONSTANCE (*taking his arm*). You are right. I am not an analyst. Not even a doctor—here. I'm not talking to you as one. (*Brulov smokes and peers at her as she continues.*) But, believe me! Not what I say—but what I feel. The mind isn't everything. The heart can see deeper—sometimes. The shock of a police investigation might ruin his chances for recovery and I can save him.

BRULOV (*quietly*). But if he killed Dr. Edwardes—how can you help him?

CONSTANCE (*passionately*). He didn't! He didn't!

BRULOV. But if it turns out he did—which I am good and certain it will—

Constance collapses into a chair. Tears appear in her eyes.

CONSTANCE. It won't! You yourself taught me what Freud says—(*gulping, unable to stop her tears*)—that a man cannot do anything in amnesia that his real character wouldn't have done.

BRULOV (*in a closeup; excitedly*). And how do you know what his real character is!

CONSTANCE (*in a closeup, her tears continuing*). I know. I know.

Brulov continues to move around his desk, waving his arm.

BRULOV. She knows! This is the way science goes backward! Who told you what he is? Freud? Or a crystal ball?

CONSTANCE (*in a closeup; sobbing*). I couldn't feel this way toward a man who was bad—who had committed murder. I couldn't feel this pain for someone who was evil.

Brulov begins to walk up and down the room, puffing on his pipe violently.

BRULOV (*roaring suddenly*). You are twenty times crazier than him! (*He begins to talk to himself.*) She couldn't love him if he was no good! This is baby-talk. . . . Nothing else! (*He looks suddenly at her.*) What do you want I should do?

He crosses over to Constance and stands by her.

CONSTANCE (*weeping*). Give me time to treat him—and cure him—before the police find him and shock him into an incurable condition.

BRULOV. This could take a year.

CONSTANCE. No, no.

BRULOV (*glaring at her*). All right, half a year. We should sit and hide for a half a year, waiting to find out if he is going to cut your throat, my throat, and set fire to the house. My dear child, even to a woman in love such a situation must seem a little unreasonable.

CONSTANCE (*looking desperately at him*). Alex—just a few days. Before you turn him over let me try—just a few days more. And if I can't do anything—if we both can't—then you can call the police. (*She holds his arm eagerly.*) You are not hiding a criminal. There is no evidence against him—except his own guilt fantasies. He is wanted only as a possible witness—as to what happened to Dr. Edwardes. But in his present condition he could tell the police nothing. (*Pleading*) Don't you see—we are doing nothing against the law. We are helping them—by investigating the patient—as doctors. Not criminals. Doctors who want the truth—even more than they do.

BRULOV (*slowly*). All right.

CONSTANCE. You'll wait?

BRULOV (*patting her shoulder and*

*smiling—and going to the doorway with her*). Go—make me 'coffee. I will pretend to myself—I'm acting sensible—for a few days.

CONSTANCE. Oh, Alex. Thank you, Alex. (*She beams at him.*) I'll make you coffee with an egg in it— (*She looks back at the sleeping J.B., and starts for the kitchen.*)

Brulov turns back into the room. We then see him going to J.B., leaning over and shaking him. J.B. stirs and looks up. Brulov watches him, and refills his pipe. The camera moves in slightly. The two men fill the screen.

J.B. (*foggily*). Who are you?

BRULOV. I am Doctor Brulov.

J.B. (*thickly*). Brulov—Oh, yes. That's right. (*He "tastes" his mouth and scowls.*) Bromides. Who's been feeding me bromides?

BRULOV. I gave you—to sleep.

J.B. (*sitting up, his head in his hands; he mutters at the floor*). Brulov. Oh —yes. Rochester.

Brulov sits down, facing him. He speaks casually.

BRULOV. What is your name?

J.B. (*heavily*). I don't know. (*His head clears—he looks up from his bent posture.*) Constance told you.

BRULOV. Nobody told me. If I don't know a patient with amnesia when I see one, what do I know? (*Brulov carries his tobacco loose in his pocket. He refills his pipe.*) You don't remember your father or mother?

J.B. (*slowly*). No.

BRULOV. Wife, or sweetheart?

J.B. (*irritably*). No!

BRULOV. Don't fight me. I am going to help you—if I can. I am going to

be your father image. I want you to look on me like your father. Trust me. Lean on me. This is a short-cut. But we haven't much time.

J.B. (*closing his eyes and hugging his head with his hands*). All right. Go on. I'm leaning.

BRULOV. Maybe you got something you want to tell me. A single thought. A few words in the corner of your head. Go on—talk to me. Whatever comes into your head—just say what it is.

J.B. (*heavily—staring at the floor— after a pause*). Nothing. There's nothing.

BRULOV. Maybe you dreamt something?

J.B. (*frowning*). Yes.

BRULOV. What did you dream?

J.B. (*scowling*). I don't believe in dreams. That Freud stuff is a lot of hooey.

BRULOV. You are a fine one to talk! You got amnesia. And you got a guilt complex. And you don't know if you are coming or going from some place. But Freud is hooey. *This* you know! (*He puffs his pipe and sneers.*) Wise guy!

J.B. looks with more interest at him. A half grin forms on his mouth.

J.B. (*smiling faintly*). You don't like me—papa.

BRULOV (*irritably*). Do you want I should help you—or not?

J.B. (*quietly*). I'm sorry.

BRULOV. I explain to you about dreams so you don't think it is hooey. The secrets of who you are and what has made you run away from yourself —all these secrets are buried in your brain, but you don't want to look at them. The human being very often does not want to know the truth about himself. Because he thinks it will make him sick. So he makes himself sicker trying to forget. You follow me?

J.B. (*in a semi-closeup, nodding slowly*). Yes.

Constance enters with coffee and toast on a tray. She comes across and puts the tray down on an end table beside the couch. The scene includes Brulov and J.B.

CONSTANCE (*looking worriedly at J.B.*) How do you feel?

BRULOV (*as he sees the tray*). Ah—coffee.

J.B. (*grunting*). Awful.

His hands clasp his head. His back is to the windows beyond, where heavy snow is falling.

BRULOV. The patient is going to tell us what he dreamt.

CONSTANCE. Fine. I'll take notes. I'll get my glasses.

Brulov eats as he talks.

BRULOV. Now here is where dreams come in. . . . They tell you what you are trying to hide. But they tell it to you all mixed up like pieces of a puzzle that don't fit. The problem of the analyst is to examine this puzzle and put the pieces together in the right place—and find out what the devil you are trying to say to yourself.

J.B. Let's see. I kept thinking while I was dreaming that all this meant something. There was some other meaning in it that I ought to find out.

CONSTANCE. We'll find out.

Constance crosses to the desk and sits

down, then takes up a pencil and paper to make notes.

J.B. I can't make out just . . .

This dissolves to a close view—a light effect against gray background.

J.B.'S VOICE. . . . what sort of a place it was.

This dissolves to a closeup of single large eyes painted on drapes of black. The camera moves in closer as still other eyes are superimposed, filling the screen. And this dissolves to a full view of a GAMBLING ROOM with painted black drapes hanging in the background. People sit at tables playing cards, J.B. and another man playing at a table in the foreground.

J.B.'S VOICE. It seemed to be a gambling house but there weren't any walls—just a lot of curtains with eyes painted on them.

We see J.B. and the man playing cards in a nearer view.

J.B.'S VOICE. A man was walking around with a large pair of scissors cutting all the drapes in half.

In the GAMBLING ROOM, a man is cutting the drapes with a large pair of scissors as the camera moves in closer. The drape falls revealing another eye. Superimposed over this we see a scantily dressed girl enter and approach J.B.'s table. She kisses his partner.

J.B.'S VOICE. And then a girl came in with hardly anything on and started walking around the gambling room kissing everybody. She came to my table first.

This dissolves to BRULOV'S LIVING ROOM disclosing J.B., CONSTANCE and BRULOV.

BRULOV. Did you recognize this kissing bug?

J.B. Well, I—I—I'm afraid she looked a little like Constance.

BRULOV. Uh-huh. This is plain, ordinary wishful dreaming. Go on.

J.B. (*closing his eyes and trying to remember*). Well, I was sitting there playing cards with a man who had a beard. . . .

This dissolves to a long view of the GAMBLING ROOM showing J.B. and his partner. The man's hand is in the foreground, holding some oversized cards. He throws the cards over. We see they are blank. A masked man enters and begins gesticulating to Dr. Edwardes (J.B.'s partner) as the camera moves in to a closeup of his masked face.

J.B.'s VOICE. I was dealing to him and I turned up the seven of clubs. He said, "that makes twenty-one—I win." But when he turned up his cards, they were blank. Just then the proprietor came in and accused him of cheating. The proprietor yelled, "This is my place and if I catch you cheating again, I'll fix you."

The scene dissolves back to BRULOV's LIVING ROOM.

J.B. I'm sorry about that kissing bug.

CONSTANCE. I'm glad you didn't dream of me as an egg-beater as one of my patients did.

J.B. Why? What would that mean?

CONSTANCE. Never mind.

J.B. Well, does it make any sense to you—what I've dreamed?

CONSTANCE. Not yet. You were trying to tell yourself something. What it is, we'll figure out later.

J.B. There's a lot more to it.

BRULOV. Go on and try to recall the details. The more cockeyed, the better for the scientific side of it.

J.B. (*leaning back and starting again to relate his dream*). He was . . .

This dissolves to an extreme long-shot of a ROOFTOP, and we see a man standing on the rooftop, leaning over the edge. The camera moves forward as the man falls off the roof and out of the picture. He resembles Dr. Edwardes, the man who was playing cards with J.B. in the earlier illustration in the dream. The masked man steps from behind a tall chimney on the roof and watches the other plunge off. He holds a small wheel in his hand.

J.B.'s VOICE. . . . leaning over the sloping roof of a high building. It was the man with the beard. I—I yelled at him to watch out. Then he went over—slowly—with his feet in the air. And then I saw the proprietor again—the man in the mask. He was hiding behind a tall chimney and he had a small wheel . . .

The masked man is laughing as the camera moves in to him. He drops the wheel on the roof and the camera pans down to it until the wheel fills the screen.

J.B.'s VOICE. . . . in his hand. I saw him drop the wheel on the roof.

This dissolves to PUFFS OF SMOKE, and the smoke fills the screen.

This dissolves to an extreme long-shot showing J.B. running down the side of what appears to be a large pyramid. A huge pair of wings appears over his head and chases him down the pyramid.

J.B.'s VOICE. Suddenly I was running. I heard something beating over my head. It was a great pair of wings. The wings chased me and almost caught up . . .

We see J.B. approaching the bottom of the pyramid, still running. He runs out of the picture just as the wings are about to catch him.

J.B.'S VOICE. . . . with me when I came to the bottom of the hill.

This dissolves to BRULOV'S LIVING ROOM and we see the three again.

J.B. I must have escaped. I don't remember. That's all there was. I woke up and saw Dr. Brulov.

CONSTANCE (*coming over with a cup of coffee*). Have some coffee.

We follow her across the room as she joins the other two.

J.B. Something—is happening.

CONSTANCE. What is it?

We see a new expression come over J.B.'s face, in a closeup. His eyes move furtively from one side to the other as though he feels something over his shoulder. The camera pulls back slowly as he turns around and rises. When he has completed his turn, we have pulled back far enough to see that the snow is falling through the window beyond. Brulov and Constance watch him in silence as J.B.'s figure begins to crumple a little. He turns back quickly from the snow. He sinks to the couch, Constance and Brulov looking down at him.

CONSTANCE (*softly, as she stares at him*). The snow.

BRULOV (*quietly*). The light frightened him. Photophobia.

CONSTANCE. No. It was the snow.

Constance looks away from J.B. out of the window. Through it she sees: three small boys appearing on a small street hill beyond. They carry a bobsled. They flop on it and race down the hill. The second group arrives at the top of the street and goes down on a sled. A

girl of twelve has a small sled of her own. She joins the coasting down the street hill.

A closeup shows Constance watching the scene, her eyes narrowing slightly, and, from her viewpoint, the camera goes forward until the windowpanes disappear from the scene so that we get just a full view of the hill and sled marks. The camera moves forward far enough so that we see nothing on the screen except snow and sharp, dark lines across it.

A closeup shows Constance still looking out. She looks down toward the coffee table, and from her viewpoint we see a closeup of the white napkin on the table.

Next, looking back toward the hill, she picks up the small sugar tongs from the table and looking down at the napkin again begins to draw lines across it, following which we get a closeup of the prongs of the sugar tongs making strong indentations on the white napkin.

Another closeup shows Constance looking from this toward J.B., and we see J.B.'s bent head from her viewpoint, while Brulov just beyond him looks at her inquiringly.

CONSTANCE (*nodding toward the snow*). That's the white he's afraid of . . . Snow . . . And those tracks.

BRULOV (*in a semi-closeup with Constance*). What tracks?

CONSTANCE. The sled tracks in the snow. The first symptom he revealed was shock at the sight of fork lines drawn on a white tablecloth. And—my white robe. It had dark lines. And last night—the white coverlet. Like those dark tracks in the snow.

BRULOV. Pull the blinds down—please!

The camera pulls back as Brulov crosses to the window blinds. He pulls one down; Constance pulls another. The room darkens.

CONSTANCE. Dr. Edwardes was fond of sports. He mentions tennis and skiing in his book, as valuable in the treatment of mental disorders. (*She straightens.*) Skiing! Ski tracks in the snow. That's what those dark lines symbolized for him. His horror of them means, of course, that they are immediately connected with the cause of his amnesia.

BRULOV (*softly*). Yes. A murder on skis.

The cup and saucer fall from J.B.'s fingers. He covers his face with his hands.

The scene dissolves back to the ROOM a little later with J.B. sitting on the couch, staring. Constance and Brulov are talking.

CONSTANCE (*tensely*). Where did Edwardes go for his skiing? We must find out. (*She leans over J.B.*) Can you tell us where? Try!

BRULOV. He has told you already. In his dream. Let me see your notes.

She hands him the notebook, and remains at J.B.'s side.

CONSTANCE. What can we do for him?

BRULOV (*staring at the notes*). You are not his mama. You are an analyst. Leave him alone. He will come out of this by himself. Hm. The sloping roof—that means only a mountainside.

CONSTANCE (*eagerly*). —They were skiing. And the father image, the bearded man, is Dr. Edwardes. It's very simple. Edwardes plunged over a precipice while skiing.

BRULOV. And then a shadow chases him up and down a hill. That could mean he was escaping from a valley.

CONSTANCE (*eagerly*). Skiing resorts are often called valleys—like Sun Valley. He was being pursued by a winged figure—a witch or a harpy.

BRULOV. No. The figure was you—if you grew wings you would be an angel.

CONSTANCE (*thoughtfully*). The dream was trying to tell him the name of the resort. An angel. Angel Valley. (*J.B. stirs beside her. She helps him sit up and speaks softly to him.*) Do you remember Angel Valley?

J.B. (*staring at her*). No.

CONSTANCE (*to Brulov*). We can call up a travel agency and check all the resort names.

J.B. (*rising—his voice low*). It wasn't Angel Valley. I remember. It was a place called Gabriel Valley.

CONSTANCE (*softly*). What else do you remember now?

BRULOV. Who was the masked figure in your dream?

CONSTANCE (*eagerly*). It was an accident. Do you remember that? A skiing accident. Dr. Edwardes went over a snow cliff.

J.B. (*staring out of the window—his voice hoarsened*). It—was no accident. (*He turns to her, his face filled with pain.*) I can't stand this any more. I've had enough of it. We've got to call the police. (*He sits down heavily in a chair—his words become inaudible. Constance is beside him.*)

CONSTANCE. No. We have to go to Gabriel Valley. You've got to go with me.

And now the scene dissolves to the POLICE OFFICE where a uniformed policeman is sitting at a side table playing "Patience." A police secretary enters with a pile of mail, chiefly police circulars.

SECRETARY. This is for Cooley when he comes in.

POLICEMAN. I'll tell him.

He lays down the mail. The policeman leans over from his side table and looks at a picture on the top of the pile. We see, in a closeup, that it is a picture of Constance, with a caption across the top reading: "Dr. Constance Petersen, Wanted by Police for Questioning."

This dissolves to BRULOV'S LIVING ROOM where Constance is talking on the telephone, just finishing a conversation. J.B. is standing looking out of the window at the snow.

CONSTANCE (*into the phone*). At four forty-five? Thank you. (*After a pause*) Goodbye.

She hangs up and goes to J.B. The camera moves in.

CONSTANCE. There's a train leaving in an hour. We can make connections for Gabriel Valley.

She pauses as she comes by his side. He continues to stare out of the window in silence. Then he turns from the window and for a moment puts his arm around her shoulder. He moves away across the room, the camera pulling back. Constance looks after him.

J.B. (*his voice tender*). I know what I have to do. (*He returns to her and takes both her hands.*) I can't go on

endangering you. I know—about last night.

CONSTANCE (*tensely*). Nothing happened.

J.B. (*softly*). But it will. I've got to end it—before it does. (*He smiles desperately at her.*) I love you. But I'm not worth loving. (*She clings to his arms. He whispers:*) Darling— you can help me—afterward.

CONSTANCE (*clinging to him, her voice low and compelling*). There's no help —afterward. If you give yourself up to the police—in your condition— there is no afterward—for either of us. I can cure you.

J.B. (*his voice low and desperate*). You can't undo a murder?

CONSTANCE (*tensely*). There is none to undo.

J.B. I killed him . . .

CONSTANCE. Stop it!

J.B. (*fiercely*). And now—you. Last night I— (*He breaks off and whispers:*) Don't try to stop me. I've got to go—

CONSTANCE (*holding him*). Guilt! Guilt! You've lived with it for a long time—haven't you?

J.B. Yes!

CONSTANCE (*sharply*). Since childhood.

A semi-closeup shows the startled expression of J. B.

J.B. What?

CONSTANCE (*in a semi-closeup; tensely, her hands gripping his arms*). Ever since your childhood you have tried to run away from something, you've always felt guilty about anything that happened around you. *What was it in your youth?* It must have been terrible, for you to prefer to think you murdered Edwardes rather than remember what happened long ago.

The camera pulls back as J.B. moves away toward the door.

J.B. (*angrily*). No.

Constance clings to him, her voice now tearful.

CONSTANCE. No. You said you loved me. Look at me then. (*She turns him from the door.*) Why am I fighting for you? Because I love you. Because I need you.

J.B. (*muttering*). I'm nothing—

CONSTANCE (*tensely*). I want you to come with me to Gabriel Valley.

J.B. (*desperately*). What good will that do!

CONSTANCE. When you see the hill where the accident happened—you'll remember it. We'll go skiing together—as you did with Edwardes.

J.B. (*in a low voice*). I was there with—I—I killed him—

CONSTANCE. You'll *see* your innocence. You'll see what really happened!

J.B. (*his voice low*). You mean—because it will happen again—

CONSTANCE. Yes.

J.B. And what if I killed him?

The camera swings over slightly to include Brulov who stands silently in the doorway. Constance looks up at him. Neither answers J.B.'s question.

J.B. (*looking from one to the other*). Isn't it true that if the episode is repeated, I'm likely to do the same thing I did before?

Constance and Brulov remain silent.

J.B. (*taking their silence for assent; turning to Constance, quietly*). Then how do you know I won't kill again?

CONSTANCE. Because I'm convinced you didn't kill in the first place.

J.B. in the foreground looks at Constance, a smile on his face.

J.B. You believe in me enough to take such a chance?

CONSTANCE. Of course I do . . . We're going back to that ski run. We'll find out what it was in your childhood that's haunted you all your life, and we'll also find out what happened to Dr. Edwardes.

She looks confidently at Brulov for his accord.—A closeup shows BRULOV turning away, and another closeup discloses CONSTANCE. Her expression of confidence falters.

This dissolves to the POLICE STATION with Lieutenant Cooley at his desk. Gillespie is talking to him. Cooley is looking through the papers left on his desk by the secretary. Cooley now has Constance's picture in his hand. He is about to throw it down on the pile, when he glances at it again.—A closeup shows Cooley's hand sketching in eyeglasses on Constance's face. Then we see Cooley and Gillespie as Cooley hands the picture over to Gillespie.

COOLEY. Ever see her before?

Gillespie looks at the picture, then the two exchange glances.

GILLESPIE. Let's go.

This dissolves to a TRAIN COMPARTMENT at night as the train is passing through a snow-covered countryside. Constance and J.B. are having dinner. J.B. sits morosely, his food untouched. Constance tries to make conversation as she eats, cheerily ignoring his mood.

CONSTANCE. I've always loved very feminine clothes—but never quite dared to wear them. But I'm going to, after this. I'm going to wear exactly the things that please me—and you.

J.B.'s eyes fasten on the knife in her hands. Constance falters, for a minute, then goes on as if everything were normal.

CONSTANCE. Even very funny hats. You know, the kind that make you look a little drunk.

A sudden roar fills the compartment as a train on the adjoining track flashes by. The lights shooting in through the window illumine wildly the knife in her hand—and J.B. continues staring at it.

The scene dissolves to a VAST SNOWY LANDSCAPE and we see two tiny figures carrying skis—Constance and J.B.—toiling up the side of a mountain. This dissolving, we see them stop at the crest of the hill. Constance kneels and begins to put on her skis. J.B. remains stiffly erect, his skis over his shoulder.

A closeup shows J.B. looking down at Constance, his face expressionless. Then we see a semi-closeup of the two as Constance, still kneeling, looks back at him, her face taut.

CONSTANCE (*sharply*). Put them on.

Without replying and almost with the manner of an automaton, he puts the skis down and commences to adjust them. Eventually he straightens up and looks at her. As though introducing a child to a lesson, she gently touches his arm. They both begin to slide away.

Next, we see them commencing to slide down the slope. Then, in a semi-closeup, we see the two, and a growing tenseness comes into J.B.'s face as he

stares ahead. Constance divides her attention between the downward slope ahead and J.B. She goes a little ahead of him, then glances over her shoulder as though urging him to follow her.

J.B., seen in a closeup, slowly turns his look from concentrating ahead over to Constance.—CONSTANCE, seen from his viewpoint, is speeding slightly ahead of him.

("Big head" of J.B.) We see his face assume a queer, distorted expression, as though his mind is trying to grope for something.

A closeup of CONSTANCE shows that her expression is one of mingled hope and fright, then a closeup of J.B. shows his expression growing more menacing.

We next see Constance looking back at J.B. as they rush down the slope. For a moment we see the white slope ahead of them and for the first time we see a precipice.

Constance, in a closeup, sees the precipice. Then we get a flash of the PRECIPICE from her viewpoint. She looks imploringly back at J.B., who is now obsessed.

We get a closeup ("big head") of J.B., and then see the slope, from his viewpoint, over which we can see the precipice in the distance begin to change. The scene changes to a balustrade of a stone front city house, and at the bottom of the balustrade are spiked iron railings. A small boy, about five years of age is sliding down and has almost reached the spiked fence.

A closeup of J.B.'s face shows him staring down from the top of the balustrade. It begins to change to himself as a boy of about seven years of age, who is sliding down the balustrade toward the other little boy. We see a look of alarm come on the boy's face. (The boy is J.B.)—And from his viewpoint, the camera (taking J.B.'s place) is now rushing toward the other little boy.— Then we get a closeup flash of the face of J.B., whose boyish face is distorted with fright.

> J.B.'S VOICE. It was something in my childhood—something in my childhood. I remember now. I killed my brother.

The camera has now rushed up to the other little boy as he bounces off the balustrade and is flung toward the spiked railings. As he hits them the screen is splashed with a dark fluid that blots the scene out.—Then we get a closeup flash of the big, distorted EYES of the boy J.B.

This cuts to the SNOWY SLOPE as in a flash J.B. flings himself in front of Constance, and the camera whips back as his arms go around her and they fall in the snow at the very edge of the drop.

We then get a closeup (the two "big heads") of Constance and J.B.

> J.B. (exultant). I didn't kill my brother! It was an accident! It was an accident.

> CONSTANCE (sobbing with joy and relief). That's what has haunted you —that was the memory you were afraid of.

They are still holding each other, and as they turn to look down at the precipice, the camera pulls back to reveal the sheer drop beneath them.

This dissolves into a TELEGRAM reading: "Dr. Constance Petersen and sus-pect File #14298 now at Gabriel Lake Lodge. New evidence uncovered makes surveillance essential until arrival officers in charge.

> Lt. J. R. Hungate by Sgt. Doan"

This dissolves to a distant view of a car driving up a road in the snow-covered mountains, and then to the lobby of GABRIEL LAKE LODGE where a log fire is burning in a rough stone fireplace. Constance and J.B. are thawing out in front of the flames.

> J.B. (his voice low). It's like looking into a picture book—an old one. And seeing the familiar pictures, one at a time. I went to Columbia Medical School. Had a girl with a giggle who, luckily, married my roommate, Ken. Oh, by the way, my name is John Ballyntine.

> CONSTANCE (smiling). I'm—very pleased to meet you.

> J.B. Another thing—my army record is—all right. I was invalided out. I ran into Dr. Edwardes when I was in the Cumberland Mountains trying to recover from some kind of nerve shock I got from the plane crash. He was on vacation, but I asked him to help me and he invited me to go skiing with him. (After a pause) We went through New York and I vaguely remember going to lunch somewhere. I'm still a little vague about that lunch part. Then we arrived here and the accident happened at that spot.

> CONSTANCE (softly). Where you saved me.

> J.B. Now, let's not have any confusion about who saved whom. (He takes her hand.) Yes—he went over there all right. I'm still a little foggy about it, but I do know that Edwardes was about fifty feet ahead of

me when he went over—I saw him plunge.

CONSTANCE. That was the thing that set you off—that stirred up your old guilt complex and made you think you had killed him. Then you had to run away from that, too. So you took on the role of Dr. Edwardes to prove to yourself that he wasn't dead and that therefore you hadn't killed him.

J.B. (*smiling at her*). Professor, I never realized in my amnesic state—how lovely you are.

CONSTANCE. Please—now that you've got your head back, you mustn't lose it again.

J.B. (*softly*). Too late. I'm beyond cure. (*He puts his arm around her.*) How does it feel to be a great analyst?

CONSTANCE. Not so bad.

J.B. And a great detective?

CONSTANCE. Wonderful.

J.B. And madly adored?

CONSTANCE. Very wonderful.

J.B. You'll look wonderful—in white —with a little orange blossom in your hair.

CONSTANCE. That sounds vaguely as if it had something to do with marriage.

J.B. Brilliant analysis, Doctor.

He is about to kiss her when he sees Lieutenant Cooley and Sergeant Gillespie entering the lobby with another man, a Captain Hickson.

Then we see the policemen moving to Constance and J.B. at the fireplace.

J. B. Hello—

CAPTAIN HICKSON (*business-like, to Constance and J.B.*). You know Lieutenant Cooley and Sergeant Gillespie, from Rochester?

J.B. Yes. Yes. We know them quite well.

CONSTANCE. How did you find us?

COOLEY. No thanks to your friend, Dr. Brulov!

GILLESPIE (*sarcastic*). We made a few inquiries at the railroad station—you left a trail a mile wide.

CONSTANCE. Well, you arrived just in the nick of time, Lieutenant.

COOLEY. I believe that's the usual expression.

There is a pause as Constance and J.B. are puzzled by Cooley's tone. Then Captain Hickson turns to J.B.

HICKSON. We've found the body of Dr. Edwardes—it's almost exactly where you told the local police it would be. You remembered the spot very well.

CONSTANCE. Well, thank goodness it's all cleared up.

COOLEY (*taking out a cigarette*). Well, not quite, Dr. Petersen. (*He lights his cigarette, calmly.*) I'm afraid a bullet was found in the body.

CONSTANCE (*shocked*). That's impossible!

COOLEY. It was in his back.

HICKSON (*rather quietly*). The case is one of murder. We shall have to detain you, sir—and it's my duty to inform you that anything you say may be used against you.

A closeup shows Constance's stricken face, then it dissolves to a series of "big heads" of Constance, each shot dissolving to another. Her voice in each

is progressively more frantic and hopeless.

CONSTANCE (*urgently pleading with
J.B.*). No, No! You mustn't say you
killed him, darling! Try to remember what happened before Edwardes
went over.

Another "big head" of Constance—
with an impression of a witness stand
in the background.

CONSTANCE (*desperately*). But when
he said he killed him, he wasn't himself! He was in a state of great mental
distress.

And this dissolves to a "big head" of
Constance—viewed through prison
bars.

CONSTANCE (*more frantic*). But you
can't put him away! You *can't*! It'll
destroy his mind! Don't you understand?

A last "big head" of Constance.—She
turns away sadly as prison doors clang
shut after J.B.

CONSTANCE. Goodbye, my dear. . . .
We won't give up hope. I'm going
to fight and fight and get you free.

This dissolves to a long view of GREEN
MANORS at night, which dissolves to the
GREEN MANORS HALLWAY. We come
upon the same scene that we saw in the
beginning of the picture. A white-
coated attendant is going down the corridor away from us.—And this dissolves to CONSTANCE'S OFFICE as Constance is pacing up and down the
room in front of the moonlit window.
A desk lamp throws a sharp light across
onto the couch. Brulov is sitting there.
His voice is kind and fatherly as he
speaks.

BRULOV (*softly*). My dear girl, you
cannot keep bumping your head
against reality and saying, "It isn't

there." The evidence was definite.
We can't remove it by wishing or
crying.

CONSTANCE (*quietly*). He trusted me
—and I led him into a trap. I convicted him. (*She stares at Brulov.*)
Is that real enough for you?

BRULOV. There is no one to blame.
The case was a little deeper than you
figured. This often happens. You
must realize now one thing—it is
over—for both of you.

CONSTANCE (*grimly*). It's not over.

BRULOV. You will have other cases.

CONSTANCE. It's not over. It never will
be. Don't ask me to stop! I can't!
(*She pauses, controls herself and
smiles wearily at the old man.*) I'm
sorry. Thanks . . . for straightening
things out with Dr. Murchison—and
everyone.

Brulov rises and goes to her and takes
her hands. (*The camera moves in until
they are both in semi-closeup.*)

BRULOV. It is very sad. To love—and
lose somebody. But in a while you
will forget. And you will take up the
threads of your life where you left
off—not so long ago. And you will
work hard. There is lots of happiness
in working hard. Maybe the most—
(*He kisses her.*) I will write to you.

CONSTANCE (*softly*). Alex, you're very
good. Thanks.

The door of the room opens and Dr.
Murchison appears.

MURCHISON. I'm sorry to hurry you,
Dr. Brulov. But your car is waiting.
You have just time . . .

Brulov smiles at Murchison, and goes
to him, Constance following.

# SPELLBOUND

**BRULOV.** Oh, thank you. I am always late. Always forgetting—

They go into the corridor.—This dissolves to a closeup of Constance at the window watching Brulov depart. Then we observe, from her viewpoint, Dr. Murchison seeing Brulov into the car. They say goodbye, the car drives off and Murchison starts back into the house.

We get a semi-closeup as Murchison enters the hall and joins Constance. They begin to walk along the hallway.

**MURCHISON.** A brilliant man.

**CONSTANCE** (*frowning*). I should have gone to the station with him.

**MURCHISON.** You are too tired. I know that feeling of exhaustion only too well. One must humor it—or it explodes. I shall try to help you—in every way.

They have stopped in front of her door, and Murchison puts a detaining hand on her arm.

**MURCHISON.** You will take care of yourself?

**CONSTANCE.** Yes.

**MURCHISON.** And try to forget—things better forgotten. You have a great career ahead of you, Constance.

**CONSTANCE.** Thank you. (*She smiles up at him gently.*) Well, Doctor, at least one good thing came out of all this—you're back at Green Manors. Who knows what might have happened to the place under Dr. Edwardes?

**MURCHISON.** I knew Edwardes only slightly. I never really liked him, but he was a good man in a way, I suppose. (*He nods to her.*) Well, good night, Constance. I hope you feel

rested in the morning. (*Murchison starts up the stairs, and Constance turns and enters her room.*)

The scene cuts to CONSTANCE'S OFFICE as Constance enters thoughtfully and closes the door behind her. (As she stands with a troubled look on her face, the camera moves in to a closer shot.) Then, very faintly, and distorted at first on the sound track, we hear a repetition of what Murchison has said in the hallway:

**MURCHISON'S VOICE.** I knew Edwardes only slightly . . . I never liked him very well. . . . (*The voice grows increasingly clearer and louder.*) I knew Edwardes only slightly . . . . Knew Edwardes slightly . . . Knew Edwardes . . . . Knew Edwardes slightly . . . . Knew Edwardes . . . . Knew! . . . (*Very loud and sharp*) KNEW!

Constance's face has grown alive and excited as the significance of the words hits her. She turns back to the door, opens it slightly, and looks up after Murchison. Then we get a long view of the HALL, with Constance's profile in the foreground seen through the partly open door. The angle is on MURCHISON's figure approaching the stair landing. An attendant is escorting a woman patient down from the upper floor. Murchison stops and speaks a few benevolent words to the patient. We cannot hear what he says. Then he passes up the stairs, out of sight.

Constance closes her door again, goes to the desk and picks up the notebook in which we have seen her take down the notes of J.B.'s treatments and the notes of his dream at Brulov's. She opens it and stares at it. Then, full of determination she crosses to the door and goes into the corridor.

We see Constance come out of the door into the HALLWAY and cross toward the stairs.—We get a closeup of Constance's face as she begins to mount the stairs. Then the camera goes up 'the stairs, showing her viewpoint. After this our eyes become level with the upper floor and we see the light under Murchison's door, the same light that we saw when she went up to Edwardes' room.

The UPPER LANDING: She reaches the top stair and crosses to Murchison's door. She rings the bell. A lock-buzzer answers. She opens the door and goes in.

Constance comes into the room and hesitates in the doorway.—From her viewpoint we see Murchison seated at his desk.

MURCHISON. Come in.

Then we get a semi-closeup as Constance closes the door behind her and approaches his desk.

CONSTANCE. I want to talk to you, Dr. Murchison.

MURCHISON (smiling). It's rather late, and you need rest, Constance.

CONSTANCE. I must talk to you.

MURCHISON (softly). Nocturnal conferences are bad for the nerves. Is it something about your work?

CONSTANCE. Yes. (She stands facing him.)

MURCHISON (smiling). Can't it wait till morning?

CONSTANCE. It can't wait.

He sighs and sits back. The light makes an eerie illumination for his face in the shadowed room. He gestures toward a chair beside the desk.

MURCHISON. Please sit down, Dr. Petersen.

The camera moves in as Constance sits down slowly, her eyes on him. Murchison smiles at her.

MURCHISON. Now. What's your problem?

CONSTANCE. It is a dream one of my patients reported.

MURCHISON. May I ask who the patient is?

CONSTANCE. The patient is Mr. Ballyntine.

MURCHISON. I fancied that. And you're still working with the possibility of his innocence. Charming loyalty—one of your most attractive characteristics, Constance. What did he dream?

CONSTANCE. He dreamed he was in a gambling house. It was full of odd people—playing with blank cards.

MURCHISON. Blank cards. Obviously the patient was trying to deny it was a gambling house—by dreaming of spurious cards.

CONSTANCE. One of the people in the place went around cutting the drapes in half. Another was a scantily dressed girl who was kissing everybody.

MURCHISON. With a little effort, one could almost imagine them inmates of Green Manors.

CONSTANCE. That's what I had in mind, Dr. Murchison.

MURCHISON. Interesting notion to play around with, isn't it? Do go on.

CONSTANCE. There were eyes painted on the curtains around the walls.

MURCHISON. Oh, the guards at Green Manors.

CONSTANCE. The patient was playing cards, now no longer blank—a game of twenty-one with a bearded man—who was evidently Dr. Edwardes.

MURCHISON. Yes. One usually dreams of one's analyst as an authority with a beard.

CONSTANCE. He dealt Dr. Edwardes a seven of clubs and Edwardes said, "That makes it twenty-one."

MURCHISON. I would say that the patient was trying to mention a locale. The seven of clubs might mean a club.

CONSTANCE. Yes. With the word "twenty-one" in it. There is such a place in New York. It's called the "Twenty-One Club."

MURCHISON. I've heard of it.

CONSTANCE. The patient dreamt that the proprietor of the place came in and began accusing Dr. Edwardes of cheating. He ordered Edwardes out, and said, "I won't allow you to play here. This is my place. I'm going to fix you."

MURCHISON. The dream gives the locale a double identity—the Twenty-One Club and Green Manors. But the proprietor seems to belong more to the latter. (*He smiles at her.*) In fact, I would say that this angry proprietor who threatened Dr. Edwardes was myself.

CONSTANCE. It seemed that way to me.

MURCHISON (*after a pause*). I presume you only arrived at this solution tonight.

CONSTANCE. Yes.

MURCHISON. And have confided your psychoanalytic findings—to nobody.

CONSTANCE. Not yet.

MURCHISON. Was there any more to the dream?

CONSTANCE. Yes. The patient dreamt he and Dr. Edwardes were on a high sloping roof—and that he saw Edwardes plunge over the edge to his death. He also saw the angry proprietor hiding behind a chimney—laughing—holding a small wheel in his hand. He dropped the wheel.

MURCHISON (*frowning*). The symbolism of the small wheel escapes me.

CONSTANCE. It was a revolver. The proprietor who threatened Dr. Edwardes' life in the Twenty-One Club dropped a revolver in the snow—in Gabriel Valley—after shooting Dr. Edwardes in the back. The weapon is still there—at the foot of a tree. With the murderer's fingerprints on it.

We get a closeup of Murchison's hand as he removes a gun from the drawer and levels it toward her. During this we hear his voice.

MURCHISON'S VOICE. I cannot agree with this part of your interpretation. For the good reason that the weapon is now in my hand. I imagined something of this sort would happen—after I made the slip tonight about knowing Dr. Edwardes. That started your agile young mind going.

We get a semi-closeup of the TWO, and then individual closeups.

CONSTANCE. You were having a breakdown, and in a state of panic you heard that Edwardes was to take your place here. You sought him out in his favorite restaurant where he was lunching with—John Ballyntine. You accused him of stealing your job. You threatened to kill him. He calmed you down—told you he was off on a skiing vacation. You followed him there—and shot him from behind a tree—

MURCHISON (*coldly*). That's enough! Your story is ridiculous. You will make a fool of yourself—a love-smitten analyst playing a dream detective—

CONSTANCE. There will be no dreams for the police. They will find out from the waiters in the Twenty-One Club that you were there. You will be identified as the man who had a row with Dr. Edwardes. There will be people who saw you on the train to Gabriel Valley—who saw you there. There will be no dreams necessary—for this case.

MURCHISON (*softly*). I see. (*He rubs his forehead vaguely.*) Please sit where you are. You are an excellent analyst, Dr. Petersen. But a rather stupid woman. (*His voice hoarsens.*) What did you think I would do—when you told me all this? Congratulate you? You forget—in your imbecilic devotion to your patient—that the punishment for two murders is the same as for one.

His face grows moist with perspiration. Constance remains motionless looking at him.

CONSTANCE. You are not going to commit a second murder, Dr. Murchison.

MURCHISON (*hoarsely*). I hadn't planned to. But—you are here. You are not leaving.

He raises the gun a little higher and points it with more deliberation at her. But Constance does not even look down at the gun, and continues quietly:

CONSTANCE. A man of your intelligence does not commit a stupid murder. You are thinking you were not mentally responsible for that other

crime in the snow. They will find extenuating circumstances—in the state of your health. They will not execute you for the death of Dr. Edwardes. You can still live, read, write, research—even if you are put away. (*She starts to rise, slowly.*)

We get another angle, shooting over the desk at Constance as she rises. In the foreground is only Dr. Murchison's hand holding the revolver. The hand keeps the revolver trained on Constance as she walks very slowly across the room toward the door.—Constance continues to talk without pause, in a calm deadly voice, hiding her tension.

CONSTANCE. You are thinking that now, Dr. Murchison. If you shoot now, it is cold, deliberate murder.

She is facing Murchison now. She walks a little nearer the door, the revolver in Murchison's hand still following her.

CONSTANCE. You will be tried as a sane murderer. Convicted as a sane man. And killed in the electric chair for your crime.

Constance is now at the door. She pauses with her hand on the knob—the gun still leveled at her.

CONSTANCE. I am going out to telephone the police now, Dr. Murchison.

Slowly, deliberately, courageously, Constance turns her back to the gun in Murchison's hand, opens the door and passes out. The door closes behind her.

The gun in Murchison's hand remains silently aimed at the closed door for a moment. Then ever so slowly his hand turns round until the revolver is pointing directly into the camera.

After a second's hesitation Murchison's finger presses the trigger and the screen is filled with the flash of the revolver's explosion.

The scene then dissolves to the TRAIN GATE in a railroad station.

Brulov is seeing Constance and J.B. off on the train. Constance is a happy bride, and J.B., the groom, beams with happiness.

BRULOV *(embracing Constance)*. Goodbye.

CONSTANCE. Goodbye, Alex.

BRULOV *(as he and J. B. shake hands)*. Goodbye.

J.B. Goodbye, Alex.

Their attitudes toward each other are now very friendly—no trace of restraint.

BRULOV *(to J.B.)*. And remember what I say—any husband of Constance is a husband of mine, so to speak.

J.B. *(laughing)*. All right—Goodbye —Good luck.

BRULOV *(as he leaves)*. Goodbye.

J.B. and Constance smiling fondly, look after Brulov as he walks out of the scene. Then they walk forward to the train gate. J.B. hands the conductor their tickets. It is the same conductor who saw them kiss when they walked through the same gate on the way to Dr. Brulov's months before. There is a faint expression of recognition on the conductor's face.

J.B. gets an idea. Suddenly, as he had done before, he pulls Constance into his arms and implants a hearty kiss on her lips—this time with more gusto. The conductor looks on in amazement. Then as Constance and J.B., smiling, go through the gates, the camera moves up to a big closeup of the conductor's bewildered expression, and the picture fades out.

# DOUBLE INDEMNITY

## (A Paramount Picture)

*Screenplay by* BILLY WILDER *and* RAYMOND CHANDLER

*From the Novel by* JAMES M. CAIN

*Directed by* BILLY WILDER

### The Cast

| | |
|---|---|
| WALTER NEFF . . . . . . | Fred MacMurray |
| PHYLLIS DIETRICHSON . . | Barbara Stanwyck |
| BARTON KEYES . . . . . . | Edward G. Robinson |
| MR. JACKSON . . . . . . | Porter Hall |
| LOLA DIETRICHSON . . . . | Jean Heather |
| MR. DIETRICHSON . . . . | Tom Powers |
| NINO ZACHETTE . . . . . | Byron Barr |
| MR. NORTON . . . . . . . | Richard Gaines |
| SAM GORLOPIS . . . . . . | Fortunio Bonanova |
| JOE PETE . . . . . . . . | John Philliber |

*Film Editor*—DOANE HARRISON

# DOUBLE INDEMNITY

## PART ONE

A DOWNTOWN INTERSECTION in Los Angeles fades in: It is night, about two o'clock, very light traffic.—At the left and in the immediate foreground a semaphore traffic signal stands at GO. Approaching it at about thirty miles per hour is a Dodge 1938 coupe. It is driven erratically and weaving a little, but not out of control. When the car is about forty feet away, the signal changes to STOP. The car makes no attempt to stop but comes on through as a light NEWSPAPER TRUCK is seen crossing the intersection at right angles. It swerves and skids to avoid the Dodge, which goes on as though nothing had happened. The truck stops with a panicky screech of tires. There is a large sign on the truck: "READ THE LOS ANGELES TIMES." The truck driver's infuriated face stares after the coupe.

The COUPE continues along the street, still weaving, then slows down and pulls over toward the curb in front of a tall office building.—The COUPE stops. The headlights are turned off. For a second nothing happens, then the car door opens slowly. A man eases himself out onto the sidewalk and stands a moment leaning on the open door to support himself. He's a tall man, about thirty-five years old. From the way he moves there seems to be something wrong with his left shoulder. He straightens up and painfully lowers his left hand into his jacket pocket. He leans into the car. He brings out a light-weight overcoat and drapes it across his shoulders. He shuts the car door and walks toward the building.

The ENTRANCE of the building comes into view. Above the closed, double-plate glass doors is lettered: PACIFIC BUILDING. To the left of the entrance there is a drugstore, closed, dark except for a faint light in the back. The man comes stiffly up to the doors. He tries the doors. They are locked. He knocks on the glass. Inside, over his shoulder, the lobby of the building is visible: a side entrance to the drugstore on the left, in the rear a barber shop and cigar and magazine stand closed up for the night, and to the right two elevators. One elevator is open and its dome light falls across the dark lobby.

The man knocks again. The night watchman sticks his head out of the elevator and looks toward the entrance. He comes out with a newspaper in one hand and a half-eaten sandwich in the other. He finishes the sandwich on the way to the doors, looks out and recognizes the man outside, unlocks the door and pulls it open.

NIGHT WATCHMAN. Why, hello there, Mr. Neff.

Neff walks in past him without answering. Then he crosses the LOBBY, heading for the elevator. The night watchman looks after him, relocks the door, and follows him to the elevator. Neff enters it.

In the ELEVATOR: Neff stands leaning against the wall. He is pale and haggard with pain, but "deadpans" as the night watchman joins him.

NIGHT WATCHMAN. Working pretty late aren't you, Mr. Neff?

NEFF (*tight-lipped*). Late enough.

NIGHT WATCHMAN. You look kind of all in at that.

NEFF. I'm fine. Let's ride.

The night watchman pulls the lever; the doors close and the elevator rises.

NIGHT WATCHMAN. How's the insurance business, Mr. Neff?

NEFF. Okay.

NIGHT WATCHMAN. They wouldn't ever sell me any. They say I've got something loose in my heart. I say it's rheumatism.

NEFF (*scarcely listening*). Uh-huh.

The night watchman looks around at him, turns away again, and the elevator stops.

NIGHT WATCHMAN (*surly*). Twelve.

The door opens. Across a small dark reception room a pair of frosted glass doors are lettered: PACIFIC ALL-RISK INSURANCE COMPANY—FOUNDED 1906—MAIN OFFICE. There is a little light beyond the glass doors. Neff straightens up and walks heavily out of the elevator, across the reception room to the doors. He pushes them open. The night watchman stares after him morosely, works the lever, and the elevator doors start to close.

The TWELFTH FLOOR INSURANCE OFFICE: (The Insurance Company occupies the entire eleventh and twelfth floors of the building. On the twelfth floor are the executive offices and claims and sales departments. These all open off a balcony which runs all the way around. From the balcony one can see the eleventh floor below: one enormous room filled with desks, typewriters, filing cabinets, business machines, etc.) —Neff comes through the double entrance doors from the reception room. The twelfth floor is dark. Some light shines up from the eleventh floor. Neff takes a few steps then holds on to the balcony railing and looks down and we see:

The ELEVENTH FLOOR, from Neff's point-of-view. Two colored women are cleaning the offices. One is dry-mopping the floor, the other is moving chairs back into position. A colored man is emptying waste baskets into a big square box. He shuffles a little dance step as he moves, and hums a little tune.

NEFF moves away from the railing with a faint smile on his face, and walks past two or three offices toward a glass door with number twenty-seven on it and three names: HENRY B. ANDERSON, WALTER NEFF, LOUIS L. SCHWARTZ. Neff opens the door.

NEFF's OFFICE: Three desks, filing cabinets, one typewriter on a stand, one dictaphone on a fixed stand are against the wall with a rack of records underneath. There are telephones on all three desks. We see a water cooler with an inverted bottle and paper cup holder beside it. There are two windows facing toward the front of the building—venetian blinds, no curtains. The waste basket is full—ash trays unemptied. The office has not been cleaned.

Neff enters, switches on the desk lamp. He looks across at the dictaphone, goes heavily to it and lifts off the fabric cover. He leans down hard on the dictaphone stand as if feeling faint. Then he turns away, takes a few uncertain steps and falls heavily into a swivel chair. His head goes far back, his eyes close, cold sweat shows on his face. For a moment he stays like this, exhausted, then his eyes open slowly and look down at his left shoulder. His good hand flips the overcoat back; he unbuttons his jacket, loosens his tie and shirt. This was quite an effort. He rests for a second, breathing hard. With the help of his good hand he edges his left elbow up on the arm-rest of the chair, supports it there and then pulls his jacket wide. A heavy patch of dark blood shows on his shirt. He pushes his chair along the floor toward the water cooler, using his feet and his right hand against the desk, takes out a handkerchief, presses with his hand against the spring faucet of the cooler, soaks the handkerchief in water and tucks it, dripping wet, against the wound inside his shirt. Next, he gets a handful of water and splashes it on his face. The water runs down his chin and drips. He breathes heavily, with closed eyes. He fingers a pack of cigarettes in his shirt pocket, pulls it out, looks at it. There is blood on it. He wheels himself back to the desk and dumps the loose cigarettes out of the packet. Some are bloodstained, a few are clean. He takes one, puts it between his lips, gropes around for a match, then lights the cigarette. He takes a deep drag and lets smoke out through his nose.

He pulls himself toward the dictaphone again, still in the swivel chair, reaches it, lifts the horn off the bracket and the dictaphone makes a low buzzing sound. He presses the button switch on the horn. The sound stops, the record revolves on the cylinder. He begins to speak:

NEFF. Office memorandum, Walter Neff to Barton Keyes, Claims Manager. Los Angeles, July 16th, 1938.

Dear Keyes: I suppose you'll call this a confession when you hear it. I don't like the word confession. I just want to set you right about one thing you couldn't see, because it was smack up against your nose. You think you're such a hot potato as a claims manager, such a wolf on a phony claim. Well, maybe you are, Keyes, but let's take a look at this Dietrichson claim, Accident and Double Indemnity. You were pretty good in there for a while, all right. You said it wasn't an accident. Check. You said it wasn't suicide. Check. You said it was murder. Check and double check. You thought you had it cold, all wrapped up in tissue paper, with pink ribbons around it. It was perfect, except that it wasn't, because you made a mistake, just one tiny little mistake. When it came to picking the killer, you picked the wrong guy, if you know what I mean. Want to know who killed Dietrichson? Hold tight to that cheap cigar of yours, Keyes. I killed Dietrichson. Me, Walter Neff, insurance agent, 35 years old, unmarried, no visible scars— (*He glances down at his wounded shoulder.*) —until a little while ago, that is. Yes, I killed him. I killed him for money—and a woman—and I didn't get the money and I didn't get the woman. Pretty, isn't it?

He interrupts the dictation, lays down the horn on the desk. He takes his lighted cigarette from the ash tray, puffs it two or three times, and kills it. He picks up the horn again.

NEFF (*his voice now quiet and contained*). It all began last May. Around the end of May, it was. I'd been out to Glendale to deliver a policy on some dairy trucks. On the way back I remembered this auto renewal on

Los Feliz Boulevard. So I drove over there.

As he goes on speaking, the scene slowly dissolves to the DIETRICHSON HOME in the LOS FELIZ DISTRICT: Palm trees line the street of middle-class houses mostly in Spanish style. Some kids are throwing a baseball back and forth across a couple of front lawns. An ice cream. wagon dawdles along the block. Neff's coupe meets and passes the ice cream wagon and stops before one of the Spanish houses. Neff gets out.

He carries a briefcase, his hat is a little on the back of his head. His movements are easy and full of ginger. He inspects the house, checks the number, goes up on the front porch and rings the bell.

NEFF'S VOICE (*synchronized with the scene*). It was one of those California Spanish houses everyone was nuts about ten or fifteen years ago. This one must have cost somebody about 30,000 bucks—that is, if he ever finished paying for it.

The DIETRICHSON HOME: We see the entrance door as Neff rings the bell again and waits. The door opens. A maid, about forty-five, rather slatternly, opens the door.

NEFF. Mr. Dietrichson in?

MAID. Who wants to see him?

NEFF. The name is Neff. Walter Neff.

MAID. If you're selling something—

NEFF. Look, it's Mr. Dietrichson I'd like to talk to, and it's not magazine subscriptions.

He pushes past her into the house, and enters the HALLWAY. It is "Spanish" in style, as is the house throughout. A wrought-iron staircase curves down from the second floor. A fringed Mex-

ican shawl hangs down over the landing. A large tapestry hangs on the wall. Downstairs, the dining room to one side, living room on the other side are visible through a wide archway. All of this—architecture, furniture, decorations, etc.—is genuine early Leo Carrillo period. . . . Neff has edged his way in past the maid who still holds the door open.

MAID. Listen, Mr. Dietrichson's not in.

NEFF. How soon do you expect him?

MAID. He'll be home when he gets here, if that's any help to you.

At this point a woman's voice comes from the top of the stairs.

VOICE. What is it, Nettie? Who is it?

As Neff looks up, the scene cuts to the UPPER LANDING of the STAIRCASE, as seen from below. Phyllis Dietrichson, a blonde woman in her early thirties, stands there looking down. She holds a large bath-towel around her very appetizing torso, down to about two inches above her knees. Her legs are bare. She wears a pair of high-heeled bedroom slippers with pompons, on her left ankle a gold anklet.

MAID'S VOICE. It's for Mr. Dietrichson.

PHYLLIS (*looking down at Neff*). I'm Mrs. Dietrichson. What is it?

Neff looks up, and takes his hat off.

NEFF. How do you do, Mrs. Dietrichson. I'm Walter Neff, Pacific All-Risk.

Following this we see PHYLLIS and NEFF alternately, each of them in the previous setting.

PHYLLIS. Pacific all-what?

NEFF. Pacific All-Risk Insurance

Company. It's about some renewals on the automobiles, Mrs. Dietrichson. I've been trying to contact your husband for the past two weeks. He's never at his office.

PHYLLIS. Is there anything I can do?

NEFF. The insurance ran out on the fifteenth. I'd hate to think of your getting a smashed fender or something while you're not—uh—fully covered.

PHYLLIS (*glancing over her towel costume; with a little provocative smile*). Perhaps I know what you mean, Mr. Neff. I've just been taking a sun bath.

NEFF. No pigeons around, I hope. . . . About those policies, Mrs. Dietrichson—I hate to take up your time—

PHYLLIS. That's all right. If you can wait till I put something on, I'll be right down. Nettie, show Mr. Neff into the living room.

She turns away as gracefully as one can with a towel for a wrapper, following which the scene cuts to the ENTRANCE HALL as Neff watches Phyllis out of sight. He speaks to the maid while still looking up.

NEFF. Where would the living room be?

MAID. In there, but they keep the liquor locked up.

NEFF. That's okay. I always carry my own keys.

He goes through the archway, while the maid goes off the other way, and the scene cuts to the LIVING ROOM, as the Narrator's Voice (that is, Neff's talking into the dictaphone) starts again:

NEFF'S VOICE (*synchronized with the scene*). The living room was still stuffy from last night's cigars. The windows were closed and the sunshine coming in through the Venetian blinds showed up the dust in the air. The furniture was kind of corny and old-fashioned, but it had a comfortable look, as if people really sat in it. On the piano, in a couple of fancy frames, were Mr. Dietrichson and Lola, his daughter by his first wife. They had a bowl of those little red goldfish on the table behind the davenport, but, to tell you the truth, Keyes, I wasn't a whole lot interested in goldfish right then, nor in auto renewals, nor in Mr. Dietrichson and his daughter Lola. I was thinking about that dame upstairs, and the way she had looked at me, and I wanted to see her again, close, without that silly staircase between us.

Neff comes into the room and throws his briefcase on the plush davenport and tosses his hat on top of it. He looks around the room, then moves over to a baby grand piano with a sleazy Spanish shawl dangling down one side and two cabinet photographs standing in a staggered position on top. Neff glances them over: Mr. Dietrichson, age about fifty-one, a big, blocky man with glasses and a Rotarian look about him; Lola Dietrichson, age nineteen, wearing a filmy party dress and a yearning look in her pretty eyes. Neff walks away from the piano and takes a few steps back and forth across the rug. His eyes fall on a wrinkled corner. He carefully straightens it out with his foot. His back is to the archway as he hears high heels clicking on the staircase. He turns and looks through the arch.

The scene cuts to the STAIRCASE, from Neff's point of view, as Phyllis Dietrichson is coming downstairs. First we see her feet, with pompon slippers and the gold anklet on her left ankle. Then the view pulls back slowly as she descends, until we see all of her. She is wearing a pale blue summer dress.

PHYLLIS' VOICE. I wasn't long, was I?

NEFF'S VOICE. Not at all, Mrs. Dietrichson.

PHYLLIS (*as the scene pulls back with her into the living room*). I hope I've got my face on straight.

NEFF. It's perfect for my money.

PHYLLIS (*crossing to the mirror over the fireplace*). Won't you sit down, Mr.—Neff is the name, isn't it?

NEFF. With two f's, like in Philadelphia, if you know the story.

PHYLLIS. What story?

NEFF. The Philadelphia story. What are we talking about?

PHYLLIS (*working with her lipstick*). About the insurance. My husband never tells me anything.

NEFF. It's on your two cars, the La Salle and the Plymouth.

He crosses to the davenport to get the policies from his briefcase. She turns away from the mirror and sits in a big chair with her legs drawn up sideways, the anklet now clearly visible.

NEFF. We've been handling this insurance for three years for Mr. Dietrichson . . . (*His eyes have caught the anklet.*) That's a honey of an anklet you're wearing, Mrs. Dietrichson. (*Phyllis smiles faintly and covers the anklet with her dress.*) We'd hate to see the policies lapse. Of course, we give him thirty days. That's all we're allowed to give.

PHYLLIS. I guess he's been too busy down at Long Beach in the oil fields.

NEFF. Could I catch him home some evening for a few minutes?

PHYLLIS. I suppose so. But he's never home much before eight.

NEFF. That would be fine with me.

PHYLLIS. You're not connected with the Automobile Club, are you?

NEFF. No, the All-Risk, Mrs. Dietrichson. Why?

PHYLLIS. Somebody from the Automobile Club has been trying to get him. Do they have a better rate?

NEFF. If your husband's a member.

PHYLLIS. No, he isn't.

NEFF (*as Phyllis rises and walks up and down, paying less and less attention*). Well, he'd have to join the club and pay a membership fee to start with. The Automobile Club is fine. I never knock the other fellow's merchandise, Mrs. Dietrichson, but I can do just as well for you. I have a very attractive policy here. It wouldn't take me two minutes to put it in front of your husband. (*He consults the policies he is holding.*) For instance, we're writing a new kind of fifty percent retention feature in the collision coverage.

PHYLLIS (*stopping in her walk*). You're a smart insurance man, aren't you, Mr. Neff?

NEFF. I've had eleven years of it.

PHYLLIS. Doing pretty well?

NEFF. It's a living.

PHYLLIS. You handle just automobile insurance, or all kinds? (*She sits down again, in the same position as before.*)

NEFF. All kinds. Fire, earthquake, theft, public liability, group insurance, industrial stuff and so on right down the line.

PHYLLIS. Accident insurance?

NEFF. Accident insurance? Sure, Mrs. Dietrichson. (*His eyes fall on the anklet again.*) I wish you'd tell me what's engraved on that anklet.

PHYLLIS. Just my name.

NEFF. As for instance?

PHYLLIS. Phyllis.

NEFF. Phyllis. I think I like that.

PHYLLIS. But you're not sure?

NEFF. I'd have to drive it around the block a couple of times.

PHYLLIS (*standing up again*). Mr. Neff, why don't you drop by tomorrow evening about eight-thirty. He'll be in then.

NEFF. Who?

PHYLLIS. My husband. You were anxious to talk to him, weren't you?

NEFF. Sure, only I'm getting over it a little. If you know what I mean.

PHYLLIS. There's a speed limit in this state, Mr. Neff. Forty-five miles an hour.

NEFF. How fast was I going, officer?

PHYLLIS. I'd say about ninety.

NEFF. Suppose you get down off your motorcycle and give me a ticket.

PHYLLIS. Suppose I let you off with a warning this time.

NEFF. Suppose it doesn't take.

PHYLLIS. Suppose I have to whack you over the knuckles.

NEFF. Suppose I bust out crying and put my head on your shoulder.

PHYLLIS. Suppose you try putting it on my husband's shoulder.

NEFF. That tears it. (*Neff takes his hat and briefcase.*) Eight-thirty tomorrow evening then, Mrs. Dietrichson.

PHYLLIS. That's what I suggested.

As they both move toward the archway, the scene cuts to the HALLWAY, and PHYLLIS and NEFF are seen going toward the ENTRANCE DOOR.

NEFF. Will you be here, too?

PHYLLIS. I guess so. I usually am.

NEFF. Same chair, same perfume, same anklet?

PHYLLIS (*opening the door*). I wonder if I know what you mean.

NEFF (*walking out*). I wonder if you wonder.

Outside the DIETRICHSON HOME, looking past Neff's parked car toward the entrance door, which is just closing: Neff comes toward the car, swinging his briefcase. He opens the car door and looks back with a confident smile. —Next we see the ENTRANCE DOOR, as the peep window in the upper panel opens and Phyllis looks out after him. NEFF sits in his car and presses the starter button, looking back toward the little window in the ENTRANCE DOOR, as the peep window is quickly closed from the inside. And then we see the STREET as Neff makes a U-turn and drives back down the block.

NEFF'S VOICE (*over the scene*). [She liked me. I could feel that. The way you feel when the cards are falling right for you, with a nice little pile of blue and yellow chips in the middle of the table. Only what I didn't know then was that I wasn't playing her. She was playing me—with a deck of marked cards—and the stakes weren't any blue and yellow chips. They were dynamite.] It was a hot afternoon and I can still remember the smell of honeysuckle all along that street. How could I have known that murder can sometimes smell like honeysuckle. Maybe you would have known, Keyes, the minute she mentioned accident insurance, but I didn't. I felt like a millionaire.

The scene dissolves to the INSURANCE OFFICE on the TWELFTH FLOOR. There is activity on the eleventh floor below: typewriters working, adding machines, filing clerks, secretaries, and so forth. Neff, wearing his hat and carrying his briefcase, enters from the vestibule. He walks toward his office. He passes a few salesmen. There is an exchange of greetings.

NEFF'S VOICE: I went back to the office to see if I had any mail. It was the day you had that truck driver from Inglewood on the carpet.—Remember, Keyes?

Just as Neff reaches his office a secretary comes out. She stops.

SECRETARY. Oh, Mr. Neff, Mr. Keyes wants to see you. He's been yelling for you all afternoon.

NEFF. Is he sore, or just frothing at the mouth a little? Here, park these for me, sweetheart.

He hands her his hat and briefcase and the scene moves with him as he continues to a door lettered: BARTON KEYES — CLAIMS MANAGER. Keyes' voice is heard inside, quite loud. Neff grins as he opens the door and goes in. Then the scene cuts to KEYES' OFFICES: It is a minor executive office, not too tidy: a large desk across one corner, good carpet, several chairs, filing cabinet against one wall, a dictaphone on the corner of the desk.—

Keyes is sitting behind the desk with his coat off but his hat on. A cigar is clamped in his mouth, ashes falling like snow down his vest, a gold chain and elk's tooth across it. On the other side of the desk sits Sam Gorlopis. He is a big, dumb bruiser, six feet three inches tall—rough, untidy hair, broad face, small piggish eyes—wearing a dirty work shirt and corduroy pants. He holds a sweat-soaked hat on his knee with a hairy hand. He is chewing gum rapidly. As Neff opens the door, Keyes is giving it to Gorlopis, the truck driver.

KEYES. Come on, come on, Gorlopis. You're not kidding anybody with that line of bull. You're in a jam and you know it.

GORLOPIS. Sez you. All I want is my money.

KEYES. Sez you. All you're gonna get is the cops.

He sees Neff standing inside the door.

KEYES. Come in, Walter. This is Sam Gorlopis from Inglewood.

NEFF. Sure, I know Mr. Gorlopis. Wrote a policy on his truck. How are you, Mr. Gorlopis?

GORLOPIS. I ain't so good. My truck burned down. (*He looks sideways cautiously at Keyes.*)

[KEYES. Yeah, he just planted his big foot on the starter and the whole thing blazed up in his face.

GORLOPIS. Yes, sir.

KEYES. And didn't even singe his eyebrows.

GORLOPIS. No sir. Look, mister. I got twenty-six hundred bucks tied up in that truck. I'm insured with this company and I want my money.

KEYES. You got a wife, Gorlopis?

GORLOPIS. Sure I got a wife.

KEYES. You got kids?

GORLOPIS. Two kids.

KEYES. What you got for dinner tonight?

GORLOPIS. We got meat loaf.

KEYES. How do you make your meat loaf, Gorlopis?

GORLOPIS. Veal and pork and bread and garlic. Greek style.

KEYES. How much garlic?

GORLOPIS. Lotsa garlic, Mr. Keyes.

KEYES. Okay, Gorlopis. Now listen here. Let's say you just came up here to tell me how to make meat loaf. That's all, understand? Because if you came up here to claim on that truck, I'd have to turn you over to the law, Gorlopis, and they'd put you in jail. No wife. No kids—

GORLOPIS. What for?

KEYES (*yelling*). —And no meat loaf, Gorlopis!

GORLOPIS. I didn't do nothin'.]

KEYES. Yeah? Now, look, Gorlopis. Every month hundreds of claims come to this desk. Some of them are phonies, and I know which ones. How do I know, Gorlopis? (*He speaks as if to a child.*) Because my little man tells me.

GORLOPIS. What little man?

KEYES. The little man in here. (*He pounds the pit of his stomach.*) Every time one of those phonies comes along he ties knots in my stomach. And yours was one of them, Gorlopis. That's how I knew your claim was crooked. So what did I do?

I sent a tow car out to your garage this afternoon and they jacked up that burned-out truck of yours. And what did they find, Gorlopis? They found what was left of a neat pile of shavings.

GORLOPIS. What shavings?

KEYES. The ones you soaked with kerosene and dropped a match on.

GORLOPIS (*cringing under the impact*). Look, Mr. Keyes, I'm just a poor man. Maybe I made a mistake.

KEYES. Well, that's one way of putting it.

GORLOPIS (*starting to leave*). I ain't feelin' so good, Mr. Keyes.

KEYES. Here, just a minute. Sign this and you'll feel fine. (*He puts a blank form in front of him and points.*) Right there. It's a waiver on your claim. (*Gorlopis hesitates, then signs laboriously.*) Now you're an honest man again.

GORLOPIS. But I ain't got no more truck.

KEYES. Goodbye, Gorlopis.

GORLOPIS (*still bewildered*). Goodbye, Mr. Keyes. (*He stands up and goes slowly to the door and turns there.*) Twenty-six hundred bucks. That's a lot of dough where I live.

KEYES. What's the matter, Gorlopis? Don't you know how to open the door? Just put your hand on the knob, turn it to the right, now pull it toward you—

GORLOPIS (*doing just as Keyes says*). Like this, Mr. Keyes?

KEYES. That's the boy. Now the same thing from the outside.

GORLOPIS (*stupefied*). Thank you, Mr. Keyes.

He goes out, closing the door after him. Keyes takes his cigar stub from his mouth and turns it slowly in the flame of a lighted match. He turns to Neff.

KEYES. What kind of an outfit is this anyway? Are we an insurance company, or a bunch of dimwitted amateurs, writing a policy on a mugg like that?

NEFF. Wait a minute, Keyes. I don't rate this beef. I clipped a note to that Gorlopis application to have him thoroughly investigated before we accepted the risk.

KEYES. I know you did, Walter. I'm not beefing at you. It's the company. The way they do things. The way they don't do things. The way they'll write anything just to get it down on the sales sheet. And I'm the guy that has to sit here up to my neck in phony claims so they won't throw more money out of the window than they take in at the door.

NEFF (grinning). Okay, turn the record over and let's hear the other side.

KEYES. I get darn sick of picking up after a gang of fast-talking salesmen dumb enough to sell life insurance to a guy that sleeps in the same bed with four rattlesnakes. I've had twenty-six years of that, Walter, and I—

NEFF. And you loved every minute of it, Keyes. You love it, only you worry about it too much, you and your little man. You're so darn conscientious you're driving yourself crazy. You wouldn't even say today is Tuesday without you looked at the calendar, and then you would check if it was this year's or last year's calendar, and then you would find out what company printed the cal-endar, then find out if their calendar checks with the World Almanac's calendar.

KEYES. That's enough from you, Walter. Get out of here before I throw my desk at you.

NEFF. I love you, too.

He walks out, still grinning, and we next see the exterior of the OFFICES. Neff comes out of Keyes' office and walks back along the balcony, where there is great activity of secretaries going in and out of doors.—Neff enters his own office. Anderson, a salesman, is sitting at one of the desks, filling out a report. Neff goes to his own desk. He looks down at some mail. On top there is a typewritten note. He reads it, sits down, and leafs through his desk calendar.

We get a closeup of a CALENDAR PAGE showing the date:

THURSDAY
23
May

and five or six appointments pencilled in tightly on the page.

NEFF'S VOICE (over the scene). I really did, too, you old crab, always yelling your fat head off, always sore at everyone. But behind the cigar ashes on your vest I kind of knew you had a heart as big as a house . . . Back in my office there was a phone message from Mrs. Dietrichson about the renewals. She didn't want me to come tomorrow evening. She wanted me to come Thursday afternoon at three-thirty instead. I had a lot of stuff lined up for that Thursday afternoon, including a trip down to Santa Monica to see a couple of live prospects about some group insurance. But I kept thinking about

Phyllis Dietrichson and the way that anklet of hers cut into her leg.

The ENTRANCE HALL of the DIETRICHSON HOME fades in. There is a moving view of Phyllis Dietrichson's feet and ankles as she comes down the stairs, her high heels clicking on the tiles. The anklet glistens on her leg as she moves. Phyllis reaches the entrance hall, and as she walks toward the front door her whole body becomes visible. She wears a gay print dress with a wide sash over her hips. She opens the door. Outside is Neff, wearing a sport coat and flannel slacks. He takes his hat off.

PHYLLIS. Hello, Mr. Neff. (*As he stands there with a little smile*) Aren't you coming in?

NEFF (*starting to go inside*). I'm considering it.

PHYLLIS. I hope you didn't mind my changing the appointment. Last night wasn't so convenient.

NEFF. That's okay. I was working on my stamp collection.

Phyllis leads Neff toward the living room, and they go in through the archway. She then heads toward the davenport, in front of which is a low tea table holding tall glasses, ice cubes, lemon and a pot of tea.

PHYLLIS. I was just fixing some iced tea. Would you like a glass?

NEFF. Unless you have a bottle of beer that's not working.

PHYLLIS. There might be some. I never know what's in the ice box. (*Calling*) Nettie! . . . . (*She pours herself a glass of tea.*) About those renewals, Mr. Neff. I talked to my husband about it.

NEFF. You did?

PHYLLIS. Yes. He'll renew with you, he told me. In fact, I thought he'd be here this afternoon.

NEFF. But he's not?

PHYLLIS. No.

NEFF. That's terrible.

PHYLLIS (*calling again, impatiently*). Nettie! . . *Nettie!* . . . . Oh, I forgot, it's the maid's day off.

NEFF. Don't bother, Mrs. Dietrichson. I'd like some iced tea very much.

PHYLLIS. Lemon? Sugar?

NEFF. Fix it your way.

She fixes him a glass of tea while he looks around. He sits down slowly. (We see them together and separately in close shots throughout the conversation.)

NEFF. Seeing it's the maid's day off maybe there's something I can do for you. (*As she hands him the tea*) Like running the vacuum cleaner.

PHYLLIS. Fresh.

NEFF. I used to peddle vacuum cleaners. Not much money but you learn a lot about life.

PHYLLIS. I didn't think you'd learned it from a correspondence course.

NEFF. Where did you pick up this tea drinking? You're not English, are you?

PHYLLIS. No. Californian. Born right here in Los Angeles.

NEFF. They say native Californians all come from Iowa.

PHYLLIS. I wanted to ask you something, Mr. Neff.

NEFF. Make it Walter.

PHYLLIS. Walter?

NEFF. That's right.

PHYLLIS. Tell me, Walter, on this insurance—how much commission do you make?

NEFF. Twenty percent. Why?

PHYLLIS. I thought maybe I could throw a little more business your way.

NEFF. I can always use it.

PHYLLIS. I was thinking about my husband. I worry a lot about him, down in those oil fields. It's very dangerous.

NEFF. Not for an executive, is it?

PHYLLIS. He doesn't just sit behind a desk. He's right down there with the drilling crews. It's got me worried sick.

NEFF. You mean a crown block might fall oh him some rainy night?

PHYLLIS. Please don't talk like that.

NEFF. But that's the idea.

PHYLLIS. The other day a casing line snapped and caught the foreman. He's in the hospital with a broken back.

NEFF. Bad.

PHYLLIS. It's got me jittery just thinking about it. Suppose something like that happened to my husband?

NEFF. It could.

PHYLLIS. Don't you think he ought to have accident insurance?

NEFF. Uh huh.

PHYLLIS. What kind of insurance could he have?

NEFF. Enough to cover doctors' and hospital bills. Say a hundred and twenty-five a week cash benefit. And he'd rate around fifty thousand capital sum.

PHYLLIS. Capital sum? What's that?

NEFF. In case he gets killed. Maybe I shouldn't have said that.

PHYLLIS. I suppose you have to think of everything in your business.

NEFF. Well, your husband would understand. I'm sure I could sell him on the idea of some accident protection. Why don't I talk to him about it?

PHYLLIS. You could try. But he's pretty tough going.

NEFF. They're all tough at first.

PHYLLIS. He has a lot on his mind. He doesn't want to listen to anything except maybe a baseball game on the radio. Sometimes we sit all evening without saying a word to each other.

NEFF. Sounds pretty dull.

PHYLLIS (*shrugging*). So I just sit and knit.

NEFF. Is that what you married him for?

PHYLLIS. Maybe I like the way his thumbs hold up the wool.

NEFF. Any time his thumbs get tired —Only with me around you wouldn't have to knit.

PHYLLIS. Wouldn't I?

NEFF. You bet your life you wouldn't. — (*After taking a sip of the iced tea*) I wonder if a little rum would get this up on its feet!

PHYLLIS. I want to ask you something, Walter. Could I get an accident policy for him—without bothering him at all?

NEFF. How's that again?

PHYLLIS. That would make it easier for you, too. You wouldn't even have to talk to him. I have a little allowance of my own. I could pay for it and he needn't know anything about it.

NEFF. Why shouldn't he know?

PHYLLIS. Because he doesn't want accident insurance. He's superstitious about it.

NEFF. A lot of people are. Funny, isn't it?

PHYLLIS. If there was a way to get it like that, all the worry would be over. You see what I mean, Walter?

NEFF. Sure. I've got good eyesight. You want him to have the policy without him knowing it. And that means without the insurance company knowing that he doesn't know. That's the set-up, isn't it?

PHYLLIS. Is there anything wrong with it?

NEFF. No, I think it's lovely. And then, some dark wet night, if that crown block did fall on him—

PHYLLIS. What crown block?

NEFF. Only sometimes they have to have a little help. They can't quite make it on their own.

PHYLLIS. I don't know what you're talking about.

NEFF. Of course, it doesn't have to be a crown block. It can be a car backing over him, or he can fall out of an upstairs window. Any little thing like that, as long as it's a morgue job.

PHYLLIS. Are you crazy?

NEFF. Not that crazy. Goodbye, Mrs. Dietrichson. (*He picks up his hat.*)

PHYLLIS (*jumping up*). What's the matter?

NEFF (*starting to leave*). Look, baby, you can't get away with it.

PHYLLIS. Get away with what?

NEFF. You want to knock him off, don't you, baby.

PHYLLIS. That's a horrible thing to say!

NEFF. What'd you think I was, anyway? A guy that walks into a good-looking dame's front parlor and says "Good afternoon, I sell accident insurance on husbands. You got one that's been around too long? Somebody you'd like to turn into a little hard cash? Just give me a smile and I'll help you collect." Boy, what a dope you must think I am.

PHYLLIS. I think you're rotten.

NEFF. I think you're swell. So long as I'm not your husband.

PHYLLIS. Get out of here.

NEFF. You bet I will. You bet I'll get out of here, baby. But quick. (*He goes out.*)

She looks after him and we then see the outside of the DIETRICHSON HOUSE, Neff's voice coming over this, as he talks into the dictaphone.

NEFF'S VOICE (*over the scene*). So I let her have it, straight between the eyes. She didn't fool me for a minute, not this time. I knew I had hold of a red-hot poker and the time to drop it was before it burned my hand off. I stopped at a drive-in for a bottle of beer, the one I had wanted all along, only I wanted it worse now, to get rid of the sour taste of her iced tea, and everything that went with it. I didn't want to go back to the office, so I dropped by a bowling alley at Third and Western and rolled a few lines to get my mind thinking about something else for a while.

As Neff bangs the front door shut, walks quickly to his car and drives away, the scene dissolves to the DRIVE-IN of a RESTAURANT, "shooting" past Neff sitting behind the wheel of his car. The car hop hangs a tray on the door and serves him a bottle of beer.—This dissolves to the interior of a BOWLING ALLEY where Neff is bowling. He rolls the ball with an effort at concentration, but his mind is not really on the game. This dissolves to the exterior of an APARTMENT HOUSE. It is late afternoon. The apartment house is called the LOS OLIVOS APARTMENTS. It is a six-story building in the Normandie-Wilshire district, with a basement garage. The view moves up the front of the building to the top floor windows, as a little rain starts to fall.

NEFF'S VOICE (*continuing*). I didn't feel like eating dinner when I left, and I didn't feel like a show, so I drove home, put the car away and went up to my apartment.

We now see the LIVING ROOM of NEFF's APARTMENT at dusk. It is a double apartment of conventional design, with kitchen, dinette, and bathroom, square-cut overstuffed borax furniture. Gas logs are lit in the imitation fireplace. Neff stands by the window with his coat off and his tie loose. Raindrops strike against the glass. He turns away impatiently, paces up and down past a caddy bag with golf clubs in it, pulls one out at random, makes a couple of short swings, throws the club on the couch, and paces again.—

NEFF'S VOICE (*continuing*). It had begun to rain outside and I watched it get dark and didn't even turn on the light. That didn't help me either. I was all twisted up inside, and I

was still holding on to that red-hot poker. And right then it came over me that I hadn't walked out on anything at all, that the hook was too strong, that this wasn't the end between her and me. It was only the beginning. So at eight o'clock the bell would ring and I would know who it was without even having to think, as if it was the most natural thing in the world.

The doorbell rings. Neff goes to the door and opens it, revealing Phyllis standing there.

PHYLLIS. Hello. (*As Neff just looks at her in amazement*) You forgot your hat this afternoon. (*She has nothing in her hands but her bag.*)

NEFF. Did I? (*He looks down at her hands.*)

PHYLLIS. Don't you want me to bring it in?

NEFF. Sure. Put it on the chair. (*She comes in. He closes the door.*) How did you know where I live?

PHYLLIS. It's in the phone book. (*Neff switches on the standing lamp.*) It's raining.

NEFF. So it is. Peel off your coat and sit down. (*She starts to take off her coat.*) Your husband out?

PHYLLIS. Long Beach. They're spudding in a new well. He phoned he'd be late. About nine-thirty. (*He takes her coat and lays it across the back of a chair.*) It's about time you said you're glad to see me.

NEFF. I knew you wouldn't leave it like that.

PHYLLIS. Like what?

NEFF. Like it was this afternoon.

PHYLLIS. I must have said something

that gave you a terribly wrong impression. You must surely see that. You must never think anything like that about me, Walter.

NEFF. Okay.

PHYLLIS. It's not okay. Not if you don't believe me.

NEFF. What do you want me to do?

PHYLLIS. I want you to be nice to me. Like the first time you came to the house.

NEFF. It can't be like the first time. Something has happened.

PHYLLIS. I know it has. It's happened to us.

NEFF. That's what I mean.

Phyllis has moved over to the window. She stares out through the wet window-pane.

NEFF. What's the matter now?

PHYLLIS. I feel as if he was watching me. Not that he cares about me. Not any more. But he keeps me on a leash. So tight I can't breathe. I'm scared.

NEFF. What of? He's in Long Beach, isn't he?

PHYLLIS. I oughtn't to have come.

NEFF. Maybe you oughtn't.

PHYLLIS. You want me to go?

NEFF. If you want to.

PHYLLIS. Right now?

NEFF. Sure. Right now.

By this time, he has hold of her wrists. He draws her to him slowly and kisses her. Her arms tighten around him. After a moment he pulls his head back, still holding her close.—Then they break away from each other, and she puts her head on his shoulder.

NEFF. I'm crazy about you, baby.

PHYLLIS. I'm crazy about you, Walter.

NEFF. That perfume on your hair. What's the name of it?

PHYLLIS. I don't know. I bought it down at Ensenada.

NEFF. We ought to have some of that pink wine to go with it. The kind that bubbles. But all I have is bourbon.

PHYLLIS. Bourbon is fine, Walter.

He lets her go and moves toward the dinette. We then see the DINETTE and KITCHEN, which contains a small table and some chairs. A low glass-and-china cabinet is built between the dinette and kitchen, leaving a space like a doorway. The kitchen is the usual apartment house kitchen, with stove, ice-box, sink, etc. It is quite small.—Neff goes to the ice-box and Phyllis drifts in after him.

NEFF. Soda?

PHYLLIS. Plain water, please.

NEFF. Get a couple of glasses, will you.

He points at the china closet. He has taken a tray of ice cubes from the refrigerator and is holding it under the hot-water faucet.

NEFF. You know, about six months ago a guy slipped on the soap in his bathtub and knocked himself out cold and drowned. Only he had accident insurance. So they had an autopsy and she didn't get away with it.

Phyllis has the glasses now. She hands them to him. He dumps some ice cubes into the glasses.

PHYLLIS. Who didn't?

NEFF. His wife. (*He reaches for the whiskey bottle on top of the china closet.*) And there was a case of a guy found shot and his wife said he was cleaning a gun and his stomach got in the way. All she collected was a three-to-ten stretch in Tehachapi.

PHYLLIS. Perhaps it was worth it to her.

Neff hands her a glass.

NEFF. See if you can carry this as far as the living room. (*They move back toward the living room.*)

The LIVING ROOM as Phyllis and Neff go toward the davenport: she is sipping her drink and looking around.

PHYLLIS. It's nice here, Walter. Who takes care of it for you?

NEFF. A colored woman comes in twice a week.

PHYLLIS. You get your own breakfast?

NEFF. Once in a while I squeeze a grapefruit. The rest I get at the corner drugstore. (*They sit on the davenport, fairly close together.*)

PHYLLIS. It sounds wonderful. Just strangers beside you. You don't know them. You don't hate them. You don't have to sit across the table and smile at him and that daughter of his every morning of your life.

NEFF. What daughter? Oh, that little girl on the piano.

PHYLLIS. Yes. Lola. She lives with us. He thinks a lot more of her than he does of me.

NEFF. Ever think of a divorce?

PHYLLIS. He wouldn't give me a divorce.

NEFF. I suppose because it would cost him money.

PHYLLIS. He hasn't got any money. Not since he went into the oil business.

NEFF. But he had when you married him?

PHYLLIS. Yes, he had. And I wanted a home. Why not? But that wasn't the only reason. I was his wife's nurse. She was sick for a long time. When she died, he was all broken up. I pitied him so.

NEFF. And now you hate him.

PHYLLIS. Yes, Walter. He's so mean to me. Every time I buy a dress or a pair of shoes he yells his head off. He won't let me go anywhere. He keeps me shut up. He's always been mean to me. Even his life insurance all goes to that daughter of his. That Lola.

NEFF. Nothing for you at all, huh?

PHYLLIS. No. And nothing is just what I'm worth to him.

NEFF. So you lie awake in the dark and listen to him snore and get ideas.

PHYLLIS. Walter, I don't want to kill him. I never did. Not even when he gets drunk and slaps my face.

NEFF. Only sometimes you wish he was dead.

PHYLLIS. Perhaps I do.

NEFF. And you wish it was an accident, and you had that policy. For fifty thousand dollars. Is that it?

PHYLLIS. Perhaps that too. (*She takes a long drink.*) The other night we drove home from a party. He was drunk again. When we got into the garage he just sat there with his head on the steering wheel and the motor still running. And I thought what it would be like if I didn't switch it off, just closed the garage door and left him there.

NEFF. I'll tell you what it would be like, if you had that accident policy, and tried to pull a monoxide job. We have a guy in our office named Keyes. For him a set-up like that would be just like a slice of rare roast beef. In three minutes he'd know it wasn't an accident. In ten minutes you'd be sitting under the hot lights. In half an hour you'd be signing your name to a confession.

PHYLLIS. But, Walter, I didn't do it. I'm not going to do it.

NEFF. Not if there's an insurance company in the picture, baby. So long as you're honest they'll pay you with a smile, but you just try to pull something like that and you'll find out. They know more tricks than a carload of monkeys. And if there's a deat'ı mixed up in it, you haven't got a prayer. They'll hang you as sure as ten dimes will buy a dollar, baby. (*She begins to cry, and he puts his arms around her and kisses her.*) Just stop thinking about it, will you.

He holds her tight. Their heads touch, side by side, as the scene slowly starts to recede and then dissolves to NEFF's OFFICE at night.—Neff is sitting in the swivel chair, talking into the dicta-phone. He has hooked the wastebasket under his feet to sit more comfortably. As he talks, a little cough shakes him now and then.

NEFF. So we just sat there, and she kept on crying softly, like the rain on the window, and we didn't say anything. Maybe she had stopped thinking about it, but I hadn't. I couldn't. Because it was all tied up with something I had been thinking about for years, since long before I ever

ran into Phyllis Dietrichson. Because, in this business you can't sleep for trying to figure out the tricks they could pull on you. You're like the guy behind the roulette wheel, watch-ing the customers to make sure they don't crook the house. And then one night, you get to thinking how you could crook the house yourself. And do it smart. Because you've got that wheel right under your hands. And you know every notch in it by heart. And you figure all you need is a plant out in front, a shill to put down the bet. And suddenly the doorbell rings and the whole set-up is right there in the room with you . . . Look, Keyes, I'm not trying to white-wash myself. I fought it, only maybe I didn't fight it hard enough. The stakes were fifty thousand dollars, but they were the life of a man, too, a man who'd never done me any dirt. Except he was married to a woman he didn't care anything about, and I did . . .

The scene dissolves back to NEFF's LIVING ROOM and the view moves slowly toward the davenport again. Neff sits in one corner with his feet on the low table. He is smoking his cigarette and staring at the ceiling. Phyllis has been sitting fairly close to him. She gets up slowly and crosses to her rain coat, lying over the chair.

PHYLLIS. I've got to go now, Walter. (*Neff does not answer. He keeps on staring at the ceiling. She starts to put the raincoat on.*) Will you phone me, Walter? (*As Neff still does not answer*) Walter! (*He looks at her slowly, almost absently.*) I hate him. I loathe going back to him. You be-lieve me, don't you, Walter?

NEFF. Sure I believe you.

PHYLLIS. I can't stand it anymore. What if they did hang me?

NEFF. You're not going to hang, baby—

PHYLLIS. It's better than going on this way.

NEFF. —you're not going to hang, baby. Not ever. Because you're going to do it the smart way. Because I'm going to help you.

PHYLLIS. You!

NEFF. Me.

PHYLLIS. Do you know what you're saying?

NEFF. Sure I know what I'm saying.

He gets up and grips her arm.

NEFF. We're going to do it together. We're going to do it right. And I'm the guy that knows how.

There is fierce determination in his voice. His fingers dig into her arm.

PHYLLIS. Walter, you're hurting me.

NEFF. There isn't going to be any slip-up. Nothing sloppy. Nothing

weak. It's got to be perfect. (*He kisses her.*) You go now. (*He leads her toward the door.*) Call me tomorrow. But not from your house. From a booth. And watch your step. Every single minute. It's got to be perfect, understand. Straight down the line.

They have now reached the door. Neff opens it. Phyllis stands in the doorway, her lips white.

PHYLLIS. Straight down the line.

She goes quietly. He watches her down the corridor. Slowly he closes the door and goes back into the room. He moves across to the window and opens it wide. He stands there, looking down into the dark street. From below comes the sound of a car starting and driving off. The rain drifts in against his face. He just stands there motionless. His mind is going a hundred miles a minute, and the scene fades out.

NEFF'S VOICE (*synchronized with the scene*). That was it, Keyes. The machinery had started to move and nothing could stop it.

# PART TWO

NEFF'S OFFICE fades in at night. Neff sits slumped in his chair before the dictaphone. On the desk next to him stands a used record. The cylinder on the dictaphone is not turning. He is smoking a cigarette. He puts it down then lifts the needle and slides it off the record which is on the machine and stands it on end on the desk beside the other used record. He reaches down painfully to take another record from the rack beneath the dictaphone, looks at it against the light to make sure it has not been used, then slides it into place on the machine and resets the needle. He lifts the horn and resumes his dictation.

NEFF. The first thing we had to do was to fix him up with that accident policy. I knew he wouldn't buy, but all I wanted was his signature on an application. So I had to make him sign without his knowing what he

was signing. And I wanted a witness other than Phyllis to hear me give him the sales talk. I was trying to think with your brains, Keyes. I wanted all the answers ready for all the questions you were going to spring as soon as Dietrichson was dead.

Neff takes a last drag on his cigarette and kills it by running it under the ledge of the dictaphone stand. He drops the stub on the floor and resumes.

NEFF. A couple of nights later I went to the house. Everything looked fine, except I didn't like the witness Phyllis had brought in. It was Dietrichson's daughter Lola, and it made me feel a little queer in the belly to have her right there in the room, playing Chinese checkers, as if nothing was going to happen.

This dissolves to a BOARD of CHINESE CHECKERS. The view then moves back and gradually reveals the DIETRICHSON LIVING ROOM at night. The checker-board is on the davenport between Phyllis and Lola. Mr. Dietrichson sits in a big easy chair. His coat and tie are over the back of the chair, and the evening paper is lying tumbled on the floor beside him. He is smoking a cigar with the band on it. He has a drink in front of him and several more inside him. In another chair sits Neff, his brief-case on the floor, leaning against his chair. He holds his rate book partly open, with a finger in it for a marker. He is going full swing.

NEFF. I suppose you realize, Mr. Dietrichson, that, not being an employee, you are not covered by the State Compensation Insurance Act. The only way you can protect yourself is by having a personal policy of your own.

DIETRICHSON. I know all about that. The next thing you'll tell me I need earthquake insurance and lightning insurance and hail insurance.

Phyllis looks up from the checker-board and cuts in on the dialogue. Lola listens without much interest.

PHYLLIS (to Dietrichson). If we bought all the insurance they can think up, we'd stay broke paying for it, wouldn't we, honey?

DIETRICHSON. What keeps us broke is you going out and buying five hats at a crack. Who needs a hat in California?

NEFF. I always say insurance is a lot like a hot water bottle. It looks kind of useless and silly hanging on a hook, but when you get that stomachache in the middle of the night, it comes in mighty handy.

DIETRICHSON. Now you want to sell me a hot water bottle.

NEFF. Dollar for dollar, accident insurance is the cheapest coverage you can buy, Mr. Dietrichson.

DIETRICHSON. Maybe some other time, Mr. Neff. I had a tough day.

NEFF. Just as you say Mr. Dietrichson.

DIETRICHSON. Suppose we just settle that automobile insurance tonight.

NEFF. Sure. All we need on that is for you to sign an application for renewal.

Phyllis throws a quick glance at Neff. As she looks back she sees that Lola is staring down at her wrist watch.

LOLA. Phyllis, do you mind if we don't finish this game? It bores me stiff.

PHYLLIS. Got something better to do?

LOLA (getting up). Yes, I have. (To Dietrichson) Father, is it all right if I run along now?

DIETRICHSON. Run along where? Who with?

LOLA. Just Anne. We're going roller skating.

DIETRICHSON. Anne who?

LOLA. Anne Matthews.

PHYLLIS. It's not that Nino Zachette again?

DIETRICHSON. It better not be that Zachette guy. If I ever catch you with him—

LOLA. It's Anne Matthews, I told you. I also told you we're going roller skating. I'm meeting her at the corner of Vermont and Franklin—the northwest corner, in case you're interested. And I'm late already. I hope that is all clear. Good night, father. Good night, Phyllis. (*She starts to go.*)

NEFF. Good night, Miss Dietrichson.

LOLA. Oh, I'm sorry. Good night, Mr.—

NEFF. Neff.

LOLA. Good night, Mr. Neff.

PHYLLIS. Now you're not going to take my car again.

LOLA. No thanks. I'd rather be dead. (*She goes out through the archway.*)

DIETRICHSON. A great little fighter for her weight.

Dietrichson sucks down a big swallow of his drink. Neff has taken two blank forms from his briefcase. He puts the briefcase on Mr. Dietrichson's lap and lays the forms on top. Phyllis is watching closely.

NEFF. This is where you sign, Mr. Dietrichson.

DIETRICHSON. Sign what?

NEFF. The applications for your auto renewals. So you'll be protected until the new policies are issued.

DIETRICHSON. When will that be?

NEFF. In about a week.

DIETRICHSON. Just so I'm covered when I drive up North.

Neff takes out his fountain pen.

NEFF. San Francisco, Mr. Dietrichson?

DIETRICHSON. Palo Alto.

PHYLLIS. He was a Stanford man, Mr. Neff. And he still goes to his class reunion every year.

DIETRICHSON. What's wrong with that? Can't I have a little fun even once a year?

NEFF. Great football school, Stanford. Did you play football, Mr. Dietrichson?

DIETRICHSON. Left guard. Almost made the varsity, too.

Neff has unscrewed his fountain pen. He hands it to Mr. Dietrichson. Dietrichson puts on his glasses.

NEFF. On that bottom line, Mr. Dietrichson. (*Dietrichson signs. Neff's and Phyllis' eyes meet for a split second.*) Both copies, please.

He withdraws the top copy barely enough to expose the signature line on the supposed duplicate.

DIETRICHSON. Sign twice, huh?

NEFF. One is the agent's copy. I need it for my files.

DIETRICHSON (*in a mutter*). Files. Duplicates. Triplicates.

Dietrichson grunts and signs again. Again Neff and Phyllis exchange a quick glance.

NEFF. No hurry about the check, Mr. Dietrichson. I can pick it up at your office some morning. (*Casually Neff lifts the briefcase and signed applications off Dietrichson's lap.*)

DIETRICHSON. How much you taking me for?

NEFF. One forty-seven fifty, Mr. Dietrichson.

Dietrichson stands up. He is about Neff's height but a little heavier.

PHYLLIS. I guess that's enough insurance for one evening, Mr. Neff.

DIETRICHSON. Plenty.

Dietrichson has poured some more whisky into his glass. He tries the siphon but it is empty. He gathers up his coat and tie and picks up his glass.

DIETRICHSON. Good night, Mr. Neff.

NEFF (*zipping up his briefcase*). Good night, Mr. Dietrichson. Good night, Mrs. Dietrichson.

DIETRICHSON. Bring me some soda when you come up, Phyllis. (*Dietrichson trundles off toward the archway.*)

PHYLLIS (*to Neff*). I think you left your hat in the hall.

Phyllis leads the way and Neff goes after her, his briefcase under his arm. The scene then cuts to the HALLWAY of the Dietrichson residence as Phyllis enters through the living room archway with Neff behind her. She leads him toward the door. On the way he picks up his hat. In the background Dietrichson begins to ascend the stairs, carrying his coat and glass. Phyllis and Neff move close to the door. They speak in very low voices.

PHYLLIS. All right, Walter?

NEFF. Fine.

PHYLLIS. He signed it, didn't he?

NEFF. Sure he signed it. You saw him.

Phyllis opens the door a crack. Both look at the stairs, where Dietrichson is going up. Phyllis takes her hand off the doorknob and holds on to Neff's arm.

NEFF (*looking up*). Watch it, will you.

Phyllis slowly drops her hand from his arm. Both look up as Dietrichson goes across the balcony and out of sight.

NEFF. Listen. That trip to Palo Alto. When does he go?

PHYLLIS. End of the month.

NEFF. He drives, huh?

PHYLLIS. He always drives.

NEFF. Not this time. You're going to make him take the train.

PHYLLIS. Why?

NEFF. Because it's all worked out for a train.

For a second they stand listening and looking up as if they had heard a sound.

PHYLLIS. It's all right. Go on, Walter.

NEFF. Look, baby. There's a clause in every accident policy, a little something called double indemnity. The insurance companies put it in as a sort of come-on for the customers. It means they pay double on certain accidents. The kind that almost never happen. Like for instance if a guy got killed on a train, they'd pay a hundred thousand instead of fifty.

PHYLLIS. I see. (*Her eyes widen with excitement.*)

NEFF. We're hitting it for the limit, baby. That's why it's got to be a train.

PHYLLIS. It's going to be a train, Walter. Just the way you say. Straight down the line.

They look at each other. The look is like a long kiss. Neff goes out. Slowly Phyllis closes the door and leans her head against it as she looks up the empty stairway.

Outside the DIETRICHSON RESIDENCE: Neff, briefcase under his arm, comes down the steps to the street, where his Dodge coupé is parked at the curb. He opens the door and stops, looking in.—Sitting there in the dark corner of the car, away from the steering wheel, is Lola. She wears a coat but no hat.

LOLA. Hello, Mr. Neff. It's me (*She gives him a sly smile.*)

NEFF (*a little annoyed*). Something the matter?

LOLA. I've been waiting for you.

NEFF. For me? What for?

LOLA. I thought you could let me ride with you, if you're going my way.

NEFF (*who doesn't like the idea very much*). Which way would that be?

LOLA. Down the hill. Down Vermont.

NEFF (*remembering*). Oh, sure. Vermont and Franklin. North-west corner, wasn't it? Be glad to, Miss Dietrichson.

As Neff gets into the car, the scene cuts to the interior of the COUPE; Neff puts the briefcase on the ledge behind the driver's seat. He closes the door and starts the car. They drift down the hill.

NEFF. Roller skating, eh? You like· roller skating?

LOLA. I can take it or leave it. (*Neff looks at her curiously, and Lola meets his glance.*)

NEFF. Only tonight you're leaving it?

(*This is an embarrassing moment for Lola.*)

LOLA. Yes, I am. You see, Mr. Neff, I'm having a very tough time at home. My father doesn't understand me and Phyllis hates me.

NEFF. That does sound tough, all right.

LOLA. That's why I have to lie sometimes.

NEFF. You mean it's not Vermont and Franklin.

LOLA. It's Vermont and Franklin all right. Only it's not Anne Matthews. It's Nino Zachette. You won't tell on me, will you?

NEFF. I'd have to think it over.

LOLA. Nino's not what father says at all. He just had bad luck. He was doing pre-med at U.S.C. and working nights as an usher in a theatre downtown. He got behind in his credits and flunked out. Then he lost his job for talking back. He's so hot-headed.

NEFF. That comes expensive, doesn't it?

LOLA. I guess my father thinks nobody's good enough for his daughter except maybe the guy that owns Standard Oil. Would you like a stick of gum?

NEFF. Never use it, thanks.

LOLA (*putting a stick of gum in her mouth*). I can't give Nino up. I wish father could see it my way.

NEFF. It'll straighten out all right, Miss Dietrichson.

LOLA. I suppose it will sometime. (*Looking out*) This is the corner right here, Mr. Neff. (*As Neff brings*

*the car to a stop by the curb*) There
he is. By the bus stop.

As Neff looks out, the scene cuts to the
CORNER of Vermont and Franklin where
Zachette stands waiting, hands in trou-
sers pockets. He is about twenty-five,
Italian-looking, open shirt, not well
dressed.

Back in the COUPE we see LOLA and
NEFF.

LOLA. He needs a haircut, doesn't he.
**Look at him.** No job, no car, no
**money, no prospects, no nothing.—
I love him.** (*She leans over and
honks on the horn.*) Nino!

We get a close view of ZACHETTE as he
turns and looks toward the car.

LOLA'S VOICE. Over here, Nino.

Zachette walks toward the car, and
the scene cuts to the COUPE: Lola has
opened the door. Zachette comes up.

LOLA. This is Mr. Neff, Nino.

NEFF. Hello, Nino.

ZACHETTE (*belligerent from the first
word*). The name is Zachette.

LOLA. Nino, please. Mr. Neff gave me
a ride from the house. I told him all
about us.

ZACHETTE. Why does he have to get
told about us?

LOLA. We don't have to worry about
Mr. Neff, Nino.

ZACHETTE. I'm not doing any worrying. Just don't you broadcast so
much.

LOLA. What's the matter with you,
Nino? He's a friend.

ZACHETTE. I don't have any friends.
And if I did, I like to pick them
myself.

NEFF. Look, sonny, she needed the
ride and I brought her along. Is that
anything to get tough about?

ZACHETTE. All right, Lola, make up
your mind. Are you coming or aren't
you?

LOLA. Of course I'm coming. Don't
mind him, Mr. Neff. (*Lola steps out
of the car.*) Thanks a lot. You've been
very sweet.

Lola catches up with Zachette, and as
they walk away together the scene cuts
to the COUPE while Neff's dictation is
heard. Neff looks after them. Slowly
he puts the car in gear and drives on.
His face is tight. Behind his head, light
catches the metal of the zipper on the
briefcase.

NEFF'S VOICE. She was a nice kid, and
maybe he was a little better than he
sounded. I kind of hoped so for her
sake, but right then it gave me a
nasty feeling to be thinking about
them at all, with that briefcase right
behind my head and her father's
signature on it—and what that signature meant. It meant that he was
a dead pigeon, and it was only a
question of time, and not very much
time at that. You know that big market in Los Feliz, Keyes? That's the
place Phyllis and I had picked for a
meeting place.

This dissolves to the SUPER-MARKET.
There is a fair amount of activity but
the place is not crowded. Neff comes
along the sidewalk into the scene. He
passes in front of the fruit and vegetable
display and goes between the stalls into
the market.

NEFF'S VOICE (*continued*). I already
had most of the plan in my head,
but a lot of details had to be worked
out, and she had to know them all
by heart when the time came.

Inside the MARKET: Neff stops by the cashier's desk and buys a pack of cigarettes. As he is opening the pack he looks back casually beyond the turnstile into the rear part of the market.

NEFF'S VOICE. We had to be very careful from now on. We couldn't let anybody see us together—we couldn't even talk to each other on the telephone—not from her house or at my office, anyway. So she was to be in the market every morning about eleven o'clock, buying stuff, and I could sort of run into her there any day I wanted to, sort of accidentally on purpose.

We see ROWS OF HIGH SHELVES in the market: The shelves are loaded with canned goods and other merchandise. Customers move around selecting articles and putting them in their baskets. Phyllis is seen among them, standing by the soap section. Her basket is partly filled. She wears a simple house dress, no hat, and has a large envelope pocketbook under her arm.—And now Neff spots Phyllis. Without haste he passes through the turnstile toward the back. Back at the SHELVES, Phyllis is putting a can of cleaning powder into her basket. Neff enters the scene and moves along the shelves toward her, very slowly, pretending to inspect the goods. A customer passes and goes on out of the scene. Phyllis and Neff are now very close. During the ensuing low-spoken dialogue, they continue to face the shelves, not looking at each other.

PHYLLIS. Walter—

NEFF. Not so loud.

PHYLLIS. I wanted to talk to you, Walter. Ever since yesterday.

NEFF. Let me talk first. It's all set. The accident policy came through. I've got it in my pocket. I got his check too. I saw him down in the oil fields. He thought he was paying for the auto insurance. The check's just made out to the company. It could be for anything. But you have to send a check for the auto insurance, see. It's all right that way, because one of the cars is yours.

PHYLLIS. But listen, Walter!

NEFF. Quick, open your bag.

She hesitates, then opens it. Neff looks around quickly, slips the policy out of his pocket and drops it into her bag. She snaps the bag shut.

NEFF. Can you get into his safe deposit box?

PHYLLIS. Yes. We both have keys.

NEFF. Fine. But don't put the policy in there yet. I'll tell you when. And listen, you never touched it or even saw it, understand?

PHYLLIS. I'm not a fool.

NEFF. Okay. When is he taking the train?

PHYLLIS. Walter, that's just it. He isn't going.

NEFF. What?

PHYLLIS. That's what I've been trying to tell you. The trip is off.

NEFF. What's happened?

He breaks off as a short, squatty woman, pushing a child in a walker, comes into sight and approaches. She stops beside Neff, who is pretending to read a label on a can. Phyllis puts a few cakes of soap into her basket.

WOMAN (*to Neff*). Mister, could you reach me that can of coffee? (*She points.*) That one up there.

NEFF (*reaching up*). This one?

She nods. Neff reaches a can down

from the high shelf, and hands it to her.

WOMAN. I don't see why they always have to put what I want on the top shelf.

She moves away with her coffee and her child. Out of the corner of his eye Neff watches her go. He moves closer to Phyllis again.

NEFF. Go ahead. I'm listening.

PHYLLIS. He had a fall down at the well. He broke his leg. It's in a cast.

NEFF. That knocks it on the head all right.

PHYLLIS. What do we do, Walter?

NEFF. Nothing. Just wait.

PHYLLIS. Wait for what?

NEFF. Until he can take a train. I told you it's got to be a train.

PHYLLIS. We can't wait. I can't go on like this.

NEFF. We're not going to grab a hammer and do it quick, just to get it over with.

PHYLLIS. There are other ways.

NEFF. Only we're not going to do it other ways.

PHYLLIS. But we can't leave it like this. What do you think would happen if he found out about this accident policy?

NEFF. Plenty. But not as bad as sitting in that death-house.

PHYLLIS. Don't ever talk like that, Walter.

NEFF. Just don't let's start losing our heads.

PHYLLIS. It's not our heads. It's our nerve we're losing.

NEFF. We're going to do it right. That's all I said.

PHYLLIS. Walter, maybe it's *my* nerves. It's the waiting that gets me.

NEFF. It's getting me just as bad, baby. But we've got to wait.

PHYLLIS. Maybe we have, Walter. Only it's so tough without you. It's like a wall between us.

Neff looks at his watch.

NEFF. Good-bye, baby. I'm thinking of you every minute.

He goes off. She stares after him, as the scene dissolves to NEFF's OFFICE. He is wearing a light gray suit and has his hat on. He is standing behind his desk opening some mail, taking a few papers out of his briefcase, checking something in his rate book, making a quick telephone call. But nothing of this is heard.

NEFF'S VOICE. After that a full week went by and I didn't see her once. I tried to keep my mind off her and off the whole idea. I kept telling myself that maybe those fates they say watch over you had gotten together and broken his leg to give me a way out. Then it was the fifteenth of June. You may remember that date, Keyes. I do too, only for a very different reason. You came into my office around three in the afternoon.

NEFF (*as Keyes enters with some papers in his hand*). Hello, Keyes.

KEYES. I just came from Norton's office. The semi-annual sales records are out. You're high man, Walter. That's twice in a row. Congratulations.

NEFF. Thanks. How would you like a cheap drink?

KEYES. How would you like a fifty dollar cut in salary?

NEFF. How would I—Do I laugh now, or wait until it gets funny?

KEYES. No, I'm serious. I've been talking to Norton. There's too much stuff piling up on my desk. Too much pressure on my nerves. I spend half the night walking up and down in my bed. I've got to have an assistant. I thought that you—

NEFF. Me? Why pick on me?

KEYES. Because I've got a crazy idea you might be good at the job.

NEFF. That's crazy all right. I'm a salesman.

KEYES. Yeah. A peddler, a gladhander, a back-slapper. You're too good to be a salesman.

NEFF. Nobody's too good to be a salesman.

KEYES. Phooey. All you guys do is ring doorbells and dish out a smooth line of monkey talk. What's bothering you is that fifty buck cut, isn't it?

NEFF. Well, it'd trouble anybody.

KEYES. Now, look, Walter. The job I'm talking about takes brains and integrity. It takes more guts than there is in fifty salesmen. It's the hottest job in the business.

NEFF. It's still a desk job. I don't want a desk job.

KEYES. A desk job. Is that all you can see in it? Just a hard chair to park your pants on from nine to five. Just a pile of papers to shuffle around, and five sharp pencils and a scratch pad to make figures on, with maybe a little doodling on the side. That's not the way I see it, Walter. To me

a claims man is a surgeon, and that desk is an operating table, and those pencils are scalpels and bone chisels. And those papers are not just forms and statistics and claims for compensation. They're alive, they're packed with drama, with twisted hopes and crooked dreams. A claims man, Walter, is a doctor and a blood-hound and a cop and a judge and a jury and a father confessor, all in one.

The telephone rings on Neff's desk. Automatically Keyes grabs the phone and answers.

KEYES. Who? Okay, hold the line. (*He puts the phone down on the desk and continues to Neff:*) And you want to tell me you're not interested. You don't want to work with your brains. All you want to work with is your finger on a doorbell. For a few bucks more a week. There's a dame on your phone.

NEFF (*picking the phone up and answering*). Walter Neff speaking.

The scene cuts to a PHONE BOOTH in the market: Phyllis is on the phone.

PHYLLIS. I had to call you, Walter. It's terribly urgent. Are you with somebody?

Back in NEFF's OFFICE: Neff is at the phone. His eye catches Keyes', who is walking up and down.

NEFF. Of course I am. Can't I call you back . . . Margie?

PHYLLIS at the phone:

PHYLLIS. Walter, I've only got a minute. It can't wait. Listen. He's going tonight. On the train. Are you listening, Walter? Walter!

NEFF at the PHONE: His eyes are on Keyes. He speaks into the phone as calmly as possible.

NEFF. I'm listening. Only make it short . . . Margie.

PHYLLIS at the PHONE:

PHYLLIS. He's on crutches. The doctor says he can go if he's careful. The change will do him good. It's wonderful, Walter. Just the way you wanted it. Only with the crutches it's ever so much better, isn't it?

NEFF'S OFFICE, Neff on the phone:

NEFF. One hundred percent better. Hold the line a minute. (*He covers the receiver with his hand and turns to Keyes, who is now standing at the window.*) Suppose I join you in your office, Keyes—

He makes a gesture as if expecting Keyes to leave. Keyes stays right where he is.

KEYES. I'll wait. Only tell Margie not to take all day.

Neff looks at Keyes' back with a strained expression, then lifts the phone again.

NEFF. Go ahead.

PHYLLIS at the PHONE:

PHYLLIS. It's the ten-fifteen from Glendale. I'm driving him. Is it still that same dark street?

Back in the office, NEFF is still watching Keyes cautiously.

NEFF. Yeah—sure.

A closeup of PHYLLIS at the PHONE:

PHYLLIS. The signal is three honks on the horn. Is there anything else?

A closeup of NEFF at the phone:

NEFF. What color did you pick out?

PHYLLIS (*seen again*). Color? (*She catches on.*) Oh, sure. The blue suit,

Walter. Navy blue. And the cast on his left leg.

NEFF (*seen again*). Navy blue. I like that fine.

PHYLLIS (*seen again*). This is it, Walter. I'm shaking like a leaf. But it's straight down the line now for both of us. I love you, Walter. Goodbye.

NEFF'S OFFICE: Neff is still on the phone.

NEFF. So long, Margie.

He hangs up. His mouth is grim, but he forces a smile as Keyes turns.

NEFF. I'm sorry, Keyes.

KEYES. What's the matter? The dames chasing you again? Or still? Or is it none of my business?

NEFF (*with a sour smile*). If I told you it was a customer—

KEYES. Margie! I bet she drinks from the bottle. Why don't you settle down and get married, Walter?

NEFF. Why don't you, for instance?

KEYES. I almost did, once. A long time ago.

NEFF (*getting up from his desk*). Look, Keyes, I've got a prospect to call on. (*But Keyes drives right ahead:*)

KEYES. We even had the church all picked out, the dame and I. She had a white satin dress with flounces on it. And I was on my way to the jewelry store to buy the ring. Then suddenly that little man in here started working on me. (*He punches his stomach with his fist.*)

NEFF. So you went back and started investigating her. That it?

KEYES (*nodding slowly, a little sad and a little ashamed*). And the stuff that came out. She'd been dyeing her hair ever since she was sixteen. And there was a manic-depressive in her family, on her mother's side. And she already had one husband, a professional pool player in Baltimore. And as for her brother—

NEFF. I get the general idea. She was a tramp from a long line of tramps. (*He picks up some papers impatiently.*)

KEYES. All right, I'm going. What am I to say to Norton? How about that job I want you for?

NEFF. I don't think I want it. Thanks, Keyes, just the same.

KEYES. Fair enough. Just get this: I picked you for the job, not because I think you're so darn smart, but because I thought maybe you were a shade less dumb than the rest of the outfit. I guess I was all wet. You're not smarter, Walter. You're just a little taller.

He goes out, and now Neff is alone. He watches the door close, then turns and goes slowly to the water cooler. He fills a paper cup and stands holding it. His thoughts are somewhere else. After a moment he absently throws the cupful of water into the receptacle under the cooler. He goes back to the desk . . . He takes his rate book out of his brief case and puts it on the desk. He buttons the top button of his shirt, and pulls his tie right. He leaves the office, with his briefcase under his arm.

NEFF'S VOICE (*synchronized with the above scene*). That was it, Keyes, and there was no use kidding myself any more. Those fates I was talking about had only been stalling me off. Now they had thrown the switch. The gears had meshed. The machinery had started to move and nothing could stop it. The time for thinking had all run out. From here on it was a question of following the time table, move by move, just as we had it rehearsed. I wanted my time all accounted for for the rest of the afternoon and up to the last possible moment in the evening. So I arranged to call on a prospect in Pasadena about a public liability bond. When I left the office I put my rate book on the desk as if I had forgotten it. That was part of the alibi.

The scene dissolves to NEFF'S APARTMENT HOUSE as Neff's coupé comes down the street, swings into the garage and goes down the ramp into the basement.

NEFF'S VOICE (*continuing*). I got home about seven and drove right into the garage. This was another item to establish my alibi.

This cuts to the GARAGE. There are about eight cars parked. A colored attendant in coveralls and rubber boots is washing a car with a hose and sponge. Neff's car comes in and stops near the attendant. Neff gets out with his briefcase under his arm.

ATTENDANT. Hiya there, Mr. Neff.

NEFF. How about a wash job on my heap, Charlie?

ATTENDANT. How soon you want it, Mr. Neff? I got two cars ahead of you.

NEFF. Anytime you get to it, Charlie. I'm staying in tonight.

ATTENDANT. Okay, Mr. Neff. Be all shined up for you in the morning.

NEFF (*crossing to the elevator, and speaking back over his shoulder*). That left front tire looks a little soft. Check it, will you?

ATTENDANT. You bet. Check 'em all round. Always do.

Neff enters the elevator and the scene dissolves to NEFF'S APARTMENT as Neff comes in. He walks straight to the phone, dials, and starts speaking into the mouthpiece, but only his dictation is heard.

NEFF'S VOICE. Up in my apartment I called Lou Schwartz, one of the salesmen that shared my office. He lived in Westwood. That made it a toll call and there'd be a record of it. I told him I had forgotten my rate book and needed some dope on the public liability bond I was figuring. I asked him to call me back. This was another item in my alibi, so that later on I could prove that I had been home.

The scene dissolves to NEFF'S LIVING ROOM. Neff comes into the living room from the bedroom, putting on the jacket of his blue suit. The phone rings. He picks up the receiver and starts talking, unheard, as before. He makes notes on a pad.

NEFF'S VOICE. I changed into a navy blue suit like Dietrichson was going to wear. Lou Schwartz called me back and gave me a lot of figures . . . . . . .

Now he is seen folding a hand towel and stuffing it into his jacket pocket. He then takes a large roll of adhesive tape and puts that into his pants pocket. —This scene dissolving, we see a TELEPHONE BELL BOX (on the baseboard) and a DOORBELL above the entrance door as Neff's hand places a small card against the bell clapper in each of these; and this dissolves to the FIRE STAIRS of the apartment house at night as the view moves with Neff going down the stairs in his blue suit, with a hat pulled down over his eyes.—And this scene dissolving, we next get a distant view of the DIETRICHSON HOME at night. There is no traffic.—Some windows are lit. Neff comes into view and approaches cautiously. He looks around and then slides open the garage door.

NEFF'S VOICE. I stuffed a hand towel and a big roll of adhesive tape into my pockets, so I could fake something that looked like a cast on a broken leg. . . Next I fixed the telephone and the doorbell, so that the cards would fall down if the bells rang. That way I would know there had been a phone call or visitor while I was away. I left the apartment house by the fire stairs and side door. Nobody saw me. It was already getting dark. I took the Vermont Avenue bus to Los Feliz and walked from there up to the Dietrichson house. There was that smell of honeysuckle again, only stronger, now that it was evening.

We see the interior of the GARAGE as Neff closes the door. A very faint light comes in at a side window. He opens the rear door of the sedan, gets in and closes the door after him. The dark interior of the car has swallowed him up.

NEFF'S VOICE. Then I was in the garage. His car was backed in, just the way I told Phyllis to have it. It was so still I could hear the ticking of the clock on the dashboard. I kept thinking of the place we had picked out to do it, that dark street on the way to the station, and the three honks on the horn that were to be the signal . . . About ten minutes later they came down.

Outside the DIETRICHSON HOUSE: The front door has opened and Dietrichson is halfway down the steps. He is walking with crutches, wearing the dark blue suit and a hat. The cast is on his left leg. There is no shoe on his left foot. Only the white plaster shows.

Phyllis comes after him, carrying his suitcase and his overcoat. She wears a camel's-hair coat and no hat. She catches up with him.

PHYLLIS. You all right, honey? I'll have the car out in a second.

Dietrichson just grunts. She passes him moving toward the garage, and slides the door open. Then we again see the GARAGE, as we get a low view from the sedan.

(The camera is very low inside the sedan, shooting slightly upward from Neff's hiding place.) The garage door has just been opened. Phyllis comes to the car, and opens the rear door. She looks down, (seen very close) and a tight, cool smile flashes across her face. Then, very calmly, she puts the suitcase and overcoat in back on the seat. She closes the door again.

Outside the garage, Dietrichson stands watching Phyllis as she gets into the car and drives out to pick him up. She stops beside him and opens the right-hand door. Dietrichson climbs in with difficulty. She helps him, watching him closely.

PHYLLIS. Take it easy, honey. We've got lots of time.

DIETRICHSON. Just let me do it my own way. Grab that crutch.

She takes one of the crutches from him.

DIETRICHSON. They ought to make these things so they fold up.

For a moment, as he leans his hand on the back of the seat, there is danger that he may see Neff. He doesn't. He slides awkwardly into the seat and pulls the second crutch in after him. He closes the door. The car moves off, and this dissolves to the interior of the CAR as Phyllis is driving and Dietrich-son is beside her. Dietrichson has a partly smoked cigar between his teeth. They are in the middle of a conversation.

DIETRICHSON. Aw, stop squawkin' can't you, Phyllis? No man takes his wife along to a class reunion. That's what class reunions are for.

PHYLLIS. Mrs. Tucker went along with her husband last year, didn't she?

DIETRICHSON. Yeah, and what happened to her? She sat in the hotel lobby for four days straight. Never even saw the guy until we poured him back on the train.

We get a close view of NEFF'S FACE, low down in the corner behind Dietrichson. His face is partly covered by the edge of a traveling rug which he has pulled up over him. He looks up at Dietrichson and Phyllis in the front seat.

PHYLLIS' VOICE. All right, honey. Just so long as you have a good time.

DIETRICHSON'S VOICE. I won't do much dancing, I can tell you that.

PHYLLIS (*as we now see their heads and shoulders as observed by Neff*). Remember what the doctor said. If you get careless you might end up with a shorter leg.

DIETRICHSON. So what? I could break the other one and match them up again.

PHYLLIS. It makes you feel pretty good to get away from me, doesn't it?

DIETRICHSON. It's only for four days. I'll be back Monday at the latest.

PHYLLIS. Don't forget we're having the Hobeys for dinner on Monday.

DIETRICHSON. The Hobeys? We had them last. They owe us a dinner, don't they?

PHYLLIS. Maybe they do but I've already asked them for Monday.

DIETRICHSON. Well, I don't want to feed the Hobeys.

We get a closeup of PHYLLIS' FACE only: there is a look of tension in her eyes now. She glances around quickly. The car has reached the dark street Neff and she picked out.

DIETRICHSON'S VOICE. And I don't want to eat at their house either. The food you get there, and that rope he hands out for cigars. Call it off, can't you?—This is not the right street! Why did you turn here?

Phyllis does not answer. She doesn't even breathe. Her hand goes down on the horn button. She honks three times. —A closeup shows Dietrichson reacting with surprise.

DIETRICHSON. What are you doing that for? What're you honking the horn for?

This is as far as his voice will ever get, as Neff starts to pull himself up. It breaks off and dies down in a muffled groan. There are struggling noises and a dull sound of something breaking. Phyllis drives on ánd never turns her head. She stares straight in front of her. Her teeth are clenched.

This dissolves to a PARKING SPACE adjoining Glendale Station, at night. The station is visible about sixty yards away. There is no parking attendant. Ten or twelve cars are parked diagonally, not crowded. The train is not in yet, but there is activity around the station from passengers and their friends, redcaps and baggage men and news vendors.

The Dietrichson sedan comes into view and parks in the foreground at the outer end of the line, several spaces from the next car, facing away from the camera. Both front doors are open. Phyllis gets out and from the other side crutches emerge, and a man (seen entirely from behind, and apparently Dietrichson) climbs out awkwardly. While he is steadying himself on the ground with the crutches, Phyllis has taken out Dietrichson's suitcase and overcoat. She walks around the car and rolls up the right front window. She closes and locks the car door. She tries the right rear door and takes a last look into the dim interior of the car. Then she and the man walk slowly away from the car to the end of the station platform and along it toward the station building. Phyllis walks several steps ahead of the man.

PHYLLIS and the MAN are then seen walking a little to one side, so that Phyllis is clearly seen but the man's face is not.

MAN (*in a subdued voice*). You handle the redcap and the conductor.

PHYLLIS. Don't worry.

MAN. Keep them away from me as much as you can. I don't want to be helped.

PHYLLIS. I said don't worry, Walter.

PHYLLIS and the MAN are now walking down the platform (facing front), and at this point it is quite clear that the man is NEFF.

NEFF. You start just as soon as the train leaves. At the dairy sign you turn off the highway onto the dirt road. From there it's exactly eight-tenths of a mile to the dump beside the tracks. Remember?

PHYLLIS. I remember everything.

NEFF. You'll be there a little ahead of the train. No speeding. You don't want any cops stopping you—with him in the back.

PHYLLIS. Walter, we've been through all that so many times.

NEFF. When you turn off the highway, cut all your lights. I'm going to be back on the observation platform. I'll drop off as close to the spot as I can. Wait for the train to pass, then blink your lights twice.

Phyllis nods. They go on. Over them is heard the noise of the train coming into the station and its lights are seen.

At the GLENDALE STATION PLATFORM: the train is just coming to a stop. The passengers move forward to the tracks. Phyllis, carrying the suitcase and overcoat, and Neff, still a little behind her, come toward us. A redcap sees them and runs up. He takes the suitcase out of Phyllis' hand.

REDCAP. San Francisco train, lady?

Phyllis takes an envelope containing Dietrichson's ticket from the pocket of the overcoat. She reads from the envelope.

PHYLLIS. Car nine, section eleven. Just my husband going.

REDCAP. Car nine, section eleven. Yessum, this way please.

Phyllis hands the overcoat to the redcap, who leads her and Neff toward car number nine. Neff still hangs back and keeps his head down, the way a man using crutches might naturally do.

Outside CAR NUMBER NINE: the pullman conductor and porter stand at the steps. The conductor is checking the tickets of passengers getting on. The redcap leads Phyllis and Neff into view. The conductor and porter see Neff on his crutches and move to help him.

PHYLLIS. It's all right, thanks. My husband doesn't like to be helped.

The redcap goes up the steps into the car. Neff laboriously swings himself up onto the box and from there up on the steps, keeping his head down. Meantime, Phyllis is holding the attention of the conductor and porter by showing them the ticket.

CONDUCTOR. Car nine, section eleven. The gentleman only. Thank you.

Phyllis nods and takes the ticket back. Neff has reached the top of the steps. She goes up after him and gives him the ticket. They are now close together.

PHYLLIS. Goodbye, honey. Take awful good care of yourself with that leg.

NEFF. Sure, I will. Just you take it easy going home.

PHYLLIS. I'll miss you, honey.

She kisses him. There are shouts of "All Aboard." The redcap comes from inside the car.

REDCAP. Section eleven, suh.

Phyllis takes a quarter from her bag and gives it to the redcap.

PORTER (*shouting*). All aboard!

The redcap descends. Phyllis kisses Neff again quickly.

PHYLLIS. Good luck, honey.

She runs down the steps. The porter picks up the box. He and the conductor get on board the train. Phyllis stands there waving goodbye as the train starts moving, and the porter begins to close the car door. Phyllis turns and walks out of sight in the direction of the parked car.

The scene then cuts to the PLATFORM as the train moves on. The light is dim.

—The conductor is going on into the car. Neff is half turned away from the porter.

NEFF. Can you make up my berth right away?

PORTER. Yes, sir.

NEFF. I'm going back to the observation car for a smoke.

PORTER. This way, sir. Three cars back. (*He holds the vestibule door open, and Neff hobbles through.*)

This dissolves to the PULLMAN CAR, which is dimly lit. Most of the berths are made up. As Neff hobbles along, another porter and some passengers make way for the crippled man solicitously.—This dissolves to the PLATFORM between two cars as the train conductor meets Neff, opens the door for him, and Neff hobbles on through. This in turn dissolves to the PARLOR CAR, where four or five passengers are reading or writing. As Neff comes through on his crutches they pull in their feet to make room for him. One old lady, seeing that he is headed for the observation platform, opens the door for him. He thanks her with a nod and hobbles through.

And now the scene cuts to the OBSERVATION PLATFORM. It is dark except for a little light coming from inside the parlor car. The train is going about fifteen miles an hour between Glendale and Burbank. Neff has come out and hobbled to the railing. He stands looking back along the rails. Suddenly a man's voice speaks from behind him.

MAN'S VOICE. Can I pull a chair out for you?

Neff looks around. He sees a man sitting in the corner smoking a hand-rolled cigarette. He is about fifty-five

years old, with white hair, and a broad-brimmed Stetson hat. He looks like a small town lawyer or maybe a mining man. Neff does not like the man's presence there very much. He turns to him just enough to answer.

NEFF. No thanks, I'd rather stand.

MAN. You going far?

NEFF. Palo Alto.

MAN. My name's Jackson. I'm going all the way to Medford. Medford, Oregon. Had a broken arm myself once.

NEFF. Uh-huh.

JACKSON. That darn cast sure itches something fierce, don't it? I thought I'd go crazy with mine. (*Neff stands silent. His mind is feverishly thinking of how to get rid of Jackson.*) Palo Alto's a nice little town. You a Stanford man?

NEFF. Used to be. (*He starts patting his pockets as if looking for something.*)

JACKSON. I bet you left something behind. I always do.

NEFF. My cigar case. Must have left it in my overcoat back in the section.

JACKSON (*taking out a small bag of tobacco and a packet of cigarette papers*). Care to roll yourself a cigarette, Mr.—?

NEFF. Dietrichson. Thanks. I really prefer cigars. (*Looking around*) Maybe the porter—

JACKSON. I could get your cigars for you. Be glad to, Mr. Dietrichson.

NEFF. That's darn nice of you. It's car nine, section eleven. If you're sure it's not too much trouble.

JACKSON. Car nine, section eleven. A pleasure.

He rises and walks into the parlor car. Neff turns slowly and watches Jackson go back through the car. Then he moves to one side of the platform and looks ahead along the track to orientate himself. He gives one last glance back into the parlor car to make sure no one is watching him. He slips the crutches from under his arms and stands on both feet. He drops the crutches off the train onto the tracks, then quickly swings his body over the rail.

We then see the OBSERVATION CAR, with Neff hanging onto the railing. He looks down, then lets go and drops to the right-of-way. The train recedes slowly into the night. Neff has fallen on the tracks. He picks himself up, rubs one knee and looks back along the line of the tracks and off to one side.

A dark landscape comes into view, and we see the RAILROAD TRACKS. Close beyond the edge of the right-of-way, the silhouette of a dump shows up. Beside it looms the dark bulk of the Dietrichson sedan. The headlights blink twice and go out.—NEFF, seen close, starts running toward the car. He runs a little awkwardly because of the improvised cast on his left foot. Then we see the CAR in the dark as the front door opens and Phyllis steps out. She closes the door and looks in the direction of the tracks. The uneven steps of Neff running toward her are heard. She opens the back door of the car and leans in. She pulls the rug off the corpse (which is not visible) and stands looking into the car, unable to take her eyes off what she sees, while at the same time her hands mechanically begin to fold the rug. The running steps grow louder and Neff comes into view, breathing hard. He reaches her.

NEFF. Okay. This has to go fast. Take his hat and pick up the crutches.

Neff points back toward the tracks. He reaches into the car and begins to drag out the body by the armpits. Phyllis coolly reaches past him and takes the hat off the dead man's head. She turns to go.

NEFF. Hang on to that rug. I'll need it.

Phyllis moves out of sight carrying the hat and rug, while NEFF gets a stronger hold on the dead Dietrichson and drags him free of the car and toward tracks. The corpse is not seen.

PHYLLIS reaches the point where one of the crutches lies. She picks it up and goes for the other crutch a short distance away. She carries both crutches, the hat and the rug toward Neff.

NEFF has reached the railroad tracks. The corpse is lying beside the tracks, face down. Phyllis comes up to Neff. He takes the crutches and the hat from her. He throws the crutches beside the corpse. He takes the hat from Phyllis and tosses it carelessly along the track.

NEFF. Let's go. Stay behind me.

He takes the rug from her and they move back toward the car, Phyllis first, then Neff walking almost backwards, sweeping the ground over which the body was dragged with the rug as they go.—Then we see the CAR as they reach it together.

NEFF. Get in. You drive.

She gets in. Neff sweeps the ground after him as he goes around the car to get in beside her. He throws the rug into the back of the car.

Inside the CAR: Phyllis is behind the wheel. Neff beside her is just closing the door. He props his wrapped foot against the dashboard and begins to tear off the adhesive tape while at the same time Phyllis presses the starter button. The starter grinds, but the motor doesn't catch. She tries again. It still doesn't catch. Neff looks at her. She tries a third time. The starter barely turns over. The battery is very low.

Phyllis leans back. They stare at each other desperately. After a moment Neff bends forward slowly and turns the ignition key to the OFF position. He holds his left thumb poised over the starter button. There is a breathless moment. Then he presses the starter button with swift decision. The starter grinds with nerve-wracking sluggishness. Neff twists the ignition key to ON and instantly pulls the hand-throttle wide open. With a last feeble kick of the starter, the motor catches and races. He eases the throttle down and slides back into his place. They look at each other again. The tenseness of the moment still shows in their faces.

NEFF. Let's go, baby.

Phyllis releases the hand brake and puts the car in reverse. Neff is again busy unwrapping the tape from his leg.— Then the car, with the headlights out, backs up, swings around and moves off along the dirt road the way it came.

We see the SEDAN driving along a HIGH-WAY in traffic, and again Neff's voice is heard over the scene. Phyllis and Neff are facing forward. Neff is bent over, peeling the towel and plaster off his foot, which is out of sight. Phyllis is calm, almost relaxed. Neff straightens up. They are talking to each other. Their lips are seen moving but what they say is not heard. They stop talking. Phyllis stares straight ahead. Neff is pulling adhesive tape off the wrapped towel that was on his foot.

He folds the adhesive into a tight ball, rolls the towel up, puts both into his pockets.

NEFF'S VOICE (*synchronized with the scene*). On the way back we went over once more what she was to do at the inquest, if they had one, and about the insurance, when that came up. I was afraid she might go to pieces a little, now that we had done it, but she was perfect. No nerves. Not a tear, not even a blink of the eyes. . . .

This dissolves to a DARK STREET near Neff's house as the sedan comes into view and stops without pulling over to the curb.

NEFF'S VOICE. She dropped me a block from my apartment house.

The car door opens. Neff starts to get out.

PHYLLIS. Walter— (*Neff turns back to her.*) What's the matter, Walter. Aren't you going to kiss me?

NEFF. Sure, I'm going to kiss you.

PHYLLIS (*bending toward him and putting her arms around him*). It's straight down the line, isn't it? (*She kisses him. He is passive in the kiss.*) I love you, Walter.

NEFF. I love you, baby.

This dissolves to the FIRE STAIRS. Neff is seen going up.

NEFF'S VOICE. It was two minutes past eleven as I went up the fire stairs again. Nobody saw me this time either.

This dissolves to a closeup of NEFF'S HAND opening the telephone bell box and the door bell. The cards are still in position. Neff's hand takes them out.

NEFF'S VOICE. In the apartment I

checked the bells. The cards hadn't moved. No calls. No visitors.

This dissolves to the LIVING ROOM, in which the lights are still on. Neff comes from the bedroom, wearing the light grey suit he wore before the murder, only without a tie. He buttons his jacket, looks around the room, and opens the corridor door.

NEFF'S VOICE. I changed the blue suit. There was one last thing to do. I wanted the garage man to see me again.

This dissolves to the BASEMENT GARAGE, where fifteen or twenty cars are now parked. Charlie, the attendant has washed Neff's car and is now polishing the glass and metal-work. Neff comes from the elevator. Charlie sees him. He straightens up.

CHARLIE. You going to need it after all, Mr. Neff? I'm not quite through.

NEFF. It's okay, Charlie. Just walking down to the drug store for something to eat. Been working upstairs all evening. My stomach's getting sore at me.

CHARLIE. Yes, sir, Mr. Neff.

He walks up the ramp toward the garage entrance, and the scene dissolves to the STREET outside the apartment house. Neff comes out at the top of the ramp and starts to walk down the street, not too fast. He walks about ten or fifteen yards. At first his steps sound hard and distinct on the sidewalk and echo in the deserted street. But slowly, as he goes on, they fade into utter silence. He walks a few feet without sound, then becomes aware of the silence. He stops rigidly and looks back. He stands like that for a moment, then turns forward again. There is a look of horror on his face now. He walks on again, and still his steps make no sound, as the scene fades out.

NEFF'S VOICE (*synchronized with the scene*). That was all there was to it. Nothing had slipped, nothing had been overlooked, there was nothing to give us away. And yet, Keyes, as I was walking down the street to the drug store, suddenly it came over me that everything would go wrong. It sounds crazy, Keyes, but it's true, so help me: I couldn't hear my own footsteps. It was the walk of a dead man.

# PART THREE

NEFF'S OFFICE fades in at night. Neff still sits before the dictaphone. There are four cylinders on end on the desk next to him. He gets up from the swivel chair with great effort and stands a moment unsteadily. The wound in his shoulder is paining him. He is very weak as he slowly crosses to the water cooler. He takes the blood stained handkerchief from inside his shirt and soaks it with fresh water.—The office door opens behind him. He turns, hiding the handkerchief behind his back. In the doorway stands the colored man who has been cleaning up downstairs. He is carrying his big trash box by a rope handle.

COLORED MAN. Didn't know anybody was here, Mr. Neff. We ain't cleaned your office yet.

NEFF. Let it go tonight. I'm busy.

COLORED MAN. Whatever you say, Mr. Neff.

He closes the door slowly, staring at Neff with an uneasy expression. Neff puts the soaked handkerchief back on his wounded shoulder, then walks heavily over to his swivel chair and lowers himself into it. He takes the dictaphone horn and speaks into it again.

NEFF. That was the longest night I ever lived through, Keyes, and the next day was worse, when the story broke in the papers, and they were talking about it at the office, and the day after that when you started digging into it. I kept my hands in my pockets because I thought they were shaking, and I put on dark glasses so people couldn't see my eyes, and then I took them off again so people wouldn't get to wondering why I wore them. I was trying to hold myself together, but I could feel my nerves pulling me to pieces . . .

This dissolves to the INSURANCE OFFICE on the TWELFTH FLOOR. Neff comes through the reception room doors on the balcony with his hat on and his briefcase under his arm. He walks toward his office, but half way there he runs into Keyes. Keyes is wearing his vest and hat, no coat. He is carrying a file of papers and smoking a cigar.

KEYES. Come on, Walter. The big boss wants to see us.

NEFF. Okay. (*He turns and walks beside Keyes.*) That Dietrichson case?

KEYES. Must be.

NEFF. Anything wrong?

KEYES. The guy's dead, we had him insured and it's going to cost us money. That's always wrong.

He stops by a majolica jar full of sand and takes a pencil from his vest. He stands over the jar extinguishing his cigar carefully so as not to damage it.

NEFF. What have you got so far?

KEYES. Autopsy report. No heart failure, no apoplexy, no predisposing medical cause of any kind. He died of a broken neck.

NEFF. When is the inquest?

KEYES. They had it this morning. His wife and daughter made the identification. The train people and some passengers told how he went through to the observation car . . . It was all over in forty-five minutes. Verdict, accidental death.

Keyes puts the half-smoked cigar into his vest pocket with the pencil. They move on.

NEFF. What do the police figure?

KEYES. That he got tangled up in his crutches and fell off the train. They're satisfied. It's not their dough.

They stop at a door lettered in embossed chromium letters: EDWARD S. NORTON, JR. PRESIDENT. Keyes opens the door, and they go in. —We then see the RECEPTION ROOM of Mr. Norton's office. A secretary is sitting behind a desk. As Keyes and Neff enter, the door to Norton's private office is opened. From inside, Mr. Norton is letting out three legal-looking gentlemen. Norton is about forty-five, very well groomed, rather pompous in manner.

NORTON (*to the men who are leaving*). I believe the legal position is now clear, gentlemen. Please stand by. I may need you later. (*He sees Keyes and Neff.*) Come in, Mr. Keyes. You too, Mr. Neff.

Neff has put down his hat and briefcase. He and Keyes pass the legal-looking men and follow Norton into his office.

In NORTON'S OFFICE: Naturally it is the best office in the building; modern but not modernistic, spacious, very well furnished; flowers, smoking stands, easy chairs, etc. Norton has gone behind his desk. Keyes has come in, and Neff after him closes the door quietly. Norton looks disapprovingly at Keyes' shirt sleeves.

NORTON. You find this an uncomfortably warm day Mr. Keyes? (*At this Keyes takes his hat off but holds it in his hands.*)

KEYES. Sorry, Mr. Norton. I didn't know this was formal.

NORTON (*smiling frostily*). Sit down, gentlemen. (*To Keyes*) Any new developments? (*Keyes and Neff sit down, Norton remains standing.*)

KEYES. I just talked to this Jackson long distance. Up in Medford, Oregan.

NORTON. Who's Jackson?

KEYES. The last guy that saw Dietrichson alive. They were out on the observation platform together talking. Dietrichson wanted a cigar and Jackson went to get Dietrichson's cigar case for him. When he came back to the observation platform, no Dietrichson. Jackson didn't think anything was wrong until a wire caught up with the train at Santa Barbara. They had found Dietrichson's body on the tracks near Burbank.

NORTON. Very interesting, about the cigar case. (*He walks up and down behind his desk thinking hard.*) Anything else?

KEYES. Not much. Dietrichson's secretary says she didn't know anything about the policy. There is a daughter, but all she remembers is Neff talking

to her father about accident insurance at their house one night.

NEFF. I couldn't sell him at first. Mrs. Dietrichson opposed it. He told me he'd think it over. Later on I went down to the oil fields and closed him. He signed the application and gave me his check.

NORTON (*dripping with sarcasm*). A fine piece of salesmanship that was, Mr. Neff.

KEYES. There's no sense in pushing Neff around. He's got the best sales record in the office. Are your salesmen supposed to know that the customer is going to fall off a train?

NORTON. Fall off a train? Are we sure Dietrichson fell off a train? (*There is a charged pause.*)

KEYES. I don't get it.

NORTON. You don't, Mr. Keyes? Then what *do* you think of this case? This policy might cost us a great deal of money. As you know, it contains a double indemnity clause. Just what is your opinion?

KEYES. No opinion at all.

NORTON. Not even a hunch? One of those interesting little hunches of yours?

KEYES. Nope. Not even a hunch.

NORTON. I'm surprised, Mr. Keyes. I've formed a very definite opinion. I think I know—in fact I know I know what happened to Dietrichson.

KEYES. You know you know what?

NORTON. I know it was not an accident. (*He looks from Keyes to Neff and back to Keyes.*) What do you say to that?

KEYES. Me? You've got the ball. Let's see you run with it.

NORTON. There's a widespread feeling

that just because a man has a large office—

The dictograph on his desk buzzes. He reaches over and depresses a key and puts the earpiece to his ear.

NORTON (*into the dictograph*). Yes? . . . Have her come in, please.—(*He replaces the earpiece. He turns back to Keyes and Neff.*) —that just because a man has a large office he must be an idiot. I'm having a visitor, if you don't mind. (*Keyes and Neff start to get up.*) No, no. I want you to stay and watch me handle this.

SECRETARY (*opening the door and ushering someone in*). Mrs. Dietrichson.

Neff stands staring at the door. He relaxes with an obvious effort of will. Phyllis comes in. She wears a gray tailored suit, small black hat with a veil, black gloves, and carries a black bag. The secretary closes the door behind her. Mr. Norton goes to meet her.

NORTON. Thank you very much for coming, Mrs. Dietrichson. I assure you I appreciate it. (*He turns a little toward Keyes.*) This is Mr. Keyes.

KEYES. How do you do.

PHYLLIS. How do you do.

NORTON. And Mr. Neff.

PHYLLIS. I've met Mr. Neff. How do you do.

Norton has placed a chair near her. Phyllis sits down. Norton goes behind his desk.

NORTON. Mrs. Dietrichson, I assure you of our sympathy in your bereavement. I hesitated before asking you to come here so soon after your loss. (*Phyllis nods silently.*) But now that you're here I hope you won't mind if I plunge straight into business.

You know why we asked you to come, don't you?

PHYLLIS. No. All I know is that your secretary made it sound very urgent.

Keyes sits quietly in his chair with his legs crossed. He has hung his hat on his foot and thrust his thumbs in the armholes of his vest. He looks a little bored. Neff, behind him, stands leaning against the false mantel, completely dead-pan.

NORTON. Your husband had an accident policy with this company. Evidently you don't know that, Mrs. Dietrichson.

PHYLLIS. No. I remember some talk at the house— (*looking toward Neff*) —but he didn't seem to want it.

NEFF. He took it out a few days later, Mrs. Dietrichson.

PHYLLIS. I see.

NORTON. You'll probably find the policy among his personal effects.

PHYLLIS. His safe deposit box hasn't been opened yet. It seems a tax examiner has to be present.

NORTON. Please, Mrs. Dietrichson, I don't want you to think you are being subjected to any questioning. But there are a few things we should like to know.

PHYLLIS. What sort of things?

NORTON. We have the report of the coroner's inquest. Accidental death. We are not entirely satisfied. In fact, we are not satisfied at all. (*Phyllis looks at him coolly; Keyes looks vaguely interested; Neff is staring straight at Phyllis.*) Frankly Mrs. Dietrichson, we suspect suicide. (*Phyllis doesn't bat an eyelash.*) I'm

PHYLLIS: You're a smart insurance man, aren't you, Mr. Neff?

NEFF: Just don't let's start losing our heads.

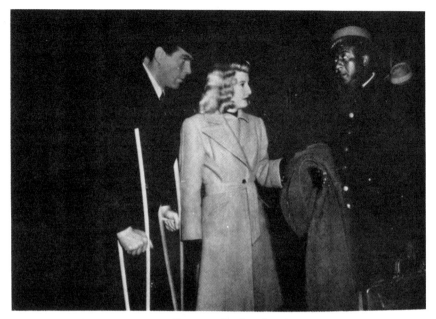

PHYLLIS: Just my husband going —

KEYES: You're all washed up, Walter.

sorry. Would you like a glass of water?

PHYLLIS. Please.

NORTON. Mr. Neff.

He indicates a thermos on a stand near Neff. Neff pours a glass of water and carries it over to Phyllis. She has lifted her veil a little. She takes the glass from his hand.

PHYLLIS. Thank you. (*Their eyes meet for a fraction of a second.*)

NORTON. Had your husband been moody or depressed lately, Mrs. Dietrichson? Did he seem to have financial worries, for instance?

PHYLLIS. He was perfectly all right and I don't know of any financial worries.

NORTON. There must have been something, Mrs. Dietrichson. Let us examine this so-called accident. First, your husband takes out this policy in absolute secrecy. Why? Because he doesn't want his family to suspect what he intends to do.

PHYLLIS. Do what?

NORTON. Commit suicide. Next, he goes on this trip entirely alone. He has to be alone. He hobbles all the way out to the observation platform, very unlikely with his leg in a cast, unless he has a very strong reason. Once there, he finds he is not alone. There is a man there. What was his name, Keyes? (*Norton flips his fingers impatiently at Keyes who doesn't even bother to look up.*)

KEYES. His name was Jackson. Probably still is.

NORTON. Jackson. So your husband gets rid of this Jackson with some flimsy excuse about cigars. And then he is alone. And then he does it. He jumps. Suicide. In which case the

company is not liable.—You know that, of course. We could go to court—

PHYLLIS. I don't know anything. In fact I don't know why I came here. (*She makes as if to rise indignantly.*)

NORTON. Just a moment, please. I said we *could* go to court. I didn't say we want to. Not only is it against our practice, but it would involve a great deal of expense, a lot of lawyers, a lot of time, perhaps years. (*As Phyllis rises coldly*) So what I want to suggest is a compromise on both sides. A settlement for a certain sum, a part of the policy value—

PHYLLIS. Don't bother, Mr. Norton. When I came in here I had no idea you owed me any money. You told me you did. Then you told me you didn't. Now you tell me you want to pay me a part of it, whatever it is. You want to bargain with me, at a time like this. I don't like your insinuations about my husband, Mr. Norton, and I don't like your methods. In fact I don't like you, Mr. Norton. Goodbye, gentlemen.

She turns and walks out. The door closes after her. There is a pregnant pause. Keyes straightens up in his chair.

KEYES. Nice going, Mr. Norton. You sure carried that ball. (*As Norton pours himself a glass of water and stands holding it*) Only you fumbled on the goal line. Then you heaved an illegal forward pass and got thrown for a forty-yard loss. Now you can't pick yourself up because you haven't got a leg to stand on.

NORTON. I haven't eh? Let her claim. Let her sue. We can prove it was suicide.

KEYES (*standing up*).Can we? Mr. Norton, the first thing that hit me was that suicide angle. Only I dropped it in the wastepaper basket just three seconds later. You ought to look at the statistics on suicide sometime. You might learn a little something about the insurance business.

NORTON. I was raised in the insurance business, Mr. Keyes.

KEYES. Yeah. In the front office. Come on, you never read an actuarial table in your life. I've got ten volumes on suicide alone. Suicide by race, by color, by occupation, by sex, by seasons of the year, by time of day. Suicide, how committed: by poisons, by fire-arms, by drowning, by leaps. Suicide by poison, subdivided by types of poison, such as corrosive, irritant, systemic, gaseous, narcotic, alkaloid, protein, and so forth. Suicide by leaps, subdivided by leaps from high places, under wheels of trains, under wheels of trucks, under the feet of horses, from steamboats. But, Mr. Norton, of all the cases on record there's not one single case of suicide by leap from the rear end of a moving train. And do you know how fast that train was going at the point where the body was found? Fifteen miles an hour. Now how could anybody jump off a slow moving train like that with any kind of expectation that he would kill himself? No soap, Mr. Norton. We're sunk, and we're going to pay through the nose, and you know it. May I have this?

Keyes' throat is dry after the long speech. He grabs the glass of water out of Norton's hand and drains it in one big gulp. Norton is watching him almost stupefied. Neff stands with the shadow of a smile on his face. Keyes puts the glass down noisily on Norton's desk.

KEYES. Come on, Walter.

Norton doesn't move or speak. Keyes puts his hat on and crosses toward the door, Neff after him. With the doorknob in his hands Keyes turns back to Norton with a glance down at his own shirt sleeves.

KEYES. Next time I'll rent a tuxedo.

They go out and the scene dissolves to NEFF at the dictaphone at night. There is a tired grin on his face as he talks into the horn.

NEFF. I could have hugged you right then and there, Keyes, you and your statistics. You were the only one we were really scared of, and instead you were almost playing on our team . . .

This dissolves to NEFF'S APARTMENT. It is almost dark in the room. The corridor door opens letting the light in. Neff enters with his hat on and his briefcase under his arm. He switches the lights on, closes the door, puts the key in his pocket. At this moment the telephone rings. He picks up the phone.

NEFF'S VOICE (*his dictation synchronized with the scene*). That evening when I got home my nerves had eased off. I could feel the ground under my feet again, and it looked like easy going from there on in.

NEFF (*at the telephone*). Hello . . . Hello, baby. . . . Sure, everything is fine . . . You were wonderful in Norton's office.

A TELEPHONE BOOTH in a drug store: Phyllis is on the phone. She is not dressed as in Norton's office.

PHYLLIS. I felt so funny. I wanted to look at you all the time.

NEFF (*at the telephone in his apartment*). How do you think I felt? Where are you, baby?

PHYLLIS (*at the phone*). At the drug store. Just a block away. Can I come up?

NEFF'S APARTMENT, with Neff at the phone:

NEFF. Okay. But be careful. Don't let anybody see you.

He hangs up, takes off his hat and drops hat and briefcase on the davenport. He looks around the room and crosses to lower the venetian blinds and draw the curtains. He gathers up the morning paper which is lying untidily on the floor and puts it in the wastepaper basket.—The door bell rings.—Neff stops in sudden alarm. It can't be Phyllis. The time is too short. For a second he stands there motionless, then crosses to the door and opens it.—In the door stands Keyes.

NEFF. Hello, Keyes.

Keyes walks past him into the room. His hands are clasped behind his back. There is a strange, absent-minded look in his eyes. Neff closes the door without taking his eyes off Keyes.

NEFF. What's on your mind?

KEYES (*stopping in the middle of the room and turning*). That broken leg. The guy broke his leg.

NEFF. What are you talking about?

KEYES. Talking about Dietrichson. He had accident insurance, didn't he? Then he broke his leg, didn't he?

NEFF. So what?

KEYES. And he didn't put in a claim. Why didn't he put in a claim? Why?

NEFF. What the dickens are you driving at?

KEYES. Walter, there's something wrong. I ate dinner two hours ago. It stuck half way. (*He prods his stomach with his thumb.*) The little man is acting up again. Because there's something wrong with that Dietrichson case.

NEFF. Because he didn't put in a claim? Maybe he just didn't have time.

KEYES. Or maybe he just didn't know he was insured.

He has stopped in front of Neff. They look at each other for a tense moment. Neff hardly breathes. Then Keyes shakes his head suddenly.

KEYES. No. That couldn't be it. You delivered the policy to him personally, didn't you, Walter? And you got his check.

NEFF (*stiff-lipped, but his voice is as well under control as he can manage*). Sure, I did.

KEYES (*prodding his stomach again*). Got any bicarbonate of soda?

NEFF. No, I haven't.

KEYES (*resuming his pacing*). Listen, Walter. I've been living with this little man for twenty-six years. He's never failed me yet. There's got to be something wrong.

NEFF. Maybe Norton was right. Maybe it was suicide, Keyes.

KEYES. No. Not suicide.—But not accident either.

NEFF. What else?

There is another longer pause, agonizing for Neff. Finally Keyes continues:

KEYES. Look. A man takes out an accident policy that is worth a hundred thousand dollars, if he is killed on a train. Then, two weeks later, he *is* killed on a train. And not in a train accident, mind you, but falling off some silly observation car. Do you know what the mathematical probability of that is, Walter? One out of I don't know how many billions. And add to that the broken leg. It just can't be the way it looks, Walter. Something has been worked on us.

NEFF. Such as what?

Keyes doesn't answer. He goes on pacing up and down. Finally Neff can't stand the silence any longer.

NEFF. Murder?

KEYES (*prodding his stomach again*). Don't you have any peppermint or anything?

NEFF. I'm sorry. (*After a pause*) Who do you suspect?

KEYES. Maybe I like to make things easy for myself. But I always tend to suspect the beneficiary.

NEFF. The wife?

KEYES. Yeah. That wide-eyed dame that ·didn't know anything about anything.

NEFF. You're crazy, Keyes. She wasn't even on the train.

KEYES. I know she wasn't, Walter. I don't claim to know how it was worked, or who worked it, but I know that it *was* worked. (*He crosses to the corridor door.*) I've got to get to a drug store. It feels like a hunk of concrete inside me.

As he puts his hand on the knob to open the door, the scene cuts to the CORRIDOR. The lighted hallway is empty except for Phyllis who has been standing close to the door of Neff's apartment, listening. The door has just started to open. Phyllis moves away quickly and flattens herself against the wall behind the opening door. Keyes is coming out.

KEYES. Good night, Walter.

Neff, behind him, looks anxiously down the hallway for Phyllis. Suddenly his eye catches a glimpse of her through the crack of the partly opened door. He pushes the door wide so as to hide her from Keyes.

NEFF. Good night, Keyes.

KEYES. See you at the office in the morning. (*He has reached the elevator. He pushes the call button and turns.*) But I'd like to move in on her right now, tonight, if it wasn't for Norton and his stripe-pants ideas about company policy. I'd have the cops after her so quick her head would spin. They'd put her through the wringer, and, brother, what they would squeeze out.

NEFF. Only you haven't got a single thing to go on, Keyes.

KEYES (*as the elevator comes up and stops*). Not too much. Twenty-six years experience, all the percentage there is, and this lump of concrete in my stomach.

He pulls back the elevator door and turns to Neff with one last glance of annoyance.

KEYES (*almost angrily*). No bicarbonate of soda.

Keyes gets into the elevator. The door closes. The elevator goes. down.—Neff stands numb, looking at the spot where Keyes was last visible. Without moving his eyes he pulls the door around toward him with his left hand. Phyllis slowly comes , out.—Neff motions quickly to her to go into the apartment. She crosses in front of him and enters. He steps in backwards after her.

NEFF'S APARTMENT: Phyllis has come a few steps into the room. Neff, backing in after her, closes the door from inside and turns slowly. They look at each other for a long moment in complete silence.

PHYLLIS. How much does he know?

NEFF. It's not what he knows. It's those stinking hunches of his.

PHYLLIS. But he can't prove anything, can he?

NEFF. Not if we're careful. Not if we don't see each other for a while.

PHYLLIS. For how long a while? (*She moves toward him but he does not respond.*)

NEFF. Until all this dies down. You don't know Keyes the way I do. Once he gets his teeth into something he won't let go. He'll investigate you. He'll have you shadowed. He'll watch you every minute from now on. Are you afraid, baby?

PHYLLIS. Yes, I'm afraid. But not of Keyes. I'm afraid of us. We're not the same any more. We did it so we could be together, but instead of that it's pulling us apart. Isn't it, Walter?

NEFF. What are you talking about?

PHYLLIS. And you don't really care whether we see each other or not.

NEFF. Shut up, baby.

He pulls her close and kisses her as the scene fades out.

# PART FOUR

The ANTEROOM of the INSURANCE OFFICE fades in. Two telephone operators and a receptionist are at work. Several visitors are waiting in chairs. Lola Dietrichson is one of them. She's wearing a simple black suit and hat, indicating mourning. Her fingers nervously pick at a handkerchief and her eyes are watching the elevator doors anxiously. (Now and then the telephone operators in the background are heard saying, "Pacific All-Risk. Good Afternoon.")—The elevator comes up and the doors open. Several people come out, among them Neff, carrying his briefcase. Lola sees him and stands up, and, as he is about to pass through the anteroom without recognizing her, she stops him.

LOLA. Hello, Mr. Neff.

NEFF (*looking at her, a little startled*). Hello— (*His voice hangs in the air.*)

LOLA. Lola Dietrichson. Don't you remember me?

NEFF (*on his guard*). Yes. Of course.

LOLA. Could I talk to you, just for a few minutes? Somewhere where we can be alone?

NEFF. Sure. Come on into my office.

He pushes the swing door open and holds it for her. As she passes in front of him his eyes narrow in uneasy speculation.—This cuts to the twelfth floor BALCONY as Neff comes up level with Lola and leads her toward his office.

NEFF. Is it something to do with—what happened?

LOLA. Yes, Mr. Neff. It's about my father's death.

NEFF. I'm terribly sorry, Miss Dietrichson.

He opens the door of his office and

holds it for her. She enters and the scene cuts to the interior of NEFF's OFFICE where Lou Schwartz, one of the other salesmen, is working at his desk.

NEFF (*to Schwartz*). Lou, do you mind if I use the office alone for a few minutes?

SCHWARTZ. It's all yours, Walter.

He gets up and goes out. Lola has walked over to the window and is looking out so Schwartz won't stare at her. Neff places a chair beside his desk.

NEFF. Won't you sit down?

At the sound of the closing door she turns and speaks with a catch in her voice.

LOLA. Mr. Neff, I can't help it, but I have such a strange feeling that there is something queer about my father's death.

NEFF. Queer? Queer in what way?

LOLA. I don't know why I should be bothering you with my troubles, except that you knew my father and knew about the insurance he took out. And you were so nice to me that evening in your car.

NEFF. Sure. We got along fine, didn't we.

He sits down. His face is grim and watchful.

LOLA. Look at me, Mr. Neff. I'm not crazy. I'm not hysterical. I'm not even crying. But I have the awful feeling that something is wrong, and I had the same feeling once before—when my mother died.

NEFF. When your mother died?

LOLA. We were up at Lake Arrowhead. That was six years ago. We had a cabin there. It was winter and

very cold and my mother was very sick with pneumonia. She had a nurse with her. There were just the three of us in the cabin. One night I got up and went into my mother's room. She was delirious with fever. All the bed covers were on the floor and the windows were wide open. The nurse wasn't in the room. I ran and covered my mother up as quickly as I could. Just then I heard a door open behind me. The nurse stood there. She didn't say a word, but there was a look in her eyes I'll never forget. Two days later my mother was dead. (*After a pause*) Do you know who that nurse was?

Neff stares at her tensely. He knows only too well who the nurse was.

NEFF. No. Who?

LOLA. Phyllis. I tried to tell my father, but I was just a kid then and he wouldn't listen to me. Six months later she married him and I kind of talked myself out of the idea that she could have done anything like that. But now it's all back again, now that something has happened to my father, too.

NEFF. You're not making sense, Miss Dietrichson. Your father fell off a train.

LOLA. Yes, and two days before he fell off that train what was Phyllis doing? She was in her room in front of a mirror, with a black hat on, and she was pinning a black veil to it, as if she couldn't wait to see how she would look in mourning.

NEFF. Look. You've had a pretty bad shock. Aren't you just imagining all this?

LOLA. I caught her eyes in the mirror, and they had that look in them they had before my mother died. That same look.

NEFF. You don't like your step-mother, do you? Isn't it just because she *is* your step-mother?

LOLA. I loathe her. Because she did it. She did it for the money. Only you're not going to pay her, are you, Mr. Neff? She's not going to get away with it this time. I'm going to speak up. I'm going to tell everything I know.

NEFF. You'd better be careful, saying things like that.

LOLA. I'm not afraid. You'll see.

She turns again to the window so he won't see that she is crying. Neff gets up and goes to her.

LOLA. I'm sorry. I didn't mean to act like this.

NEFF. All this that you've been telling me—who else have you told?

LOLA. No one.

NEFF. How about your step-mother?

LOLA. Of course not. I'm not living in the house any more. I moved out.

NEFF. And you didn't tell that boy-friend of yours? Zachette.

LOLA. I'm not seeing him any more. We had a fight.

NEFF. Where are you living then?

LOLA. I got myself a little apartment in Hollywood.

NEFF. Four walls, and you just sit and look at them, huh?

LOLA (*turning from the window with a pathetic little nod; through her tears*). Yes, Mr. Neff.

The scene dissolves to LA GOLONDRINA at night. In the foreground, Neff and Lola are having dinner. In the background the usual activity of Olvera Street—sidewalk peddlers, guitar players, etc.—This dissolves to NEFF'S COUPE. Neff and Lola are driving along the beach near Santa Monica. Neff is wearing a light summer suit, very much in contrast to Lola's mourning. Apparently she is telling him a story and now and then she laughs, but there is no sound. (The view moves past her to a closeup of Neff behind the steering wheel.) He is only half listening to Lola. His mind is full of other thoughts.

NEFF'S VOICE (*synchronized with the above scene*). So I took her to dinner that evening at a Mexican joint down on Olvera Street where nobody would see us. I wanted to cheer her up . . . Next day was Sunday and we went for a ride down to the beach. She had loosened up a bit and she was even laughing . . . I had to make sure she wouldn't tell that stuff about Phyllis to anybody else. It was dynamite, whether it was true or not. And I had no chance to talk to Phyllis. You were watching her like a hawk, Keyes. I couldn't even phone her for fear you had the wires tapped.

This dissolves to the INSURANCE OFFICE as Neff, with his hat on and no brief-case, is walking toward Keyes' office. As he comes up close to the door, he stops with a startled expression on his face. On a chair beside the door sits a familiar figure. He is Jackson, the man from the observation platform of the train. He is wearing his Stetson hat and smoking a cigar. He is studying something in the file folder. Neff recognizes him immediately but Jackson does not look up. Neff controls his expression and goes on to open the door to Keyes' office.

NEFF'S VOICE (*over the above scene*).

Monday morning there was a note on my desk that you wanted to see me, Keyes. For a minute I wondered if it could be about Lola. It was worse. Outside your door was the last guy in the world I wanted to see.

Inside KEYES' OFFICE: Neff is just closing the door from the inside. Keyes, his coat off, is lying on his office couch, chewing on a cigar, as usual.

KEYES. Come in. Come in, Walter. I want to ask you something. After all the years we've known each other, do you mind if I make a rather blunt statement?

NEFF. About what?

KEYES. About me. Walter, I'm a very great man. This Dietrichson business. It's murder, and murders don't come any neater. As fancy a piece of homicide as anybody ever ran into. Smart and tricky and almost perfect, *but—* (*bouncing off the couch like a rubber ball*) —but, I think Papa has it all figured out, figured out and wrapped up in tissue paper with pink ribbons on it.

NEFF. I'm listening.

KEYES (*levelling a finger at him*). You know what? That guy Dietrichson was never on the train.

NEFF. He wasn't?

KEYES. No, he wasn't, Walter. Look, you can't be sure of killing a man by throwing him off a train that's going fifteen miles an hour. The only way you can be sure is to kill him first and then throw his body on the tracks. That would mean either killing him on the train, or—and this is where it really gets fancy—you kill him somewhere else and put him on the tracks. Two possibilities, and I personally buy the second.

NEFF. You're way ahead of me, Keyes.

KEYES. Look, it was like this. They killed the guy—the wife and somebody else—and then the somebody else took the crutches and went on the train as Dietrichson, and then the somebody else jumped off, and then they put the body on the tracks where the train had passed. An impersonation, see. And a cinch to work. Because it was night, very few people were about, they had the crutches to stare at, and they never really looked at the man at all.

NEFF. It's fancy all right, Keyes. Maybe it's a little too fancy.

KEYES. Is it? I tell you it fits together like a watch. And now let's see what we have in the way of proof. The only guy that really got a good look at this supposed Dietrichson is sitting right outside my office. I took the trouble to bring him down here from Oregon. Let's see what he has to say. (*Keyes goes to the door and opens it.*) Come in, Mr. Jackson.

JACKSON (*entering with the file folder*). Yes sir, Mr. Keyes. These are fine cigars you smoke. (*He indicates the cigar he himself is smoking.*)

KEYES. Two for a quarter.

JACKSON. That's what I said.

KEYES. Never mind the cigar, Jackson. Did you study those photographs? What do you say?

JACKSON. Yes, indeed, I studied them thoroughly. Very thoroughly.

KEYES. Well? Did you make up your mind?

JACKSON. Mr. Keyes, I'm a Medford man. Medford, Oregon. Up in Medford we take out time making up our minds—

KEYES. Well you're not in Medford now. I'm in a hurry. Let's have it.

JACKSON (*indicating the file folder he is holding*). Are these photographs of the late Mr. Dietrichson?

KEYES. Yes.

JACKSON. Then my answer is no.

KEYES. What do you mean no?

JACKSON. I mean this is not the man that was on the train.

KEYES. Will you swear to that?

JACKSON. I'm a Medford man. Medford, Oregon. And if I say it, I mean it, and if I mean it, of course I'll swear it.

KEYES. Thank you. (*Turning to Neff*) There you are, Walter. There's your proof. (*Keyes remembers he forgot to introduce Jackson.*) Oh, Mr. Jackson, this is Mr. Neff, one of our salesmen.

JACKSON. Pleased to meet you, Mr. Neff. Pleased indeed.

NEFF. How do you do?

JACKSON. Very fine, thank you. Never was better.

KEYES. Mr. Jackson, how would you describe the man you saw on that observation platform?

JACKSON. Well, I'm pretty sure he was a younger man, about ten or fifteen years younger than the man in these photographs.

KEYES. Dietrichson was about fifty, wasn't he, Walter?

NEFF. Fifty-one, according to the policy.

JACKSON. The man I saw was nothing like fifty-one years old. Of course, it was pretty dark on that platform and, come to think of it, he tried to keep his back toward me. But I'm positive just the same.

KEYES. That's fine, Jackson. Now you understand this matter is strictly confidential. We may need you again down here in Los Angeles, if the case comes to court.

JACKSON. Any time you need me, I'm at your entire disposal, gentlemen. Expenses paid, of course.

KEYES (*picking up the telephone on his desk and speaking into it*). Get me Lubin, in the cashier's office.

Meanwhile, Jackson crosses over to Neff and, during the ensuing dialogue between him and Neff, we hear Keyes' low voice on the phone in the background. We do not hear what he says.

JACKSON (*to Neff*). Ever been in Medford, Mr. Neff?

NEFF. Never.

JACKSON. Wait a minute. Do you go trout fishing? Maybe I saw you up Klamath Falls way.

NEFF. Nope. Never fish.

JACKSON. Neff. Neff. I've got it! It's the name. There's a family of Neffs in Corvallis.

NEFF. No relation.

JACKSON. Let me see. This man's an automobile dealer in Corvallis. Very reputable man, too, I'm told.

KEYES (*rejoining them at this point*). All right, Mr. Jackson. Suppose you go down to the cashier's office—room twenty-seven on the eleventh floor. They'll take care of your expense account and your ticket for the train tonight.

JACKSON. Tonight? Tomorrow morning would suit me better. There's a very good osteopath down here I want to see before I leave.

KEYES (*having opened the door for Jackson*). Okay, Mr. Jackson. Just don't put her on the expense account.

JACKSON (*doesn't get it*). Goodbye, gentlemen. A pleasure. (*He goes out.*)

KEYES. There it is, Walter. It's beginning to come apart at the seams already. A murder's never perfect. It always comes apart sooner or later. And when two people are involved it's usually sooner. We know the Dietrichson dame is in it, and somebody else. Pretty soon we're going to know who that somebody else is. He'll show. He's got to show. Sometime, somewhere, they've got to meet. Their emotions are all kicked up. Whether it's love or hate doesn't matter. They can't keep away from each other. They think it's twice as safe because there are two of them. But it's not twice as safe. It's ten times twice as dangerous. They've committed a murder and that's not like taking a trolley ride together where each one can get off at a different stop. They're stuck with each other. They've got to ride all the way to the end of the line. And it's a one-way trip, and the last stop is the cemetery. (*He puts a cigar in his mouth and starts tapping his pockets for matches.*) She put in her claim and I'm going to throw it right back at her. (*Patting his pockets again*) Have you got one of those?

Neff strikes a match for him. Keyes takes the match out of his hand and lights his cigar.

KEYES. Let her sue us if she dares. I'll be ready for her—and that somebody else. They'll be digging their own graves.

The scene dissolves to a TELEPHONE BOOTH in Jerry's market. Neff is in the booth dialing a number, and as he waits he looks around to make sure he is not watched.

NEFF (*into the phone*). Mrs. Dietrichson? . . . This is Jerry's market. We just got in a shipment of that English soap you were asking about. Will you be coming by this morning? . . . Thank you, Mrs. Dietrichson. (*Neff hangs up.*)

This dissolves to the exterior of JERRY'S MARKET. The LaSalle stops in front of the market. Phyllis steps out and goes into the market, looking around. Then we see the SHELVES in the rear of the market.

Neff is moving slowly along them, outwardly calm but with his nerves on edge. From beyond him Phyllis approaches. She stops beside him, facing the same way, with a couple of feet separating them.

PHYLLIS. Hello, Walter.

NEFF (*in a harsh whisper*). Come closer.

PHYLLIS (*moving closer to him*). What's the matter?

NEFF. Everything's the matter. Keyes is rejecting your claim. He's sitting back with his mouth watering, waiting for you to sue. He wants you to sue. But you're not going to.

PHYLLIS. What's he got to stop me?

NEFF. He's got the goods. He's figured out how it was worked. He knows it was somebody else on the train. He's dug up a witness he thinks will prove it.

PHYLLIS. Prove it how? Listen, if he rejects that claim, I *have* to sue.

NEFF. Yeah? And then you're in court and a lot of other things are going to come up. Like, for instance, about you and the first Mrs. Dietrichson.

PHYLLIS *(looking at him sharply)*. What about me and the first Mrs. Dietrichson?

NEFF. The way she died. And about that black hat you were trying on— before you needed a black hat.

A customer comes along the aisle toward them. They move apart. The customer passes. Phyllis draws close again.

PHYLLIS. Walter, Lola's been telling you some of her cockeyed stories. She's been seeing you.

NEFF. I've been seeing her, if you want to know. So she won't yell her head off about what *she* knows.

PHYLLIS. Yes, she's been putting on an act for you, crying all over your shoulder, that lying little—

NEFF. Keep her out of it. All I'm telling you is we're not going to sue.

PHYLLIS. Because you don't want the money any more, even if you could get it? Because she's made you feel like a heel all of a sudden.

NEFF. It isn't the money any more. It's our necks now. We're pulling out, understand.

PHYLLIS. Because of what Keyes can do? You're not fooling me, Walter. It's because of Lola. What you did

to her father. You can't take it that she might find out some day.

NEFF. I said, leave her out of it.

PHYLLIS. Walter, it's me I'm talking about. *I* don't want to be left out of it.

NEFF. Stop saying that. It's just that it hasn't worked out the way we wanted. We can't have the money. We can't go through with it, that's all.

PHYLLIS. We have gone through with it, Walter. The tough part is all behind us. We just have to hold on now and not go soft inside, and stick together, close, the way we started out.

Phyllis takes his arm, forgetting where she is. He pulls away.

NEFF. Watch it, will you. Someone's coming.

One of the market help, pushing a small hand-truck loaded with packaged goods, comes along the aisle. He stops and begins to restock a shelf very close to Neff and Phyllis. They go off slowly in opposite directions. The view moves with Neff as he walks toward another shelf, one that stands away from the wall. Phyllis appears on the opposite side of the shelf and stops, facing him. They now continue their low-voiced dialogue through the piled-up merchandise.

PHYLLIS. I loved you, Walter. And I hated him. But I wasn't going to do anything about it, not until I met you. It was you had the plan. I only wanted him dead.

NEFF. Yeah, and I was the one that fixed him so he was dead. Is that what you're telling me?

Phyllis takes off her dark glasses for the first time and looks at him with cold, hard eyes.

PHYLLIS. Yes. And nobody's pulling out. We went into it together, and we're coming out at the end together. It's straight down the line for both of us, remember.

Phyllis puts the glasses on again and goes out.

This dissolves to NEFF's OFFICE where Neff is dictating into the dictaphone.

NEFF. Yeah, I remembered it all right. Just as I remembered what you had told me, Keyes, about that trolley car ride, and how there was no way to get off until the end of the line, where the cemetery was. And I got to thinking what cemeteries are for. They're to put dead people in. I guess that was the first time I ever thought about Phyllis that way. Dead, I mean, and how things would be if she was dead. Because the way it was now she had me by the throat. She could hang me higher than a kite any day she felt like it. And there was nothing I could do, except hold my breath and watch that day come closer and closer, and maybe pray a little, if I still knew how to pray . . . I saw Lola three or four times that week. I guess it sounds crazy, Keyes, after what I had done, but it was only with her that I could relax and let go a little. Then one night we drove up into the hills above Hollywood Bowl . . .

This dissolves to HOLLYWOOD HILLS. Neff and Lola are climbing over a low hill in the foreground. The sky is starlit and music from the Bowl comes over the scene from below. As he helps her climb up, the view moves with them and shows the expanse of the

Bowl below, a packed audience, and the orchestra on the lighted shell. They sit down on the grass. Neff sits near her, not too close. It is very dark and they are silhouetted against the shell lights. Neff puts a cigarette in his mouth and strikes a match. The flame lights up Lola's face. Neff glances at her. She is crying. He lights his cigarette and blows out the match. A pause follows.

NEFF. Why are you crying? (*As Lola doesn't answer*) You won't tell me?

LOLA (*in a choked voice*). Of course I will, Walter. I wouldn't tell anybody else but you. It's about Nino.

NEFF. Zachette? What about him?

LOLA. They killed my father together. He and Phyllis. He helped her do it. I know he did.

NEFF. What makes you say that?

LOLA. I've been following him. He's at her house, night after night. It was Phyllis and him all the time. Maybe he was going with me just for a blind. And the night of the murder—

NEFF. You promised not to talk that way any more.

LOLA. —he was supposed to pick me up after a lecture at U.C.L.A.—but he never showed up. He said he was sick. Sick! He couldn't show up, because the train was leaving with my father on it. (*She begins to cry again.*) Maybe I'm just crazy. Maybe it's all just in my mind.

NEFF. Sure, it's all in your mind.

LOLA. I only wish it was, Walter, because I still love him.

Over Neff's face, as he listens to the music comes the dictation:

NEFF's VOICE. Zachette. That's funny. Phyllis and Zachette. What was he doing up at her house? I couldn't figure that one out. I tried to make sense out of it and got nowhere. But the real brain-twister came the next day. You sprang it on me, Keyes, after office hours, when you caught me down in the lobby of the building.

This dissolves to the LOBBY of the Pacific Building, about 5:00 P.M. or a little later. A stream of office employees is coming out of an elevator; a second elevator reaches the lobby and some more office employees come out, among them Neff, wearing his hat and carrying his briefcase. The view precedes him as he walks toward the entrance doors. He is stopped by Keyes' voice, off to one side.

KEYES' VOICE. Oh, Walter, just a minute.

Neff stops and looks toward the cigar counter, as he moves toward him. Keyes is standing there buying cigars. He is stuffing them into his pockets.

NEFF. Hello, Keyes.

KEYES. Hang onto your hat, Walter.

NEFF. What for?

KEYES. Nothing much. The Dietrichson case just busted wide open.

NEFF. How do you mean?

KEYES. The guy showed. That's how.

NEFF. The somebody else?

KEYES. Yeah. The guy that did it with her.

NEFF. No kidding?

KEYES. She's filed suit against us, and it's okay by me. When we get into that courtroom I'll tear them apart,

both of them. Come on—I'll buy you a martini.

NEFF. No thanks, Keyes.

KEYES. With two olives.

NEFF. I've got to get a shave and a shoeshine. I've got a date.

KEYES. Margie. I still bet she drinks from the bottle.

He bites off the end of the cigar and puts the cigar into his mouth. He starts tapping his pockets for a match, as usual. Neff strikes a match for him.

NEFF. They give you matches when they sell you cigars, Keyes. All you have to do is ask for them.

KEYES. I don't like them. They always explode in my pockets. So long, Walter.

Keyes goes toward the street and out of the scene. Neff moves back into the lobby. As he reaches the elevator, he looks back over his shoulder, to make sure Keyes is gone, then steps into the empty elevator.

NEFF (*entering the elevator*). Twelve.

This dissolves to the ENTRANCE of the office on the 12TH FLOOR as Neff comes out of the elevator. The receptionist is just tidying up her desk. She has her hat on and is preparing to leave. Neff passes on through the swinging doors to the twelfth floor balcony.—This cuts to the 12TH FLOOR BALCONY as Neff enters from the reception room. A couple of belated employees are leaving for the day. Neff goes toward Keyes' office, looks around to make sure he is unobserved, and enters.

KEYES' OFFICE: Neff has just come in. He goes over to Keyes' desk and searches the papers on it. He tries the desk drawers and finds them locked.

His eye falls on the dictaphone on the stand beside the desk. A record is on it, the needle is about two thirds of the way toward the end. He lifts the needle and sets it back to the beginning of the record, sets the switch to play-back position. He lifts the arm off the bracket and starts the machine. Keyes voice is heard coming from the horn:

KEYES' VOICE. Memo to Mr. Norton. Confidential. Dietrichson File. With regard to your proposal to put Walter Neff under surveillance, I disagree absolutely. I have investigated his movements on the night of the crime, and he is definitely placed in his apartment from 7:15 P.M. on. In addition to this, I have known Neff intimately for eleven years, and I personally vouch for him, without reservation . . . .

Neff stops the machine. He sits down slowly, still holding the horn. He is deeply moved. After a moment, he presses the switch again.

KEYES' VOICE (*from the dictaphone*). . . . . Furthermore, no connection whatsoever has been established between Walter Neff and Mrs. Phyllis Dietrichson, whereas I am now able to report that such a connection has been established between her and another man. This man has been observed to visit the Dietrichson home on the night of July 9th, 10th, 11th, 12th and 13th. We have succeeded in identifying him as one Nino Zachette, former medical student, aged twenty-eight, residing at Lilac Court Apartments, 1228½ N. La Brea Avenue. We have checked Zachette's movements on the night of the crime and have found that they cannot be accounted for. I am preparing a more detailed report for your consideration and it is my belief

that we already have sufficient evidence against Zachette and Mrs. Dietrichson to justify police action. I strongly urge that this whole matter be turned over to the office of the District Attorney. Respectfully, Barton Keyes.

Neff sits, staring blankly at the wall. The cylinder goes on revolving, but no more voice comes—only the whir of the needle on the empty record. At last he remembers to replace the horn. He hangs it back on its hook. The machine stops. Neff gets up from the chair, walks slowly to the door and goes out.

We see the 12TH FLOOR BALCONY as Neff comes out of Keyes' office. He walks slowly back toward the reception room entrance, then stands there looking out through the glass doors. All the employees have now left. Neff is entirely alone. He moves as if to go out, then stops rigidly as his face lights up with excitement at a sudden idea. He turns quickly and walks on to his own office and enters.—Then NEFF'S OFFICE comes into view as Neff walks across to his desk, lifts the telephone and dials a number. (During the ensuing telephone conversation, only what he says is heard. The pauses indicate speeches at the other end of the line).

NEFF. Phyllis? Walter. I've got to see you . . . Tonight . . . Yes, it has to be tonight . . . How's eleven o'clock? Don't worry about Keyes. He's satisfied . . . Leave the door on the latch and put the lights out. No, nobody's watching the house . . . I told you Keyes is satisfied. It's just for the neighbors . . . That's what I said. Yeah. Eleven o'clock. Goodbye, baby.

Neff hangs up and stands beside the desk with a grim expression on his face, takes a handkerchief out and wipes perspiration from his forehead and the palms of his hands. The gesture has a symbolic quality, as if he were trying to wipe away the murder.

NEFF'S VOICE. I guess I don't have to tell you what I was going to do at eleven o'clock, Keyes. For the first time I saw a way to get clear of the whole mess I was in, and of Phyllis, too, all at the same time. Yeah, that's what I thought. But what I didn't know was that she was all set for me. That she had outsmarted me again, just like she always had . . .

This dissolves to the HALL STAIRWAY of the DIETRICHSON HOME at night. The lights are turned on. Phyllis is coming down the stairs. She wears white lounging pajamas, and she is carrying something small and heavy concealed in a scarf in her right hand. She reaches the front door, opens it slightly, fixes the catch so that the door can be opened from the outside. She switches off the porch light and the hall light. She moves toward the living room, where there is still a light on.

NEFF'S VOICE. She was all set and waiting for me. It could have been something in my voice when I called her up that tipped her off. And it could have been that she had the idea already. And an idea wasn't the only thing she had waiting for me.

The scene cuts to the LIVING ROOM. On the long table behind the davenport, one of the lamps is lit. The only other light in the room is a standing lamp beside the desk. A window toward the back is open, and through it comes the sound of music, probably a neighboring radio.—Phyllis enters and crosses to the table. She puts out the lamp, then moves over to the desk and puts out the lamp there. The room is filled with bright moonlight coming in at the windows.—Phyllis crosses to the chair by the fireplace (the one she sat in the first time Neff came to the house). She lifts the loose cushion and puts what was in the scarf behind it. As she withdraws the scarf, there is a brief glint of something metallic before she covers the hidden object with the cushion again.—She turns to the low table in front of the davenport and takes a cigarette from the box. She takes a match and is about to strike it when, just then, she hears a car coming up the hill. She listens, motionless. The car stops. A car door is slammed.—Calmly, Phyllis strikes the match and lights her cigarette. She drops the match casually into a tray, goes back to the chair, sits down and waits, quietly smoking. There are footsteps outside the house.—Over the chair in which Phyllis is sitting the hallway is visible through the arch. The front door opens. Neff comes in. He is silhouetted against the moonlight as he stands there. He closes the door again.

PHYLLIS (*in the foreground*). In here, Walter.

Neff comes through the arch and walks slowly toward her.

NEFF. Hello, baby. Anybody else in the house?

PHYLLIS. Nobody. Why?

NEFF. What's that music?

PHYLLIS. A radio up the street.

NEFF (*sitting down on the arm of the davenport, close to her*). Just like the first time I was here. We were talking about automobile insurance. Only you were thinking about murder. And I was thinking about that anklet.

PHYLLIS. And what are you thinking about now?

NEFF. I'm all through thinking. This is goodbye.

PHYLLIS. Goodbye? Where are you going?

NEFF. It's you that's going, baby. Not me. I'm getting off the trolley car right at this corner.

PHYLLIS. Suppose you stop being fancy. Let's have it, whatever it is.

NEFF. I have a friend who's got a funny theory. He says when two people commit a murder they're kind of on a trolley car, and one can't get off without the other. They're stuck with each other. They have to go on riding clear to the end of the line. And the last stop is the cemetery.

PHYLLIS. Maybe he's got something there.

NEFF. You bet he has. Two people are going to ride to the end of the line, all right. Only I'm not going to be one of them. I've got another guy to finish my ride for me.

PHYLLIS. So you've got it all arranged, Walter.

NEFF. You arranged it for me. I didn't have to do a thing.

PHYLLIS. Just who are you talking about?

NEFF. An acquaintance of yours. A Mr. Zachette. Come on, baby, I just got into this because I knew a little something about insurance, didn't I? I was just a sucker. I'd have been brushed-off as soon as you got your hands on the money.

PHYLLIS. What are you talking about?

NEFF. Save it. I'm telling this. It's been you and that Zachette guy all along, hasn't it?

PHYLLIS. That's not true.

NEFF. It doesn't make any difference whether it's true or not. The point is Keyes believes Zachette is the guy he's been looking for. He'll have him in the gas chamber before he knows what happened to him.

PHYLLIS. And what's happening to me all this time?

NEFF. Don't be silly. What do you expect to happen to you? You helped him do the murder, didn't you? That's what Keyes thinks. And what's good enough for Keyes is good enough for me.

PHYLLIS. Maybe it's not good enough for me, Walter. Maybe I don't go for the idea. Maybe I'd rather talk.

NEFF. Sometimes people are where they can't talk. Under six feet of dirt, for instance. And if it was you, they'd just charge it up to Zachette, wouldn't they. One more item on his account. Sure they would. That's just what they're going to do. Especially since he's coming here tonight . . . Oh, in about fifteen minutes from now, baby. With the cops right behind him. It's all taken care of.

PHYLLIS. And that'd make everything lovely for you, wouldn't it?

NEFF. Right. And it's got to be done before that suit of yours comes to trial, and Lola gets a chance to sound off, and they trip you up on the stand, and you start to fold up and drag me down with you.

PHYLLIS. Listen, Walter. Maybe I had Zachette here so they won't get a chance to trip me up. So we can get that money and be together.

NEFF. That's cute. Say it again.

PHYLLIS. He came here the first time just to ask where Lola was. I made him come back. I was working on him. He's a crazy sort of guy, quick-tempered. I kept hammering into him that she was with another man, so he'd get into one of his jealous rages, and then I'd tell him where she was. And you know what he'd have done to her, don't you, Walter.

NEFF. Yeah, and for once I believe you. Because it's just rotten enough.

PHYLLIS. We're both rotten, Walter.

NEFF. Only you're just a little more rotten. You're rotten clear through. You got me to take care of your husband, and then you got Zachette to take care of Lola, and maybe take care of me too, and then somebody else would have come along to take care of Zachette for you. That's the way you operate isn't it, baby?

PHYLLIS. Suppose it is, Walter. Is what you've cooked up for tonight any better?

NEFF (*getting up from the davenport, listening to the music for a moment*). I don't like this music anymore. It's too close. Do you mind if I shut the window?

Phyllis just stares at him. He goes quietly over to the window and shuts it and draws the curtain. Phyllis speaks to his back:

PHYLLIS (*her voice low and urgent*). Walter!

Neff turns; something changes in his face. There is the report of a gun. He stands motionless for a moment, then very slowly starts toward her. Phyllis stands with the gun in her hand. Neff stops after he has taken a few steps.

NEFF. What's the matter? Why don't you shoot again? Maybe if I came a little closer? (*Taking a few more*

*steps toward her and stopping again*) How's that. Do you think you can do it now?

Phyllis is silent. She doesn't shoot. Her expression is tortured. Neff goes on until he is close to her. Quietly he takes the gun out of her unresisting hand.

NEFF. Why didn't you shoot, baby? (*In reply Phyllis puts her arms around him in complete surrender.*) Don't tell me it's because you've been in love with me all this time.

PHYLLIS. No. I never loved you, Walter. Not you, or anybody else. I'm rotten to the heart. I used you, just as you said. That's all you ever meant to me—until a minute ago. I didn't think anything like that could ever happen to me.

NEFF. I'm sorry, baby. I'm not buying.

PHYLLIS. I'm not asking you to buy. Just hold me close.

Neff draws her close to him. She reaches up to his face and kisses him on the lips. As she comes out of the kiss there is realization in her eyes that this is the final moment.

NEFF. Goodbye, baby.

Out of sight the gun explodes once, twice. Phyllis quivers in his arms. Her eyes fill with tears. Her head falls limp against his shoulder. Slowly he lifts her and carries her to the davenport. He lays her down on it carefully, almost tenderly. The moonlight coming in at the French doors shines on the anklet. He looks at it for the last time and slowly turns away. As he does so, he puts his hand inside his coat and it comes out with blood on it. Only then is it apparent that Phyllis' shot actually did hit him. He looks at the blood on his fingers with a dazed expression and quickly goes out of the room, the way he came.

And now Neff comes out of the DIET-RICHSON HOME. He closes the front door with his right hand. His left arm hangs limp. He takes a few steps down the walk, then suddenly hears somebody approaching. He moves behind the palm tree near the walk.

A man comes up the steps toward the front door—Zachette. Just as he reaches the door, Neff calls to him.

NEFF. Hey you. Come here a minute. I said come here, Zachette. (*Zachette turns and approaches him slowly.*) The name is Neff.

ZACHETTE. Yeah? And I still don't like it. What do you want?

NEFF. Look, kid, I want to give you a present. (*He takes some loose change out of his pocket and holds out a coin.*) Here's a nice new nickel.

ZACHETTE. What's the gag?

NEFF. Suppose you go back down the hill to a drug store and make a phone call.

Neff starts to drop the nickel into Zachette's handkerchief pocket. Zachette knocks his hand away.

ZACHETTE. Keep your nickel and buy yourself an ice cream cone.

NEFF. The number is Granite 0386. Ask for Miss Dietrichson. The first name is Lola.

ZACHETTE. Lola? She isn't worth a nickel. And if I ever talk to her, it's not going to be over any telephone.

NEFF. Tough, aren't you? Take the nickel. Take it and call her. She wants you to.

ZACHETTE. Yeah? She doesn't want any part of me.

NEFF. I know who told you that, and it's not true. She's in love with you. Always has been. Don't ask me why. I couldn't even guess.

Zachette just stares at him. Neff moves again to put the nickel into Zachette's pocket. This time Zachette allows him to do it.

NEFF. Now beat it. Granite 0386, I told you. (*He motions toward the street below.*) That way.

Zachette goes slowly past him. Neff grabs him and pushes him almost violently down the walk. Zachette goes out of view. The sound of his steps dies away as Neff looks after him, and, far off in the distance, the siren of a police car is heard. Then Neff moves off through the shrubbery toward the side of the house where he parked his car.

This dissolves to NEFF'S OFFICE at night. The desk lamp is still lighted; outside the windows, the dawn is slowly breaking. Neff is still clutching the horn of the dictaphone. There are eight or nine used cylinders on the desk beside him. A widening stain of blood shows on the left shoulder of his gray jacket. He is very weak by now, and his voice holds a note of utter exhaustion.

NEFF. It's almost four-thirty now, Keyes. It's cold. I wonder if she's still lying there alone in that house, or whether they've found her by now. I wonder a lot of things, but they don't matter any more, except I want to ask you to do me a favor. I want you to be the one to tell Lola, kind of gently, before it breaks wide open . . . Yes, and I'd like you to look after her and that guy Zachette, so he doesn't get pushed around too much. Because . . .

Suddenly he stops his dictation with an instinctive feeling that he is not alone in the room.

As he turns in his chair the view draws back slowly. The office door is wide open. Keyes is standing a few steps inside it. Behind him, on the balcony outside, stands the night watchman and the colored janitor, peering curiously into the room over Keyes' shoulder. Slowly, and without taking his eyes off Neff's face, Keyes reaches back and pushes the door shut.—*Neff hangs up the dictaphone horn. He looks at Keyes with a faint, tired grin and speaks very slowly.*

NEFF. Hello, Keyes. (*Keyes moves toward him a few steps and stands without answering.*) Up pretty early, aren't you? I always wondered what time you got down to work. (*Keyes, staring at him, still does not answer.*) Or did your little man pull you out of bed.

KEYES. The janitor did. Seems you leaked a little blood on the way in here.

NEFF. Wouldn't be surprised. (*Neff makes a motion indicating the used cylinders standing on the desk.*) I wanted to straighten out that Dietrichson story for you.

KEYES. So I gather.

NEFF. How long have you been standing there?

KEYES. Long enough.

NEFF. Kind of a crazy story with a crazy twist to it. One you didn't quite figure out.

KEYES. You can't figure them all, Walter.

NEFF. That's right. You can't, can you? And now I suppose I get the big speech, the one with all the two-dollar words in it. Let's have it, Keyes.

KEYES. You're all washed up, Walter.

NEFF. Thanks, Keyes. That was short anyway.

They stare at each other for a long moment, then, with an intense effort Neff gets up on his feet and stands there swaying a little. His face is covered with sweat. His shoulder is bleeding. He is on the verge of collapse.

KEYES. Walter, I'm going to call a doctor.

NEFF (*bitterly*). What for? So they can patch me up? So they can nurse me along till I'm back on my feet? So I can walk under my own power into that gas chamber up in San Quentin? Is that it, Keyes?

KEYES. Something like that, Walter.

NEFF. Well, I've got a different idea. Look here. Suppose you went back to bed and didn't find these cylinders till tomorrow morning, when the office opens. From then on you can play it any way you like. Would you do that much for me, Keyes?

KEYES. Give me one good reason.

NEFF. I need four hours to get where I'm going.

KEYES. You're not going anywhere, Walter.

NEFF. You bet I am. I'm going across the border.

KEYES. You haven't got a chance.

NEFF. Good enough to try for.

KEYES. You'll never make the border.

NEFF. That's what you think. Watch me.

Neff starts to move toward the door, staggering a little, holding himself upright with great effort.

KEYES (*in a voice of stony calm*). You'll never even make the elevator.

Neff has reached the door. He twists the knob and drags the door open. He turns in it to look back at Keyes' implacable face.

NEFF. So long, Keyes.

Neff goes out, leaving the door wide open. The view follows his staggering walk along the balcony toward the elevator lobby. The sound of his breathing is so harsh and loud that for a moment it dominates the scene. Finally he reaches the swing doors leading into the lobby and starts to push them open. At this moment he collapses. He clutches the edge of the door and as it swings around with him he falls to the floor. He tries to struggle up but cannot rise. In the background comes the sound of a telephone being dialed.

KEYES' VOICE. Hello . . . Send an ambulance to the Pacific Building on Olive Street . . . Yeah . . . It's a police job.

There is the sound of the phone being replaced in its cradle. Then there are footsteps growing louder along the balcony and Keyes walks slowly into view. He kneels down beside Neff.

KEYES. How you doing, Walter?

Neff manages a faint smile.

NEFF. I'm fine. Only somebody moved the elevator a couple of miles away.

KEYES. They're on their way.

NEFF (*slowly and with great difficulty*). You know why you didn't figure this one, Keyes? Let me tell you. The guy you were looking for was too close. He was right across the desk from you.

KEYES. Closer than that, Walter. (*The eyes of the two men meet in a moment of silence.*)

NEFF. I love you too.

Neff fumbles for the handkerchief in Keyes' pocket, pulls it out and clumsily wipes his face with it. The handkerchief drops from his hand. He gets a loose cigarette out of his pocket and puts it between his lips. Then with great difficulty he gets out a match, tries to strike it, but is too weak. Keyes takes the match out of his hand, strikes it for him and lights his cigarette. The scene fades out.

# A TREE GROWS IN BROOKLYN

*(A Twentieth Century–Fox Production)*

*Screenplay by* TESS SLESINGER *and* FRANK DAVIS

*Adapted from the Novel by* BETTY SMITH

*Produced by* LOUIS D. LIGHTON

*Directed by* ELIA KAZAN

## The Cast

| | |
|---|---|
| KATIE . . . . . . . . . | Dorothy McGuire |
| AUNT SISSY . . . . . . . | Joan Blondell |
| JOHNNY NOLAN . . . . . | James Dunn |
| MCSHANE . . . . . . . . | Lloyd Nolan |
| FRANCIE NOLAN . . . . | Peggy Ann Garner |
| NEELEY NOLAN . . . . . | Ted Donaldson |
| MCGARRITY . . . . . . . | James Gleason |
| MISS MCDONOUGH . . . . | Ruth Nelson |
| STEVE EDWARDS . . . . | John Alexander |
| GRANDMA ROMMELY . . | Ferike Boros |
| CARNEY . . . . . . . . | J. Farrell MacDonald |
| MRS. WATERS . . . . . | Adeline De Walt Reynolds |
| MR. SPENCER . . . . . | George Melford |
| HENNY GADDIS . . . . . | Vincent Graeff |
| FLOSSIE GADDIS . . . . . | Susan Lester |

and others

*Film Editor*—DOROTHY SPENCER

# A TREE GROWS IN BROOKLYN

## PART ONE

A short montage of current newspaper headlines fades in:

INVASION JITTERS

HEAVY CASUALTIES EXPECTED

ITALIAN FOOTHOLD THREATENED

Over these comes a woman's voice:

VOICE. One small paragraph in this morning's news of death, and blood, and tears—and a sudden wave of nostalgia swept over me. I found myself remembering sharply the Brooklyn of my childhood. And why? The paragraph had nothing to do with me, nor even with Brooklyn. It told of an American soldier in Italy, a Texas boy. They were in danger of being swept into the sea, when the soldier took from his pocket a small box and spilled its contents on the Italian earth. "That's dirt from Texas," he said. "Now I'm standing on Texas soil, let's see them push me off it." As simple as that, but infinitely deep. For that single moment I could not understand why it should take me back to Brooklyn. And then I knew. In the end, that is the true thing for which men so bravely die—not the pretentious phrases, but for that place which is their own, where grew their roots. It makes no difference where the place is. Most families have their roots in soil; we Nolans drove our roots down through the cement of the Brooklyn sidewalks—like the occasional miraculous tree—but no matter. It is all the same. Saturdays were the same, for children in Brooklyn or in Texas—we were free—free from school. There was never anything finer than the beginning of a Saturday in Brooklyn.

Over this, the headlines dissolve first to the Williamsburg Bridge, and then back through views of modern Brooklyn into the Brooklyn streets of a generation ago. We see horse-drawn beer trucks; the swinging doors of a saloon; a street sweeper; bedding piled on fire-escapes; a wooden cigar-store Indian; the tree near the Nolan tenement and finally the Nolan street and tenement.

This dissolves to the NOLAN KITCHEN. It is early Saturday morning. Katie and Francie are finishing cleaning up the breakfast dishes. Neeley is struggling in from the hall with Katie's scrubbing pail and cloths and mop. He sets them down inside the door.

KATIE, the mother of the family, is in her early thirties, still young enough to be quick and alive to life. She is attractive, but is always so busy that she never has time to pay much attention to herself. The flat is a small one, on the second floor back, sparsely furnished, but its spotlessness reflects Katie's passion for cleanliness.

FRANCIE, her daughter, is about thirteen. She is a rather quiet child. She has inherited from Johnny, her father, a sensitiveness and an imagination that make her by far the more difficult problem in parenthood for the Nolans.

NEELEY is a year younger, and is completely a normal, healthy boy. He is much more Katie's child, while Francie was born with something of both of them.

NEELEY (*setting down the bucket*). Is that all, mom, can we go now?

KATIE. Not so loud, Neeley, you want to wake papa?

NEELEY (*much quieter, to Francie*). Gosh, ain't you through with them ole dishes yet?

KATIE. She'll only be a minute. My, I wish you was as anxious to get going on a school morning as on a Saturday.

FRANCIE (*wiping the dishes*). Papa was late last night.

KATIE. I was dead asleep when he come in, I guess.

FRANCIE. He says if people didn't like to make speeches so much at dinners, waiters could spend more time with their families.

KATIE. Wasn't much of a job, I guess. Them club dinners don't tip much.

FRANCIE (*finishing*). Is that all, mama?

KATIE. Yes, yes, go on, and I'll do the rest. (*She indicates the sack Neeley has dragged out.*) Don't look like you got much in there this week.

NEELEY. One of these days Mrs. Gaddis is goin' to throw away that ole wash boiler of hers. Carney will pay us plenty for the copper bottom off of that.

KATIE. He won't pay you any more than he has to. You watch him on the weighin'.

NEELEY (*in a hurry*). Yes'm. Goodbye, mom.

KATIE. Parents ought to have a day that's like Saturday for kids. Maybe if I start in the lower hall and scrub my way up today it'll make somethin' special out of it. Keep an eye on him now, Francie.

FRANCIE. Yes, mama.

NEELEY. Aw, come on.

Their exit has been a scramble of getting their coats on, and hardly being able to wait to get outdoors. When the door slams behind them, Katie looks after them a second with a little smile, half-envious of their childhood. Then she starts to get her implements together to begin her day's work as janitress, and the scene dissolves to Francie and Neeley pulling their sack of junk along the crowded street. The street is alive and vital with activity, but Francie and Neeley pay no attention to it.

NEELEY. Well, he was silly to stay down there that long. I'd've kicked and kicked that ole whale's stomach good, so he'd have got sick right off. I wouldn't have waited like Jonah did. (*To a passing boy*) Hi, Snozzy.

SNOZZY (*matter-of-factly*). Hi yourself and see how you like it.

This brief exchange of courtesy is quite routine. Neeley stops suddenly as he sees something about to happen down the street.

NEELEY. There she comes!

From their angle we see a big garbage wagon swing around a corner. Four boys are waiting matter-of-factly, and just as the wagon swings around the corner, they throw a chunk of wood under its rear wheels. It makes the truck take quite a bump, and shakes off some of its cargo. The boys are on this like a shot to redeem anything of value. The driver yells back at them and they shriek answering derision.

CHORUS OF BOYS. Aw, go chase yourself. It's a free country, ain't it? Stick in the mud, and so's your ma. It's a free country.

One of the boys shies a can at the driver. The wagon goes on and the brief exchange is over.—Neeley and Francie make no effort to horn in on the other kids' beat, but watch with a detached interest.

NEELEY. They done good today.

Neeley and Francie start on down the street. At that moment a man passes, takes the last cigarette out of a package and throws the empty package into the gutter. Francie and Neeley dive for it. So does another boy. The Nolan teamwork shows long practice. Francie dives onto the other boy, and they go down together while Neeley retrieves the package. The boy scrambles up, ready for battle, but thinks better of it when he sees there are two of them.

BOY (saving his dignity). Aw, rag pickers! Rag pickers!

He beats it. Francie picks up the junk sack. Neeley separates the tinfoil from the paper. Neeley then becomes fasci-

nated as he drops the paper through the grating into the sewer.

NEELEY. You know somethin', I bet she goes clear down to the river.

FRANCIE (joining him). Maybe clear to the ocean—Maybe clear over to foreign climes. (Neeley just gives her a "You're nuts" look; and she adds matter-of-factly:) It stinks awful, don't it?

NEELEY. Yeah.

FRANCIE. I bet that's the worst stink in the whole world, don't you?

NEELEY. I don't know. I can't remember everything I smell.

They pick up their sack and move on; the view moving with them.

NEELEY. You know what, I'm goin' to get a job cleanin' up over to the fights. Skinny's cousin's doin' that and you'd ought to see alla stuff he finds—joolry and pocketbooks and alla candy he can eat.

FRANCIE. Thou talkest very big.

NEELEY. You talk crazy.

FRANCIE. I do not. I talk like God talks.

NEELEY. How do you know how God talks?

FRANCIE. Well, it's in the Bible, and I guess it's His Bible isn't it, and so that's the way He talks.

NEELEY. Aw, you talk crazy.

Neeley changes the subject rather than admit defeat. They have reached an old stable which carries the sign "CARNEY'S, GOOD PRICES FOR JUNK." Beyond them, inside the old barn, CARNEY can be seen weighing out the junk that some of the children have brought in. Neeley stops Francie and addresses her with male authority.

NEELEY. Now look, stand on the same side as him when he weighs it so's he can reach you, and don't forget to stand there after he pays you, you forgot that last time, and a penny's a penny, ain't it?

FRANCIE. Well, I guess I know it is.

NEELEY (*triumphantly*). Well, all right then.

As Francie starts dragging the sack inside, a boy who has sold his junk comes out past them. "Rag pickers, rag pickers!" he jeers. But Neeley passes this insult, being more interested in watching Francie.

Francie drags the sack in and gets next in line. Carney is paying off the kid who preceded her, counting pennies into his hand.

KID (*starting to protest*). Look—

CARNEY (*interrupting*). Shut your trap. I say what things weigh around here. Who's next?

The kid subsides and goes out. Francie moves up.

CARNEY (*seeing her*). Oh, hello, little girl.

Francie gives him a mechanical smile in answer. His manner is somehow different with girls. He dumps out the contents of the junk sack, starts to sort and weigh them.

Francie shoots a look at Neeley. He motions her to edge closer. And as she obeys, Carney finishes the weighing.

CARNEY. You done pretty good. Nine cents.

He counts the pennies into her hand. Francie stays there. Carney chuckles a little and reaches out and pinches her cheek. Having done this, he brings forth another penny. Francie's hand is out immediately.—Neeley is well-satisfied.

CARNEY. And there you are, an extra penny because you're a nice little girl.

The very matter-of-factness of all this is somehow worse than if it were an ordeal to Francie. The moment she has the penny, she runs out and joins Neeley. His manner is approving.

NEELEY. That's better. Gosh, I wisht Carney liked to pinch boys.

FRANCIE. Nine, and my pinchin' penny. That's five for us, and five for the bank.

NEELEY. Now wait a minute. The pinchin' penny don't count, it's yours by rights.

FRANCIE. Well, I don't know, Neeley, if you got somethin' it counts, don't it?

NEELEY. Sure it don't. Look, half what we get for the junk is for the bank, that's what mama says, ain't it?

FRANCIE. Well, yes, but—

NEELEY. Well, we didn't get that penny for junk, we got it for pinchin', so it's yours, so there ain't any use in talkin' any more about it.

FRANCIE. Well—

NEELEY. Anyway that leaves nine, don't it, and now you tell me how we're goin' to divide nine in half, go ahead.

FRANCIE. Well, we could put—

NEELEY. You can't do it, not without splittin' a penny in two, and then it wouldn't be any good. So we got an extra penny, and by rights it's mine, cause you already got one.

FRANCIE. But Neeley, mama said—

NEELEY. All right, wisenheimer, you show me how to split a penny!

FRANCIE. Well, I guess—Well, maybe the next time it don't come even the bank gets it—

NEELEY. Sure, ain't that just what I been sayin'. And that leaves eight—two more for me, two for you, and four for the bank. (*Francie divides the pennies.*) You see, it comes out just right. I don't see why you got to be so dumb.

He leads the way as they start on down the street, while other children come up with some junk.

FRANCIE AND NEELEY (*as scornfully as they were yelled at*). Rag pickers! Rag pickers!

As they go on down the street the scene dissolves to the exterior of CHEAP CHARLIE'S, a neighborhood store, one of the places where the boys hang out. —Francie and Neeley come down the street, kicking a little block of wood down the sidewalk, and trying to keep it on the sidewalk. The game automatically ceases as they come to the door of the shop.

NEELEY. Now wait a minute! Don't go in like you was with me.

FRANCIE. Well, hurry up then.

Neeley swaggers in and in a moment Francie follows him into CHEAP CHARLIE'S. Neeley joins some boys before a form of punchboard, the prizes hung on the wall—a few good ones—a catcher's mitt, a pair of roller skates, a doll. This is the sort of place that is the forerunner to the poolhall where the boys will hang out when they are older. One of the boys puffs a cigarette

self-consciously.—Francie lingers near the cash register.—One of the boys has just taken a chance on the board and is opening the envelope.

CLAMOR OF VOICES. Fourteen! A pencil! It's a gip! Looka the sucker thinks he can win somep'n! Gimme a drag, Red. Get away, I got dibs on butts.

Neeley dives for the board immediately. and pulls a number.

NEELEY. Twenty-six! (*He looks at the board.*) A penwiper!

CHEAP CHARLIE. Prize or candy, mister?

NEELEY. Candy—a lickorish whip.

Charlie hands him one, which Neeley wraps around his wrist. Charlie starts toward the register to wait on Francie, but keeps an eye on the boys.

BOYS. It's a gip! Aw, there ain't no numbers for them good prizes!

CHEAP CHARLIE (*as he passes them*). All of life's a gamble, gentlemen, you never win if you don't keep on takin' chances. (*Coming to Francie*) What's yours, young lady?

FRANCIE (*counting out five pennies onto the counter*). Change to a nickel, please.

CHEAP CHARLIE. Well, I'll get fat on that kind of business.

But he grudgingly takes the pennies and gives her a nickel from the cash register. She slips out without answering, and Cheap Charlie looks after her a second before he starts back to the boys.

Francie hurries down the street. A group of girls are playing pottsie—a form of hopscotch—on some marked-out squares on the sidewalk. Francie has to pass near them.

GIRLS. Hi, Francie. How much did you get? Want to play, Francie?

FRANCIE (*hurrying past them*). I can't. I'm in a hurry.

This dissolves to a FIVE AND TEN CENT STORE, where Francie is seen wandering languidly down an aisle. She is in the midst of the beauty of the world. Her longing to be here is not at all the desire for acquisition; there is nothing wistful or envious about her. Being here is complete fulfillment. She pauses a time or two to look at or touch something as if she were in fairyland.— A floorwalker observes her curiously.— Unaware of him, she continues to look her way down the counter. She is fascinated by a pile of colored bathing caps and picks one up tentatively. A salesgirl steps up and Francie puts it down quickly.—The floorwalker steps up to her.

FLOORWALKER. Do you want something, young lady?

FRANCIE (*with great dignity, opening her hand to display the nickel*). I'm merely looking, thank you. I got a right. I got money.

Her confidence that the money justifies her being there is complete. She goes on her way. Her attitude rather than the nickel defeats the floorwalker. He looks after her as she stops again to look at something and then moves on unhurriedly to the door.

Francie emerges from the store replete with the fulfillment of the adventure. She gives a deep and happy sigh, then starts down the street. She has only gone a few feet when a fragrance strikes across her dream world and penetrates to her healthy child's stomach. The stomach wins hands

down over the dream. Her manner changes completely as she turns to the window and sees the candy. She looks at it for a moment and goes in.

Inside the CANDY STORE, Francie presses close to the case to make her important choice. The proprietor comes up.

FRANCIE (*deciding*). Three cents worth of peppermint drops, please.

The proprietor isn't particularly pleased by the magnitude of the sale but reaches for a sack as the scene dissolves to the STREET. The bag of candy in one hand, her mouth full of peppermint, Francie is absorbedly trying to avoid stepping on the cracks in the sidewalk.

FRANCIE (*to herself*). Step on a crack, break your mother's back.

She pauses to readjust the peppermint drop in her mouth. You don't chew these, and if you suck them just right they last longer. In the midst of this process of careful adjustment, she hears the shrill yelling of some boys, and looking off she sees a CAR TRACK where Neeley and a gang of boys are putting a tin can on the track so that the streetcar will smash it.—Francie comes into the scene and watches.

BOYS (*seeing the car approaching*). Here she comes! Cheese it!

They tear to the sidewalk.—The streetcar rolls over the tin can without a tremor.—The boys emerge cautiously, as though they had done something very daring.

BOYS. That ole can's mashed good and flat. Boy, did you see the look on that motorman's face. That ole car came near jumpin' the track, I bet.

They retrieve the can and study it.

FRANCIE (*from the sidewalk*). Neeley, we got to go home.

The boys turn. They are aware of her for the first time. Neeley is in a spot, in being told what to do by a mere girl.

NEELEY (*uncomfortably*). Beat it.

FRANCIE (*firmly*). Mama *said*.

BOYS (*derisively*). Mama said! Go on, we don't want no skirts around! Look who's got to do what his mama said!

Neeley is definitely in a spot. Keyed by the situation, one of the boys gets a new idea. He staggers as if drunk.

BOY (*walking drunkenly*). Look at me, I'm Neeley's old man.

There is laughter. Both Nolans stiffen. They are together now. Neeley unwinds what is left of the licorice whip and gives it to Francie to hold.

NEELEY (*ready for battle*). Do that again!

BOY. Do what?—Auggie pushed me.

NEELEY. Go on, I dare you.

AUGGIE. He didn't say nothin'. It's a free country, ain't it?

NEELEY. I never said it wasn't.

FIRST BOY. Then the sidewalk's free, too!

NEELEY. I guess what I'm standin' on is mine while I'm standin' on it.

AUGGIE. Then I guess what he's standin' on is his.

FIRST BOY. Sure, and I can do what I want to on it.

NEELEY. Well, let him come over on *my* piece and say somethin', I dare him.

BOY. Well, who wants your old piece?

NEELEY. Well then, don't talk like you was on my piece.

BOY. Well, who wants to.

NEELEY. Well, all right, then.

This procedure doesn't make much sense but it seems to satisfy the immediacies. Neeley is victorious. With a lordly air he walks over to Francie and takes back his licorice whip and starts to wind it around his arm again.

NEELEY (*to Francie*). Come on.

They start down the sidewalk together and the scene dissolves to the TENEMENT HALL as Francie and Neeley come up the stairs to where Katie, their mother, is on her knees beside a bucket, scrubbing the floor.

KATIE. Heaven's sake, is it that late already? I'll have to leave these stairs go till later. (*She gets to her feet.*)

FRANCIE (*showing the pennies*). Four cents.

KATIE. Pretty good. Dump the bucket, Neeley.

NEELEY (*tentatively*). Mama, can I—

KATIE. No. Bring the bucket and dump it. (*Starting up the stairs*) It's the day for the insurance collector. I don't want him to catch me lookin' like this.

They go up the stairs, Neeley struggling with the bucket. They pass a blowzy woman going down with a basket on her arm.

WOMAN. Hot, ain't it?

KATIE. Yes, but Christmas'll be here before you know it.

WOMAN. I got enough troubles without thinkin' about that.

They go on down the hall toward the flats at the back. Neeley disappears into the lavatory to dump the bucket.— Katie stops at the door to search for their key. A boy, HENNY GADDIS, comes out of the door across the hall.

KATIE. How's your sister today, Henny?

HENNY (*matter-of-factly*). Poorly, thank you.

Just as he answers, Neeley comes up with the bucket. His answer means so little to him that almost simultaneously Henny kicks the bucket out of Neeley's hand. It clatters to the floor. Henny beats it and Neeley gives chase.

Katie unlocks the door just as Flossie, Henny's sister, appears in the doorway. She is pathetically thin, with dark, luminous eyes; and is dressed unlike any other occupant of the tenement in a soft, feminine dress. She is very conscious of the dress as she smiles shyly at them.

KATIE. Why hello, Flossie dear.

FLOSSIE. Hello, Mrs. Nolan. (*Then, shyly*) Don't—don't you notice somethin'?

KATIE (*not getting it*). Why, seems to me you look mighty well. Much better, don't she, Francie?

FLOSSIE. No I don't, I don't—

This is not what she wanted to hear. She slams the door shut quickly. The sound of coughing can be heard. Katie stares at the door for a second without understanding and then unlocks her own door and goes in.

The NOLAN KITCHEN as Katie and Francie enter: The kitchen is the most used room of the flat. They cook and eat and live here. It is bare but clean and neat. It has an iron stove. A fire escape can be seen past the window. Beyond this we get a glimpse of the scraggly tree in the yard.

KATIE (*as she crosses to the bedroom*). Heat up the coffee while I fix up.

Francie starts to make the fire. Neeley appears in the doorway, triumphantly, with Henny meekly carrying the bucket. He sets it down inside the kitchen.

NEELEY (*victoriously*). That's better.

Neeley pushes Henny outside and shuts the door. Being always hungry, Neeley starts to look for something to fill in until dinner is ready and finds a few crumbs in a cracker box on the table. As he does so, he sees the four pennies where Francie has put them down. He stares at them a moment, and an idea takes shape in his mind.

NEELEY. Mom!

KATIE (*from the bedroom*). Yes, Neeley.

NEELEY (*craftily*). Mom, if there was a rule about somethin', that doesn't mean you couldn't do somethin' else once in a while, I mean if it was important, does it?

KATIE (*offscene*). No, Neeley.

NEELEY. If it was important, I mean, people could change their minds about somethin', and it's all right, ain't it?

KATIE (*still offscene*). Yes, I guess so.

NEELEY. Well, mom, I was just thinkin', you know I never smoke cigarettes because you said I mustn't, even if some of the fellers make fun of me. I don't but, it's been kinda hot lately, and—

KATIE (*interrupting, quite pleasant about it*). Neeley, you cannot have any of those pennies to buy an ice-cream cone. They go in the bank, same as usual.

Neeley gives, this a quick, startled reaction. How in the world did Katie know what he was trying to do before he really got to his point? It is a distinct letdown.—Francie, busy at the stove, smiles at his reaction.

KATIE (*from another room*). Bring 'em in here, Neeley.

Dutifully Neeley picks them up and starts for the other room, and the scene cuts to the BEDROOM, which is small, with a lumpy double bed and an old bureau with a wall mirror. Katie is primping before the mirror, and you have to be rather careful to look in the right place or it will distort. Neeley enters with the pennies. Katie goes to the closet, and Neeley follows her.— The closet contains very little in the way of clothes. The condensed milk can, used as a bank, is nailed to the floor.

KATIE. Half of everything we get goes into the bank. That's the way it is, and that's the way it's going to stay. Now put 'em in there.

NEELEY (*obeying*). Gosh, I bet we got about a hundred dollars in that ole bank by now!

Katie comes out of the closet and returns to the mirror.

KATIE (*dryly*). Nine's more like it.

There is a sound outside of a limb of a tree splitting. At this the scene cuts to the KITCHEN where Francie has turned from the stove in time to see the limb outside the window sway and disappear from view.

FRANCIE. Mama—they're cutting the tree!

Neeley tumbles into the kitchen followed by Katie carrying her hairbrush. They crowd behind Francie at the window to look out.

Looking out the window from their angle, we see two men sawing the limbs off the tree. Katie stares at it a moment.

KATIE. Oh, that's too bad, it was kind of pretty there, and the birds sittin' in it sometimes like they do.

FRANCIE. Papa loved that tree.

KATIE (*abruptly*). Oh, quit moonin' over it, it got in the way of the washing. A tree ain't goin' to put no pennies in the bank.

She starts for the bedroom. Francie is mildly bewildered by this sudden change. Katie is a little sorry for her abruptness, but before she can say anything there is a knock on the door.

KATIE. It's Mr. Barker. Get out the saucer and give it a wipe. I think there's matches in it. (*Then, as a small apology for her outbreak*) If— if you want you can stay in the room while he's here.

Katie hurries back into the bedroom. Francie gets the saucer out, sets it down, and then hurries to the door to admit Mr. Barker. Mr. Barker is a kindly enough little man, rather old, but with the soul of a busybody. He is an important visitor, since in making his collections he sees almost everyone, and is a sort of newspaper for the neighborhood gossip. Consequently the Nolans treat him with their best manners.

FRANCIE (*with her best book-manners*). How do you do, Mr. Barker. Mama is temporarily detained, but will join you directly. (*Neeley gives her a withering look.*)

MR. BARKER. You got manners right out of a book, Francie. (*To Katie as she enters*) And company or no company, Mrs. Nolan always looks the lady. You should see some of my people, even ladies with husbands that work steady—

He stops, realizing this is not a very good point to bring up. Katie stiffens a little.

KATIE (*with dignity*). Won't you come in the parlor and have a cup of coffee.

MR. BARKER. That I will, and your hospitality is very kind, Mrs. Nolan.

They start for the parlor. Mr. Barker bows gallantly for Katie to precede him through the door. She pauses to take some coins out of an old cup on a shelf. Francie automatically starts to get the cup of coffee.

The PARLOR is dark, small, and stuffy. It is seldom used. The couch that serves as Francie's bed is under the window.— Katie and Mr. Barker are followed by Neeley. Mr. Barker seats himself in the best chair, and takes out his fountain pen to write the receipts. He talks steadily.

MR. BARKER (*cheerfully*). Well, old man Gentry's off to jail again.

KATIE. That's too bad.

MR. BARKER (*hurriedly*). But she's keepin' up his insurance just the same.

KATIE. And here's ours—ten cents for me, ten for Mr. Nolan, a nickel for each of the children.

MR. BARKER. And you'll never regret it. A fine funeral for every member of the family, heaven forbid.

He is busy writing the receipts as Francie appears with the cup of coffee and can of condensed milk. Mr. Barker accepts it and pours the condensed milk lavishly.—The Nolan family watch

fascinated as he continues to pour the milk.—Mr. Barker finally ceases pouring, and the Nolans are relieved. He talks steadily as he does this.

MR. BARKER. Thank you, Francie. And your weekly receipts, Mrs. Nolan. (*He gives them to her.*) Now there's one party, not far from here, I wouldn't like to say who, that didn't get no receipts this week. And not naming any names, I will say that it's a family that the Angel of Death has marked on its invitation list, heaven forbid.

NEELEY. Henny says his sister's got one leg in the grave.

KATIE. Neeley!

MR. BARKER. It'll mean Potter's Field, most likely. Well, that's what people get, wastin' good money to give her dresses instead of insurance, dresses that'll last longer than she will. It all depends on what folks thinks is important.

FRANCIE. But papa says that sometimes—

KATIE. That's right, Mr. Barker, it all depends on what folks think is important.

MR. BARKER. And how *is* Mr. Nolan, is he working or not working, some tell me one thing, some another—I don't listen.

KATIE. Mr. Nolan bein' a singing waiter, Mr. Barker, and what you might call an artist, his work don't come steady like other peoples'. But I'm sure you'll remember, when you talk to folks, that the Nolans have always paid their insurance on the dot.

Francie gives her mother an admiring look for this defense of Johnny.

MR. BARKER (*retreating*). You surely don't think I'd go around spreadin' gossip about my clients, Mrs. Nolan?

KATIE. Oh, sure not. How is my mother, Mr. Barker?

MR. BARKER. In the prime, Mrs. Nolan, fine as can be, she says to tell you she'll be over tonight the same as usual. (*Then, with relish*) And I trust you're happy with the news about your sister.

Katie is instantly alert. It is quite evident that here is news she does not know, but she does not like to admit it.

KATIE. Just which news do you mean, Mr. Barker?

MR. BARKER. Well, it must be she's savin' it to surprise you with tonight when the family's all here together.

KATIE (*apprehensively*). I'd take it kindly if you told me what you mean.

MR. BARKER (*warming to his work*). Well, I trot around the same as usual to collect her weekly dime, and what do you think happens—well, sir, she gives me *two* dimes. (*He pauses for effect.*) Yessir, she's done it again, she's got herself a brand-new husband, and—

KATIE (*startled*). Oh, no!

She breaks off abruptly. It is none of Mr. Barker's business that Sissy had never been divorced from her last spouse. The children are fascinated. Mr. Barker is in his element. Katie's worry about the marriage will make a fine story indeed.

MR. BARKER. Well, now, I suppose you mean about her still bein' married. I don't mind sayin' the same thought occurred to me. But I'm sure it must be all right, she must have made some arrangement, but—

KATIE. I'm quite sure she did, Mr. Barker, I'm sure that—

NEELEY (*fascinated*). Does she call this one Bill, too?

His question makes Katie sharply aware of the presence of the children. They shouldn't be hearing such a discussion.

KATIE. You children run along now, and do the marketing. Take some money from the cup—

NEELEY. Aw, but mom! I want to hear about Aunt Sissy!

KATIE. Take the money and get a five-cent soup bone off of Hassler's; *don't* get the chopped meat from him though, he grinds it behind closed doors, and heaven only knows. Go to Werner's for the meat, get round steak chopped, ten cents worth, and don't let him give it to you off the plate. Take an onion with you and ask him to chop it in. And don't forget, just at the last, to ask for a piece of suet to fry it with.

During this domestic discussion, Mr. Barker does a little snooping. He tries, with his finger, to see if there is any dust on the table, and is disappointed when there is none. Then he moves a small hassock with his foot and is delighted to discover, as he suspected, that it covers a hole in the carpet. The Nolans are unaware of this.

FRANCIE. He won't always do that, mama, he—

KATIE. Tell him your mother *said*. And then go for the bread.

NEELEY. It's Saturday, mom, can we—

KATIE. All right, all right. Ask for a nice pie, not too crushed, and go on now and do it.

FRANCIE: I'll take him home, he's my father.

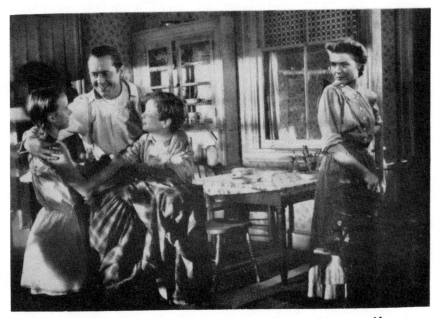

JOHNNY: I'm goin' to take you to see the ocean for yourself.

KATIE: We got to save where we can . . . I don't mind the extra stairs.

SISSY: That's for nothin', Johnny — except maybe bein' a nice guy.

FRANCIE (*reluctant to go*). Mama, we know Aunt Sissy's been married before.

NEELEY. Sure, I can remember two Uncle Bills.

KATIE. That's nothing for you to talk about; go on now and get things done.

Reluctantly they leave. Katie turns back to Mr. Barker.

KATIE. You got no right, Mr. Barker, to be carryin' tales about my sister as though there was somethin' wrong. She's funny some ways, maybe, but she wouldn't do nothin' wrong. So I'd like it if you didn't talk to anybody about it like it was.

MR. BARKER (*lying, of course*). Strike me dead if I'd ever think of mentionin' it to anybody but you.

KATIE (*dryly*). Yeah, sure, I know. (*She sits down.*) Well, you might as well go on and tell me what you do know. No point in my bein' the only one that don't hear it.

MR. BARKER (*eagerly starting his story*). Well—

The scene dissolves to WERNER's BUTCHER SHOP, with Francie and Neeley in front of the counter. Werner is waiting on them.

WERNER. Ten cents worth of round steak. You want it ground?

FRANCIE. No.

WERNER. You're sure now? Wasn't twenty minutes ago I ground that whole plateful fresh.

FRANCIE. No, thank you.

Werner takes some chunks of meat out of the case and starts to wrap them.

FRANCIE. Oh, I forgot. My mother wants it ground.

WERNER (*giving her a dirty look*). You don't tell me!

The children make no answer. He gives an angry exclamation and gives up—starts to grind the meat. Francie reaches timidly across the counter with her onion.

FRANCIE. Mama said to chop up this onion in it.

WERNER. Oh, she did!

But he takes the onion angrily and puts it in the grinder with the meat. He starts again to wrap the ground product. At this point Francie takes a deep breath and blurts out the last instructions.

FRANCIE. And-a-piece-of-suet-to-fry-it-with-mama-said.

Werner stands for a moment as though turned to stone.

WERNER. Sweet jumpin' Christopher!

But he takes the piece of suet and puts it on top of the meat as he folds the paper around it. The Nolans have won.

This dissolves to HASSLER's BUTCHER SHOP. Neeley is peering through the window to watch Francie, on the inside, make her purchase. He is taking pains to keep himself and the package of ground meat out of sight.

Inside the BUTCHER SHOP, Hassler, a kindly man, is exhibiting a husky-looking soup bone before he wraps it up for Francie.

HASSLER. Ain't that a beauty, though? Now you tell your mama when she cooks it, tell her to take the marrow out and spread it on a piece of bread for you. That's good, and you need to get some meat on your bones. (*He laughs at this joke as he slaps the package down.*) And here. (*He slices off a thin slice of liverwurst and offers it to Francie.*) Do me a favor —try this and see if you think it's all right for my customers.

He is "thin-make" covering up a good deed and Francie knows it. She takes the slice of liverwurst and tastes it.

FRANCIE. Yes, sir.

HASSLER. Well, that's fine. Now you finish that before you get home. How's your papa?

FRANCIE. He's fine, sir! (*Francie exits, Hassler smiling after her.*)

Outside the butcher shop, Francie joins Neeley and they start down the street. She breaks the piece of liverwurst in two and gives Neeley half. He wolfs it.

NEELEY. Free?

FRANCIE (*moved by the kindliness of the world*). He made out he wanted me to tell him did it taste all right. (*She blurts out with sudden passion:*) I wish we could buy all our meat from Hassler's. I *wish* he didn't grind his meat behind closed doors.

NEELEY. Well, you don't have to bawl about it. (*Francie isn't really crying, but she could.*)

This dissolves to the exterior of LOSHER'S BAKERY and STALE BREAD STORE. A sign reads "NOT QUITE FRESH BREAD, 2 LOAVES FOR 5¢." A long queue is waiting patiently for the doors to open. The scene moves to the bakery window next door where Francie and Neeley, meat packages tucked under their arms, are gazing longingly into the window at a huge chocolate cake on display.

FRANCIE. You know, mama thinks we don't know *anything.*

NEÉLEY (*getting the drift at once*). Yeah, she acts like we were kids or

somethin'. (*They edge along to a platter of cream puffs and stare.*) I bet she has a fight with Aunt Sissy tonight.

FRANCIE. It's got something to do with men like Aunt Sissy too much.

NEELEY. Papa says we'd ought to make everybody like us.

FRANCIE. I guess maybe ladies shouldn't. (*Then, thoughtfully*) Maybe Aunt Sissy wouldn'ta changed husbands so much if any of her babies had lived. She's crazy about babies.

NEELEY. Look who's talkin' about babies! A lot you know!

FRANCIE. I know as much as you do!

NEELEY. You don't know nothin'.

FRANCIE. You think you're so smart. Boys make me sick!

NEELEY. Well, what do ya think girls make people, you think—

But there is a sudden interrupting shout from the crowd as the stale bread store door is thrown open and the people push forward.

Francie and Neeley, their argument forgotten at once, adjust their packages and stalk toward the entrance. Their eyes flash with the light of battle, like a fighter advancing across the ring to engage his opponent.

At the entrance the crowd is pressing forward. A kid dashes out of nowhere to the head of the line and worms his way through the door. This seems to be the signal for the disappearance of all semblance of order. Neeley fights his way in; Francie follows through the hole made by him. The crowd is storming the counter behind which two harassed clerks dole out the bread and collect the money.

AD LIBS. Two loaves! I was first! Four loaves! Quit shovin'!

Neeley squirms, pushes, fights his way to the counter; Francie is right behind him.

NEELEY. Six loaves.

FRANCIE. And a pie not too crushed!

This dissolves to the NOLAN KITCHEN where the children are just dumping their packages onto the table. This marks the end of their chores, and the beginning of that part of the day which is theirs. Katie examines the bread.

KATIE. This bread's fine. I wouldn't be surprised if it wasn't more'n three days old.

NEELEY. Is that all, Mom? Can we go now?

KATIE. Yes—you're free.

Neeley bolts for his room and Francie for the parlor, while Katie starts to put the things away. In a moment Neeley reappears with a baseball glove, and heads for the door. Francie emerges more quietly with a library book.

KATIE. Where's the fire?

NEELEY (*on his way*). There's a Dodgers scout around.

He disappears and the door bangs behind him.

KATIE (*to Francie*). Where you goin'?

FRANCIE. Oh, no place much.

KATIE. Well, don't go dream walkin' crossin' the streets.

Francie is gone too, and as Katie smiles after them the scene dissolves to the exterior of the PUBLIC LIBRARY.

It's a rather small library, but it has dignity. Francie hurries down the street, her attitude and pace changing as she arrives. She stops a moment, then starts slowly and reverently to mount the shallow steps as the scene dissolves through to the interior. Francie enters into the hush of the room, the door closing soundlessly behind her and she advances to the librarian's desk. A few people are reading at the tables or are at the stacks.

At the desk she offers her book. The librarian takes the card, stamps it mechanically, returns it without once looking at her. Francie meantime has reverently touched the blue bowl with yellow flowers and the polished desk. Now she takes her card and almost tiptoes to the shelves. The librarian stacks the returned book; we see it is by Browning.

FRANCIE, passing the shelves, lingers at the C's. Then she turns dutifully to the B's, runs her finger through the Brownings, and chooses the volume which comes next. She goes back to the desk.

At the desk, she offers the B book. The librarian stamps mechanically, then notices the title: Burton's *Anatomy of Melancholy,* and for the first time looks curiously at Francie.

LIBRARIAN. Burton's *Anatomy of Melancholy!* Are you sure you want this?

FRANCIE. Yes, ma'am.

LIBRARIAN. Don't you think it's a trifle over your head?

FRANCIE. Yes, ma'am—I mean, yes, ma'am.

LIBRARIAN. Well, why did you select it?

FRANCIE. Well, I—I read all the authors that far, all the ones that begin with A and then the B authors up to Burton. It's next.

LIBRARIAN. You don't mean you're trying to read your way straight through the library?

FRANCIE. Yes, ma'am.

LIBRARIAN. But a book like that, you'll only be confused and—

FRANCIE. Please, I want to go on, through the alphabet—I want to get to know everything in the world.

The librarian stares at her a moment. It is evident that Francie means it.

LIBRARIAN. Well, all right. (*She marks the book—then before she hands it to Francie she adds:*) Only—look, do something for me, will you— take another one too—here, *Lavender and Old Lace*—just for fun. It's Saturday. I'll have a headache thinking about you wrestling with *The Anatomy of Melancholy* all weekend. Will you?

FRANCIE (*smiling shyly*). Yes, ma'am.

The librarian marks the book and Francie starts out with it, the librarian smiling after her.

This dissolves to the YARD of the NOLAN TENEMENT in the afternoon. The tree, shorn of its limbs, stands like a scarecrow. A man is mounted on a ladder retying the clotheslines. Women hang from the windows giving free advice and gossiping.

WOMEN. A little to the left, Mrs. Crackenbox! You think I want for Mrs. Wittely's baby-clothes to drip on my good sheets? Why don't you try oil of cloves? Nothin' won't make her stop, she's cuttin' her teeth. Didja hear old man Hammerslaw

taken out last night? They'd oughta make the stairs wider or the coffins narrower . . . (*Mixed with this are the sounds of a buby crying and the shouts of kids.*)

The camera moves steadily past this bedlam and up to the second-floor rear fire-escape outside the Nolan window, to discover Francie, completely oblivious to all the noise, eating peppermints and having "fun" crying pleasurably over the sorrows of her book. The bedlam continues over her but she hears nothing. She comes to a pausing place where it is just too beautiful to go on, closes the book, and sits reveling in its tragedy—but managing to take another peppermint through the tears.— Suddenly her head lifts as she hears singing, faint at first, then stronger. It is her father's voice, singing "Molly Malone." As soon as she is sure, she is galvanized into action and scrambles toward the kitchen.

The KITCHEN: Francie rushes to the door and throws it open as the singing comes closer. She gets it open before the last line is finished, and Johnny, her father, is revealed. This is a game of long-standing, to try to get the door open before he finishes the last line. Johnny holds out his arms and Francie flings herself into them joyfully.

FRANCIE. I won, I won!

Johnny laughs and holds her for a moment. Johnny is nice-looking, debonair. He is a free soul who could give and take superb happiness if only the world contained no economic problems, no responsibilities beyond the joy of living. It isn't so much that he shirks the responsibilities of a family man, as that he simply cannot cope with them. He is man enough to be bitterly ashamed of his weakness, but not quite man enough to overcome it. The truth is that Johnny has never quite grown up. His charm and his gift of play are something like those of a child. His moods are extravagant and volatile, like a child's. He wears the only suit he possesses—a shabby Tuxedo, badge of his trade, with it a derby, jauntily worn. At the moment he is in a very high mood because he has a job for tonight, so that momentarily he feels more like the head of his house than he ordinarily does.

JOHNNY. Well now, I wouldn't be so sure o' that if I was you.

FRANCIE. But I did, I got it open before you finished, that's the rules!

JOHNNY. But I come up one flight two steps at a time before I remembered. Don't that make a difference?

FRANCIE. No sir, the rules—

JOHNNY. And in a manner of speakin', you never stopped me at all, because my heart kept right on singin'.

FRANCIE. Oh, papa, you're joking.

JOHNNY. Well, maybe I'll let you get away with winnin' this time, Prima Donna. (*Looking around*) And where's your beautiful mama?

FRANCIE. Finishing the halls. She must be up on the top floor or she'd have heard you.

Unconsciously and almost imperceptibly, Johnny relaxes. He is instinctively more at ease with Francie than with Katie.

JOHNNY. Well, in that case you'd better be gettin' busy. Why aren't you layin' out my clothes?

FRANCIE. You're always makin' fun, papa, you know you haven't any more clothes.

JOHNNY. What's this, then?

FRANCIE. A tie.

JOHNNY. What's this?

FRANCIE. A dickey.

JOHNNY. And this?

FRANCIE. An apron.

JOHNNY. Them's clothes, aren't they? And you'd better be gettin' that apron ironed.

FRANCIE. Oh, papa, you've got a job for tonight?

JOHNNY (*savoring his good news*). Do you see the palm o' that hand? That's right where I got the world, tonight.

FRANCIE. Where is it, papa?

JOHNNY. Klommer's—big wedding party. There'll be lots of tips.

FRANCIE. Singing or waiting?

JOHNNY. Both.

FRANCIE. Oh, papa, maybe tonight will be it, maybe he'll be there, the impresario, and he'll hear you and put you on the stage.

JOHNNY. Why not, ain't I the Brooklyn thrush? Only if that's the case, hadn't you better be gettin' that apron ironed?

FRANCIE. I'll have it in a jiffy, papa. And the coffee's on.

JOHNNY. That's my Prima Donna. (*Then, teasing her*) "I've got a lassie, a bonny, bonny lassie, She's as fair as—as—" (*He pretends not to remember.*)

FRANCIE (*fussed*). Oh, papa, I can't sing.

JOHNNY. Come on, you're holdin' up the singin'.

FRANCIE (*shyly*). "As fair as the flowers in the dell—"

JOHNNY. Better singin' I never heard.

FRANCIE (*shyly*). I love to iron for you, papa.

JOHNNY (*pouring the coffee and bringing it down to the table*). You know, a day like this is like somebody givin' you a present, everything just right. I wonder how did folks get on before coffee was invented. Ah, the world would be a fine place if—(*He gets away from this thought as quickly as possible.*) Prima Donna, do you know you're gonna make a mighty nice wife for somebody some day.

FRANCIE. Oh, papa!

JOHNNY (*teasing*). And pretty, too— that is if your nose don't grow crooked.

FRANCIE. Could it really—honest?

JOHNNY. Ah, it's the prettiest nose in Brooklyn.

FRANCIE. Oh, ʀapa, it isn't!

JOHNNY. Who says it isn't? You just tell me who says so and I'll take care of him.

FRANCIE. Papa, you're crazy.

JOHNNY. You know somethin' else, you ain't gonna be ironin' like that no more when that impresario comes around. Things are gonna be different around here, you wait and see.

FRANCIE. Yes, papa.

JOHNNY. What's the wish you wish the most, when our ship comes sailin' in?

FRANCIE (*not looking at him*). It already came true.

JOHNNY. What was it, baby? (*She irons, and won't look at him.*) Come on, tell me now.

FRANCIE. I—I wished when you came home today, you wouldn't be—sick.

JOHNNY (*moved*). Who told you to call it sick, baby? (*Then, trying to get away from this*) Ah, now, you shouldn't be wastin' wishes like that; you ought to be savin' them for a silk dress or somethin'. Haven't you got a better wish than that?

FRANCIE (*hesitantly*). Well—

JOHNNY. Come on.

FRANCIE. I wish mama won't be too mad with Aunt Sissy.

JOHNNY. What about Aunt Sissy?

FRANCIE. She's gone and got herself a new husband again.

JOHNNY (*laughing*). No! If there ain't a woman for you—If one husband don't suit her, she keeps right on lookin' for the best. Uh—what did your mama say?

FRANCIE. Well—she didn't like it.

JOHNNY. Yeah, I wouldn't be surprised.

FRANCIE. Couldn't you—sort of say something to mama, not to be too mad.

JOHNNY. Why, sure I could, Prima Donna—and I will.

FRANCIE. Oh, thank you, papa.

JOHNNY. Now ain't you got a real wish—one just for you?

FRANCIE. Well—did you see it, papa?

JOHNNY. What?

FRANCIE. Out the window—our tree, they've killed it. (*He crosses to the window, and she follows.*)

JOHNNY (*looking out*). Well, look at that now.

FRANCIE (*fiercely*). They didn't have any right to kill it, did they, papa?

JOHNNY (*sensing how serious it is with her*). Wait a minute now, they haven't killed it. Why, they couldn't kill that tree!

FRANCIE. Honest?

JOHNNY. Why sure, baby. Now look, don't you tell me that tree's goin' to lay down and die that easy. You look at that tree, see where it's comin' from—right up out of the cement. Didn't anybody plant it, it didn't ask the cement could it grow, it just couldn't help growin' so much it pushed that ole cement right out of the way. When you're bustin' with somethin' like that, can't anybody stop it. Like that little ole bird, listen to him—(*He imitates a bird.*) He don't ask nobody can he sing. He don't take no lessons, he's just so full of singin' it's got to bust out someplace. Why, they could cut that tree way down to the ground and the root'd shove up some place else in the cement. Just you wait until next Spring, and you'll see, Prima Donna. (*Their eyes meet and Francie's worry is laid to rest.*) Well, now, this ain't earnin' the family bread. (*He gets his hat and brushes it carefully with his sleeve.*) Haven't you got one little wish that's just for you?

FRANCIE. No, papa. I—I just—

JOHNNY. Just what?

FRANCIE. I just love you so much, papa!

She clings to him, tightly. Johnny holds her.

JOHNNY (*gently, moved*). Well, what do you know. Listen, if I get a lot of tips tonight, you know what I'm gonna do? I'm gonna put two bucks on a horse I know runnin' Monday. I'll win ten, then I'll put the ten on another horse. If I use my head and have any luck, maybe I'll run it up to five hundred. Then you know what I'm gonna do?

FRANCIE. What, papa?

JOHNNY. I'm gonna take you on a trip, just you and me, on a regular train. Maybe we'll go down South, and see where the cotton grows. You know, "Down where the cotton blossoms blow."

To make her laugh, he does a little step with this.

JOHNNY (*very gently*). You're a nice girl, baby. Come on, we better go tell your mama the news about my job.

He puts his derby on at a rakish angle, and Francie gives him the package with the apron. They go out together.—We then see them in the HALL. Johnny is feeling very good indeed, and he deliberately turns on the charm as he calls up the stairs.

JOHNNY (*calling*). Anybody seen Johnny Nolan's wife?

He starts gayly up, Francie looking after him, adoringly, and the scene cuts to the UPPER HALL where Katie is on her knees on the stairs, scrubbing her way down. She is slightly apprehensive as she looks down quickly.

KATIE. Johnny! You all right?

JOHNNY (*coming up the stairs*). And why wouldn't I be, married to the most beautiful woman in Williamsburg, Brooklyn?

KATIE (*relieved*). You're shoutin' it so, they'll hear you over to Manhattan.

JOHNNY. Don't you get fresh with me tonight! Happens I'm workin' at Klommer's—big weddin' party.

Katie is pleased in a maternal way, but values the news for what it is—a one-night job—whereas to Johnny it changes the complexion of his world and ought to change *her* world. To Katie his enthusiasms are an old, and now a somewhat humorous, story; her humor is a necessary defense against disappointments.

KATIE. I thought you was kinda extra dressy! Well, looks like you won't get home before the sun comes up.

JOHNNY. The later the better; the more tips the more fine silk stockings for my wife's pretty legs.

KATIE (*smiling*). Silk stockin's is just what I need.

She turns away to go on working. A man comes up the stairs past them and a couple of tenants look out from their doors to see what's going on. An audience always inspires Johnny.

JOHNNY. Just a minute, Mrs. Nolan. Don't you think you better kiss me for luck?

KATIE. The whole house is lookin'!

JOHNNY. Who cares! (*But he draws her back, then speaks softly:*) This is the best job I had in a couple a months. Maybe I'll get more, from tonight.

He puts his arm around her. She pretends to be out of patience with him, but she is pleased. None of the other women in the tenement get treated like this by their husbands.

KATIE. You better get on then, good jobs don't wait—

JOHNNY. A job's no good without you kiss me.

She lets him kiss her, and is warmed in spite of herself. Then she gives him a playful push, and speaks almost ruefully.

KATIE. Well, you still got a way with you, Johnny Nolan! Go on now, before you know it those folks at the weddin' will be an old married couple.

JOHNNY. Before you know it, I won't go at all. Theirs ain't the only weddin' that counts.

KATIE (*smiling*). Put your hat on now and get out of here before somebody else cops that job!

He puts his hat on jauntily, grins, and comes to the head of the stairs. But he catches Francie's eye fixed on him from the bottom. He turns back to Katie, outwardly jaunty but actually a bit awkward.

JOHNNY (*hesitantly*). Oh—Francie tells me Sissy's gone and done it again. Don't—I mean, maybe he's a nice fellow—don't be too hard on her, huh?

KATIE (*dryly*). They've all been nice fellows. Beat it now, Johnny.

A little lamely, Johnny turns away. He is glad to have this over with. His jauntiness returns. He tips his hat to Katie elaborately.

JOHNNY. That's just a sample, Madam. If you like my stock, drop me a card and I'll be around again.

Katie has to smile. Johnny starts down the stairs, pretending to be aware for the first time of his small audience. He tips his hat again.

JOHNNY. Oh—evening, folks.

At the foot of the stairs Francie, delighted by the whole scene, slips her hand into his and accompanies him proudly.—The view moves with them and "picks up" Flossie Gaddis, still in her pretty dress, shy and wistful in her doorway. When she sees him, she starts to smile. Johnny stops.

JOHNNY. Well, will you look at our beautiful princess tonight, in a brand new gown.

FLOSSIE (*shyly, but infinitely pleased*). It's made out of silk.

JOHNNY. Why, let's see. Silk! Why, don't you tell me that—that dress is made out of flower petals and birds' wings and a little old piece of cloud. Anybody could tell *that!*

Flossie laughs softly, and it is beautiful to see. Johnny laughs too, pats her head and starts on.—Francie's reaction marks her worship of this father of hers. The scene moves on again as they go on down the stairs. They pass two old ladies who are standing in the doorway. On the door is a sign: Piano and Vocal.

JOHNNY (*tipping his hat*). Evening Miss Lizzie, Miss Maggie.

THE MISSES TYNMORE. We wish you well, Mr. Nolan.

JOHNNY. Thank you, ladies. Evening, Mr. Spencer.

MR. SPENCER (*going up stairs*). Working tonight, Johnny?

JOHNNY. Sure, big weddin' party. (*They pass through the front door and on to the street.*)

We get a glimpse of Katie looking down for a moment after Johnny. Her face shows the mixture of her feelings. She sighs a little and turns back to work.

The STREET: Johnny and Francie come down the front steps, and what is, to her, a small triumphal march, continues. She holds onto his arm and is enormously proud. A couple of young girls are sitting on the steps.

JOHNNY (*tipping his hat again*). Good evening, young ladies.

GIRLS. Good evening, Mr. Nolan.

They giggle, a little flirtatiously. Johnny is unaware but Francie gives them a look. Her head goes higher and she holds tighter to Johnny's arm.

FRANCIE. What did mama say about Aunt Sissy?

JOHNNY. Don't you worry—it'll be all right. Your Aunt Sissy's a fine woman, Francie.

Suddenly he stops at the window of the hardware shop as they pass it.

JOHNNY. Look at all the things they got. No use talkin', some day I'm gonna get you them skates.

FRANCIE (*maternally*). Mama said not to be late, papa.

JOHNNY. God invented time, Prima Donna, and whenever He invents somethin' there's always plenty of it. (*Moving down the window*) Look at them knives!

FRANCIE (*gravely*). Mama says time is money.

JOHNNY. Well, I guess maybe He wasn't worryin' about money right then.

FRANCIE (*a little worried*). There's your car, papa.

JOHNNY (*looking, and grinning at her*). Might as well catch it, I guess.

He kisses her quickly and goes toward the car. Francie calls "goodbye" after him and stands watching anxiously.

Johnny swings onto the car just as it starts to move on. He smiles back, then tips his hat with a fine flourish to Francie.

Nobody but papa has ever yet tipped his hat to her. She is so proud her eyes glisten suspiciously. Her concern is gone and nothing is left but worship. She waves till the car is out of sight. And the scene fades out.

# PART TWO

The NOLAN KITCHEN fades in. It is evening. First we see FRANCIE setting the table but more concerned with reading her book, which is open on the table. Then the scene pulls back to reveal Neeley washing at the sink, and Katie transferring the food from the stove to the table.

KATIE. Now tomorrow this bread'll make up real nice with a sauce of ketchup and coffee. Use soap, Neeley. Monday we'll slice it and fry it in bacon fat and—Francie, you're not listening, put up that book.

FRANCIE (*obeying*). Yes mama . . . bacon fat.

KATIE. Supper's ready.

She and Francie sit while Neeley, having splashed his face with water, dries it with a dish towel, looking over longingly.

NEELEY. Oh boy, we won't have to play no North Pole this week! Hey! Am I hungry! (*He comes to the table, starts wolfing his food standing up.*)

KATIE. And when weren't you?

FRANCIE. Mama.

KATIE. Yes, Francie.

FRANCIE (*dreamily*). What does white mean?

KATIE. Just white, I guess. What do you mean, what does it mean? Neeley, sit down at your place. (*He sits down.*)

FRANCIE. Well, what do girls always wear it for when they get married, and when they're confirmed, and when they graduate—why does it always have to be white?

KATIE. I don't know, somebody just started it I guess. Lots of things like that.

FRANCIE. Will I have a white dress when I graduate?

KATIE. We'll see. Neeley'll probably need shoes by then.

FRANCIE. But mama.

KATIE. Talk to him about it. If you can get him to quit always comin' through his soles . . .

FRANCIE. Just because he's a *boy* . . . (*She changes; right out of her book.*) All right, mama. I will gladly do without so my little brother can be happy with new shoes.

NEELEY. Little brother my eye, you—

KATIE. That'll do. (*To Francie*) You read too much.

The door suddenly bursts open and Aunt Sissy comes in—but she gives the impression of blowing in, like a fresh breeze. She is a couple of years older than Katie, lively, completely natural, looks not unlike a street-walker, but is actually a simple, direct, earthy woman. She carries some magazines.

SISSY. Well, hey, everybody!

THE CHILDREN (*with cries of delight*). Aunt Sissy, Aunt Sissy! What did you bring us, Aunt Sissy?

They fly into her arms and she embraces them warmly, magazines, and all.

SISSY. I brung myself, chickabiddies, ain't that enough! Oh—and a couple magazines from the dentist's—what does he need 'em for—or me either, I can't read like my eddicated little niece here!—(*Francie takes the magazines, Sissy looks at Katie.*) Hello, Katie my darlin'!

KATIE (*a little stiffly*). Good evening, Sissy.

SISSY (*getting the fact that there's a chill on*). Well, you look fine, Katie.

KATIE. Yes, I look fine.

SISSY (*with rueful humor*). Who spilled the beans—oh, that's right, I forgot it was old Barker's day here. Where's Johnny? I was kinda countin' on him to be in my corner!

KATIE. Oh, sure, you and Johnny.

SISSY (*abruptly putting her arms around Katie*). Aw. look Katie, I didn't tell you because I wanteơ to bring Bill around, but I couldn't, he's home sleepin', he's a milkman, see . . . Ah listen, you're goin' to wish me happiness, ain't you?

KATIE. Naturally I wish you happiness—*this* time, too.

SISSY. Oh, golly—can't you just skip to the place where you forgive me. You're goin' to before you're through, you know I'll get around you in the end. Why can't you just be human now and get it over with?

KATIE (*laughing in spite of herself*). Well, I'll say that much, there ain't anybody in the world like you to get around a person—unless it's Johnny. You better sit down, you're in time for pie.

SISSY. Now that's more like it, that's my kid sister talkin'. Just coffee for me. I gotta get home soon and make breakfast for Bill.

NEELEY. Breakfast? At night?

SISSY. Yeah, ain't it a riot. We sleep all day with the shades pulled down to keep out the sun and the windows shut to keep out the noise. It's fun, you don't live like nobody else.

KATIE (*dryly*). No, you sure don't.

SISSY. Easy on the whip, kid. Ah, wait'll you meet my Bill—you and him will—

NEELEY. Wouldn't you marry nobody that they wasn't named Bill, Aunt Sis?

KATIE. She mightn't remember 'em if they wasn't.

SISSY (*laughing*). Oh, Bill's got some other name—Steve I think it is—but I always like Bill. A good man's name with no stuck-up about it. Ah, like I say, you'll be crazy about him, Katie.

KATIE. Yeah . . . but the question is, how'll him and *you* get along? (*Genuinely troubled*) It's wrong, Sissy, it's . . . I mean, the other ones, and—

SISSY. What's wrong about it? The others was wrong. What's right about keepin' on with a guy when you don't love each other any more?

KATIE. But it ain't just as easy as that, it—

FRANCIE (*earnestly—dreamily*). I think Aunt Sissy is right about when love is dead.

KATIE (*to Sissy*). Now look what you started. It ain't anything to talk about in front of them. Every time you come around you fill their heads with—

SISSY. All right, kids, you go on downstairs awhile. Your mama's got a spankin' up her sleeve, and she ain't gonna feel right till she gives it to somebody. Might as well get it over with.

Neeley and Francie start out. Francie turns at the door, a little worried about her aunt and mother.

SISSY. You don't want to frown like that, snuggle-pup. The fellows don't go for that at all.

Her grin is contagious and Francie is relieved. She follows Neeley out. Sissy turns back to Katie with a grin.

SISSY. All right, kid, let's have it, the works. I'm a disgrace, you don't know what you're goin' to do with me, you can't hardly face the neighbors with what they must be sayin', I'm old enough to know better.—Go on, get it all off your chest, and then we can make up and forget about it.

KATIE. That's right, talk your way out of it, and you probably will, too. What did mama say?

SISSY. Oh, you know mama, she don't say much, but—

KATIE. Yeah, I know. (*Imitating her mother*) "Sissy is bad only where the men are concerned, but she is good in the heart." (*Her smile dies.*) But that ain't it. You make me ashamed,

Sissy. Folks got a right to talk, and the kids are bound to hear. It ain't right for them. And you can get in trouble. You ain't real sure what happened, and there's laws about things like that.

SISSY. Look, Katie, so help me, this time it's for keeps. I ain't even goin' to look at another guy. And as for the last one, he can't be alive, or I'd have heard from him. I been pretty good. Seven years is a long time for me to wait around, not bein' married —they said seven years was all you had to wait, and I waited. Where would I get the money for a divorce?

KATIE (*Sissy is hopeless*). Well, for the life of me, I don't know what you've talked yourself into—but I got a feelin' it ain't right.

SISSY (*on the level*). Look, kid, all I know is, it can't be wrong, or I couldn't feel like I do about it. I'm dumb, sure—but I know this much, if I feel bad about somethin', it's wrong, and if I feel good, it's right. Ah, you couldn't get it, Katie, you got all the breaks I never had—you got the kids, and you got a guy you're clear overboard about. You're lucky.

KATIE (*with a touch of bitterness*). Yeah, I'm that, all right.

SISSY. Sure, you are. And that makes all the difference. You got somethin' to stick to, you—

KATIE (*with a sudden flare she didn't know was in her*). All right, and where does crazy over somebody get you! It don't put no pennies in the bank, it don't buy no clothes for the kids to go to school—Maybe you got it better, not stickin' to one man. I wish I wasn't crazy over him some-times—

SISSY. Hey, Katie—

KATIE (*unconsciously her voice rises*). —And I won't have the kids takin' after him either, him and those dreamy ways I used to think so much of—not if I got to cut it right out of their hearts!

There is a pause that means a lot. Katie hadn't the least intention of saying that. Sissy stares at her. It is the first knowledge Sissy has had that there was something deeply wrong between Katie and Johnny.

SISSY. Hey, kid, what're you sayin'?

KATIE. Nothing, I—

SISSY. Yes you are, you're sayin' plenty. What's happened between you and Johnny?

KATIE. I don't know what I'm sayin'. I don't know what come over me.

SISSY. Well, look, hon, we better find out. Sure, we got somethin' to talk about now.

KATIE. No, I don't want—

SISSY. Uh-uh, you're the kid sister, you listen now. Look, you was awful crazy about Johnny—Don't tell me, I seen you: it was like every woman wants to be with a guy.

KATIE. Yeah, I know, but—

SISSY. All right, maybe Johnny didn't turn out just like you figured; sure, he drinks and all, and you're the one has had to make most of the livin'. But everybody's got somethin'. And you wasn't crazy about Johnny because he was goin' to be a banker. It was on account of—well, how he laughed, and how he could talk about things, and—and how you felt walkin' down the street holdin' on to him and havin' other women look at you —and the way he had of sayin' hello to everybody like—like he was givin' away somethin'. That's what you was crazy about, and that ain't changed; I don't know, them things couldn't change in Johnny, not even if he tried, he's just—different. And that's what you was crazy over. If there's been any changin', maybe it's you, kid. You still got all you was crazy over, ain't you?

KATIE (*moved, looking away from Sissy*). Yeah, I—

SISSY. Then you thank your lucky stars for what you got, Katie Nolan, and take the rest along with it. And take it from me, you got a lot, and don't think you haven't.

There is a pause. Sissy really means it. And it has moved Katie enough to make her very near tears, but she would not show this for anything in the world. She manages a little grin.

KATIE. I might've known, startin' out to take you apart, I'd wind up with you workin' me over.

It is as close as she can come to acknowledging in words the truth of what Sissy has said. But their eyes meet, and there is a nice moment between them. These two sisters like one another at that moment as well as they have in a long time.

SISSY. Nice goin'—You're a nice girl, Katie.

The warmth between them holds as the scene dissolves to the NOLAN TENEMENT BUILDING: First we see NEELEY, bent over with his hands on his knees, playing he's an infielder. He's playing all by himself. He throws a small ball against the wall, feels it as it bounces back to him and tags out an imaginary runner on second base. He's very intent on all this. Evidently there's some question about the decision. Neeley speaks to the imaginary umpire with righteous anger.

NEELEY. Aw, he was out a mile, I tell you. Don't give me that—well, that's better.

Evidently he wins the argument with the umpire, because he is mollified and returns to his fielding position. The camera pulls back to reveal the front of the tenement just as Sissy emerges from the front door. Francie is sitting quietly on one of the doorsteps fingering a pair of roller skates. A man and his wife are on the steps higher up, and Sissy has to step over them to get down.

SISSY (cheerfully). Don't stir yourself, Pal.

She steps over him with a grin. He grins in answer. The wife recognizes Sissy.

SHEILA'S MOTHER (stiffly). We better go in, Alfred.

Sissy gets it but doesn't care. Francie looks up eagerly, and Neeley quits his ball game to come over to Aunt Sissy.

NEELEY. How'd you come out, Aunt Sissy?

SISSY (grinning). No decision. It was a draw. (She smiles at them.) Ah, your mom's bark is worse than her bite—you know. Look, tell me somethin', when papa's home, I bet him and mama laugh a plenty, don't they —you know, like they always did.

NEELEY. Sure, pop can make anybody laugh when he wants to, except when he's drunk.

FRANCIE. Sick, Neeley, mama says to call it.

NEELEY (returning to his ball game). Okay, sick then. Funny, he ain't like

other guys when he gets that way, he gets all quiet. (He tags another runner.) That'll teach you to steal a base on, I guess.

FRANCIE (to Sissy). Mama kind of doesn't want to, sometimes, but after a while mostly she does.

SISSY. Sure, I'll tell you somethin' you can do for me; do all the laughin' you can—you know, keeps everybody healthy.

NEELEY. Okay.

FRANCIE (quoting from a book again). Laughter is the singing of the angels.

SISSY. You're a funny kid, head full of all them things, kind of like your pop.

NEELEY. She tells lies like pop, too.

FRANCIE (quickly). He doesn't tell lies.

NEELEY. Well, I don't know what you'd call it, he—

SISSY (averting war). Hey, time out, I've had enough battlin' to last me today. (Then to change the subject) Where'd you get the skates?

FRANCIE. Oh, they aren't ours. Papa said he was going to get us some, though.

NEELEY. Aw, he didn't mean it, he just said that and I'd like to know what you call that if it ain't lies.

FRANCIE. He did so mean it, Neeley Nolan.

SISSY. Easy, now. (To Francie) Kind of like your papa, don't you, lamb?

FRANCIE. He does mean it, doesn't he, Aunt Sissy?

SISSY. Sure he means it, hon, he means it every word. Only—well, sometimes things, you know, happen. But it kind of ain't his fault, he—(*Realizing she is becoming more and more involved she changes the subject.*) I tell you what—let's make out Johnny gave you them skates like he said, and they're yours, it won't hurt nobody.

FRANCIE. But Aunt Sissy, we couldn't, it—

SISSY. No sense things standing around and nobody using them.

She starts to strap the skates on. Neeley leaves his ball game to come over for this new excitement.

NEELEY. Hey, can I put 'em on next?

SISSY. All right, now. Take it easy.

Francie laughs in high enjoyment as Sissy steadies her. The front door of the tenement flies open and the little girl, who is the owner of the skates, shows up.

SHEILA. Hey, you come back here with my skates. Mama!

SISSY. It's all right honey, we ain't gonna hurt 'em.

Sheila's mother appears. She's the woman who was sitting on the step.

SHEILA. Ma, they stole my skates.

The child's father appears in the doorway. The woman advances down the steps.

SHEILA'S MOTHER. You bring them back. You put them kids up to it, you—

SISSY (*facing her*). Easy now, nobody's hurt. I only borrowed 'em.

SHEILA'S FATHER (*mildly*). She isn't going off with them, Effie, just—

SHEILA'S MOTHER (*to her husband*). Don't you take up for that woman like that, you—

SISSY (*smiling at the husband*). You poor little guy, you got to put up with that all the time?

The clamor of the argument has brought forth other neighbors.

WOMAN (*horning in*). Ask her whose husband she'd like to borrow.

SHEILA (*to Francie*). My mother says your aunt's got dyed hair.

NEELEY (*belligerently*). Yeah!

A KID. Hey, the cop!

The hubbub ceases. McShane, a rather young and nice looking cop, comes in.

MCSHANE. Come on, break it up, break it up now, take it easy.

SISSY (*smiling full at him*). Well, I'm sure glad you come along, handsome. You look like you ought to be able to whip a bunch of women into line.

MCSHANE (*making no response to her impertinence*). That's fine, but maybe somebody better tell me what all the excitement's about.

SHEILA'S MOTHER. She tried to steal my little girl's skates.

WOMAN. She tried to vamp her husband.

FRANCIE. We only borrowed them for just a minute, honest.

SISSY. That's right, there wasn't nobody usin' 'em, and a little fun and frolic on a Saturday never hurt anybody. I'll bet you know all about that, don't you?

MCSHANE. It's kind of you to ask, but I'm afraid I don't, lady.

SISSY (*studying him*). You mean it, too, don't you. Yeah, I should've known you weren't the type. That's kind of nice, handsome.

SHEILA'S MOTHER. If you think you're goin' to get out of it makin' eyes at the law—

SHEILA. Your aunt's goin' to the station house, your aunt's goin' to the station house!

Bedlam breaks loose again. It is at this point that Katie comes out the door and hurries forward.

KATIE. Officer, please. (*As she comes up to him*) This lady's my sister. She didn't mean any harm, I'm sure she didn't.

McSHANE (*studying her a moment—impressed*). Sure, and it doesn't look to me like any harm's been done. (*To the crowd*) Clear the streets now, all of you.

His tone is authoritative, and the crowd starts to disperse.

McSHANE (*turning to Katie*). I'll see you ladies to your door.

SISSY (*with a grin*). Thanks, handsome.

KATIE (*in reproof*). My sister is always trying to be funny, officer, she doesn't mean anything by it. (*They pause at the door.*) I'd like you to know this is the first time my family ever got into any trouble on the streets—(*looking at Sissy*) and I'll see it don't happen again.

McSHANE. I guess I know a lady when I meet one, ma'am—My name is McShane and I'm glad I could be of service to you, ma'am. (*He turns and goes.*)

SISSY (*grinning*). He sure took a shine to you, Katie.

KATIE. Go on! (*Fussed*) Who'd look at me?

SISSY. He would.

KATIE (*in an odd mood for a moment—looking at her hands*). Funny, you kind of forget sometimes that you're a woman.

FRANCIE. He wasn't going to arrest us, mama. Aunt Sissy talked him out of it. And we got to skate on 'em anyway, didn't we, Aunt Sissy?

This makes Katie look at Francie. Francie has evidently enjoyed the excitement from the adventure, and this disturbs Katie.

KATIE. You go on down the street and tell Sheila and her mama you're sorry now, Francie.

FRANCIE. Do I have to, mama?

Katie doesn't answer, and Francie starts reluctantly down the street. Katie watches her go a minute, and then turns back to look at Sissy levelly.

KATIE. I don't like sayin' what I'm goin' to, Sissy.

SISSY (*ruefully*). Oh, golly, are we off again?

KATIE. You're the only sister I got, but—I don't care for myself, what people think about you, only—I got the kids to worry over, and if I don't do it nobody else will. You're bad for 'em, Sissy, you got Francie in trouble right on the street. You—you might even make 'em trouble at school.

SISSY (*very quietly*). What is it you're tryin' to say, kid?

KATIE. Sissy, I'm askin' you not to come around any more. My mind's made up, and don't try changin' it with any more of that soft talk.

SISSY. I won't, Katie, not if you mean it. But let's keep on talkin' about you. Soft's one thing, kid, but—bein' too hard is another.

KATIE (*flaring*). All right, it ain't nice to be hard, but my children are goin' to be somebody if I got to turn into granite rock to make 'em!

Sissy studies her for a long moment. Their eyes hold. Katie doesn't yield.

SISSY (*with a funny little smile*). I kind of wish you hadn't said that, kid. (*She turns.*) So long, Katie. I'll give your love to Bill.

She goes. Katie stares after her. Some of the inflexibility leaves as she watches Sissy go. She is bewildered, mixed up with the inner conflict; she turns abruptly to go into the tenement.

The scene dissolves to the NOLAN KITCHEN at night. First the cover of a Gideon Bible in Neeley's hands comes into view, then the scene pulls back to reveal Neeley, ready for bed, reading aloud. Francie sits near, holding a volume of Shakespeare. Katie is remaking a dress of hers for Francie. Grandma Rommely sits quietly listening. Grandma Rommely is of Austrian peasant stock, old, given much to silence. She has a faraway look, and nods occasionally while she listens to this reading, which is very important to her. It is a good thing.

NEELEY (*reading*). "—and Nahor lived nine and twenty years and begat Terah, and Nahor lived after he begat Terah an hundred and nineteen years."—boy, that's older'n Grandma, ain't it?—"and begat sons and daughters"—Okay, that's the end of the page.

FRANCIE (*reading immediately*). "And dreaming night will hide our joys no longer, I would not from thee. *Cressida:* 'Night hath been too brief.' *Troilus:* 'Beshrew the witch with venomous' "—

NEELEY (*interrupting, disgusted*). Aw, that ain't even English.

FRANCIE. It is *so*. Shakespeare wrote the best English of anybody.

NEELEY. All right then you tell me what it means, you're so smart.

FRANCIE. I didn't say I know what it means, I said I liked it.

KATIE. That'll do, now.

NEELEY. Okay, but I bet you don't know what it means either.

KATIE. Maybe not, but I know it's good for you.

FRANCIE (*resuming her reading*). " 'Beshrew the witch' "—

NEELEY (*grumbling to himself*). She don't know what it means, *mom* don't know what it means, grandma can't even read, and gosh knows *I* don't know—

FRANCIE. Mama, I can't read if he—

NEELEY. —Just wastin' time every night readin' stuff *nobody* knows what it's all about.

KATIE. Well, it ain't as bad as that, I get *some* of it. That about nights is too brief, that means short, and goodness knows they are, and the days too. (*She measures the dress against Francie as she speaks.*) Hold still a minute. Now listen, Aunt Sissy brought us that Bible from Sheepshead Bay, and papa blew in all his tips one time on that Shakespeare because Grandma said they was the greatest books and we should read a page every night. So we ain't gonna waste 'em. And I don't know, sometimes it does seem kinda foolish but —I guess it gets you somewhere, might help you find a job someday, you can't tell.

Her defense of the custom winds up a little lamely, but it is the best she can muster. None of them notices Grandma until she speaks abruptly.

GRANDMA ROMMELY. This reading will not stop. I say this thing.

This is said quietly, but with so much determination that all three turn toward her. She is completely immobile as she tries to gather words, which are difficult for her.

GRANDMA ROMMELY. In the steerage we come, to this new land, your grandfather and I. Hard we work, but there is something we look for that we do not find. So this is not different, I think, from that old country. And then I watch my children, and then their children. And then I know, when I am old, I know. In that old country, the child can rise no higher than his father's state. But here, in this place, the children need not to walk out their lives in the shoes of their elders. And this has to do something with the learning which is here free for all people. This is the thing, that with this learning each one is free to go so far as he is good to make of himself. This way each child can be better than the parent, and this is the true way things grow better. This, to me who am old, is the great wonder of this country, in this way to be free. I have missed this thing, and I have let my children miss it, but this shall not be so for my children's children. This reading will not stop.

Probably never before has Grandma Rommely put so many words together. She is lost in them, almost transfigured, there is deep strength behind her feeling. The others are silent, a little awed by the unaccustomed speech. The argument about the reading is ended forever.

GRANDMA ROMMELY. And you, Katie. It is not just for the job. You do not think well about this, nor about what you do with your sister. You have forgotten to think with your heart. There is a coldness growing in you, Katie.

She has finished; and she retires inside herself again, settling back in her chair. There is a pause, and there is definitely nothing more to say. It has had an effect on Katie. Francie looks from one to the other.—Finally Katie's eyes leave her mother and meet Francie's. Katie nods. Francie resumes the reading.

FRANCIE. " 'Beshrew the witch! with venomous wights she stays As tediously as—' "

Katie's eyes go back to her mother. The old lady does not look at her, but nods again, almost imperceptibly. It is good. But her words, coming on top of Sissy's, have shaken Katie.

The scene dissolves to a STREET late at night. It is practically deserted. The shadowy figure of Johnny, carrying a couple of paper bags, comes down the street from the carline. He is singing "Call Me Up Some Rainy Afternoon" to himself. Thereupon the scene cuts to the NOLAN PARLOR where Francie is on her couch under the window. The faint sound of Johnny's singing awakens her. Her face lights up. She looks out the window. Then, in her nightgown, she scurries for the kitchen.

In the KITCHEN Katie is asleep with her head on her sewing on the table as Francie enters. Francie is startled at seeing her mother there. As she hesitates, Katie stirs and lifts her head. The sound of the singing is closer as

Johnny comes up the stairs.—Katie's and Francie's eyes meet and there is a sense of understanding between these two who wait. Instinctively Katie's hands start to fix her hair.

FRANCIE. He's all right, mama. I don't think he's sick.

The singing approaches the door. True to their game, Francie goes to open it before the song finishes. The open door reveals Johnny and his paper bags. There is a second of relief for both women when they're sure he is sober.

FRANCIE. Papa!

JOHNNY. Well, what do you know, if it isn't my beauty. (*He is a little surprised at seeing Katie still up.*) Hey! What're you doing up this time of night?

KATIE (*a little awkwardly*). Oh, I made up my mind to sit up for you. But I guess I ain't used to the hours, any more.

Johnny sets his bags on the table. Katie resumes adjusting her hair.

JOHNNY. Leave it, it's nice.

KATIE (*pleased*). Go on. What you got in them bags? Francie, the coffee.

FRANCIE (*going to light the stove*). Is it something to eat, papa?

JOHNNY. And what else, with me comin' from a grand banquet? (*And he empties the bags.*) French rolls, a whole half of lobster from the shores of Maryland, caviar all the way from sunny far off Russia, fried oysters, cheese—from—from the mountain fastnesses of la belle France.

KATIE. What do you know about the mountain fastnesses of France?

FRANCIE. Is it better comin' from there, papa?

JOHNNY. Supposed to be mighty good. (*Looking at Katie.*) But comin' home like this—I know that's good.

KATIE (*a little awkwardly*). Well, let's eat it, no reason we shouldn't have a party of our own.

Abruptly Katie turns from setting the table and, without explanation, disappears into the bedroom. At the same time a very sleepy Neeley appears from the other bedroom.

NEELEY. I'm hungry.

KATIE (*from the bedroom*). Is that all you got to say to your papa?

NEELEY. Hello, papa. (*He starts immediately pulling a chair up to the table.*)

JOHNNY (*laughing*). His stomach's like the Irish sea, no bottom to it.

Katie reappears, shy and pretty, her hair arranged and held in place by a tortoise shell comb. Johnny looks at her, moved.

FRANCIE. Mama, your wedding comb!

KATIE (*a little shy at her own sentiment*). Well, ain't this a kind of wedding party.

JOHNNY (*pulling out a chair, playing up to the mood*). You bet it is. I wish I could've swiped some champagne. (*Then, as he meets her eyes*) No, I don't, coffee's better.

Francie brings the coffee to the table and sits down next to her father. Neeley is already eating.

JOHNNY (*looking at Katie; teasing*). Only will you look at who's tellin' me I don't know about the mountain fastnesses of France.

KATIE (*looking down, fussed*). Oh, that.

JOHNNY. Yeah, that—imagine you forgettin'.

KATIE. Well, I didn't, not exactly, only that was a while back and—

JOHNNY (*to the children*). What do you think of havin' a mama that'd forget where we went on our honeymoon.

FRANCIE. Did you really go there, mama?

KATIE. O' course not, papa's joking.

JOHNNY. Sure we did—or just the same as. We spent our honeymoon in a school, was as big as a palace, and—

KATIE (*interrupting*). We just worked there nights, cleanin', the both of us. It was right here in Brooklyn, before you was born.

JOHNNY. Well, that wasn't what you said then. You mean to tell me, when we was havin' our supper all alone there, and I used to pull down them maps and take the teacher's pointer and pick out the places we'd pretend we was that night—you mean to tell me we really wasn't there? You mean you forgot that sunny France was where we liked the best, and all the laughin' we done there, and you goin' to sit right there and tell me we wasn't even there?

He is making arrant love to her with this. Katie is stirred.

KATIE (*finding this rather trying*). Yeah. I guess we kind of was, at that.

JOHNNY. And you're askin' how I know about the mountain fastnesses of France. I'm ashamed of you, Katie Nolan.

Francie has been watching this between her father and mother; she doesn't quite understand the mood between them, but she is fascinated.

FRANCIE. Wasn't there anybody in the school but you, papa?

JOHNNY. No sir, we—

KATIE (*interrupting*). Your papa better quit talkin', he'll have you believin' you was in France too.

FRANCIE. No, talk some more, papa—

NEELEY. What's this here stuff?

JOHNNY. Caviar, that's fish eggs come all the way from Russia.

NEELEY (*appalled*). Fish eggs!

JOHNNY (*as he and Katie laugh*). Tell the truth, I never could get the idea myself why they like it, except it's hard to get and costs a lot.

FRANCIE. And that makes it good, papa?

NEELEY. What about the Russians—it ain't hard for them to get—do they like it?

JOHNNY (*to Katie*). Can you tie that, ain't we got the smartest kids?

FRANCIE. Papa, talk some more, tell us about the party tonight, don't leave out anything.

JOHNNY. Oh, that can wait. (*He lays three dollars before Katie.*) How's that?

KATIE. Three dollars! That's good wages.

JOHNNY (*jingling his pocket*). Good tips, too.

FRANCIE. Papa, start. Was there music? Did they dance?

JOHNNY. Aw, your mama's got no time for all that.

KATIE (*softly, not looking at him*). You—you could tell me. You used to.

Johnny starts uncertainly at first, watching Katie. Neeley continues to eat. Francie listens to her father with her elbows on the table.

JOHNNY. Well, it was pretty swell. Klommer's best room, all fixed with white flowers—flowers on the table, on the chandeliers, even on the floor. There was a big horseshoe table, and lots of people, and right in front was a big tall wedding cake, must have been two feet high.

NEELEY. Why didn't you bring home some of that?

KATIE. Was the bride pretty?

JOHNNY. Well, she was maybe not so young, but—

Johnny cannot spoil a moment like this with the truth. Everything must be perfect, so he improves on the bride a little.

JOHNNY. Sure, she was awfully pretty, in that blue dress and all. She had diamonds on her hands and even in her ears so she kind of glittered, and when she walked her clothes swished, kind of. Well, sir, the champagne flowed like water, and the smell of it got all mixed with the flowers and the powder the ladies wore and it was like a wonderful new kind of perfume, made you feel good just to smell it.

FRANCIE (*with a little shiver of delight*). And did you sing for them, papa?

JOHNNY. Sure thing, I was comin' to that. I got three encores for "My Wild Irish Rose," and—everybody clapped and clapped so I did "Irish Eyes Are Smiling" *four* times.

KATIE. It must have been awful nice.

JOHNNY. It was all right. And when it was time to cut the wedding cake

the band played "Kiss Me Again" and she put her arms around him and boy, did he look scared!

NEELEY. What was he scared of, papa?

JOHNNY. Huh?

KATIE. You kids ask too many questions. Go on, you heard the story, go back to bed now, it must be three o'clock.

NEELEY (*matter-of-factly*). I got a bellyache.

KATIE. Lay on your right side.

NEELEY (*kissing her*). Goodnight, mom.

KATIE. Goodnight, Neeley.

FRANCIE (*a little stiff—not kissing Katie*). Goodnight, mama.

KATIE. Goodnight, Francie. (*Laughing awkwardly*) Francie's kind of mad at me because Sissy made a scene of herself out on the street and I—I told her to stay away.

FRANCIE. Papa—

KATIE. Run along now, both of you.

Both of the kids start to obey. The small incident has broken the perfection of the evening, and this disturbs Johnny.

FRANCIE. Goodnight, papa. (*Kissing him, then whispering*) Was—was there an impresario there?

JOHNNY. Not tonight there wasn't, Prima Donna. Come here. (*Awkwardly*) You got no call to be mad at your mama, Francie, she—she always got a reason for what she does.

Johnny means this. Unaccustomed to reproof from Johnny, even as gentle as this is, has its effect on Francie. She hesitates, then goes over and kisses her mother with some restraint. Katie, who is feeling more deeply than she has felt in a long time, holds her close for a moment. Suddenly Francie flings her arms around her mother, and they are very close for a moment.

FRANCIE (*in a completely different tone*). Goodnight, mama.

Francie hurries into her room and shuts the door. Her going makes a little awkward moment between Johnny and Katie, who are left alone, each lost in his own thoughts.

KATIE (*after another little pause*). Johnny. What else happened at the party—tell me.

JOHNNY. Well, it was nice like I said it was, awful nice—the bride all dressed up and all, and—

But he cannot get going again. And Katie hasn't really heard.

KATIE (*interrupting*). Johnny.

JOHNNY. Yeah.

KATIE. Do you think—I mean, have I—well, changed a lot—you know.

JOHNNY (*misunderstanding — quickly*). Changed, why, she couldn't hold a candle to you. She wasn't so hot, I just said that, for the kids. No sir, you're—

KATIE (*interrupting*). No, I mean—am I gettin' you know, hard?

She is troubled, inarticulate. Johnny is bewildered.

JOHNNY. Why, where'd you get hold of an idea like that, hard?

KATIE. I don't know, I don't want to be, but—well, there's the kids and all, I want to do what's good for them—and maybe sometimes—

JOHNNY. Aw, baby, don't talk like that. Why, you know something,

you're prettier than you ever was. I come near tellin' it to the whole party tonight—hey, you ought to see *my* bride that's waitin' home for me. (*Softly, looking straight at her*) And you *was* waitin'. That was—nice, Katie, it was—like it used to be.

KATIE. You—you told about the party nice, Johnny. I—I should've waited up more, I guess.

JOHNNY. Aw, it ain't your fault, baby, you workin' like you do. (*He touches the comb.*) I—I wish I'd bought you the rest of that set when we was married, the man said it came all the way from Spain.

KATIE. What else was there to it?—You ain't told me for a long time.

JOHNNY. There was two little side combs and a locket on a chain.

KATIE. And a bracelet, you said.

JOHNNY. You know what, I'm gonna look up that man some day and get you the rest of that set.

Johnny is deeply moved. This is the closest that he and Katie have been in a long time. If things were entirely right between them, most of all if they were entirely right between Johnny and himself, this is the moment in which he would take her in his arms. Subconsciously, both of them know it. They enjoyed perfection, when they were young together, as closely perhaps as people come to it. Life together, when they were young, was very right between them. This day has moved Katie to an instinctive reach back toward that old perfection, which they have not felt in a long time. This is what she is subconsciously asking from Johnny. And subconsciously he realizes this. And because of his failures, he has not quite the feeling of this perfection, this completeness, to give her. This feeling is taut between them for a moment. And then Johnny feels instinctively the necessity of talking a little more, to try to reassure himself, to try to build with his words something more of reassurance that everything is all right within him. This very feeling is an acknowledgment that he no longer has that perfection to offer her. So, with his words, they go past the perfect moment. Katie senses this. There is a desperate need in her for Johnny to take her in his arms, without any more words, as he would do if their world were right. She is trying to hold on to this moment, not to let it get by, when after a moment she speaks.

KATIE. That's nice, Johnny, but—

JOHNNY (*eagerly, working himself into believing*). Ain't no buts about it, I mean it. Things are goin' to be different around here, you—you got no business workin' like you do.

KATIE. I don't mind the work, I—

JOHNNY. No sir, I ain't goin' to have it. Look at them pretty hands, they got no business bein' in water all the time. I'm goin' to change a lot of things. I'm goin' to quit the drinkin' too. And just to show you, here's my tip money, you can—

KATIE. No, Johnny, the tips are yours —you take all a man's money, it ain't right.

JOHNNY (*accepting this a shade too easily*). Well, there's a dime anyway. I—I had to take a nickel out of the bank for carfare, you can put a dime back. But I'm goin' to keep at 'em down at union headquarters and make 'em get me jobs. Tonight's the beginning of somethin' new, Katie— you believe me, don't you, Katie?

KATIE (*wanting to*). Sure, Johnny, sure I do.

JOHNNY. I'll be singin' all over Brooklyn and maybe Manhattan too. Have you heard Johnny Nolan sing, they'll say. Yes sir, our luck's turned, and some day—

KATIE (*from her heart*). Ah, stop it, Johnny, stop it, stop talkin'!

He looks at her, hurt, amazed. Katie has had all she can stand. It isn't any good, it's phony.

KATIE (*bitterly*). Talkin' like that only makes it worse! We ain't got a chance, who are we tryin' to kid!

There is a long pause. The truth that has been torn from Katie is the last thing either of them wanted to face— it is the sort of thing people try the hardest to keep from facing. But it is here. All Johnny's desperate effort to kid himself dies within him. He stares out the window. He could not possibly look at Katie in this moment.

JOHNNY (*very quietly*). Yeah. That's right, sure, who am I tryin' to kid.

Katie feels sorry for him, for them both, but there is no use in weakening— you can no longer evade the hard truth.

KATIE. I didn't go to hurt you, but it's the truth, I can't change it, Johnny.

JOHNNY. Yeah, and I can tell you somethin' else, too. All that baloney about the encores tonight—that was just because they was a little drunk and feelin' good. I wasn't so hot.

KATIE (*dry and hard*). No use talkin' like that, it won't help any.

JOHNNY. I don't know, as long as we're on the truth, let's keep lookin' at it. I'm the one ought to be kicked out, not Sissy. I got a wife and kids and I don't take care of 'em, I don't know why. I didn't want the kids when they come, but I love 'em—

how could you help it—sure, I love 'em a lot, but I just can't seem to turn into a hard-workin' man to take care of 'em. What sense does that make, all I want to do is sing, I don't know why. And I guess that's right, I ain't ever goin' to be able to change it. Sure, you're right, who am I tryin' to kid.

This comes so quietly from Johnny that it is frightening. For the first time in his life he has faced himself. Katie made him do it, even if she did not intend to. They have both faced him. So these two will never again feel quite the same about one another. What he has said is bitterly true, there is no answer to it.—Katie slowly picks up some of the dishes from the table, as though she would take them to the sink. But

even lifelong habit is no good, and she sets them back on the table.

KATIE (*dully*). We better get some sleep.

JOHNNY (*without turning*). Yeah.

Katie stands helplessly a moment, and then starts toward the bedroom. Johnny doesn't move.

In the PARLOR Francie is lying on her bed beside the window, illumined by the faint moonlight. She is awake, staring at the ceiling, as if feeling a presentiment about the next room. Outside the window stands the Tree in the backyard, bereft of most of its branches, but stark and strong in the moonlight. The scene fades out.

# PART THREE

MCGARRITY'S SALOON fades in, in the early morning. It is a small corner saloon. Next to a big free lunch sign is a cigar store with a wooden cigar store Indian.— McGarrity, the proprietor, is just finishing sweeping the sidewalk.

PASSING MAN. Morning, Mac.

McGarrity waves in answer and goes inside.—The place is deserted except for Johnny, who is sitting at a table, head down on his arms at a table. Before him is a whiskey glass and a litter of cigarettes. McGarrity studies him compassionately, then goes over and shakes him gently by the shoulder.

MCGARRITY. Seven o'clock, Johnny, better be goin' home.

Johnny raises his head wearily. He has not been asleep. And he is not as drunk as he would like to be, although he has tried hard to drink enough so that he would stop thinking.

JOHNNY (*wearily*). Sure, sure, home.

(*Singing*) "Home is where the heart is—"

He pulls himself to his feet and moves somewhat uncertainly to the bar. Automatically, McGarrity goes behind the bar, and just as automatically wipes the polished surface.

JOHNNY (*tonelessly*). Write nice songs about it, don't they, Mac?

MCGARRITY. Sure, Johnny.

JOHNNY. I sing 'em good, too, don't I, Mac?

MCGARRITY. Sure, Johnny, sure.

JOHNNY. Don't just sure me like that, Mac. You're wrong about somethin', you don't know it, but you're wrong. I'm not ever goin' home any more.

MCGARRITY. Sure you are, Johnny, you got a mighty nice family to go home to.

JOHNNY. You don't get it. I'm goin' there, I'm gonna walk down the same street, I'm gonna turn in the same door, and there'll be my nice family, but I won't ever be goin' home again. Give me a drink, Mac.

MCGARRITY. I don't get you, boy.

JOHNNY. Sure you don't, I don't get it either. I pretty near did, sittin' there thinkin' about it. Listen, Mac, listen good now. (*Singing*) "Maxwellton's braes are bonnie, where early fa's the dew—" (*Stopping*) What did you hear, Mac?

MCGARRITY. You always sing good, if that's what you mean.

JOHNNY. If that's what I mean? I don't know what I mean. What good is singin'—you feel somethin', but there ain't nobody *hears* what you feel. It's no good—she used to hear, but not any more. So I won't ever be goin' home again. I hate singin'. I should've been tendin' bar like you. Don't ever sing, Mac.

McGarrity studies Johnny closely. He knows Johnny is in pain about something, but he isn't quite sure what.

MCGARRITY (*polishing the bar*). Lots of angles to it, boy. You wouldn't be any good tendin' bar. You're a funny fellow, Johnny.

JOHNNY. Sure, sure, I'm funny. I want a drink, Mac.

MCGARRITY. I don't know if I'd trade with you—a poet that can't write, that's bad. But it takes all kinds of people, maybe some of 'em just wasn't meant to make a livin'. And maybe I would trade, at that. And now you

better get home to that nice family, your missus will be worryin'.

JOHNNY (*flaring up*). All right, it's the nicest family in the world, you think I don't know that. Give me a drink, I said.

MCGARRITY. Easy, Johnny, easy. (*He sets out a drink.*) Have one on the house.

JOHNNY (*bitterly*). Sure, that's better, and I'll sing for it, that's what I'll do, I'll sing for it.

McGarrity studies Johnny compassionately as Johnny pours the drink. Johnny's bitterness toward life, and most of all his hatred for himself and what he is, is at its peak.

The scene dissolves to the NOLAN TENEMENT as Francie emerges with pencil box and books, starting out for school. In a moment the door bursts open and Neeley emerges, always a little late. He has his books in a strap. As he joins her, Neeley starts to rip off the tie he is supposed to wear to school.

FRANCIE. Neeley Nolan, you stop that.

NEELEY. Aw, I don't want to wear no old tie, it's—

FRANCIE (*maternally*). Mama *said*.

NEELEY. Aw, go chase yourself.

But he submits to her mothering as she starts to pull the tie back into place. Suddenly they hear a clamor off scene —and we then see what they see: Johnny, drunk and unsteady, is just coming around the corner surrounded by a swarm of derisive kids. Johnny pays no attention to them.

THE KIDS. Just pickle my bones in alcohol. He's stiffer than a goat, look how he walks.

Francie and Neeley run to their father.

Francie pushes her way to him and tries to take his arm.

FRANCIE (*fiercely*). You leave him alone! Papa—come on, let's go home, let's hurry, papa.

Johnny tries uncertainly to smile, but he is pretty far gone.

NEELEY (*to the kids*). You leave him alone or I'll bust you one.

The kids pay no attention. Neeley socks one of them and a fight is on. Francie tries desperately to help Johnny toward their door.

McShane enters from across the street, and breaks up the fight.

MCSHANE (*to the kids*). Come on now, quit it—quit it or I'll run you in. Beat it now.

The kids break and beat it, still yelling derisively. Francie and Neeley remain and McShane turns back to them.

MCSHANE. Now, my lad, where do you live?

FRANCIE (*fiercely*). I'll take him home, he's my father.

MCSHANE. I expect you'd best be gettin' on to school, hadn't you? I'll look after him for you. (*Francie hesitates.*) Don't you worry, he ain't in any trouble, I'll take good care of him. This the building?

FRANCIE (*nodding*). Second floor back. If—if you talk to him, he—he's always all right and you'll—

MCSHANE. Don't you fret a minute. (*He takes Johnny's arm.*) Come on now—we'll make it, lad.

Johnny gives him a blurred look but submits to being led up the steps, and as Francie stands looking after them, miserable, the scene dissolves to the TENEMENT HALL where McShane helps Johnny toward the Nolan door. Johnny only half-coherently tries to sing.

JOHNNY. "When Irish eyes are smiling—"

MCSHANE. Quiet, now, quiet does it.

JOHNNY. Got to sing, don't you, very important, and she'll hear you, but you got to sing ju-u-st right, so she can get the door open first, very important.

MCSHANE. All right, sing then, if it eases what's hurtin' you.

JOHNNY. "When Irish eyes are smiling—"

The noise causes a couple of neighbors, who open their doors, to look out. McShane knocks at the Nolan door, and Katie appears, just ready to start her morning's janitor work. McShane is surprised to see her.

KATIE. Johnny!

Scarcely noticing McShane, she starts to help Johnny into the kitchen. McShane helps.—The scene cuts to the KITCHEN as they get Johnny into a chair at the table. McShane studies Katie, who is busy with Johnny.

MCSHANE. I—I didn't—I didn't expect to see you, ma'am. Is there anything I can do?

KATIE. He's my husband, I can take care of him. (*To Johnny*) It's all right now, Johnny, I'll get you a nice cup of coffee.

JOHNNY (*blurred*). Nice cup of coffee, nice cup of coffee.

Katie goes to the stove. McShane stands awkwardly for a moment.

MCSHANE. I just wanted to tell you, the gentleman wasn't makin' no trouble, just—needed a little help.

Katie stops pouring the coffee to look at him. She is instinctively defensive about Johnny, so her look is antagonistic at any intrusion into their family troubles.

MCSHANE (*awkwardly*). If—if there's anything I can do, ma'am—

Katie comes over and puts the coffee down in front of Johnny.

KATIE. There, Johnny, drink it. (*Then, turning to McShane*) If you wasn't new on the beat, Mr. McShane, you'd know Johnny never makes trouble—and you'd know the whole Nolan family don't need anybody's help, and—and I'd thank you very much, Mr. McShane, to mind your own business. (*Her eyes meet his squarely.*)

MCSHANE (*after a moment*). Sure— Mrs. Nolan.

He turns and goes, closing the door behind him. Katie turns to Johnny.

Out in the HALL, McShane pauses a moment beside the door and looks back toward the room a little ruefully. He sure caught hell. He grins in admiration, then starts down the stairs.

The scene dissolves to the PUBLIC SCHOOL. The school yard is swarming with children. The bell is ringing, and the youngsters start to form lines to march in. This dissolves to the EIGHTH GRADE CLASSROOM. The view is focused on one group and then moves past the intent, struggling faces of other children as they recite in unison, with a curious cadence with which poetry is scanned.

KIDS. "*Beau*-ty is *truth* truth *beau*-ty that is *all* Ye *know* on *earth* and *all* ye *need* to *know*."

The camera comes to Neeley, and then Francie; then pulls back to reveal a classroom so crowded that some of the children have to sit in the aisles in chairs without desks. The teacher, MISS TILFORD, middle-aged, and tired, is at the blackboard, marking off with chalk the metric divisions of the lines which are written on the board. Miss Tilford is repeating it with them.

MISS TILFORD (*as they finish*). Now, who knows the name of the meter? (*Looking at the class; Francie's hand is up.*) Frances Nolan?

FRANCIE (*standing up*). Yes, but—

MISS TILFORD. You can't "know but." You either know or you don't know.

FRANCIE. I know it's iambic pentameter, five metric feet, with a long syllable coming after a short one, but—I only meant to say—I was thinking about the words, what they mean, and I wondered—

MISS TILFORD. You don't have to know the words, Frances, only the meter. And we're late now for our arithmetic. The class will get their arithmetic books.

She moves to the desk. There is a general rustle in the class as the exchange of books is made. Francie sits down slowly.

MISS TILFORD (*opening her book*). Now then! The farmer has a hundred and sixty-nine apples in a barrel. He wants to divide them into equal piles, with as many apples in each pile as there are piles of apples. How would he go about it? (*As there is no answer, she goes on.*) What method would he use—What is the latest process we've been studying?

FRANCIE (*with hand raised*). Miss Tilford—

MISS TILFORD. Yes, Frances.

FRANCIE (*rising*). If beauty is truth and that's all ye need—I mean all you need to know—Then that means it's the most important thing, and if a man—I mean somebody—spent all their time just trying to live like that —Well it's hard to put, but no matter what else he did, then—then—

She falters, feeling strongly what she wants to say, but unable to say it. Neeley knows what she is getting at.

MISS TILFORD. Then *what*, Frances?

FRANCIE (*lamely*). Then—it would be all right, wouldn't it—I guess.

MISS TILFORD. I'm afraid I haven't the slightest idea what you're talking about, Frances, but I *do* know we're disrupting the arithmetic! Now, class! Square root! Does no one remember square root!?

As Francie sits down, deeply humiliated, the scene dissolves to the CLASS-ROOM while the children are filing past a doctor and a nurse, who examine briefly the head of each child, looking for lice. As they finish, the children are free to leave. Francie and Neeley are in line. The doctor is examining a boy, and indicates for the nurse to look.

DOCTOR. Report to your principal and give him this card.

The boy goes on with the card non-chalantly, but as he leaves some kids who successfully passed the examination, jeer:

KIDS. Mickey's lousy, Mickey's lousy!

Neeley, next in line, submits indifferently, and dashes to his cronies as soon as the doctor murmurs "All right." Francie steps up. She offers her head,

enduring the examination as a necessary evil, but clearly knowing it is not necessary in her case. Miss Tilford, checking the line, observes her.

DOCTOR. All right.

He has turned to the next child and misses Francie's scornful glance—as much as to say "I know that"—but Miss Tilford sees it, and suddenly feels a compunction.

MISS TILFORD (*as Francie passes her*). Frances..

FRANCIE. Yes, Miss Tilford?

MISS TILFORD. Er—maybe I was a little too abrupt with you this morning—I mean, you *are* a smart girl and —it's just that you must learn to stick to the point and not go wandering off the subject.

FRANCIE. Yes, Miss Tilford.

MISS TILFORD. If you'll do that, you needn't worry about passing.

FRANCIE. I wasn't worrying about— (*Giving up; meekly*) Yes, Miss Tilford, thank you, Miss Tilford.

As she wanders out, completely lost, the scene dissolves to the SCHOOLYARD. Neeley has waited for Francie and they are now walking across the yard toward the gate. Francie is vaguely troubled.

NEELEY. How should I know if they knew you was talkin' about him. I don't see what for you want to talk so much anyway. Pop was just a little drunk, that don't hurt nobody. (*He breaks off as he sees something off-scene.*) Hey, look!

We then see SISSY, from their angle, waiting at the corner for them. She waves.—The children stop short in a quandary.

NEELEY. What'll we do? We ain't supposed to talk to her.

FRANCIE (*troubled*). I don't know—(*She has an idea.*) Neeley, that's all they said, we was only supposed not to *talk* to her.

Neeley's face brightens. Francie hurries toward Sissy and Neeley follows.

Sissy embraces them both, and doesn't notice their silence.

SISSY. Chickabiddies! I couldn't stand it no longer! I just *had* to get a peek. Man alive, you both look good enough to eat!

NEELEY. Gee, it's—

Francie shakes her head warningly. Sissy doesn't notice.

SISSY. Well, how are you anyway? (*No answer—Francie stares at her miserably.*) Tell me all about it, how's things at home? (*There's a miserable silence.*) Well, you're not lettin' me get a word in edgewise. Oh—I catch! You ain't allowed to talk to me, huh? (*They nod—she laughs and ·hugs them.*) Well, you do just like your mama said. But there ain't nobody said anything about me talkin' to you, is that it? (*They nod and shake their heads in happy confusion.*) Smart enough for lawyers, the both of you! Well, let's see, you can nod and shake and make faces, can't you? . . . How's Katie? (*They nod.*) And your papa? (*They hesitate, then nod uncertainly.*) Not workin' much? (*They shake their heads sadly.*) Well, don't you worry, he will. (*They nod; then tentatively*) Any sign of the ice meltin' in my direction yet? (*They shrug and Sissy sighs humorously.*) Guess I'll have to tell Bill you still got scarlet fever, he's kinda wonderin' . . . Oh, well. And how's school?

There is a divided opinion on this. Neeley's shrug implies that it's okay enough, but to hell with it. But the question has revived Francie's problem, and her shake of the head is troubled. Sissy's interest centers on her.

SISSY. What's wrong, ain't you doin' good? (*Francie shakes her head.*) Well . . . got in any trouble? (*There is a confused shrug.*) Teacher mean to you? (*There's a division of opinion—a half-hearted negative from Francie, a nod from Neeley. Sissy is puzzled.*) I don't get it, lamb, somethin's troubling you, maybe I ain't askin' the right questions.

Francie looks at her miserably, wanting terribly to talk to Sissy, to someone, about it. For a moment the scene is at an impasse. Then Francie has an idea.

FRANCIE. Neeley. (*He looks at her.*) Neeley, Aunt Sissy wants to know if it's because the teacher's mean to us.

NEELEY. Sure she is, she—

Francie touches his arm, shakes her head, indicates that he is to talk to her, not Sissy. The great light dawns on Neeley.

NEELEY. Oh—was you speakin' to me, Francie? Why yes, Francie, I'd say that teacher was pretty mean, wouldn't you, Francie? I'd say all teachers was pretty mean, Francie.

FRANCIE (*as Sissy grins at this subterfuge*). Well, Neeley, I wouldn't say that she was mean, exactly. That isn't what we mean, Neeley, is it?

NEELEY. Ain't it, Francie?

FRANCIE. No, what we mean is, Neeley, school's to learn things in, that's what it's for, isn't it, and if you got questions—

NEELEY. Well now, look, Francie—if

you mean all that talkin' you did about pop, then I don't know—

FRANCIE. Neeley Nolan, you don't understand anything. You got to know things, if they're important, that's what school's for, isn't it? It's just if she'd tell you things, not just the meter but what they mean, that's what teachers ought to do—Isn't it, Neeley?

NEELEY (*giving up*). Well, Francie, maybe you know what you're talkin' about, but if you ask me, you just talk but don't say nothin'.

FRANCIE. But, Neeley—

SISSY (*gently*). It's all right, lamb. I can't say I could draw a map of it, but I get some of it. (*She draws Francie to her.*) You quit worryin' about it, hon, and run along home. Maybe your old Aunt Sissy can do somethin' about it. (*She hugs them both tightly.*) Look, maybe it's just as well if you don't say nothin' at home about seein' me—you know, it ain't lyin' as long as nobody asks you.

NEELEY (*lightly*). I guess we can't help it, Francie, if people listen to us in the street.

He is off like a shot, calling to a group of boys. Francie smiles gratefully into Sissy's eyes. Sissy watches after her a moment, and then her face hardens. Nobody is going to make Francie suffer because of her father's weakness, or for any other reason, whatever it may be. She starts toward the school.

The scene dissolves to a CLASSROOM. Sissy is standing belligerently in front of a bewildered Miss Tilford's desk.

SISSY (*belligerently*). What I'm sayin' is, whatever it is you're teachin' the other kids that Francie ain't gettin'—I ain't gonna have it!

MISS TILFORD. But I assure you that your daughter is being taught exactly the same as the other children. If you could just tell me what it is that you mean—

SISSY (*interrupting; humbly*). Look, lady. I don't know myself what we're talkin' about. I ain't very smart, I guess you seen that. But somethin's eatin' that kid, and she's a good kid and—don't you hold out nothin' on her, don't you teach the other kids nothin' she ain't gettin', or—(*Confused*) Well, you see that you do like I said. (*She attempts belligerence again.*) Or I'll call a cop, and that ain't kiddin' either. I used to be married to one!

With this last lame threat she stalks out, leaving Miss Tilford shaking her head in relief as though at a lunatic who hasn't affected her at all.

The scene dissolves to the NOLAN KITCHEN where we get a close view of the Sunday funny paper spread on the floor. The text is the Katzenjammer Kids. This dissolves to a full view of the kitchen to show Neeley sprawled on the floor with the funny paper. Francie is quietly staring out the window, preoccupied, drumming on it idly. Katie enters from the hall, with a few clothes over her arm that she has just brought in from the line to be ironed. She stops abruptly when she doesn't see Johnny in the room. Her question carries quick, instinctive apprehension that Johnny may have gone out to get drunk again.

KATIE. Where's your papa, did he go out?

NEELEY. No'm, he—

Johnny appears from the bedroom. He has heard.

JOHNNY (*with quiet bitterness*). No, he didn't go out.

KATIE. Oh. I thought—

JOHNNY (*quietly*). I ain't goin' to McGarrity's, if that's what you mean. (*To Francie*) Them's fine compositions—they read nice, Prima Donna.

FRANCIE (*absently*). Thank you, papa.

Johnny has the compositions in his hand. He goes over to the table and puts them down. He isn't looking at Katie. This Sunday is a hard day for Johnny. With what has happened between him and Katie, it is very difficult to be shut in these small quarters with his family, with something dead between them. Life is at low ebb for Johnny. He picks up a piece of the newspaper and studies it absently, to avoid looking at Katie. Katie studies him for a second. She, too, is aware of the tension, but life has to go on. She puts the clothes into her work basket and starts to mend some of them. There is a little silence.

NEELEY (*quite unaware of all this*). Pop, why don't the Katzenjammer Kids talk plain English?

JOHNNY. Supposed to make it funny, I guess.

KATIE. Francie, you been staring out that window for half an hour. Can't you make up your mind to do something?

FRANCIE. What shall I do?

KATIE. You used to like to do your homework Sundays.

FRANCIE. I—I don't know, I don't like school as much as I used to.

NEELEY. Now you're gettin' some sense!

KATIE. School's just the same this year as it was last.

FRANCIE. Mama.

KATIE. Yes.

FRANCIE. You know that big market on Clancy Street, down the hill?

KATIE. We can't deal there, if that's what you mean. That neighborhood's expensive.

FRANCIE. Well, I wasn't talking about the market.

KATIE. You said did I know that market. Neeley, don't just lie there and scuff your shoes out.

FRANCIE. Well, I meant, the other day I walked home that way, and— and do you know what's just a couple of blocks away from that market?

KATIE. Another market, I guess, and am I supposed to guess what's two blocks away from that. Why don't you say what you mean, Francie?

FRANCIE (*discouraged*). I didn't mean anything, I guess.

From behind his paper, Johnny gives her a quick look. He knows Francie has something on her mind, and is getting no place with it. He is very much aware of the unconscious duel between the two.

KATIE. Sometimes it looks like you make these holes on purpose, Neeley.

NEELEY (*grinning*). Aw, can I help it if things just happen?

FRANCIE. Papa.

JOHNNY. Yes, baby.

FRANCIE. You know what I read in a magazine once?

JOHNNY (*getting a look from Katie*). What was it, Francie?

FRANCIE. Well, it said walking is a good thing, it said people would look and feel better if they walked a lot. "Walk and put rose petals in your cheeks," it said.

KATIE. Then I ought to be a ravin' beauty with all those stairs.

Francie wanders over to her father's chair, and stands in back of it. As she talks it is clear it is for his benefit.

FRANCIE. It didn't mean that. It meant—Well, like on a Sunday, people would feel lots better if they took a long walk or something, instead of just sitting around and—

KATIE. Francie, I want you to stop talkin' around things like that. It ain't right. If you got somethin' to say, I want you to say it right out, plain.

FRANCIE (*defeated, starting back to the window*). I wasn't going to say anything. I was just talking about walking.

Johnny, from behind his paper, shoots a quick look at Katie and then at Francie. He lays down his paper, gets to his feet and stretches himself. When he speaks, it is indirectly a reproof to Katie.

JOHNNY. Been so much talk about walkin', I think I'll take one. Come along, Prima Donna.

Francie's face lights up, but she restrains herself quickly.

FRANCIE. Oh, yes, sure, papa.

Johnny grins at her and starts to pick up his coat. As Katie looks sharply at him the scene dissolves to a STREET in a BETTER NEIGHBORHOOD: Francie and Johnny are walking together. She has hold of his arm proudly.

JOHNNY (*teasing*). Must be pretty special, this place you walk to that's two blocks from a market.

FRANCIE. This way, papa.

They come to a corner and Francie stops. Johnny looks around, but can't make out just what it is.

JOHNNY. Is this it, Prima Donna?

FRANCIE (*shyly*). Yes, papa.

Johnny looks where she points, and we next see the new school from their angle. It is a long way from being the best school you ever saw, but it is different from the old one—a bigger yard, a few trees, less dingy. Johnny looks from the school back to Francie. It doesn't make sense, somehow.

JOHNNY. The school? (*Francie can only nod.*) I don't get it, baby.

FRANCIE (*hesitantly*). It must be just as nice inside, don't you think? The teachers and all, and—(*She falters to a stop.*)

JOHNNY (*gently*). What are you gettin' at, Prima Donna?

Francie can't look at him. It is such a hard thing to explain, even to papa. Her reply is almost a whisper.

FRANCIE. Bend down, papa. (*He does.*) I wish I could go to that school, papa.

The strange intensity of her feelings touches Johnny. He doesn't want to let her down, but he doesn't know quite what to do about it. He puts his arm around her.

JOHNNY. I don't know. It would be awful nice but they got rules, honey, you got to go to the school where you live.

Francie's face falls. She knew that this was the answer.

FRANCIE. I know. I didn't really— (*She can't go on.*)

JOHNNY (*he can't stand it*). Wait a minute, maybe there's a way, it's a free country, ain't it? (*As he sings*) "School days, school days—" Maybe we could move near to here.

FRANCIE (*like a shot*). When?

JOHNNY (*taken aback*). Well, not just yet, Prima Donna, not for a while. But just as soon as our ship comes in, you'll see.

FRANCIE (*let down*). Oh, only by that time I'll—

JOHNNY. You want to go there awful bad, don't you, baby? (*Francie nods.*) Then, look, we're goin' to find a way.

FRANCIE. Honest?

JOHNNY. Well now, I've got to turn this thing over some. Let's us do a little more walkin', it's—maybe it's good for thinkin' too.

With complete faith in this, Francie takes his arm again and as they start to walk the scene dissolves to a RESIDENCE STREET composed of small houses, fairly attractive. Johnny and Francie come down the sidewalk. They are walking slowly.

JOHNNY (*making conversation*). That's not a bad house, how'd you like to live there? Nice little porch.

FRANCIE (*shaking her head*). I don't like brown houses.

JOHNNY. Well, maybe a coat of paint.

FRANCIE (*seeing the next house*). Oh, papa! (*Johnny looks, Francie goes on:*) That's it.

Johnny looks and we get a view of the next house—small, white, a neat white fence, and flowers.

JOHNNY. Yes sir, that's it.

FRANCIE. If we only could!

JOHNNY. Well, why can't we. Our luck's bound to turn, and the first thing we'll do is buy that little house when—(*lamely*) some day.

The fairy tale is back, and Francie's elation is gone. Johnny looks at her, cornered.

JOHNNY (*in desperation*). Look, as long as we're goin' to buy that house some day, why can't we maybe borrow it for now? Like—say we make out it's ours, then your address is—(*looking*) 98 Hibbard Avenue—startin' right now! Then, you see, you got to transfer from your old school.

FRANCIE (*it is too much to understand all at once*). How do you *mean*, papa?

JOHNNY. That's it . . . We could say you come here to live with your aunt, your rich old aunt. She's lonely and she's goin' to leave you all her money.

FRANCIE. Oh papa, could we *really!*

JOHNNY. Sure we could, it's nobody's business. And every day you eat off real china dishes with little cherries painted onto 'em, and when you drink coffee, you have a cup and saucer to match, and a plate too, like they come from a restaurant.

FRANCIE (*ecstatic*). Sometimes I forget to water the geraniums and you ought to hear Auntie scold me!

JOHNNY. You got to put up with her crotchets—after all, you're her heir.

FRANCIE (*pointing*). That—that could be my room up there where the little window is.

Johnny, watching her, suddenly becomes troubled by the enormity of what he is doing.

JOHNNY. Now look, Prima Donna,

you know what we're doin' ain't exactly accordin' to the rules.

FRANCIE (*fearfully*). You mean it's wrong?

JOHNNY. Not by a jugful it ain't wrong. See, the house is here, and we're here, and the school—we wasn't all brought together like this just for no reason. *But* . . . we'll have to keep it a kind of secret, you won't be able to tell anybody, and you'll have to be extra good to make up for it.

FRANCIE (*relieved*). Oh, I will! (*She looks around.*) I think here comes auntie now.

An elderly man and woman, coming down the street, turn in at the gate. They are very nice looking.

JOHNNY (*whispering*). I see you got an uncle too. (*They both laugh; everything is settled.*) Now, I'm goin' to show you a way to your new school through a little park. I know right where it is, and you can see the seasons change on your way.

He has taken her by the arm and they are moving again down the street.

FRANCIE (*trying to speak*). Papa—bend down. (*But she is too moved for mortal words.*) My cup runneth over. (*Her eyes glisten softly.*)

The scene dissolves to the NOLAN KITCHEN at night. Francie is helping Katie with the dishes, but hovering over Johnny who is laboriously writing a letter on the kitchen table. Across from him Neeley scowls over his homework.

KATIE. It's dishonest, that's what it is. You're settin' the child an awful bad example.

FRANCIE. Papa says if it doesn't hurt anybody, and you're not dishonest in your heart—

KATIE. You two with your fancy words—

JOHNNY (*paying no attention*). How you spell "transfer," Prima Donna?

FRANCIE. T-r-a-n-s-f-e-r.

NEELEY. I'd ruther be shot than do this arithmetic.

KATIE (*mechanically*). It'll come to you, sonny . . . And another thing. We kept Francie out a year so's she and Neeley could be in the same class, so's she could look after him, and here just the year they're gettin' ready to graduate, you go and—(*She breaks off, exasperated.*) It's against the law and it's makin' her live a lie and—I won't have you doin' it.

Johnny stops writing. For the first time he turns and looks squarely at her, speaking very quietly.

JOHNNY. I'm goin' to do this for her, Katie. Maybe it's my fault or not there ain't much I can give her—but this is one thing she's goin' to have.

There is a pause. Katie is surprised by his firmness. She is the first to falter.

KATIE (*yielding*). It'll make an awful long walk for you, mornings.

FRANCIE (*with a gleam of hope*). I don't mind gettin' up early.

KATIE. It'll be lots harder on your shoes, and you won't have dresses like the other children.

FRANCIE. I'll wash and iron my dress every single night.

JOHNNY (*writing again, with a funny little smile*). How do you spell appreciate, Francie?

FRANCIE. A-p-p-r-e-c-i-a-t-e.

KATIE (*awkwardly*). If the principal of the school swallows that story—which I don't think he will—I'll see what I can do about makin' over that checked dress of mine.

Katie goes on washing the dishes to cover her surrender. Francie's face is radiant. Johnny smiles a little to himself as he writes.

The scene dissolves to the PRINCIPAL's OFFICE where Francie is standing anxiously before the principal as he reads Johnny's note. At length he looks up from the note.

PRINCIPAL. Why not? My school's overcrowded as it is.

Francie smiles tremulously. It is almost too good to be true.—This dissolves to "FRANCIE'S LITTLE HOUSE." Francie, her coat over the new plaid dress, approaches the little house. She pauses near the gate, looks in. It is a miracle, this little house of hers. She sees a scrap of paper, and a broken dead flower stem inside the fence. Making sure no one is looking, she slips through and picks these up. It is her gesture of serving the little house. As she starts out the gate again, her manner changes and for a fleeting moment she has the job of pretense that it is really hers, and she is emerging to start to school. She walks through the gate with something of the manner of a princess. The gate squeaks a little. She tries it again.

FRANCIE (*proprietary*). Dear me, I must remember to oil that gate.

As she goes on down the street, completely happy, the scene dissolves to a CLASSROOM in the NEW SCHOOL. The room is different, less crowded, cleaner. Class has just taken up. Miss McDonough, the teacher, is standing beside her desk, her arm around Francie's shoulder.

MISS MCDONOUGH. This is Frances Nolan, class. I'm sure you'll all make her welcome to our school. Now this will be your desk, Frances. (*She takes Francie to the desk.*) And one more thing, Frances. Don't worry about marks at first. I've told the class, often, it isn't the marks that count, it's the knowledge that you make your own, that you make forever and forever a part of you. Now you may go to your desk.

Miss McDonough turns to her desk. Francie stands a second. For a moment it is too good to be true. Then she slips down into the desk. It is hers. She begins to smile.

The scene dissolves to the NOLAN KITCHEN where we first see Francie ironing her school dress as she talks. She is thrilled over her first day at the new school. Then the scene pulls back to reveal Johnny and Katie also in the kitchen. Katie is laying the table for supper. Johnny is finishing getting dressed to go out on another job.

FRANCIE. And oh, Miss McDonough is just wonderful. She said we could choose anything in the world to write this composition about, just anything. She said it was good for us to choose our own subject.

JOHNNY. Well, that's mighty fine, Prima Donna. What did you decide on?

FRANCIE. She said it'd be nice if we wrote about something in nature. But we don't know much about nature, do we, papa?

JOHNNY. Well, your tree's nature.

FRANCIE. But just one tree for a composition, it'd be awful short. What else is nature?

JOHNNY. Grass, wind, dogs—why don't you write about a dog?

FRANCIE. Are dogs nature?

JOHNNY. Sure.

FRANCIE. But I'd like this to be kind of a—special composition. She was *so* wonderful.

JOHNNY. I'll tell you what then— what am I doin' tonight but goin' to sea on the good ship Governor Clinton, and the ocean's nature, ain't it? I'll keep an eye on the sea tonight, and tell you all about that.

Through this, Katie busies herself with the scanty preparations for the meal. Johnny is getting a warm glow out of Francie's happiness over the new school that he has given her. Katie knows deep inside herself that she never would have given Francie this odd gift, so there is an instinctive little resentment of the closeness between father and daughter. None of it is lost on her.

KATIE. Bein' a waiter on a little excursion boat goin' up the Hudson River ain't exactly goin' to sea.

JOHNNY. Sure it is, it's a kind of a sea, it's water. I'll remember everything about it, so you can write about the bright blue sea, Prima Donna. How's that?

FRANCIE. I think that would be kind of special.

KATIE (*drily*). Your Miss McDonough bein' so wonderful, she didn't happen to mention where our supper was comin' from tonight, did she?

NEELEY (*appearing suddenly from his bedroom, on cue*). Did you say supper, mom, I'm hungry.

KATIE. There ain't much, sonny. But maybe we can fill out with one o' them compositions about the bright blue sea.

JOHNNY. Prima Donna, you know what—this ought to be extra special for your new school. You know what we're goin' to do?

FRANCIE. What, papa?

JOHNNY. If there's tips enough on this job tonight, come Sunday, I'm goin' to take you to see the ocean for yourself.

FRANCIE. The really ocean?

NEELEY. Me, too, pop?

JOHNNY. You bet. It ain't right livin' this close and you never even seen it. People ought—

KATIE (*sharply*). Johnny!

JOHNNY. Yeah.

KATIE (*changing her mind*). Nothing. Maybe at that it's better than that McGarrity gettin' your tip money.

JOHNNY. Yeah. I get it—I—I wasn't thinkin'. (*To the children*) Sure, your mama's right, we better get a little bread and bacon in that old cupboard before we go to takin' fishin' trips. But we'll go one of these days, when—well, you wait and see. (*He takes his hat.*) Well, this ain't earnin' the family bread. (*Ready to go, grateful to escape this*) Needn't wait up. If I know the Governor Clinton, I won't be bringin' home no caviar. Goodnight, my hearties.

FRANCIE. Goodnight, papa.

NEELEY. Goodnight, pop.

JOHNNY. I'll keep an eye out good, Prima Donna, and tell you all about it.

He is gone. There is an odd little tension in the room for a moment. Katie sets the last things on the table.

KATIE. All right, men, step right up and get your rations.

NEELEY. Oh, golly, mom, you mean we got to play North Pole again?

KATIE (*quickly*). I couldn't help it, son, there wasn't a penny in the pitcher.

FRANCIE. Look, you can be captain, Neeley, and when we find the Pole you can drive in the stake with your name on it.

The children sit down and Katie pours the coffee. What food there is, is on the table—a heel of bread, a bit of cold potato, cracker crumbs.

NEELEY (*glumly*). Gosh, even caviar would look good, lookin' at that stuff.

FRANCIE. My, fish from Alaskan waters and chopped Eskimo whale.

KATIE (*bitterly*). That's right, knowin' about all them ocean things sure helps to keep you from feelin' hungry, don't it?

NEELEY. I'd rather think about all that free lunch down at McGarrity's. Mom, how much longer do I got to be a minor?

KATIE. You ain't ever goin' to start takin' anything from that place.

FRANCIE. I bet papa'll bring home some swell food, nice rolls and—

NEELEY. Aw, quit it. Mom—I'm hungry.

KATIE. Steady, captain.

Neeley's eyes meet hers, and he gets hold of himself, and gulps some coffee.

FRANCIE (*watching this*). Mama, you'd rather do anything than break into the star bank, wouldn't you?

KATIE. Just about. Bein' a little hungry ain't never as bad if you know you got a little somethin' in the bank.

FRANCIE. Mama. (*Katie looks at her.*) When explorers get hungry, there's a reason, something big comes out of it, like they discover the North Pole. But what's the big thing comes out of us bein' hungry.

KATIE (*wearily*). You found the catch in it, Francie. (*Then, ashamed of admitting it*) Aw, that's no way to talk. Sure, somethin' comes out of it. Courage, my men, the Spring thaws will be here before you know it.

She roughs Neeley's hair affectionately as she goes to get some more coffee. The scene fades out.

# PART FOUR

The BEDROOM CLOSET fades in. Katie is prying the star bank loose. Neeley, loaded down with blankets and frying pans, watches avidly.

KATIE. Run along, sonny—I ain't goin' to spill a penny!

She slides a paper under the bank, lifts it, and wraps it quickly in a dish towel, keeping her word. They go out through the now bare bedroom.

The scene cuts to the KITCHEN, which

is empty of everything but the stove. The Nolan bedstead is just going through the door, borne out by Charlie, whose cap bears the simple legend "Ice."

KATIE (*taking a last look around*). I guess we got everything.

Out in the HALL, Charlie, carrying the bed up, and Mr. Crackenbox, carrying a trunk down, have difficulty passing each other on the stairs, and Katie and Neeley have to wait. A humble bit of crepe hangs on the Gaddis door; Katie straightens it.

KATIE. Poor Flossie.

A couple of women tenants peer out their doors at the moving.

FIRST WOMAN. Johnny ain't doin' too well, eh, Mrs. Nolan?

KATIE (*starting up the stairs*). Just movin' nearer to the sun. Soon's we heard Mrs. Waters was vacatin', we made up our minds. (*She goes on up determinedly with Neeley.*)

Next, on the FOURTH FLOOR, Francie is seen leaning excitedly over the banister, as Charlie struggles up the last of the stairs and through the door of a rear flat, just over the Nolans' old one.

FRANCIE. Neeley, our new fire escape leads right up onto the roof.

NEELEY (*coming up*). Whoever lives on the top floor gets dibs on the roof!

As Katie follows him up, Mrs. Waters, the vacating tenant, comes out of the flat, and addresses her anxiously. The children fly into the flat.

MRS. WATERS. I been waitin' for you, Mrs. Nolan. There's somethin' I got to ask you—a favor. I—I better show you.

She leads the way into the KITCHEN of the NEW FLAT. This is a little smaller, darker, meaner. Some of the Nolan belongings are in place, some in a tangle. Mrs. Waters leads Katie to the parlor. Francie and Neeley climb in the window from the fire escape and follow. The scene cuts to the PARLOR, which is empty of furniture except for a small, old-fashioned upright piano. Mrs. Waters touches it lovingly.

MRS. WATERS. The late Mr. Waters gave it to me for a wedding present. It won't go down the stairs, and— they want fifteen dollars to move it lowerin' it out the window. Do you mind my leavin' it, Mrs. Nolan? It don't take much room, and some day, when I get the fifteen dollars, I'll send back for it.

KATIE (*touched*). Why, sure I don't mind, Mrs. Waters.

FRANCIE (*to Mrs. Waters*). Can you play it?

MRS. WATERS. No, neither one of us could. (*To Katie*) And if it ain't too much trouble, you could dust it off once in a while and leave the kitchen door open a little so it won't get cold or damp.

KATIE. Sure I will. And I hope it won't be long until you can send back for it.

She follows Mrs. Waters out and both children cross their fingers instantly, showing they don't share their mother's "hope." Then, reverently, each strikes a note.

The scene cuts to the KITCHEN as Mr. Crackenbox comes out of the smaller bedroom carrying the last of Mrs. Waters' possessions, topped by a small, cheap, old bassinet. Mrs. Waters is about to follow him out, when Katie sees the bassinet. (Charlie is heard putting up the bedstead in the bedroom.)

KATIE. Mrs. Waters. That—that—is it a . . .

MRS. WATERS (*smiling*). Yeah, we kept the baby in it—about thirty years ago.

KATIE (*with difficulty*). I was just thinkin' . . . if you don't need it. . . . Make a nice handy little washbasket. I'd be glad to give you a quarter for it.

MRS. WATERS (*looking at her curiously*). Why sure. My Edgar's kids is even too old.

Tenderly the two lift the thing down, and Mr. Crackenbox goes out with the rest of the load. Katie gets a quarter out of the bank, then quickly wraps it up again.

MRS. WATERS (*touching her; softly*). Excuse me for askin', Mrs. Nolan, but—it won't really make a very handy washbasket? (*Their eyes meet.*)

KATIE (*nodding; quietly*). Please don't say nothin'. I—I ain't told nobody yet.

MRS. WATERS (*with deep feeling*). I know it ain't always easy, when you're poor, but—it'll be a blessin' to you.

KATIE (*very low*). Yes, sure—sure it will—

The children, starting to run in, rouse her, and she nods a hasty farewell to Mrs. Waters as she hurries with the bassinet into the bedroom. Mrs. Waters understands and goes.

NEELEY (*gleefully, to Francie*). I tell you, there ain't!—

He runs into the smaller bedroom, as

Katie comes back carrying only the bank. Charlie emerges sweating.

FRANCIE (*in a low tone*). Don't forget we're supposed to give him a beer—or the price of one.

Charlie wipes his sweating brow significantly, hopefully.

CHARLIE. I'm done.

KATIE. I can't thank you enough, Charlie.

CHARLIE. Always glad to do my customers a favor, of course. (*He doesn't move.*)

KATIE (*firmly*). We're real grateful, Charlie.

CHARLIE. It ain't as though I was in the regular movin' business.

KATIE. We'll be takin' ice, once a week, same as usual.

CHARLIE (*after a pause; grimly*). Well, goodbye.

KATIE. Goodbye, Charlie.

He goes out, slamming the door. Francie looks reproachfully.

FRANCIE. He worked awful hard, Mama!

KATIE (*hardening*). We moved to this flat to save money. We're not goin' to make a start by throwin' away dimes.

NEELEY (*entering joyfully*). No-sir, there ain't a bathtub anywhere, I looked all over.

Katie grins, leads him to the kitchen sink and lifts out a partition by which a tub can be improvised.

KATIE. That's the tub, young man— every Saturday and Wednesday, same as always.

A knock causes Katie to breathe "Mr.

Barker!" She sets the bank down and quickly puts her hand to her hair as Francie opens the door. Mr. Barker enters, looking around for gossip.

MR. BARKER. Well, seems like the Nolans have come up in the world. (*He means "down."*)

FRANCIE (*glibly, like Katie*). Yes, we're so very very fond of the sunshine.

KATIE (*polite but hasty*). Sorry I can't ask you to sit, Mr. Barker. I ain't even got the coffee on yet. But I got the insurance money handy. (*She reaches in her pocket.*)

MR. BARKER (*taking out his pen*). Smaller'n your old flat, ain't it?

Suddenly Johnny's voice singing "Molly Malone" is heard.

KATIE (*quickly, to Neeley*). Run down and catch him before he goes in the old place. (*To Mr. Barker, defensively*) Mr. Nolan happened to be—*working* when we found we could make the move. (*Neeley goes out.*)

MR. BARKER (*dubiously*). I suppose you're too busy to listen to a bit of news—about your sister. (*He pauses for effect.*) She's goin' to have a baby.

Katie stares. After a moment, she speaks.

KATIE (*quickly*). Tell her—please tell my sister she shouldn't make herself such a stranger.

MR. BARKER (*in his best manner*). I shall be very happy to render your message. Your receipts, Mrs. Nolan.

FRANCIE (*delighted*). Be *sure* to now, Mr. Barker.

Johnny appears in the doorway with Neeley. He is a little bewildered by the move, can't say anything to Mr. Barker.

MR. BARKER. Good day to you, Mr. Nolan. Well, I'm not one to spoil a family party. I'll be on my way.

He scurries out. Johnny looks around the cheap little flat.

FRANCIE. Surprise, Papa! Welcome to your new home.

JOHNNY. Yeah, it's kind of a surprise, all right. (*After a moment, to Katie*) Did you move up here because it was cheaper—I mean, because—

KATIE (*not looking at him*). We got to save where we can, somebody's got to. I don't mind the extra stairs.

JOHNNY (*very quietly*). Yeah.

He goes dejectedly to the window, accepting the full measure of his defeat. The children, lost in this adult mystery, only know that Papa needs cheering.

FRANCIE. We can still see the tree.

NEELEY. Pop, the top floor tenants, the roof is theirs, and I ain't goin' to let anybody up there except Henny Gaddis because—Hey, does Pop know?

KATIE. Flossie Gaddis died last night.

JOHNNY (*instinctively*). Ah, the poor baby.

FRANCIE. Everybody says it's a mercy, but I think it must be awful sad to die.

JOHNNY (*touching her hand*). Well, I don't know, baby. Maybe not, if you get to a place where things are goin' to keep gettin' worse for you instead of better. Nice her mama got her all them pretty dresses.

KATIE (*impulsively*). Only now it'll mean the poor thing'll have to lay in Potter's Field.

JOHNNY (*quietly*). Yeah, but she *had* the dresses.

Katie doesn't like this kind of talk, that makes her kids brood over things "way over their heads."

KATIE (*abruptly*). You better show your papa the piano.

JOHNNY. Yeah, we better look at the piano, Prima Donna.

FRANCIE (*going into the parlor*). The lady that was here left it—

Alone, Katie picks up the bank, and the scene cuts to the PARLOR. Johnny, under the fascinated gaze of his children, strikes a chord.

JOHNNY. Good tone. It's nice. (*He sits down, his spirits rising.*) It'd be nice if you kids had some lessons, now we got it. Maybe—

It isn't any good. His fingers move over the piano and strike a note or two which suggest a song to him. He starts to sing "Annie Laurie," simply, beauti-fully. The children are spellbound. Katie appears in the doorway and listens a moment. She is moved, not only by the singing, but by an obscure sense of guilt. She speaks softly.

KATIE. I never heard you sing that before. It's—pretty.

He doesn't look at her but goes on singing. As though it were a reproof, Katie shrugs, and leaves the doorway.— Johnny's song goes on, all his longing and defeat pouring out. Francie watches and listens with all her heart.— After a moment, a faint sound of hammering comes from the bedroom and we next see the BEDROOM CLOSET and Katie kneeling, hammering down the bank with an old shoe, fastening it to the floor exactly as it was in their old closet. In a dark corner the little bassinet stands hidden, waiting. The song drifts in. Katie pauses almost imperceptibly, listening. Her eyes rise to the bassinet. She goes back determinedly to nailing down the star bank as the scene fades out.

# PART FIVE

FRANCIE'S CLASSROOM fades in, and we first get a close view of a well-filled Christmas basket on Miss McDonough's desk and "A Merry Christmas" card from the Eighth Grade. Then the camera pulls back to reveal Miss McDonough finishing tying a bow on the basket, and the class in their seats. The room has some decoration for the Christmas season.

MISS MCDONOUGH (*brightly*). Well. This winds up a very pleasant term. And I'm sure we'll all enjoy our holidays more, knowing we've helped some unfortunate family who'd have had no Christmas dinner without this basket. (*She turns to the class to dismiss them.*) And so a very Merry —Oh, one last thing. This little pie Miss Shilling brought up was left over. It's a bit crushed, but—anybody want it?

There is no answer from the class. They are all anxious to get going.— Francie has the impulse to speak, but is afraid to. Her mouth waters for the pie.

MISS MCDONOUGH (*smiling*). My, what well-fed boys and girls . . . All right, class—

FRANCIE (*unable to stand it*). Miss McDonough.

MISS MCDONOUGH. Yes, Frances.

FRANCIE. I—I just remembered—I know a *very* unfortunate family— They live in a—a hovel, and there are two children, little golden-haired twins, and they're all starving! The pie will—will probably save their lives.

Miss McDonough knows the story is phony. She eyes Francie with a barely perceptible compassion.

MISS MCDONOUGH. Then you shall take the pie, by all means. You can come and get it after class is dismissed—(*smiling*)—which is now. Merry Christmas to you all.

CLASS. Merry Christmas, Miss McDonough.

The class breaks up and stampedes for the door, some of the youngsters coming past Miss McDonough's desk, wishing her an added Merry Christmas.— This dissolves to FRANCIE standing in front of MISS MCDONOUGH'S DESK.

MISS MCDONOUGH (*very kindly*). That was a very fine Christmas spirit, Frances, but—it seems such a tiny pie to save so many lives.

FRANCIE. It won't seem small to them, Miss McDonough; even a little pie can look awful big if you haven't had very much to eat for days and days. I'll have to tell them to eat it slowly because if they eat it too fast on an empty stomach—they'll—they'll—

Miss McDonough doesn't say a word through this, but her level gaze is too much for Francie.

FRANCIE (*miserably*). It isn't true, it's all a lie. I wanted it for myself. (*Desperately*) I'll stay after school, I'll do anything, but don't send a note home.

Francie is near tears. Miss McDonough takes her hand consolingly.

MISS MCDONOUGH (*gently*). I'm not going to punish you, child, for being hungry—or for having an imagination.

At these magic words, Francie looks at the teacher incredulously. There is a little pause.

MISS MCDONOUGH (*with a little twinkle*). You know, that's something very few people have. It's very precious. (*A trifle more seriously*) But it can also be dangerous, unless we learn how to use it. Our everyday lives are real and true, aren't they? But all the stories in the world, all the music, came out of someone's imagination. So if we *tell* the truth and *write* the lies, then they aren't lies anymore, they become stories. Like some of the very nice compositions you've written, Frances.

FRANCIE (*carried away*). Like the one about my father taking me to see the cotton fields down South? We didn't really go.

MISS MCDONOUGH. Well—I rather guessed you hadn't. But don't you think it would be still better if you'd write about the things you really know about, and then add to them with your imagination? Even stories shouldn't be just—well, pipe dreams. Pipe dreamers can be very lovable people but—they don't help anybody, not even themselves. (*Patting the wondering Francie*) Think about it a little. And now enjoy your pie and have a Merry Christmas.

FRANCIE (*in a daze*). Yes, Miss Mc-Donough. Thank -you, Miss Mc-Donough.

She goes, so entranced that she is quite unaware of the pie she is carrying. Miss McDonough looks after her affectionately.

The scene dissolves to a STREET with Francie walking home so beautifully deep in thought that she is still completely unaware of the pie. As she comes to a corner she is met by an impatient Neeley, who has been waiting for her.

NEELEY. For gosh sakes, where you been? You was supposed to meet me at—(*Seeing the pie*) Where'd you swipe that?

FRANCIE. Neeley, I'm—I'm going to be a writer!

NEELEY. All right, but let's eat the pie.

Francie looks at the pie, surprised that she has it. Neeley promptly takes it and breaks it in two—gives her half and starts on the other half himself.

NEELEY (*his mouth full of pie*). Come on, we got to get there about our Christmas tree!

FRANCIE (*coming back to earth*). Oh, golly, it isn't gone, is it?

Neeley shakes his head, already moving on. Francie starts to eat her part of the pie as she follows, and the scene dissolves to a CHRISTMAS TREE STAND in the afternoon. There's a rather small selection of Christmas trees near the sidewalk. The Christmas tree vendor, a big man, is trying to keep warm by flapping his arms as he waits for customers. He has a head cold. A few other kids are hanging around.—Francie and Neeley appear and go straight to the biggest tree.

NEELEY. Yeah, it's still here. He ain't got much time left to sell it.

The vendor comes up, a woman customer with him.

VENDOR (*to all the kids*). Go on, beat it, you know I ain't goin' to throw 'em till midnight. You tryin' to block the sidewalk—keep customers out?

NEELEY AND FRANCIE. Aw, you don't own the sidewalk. It's a free country, ain't it?

WOMAN CUSTOMER (*indicating "their" tree*). No, that one's too big. I want a small one,

As the woman leaves their tree, Francie and Neeley breathe again.

NEELEY (*looking at the tree*). It's awful big, to get throwed at you. Why does he have to throw 'em at us anyway? Why can't he just give 'em to us if he don't sell 'em?

FRANCIE. If he just gave them away everybody'd wait and he'd never sell any of 'em. (*She touches the tree gently.*) Gee, it smells good.

As they settle down to wait the scene dissolves to the CHRISTMAS TREE STAND at NIGHT. A number of excited kids are standing in two lines, forming a sort of lane, at one end of which stands the Christmas tree vendor, ready to throw the trees. At the other end of the lane stands a ten-year-old boy.—The vendor lets go with the tree, hits the boy with it and he goes down. There is laughter and jeers.—The kid gets up, scratched and almost crying with disappointment.

KID (*almost crying*). I—I stumbled, I could've—

ANOTHER KID. Gimme a try, I'm next.

The boy who failed is shoved aside;

the new boy takes his place. The tree is passed back. The vendor heaves it, and the boy holds his feet. There are cries of triumph.

VENDOR. All right, take it and get out. (*He picks up the big tree.*) Now, who's man enough to take a chance with this here one.

Francie pushes forward eagerly, but a bigger boy shoves her out of the way and gets there first.

LARGE BOY. I can take anything you got, mister, let her fly.

FRANCIE (*fiercely*). I'm next, that's my tree!

VENDOR. Aw, go on, you're too little.

FRANCIE. Me and my brother—we're not too little together.

VENDOR (*grinning*). Spunky, huh? (*He picks up the tree.*) All right, but if one of you goes down, you lose the tree.

LARGE BOY. That ain't fair, the two of 'em.

VENDOR. Shut your trap! Who's throwin' these trees.

Neeley and Francie take their places, holding hands to brace themselves. The vendor raises the tree and lets it fly. Neeley would have gone down but Francie catches him. Together they manage to stay on their feet. There is an approving yell from the crowd.

VENDOR (*in gruff admiration*). All right, take it and get out. You got it comin'!

The two come to, a little dazed. Then they grin proudly and start to drag the tree away.

The scene dissolves to the KITCHEN at NIGHT, with Katie, Johnny, Sissy, Steve (*her husband, to whom she refers as Bill*) and Grandma Rommely in the room. They are drinking coffee, waiting for the children to come home. There is an awkwardness and constraint over the whole scene. It is Christmas Eve, which should be a very happy time, but conversation has been lagging. —Johnny is playing solitaire, and not looking at anyone. Sissy is watching first one and then the other, as she tries to carry the burden of the conversation.

SISSY. Bill thinks the same as me, we're goin' to keep ours believin' in Santa Claus as long as we can.

GRANDMA ROMMELY (*nodding*). Is good, yes.

Katie has gotten up restlessly, and gone to the window to look out. She has scarcely heard what Sissy has been saying. Sissy watches her narrowly.

SISSY. Quit worryin' about 'em, Katie, they'll be here pretty quick.

KATIE (*from the window*). They ain't old enough to be out this late. Johnny should've made 'em tell what they was up to. No tellin' what kind of notion Francie's likely to get in her head.

SISSY. They'll be all right.

There is no answer from Katie. There is silence for a while. Then Steve yawns.

SISSY (*a little uncomfortable*). Maybe we better be gettin' on home and see 'em tomorrow.

JOHNNY (*quickly*). Don't go.

Sissy gives him a quick look. There is another little silence. Then it is broken by cries from outside.

VOICES OF FRANCIE AND NEELEY. Pop, hey, mom! Papa!

Katie turns back to the window. Johnny hurries across to join her, and the others follow. They look down, and from their angle we see, at the street entrance, Francie and Neeley, dragging the Christmas tree. They have stopped to call up to their parents. They wave and start on.

The scene cuts back to the PARLOR. Johnny's spirits lift.

JOHNNY. Holy smokes, will you look what they went and done!

He dashes out to help them bring the tree up the stairs. Katie is relieved that the youngsters are all right. Johnny's exit gives Sissy a little moment alone with Katie.

SISSY. They're tryin' to make a Christmas. Help 'em, kid.

Her eyes meet Katie's levelly. Katie smiles in answer—a reassurance that she will try to make Christmas what it should be for them in spite of the constraint within their house.

In the NOLAN TENEMENT VESTIBULE Francie and Neeley are now seen dragging the tree through the door. Officer McShane comes in and starts to help.

FRANCIE (*defensively*). It's ours, we won it.

NEELEY (*proudly*). Looka my face, we got it throwed at us.

MCSHANE. I was only wonderin' if you couldn't use a little help.

He picks up the other end of the tree and helps them along with it. Francie accepts his geniality with just a trace of surprise. Next we see the HALL as Johnny comes running down the stairs. He opens the door and the children come in. All speak at once.

JOHNNY. How in Jerusalem—?

FRANCIE. We won! We stood up to 'em!

NEELEY. Looka my face, Pop, looka my face!

McShane, helping with the tree, comes through the door.

JOHNNY. Nobody around here ever saw a tree like that!

FRANCIE. We won it fair.

NEELEY. Looka my face if you don't believe me.

JOHNNY. I see you got the law on your side, too.

MCSHANE. Merry Christmas to you, Mr. Nolan, and it looks like you're going to have one.

JOHNNY. Same to you, Mr. McShane, and thanks.

TYNMORE SISTERS (*having opened their door*). Merry Christmas, Mr. Nolan. Merry Christmas, children.

JOHNNY. Merry Christmas, Miss Maggie. Merry Christmas, Miss Lizzie.

FRANCIE. Isn't it a wonderful Christmas, papa?

JOHNNY. Well, it is now, Prima Donna. Imagine us having a tree like that—and the nicest kids in the world, I guess.

Johnny and the youngsters have started up the stairs, dragging the tree. The racket brings the neighbors to their doors.

JOHNNY (*out of pure exuberance he starts singing*). "Silent night, holy night—"

As they mount the stairs, another door or two open. Some of the neighbors have been in bed, some are still dressed —Mrs. Gaddis, at her door, joins in the singing.—A man starts to sing.— McShane opens the door from the street and stands looking up after them, listening.—A little girl claps her hands delightedly.—More singers join in.

SISSY (*to Katie*). He ain't any older than they are.

Katie is at the head of the stairs. With her is Sissy, Sissy's husband Steve, and Grandma Rommely. A man from the fourth floor joins them. He sings.— Katie is moved, and starts to sing. As she does, tears glisten in her eyes.— Sissy is also moved. Her tears are more uninhibited than Katie's.—Grandma Rommely joins in, in German.—Johnny and his children struggle their way up the stairs. Several people are singing now.—Neeley's excitement somehow subdues. He finds himself singing with the others.—But Francie is too thrilled and awed to sing. Her eyes are wide with the wonder of her father—of what he has done to these people.

This dissolves to the NOLAN PARLOR somewhat later. The tree, braced in Katie's scrub bucket, stands in the middle of the room, pretty well filling it. The family is gathered round the tree, and have been opening various small presents. Grandma Rommely sits in her chair near the window. Sissy is on the floor with the children. Neeley has several strips of court plaster on his face. The tree is sparsely decorated, principally with strips of colored paper the children have torn. Uncle Steve is standing on a chair, hanging a few candy canes. The usual evidences of coffee and cups are about.

KATIE. Can you put it higher, Bill?

STEVE (*mildly; obeying*). Steve's the name.

SISSY. That's better, Bill.

KATIE (*with a deliberate effort for Johnny*). It was real nice of your friend—of Mr. McGarrity, sendin' the kids them canes.

JOHNNY. Yeah.

But Neeley, opening a package, breaks across.

NEELEY. Aw—old itchy underwear.

JOHNNY. Think of all the, fun you can have, scratchin'.

FRANCIE (*taking out an identical pair*). Thank you, mama. They— they're just fine.

KATIE (*smiling*). You know you hate 'em.

FRANCIE (*a little shyly*). I got something for you too.

She goes to her couch and starts pulling out the large box from under it in which she keeps her treasures. During this, Steve has dismounted, and Grandma now takes out of her bag a thick, home-made candle.

GRANDMA ROMMELY. I have made this candle for today. It is time now to light it.

Steve and Johnny take and light it. Francie has pulled out two small packages from her box, and gives one to Katie.

FRANCIE. Merry Christmas, mama— from Neeley and me.

KATIE (*opening it*). Rose water and glycerine. It's pretty—what is it?

FRANCIE. You rub it on your hands.

NEELEY. I think it's silly. But Francie said papa was always talkin' about what nice hands you got. It cost a dime, but we had a seltzer bottle top in the junk.

KATIE (*rubbing some on awkwardly*). My, I'll be quite the thing, won't I?

FRANCIE (*giving the other package to Johnny*). This is for you, papa, from me and Neeley.

Johnny opens it and holds up a rather odd-looking affair—a watch fob made out of braided shoelaces.

FRANCIE. It's a watch fob. It's made out of shoelaces. I wove it on a spool with nails.

JOHNNY (*touched*). Well now, if that ain't about the nicest thing I ever saw.

He takes his union button from his lapel and pins the fob on his trousers as if he had a watch. He makes a little show of parading up and down with it, then tosses a handkerchief over his arm like a waiter's napkin.

JOHNNY (*bending over Francie*). We're all out of mushrooms under glass, madam, but I can tell you the time.

FRANCIE. Maybe it's kind of silly, with you not having a watch.

JOHNNY (*holding her to him*). Prima Donna, it's the nicest present I ever got. And thank you, son.

NEELEY. You're welcome. I guess the shoelaces was mine. (*Everybody laughs.*)

FRANCIE. It *was* silly . . .

SISSY (*gaily*). Ain't nothing silly on Christmas.

Steve clears his throat, and reaches into his inside pocket, half pulling out a parcel.

STEVE. I—I got a little present here—

He is interrupted by a knock on the door. Everyone is a little startled.

Francie goes out to the kitchen to open the door.

STEVE (*trying again*). Like I was sayin', I got—

But he is interrupted by Francie, returning with McShane, who is carrying a bag of candy canes. He makes no attempt to come in, but takes in the scene appreciatively.

MCSHANE. Merry Christmas, folks.

CHORUS OF ANSWERS. Merry Christmas.

SISSY. Hello, handsome!

MCSHANE. I was passin' and saw your light was still on and—I got to thinkin' I'd like a hand in fixin' that fine tree—but I see somebody's already provided you.

KATIE (*charming and shy*). We can always use more of 'em, Mr. McShane, and we thank you kindly. (*She takes the candy canes.*)

JOHNNY. Would you come in and have a cup of coffee with us?

MCSHANE. Thank you, but this evenin' is for families. I got to be gettin' home myself, so I'll be sayin' goodnight, and Merry Christmas to all.

AD LIB. Merry Christmas. Good night.

Johnny follows him out to see him to the kitchen door. Everyone is silent for a moment, touched by the little visit.

JOHNNY. That was mighty nice of him.

SISSY. He's cute.

KATIE. Mr. McShane is a fine man.

GRANDMA ROMMELY. He is, I think, sometimes a lonely man.

STEVE. Like I was sayin', I—I got somethin' here—I mean I gotta present for—for somebody that ain't exactly here. (*He extracts a tiny baby sweater from his parcel.*) Grandma helped me pick it out. It's for—you know who.

SISSY (*deeply touched*). Aw Bill, it's beautiful. Look, everybody, look at the size of them little sleeves! Aw gee, I ain't never been so happy, Bill, honey—

Katie turns from the tree and looks at the sweater with a strange expression.

KATIE. I'm goin' to get some coffee. (*She turns abruptly and goes into the kitchen, closing the door.*)

SISSY (*on whom the impression is not lost*). I better see if I can help. (*She follows Katie.*)

This cuts to the KITCHEN. Katie is not bothering with the coffee. She is staring out the window as Sissy enters. When she hears Sissy, she turns quickly to the stove and pretends to be busy.

KATIE (*dissembling*). I just wanted a breath of air for a minute, I—

SISSY (*quietly*). Katie.

KATIE (*after a pause*). Yeah.

SISSY (*coming closer to her*). I'm glad for you.

Katie meets her eyes for a moment in acknowledgment of the truth.

KATIE. I don't know. I—I'm scared, I guess.

SISSY. You got no call to be. Look at how swell them two are.

KATIE. Yeah, I know.

SISSY. Have you told Johnny? (*Katie shakes her head.*) You'd ought to, maybe it'd help him.

KATIE. Yeah. (*She gives Sissy an affectionate smile.*) We better take the coffee in.

SISSY. You're a fine girl, Katie. I never said any different.

Their eyes hold for a minute with a feeling of understanding between them. Then Sissy picks up some cups and takes them into the other room. Katie prepares to follow.

This cuts to the PARLOR as Sissy comes in with the cups. Johnny is picking out a tune on the piano; the children are beside him.—Sissy pauses for a moment and looks at Johnny, with Francie leaning close against him. To Sissy, it looks like a portrait of a good enough parent.—She sets the cups down on the piano. Then she bends over suddenly and kisses Johnny on the top of his head.

SISSY. That's for nothin', Johnny—except maybe bein' a nice guy.

Johnny looks up and smiles at her. Then Sissy breaks the little moment of feeling between them.

SISSY. Coffee, everybody!

As she starts to set out the cups and Katie comes in with the coffee, the scene dissolves to the KITCHEN where the cups are being put into the sink. It is late, and the family is alone, carrying things into the kitchen, straightening up after the party. Katie is getting ready to wash the dishes.

JOHNNY. Don't do 'em tonight, it's Christmas. I'll give you a hand tomorrow.

KATIE (*with a little smile*). You better give me a hand right now, before it slips your mind.

JOHNNY (*grinning*). Yeah, I guess you're right.

KATIE. And you better get to bed, son, before you go to sleep standin' up.

NEELEY. Okay. Goodnight.

He goes to his bedroom, practically asleep. They smile. Katie starts to wash the dishes, and Johnny and Francie pick up cloths to wipe them.

JOHNNY. Bill was funny, wasn't he—nice, I mean.

KATIE. Yeah, Sissy's awful happy.

JOHNNY. There's somethin' good about Christmas, everybody was swell.

FRANCIE. Papa, why did Grandma say Mr. McShane was lonely.

JOHNNY. I don't know, maybe he is at that.

KATIE. How do you mean, Johnny? What do you know about him?

JOHNNY. Oh, some. He's a fine man.. Come to this country with nothin', worked hard, studied to get on the force. Some folks was kind to him when he first come, he lived with 'em, and then their daughter was in trouble, her husband ran off and left her when she was goin' to have a kid. So McShane married her to take care of her.

KATIE. Have they got—children?

JOHNNY (*shaking his head*). There was a couple, but they died when they was young with lung trouble they took from their mother. He don't ever talk about it, but I guess he is kind of lonely.

KATIE (*abruptly*). It ain't right.

JOHNNY (*quietly*). No, I guess it ain't.

KATIE. It ain't right. Why did she have to put her troubles off on him. A fine man like him, steady and all, he ought to have a fine home, and

children, that's every good man's right.

Katie had no intention of saying this. It comes from her a little too violently, born of her feeling of desperation. But once said, it hangs between them like a shadow. There is a little pause. Johnny grows very quiet and the gaiety of the Christmas is gone.

Francie, wide-eyed, looks from one to the other. She senses that Johnny has been hurt. Instinctively, she slips her hand into his.

Johnny, suddenly aware of the touch, looks down at her and smiles thinly, his hand tightening on hers.

JOHNNY. That's about all the dishes, baby, you better get to bed.

FRANCIE. Yes, papa.

KATIE. And go to sleep—don't just lie there lookin' at the tree all night.

FRANCIE. I won't, mama. Goodnight, papa.

JOHNNY. Goodnight, baby.

Francie goes into the parlor and closes the door. Left alone, there is an awkward little pause between Johnny and Katie.

JOHNNY. They're fine kids.

KATIE. Yes, they are.

JOHNNY (*hanging up the dish cloth*). That's about all, I guess.

There is a moment's pause, but Katie makes no move to go. Johnny stands uncertainly. Then abruptly Katie turns to him.

KATIE. Johnny, I got to tell you somethin', maybe it ain't the best time, maybe it is. The reason I moved us up here—we're goin' to have a baby,

Johnny, that's why I been scrimpin' so much and tryin' to save.

Johnny feels that he ought to take her in his arms—he would have if everything were really all right between them. But instead, there is a little pause.

JOHNNY (*quietly*). That's—I mean, I'm awful glad, Katie, if—if you are.

KATIE. There's a lot we got to think about, Johnny.

JOHNNY. I know, but—we'll manage. Maybe things'll be—better, havin' one to kind of grow up with again.

KATIE. I got things all figured out. I oughta be able to keep on workin' till anyway April. Then Francie'll have to leave school and get her workin' papers. She's young, but with what she can make, we can make out, and—

JOHNNY (*instinctively*). Aw, no, Katie, we can't—

KATIE (*quickly*). I don't like it any better than you do, but I thought and thought, and there ain't any other way. And you got to help with somethin', Johnny. She listens to you, you got to quit keepin' her all so excited about her school, and—

JOHNNY. But Katie, why does it have to be Francie? Neeley's the boy, and he don't care like she does.

KATIE. Maybe that's why, maybe it'll do her good to get out in the world and learn how to take care of herself, learn somethin' practical while she's young. She's got to learn some day.

JOHNNY. There—there must be somethin' else, Katie—Don't tell her yet, Katie, there's time till April. Maybe I—I'm goin' to try to swing somethin'.

KATIE. We can't count on that,

Johnny. (*Then, defensively*) School ain't everything, maybe sometime she can go back. (*She can't stand his look.*) Don't look at me like that! It ain't my fault! (*She manages to get hold of herself a little.*) It ain't yours either, I guess, I don't know. (*Turning away*) Anyway, one member of the Nolan family will get to graduate, and she come close, that's somethin'.

This small effort at optimism gets no response from Johnny. Katie hardens.

KATIE. You better put out the light, and let's try and get some rest.

She goes into the bedroom without looking at him again. Johnny stands alone—looks after her a moment, brooding. His hand plays with the watch fob, and he looks toward Francie's door. After a moment he crosses the room and very gently opens the door to the parlor.

Johnny closes the door and moves softly to Francie's couch. The light from the window shows her wide awake, looking up at him.

JOHNNY. I thought you'd be asleep, Prima Donna.

Francie is in a new mood, a little girl just stepping over the line into wondering adolescence. They both talk softly, secretly, alone in the world. He sits on the edge of the bed.

FRANCIE. Uh-uh. I been—thinking.

JOHNNY. Well now, you ought to be careful about that, so many things in this world to think about you might never get to sleep.

FRANCIE. Papa. I might be going to be a writer. I—I've just about decided.

JOHNNY (*gently*). I knew you when

you was goin' to be a lady fireman.

FRANCIE. Don't joke, papa, I'm serious.

JOHNNY (*gently*). All right, baby. All I meant, maybe it's better sometimes not to get your heart set on—on just the one thing, oh, in case somethin' happens, or—

FRANCIE (*scarcely hearing him*). She said, Miss McDonough, I mean, she said maybe I could be. She says I have imagination. Do you think I have, papa?

JOHNNY. Sure I do, baby. Those compositions of yours, they been fine. But—

FRANCIE. She said I'd have to work hard; she said imagination wasn't any good if you were just a pipe-dreamer about it, you didn't help anybody that way, not even yourself.

JOHNNY. I see, yeah, a pipe-dreamer.

FRANCIE. I'm not putting it good like she did—Oh, I just understood everything she said, and now I don't, but—I kind of still do. I wish you could've heard her, she was wonderful. Forever and ever I'll be glad you helped me go to that school.

JOHNNY (*finding it pretty tough*). You kind of like that school, don't you, baby?

FRANCIE. Yes, oh yes. And she said lots more. I've been trying to remember—she said even if you have imagination it's better to write about things you know about, so it will be true, and—and the way things are. I've been looking at things all day, to see them that way, only—

JOHNNY. Only what, baby?

FRANCIE. Papa, the people in the hall when we brought up the tree, the look on their faces, all friendly and nice—why aren't people like that all the time, not just Christmas?

JOHNNY. Well, I'd say it was—I don't know. Maybe it's just they take time at Christmas, or—or maybe you oughtn't to think like that, baby. Maybe Christmas is like people really are, and the other part ain't true, and with all that imagination you got, maybe if you just think about it hard enough that way, you know, like it ought to be— (*He flounders to a stop.*)

FRANCIE. But when you get to *thinking*—papa, the people in Aunt Sissy's magazines, they don't just live happily ever after, do they?

JOHNNY. No, baby.

FRANCIE. Well, the trouble is—it doesn't *feel* good when you think about things like that—I mean, the way they really are.

She is really troubled. Johnny's smile as he looks down at her is curious, gentle, and somehow infinitely sad.

JOHNNY. You better stick out your tongue, baby. (*As she obeys him*) Just what I was afraid of. You got a bad case, a very bad case.

FRANCIE. Case of what, papa?

JOHNNY. You got a very bad case of growing up, Prima Donna.

She realizes he is joking, and smiles shyly.

JOHNNY (*gently*). That's all it is. It ain't fun sometimes, but don't you be afraid, I don't want you should ever be *afraid*.

Francie smiles, then settles back, relaxed. Almost as if in confirmation of his words, she makes a small, almost unconscious movement of pulling the covers up higher—the first subconscious awareness of herself as something more than a child. It is not lost on Johnny.

FRANCIE (*sighing deeply*). You're so nice, papa. I was feeling kind of—funny before you came in. Now I feel good. (*She yawns contentedly.*) I guess it's better if you don't just stay young all your life; it will be nicer growing up.

Johnny looks at her for a long moment, then gets to his feet. He has had about all he can take, and there is a weariness about him. His eyes are shadowed by the vision of that not far distant day when Francie will no longer look at him with the eyes of a child, but will see him as Katie sees him, and as he sees himself.

JOHNNY (*very quietly*). Yeah. When you begin to see things like they really are.

The bitterness of his meaning is lost on Francie. He bends down and kisses her gently.

JOHNNY. Goodnight, baby.

FRANCIE (*drowsily*). Goodnight, papa. I'm sleepy now.

JOHNNY. That's fine, baby, that's fine.

He goes out and closes the door quietly. Francie is half-asleep.

Back in the KITCHEN, Johnny stands a moment near the door. Then mechanically he turns off the gas. There is a light from Katie's bedroom. He crosses to the door and stops at the bedroom. Katie is in bed in the background, an arm over her eyes to shield them from the light. A feeling of revulsion comes over Johnny. How can she lie there so peacefully, so soon after making her decision about Francie? At that moment it would be inconceivable for Johnny to go into that room and lie down beside her. He turns abruptly and starts to go. Katie stirs.

KATIE (*sleepily*). Ain't you comin' to bed, Johnny?

JOHNNY. I'm goin' out for a little walk.

He moves out into the kitchen. Katie sits up.

KATIE. Don't start drinkin', not to-night, Johnny.

JOHNNY, near the door leading to the hall, is taking down his hat.

JOHNNY (*quiet, strained*). I won't, Katie—I won't.

KATIE (*from the bedroom*). Well—take your muffler, it's cold.

JOHNNY. Yeah.

He goes out. Katie is troubled for a moment, then gives it up and lies down wearily.

The HALL is dark and deserted. Johnny starts down the stairs mechanically, slowly putting the muffler around his neck. His eyes are desperate as the scene fades out.

# PART SIX

The SIGN of the WAITERS' UNION HEADQUARTERS fades in. Above it is a banner with the legend "Happy New Year." This dissolves to the UNION HEADQUARTERS in the late afternoon. Katie is at the desk talking to the man in charge.

MAN. No ma'am, Mr. Nolan hasn't been around for several days.

KATIE. Is he out on a job, do you know?

MAN. If he is, he didn't get it through us.

KATIE. Thank you.

As she starts out, the scene dissolves to MCGARRITY'S SALOON. Katie enters, hesitates, decides to go on, passes the sign at the side that says "family entrance," hesitates again and goes in.

This in turn dissolves to MCGARRITY'S SALOON disclosing several customers, and quite a bit of noise. McGarrity is behind the bar. A boy comes in from the back room, speaks to him, but we cannot distinguish what he says. McGarrity looks surprised, and starts for the back room.

We see the BACK ROOM as McGarrity enters from the saloon. There are a few people in this room. Katie is standing just inside the street door, a little uncomfortable. McGarrity goes to her.

MCGARRITY. How are you, Mrs. Nolan, and Happy New Year.

KATIE. The same to you, Mr. McGarrity. I—I just came to—(*She can't make it—to ask about Johnny.*) I just happened to be passin' and I thought I'd run in and thank you for the candy canes. It was nice of you.

MCGARRITY. That's all right. It wasn't much.

KATIE. Well, it was nice of you anyway. (*Then, after an awkward pause, she turns to go.*) Well, goodnight, Mr. McGarrity.

MCGARRITY. Goodnight, Mrs. Nolan.

She gets the door open, and then McGarrity stops her.

MCGARRITY. Mrs. Nolan. (*Katie turns.*) Johnny ain't here—he hasn't been in since before Christmas.

Katie stands for a moment, caught between gratitude for his understanding and the stubbornness of her pride. The latter wins. She hurries out, and the scene dissolves to the NOLAN TENEMENT at night. Most of the lights are out, but the light is still on in the Nolan kitchen. This dissolves to the NOLAN HALL as McShane's feet are seen mounting the stairs, and then to the NOLAN DOOR as McShane comes into view. He stands for a moment before he knocks. Almost immediately the door opens to reveal Katie, still dressed and anxious eyed.—Behind her Francie appears, in her nightgown, from the parlor, and stands wide-eyed and apprehensive.

MCSHANE. I'm afraid it's bad news I'm bringin' you, Mrs. Nolan. Our station got a report that Mr. Nolan was found over in Manhattan very sick. He's been taken to the hospital.

Francie's eyes are tragic but she makes no sound.—Katie turns without a word and picks up her coat. Then she sees Francie.

KATIE. See that Neeley gets to school in time in the morning. There's an apple for your lunches.

Francie stares at her as Katie struggles into the coat.

MCSHANE. The report was that he just collapsed right in the doorway of an employment agency. He was just goin' out on a job, sand hog in a tunnel, they said. He hadn't been drinkin', ma'am, he'd been waitin' there a long time for the job—he was just sick.

Katie is going out past him as he finishes. McShane follows and closes the door, shutting out the tragic little figure of Francie.

This scene dissolves to a HOSPITAL CORRIDOR as Katie comes out of a ward accompanied by a nurse. The nurse closes the door.

NURSE. We did everything we could.

KATIE. Yeah, I know.

As she starts walking down the hall, the scene dissolves to the HOSPITAL DOCTOR'S OFFICE, where Katie is standing in front of the doctor at his desk.

DOCTOR. Just a few questions, Mrs. Nolan—date of birth and so on.

KATIE. What are you writin' down that he died from?

DOCTOR. Acute alcoholism and pneumonia. One led to the other.

KATIE. I don't want you to write down that he died like that. Put just the pneumonia, doctor.

DOCTOR. I can't do that. Pneumonia was the direct cause of death, but the alcoholism—

KATIE (breaking through). Look, he's dead. I got two nice kids. They're goin' to grow up to amount to something. Why do you have to make it harder, sayin' their father died because of the drink, when that—that's only a little piece of the truth. He wasn't drinkin', they said so, he was out looking for work, why don't you put that down?

DOCTOR (after a moment). Cause of death, pneumonia. Date of birth?

There are tears in Katie's eyes, but something fierce, too, shines through them, as the scene dissolves to the KITCHEN. We get a close view of Francie, dry-eyed, staring out of the window. She is looking down at the tree, hardly aware of the sordid conference with the undertaker that is going on in the room. Then the camera pulls back over the dialogue to reveal Katie, Sissy, Grandma Rommely, Neeley and the undertaker. Neeley is crying. He stands next to his mother's chair. Her arm is around him, and from time to time she gives him, half automatically, a comforting pat.

UNDERTAKER.—It's a first-class funeral, with nickel handles on the coffin, and for two hundred dollars it includes—

SISSY (bitterly). Ain't it odd that the best you can do comes to just what his insurance amounted to.

UNDERTAKER. I'll make it one eighty five, and I won't be makin' hardly a cent.

KATIE (dully). All right.

UNDERTAKER (producing pen and printed form quickly). Sign here, please. That gives me the right to collect the insurance, and I'll give you the fifteen dollars in cash now.

GRANDMA ROMMELY (as Katie takes

*the pen*). Read it before you sign.

Katie pauses, and stares at it for a moment. She looks at Neeley, who is sniffling. Then she looks around for Francie and sees her at the window.

KATIE. Francie. (*Francie turns slowly.*) You're the best reader.

Francie comes down slowly, not looking at them. She takes the paper and studies it, dry-eyed.—Sissy studies this strange shut-in quality in Francie with compassion.

FRANCIE. It says what he says.

She hands it back, and goes back to the window.—Katie signs the paper. The undertaker takes it from her.

UNDERTAKER. And now, Mrs. Nolan, if you have the deed to the funeral plot.

KATIE. Plot? We don't own no plot. I thought—

SISSY. You was awful careful not to mention it till she signed.

UNDERTAKER. But, Mrs. Nolan—

KATIE. Never mind. How much is a plot?

UNDERTAKER. All prices. Twenty, thirty—the least would be twenty.

There is a silence. Then Katie gets wearily to her feet, and crosses to the bedroom. As she passes Francie, Francie does not turn, but continues to stare at nothing out the window.

Once in the BEDROOM, Katie picks up a shoe-horn from the dresser, goes to the closet, and as she starts to pry up the star bank the scene dissolves to a CEMETERY where Johnny's coffin is in place over the grave. There are quite a number of people, and quite a number of floral offerings, some large and some very small. The priest is reading the service for the dead as the view moves down the line of the Nolan family, successively disclosing: Grandma Rommely, eyes closed, lips moving in silent prayer; Uncle Steve, his honest face full of emotion; Sissy, crying openly, the tears welling straight from her warm heart; Neeley, awed, sniffling a little, standing close to his mother and holding on to a fold of her coat; Katie, moved, feeling strange things at the sight of all the flowers, and all the people who have turned out to offer their affection to Johnny's memory.

We get a view of the people, and the flowers, as she sees them—McGarrity, the man from the union headquarters, several recognized neighbors from the tenement, and quite a number of people we have never seen before. The feeling of all of them is so apparently genuine. Johnny's coffin is covered with their flowers.

Katie, seen close, is a little bewildered. So many people loved Johnny, he must not have been just a failure to them. She looks down at Neeley, and then on the other side, at Francie.

Francie stands, unlike Neeley, quite apart from Katie. She is still dry-eyed, lost. If Neeley has lost a father, and Katie a husband, Francie has lost her whole world. And in her loss, she has no inclination, as has Neeley, to reach toward Katie.

Katie's eyes are troubled, a little puzzled, as she watches her daughter—and the scene dissolves to the FUNERAL CARRIAGE disclosing KATIE, FRANCIE, SISSY, NEELEY. The carriage is coming down the street toward the tenement. Francie sits dry-eyed and aloof. Katie, still in the bewildered mood of the funeral, is trying to puzzle things out.

KATIE. All them people, and the flowers—some of 'em from people I never heard of even. Who'd've thought that many folks—I mean, they was carryin' on like—like they was his family, or—I don't know.

Katie is so intent on her own troubled problem that she is quite unaware of Francie. But Sissy is aware of what both of them are feeling. She sees that Francie's eyes hold something like the beginning of hatred for Katie.

SISSY. Yeah, he took the time to make a lot o' people love him, all right.

KATIE. It's hard to figure, so many of 'em showin' up, and they was feelin' somethin', there wasn't no reason for 'em to put on. I mean, he wasn't nobody big, he was just—

SISSY (*putting her hand quickly on Katie's arm*). I wouldn't talk about it no more now, kid.

She has seen Francie turn bitterly away from her mother. Quite unintentionally Katie's words have been a violation of Francie's feeling about her father.

This dissolves to the NOLAN TENEMENT, the carriage just stopping. Francie, still bitterly tense, gets out first and starts swiftly down the street. Katie, climbing out with Neeley, sees this.

KATIE. Francie!

SISSY. Best leave her go, Katie. She maybe wants to be by herself.

KATIE (*watching Francie go, troubled*). She's takin' on kind of—funny. She ain't even cried.

SISSY. Best leave her come out of it her own way.

KATIE (*not even hearing*). They was always funny together—nice, I mean. They was like kids, they never ran out of talk. (*After a little pause*)

Well, one thing—he never lived to see that change; he beat that one.

SISSY. You want for me to come up with you?

KATIE (*as Sissy watches her trying to puzzle it out*). And there's somethin' else, maybe that was it—he wasn't drinkin', they told me, there was somethin' drivin' him—maybe that was it, maybe he was tryin' to be different like—like—(*She turns this over for a moment, then gives up.*) I don't know.

She turns abruptly, without even saying goodbye, and starts into the house. Neeley follows. Sissy watches after her with deep compassion as the scene dissolves to a STREET and we see Francie, all alone, coming down the street. She pauses in front of a little barber shop, and then goes in.

In the BARBER SHOP: The head barber, a little Italian, is half-asleep in the first barber chair. The other barber is working on a customer. Francie enters, and goes to the head barber.

FRANCIE (*hesitantly*). I'd like my father's shaving cup, please. (*Pointing to it*) It's that one.

BARBER (*looking up*). Oh. (*He takes down the cup with Johnny's name.*) You're the little girl. Yes, I'll clean it up for you. (*He starts to clean it.*) He was a fine man. Tell the mama that I, his barber, said this.

Francie watches as he finishes cleaning the cup and hands it to her. She starts to turn away, and then asks—

FRANCIE. Is—there isn't anything else of my father's here, is there?

BARBER. No, that's all he had.

As Francie turns and goes, the scene dissolves to the NOLAN KITCHEN. Katie is alone in the kitchen. The door opens and Francie comes in carrying the mug. Without looking at her mother she goes straight into the parlor. Katie looks after her, forcing herself not to stop her.

In the PARLOR, Francie pulls out her box from under the couch, adds the shaving mug to a carefully put away collection of memories of Johnny: his tuxedo shirt, his waiter's apron, his union button, the whisk broom with which he always brushed himself before going out. Her face never changes as she slides the box back under the couch, rises and goes into the kitchen.

The KITCHEN: Again not meeting Katie's anxious eyes, she crosses the kitchen toward the door into the hall. Katie can contain herself no longer.

KATIE. Francie.

FRANCIE (*stopping, but without turning*). What?

KATIE. Francie dear . . . Where you going?

FRANCIE. No place. (*She gets as far as the door.*)

KATIE. Francie.

FRANCIE (*still not turning*). Yes, mama.

KATIE. The neighbors were awful nice, leavin' all this food. Don't you want a little somethin'?

FRANCIE. No, mama.

KATIE. Well, I—I wanted to talk to you. I want things to go on, the reading and all, just like—I want to do—(*Desperately*) I got to be mama and papa both to you now—

She has said the impossible. Almost imperceptibly Francie stiffens.

FRANCIE. Yes, mama. Is that all, mama?

KATIE (*sheepishly*). Well—(*Francie starts to go out.*) You got to go right now, Francie, I—

FRANCIE (*desperately*). I'll be back, honest I will.

She goes out. Katie sighs, defeated, and sinks into a chair by the table. After a moment Neeley's door opens. He wants to comfort her, and boyishly says the only thing he can think of.

NEELEY. Mom, I—I guess I'm a little hungry.

Katie manages a smile, and reaches out a hand to pull him to her.—Next the ROOF of the NOLAN TENEMENT comes into view. At the edge of the parapet overlooking the city and the harbor Francie stands, living out her own private ceremony for her father. She is unaware of the street noises which float up, unaware even of a woman hanging out wash to dry on the roof behind her. She doesn't even know that tears are in her eyes, because they are not the burning tears that give relief. She might be a very young and bitterly passionate priestess, dedicating herself. After a long moment of silence she lifts her head and looks up.

FRANCIE (*very low, half in a whisper*). Look—he can't be gone, he can't. They don't understand. Maybe—maybe you could let me have a baby some day, and it could be a boy, so—so it could be just like him. It would have to be me, nobody else loved him like—like I do. Maybe you could do that for me, and if you could—he wouldn't even—die.

She can't go on, as the scene fades out.

# PART SEVEN

The KITCHEN fades in. Francie is ironing her school dress. Katie is just admitting McGarrity. He is constrained, has something to say and doesn't know quite how to go about it. He is in his best suit.

MCGARRITY *(as he enters)*. I hope you don't think I'm forward just comin' in like this. Oh, how are you, Francie?

FRANCIE. I'm well, thank you.

KATIE. Have a chair. Francie, see if Mr. McGarrity won't have some coffee.

MCGARRITY. Not for me, thank you.

He does not sit down, but stands turning his hat. There is an awkward little silence. Francie keeps on with her ironing.

MCGARRITY *(ill at ease)*. I—I figgered I'd ought to come. You might say I knowed Johnny pretty well, in a manner of speakin'.

KATIE *(with a flicker of humor)*. Yes, I guess that's right.

MCGARRITY. Well, the first thing is, I guess you know how Johnny and I done business. He used to give me money sometimes to keep and then draw against it, and when he—I mean, I got to lookin' around, and what do you think, I had pretty near five bucks in his box. I—I figgered it belongs to you.

He ends very lamely. McGarrity is not a facile liar. It doesn't fool Katie, but she is touched by his intent.—Francie, unnoticed, stops ironing at the mention of her father's name.

KATIE *(with a little smile)*. If you told the truth, it'd more likely be that he owed you. But I thank you very much.

McGarrity shifts uneasily. He does not like being caught at being a good man.

MCGARRITY. Well, I—I just thought—

KATIE *(quietly)*. We'll make out.

McGarrity uncomfortably returns the bill to his pocket.

MCGARRITY *(examining his hat intently)*. Well, there was somethin' else. I was thinkin'—you know, I try to run a nice place, clean, so nice folks can—Well, who I hire is important, they got to be nice too, and I was thinkin' that—that maybe you wouldn't mind if the kids come to work for me, afternoons like. I mean after school, and Saturdays. Maybe it ain't just the kind of place you'd favor 'em workin', but I'd keep an eye on 'em. I could pay 'em two dollars a week a piece and—I'd take it as a real favor, ma'am.

McGarrity runs down lamely. Katie is really touched.

KATIE *(after a moment)*. You're an awful bad liar, Mr. McGarrity. But you're a very good man. I'm ashamed I didn't know it before.

MCGARRITY *(uncomfortably)*. No ma'am, it ain't that. Johnny was—I don't know, Johnny was always talkin' about his family like—like folks ought to, only they don't;

funny, the things he talked about pretty near always made you feel better, or laugh, like a sea shell I had down there he was always listenin' to and tellin' you what it was singin'. He was always givin' things like that to people. He—he was a fine man, Mrs. Nolan.

McGarrity's tribute to Johnny is somewhat confused, but the feeling behind it is so earnest that it cannot be mistaken.—Francie listens intently. McGarrity's whole wish to do something for them is because of his feeling for her father.—Katie too is moved. Enough that she forgets momentarily that Francie is in the room.

KATIE. I'd be glad for the children to work for you, Mr. McGarrity. Four dollars a week will keep us until the baby comes, and Francie won't have to quit school; she can keep on and they can both—

She stops. She had not intended to say this. She looks quickly at Francie.—Francie's eyes refuse to meet her mother's. She turns back and starts ironing again.

MCGARRITY (*sensing tension he does not understand*). It's a deal. Tell 'em to come to the family entrance tomorrow right after school. Is that all right with you, Francie?

FRANCIE (*not looking up*). Yes.

MCGARRITY. It's all settled then. Well —goodbye, Mrs. Nolan.

KATIE (*gratefully*). And thank you again, Mr. McGarrity.

McGarrity goes a little awkwardly. Francie and Katie are left alone, and there is a sharp constraint between them. Francie does not look at her mother. Katie studies her, troubled.

KATIE. Francie.

FRANCIE (*ironing*). Yes, mama.

KATIE. I—I'm glad you can keep on with your school. I didn't tell you because I was hopin' somethin' would happen. I didn't want to say anything until the time came. But there were reasons, your papa and I talked it over, there wasn't any other way—

Francie still avoids looking at Katie.

FRANCIE (*quietly*). It doesn't matter. Papa saved me from it.

She turns and goes into the parlor, closing the door on Katie as the scene dissolves to MCGARRITY'S SALOON. Sissy enters down the street. She doesn't bother going around to the family entrance, but barges nonchalantly through the swinging doors.

Two or three customers are visible. McGarrity is behind the bar. Neeley is putting a ham and some other things from a tray onto the free lunch end of the bar. The men look up, surprised at seeing a woman enter the bar.

SISSY (*to Neeley*). Hi, kid. They're takin' chances I wouldn't, leavin' you handle the eats. Where's Francie?

NEELEY (*with a full mouth*). Kitchen.

SISSY. Thanks. Hi, Mac.

She waves nonchalantly to McGarrity, and disappears through the family entrance toward the kitchen. The men look after her approvingly.

In the KITCHEN, Francie is dispiritedly cutting some dill pickles into long lengths as Sissy enters.

SISSY. Hello, lamb.

Francie looks around, but does not light up as she generally does when she sees Sissy.

FRANCIE. Hello, Aunt Sissy.

SISSY (*taking a paper from the top of her stocking*). How are you, kid? Look, you got to help me with somethin'. This was in the paper and I cut it out. You got to read it to me and—(*She is suddenly aware of Francie's mood.*) What's the matter, hon?

FRANCIE. Nothing. I'm all right, Aunt Sissy.

SISSY. No you ain't, kid, you ain't been since—Look, hadn't you better spill it to your Aunt Sissy.

FRANCIE (*on the defensive*). What is it you want me to read to you? Let me read that, Aunt Sissy.

SISSY. Well, we'll get that out of the way first. Look, here it is, likely you don't remember him, but it's my last husband, Bill—the one I thought was dead. But he ain't, he's got his picture in here, and I got to know what it says. (*Francie takes the clipping and studies it.*) Maybe it'll tell where he is, so I can write to him about gettin' a divorce or—or somethin'. I don't want this here one bobbin' up and makin' no trouble. He's a fireman somewhere, I can tell that by the clothes. He was just startin' out in the fireman business when—

FRANCIE. It says here he's a hero, Aunt Sissy. He saved some people in a fire.

SISSY. Does it say where?

FRANCIE. The Ninth Precinct, Manhattan.

SISSY. Manhattan, huh—couldn't make the grade in Brooklyn, I guess. Now listen, Francie, I want you to write him for me. Write this, "Dear Bill—"

FRANCIE. This says his name is Roland Pulaski.

SISSY. That's right, I remember. Make it "Dear Mr. Pulaski: Being I'm now married to somebody else, I want you to see about gettin' a real legal divorce because I thought you was dead, and because you got the money now on account of the reward. Yours very truly, Sissy." Something like that.

FRANCIE. But Aunt Sissy, he must have already done that, because it says here he's married again.

SISSY. It does!

FRANCIE (*reading*). "On the human interest side of the story, Mrs. Pulaski had returned home only the day before from the hospital, after presenting Mr. Pulaski with a brand-new son, the fourth child of the marriage. Perhaps it was his pride that—" (*Looking up*) So if he got a divorce that long ago, you don't have to.

SISSY. Then my bein' married to Bill—this one, I mean—is all legal.

Francie nods, and turns back to slicing the pickles.

SISSY. Well now, if that ain't a load off my mind. You know, I think I'll send Bill Pulaski a weddin' present.

FRANCIE. But you can't, Aunt Sissy, he's been married for years.

SISSY (*this news bothers her*). Four kids, huh? (*Then, trying to comfort herself*) Must be a pretty sickly woman, this Mrs. Pulaski, goin' to a hospital just to have a baby.

FRANCIE (*dully*). No. Lots of people go there now to have babies. It's better.

SISSY. Sure enough? (*Francie nods.*) You know somethin', I'm goin' to cash in my funeral policy and have my baby in the hospital. And when my baby is born and lives, I want you to write to that R. Pulaski and —and announce it! (*She takes a deep breath.*) Hey, do I feel better!

Francie turns back to her work. Sissy has been so concerned with her own problem, that she has hardly been aware of the apathy with which Francie has shared it. But now, her own problem settled, she looks down at Francie's miserable little figure, her back turned as she works away at the pickles. Sissy suddenly pulls up a chair beside Francie and sits where she can see Francie's face.

SISSY. And now, chickabiddy, we're goin' to talk about you. Can't your Aunt Sissy help any? (*Francie shakes her head miserably.*)

FRANCIE. I'm all right.

SISSY. But you ain't, honey, not all shut up like that. (*Francie doesn't answer.*) I know how you feel, but you can't just keep hangin' on to it.

FRANCIE. I'm all right, I don't want to talk about it.

SISSY. All right, baby, sure. But I tell you what, you can do somethin' for me. Look—your mama feels awful bad too. She needs you. Why don't you talk to her about it—

FRANCIE (*with sudden bitterness*). She doesn't need me.

SISSY. Why, yes she does, hon, she—

FRANCIE. No, she doesn't. She's got Neeley. Why wasn't it Neeley she was goin' to make quit school, he never cared about it. She doesn't love me like papa did. And she didn't love him, either, not really. She hurt him. I saw her. And he never hurt anybody. I'm going to finish this grade because he gave it to me, and then

I'll work for her, but she can't be papa to me, she can't ever!

This pent-up feeling blazes out of Francie with so much passion that it frightens Sissy. When it is over, Francie turns blindly back to her work, shutting out even Sissy. Moved, Sissy puts an arm around her and tries to draw Francie to her.

SISSY. Aw, baby, don't feel like that, don't—

FRANCIE (*twisting away from her*). Leave me alone, I'm all right. Please go away and leave me alone.

Rebuffed, Sissy is at a loss as to what she can do. The feeling is so fierce that it frightens Sissy. Francie is crying, but it is hard and dry, not like a child ought to cry. She is fighting it terribly, instead of giving way to it.

SISSY (*helplessly*). All right, chickabiddy, all right.

Sissy turns helplessly and goes out. Shaken with her feeling, Francie tries to go on with her work as the scene dissolves to a SCHOOL ROOM where Francie, standing by her desk, is reading a composition in the English class.

FRANCIE (*reading*). "But when he died, although many of the older people said he drank too much and was a failure, the little children took their pennies and built this monument to him, because he was so good in his heart and they loved him best of all. And after a time—"

Francie is very earnest as she reads this, carried away with this attempt at justification of Johnny. To the children, it is pretty dull. But Miss McDonough watches her curiously, unable to understand quite what this is all about, as the scene dissolves and the CLASSROOM is seen after the others have gone and

Francie is standing again in front of Miss McDonough's desk. She is troubled. Miss McDonough holds the composition.

MISS MCDONOUGH. —And the sentence structure is excellent, Francie, but—there's something else that worries me. If we are going to write, the choice of subject—what we write about—is just as important as the writing itself. We ought to write about the best of things, we shouldn't choose a subject that is ugly and sordid, like—

Francie has been listening miserably, and not looking at Miss McDonough. But with this her head comes up.

FRANCIE. It isn't sordid, it isn't.

MISS MCDONOUGH (surprised). But, Francie, I only meant—

FRANCIE (interrupting). Maybe I didn't say it right but it isn't sordid. I won't write about it any more if you don't want me to. I don't care if I don't write anything any more.

She turns quickly to go. Miss McDonough is bewildered by this outburst and would like to get to the bottom of it.

MISS MCDONOUGH. Francie—

But Francie hurries on out, and Miss McDonough knows there is no use in trying to stop her.

The scene dissolves to the PARLOR. Francie has the box of her treasures pulled out from under the couch. She puts alongside the apron and the shaving mug and the other treasures, the composition about Johnny. Her face is hard and set. She shoves the box back under the couch. Then she pulls out another smaller box which she has kept here for English compositions. She picks this up and marches toward the kitchen.

Francie enters from the parlor and carries the box of papers to the garbage can in the KITCHEN. Fiercely she starts to tear them up and stuff them into the garbage can . . . She is never going to write anything again.—The scene fades out.

# PART EIGHT

A HOSPITAL room fades in, and we get a close view of a white-robed doctor bending over a table out of scene. The sound of his slapping a baby to try to start it breathing can be heard. We get a closeup of SISSY in bed, half-conscious, as she turns her head to look in the direction of the sound. A nurse comes into the scene and stands near the doctor.

DOCTOR (quickly). Oxygen. (The nurse goes out quickly.)

We again get a closeup of SISSY, and over it the baby beginning to cry as the scene dissolves to a HOSPITAL WAITING ROOM where Steve, Katie, Neeley, Francie and Grandma Rommely are

waiting, ill at ease. There are a couple of other expectant fathers in the room. Steve gets up and paces a little and then sits down again, but nobody pays any attention to him.—Neeley is sitting next to Katie, and Katie is watching Francie, who is quite apart from the rest of them, staring at nothing out of the window. The hospital and the coming of Sissy's baby have made Katie very much aware of the imminence of her own motherhood.—In a moment Katie gets up and moves over near Francie.

KATIE (*hesitantly*). Francie.

FRANCIE. Yes, mama.

KATIE. I—I wanted to talk to you, Francie.

FRANCIE. Yes, mama.

KATIE. It isn't going to be long now —for me. I mean, my baby. We can't come to the hospital—there isn't goin' to be money enough even for the woman to help.

For the first time, Francie looks at her.

KATIE. I'm goin' to need you, Francie, don't ever be far away. Neeley, he's— a boy ain't no good at a time like this, I'm countin' on you. You—you won't forget that, will you, Francie?

It is hard going for Katie to put this much into words. For this very reason, it is so real that for the first time Katie's need of her stirs something in Francie. She looks at Katie a little wonderingly. In the background Grandma Rommely watches, missing nothing.

FRANCIE. All right, mama. I—I'll remember.

In that moment they are closer than they have been in a long time. But the mood of it is broken by the entrance of the doctor. Through the open door a baby's crying can be heard.

DOCTOR. Which one of you is Mr. Stephen Edwards?

STEVE (*rising weakly*). That's— that's me.

DOCTOR (*to Sissy's husband*). Well, there are three in your family now. You're the father of a pretty fine boy.

GRANDMA ROMMELY (*quickly*). Alive?

DOCTOR. Very much so. He was a little reluctant about it at first, so I had to rouse him with a little oxygen. Now he's mad at me—hear him?

STEVE (*hardly able to talk*). I got to see him.

DOCTOR. Well, neither of them are quite up to a visit just now. In a little while. (*He goes out.*)

GRANDMA ROMMELY (*quietly*). The learning. It is the learning that has saved this baby.

KATIE. That's fine, Bill.

Steve is so excited that he doesn't know what to do. Suddenly he grabs up his hat and starts out.

NEELEY. Where you goin', Uncle Bill?

STEVE (*stopping*). I'm goin' out and get some strawberry ice-cream and a rattle for my son. And what's more my name ain't Bill, it's Steve. Do you hear that—I'm a papa, and my name's Steve. And it's Uncle Steve too—Steve, Steve!

He goes out and slams the door. The little family look at him in surprise.

GRANDMA ROMMELY. So! We have a man in the family.

She nods, well content, as the scene fades out.

# PART NINE

The NOLAN TENEMENT fades in, in the afternoon, as Francie and Neeley, with their school books, come down the street. Francie stops on the steps of the tenement. She takes Neeley's books.

FRANCIE. As quick as we see if she's all right, you go on down to Mc-Garrity's and see if you can do my work too. I'm going to stay here.

NEELEY. You're just gettin' out of work, that's what you're doin'.

FRANCIE. No, I'm going to finish the scrubbing for her. She oughtn't do anymore, she wasn't feeling good this morning.

There is a new little note of authority in Francie's manner. She leads the way into the tenement and Neeley follows as the scene dissolves to the UPPER HALL, and we see Francie and Neeley come up the stairs.

FRANCIE (calling). Mama?

We get a view of the KITCHEN as Francie and Neeley come in. Katie is nowhere in sight.

FRANCIE (apprehensively). Mama!

KATIE (from the bedroom). In here, Francie.

FRANCIE (quickly, to Neeley). You wait.

She goes into the bedroom.—In the BEDROOM, Katie is lying down on the bed. She is ill, and knows that the time for the coming of the child is near. Francie enters, and stops, worried, as she sees her mother.

FRANCIE. You—you all right, mama?

KATIE. Give Neeley a nickel to go after Grandma and Sissy. He can walk home after. Tell him to stop at McGarrity's on the way back and explain.

FRANCIE (gravely). Yes, mama. (She starts out, but Katie stops her.)

KATIE. Get me a nightgown—the bottom drawer.

Francie obeys, and puts it on the bed. Katie gets up. Francie stands staring at her, worried.

KATIE. Hurry, don't stand there staring.

Francie turns quickly and goes out.— Katie laboriously starts to stir herself to get into the nightgown.

Francie enters the KITCHEN. Neeley is very frightened by what he has heard.

NEELEY. Is she goin' to die?

FRANCIE (in a tone of assurance she does not feel). Of course not. It's the baby. (She gets the nickel.) You heard what mama said. And hurry. And don't forget stopping at Mc-Garrity's on the way back. We can't lose the work. (With a strange little pride) She—she just wants me now.

Awed, Neeley starts out. When he is gone, Francie is lost. She doesn't quite know what to do next. She starts to light the fire under the coffee, then listens for any sound from the other room. There is none.

FRANCIE. Mama?

KATIE (*from the bedroom*). What is it?

FRANCIE (*relieved*). Oh. I'll be there in—in a minute.

She gets the coffee started, and then goes into the bedroom.—The BEDROOM: Katie is in bed as Francie comes in. Francie is helpless now, doesn't know what to do next.

KATIE. Francie.

FRANCIE. Yes, mama.

KATIE. Don't go away, stay close by me.

FRANCIE. Yes, mama.

KATIE. I don't want to be alone. What time is it?

FRANCIE. Five to four. I'm—I'm fixing you some coffee, mama.

KATIE. That's nice.

Francie stands helplessly for a moment, then goes again to the kitchen.—Francie feels the coffee pot to see if it's hot enough, then gets a can of milk and a cup. She picks up the coffee pot and starts in with it, then decides to put it on a kitchen chair for a tray, and starts with the whole thing into the bedroom.—Back in the BEDROOM, Francie puts the improvised tray beside the bed, and then waits.

KATIE. You pour it. (*Francie obeys.*) Is it dark out?

FRANCIE. No, mama.

KATIE. It's dark in here.

FRANCIE. I'll light the gas.

KATIE. No, it'll hurt my eyes.

Francie puts the cup of coffee on the side of Katie's bed and puts milk in it. Then she goes to Katie's dresser and gets what is left of the Christmas candle

and starts to light that.—Katie takes a deep sip of the coffee.

KATIE. Tastes good. (*She sees what Francie is doing.*) You're takin' real good care of me.

FRANCIE. Am I, mama?

She puts the candle near the bed. She wants so desperately to do something more, but doesn't know what.

FRANCIE. Can I—can I get you a glass of water, mama?

KATIE (*with sudden irritation*). When I want something, I'll ask for it.

FRANCIE. Yes, mama.

KATIE. Don't just throw questions at me, I'm too tired. You better have some coffee too.

Francie obeys mechanically. She is hurt.

FRANCIE (*after a moment*). Mama, —even if Neeley is a boy, wouldn't you rather have him here, he's always such a comfort to you.

KATIE. No, it's you that's the comfort now. What time is it?

FRANCIE. I don't know, mama.

KATIE. Get the clock.

Francie obeys and goes to the kitchen. —Katie turns restlessly as there is a spasm of pain.—In a moment Francie returns with the clock and puts it down beside the bed:

FRANCIE. One minute to four, mama.

KATIE. Are you sure it isn't slow?

FRANCIE. No, mama.

KATIE. Maybe it's fast then.

FRANCIE. I'll look at the jeweler's clock out the parlor window.

She starts to go, but Katie hasn't even heard her.

KATIE. The candle is pretty. Like Christmas. That was the night I told him. (*After a little pause*) It's—nice, havin' a visit with my daughter. Hey, that's funny, you're drinking your coffee.

FRANCIE (*who hadn't known she was*). Yes, mama.

KATIE. I didn't want for you to have to grow up so soon. I didn't want for you to quit school, I tried to tell him that. He didn't mind about the baby, but he never forgive me for wantin' you to quit school. I told him and he just went out. You never forgive me either.

FRANCIE. Please don't, mama.

KATIE. He woulda bought you dolls insteada milk, and I don't know, maybe you woulda been happier, I don't know. I never woulda thought of givin' you that school like he did. And all them fine compositions of yours, I never read any of 'em. I should've had time, Johnny did. (*She stirs restlessly.*) But I couldn't do any different, I don't know how I could do any different. What time is it?

FRANCIE. Five after four.

KATIE. Wring a cloth out of cold water and wipe my face.

She turns restlessly. Francie, awed and frightened, gets up and goes to the kitchen again.—She gets a cloth and starts to wet it and wring it out in the sink. She is frightened and terribly moved.

FRANCIE (*half under her breath*). Don't let her die, please don't let her die. I'll give you anything, I'll—I'll give you my writing, I'll never write

anything again, if you just let her live.

This is only half-articulate. She hurries back to the bedroom.

In the BEDROOM, Katie is quieter again; Francie wipes her face with the cloth, and it soothes Katie so that she smiles a little.

FRANCIE. Mama, suppose the baby comes before Grandma and Aunt Sissy get here—What—What—

KATIE (*dryly*). I wouldn't be that lucky.

Her eyes close for a minute. Francie watches her helplessly. In a moment Katie's eyes open again and she looks at Francie.

KATIE. You can see I couldn't do any different. Neeley—he doesn't like school, if he stopped he'd never go back again. But you—No matter how hard it was you'd find a way to go back, you'd fight to go back. You can see that, can't you?

FRANCIE. I—Yes, mama.

KATIE. Read me something, Francie.

FRANCIE. Yes, mama.

KATIE. Read me one of your compositions. I never read any of your compositions, it's on my conscience.

FRANCIE. I tore all those up.

KATIE. No you didn't, not all of 'em.

FRANCIE. Can't I read you the Shakespeare, it—it's better.

KATIE. Read about " 'Twas on a night like this." I'd like to have something pretty on my mind. (*Francie gets the book from the dresser and opens it.*) Sit by the candle.

FRANCIE. "The moon shines bright!—
In such a night as this
When the sweet wind did gently kiss
the trees—"

KATIE. Did you ever find out who
Troilus was, and Cressida?

FRANCIE. Yes, mama. Troilus was—

KATIE. Some other day, when I got
time. Read me one of your compositions now.

FRANCIE. You won't like them, mama.

KATIE. You thought about them, and
wrote them, and got good marks on
them, and I never read one of them.
(*A little petulantly*) Get them, I said.

Reluctantly Francie goes to get them.
Katie stirs restlessly. The pain is getting worse.

We see the PARLOR as Francie comes in,
pulls out the box from under the couch
and reluctantly takes out one of the
compositions. She starts, back to the
bedroom with it.

In the BEDROOM, Katie's eyes are closed
as Francie comes in. Seeing this, Francie moves very quietly, a little relieved
that she may not have to read the composition. But Katie's eyes open.

KATIE. Sit here. (*Francie obeys, but
does not start immediately.*) Go on.

FRANCIE (*not looking at her*). It's
called "The Man People Loved."
(*Breaking off*) Please don't make me
read it, mama.

KATIE. Read it.

FRANCIE (*reading*). "Perhaps many
people might have said of him that
he was a failure. It is true that he
had no gift for making money, but
he had a gift for laughter, and for
making people love him. He had the
gift of making you feel proud to
walk down the street with him. He
had nothing to give but himself, but
of this he gave generously, like a
king. And—"

KATIE. Like a king, that's right,
walkin' down the street with him
you always felt like that.

FRANCIE. Did you, mama?

KATIE. You were real smart to write
it down like that, that's like it was.
Oh, Francie, I miss him so much.

There is a new light in Francie's eyes
as she looks at her mother. Katie stirs
restlessly. Hardly knowing she is doing
it, she reaches out a hand to Francie,
and hangs on to her hard. She is more
than half delirious now, so that her
speech is disjointed. But at last Johnny,
and their feeling for him, is in the open
between these two.

KATIE. If the baby's a boy, we'll call
him Johnny. Where's Sissy—Neeley's
been gone a long time. Wipe my face,
Francie—No don't let go my hand.
Everybody loved him, you could tell
that at the funeral. Maybe if it's a girl
we'll call her Annie Laurie—remember that tune he played? You oughta
have music lessons, maybe we can
manage it. You won't forget to dust
the piano, will you, Francie? Who'd
cry about me like that if I died. I
never done a wrong thing in my life,
but that ain't enough. I didn't mean
to be hard, Sissy, like you said. If
Johnny was here, he could go to
your graduation and I'd go to
Neeley's. I can't tear myself into two
pieces, how am I goin' to go to both?
Where are you, Francie?

FRANCIE (*frightened*). I'm here,
mama.

KATIE. You're such a comfort. I'm so
tired, leave me sleep now.

Her eyes are closed in half-sleep, half-unconsciousness. Francie, awed, sits holding on to her hand and staring at her as the scene dissolves to the KITCHEN, which Aunt Sissy and Grandma Rommely have just entered from the hall. They cross immediately to the bedroom.—Here, Francie is still holding on to the restless, fretful hand. She stands up as Sissy and Grandma come in. She is frightened. Sissy and Grandma take off their coats and get ready to go to work immediately.

SISSY (*noticing Francie's fear*). You better go out and start some water boilin', chickabiddy. We'll call you if there is anything we need.

KATIE (*eyes opening*). I thought you was never comin'.

SISSY. You quit worryin' now.

She motions to Francie with her head to go on into the kitchen. and the bewildered Francie obeys. Sissy starts looking in the dresser drawers for cloths and the baby's clothes.

The scene dissolves to the KITCHEN, where Francie is mechanically tending the water on the stove. The door from the bedroom opens and Sissy hurries out. She tests the water with her hand.

FRANCIE. It isn't boiling yet.

SISSY. You let me know when it is, I'll take it in. You're to stay out here.

FRANCIE (*wanting to help*). She—

She doesn't want any light, just the candle.

SISSY. She's goin' to be all right, baby. (*Sissy starts back to the bedroom.*)

FRANCIE (*troubled*). Aunt Sissy? (*Sissy stops.*) I just wanted to know —Did she want me to stay out—or—

The question means so much to her, in her uncertainty, that she can't go on. Sissy understands, and comes back to her.

SISSY (*gently*). She said you was to stay out, kid. People always want to spare the ones they love.

She looks at Francie for a long moment, and then turns and goes on into the bedroom closing the door behind her. Francie stares at it, then turns to the window and stares out. Next, from Francie's point of view we get a view of the tree, struggling into life again. —As Francie stands looking out at it the scene dissolves to the KITCHEN, and we get a close view of the bedroom door as it opens and Grandma appears. Francie turns quickly.

GRANDMA (*smiling*). The baby is here. And the mama does good, she sleeps. A very small baby sister it is. (*Francie is infinitely relieved.*)

FRANCIE (*tremulously*). Annie Laurie. Papa would have liked that.

As Grandma smiles at her gently, the scene fades out.

# PART TEN

The exterior of FRANCIE's SCHOOL fades in as children, dressed for their graduation, are going inside with their parents, and this scene dissolves into the SCHOOL CORRIDOR, where Sissy is waiting for Francie, who comes out of the girls' washroom and joins her. Francie has on a very simple white graduation dress. Excited girls are milling back and forth in the corridor.

FRANCIE. Where's Grandma?

SISSY (*chuckling*). I got her into a front seat so she won't miss a thing.

As they talk they go on into the classroom. The exercises have not yet begun. There are flowers on a number of the girls' desks. As Sissy and Francie enter, one girl calls to Francie.

BERNICE. Hey, Francie, you better come get your flowers.

She indicates some roses on Francie's desk. Francie knows they can't be for her.

FRANCIE (*calling back*). They aren't mine, I'm not wearing flowers tonight. (*Then, to Sissy*) Some of the girls, their families send them flowers.

SISSY (*with a little smile*). They're on your desk, lamb, I'd go see.

Francie hesitates. She would rather not.

FRANCIE. Well, I've got to get my things anyway.

She goes toward her desk. Sissy watches her. Francie comes up to her desk. She makes a show of starting to get her things together from the desk. As she does this, she looks down at the flowers. —We then see a card on the flowers. It reads: MISS FRANCES NOLAN.—Francie can't believe it. Then she opens the little envelope and we see that the card, which is in it, reads: "To Francie on graduation day. Love from Papa."— Francie stares, awed and frightened. She does not know what to believe, and a wave of emotion catches her. Anticipating this, Sissy steps in 'beside her quickly.

SISSY. He gave me the money to buy 'em, way before Christmas. To make sure of havin' it, he said. And he wrote out the card.

Francie stands unbelievingly for a moment. Then it is too much for her. A wave of feeling catches her, and her face goes down into the flowers. Sissy knows that in a moment there will be a flood of tears.

SISSY (*quickly*). Come on, kid.

An arm around Francie's shoulders, she hurries her up the aisle as the scene dissolves to the GIRLS' WASHROOM. A girl is just leaving as Sissy leads Francie in. Sissy closes the door, and they are alone.

SISSY. Now, let it go, baby.

Francie looks at her and the emotion is too much. A sob catches in Francie's throat.

SISSY. There, nobody won't hear you and I won't let nobody in. You just have it out.

Francie stands clutching the flowers to her, and then the flood of tears breaks.

FRANCIE. Papa, oh papa—

She starts to cry as she should have long ago, and as Sissy comforts her, the scene dissolves to the SCHOOL AUDITORIUM where we see a line of children filing by to get the diplomas which are being given out by the principal. There is applause at each name.

PRINCIPAL. Eugene Bricker! (*Holding out the next diploma*) Frances Nolan!

Francie, eyes shining, receives her diploma.—Sissy applauds vociferously.—Miss McDonough applauds too, and her eyes are a little misty.—Grandma Rommely is too moved to applaud. She has lived for this moment. This is fulfillment.

This dissolves to an ICE CREAM PARLOR with several marble-topped tables. The Nolans are occupying one—Francie, Neeley, Katie and Sissy. They are having ice cream. Francie still has her flowers. Sissy is talking but Katie is watching Francie and the flowers.

SISSY. Well sir, I don't think Grandma spoke one word the whole time, and from the looks of her when I put her on the streetcar, she'll probably ride clear out to Coney Island and never know the difference. Heaven only knows what she'd have been like if she could've got to both graduations.

KATIE (*looking at Francie*). Looks to me like it was a pretty good day. Your soda all right, Francie?

FRANCIE (*looking at her shyly*). Pineapple's not as good as chocolate.

NEELEY. Then what did you order it for?

FRANCIE. Because I'm up to the P's. I'll try raspberry next.

SISSY (*laughing*). There's somethin' to that idea—Try everything once.

(*At this, Katie gives her a significant look.*)

At the table behind them a man pays his check and gets up.

MAN (*to the waiter*). And a dime for you, my boy. This is a special night.

His party goes out. Their boy too has a diploma.

KATIE (*smiling*). He don't know how special—Two diplomas in the Nolan family all in one day.

FRANCIE (*leaning close to her mother; whispering*). Mama. (*Katie leans closer.*) I got a nickel if you want to leave it. People do.

KATIE. It'll be all right, Francie. (*She leans back.*) You know somethin'! They ain't goin' to be the last diplomas, either. I don't know how we're goin' to work it, but—

Her speech is interrupted by the arrival at the table of two boys, one Auggie, whom we have seen before, about Neeley's age. The other, a little older.

AUGGIE. Hi, Neeley, how you doin'?

NEELEY (*indicating his diploma*). Okay, I got out o' jail.

HERSCHEL (*Auggie's older brother*). Nice goin'. Say, wasn't it you I saw workin' behind the bat the other day?

NEELEY (*flattered*). Yeah, but—

HERSCHEL (*with phony enthusiasm*). Say, you were pretty good. You know what, I'm comin' out and give you some pointers some day.

NEELEY. Honest?

HERSCHEL. Sure I will. (*Looking at the others*) That is, if your ma don't mind.

NEELEY. Naw, she won't mind.

The obviousness of his attempt to get introduced is apparent to both Katie and Sissy. It amuses them.

HERSCHEL. Well, I'll see you on the lot. (*Stalling*) Maybe you better ask your ma. I don't want to do nothin' she wouldn't want me to.

NEELEY. Aw, she wouldn't care.

SISSY (*grinning and coming to Herschel's rescue*). Maybe you better ask her yourself, just to make sure. I'm Neeley's aunt, and this is his ma, but this is his sister. What's your name, big boy?

HERSCHEL. Herschel Knutsen.

SISSY. Mr. Knutsen, I'd like for you to meet my niece, Miss Francie Nolan.

HERSCHEL. Pleased to meet you.

FRANCIE. Hello.

SISSY (*to break the silence that has ensued*). Nice night if it don't rain. Why don't you sit down, Herschel? (*Herschel does so promptly, next to Francie.*)

HERSCHEL. Doin' anything tomorrow afternoon, Miss Nolan? It's Saturday.

FRANCIE. I don't know. Why?

HERSCHEL. There's a swell picture, Bill Hart. Maybe you'd like to go.

FRANCIE. Who with?

HERSCHEL. Me.

FRANCIE. Oh.

It is Francie's first date. Sissy and Katie are amused and interested. Francie hesitates and then passes the feminine crisis beautifully.

FRANCIE. Well, I—I might be busy. I'll let you know.

HERSCHEL (*docilely*). Well, I'll come around and see.

NEELEY. I thought we was goin' to play ball tomorrow.

HERSCHEL. We can do that any time, sure. There's lots o' time.

Both Neeley and Auggie are overwhelmingly disgusted with the feet of clay that Herschel has shown.

AUGGIE (*disgusted*). Aw, come on, Hersch.

HERSCHEL (*getting up*). Well, I'll be seein' you, Miss Nolan.

Francie smiles, but doesn't answer and Herschel and Auggie leave. Francie has made her first conquest.

NEELEY (*in pain*). Him, mushy!

SISSY. I'm proud of you, chickabiddy. You handled him fine.

Francie is flustered, but it is very pleasant.

KATIE (*smiling*). It's the hair that done it. (*Then, reluctantly*) I hate to bust up the party, but—them babies got to be fed.

SISSY. Steve will need a little somethin', too—Three hours with the both of 'em.

They make preparations to leave. The waiter enters with the check. Katie puts a half dollar on the table.

WAITER. Thirty out of fifty.

He starts to take out some change. Katie hesitates, looks at Francie, and then at Johnny's roses. Then she gets to her feet.

KATIE. Keep the change.

It is a decision monumental in its importance. Francie's eyes shine as she looks at her mother.

WAITER (*surprised*). Thank you, Ma'am.

SISSY. Why, Katie Nolan!

KATIE. I don't care! There's times when feelin' good and—and things like that is important. I don't care.

They gather their things and start out. Neeley takes a last noisy pull at the straw in his drink. As they start out, Francie walks next to Katie.

As they get to the door, and the others pass through, Francie hesitates a moment.

FRANCIE (*shyly, to Katie*). You—you want to carry my flowers, mama?

Katie looks down at her, a little tremulously. Their eyes meet, and things are fine. Katie takes the flowers a little awkwardly. It is the measure of their sharing of Johnny. They start out together. Francie is close beside her as the scene dissolves out.

The NOLAN KITCHEN dissolves in as Katie, Sissy, Francie and Neeley are just entering. Their spirits are high.

AD LIBS. You missed it, Steve. How are the babies?

They stop short as they see McShane sitting at the table with Uncle Steve. Each holds a sleeping baby. McShane gets to his feet, embarrassed.

MCSHANE. I'm beggin' your pardon, ma'am, but I just dropped in, and your brother-in-law seemed to be needin' a little help, and the baby didn't seem to mind. I hope I'm not intruding.

KATIE. Not at all, Mr. McShane.

SISSY. Sit right down, we're just goin'. (*She takes her baby.*) Come along, Steve.

KATIE (*to McShane*). I'll take her, Mr. McShane.

MCSHANE. I'd like it if you'd leave her. Her and me has got to be good friends.

Katie hesitates and then complies. Francie moves about putting her flowers in water. Sissy and Steve are getting ready to go.

KATIE (*to Sissy*). I wish you wouldn't hurry.

SISSY. Got to get this family of mine home. Steve's got his milk to deliver to a lot more babies that like that bottled kind.

They move toward the door. Katie goes with them.

SISSY (*grinning, and whispering to Katie*). Quit frownin', Katie. The fellers don't go for that at all.

Katie flushes but has no answer. Sissy is enjoying the situation thoroughly.

SISSY (*to the others*). Goodbye, kids. So long, Mac.

MCSHANE (*grinning a little*). Goodbye, Mrs. Edwards.

FRANCIE (*coming closer*). Thank you, Aunt Sissy.

Sissy ruffles her hair a little, then suddenly bends and kisses her. Sissy and Steve go. Suddenly there is a little constraint in the room.

KATIE. Well, I—I'll take the baby off you now, Mr. McShane.

She does, and sits down across the kitchen table from him. McShane doesn't know quite what to do with the blanket that has been across his lap. Conversation lags for a moment.

MCSHANE. You—you got a nice family, Mrs. Nolan.

KATIE. Thank you, Mr. McShane.

There is another silence, and then Mc-Shane gets to his feet. He has something to say, but doesn't know how to go about it. Then he takes a long breath.

MCSHANE. Mrs. Nolan, likely you're wonderin' why I came here tonight. Let your wonderin' be over. I came on a personal matter.

He pauses and clears his throat. Francie looks at her mother uncertainly.

FRANCIE. Mama, shall I go and—

MCSHANE. No. Don't be leavin', children. My conversation would be concernin' you as well as your mother. (He clears his throat again.) Mrs. Nolan, I feel it is no disrespect to speak my mind at this time. The last thing I'd intend would be any disrespect. But—I mean, I'm in line for a sergeancy now, and I feel that it has been a decent interval since the passin' of Mrs. McShane, God rest her soul—

KATIE. I didn't know, Mr. McShane, I'm sorry.

MCSHANE. I said nothing, Mrs. Nolan, because it was near the time of your own bereavement, and I didn't wish —that is, I know it is barely six months now since your husband too, left this world, rest his soul—But intendin' no disrespect—and even without the sergeancy, I feel I'm in a position to—speak my mind now. So that when you feel a decent interval has elapsed, I'm—I'm askin' to start keepin' company with you, Katharine Nolan, with the object of a weddin' when—when a decent time has elapsed.

There is a silence. Katie looks first at

Francie. Francie smiles a little. Then Katie looks up at McShane.

KATIE (very simply). For my part, I will be glad to keep company with you, Mr. McShane. Not for the help you offer, because I know we'd manage some way. But because you are a good man, Mr. McShane.

MCSHANE. There's one more thing. There's little enough I can be offerin' to such a fine family, but it's little enough I'd be askin' of the children. Their father was a fine man, and I'd have no wish to be tryin' to take his place. It would be my intention to be more like—like a real good friend. (Directly to Francie) As the eldest, could you be approvin'?

His understanding about her father has been the winning stroke with Francie. She looks at him squarely.

FRANCIE. Yes, Mr. McShane.

MCSHANE. I was thinkin' it wouldn't be right that I should ever ask the two oldest to take my name. But the little one—the one that never looked on her father—Would you think of lettin' me legally adopt her?

KATIE (smiling ever so little). If that time comes, the child shall have your name.

MCSHANE (drawing a deep breath of relief). Now I'm wonderin' if I could smoke my pipe?

KATIE. You could have smoked any time, Mr. McShane.

MCSHANE. I didn't want to be takin' privileges before I was entitled to 'em.

He fishes for his pipe with enormous relief.—Francie comes to her mother and starts to take the baby from her.

FRANCIE. Help me put her to bed, Neeley.

NEELEY. Why?

FRANCIE. To fix the blankets.

She starts for the bedroom, giving Neeley a gesture with her head for him to follow. Left alone with McShane, Katie goes to the stove.

KATIE. I'll just heat up the coffee. Will you join me in a cup, Mr. McShane?

MCSHANE. Thank you, Katharine, I will.

In the BEDROOM, Francie and Neeley are putting the baby in the basket.

FRANCIE (*with a superior air*). They want to be alone. They've got things to talk over.

NEELEY. Oh.

They finish tucking in the sleeping baby. Francie goes to the window and looks out. She is in a strange mood.

FRANCIE. Neeley—let's go up on the roof?

NEELEY. Okay. (*He laughs.*)

FRANCIE. What's the matter?

NEELEY. He called her Katharine.

Francie smiles too, and as they start out, the scene dissolves to the ROOF, where Francie and Neeley are leaning against the parapet, looking out at the world.

FRANCIE. Annie Laurie McShane.

NEELEY. Yeah.

FRANCIE. She'll never have the hard times we did, will she?

NEELEY. She'll never have the fun, either.

FRANCIE. We did have fun, didn't we, when we were young?

NEELEY. Yeah.

FRANCIE. Remember those olden days when we collected junk?

NEELEY. Poor Laurie.

FRANCIE. Neeley, look at the tree, it's growing again just like papa said. (*After a little pause*) I—I feel kind of sad, like—like we're saying goodbye to something.

NEELEY. Yeah. (*Again there's a little pause.*)

FRANCIE. Neeley?

NEELEY. Uh-huh.

FRANCIE. Am I good looking?

NEELEY. Aw, what's eatin' you?

FRANCIE. No, honest, Neeley, I want to know.

NEELEY (*grudgingly*). You'll pass.

This is high tribute from Neeley. Francie smiles happily.

FRANCIE. You're sweet, Neeley.

NEELEY. Aw, cut the mush.

Content, they gaze out over the world which their diplomas have made theirs as the scene fades out.

# NONE BUT THE LONELY HEART

*(An R.K.O. Radio Picture)*

*Screenplay by* CLIFFORD ODETS

*From the Novel by* RICHARD LLEWELLYN

*Produced by* DAVID HEMPSTEAD

*Directed by* CLIFFORD ODETS

## *The Cast*

| | |
|---|---|
| ERNIE MOTT . . . . . | Cary Grant |
| MA MOTT . . . . . . | Ethel Barrymore |
| TWITE . . . . . . . | Barry Fitzgerald |
| ADA . . . . . . . . | June Duprez |
| AGGIE HUNNER . . . | Jane Wyatt |
| JIM MORDINOY . . . . | George Coulouris |
| LEN TATE . . . . . . | Dan Duryea |
| DAD PRETTYJOHN . . | Roman Bohnen |
| IKE WEBER . . . . . | Konstantin Shayne |
| MA CHALMERS . . . . | Eva Leonard Boyne |
| TAZ . . . . . . . . . | Morton Lowry |
| SISTER NURSE . . . . | Helen Thimig |
| KNOCKER . . . . . . | William Chalee |

*Associate Producer*—SHERMAN TODD

*Film Editor*—ROLAND GROSS

*Production Designer*—MORDECAI GORELIK

# NONE BUT THE LONELY HEART

## PART ONE

A long view of the city of London at night fades in. The famed Big Ben booms out 2:00 A.M. Then we see the THAMES EMBANKMENT as a man moves through the murky, fog-streaked November night, a dirty white bull terrier straggling wearily behind him. The man's dress and manner mark him as a cockney; his feet crunch dead leaves. We get a close view of the man, ERNIE MOTT, as he stops and fishes in his pocket for a cigarette, which he lights, the flame showing more of his face. Then in a wider angle we see, in the background, several homeless men sprawled in dejected attitudes on a stone bench. One of them hopefully lifts his head and calls out hoarsely:

MAN. Spare one of them fags, can you. . . ?

ERNIE (*staring at the man in silence, puffing his cigarette; mockingly*). Stand back! Let the man see the rabbit!

Then he throws the entire pack to the man and moves on. He climbs a flight of stone steps and stands now at the head of a street. Fifteen yards away a large church door is open, its light thrown outward.

We see the façade of WESTMINSTER ABBEY as ERNIE wonders what is up. Then the view moves with him as he walks to the door of the Abbey and stands there. A woman comes out, her eyes red with weeping; a man enters gingerly.

Ernie slowly saunters into WESTMINSTER ABBEY, while the dog waits outside. Ernie looks around, puzzled and scornful. He sees a dozen people scattered around the dimly lighted church, in attitudes of prayer and contemplation.

Ernie moves left to an old man, TWITE, who is looking down at a slab in the floor.

ERNIE. What's this? What's this tonight?

MAN. Memorial services. Armistice Day tomorrow, you know.

Ernie gives a knowing grunt and follows the man's eyes down to the slab. —We get a closeup of the TOMB OF THE UNKNOWN WARRIOR in the Abbey, then return to the scene. The man is looking down at the slab with a sorrowful face. Ernie is hard about it all.

MAN. It might be my boy Alf . . .

ERNIE. Might. (*Then*) It might be me old man.

MAN. Might.

ERNIE (*after a pause*). 'Night.

MAN. 'Night.

The scene widens as Ernie leaves the church, disappearing into the fog as Old Twite looks after him. A narrator's voice accompanies Ernie's exit.

NARRATOR (*who is not seen*). When Ernie Mott—humble citizen of the city of London—saw for the first time, the tomb of the Unknown Warrior, he little realized that he might someday become the Unknown Warrior of the Second World War.

This dissolves to a LONDON STREET at night. It is still foggy as Ernie is seen moving along. He is passing a monument, and his face is scornful and lowering. He notes homeless men sleeping in corners. He turns, and the scene dissolves to "THE ROAD," Ernie's home street. Ernie appears at the head of the street, entering from a tunnel. He looks down the dark street, glad, as his tired dog is, to be home.—The narrator's voice continues to be heard.

NARRATOR. Yes, someday soon, he might become a glowing legend for happy boys and girls, living a life he merely dreamed about.

We get a moving view of Ernie and the dog as they start down the street. They pass a house showing some light under a blind. Ernie passes the window, changes his mind, and steps back for a close look into the window. He is coolly interested in what he sees. He grins and crosses the street to a house ten yards down.

NARRATOR. High destiny for quiet Ernie Mott who quarreled, hungered and loved. For this is his story — —

We next see the exterior of ERNIE MOTT'S HOME. Ernie in full view is seen in front of his home, looking up with some satisfaction at a sign which reads: "Mott's. Furniture, etc. Bought. Sold. Exchanged." Ernie moves in closer to the door and opens it quietly with a key.

NARRATOR. —the story of Ernie Mott, who searched for a free, a beautiful and noble life in the second quarter of the twentieth century.

The dog disappears into the house. Ernie is about to follow, but changes his mind, turns, and scrawls on the pavement with chalk: "Ernie Mott is home again." Then he dusts his hands off, lights a fresh cigarette, inhales deeply, and slowly saunters into the house and closes the door behind him, as the scene fades out.

ERNIE'S MA'S BEDROOM DOOR fades in. The door opens and Ma comes out, dressed for the day's work. Once she was very handsome. The face is tired, a little grim, but plenty of character there. Ma is startled at what she sees.— At the other end of the short corridor (as seen from her position), the dog is lying in front of Ernie's door; it sighs and breathes deeply. The dog looks up at Ma, vigilant, uninterested in her.

MA looks at the dog mutely, not much interested in it. But the dog indicates to her that Ernie is home again, and she quietly walks down the stairs.

This dissolves to MA's combined KITCHEN and LIVING ROOM. First we get a close view of Ma at the stove, turning over some sausage in a pan. She puts the sausage on a plate and turns, the view moving with her, as she crosses to the table where she sits with her meal. In background is the front room, which is used as a furniture shop; it is a jumble of secondhand furniture, curios, and household trash. A clock is heard whirring and striking the early hour of nine with a high tinkle. Two other clocks join in, like a musical round, and the view cuts around, revealing the various sounding clocks, following which we again see MA's

KITCHEN, with Ma at the table. She looks upward to Ernie's room. Her face is grim, promising a scene with Ernie.

MA (*raising her voice*). Ernie? Grub's ready, an' don't be all year about it or you'll have to fight the birds for it!

This cuts to ERNIE'S BEDROOM, where Ernie is sitting on the edge of the bed in his long underwear.

ERNIE (*calling down*). Won't be but a minute, Ma.

A clock behind him sounds off nine as the scene dissolves to MA'S KITCHEN, where Ernie is now unconcernedly packing away his food, while the dog sits phlegmatically in the background, waiting for an occasional scrap. Ma brings the teapot to the table and refills Ernie's cup. She returns to the stove as Ernie throws the dog a tidbit.

MA. Don't think pork sausage a bit too good for the beast, do you?

ERNIE (*sarcastically polite*). Nothing too good for this dog, Ma—part of myself, he is. Don't like him, do you?

MA (*after a pause*). Where you been, Ernie?

ERNIE (*lightly*). Oh, knocking about, north an' south, all over the shop. (*Ernie looks up, disturbed by Ma's intent, brooding silence.*) What's up?

MA (*coldly*). Why?

ERNIE. You're standing there as if I jabbed you with your own hatpin or something.

MA (*dryly*). What you come back home for, son? Miss me?

Ernie grins easily as he reaches into his pocket and brings out a stub of a cigar and a holder, and begins smoking.

ERNIE. Can't say as I did, Ma. You know me, duckie—tramp of the universe.

Ernie laughs as Ma moves to the sink with several dishes. Seeing he has hurt her feelings, he now adopts a conciliatory tone.

ERNIE. Nothing in the shop needs mending, Ma?

MA (*stiffly*). No need for your help, Ernie sweets. 'Sides, it's Sunday.

ERNIE (*crossing*). Painting, polishing, putting a spade to the garden? Mean to do me best by you, ma gel.

She suddenly slaps him violently across the face as he attempts to put an arm around her. The dog hurls itself into the scene, and but for Ernie's "Down" might well tear Ma's arm off.

ERNIE (*sarcastically*). Happy couple, aren't we?

MA. A bit of proper respect is what's needed from you, but I expect it no more than I got it from that father of yours!

ERNIE (*cool and mocking*). An' that's that!

MA. An' that's that! So you got your choice, Ernie.

Ernie crosses the kitchen to the shop door and turns there.

ERNIE. What choice . . . ?

MA. Stay or get out. Take hold here an' do a man's work, or don't come back. Stay put, so I don't have to keep frettin' my fat about you. What call've you got anyway, to be wandering around the country, year in an' out, like some homeless breath of wind? Don't I treat you right, or what?

ERNIE (*darkly*). If noise was a penny, you'd have a fortune.

MA (*grimly*). Well, I told you *your* fortune now.

ERNIE. Okeedoke. I'll be off in the morning.

Mother and son look at each other intently. To one side two of the clocks sound off. In the ensuing silence Ernie snaps his finger at the dog, turns and walks out, the dog following him.

We get a close view of MA. Her face seems relentless as she turns to the dishes in the sink. A faint wince of pain shadows her anger.

Outside ERNIE'S HOUSE: Ernie is seen coming out of the house and looking down the street with disgust. This is followed by a long view of "THE ROAD" as seen from Ernie's angle. It is a narrow slum street, hemmed in by oddly assorted two-story houses; some of the front rooms have been made into shops; there is a brewery at one end. A cat streaks away to one side; filth and squalor are everywhere. An old lady in a black shawl is hobbling down one side; three children are playing a game; opposite, an old man sits on his steps in the sun. A few pigeons whirl overhead.—Then we see Ernie turning to greet Ma Chalmers coming out of the next house. Organ music is heard, apparently coming from her house.

MA CHALMERS. How is it, Ernie boy? Home for a time?

ERNIE (*pleasantly*). How'd you know I was back, Ma?

MA CHALMERS. Live so close, I can fair hear you part your hair.

ERNIE. Nice music on your wireless.

MA CHALMERS. Don't know what I'd do without it. (*Slyly*) The piano needs tuning, too.

ERNIE. I'll look in at it around tea-time, Ma.

The view moves with Ernie and the dog as they drift down "The Road" toward the tunnel. Two gossiping crones glance at Ernie as he passes. He slows down near an old man who is leaning on his gate, smoking a pipe.

ERNIE. When you mending that window, Dad?

DAD FITCHETT. Catch me muckin' about with a window, Ern boy. Life's much too short.

ERNIE (*moving on*). You're a man after me own heart, you are, Dad!

Ernie starts across the street, heading for Aggie Hunner's house, the dog behind him, following which the scene cuts to the FRONT ROOM of AGGIE HUNNER'S HOUSE, where Aggie is playing the cello. She looks up through the window and sees Ernie. She quickly puts the cello aside and starts for her door.—And this scene cuts to the exterior, to the door and steps of Aggie's house, including the pavement. Aggie enters the scene, calling to Ernie in the background. There is something simple, normal, earnest and extremely likeable about her.

AGGIE. Ern! (*Devouring him with her eyes*) Been home long? Bring yourself in for a spot of tea.

ERNIE. My basket's full of breakfast.

AGGIE. Come in anyway, Ern . . .

He starts up the steps, followed by the dog and Aggie, and the scene cuts to AGGIE'S studio-like FRONT ROOM as Aggie and Ernie enter, followed by the dog. Ernie plucks a string of the cello.

ERNIE. Practising?

AGGIE. It's a living, and it pays to keep your tools sharp.

ERNIE (*looking around*). Nicest drawing room in the neighborhood, this.

AGGIE. It's yours, whenever you want it . . .

ERNIE (*moving over to the piano and fingering the keys*). Have to take you with it, do I?

AGGIE (*smiling*). Want me to move out?

Ernie sits at the piano and improvises a little ditty, mockingly singing the words.

ERNIE (*singing*). He's the boy for me, I'm the gel for him, He's a lump of toffee, cake an' pudding . . .

Aggie comes up behind him and puts her arms around Ernie. He stops, looks up and grins in a friendly way.

ERNIE. You're the biggest fool I ever met, Aggie. I'm black as the ace. . . . Don't you know it yet? Matter of fact, Ma give me the ultimatum today. "Stay put or stay out," she says. (*At the same time Ernie swings Aggie around so that she is now sitting in his lap.*)

AGGIE (*with concern*). What will you do?

ERNIE. Hmmm . . . something.

AGGIE. What?

ERNIE. Something . . .

Now Ernie abruptly puts his arms around Aggie and kisses her.

[Back in MA'S SHOP we get a close "shot" of her looking out of her shop window at Aggie's window across the street. A sharp voice calls her to attention.

VOICE. Well . . . ?

The scene widens as Ma turns and faces Mrs. Snowden, a smartly dressed visitor who has entered the room and now stands impatiently tapping a large umbrella.

MA (*shaking her head*). No bid, Mrs. Snowden. Second place, wish you'd stop bothering me. It's thieving, just like I took them myself!

MRS. SNOWDEN. No, it ain't. Me and my friends do the lifting—you just do the selling.

MA. It's shoplifting, that's plain. Save your breath!

MRS. SNOWDEN (*stopped*). Settled, is it?

MA (*emphatically*). Settled years ago!

MRS. SNOWDEN. One of these bright days you'll change your mind. (*She slowly starts for the door and turns there.*) And you want to be more careful, you do. You called me a thief.

MA (*dryly*). What did I ought to do then? Say me prayers?

Mrs. Snowden's answer is to exit and slam the door behind her. Ma turns and looks at Aggie's house across the street again.]

Inside AGGIE HUNNER'S FRONT ROOM: Ernie is lying on the couch, staring up at the ceiling. Aggie is playing "None but the Lonely Heart" on the cello.

ERNIE (*reflectively*). Some blokes is never happy unless they got a hammer walloping away at something, or digging up a bit of grass, or fiddling about with a lump of wire or some bright thing or other. Get proper wore out and say they got a hobby. I believe in letting things alone, and if they're broke, they are broke, and that's it. (*Ernie listens some time in silence.*) You're a little flat, there, Aggie. F-sharp instead of F. What's the music called?

AGGIE. "None but the Lonely Heart."

ERNIE. Italian?

AGGIE (*playing*). Russian.

Now the song is finished, and Ernie, murmuring, "Nice," gets to his feet. Aggie lays the cello to one side.

AGGIE. See you tonight?

ERNIE. Might.

AGGIE. Around nine?

ERNIE (*suddenly irritated*). All alike, you women. I don't go on the time-tables like a train. I'm Ernie Mott, citizen of the Great Smoke, and I don't stay put!

AGGIE. I understand . . .

ERNIE (*somewhat mollified*). Do you?

AGGIE. Of course.

ERNIE (*grinning, after a pause*). Then maybe I'll see you tonight, Nipper. (*Then*) Maybe I will . . . Or maybe I won't.

He starts to go but is stopped by Aggie.

AGGIE (*fondly*). Who give you that?

ERNIE. What?

AGGIE. The dimple in your chin.

ERNIE. Present from me Pa. 'Bye, Aggie.

AGGIE. 'Bye, Ernie boy . . .

Ernie goes out with the dog, and Aggie goes to the window and looks out after him, following which we see Ernie coming out of the house and slowly crossing the street, starting up "The Road."

Outside TATE'S FISH AND CHIPS SHOP: Ernie enters the scene, whistling "None but the Lonely Heart." Through the shop window he is being observed by Len Tate and his scrofulous mother, smug citizens. Their disapproval of Ernie is quite evident as they nudge each other. Ernie waves at them, albeit with a grimace. They stare back coldly. —Then the view moves with Ernie up the road, as he stops and knocks at the door of Dad Prettyjohn's General Store. A blustering voice is heard from inside.

DAD PRETTYJOHN'S VOICE. What's coming off? Sunday, or ain't it? Nobody home! Nobody home!

ERNIE (*grinning*). It's me, Dad. Ernie Mott.

At this, Dad Prettyjohn opens the door, mollified, looking over his glasses.

DAD PRETTYJOHN. Oh, you, is it? . . . Ain't seen you in three months, have I?

ERNIE (*grinning*). You're blocking the door, Dad. (*Ernie enters the shop and Dad, who is very fond of him, closes the door.*)

Inside DAD PRETTYJOHN'S GENERAL STORE:

ERNIE. Miss me, did you?

DAD. Had your post card from up north. Don't let no grass grow under your feet, do you?

ERNIE. Dad, how do we go for some smokes today? I'm so broke, I'm two halves.

DAD. What, again? Guess you think it grows on trees.

ERNIE (*sternly*). Oh, now, Dad, you're not giving me the boot, are you? Now, what cigars you got?

DAD. Cigars? Got a very doubtful stock of them, Ern. Can't make out what happens to things lately. But I got a good Burma cheroot.

ERNIE. Got more respect for my guts, I have. Give us a large Rigby's.

DAD (*wincing*). Large Rigby's it is!

ERNIE (*lighting a cigarette*). Proper lovely to be alive and have friends like you, Dad. Remembering you in my will, I am.

DAD. Don't think I'll live to see the day, do you? (*Dad accompanies Ernie to the door and opens it for him.*) How's your Ma?

ERNIE. Ma goes on like an engine. Tower of London don't do better. 'Bye . . .

DAD. Drop in again, Ern.

This dissolves to "THE HIGH ROAD" as Ernie is going down the main street with much traffic and tram lines. Ernie is walking along, dog beside him, enjoying the sun. He stops at a shop window filled with girl dummies, a beautiful dummy in front, wearing a sign which reads, "Take me home for 28 shillings." Ernie looks very arch as he moves on, the scene dissolving to the exterior of the FUN FAIR (penny arcade): A drunkard is standing to one side, muttering to himself, as Ernie walks into the scene, Nipper behind him; they enter the Fair.

The FUN FAIR: The large room sparkles with electric lights, mirrors, chromium and glass. The place is crowded with men and a few girls in giggling, excited pairs. A loud-speaker is blaring out dance music in competition with a mechanical piano across the room. There are games of darts, their various prizes of dolls, silver spoons, vases and clocks displayed to one side; likewise

with a rifle range. A mechanical crane, weighing machines, strength and grip testers, distorting mirrors, peep-o-scopes, etc., are scattered around. A "Bloke" is heard shouting "Here you are—three for a penny."

One aisle leads through a large arch, painted to look like natural stone. The main feature of the place consists of two long rows of pinball machines. In the middle of one row, on a raised platform, sits ADA, who makes change for the customers. At the end of this aisle is the booth of "Madame La Zaka, Fortunes."

Ernie moves up the aisle leading through the stone arch, looking around with amused unconcern. He stops at the jangling mechanical piano, which is next to Madame La Zaka's booth. Madame is standing there.

ERNIE (*with a grimace*). Out of tune.

MADAM (*with a shrug*). Don't worry me, duckie. 'Ave your fortune told? Reveal the future?

ERNIE (*grinning*). I know me future, Madame—it's fruit cake with nuts, ending with a gas supper.

The view moves with Ernie as he slowly wanders past the dart games. One man has just won a clock.

DARTS MAN. There you are, folks! Knows how to do it, a gent! Wins his self a darling clock!

Ernie crosses over to the active rifle range and stops behind a few on-lookers. Three men, with their backs turned, are shooting. Then we see Ernie and other on-lookers, including the Bloke who runs the range, near the rifle range counter.

BLOKE. Try again! Practice makes perfect! Try again! Nothing to lose but a tanner! (*The Bloke suddenly spies Ernie among the on-lookers.*) Here he is, gents! Best shot of the district an' all done here! He can take care of his self an' his family any time there's a bit of barney anywhere! Safe all over the world, he is, an' respected. Kindly note the last word—I said respected!

A closer view shows the Bloke reaching across the counter, offering Ernie the rifle. Ernie takes it, handling it professionally, getting his elbows set on the counter. The three men who have been shooting are stopped, for Ernie has pushed his way between them with a smiling remark:

ERNIE. Stand back! Let the man see the rabbit!

The remark amuses the well-dressed Jim Mordinoy, one of the three men; but his two lieutenants, Cosh and Slush, are less amused by Ernie's charming insolence.

BLOKE. Now watch the fur fly, gents. Quiet, please, while the shots are took. (*In a dramatic whisper*) All paid an' all weighed? Eyes down, lookin' in . . .

Twice Ernie fires and twice the bull's-eye is hit. Jim Mordinoy and his lieutenants are impressed. Now come eight more perfect shots. The Bloke reels in the target, holding it up.

BLOKE. There! Ten shots an' all of them where they should be, in the little black hole of Calcutta. I told you who he was, an' this is him! (*Handing Ernie a prize*) Your fags, governor, and good luck to you.

Ernie takes the fags, but a closer view reveals that the Bloke is handing him some coins, too, for helping drum up business. People are pushing forward to try their skill with the rifles. Ernie

slips gracefully away. Mordinoy follows him, leaving his lieutenants behind.

The view then moves with Ernie walking up the aisle, the dog after him. He comes to the piano, looks it over, finds and kicks away the electric connection. The piano stops and goes dark. Mordinoy sees this.

MORDINOY. Don't like music . . . ?

ERNIE. This thing is out of tune.

MORDINOY. An' why let that bother you?

ERNIE. 'Cause it gets in my ear and agonizes around in there, that's why! Perfect pitch I got, that's why!

MORDINOY. What's perfect pitch?

A rifle shot sounds from the range. It strikes a metal target with a musical clang.

ERNIE. Hear that? C-sharp! (*As another sounds*) Upped a half note—D! When I recognize the sound, that's it—that's perfect pitch!

MORDINOY. Easy as eatin' breakfast, ain't it? I'm Mordinoy. Jim Mordinoy.

ERNIE. Am I supposed to know you?

MORDINOY (*smiling faintly*). Thought as how you might . . . (*Then, bending down to stroke the dog*) Ever fight your pup?

ERNIE. Never. What about the piano?

MORDINOY (*surprised*). What about it?

ERNIE (*twinkling*). Do I tune it or do I don't? Cost you only half a quid.

MORDINOY (*with a slow smile, and bringing out a wallet*). Life's easier 'an that. Take a quid an' leave the pianner undisturbed.

ERNIE (*suspiciously*). Now why would I take your quid?

MORDINOY. Just to be a pal . . .

In a moving view we see Ernie and Mordinoy going toward the front of the room. Ernie slowly takes the bill.

ERNIE (*examining him*). What's that I smell on you? Hair oil?

The men come to a stop at a section of the pinball row. Ernie's back is to Ada, sitting on her dais in the background. Mordinoy is looking Ernie up and down.

MORDINOY. Can't understand why a man of your particular talents wears them rags.

Ada, on her dais, is looking Ernie over, too, listening. She seems cold, bored, diffident.

ERNIE. Clothes is a lot of bleeding excitement about nothing most of the time. As to what you call my "rags," they are the uniform of my independence.

MORDINOY (*still smiling*). Clothed in your perfect pitch, you are, I suppose.

ERNIE. Now you understand me, Mr. Mordinoy.

We now get a close view of Ada on her dais; Ernie seems to be arousing her interest. Then we see Ernie and the coldly affable Mordinoy close together.

ERNIE (*with a mocking undertone*). Life is a piece of meat, when you know how. What's most of them floatin' around in here? Victims! Hurry, worry an' scurry to make a bit of brass. Right? Right! Now

what's your kind, Mr. Mordinoy? Wilful an' deceitful. Take what you want. Right? Right! So that's what it's all about—either be a Victim or be a Thug. But suppose . . . (*Drawing him closer and turning Mordinoy around; now it is Ernie who faces Ada.*) Suppose you don't want to be neither. Not the hare an' not the hound. Then what?

The angle widens, to include Ada in the scene.

ADA (*with a delicate smile of encouragement*). Then what . . . ?

Ernie looks up and gives Ada a cold stare which slowly changes to one of appreciation.

ERNIE (*to Mordinoy*). Oh . . . Who's the piece of pastry in the jersey?

MORDINOY. Ada Brantlin . . .

ERNIE. Fair blinds you with science, don't she?

Ada doesn't like this fresh outburst and shows her displeasure by turning away.

MORDINOY. She don't like the rough stuff.

ERNIE (*not taking his eyes off her*). Have to box clever there?

MORDINOY. Yes, I suppose you would.

ERNIE. I see . . .

Mordinoy looks steadily at Ernie, then at Ada. He drifts away without looking back. Ernie moves to Ada's change counter. He puts the pound note in front of her.

ERNIE. Change, please, miss. (*As she coldly changes the bill*) Who's this Mordinoy? Runs this place, does he?

ADA. Wouldn't dirty his hands on it.

ERNIE. Then what's he doing here?

ADA. It happens the gentleman came in to converse with me. Now kindly move on.

Ernie solemnly moves to a pinball machine next to Ada's dais, never taking his eyes off her. He drops a coin in the machine and expends all the balls without looking down. She keeps her composure. He drops in another coin.

ERNIE. How do I get into your good books, Ada? (*Getting no answer*) Lovely fingernails . . . (*As she haughtily tries to stare him down*) You are looking at a goldfish as got himself lost among a pack of oily sardines.

ADA (*stiffly*). What's up. Don't you know when your health is good?

ERNIE. Wished I was a painter.

ADA (*defiantly*). An' you'd do what?

ERNIE. Well, what's a painter do?

A pause, then a smile from her as she holds up a novel she has been reading.

ADA. In this book a painter does some very strange things. Calls it art, too, he does! (*After a laugh*) You an artist?

ERNIE (*raising his eyebrows*). Me?! Tune pianos, that's me. Play the piano by ear. Polish furniture, shoot rodents with a rifle and exterminate other pests with sulphur and arsenic. Are there bugs in your house? Send for Ernie Mott. Know how to medicate dogs or cats. Excellent at repairing clocks and other delicate machinery. I invent inventions.

ADA (*liking his blarney*). What you invent?

ERNIE (*with a vague gesture*). Ohh . . .

ADA (*archly*). I see.

ERNIE. I happen to be working on my greatest invention at the present time. A human animal which don't look for a master . . . (*Grinning*) Ain't easy!

Ada gives him an intent look, and crooks a finger at him.

ADA (*dropping her voice*). Listen, come closer. (*After Ernie moves in*) I like that kind of talk.

ERNIE (*whispering*). You do?

ADA. Sounds barmy as the muffin man, but I like it.

We get a close view of MORDINOY and his lieutenants at the dart game. They are looking over at Ernie and Ada. Then the scene cuts back to the couple.

ERNIE. Well, that brings up just one question, Ada dear.

ADA. What?

ERNIE. What time you get off?

An arch pause from Ada; she pulls her sweater down.

ADA. Half six. Round the back.

ERNIE. Thank you.

He looks at her again, turns and walks toward the exit, followed by Nipper. Ada looks after Ernie. A man comes into the foreground for change, and Ada turns to business.

This dissolves to an ALLEY STREET at NIGHT—a dark street at the mouth of the back of the alley which leads to the back of the Fun Fair. Ernie Mott, followed by his dog, passes and enters the alley.—Then we see him walking up the narrow, squalid alley. He is about to pass a homeless man who is grubbing through a rubbish can. He stops, pulls a coin out of his pocket, and tosses it to the man.

ERNIE. Oh . . . Catch!

MAN. Thank you, sir.

Ernie then continues up the alley, looking for the back entrance to the Fun Fair. He seems unable to find the door. Ada, leaning against a bill-posted fence, has been watching him all the time. Now she calls softly:

ADA. Here . . .

Ernie turns and quickly moves to her. He looks at her for a silent moment. She is very beautiful to him and he is in no mood for jokes.

ADA (*quietly*). Charitable sort you are . . .

ERNIE. Oh, that . . . Friend of mine. Knew him "when."

ADA. When what?

ERNIE. When he was a man . . .

They look at each other in dead silence. Ernie puts one hand on each side of her head, bracing himself against the fence but not touching her.

ERNIE. Old Ike Weber, friend of my Ma's, told me this, "As I was out walking, I saw in the distance what seemed an animal. Come up closer an' see it was a man. Come still closer and see it was my brother . . ."

Ada looks at him in silence, her face soft, responsive; this is a new kind of man for her; she looks dead at him, immobile.

ERNIE (*quietly*). Tired . . . ?

ADA (*nodding*). Umm . . .

Not dropping his hands, Ernie's face moves in and he kisses her yielding mouth, all very quietly and special; it lasts a full moment, then:

ERNIE. Quiet as mice, ain't we?

ADA. Umm . . . (*After a pause*) What you looking at?

ERNIE. Nothing.

ADA. Tell us . . .

ERNIE. Tired, ain't you . . . ?

ADA. Always tired. (*And the spell is suddenly broken.*) My feet's just about wore off. Let's go. Nice strong cup of tea for two.

She pushes his hands down and starts for the mouth of the alley. Ernie slowly follows her, the dog behind him.

ADA. What's the dog doing 'ere? (*Surprisingly cold now*) I don't go out with dogs, you know!

ERNIE. All right. I'll drop him off on the way.

He takes her arm and hurries her away. The view moves to Jim Mordinoy sitting in his car across the street. He watches them go off, his face expressionless.

The scene dissolves to a CAFE at night. First we see (in a "close shot") Ernie's and Ada's feet under a cafe table. Her feet are comfortably out of their shoes, and in a moment, one is used to scratch the other. The following dialogue is heard during this scene.

ERNIE'S VOICE. Not much on talking either, are you?

ADA'S VOICE. Not much. Have to excuse me, I'm a bag of nerves.

ERNIE'S VOICE. My own Ma's that way, so it's nothing new to me.

And now we see Ernie and Ada sitting at a table. Ernie is eating most of the food on the table, meat pie, doughnuts and tea.

ADA. You saved me a bit of a fuss

tonight. Mr. Mordinoy wanted me to go out with him . . . (*Then*) Kissing me like that, the first meeting—I never done a thing like that before in my life.

ERNIE (*smiling*). Lucky me.

ADA. Lucky you?

Ernie takes her hand while reflectively drumming the fork with the other hand.

ERNIE. Five red beetles on the end of your fingers . . . (*Looking straight at her, Ernie now remarks of the silver chime of the fork.*) G-sharp. (*Answering her puzzled look*) The pitch of this—G-sharp. Perfect pitch, that's me. Not one in a million's got that, didn't you know? Very unusual person. Didn't you know?

ADA (*smiling faintly*). Are you?

ERNIE (*grinning*). Yes, and all I want is to put my arms around you and hold you tight and murder anyone who says a blind word to you!

ADA (*withdrawing her hand*). Interesting program, but what's it get me?

ERNIE. Only trouble.

ADA (*smiling*). That's what worries me. (*Then*) I like you. You're quiet and you don't chuck your weight about. Just nice quiet little Ernie boy, with a look in his eye. Interested in perfect pitch and that sort of thing. I ought to like you, didn't I? Well it's been a long day.

ERNIE (*alertly*). Want me to take you home?

ADA. No, thanks. I'll hop on a tram, if it's all the same to you.

ERNIE. Don't want me to come along?

ADA. No, it ain't far, and you've give me a lovely evening. I wouldn't bother you.

ERNIE. The less said the better, Ada dear.

He stands up, drops some coins on the table and they start out of the scene. This then dissolves to a STREET, where Ada and Ernie are walking between shabby flats.

ERNIE. Why don't you put your hat on?

ADA. I don't want to spoil my hair. (*She puts her hat in her coat pocket.*)

ERNIE. Meetin' someone.

ADA. It's late. It's later than I thought.

ERNIE. Time is not of the essence with me. No place to go, and going there tomorrow.

ADA. I don't pretend to know what that means.

ERNIE. Never see my happy home again. Fight like cats with Ma. Told her off today, I did. So it's the end. She don't know they milk the cow that stands still. Wants me in that silly dusty business of hers, squeezing pennies out of paupers. (*Vehemently*) No, thanks! No, thank you!

Outside ADA'S HOUSE, as Ada stops at the entrance to a dingy basement apartment.

ADA. You mean you're leaving London in the morning?

ERNIE. Can't think of any reason not to, can you? (*After a pause*) Inviting me in?

ADA. No. My Aunt and Uncle's asleep in the back. (*Suddenly hefting her handbag*) I'd like to smash you one with this!

ERNIE. Why?

She scornfully moves down to a basement entrance under the steps. Ernie follows her.

ERNIE (*after a wait*). Why?

ADA (*all the fight suddenly gone*). Never mind . . .

ERNIE. Blow hot—blow cold, don't you?

ADA. Blow any bloomin' way I please, and it's not your business! (*Coldly*) Take you an hour to get home, won't it?

Ernie's answer is to try to put his arms around her. But Ada won't permit this.

ADA (*coldly*). I don't like to 'ave you touch me.

ERNIE (*quietly*). Feel like I know you a whole lifetime, Ada dear . . .

ADA (*her mood abruptly changed*). You want to see me cry?

ERNIE. No.

ADA. Then say goodbye and go away.

Ernie answers by gently embracing and kissing her. Ada, properly tamed, moves her mouth away after a moment.

ADA. No sense to this, is there? We're just wasting our time, that's all. You're a stranger. I meet you . . . Suddenly . . . You ever been in love, Ern? I mean you make me feel twelve years old again. I don't know why . . . You're the only man I've met in a million years gives me the slightest sort of feeling. Say goodbye now, and that's the end of it.

ERNIE (*pausing soberly*). I'll drop by the Fun Fair tomorrow.

ADA. Don't.

ERNIE (*after a pause*). Good night, Ada dear.

ADA. Goodbye, Ern boy . . .

He is just about to reach out and kiss her, but adroitly she has suddenly slipped behind the grille door. They are now looking at each other through bars.

ADA. In the end you wouldn't give me what I need. Confidence, that's what a woman needs.

ERNIE. Confidence?

ADA. Yes . . .

ERNIE (*after a pause*). Good, then you won't see me again. Black as the ace I am, Ada girl. No future in me for anyone like you. No confidence. (*Then*) 'Night.

ADA. 'Night.

He turns and goes. Ada, a beautiful, yearning prisoner behind the bars, looks after him as the scene fades out.

[We see "THE ROAD" as Ernie is returning home. He walks under the tunnel at the head of "The Road" and emerges from the other side. He is smoking a stub of cigar in the holder, thinking of Ada. He snorts out one word to himself, "Confidence." He passes Aggie's house, pausing only briefly, and then continuing on across to his own door. Here he opens the door with a key, but his concentration is decidedly on Aggie's window across the street.—The dog appears, its eager snuffle and shuffle heard at Ernie's feet. He absent-mindedly reaches down and speaks to the dog in a stern whisper.

ERNIE. Yes, I know . . . know all about it, how you like me. Scamper about now and don't be all night about it!

Ernie leans against the wall, waiting for the dog, his concentration meanwhile on Aggie's window.—A close view of Aggie's window shows the shade lifting slightly in the breeze. Then we get a close view of ERNIE still looking across at the window. In the meantime the iron shutter of a warehouse at the other end of The Road goes up. Four ghostly push-cart men roll out their carts and parade down toward the tunnel. Ernie snaps his fingers and the dog returns.

ERNIE (*softly*). In the house . . .

Ernie softly closes the door behind the dog. He starts across the street to Aggie's house, and the scene fades out.]

# PART TWO

MA'S SHOP fades in. It is morning, and Ernie's MA and IKE WEBER are standing before a tall, elegant antique clock, Ike examining it with the eyes of a connoisseur.

IKE. No question, Mrs. Mott, it's worth every farthing you ask. Irregardless. I'll send my Mr. Lesser for it this afternoon. Where could I find the heart to sell an object like this? It goes in my private collection.

MA. Good enough, Ike, if you can afford it.

IKE. The trouble is, I can't . . .

Ike Weber is an elderly Jewish pawnbroker with a Rembrandt face; he has much appreciation and feeling for fine antiques and gems, plus real perception about people.

IKE. Maybe your son would like to clean the mechanism? He's got a real talent for such things. (*Ma's answer is a grim snort. He continues gently.*) Still the same old trouble? He won't stay home?

With some agitation Ma sits in a rocker near the counter. She begins to rock herself violently, the feather on her hat waving.

MA. There's a business here to be run. He might line his pockets if he knew the ins and outs. But the boy simply won't settle down! Says he won't be "victimized," whatever that means. Says the meek never inherited nothin' but the dust of the road. It all makes him want to howl, he says! Don't ask me who he takes after. His father maybe drank, but he always come home. His father would have jumped at the Dole like a shot. Not Ernie. Proud as the Queen's carriage he is, and independent. Catch him being a number on a Minister of Labour card! Not much! (*After a pause, shaking her head*) He's leaving home for good today.

Ma rocks in silence for a moment. Ike is thoughtful.

IKE (*finally*). Excuse me for mentioning it, but why don't I talk to him?

MA (*unhearing*). You'll have to help me, Ike.

IKE. But of course . . . irregardless.

MA (*fingering her diaphragm*). I'm sick . . .

IKE ? ? ?

MA. What your wife up and died of.

IKE (*very softly*). Oh . . .

MA. It might happen sooner than I think. See Ernie gets it all. He'll probably want to sell the place. Do the best you can for him.

IKE (*softly*). But Mrs. Mott, you know I will.

MA (*looking at him*). Yes, you're a good boy, Ike.

Very moved, Ike goes to the window where he looks out. Ma blows her nose vigorously. Ike turns to face her again.

IKE. Thinking out loud, it would be very fine if you had him with you for the next few months. You need sleep and special considerations . . . that's impossible with him walking around the country. (*After a pause*) Why don't you tell him? . . . (*Ma's answer is to turn a stern eye on Ike.*) No . . ? (*With mild protest*) But isn't it possible, Mrs. Mott, that maybe you exaggerate his feelings?

Again Ma's answer is a grim snort. A shadow falls in the doorway and Ike looks up. An incredibly ragged little woman, MA SEDGWISS, has just entered the shop and is standing in the doorway, a canary bird in a cage in one hand.

MA SEDGWISS. I brought Joey round again.

IKE (*leaving*). Remember, Mrs. Mott, I'm always at your service . . .

[Ma Sedgwiss has gone to the counter with the cage.

MA SEDGWISS. I'll have me Joey out again soon as I draw me pension. Go three an' a tanner on him, Mrs. Mott?

MA (*behind the counter*). You know he never gets more than two shillings.

MA SEDGWISS. Just this once, will you? Three an' a kick?

MA. Half a dollar, take it or leave it.

The old woman slaps the counter and shakes the curlers in her hair.

MA SEDGWISS (*shouting*). Now what can I do with half a dollar? Shilling for coal an' I got one an' six. What can I get for one an' six? What about me tea an' bread?

MA (*firmly*). No use your carrying on there. I'm used to it by now. Half a dollar or don't waste me time.

Unseen, Ernie has been standing in the background for some time, disgusted with this bickering.

MA SEDGWISS. Three an' odd an' leave him here till tomorrow. See, I got his birdseed here. Now give me my three an' a tanner an' I'll go out an' get meself some grub.

MA (*stolidly*). Half a dollar.

ERNIE (*in the background*). Why not give her the extra bit?

Ma turns, sees Ernie and silently obeys.

MA SEDGWISS (*overjoyed*). Now I'll have me eats! An' don't you worry, Mrs. Mott. You'll see me tomorrow, you will, when I get Joey back.

MA (*calmly*). You're a liar, Ma Sedgwiss. Take Joey an' get out!

Ma Sedgwiss takes the money and the cage, and goes. Ma makes an entry in a book, pretending to have forgotten Ernie who is still in the doorway, in the background.

ERNIE (*finally*). Anything to eat in the house?

MA (*not turning*). Sit down an' you'll get it.

The scene cuts to MA'S KITCHEN as Ernie comes to the table and sits down, his dog in the background. Ma comes in and goes to the stove in silence, stirring something already prepared in a pan. The mood between mother and son is a tense one.

MA (*not turning*). I'd like to know how you'd got on as a boy if I'd kept shelling out those extra pennies.

ERNIE (*pushing back his chair*). Are we off again? Or do I eat my meal in the peaceful hush of this late Monday morning?

MA. Do as you see fit, son.]

MA'S KITCHEN: Ma goes from table to stove and returns with the tea. Ernie throws a piece of meat to the dog behind him; it is quickly gulped up. Ernie begins packing in the food and tea. Ma goes to a shelf and takes two pills out of a bottle, swallowing them. Ernie looks up and sees this. Ma puts the bottle back on the shelf.

ERNIE. What are them pills for?

MA. Yeast tablet.

ERNIE. Don't think they'd do much good, do you?

MA. Do me at least as much good as *you* do.

Ernie drops his knife and fork. There is a pause. Ernie decides to settle this whole business; he stands up.

ERNIE. See—that's what I mean. Never an hour of peace between us! (*Going to the door and turning*) Reckon the stork brought you the wrong sort of a son.

MA (*bitterly*). I wouldn't be surprised.

ERNIE. You'll never get me to stay here an' run this shop! Not if the sky fell. I'm not in the business of sweating pennies out of devils poorer than meself. Not if they brought me home with both me legs cut off! I'd

crawl out into the street again, I would!

Ma, at the table, is facing Ernie; she is pale and intensely dignified.

MA. Some day you'll know I'm the only friend you got.

She slowly sits down at the table, unable to say more, wanting to cry, a bitter taste in her mouth.

ERNIE. Less said, the better.

MA. Eat your breakfast.

ERNIE. Goodbye. (*He calls "Nipper," goes around the table to the doorway, and turns back to Ma.*) I'll drop you a postcard from the seaside.

For a moment it seems as if Ernie is about to change his mind, as if a sudden wave of affection for Ma is going to engulf him. Instead he turns abruptly and goes out, the dog after him, leaving Ma sitting dejectedly in the kitchen.

Ernie comes out with the dog, stands there blinking in the sunlight, and tightens his belt and sets his cap at a jauntier angle. Then we see a section under a tunnel on "THE ROAD": Ike Weber is standing there, looking down "The Road." Suddenly he sees Ernie come out of his house. Slowly Ike begins to amble toward him.
The view moves with Ernie up "The Road," toward the tunnel. He looks across and sees Aggie leaving her house, cello under her arm. She turns as he crosses to her.

ERNIE. Where you off to?

AGGIE. Rehearsals. Had some breakfast?

ERNIE (*gloomily*). This street makes me sick. All the people in it, too. I'm leaving for good now. (*In his mocking tone*) Miss me, will you?

AGGIE (*seriously*). It's nothing to do with me, mind, if you quarrel with your Ma. Only thing, I'll miss you. Marry you quick, if I had the chance.

ERNIE. What about money? Money talks, they say. All it ever said to me was "Goodbye." Support me, would you?

AGGIE. If you wanted me to.

ERNIE (*archly*). Think you could handle me, Aggie?

AGGIE (*seriously*). I know how to handle you—not handle you at all—leave you be.

ERNIE (*grinning*). I've never been so tempted in all me born days!

AGGIE (*picking up the cello*). Think about it . . . you know the address . . . I'd better hurry—got to get my collars washed. 'Bye, Ernie.

ERNIE. Goodbye, Aggie.

She goes down the street, leaving Ernie gloomily gaping after her, impressed by her simple clarity. Then the view moves with Ernie, as he starts up "The Road" again, crossing the street, heading for TATE'S FISH AND CHIPS SHOP, from which singing is heard. Through the glass we see Ike Weber sitting at the counter, nibbling.

Inside TATE'S FISH AND CHIPS HOUSE: Ernie comes to the counter. Behind it are the usual paraphernalia. Ma Tate and her son, Len, a smug and unpleasant fellow, are leaning on the counter, Len picking his teeth.

ERNIE (*throwing a coin*). A big six-penny bit, chips on the side. Looking very prosperous there, Len—new fixtures and all.

LEN (*lazily, lofty*). Yes, I got mine.

ERNIE (*disliking him*). Looks as if it's all in your teeth.

Ike, at the window end of the counter, is furtively watching Ernie. Ma Tate, who dislikes him, puts the food in front of Ernie, who takes it to a corner bench against the wall.

MA TATE (*gossipy*). Ain't it time you stayed home and settled down in business for yourself, son?

ERNIE (*eating*). Me? If it's what you happen to want.

LEN (*"lord of creation"*). It's safe, that's what it is—safe.

ERNIE (*sardonically*). Envy you, Len, I must say!

LEN (*wiping his face with a dirty apron*). Course you do, Ern, course you do.

Ernie throws the dog a piece of fish. Ike Weber turns around, revealing his face to Ernie.

ERNIE. Well, here's Ike Weber! What brings you in the neighborhood, Ike?

IKE. And how is Mr. Mott today? What an honour, Mr. Mott!

Ike goes over to Ernie and shakes his hand.

ERNIE. Come down for some of Tate's famous chips?

IKE (*smiling*). Everything with a kiss. I'm glad I ran into you.

ERNIE (*pertly*). Are you?

IKE. Yes. I need two pounds' worth of clock repairs.

ERNIE (*after a quizzical glance*). I'm on my way to Liverpool.

IKE. Don't they use money in Liverpool any more?

Ike waits for an answer. Ernie stands,

and looks at him for a reflective moment, and slowly smiles as the scene dissolves to IKE'S PAWNSHOP. At first we see only Ernie's hands working skillfully on a clock mechanism. Two other clocks are on a wooden work table. Then the view draws back to a section of the back of Ike's pawnshop, which shows fur coats hung on a rack, a stack of pawned luggage, etc. Ike himself stands in the background at a sort of bookkeeper's stand, in his shirt sleeves, pen on one ear, wearing his usual black homburg hat. He occasionally scratches a figure in a ledger, but he is really examining Ernie.

ERNIE (*looking through his glass at a watch*). Ah . . . ancient history: "To Edward from Mary, with love." (*He takes the glass from his eye, puts it down on the table, and looks at the watch as he talks.*) No, Ike—give me good old quiet machinery any time.

[ERNIE (*relaxing*). After a while, you don't respect men, just machinery. Clocks, motors, that sort of thing.

IKE (*interested*). What makes you say such a thing?

Ike comes closer to the table, putting his pen on his ear.

ERNIE. How many wars you see go by?

IKE (*thoughtfully*). Wars? Quite a few . . .

ERNIE. Quite a few! An' you're still only a boy! An' maybe you think a new one ain't around the corner?

IKE. To tell the truth, who can see so far ahead?

ERNIE. Well, how about what's under that inelegant nose of yours? See that far ahead, do you? See far ahead as two million unemployed? Two million lads an' lassies so ruddy gutted, they'd knock each other down to get a bit of roast an' boiled! But "Safe," he says, that soppy Len Tate! See how safe he is when he gets his blinkin' eyes shot out!

IKE. And what is the remedy for all these evils?

ERNIE. Don't victimize your own kind! An' don't be victimized yourself!

IKE. And if a war comes?

ERNIE (*promptly*). Don't fight!]

Ike's assistant, little Mr. Lesser, comes in from the shop, a ring in his hand.

LESSER. She wants a quid on this—an old lady.

IKE (*looking at the ring*). Give it to her—an old lady, Mr. Lesser. (*Sighing*) Everything with a kiss.

LESSER (*shaking his head as he walks out*). Clocks, clocks . . . tick tock.

IKE (*sadly*). Tick tock, tick tock . . . (*To Ernie*) Is that one finished?

ERNIE. Best I could do with that old main spring.

IKE (*as he picks up the clock, looks it over, and puts it down*). Tick tock, tick tock . . . (*Then*) Did you ever realize your mother was once upon a time maybe the most beautiful woman in the East End of London? (*Ernie looks up, surprised at this irrelevancy. Ike continues soberly and shrewdly.*) In the old days, I mean.

ERNIE (*puzzled*). What about it?

IKE. Excuse me if I put a flea in your ear. Your mother is a very sick woman . . .

Ernie slowly stands up. He looks tightly at the old man.

ERNIE. You owe me two pounds, Mr. Weber. Pay it an' I'll be on my way.

Silently Ike takes some bills from his pocket and gives them to Ernie. Ernie puts on his cap and starts out through the front of the shop, the dog after him. He passes the counter where Lesser is polishing some rings. About to leave the shop, Ernie stops with his hand on the doorknob. Then he slowly turns, calling back sarcastically, hand still on the knob.

ERNIE. What's it she's got? A pain for her no-good son?

Ike slowly comes out and advances to a position behind the counter. He speaks quietly.

IKE. Your mother's not a superficial woman, Mr. Mott. When she gets sick, she gets sick . . . (*Ernie stands undecisively at the door, waiting for more. Ike continues after a pause.*)

I thought her only living relative should know about it.

Ike waits. Ernie is still and somber; his face suddenly snaps.

ERNIE. No thanks! Don't tell me!

Ernie opens the door and goes out. The door closes behind him. He stops, then turns and looks at Ike through the pane of glass.—Then we see Ernie outside, as seen by Ike. Ernie slowly opens the door, comes in, and advances to Ike.

ERNIE. What is it?

IKE. Cancer. (*After a long pause, as Ernie stands there, stunned*) I recommend you not to say a word to her.

Ernie leaves the shop, the patient dog behind him. Ike stands in his place, looking after him until he has disappeared, as the scene fades out.

IKE (*softly*). Everything with a kiss . . .

# PART THREE

A BRIDGE fades in at night. ERNIE, seen close, is standing on a parapet, looking down at the water. He is in a brown study, frowning, making small sounds to himself. The dog is patiently seated at his feet.

We get a close view of Henry Twite: He is about ten feet away from the bridge, and is watching Ernie. Twite is wearing a crushed grey top hat, a high collar and cravat and a swallow-tailed coat over striped trousers. A big umbrella and old doctor's bag complete the ensemble.—Then we see Ernie and Twite, with Ernie in the foreground. He snorts bitterly to himself, unaware of the watchful Twite in the background.

TWITE (*clearing his throat*). What

you laughing about, son? Are you laughing?

ERNIE (*turning; as if dazed*). What?

TWITE (*moving in*). Thought I heard you laughing . . . (*Ernie looks down at the water again, paying no attention to Twite who has snuggled in beside him.*) Seems as I've seen you before. Wasn't it the other night, in Westminster? What's your name, son?

ERNIE (*still dazed*). What?

TWITE. Who are you?

ERNIE (*irritably*). Ernie Mott.

TWITE (*smoothly*). As the bacon said to the egg, "So pleased to meet you." Henry Twite's my name.

ERNIE (*bitterly*). Ernest *Verdun* Mott, if you want it all!

TWITE. How'd you come by a rare old title like that?

ERNIE. My father rolled up there, at Verdun, in the last war. A friend of mine put something in my ear and I can't get it out.

TWITE (*sympathetically*). Been drinking, have you?

ERNIE (*gloomily*). What's your opinion of mothers?

TWITE. Mothers? Wonderful!

There is a brief silence. Then a train is heard. Twite, not losing his humour, is examining Ernie from the corner of his eye.

TWITE. Lor' lummey, you got it bad! Know all about trouble, I do. Son of my bosom, that's what you are.

ERNIE (*lashing out*). Son of your nothing! I'm a lone wolf, barking in a corner, plain disgusted with a world I never made nor don't want none of!

TWITE (*complacently*). There's the river, boy—help yourself. (*After a pause*) Don't care for water neither, I see.

Then suddenly Ernie, elbows up on the parapet, puts his face in his hands. Twite watches him for a silent moment.

TWITE. Ah, that's different, that is. Sweating like that on a night like this, you'll catch your death of double ammonia. Scarper 'long with me to a place where it's snug and dry—give you a chance to rub yourself down a bit.

Ernie lifts his face and looks at him in brooding silence. Then he starts walking. Twite starts after him, the dog behind them as the scene dissolves to the inside of a PUB at night. At the bar, two men and the barmaid are listening to Ernie, heard playing a homemade but feelingful piano rendition of "None but the Lonely Heart."— [We get a close view of two old cronies, playing checkers; they pause and listen. Another old man is asleep in the background, his mouth hanging open.—Then TWITE is seen listening, sitting at a table, reconverting hundreds of old cigarette butts into fresh cigarettes with the aid of a small hand machine on a spread newspaper. Sitting to one side of Twite is a smallish old knave named Marjoriebanks.—Finally, we see a full view of the pub with Ernie playing the piano. Ernie finishes the song with embellishments, and then turns to Twite with a smirk, charmingly drunk.

ERNIE. An' that's it! Definitely it! Constructively an' sincerely it!

TWITE (*with a sage shake*). A right packet of grief in that little piece!

MARJORIEBANKS (*helping himself to a cigarette*). Makes you want to yell away like one o'clock, don't it?

Ernie stands and smiles at the barmaid as he finishes his swallow of gin.

ERNIE. Stand back, stand back, let the man see the rabbit! (*Crossing to the barmaid*) Someone's threaded a needle and it's gone in one ear an' being pulled out the other! Wasn't you who done it, was it?

BARMAID (*amused, to Twite*). Best

get your young friend home, Henry.

Twite, in the background, has been packing his paraphernalia into the doctor's bag. He is slightly oiled, too.

TWITE. Right. Verdun! Let's hop it—tomorrow's another day!

ERNIE. Hop it we do! (*Tucking in his shirt*) Showing a bit of laundry. Nipper! 'Night all!

OTHERS. 'Night!

Ernie goes to the door with the dog. In the meantime Twite has hastily been dropping cigarettes in front of some of the customers. He looks sternly at Marjoriebanks, giving him some cigarettes.

TWITE. Couldn't forget you, could I? You're an east wind, that's what you are—always with us! (*To the others*) 'Night!

OTHERS. 'Night!

Twite, tipping his hat around, follows Ernie, who has already walked out with the dog. Marjoriebanks scurries after them.—Then outside the PUB, we see Ernie standing indecisively as Twite and Marjoriebanks come out of the pub. Marjoriebanks, smoking a cigarette with each hand, addresses Ernie.

MARJORIEBANKS. Are you educated? Something you could help me in.

TWITE. I'll 'elp you with a smack aside the earhole, you wormy old fluff!

MARJORIEBANKS (*ignoring Twite*). What's percentage?

ERNIE (*puzzled*). What's percentage? What?

MARJORIEBANKS. Per cents. Supposin' I say fifty per cent, talking big, see? What am I talking about?

TWITE (*annoyed*). Per cents is a way of sayin' something, like, "The Above Have Arrived," or "Bob's Your Uncle," or "Have A Banana!" Now push off, you! (*To Ernie*) What an aggronoying boy, eh?

MARJORIEBANKS (*craftily*). Yes, but what's per cents?

ERNIE (*swaying*). It's a hundredth part. One per cent is one hundredth part of anything or something.

TWITE (*brightly*). There you are! That's it!

MARJORIEBANKS (*boring in*). Yes, but what's a hundredth, while we're at it?

Twite lets out a roar and lifts his umbrella as if to strike the little man.

TWITE. He just told you, didn't he?!

Marjoriebanks runs out of range, into the gutter, and calls from there.

MARJORIEBANKS (*sarcastically*). Everybody chucking per cents and hundredths around the shop and they don't even know how it starts!

TWITE (*shouting*). How what starts, you stoopid old crab?!

MARJORIEBANKS. Per cents! Now who's stoopid? A black cat ain't white, is it?

Marjoriebanks goes off into the dark, laughing so hard that he begins to cough. Twite shakes his head in disgust.

TWITE. Know some strange ones, don't I? (*Then*) Get home awright, can you?

ERNIE. Easy as oiling a bike, Dad.

TWITE. Use half a bar?

ERNIE (*refusing it*). Don't need

money now. Start fresh in the morning, I do. Take it off little kids an' old ladies. In business, I'll be. Phew, what a stencho! (*Taking Twite's arm*) Walk up a way, Daddykins . . .

The view moves with them as they start up the street.]

The scene dissolves to THE TUNNEL at night as Ernie, Twite and the dog are seen coming up under the tunnel at the head of "The Road." Ernie is softly whistling "None but the Lonely Heart." They stop in the tunnel.

ERNIE. 'Ere we are. (*Referring to the hollow tone in the tunnel*) Echo! Echo, echo . . .

TWITE. Well, see you again soon?

ERNIE. What for, Dad? Echo, echo, echo!

TWITE. Maybe help you get more adjusted to your environment.

ERNIE. Now wait! Why not help my environment get more adjusted to *me!* Follow that?

TWITE. Verdun, you're drunk, you are!

ERNIE (*with a sigh*). Dad, I am . . . Echo, echo, echo!

TWITE. Say good night. See you soon. (*Snorting*) What's per cent! (*Then*) Feet's killing me!

ERNIE. 'Night, Dad.

TWITE. 'Night, Verdun . . .

They shake hands. Old Twite goes, disappearing in the dark, Ernie peering after him. Then he starts down "The Road," toward his house, and we next see Ernie walking with a limping gait, one foot on the sidewalk, the other off the curb. He reaches the front of his house. Quite drunk, he peers into the small shop window, shading his eyes. Then he retreats backwards and looks up to see if any lights are on. The house is totally dark, as are all of the others on "The Road." And now Ernie is fumbling, trying to insert the key. He mutters under his breath and at last turns the lock. The door pushes open more easily than he expects: he almost falls through, the dog after him.

Inside MA'S BEDROOM at NIGHT: We get a close view of Ma asleep in her bed upstairs. A crash is heard below. Ma opens her eyes. Another crash is heard below. Ma slowly sits up, listening intently. Then she slips out of her bed, puts on a robe and goes to the door. She opens it a few inches and looks out. And this cuts to the STAIRWAY and HALL, as seen by her, the shaft of light from her room spotting Ernie. He is coming up the stairs on all fours, like an animal, one shoe in his hand. He stops and peers at his mother. His mother peers back at him. There is a long pause.

MA (*finally finding her voice*). What's up?

Ernie stands up, wavering but making an effort to steady himself. He wants to look respectable and dignified in his mother's eyes. He drops the shoe.

ERNIE (*finally, with desperate dignity*). Changed me mind. 'Ome to stay . . . Late at night, it is. Less said, the better.

Ernie now navigates the ten steps to his room, concentrating on appearing sober. Ma's eyes follow him until he disappears into his room and his door closes.

This cuts to ERNIE'S BEDROOM, where Ernie is flung face down on his bed,

fully dressed. He is shaking with muffled sobs. Then we see MA standing in
her doorway. Her hard face softens.
Tears appear in her eyes. She steps back
and softly closes her door. The small
hall is dark again. The relaxed dog
sighs outside Ernie's door as the scene
fades out.

# PART FOUR

MA'S SHOP fades in. Ernie is on top of a ladder outside the shop, freshly painting
the shop's sign in several colors. He is whistling to himself as he works, evidently enjoying himself. It is some weeks later. The views moves down to sidewalk level with Ernie. The cheaper pieces of furniture—dressers, chairs, tables,
etc.—are outside the front of the shop, all of them priced by chalked figures.
Then the view moves with Ernie into the shop, which has obviously been freshly
painted and scrubbed clean. He is whistling brightly, to the abstracted annoyance
of Ma, who is adding up a column of figures behind the counter.

MA. Ernie boy! Knock off that piping,
will you? Time to make a move anyhow. So up to Ma Tates an' get
some grub.

Ernie is very cheerful with Ma now,
humours her, trying to be a good son.
Irked or depressed, he never shows this
side of himself to her. Instead he shows
his best characteristics—he is cheerful,
industrious, loyal and open-minded
with her. He has really pitched in and
is keeping things going. In his own
mind *she* has become the child and *he*
the mother!

ERNIE. Spirit of the morning, Ma!
Here's you and here's me, all in one
piece and working order!

MA (*speaking gruffly but well pleased
with her son these days*) Go and
get your dirty dial washed.

ERNIE (*extending paint-stained
hands*). Ain't I lovely, eh?

MA (*dryly*). Proper dream, you are.

He goes into the kitchen, Ma looking
after him with hungry fondness. She
tries to go back to her figures, but momentarily loses herself in a smiling
daydream. Then she comes to with a
start, rubs away a twinge of pain and
follows Ernie into the kitchen.

Inside MA'S KITCHEN: Ernie is washing
his hands and face at the sink as Ma
enters. Nipper is lying at the door,
which leads to the backyard.

ERNIE. All blistered up from weeks of
work. I'm going to need some more
paint for that sign.

MA. Pick it up at Dad Prettyjohn's.

ERNIE (*noticing her dress*). Where
you off to?

MA. I'm doing a bit of business in
the city. Don't know how long I'll
be, but you take charge of the shop,
see? Let's see how you go.

ERNIE (*solemnly*). Makes me proud
you think I can do it, Ma love. (*He
winks at her.*)

MA (*with a mock threatening gesture*). Slosh you one! Ain't so long
ago since I was washing out your
baby napkins, you!

Laughing, as much as she ever laughs,
she jabs her hatpin tighter into her hat
and jabs a finger at Nipper.

MA. Out to the front and wait there for me.

To Ernie's surprise, the dog obeys Ma's instructions.

ERNIE. Taking Nipper with you?

MA. And why not? Cradled him, didn't I? (*Giving the grinning Ernie a bill*) Stick this in your sky and see how you like it.

ERNIE (*laughing*). Right, Ma.

MA (*again the mock blow*). Slosh you one! . . . .

And she marches out through the shop like a major-domo, Ernie laughing at her new spirit. Three clocks are heard chiming together.

[This dissolves to the exterior of MA's SHOP: Ernie is now selling an arm chair to a defeated-looking man.

MAN. Don't think four bob's too stiff, do you?

ERNIE. Me? Think it's way too stiff. But it's these lovely tassels makes it that expensive.

MAN (*hopefully*). Can't take them off, can you, the tassels?

ERNIE (*fingering the tassels*). Where'd we put them, on a hat?

MAN. My wife'd like a chair like this.

He looks at the chair with considerable tenderness; Ernie does not miss this.

MAN (*finally*). Think I better not then . . .

ERNIE. How much you got to spend?

MAN. 'Alf of what you're asking.

ERNIE. Take it an' run, before me Ma returns.

The man brightens and puts the money in Ernie's hand, following which the scene dissolves quickly to MA's SHOP, later in the day. Ernie is standing behind the counter of the shop talking to a little lame girl, an old tin alarm clock in her hands.

GIRL. Me mum says I'm to get one an' six for this, sir.

ERNIE. Your mum says that, does she? Putting it in for a week?

GIRL. For a week, yes sir.

ERNIE (*looking thoughtfully into the ledger on the counter*). Well, *my* mum don't usually pay out more than one naked shilling for an object like that.

GIRL. Can't you make it one an' six, sir?

ERNIE (*weakening*). Not supposed to, Peggy . . .

The silent child looks at him appealingly. Suddenly the clock begins to ring its alarm bell. Ernie stops the bell, sets the clock on the counter and counts out the money.

ERNIE (*weakly*). Bang! One an' six it is!]

This dissolves to MA's SHOP. Ernie is in a corner of the shop, vigorously polishing the top of a table. Finished with this, he caps up the polish bottle. His eyes fall on a stack of framed pictures in one corner. He picks up a dust rag and moves to them. The pictures are those of classic lovers: Leda and Swan, Pygmalion and Galatea, Beatrice and Dante, etc. Ernie dusts them vigorously, but gradually slows down as he notices the subjects. He holds up the picture of Leda and Swan.

Ma is seen entering the shop, a heavy bundle under one arm. Ernie does not notice her until she comes up to him; he quickly lowers the picture, for

Leda has reminded him of Ada. The dog, behind Ma, drops to one side as Ma, tired out, sits in her rocker.

ERNIE (*sheepishly*). How's your poor old feet, Ma?

MA (*grunting*). Old.

ERNIE (*holding up the picture for Ma's inspection*). Thought I'd hang her up in my room.

MA. What for, son?

ERNIE. Reminds me of a person.

MA. Reminds me of a Christmas goose. (*Picking up the bundle on her lap*) Take this with you. (*Then, casually*) Hop it now. Up to your room.

ERNIE (*taking the bundle*). What is it, Ma?

MA (*not answering*). There's sausage and mash for supper, so don't be late coming down.

Ernie looks at her, then goes out with the bundle. Ma begins to hum to herself as she rocks in the chair, stroking the dog.

ERNIE'S BEDROOM now comes into full view. It is clean and bright with its new furniture and curtains. Ernie opens the door and enters; he puts the bundle on the bed and opens it. Then he slowly moves to the window and leans against it, looking out, thinking, remembering, feeling a great tenderness for Ma.—This is followed by a close view of the package on the bed, disclosing two new suits, two pairs of shoes, several new shirts, ties and socks. Then we see Ernie at the window, his back to us. He slowly turns and walks toward the bed, a quizzical, mysterious smile on his face. He slowly begins to unbutton the shirt he is wearing.

The scene dissolves to MA'S KITCHEN in the evening. Ma, at the stove, is cooking, her back to us. She slowly turns when she hears Ernie calling to her.

ERNIE'S VOICE. Ma . . ?

Ernie appears in the doorway. He is dressed in one of the new suits.

ERNIE. Makes me give at the knees, this surprise of yours . . .

Ma looks across the room at Ernie. Her mother's heart is full. There is a long pause, then:

MA. Glad you like it, son. (*To cover her feelings, turning back to the stove*) Supper's 'bout ready.

ERNIE (*moving to a position behind her*). Ever kiss you, did I, Ma gel? Turn around . . .

She turns around, loaded frying pan in one hand, a fork in the other. Ernie gives her a good kiss.

MA (*quietly*). Sit down and have your supper, Ern.

Ernie sits down. The table is already set. Ma puts most of the food on his plate, little on her own.

MA (*almost to herself*). Wish you'd walk by "Fish and Chips" an' let that Mrs. Tate see you now. (*Walking back and forth from the stove to the table*) Not to mention dear Ma Fadden an' her plaster-haired Alf!

ERNIE. Surprise 'em all, won't I?

MA. Surprises me the most. Look just like your father did. In his best days, that is.

Ma sits down at her place. Ernie bends over his food but he is really slyly looking Ma over.

ERNIE. Lóve my pa, did you?

MA (*tightening*). Love's not for the poor, Ern. No time for it.

They eat in silence for a moment, both of them furtively eyeing each other from time to time, wanting to say a good deal which, however, goes unsaid.

ERNIE (*finally*). Expecting you to do something for me.

MA. What?

ERNIE. Stroll about a bit with me tonight—maybe visit a cinema, the one an' six seats.

MA (*flushing pleasurably*). Go on, sauce. Don't you try any of them larks on me! Why, I'm old enough to be your mother!

ERNIE (*grinning*). Come on, do it, Ma!

MA. Couldn't, son.

ERNIE. Why not?

MA. Sleep's a blessed thing, son, something I can't afford to miss, an old lady like me. Wished I had it to live all over again.

Ma suddenly stands up—a look of repressed pain on her face—with a certain awkward stiffness. Ernie starts up in his seat.

ERNIE. What's wrong? Something hurt you?

MA (*slowly*). Nothing of the sort . . . (*Taking a deep breath*) What give you an idea like that?

She slowly sits down. Ernie just as slowly moves back to his place. He toys with the food, pretending to eat, but his inner concentration is all on Ma. But Ma is looking at him too, wondering if and what he knows about her.

ERNIE (*trying to cover the situation*). Got a funny story right on the tip of me tongue. A little man is sitting in the park—

Ernie stops abruptly, for a soft moan has come from his mother's lips.

MA (*in a hushed but horrible voice*). Get me those yeast tablets, Ern . . .

Ernie quickly brings her the bottle and she takes one of the pills with her tea. Then she slowly caps the bottle.

MA. Tummy ache . . .

Ernie is helpless. He reaches over and picks up the yeast tablet bottle, so marked on its label.

ERNIE. Good for headaches, too, are they? Might try one myself.

He begins to uncap the bottle, but Ma roughly snatches it away from him.

MA. What about that funny story, son . . . ?

ERNIE (*ransacking his brain*). Yes . . . well . . . this man, I said . . . in the park . . . Slipped my mind, it did! (*Then, contritely*) Ache all gone?

She dismisses the matter as Ernie stands, wiping his mouth.

MA. Nothing to it. Sausage ain't for delicate appetites.

ERNIE. You cook them a treat, Ma.

MA (*smiling faintly*). Me? Worse cook in London town! Don't you go buttering me up on my cooking. If it's a pound you want, to have a good time, why there it is, on the mantelpiece, under the vase.

ERNIE (*taking the pound note and laughing over-brightly*). That's it, Ma! Seen right through me, you did!

MA. Off you go then. Tomorrow's Sunday. Don't care how late you come in—just don't wake me.

ERNIE. Right, Ma.

MA. Leave Nipper here.

ERNIE (*over-brightly*). Right, Ma!

Ernie walks to the door. He has been dismissed; doesn't want to leave but does not know how to stay without revealing to Ma that he knows her secret. He hesitates.

ERNIE. Well, I'm off, Ma . . .

MA. Have a good time, boy.

ERNIE. Thanks, Ma . . .

Ernie goes through the shop to the street, following which we see Ma in her room sitting at the table and putting her hand to her head in agony. [Ma stands stock still a moment. Then she picks up the dog in her arms and goes to the door, the view moving with her as she enters the shop.

We get a close view of Ma sitting in the rocker, the dog in her lap. She is rocking herself quietly, staring ahead at nothing; the morphine pills have quieted her down. The shop is dark, ghostly shadows of furniture are all around. Then the view widens to include a woman looking in through the closed door. She scratches timidly and then opens the door, standing there, uncertain. Ma does not move now nor through the following scene, rocking quietly, her face expressionless.

MA. Who's that . . . ?

WOMAN. Me, Mrs. Mott, Millie Wilson. (*In a timid whisper*) Alone, are you?

MA. You drunk?

MILLIE (*timidly*). No, give it up, I did—give it up.

She advances into the room, an incredibly nervous and spidery woman, a chronic inebriate, bird-like and timid.

MILLIE. Ma Snowden sent me. (*Waiting*) She got herself a half dozen down pillows . . . soft enough for aristocracy . . . never slept on neither.

MA (*immobile*). Where they from? Usual place?

MILLIE. Yes.

MA. I don't handle stolen goods, Millie.

MILLIE. She'd sell them cheap, she would, dearie, Mrs. Mott.

MA (*tonelessly patient*). No.

MILLIE (*after a helpless pause*). Three or four fine woolen blankets, too, dearie, Mrs. Mott . . .

MA. No.

MILLIE. Five bob apiece gets the lot . . .

MA. No.

Inexplicably the dog, without moving, begins to growl at the intruder. Ma says simply, "Quiet," and the dog subsides. Millie retreats sideways to the door.

MILLIE. Sorry, Mrs. Mott . . .

She vanishes rather than goes out, and Ma, seen closely, does not move, rocking a little in the chair. Then she slowly closes her eyes, still rocking quietly.

This dissolves to the FUN FAIR at night. Ernie is standing in the entrance of the Fun Fair, looking around. The scene moves with him as he walks down and around to Ada's seat, and then we see Ada on her dais. Ernie stands looking at her in silence. Her eyes are lowered to a book which she pretends to be reading. She slowly looks up at Ernie; he moves in closer; she looks at his new clothes.

ERNIE. Beetles . . .

ADA (*casual*). Oh, it's you, is it?

ERNIE. It's me, being blinded by science.

ADA (*eyeing him*). Why'd you come back . . . ?

ERNIE. See you later?

ADA. I've an appointment for the evening.

ERNIE. I don't believe it.

ADA (*severely*). Appointment with a girl friend, if you don't mind, Mr. Mott.

ERNIE (*grinning*). Break it!

ADA (*After a pause*). Half nine, around the back. (*Shaking her head with a faint smile*) More sauce than a bottling factory, you have!

ERNIE (*grinning*). That's right—noted for it. Half nine, then, around the back.

He walks away down the aisle. He turns; they are looking at each other. He executes a little jig to show her his jubilation. Then he goes, leaving a smiling Ada behind him. But she quickly resumes her public attitude as the scene dissolves.]

Ada and Ernie appear down a shabby street. Ernie is puzzled by her restraint and silence.

ERNIE. Quiet as a little mouse . . .

Ada looks up at him and suddenly stops in her tracks.

ADA. Listen, Ernie, I'm sorry you've come back.

ERNIE (*with humorous shock*). Ow! Rolled an ice-cold pickle jar down my back, you did!

He looks at her and sees her intent seriousness; he meets her mood now.

ERNIE. You mean it, Ada girl?

ADA. You're not serious. I'm not an apple, you know, to take a bite of and throw away!

ERNIE. I thought about it, for five weeks—whether or not to see you again. That's serious . . .

She looks at him deeply, trying to read into him.

ERNIE (*softly*). What are you looking at Ada? See a parade going by . . . ?

ADA (*slowly*). Yes. Maybe a whole bloomin' parade of troubles . . .

A policeman saunters through the scene, majestic and imperturbable, not even stopping as he says:

POLICEMAN. You can't fight it out 'ere, you know. There's places for such things. Best to find one . . .

The policeman disappears, and after an intent moment Ernie takes her arm and they start walking away as the scene dissolves to ADA'S GRILLE DOOR under the steps. Ernie and Ada are both puffing cigarettes silently. Ada takes a deep final puff of her cigarette and steps on it before she gently pushes Ernie away, saying:

ADA. Now be a good boy, Ernie, and say good night.

ERNIE (*taking her arms*). What a way you have of making simple things difficult!

ADA. Think so? But suppose a certain party don't happen to like me seeing you.

ERNIE. An' who would that be?

ADA. Jim Mordinoy . . .

ERNIE. Mordinoy, the flash boy? How's he crept into your young scientific life?

ADA. Didn't say he had, did I? There's about twenty good kisses left in me, but he'll never get one!

ERNIE. Told him so?

ADA. More than once.

ERNIE. Then that's that!

ADA. According to whose book?

ERNIE (*promptly*). Ernie Mott's! I'd blind him out of two eyes quick as see him!

ADA. Here's hoping you don't try! Now say good night an' forget it all.

ERNIE. We all right for next Wednesday night?

ADA (*coquetting*). Take me dancing?

ERNIE. Anything you like, Ada.

ADA. Here's five beetles on it . . . (*She gives him her hand but instead he puts his arms around her and kisses her strongly.*) Give over, boy. You'll mash me to a pulp!

ERNIE (*as he releases her and looks her square in the eyes*). Next Wednesday, half nine, then.

ADA. That's it.

He turns and goes, she looking after him. Then she enters the grille door. This dissolves to the ROAD SIDE of the TUNNEL at night as Aggie Hunner comes into view, her cello under her arm, wrapped in a heavy cloth case. She stops, alarmed, hearing footsteps

behind her. In a few seconds Ernie steps up, coming from the tunnel.

ERNIE. Okeedoke, Aggie—it's a friend.

AGGIE (*relieved*). Oh, what you doing out at this time of night?

ERNIE. Bit of fresh air. (*As he looks her over*) Tall tonight . . .

AGGIE. High-heeled shoes!

The view moves with them as he takes her cello and they walk toward her house. Ernie is in a dreamy mood.

AGGIE. I've just finished playing at a club dinner—you know what they're like. A lot of men smoking their annual cigars and getting tight and showing off. I get sick of it. (*Then*) Thought you'd forgotten me.

ERNIE (*dreamily*). No, not at all.

She glances at him sideways but says nothing, and by this time they are up to her door.

AGGIE'S FRONT ROOM: Aggie enters, a lighted match in her hand. Ernie, behind her, walks to the low studio couch and puts the cello there. She, in the meantime, lights a candle.

AGGIE. Like some coffee?

ERNIE (*abruptly*). Are you a fortune teller, Aggie?

AGGIE. Somewhat . . .

ERNIE. I'm on the fringes of a great romance. What shall I do?

AGGIE (*promptly*). Have it!

ERNIE (*after looking at her a long time*). But it's not you, Aggie . . .

AGGIE (*smiling*). That's no news, is it?

ERNIE. I know you like it honest.

AGGIE (*gallantly*). Don't often meet a cavalier this late at night.

ERNIE. It's not fair to you, these sort of meetings—

AGGIE (*wryly*). Oh, really, Ern, you're a fool, a moody, clever human fool! Why, you're trying to tell me you love another girl, that it? Is that why you're home to stay?

ERNIE. No. That isn't why. (*Suddenly blurting it out*) Me Ma's ill. Last card in the pack, it looks.

AGGIE (*distressed for him*). Oh!

ERNIE (*unhappily*). All roads lead to Ma this year. (*Then*) What we start talking about?

AGGIE (*all sympathy and love*). Nothing that won't keep.

ERNIE (*irresolutely*). I'd better make a move . . . (*Then*) I get an idea of a sudden she don't sleep every night.

The view moves with Ernie as he goes to the small foyer, Aggie behind him.

AGGIE. Mind the step.—Wait a minute, Ern. Don't worry for me.

We get a close view of ERNIE and AGGIE just inside the door.

AGGIE (*warmly*). I'm here if you need me. I can't help my own nature. If I love you, it's something I can't help and something I need. People are what they are and love what they love, and I don't see any sense in trying to be something else. I wouldn't trade it for a symphony orchestra, the thing I feel for you. And you can't change it or take it away from me. So there you are, Mr. Jack-in-the-box! (*Opening the door*) Now, cross over and sleep well . . . (*She kisses him with feeling, he responding solemnly.*)

ERNIE. Well, I'd better make a move.

He starts down the steps as the scene fades out.

# PART FIVE

MA'S SHOP fades in. Ike Weber and Ma are in the shop, moving from piece to piece, while he silently makes an inventory, listing the value of each piece on a paper slip. Now he stops to touch and admire an antique mirror marked "16s" in chalk.

IKE. Sixteen shillings? That's very cheap for such a good piece. I'd put it down for at least two pounds.

MA (*hopefully*). You would?

IKE (*noting it*). Why not? It's worth every penny of it.

Ma follows him, watching anxiously, as he jots down a few more values. She now objects to one of his estimates.

MA. You don't think that's worth more, Ike?

IKE (*delicately*). To my mind, no, Mrs. Mott.

MA (*sighing*). All right . . .

Ma watches Ike as he makes a rapid calculation of his figures.

IKE. It adds up just under two hundred pounds, the piano not included.

MA (*pausing*). Very disappointing . . .

IKE (*sympathetically*). You expected it to be more?

Ma sits silently in her rocking chair, the feather waving in her hat. She nervously pulls out her hatpin and then plunges it in more securely.

MA. That's nothing. It would go through his generous hands in a year. (*Waving her hand*) Look at him out there—

Looking out through the window, from Ma's angle we see Ernie vigorously sweeping the pavement in front of the shop.

MA'S VOICE. Wouldn't know it was the same boy, would you?

We get a close view of Ma and Ike.

MA. There is such things as prayers being answered, you know.

IKE (*smiling quietly*). Yes, the places of the world are empty, and the human heart is everything. (*Embarrassed*) That's a speech. (*Then*) Well, I'll go.

MA (*giving her hand*). Thanks, Ike, you're a sport.

IKE. Any time, Mrs. Mott. A pleasure to serve you. Irregardless.

She looks affectionately after Ike as he walks out and exchanges a few words outside with Ernie.

This dissolves to the TUNNEL and "THE ROAD." Henry Twite, dressed as usual, is driving a little pony and cart. There are ribbons in the pony's hair and its ears stick through a straw hat decorated with rosettes. The view moves with the cart as it comes down "The Road," going toward Ernie's house. A few of the locals stop and gape; a child turns with wonder and entertainment. To all of them Twite politely doffs his topper. Then he drives right up to Ernie, who, broom in hand, is about to enter the shop.

TWITE. What, me Verdun boy! How's your Ma and other relatives?

ERNIE (*surprised and amused*). What you got there? Couple of tons of coal?

TWITE (*getting down*). Thought you'd lost me, did you? Selling fruit around the pubs at the minute—doing a rare old trade an' all.

Ma is looking out of a window in the background. From her house next door, Ma Chalmers is doing the same. So are the jealous Tates.

TWITE (*pointing*). That your Ma playing peek-a-boo in there? Bring her out, boy, a person of me own generation . . .

Ernie turns and signals to Ma, who comes out. Twite takes a small basket out of the cart.

ERNIE. Ma, want you to meet a friend of mine, Henry Twite.

Ma nods to Twite. A lone child watches from the side. Ma Chalmers comes out of her house and stands in the background.

TWITE (*to Ma, basket in hand*). Asked how I was, did you? Can't grumble. Been worse, been better. Awright with you, me old China?

MA (*solemnly*). Ain't bad, Mr. Twite. Could be better.

TWITE (*handing her the basket*). This is from your hopeful here.

MA. This for me . . . ?

TWITE (*wagging away*). I should shay sho! A pine an' a half a dozen glass growed peaches, pride of the Kentish Gardens—nothing better on the board of any Duke. Sent by a dutiful son!

Twite slaps the surprised Ernie on the back. Ma doesn't know what to say. Ma Chalmers has moved in closer. Twite picks out the pineapple and holds it under her nose.

TWITE. Sweets of nature. All you get to do is eat 'em. Anything hard about that? Smell it, nature in the raw. Lovelyhee! Sent by a dutiful son who's looking after his Ma while she's still here to be looked after!

There is a moment of silence. Ma is too moved to say anything. Ernie looks down at his broom, embarrassed.

MA (*not looking at Ernie*). Buy these for me . . . ?

ERNIE. Umm . . .

Basket in hand, Ma suddenly darts into the shop and disappears. Ma Chalmers sighs. The child skips away with a bored exclamation. Ernie looks at Twite in grateful silence.

TWITE (*less waggish now*). Looks like you made a hit there, son.

ERNIE (*wryly*). Looks like I did . . . Thanks. (*Twite climbs back into his cart and takes the reins.*) Where you off to? Stay for some supper.

TWITE (*shaking his head*). Look me up at Tiger's, most any night. Can't dally with friendship when making a living's in the air. Well, I should shay sho! (*He doffs his hat, snaps the reins and pulls away down the street.*)

MA CHALMERS. Lovely man, that.

ERNIE. I should shay sho!

MA CHALMERS (*wistfully*). Never had nothing like that give me. (*A sly addition*) People don't even tune a piano for me when it's promised to.
ERNIE (*remembering*). Anyone so thoughtless ought to get his bottom smacked! (*Giving her a hug*) I'll do it before the sun is down, Ma. (*He turns and goes into the shop.*)

MA'S KITCHEN: Ma is at the sink, her back turned as Ernie enters. The basket of fruit is on the table.

MA (*turning slowly*). Nice man, that Twite . . .

ERNIE. Best of the best. Had a quiet sniff, did you?

MA. Best change the subject or I'll howl out, I will. (*Looking over his shoulder*) Someone in the shop.

ERNIE. Promised to tune Ma Chalmers' pianner. (*As Ma starts for the shop, he calls to her softly.*) Ma (*As she turns*) Come here . . .

She does and he kisses her. Then he leaves through the back door. Ma stands still, looking after him. The dog looks up at her and then follows her into the shop.

Inside MA'S SHOP: Mrs. Snowden is standing there, tapping her foot impatiently, looking around the shop with a professional eye. She is a small, bustling woman, her tongue sharp, extremely practical and sure-footed.

MRS. SNOWDEN (*as Ma enters*). What you think you're doing with my Millie Wilson?

MA. Your Millie Wilson? (*Puzzled*) Doing what?

MRS. SNOWDEN. Three four nights ago you set the dog on her.

MA. You're as daft as she is!

A few piano chords sound from next door where Ernie is beginning to tune the piano. From now on until the end of the scene, the piano notes go up higher and higher, as if pacing the scene and underlining it.

MRS. SNOWDEN (*turning at the door*). Come in here, Millie . . . (*The creature comes sidling in.*) Didn't you say she set the dog on you?

MILLIE (*nervous and timid*). She did—that one—the white one—him.

MA (*sitting grimly in her rocker*). Wish I had, that's what.

MRS. SNOWDEN (*scathingly*). Wish you had? That's the trouble with you, Mother Mott.

MA. Don't you "Mother Mott" me, Jane Snowden. Two ticks an' I'll have you both in the gutter if you raise your voice to me!

Ma rocks violently in her chair. Millie hides behind her protectress.

MRS. SNOWDEN (*after a pause*). No reason to fight, is there? Worth your mint of money, ain't you? Don't need what I can turn your way, do you?

MA. No, I don't.

MRS. SNOWDEN (*silky and purring*). An' that's the end of a perfect day, is it?

MA. No more talk, please.

MRS. SNOWDEN (*easily*). I can see you don't realize what's involved here.

She picks up a piece of Ma's marking chalk, and with a flourish chalk-writes "£500" on the top of a low wash basin stand. Then she throws the chalk away and dusts off her hands.

MRS. SNOWDEN. Not three or four—*five hundred* pounds a year! Tidy little nest egg, it looks to me.

MILLIE (*a faint echo*). Tidy . . .

Silence ensues. Ma is rocking, and hasn't turned her head to look. Next door, Ernie's piano notes mount higher and higher.

MRS. SNOWDEN. What's the income of your shop compared to sums like that?

MA. It's shoplifting—that's plain. Save your breath.

MRS. SNOWDEN. Shoplifting is only taking your rights from them as has more than they can handle. Like you go in an orchard and pick apples. What's wrong on that? (*Suddenly belligerent again*) Or are you calling me a thief again!

MILLIE (*a faint echo*). Called you a thief.

MA (*tired now*). No bid, no bid, Mrs. Snowden. You tire me out, you do.

MRS. SNOWDEN (*stepping back*). Well, I won't waste me time again. (*Indignantly to her stooge*) Here's Ma Mott, I thought. Growing old, needing rest, I says. Let her make enough, I says, to live out her days in peace. Maybe leave a bit behind for her boy, I says. Good old Ma Mott, I says! An' that's the gratitude, Millie! Called a thief!! (*Rolling her eyes*) Somethin' for the book, that's what it is! (*Turning at the door*) But I've got nothing more to say. But if you happens to change your mind, you know where I'll be. Five hundred pounds, I says! Not less!

Mrs. Snowden sweeps out, Millie quickly after her. Ma slowly looks over at the wash basin stand. Next door the piano tuning mounts higher. Ma slowly walks over to the stand and looks down at the figures.—We get a closeup of the figure on top of the stand: "£500", and then get a close view of Ma's thoughtful face. But Ma decides against dishonesty. She runs a hand across the figures, obliterating most of them as the scene fades out.

# PART SIX

[FUN FAIR ALLEY fades in at night. Ernie dressed in the other new suit, is just swinging up to the alley that leads to the back of the Fun Fair. He is full of jaunt, whistling brightly, carrying a small box under one arm, when someone calls out to him.

VOICE. Mott!

Ernie stops dead in his tracks. The view moves over to a black sedan. Ada is sitting next to. Jim Mordinoy at the wheel, the latter dressed in evening clothes to match Ada's gown.

ADA. Ernie? Here we are . . . (*As Ernie slowly walks to the car, Ada leans out.*) We got a lift. This is Jim Mordinoy.

ERNIE (*bristling*). Had the pleasure, if memory serves . . .

ADA. Get in the back. You're late.

Ernie looks at Ada and slowly gets into the car. It starts off. Jim smiles softly, sleepily, looking very much the killer bull-terrier that he is. Ernie is sitting stiffly in the back. Ada turns to him, noting the box.—

ADA. Brought your lunch, have you?

ERNIE (*giving her the box*). Something for you . . .

ADA (*after a quick glance*). Oh! Gardenias!

JIM (*patronizingly*). He's after you, Battler Girl, he's after you! Want to watch him—he's a boy!

ADA (*smelling them*). I don't know what to call them, they're that lovely!

JIM. Watch out, Ernie boy! She's a killer when she starts!

Ernie is staring ahead, stiff and silent. He doesn't like this whole business. Ada reaches across the back of the seat and gives him her hand. He takes it stiffly as the scene fades out.]

The interior of the LUCKY SEVEN CLUB fades in. Jim Mordinoy is sitting alone at a table, his eyes following Ada and Ernie on the dance floor. Rossi, the headwaiter, is opening a second bottle of champagne. We can hear the typical music and hubbub of a small, crowded night club, with an exclusive clientele.

JIM. How's business tonight?

ROSSI (*timid but self-respecting*). Could not be better, Mr. Mordinoy. (*More confidentially*) Bert Marks in the house, with two boys, down left.

JIM (*immobile*). By theirselves?

ROSSI. With three girls.

JIM (*relaxing*). No trouble then.

Rossi takes the empty bottle and leaves. Jim looks out at Ernie and Ada on the dance floor.—Then the crowded dance floor, featuring Ada and Ernie, is seen from Jim's view. He is in the same mood as when last seen; the mood is heightened by the half bottle of champagne under his belt. Jim's lieutenant, Cosh, dances by with a girl. He winks at Ernie who merely stares at him in return.

We get a close view of Jim at the table, as he is approached from behind by the other lieutenant, Slush, who whispers something in his ear. Jim merely nods without turning, his eyes still on Ada as Slush leaves.

Ernie and Ada are seen dancing. She is dressed in a beautiful gown; she is playful and coquettish, but Ernie won't respond.

ADA. Like me, Ernie?

ERNIE (*coolly*). A bit. (*Then*) There's three reasons I don't care for this dancing. One: I don't dance good enough. Two: It's too hot, and three: what's Mordinoy doing here?

ADA. He owns this place.

ERNIE. An' what makes that tie the lamb's tail?!

ADA (*catching his mood*). Want to stop?

ERNIE. Suits me.

ADA (*avoiding a quarrel*). Now don't you think I know three's a crowd? He sort of invited his self. It's most important.

ERNIE. I can hardly keep my hands off him.

ADA (*swiftly, earnestly*). Listen, twenty boys here'd carve you up like a side of beef if he so much as said the word! Now don't be romantic, Ernie dear. (*Archly*) Save it for me. The evening's young, don't forget. Sit down now, shall we?

She starts for the table and after a moment's hesitation, Ernie follows her.

A fairly close view of Jim's table discloses an important-looking man sitting with Jim, deferentially whispering in his ear. Jim merely nods, his eyes on Ada who is approaching the table. Jim stands as Ada comes toward him. The man sees he is not wanted and apologetically leaves. Ada and Ernie sit down, and Jim immediately fills their glasses.

JIM. What about me, Ada? Do I get the next one?

ADA. Let's get me breath. Think I'm made of?

JIM (*smiling sleepily*). I couldn't give it a name. But I'll find out one of these days.

ADA (*to Ernie, heading him off*). Kids himself something cruel.

They sip their champagne silently. Ada enjoys the music.

ADA. I love the way those saxes come out, sort of in kid gloves, just loud enough to be heard. (*Dreamily*) I wish I could live out my time like this.

JIM (*affably*). Perfect Pitch don't hear a word you're saying, Battler.

ERNIE (*abruptly, of the champagne*). What's this stuff called? (*Jim laughs.*) What's funny?

JIM. I thought everyone over sixteen knew champagne when he felt it hit his gizzard.

ERNIE (*gloweringly*). I won't be sixteen till next March.

JIM. You're well developed for a boy.

ADA (*sharply*). I don't want no quarrels here!

JIM. Quarrels? Mott likes me. He won't fight with me. Don't you, Mott? Don't you like me?

ERNIE. Why should I like a mugg like you?

ADA (*quickly, covering Ernie*). Half

a spoonful of lemonade and he's bandy-legged!

ERNIE. I'm not bandy-legged!

JIM (*laughing heartily*). That's what I like about you, Mott—your attitude. It'll kill you or make you.

A friendly, rolypoly man comes to the table and puts his arm around Ada's chair.

MAN. Ada, been waiting years for this! How about a turn or two?

The man gets a sickly look when Jim glances up and reveals his face.

MAN. Oh, sorry, Mr. Mordinoy . . .

ADA (*standing*). Mr. Mordinoy don't mind, Sid.

Ada gives Ernie a glance and drifts away with Sid. After some silence, Jim speaks.

JIM. How's your Ma do in that shop of hers?

ERNIE. Who told you that?

JIM. Interested me to find out. Why? You're a cut above the usual article floats around.

ERNIE. Only a cut?

JIM (*smiling faintly*). There's that attitude again . . . (*Then*) Ada's interested in you, it seems.

ERNIE (*warily*). Nothing special . . .

JIM. An' I'm interested in Ada. Very special. (*Then*) I'm going to do something for you, Mott. Like to line your pockets?

In the background, Rossi is fussing around with another bottle of champagne. The cork pops.—The scene cuts to Ada anxiously watching them from the dance floor, then to Rossi leaving Jim's table.

JIM. You know where Ermington Street is? Tattamy's Garage? I'm there any morning. Live up to that attitude of yours and do yourself a piece of good. You've got talents and imagination—work hard for me an' you'll start at fifty pounds a week.

ERNIE (*looking at Jim*). Breaking whose neck?

This cuts to Ada watching them from the dance floor; her partner, Sid, would get out of this mess if he could! Then we get a close view as Jim sits back, angered by Ernie's last remark. But he speaks quietly.

JIM. Don't you think you're being rude?

ERNIE (*pausing*). What about Ada?

JIM (*withdrawing*). Quite a girl, quite a girl . . . (*In a voice edged with violence*) I been after Ada too long to lose her for even a second. She knows it an' now you know it!

ERNIE. But she won't wear you, seems like.

JIM. Ada was always a bit giddy. I recall a couple of week-ends at Brighton, a few years ago. We shared adjoining rooms and she . . .

ERNIE (*blazing with indignation*). Now look here . . .

Jim looks at Ernie and rises.

JIM. What's the matter with you? What are you interrupting me for? I remember, it used to give me a special sort of pleasure to choose her clothes. (*As Ernie starts to rise*) Now wait a minute.

The scene cuts to a view of the dancers and we see Ada glancing toward Jim and Ernie; then we see Ernie standing up and looking down at Jim who is now seated.

JIM. You're young and excitable, Mott. Sit down.—Ada is Mrs. Mordinoy.

Ernie can't believe his ears. Ada hurries into the scene. She looks silently from Jim to Ernie and back again. The man, her dancing partner, gets out quickly.

Abruptly Ernie cuts out of the scene, starting for the stairs. Ada looks bitterly at Jim, grabs up her purse, and then goes after Ernie.—We then see Ernie moving out through a section of the foyer of the club as Ada catches up to Ernie and grabs his arm.

ADA (*out of breath*). Ernie, wait a minute!

ERNIE (*stopping and staring at her*). Mrs. Mordinoy . . .

ADA (*defiantly*). Used to be me name. What'd you want? My whole history in a flash?

ERNIE. Might have told me it was a family quarrel.

ADA (*desperately*). 'Cause it isn't. Be two years next month, we're divorced.

ERNIE (*shaking his head*). No, that won't wash, Ada ducks!

ADA. What won't wash?

ERNIE. Less said the better!

ADA (*angrily*). Quick's the word then! There's the door!

Ernie's face is set. Ada's eyes are blazing. Ernie turns and goes out. Ada stands there for a moment, her spunkiness punctured by his departure. In the background Jim is seen coming up the stairs. Ada turns, ready to cry, and enters a door marked "Ladies," as the scene fades out.

# PART SEVEN

MA'S KITCHEN fades in. It is morning and Ernie is washing at the kitchen sink. He dashes cold water into his face, wincing with a hangover. Ma enters from the shop, through the curtains.

ERNIE. Morning, Ma . . .

MA. Good morning, son.

Ernie sits down to breakfast, everything already in place. Ma brings a hot dish to the table, looking him over.

MA. What happened to you last night?

ERNIE (*humourlessly*). Hit by a train. Head-on collision. Half the wheels still spinning in me head. (*Wincing, he looks down at his food and pushes the dish away.*) Oh my—sheep's heart again! Are we that poor, to be eating the guts and entrails of cows and sheep, day in, day out?

MA (*quietly*). Millions more worse off, son.

ERNIE. Poor, putrid millions!

At this point, a man's voice calls from the shop.

VOICE. What's the price of this one, Mrs. Mott.

MA (*to Ernie*). Percy Floom an' Flo, looking over some wedding stuff on his day off. (*Ernie looks toward the shop disgustedly.*)

[The view moves with Ma as she hurries into the shop. Percy is clerkish and prissy, but his bride is big and lusty.

FLO (*slapping a brass bed*). This is the one I'd have if it was me.

MA. Always get your money back on that, Percy. Lovely springs an' all. Cost you three quid, it would.

PERCY. Well, at that price, I'd be afraid to get in it!

FLO. You'd what? (*To Ma*) Hark at him . . . an' he's being married next week!

PERCY (*testily*). Would you mind getting on with the business, Mrs. Mott? We can't keep Mum's dinner waiting.

FLO (*with mock astonishment*). Well, catch me a cold, if he ain't started to tone me down already!

MA (*smiling*). Well, what else you want?

PERCY. What about a washing-stand an' things?

FLO. But the bed's the most important.

PERCY. I believe you have already referred to that article, Flo!

Flo laughs. Ma soothingly puts her arm around the bridegroom.

MA. Got all your kitchen stuff, 'ave you?

PERCY. No. Mum's giving us a bit here an' there, but we'll have to buy most.

MA. You'll have to start a book, Percy. Pay in so much a week, so it don't come hard on your pocket, see? Leave it to me, dear.

Ma is walking to the street door with Percy and Flo.

FLO. An' don't forget the bed!

PERCY (*mortified*). I wish you'd give over, you!

FLO (*slapping him on the back*). Oh, getting personal, eh?!

Percy stares at his brazen bride and hurries out of the shop. Flo howls with delight.

FLO. So long, Ma. I'll train him right. See you!

Laughing, Flo goes out. Ma closes the door and turns back to the counter where she jots down some notations.] Ernie has come in during this and is now standing behind the counter, paring his nails. He remains in the background.

MA. Make a lovely match, they will.

ERNIE (*uninterested*). She's a proper case, ain't she?

MA. Nice, sensible head on her, for all that. He'll have a happy life.

ERNIE (*bitterly*). Blinking idiots, the pair of them!—Getting married.

This cuts to MA standing behind the grating in the store. She gives Ernie an intent, searching glance.

MA. I'd like to see a nipper or two of yours 'fore I get took off. Shan't be here always, you know.

ERNIE. Go out, Ma! Who am I going to marry? Who'd have me?

MA. You'll have this business of your own—you're fixed up for your home. Have a look around.

ERNIE. Had too many looks around. What an ugly unsanitary life it is!

MA. Needn't be.

ERNIE. But it is.

MA (*shrewdly, pausing*). Lots of love in you, Ernie. Needs an object, something to lavish it on.

ERNIE. What's wrong with *you*, Ma? You're an object.

She looks at him; he looks at her. She takes the hatpin out of her hat and plunges it back. She smiles at him, he smiles back; they are very fond of each other.

This dissolves to a series of spot scenes of MA'S SHOP.—Ernie behind the counter, a cigar stub in his mouth.—Another day: A little girl standing in the foreground (her back to the camera). She puts two small coins on the counter. She keeps watching the bird in the cage at the left as the bird is singing.

CHILD. For Keats, please . . .

ERNIE. Which book, nipper?

CHILD. Boot club.

ERNIE. Boot club. Keats . . . Keats . . . Keats (*Opening the book*) Saving up for a pair of boots, are you?

CHILD. Yes sir, Mr. Mott.

ERNIE (*finding her name and checking it*). One an' two, right.

He closes the book and looks at the child. She is particularly fragile and appealing.

ERNIE. That makes two and three-pence so far. Right?—How long's it take to save for the boots?

CHILD. Twenty-seven weeks, sir . . . Good-day.

ERNIE. Good-day . . .

We get a close view of Ernie's pitying face looking after the child as the scene dissolves.

MA'S SHOP again: Ernie is at the counter. Ma Sedgwiss is in front of the counter, her caged canary between them. She is a little drunk, her hair done up in paper curlers.

MA SEDGWISS. Your Ma always goes three an' a tanner on him an' you know it!

ERNIE (*kindly*). Sorry, but I can't pay you more than what the book says.

MA SEDGWISS (*grandly now*). Then you can take it or leave it, you an' your Ma.

ERNIE. Sorry.

We get a close view of the bird in its cage. It is obviously going to keel over any minute. Without a sound, the bird rolls over and is dead. Then we see Ernie, and Ma Sedgwiss glaring at him; this is an impasse.

MA SEDGWISS. So, you're throwing me out, are you?

ERNIE (*tired but patient*). No, I'm not throwing you out, but I can't give you more than half a crown for him, that's all.

MA SEDGWISS (*after a pause*). Well, I'll take it! An' I'll tell your Ma about you, you wait! No feelings nor nothing, you young blokes! Don't matter to you what we has to go through, does it?

ERNIE. Here's your money . . .

She is about to take the money when her eyes shift to the cage. Ernie is struck by the awful freeze that hits her face; then he, too, sees the dead bird.

MA SEDGWISS (*whispering*). Joey . . . ? Joey? What's up with you, ducks? (*Raising the cage up in one hand*) Eh, lovely? What's up then, eh? What's up, boy . . . ?

Ernie looks at her through the bird cage; she stares back at him. Then she shakes the cage frantically.

MA SEDGWISS. Joey! Joe boy! Joe . . . ? . . . Speak to your mum, boy! Speak to her, ducks! Here, Ern. You reckon he's all right, do you? Do you, Ern?

Ernie opens the cage and brings the dead bird out. Ma puts both her fists to her cheeks and begins to scream.

Ma Sedgwiss, still screaming, runs out of the shop and down the street. Ernie stands there, bird in hand, helpless. Abruptly he starts after her, and we see Ernie, in front of the shop, looking up "The Road." Ma Sedgwiss is twenty yards away, staggering and screaming. People are looking out of windows and doorways. Then the scene moves with Ernie as he starts up "The Road," the bird carefully carried in his hand; he reaches the woman. Dad Prettyjohn comes out of his shop, wearing a trick hat, watching grumpily. A passing train makes it necessary to shout.

ERNIE. Here you are, old girl. Take half a crown . . . here's Joey . . .

He gives her a large coin and the dead bird. She takes one in each hand, tears streaming down her face. Dazed, she starts for the tunnel. Ernie stands looking after her horrified. Her screaming vibrates out from under the tunnel.

DAD PRETTYJOHN (*grumpily*). What's up now? Pinched something, has she?

ERNIE. Canary's kicked it.

DAD PRETTYJOHN (*shaking his head and spitting*). Ain't too comic for the old mare, is it?

The screaming dies away. The train sounds fade. Ernie slowly starts back to the shop, shaken. Aggie calls from her window.

AGGIE. What happened, Ern?

Ernie looks at her but doesn't answer. He reaches the shop, enters, then walks to the counter and in a burst of fury smashes the wire bird cage.

[The scene dissolves to the TABLE in MA'S KITCHEN after supper, Ma is going over some of her account books. Ernie is hidden behind a newspaper. Ma looks up.

MA. Ern . . . I make you four an' eightpence out on your cash.

Ernie lowers his paper and looks across at her; he is still shaken. He drops a coin in the gas meter as he talks.

ERNIE. Ma Sedgwiss had two an' six for Joey.

MA. Where's the bird then? Hid in the coal hole?

ERNIE. Rolled up. She rushed off screaming the place down. Had to do something—I give her half a crown.

MA (*studying his face*). Made you unhappy?

Ernie doesn't answer. Ma takes pen, ink, and ledgers to a shelf. She turns and looks at him. Suddenly she has poked the feather of her hat into a lighted gas mantle and the feather is blazing away. Ernie jumps to his feet and has the burning feather and hat at the sink in a flash.

ERNIE (*crossly*). Wouldn't happen if we had this place electrified!

MA (*fixing her hair*). What give you that foolish idea, son? Who's got the money for it . . . ? (*She comes over to Ernie as he is drying his hands.*) Bit sick at heart tonight, ain't you?

ERNIE. The lowly will inherit the dust of the road—that's what I'm thinking. It's a sell-out, Ma . . . it's all a sell-out, for a bit of sheep's heart an' a place to sleep! Cheap—they get us cheap, how cheap!

MA. What a boy you are . . .

He is about to say more, when Ma abruptly pricks up her ears.

MA. That the knocker? (*Before Ernie can answer, the knocker sounds double at the shop door.*) I'll go.

Inside the shop door next, two policemen are seen standing outside, behind them a few curious passersby. Ma comes in, stops, peers through the glass, and then unbolts and throws open the door. We get a close shot of Ernie at the kitchen table, idly leafing through the newspaper, scornful of the news. Suddenly he looks up and then we see Ma standing near the door, the two policemen with her. The Policeman with stripes comes forward and seats himself, opening a pocket notebook.

MA (*to Ernie*). It's about Ma Sedgwiss.

POLICEMAN WITH STRIPES. All friends here. Just want to know what happened here this afternoon.

MA. Went an' took herself a gas supper, poor old girl . . .

Ernie is silent. Then he puts his folded hands on the table, like a boy in school. He looks at his hands as he speaks.

ERNIE. She come in here to take a loan on her canary bird. Then she see it kicked it, an' begins to scream. I caught her down "The Road" a bit —give her back the bird. That's all . . .

The Policeman with stripes is making a few notes. He puts the book away.

POLICEMAN WITH STRIPES. Right. That's the four sides of the picture.

POLICEMAN (*in the background*). Sorry to give you all this trouble.

MA. What about a little drop of something before you go?

POLICEMAN WITH STRIPES (*on the verge of acceptance*). Well . . .

ERNIE (*with abrupt harshness*). Coppers don't drink in this house!

The Policeman with stripes looks shocked. Then he turns and speaks to Ma.

POLICEMAN WITH STRIPES. Thank you, Mother.

He leaves, followed by his assistant and Ma. Ernie ties a scarf around his neck and puts on his coat. Ma returns and looks at him in silence. Ernie goes to the table. Ma looks at him. He suddenly bangs his fist on the table.]

The scene dissolves to MA'S KITCHEN as Ernie stands talking.

ERNIE. Peace! That's what I'm looking for. I want peace with happy hearts and straight bones—without dirt an' distress. Surprises you, don't it? Peace! That's what us millions want—without having to snatch it from the smaller dogs. Peace—to be not a hound and not a hare. But peace with pride and a decent, human life, with all the trimmings!

MA (*shaking her head*). Won't find nothing in this world like that. Not in our day, son. No way to beat it, boy.

ERNIE (*darkly*). There's a way—travel with the hounds!

MA. I don't like your looks, Ernie. Where you off to?

ERNIE. A walk around. (*He snaps his fingers at the watchful dog.*)

MA. Leave Nipper here.

ERNIE (*after a pause*). Right . . .

He leaves the scene. For a second Ma is immobile, then the front door can be heard closing.

[A close shot shows Ma standing there, one hand leaning on the table. Suddenly she is struck by fear. She hurries after Ernie.—We get a fairly close view of the door outside the shop as Ma opens it, steps out quickly, then looks in both directions. The dog is with her.

MA (*calling*). Ernie! . . .

She listens. There is no answer. She begins to run toward the tunnel. Gay radio music is coming from one of the houses. A train begins to go by.—We see MA moving along calling "Ernie" and then see the other side of the tunnel as Ernie comes out from under it. He hears his mother and stops. There is a sound of running steps and Ma runs into view. Breathless, she clutches Ernie by the arms, waiting till the train clatter passes by.

MA (*dropping her voice*). Ernie . . . you coming back?

ERNIE. Yes, Ma . . . I'm coming back.

He lifts a finger in goodbye and disappears into the fog. His mother does not move for a moment. Then she turns and starts back, the dog with her.— Her face expresses a double agony. A cancerous pain has begun to grip her— she puts her hands to her diaphragm. She hurries, reaches the shop, and enters.]

Inside MA's SHOP: The shop is lighted by a shaft of brightness from the kitchen. Ma comes into the scene as she quickly goes to a drawer and finds the yeast tablet bottle. She takes two of the pills. She is in bad pain, a veritable spasm. She puts her hand on a piece of furniture for support.—Then we see her closer, as with her eyes closed and breathing heavily she rests her hand on the wash-stand. She is in the shaft of light from the kitchen.— We next see Ma's hand on the wash-stand. The fist clenches with pain, holds, then slowly unclenches. Half obliterated chalk marks read "£500." —Ma, seen closely, slowly opens her eyes. She wipes the perspiration off her forehead with the back of her hand. Then she looks down and sees the chalked "£500." She stares at the ciphers. Her face is intense but growing more quiet. Her lips silently form the words, "Five, five . . ." Now her face is calm; she has arrived at a decision, and her pain is almost completely gone.—She goes to her rocker. Her coat is there. She puts it on, and speaks in a low voice to the inquiring dog.

MA. Mind the house, boy.

She leaves the shop through the front entrance. The view moves to the shop window. Ma passes the window and disappears into the fog as the scene dissolves.

[The HIGH ROAD at NIGHT: Ernie is seen walking, cigar holder and stub in his mouth. His mood has not left him. He stops, looking at a shop window.

The window contains a display of electric articles, irons, lamps, radios, heating bowls, a refrigerator, etc. Above them a sign boldly says: "Why not ELECTRIFY now? Why let MOTHER SLAVE away? Easy terms arranged!"

Ernie stares into the window, standing beside a married couple; the woman is old at thirty, but her face is rapturous now.

WOMAN. Oh, what a stack of lovely things!

MAN (*gruffly*). Want everything you see, do you?

WOMAN. Electrification of the home! It's a dream, that's what it is! A perfect dream!

MAN (*stiffly*). Don't doubt it, me girl, don't doubt it!

WOMAN. An' there's 'appiness in all these things, don't forget it!

MAN. Wouldn't 'ave your eye on Windsor Castle while you're at it, would you now?!

Disgusted, he takes his wife's arm and literally has to drag her away. Ernie looks after them, thoughtfully, then turns back to the sign, and we see a portion of the SIGN reading: "Why let MOTHER SLAVE away?"—

Ernie slowly turns away from the window and starts off, as the scene fades out.]

The front of ADA'S HOUSE at night, featuring the grille door and adjoining window, dissolves in. Ernie is standing there, looking and listening. Now he throws away his cigar stub and taps faintly on the blinded window. In a moment, a dim light appears behind the grille door and Ada looks out cautiously. She slowly opens the door and he steps just inside. Ada shakes her head, unable to speak for a moment. Too much has welled up in her throat.

ERNIE (*whispering*). Open it quick.

ADA (*softly*). I don't want no more trouble in my life, Ern. I've had a big packet of it in my time. No more,

Ern. Not from you, an' not from Jim. I'm leaving there as soon as I find another job.

He is staring at her. Modesty makes her draw her kimona closer.

ERNIE (*softly*). I was feeling as if I'd just started living . . .

ADA (*after a searching pause*). Were you? I ought to hate you, didn't I? But I don't . . . Want to come in 'alf a minute?

ERNIE (*shyly*). Want me to?

ADA. There's something that I'd like you to see.

She enters and he follows, closing the door behind him, as the scene cuts to a full view of ADA'S ROOM. Ernie and Ada tiptoe in. Ernie looks around the room, the essential meanness of which is covered with feminine frills. Two doors lead to the back of the house; Ada tiptoes to the open one and closes it as she counsels quiet.

ADA. Aunt and Uncle . . .

ERNIE (*whispering*). Very mysterious, the room of the girl you love.

Ada, beckoning for Ernie to follow her, tiptoes to the other door and opens it and next, from their angle we see a BABY'S ROOM. It is closetlike with a child's blackboard and two absurd paper rabbits pinned to the wall. Under them, sleeping on a cot, is a three-year-old girl with Ada's golden hair. She stirs and sighs deeply in her sleep.

ERNIE (*awed*). Yours . . . ?

ADA (*whispering*). Yes, that's my kiddie. That's the little girl of all my dreams . . .

The scene then cuts back to ADA'S ROOM

as Ada slowly closes the door. Ernie looks at her, very moved.

ADA. Bright as a gem, too.

ERNIE (*softly*). What a wallop you give me, Ada dear. (*Then*) Put your face up half a mo . . .

She puts up a small, appealing face which he kisses.

ADA. Put your arms around me . . .

Ada senses something strange and strained in his attitude. She looks up at him anxiously.

ADA. Aren't you happy to see me?

ERNIE. You make me very happy, but I have to tell you . . . (*After a pause*) I'm thinking of going in with Mordinoy.

She looks at him as if uncomprehending, titters nervously, and then moves off and sits down.

ERNIE. I want some money and don't know how to get it sooner.

A certain pallid bitterness appears in Ada's face before she finally speaks.

ADA. Really, I'm sorry. I'm sorry I ever see you. You'll do time.—He'll see you will. Jim will. I'm sorry I ever see you!

ERNIE. My eye, what a girl!—Don't she get tired of saying goodbye?

They are quiet as Ernie sits on the couch beside Ada, picking up a music box which softly begins to tinkle, "London Bridge Is Falling Down."

ADA (*bitterly*). That's right, wake my kiddie.

ERNIE (*unable to stop it*). Sorry.

ADA (*with hushed vehemence*). You got any sense in you? I could murder you myself! What would you want me for? Be your girl? Your wife? And the next week be poking you bananas through the bars?

In the ensuing silence, the music box slowly runs out. Ada stands, as if to terminate the interview, Ernie following suit.

ERNIE. I see your point, Ada child, but I'll never let you go.

She is standing there as if at bay, vulnerable, vivacious and tragic. He makes a step towards her, but she stops him.

ADA. No, you don't. You don't touch me ever again. No, you don't!

ERNIE. Ada child, don't die on me. What can I lose if I do a job or two for him?

ADA. Me! Do you hear that? Me! Listen, Ernie Mott, the world I want can be as small as this one room, but I have to know it's there tomorrow, too. Yes, I'm as old-fashioned as sealing wax. I believe every girl should be married. See? But it wants a solid base, not police and being slashed about. See? Tile baths and all, silks and jewels, that's why I left him. See? (*Then*) I'll only start crying. So give over now. Say goodbye.

ERNIE. I'll say good night. Good night, Ada dear.

Again he tries to touch her, but she shakes her head and leads him out of the grille door. He is unaware of the music box in his hand. He is both ashamed and defiant. He looks at her earnestly, but she shakes her head, unable to speak. He falters a moment before he leaves. Tears in her eyes, she stands looking after him from behind the bars.

The scene dissolves to "The Road" side

of the tunnel. The delicate tinkle of the music box is heard as Ernie comes into view. The nightly caravan of push-cart peddlers is moving the other way.

Ernie looks at them for a moment, and moves down the street toward his house as the scene fades out.

# PART EIGHT

The COBBLED INNER COURTYARD in front of TATTAMY'S GARAGE fades in. An archway, between backs of shops, leads to the street. Jim Mordinoy and two men in dungarees are standing around an expensive car minus a back wheel. Jim is eating a handful of raisins, chatting quietly about the car.—

In the background Ernie appears in the archway. The men around the car don't see him, but it is only a moment before two other quiet men notice him. —We then get a closer view of Ernie as he is stopped by the two men.

MAN. Where you going, Happy Face?

ERNIE. Here to see Mr. Mordinoy.

MAN (*calling*). Customer here.

Jim and his friends turn at the car. Jim smiles and signals for Ernie to be brought in.

JIM (*greeting him*). Ah . . . (*To Slush*) This is the lad I was telling you about. Name of Mott. Ernie boy, this is Slush Yatley.

SLUSH (*wearing gloves, winking*). How she go, Ernie boy?

JIM (*thumbing the other man*). This is Cosh Simmons.

Ernie smiles acknowledgment of the introduction, shaking hands with Slush. Cosh is unfriendly. The other two men have disappeared.

JIM (*referring to Cosh*). He never shakes hands.

SLUSH. Is Ernie a buyer, Jim, or join-ing the riding academy?

JIM. Joining the academy. Going to

learn something off of you, I hope. Or maybe teach you something—you never know with Mott.

COSH (*slowly*). Then seven o'clock tomorrow morning, Ernie boy. We don't keep gentlemen's hours here.

ERNIE (*soberly*). Okeedoke.

SLUSH. Better come on around an' see what's going on, eh?

ERNIE. Right.

Slush starts for the garage door, Ernie about to follow. But Jim stops him for a moment.

JIM. How's Ada . . . ?

ERNIE. Don't see her too often, Mr. Mordinoy.

Ernie turns and follows Slush who is already in the garage. Jim smiles sleepily and the scene fades out.

MA'S KITCHEN fades in at night. Many guests are standing around, awed. Some of them are drinking beer, there being bottles on the table. The house has been completely electrified. A radio is spewing out music. When it is turned off, music and noise are heard from the street where Percy's and Flo's wedding is being celebrated. But the focus of all eyes is the white refrigerator crowded into the small room. No one present has ever stood so close to such a wonder. Ma is tired, but she is both proud and amused at the attention she is getting. She is beautifully dressed for the wedding party. Ma Tate and Len are particularly envious, as they open and close the "frig" door.

MA TATE. But nothin' won't never take the place of ice, it seems to me.

LEN (*loftily*). I would say the same.

MA CHALMERS. Well, I never seen nothing to beat this—nothing on land or sea!

MAN. Mixes its own ice—why, that's magic!

LEN. Money belongs in the bank, don't it, Ma?

MA TATE. In the bank, that's what. That's where you want it. Sticking it up on the wall or on your back don't get you nowhere! (*To Len*) You'll catch it, my lad, if you ever go buying me any presents. Huh.... Come on, son.

She sweeps out grandly, Len after her.

MA CHALMERS. Jealous, she's jealous.

MA (*amused*). Clara Tate's a copyrighted nuisance. Just the smell of her's a meal.

[In the meantime several more neighbors have drifted in and are staring with awe at the white box. Amelia, the crippled girl, says:

AMELIA. It's wonderful, Mrs. Mott!

MAN'S VOICE (*from outside*). Party's begun! Lots to eat and drink out there!

Many of the guests make a rush for the door. Ike Weber is seen, sitting on a chair in the shop.

"The ROAD" now comes into view. Ernie is merrily playing the piano, which was placed near Aggie's house, for the dancing couples. A child watches his dexterity. "The Road" is in ferment. Many chairs and tables are out along the curb. Stretched across the street is a crudely painted sign reading, "Hope It's Twins, Percy Boy!" Neighbors sit on steps and chairs, drinking and eating. The bar table in front of the grocery shop is being supervised by Dad Prettyjohn, wearing an old Admiral's hat, a coat tail and a collarless shirt. Children are under everyone's feet, particularly running up and down the railroad stairs. A baby is crying in a perambulator. Three old women sit to one side, fanning themselves with newspapers. The man with the gramophone stands by, hoping his services will be needed. Near the tunnel the ice cream man waits with his bicycle cart. Dogs and cats are present, some of them chewing on scraps. Lines of candles are lighted in many of the windows. A child runs by, waving a small flag. A man is lighting the second of two Chinese lanterns hung up in front of his home. Aggie is sitting on her front steps; Ma Chalmers comes out of Ma Mott's shop and crosses to her. Two beggars are watching from under the tunnel. A woman knits. Another wheels her baby's perambulator up "The Road." A blind man is enjoying the sounds and the beer, head lifted. Pa Floom, still in church clothes, emerges from his shop, carrying an armful of glasses to Prettyjohn's table. He drops a few which break.

DAD PRETTYJOHN. Pa Floom's drunk already!

PA FLOOM. No I ain't!

His shrew of a wife flies out of the door into the scene.

MA FLOOM. Told you to be careful, you big wet drip!

DAD PRETTYJOHN. That's the way to start it! A big smelly row! Clear the air! Call in the militia!

MA FLOOM. You mind your own business! Bet I know whose son was married today!

DAD PRETTYJOHN. Bet you do, Mrs. Floom!

Ma Chalmers approaches the laughing Ernie at the piano. Ernie calls to her to relieve him at the piano.

ERNIE. Help, help! I'm melting to an inkspot!

MA CHALMERS. Let me worry them piano keys a minute.

Ernie gladly changes places with her. She slips into a waltz while he stands, finishing his beer and looking down "The Road" toward his house.

ERNIE. Ma inside?

MA CHALMERS. Bring 'er out for a waltz, Ernie dear.

ERNIE. Ar! Get a breather!

Ernie starts for his house. Len Tate stops him. We see them in front of Aggie's house.

LEN. Glad you're settled down in business for yourself, Ern. Put you in with the quality it do, a smart shop like that one. Changed man if I ever see one, Ern!

ERNIE. Don't see any difference in the mirror. What happens when *you* look in the mirror, Len? See something monumental, do you?

LEN (*slow-witted*). How's that?

Ernie winks at Aggie in the background, and crosses to his house. Ike is

sitting at the door in front of the shop.

ERNIE. My daughter inside, Ike?

IKE (*smiling*). She's coming out.

Ernie goes into the shop.

Inside MA'S KITCHEN: Ma is there with an old woman who is about to leave. Ernie enters.

OLD WOMAN (*pensively*). An' this is the boy who done it. Thought of his Ma. Didn't buy hisself a motor car —thought of his Ma.

She turns sadly and goes out. Ma turns off the radio.]

We see MA and ERNIE, as Ma sits, Ernie behind her.

ERNIE. How's my daughter?

MA. Splitting headache . . .

ERNIE (*cheerfully*). Find a seat out there with Ike. I'll bring you a glass of stout. Say, where's Nipper?

MA. Put him upstairs for the night.

ERNIE. Happy, Ma?

MA (*pausing*). Where'd the money come from bought all this?

ERNIE (*evasively*). Money . . . ? Where's money come from, Ma? You earn it, you steal it, you find it . . . someone leaves it to you.

MA (*a pause*). Find yours under a tree?

ERNIE. That's it, Ma.

MA (*wryly*). Hope you won't find any more . . .

She looks at him intently and then goes out. Ernie switches the kitchen into darkness and follows her, as the scene dissolves out.

[In front of MA'S SHOP, at night: In a

fairly close view we see Ma, Ike and Ernie sitting before the shop, the party going on in the background. Ma quietly sips her stout.

ERNIE. What you thinking, Ma?

MA. Only one thing I'd be thinking on a night like this. Where's the girl for Ernie Mott?

IKE (*a soft echo*). Where is she?

MA (*waving her hand around*). You'll have a better do than this, I can tell you!

ERNIE (*grinning*). Stand back—let the man see the rabbit!

MA (*seriously*). There's young Doris Hurley, for instance. She knows her business.

ERNIE (*mockingly*). That skinny bit? While I'm at it, I'd like to find something with a bit of shape.

Ma looks over at Aggie's house, and we get a close view of Aggie on her step. She is looking over at Ma.

MA (*flanked by Ernie and Ike*). Shape ain't everything. Never got *me* much. Had a shape, didn't I, Ike?

IKE (*softly*). Like a melon, Mrs. Mott . . .

Ma sighs. Ernie has quieted down. There is a pensive silence. Ernie stands.

ERNIE. What you need, Ma, 's a nice drop o' rum. You, Ike?

IKE. Make it double.

MA (*as Ernie enters the shop*). On the table, Ern.

An old waltz plays. Ike looks at Ma with great regard.

IKE. I have an idea, Mrs. Mott . . .

MA. Yes?

IKE. But I could never tell it to you, my idea.

MA. Then I'll never know . . .

IKE. You'll never know . . .

Ma slowly turns and looks at Ike. He looks at her a second and then drops his eyes: Ma knows his idea.

A young dancing couple comes down the street, waltzing beautifully. Ma and Ike watch them. Ernie comes out and is seen pouring rum for them. Then we see Ernie lifting his glass in a toast, Ike joining him.

ERNIE. My best respects, Ma girl.

MA. Same to you, son.

They drink the rum in silence. The dancing couple flits back and forth in the street in front of them.—We get a close view of Ernie pensively watching the dancers, the blonde girl reminding him of Ada.—ERNIE sips his rum. MA watches him thoughtfully.

ERNIE. Think this'll last?

MA. All night. When you going to have a dance?

ERNIE. Going to find somebody. Shan't be long.

MA. Take your time, son.

ERNIE. Keep my place warm.

The dancing couple glides away. Ernie starts up "The Road." Ma is looking after him. Aggie crosses the street and sits next to Ma. Ma gives her a friendly look. Both women look up "The Road" after the disappearing Ernie. Ma looks sympathetically at Aggie, knowing what the young woman is thinking, as the scene fades out.]

The scene dissolves to FUN FAIR ALLEY at night, and we get a close view of Ernie and Ada against a billboard. He is pleading against her fatigue. Literally and figuratively, she is backed against the wall, loving him and yet feeling she must give him up.

ADA. Working for Jim now, ain't you? You were down at the Club Monday. Doing what? Can I trust you now?

ERNIE. Do you want me to shout?

ADA. Oh bash me one and get if over with!

ERNIE. I'll shout if you want me to!

ADA. Bash me proper, so's I don't never wake up again!

She suddenly relents, moving and throwing her arms around him and crying out wildly:

ADA. I don't know what we're in for, you and me! Don't you see I love you? But don't you see you can't eat your cake an' have it, too? It's me or him! And if it's me, we'll have to go away!

ERNIE. Why go away?

ADA. What about *him*? He watched me from the office balcony all the afternoon. Called me in at supper time. Yelling away like one o'clock —I never seen him that way before. Jealous. On and on, like a piece of music!

ERNIE (grimly). Reminds me—I owe your kiddie a toy.

ADA. What about him? He pops a few raisins in his mouth an' has us done away with!

ERNIE. Ada dear, quiet down . . . you talk so wild.

ADA. Oh, I won't be wild somewhere far away. And the sooner we went the better.—I'd have my kiddie an'

you'd have me. We'd have a future!

ERNIE (uneasily). Ada girl, Rome wasn't built in a day.

ADA. It's yes or no, Ernie Mott—no two ways about it! (Abruptly) What worries you? My kiddie . . . ? I could leave her with my Aunt . . .

ERNIE (gently). It's not the kiddie, Ada. My ma's been took queer—she's very sick. I couldn't leave her.

That stops Ada! She is repressing her wildness, but wrings her hands nervously, silently.

ADA (finally). That's the end then . . .

ERNIE (violently). No! Give me time to use my brain and look about!

ADA. But what's the use of that?

ERNIE. Ada, look—it's my birthday tonight. Just give me a bit of time for a gift!

Ada looks earnestly at Ernie. After a pause, her mind made up, she takes his arm and speaks in a low voice.

ADA. See me home, then. I'm freezing here.

A cat scoots off as they start away. Ernie mutters to himself:

ERNIE. Give me time to think . . .

The scene dissolves to MA's SHOP as Ernie enters from the street. He is surprised to see the light on in the kitchen. He bolts the door. Then he looks in at the entrance. Ma has left a lamp lighted. On the kitchen table is a small package and a note. Ernie walks to the table and picks up the note.—The writing on the NOTE reads:

"To my dearest Ernie for his Birthday with the hope he never leaves his, Loving Ma"

Ernie opens the package and brings out

what seems to be a silver cigarette case. He opens it—it is filled with cigarettes. His face is a painful study. Suddenly he snaps the case shut as the scene fades out.

# PART NINE

JIM MORDINOY'S OFFICE in TATTAMY'S GARAGE fades in. We get a full view of the cars as seen through the door, in the background, which opens out into the courtyard. It is a mere cubby hole, filled by a rolltop desk and several chairs. Cosh, Slush, and Knocker are listening to Jim, who is sitting at the desk.

JIM. You'll want three cars, Cosh boy.

COSH. Done!

KNOCKER. Where's Mott, Jim? Don't he go with?

COSH. That's right—where's Mott?

Ernie appears in the doorway, late.

ERNIE. I miss anything . . . ?

COSH (*sourly*). Buy yourself an alarm clock, Mott.

JIM. Cosh likes everything in order —punctuality is the essence of our business. (*To the others*) See you all later.

Slush and Knocker go, Cosh after them looking back sourly at Ernie whom he doesn't like. Out in the courtyard a mechanic is tuning up a motor; racing and roaring fill the silence while Ernie looks at Jim, seeing in him for the first time a deadly enemy.

JIM. It's skins tonight. Belnic's Fur Shop in the Brompton Road. Meet here at six tonight. (*Seeing Ernie staring*) Didn't hear me?

ERNIE (*with a start*). Okeedoke!

JIM (*standing*). Better stroll up there an' have a look in daylight.

ERNIE. Okeedoke.

Jim goes out, Ernie following him, and the scene cuts to the COURTYARD, filled with the sound of motors. Jim is aware of Ernie staring at him.

JIM (*sharply*). Something in your eye, Mott?

ERNIE (*shouting over the roar*). What?

The motor roar coasts down to a whimper. There is something very sinister about the scene suddenly, the motors purring like "scare" music.

JIM. Something you wanted to say, Mott?

ERNIE. Me? Not a thing at the moment.

The scene moves with Jim as he starts toward the front, Ernie going with him. A running motor back-fires. Ernie brings out his new cigarette case and offers one to Jim.

JIM. Never smoke in the afternoon, thank you.

Jim takes the case and looks at it as Ernie lights up.

ERNIE. Present from me Ma.

JIM (*giving it back*). Platinum.

ERNIE. Silver, she said.

JIM. Platinum. Your Ma knows what's what.

ERNIE. As a matter of fact, something I *did* want to say. (*As they stop momentarily at the edge of a greasing pit, lighted up from below*) Friend of mine's in trouble . . .

JIM. Coppers?

ERNIE. Girl.

Jim takes Ernie's arm and leads him to the main gate. Behind them a two-toned horn bleats out.

ERNIE. He loves a girl, and she loves him.

JIM. All happy, then.

ERNIE. No, that's the trouble. A third party there, acting like a dog in the manger. The girl don't like him, but he's a big boy, an' he's promised to make enough trouble for my friend to start a business.

JIM (*pausing*). What's your friend's name?

ERNIE. Name of Ernie.

JIM. Oh—like you. (*Then after a pause*) What's the big boy's name?

ERNIE. Name of Jim, like you.

A moment's silence is punctuated by a motor abruptly roaring to its peak and then tapering down to dead silence. Ernie flips his cigarette away.

JIM (*quietly*). Well, if ·your friend's as good looking as you, what's he want to get married for? Waste of time, ain't it?

Jim looks up. One of the "academy" boys, Knocker's brother, runs into view and comes to a respectful, deferential stop in front of Jim.

JIM. What's up, Taz?

TAZ (*excitedly*). I pawned a ruby ring last week, Jim. Just went there to get it out, an' they says the police took it.

JIM. Why?

TAZ. Stolen property, they says.

JIM. And is it?

TAZ (*indignantly*). How could it be? Me married sister give it me last year!

JIM (*smiling faintly*). The old lark —it's been worked before. Tell Slush to heat up a car. And get Cosh.

TAZ. Oh, thanks, Jim—that's grand!

The excited Taz runs into the garage, calling for his brother: "Knocker? Knocker?" Jim in the meantime straightens out his tie, tightening the knot.

JIM. Can't treat the family like that, can they, Mott? Have to go down an' show 'em.

ERNIE. Don't figure you'll want me along, do you?

JIM (*with mock surprise*). Ain't you one of the family anymore . . . ?

Unanswered, Jim starts out across the courtyard; Ernie slowly follows him, and the scene dissolves to a WHITE-CHAPEL STREET as Jim's car pulls up to the curb. Jim, Cosh, Taz, and Ernie pile out of the car and are face to face with the side entrance of the pawnshop.

JIM. Got the ticket, Taz?

All start for the side door, a sign above it saying: "Pledges." Ernie stops at the door—the others have already entered—as he realizes this is Ike Weber's shop. Then he enters.

We get a full view of IKE WEBER'S PAWNSHOP as Cosh, Taz, and Jim go right up to the counter; Ernie lingers behind, half-hidden by a rack of old overcoats. Jim daintily taps the bell on the counter. Little Lesser hurries out, scenting trouble, recognizing Taz.

LESSER. Now then, what's the matter?

Jim leans over and grabs him by the shirt front.

JIM. What's your game, you slimy stink?!

LESSER. What did I do?

JIM. Where's my friend's ruby ring? Here's the ticket, an' here's the money! Go an' get it!

LESSER. Oh, the ring. I give you my honest, solemn oath the police took it.

Jim puts his big hand in Lesser's face. The little man goes down, scrambles to his feet, and runs behind a grille partition. Ike Weber steps out of the archway of luggage and old clothes; he takes the ticket out of Lesser's hand and comes forward.—

A close view of Ernie at the rack of coats shows him shrinking back at the sight of Ike at the counter.—Ike, not afraid, waves the ticket at Jim.

IKE. My Mr. Lesser told you the truth. The ring was stolen property—

JIM. You're a dirty, connivering, ignorant crook! Nip over the back, Cosh—you, too, Taz—have a look around! Go with them, Ernie!

A wider angle shows Jim turning as Ernie slowly emerges from his hiding place, stupefied by the situation. Ike sees Ernie; Lesser, in the background also sees him. Cosh comes in and knocks Lesser down as he and Taz pass by the grille. Ike turns to Lesser, helping him to his feet. Both old men stand looking at Ernie.

JIM (*sharply*). Well, Mott, don't take all day.

Ernie slowly scales the counter and silently walks past Ike and Lesser.

Cosh is sniffing his way, like a hunting dog, through an archway which ends in a dump of tools. Ernie comes in behind him. Cosh helps himself to a pocketful of braces and chisels.

COSH. Come in very handy, they will. My fee for coming.

Jim is sitting on the counter, calmly eating, picking raisins out of his pocket. Lesser is sitting in a chair now, face in hands, trembling with fear and pain. Ike, white-faced, stands behind him, a comforting hand on the little man.

A full view of the BACK ROOM of IKE's SHOP shows it to be full of jewelry, watches, etc., on little hooks and shelves. Taz and Cosh are tearing down everything in their search. Ernie is pretending to assist them, but he is sick at heart. Cosh shakes the inner door of a big open safe; it's locked.

COSH. Locked. The key's what's needed here!

Cosh strides out. Taz is actually panting with excitement.

TAZ. See anything like my ring, Mott?

ERNIE. Huh? No, I don't . . .

Taz keeps on plowing around, but Ernie, ready to kill or vomit, turns and listens. Someone is being hit up front, from the sound of it. Cosh runs back into scene with a ring of keys, happy as a lark.

COSH. That old one's got to be walloped before he sees the light . . .

TAZ. I wish my brother was here. He's missing all the fun!

Ernie's face is growing tighter by the moment. The heavy inner safe door now swings open.

In the FRONT ROOM, Ike, mopping his face with a bloody handkerchief, is standing straight as a tree, shirt spattered with blood. Lesser is on the floor, knocked out and bleeding. Jim is calmly eating raisins, throwing one or two in the air and catching them in his open mouth.

We again see the BACK ROOM, from Ernie's angle, as he watches Cosh and Taz burrowing into the safe. Cosh is filling his pockets.

TAZ (*suddenly*). Here it is! Ask me brother Knocker—the very one me sister give me!

COSH. Lucky boy—found his ring. (*Bringing out a handful of pound notes*) Come in very handy for the Sunday collection, this will. Let's go.

They hurry out, Ernie a reluctant, sickened last. The scene then cuts to the FRONT ROOM, the section at the counter. Jim turns as the others come in. Ernie steps to one side, near a pile of luggage; he is horrified at the sight of the bleeding men.

COSH. Jim, he's got it!

JIM (*smiling*). Yes? Let's see (*Admiringly*) Your married sister's got her taste, Taz boy.

ERNIE, seen close, is watching them with loathing; he is helpless, but his mind is clicking fast. Then we see Ernie moving intently to the counter as Jim turns to Ike.

JIM. Listen, you! Didn't you say the ring was gone?

IKE (*still dignified*). The boy lies—

now stop this stupidity and leave my shop.

ERNIE (*abruptly*). We'll have the police here any minute.

JIM. What do we do with them, Cosh?

Lesser staggers to his feet, clinging to a chair.

LESSER (*thickly*). Misser Web . . . call police . . .

Laughing, Cosh swings a blow, and Lesser falls unconscious, his jaw broken, the chair down with him.

IKE (*in a terrible voice*). Stop this! Stop this!

Jim abruptly starts to his feet and pushes Ike against the grille partition. He swings several times, and Ike is on the floor, in a sitting position, blood streaming from his chin. Jim wipes his hands on a curtain.

COSH. Don't I get a bash, then?

JIM. Help yourself.

TAZ (*bright-eyed*). Oh, my brother's missing all this!

Cosh comes forward and lifts Ike to his feet. Jim stands off like an expert, his head cocked to one side.

JIM. Watch this, Mott—style's everything. Old Cosh'll learn you, won't you, Cosh?

COSH. Course!

ERNIE (*frigidly*). Someone's in line to get his head tore off!

Cosh, his authority challenged, turns and deliberately cracks Ike in the jaw. (*Jim is watching Ernie with a sardonic smile.*) At this Ernie cracks Cosh in the jaw, knocking him down.

ERNIE (*looking at the others wildly*). Who's next? Who wants it next?

ERNIE: What's the music called?

MA: You'll have to help me, Ike.

JIM : I'm a machine, Mott . . . I ain't human — you can't beat me.

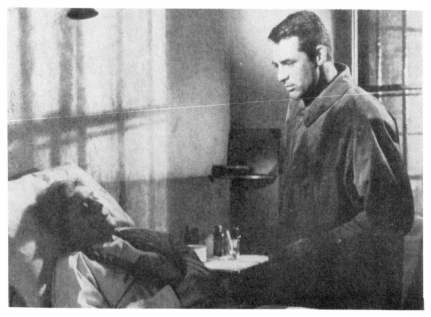

ERNIE : I can't understand, Ma . . . what you in here for?

Jim has quickly pulled back. Now he speaks coldly, as Cosh starts to rise and fight back.

JIM. Stay where you are, Cosh. Let's get out of here.

Cosh, breathing heavily, wipes his face. Taz has turned white, his entire world upset. Ike is helplessly hurt, but his eyes are clear and seeing as he looks from Jim to Ernie and back.

JIM (*to Ike*). Listen, Yikyak, blow the gaff about this an' I'll fix you right. An' your families, too.

Jim walks across, passing Ernie, who doesn't move. He disappears through the side entrance and is quickly followed by the others. Ernie slowly follows them out.

Outside IKE'S SHOP: We get a full view of the sidewalk and an auto at the curb. Jim is already in the car, in the driver's seat. Taz is sitting in the back, and the front door is open, waiting for Cosh to get in. The murderous mood has not left Ernie as he comes out. Jim, slamming the door shut, leans across Cosh and calls softly:

JIM. What happened in there, Mott? Sort of turned your stomach, did it? (*Then*) Think what you'd do if it was someone like your friend's girl . . .

Ernie, standing near the door, silently stares at Jim. Jim is looking out at Ernie . . Cosh sits there with an Indian fixity. Jim smiles coldly, then turns to the car; it pulls away.—Ernie seen closely, is motionless as the car pulls away and the scene dissolves. MA'S KITCHEN, at night, fades in. Ma is ceremoniously writing a post card at the table. Nipper is watching her with one open eye. Ma keeps a corner of one eye on Ernie as he goes to the sink

and begins to wash and dry his hands.

MA. Washing your hands again? Tenth time you done that tonight.

He doesn't answer. She corks the ink bottle and stands up, the post card written.

MA. Going for a stroll, son?

ERNIE. Might. Why?

MA. Wish you'd post this then. To Ike Weber.

ERNIE. Ike?

Ma misses his start as he takes the card and puts it in his jacket.

MA. Don't forget now. I want him to price a lovely antique piece for me.

ERNIE (*wincing*). No, I won't forget, Ma.

Ernie crosses to the table. As he is about to sweep some clock parts together, there is a sharp knock at the shop door. Ma notes how Ernie freezes. The dog looks up sleepily.

ERNIE. Don't know who it can be . . .

He goes into the shop. Ma stands to one side, looking after him, listening. The ENTRANCE to MA'S SHOP: We get a fairly close view of the inside door of the darkened shop as Ernie enters cautiously. He sees Twite peering through the glass, and slowly opens the door. Marjoriebanks is behind Twite.

ERNIE. What's the Commodore of the Rubbish Fleet and his first mate doing out of his cab on a night like this?

TWITE (*whispering*). Your Ma in store?

ERNIE. Come in. No.

Twite steps in, and Ernie closes the

door, looking over his shoulder and dropping his voice to make sure Ma is out of earshot.

ERNIE. What's up, Dad?

TWITE. You're in trouble, son. Mordinoy's right-hand man after you—heard about it down Tiger Collis's place. Some sort of plans to slash you about a mite—you an' some girl, I heard. Who's the girl?

ERNIE. Name of Brantlin, Ada Brantlin . . .

TWITE. Can't say I know the name.

ERNIE. Former Mrs. Mordinoy . . .

TWITE. Stone the Crystal Palace!

Ma, in the kitchen, is seen listening intently. Then we again see Ernie and Twite at the shop door.

ERNIE. Tell you what, Dad, wait up the tunnel a bit—just half a mo.

TWITE (earnestly). I should shay sho!

Ernie lets Twite out and turns back to the kitchen.

In MA'S KITCHEN: Ma hears Ernie coming and pretends to be busy at the table. Ernie enters and puts on his coat.

ERNIE. Friend of mine, Ma, needs some advice on cleaning out his dog's ears—long-eared breed, canker an' stuff.

MA (soberly). Be home late . . . ?

ERNIE. Can't say, Ma. So long.

MA (steadily). So long, son.

They look at each other in silence. Ernie smiles in a sickly way and starts to the shop. Ma stops him abruptly.

MA. Ernie . . .

ERNIE. Yes?

MA (pausing). Take Nipper with you.

ERNIE (pausing). Right, Ma.

Again mother and son look at each other in silence. Then Ernie snaps his fingers; the dog immediately heels in behind him. They leave and in a moment the sound of the shop door closing is heard.—The scene moves with Ma as she enters the shop and goes to the door, following which we see Ma's face pressed against the pane in the door. She is looking into the dark after Ernie, her face worried but strong. Far away a boat whistles sadly.

This dissolves to the interior of the FUN FAIR, where a watchful, wary Twite is standing on guard for Ernie, in front of a dummy old witch in a glass case who is grinding out fortunes in a mechanical voice. We see Ernie talking to Twite, and the scene moves with Ernie, Twite and the dog as they walk on. They pass the mechanical piano.

ERNIE. Out of tune . . . agonizing!

They stop at the piano as Taz comes into the scene and says deferentially:

TAZ. Jim like to see you, Mott . . . you an' Miss Brantlin. Up in his office.

ERNIE (pausing). Who else is up there besides Jim?

TAZ (hastily). We're all on our way down to the Lucky Seven Club. Expectin' some trouble there, they are, with Bert Marks' boys. (He starts away, stops and calls back:) Don' forget Jim.

ERNIE (sardonically). Almost slipped my mind . . .

TWITE (soberly). Count you as one

of the most sensible boys ever put his foot inside a boot. Be careful . . .

ERNIE. Wait around the back, Dad. Won't be too long.

TWITE. Very aggranoying thing, love.

Twite shakes his head and starts for the main entrance. Pausing, Ernie and the dog start across toward Ada's dais. —Then the scene cuts to JIM's OFFICE in the FUN FAIR: a cubicle, decorated with boxing and greyhound pictures— a couch, chairs and a desk. Jim is dropping coins into a private gambling machine. Slush is asleep on the couch and throughout the following scene mutters, grunts and cries out in his sleep. Now a knock sounds at the door. Jim calls over his shoulder:

JIM. Come in.

Ernie, Ada and the dog enter. Seeing Jim attentive only to the machine, they sit down. Ada's mood is one of defiant hopelessness. Finally Jim turns lazily.

ERNIE. I think you asked to see me, Mordinoy.

JIM. Fascinating symbols—you can't beat a machine. Ever fight your pup, Mott? Or did I ask you that before?

ERNIE. You asked me that before.

JIM. How's the girl, Battler?

ADA. (*bitterly*). Which girl? Me or your kid?

JIM (*smiling faintly, to Ernie*). Been trying to make this girl nervous for years—nigh on impossible, seems.

ERNIE. Why should you want to make her nervous?

There is a short silence. Jim, behind his desk, begins to eat raisins.

JIM (*casually quiet*). I'm a machine, Mott. I ain't human—you can't

beat me.—Do you believe in astrology, Mott?

ERNIE. No.

JIM. Neither do I. But in April, 1912, the Titanic sank. Me own father was on it, polishing brass, and an old lady told him it would sink—claimed she read it in the stars. Comin' back to you—I'll sink you worse than any Titanic if you don't stop seeing Ada.

ERNIE. See that in the stars?

JIM. I seen it in me mirror.

ERNIE. An old lady told me how to keep young once: know some funny stories an' tell them to yourself.

JIM (*coldly*). What about Ada?

ERNIE. What about her?

JIM (*starting to rise*). The holiday is over. For both of you.

ADA (*bitterly*). St. Patrick drove 'em out and they're all in Mordinoy's pocket!

JIM. I don't want you two meeting again, see?!

ERNIE (*softly*). That's the way—appeal to me—I might be dissuaded. I'm a reasonable man.

The desk phone rings. Jim picks it up. Slush abruptly sits up.

JIM (*angrily*). Hello— Well, don't raise the dust, Rossi. I'll be down the Club in twenty minutes! (*Banging up the phone and taking his coat from a rack*) You understand me, don't you? Go to the films, if it's love you're looking for! Personally, I don't believe in it!

ADA (*flaring out*). What *do* you believe in?

JIM (*putting his coat over his arm*).

Nothing. Simple, ain't it? Nothing in the whole wide world! An' don't appeal to me—I won't be persuaded!

He turns, and goes out, leaving silence behind them. Outside the radio is heard playing.

ERNIE (*softly*). First thing in the morning we're taking out the marriage license.

ADA. Are we . . . ?

ERNIE. I wonder what the weather man promises for tomorrow?

ADA (*hopelessly*). Likely rain, followed by suicide in bed . . . (*Then*) Let's get out of 'ere.

Ernie gravely looks at her, opens the door and they start out as the scene dissolves to the ALLEY back of the Fun Fair where Twite is waiting in the dark. Ada and Ernie come out of the Fun Fair. A light rain is falling.

ERNIE (*cautiously*). Dad . . .

TWITE. Verdun . . .

ERNIE. Dad, like you to meet the future Mrs. Ernest Verdun Mott.

Twite looks at Ada closely and then stamps his umbrella.

TWITE (*looking at her, chuckling approvingly*). So this is the future Mrs. E. V. M.? Well, stone the Crystal Palace! I'm for it.—Wait here.—It wants a cab, don't it? I should shay sho!

He trudges away down the dark alley, and now Ernie and Ada are alone, with the dog.

ERNIE (*putting an arm around her*). Don't be nervous, Beetles.

ADA (*who is somewhat hysterical*). Up to your knees in dreams, are you?

ERNIE (*emphatically*). We're starting tomorrow with five or six pounds an' a sunny personality!

ADA (*strained*). Are we . . . ? Supposing I went off with Jim?

ERNIE. What a thing to say? Supposin' I flew off to the North Pole an' back in a twinkle?

He reaches for his cigarette case. A sudden outburst comes from Ada.

ADA. I don't know what I'm saying anymore. Ernie, dear, why don't we go away somewhere, just the two of us? Please!

Ernie looks at his cigarette case and slowly shakes his head. Twite hails them from down the alley, calling out "Verdun."

ERNIE (*calling*). Right, Dad.

ADA (*holding him*). Ernie, please!

ERNIE (*shaking his head*). Couldn't do it, Ada.

Then they start down the black, wet alley, the dog patiently following them. Now we get a fairly close view of Twite waiting at the cab. Ada and Ernie enter. Twite opens the door of the cab. Ernie snaps his finger at the dog, gesturing for him to jump into the cab and after an inquiring look, the dog obeys.

ERNIE. Go with her, Nipper, with Ada.

Ada is looking at Ernie in inquiring silence. Her face is delicate and white, full of conflicting emotions—love and despair.

ERNIE (*gently*). Nothing'll harm you while the dog's with you. (*To Twite*) Dad, you go with her too, would you?

TWITE. Pleasure . . .

ADA (*to Ernie*). Where you off to?

ERNIE. Something to be said to Mordinoy. Couldn't be said in front of ladies.

Ada is looking at Ernie through unshed tears. Abruptly she puts her arms up around his neck and kisses him passionately. Twite turns away.

ERNIE (*softly*). Every time you kiss me, it gets deeper.

ADA. Does it . . . ?

ERNIE. See you in the morning . . .

He turns her around and she enters the cab, Twite after her. The cab starts off, following which we get a close view of Ada's small, white face, framed in the glass at the back of the cab, looking out at Ernie. Then we see Ernie's intent, loving, brooding face as he watches the cab off. Now Ernie shakes himself out of his mood and briskly starts back up the alley as the scene quickly dissolves to the FUN FAIR at NIGHT. Ernie, at the counter of the Rifle Range, has a rifle in his hand. The Bloke is shaking his head violently.

BLOKE. How many cartridges do you want?

ERNIE. Eight or ten will be enough. Lend us your newspaper.

BLOKE. Yeah. (*Handing Ernie the cartridges as he wraps the rifle in the newspaper*) Careful goin' out.

ERNIE. Leave it to me . . .

Winking, Ernie slides away from the counter.

[The scene dissolves to a short STREET at night. At the head of the street we see an electric sign reading: "Lucky Seven Club." Ernie comes into the foreground. He pauses for a moment. Then he moves forward and disappears around one side of the building.

At the SIDE ENTRANCE of the LUCKY SEVEN CLUB: Ernie comes into view, softly whistling. He marches straight in through the door and we get a full view of the narrow passage leading to the kitchen. Double doors with port holes in them are visible. Ernie comes into the passage and walks to the doors. He pushes one open and reveals a flurry of kitchen activity. The door swings violently after him, and we get a view of the length of a narrow wine cellar as Ernie cautiously walks through to an open door at the end. And we see the CELLAR ROOM of the LUCKY SEVEN CLUB. The room on which the door opens is small. Two youths are sitting at a small table, eating and drinking. A bald gnome in a black apron is serving them. Ernie stops short as he sees them. One of the boys, Thirsty, scrambles to his feet defensively; the other, Rush, restrains him.

RUSH. Here, Thirsty boy, it's only Mott!

THIRSTY (*drunk*). So it ain't! Had your supper yet, Mott?

ERNIE. Twice tonight's enough.

The little gnome pushes out a chair for Ernie and leaves. Ernie sits down, hunching to hide the gun, but the others are interested only in their food.

RUSH. What you doing here, Smash boy? Got a telegram like us?

ERNIE (*not quite sure of his ground*). Bert Marks' lot expected, that it . . . ?

THIRSTY (*excitedly*). Better join in—bags of sport to it. Two dozen of our blokes upstairs already!

A sudden commotion brings after it

three club girls, on their way to the street, birds before the coming storm.

THIRSTY (*gleefully*). Yvonne, Lola and Mabel.

Three more girls scoot through and disappear, furs and handbags flying. Rush, delighted, pounds the table.

RUSH. Mary, Gertrude and Phoebe!

THIRSTY. Getting the brides out before it all begins.

Ernie stands and starts for the opposite entrance.

THIRSTY. Better get something to play with.

Ernie smiles and pushes the rifle in closer. A last girl flies through, almost knocking him over, disapppearing through the other entrance without a word.

RUSH. Ruthie Mackinac!

The FOYER of the LUCKY SEVEN CLUB: We get a full view of a wide landing at the head of the stairs. Behind the heavy door is the big room. Ernie tiptoes to the door and pushes it open cautiously. Music comes up fuller than before.—Ernie slides through and lets the door shut softly. He is looking at— the MAIN ROOM of the LUCKY SEVEN CLUB and in a slow moving shot, from Ernie's angle, we see groups of silent, sinister men sitting at all the tables, waiting, smoking. Rossi is sending out two waiters. The orchestra men are playing weakly, frightened.

The scene moves with Ernie as he walks down the left side of the room. Men look at him in silent appraisal as he goes to a table left of the bandstand. He slides into his seat against the wall. —Ernie, behind the table, appears uneasy as he looks around; he shifts the

bulky rifle, finally has to put it under his feet. When he looks up, a tough man is staring at him. Ernie stares back, ready for anything.

MAN. You Jim Mordinoy's lot . . . ?

ERNIE. Yes.

MAN. I thought you was Chick Malone a minute.

Satisfied, the man goes back to his seat, Rossi, in the background is now up on the bandstand, whispering. The band breaks off; the men scramble off the stand, and we get a full view of the room from Ernie's angle. Suddenly there are some muffled shouts and sounds of rushing about from outside. A few of the men quietly get to their feet and stroll out of the main door.— Ernie gets to his feet, looking around. There is a loud burst of mingled screams, shouts and breaking glass from outside.

We see the main door as it bursts open. A mass of struggling, cursing men begins to push in. They are using every sort of weapon, razors, bottles, blackjacks, hammers, etc.—A wider view shows all the men in the room springing into action. The blot of fighting men widens out to fill the room. Cosh and the academy boys are there, fighting with animal zest.—A close view of Ernie shows him standing on a chair, looking for Jim. He turns and runs up to the balcony.

Jim is seen fighting with an Italian, in front of the door which leads to the kitchens.—Ernie on the balcony, spots Jim. He hugs his rifle and starts down for 'him.

A moving view of Ernie shows him struggling to get through the fighting men. He is hit and begins to hit back, literally clubbing his way through. He loses his rifle.

Jim, his face bleeding, is fighting two new men at the kitchen door. Ernie enters the scene, variously mussed up. Police whistles cut through the din. One of the men turns on Ernie who fights him off and knocks him down. Jim's other assailant slips away, his work done. Jim is on the floor, badly beaten and bleeding. Ernie looks down at him. Throughout the room a shout of "Coppers! Coppers!" goes up.

We get a wider view of the room. The fighting has abated only slightly, but already many men are hastily leaving through the various exits. Ernie, in the foreground, looks around. Then he bends and pulls Jim through the kitchen door.

In the FOYER of the LUCKY SEVEN CLUB: Ernie sets Jim to rest at the top of the stairs. He straightens up, in a quandary. A mobster comes through, on his way down.

ERNIE. Lend a hand here, please.

MOBSTER. There's coppers there!

He runs down the stairs. After a quick moment of deliberation, Ernie picks up Jim and begins to lug him down the stairs into the white kitchen. A trembling cook is hiding in the corner.

Outside the LUCKY SEVEN CLUB, behind the club building: Police whistles and battle sounds roar in the air. A man staggers past, hands up to a bleeding face. Ernie comes into view, staggering with Jim's dead weight. He looks around for direction, then quickly heads for the mouth of an alley.—This cuts to a STREET ending in a flight of

steps. Ernie comes in with the body. The battle sounds are more distant now. Ernie hears running footsteps behind him. He stops at the foot of the steps, stepping into shadows. Slush flashes by, stops dead.

SLUSH. Who's it?

ERNIE. Jim Mordinoy, of course! (*Stepping into the light*) Here's your fallen hero, Slush. Before he bleeds to death.

SLUSH. Ar! (*Then*) Up the steps, Mott! Quick!

Slush starts up the steps. Ernie slowly shifts Jim to his back and starts after him, following which we get a full view of the top of the steps and the street beyond as Slush comes in and hurries to a parked car. Ernie follows.

SLUSH. Get him in there, behind! Ar!

ERNIE (*shoving Jim in the car*). Get him to the doctor's.

Ernie closes the back door, his task done. Slush runs around to the driver's seat, calling to Knocker.

SLUSH. Knocker!

A wider angle discloses Knocker and Taz waiting at an expensive car, ten yards away. Knocker hurries up.

SLUSH (*to Ernie*). They'll drive you down a way. (*To Knocker, entering*) Drive Mott down.

KNOCKER (*as Ernie goes to the other car; hurriedly*). Anything else, Slush boy?

JIM (*his eyes open now*). Yes. Get rid of him. Don't bring him back!

Knocker's eyes widen, but he gets the idea and nods assent, hurrying away. Slush looks at the stone-faced Jim, puts the car in gear and starts off.]

THE ALLEY: We see two men in a luxurious car. Taz is at the wheel; Knocker, in the back, is lighting Taz's cigarette.—Ernie is now seen coming out of the doorway in the background. He is putting a package under his arm.—We see the two men in the car again, watching him. Knocker calls out "Mott."—Ernie goes over to them.

ERNIE. Ah, the brothers Jones! Good evening!

TAZ (*softly*). No offense about anything, I hope.

ERNIE. Nice car. Steal it?

KNOCKER (*proudly, turning*). Picked this one up in Newman Street, Mott. One of them big new Yanks.

TAZ. We're on our way down to the club.

ERNIE. Uh—huh. Meeting Jim down there?

KNOCKER. Yes, bags of sport down there tonight.

ERNIE. I'm in the mood for sport tonight. (*He opens the back door of the car and gets into the back seat.*)

TAZ. Don't want to sit in the front?

ERNIE. (*carefully*). I'd be more comfortable back here.

We see the CAR moving along, with Taz driving and Ernie and Knocker in the back.

TAZ. It's been a long day, ain't it?

ERNIE. That's just what I was thinking.

KNOCKER (*throwing his cigarette away, calling out*). Watch the red light, Taz.

The CAR goes past a STOP SIGNAL; brakes squeal as it dodges through traffic.— We then see a POLICE CAR, an officer

getting in, and the car roaring out of sight, following the men.—We follow the chase, and then see the car again at close range.

KNOCKER (*looking out of the rear window*). Coppers up, Taz. Right behind us.

TAZ. You're crazy.

ERNIE (*looking out*). He's right. It's a police car.

KNOCKER. Spread 'em. Taz! Don't spare the horses.

Looking through the mirror above Taz's head we see the headlights of the police car. (The scene pulls down to Taz.)

TAZ. Any bets I can't lose 'em inside five minutes?

The car leaps ahead into the dark.— Around corners, up little roads; past back gardens, knocking over clothesline props; over bumps and holes in dirt roads, and finally through a "road closed" sign.

ERNIE. B flat . . .

TAZ (*shouting*). We got the tunnel coming!

Outside the TUNNEL: the car whams in. Two seconds later, the police car whams in.—Inside the TUNNEL: The two cars flash by the white tiles. The roar and clanging are something out of hell. The police car is gaining rapidly.—In the CAR we see KNOCKER looking back and TAZ growing desperate at the wheel.

TAZ. I can't get no more out of this— foot's flat on the road! Jump right outside the tunnel, do we?

We get a full view outside the tunnel as the Cadillac whizzes out. The police car follows, thirty yards behind. A steep hill is visible ahead. The police officer is shouting into the microphone indistinctly.

OFFICER. This is a police car.

Inside the car Ernie has joined Knocker in looking back.

KNOCKER (*suddenly jubilant*). We're gaining up the hill! They got too much weight there!

TAZ. We might do it yet!

This scene quickly dissolves to the CAR. Ernie and Knocker are looking back.

TAZ (*fiendishly*). How are we, Knock?

KNOCKER (*relieved*). You done 'em again! Proper stone cold, you have!

TAZ (*proudly*). They always fall off in the stretch. I've noticed it before, I have.

Taz is curving in and out, behind lorries and around vans.

TAZ (*suddenly*). Oh, Lordy!!

Taz wrenches the wheel to the right. The car screams! Then we see an outside section of a ROAD. We get a full view of another police car as it comes out from the opposing left and has forced the car into a stone wall. There is a sickening crash with an ice truck. Traffic stops like magic; flames shoot up in the background, people begin to run into the scene.

A closer view shows that the two right wheels of the car are off. The motor is half ripped out of the hood. And a close view of the inside of the car shows Taz pinned behind the wheel, chin on chest. Ernie and Knocker are on the floor in the back. Policemen are already at the jammed windows, flashing lights into the car.

SERGEANT. Come on, open this door!

Ernie sits up. People are trying the handles of the doors but can't open them.

KNOCKER. It's a dead pinch . . . (*Then*) Taz . . . ? (*Shaking his shoulder*) Taz boy?! (*Shouting now*) Quick! Open a door! Any of 'em!

VOICE (*outside the car*). Turned your petrol off in there?

ERNIE. Turn it off, Knocker.

Knocker is hysterically shouting, "Open a door, open a door, get him out!" Ernie tries to get to the ignition switch but Knocker is in the way.

A policeman and a sergeant are at the right windows of the car. The fire is heard burning.

SERGEANT. Here, you—you hurt? (*They smash the two windows and reach inside.*) Come on, I want all of you.

Ernie is dragged out and stands there numbly, shaking a temporarily sprained hand.

SERGEANT. Hold onto him.

A wider angle now includes people watching, horrified, their blood quickened by the wreck. Two more policemen bustle in and assist the others. Knocker is pulled out.

SERGEANT (*to Knocker*). Let's have you out of the way. Come on, step lively, son!

KNOCKER (*frantically*). Get him out! He's hurt. Get me brother out—he's hurt!

Ernie, looking into the car, realizes that Taz is probably dead. He walks in and tries to help the policemen.

SERGEANT (*to Ernie*). Get your body out of it!

ERNIE. Don't you see the wheel's pinned him in?

KNOCKER (*in the background*). Get him out, get him out!

A small orange flash puffs up in the wreckage. The Sergeant raises both hands and shouts:

SERGEANT. Watch yourselves! Look out! The petrol!

POLICEMAN. The petrol!

Everyone moves backwards quickly, eyes big with horror. A policeman drags Knocker back. The orange flash balloons up into a large flame.

Knocker, hysterical, is burrowing his way through the crowd until he stands in the clear.

KNOCKER (*screaming*). Get my brother out of there! Get him out!

Two policemen are having a difficult time holding him.—A wider angle shows the blaze growing higher; there is a soft whoomf of an explosion. Two men come in as closely as possible with inadequate fire extinguishers.

Ernie, seen closely, looks at the funeral pyre; he turns his head away. Knocker, held by two policemen, is raging and tearing.

KNOCKER. Let me get him, let me get him, let me get him!!!

The police sergeant crosses himself.

SERGEANT (*softly*). Oh, God Jesus Christ . . .

A little wrinkled crone, munching her toothless gums, says:

CRONE. What's his mother going to say . . . ?

We see the burning car, black smoke billowing upward from the heart of the flame. Knocker's screaming is mere gibberish now and he is tearing and pulling like a senseless animal.—Then we see Knocker, in the middle, Ernie to one side. The policemen are helpless. Ernie suddenly turns and hits Knocker on the jaw, knocking him unconscious.

ERNIE (*unhappily*). I'm sorry, but someone had to do that . . .

SERGEANT (*gruffly*). Sensiblest thing tonight . . .

Two policemen pick up Knocker. The crowd opens, making an aisle which leads right to a police car in the background. The sergeant touches Ernie's arm and he follows, his head down.

The scene dissolves to the CHARGE ROOM of the POLICE STATION at night. The total contents of Knocker's and Ernie's pockets, including Ernie's platinum cigarette case, a handful of rifle bullets and Ma's unposted card to Ike are on the desk. The view pulls back as the articles are examined gravely by a police sergeant at his desk. Now he hefts the case in his hand.

SERGEANT. An' what have we here? None of that cheap nasty silver or gold, eh? Platinum, just the bare platinum . . .

The view moves around the usual bare police room. Ernie and Knocker are sitting on a bench, under a round clock; Knocker's face is in his hands. Ernie is silent, the empty cigar holder in his mouth.

SERGEANT'S VOICE. Still wouldn't care to say a word or two, either of you, eh?

Knocker doesn't move. Ernie's eyes roll slightly but he remains silent. The view slowly moves back, taking in the grim, solemn faces of several policemen before coming to: A close-up shot of the sergeant, majestic at his desk. He picks up the post card addressed to Ike.

SERGEANT. Hmm . . . not posted. I. Weber, Esquire. (*To Ernie*) Well, we'll find out who *you* are soon enough. (*Smartly, to a cop*) Lucas, ring up this Mr. Weber. I'll talk to him.

LUCAS. Yes. Sir.

A close shot of Ernie on the bench: He nervously toys with the cigar holder; he is worried now. Beside him Knocker is softly sobbing in his hands as the scene fades out.

[The scene dissolves to a CELL BLOCK at the POLICE STATION at night. We see a passageway in front of a block of four cells. A kindly policeman is just locking in Knocker, already out of sight. He beckons to Ernie, who is standing there. They move down to the third cell, a snoring old man asleep in the cell in between.

POLICEMAN. They've gone to do your drum.

ERNIE. Do me drum? What's that?

POLICEMAN (*opening the door*). They'll search your house.

ERNIE. Why?

Ernie steps into the cell. The kindly policeman closes the door on him.

POLICEMAN (*sadly*). A lot of money in your pockets wants accounting for. And a platinum cigarette case, an' the ammunition. A joy ride in a stolen car an' a dead youth of nineteen. But if you're a respectable kind of a lad . . .

He finishes with a shrug and goes out. We get a close view of Ernie in his cell. He slowly sits down on the bunk; the scene is illuminated by a small gas flame in a wire cage. He is thinking of his Ma. Softly, reflectively, he begins to whistle, "The Very Thought Of You."—Next in the CELL BLOCK we get a close view through the bars of Knocker's cell. The boy has thrown himself face down on the bunk; he is sobbing. —And then we see Ernie through the bars, on his bunk. He can hear the sobbing. The future looks black from where he sits.]

# PART TEN

The CHARGE ROOM at the POLICE STATION fades in. Ike Weber is standing at the desk, signing a paper. His hat and mackintosh are wet, an umbrella is over one arm. A cop in a dripping rubber cape sloshes through. Ike hears a sound and turns.

At the door Ernie is being led in by a policeman. He stops dead in his tracks when he sees Ike and his badly bruised face. Ike looks at him in silence before starting for the door to the street. The policeman behind the desk speaks to Ernie.

POLICEMAN. You can go now.

Ernie looks at him and then follows

Ike.—We then see them outside the POLICE STATION as Ike comes out of the station and stops on the steps, Ernie right behind him. It is raining.

ERNIE. Ike . . . paid the bail, did you? (*Ike shrugs but is silent.*) I shan't forget you. Nor will Ma . . .

IKE (*opening his umbrella*). Everything with a kiss . . .

ERNIE (*ashamed*). How's Mr. Lesser?

IKE. In the hospital. I stood you bail for one hundred pounds. You'll have to be at Bow Street, in the court, day after tomorrow, nine fifteen.

That seems to be all Ike has to say. He starts down the steps but changes his mind.

IKE. Listen, Mr. Mott, you're frying yourself in your own fat. You realize that? (*Then, giving him some bills*) You'll need a few quid for incidentals.

ERNIE (*returning some of the money*). One's enough. Thanks again . . .

IKE. And no matter what anyone says, your mother's a wonderful woman!

Abruptly Ike walks away. Ernie looks after him, the money in his hand. Then he bends his head to the rain and goes up the street, as the scene dissolves to DAD PRETTYJOHN'S SHOP. Dad Prettyjohn is behind the counter of his store. Aggie is standing by the window.

DAD. No sign of him yet?

AGGIE. No.

Twite, the dog with him, comes into view, eating soda crackers. Aggie is silent and unhappy.

TWITE. Who's to tell him? You or me?

DAD PRETTYJOHN. Don't know.

TWITE (*disgusted with the crackers*). Stale as an old debt, they are.

Prettyjohn offers Twite a second box of biscuits.

DAD PRETTYJOHN. Well, try these then.

TWITE (*refusing them*). They're just as worse—my eye tells me.

DAD PRETTYJOHN (*expostulating*). Stone the pigeons of St. Paul's! Me whole stock ain't stale, is it?

TWITE (*mildly*). Dessay it is.

Across the street: Ernie is going down "The Road." Now he cuts across the street to this side, eyes to the ground.

AGGIE. Here he is.

Aggie taps on the window pane. Dad Prettyjohn rushes to the door and opens it calling "Ernie." Ernie appears at the door.

DAD. Come in, son—come in.

ERNIE. What's this—a gathering of the clans . . . Nipper!

DAD PRETTYJOHN (*opening the door*). Where you been all night?

ERNIE. Why? Ma worried about me?

Ernie comes into the shop. He is surprised to see Aggie there, and Twite complacently munching dry biscuits. The dog fusses over Ernie. Prettyjohn is closing the door.

DAD PRETTYJOHN. Been in a right stew about you, all of us, we have. (*Indicating Twite*) Friend of yours. Dropped in, don't know why. Eatin' through me stock like a flock of mice on wheels, he is!

TWITE. Just brought the dog back, Verdun . . .

Aggie comes up behind him.

AGGIE. Off with the wet coat, Ern. Let's have you.

Aggie helps him off with the coat, putting it on a chair. Ernie gratefully warms his hands at the stove.

DAD. Your Ma's gone out for a bit.

AGGIE. Where you been, Ern?

ERNIE (*wearily*). Seeing how the other half lives. Where's Ma?

The quality of the silence which answers this question makes Ernie turn and look at the faces of his friends.

DAD. Nice egg an' a sausage left over if you care to take it.

ERNIE (*slowly*). Where's Ma, Aggie? (*Then, to Twite*) Where is she?

TWITE. No good standing. Put your feet up.

ERNIE. What's happened, will you?!!

Prettyjohn doesn't know how to begin, confirming Ernie's worst fears. Pretending to pare his nails, he plunges in.

DAD PRETTYJOHN. Well, I'm in bed an' a copper comes along an' gets me out to go down your house with him. So down I go an' there's a dozen of them there.

ERNIE. Dozen who?

DAD PRETTYJOHN. Coppers. Your Ma's just sitting there, letting 'em have the run of the house. She can't explain your . . . cigarette case—where it's from . . . Then they find some other stuff . . .

ERNIE. What stuff?

DAD PRETTYJOHN. Couldn't tell you, boy—stuff dragged out of cupboards. [She never told me neither, 'cept to go get Ike Weber to pull you out today. Which I done.]

ERNIE. What about Ma?

PRETTYJOHN. She told me to tell you don't worry, see?

ERNIE (*insistently*). But where *is* she?

PRETTYJOHN. They took her in with Mrs. Snowden and the others.

TWITE. Poor girls.

PRETTYJOHN (*suddenly throwing the knife away, infuriated*). Done me nails four times today!

TWITE (*solemnly*). Biggest shop-lifting gang this side of the river, a copper said.

ERNIE (*incredulously*). They've got her inside, you mean? Pinched?!

Prettyjohn nods and glowers, holding back the wash of tears behind his half-moon spectacles. Aggie turns away. The scene moves slowly with Ernie as he walks to the window and looks out, his heart heavy. The dog stands with him. The rain is whipping against the glass as the scene dissolves out.

A SMALL GATE HOUSE of the HOLLOWAY PRISON dissolves in. The windows are rain spattered. The scene moves back to a full view of the reception desk. Ernie and Twite are standing there, waiting.

TWITE (*whispering*). There's a smell to these sort of places, official sort of smell . . .

Ernie is silent, smoking a bit of cigar in his holder. The uniformed guard returns through a small back door, another guard behind him.

GUARD. He'll take you down there. (*Filling out a pass*) Got any proof you're Mrs. Mott's son, have you?

ERNIE. She'll tell you when she sees me.

GUARD. You'll do. Follow him. You've got ten minutes.

TWITE. Be here when you get back, Verdun boy.

Ernie follows the second guard, and the scene dissolves to the interior of the PRISON HOSPITAL as the guard and Ernie come in through the doorway. Ernie turns to the guard, puzzled.

ERNIE. Hey, what's this?

GUARD. Why, the old girl's in the hospital here. Don't you know that?

ERNIE. She is?

GUARD. The sister'll tell you everything, I expect.

A sister-nurse joins Ernie as they enter a CORRIDOR. The nurse looks at him intently and sees that he is well-intentioned. She turns and starts down a passage. The view moves with her down the passage, Ernie following, very sober, nervous and soft-treading. They stop at a door.

ERNIE (hesitantly). How much time . . . do they give her?

NURSE. It might be tonight. May be a week. (The nurse pushes back the door very quietly, beckoning Ernie in.)

MA'S HOSPITAL ROOM: Ernie takes his cap off as he enters with the nurse, who goes over to Ma's bed.

NURSE. Mrs. Mott, here's your son to see you. Just ten minutes and you mustn't upset yourself.

Ma looks up; her hair is down and in two braids. Ernie slowly walks to the bed. (The nurse leaves the room.) He sits and takes one of Ma's hands in his.

ERNIE (softly). How's my daughter today . . . ?

MA (weakly). Hullo, Ernie. Where you come from?

ERNIE (delicately gay). Just thought I'd pop in an' have a look at you.

MA. Raining out?

ERNIE. Wet as water.

MA. See Ike this morning . . . ?

ERNIE (nodding). Umm . . .

Apparently this has exhausted the conversation. Finally:

ERNIE. What I can't understand, Ma . . . what you in here for? What's the matter with you?

MA. Tired out . . . machinery run down, you know. (Then) If you get in any trouble, see Ike. Been a good friend to me.

ERNIE. Well, don't be in here long. I got to get married, don't forget.

MA (looking past him). That's right. Find a nice girl . . . look after you. A good girl, son, something steady, nothing cheap . . . head on her shoulders.

ERNIE. Umm . . .

MA (after another pause). Love me, son . . . ? (Before he can answer) Disgraced you, Ernie boy!

ERNIE (with mocking tenderness). Disgraced? Why, Ma!

And now she is trying to lift herself from the pillows, holding on and almost clambering up his arms, suddenly gushing bitter tears.

MA. It was all my fault . . . my fault . . .

ERNIE (his arms tightly around her). Didn't disgrace me, Ma. This is your son, Ernie Mott, Ma! This is the boy who loves you, needs you, wants you!!

The nurse glides in, shocked and peremptory.

NURSE. There, after all I've told you! Outside now!

Ernie ignores the nurse as he gently eases Ma back.

ERNIE. I'll be back tomorrow, Ma. Be quiet, an' get a good night's sleep.

But Ma is sobbing into her pillow. The nurse makes a vigorous signal for Ernie to leave; he does so, looking back from the door before he goes. Then we see the CORRIDOR as Ernie comes in with the guard. Ernie leans against a wall, his arm over his face as he sobs.

The scene dissolves to a PUB where Ernie and Twite are sitting at the cheap cafe table, drinking tea. The window is spattered with rain. A loosely wrapped package is on the table, Ernie playing with the string.

TWITE. What you thinking, Verdun boy . . . ?

ERNIE (*sighing*). I'd best be off to Ada's—she's expecting me and she'll be worried. (*Referring to the package*) Got a nice toy for her kiddie here . . .

Twite looks sympathetically at Ernie before he draws an envelope from his pocket.

TWITE. She give me that to give to you last night . . . Ada did.

Twite holds up the envelope. Ernie stares at it but doesn't touch it; instead he tensely snaps the string on the package.

ERNIE. Read it, Dad . . .

Twite opens the envelope, clears his throat and solemnly reads:

TWITE. "Dear Ernie Mott—I just couldn't face it, for your sake and mine. I am going back with Jim. The only other choice is to make our bed in the river and that is something I could not face."

The toy package is open now, revealing a tin ballerina on top of a tin music box. Ernie pushes a lever; the ballerina dances jerkily, the music box tinkling out sweetly, "Parade of the Wooden Soldiers." Twite reads on, softly:

TWITE. "I tried to do different, but it is best this way all around. I hope and pray you will forgive and forget, Ernie Mott. Sincerely, Ada Brantlin." (*Pausing*) "P.S. Please excuse paper."

ERNIE (*standing up brusquely; bitterly*). Stand back. Let the man see the rabbit.

There is silence but for the tinkly music. Ernie slowly takes the note and puts it in his pocket. Tight-lipped, he stares at the rotating ballerina.

The scene dissolves to a view of ERNIE and TWITE on the ROOF of the building, with Twite holding an umbrella over his head.

TWITE (*closing the umbrella*). Hmm. Stopped raining.—What you thinking, Verdun boy . . . ?

ERNIE. I'm dreaming, Dad . . . "dreaming the better man." What a go—what a rum go it is! Where's the decent, human life the books tell us about? When's the world coming out of its midnight? When's the human soul getting off its knees?!

TWITE. I'm too old, Verdun, to tell you that . . .

Both stop and look up. High up, a plane is flying down the river, its motors making a great humming; loud, soft, softer, silence.

TWITE. Something shuddering in the air these days, son . . . ever notice it? (*Sighing*) If there's a better world to be had, son, you'll have to make it.

ERNIE. Yes, I have, dad. Sometimes late at night I hear it say: "Wake up! The world needs happiness."

TWITE. Well, the world finds something if it needs it bad enough. But sometimes it takes a war. So if there's a better world to be made, you young ones will have to make it.

ERNIE. That's it dad, one thing is left. I see it plain as London town! Fight with the men who'll fight for a human way of life.

TWITE (*heartily*). I should shay sho!!

Twite locks his arm in Ernie's and they vigorously start off as the scene dissolves to LAMBETH BRIDGE.

TWITE. Well—here's where I leave you . . .

ERNIE (*affectionately*). Leave me— you'll never leave me, you old lopsided muggins!

TWITE (*winking*). Well, see you sooner!

ERNIE. How sooner?

TWITE. Who knows. It's all written in the book.

ERNIE. Right, Dad.

They clap each other on the back. Ernie goes off, Twite looking after him with much affection, waving his rolled-up umbrella. Then the scene dissolves to a STREET, as a lamplighter comes in and lights the street lamp. Ernie walks by in the opposite direction, slipping around the lamp post. Then we see him walking home.—He is outside TATE's FISH AND CHIPS, Len Tate and his Ma watching him from inside.—He walks on, passing people, stops by a window and looks at the flowers in the window box. He is listening to Aggie playing, "None but the Lonely Heart."

[We see Aggie playing her cello in the front room. Ernie's dog is sitting by her side.—Aggie doesn't look up, not seeing Ernie. There is a world of goodness and love in her face.—A close view shows Ernie looking at Aggie, listening to the music, warmed by her goodness.—We see Len Tate and his scruffy Ma. From inside their shop window they are watching Ernie disapprovingly.] Ernie looks up at the door. He shakes himself and slowly walks toward the steps, while the music continues and the scene fades out.

# THE SOUTHERNER

*(A Loew–Hakim Picture)*

*Screenplay by* JEAN RENOIR

*Adapted by* HUGO BUTLER *from the Novel*
HOLD AUTUMN IN YOUR HAND, *by* GEORGE SESSIONS PERRY

*Produced by* DAVID L. LOEW *and* ROBERT HAKIM

*Directed by* JEAN RENOIR

## *The Cast*

| | |
|---|---|
| SAM TUCKER . . . | Zachary Scott |
| NONA TUCKER . . | Betty Field |
| DEVERS . . . . . | J. Carrol Naish |
| GRANNY . . . . . | Beulah Bondi |
| HARMIE . . . . . | Percy Kilbride |
| TIM . . . . . . . | Charles Kemper |
| MAMA . . . . . . | Blanche Yurka |
| FINLEY . . . . . . | Norman Lloyd |
| LIZZIE . . . . . . | Estelle Taylor |
| RUSTON . . . . . | Paul Harvey |
| BECKY . . . . . . | Noreen Nash |
| DOCTOR . . . . . | Jack Norworth |
| BARTENDER . . . | Nestor Piva |
| UNCLE PETE . . . | Paul Burns |
| JOT . . . . . . . | Jay Gilpin |
| DAISY . . . . . . | Jean Vanderwilt |

*Associate Producer*—SAMUEL RHEINER

*Assistant Director*—ROBERT ALDRICH

*Film Editor*—GREGG TALLAS

# THE SOUTHERNER

## PROLOGUE

As the film fades in we see the pages of an album being turned, and over the various pictures we hear the voice of TIM, our unseen narrator. "This here is a little souvenir, a picture of my best pal, Sam Tucker, and his folks. Believe me, they don't come no better. When old Sam here gets an idea in that hard head of his there ain't no room for nothin' else. This is Nona, Sam's wife. Here's Sam's Ma, widow woman. Not so young but her heart's still full of fire. Harmie here ain't no Tucker, just a good friend. If he looks kind of sheep-eyed, it's 'cause he's all lit up with that flame in Ma's heart. These are the youngest of the Tucker clan . . Sam's kids . . Daisy and Jottie. And here's Sam's Granny. She didn't like havin' her picture taken neither. This one's me. I'm a town man myself. Only come home for burials, weddings and such. That's how come I cherish these pictures so. Makes me feel close to my friends to look at 'em." (*The scene dissolves, and the story begins.*)

## UNCLE PETE

The scene is a cotton field during the harvesting of the crop. We get a long view of an ENSEMBLE of COTTONPICK-ERS. There are about two hundred pickers scattered over the field. They work in groups, usually families, each individual following along his separate row. Men, women, children, old and young, they all started at the same time, each in his separate row; but the fastest pickers have, of course, covered more ground than the others, so that after two or three hours, they are scattered.

A NEGRO FAMILY is seen picking cotton; the father, the mother, some children, and a very old lady.

A MEXICAN FAMILY: A middle-aged Mexican couple and several children between fourteen and eighteen years of age are picking cotton.

An OLD COTTON PICKER is seen picking cotton. He is a dignified old man, who looks very tired and worn.

We get a close view of ZOONIE, the old man's little dog, who is lying on the ground watching his master work, and this cuts to the OLD COTTON-PICKER: He is obviously tired and ill. He stops picking, lets go of his sack, and straightens up with difficulty. His hand goes up to his forehead, and involuntarily knocks off his hat. Finally, he decides to call his neighbor in the next row.

OLD COTTON-PICKER. Sam . . .

We then see the OLD PICKER, SAM, NONA, OTHER PICKERS: In the foreground, the old man gives signs of being more and more ill at ease. In the background, another picker has straightened up to respond to his call. Then a young woman also straightens up and looks over. They are Sam Tucker and his wife, Nona. Sam is between twenty-eight and thirty. He is a long-legged, hard, sinewy, strong man. His hands are large and capable. His face is tanned, the face of a man who works outdoors in all seasons. Nona Tucker is a young woman about twenty-five, very pretty and at the same time very energetic. Everything about her shows that she is a hard worker, who assumes a definite part in managing her family.

OLD COTTON-PICKER (*suffering*). Sam. . . .

Sam, after watching him an instant, steps quickly through the stalks and comes to help him. Nona and a few other pickers are still looking toward him.

SAM (*anxiously*). What's the matter, Uncle Pete?

UNCLE PETE. It's awful hot . . .

The old man, staring about, dazed, totters. Sam grasps him quickly. As he does so, the old man collapses. Sam lowers him to the ground.

SAM (*turning his head*). Nona . . . (*Nona approaches as Sam helps him to lie flat in the cotton-row.*) That's right. Lay still now. I'll git you some water.

UNCLE PETE (*fumbling weakly*). My hat . . .

NONA (*giving him the hat*). Here it is.

Sam picks up a bottle of water which is lying in his row on the ground. Then the scene cuts to a fairly close view of SAM, UNCLE PETE and ZOONIE. Sam gets Uncle Pete settled on the ground. Zoonie, the old man's dog, comes over and licks his hand. Automatically, the old man strokes the dog. Nona has taken the bottle of water from Sam and helps Uncle Pete to take a drink.

UNCLE PETE. It's my durned old heart.

SAM. You better lie quiet 'n try to sleep. . . . I'll finish yer row fer ya.

UNCLE PETE. Much obliged, Sam.

SAM (*to Nona*). I gotta take my cotton over now . . .

NONA (*squatting near Uncle Pete*). I'll take care o' Uncle Pete . . .

Sam returns to his row, picks up his sack full of cotton and walks away, following which we see the FOREMAN and several COTTON-PICKERS. The foreman, after having weighed a sack of cotton, writes a number down on a record sheet that a picker has given him. Sam arrives in the background. Next, we get a close view of SAM and OTHER COTTON PICKERS standing in line, waiting for their cotton to be weighed.

A PICKER (*to Sam*). Where ya goin' after the crop's over?

SAM. I figure I might stay here. Get me a bulldozin' job. Where you goin'?

PICKER. Oh, I think I'm goin' North from here.

THE PICKER empties his cotton, which has already been weighed, into the truck, which then drives away.

SAM is then seen returning to the field with his empty sack. NONA gets up from next to Uncle Pete. The latter and Zoonie are not visible, being hidden by the cotton.

SAM. How is he, honey?

NONA. Sam—he ain't so good.

Sam puts his sack down and goes toward Uncle Pete. Then Sam and Nona are seen squatting down next to Uncle Pete. The latter looks really very ill. With a weak stroke of his hand, he caresses Zoonie.

UNCLE PETE (*in a very weak voice*). Don't do that . . . Don't work for others—work for yerself . . . grow yer own crops.

SAM and UNCLE PETE: Sam tries to give him another drink.

SAM. Want some more water, Uncle Pete?

But the old man is too weak, even to drink. In an almost inaudible voice, he repeats his advice.

UNCLE PETE. Grow yer own crop . . .

His head falls against Sam who holds it up on his shoulder.

A close view of NONA shows her eyes, huge with fright.

NONA. Oh, my goodness! Uncle Pete . . . Uncle Pete.

We begin to hear Zoonie's whimpering. We see SAM, NONA, UNCLE PETE and ZOONIE closely as Sam lays the old man down on the ground. Uncle Pete's face is hidden by Sam's action, and by Nona who helps him. But the immobility of his body makes us understand that he's dead.

ZOONIE, seen closely, is next to her old master's hand—her whimpering changes to sad wailing as the scene fades out.

## UNCLE PETE'S FUNERAL

A close view of a CROSS fades in. This cross was crudely made by hand—no doubt by Sam. Sam's hand is visible, holding a big rock with which he forces the cross into the ground. On the cross, written by hand, we read: PETER TUCKER.—ZOONIE is then seen closely.

The little dog is whimpering at the foot of the cross. The movement and the noises of the rock indicate that Sam is still planting the cross into the ground.

In a fairly close view we see SAM, NONA and some NEIGHBORS in the background. Sam finishes sticking the cross into the ground and throws the rock away.

NONA. Pore Uncle Pete . . .

SAM. Yes—pore ol' man . . .

NONA. I wish we could rise him a tombstone . . .

SAM. That's fer folks who got money. —Come here, Zoonie. Jottie . . .

SAM, NONA, GRANNY, DAISY, JOT, and some CAMP PEOPLE are seen together. Uncle Pete's cross is standing in a poor, isolated corner òf the cemetery. In the background we just see four or five wooden crosses, very crude, and behind them, the fields. A mule-drawn wagon is also seen. Nona puts a little bouquet of flowers at the foot of the cross. Then they all go off. Around Sam and Nona, an old lady (whom we shall know later as Granny), Daisy and Jot, the little Tucker girl and boy, are all together. Their grouping makes us understand that they are all one family. Sam comes back and picks up Zoonie, who had stayed behind at his master's grave.

This dissolves to a fairly close view of the TUCKER FAMILY and some CAMP PEOPLE. They go back to the camp, on foot, along a little path through a field of wild flowers. The wagon, drawn by mules, which no doubt had brought the coffin, passes them.

JOT. Papa, my foot hurts.

Jot is a small boy, thin and sickly looking—about four years old. Sam gives Zoonie to Nona, and carries Jot. This action has caused them to stop a moment, and has permitted Daisy to notice something interesting in the field.

DAISY. Oh—see the fox-grapes . . .

She runs toward the fox-grapes. A close view of DAISY shows her to be a little girl, about six and a half years old.

DAISY. Granny—Granny—look at the fox-grapes. Don't you want any good fox-grapes, Granny?

We get a close view of GRANNY. She is a very old lady, still strong, but with a disgruntled air about her.

GRANNY. No sir! An' you come out of them snaky vines, too. I don' wanna git mixed up with no copperheads—I'm awready wearin' one crooked toe one o' them scoundrels ruint.

DAISY (*seen closely, eating a foxgrape*). Yum-yum . . .

GRANNY, seen close, looks at Daisy, her eyes shining with greed; following which we get a moving view of the FAMILY. In the foreground, Sam is carrying Jot, and Nona is carrying Zoonie. They start walking, paying no attention to Daisy and Granny. In the background, Granny joins Daisy to pick grapes. The people who attended the funeral continue to pass on the road.

GRANNY. Don' be a hog, Daisy. Leave a few fer the next feller.

DAISY. I thought you was afeared o' snakes.

GRANNY (*eating greedily*). I am. But that ain't no sign I gotta starve to death, is it?

SAM, JOT, NONA and ZOONIE are continuing to move ahead.

NONA. Why didn't Ol' Uncle Pete, who was always tellin' us that a man ought to work fer hisself, grow his own crop—why didn't he ever try it hisself?

SAM. Cause he was all alone in life— since Aunt Vittie passed on—long before I was ever born. Y'know, honey, when a man's got no folks to work fer, he's apt to kinda give up. Ya gotta be hardy an' full o' fire to work fer yourself. After all, when ya work fer a big outfit, ya mebbe don't make very much, but ya still git yer pay, even if the crop is bad. The guy what grows his own crop— if his crop gits ruint—he's got nothin' left to do but tighten up his ol' belt. But I still think it's crazy to spend yer whole life sellin' yer sweat fer six bits a day . . •. Ya know the l'il San Pedro place near the river?

NONA (*as she turns around to see what Daisy is doing*). Yeah, I know where it is . . . I ain't never seen it.

SAM. Well, it b'longs to the boss-man, too. Lige, at the commissary, told me it's fer rent. It's been laying out fer three years now, ought to be rich as mud. In the old days, Old Man Corinth used to make the best crops in this country on it.

NONA. If it's bin layin' out all that time, it'll take a whole year to clear it off.

The scene cuts to GRANNY and DAISY: Granny is eating grapes greedily. She pushes Daisy away so as to have them all to herself, but from behind her back, Daisy brings out a little dead snake which she dangles in front of Granny's nose.—Granny leaps back. Daisy takes her place and starts eating grapes.

GRANNY. Oh! . . . Nonie . . Nonie . . . come here right this minute 'n spank this outrageous vilyun, or I'll do it myself! Help . . . Help . . . Nonie!

Nona comes to Granny's assistance, calling to Daisy.

NONA. You behave yourself, Sis. Don't you always be teasing Granny.

In the background we see Daisy throwing the snake away, reluctantly leaving the grapes, and coming to join Sam and Nona in the foreground. Granny picks a few last grapes and starts walking towards the others.

SAM. I reckon I could ast old man Hewitt for his mules—he don' hardly ever use 'em nohow. I'd pay him with a bit o' the crop. 'Bout the seed 'n fertilizer, bet I could make a deal with ol' Harmie . . . Pa's ol' plow's still in Ma's backyard—with the chickens roostin' on it now, since Pa died . . . I'm goin' to talk to the boss about it! . . .

NONA (smiling up at him). Askin' don' do no harm.

SAM. No. Askin' nor work either don' harm a man. After all, the boss is a purty good guy . . . we allus got along.

NONA (hurrying the laggard members of her family). Jottie . . . Sis . . . Granny . . . come on.

The scene then dissolves to the OFFICE of the boss, RUSTON, where SAM is concluding his visit.

RUSTON. It's okay with me, Tucker, I ain't interested in that piece of land . . too far away from my other property. But just remember this . . if I ain't satisfied with the way you're workin' I aim to break that contract any time I like.

SAM. That's all right with me, boss.

RUSTON. I like you, Tucker . . you're a good hard worker. An' that's why I'm botherin' to warn you. And I'm tellin' you again . . if you're workin' for a big outfit, maybe you don't git rich, but you still git your pay even if the crops is bad. But the little guy who's growin' his own . . if his crops is ruined he's got nothin' left. (Seeing that Sam is resolved) Well, I see you've made up your mind. You got some way of movin' your things?

SAM. Yes, sir, Carillo said I could borrow his truck.

RUSTON. Okay . . Good luck, Tucker.

SAM. Thank you, sir.

## THE FAMILY MOVES

A long view of the CAMP: Workers and their families are preparing to leave the camp to go on to other places. They are piling their household effects into old dilapidated cars. Others are packing old baby carriages full of various things; still others are filling old gunny sacks. A very old little truck drives through the camp, raising a cloud of dust.

We get a close view of SAM, NONA, DAISY, JOT, ZOONIE: Sam is at the wheel of the moving truck. We understand, from the various packages and bundles on Nona's lap and in the children's arms, that the Tucker family is also moving out.

GRANNY is seen sitting on her rocking-chair in the back of the truck. All around her there are unassembled beds, mattresses, a table—all the meagre furniture of the family. The wind bothers her and she looks very disgruntled. In some strange way, she dominates the entire country-side.

The TRUCK drives out of the camp and goes off on the highway, and then SAM, NONA, DAISY, JOT and ZOONIE are seen close.

NONA. When d'ya hafta git the truck back, Sam?

SAM. Tomorrow mornin' 'll do—Olivera's leavin' camp tomorrow evenin'.

NONA. That's jes' fine, honey—gives us the whole day fer movin' 'n gittin' settled in the house. Where the Oliveras aim to go?

SAM. North, he tole me—wants to try the wheat-fields nex' year.

DAISY. How far's our house from the river, papa?

SAM. It's almost jes' right nex' to the river, honey.

Daisy, Jot and Nona are obviously excited about the adventure of moving to their new place.

DAISY. Oh, goody—goody—

We get a distant view of the TRUCK ON THE ROAD as seen from behind. An old shawl which Granny has around her neck is flying in the breeze like a flag. The truck passes a Negro boy on his way back from fishing, his pole on his shoulder. The scene shows a black stormy sky.—A close view of the NEGRO BOY shows him staring at Granny in astonishment as the scene dissolves.

And now the truck pulls up in front of the house, which is a pretty sad spectacle under the cloudy sky. It is leaning strangely over to one side, almost as if it were ready to fall. Some birds, startled by the noise, fly away. Then we see the family looking at the HOUSE as Sam helps Nona, the children and Zoonie get off the truck, first taking their packages from them. Granny, on her rocking chair, does not stir.

SAM. Well, here we are . . . Mind there, l'il brother, don't fall—jump down like a man!

We get a close view of GRANNY on the rocking chair. She is knotting and unknotting her shawl, shaking her head disapprovingly, and muttering to herself in great distress while the family moves its possessions from the truck and ignores her.

GRANNY. Don' look like no house at all to me . . . huh . . . looks more like a sow's nest. Why, I'd ruther live back in that there dirty ol' camp than in a heap o' junk like that. You ain't never goin' to get me to go into that old sinkhole. Bringin' their old Granny to this scrubby place . . . must be they don' love me no more than if I was a yellow dog.

Sam takes a package from Daisy. Nona is looking at the house, unable to hide her disappointment. The children, on the other hand, are looking toward the river.

SAM. Look out with my gun, Daisy—Mind ya don't drop it—Need that ol' friend there fer gittin' good fresh meat . . .

DAISY. Oh, look at the river, look at the river!

JOT. Oo-o-o! Look at the river.

DAISY. Mamma, when kin we go fer a good swim?

We get a close view of NONA and SAM facing the house.

DAISY'S VOICE (*insisting*). Mamma, when kin we go in swimmin'?

NONA (*unable to take her eyes from the house*). When it warms up, sister. (*To Sam, in dejection and despair*) Oh, Sam . . .

SAM (*attempting buoyancy*). Come on, let's go look at it.

They get near the house, which, seen from up close, looks even more dilapidated and miserable. Sam goes in. Then we see him in the house. He steps on the end of a broken floor board which flies up, almost hitting him in the face, then falls back with a bang. This noise startles a family of bats and they fly away. Nona tries to open a door, which undoubtedly leads to another room, but the door won't open. She goes out, intending to go around the house and come in from the outside. Sam succeeds in opening the door, which causes a whole cloud of dust to rain down. He has lost much of the confidence he had upon arriving at the farm, understanding Nona's great disappointment.

Nona, outside, having gone around the house, arrives at the exterior of the second room. The walls and part of the roof are almost completely demolished. Only a door seems to be solid. Nona opens it, but only succeeds in loosening a part of the roof which falls in.

SAM'S VOICE (*from inside*). Here! Look out!

Sam comes out through the mess that Nona has caused. Then SAM and NONA are seen together in the house.

NONA. I allus hoped we could have a room to ourselves someday. I think lots o' times that Granny ain't sleeping when she lets on to be . . .

SAM (*almost hopelessly trying to justify himself*). Well, we kin have, when summer comes. Let Granny and the kids sleep in here, and move our bed out on the porch . . . and have everything real nice.

NONA (*looking around*). Oh, Sam, the house don't seem like nothin' extra.

SAM. Seems like extra one thing . . . pretty durn extra bad. I reckon I was thinkin' too hard 'bout the land . . . I plumb forgot about the house. Sure be some patchin' to do. More than a little . . .

NONA. What about the well, Sam?

Sam and Nona go outside the house and come up to a well in the foreground. In the background the children are playing with Zoonie, and Granny is still on her rocking chair in the truck.

GRANNY (*repeating herself*). Don' look like no house 'tall, looks more like a sow's nest.

Nobody pays any attention to her. In the sky, the clouds get more and more menacing.

SAM and NONA: Sam looks down into the well which appears to be in as bad condition as the rest of the property. He pulls out a piece of broken beam. Now, completely desperate over Nona's disappointment, Sam doesn't try any longer to cover up his feelings.

SAM. Yes, honey—I was crazy to think we could live in this place . . . It'd take me at least two weeks to dig this well again.

NONA. 'Thout even talkin' 'bout the money the planks 'n beams'd cost . . .

GRANNY is seen rocking furiously in her rocking chair.

GRANNY. Tain't much o' a man that brings his babies 'n womenfolk to soak 'n freeze in no sech sump hole as this.

SAM and NONA: Sam keeps looking at the well.

SAM. Think mebbe she's right . . . Water from this here river fer the kids—be jes' like servin' 'em up a dish of typhoid.

GRANNY'S VOICE. Tain't much o' a man, I say.

Sam reflects a moment, then turns toward Nona.

SAM. Look, honey, we kin still go back to camp, if you want to. The boss couldn't a rightly knowed how bad the place wuz. I could talk to him again, 'n mebbe still get my bulldozer job fer the winter.

NONA (after some hesitation). Well, how's the ground?

SAM. Oh, it's good earth, all right.

He takes a knife from his pocket, opens it, and kneels down. We then see him digging a little with his knife, picking up a handful of dirt, and getting up.—ZOONIE is seen closely, as the little dog continues digging in the dirt when Sam stops digging with his knife.—Sam looks at the earth in his hand and spreads it around his palm with a finger.

SAM. You know with dirt like this a fellow could raise the best crop in the country—'n almost without no fertilizer, hardly. Been layin' out all these years. The Earth is like men—it needs a rest once in a while. Maybe that's the reason the Lord invented Sunday.

NONA (indicating the place around them). But Sam, how 'bout all this brush 'n Johnson grass? Y'll kill yerself cleanin' it off 'fore the plantin'!

SAM. I ain't all alone, honey. I ain't like pore Uncle Pete. Every time I get plumb wore out, I think about you and Jottie and Daisy, and I ain't quite so tired no more.

Nona, greatly moved, approaches Sam, who puts his arm around her shoulder. There is a great tenderness between them.

NONA. Oh, Sam . . . Sam . . . I jes couldn't never git along without you . . .

SAM. Me, too, honey . . . I couldn't live without you.

NONA. The thing'd be good 'bout livin' here, we'd allus work together. When you clear off the brush, I could burn it fer you—When you did the plowin', I could lead the mules. An' in the summertime, we could lie in the grass 'n watch the kids swimmin' in the river . . .

SAM. Yeah, that'd be fine, honey . . . But what worries me is that busted well.

NONA. Sam, we could surely borrow water from the neighbor yonder. Ain't nobody refuses water.

SAM (shyly, but with hope). Yeah. I heared he's got a good well.

NONA (thinking for a moment, then suddenly). Sam, I reckon we oughtta stay.

SAM (his face lighting up). Ya really mean that, honey? Ya ain' just sayin' it to make me feel good?

NONA. No, Sam. I'm sayin' it 'cause I b'lieve yer as good as any man—

'n it's right fer you to be yer own boss.

As Sam, deeply touched, looks at her warmly and presses her to him, the scene cuts to GRANNY, THE CHILDREN and ZOONIE. The children are amusing themselves by seeing who can spit the farthest. Granny looks furiously towards Sam and Nona.

GRANNY. Hey, you two, ya ain't all alone here, you know!

SAM and NONA don't even hear Granny. Having broken their embrace, Sam runs toward the truck.—Zoonie stops digging in the ground and barks joyously, following Sam. We see the WHOLE FAMILY as Sam is running toward the truck, Nona following him, more calmly, but happy.

SAM (shouting to the children). Hey, there—we gotta house—we're movin' in and it's all ours. C'mon, ya 'possums, and help me. Give me a hand.

He takes something very heavy from the truck. Nona follows the action, and an excited Zoonie jumps around, barking loudly.

NONA. You take the pictures, sister, don't drop them.

JOTTIE. I want my teddy-bear.

We see SAM closely as he takes different things from the truck, among them a long piece of cable. This last gives him an idea and he looks toward the house before continuing to unload the truck. He begins to whistle, joyfully.

GRANNY is seen closely. She watches the scene angrily, as all the household effects—beds, table, packages—pass her by. Then we see SAM trying to get her down from the truck, holding out his hand cheerfully.

SAM. Come on, cutie, I'll help you down.

GRANNY (fighting him off). No, you don't. I don't aim to go into no slew-footed—cain't even say it, bein' I'm a lady.

SAM (turning away, to complete his labors). All right, old lady, but you better be down before morning or you'll go right back to camp on this truck. Old Man Carillo mightn't like that so much neither.

GRANNY (muttering on). Huh . . Sam Tucker, my own grandson, gone crazy as a bedbug. Pure plumb crazy I tell ya. Crazy as a bedbug . . he's going completely crazy . . that boy. Loonier than a coot. He's jes' plain outten his mind, I tell ya, what little mind he ever done had. If he thinks he's going to stick his old Granny in a trash box like that which ain't fitten for nothin' more than kindlin' . . he's sure got another think comin'. No, sir . . I don't aim to spend my last days on this here earth in no dirty ol' garbage pile. There's some whut's jes downright mean an gotta take out their cussedness on helpless ol' folks! Well, I done had my share . . an' I ain't takin' no more, nohow, I tell ya . . no more.

## THE FAMILY GETS SETTLED

We see a corner of the roof of the house in a stormy sky. The cable that we saw Sam take off the truck in the preceding scene has been attached to this corner of the roof. Its agitation makes us realize that someone is pulling it from below, so as to make the house firm. A clap of thunder is heard;

a flash of lightning crosses the sky. Then we get a close view of SAM as he finishes stretching the cable, the other end of which is attached to a tree. Having finished stretching and attaching the cable, Sam walks away, as another clap of thunder is heard.

Sam goes up the porch steps which Daisy is finishing sweeping. Nona comes out of the house, followed by Jot who won't leave her for a moment, fearful of the storm. Another clap of thunder sends the little boy scurrying to his mother's skirts.

SAM (*to Nona*). Tain't exactly a veranda, honey, but to me it's the porch that makes a house a home.

NONA. Sam, I think I've got the stove working.

SAM. Oh, did you?

This cuts to the interior of the house. Sam and Nona, with the children in the background, are gathered near the stove.

NONA. We'll all light it together. (*Lighting the stove*) It's our first fire in our own house.

SAM (*watching the stove*). Yeah . . . you sure made a good job of that stove, honey.

NONA. It won't be long before we'll have a good hot cup of coffee. You get some water, Sam. Jottie . . . Daisy . . . get the cups and put them on the table. (*To Sam*) Do you reckon Granny's gonna stay out there all night?

SAM (*indicating the sky*). I think that'll be took care of.

The rain starts to fall and is visible on the window-pane in the background and in the foreground, in front of the porch.

NONA. Sister, you go call Granny.

The scene cuts to GRANNY, still rocking herself furiously, as DAISY comes up to her.

DAISY. Granny . . . do you want some good hot coffee?

GRANNY. No, sir. Nothin' whut comes outta that ol' pot don't tempt me none at all.

Daisy returns to the house.

DAISY. Mama, it's rainin' and Granny won't come in.

JOTTIE. It's rainin'. It's rainin'. Granny won't come in.

NONA. Well, we'll have our coffee anyway.

SAM. You sit down, honey, I'll get it.

In the foreground is the table where Nona has placed the coffee-cups. In the middle of the table is a small jar of honey. In the middle of the room is the stove, roaring cheerfully. Nona takes the coffee from the stove and goes to the table to serve it. In the far background we see the truck in the pouring rain, and on the truck, a stubborn Granny who continues rocking on her chair. At the moment when Nona serves the coffee, rain leaks from the roof onto the table. Sam and Nona pick up the table and move it out of the way of the leaking water. This incident takes nothing away from Sam's good humor, who, since the beginning of the scene hasn't stopped whistling joyfully. The children are very much amused by the incident.

DAISY (*clapping her hands merrily*). Oh, Papa—there's a hole in the ceilin'—

JOT (*who likes to repeat Daisy's words*). Oh, Papa, there's a hole in the ceilin'!

Daisy and Jot start amusing themselves by running back and forth under the leak. Nona and Sam again push the table away from the leaking spot.

NONA. C'mon to the table, everybody.

Sam picks up a bucket and places it under the leak in the roof.

SAM. Well, we don't have to ask our neighbor for good water today.

NONA. Here's some honey, Jottie.

We again get a close view of GRANNY as she stubbornly stays on her rocking chair. The rain begins to get her really wet. No longer able to hold out, she gets up to go into the house.

Inside, in the foreground, Sam, Nona and the children start to drink their coffee. Nona sweetens the coffee with honey. In the background, Granny suddenly gets off the truck, using the box that Sam placed beneath it for a step, and runs toward the house, holding her skirts up. Sam gets up and goes toward the door.

Granny runs into the house. Sam waits for her, his hand on the doorknob. She walks toward the table. Sam closes the door with a broad grin on his face, and the children greet her excitedly.

DAISY.     Oh,     Granny—Granny's changed her mind. She's changed her mind.

DAISY and JOT (calling out together). Granny! Granny! She's changed her mind. Hey, Granny!

SAM (picking up a blanket and putting it on her). Come on, Granny. Here, I've got your good blanket. Now put it around you before you catch your death of cold.

NONA (handing her some honey). Here's some honey, Granny.

GRANNY (reaching for it greedily). Honey! Ha . . . they not only let me die o' the cold, but they hide out the goodies from me.

And now we see the alcove in which Sam and Nona's bed is made up. Sam and Nona haven't undressed yet, but are stretched out on the bed with all their clothes on, dreaming of this day which has marked such a great change in their lives. Nona leans her cheek on Sam's shoulder. Sam looks in the direction of Granny.

SAM. D'ya think we kin spare a cover, honey?

NONA. Sure—with the fire agoin', it's nice 'n warm in here.

Sam rises. He takes a quilt made of old flour sacks from the bed, and goes to hook it across the front of the alcove, so as to give them a little privacy. He flashes a quick look toward Granny, and returns to his bed, passing under the hanging quilt.

NONA (calling to Granny). Good-night, Granny.

GRANNY opens one eye stealthily, devoured by curiosity, and looks in the direction of Sam and Nona, as the scene fades out.

## DEVERS

SAM, up to his waist in the river, is ready to pounce on a fish. With a rapid movement of his two bare hands, he grapples it and takes it out of the water. It is a rather big fish which struggles hard.

We get a fairly close view of SAM, NONA, JOT and ZOONIE by the river. In the foreground, Sam is struggling with the fish. In the background, Nona is gathering wood from a tree that Sam has chopped down and made into firewood. Jot is with her. Sam, with the big fish in his hands, goes over to a crude, home-built slatted box, half-submerged in the river. Zoonie is at his heels.

SAM (*calling*). Nona . . . C'm here.

NONA (*approaching*). Oh, that's a pretty one, Sam.

SAM. Yeah, honey, that's a mighty fine fish.

NONA. It'll make us a good dinner.

SAM (*embarrassed*). Oh, I figgered I'd take this one to Devers, that neighbor of ours down the road with the good well. (*Indicating a fish in the bucket*) That little one in the bucket's for us. (*We see a small fish in the bucket and Nona's disappointment.*)

Sam wraps the big fish up in some leaves and grass.

NONA. Ain't ya gonna put some dry clothes on?

SAM. Oh, I'll dry off walkin' over. Won't be gone long. Better keep Zoonie here.

Nona leans over the box to pick up the small fish.

NONA (*as Sam is leaving*). This one ain't so big, honey—Come on, Jottie . . . Zoonie.

SAM. Well, I'll catch us another one tomorrow . . . a big one. We'll keep it. (*To Jottie, as he goes past him*) Run along with your mother, Jottie.

We get a close view of NONA and JOT.

JOT. Does fish like bein' caught?

NONA. I guess not . . .

JOT. Why does papa catch 'em?

NONA (*smiling*). We got to eat, brother—that's why.

JOT. But fish don't like it . . .

NONA. Look, brother—it's fish or folks—if you had to choose which was to stay alive, what would you say?

JOT (*finally*). Fish.

The scene dissolves to a close view of BECKY. Becky is a very innocent-looking young girl. She is the daughter of Henry Devers, and life on her father's farm cannot be too easy. She is possessed by a terrific desire to know the world outside. At the moment, she is in the act of taking water from a well. The well-rope, as we can see, is extremely worn. The sound of a rustic flute is heard.

BECKY. One o' these days, this ol' rope is shore to break and we'll lose this bucket in the bottom o' the well.

FINLEY appears, blowing into a piece of corn-stalk out of which he has made himself a flute. He doesn't reply to Becky's statement, interested only in making her admire his music. He is a young man of about twenty with rather a blank look on his face. He is dressed in very old tattered clothes.

BECKY. You better git back to yer work right now. If my daddy sees ya loafin', he'll take the switch to ya.

Finley passes to the other side of the girl, continuing to play his simple melody.

BECKY. 'N anyhow, you're makin' me deef with that there squawkin'.

FINLEY. Don't ya like my music?

BECKY. Cose not . . . sounds silly.

FINLEY. All right, Becky. (*And he flings the instrument away over his shoulder.*)

We get a fairly close view of BECKY, FINLEY, DEVERS and later of SAM. In the background, Devers' truck appears. In the foreground, Finley runs back to his work, which turns out to be the week's washing. Becky goes off toward the house carrying her bucket of water. Devers gets out of his truck carrying an iron rod in his hand and goes toward a shed. Sam appears and starts toward Finley. At the door of the house, Becky, carrying her bucket, stops a moment before entering to look at Sam, interestedly.

SAM. Howdy. You the owner here?

Finley, surprised, turns around, but doesn't answer. Sam advances toward him, obviously friendly.

SAM. Shore is a fine place ya got here . . . (*He looks around him with admiration.*) Are you Henry Devers?

FINLEY. Nope. Folks call me Finley —He's my uncle—He's over yonder in the shed. (*He goes back to his washing with vigor.*)

SAM (*after staring curiously at Finley a moment*). Much obliged.

Sam goes toward the shed which Finley has indicated. In the background Becky comes out of the house to get some wood.—BECKY is seen closely as she picks up her wood, then looks at Sam with great interest.

Sam arrives at the shed, stops and looks at Devers who is heating the metal rod in a forge. In the shed there are quantities of old junk picked up from here and there; old automobile wheels, old pieces of cable, old pipes. All this is stacked and hung neatly, and we feel that this man, when he is out on the road, picks up any old thing that he thinks might come in handy some day.

SAM. Howdy!

We now get a close view of DEVERS. Devers is a big strong middle-aged farmer, with a stupid stubborn face, who always seems to distrust the person he is speaking to. He is wearing very old clothes, patched, but well kept and clean like his farm . . . At the moment he is encouraging the fire with an old pair of bellows.

DEVERS. Whut d'ya want?

SAM advances toward Devers inside the shed.

SAM. I'm yer neighbor. Name's Tucker. Brought you a fish.

DEVERS looks at Sam with suspicion, and then takes the metal rod and a hammer and starts forging on an anvil.

DEVERS. Ya mean do I wanna buy it?

SAM. Oh, no—it's a present.

DEVERS. All right—leave him if ya ain't got no use fer him . . .

He goes back to his forging without paying any more attention to Sam.

SAM. Where should I put him?

DEVERS. Oh, anywhere . . . on the table.

Sam puts the fish down on a work-table, then looks interestedly at the work that Devers is doing. The metal rod has now become an enormous fish-hook.

SAM. That's a mighty queer fish-hook y're making there . . .

DEVERS (*evasively*). I ain't no grabbler . . . I fish hook 'n line.

SAM (*becoming more curious*). Ya figger on usin' it in this river?

DEVERS (*annoyed*). I figger on usin' it wherever I feel like it.

Devers plunges the red-hot hook into a bucket of cold water, which creates a cloud of steam. Then he calls.

DEVERS. Finley!

He whistles at his nephew as he would to a dog, and Finley appears immediately.

DEVERS. Here, Finley. Take this here fish and give it to Becky to cook fer dinner.

Finley picks up the fish from the table. Becky appears and looks at Sam.

BECKY. You the new neighbor? I'm Becky Devers . . .

SAM. Yes, ma'am—we're the Tuckers—

BECKY. Be right nice to have folks nex' door—It's lonesome here.

DEVERS. What are you doin' here? I never called ya . . .

BECKY. But, Papa . . . I thought. . . .

DEVERS. You don't need to think. Take this here fish and git back to the house.

BECKY. All right, Papa. . . .

She takes the fish and walks away. Finley, realizing that his uncle is angry, tries to be friendly.

FINLEY. Oh, that there's a real fine fish . . . it's a beauty.

DEVERS (*impatiently*). Hurry up— git back to yer washin'. (*Finley exits hurriedly.*)

SAM and DEVERS appear close. Sam finally decides to speak.

SAM (*after a moment*). My wife'll likely be over here 'fore long to borrow water from yer well.

DEVERS (*turning, after a moment*). So that's what ya come for. . . .

SAM (*quietly*). That's right. My well ain't no good.

DEVERS (*fixing the hook with a vise*). I could have told ya that.

SAM. So kin I . . . now. What about the water?

DEVERS. Why don'tcha git it at the river?

SAM. River water ain't no good for the kids to drink . . .

DEVERS (*taking up a drill to make a hole in the hook*). Well, all right— long's there's plenty o' water. But when summer comes, you'll have to make other arrangements . . . gits purty weak in dry weather. (*He starts to drill—Sam watching.*) We'll take turns about replacin' the woreout rope.

SAM, seen close: he is more and more amazed by his neighbor's strange manner.

SAM (*somewhat reluctantly, looking toward the well*). Seems like it's purty wore-out already . . .

DEVERS (*seen close*). If ya don't like it, nex' well's five mile down the road.

SAM is seen close. He is determined to remain calm so as to get the water.

SAM. All right. It suits me.

Devers picks up a file and begins to work on the hook. He suddenly looks at Sam now, whereas in the beginning of the scene he seemed, for the most part, to be watching only his work.

DEVERS. Yer likely gonna fix yer own well, ain'tcha? If yer rentin' ya must have some savin's put aside.

SAM (*looking back at Devers with defiance*). I got two strong arms—that's worth more than savin's . . .

DEVERS (*with a little laugh*). There's folks think they kin be farmers jes' like that—with their bare hands! Ya got tools—a tractor?

SAM. I got no tractor—but I got two mules, and a good old plow—friend o' mine's lendin' the seed.

DEVERS. 'N Ruston furnishes the fertilizer—don' need much fer good muddy land like that—'n he gives you the poison for the weevils; pays the cottonpickers 'n even lets you draw grub from his commissary after you git the ground broke—yeah—he furnishes 'most everything but the sweat. 'N if ya git through the year he generously leaves ya take your share o' the crop—ain't that right?

SAM. Why ask me? Seems like you already know it . .

DEVERS. No . . . but I know Ruston. This ain't the fust time he's gitten a piece o' land cleaned off fer nothin' . . An' till ya start plowin' and kin draw rations from him, how ya aim to eat?

SAM. I aim to fish, 'n hunt varmints 'n sell a few skins. Lots o' folks live like that 'round here, 'n lots of 'em done it b'fore.

DEVERS. That's up to you—you go ahead 'n clear that land, 'n when ya get it cleared off mebbe Ruston'll sell it to me—'n I'll git it like I always wanted it, ready for plowin' 'n plantin'.

SAM. Too bad fer you—but I got a deal—'an nothin's gonna stop me from growin' my own crop. . . .

DEVERS. We'll see 'bout that. . . .

SAM (*seen close*). 'N how 'bout you? How'd you git started?

DEVERS (*seen close*). Share-croppin'.

Since the tone of the conversation has risen, Devers has completely stopped his work on the fish hook. His tone of voice is now passionate.

DEVERS. The fust year my whole crop wuz ruint by the hail. The second year, the hoof 'n mouth took my cow 'n pig I'd spent all my savin's fer. My woman caught a cold 'nd she died. Two years later, one of my kids died, the boy, from spring sickness—mebbe I lost em both, my wife 'n kid, cause I didn't have no money fer doctorin'.

SAM, seen close, listens, struck by this account of catastrophes, which somewhat explains his neighbor's strange character.

DEVERS. 'N here I am—with a good farm—b'longs all t' me—'n it's wuth lots o' money—only, I know what it cost me. So when I see young folks like you, with their plumb sureness 'n their noses in the air—it jus' makes me laugh.

SAM. Well, much obliged fer the water . . good luck with the fish hook. (*Sam exits. Devers stands in deep thought.*)

SAM and FINLEY: In the foreground, Finley is hanging up his washing to dry. As Sam passes near him, he gets an idea. He goes up to Finley.

SAM. Whut's that great big ol' fish hook yer uncle's makin'? Any whale in this river?

NONA: It's our first fire in our own house.

SAM: Hold on, everybody, there's goin' to be a blessing.

NONA: Sam . . . I'm afraid.

SAM: 'N now, Devers, I'm goin' to break yer neck.

FINLEY. That's fer Lead Pencil.

SAM. Lead Pencil? What's that?

FINLEY. A catfish—he's got chin whiskers like lead pencils—the bigges' durndes catfish ya ever seen in the river.

We now get a long view of SAM, FINLEY, DEVERS and BECKY: In the background Becky appears on the doorstep and looks at Sam and Finley. Then Devers comes out of the shed and sees that Finley has stopped working.

DEVERS. Finley, ain't ya finished the washin' yet?

FINLEY. Right away, Uncle Henry.

DEVERS. Hurry up, then, 'stead o' gabbin' so much.

Devers goes back into the shed. Finley hurriedly goes back to work again. Becky, at the door of the house, waves in a friendly manner to Sam who responds politely and goes off as the scene fades out.

BECKY. Come over again.

SAM. Thank you, Ma'am.

## DAISY'S COAT

It is the end of day, and there is a violent wind. We see some leafless branches blowing in the wind. Next we see a PUDDLE OF WATER, covered by a thin layer of ice, as a heavily shod foot breaks the ice.

Sam, followed by Zoonie, is going toward the house, which appears lugubrious in the winter wind. A bare tree is shaking violently. Clouds of smoke are coming out of the chimney like little whirlwinds.

Sam goes up the porch steps and opens the door. The wind causes many things inside to blow around. In the background, we see the rest of the family. Sam enters quickly.

INSIDE THE ROOM, Sam closes the door. Daisy runs after the pages of an old catalog that the wind has blown in all directions. Jot helps her. Zoonie hurries over to the stove. Nona and Granny look at Sam. Nona gets up, and approaches Sam who hangs up his gun in the foreground. In the background, Daisy and Jot are watching.

NONA (*in a low tone*). Nuthin? . . . (*Sam replies with a shake of his head which means no.*) Must be the wind . . .

SAM. It's more the signs—Fer days now, the moon's been risin' closer and closer to the north star—animals don't like that—they hide out. It's foolish to go against the signs . . . but what can we do . . . gotta try to get food.

NONA (*thinking a moment*). Daisy, honey, why don' you 'n I'll brother go to sleep? It's nice 'n warm in bed.

In the background we see Daisy and Jot, disappointed, going toward their bed. In the foreground, Sam approaches the stove to get warm. Nona puts some wood into the fire.

SAM. You have a good day in school, sister?

Daisy, beside her bed, starts to answer, but Nona cuts her off.

NONA. She didn't go . . .

SAM. Why not?

NONA. It's too cold, Sam—she ain't got no coat. I'm scairt she'll ketch her death . . . .

SAM. Daisy's gotta go to school! Jes'

cause we're havin' hard times right now—ain't no reason to stop nothin'. Things gotta go on—once we give up, jus' won't have the courage to git ourselves back to good times . . .

DAISY, JOT and GRANNY: In the foreground, Daisy and Jot get into their bed. In the background, Granny rocks suspiciously in her rocking chair—she has a blanket over her knees.

GRANNY. As I see it, ain't gonna have no supper again tonight. . . .

We see SAM and NONA closely. Sam stirs the fire as he reflects.

NONA (attempting buoyancy). To-morrow for breakfast, we'll have a nice big bowl o' cornmeal mush.

GRANNY. When y' all look on my col' dead face in that county pine box, mebbe ya'll be sorry then.

NONA (furious at Granny's ranting). Ya keep on promisin', Granny, but ya don't never deliver the goods.

GRANNY. You hush your mouth. Cain't talk t'me like that—You ain't even a real Tucker!!

NONA. Well, you ain't either, Granny . . .

Sam makes a gesture for Nona to be quiet. We understand that he has an idea.

SAM. Daisy's gotta be coated—she gotta go to school. (He moves toward Granny.)

In the foreground we see the children in bed—Granny in the background. Sam approaches Granny and, with a quick motion, takes her blanket off her lap. She tries in vain to hold on to this treasure.

GRANNY. Don't you touch my blanket,

Sam Tucker! Don't you touch my blanket.

Without getting disturbed, Sam, holding the blanket, goes toward the children's bed.

SAM. Git up, sister. (Daisy gets up in bed.)

GRANNY. Sam Tucker—if you touch one thread of my bes' blanket—you'll be punished for it . . .

NONA (violently, to Granny). Granny, ain't you got no heart?—Do you want Daisy to ketch her death? Don't you want her t'have no coat? There'll be enough blanket left to keep you warm . . .

GRANNY (just as violently). I like it big.

In the foreground, Sam is measuring Daisy's shoulders on the blanket; he takes his knife out of his pocket and starts to cut.

GRANNY. Cuss you—Sam Tucker— My bes' blanket . . . Cuss you . . .

NONA (talking at the same time). Hush your mouth, Granny—Yer grandson Sam Tucker's the boss 'round here . . . kin cut up all the blankets he wants—kin bust up anything he likes in this here house . . . Sam's the boss—hear?—the boss . . . (Now trying to calm her and console her) Oh, Granny, don't take on so. Look, I think I know where there's a ·nice swarm o' wild bees. Maybe tomorrow I'll go out and get you some honey . . . maybe.

GRANNY. Wild bees . . . wild bees don't care much fer folks coming and helping theirselves, ya know.

NONA. Now, don't you worry. I'll git yer honey.

GRANNY. I guess you're rightly a Tucker, after all.—An' that Sam of yours . . . he's most as good a man as Fayette.

In the foreground, very quietly, Sam goes ahead with his tailoring. Jot seems frightened by all the fracas.—Sam calms him with a gesture and continues his work, And now he has a coat wrapped around Daisy, and even Granny admires it as the scene fades out.

## THE 'POSSUM

A close view of ZOONIE and of SAM'S HANDS fades in.

Zoonie is barking furiously at the foot of a tree in which there is a hole. Sam's hands have finished preparing a bonfire of leaves which he lights. He watches the fire getting started. Then the view moves toward the top of the tree. A little smoke begins to rise and shoots up through the top of the tree. A little animal appears. Its back can barely be seen through the branches. SAM takes aim, fires and follows with his eyes, the 'possum which falls out of the tree.

SAM (*with great enthusiasm*). Yippee!

ZOONIE runs over and picks up the 'possum. He barks joyously.

SAM: Hey Zoonie, come here. (*Taking the 'possum from Zoonie*) Come here.

SAM looks at the 'possum, which is very fat. On Sam's face, there is an expression of great joy.

SAM (*looking at it*). Yes, that carcass of yours is sure gonna make four more Tuckers mighty happy. (*Starting forward*) Come on, Zoonie. (*Looking at the 'possum again*) Yes,

sir, your hide will just about bring the price of a pair of silk stockings for Nona . . . nice an' shiny.

Followed by Zoonie, who is jumping and barking, SAM goes quickly off toward the farm, and the scene dissolves to another view of SAM and ZOONIE in another part of the woods. Sam starts to run. And the scene moves on to show Sam jumping over a ditch and shouting with delight. This again dissolves to a view of Sam sliding down a little slope, and then to the INTERIOR OF THE HOUSE. In the foreground, Nona is nailing a sole onto one of Sam's shoes. Jot is sleeping on his pallet. Granny is stretched out on hers, and the remaining half of the cover is over her. We hear Zoonie barking and Sam shouting. Nona gets up, deeply moved. Then Granny gets up too, and Jot gets on his knees in his bed. The door opens and Sam appears, holding the 'possum in his hands. Zoonie continues to bark. Sam is silent.

We get a close view of NONA as she looks at Sam and then for one moment looks as though she is going to faint with joy. She gets hold of herself and walks solemnly over to a crude shelf. The view moves with her as she picks up a kitchen knife and a whet-stone and starts sharpening the knife vigorously.

NONA (*smiling happily*). Reckon we kin eat purty soon, folks.

## THE DINNER

The 'possum is cooking in a pot on the stove, and we hear the noise and voices of the family taking their places around the table. A hand picks up the pot and takes it off the stove. The view moves to Nona who has put the pot on the table. Everybody is awaiting the feast with great excitement. A respectful silence welcomes the long awaited food. Granny is beaming from ear to ear. Before anybody else, she sticks her hand out to grab a piece of meat. Nona stops her. This gesture breaks the silence. Jot, on Sam's lap, begins to tap the table with his spoon to attract his mother's attention. Daisy points to the piece that she wants.

DAISY. I wanna leg, mama; I wanna leg.

NONA. Easy, you'll all get your share.

SAM. Hold on, everybody, there's goin' to be a blessing. (*He bends his head low, and the others follow suit.*) Much obliged, Lord. Looks like the Tuckers are going to make the grade after all. Amen.

NONA (*putting a piece of meat in Granny's plate*). Granny! . . .
Granny gets the first because she's the eldest.

We get a close view of GRANNY and of NONA's HAND. Nona's hand puts a second piece of meat in front of Granny. Granny looks at her food. Her face becomes serious and she starts bolting her food ravenously.

GRANNY. I'd taken the Lord to be a stranger in this house.

NONA's VOICE. Then comes Jottie, 'cause he's the littlest.

SAM and JOT: Nona's hand puts a piece of meat on the plate in front of Jot who is on Sam's lap. Much to Sam's amusement, Jot takes the piece of meat in his hands and starts biting into it.

NONA's VOICE. Then comes Papa, 'cause he caught the 'possum.

We see ZOONIE and NONA's HAND: Nona's hand gives Zoonie a meaty bone.

NONA's VOICE. And this one's for Zoonie, 'cause he helped.

NONA and DAISY are seen closely as Nona sits down next to Daisy and continues serving.

NONA. Last of all come Daisy 'n me, 'cause we're the women-folk.

DAISY (*as she eats, cheerfully*). At school they say this kin' o' food's bad fer ya all the time. (*She takes a big mouthful.*) They say ya gotta eat vegetables. Too much meat's bad.

NONA. Vegetables—in winter?

DAISY. If ya don'—they say—ya git—pella—pellagra.

NONA. That must be spring sickness, Sam.

SAM (*disbelievingly*). Why, it's eatin' vegetables that causes spring sickness. That's when ya git it. Right 'bout the time ya start eatin' vegetables.

We get a close view of GRANNY, who nods sagely.

GRANNY (*her mouth full*). I ought to know. I lost three o' mine from it. (*To Sam*) Yer Uncle Walter—yer Aunt Bet and Sue. And not one of 'em wuz over six.

Sam stops eating for a few seconds, then he looks at Jot who is silently and delightedly gnawing at a bone. He also looks at Daisy. Sam waves his hand in a gesture of doubt.

SAM. Shucks. Look at them! Anything a body likes as good as that couldn't be bad fer 'em. (*Turning toward Nona*) Ain' that true, Nona?

NONA, seen closely, has already started to eat. She stops and looks at Sam, smiling confidently.

NONA. That's right, Sam.

[We get a close view of GRANNY as she stops eating for a second and looks at Nona and Sam.

GRANNY. I s'pose t'night the blanket'll go up on the wall again.

Granny returns to her eating seriously as the scene fades out.]

## SPRING

A close view of a BRANCH of A TREE in bloom fades in, and in a series of fairly close views we see some BIRDS; some FISH in the river: and finally SAM as he is clearing the brush with a machete. —This dissolves to a scene in which SAM and NONA are burning piles of the cut brush and big flames flare up. This dissolves to a close view of SAM as he presses down on the plow-handles, following which we see NONA, up at the mules' heads, helping get them started off.

Finally we get a view of a PLOWSHARE. The plowshare is ready to cut into the earth. We hear Sam's voice, then Nona's rein egging the mules on. The plowshare starts, cutting open the earth.

Next, the plow traces a furrow where before there was only brush. This dissolves to a long view of SAM, NONA and ZOONIE, and we see that half of the field has been plowed. And this dissolves to a long view of SAM, NONA and ZOONIE when the entire field has been plowed. Sam stops the plow and approaches the mules.

We then see SAM, NONA and the MULES at close range as Sam and Nona stroke the mules' noses and look at the field. As they did in the beginning when they arrived at the farm, Sam puts his arm around Nona.

SAM. We done that all ourselves. Kept workin' and pluggin' away, an' by gosh, we done good. 'Fore long now, we can start plantin' our cotton . . . round about the Twin Days. Then our crop will really get started. (*On this the scene fades out.*)

## JOT IS ILL

We see SAM fishing in the river while NONA and JOT are watching. The river is broad and gleaming.

SAM (*pointing to the tree whose branches hang over the river*). See those little green woolly worms falling out of that tree? They're all drifting down together to the same place. Now, some folks might think that that was what Lead Pencil's after. But they'd be wrong. 'Cause he's after somethin' else. He ain't interested in no worms. Old Lead's a pretty smart old guy. Wouldn't hardly live to be as old as he is if he wasn't. I bet you old Lead waits for his dinner right over yonder by that there drift. It's like a trap on the river bottom.

JOTTIE. Is Lead Pencil older than Granny, Papa?

SAM. Yes, he's older than Granny. Yes, sir. It must be yonder Old Lead Pencil's got his cover. (*Throwing Nona a fish*) Here you are, honey.

The scene dissolving, we see Granny coming out on the porch and calling out as Nona and Sam are busy planting cotton seed.

GRANNY (*very loudly because of the distance*). Sam, Nonie—y'all come here quick.

We see SAM, NONA and ZOONIE as Sam and Nona continue to sow their seeds as they look toward Granny. Zoonie follows them.

SAM (*shouting*). What're you sayin', Granny?

They continue their work, without paying much attention to Granny.

GRANNY (*very proud to have such important news; shouting*). Jot's ailin'. (*Sure of the effect*) Reckon he's got the spring sickness!

The scene cuts to NONA, SAM, the MULES and ZOONIE: Nona stops and looks toward Granny with terror.

NONA. Whut ya sayin', Granny?

Sam stops the mules and comes over to Nona, followed by Zoonie.

SAM (*shouting*). Spring sickness? How d'ya know?

GRANNY'S VOICE (*very sure of herself*). I say it's the spring sickness! Who'd know it quicker 'n me, that's already lost three from it?

Nona and Sam look at each other and start toward the house. Before walking away, followed by Zoonie, Sam calls to the mules.

SAM (*to the mules*). Y'all stay here . . .

NONA. Sam . . . I'm afraid.

## THE DOCTOR

We get a fairly close view of a DOCTOR, NONA and JOT in the doctor's office.— The doctor is a very old man, dressed in somewhat old-fashioned clothes, which hardly express comfort or wealth. He is holding Jot on his knees, wiping his face with cotton. Nona is standing facing them. The room is very simple. Through the window we see people

going to a carnival and we hear the music of the merry-go-round.

NONA (*embarrassed*). I didn't see no reason to bother you, doctor—(*Looking at the child's face*) It wuz jes' a l'il sore—'n sonny ain' really been sick all his life—but I got to watchin' it day by day—'n it grew 'n spread 'til it seems like now it's jes' plumb gonna possess him . . .

The doctor gets up and hands the baby over to Nona who continues to explain. Then he goes over to a medicine cabinet which he opens.

NONA (*frantically*). Ya see, doctor, it's like as if there wuz some kin' o' evil crawlin' worms eatin' up our baby—I jes' can't stand t'watch it no more—gotta do somethin' to stop it.

DOCTOR (*looking for something in the medicine cabinet*). You don't have a cow, do you?

NONA. No, sir.

DOCTOR. Well, you better tell Sam to get one.

NONA (*in despair*). How could we get a cow?

DOCTOR. Borrow one; let Sam raise a heifer for somebody. Or borrow some milk, anyway. A pint a day—or better still, a quart. Any neighbor with a cow can spare you that.

NONA. I'll try, doctor. What medicine?

The doctor, without answering, takes all the necessities for a hypodermic out of the cabinet.

DOCTOR. Undress the boy . . .

Nona goes to an operating table, puts Jot down and proceeds to undress him. The doctor comes over to them.

DOCTOR. What vegetables have you been eating lately?

NONA. Vegetables? Couldn't grow vegetables in winter.

The doctor takes the hypodermic syringe out of its box.

DOCTOR. Have you got any money?

NONA. Yes, doctor. I got yer two dollars. (*She fumbles in her worn purse.*) And Sam has a dollar and thirty-five cents more. (*She offers the doctor the two dollars; he thrusts it aside, disguising his pity and exasperation with rudeness.*)

DOCTOR. Keep it. Where's Sam?

NONA. He's waitin' fer me at Harmie's store.

DOCTOR. You take all yer money and spend it all on vegetables, and get some lemons; give him a glass of lemonade twice a day. And get that milk, do you hear? (*The doctor shows Nona the hypodermic which is now ready.*) If you don't give him milk and vegetables, anything I can do will be just plumb wasted.

NONA. And with the milk and vegetables?

DOCTOR (*pensively*). I think he's got a chance.

The doctor fills the hypodermic with the contents of a glass tube.

## HARMIE'S GROCERY STORE

We now get a view of the interior and exterior of Harmie's Store. It is a typical village general store in which a little of everything is sold. Then we see HARMIE and some CUSTOMERS: Harmie is a simple man, happy and full of the joy of living. He looks very good-natured. He is eating cherries. From outside, in the street, we hear the noise of the carnival.

HARMIE (*to a customer, giving him change*). Thank you, call again. (*Turning to a group of listeners*) Me, I know—I know what war is . . . When we was right close to Chateau-Thiery—the Old Cunnel, he brung us all together—'n he said . . .

We get a close view of TIM, one of the listeners. He is a stocky, young blade, with apparently not a worry in the world. He is dressed like a city worker, but has retained his village accent. He is seated on the counter with his legs hanging. He, too, is eating cherries.

TIM. He said: Young men—in civilian life, don't brag about your conquests whether it be love or war.

We get a fairly close view, from the counter, of HARMIE, TIM, and some VILLAGERS, with Harmie and Tim in the foreground. In the background through the door and window we see the street. Some villagers listen to the conversation. A lady, elderly and rather severe looking, is serving herself, filling a shopping bag with all sorts of things.

HARMIE. Aw, shut up, feller—I'm tellin' ya—I know . . . and I know I know . . .

In the background we see Sam coming into the store.

LADY. How much for these here pipe cleaners?

HARMIE. Ten cents a package.

LADY. Ain't they gone up? Usta be a nickel . . .

HARMIE (*bored*). No, Ma'am.

LADY. They're fer my husband. . . .

HARMIE. Ol' Zeke'll be mighty pleased with 'em, ma'am. (*Turning to Sam and indicating Tim*) He jes' came back to show off his city clothes . . .

A CUSTOMER. Yeah . . . take a look at that fancy tie. . . .

ANOTHER CUSTOMER. An' how!— Seems like in the city, dollars grows faster than beans in the fields. . . .

TIM. Don't pay them yokels no mind, Sam. I been lookin' fer you—C'mon over to Seaman's—I'll buy us a beer 'n tell ya all 'bout it.

SAM. Man, I'm with ya any old time for a beer—(*To Harmie*) Nona 'n the baby are over to Doc White's, Harmie. When they come over, tell 'em I'll be back in a minute, will you?

HARMIE. Yeah—I know whut a minute means when yer drinkin' beer with ol' Tim there. (*Sam and Tim exit toward the door.*) That ol' cunnel! Jes' a l'il ol' guy—but he sure was one with the ladies—Ooh la la! Them French gals. . . .

We get a close view of a LADY as she holds up a pair of eyelash curlers.

LADY. How much for this eyelash curlin' machine?

HARMIE (*seen closely*). That fer yer husband?

LADY. How much for this pair of garters, please?

In a moving view outside HARMIE's STORE we see Sam, Tim, villagers and several Negroes. Sam and Tim close the door. There is much activity in the street due to the carnival. A group of children pass by, eating ice cream cones.

Two young girls pass by, accompanied by two young men. A child pulls its mother by the hand and insists:

CHILD. Mama—I wanna ride on the merry-go-round—I wanna ride—

The view moves and shows the little carnival in the background. Sam and Tim go toward the bar; from time to time, they interrupt their conversation to say, "Howdy" to an acquaintance.

TIM. Did Nona and Jottie go over to Old Doc White?

SAM (*worried*). Yeah.

TIM. What's wrong, Sam?

SAM. Oh, Jottie's ailin'. Granny says it's spring sickness. Poor Nona. With a sick kid, she don't hardly get a wink of sleep.

TIM. Gee, that's tough, Sam.

SAM. My ma came out to my place yesterday to help. Harmie brought her out in his truck. That's kind of a relief.

TIM. Sam, you be interested in comin' to work in the factory with me?

SAM. You gone crazy? What would I be doin' in a factory?—I'm a farmer . . .

TIM. They just opened a new plant. They're cryin' for men—don't even hafta be skilled—I know the foreman—could git ya on in a minute . . .

SAM. They pay much?

TIM. Seven bucks a day.

SAM (*impressed*). Seven bucks a day! (*They go into the saloon.*)

## THE BAR

We now see the interior of SEAMAN's

BAR: SAM, TIM, the BARTENDER, a GIRL and SEVERAL CUSTOMERS are in it.

It is a large, dark, dank place with soap-lettering on the mirror behind the bar and sawdust on the floor. As Sam and Tim enter, two men who have been playing dominoes get up and leave. An Old Mexican, standing at the bar, is drinking methodically. He continues during the entire scene, without paying attention to any of the action. A sad-eyed blonde, named Lizzie, who leans against the bar filing her nails, looks up at them. They ignore her and go to the middle of the bar. The bartender, a large man with drooping chins, turns from figuring in a book and approaches them.

BARTENDER. Hello, gents. What'll it be?

TIM (*affably*). Ain't ya new here?

BARTENDER (*ignoring him*). What'll it be?

TIM (*eyeing him*). Okay, Big Shot. Two bottles o' beer.

The bartender turns, takes two wet bottles from the ice and, levering off the caps, sets them on the bar. Lizzie edges up to Tim.

LIZZIE (*seen close with Tim*). Shore is hot in here—How 'bout a beer for me? I'm mighty thirsty.

TIM. Why don't ya ask yer sweet papa there? He gits it wholesale.

LIZZIE. Oh, him—this ain't one o' his good days—musta got outta bed on the wrong side.

TIM. Well, I got out on the right side —Bartender! Another beer.

The bartender looks furious at this conversation. He puts a bottle of beer in front of Lizzie, who sits down next to Sam.

Lizzie tries to be friendly to Sam, who is thinking of what Tim told him in the street and pays no attention to the girl.

LIZZIE. Ain't I seen you somewhere before?

SAM (*who doesn't reply at first*). Huh? What'd you say?

LIZZIE. I ast ya ain't I never seen ya before?

SAM. Could be—I don't know.

LIZZIE. You in town all alone?

SAM. Nope—like ya see, I'm with my friend here—'n my wife's waitin' fer me at Harmie's store. . . .

LIZZIE. Oh! So you gotta wife. . . .

SAM. Yep—I gotta wife.

LIZZIE. There's some what's got wives' an' are still nice an' friendly. . . .

SAM. I'm sorry, ma'am—I was studyin' 'bout somethin'.

SAM, TIM, LIZZIE and the BARTENDER are seen together. Tim is annoyed by the girl's advances to Sam.

TIM (*to Sam*). Let's go down to the end o' the bar, pal. We cain't talk here.

They pick up their beer bottles and go off. Lizzie looks insulted. As he passes by her, Tim speaks:

TIM (*to Lizzie*). I ain't got no wife waitin' fer me, baby—how 'bout a date tonight?

LIZZIE (*furious*). You big fat hog— you know what you kin do with yer date . . .

TIM. Okay,—okay, Baby. We'll talk about it later. (*Sam and Tim sit down at the other end of the bar.*) To yer kids, Sam. (*They both drink.*)

SAM (*pensive*). Seven bucks a day. . . .

TIM. So it's yes? You'll come?

SAM (*shaking his head*). Don't rightly see how I could. . . . Made a deal with Ruston. . . . I awready got some credit at his commissary . . .

TIM. Man, with seven bucks a day, wouldn't take long to pay him back.

SAM. Yeah, but I'll tell ya, Tim— this is the first time I'm growin' my own crop—jes' the way I want to. That's somethin' I couldn't give up jes' like that.

TIM. How much kin ya make on yer crop?

SAM. Man, with that there ground I got, it'll be the best crop in the country.

TIM. What does that mean, the best crop in the country?

SAM. With any luck I could hope to make two bales per acre.

TIM. How much will that make fer you?

SAM. That'll make more than fifty bales!

TIM. I mean how much money?

SAM. Do you know that on that ground that I've been workin' on now, Old Man Corinth made a fortune in the last cotton boom—a real fortune!

TIM. Oh . . . so that's the idea . . . all you farmers is jes' the same— gamblers is whut y'all are—to a man. Year after year ya starve to death in the hope that *some* fine day. . . . Well, I think you're nuts! Me, I'd ruther be safe first . . .

SAM. Me, I'd ruther work in my fields—I feel better there that way. I feel more free. . . . .

TIM. Free . . . . free. . . . . With money in yer pocket, yer free as the wind. (*He takes a money clip full of bills out of his pocket.*) With this, if ya want a good meal, ya go to a restaurant—a good room, ya go to a hotel. All ya gotta do is flash yer greenbacks 'n ya kin have anything ya want.

Tim slips a five-dollar bill from the clip and puts the clip back in his pocket. During the rest of the scene he plays with the bill he has in his hand, ready to pay for the beer.

TIM. Ya call that free—sweatin' from mornin' till night, in that bakin' hot sun, workin' in them fields?

SAM. Oh, I 'low as how it's some- times purty hard—but whut I mean is, bein' able to decide things fer myself.—(*He is now seen close.*) To know that I kin choose my own time fer plowin', 'n sowin' the seed, 'n harvestin' my crop—'n that I kin do it all my own way—'n not have to answer to nobody. I mean fer me alone to be 'countable fer it, no mat- ter if the weevils strip it clean, or if it's the best crop in the country.

We get a close view of TIM. He is drinking beer and listening to Sam as though he were slightly demented.

SAM'S VOICE. If I gotta be told whut to do—when to start, when to eat, and when to stop at night, and go home—If I hafta punch a clock 'n 'bide by the will o' machines—If I don't feel really 'countable fer things I raise with these here hands, then it seems to me like I ain't rightly a man no more.

We get a close view of SAM and TIM.

SAM. Shore, my mules is happy thataway. They don't bother their heads over nothin'. I tell 'em what to do, to pull the plow or cart the wood—'n when they're tard I'm the one decides when they git a rest. 'N as long as I feed 'em good, they're happy.

TIM. Then—all that baloney . . . that means No?

SAM. I'm afraid so, Tim.

TIM. Ya want another beer?

SAM. No, thanks jes' the same.

Tim pounds on the counter. His hand is holding a five-dollar bill. The bartender takes the bill from Tim and gives him some change.

TIM. Well, pal—I think you're makin' a big mistake.

SAM. Mebbe so—but you don't really b'lieve that money is everything? Shore, man, I like to have money— I work real hard fer it, but I like to live on my farm 'n be happy with Nona 'n the kids too. . . .

TIM. Man, you got ideas from outen a different world—you been in the sticks too long. Well, if ya ever change yer mind, you know where to find me—(*Noticing the change the bartender has given him*) Hey, bartender—where's my other four dollars?

BARTENDER. What four dollars? (*He turns to Lizzie.*) Lizzie, you seen that was a one!

LIZZIE. 'Course I did. That pretty boy that's goin' back to his wife . . . he seen it too!

TIM and SAM look at Lizzie, then at each other.

TIM. Well, I'll be doggoned! So that's

how it is! Nothin' but a hicky ol' farmer, 'n yet the gals fall fer ya like a ton o' bricks! What in heck you got that I cain't buy with my dough?

SAM (*politely, to the bartender*). I'm tellin' ya, mister—I seen that bill— it was a fiver.

TIM. An' how that was a fiver!

His anger becomes uncontrollable.

TIM (*roaring at the bartender*). Gimme that four dollars, ya big double-jointed son o' a skunk! Or I'll tear this joint down.

The bartender's hand rises above the level of the counter. It holds a forty-five revolver.

BARTENDER (*threateningly*). Outside.

Sam and Tim stand still, watching the bartender.

TIM (*finally*). Okay, brother—but I hope it's goin' t'be wuth four dollars to you. (*He turns and Sam follows him outside.*)

Tim and Sam come outside. Tim shoves his hands in his pockets and starts to walk up the street, toward some piles of sand and granite, tools and concrete mixer. The Carnival music is heard clearly. In the middle of the street repairs, some children are playing "War." There is much activity due to the Carnival.

SAM. Whut're you aimin' to do?

Tim, bursting with anger, does not reply. He stops at the pile of sand and granite and fills his shirt and pockets with big chunks of granite.

TIM. I ain't askin' ya to help, Sam. Ya gotta family. (*He leaves Sam and starts to go behind the concrete-mixer.*)

SAM. I wouldn't start no trouble, Tim.

TIM. Now don't stay here, Sam.

SAM. This is apt to cost ya more'n four dollars.

TIM. I'm askin' you please not to stay here.

Sam, torn between the desire to avoid trouble and the desire to help his friend, takes a few steps toward an empty lot next to the saloon. This lot is used as an unloading place for the saloon. In it, there are a truck, some cars, some old barrels, and so on.

TIM is seen closely as he throws a rock. —The windows of the bar smash to bits—glass flies about. In the foreground, Tim is throwing rocks.—The bartender comes running out. The children, playing "War," run away. Passersby start running also.

BARTENDER. Hey . . hey . . what're you doing? Hey . .

The Carnival music continues to be heard. In one moment, the street is cleared, except for Tim, Sam and the bartender. Tim is attacking vigorously with big rocks and the bartender runs back into the saloon. Sam, in the empty lot, is witness to the fight.

In the foreground, in the vacant lot, Sam watches. In the background, at the left, Tim picks up as many rocks as he can and advances toward the door of the bar, determined to demolish the place. In the background, right, the bartender goes out of a side door, opening onto the vacant lot, intending to take Tim by surprise, from behind. He has his revolver in his hand. Sam, seeing his friend in danger, picks up some stones and throws them at the bartender. The latter falls from a blow from Sam's rock. Lizzie comes out

screaming. In the background we see the Sheriff arriving and some villagers who want to stop the fight. Sam signals to Tim, who joins him. They run toward the back of the vacant lot—the view moving with them. They climb over a high fence and disappear. The merry-go-round music continues.

[The scene dissolves to a fairly close view of HARMIE, NONA, SAM, TIM, and some CUSTOMERS inside the store and, next, Harmie is hustling Nona out toward the yard which we can see in the background, and where Sam and Tim are preparing to get into Tim's car. The merry-go-round music can be heard. Nona is carrying Jot, who is crying.

HARMIE (to Nona). Here's five cans o' milk, Nona. That's even better than if it comes straight from the cow. (He hands Nona the milk and other packages.) Gimme that boy!

He helps her into the car, puts Jot in after her and they drive off. The customers have watched this whole scene with avid interest as the scene fades out.]

## THE VEGETABLE GARDEN

A "TRAVELING" view of Sam's FARM fades in, featuring SAM, NONA, JOT, GRANNY, MA, and ZOONIE.

The scene shifts to a close "shot" of JOT, in the arms of an unknown person, later identified as Ma. In spite of the heat, Jot's face is covered with a rag. He whimpers constantly. The person who is carrying him walks back and forth to quiet him. At this point we see the face of the person who is carrying him. It is Ma. She is about

fifty years old. Her usual aspect is
kindly and smiling. At this moment,
however, she is very much worried by
Jot's condition. She walks along the
river, trying to calm the little boy.—
Then we see the Tucker family planting the vegetable garden that the doctor ordered. Sam and Nona are digging
vigorously. Even Granny is helping.
She is carrying a bucket of water from
the river.

GRANNY (*lugging her bucket*). Milk
'n greens! Humph! That's whut that
doctor-man done said fer l'il Jot. Jes'
like to see *him* git them vegetables
to grow—'n where's he figger we're
gonna git that there milk! Jes' like
that—outten the sky—Why shuckins!
(*Noticing Ma*) Oh . . . seems like
Sam ain't the only pig-headed one
around here. That Ma of his . . .
humpf! Thinks she kin cure the
spring sickness with fresh air. A
widow-lady her age oughta have better sense. Me, I say that baby'll just
ketch his death in this here wind.

In a fairly close view we see SAM, NONA,
GRANNY, MA, JOT and ZOONIE.
Sam has just finished digging a row.
He leans on his spade and thinks. Sud-
denly, he sticks his spade in the ground
and starts off.

NONA. Where are you goin', Sam?

SAM. I'm goin' to git that milk . . .

Sam and Nona look haggard—We feel
that they are at the end of their courage. Ma passes in the background, carrying Jot, who is still crying. Sam stops
to look at his son as he leaves.

MA (*looking after him*). Poor Sam.

GRANNY (*watching Sam go—to Ma*).
Males in this here Tucker family jes'
ain't strong—my ol' man, Fayette

Tucker, upped 'n' died—jes' like
that—'n' son Lee—yer own husband
—he shore didn't live to git old—
Grandson Sam—seems like he's
strong—but you wait 'n' see. (*Pointing to Jot*) That li'l boy—I know
what I'm talkin' about—buried three
of 'em—fust they don't wanna eat—
then they cain't walk—'n' then one
fine day—(*With a gesture of finality
with her hand*) Pft! 'N' I say ain't
nuthin' a body kin do about it—no
doctor, no nothin'.

MA. You say nobody, Granny? Well!
—I say the Lord kin help him.

GRANNY (*defiantly*). The Preacher?

MA. I never said the Preacher—I said
the Lord. Can't afford to pass Him
up at a time like this.

NONA, seen closely, is working hard in
the garden with a hopeless expression
on her face as the scene dissolves.

## THE MILK

Devers' Farm dissolves in. In the foreground, Devers is talking to Sam. In
the background, Becky is finishing
milking a cow. Finley is preparing food
for the pigs. We are outside, in front
of Devers' pigpen.

DEVERS. No, sir, just like I tole you,
Tucker, I don't need no extry help—
I got Finley—'n my gal Becky. Too
bad about your boy—I know what
that is, a sick kid—very sorrowful!
Becky, you take that there milk over
to Finley.

Becky takes the bucket over to Finley.
—Sam listens solemnly to Devers, understanding that he's lost his plea.

DEVERS. But I tole ya before—it's
wrong for a man to be too big fer his
britches—When ya got no money, ya

work fer them what's got it—that there's the rule. Why don't ya go back to Ruston's? You'd git yer six bits a day—some milk fer yer chap—'n mebbe some doctorin' even . . .

Devers takes the bucket Becky has brought to Finley and pours the milk into the pigs' food.

DEVERS. 'Bout the milk—like ya see —it's too bad, but I cain't rightly spare ya a drop—

SAM, seen closely, listens, almost without a reaction of any kind. Devers' words place him once again before the awful dilemma—should he continue working for himself or not?

DEVERS' VOICE. Me, ain't got no milk fer myself—it's all fer the pigs.

We get a close view of DEVERS mixing the milk deliberately into the pig-food.

DEVERS. 'N yer cotton? Is it comin' along? Not too many bugs? I seen ya the other day in the field—ya was shavin' that cotton so close with yer plow, it scairt me. That's the best way to git rid o' the bugs—rolls 'em right out into the sun, 'n the heat kills 'em better'n any poison. But ya shore gotta have a good eye—'n a good steady hand. You're a fine worker, all right—if I was you I wouldn't think twice—I'd go back to work for Ruston.

SAM (seen closely). If I wanted to give up, wouldn't hafta go back to Ruston's . . .

DEVERS (very curious). Ya got somethin' better?

He pours the food to the pigs, and adds more milk.—SAM watches Devers but controls himself.

SAM. Yep—somethin' much better—but I already done tole ya—I wanna

grow my own crop an' I aim to do it!

DEVERS. If yer so sure o' yerself, how come ya allus comin' around askin' yer neighbors for help?

SAM. That's jes' whut I'm wonderin' —why I ever ast you fer anythin'— likely some old-fashioned idea I had 'bout neighborliness. . . . Well, s'long, Devers—take good care o' them pigs. . . .

DEVERS. That's sure whut I'm going to do. Finley, see that that black hog eats all his dinner, do you hear.

Sam goes off. Becky who has returned to the cow with a clean bucket, sits down to continue her milking. Devers goes into the house, leaving Finley to take care of the pigs.

BECKY is seen closely as she looks toward where Sam went off, and continues to milk the cow. Then the scene dissolves to a fairly close view of SAM and BECKY as Sam is walking along the river. He hears Becky calling him and stops. Becky joins him.—Becky is holding out a tin can full of milk.

BECKY. Here, take it—it's fer Jot. I kin git ya some more onct in a while —my daddy won't never see.

SAM. Oh, much obliged—I'll take it 'cause my boy's really bad off—but I'll pay ya fer it. . . . .

We see SAM and BECKY, and then FINLEY as Finley runs in and gets between Sam and Becky at the very moment when Sam was going to accept the milk.

FINLEY. Becky . . . Becky . . . I seen you . . . I seen what ya done . . .

SAM (angrily). I feel just like breaking somebody's neck today.

FINLEY. I'm gonna tell yer Paw yer

stealin' his milk . . . I knowed ya wuz hankerin' after this feller . . . I seen ya lookin' at 'im before. . . . Yer a hussy, that's whut ya are. I'm gonna tell yer Paw . . .

He snatches at the can of milk.—Becky tries to hold on to it. It falls on the ground, the milk spills and is lost. The fighting stops.—There are tears of anger in Becky's eyes.

BECKY. Oh Finley! You . . . . you . . . What'd you do that for? I ain't never goin' to speak to you again. . . . . .

FINLEY. An' if I see you talkin' to him again, you'll be sorry.

SAM (driving him off). Git, Finley. (He speaks kindly to Becky, as Finley runs away.) Don't you fret, Becky. I'll find some milk somehow . . . You're a good gal. 'N thanks jes' the same.

He exits as the scene dissolves to a fairly close view of SAM outside, then inside his farm.

Sam, returning from Devers' place is walking up the steps of the porch. He arrives at the door but hesitates to open it. On the porch wall there are some animal skins drying, and on the porch there is a bed. We hear Jot crying inside the house.

Sam hesitates a moment, then opens the door. Through the open door we see Nona, Granny, and Ma who is carrying the crying boy.

NONA. I can't listen to him cry no more, Sam.

Her face is wracked—we feel that she is at the end of her wits. She goes off toward the cotton field. Sam follows her, wanting to console her.

SAM. Honey . . . Nona—Nona—honey.

Nona, followed by Sam, walks in the middle of the young cotton. Sam is helpless before her misery.

SAM. Nona—Honey—Nona—

Nona replies by shaking her head hopelessly. We see only their silhouettes.— Suddenly, Nona is no longer able to control herself. She throws herself on the ground, face down; and we get a close view of NONA lying among the young cotton plants. She sobs and digs into the earth with her fingers.

We get a moving view of SAM and NONA.

The scene starts with a close-up of SAM looking helplessly at Nona. Suddenly, he turns his back and goes off in the cotton-field, and the scene shifts to Nona lying on the ground, sobbing.

Now Sam is seen in the foreground. In the background we see Nona lying on the ground. Suddenly, he stops and looks toward the sky.

SAM. Oh, Lord—How come You put that sky up there, 'n this ol' mud down here? . . . 'n made it so purty . . . if You don't want us to love it? Mebbe Ya changed Yer mind— Mebbe You want fer all Yer creatures to go live in the towns 'n work in the factories with the machines. Mebbe Tim's right—'n I oughta git in line 'n make my seven bucks a day—under a roof what hides Yer sky and puts out Yer light . . . Tell me, Lord—help me to know—

At this, the scene dissolves, and we see Harmie's truck driving up in front of the house. It stops. Tim, Harmie and Daisy jump out, all looking excited and very happy over the surprise they have in the truck. They go behind the truck, just below a cow which is standing in the back of it. Daisy has her school books in her arms.—Then we get a closer view of TIM, HARMIE, DAISY, and then the cow as Tim and Harmie start preparing to get her off the truck.

HARMIE (*to the cow*). Hi, Lady! Ja have a good trip? (*To Tim*) Come on, Timmy, 'n hep me with her—

TIM. Say! I'm leery o' them things. . . .

HARMIE. Waal I'll be a. . . . . This nice ol' gal won't never hurt ya— b'lieve you me, she's a lot more gentle than that Lizzie at the saloon. . . . . .

DAISY. Papa! Mamma! Tim 'n Harmie's brought a cow fer Jot—We gotta a cow fer Jot. . . . .

The scene dissolves to a close view of NONA sitting on an old packing box, milking the cow. The milk is pouring into a bucket. Her face is radiant with happiness.—This cuts to a view of SAM carrying JOT, who strangely enough has stopped crying. Sam is so happy he is speechless. He hugs the boy to his chest.—

ZOONIE, seen closely, is at Sam's feet. —Then we see everybody standing around Nona, watching her milk the cow.

GRANNY and DAISY are seen together; Daisy has gotten up on a fence, the better to see.

GRANNY (*grudgingly*). That Harmie! Wuz he to come waggin' in one o' these days with a boa-constrictor, I wouldn't be one bit surprised.

DAISY (*to Harmie*). Whut's her name, Uncle Harmie?

[HARMIE. Oh, I reckon she ain' rightly got no name.

Ma is holding Harmie's hand and is looking at him tenderly.

MA. I'd like to call her "Mercy o' God"!

SAM, TIM and JOT are seen closely.

TIM. All cows is called "Bossy," ain' they, Sam?

SAM. Sure, "Bossy" is a good name.]

DAISY. I'm gonna call her "Uncle Walter."

The scene fades out.

## LEAD PENCIL

[A fairly close view of MA and JOT, inside Sam's house, fades in. Ma is sitting on Granny's rocking-chair. Jot is asleep on his pallet.—It is very hot, and we are aware of the many flies buzzing around Jot, which Ma is shooing away. Suddenly she dozes off in her chair.—We get a close view of JOT as a fly wakes him up. He pushes off his blanket, sits up, shakes his arms and legs and decides to try to get up off his pallet.

JOT moves painfully, slowly, as he is still very weak on his legs. He goes haltingly toward the table.—On the table there is a dish full of berries. Jot pulls this dish toward himself. He fills both his hands with the berries and starts stuffing them into his mouth, getting them all over his face.

The noise of the dish moving on the table wakes MA. She looks anxiously towards Jot's pallet and is astonished at not seeing him. She looks around and discovers him at the table. Her face lights up.

MA. Jot! Baby! Jottie's walkin'!!!

MA gets up, hurries toward the little boy and takes him in her arms. She covers him with kisses thereby getting her own face smeared with blueberries. Then in a rush of wild joy, she hurries toward the door.—We next see her out on the porch, still carrying Jot. Ma looks to see where Sam and Nona might be in the fields.

MA. Sam . . . My boy . . . Nona . . . Granny . . . Jottie's walkin'! Everythin's fine again! Our l'il feller's cured!

This dissolves to a close view of a HAND. It is forging a big fish-hook on a small home-made anvil. And this dissolves to a fairly close view of NONA, JOT, GRANNY, and later on, SAM, DAISY and ZOONIE.

Nona is in the act of bathing Jot in a washtub. The little boy is covered with soap.

NONA. C'mon, brother—gimme yer nose! Now yer ear . . . 'n now that other ear. . . .

She is humming lightly as she scrubs Jot with a soapy cloth. Sam appears, followed closely by Daisy and Zoonie. In his hand he holds the big fish-hook we saw in the preceding scene.

SAM. Y'know, honey—while that l'il feller was sick, I plumb fergot 'bout that big catfish—but now that he's better—we'll have us some fun—'n mebbe even git back at that neighbor o' ourn what figgers he's the only one 'round these-here parts!

NONA. Oh, Sam—now that Jottie's cured, I'm so thankful cain't even hate Devers.

In the background, Granny has been fast asleep in her rocker during the whole scene. Suddenly she opens her eyes.

GRANNY. Devers is real nice—he got good sense. The other day, when we met up with each other in them fields, he says to me, "Nobody 'preciates their ol' folks till they're dead 'n gone—'n then it's too late."

This dissolves to a fairly close view of SAM, DAISY, NONA, JOT and ZOONIE. Daisy and Jot stand transfixed, avidly watching Sam as he takes the cable off the porch, which he had put up when they arrived at the farm, to make the house firm. Zoonie is also watching. Nona passes by carrying some laundry. She stoops to kiss Jot and joyfully goes towards the background, where she starts hanging the laundry on a clothes-line. She hums as she works.

SAM. It ain't that I'd b'lieve what goofy Finley says—but Becky, she tole me too that that there catfish is bigger'n a hog. Yessir, sister, if I could ketch that there monster, I'd sell 'im in town and with the money I'd buy yer mamma some purty silk stockin's . . . some shoes for you kids—and a big box o' snuff fer Granny.

This dissolves to a "close medium shot" of SAM, DAISY, JOT and ZOONIE.

The river is in the background. Sam is fixing a piece of bait on the big fish-hook, now attached to the cable. The two children are literally eating up his action with their eyes.—Then SAM is seen closely as he points with his finger towards the different spots in the river of which he is speaking, anxious to make the children see clearly what he means.

SAM. Ya see them little green, woolly worms that're fallin' into the river from the trees—ten a minute?

They're all goin' 'long the stream to the same place. Well, some folks might think that they're what Lead Pencil's after—but they'd be wrong. Lead Pencil, he wants the perch— don't care nothin' 'bout the worms.

We get a close view of DAISY, JOT and ZOONIE. They are all listening intently to Sam.

> SAM'S VOICE. Ol' Lead's a smart guy —wouldn't a hardly lived to be so old if he wasn't. I betcha he waits fer them perch over yonder at the tail end o' that little drift . . . it's kinda like a trap that Nature made in the river-bottom.

> JOT. Is Lead Pencil older than Granny, papa?

> SAM (seen close). Yep, sonny—he's older'n Granny—but he shore kin run faster!

We get a fairly close view of SAM, DAISY, JOT and ZOONIE.

> SAM. Must be yonder ol' Lead's got his cupboard. . . .

He gets up with his line, walks into the water and goes in the direction that he had indicated. And this cuts to a view of FINLEY, hidden in the bushes along the river; he is watching the scene, as it fades out.]

# DESTRUCTION OF THE VEGETABLE GARDEN

A fairly close view of SAM and NONA fades in. They are asleep in their bed on the porch. We hear Zoonie barking violently. In the background we see the cotton, almost ripe now.—Then we see them closely as Zoonie's barking wakes SAM. Sam's movement awakens Nona.

> NONA (crying out). Our vegetable garden!

This cuts to a view of Zoonie battling heroically with Devers' cattle, but in vain. They are too much for her. The cows and pigs are trampling over the vegetables, and eating them as fast as they can.

Sam and Nona, armed with sticks, appear. They manage to chase Devers' stock back to the other side of the broken fence. Sam notices Finley, who, attracted by the noise, had come over to see what was happening.

> SAM (to Nona, as they come running). That's Finley, and there's Devers' cattle.

> FINLEY. Aha . . . Sure looks like the end o' yer vegetables!

> SAM (violently). Get out of here. Get out of here.

But Finley picks up a stick and starts to help Sam and Nona. The last animal having been shoved across, Sam and Nona leave Finley to get them back to where they belong. Sam pulls up the broken part of the wire fence, and fixes it as well as he can. Nona goes off toward her ruined garden, and sadly looks at the devastation.

SAM, in a closeup, kneels down to inspect the wooden post to which the broken wire of the fence was attached. He sees that something more than cattle made the break.

> SAM. Sure looks like somebody helped 'em!

NONA and ZOONIE are seen together as Nona stands in the middle of her wrecked vegetable garden.

> NONA. Oh, Jottie! . . . Jottie . . . (Zoonie, as if to console her, comes

*close to her side. Nona strokes him.*)

In a fairly close view of SAM, NONA and ZOONIE, Sam is seen still squatting near the broken fence post. He gets up. On his face there is an expression of fury.

SAM (*to Nona*). You go back in the house, honey. (*As she hesitates*) Go on back in the house. (*As she turns to go; advancing to Finley*) Finley, what do you know about this?

FINLEY (*protesting*). I don't know nothin'. I didn't do it.

SAM. No, not by yourself. But we both know who did. (*Getting hold of him*) Come on, we're goin' to your place.

## THE FIGHT

Devers' Farm dissolves in. The river bank is visible. In the background, Finley is just getting the last of the animals back into the corral, with the aid of his stick. In the foreground, Sam approaches Devers. He is at the height of his fury, and it is obvious that he is controlling himself with great difficulty. Devers seems to be enjoying the situation fully.

SAM (*striding over to Devers*). Devers, look, I say—why did you do it?

DEVERS. What do you mean, why did I do it?

SAM and DEVERS are seen closely.

DEVERS. Ya cain't prove anything. The law will call it an Act o' God. As for yer garden, ya kin plant it again, cain't you?

SAM (*bitterly*). Plant it again!

DEVERS (*sarcastically*). Or did you come to borrow some seed?

SAM (*furiously*). I wouldn't borrow from you . . .

We get a fairly close view of DEVERS, SAM and FINLEY, as Devers goes to the well. Sam remains stubbornly in the middle of the yard. Finley who has gotten the animals all into the corral, approaches the two angry men, but stops a safe distance away. He is still holding the stick in his hand.—Then we get a close view of DEVERS AT THE WELL. He takes hold of the well rope and studies it.

DEVERS. Wait a minute . . . speakin' of borrowin' . . . This rope's plumb ruint. (*He takes a knife out of his pocket and opens it.*) Ya 'member whut we agreed on when ya came 'n ast fer water?

In spite of his terrible anger, SAM is utterly aghast at such out and out meanness in his neighbor.

SAM. Ya mean 'bout replacin' the rope?

DEVERS. Yep. Time fer ya to do it now . . . I don' aim to use this one no more. (*He cuts the rope with his knife.*) . . . And I'm sick and tired of you comin' around here askin' fer water.

We get a close up of SAM. This last is too much. His fury gets the better of him. Sam rushes at Devers, grabs him by the neck, shakes him, and sends him flying back against the pigpen fence.

SAM. 'N now, Devers, I'm goin' to break yer neck.

DEVERS (*self-confident because of his knife*). I'm mighty glad ya started this—'specially with Finley here fer a witness—That makes two o' us now kin talk to the law.

Sam rushes at Devers again, and starts attacking him. Finley is an interested spectator. Sam manages to give Devers several good blows with his fist, and to avoid Devers' knife. In the background, Becky comes out of the house, attracted by the noise of the fight.— DEVERS and SAM are seen close, as Devers, breaking Sam's blow, attacks with his knife. Becky rushes over.

BECKY. Pa . . . don't!

DEVERS. Shut your mouth'n git back in the house.

Sam succeeds in getting in a blow which sends Devers sprawling on the ground. Sam tries to jump on top of Devers, but Finley throws his stick which trips Sam, and he falls before he can get to Devers.

We get a close view of DEVERS as he gets up and starts towards Sam.— Devers attacks Sam with his knife, just at the moment that Sam is getting up. Sam is wounded, but manages to strike a blow at Devers' face.—Sam is holding his side which has been wounded, and which is hurting him. He picks up the stick and staggers towards Finley, who has been watching the fight passionately. Finley, frightened, jumps back out of Sam's way. During this time, Devers has gotten up and is going toward Sam to attack him in the back, but Sam turns around, sees him, and begins striking furiously at Devers' arm with the stick. Devers drops the knife, and Sam grabs Devers by the neck.—And now we see Sam pushing him up against the pigpen. It looks as though he is going to hurl him to the pigs, but he changes his mind.

SAM. You'd like to see me leave here, wouldn't ya?

DEVERS. Yeah . . . of course I would. . . .

Sam, amazed at his neighbor's frankness, lets go of him.

SAM. How come? What'd I ever do to you?

DEVERS. It's like I tole ya, the fust time ya come to ast fer water—jes' don' like to see folks tryin' to be somethin' better than they are. In this world, gotta be some whut gives orders 'n some whut takes 'em.

SAM. An' you figger you was made to give them orders and I'm made to take 'em? Why?

DEVERS. 'Cause I've worked hard all my life. . . .

SAM. I work hard too . . you know that. . . .

DEVERS. But why here an' not someplace else? Before you-all come, I wuz 'lone around here. Whole country wuz mine. I wuz fixin' to buy yer farm—it wuz cheap then. Now. . . . (*He gestures with his hand.*)If it goes on like this, everythin's gonna be yourn 'round here— All I ever see is you—wherever I go —in the woods, killin' the varmints —at the river, catchin' the fish. . . . Finley told me ya set a line fer Lead Pencil.—And my gal, Becky— ya heard what she said.

During this last conversation, Devers has gone farther and farther away from Sam. The latter, stupefied by this outburst of hatred, pays no attention to the fact that Devers has moved away from him.

And now we see FINLEY approaching the knife quietly. He suddenly picks it up. He starts to hand it to Devers.— But BECKY, seen close, starts yelling "Sam! Sam!"—And Sam, warned by Becky's outcry, sees Finley's movement. He takes a step toward the young man, who, terrified, moves back. Then he moves toward Devers, and with a blow, sends him rolling among the pigs in the pen.—Next, Sam starts off and Becky advances toward him.

BECKY (*indicating Sam's wound*). You better take care o' that cut . . .

SAM. Go back to yer house, Becky—best not bother 'bout me anymore.

He goes off, passing by Finley, who, frightened, jumps into the middle of the pigpen. Becky hides her face with her hands and goes over to lean against the wall.

And now we see DEVERS coming out of the pigpen. He calls Finley by whistling, and Finley approaches him eagerly.

DEVERS. Finley!—Get my gun!

Finley runs into the house, and brings out the gun.

DEVERS. Where'd he go?

FINLEY. He follered the crik . . .

DEVERS. C'mon!

He goes off in the direction indicated, followed by Finley.—A close view discloses BECKY, who has heard everything. She starts to run.

## THE MIRACULOUS CATCH

SAM, seen close, is at the river's edge, washing his wound. We are right at the place where we saw him install his fishing line for Lead Pencil, with Daisy and Jot. We see the river in the background. Then in a reverse view we see SAM, DEVERS, and FINLEY. In the foreground, Sam is washing his wound. Quite far in the background, we see Devers and Finley arriving. The cable

which is now the line for Lead Pencil starts agitating and attracts Sam's attention. In the foreground, now, Sam looks at the middle of the river, where the end of the line agitates curiously. Then we again see DEVERS and FINLEY. Devers, at the height of his fury, stops. Finley is terrified . . .

FINLEY. Uncle Henry . . . Uncle Henry!

DEVERS (*taking aim*). Shut up!

SAM is now seen pulling on the cable. Then we see a BIG FISH, in the middle of the river, leaping around, trying to free himself from the hook, as the scene cuts to a close view of DEVERS and SAM: Fascinated by this spectacle, Devers looks on, all attention. He has forgotten everything, his idea of murder, his fury—Only one thing interests him now—the big fish.

DEVERS. Holy Smoke!—It's Lead Pencil!

He automatically hands his gun to Finley and goes toward Sam, followed by Finley.

In the background, SAM is pulling the big fish, which we can't see now but which we realize is at the end of the line in the river. DEVERS approaches him, followed by FINLEY. Sam sees him, but their common passion for fishing has now changed the situation entirely.

DEVERS. Shore—it's Lead Pencil.

SAM. Shore is—it's ol' Lead himself.

DEVERS (*timidly*). Kin I help ya?

SAM. Jes' hold on to this line for a minute . . .

He gives the line to Devers to hold—He wraps his handkerchief around his hand so as to be better able to pull the cable, and begins once more to pull on the line, aided by Devers.

The scene dissolves to a close view of LEAD PENCIL, who is lying on the river bank, and then we see the three men squatting around the fish. Sam is winding up the cable which has served as a line to catch Lead Pencil. Devers is looking at the fish in almost insane admiration. Finally, unable to control himself any longer, he speaks.

DEVERS. Tucker. (*As Sam doesn't answer*) That's my fish.

SAM. So ya own the river too, huh? But maybe the Law will call my hook 'n line an Act o' God.

DEVERS. Ya gimme that fish, 'n swear never t'tell ya caught it, 'n I'll give ya (*hesitating*) a dollar.

SAM (*busy with the fish-line*). I don' need no dollar. My folks likes fish.

DEVERS. All right. I'll keep the fish long 'nuf to take it to the store 'n show it fer a day or two, and you kin have it back.

SAM (*still busy with the fish-line*). It ain' likely to be very good eatin' after that.

DEVERS. All right. Lemme have the fish 'n ya keep yer mouth shut, 'n ya kin use outta my whole garden.

SAM is seen close, working the hook out as delicately as if the fish were the frailest gossamer.

SAM (*pleasantly*). He sure taken a holt of it, didn't he?

DEVERS (*frantic*). All right, then. You kin have the whole durn garden.

SAM (*looking up*). 'N the well rope? How we gonna draw water?

DEVERS. All right, durn it. I gotta another rope in the barn.

Sam rises. Devers and Finley are looking at him anxiously. In the background, Nona and Becky come running. We understand that Becky had gone to get Nona. Sam looks at them. The two women stop short, amazed at the friendly attitude of the men.

NONA. Sam! What's happened? Becky tole me. . . .

SAM (*nonchalantly*). Oh, it ain't nothin! I wuz jes' helpin' Devers here pull this big catfish outten the river! He done caught Lead Pencil!

DEVERS (*after a pause*). Yeah.

Devers looks closely at Sam, gratitude and friendliness in his eyes, as the scene fades out.

## MA AND HARMIE ARE ENGAGED

A close view of beautiful RIPE COTTON on Sam's Farm fades in. Then in the background we see the house. Sam and Nona are walking in the middle of the cotton-field. We hear the strumming of a guitar, not really playing a tune, but rather vaguely picking the music out. Sam feels, with his hand, a ripe cotton bloom.

SAM. It feels good—

NONA. Yes, Sam—I b'lieve we got a fine crop.

They walk. We feel that they are perfectly happy, that they love each other, and that the future is all theirs. The guitar is now heard a little more strongly. Sam winks at Nona. They go toward the place where the music is coming from. The view moves with them and shows Harmie and Ma, lying on the ground, at the edge of the field, and hidden by the cotton plants. Ma, stretched out on the ground, is chewing on a long blade of grass. Harmie is also stretched out, his head on Ma's shoulder. Ma strokes his hair. He is toying with his guitar.

We get a close view of SAM and NONA smiling knowingly. They look at Harmie and Ma, as they themselves have their arms around each other's waists. This is followed by a close view of HARMIE and MA: They smile, Harmie very proudly, Ma somewhat embarrassed.

MA. Oh, I forgot to tell y'all.

HARMIE (*beaming*). Yeah, we plumb forgot.

MA. You tell 'em, Harmie.

HARMIE. Well, we're goin' to get married Sunday. (*Laughing with embarrassment*) Ha . . . ha . . .

# THE WEDDING PARTY

A close view of an enormous WEDDING CAKE fades in. A hand is cutting into it. The scene is Harmie's Store.—Then we see HARMIE cutting the cake into slices. Ma is serving them. She is dressed in a pretty dress and seems very happy.

MA (*as we get different "shots" of the wedding guests*). I'm jes' studying 'bout how blessed us Tuckers is! An' I cain't help wonderin' why. I get the man I want. (*This is greeted with laughter.*) 'N now, here we are all together, all my loved ones around me—Jottie, my own l'il grandson's cured 'n happy once more— Daisy's so good at her book-larnin' she's gonna git a prize at school— Sam . . . My Sam's growed the bes'

crop in the country—'n mebbe even buy his own place with whut he makes offen it. Yep, I been studyin' 'bout why Almighty blessed us Tuckers so generous! But I reckon I know . . . It's because o' Sam 'n the way he worked that farm of his —'n the crop he done growed. Must be jes' the way the Lord wanted him to do it.

A close view shows SAM and NONA receiving their pieces of cake.

NONA. Oh, Ma—You're shore right— only if Sam's like he is, it's cause he's got such a good Ma.

SAM. Yes, I got somethin' to say, too —that there ain't no other feller I'd ruther have than Harmie for my new Pa.

We see the whole TUCKER FAMILY and THE GUESTS in Harmie's store, and all seem very gay and excited. Many of the men have taken off their coats. We understand that the party has been going on for several hours. A few men pass each other pints of whiskey and furtively take drinks from the bottle. Sam, moved, kisses his mother. In a comical manner, Harmie tries to push him away, and kisses his new wife. The guests laugh merrily.

HARMIE (*to Sam*). Hey, son—ya ain't a baby no more—leave yer Ma alone —she's mine now . . .

NONA (*pulling Sam*). Oh—she's yours, eh? What do you think you are—a Indian chief? She's part ours too, y'know . . .

MA. Well—at least I *ain't* like that there weddin' cake—cain't cut me in pieces . . .

HARMIE. C'mon, Ma—let's leave these kids . . . they don't know nothin' . . .

NONA. C'mon, Sammy . . . let's leave them lovebirds alone . . . they'll come down to earth later . . .

Sam puts his arm around Nona's waist. Everybody has a mouthful of cake, and looks happy.

A GUEST. Hey, Harmie—S'pose now that you're married, I suppose you're goin' on the wagon . . .

HARMIE. I was jes' thinkin' I'd start that tomorrow.—But it ain't tomorrow yet . . . (*He winks.*) C'mon in here . . .

The men follow Harmie.

A GUEST. Aha . . . Now we're gonna find out where he caches his stuff.

Tim, a whisky bottle in his hand, is standing next to a young girl. He leaves her and joins the men.

TIM. Hey! Wait fer me—I could use another one.

He shows that his bottle is empty and joins the men who exit toward another corner of the store.

The women and children have stayed around the counter where Ma finishes giving them wedding-cake. We make out Granny who is eating heartily, Daisy who shares her piece of cake with Zoonie, Jot to whom Ma gives the little bride and groom from off the top of the cake.

MA. You havin' a good time, Granny?

GRANNY. A fine time—but I'd like to hear some purty music—

MA. You heard some durin' the dancin'—

GRANNY. No—no—When we git rich —when our ship comes in, I want us to git one o' them talkin' machines 'n a lotta good sacred records.

The old lady, having finished her cake, starts fanning herself with a fan.—And we get a close-up of GRANNY'S FAN. It is an advertisement for a local funeral parlor. Then we again see GRANNY addressing a group of guests and Ma.

GRANNY. I wanna set on the gallery 'n drink lemonade with ice in it—'n hear "Beulah Land" . . .

Ma stoops down to calm a little dispute between Daisy, Jot and Zoonie. Daisy is trying to get the little bride and groom away from Jot, who refuses to give them to her. Zoonie is trying to get at the cake that is stuck to the little statues. In the background, Nona has joined a girl who is trying on big straw hats, of which there is a high pile in the corner of the store.

We get a close view of MA, JOT, DAISY and ZOONIE as Ma picks Jot up in her arms and gets up, having saved the little statues.

GRANNY'S VOICE (*singing*). "I'm drinkin' at a fountain—Underneath a cloudless sky—Praise God . . ."

In the foreground, Nona and the girl are next seen trying on the straw hats. Nona puts one on back to front, looks at herself in a mirror, and both women burst out laughing. In the background, Granny, next to Ma, continues to sing.

GRANNY. "I'm drinkin' at a fountain —that never shall run dry—Hallelujah!"

And now we see SAM, TIM, HARMIE and several OTHER MEN, in a corner of the store. The men pass Harmie's jug back and forth and drink out of it.

A GUEST. Say, Harmie—didn't ya ketch cold the night ya made this?

HARMIE. Don't ya know that this is

jes' the stuff to keep ya warm . . .

ANOTHER GUEST. Hey, Harmie, wasn't ya afeared o' the law?

HARMIE. Are you kiddin'? The law was right there waitin' fer the finished product . . .

We get a close view of SAM and TIM. They have just finished drinking and pass the jug to the others.

TIM (*winking*). Sam—c'mon with me—got somethin' to show you. (*They start to go out.*)

A GUEST (*turning the empty jug over*). Well—that kills that . . .

HARMIE. Don't you worry—I'll git her sister . . .

A guest begins singing "Rye Whiskey, Rye Whiskey. Rye Whiskey I cry, Rye Whiskey till I die." This cuts to SAM and TIM as they enter the now empty kitchen. Tim approaches his coat, hanging on a nail in the wall. From the pocket, he takes out a bottle. We hear the noise of the conversation in the store, and the somewhat drunken guest singing "Rye Whiskey."

TIM. It's real city stuff, Sam—like they drink in those hot-shot night clubs. (*He uncorks it.*) Just lay yer nose on that. (*Sam takes the bottle and drinks.*)

TIM. Smell it, Sam, smell it. (*Sam does as he's ordered.*) Ain't that something?

SAM. Sure is—

TIM (*proudly*). Three bucks a quart.

Sam looks at the bottle with profound respect and hands it back to Tim, who drinks. In the background, an old man,

whom we had seen among the guests, enters the back room with a fiddle. Harmie is with him.

HARMIE. We're gonna have a square dance now, folks.

Nona and the young girl of the hats enter, running.

NONA (*running in*). Oh, yes—yes—a square dance.

MA (*coming in, happily*). Oh—that'll be fun—let's have a dance—

The old fiddler starts playing an introduction. Soon the whole room is full of people ready to dance. In the foreground, Tim, having finished drinking, looks at the crowd.

TIM. Gotta find me a good hidin'-place—(*He looks around.*)—That's it—

He goes over to the stove and hides his precious bottle inside. The girl who was with Tim before, notices Tim and Sam, comes into the kitchen and pulls Sam by his arm.

We get a close view of SAM and the YOUNG GIRL.

YOUNG GIRL. C'mon, honey—You dance with me . . .

SAM. You're very kind, ma'am—but I gotta partner—

YOUNG GIRL. After the dance, we could go outside, honey—I got some mighty fine drinkin' liquor out in my car—

SAM. I'm sure sorry—but . . . No thanks.

The girl looks at him angrily. Disappointed, she takes Tim's hand.

YOUNG GIRL. You—you'll dance with me?

TIM. Sure, honey chile—'n after the dancin', we'll go out to yer car . . .

Sam joins Nona in the background. She had been looking for him. The dance starts. Tim and the girl, at the kitchen door, pass Granny, who enters the kitchen. Her furtive looking around makes us understand that she intends to take advantage of the dancing in the other room, to give herself a treat.

She takes an old coffee pot, a package of coffee, and lights the fire in the stove. The dance continues.—We get a close view of the FIDDLER playing, and then see the square dance; MA and HARMIE, SAM and NONA, DAISY and JOT trying to dance like adults, and others dancing. And throughout this the CALLER is singing out:

CALLER:

All join hands, circle down South,
Let a little sunshine down ya mouth.
Come back home, and all eight swing,
Promenade single file, ladies in the
  lead,
Indian file.
Swing that girl behind you.
Promenade single file, ladies in the
  lead,
Indian file.
Swing the girl behind you.
Swing the girl behind you,
First and third out to the right.
Chase the rabbit, chase the squirrel,
Chase that pretty girl round the
  world.
Chase the baboon, chase the coon,
Chase that pretty boy around the
  moon.
Four hands up and around you go
Round, round, and don't be slow.
Do si, do, chicken in the bread pan
Picking out dough.

Grab your partner, and on you go.
Chase the rabbit, chase the squirrel,
Chase that pretty girl round the
  world.

Suddenly TIM stops dancing and looks anxiously toward the kitchen. Then we see him hurrying toward Granny, whom we see in the foreground, making her coffee at the stove. He opens the stove and tries to save his bottle.

GRANNY (yelling). Man—You leave me make my coffee—I don't drink no hard liquor like you-all—I want my coffee—Git—outen here! . . .

TIM. Granny, mind what you're doin'. I've got my bottle stached in there. Now ain't that somethin'.

He manages to get the bottle out, but it is very hot and he burns his fingers. This provokes a little dancing and hopping around on Tim's part, with all sorts of exclamations . . . All this noise attracts the attention of the dancers. The dancing stops and everybody comes to the kitchen door to look at Tim and Granny. In the first row are Sam and Nona, who laugh.

Tim puts the bottle on the table. The heat makes the cork pop out and the liquid flows out of the bottle. Tim tries to save what he can with a pan.

GRANNY. That serves ya right!

We see SAM and NONA laughing as hard as they can; then TIM, who sees Sam laughing and is furious.

TIM. You think that's a joke? . . .

He advances toward Sam and gives him a push. Sam goes reeling back into the room where the dancing had gone on, and falls, sprawling, across the bed. We see the GUESTS laughing at Sam's comic position. Sam gets up and in turn shoves Tim. This friendly fight continues for a while. No sooner is one of them up than he pushes the other one down.

This cuts to a close view of the YOUNG GIRL, who had been refused by Sam in the kitchen. She watches the fight with a somber air, standing by the kitchen door.

Sam now pushes Tim, who falls on the bed and stays there, asleep. Sam, very proud, goes to kiss Nona and receive congratulations from the others who salute him comically. But suddenly the young girl takes the top of a wooden box from the floor, and hits Sam over the head with it. He turns 'round two or three times, and falls down next to Tim. And the next scene shows SAM and TIM lying together. Tim, awakened by Sam's falling next to him, opens his eyes and recognizes him vaguely.

TIM. Sam . . . my ol' pal. . . .

SAM. Tim . . . ol' friend!

They smile at each other, close their eyes and go to sleep, as the scene fades out.

The back room then dissolves in: Some time has elapsed. Sam and Tim are sleeping on the bed against the wall of the back room, which is almost empty now. They are covered with a blanket. Harmie, Ma and Nona accompany the last guests to the back door. In another corner of the room, Granny, Jot and Daisy have been installed on a mattress on the floor, and are sleeping. A loud clap of thunder is heard, followed by a flash of lightning. Harmie opens the door and the others go out toward their car in the yard. Harmie, Ma and Nona take a few steps with them. Through the door, the guests can be seen getting into their car with difficulty—due to their drunkenness.

THE FIDDLER (*quite drunk*). Yep—that was a fine party—best weddin' I ever saw—'n b'lieve me—I seen lotsa weddin's in my day . . .

MA. You-all be careful—don't have no accidents . . .

The two other guests sing "Sweet Adeline" during this last dialogue.

FIDDLER. Yeah—man—a fine weddin'—You-all gonna have a happy life . . . Yes, sir! Best weddin' I ever seen . . .

Very much moved, Harmie and Ma look at the others drive away. But Nona, worried, looks at the sky. There is another clap of thunder followed by a flash of lightning.

NONA. My goodness! It's startin' to rain.

By the sound we understand that the car has left the yard. Harmie and Ma don't hear Nona's reflection.

NONA (*as we see the rain drops starting to fall*). Ma—It's rainin'! What's gonna happen to our cotton?

HARMIE (*somewhat sobered*). Sure is a bad time for rain to come . . .

MA. We better git back in—Won't do no good fer us to git wet . . .

They go back into the house, of which we see the door and window lighted in the background. Harmie closes the door—then he pulls the shade down. All is dark as the scene fades out.

## THE STORM

A long view of the COUNTRYSIDE fades in. A violent storm is raging—great gusts of wind blow the trees wildly. The rain is coming down in torrents. This dissolves to a view of the TREES tossing violently in the wind and rain; to some VILLAGE ROOFS in the storm; to a full view of HARMIE'S BACKYARD. Some clothes, drying in the yard, blow noisily in the wind.

NONA, inside Harmie's house, looks at the weather through the window. The rain is beating so violently against the window-panes that it looks as though they might break. Nona's face is hopeless. Suddenly, she makes a decision—goes away from the window and approaches the corner where Sam and Tim are asleep. She shakes Sam to wake him up.—SAM wakes up and looks at Nona without understanding what it's all about.

NONA. Sam—there's a terrible storm —we gotta go home . . .

Sam looks toward the window, and realizing what is going on, he gets up suddenly.

SAM. Oh, my gosh!!! (*This action awakens Tim.*)

TIM. What goes on—what's the matter? (*He gets up also and joins them.*)

Sam, followed by Nona, arrives at the door and opens it. A great gust of wind and rain enters the room. Sam closes the door. He turns toward Tim, now next to him.

SAM. Tim—lend me your car—I gotta go see my cotton . . .

TIM. Sure, pal—I'll go with you.

Nona wants to go, too—but Sam stops her.

SAM. You better stay here with Granny and the kids . . .

He opens the door and goes out into the storm, followed by Tim. Nona closes the door with difficulty, and through the window watches them leave. Tim's car is in water up to the hub-caps. It drives away and disappears.

[This dissolves to a close view of SAM and TIM behind the car window, although they can barely be seen through the heavy downpour on the window.

We get a fairly close view of a MAN and WOMAN on the road. They are signaling for Tim to stop. The storm is fierce by now, and the wind is blowing even more violently than before. They are gesturing and pointing to something up ahead on the road. Due to the noise of the rain and the wind, we can't hear what they are saying.

In a long shot—we see ANOTHER CAR up the road a little way. It is stuck in a sea of mud.

We see SAM, TIM, the MAN and WOMAN closely.

MAN. Ain' no use y'all tryin' t' go on—road's plumb out . . .

SAM (*to Tim*). Go on—drive around it—that ditch ain't deep . . .

TIM (*with a gesture of fatalism*). Okay, we can't do no more than git stuck too! (*To the man*) Y'all wanna come with us?

MAN. No, sir. Much 'bliged—we jes' come from there . . .

Tim's car drives away, leaving the man and woman in the rain. Then the view moving with TIM's CAR, we see it on the flooded road lurching down into ditches.

Tim is driving very carefully. By his expression we can see that he is very unsure of getting through. The car starts sputtering and is about to stop dead, but moves on until the car enters a deep pool of water and stops right in the middle of it.]

We next see a road in the midst of the fields. Sam is getting out of the car, followed by Tim. Knee deep in water, they start walking ahead. The rain has stopped, but the spectacle is one of complete devastation. On both sides of the road the cotton has been completely flattened by the wind and the rain. The road itself has been transformed into mud. Sam and Tim advance with difficulty, not even trying any longer to avoid the mud. In the background, Harmie's truck appears—the two men get out of the way to let it pass, but it stops when it gets to them. Nona is driving—Next to her are Granny, the children and Zoonie. The truck is all muddy.

We get a long view of the TUCKER FAMILY in the COTTON FIELD. Sam's entire cotton field has been flattened out by the storm. In the foreground, the house is leaning over precariously. A part of the roof is completely off. Nona, without leaving the wheel, looks around in consternation. In the background, Granny and the children are asleep.

Sam is next seen advancing toward the flattened cotton, with Zoonie after him. Nona gets out of her seat and follows him.

They arrive at the cotton. Sam tries to raise a completely broken plant. Zoonie looks at the plant.

NONA. Oh, Sam . . . Sam . . .

Sam does not reply. He is so struck by his misfortune that all he can do is to look around him. He needs some time to realize the extent of the disaster.

The scene then cuts to GRANNY, DAISY and JOT. Granny gets out of the truck and takes a few steps. She looks around furiously.

GRANNY. Sam Tucker, I ain' stayin' here one minute longer—I'm takin' this weary ol' body d'rect to the cemetery . . . don' even have a decent place to set 'n wait fer my call to glory. Yer a criminal, Sam Tucker —treat yer ol' Granny like this.

SAM and NONA: Sam hasn't even heard Granny. Nona turns toward the old lady, as she turns around and goes off down a path with the air of one who never wishes to lay eyes again on this awful place.

GRANNY (*yelling*). Yeah, yer nothin' but a criminal, Sam Tucker. A mean, mean criminal.

Sam is completely detached from this scene. He looks around him, weighing the disaster in his mind. Suddenly he notices something.

SAM. "Uncle Walter" . . .

He goes away. Nona does not follow him, but goes after Granny, who passes by the truck, continuing to shout.

GRANNY. Sam Tucker's a criminal, I tell ya, a mean criminal.

TIM notices Sam going down toward the river and starts to follow him.

TIM (*calling*). Sam . . . Sam . . .

NONA and GRANNY: Nona catches up to Granny. She picks up a thin branch from the ground and stands doggedly in front of the old woman.—Nona's attitude is menacing. She will stop at nothing, so wounded has she been by the insults to her husband at a time like this.

NONA (*threatening with the stick*). Granny, ya'll stay right here—a time like this, folks gotta stick t'gether— ya'll stay right here with the rest o' us.

Granny stares at Nona and realizes that she means every word she says.

GRANNY. All right—I'll stay—but if I do, it's 'cause yer trappin' me like ya allus do—yer big 'n strong 'n ya gotta stick. Whut kin an ol' 'crepit Granny do 'gainst the likes o' you?

NONA. Ya come right back to the house with me. We got work to do.

At this, Granny turns around and goes toward the house, followed by Nona. Then the scene cuts to SAM and TIM. Sam arrives at the spot where he had tied "Uncle Walter" up the day before. In the far background, we see Harmie's truck and Nona and Granny advancing toward the demolished house.—Then we get a close view of SAM and TIM: The fence-post is there, but the chain, which haltered "Uncle Walter" to it, is broken. Sam picks it up and examines it carefully.

SAM. I'm gonna look fer "Uncle Walter"—

He is ready to start without Tim, who stops him with a gesture.

TIM. Look fer "Uncle Walter"? Where do you reckon she might be?

SAM. There ain't no tellin'. But I just got to find her, Tim. The pasture down by the river is all under water.

TIM. Sure hope she ain't in the river. There ain't no cow's worth gitten drowned fer!!

SAM (*starting off*). I ain't askin' you to help.

After a gesture of impotence, Tim follows him.

The countryside is completely flooded. There is desolation everywhere. Trunks of trees, parts of houses, other debris are being carried down the current.— Sam is walking ahead, followed by a resigned Tim. Both of them are looking toward the river, on which various scenes are enacted. We see: a WAGON being carried down the current; some PILES OF STRAW floating in the river; some FARM ANIMALS carried along the current on part of a roof; SAM and TIM continuing their search:

And now SAM, who is looking on all sides, suddenly designates something to Tim, and we next see: "UNCLE WALTER" in the distance—in the middle of a little island that the over-flowing river hasn't as yet completely submerged. She is up to her belly in water, but she is alive.—We get a fairly close view of SAM as he starts running. "UNCLE WALTER" is seen again. She looks very uncomfortable on her island. The broken chain is hanging around her neck. Then we see SAM and TIM approaching.

SAM. I'll go over 'n bring her back.

TIM. Why don' ya wait for the water to go down?

SAM. That river's gonna keep right on risin'.

TIM. Okay, pal, I'll give ya a hand.

SAM enters the water, and Tim follows him hesitantly. In the foreground, "Uncle Walter" is waiting patiently to be rescued. In the background, Sam starts crossing a very wide, deep fork of the river, formed by the flood. He has to keep avoiding debris which is being swiftly carried down the current. He gets close to "Uncle Walter" before Tim, hesitant, has even gotten well into the water. Sam pulls the resisting "Uncle Walter" toward the water.

SAM. Okay, I am goin' on alone.

TIM. No, you ain't. I'm goin' along with you.

SAM. Better stay here. (*But Tim plunges into the stream with Sam.*)

And we get a close view of TIM, who has been making an effort to reach Sam, in order to help him. Suddenly he comes to a very deep spot. A tree trunk in the current strikes him and he loses his footing.

TIM (*yelling*). Help, help . . . Sam!

SAM and "UNCLE WALTER" are then again seen in the water. Sam is employing all his strength to keep the cow from being swept away by the current. He hears another cry from Tim and looks over at him.—We see what Sam sees: Tim is struggling hard, now disappearing under the water, and then reappearing.

Sam lets go of "Uncle Walter" and swims toward Tim. The current takes "Uncle Walter." We then see SAM and TIM. Tim is overcome by a great swell of water and has to let go of the board. Sam gets to him just in time to catch him by his shirt. Another board is swept toward the two men. Sam grabs it and manages to pull Tim's head out of the water.

And now we see "UNCLE WALTER" being swept away by the current, down the river, and when this scene dissolves, we see Sam and Tim walking in the flood, waist-deep in water. In the background, a pile of debris collected in one place in the river indicates that Sam and Tim have been forced to this spot by the swift current.

TIM. Ya got any liquor at yer place?

SAM. Use t'have a l'il jug o' Harmie's, but now it likely's all busted up.

TIM. Le's go see.

And now we see them moving toward the house through the mud and the destroyed cotton. Sam looks at the ruined cotton and is overwhelmed with his sense of losing everything. He can contain himself no longer as they walk toward the wrecked porch. The windows and doors have been destroyed by the tilt of the house, leaving only openings in their places.

SAM. I'm comin' to town with you, Tim. I'll gather up my few measly belongin's that's left and pack up my whole bunch and get out. All these fields and the trees an' the river . . I just can't look at them no more. I gave 'em everything I had to give . . honest . . and what do they give me back? Nothin'. Nothin' but trouble and misery. I'd be crazy to stick any longer. A feller ought to know when he's beat. When he ain't wanted on a place, there ain't nothin' for him to do but pack up and get out. Come on, let's go.

At this point, however, we see NONA coming out of the wrecked house, bending down to avoid the wreckage. She takes Sam's hand and leads him to the end of what had been the porch. We see Granny, who is hanging out some covers and clothes, Daisy and Jot helping her. The remarkable old lady has put up a line between two trees and she is energetically trying to get the things dry.

NONA. Sam, I can hardly believe the house is still standin'..Sam, your gun is safe, and lots of other things too. Lots of Jottie's vegetable jars are still whole. 'Course the pictures got kinda broke, but once I get them straight on the wall they won't look so bad. Course the worst of all was this stove pipe. But I got it back up again and I think it'll work all right now. How do you like that, Sam?

SAM (*moved; tenderly*). I like it fine, honey.

And now Granny, surrounded by the two children, turns toward Sam and speaks in a loud voice.

GRANNY. Hey, Sam Tucker. Ya know whut this reminds me of? Reminds me o' forty-three years ago, with your gran'pappy Fayette—Same thing happened to us—only it wuz much wuss—The roof come clear down to the floor 'n the walls wuz plumb caved in. Fer a whole week, we had to crawl in 'n out on our hands 'n knees, jes' like prairie-dogs in their holes. But ol' Fayette, he jes' says, "it 'could be lots wuss, sugar, if the Injuns attacked us." Ha . . .

We get a close view of SAM and NONA. They are listening to Granny. Nona is smiling and calm; Sam serious and thoughtful.

SAM. Nona, we .was fools to make the deal with Ruston fer only plantin' cotton—L'il guys like us jes' cain't 'ford to plant cotton alone—Gotta have 'taters 'n corn 'n beans—l'il bit o' everythin'—

He goes into the house. We see him searching for something there, and he finally pulls out the cable with which he had caught Lead Pencil. Then he comes out of the house and throws the cable like a lasso. The end of it catches on to a corner of the roof, and Sam begins to pull . . .

Then we see SAM and NONA closely as Nona joins Sam and helps him pull the cable. Sam turns around.

SAM. Hey, Tim, come give us a hand!

We get a close view of TIM, who has watched this whole scene as though they were all lunatics. Now he goes toward Sam.

We get a close view of GRANNY as she leaves the clothes line and also starts toward Sam.

We then get a fairly close view of SAM, NONA, TIM and GRANNY pulling on the cable with all their might. Daisy and Jot, very much excited, are watching them.

We now get a close view of the ROOF of the HOUSE. It seems a little straighter than before.

And, again, fairly close, we see SAM, NONA, GRANNY and TIM with DAISY and JOT in the background. By the expression of the "pullers," we understand that the house is now somewhat more solid. Sam fastens the end of the cable to a tree, as he did in the beginning of the picture. Tim helps him. Having finished, Sam turns toward Tim. Granny and the children go off toward the background to continue gathering up their lost belongings.

TIM (*approaching him*). Sam, ya said ya was comin' to town with me—

SAM. Yeah, yeah, I said it.

TIM. Ya said it—but ya ain't comin' now, huh?

SAM. I was so plumb wore out. I jes' didn't seem to b'lieve in nothing no more. Now that my clothes is startin' to dry, I'm beginnin' to b'lieve again. Reckon that's the way the ol' dirt feels when she's so wet. But the sun'll dry her out an' she'll start a-callin' me, jes' the way Nona does sometimes.

TIM (*resigned*). I knowed it all 'long that you'd never leave here.—Man, if there was only one farmer left on this here earth, that'd be you . . .

SAM (*as we see him and Tim close*). Quit yer kiddin, Tim. Them machines o' yourn, they're purty fine—I realize that—but you shore can't eat 'em. Once in a while, you gotta have ya a hunk o' beef an' a few ears o' corn to fill up yer belly. You're purty smart, you town folks, but without us farmers, I'm afraid you'd git awful skinny.

TIM. 'N without us workers, I jes' wonder how you-all would git along! Yer plow—she shore didn't grow on no tree! 'N yer gun, that ya feed yer bunch with in winter—ya never planted no seed to git that! 'N some day when, like I hope, ya git ya a tractor, where d'ya reckon that'll come from? B'lieve me, friend, takes all kinds to make up this ol' world . . . You love yer farm—it's right that ya stay. But I like the work in the factory 'n that's why I wanted to take ya back there with me, Sam. . . .

Well, you know whut I'm talkin' 'bout—'n I don't mean no harm— if ya ever need me, ya know where to find me . . .

SAM (*kindly*). Yeah, I know, Tim . . thanks.

And now NONA comes out and calls to them: "Coffee's all ready," and the scene cuts to the interior of the house, where the family is seated.

DAISY and JOTTIE. I want some honey. I want some honey.

TIM (*contentedly*). Boy, nothin' could taste better than this.

SAM. Just what we needed, all right.

GRANNY (*enjoying her coffee*). This is the first time you made anything in that old pot fitten to drink, Nonie. Ha . . ha . .

NONA (*smiling*). Thank you, Granny.

SAM. Thank you, honey.

NONA (*reflecting*). Tomorrow, I guess we'll be thru with the ploughin'.

GRANNY. Thru with the ploughin' . . How ridiculous . . as if we ever get thru with the ploughin'. I'm going back to the house, and just sit, and wait for my call to Glory.

SAM (*full of resolve; eager to get started*). Yeah . . spring's gonna come a little early this year, honey. I reckon we kin start our seedin' even before the Twin Days.

# EPILOGUE

The scene is in the storm-swept field. And we get a close view of NONA and SAM, as aided by Nona, Sam is hitching up the mules to the plow. She helps him put the bit in the mules' mouths. As he finishes fastening the leather strap, Sam takes Nona in his arms and kisses her tenderly. Then he leaves Nona at the mules' heads.—Nona takes the reins to help get them started. Sam goes off back of the plow, ready to start and presses down the handles, and the plow and the mules, with Nona up ahead, and Sam in the back, once more begin their labor in the devastated field as the scene fades out.

ERNIE PYLE'S

# STORY OF G. I. JOE

*(A Lester Cowan Picture)*

*Screenplay by* LEOPOLD ATLAS, GUY ENDORE, PHILIP STEVENSON

*Produced by* LESTER COWAN

*Directed by* WILLIAM A. WELLMAN

## The Cast

ERNIE PYLE . . . . . . . Burgess Meredith
LIEUTENANT WALKER . . . Robert Mitchum
SERGEANT WARNICKI . . . Freddie Steele
PRIVATE DONDARO . . . . Wally Cassell
PRIVATE SPENCER . . . . Jimmy Lloyd
PRIVATE MURPHY . . . . Jack Reilly
PRIVATE MEW . . . . . . Bill Murphy

And, as themselves, combat veterans
of the campaigns in Africa,
Sicily and Italy.

*Associate Producer*—DAVID HALL

*Supervising Film Editor*—OTTO LOVERING

*Film Editor*—ALBRECHT JOSEPH

*Assistant Director*—ROBERT ALDRICH

*Research*—PAIGE CAVANAUGH

# STORY OF G. I. JOE

*Over the title of the picture come the words of a song "I've gone away for to stay a little while but I'm coming back—I'm coming back if it be one-thousand miles."*

## PART ONE

The BIVOUAC in the desert fades in. Dawn is just beginning to break over the distant hills. The chill and half-dark of the night is still on the scene. But now there's a great sense of stir and activity. There is a grinding roar of motors as troop trucks, jeeps and armored cars maneuver about, taking on their loads of men and artillery and uncoiling to form a thin snake of a line that is just beginning to head off across the desert floor to the distant hills to the right. A Sergeant is supervising. Next the view weaving through the movement of the convoy, discloses some of its action: Trucks loaded with men and supplies grind past as they swing into line; a jeep jouncing down the line like a shepherd dog; men on the double-quick run toward trucks that are loading up while still waiting their turn in line. Then we see the TROOP TRUCK as several GI's pile into it and move to the fore. Foremost is Gawky, with a pup still cuddled in his arms. Behind him pile in several other GI's, among them Murphy, Lopez, Mew, Dondaro. As they do so, Lieutenant Walker, a raw-boned, business-like fellow of twenty-six, strides into the scene from the right. Gawky's pup, in its exuberance, lets out a yip. Without breaking his stride Walker scans the truck and heads toward Gawky, the view moving in.

WALKER (*with a sharp, between-the-teeth whistle at Gawky*). Hey you—! Hey you! Get that pooch out of there. Whataya want to do, get him killed? (*Gawky looks up, disturbed; he hesitates for a moment.*) Awright! Awright! Quit stalling!

He goes on, not waiting to see whether his order will be carried out; he knows it will.

WARNICKI. All right, all right, you heard the lieutenant.

We get a close moving view of the GI's and the PUP. Reluctantly, hungrily, Gawky passes the pup on to the next man, who now silently passes it on to Murphy, who hands it on to another GI, who then nudges Mew, whose back is turned. Mew, having missed Walker's order, delightedly receives the dog and starts to pet it. The man beside him nudges him and gestures "out." Mew's face falls; he pulls the pup apart from a button the mutt's playfully begun to chew and reluctantly hands him on to the next man, who silently passes him down the line. As the hands of each man leave the dog, there's a lingering reluctance in their gesture, as if the very warmth and furry softness of the little animal body gave them a sense of something they knew they'd never find again in this arid desert—something they'd want to cling to.

Dondaro, receiving the pup at the end of the truck, hasn't got the heart to toss it away. For a moment he doesn't know what to do. Suddenly he drops it to someone off the truck. The view moving and stopping on Ernie, who had approached the truck a moment before, we see him lugging his bedroll and duffle bag. Somewhat startled, Ernie holds the pup and looks up—just as the view widens to include Walker coming into the scene.

We then see the BACK of the TRUCK, the view featuring WALKER and ERNIE—with the GI's in the background. Walker is about to order Ernie to get rid of the mutt, but at the same instant he catches a glimpse of the GI's, their eyes all hungrily directed at the pup in Ernie's arms. His eyes shift away. A little smile plays about his lips. He seizes on Ernie's armband as an excuse to countermand his order without seeming to do so.

WARNICKI. Ah, you poor little fella, you're going to freeze out there.

ERNIE. What do you want me to do with it?

WALKER (briskly). Correspondent, huh? Well, you want to get up to the front, don't you? (Over his shoulder) Here, make room for this man.

Remembering Walker's former order, Ernie starts to set the pup down, but Walker intercepts him.

WALKER. Well, get in, get in! Make it snappy!

For an instant the two men's eyes meet. A flash of understanding passes between them. Walker briskly turns and walks away—"the cop who wasn't there."

WALKER (going off toward his seat in front). All right, let's get moving.

Ernie quickly starts to scramble up the truck, pup in one arm, bedroll and duffle-bag dragged behind him with the other. He hands the pup on to Dondaro, who quickly passes it on and cheerfully gives Ernie a lift.

For a brief instant Ernie looks resentfully at Dondaro. This is the second time this guy's called him "Pop." But he grins as he sees, in a close, moving view the pup being passed back from hand to hand on its way to Gawky. The rhythm of the camera movement has a quicker, more joyous tempo this time. The view stops on Gawky as he finally gets the pup. Gawky, in his delight, quickly reaches in his pocket for a can of C rations, and he holds it out to the pup. The pup sniffs it and growls at it.—The boys' laughter is free, easy, exuberant now. The tension is broken. All's well with the world. They and Gawky have their pup back.

We get a close view of the TRUCK WHEEL. It spins in the sand as the motor is heard starting. Perhaps that yelp of delight that comes over the scene is from the pup—or perhaps it's just the truck wheel biting into the sand and starting forward. Next, the view moves up slightly as the truck spins around, bringing the rear of the truck into focus and we see Ernie, still being hauled onto the truck by the seat of his pants. Then as the truck moves on and off into the desert the scene dissolves to a long moving view of the convoy rolling along a desert road. It's mid-day and the sun beats down on the GI's.

Inside the TROOP TRUCK: Ernie is seated next to Dondaro. Opposite and alongside are the rest of the gang. Although his presence is accepted he's still outside their tight little clique. He listens with amused interest to their jabber. The boys are keyed up, not tense—but full of the fizz and vinegar of young healthy animals confined in a small space on their way to "the big game."

DONDARO. Got a cigarette?

Ernie reaches into his pocket and hands Dondaro a pack. Dondaro takes one and without thinking twice, passes the pack along to the rest of the boys. Ernie watches the progress of the pack around the truck.

MEW. Hey, Gawky, what're you going to call that purp? Betty Gordon?

Gawky grins as everyone laughs. Their spirits have risen again.

DONDARO (calling down the line). Lay off the Gawk. He's my territory.

ERNIE and DONDARO are seen closely.

ERNIE. Who's Betty Gordon?

DONDARO (shaking his head; laughing amiably). Ah, the kid's been waiting for a letter from her ever since we left the States.

Warnicki leans over and returns Ernie's pack. It's empty. He looks at it wryly. Dondaro notices it.

DONDARO (with a nod toward the boys). Chain smokers. (Then) Guess you're getting off at the first airbase, ain't you, Pop?

ERNIE. Why?

DONDARO (ironically; with a touch of bitterness). Correspondent, ain't you? The fliers are the guys you guys always write about. The Hollywood heroes. We're just the mugs along

for the ride, that's all. Just for the ride. (He looks across.) Ask Wingless. He'll tell you.

The view widens to include the others.

MURPH. Yeah? Just one plane and you're all dead ducks. Just one plane and z-z-z-ang!

Almost simultaneously with his voice, a sharp screech of brakes is heard. The boys lurch forward. Several automatically look up as if expecting a plane.

WALKER. All right, men. This is a break—unload.

And we see the rear of the truck as the boys, Ernie among them, scramble off the truck. Walker comes toward Ernie.

WALKER. How far up you going, Mr. —Mr. . . .

ERNIE. Pyle. End of the line. If it's okay with you.

WALKER (starting on). Sure. (Then, suddenly turning) Pyle? You say Pyle? (Ernie nods.) Say, aren't you the guy that runs that column about week-end trips or somethin'?

ERNIE (grinning). Mostly—or something—(Nodding toward the boys) Pretty good-looking outfit you got.

WALKER. We're not an outfit yet— (Glancing at his watch) Maybe by this time tomorrow we will be. Say, come to think of it, my old man reads your column. He thinks it's great.

Ernie looks up quickly at him. The sharp piping of whistles are heard all down the road.

ERNIE. Well, I'll be darned!

WALKER. All right, men—let's get going—

The DESERT dissolves in at night: First we get a close view of the RADIOMAN on the JEEP. He is sitting hunched up, blanket around his shoulders, phones pressed to his ears, listening to the radio. A smile comes to his face as if he were hearing something delightful. Grinning, he removes the earphones, snaps on th loudspeaker so that the soft, rhythmi strains of a popular band orchestra can be heard.

RADIOMAN. Hey, fellas, get a load of this—Artie Shaw—

The view moves to the right, disclosing in a medium long shot a convoy bivouacked for the night. Scores of pup tents, interspersed with trucks, jeeps, armored cars, are spread irregularly across the bright moonlit desert. In the distance only mountains and sky are visible.

As the music softly floats across the night, the view moves in closer, weaving past tents, revealing the various activities of the men preparatory to "blanket drill." Many have their heads sticking out of the tents. Others are reclining in various stages of relaxation.

The camera comes to a halt on a pair of enormous feet, sticking out of a tent flap. Their owner evidently is too big for the normal sized tent. The view moves along the wall of the tent to the front flap, which is open. The GI's head extends beyond that too. He keeps staring at the star-studded sky.

AD LIBS. Out of this world. Solid Jack—

Looking into the tent we see Murphy in the foreground. Within, a thin, medium-sized youngster, his bunk mate, is huddling with the cold, for the tent flap is open. This is Charley Mew, an Ohio farm boy, a child of neglect, naïve and wondering.

MEW (*not really complaining*). Gee

whiz, Murph—I wish you weren't so long—it's sort of cold out here in the open.

MURPHY (*without turning*). I'll cut my legs off.

MEW (*almost apologetically*). No, geez, you don't need to do that . . . (*Then; something on his mind*) I hear we're getting into the real business tomorrow.

MURPHY. Well, so far as I'm concerned, they can deal me out.

MEW (*concerned*). The infantry ain't so worse—

MURPHY (*cutting in; tersely*). Look, this is a modern war, ain't it? I'm a modern guy—the modern age is up in the air. That's where I belong. Not down here.

MEW. They only washed you out because you're too big. It ain't your fault.

MURPHY. I'll cut my legs off.

MEW. Me, me, me.

Inside another TENT: In the tent are Lopez and Sgt. Warnicki. Lopez is obviously of Mexican extraction; Warnicki, a muscular ex-coal miner. He is stolidly polishing his tommy-gun. The music comes over.

LOPEZ. What do you think I ought to bring Maria and the little fellow when I go back?

Warnicki looks up abruptly from his gun polishing.

WARNICKI. When you go home! (*Grimly, he sets about polishing his gun again.*) If, and when, you mean.

The gun catches a glint of the moonlight; Lopez catches a glint of his meaning and nods solemnly.

From another angle, the view favoring GAWKY, we see the mutt licking Gawky's face. He grins down at it.

DONDARO. If you had to sneak something out of that village, why'n't you bring something in skirts—?

Gawky is about to speak, but Dondaro shushes him as a long silvery trumpet note arrows softly into the night sky.

DONDARO. Sh—! Listen—don't interrupt the music— (*In ecstasy*) Murder—!

The announcer's voice is now heard coming over the radio jeep. It is a husky, feminine, seductive voice. The radioman listens delightedly.

VOICE. This is Berlin playing the jive music of Artie Shaw—

RADIOMAN. That's our Sally—

VOICE. Nothing sweeter 'n hotter in the world, is there . . . Remind you of Rosalind, Sylvia, Phyllis, Nancy, Mary, Ellen, Daisy . . . . yes, you bet it does . . . summer nights . . . the juke-box down the road . . . cokes, double malts . . . a girl's soft laughter in the moonlight. . . . Tomorrow, you boys of the 18th Infantry will meet our armies for the first time . . . the armies that have beaten the world—the French, the British, the Russians—What chance do you stand—

SOLDIER (*reacting to her propaganda*). Sez you—Bring 'em on—

The view moves past the faces of the soldiers as they listen.

VOICE. Why not be sensible—be sensible and surrender!

SOLDIERS (*ad lib*). Oh, yeah!

VOICE. Be my guests in Germany. . . . Dance with our lovely girls—

They know how to entertain . . . nice young men like you.

SOLDIER (*calling out*). Save one for me, sister, I'll be right there.

MEW. What a voice—what a bedroom—what a—(*He clucks.*)

VOICE. I will now sing Germany's latest hit, with lyrics written especially for my *nice* handsome American friends. . . . (*Now heard singing.*)

Light for me a cigarette
In that small café where we met.
Let me feel your finger tips,
Linda, Linda, on my lips.
Where two lovers used to be
Are these echoes waiting for me,
And do you still wait for me too,
As Linda, my love, I wait for you.

The view focusses on DONDARO and others in scattered tents.

DONDARO. There's a piece of furniture I'd like to push around.

SERGEANT'S VOICE (*rasping*). Turn that radio off.

The radio is instantly clicked off. In the ensuing silence some of the GI's quickly pull back into their tents. And we see the group fairly closely, the view favoring Lopez as he picks up his guitar.

LOPEZ (*as he strums*). It was Nazi music. Now it's mine—our first German prisoner.

We get a long view of the mountains, sky and desert. And over it comes Lopez' soft strumming of "Lili Marlene" as if the melody haunted the scene. The view moves slowly away from the landscape to the bivouac, passing a lone sentry pacing up and down, then resting for a moment on Dondaro, his feet out of the tent. He hums as he gazes dreamily at the sky. A little beyond him is Gawky, fast asleep, a smile on his grimy face as the mutt snuggles its muzzle under his chin.

DONDARO (*after humming some more*). Pst—hey, Pop! (*Ernie turns instinctively, though resentfully at this designation; but Dondaro continues brashly:*) Why wasn't you born a beautiful dame? (*Then, as an afterthought*) Or even an ugly one.

Ernie, half grinning a little uncomfortably, a little nervously, doesn't quite know how to take it.

VOICES (*ad lib*). Hey, why don't you guys pipe down?

DONDARO. Awright! Awright! (*And we see him closely as he turns over, gazing at the sky.*) Tonight, boys—tonight, I dream in technicolor.

We get a fairly close view of Ernie, still cold and uncomfortable, lying on the ground for the first time as the scene slowly dissolves to a CURVE of ROAD. The convoy of trucks is still moving forward. The vehicles go past the camera at short intervals. The truck carrying Ernie swings into view. Bill Walker and the driver can be seen in the cab. As the van of the truck bounces by, the view moves with it a little way. It is nearing sundown and the boys aren't quite as full of fizz and vinegar as they were at high noon and it's hot.

Inside the TROOP TRUCK: The view favors the Air Guard who is stolidly chewing gum as he keeps his eye on the sky. Warnicki looks up to him.

WARNICKI. Hey, how much further we got to go?

AIR GUARD (*stolidly*). About twenty miles.

The view slowly pulls back to include the others.

LOPEZ. How far?

AIR GUARD. Twenty miles. Then you get out and walk another ten—you know, to get the stiffness out of you.

SPENCER (*indignantly*). Where we going? China?

Several sudden dull thud-thuds from the distance interrupt him. They're repeated. Everyone grows still—look at each other.

SPENCER (*excitedly*). Hey—that's ours —105's—

AIR GUARD (*laconically*). Theirs— 88's—

They all grow tense. The artillery fires again. They all look off toward the horizon, following which there is a distant view of the HORIZON; with the darkening hills illumined by flashes of artillery fire. Then we again see the group, the view favoring the AIR GUARD.

WARNICKI. Thought you said twenty miles—

AIR GUARD. That's what I said— twenty miles—

Suddenly without warning, he pounds the cab-roof with his rifle butt. There is a shriek of brakes and the men are half-thrown off their feet as the truck stops. Whistles and cries are heard. The men are half petrified.

Inside the CAB: There is a pounding on the roof. Walker has already jumped on the seat and is opening the cab skylight. The driver is hunched over the wheel, face down.

We get a fairly close view of the TRUCK as an explosion shakes it. The men scramble over its sides and we next see the HIGHWAY at a low angle, with the men jumping forward and out of sight, as other, closer explosions shake the earth.

A close view of the TRUCK discloses WALKER firing at the diving but still distant Stuka. He is alone, utterly exposed.

In a series of "flashes" we see the various GI's hitting the dirt: Dondaro and Newman; Warnicki and Spencer; Mew alone; Lopez and Murph; Ernie, near Gawky who is hugging his dog close. We just get a glimpse of Gawky as he picks up the dog and runs for the ditch. There is the splatter of the machine gun and the terrifying whine of the Stuka as it dives closer.

WALKER, seen closely, is firing away at the fast approaching Stuka. As the plane's engine swoops down, reaching its most unbearable pitch, Walker swings around, firing at the plane. His face is gutted, hard, perspiring. The sound of the Stuka recedes.

We see WARNICKI and SPENCER on their knees:

SPENCER (*looking, bewildered, up at the sky*). I—I didn't even see him.

We see DONDARO getting to his feet. Then as he suddenly realizes he's alive, his face lights up with the exhilarated exultance of survival. He laughs a little hysterically and looks around. The view widens as several of the others gather. They look at each other for a moment, unable to speak with joy at having come through their baptism of fire alive.

MURPHY (*excitedly*). Hey—what'd I tell you guys about the Air Corps.

WARNICKI. They stink!

MEW. Look at 'em scram!

DONDARO. The yella bellies!

Dondaro stands there giving the Italian elbow business. They all start toward the truck. Dondaro turns around looking for Gawky. They all look around and in the expressions on their faces we know what they see off scene. There is a moment's still tableau. Lt. Walker comes into the scene with the dog under his arm—he hands the pooch to Warnicki.

WALKER. Okay, fellas—in the truck— in the truck. (*As they slowly start climbing in—softly*) The medics will take care of him. (*Harsh again*) Come on, get movin', get movin'.

Ernie comes. He and Walker exchange looks.

WALKER (*quietly*). First dead's always the worst.

ERNIE (*without conviction*). I suppose so.

Walker walks away. Ernie looks after him with a deep understanding. We then see the TRUCK as Ernie climbs into it and it starts off. Ernie takes his place between Mew and Dondaro. The men are saddened, silent, gazing in the direction of Gawky, and we next see GAWKY lying in the distance against the background of a burning truck, and a lone medic making his way toward the figure on the ground. A little gust of wind is blowing sand toward the body.

The scene cuts back to the GROUP on the truck.

MEW (*quietly*). Guess he won't never get that letter from that Gordon dame now.

DONDARO (*spitting; harshly*). That makes 'em even. She won't get no more from him neither.

Silence—except for the spaced thud of shells in the distance. Ernie looks around at the men, and we see that they are subdued, quiet, tense. The dusk deepens. The burst of shells comes closer, louder. Then we get a close view of ERNIE and DONDARO.

ERNIE (*quietly*). What was Gawky's last name?

DONDARO (*simply*). Henderson.

The scene dissolves to a long view of a DETRUCKING POINT at gray dawn. A steady, bone-chilling rain comes down as the trucks disgorge their men. Jumping off from the rear of one of the trucks into the splashing mud, our boys form up into the lines off scene. Walker is standing by the truck. Continued thud of shells throughout—much closer now. Shivering, he takes his place in line. He's followed by Mew, then Warnicki and the pup, then Ernie. Ernie looks like a wet cat. As he piles off, Walker turns to him.

WALKER. Well, Mr. Pyle—this is the end of the line. We're liable to run into a little trouble from here on . . . We've got a couple of jeeps going back—

ERNIE (*hesitating for a moment, fully aware of the others waiting for his reply*). Do you mind if I go all the way?

WALKER (*after a brief pause*). Well, it's your funeral—

Ernie falls into line, as we hear shouts of "All right, fall in" and "Is this trip necessary?"

There is a close moving view of the men in files moving up, past the rain drenched trucks, as one soldier declares "Here we're getting amphibious." Dondaro and Warnicki exchange a glance

of jocular respect in Ernie's direction. The thunder of the guns momentarily grows louder. The men's glances stray upward. Their expressions turn grim as they look—toward the HILLS which flare up with a spasm of artillery fire.

This dissolves to a picture of GI BOOTS in the RAIN picking up wads of muck as they slog on through the mud. The view moves up to the bowed heads of Mew and Dondaro. The rain falls with constant, steady penetration.

DONDARO (*half-looking about*). Hey, where's the little guy?

MEW. Pop?

DONDARO. What d'ya mean, Pop. Ernie.

MEW. Ernie's a little way back—

They turn and look over their shoulders, and we next see—plugging his way up the incline—a small, drenched figure, falling slowly but steadily behind, despite his effort to keep up. The scene then cuts back to DONDARO and MEW shaking their heads as they plow on.

DONDARO. He's over thirty-eight. He don't need to be here.

MEW. Be here! He can even go home!

But there is a wry respect in their tone. The artillery fire comes closer as they slog on, and the scene dissolves to a long view of the TROOPS marching endlessly in the rain. They are more tired and their tempo is slower now. The company commander is seen in the background.

COMPANY COMMANDER (*yelling*). Okay, men. Fall out and take a break.

We see DONDARO, MURPHY, MEW and ERNIE slump to the ground exhausted.

This cuts to a close view of a GI's HEAD and SHOULDERS. Forked around his neck is a heavy machine-gun tripod. As he staggers to the side of the road it is as if he were undergoing some medieval torture. Sweat pours down his deep-lined, unshaven face as he removes the tripod and wearily sinks in the mud with it.

This cuts to a long view of the BOYS. They are seated and lying in various postures of complete exhaustion. The same company commander rises in the foreground as a runner comes up to him.

COMPANY COMMANDER (*in a matter-of-fact tone*). Okay, men, let's get going.

As they all start to rise, JOE, the eternal soldier, meekly takes up the tripod, slings it over his neck, pulls himself up and slogs on.

The scene dissolves to a view of the MARCHING TROOPS: then to ERNIE as he drags himself up to a stone on the side of the road and sits down! He's pooped. Despite the cold rain, he takes his helmet off and wipes the perspiration from his brow. He looks over his shoulder and waves the gang on. The angle widens, keeping ERNIE in the fore. Quite a distance off now, Walker's company is heading up through a defile. A couple of the boys turn and wave back to Ernie before they disappear around a bend.

ERNIE, seen closely, reaches into his pocket for a cigarette. Wet-fingered, he finally gets a cigarette out and then vainly tries to light a match in the rain. After some effort, he gets the precious flame lit and is bringing it up to the bedraggled cigarette when the water pouring down from his helmet drenches everything. He dashes the limp cigarette to the ground. There is the sound of troops moving off. Ernie turns and, in a fairly long view, as seen from his angle, we see: coming up the narrow road another line of troops approaching Ernie and going in a direction at right angles to that taken by Walker's company. They too are mud-caked, weary looking, but with a certain cockiness about them. They call out jauntily as they pass Ernie.—One of the men falls slightly out of line.

GI. How about getting my name in the paper? Harry Fletcher, Ashtabula, Ohio.

ERNIE (*grinning*). Sure. What'll I say?

The angle widens to include the SOLDIER as he moves on.

GI (*yelling back*). . . . Anything, just so the folks back home see my name in the paper . . .

And now another soldier calls out to him.

GI. Hey, Ernie. Tell Cleveland, Joe McCloskey is winning the war—single-handed.

We get a close view of ERNIE as he watches the soldiers moving on.

ERNIE'S VOICE. Winning the war single-handed—Joe McCloskey who mixed sodas in the corner drugstore and Harry Fletcher who just hung out his law shingle—Danny Goodman who checked your oil in the summer and studied medicine in the fall, and here they are, facing a deadly enemy in a strange and far-away land. This is their baptism of fire—with chaos—in defiance—Going up the brink of death in the night time — puzzled — afraid — each boy faced the worst moment of his life—

alone—It was a battle without let-up —and it was going against us.

He wipes his face thoughtfully and

then gets up to join the line as the scene fades out.

# PART TWO

The interior of a FARMHOUSE fades in. It is dusk. The old battered farmhouse has been converted into a command post. Lieutenant Strobel, his face strained to the point beyond exhaustion, is at the phone which has been set up on a box. On the wall behind him is a torn field map; Sergeant Fleers near it. Several men lie huddled in sleep in the shadows of the room. Lt. Wilson sits slumped on a box. Dusk is rapidly falling and there is a chill and spiritual darkness about the scene which is sensed more in the weariness of the men's faces, bodies, and dust and sweat-clotted uniforms, than in the failing light. It is that final weariness which men can endure while they still move, talk when they have to, or even fight again when they must. Continuous sound of gun fire is heard throughout.

[STROBEL (*half-asleep at the phone*). Two days ago we were doing fine . . . going to kick the . . . 'n' parade into . . . parade into . . . .

Dozes off without finishing. Suddenly he jerks awake and grabs the phone.

STROBEL (*into the phone; automatically*). First Battalion . . . First Battalion.

He looks a bit bewildered as he hears no reply—and hangs up.

STROBEL (*smiling wanly*). Keep hearing it all the time. . . . (*Then*) Try to reach Walker again . . . See how he's . . . Strobel to Walker. Over. (*A burst of shell fire blots out his words.*)

From another angle, which includes the DOOR, we see Ernie as he enters, battered and worn. He limps over to Sgt. Fleers, who is marking his map with the aid of a flashlight.

STROBEL. Shut that door!

ERNIE (*wearily*). Sorry. How we doin'?

FLEERS (*after a pause; morosely*). It's not so good. . . . Got us "zeroed" in with artillery on two sides . . . They can fan a fly's tail in mid-flight if it's dumb enough to show. . . .

A terrific explosion bursts directly overhead. The two men instinctively dive to the floor.—We see the two men on the FLOOR as they are about to rise, but before they can do so, a second explosion shakes the house. Fleers looks over at Ernie.

FLEERS (*a little angrily*). You're a correspondent. What in hell d'ya want to get up so close for?

Ernie is a little apologetic at his lack of good sense.

ERNIE. You got me!

They start to rise shakily, the angle widening.

FLEERS (*spitting*). If I was out there and I wasn't scared—I'd get scared now . . .

Suddenly there's a burst of gun fire, flatter and nearer than the shell fire.

FLEERS (*laconically*). Sending in their heavies.

LT. WILSON (*limping over*). Lousy Krauts. Sneak out, fire a few rounds at our lighter stuff and then chase back to cover. . . .

Fleers glances at the map, the view moving in.]

FLEERS. Only thing between us and them is Walker's gang.

STROBEL. Not many men.

FLEERS (*pointing to the spot on the road*). Yeah—it's a lucky thing them Huns don't know it—yet.

STROBEL (*into the phone*). First battalion . . . Right. . . . Withdraw Somers position to Hill 362. . . .

Fleers does so. His new pencil mark makes a definite dent in the right flank.

STROBEL. Strobel to Walker. Strobel to Walker. Over . . . Can't seem to reach Walker . . .

The three men exchange silent glances. They turn away. The phone rings.

STROBEL (*answering it*). First Battalion . . . D company. Yes, sir, . . . I see . . . No, sir, Colonel Hunt hasn't got back yet from his reconnaissance . . . He . . .

COL. HUNT'S VOICE (*cutting in*). Who is it, Ralph?

The angle widens revealing Colonel Hunt standing in the doorway. A PFC closes the door behind him. Hunt's tired old-young face, lean as shell splinters, is rowelled with exhaustion.

STROBEL. Captain Horton, sir. . . . Reporting four of his mortars knocked out. . . . He's pretty badly shot up.

All stare at Hunt. After a moment he makes his decision.

HUNT. Tell him to pull back to Hill 148 and dig in.

STROBEL. Right, sir. (*Over the radio*) D Company. Hello. . . . D Company. Hello . . . (*His voice frantic*) They don't answer, Colonel . .

COL. HUNT. Keep trying.

STROBEL. Right, sir.

Silence—the significance of Horton's sudden silence sinks in. Hunt stares singly at the men in the room. They stare back at him through the half-light. When he comes to Ernie, he pauses.

FLEERS (*quietly explaining*). Correspondent . . . Hello . . Ernie. Hi!

STROBEL (*still trying to make contact*). Hello—hello.

Hunt just looks at Ernie and then goes over to the map, swaying slightly from exhaustion as he goes.

We see the men grouped around the map, the view favoring HUNT. The men have gathered around Hunt. He closes his eyes for a moment and then opens them.

HUNT. Both flanks are gone. Our center's weak. We're just spread too thin . . . They threw us in to try to bluff and hold them. The lousy Krauts are beginning to find out . . .

The men listen; the shadows in their exhausted faces are deepened by the flashlight held under them.

HUNT. They're pouring more and more strength through the pass. Yeah, and despite all the fairy stories, a good green man can't beat a seasoned, crafty veteran—especially when the veterans get thrown together.

STROBEL (*quietly*). Benson's through, sir—they knocked him out when they came through the pass. . . .

HUNT (*his lips pressing together; shrugging*). Well, there it is. All we got in front of us is Robert's and Walker's outfits. A little more than a company. They're not enough to hold the Jerries back. . . . But if the infantry sticks it out—(*decisively*)— we will too.

He looks around for any contrary opinions. There are none. The men move silently away. Lang comes in from the next room.

LANG. There's some hot coffee and beans on the fire, sir . . .

HUNT. No, thanks.

FLEERS. I could use some.

He looks inquiringly at Hunt. Hunt sinks to a box without replying. There is a shell burst close by. The men hunch within themselves. The building trembles and subsides.

ERNIE. Me, too.

STROBEL (*trying the phone*). D Company—hello, hello.—They don't answer, Colonel.

HUNT. Okay.

They follow Lang toward a side doorway, following which we see them flashlight their way down a narrow passageway toward the kitchen. Two more shells burst just overhead. The passageway is too narrow for them to do anything but huddle against the wall until the trembling building subsides.

FLEERS. He's beginning to split the plate.

The view moves with them down a stairway leading to the kitchen on the ground level. Next we see them in the KITCHEN moving across to the stove and being forced to step across a young girl's legs as they go . . . Then we see the GIRL from Ernie's angle. Only a slight trembling of her body and a tighter gripping of her chair reveal any reaction. Her eyes still remain fixed into space. There is the sound of the door opening.

The scene cuts back to the main room of the farmhouse, the officers' dugout, where COLONEL HUNT is seated in the foreground. The door opens. Hunt looks up. Walker enters the room and comes toward him. Walker's unshaven face is gaunt with weariness; his uniform gray with caked mud.

WALKER (*tensely*). How's it going, Walker?

WALKER (*his voice deadly tired*). Oh —we're holding out okay, sir . . . Our phone went dead . . . Captain Roberts sent me up to see if there was any—any change in plans—or— or what . . . well, if there was—

Hunt glances over to Strobel, who is listening intently at the phone. Strobel shakes his head.

HUNT (*to Walker*). No. No change— yet—Better stick around for a while.

Walker turns away, the scene moving with him as he goes wearily toward a box. Ernie, preceded by Lang, comes out of the passageway. Ernie and Walker stare at each other for a moment, their eyes expressive of all their thoughts. Behind them, in the shadows, Fleers and Wilson return to the room. Suddenly, as Walker sinks to a box, all sound of gun fire ceases outside.

A deadly and ominous silence falls over the room. The men lift their heads, straining their eyes, their bodies tense. The silence is sharply cut by the jangle of the phone.

VOICE OVER RADIO. Day to Hunt . . Day to Hunt . . . Over

STROBEL (*who has lifted the phone*). Hunt to Day. Over.

VOICE OVER RADIO. Withdraw tank positions—Zebra 87. Zebra 87. Over and out.

Hunt's lips tighten. There's a brief pause. Then he speaks:

HUNT. Fleers—put all these papers in the fireplace.—

FLEERS. Burn 'em, sir?

A wider angle shows everyone tensely watching Hunt, waiting for his decision. Hunt's face mirrors his brief hope that he can still hold.

HUNT. Not yet.

Fleers quickly goes about the business of gathering up the company documents lying on boxes near Strobel, taking them to a small fireplace at the right. Suddenly the sound of shell fire starts again in the distance. And as suddenly the door bursts open and a worn and bloody soldier staggers into the room. Several flashlights turn on him as the view swiftly moves in to him. It is Warnicki, bleeding profusely from a cheek wound, his eyes glazed, his tongue thick with shock.

WARNICKI (*panting; thickly*). Lieutenant Walker—Lieutenant Walker—

WALKER (*who is at his side*). What is it, Sergeant?

In his shocked state Warnicki doesn't recognize him. He starts moving on.

WARNICKI. Lieutenant Walker . . . Got to see Lieutenant Walker . . .

Walker holds him, turns him around. The others gather around.

WALKER. Here I am, Warnicki!

WARNICKI. Never saw anything like it. Never saw anything like it in my life.

A faint look of recognition flickers in Warnicki's dazed eyes. He tries to talk, but his tongue is too thick with shock.

WALKER (*soothingly; his voice surprisingly soft*). Take it easy. Easy—boy—easy. . . . .

Someone—Lang—comes up with a drink. Warnicki gulps it; seems to revive—recognizes Walker's friendly face for the first time. He begins to talk, his lips still stammering.

WARNICKI. Th-their heavy t-tanks overran our position—p-point blank! Point blank, sir . . . had to get out . . . had to get out. Got some of the men behind the hill. Did the best I could, sir . . . did the best I could.

The men are seen closely, the view favoring HUNT, as he watches Warnicki's agonized face and hears his words.

HUNT (*decisively*). Fleers, burn the papers . . .

An officer at his side starts to protest.

HUNT (*a little sharply*). This'll be the first time I ever ordered any outfit out of anywhere. I wonder when we're going to start winning this war.

He turns to the others, the angle widening. The flames of the company papers cast an eerie dancing light over the scene.

HUNT. Strobel, notify the company

commanders we're pulling out. (*Grimly*) We'll save what we can for another day. All right, men, on your feet.

STROBEL. Strobel to Day. . . . Come in. Over.

VOICE OVER RADIO. Day to Strobel. Over.

STROBEL. Scram . . . Scram. . . . Over and out.

Hunt starts toward the door, followed by the various officers and men, the view moving with them to the door.

FLEERS (*to Ernie, nodding toward a "sleeping" man*). Come on . . . he's dead.

The view "holds" on the door, as the men hurry, limping grimly into the night. The dancing flame of the burning papers is reflected on the door as the scene fades out.

# PART THREE

A rocky landscape fades in. There is a long view of the countryside as soldiers are winding over a hill and coming forward. Then we see ERNIE seated at a typewriter in the foreground. As he types, he is seen drinking coffee from a flask and soaking his feet in a helmet filled with water.

ERNIE (*as he types*). American boys —beaten—beaten badly. One of the few times in our history. It was a bitter and humiliating experience, and Joe McCloskey was wondering what the folks back home in Cleveland were thinking of him now.—As we look back on that first defeat and the bloody victories that followed we realize that only battle experience can make a combat soldier. Killing is a rough business—men live rough and talk tough.—Jimmie O'Brien— 1918—State . . .

We see a GI standing near Ernie, looking over his shoulder.

JIMMIE. Hi, Ernie, thanks for putting my name in the paper—I believe I'll get a commission—

ERNIE. Selling what?

JIMMIE. Me and my buddy—E-l-b-r-i-g-h-t . . .

ERNIE. That was cute the way he told the joke.

JIMMIE. Best outfit in the whole army.

ERNIE (*continuing to type*). On a dull day you can always get a fight in the Army by arguing which is the best outfit. In a year I've been to a lot of places and learned to love a lot of men. One special place in my heart was with the boys I'd started with. Everybody else had a company and I felt I had one too— Company C—18th Infantry. And I was wondering about Wingless Murphy, Sergeant Warnicki and Lt. Bill Walker and a funny little mutt named Ayrab.

The scene dissolves, showing the BOOTS OF GI'S ON A DUSTY ROAD. The boots, hard and encrusted, look as though they've been slogging over three of the five continents and are well on their way over the next two. Tagging along with them, like a lean, graydusted veteran, is Ayrab, the company pup. As the swirls of dust rise, the view moves up and reveals Dondaro and Murphy. They look tough, whiskery, hard-shelled—and weary as they march on.

MURPH. Hey, Dondaro . . . What town do we take today?

DONDARO. San Raviolo.

MURPH. Didn't we take that one yesterday?

DONDARO. Naw, that was San Something Elsio.

They walk on for a few moments.

ERNIE'S VOICE (*coming over the scene*). Hadn't seen 'em in a long time—now I set out to find 'em. They'd been through a lot by now—Conquest of Sicily—murderous landings in Salerno—hammering down the long hard road to Rome.· . . .

We now see a STEEP HILL as our men slog up a few steps, reaching a level spot. Walker climbs into view.

WALKER. All right, men. Fall out. Chow up. (*The men flop wearily to the ground.*)

MURPH (*as he stretches out*). You know after this war is over I'm gonna get me a map and find out where I've been.

Mew, nearby, glances off and grins. He nods across the road, whereupon the view moves slightly to include a windmill standing in a field. It bears the manufacturer's sign: "Meline Company, Illinois."

The GI's on the GROUND are startled by a loud, but distant reverberation which shatters the otherwise peaceful scene. Spencer, who has been dozing, wakes up, alarmed. As the boys sink back and relax again, we hear the noise of trucks grinding up the hill, immediately followed by a cry of "Mail Call." Spencer and the others instantly come awake and run off in the direction of the cry, and we next see them gathered around the jeep waiting for their mail. The jeep is one of several other supply trucks that are still coming up and parking. As the lucky ones get their letters, they go off by themselves to read them.—As the ·view moves past them at the various boys. One kisses his letter surreptitiously; another frowns; a third, Dondaro, laughs aloud. As he continues to read, the camera moves on past Lopez whose smile-wreathed face nods, "Si, si, si," as he reads, then pauses on Mew who seems puzzled as he turns an official looking paper over.

MEW. Hey, what's this?

SPENCER (*looking over*). Your insurance form. What's the matter with you?—You forgot to put in the beneficiary's name.

MEW. What's that?

SPENCER. Anybody whose name you put in there gets the 10,000 semoleos.

MEW· (*a little taken aback*). Anybody whose name *I* put there gets . . .

SPENCER (*laconically*). Yeah. And you'd better put it in before the next shindig, bub, or there won't be no dough. Stick your old lady's name down and you're okay.

MEW. I ain't got no—

SPENCER (*shortly*). Your old man, then. (*As Mew shakes his head*) Ain't you got no relatives?

Mew grins and again shakes his head.

SPENCER (*a little impatiently*). Well, stick anybody's name down. You don't wanna let all that dough go to waste.

He goes, leaving Mew grinning like a potential millionaire. But suddenly a worried look appears on Mew's face. Whom shall he put down? Here he has all this bounty to dispense but— Suddenly his face lights up. He starts to put a name down—then changes his mind. He's in a quandary. He looks around and suddenly spots Warnicki. His face lights up as he hurries over to him.

MEW (*elatedly*). Hey, Sarge—what do you know! Yesterday I ain't worth a plugged nickel, today I can throw ten thousand bucks away just like that.

But Warnicki has his own little problems. He's holding a large flat cardboard package and he doesn't know what to make of it. He keeps turning it over. Ayrab keeps leaping around him, thinking the package is something for him.

MEW (*suddenly caught by Warnicki's package; inquisitively*). What've you got there? Somethin' to eat?

WARNICKI. I dunno.

MEW. Well, open it. How're you gonna find out unless you open it?

WARNICKI. That's an idea.

His dirty, claw-like hands rip the wrapping off and it's wrapped better than an onion. Warnicki finally reaches the bottom layer, revealing—a phonograph disc. He quickly reads its label and his grizzled pug's face lights up.

WARNICKI. It's from the old lady! Look what she done. She had the kid's voice put on a record. Junior's voice. He couldn't even say ma-ma when I left.

MEW (*delighted for him*). Geez. Let's listen to it.

WARNICKI. Who's got a phonograph around here?

MEW. Maybe they got one in the next town.

WARNICKI. Yeah! What are we waiting for! Let's get going!

As he whirls off with no other thought than getting to the next Italian town as quickly as possible, there is a sudden shriek of brakes near him. He almost drops the record.—A jeep has nearly run Warnicki down. Warnicki turns in sudden murderous anger. His expression has swiftly changed. There's really a killer in his expression.

WARNICKI (*starting toward the jeep; humorlessly*). Why don't you look where you're going you—

We now get a close view of the jeep and its occupants: the driver and Ernie. Ernie looking haggard, worn, combat-strained, starts to smile, but suddenly he becomes anxious as this murderous looking animal in khaki bears down on him.

WARNICKI (*glowering*). Get outa that jeep'n I'll beat your brains out— (*Suddenly he stops.*) Hey, it's Ernie! It's the little guy!

Ernie relaxes. It was a bad moment. But he doesn't have a chance to savor his relief, for others have come crowding up.

DONDARO. It's Pyle.

Ernie beaming, shakes hands on all sides.

GI's (*ad libbing*).

Seen any dames?

What's been keeping ya?

Good to see you, Ernie.

Been saving sugar for you, Ernie.

At last I met Ernie Pyle, now I can write the old man and he can relax.

BENEDICT. Here we go again. Every time you show up there's a big battle. That's the way it was in Tunisia. You better check your dog tags, boys. You know something—my old man says I look like you!

ERNIE. Yeah, that's me. I go around starting wars. A guy's gotta make a living. Gotta have something to write about. Good to see you boys again.

At this point, Walker appears, bringing the expected news.

WALKER. On your feet, men, we're pulling out. . . .

ERNIE (*seeing Walker, who is a Captain now*). Hi, Bill.

WALKER (*warmly*). Hi, Ernie.

The sergeant's voice rings out—and is echoed down the line. The GI's slouch off, obeying the whistle. Ernie gets out of the car, and we see him with Walker.

ERNIE (*grinning; with a glance at Walker's bars*). Well, I see you've been going up in the world—congratulations.

WALKER (*glancing at his shoulders*). Oh, these. Thanks. (*With a grim smile*) You know that's because I survived longer than the other Looey's, I guess. Okay, Sergeant. Move 'em out!

Ernie and Walker start moving down the line as the sergeant's whistle blows again.

ERNIE. How are you, Wingless. How's the Air Corps?

MURPHY. 'Fraid the Buddy system's got me.

ERNIE. Me too. (*Ernie glances off to-*

*ward the men; grinning, to Walker:*) Well, you got an outfit now?

WALKER (*grimly*). You bet your life we're an outfit.

Ernie again looks off toward the men, and we see, from his and Walker's angle, the GI's slogging down the road. There is something about their slouching stride, their cold, intent, impersonal movements, the way they carry their rifles, the slant of their shoulders that characterizes them, sets them apart.

ERNIE. They look tough.

WALKER. They *are* tough . . . (*Quietly; grimly*) They're killers.

Something in Walker's tone makes Ernie look up. He looks directly ahead. The reverberation of heavy shelling comes from the not too distant right. Walker looks off, his lips compressed.

WALKER (*grimly*). And they'd better be.

Ernie glances up at Walker. His face too is grave, as the two slog on and disappear. The scene dissolves to a BATTERED SIGNPOST, with GI's marching in the foreground. The Signpost reads:

| Roma | 188 Km. |
| Cassino | 19 Km. |
| San Vittorio | 3 Km. |

We see a long view of SAN VITTORIO under heavy artillery bombardment, then a SAN VITTORIO STREET. Slam-banging furiously through the battle-clouded piazza, an Anti-Tank 37 swings into action against a shell-splitting pillbox blocking its way. With workmanlike precision the five-man team blasts shell after shell at the pill-box . . . in the background a pack of wild dogs run howling through the street . . . (*Throughout the following sequence of street fighting, there is the continuous* rat-tat of machine-gun fire, ping of sniper bullets and the blast and boom of shells.)

BEFORE A THEATER: A Bazooka team dives through enemy fire to the protection of some rubble. They wham away at a shell-torn, sniper-infested theater. As they inch forward the rear man is hit by machine-gun fire. Glancing back only momentarily, the front man carries on alone amid the machine-gun fire from the theater. . . .

A NARROW STREET: A tank plows through a narrow street blasting at the houses on either side. Its sides seem to swell with each shell burst. Half-exposed, the Tank Guide blazes away in a circular fire. Now coming into the clear, guns ablaze, the tank sprints across an avenue, nimbly crunches up the steps of a public building and smashes through its walls—and continues on . . .

A SHELL-TORN STREET: A squad of GI's whirl around the corner in the background only to be pinned down by a rain of machine-gun fire from a roof-top in the foreground. They swiftly dive behind some rubble on the ground. One of the GI's (Murph) in the rear, slinks off to the right.

A CORNER BUILDING: Pressed against the walls, Murph comes around the corner of the building in an almost careless slouch.

We get a close view of MURPH unpinning a grenade. He hurls it with an over-hand motion to the roof-top above him. And waits—with an almost comically meditative patience. There is a blast above him. Smoke and powder billows out of the smashed window. Murph kicks open the door and peers

in. He pops out again, his mud-caked face split in a grin as he holds up three fingers.

We see ERNIE peering out cautiously from behind some rubble in the direction of the street fighting. He's evidently making up his mind to dash across the street. Bullets spatter all about. Suddenly there's a lull—and he chances it.—As he darts across, doubled over, several rifle shots ping at him. He reaches a wall, from behind which Walker is covering him, firing with cold precision at the sniper.

We get a close view of ERNIE and WALKER: Ernie is panting and sweating.

ERNIE. When you're in the Infantry—there's no way to reach a ripe old age.

Several bullets splinter the brick above them. Walker swiftly fires back. The enemy is silenced.

WALKER (his eyes glinting). I'm gonna build me a highway to Berlin over them . . .

The rattle of machine-gun fire cuts his words. This is immediately followed by a cry of "Medic! Medic!"

From another angle we see Mew and Spencer hiding behind some rubble. With them is a Medic who has just finished bandaging a wounded GI. The cry of "Medic!" comes over. The Medic exchanges a short swift glance with Mew and grimly crawls off in the direction of the cry. Suddenly Spencer raises his rifle upward.

Next we see Dondaro, sweating and breathing hard, breaking into a small café where there is a sudden scream. He is about to shoot when he sees a young, disheveled, frightened, but obviously handsome, woman backing away in a corner.

DONDARO (*almost to himself*). The Promised Land. (*Grinning; softly*) Hiya, babe—

As he approaches, she backs away slightly. Her look of fright has disappeared; her lips part in a soft, sultry smile. They are both breathing hard, their eyes fastened to each other. The war outside has vanished, has been forgotten completely—if anything, enhancing and adding excitement to their meeting.

DONDARO (*in Italian, softly*). My bones told me all the time you were waiting right here for me, babe—

AMELIA (*her eyes suddenly widening with a new delight; in Italian*). You —Americano—! You speak beautiful Italian—!

DONDARO (*as he moves closer to her; in Italian*). Yes, from Brooklyn . . . gift to Italian womanhood. The liaison officer. Your long lost cousin.

AMELIA (*delighted with his Italian*). Bello! Bello! You speak my language!

His hand strays to her hip.

DONDARO (*half Italian, half English*). Listen, Rainbow, even if I was dumb, I'd still speak your language. Si?

Her eyes glance sidelong down at his hand and then back at him.

AMELIA (*softly*). Si.

With a throaty little laugh, she slips excitingly away from him to behind the counter. He swiftly follows her. Suddenly they look at each other and words are superfluous. He grabs and kisses her fiercely—pouring all his hunger, loneliness, anguish, dreams in that kiss. She yields, returning his kiss with the same intense hunger. As he bends her back, their figures are hidden by the counter. The view holds on the half-shattered shelves with broken wine bottles. The beat and throb of the battle outside comes over.

Machine gun fire suddenly rakes the wall, sending down a shower of glass. But still they don't come up for air. Suddenly there's a burst of nearby shellfire, shaking the house. Dondaro lifts his head, dazed. He slowly seems to remember where he is, what's going on outside. He shivers as if pulling himself together.

DONDARO (*disgusted*). There's that . . . (*another shell burst*) . . . war again. Sounds like they're paging me—

He releases her and hurries toward the spot where he dropped his rifle. Amelia, trembling, clings to him.

AMELIA (*in Italian*). Oh—no! Don't go!

DONDARO (*in English; half tempted*). Honest, Rainbow, this hurts me more than it does you—

He kisses her again; quickly this time— and picks up his rifle.

DONDARO (*in English*). I'll be back, don't worry—

He starts toward the door.

AMELIA (*shaking her head; in Italian*). I don't understand what you mean—

DONDARO (*stopping; with a grin; in Italian*). When I get back—you'll understand — (*in English*) — okay, okay—(*He gestures; in Italian.*) You wait here. Si?

She nods with a little laugh.

AMELIA (*in broken English*). Okay— Okay.

As Dondaro hurries toward the door, he turns. Amelia smiles and nods eagerly. Dondaro opens the door. The sound of battle grows louder. Grinning, he pauses only long enough to note the number "29" on the door, and ducks into the battle-riddled street.

The TOWN SQUARE: In the foreground, Warnicki, Walker and Rogers, grimly move down the rubble-strewn square seeking out snipers. Suddenly Rogers, bringing up the rear, steps on a hidden mine. There's a terrific explosion. Warnicki and Walker flatten out.

As the shower of rocks and smoke subsides, they look back. Rogers has completely disappeared from the face of the earth. Their lips frame soundless curses. Grimly they start forward again, only to be suddenly pinned down by a sharp hail of bullets from the right. Swiftly they dive behind some rubble and peer in the direction of a half-ruined church diagonally across the street.

WALKER. Where's our platoon?

WARNICKI. Up the street.

WALKER. Looks like this one's on us.

WARNICKI. Okay. I'll cover you.

The CHURCH BELFRY comes into view and we see a pair of German snipers firing down at Warnicki and Walker from the windows, following which WARNICKI and WALKER are seen firing back futilely.

WALKER. Let's go to church, Warnicki.

WARNICKI. Okay. Wait a minute.

Walker nods and keeps firing as Warnicki quickly unloosens a smoke-grenade from his belt. The two men act in accord, as a team, without words. Warnicki removes his carefully

blanketed record and lays it in a little cache amidst the rubble.

WARNICKI (*patting it as he might a child*). You stay there, Junior. Papa'll be right back.

He hurls the grenade into the street.— We see the STREET as it is instantly filled with obscuring smoke. Warnicki and Walker dive into it. A frantic spray of bullets from the church seeks them out.—Through the thinning smoke, Warnicki and Walker, uninjured, are revealed tensely flattened against the wall. Walker is about to dash into the church. But Warnicki checks him. He loosens another grenade and hurls it through the door. Again smoke blots out the scene; again the excited searching spray of tommy-gun fire.

Inside the CHURCH: Smoke still fills the scene. But the sound of the gunfire is strangely different. It echoes and re-echoes eerily through the cavernous building. Suddenly it ceases. The scene is filled with a deathly stillness as the last echo dies away. As the smoke thins we see Warnicki and Walker hidden behind a pile of rubble. They listen tensely. They scarcely dare breathe as they peer about cautiously.

There is not a sound, not a movement in the half-demolished church. A single fading ray of sunlight shoots down through the torn roof. The rest is in massive shadows. The statue of an angel stands like a ghost in the half-light. Before the altar lies a heap of rubble. The stillness is filled with an awesome terror; death may spit instantly from any shadowed niche or crevice.

WALKER (*barely audible*). Pst! (*Suddenly he shouts out a taunting insult.*) Lousy Kraut schwein!

As the shout echoes and re-echoes against the walls, from somewhere another shout comes over.

SNIPER'S VOICE. Americanische Schiese!

The shouts and the echoes intermingle in weird and bewildering reverberations. Walker, ready to shoot, doesn't. The echoes are too bewildering. Warnicki grimly realizes something must be done to get the snipers to disclose their position. Silently he gestures his intent to draw the German's fire by dashing across to a pillar toward the alter. As he does so, Walker is to cover him. Walker nods. Warnicki tensely sets himself.

We get a wider angle of the CHURCH, with Warnicki and Walker in the foreground. As Warnicki with a cry of "Lousy Kraut Swine!" exposes himself by swiftly diving across from the rubble heap to the pillar, a shot rings out. Shot and cry reverberate.

We see WALKER swiftly firing toward the gallery, and then the GALLERY as a sniper tumbles forward, following which the view widens to disclose Warnicki, hidden behind the pillar, indicating he's all right. They grin at each other. They are breathing hard with the tension. Walker lifts his fingers indicating "That was one, but there are two." He gestures it's his turn now to try Warnicki's trick. Warnicki grins and bows his acquiescence.

We get a close moving view of WALKER as he dives with a cry toward another rubble heap near the altar.—But there is no revealing shot. Warnicki tensed to fire, looks puzzled. He looks across at Walker. They look troubled, let down. Where is that other German? Warnicki shouts again. But only his own voice echoes through the church. Stillness again. A more ominous stillness.

Slowly a rifle barrel appears between the wings of the STATUE OF THE ANGEL, aiming downward.—WARNICKI swiftly fires at the angel, and we see it, then, toppling with the sniper. Warnicki and Walker rise from their places with audible sighs of relief.

WARNICKI. It's a funny place to be killing men in, isn't it?

And on these words Walker goes toward the sniper near the angel, while Warnicki, in his simple gratitude, picks his way over the rubble to the altar.

Through a narrow break in the debris —a perfect sightline for a sniper— Warnicki can be seen kneeling to cross himself in devotion. A shot rings out.— Simultaneous with the shot, Warnicki bows his head. The bullet pierces through the top of the helmet, missing his skull by the fraction of an inch, caused by his bowing.

Thereupon the scene tilts upward past Warnicki to the belfry. Warnicki swiftly swings around. He fires at a sniper exposed in the belfry. He hits him. The sniper staggers and grabs at the bell-rope to steady himself. The bell begins to toll—slowly, with a death-like knell. Warnicki and Walker drill steel at the swaying body, until the German's grasp loosens and his body plunges downward. As he falls, his plunge gives momentum to the swinging bell, and its rhythm accelerates into a joyous, triumphant ring, echoing and re-echoing through the church as the scene fades out.

# PART FOUR

A WINDOW fades in; the sound of the church bell still ringing over the scene. An old, wrinkled woman timidly peers out from behind the battle-scarred, shattered window. She looks uncertainly up and down the street. Evidently reassured, she sticks a small American flag in a corner of the window, a broad smile wrinkling her face.—Fresh American troops pour across the PIAZZA. Several ambulances of the Surgical Unit drive by. Old Italian villagers with children and bundles trudge back wearily but happily, to their homes. In the foreground the engineers have begun to repair the shattered bridge.—Outside the CITY HALL, a vociferous crowd is angrily milling around the shattered doorway. They drag out a rat-faced civilian from his hiding place. They shower him with blows, cursing: "Fascista Manure Traittore!" as he coweringly runs their outraged gauntlet. Several MP's enter the scene and take the Fascist in tow.

MP SERGEANT. Okay, guys! We'll handle him from here on!

As the MP's drag him off, the villagers still spit and hurl their curses in the traitor's face.

We next see a STREET CORNER where GI's are distributing hot soup and bread from a food truck to a long line of women, children and old men. The children gulp their food down without chewing, as if they had never eaten before. Grins gradually suffuse their faces as the hot food begins to take effect. One little girl looks up at the ladling GI. Cries of "Viva Americano, Viva Americano" are heard.

A STREET INTERSECTION comes into view. A double file of German prisoners, guarded by GI's, come down a side street. Some are still a surly, arrogant-looking lot. Others are beaten to a point of cretinism. A couple of Signal Corps cameramen run up and take pictures of them.—The view swings sharply toward a side street where several returned villagers are poring over the rubble in the middle of the street.—A MIDDLE-AGED COUPLE stands forlornly looking at the wreckage of a shop. The man holds a child in his arms; beside the woman stands a little ragged girl—obviously their children. There is a black armband around the man's sleeve.—Tears fill their eyes as they view the wreckage of their life's work. He looks up at the ruined building. They all follow his gaze, and we see American flags appearing in many windows.—Smiling through their tears, the little group enters their wrecked shop and starts to straighten it up.—Then we see ANOTHER STREET as the fresh GI's march down, a bunch of children tagging after them, brashly importuning.

CHILDREN. Americano cigarette! Gimme!

One, a ragged boy in a GI barracks bag with name, serial number, etc., imprinted across the seat, is particularly persistent.

BOY. Gimme Americano cigarette! Gimme.

GI. Cigarettes are no good for children—go away—go away.

BOY (pleading). Gimme! Gimme! Me Americano!

GI. Sure. Your name's GI Joe, ain't it.

BOY. Si, si! Me. GI Joe! (*As the GI laughs*) Cigarette! Cigarette!

GI (*reaching into his pocket*). Cigarettes no bono for kids.

He throws the child a small package, and the boy expertly catches it. It's a bar of chocolate. The boy bites into it and grins. Then he runs after the GI; and in the distance we see him take the GI's hand and go off skipping as the scene dissolves to the OUTSKIRTS of the TOWN. Lying around in various stages of exhaustion, on both sides of a tree-lined road, are our GI's. Dondaro has taken off a mud-caked shoe and is examining his arch. Nearby Ernie is washing an extra pair of socks in his tin helmet. Warnicki is lying back on his equipment staring at the sky, a wisp of grass between his teeth, Ayrab at his feet. Mew keeps polishing his rifle; Murph is yawning.—Dondaro lets out a groan.

DONDARO. If this war don't kill me first, my feet will.

WARNICKI (*with a jaw-cracking yawn*). Me, I feel like forty-five.

Ernie wrings out his hose.

ERNIE. I feel like I was too. And I damn near am.

MEW. How old are you?

ERNIE. Forty-three.

DONDARO. I'm twenty-six. If I knew I'd live to be forty-three I wouldn't have a worry in the world.

ERNIE. Oh, yes you would. (*He empties his helmet.*) You'd be just like me. Worrying whether you'd ever get to be forty-four.

Spencer comes into the scene.

SPENCER. Hey, guys—we got twelve hours rest until they rebuild that bridge—

DONDARO (*leaping up as a bright idea suddenly strikes him*). Stop pooch!

ROSS. Where's that whizz bang going?

ERNIE. I know I'm going to get some sleep.

Dondaro hops around on one foot, trying to get his shoe on and laced in a hurry. Warnicki has a bright idea of his own. He reaches under his equipment for Junior's blanketed record. Murph just relaxes.

SPENCER (*swinging into the scene*). Hey, Murph—hey, Murphy. That red-headed nurse of yours is in town —you know, your financee!

MURPH. Is she?

ROSS. What a lucky guy you are— meeting a girl you're engaged to in the States way over here.

MURPH (*sitting up, leaden-eyed*). Hey, did you hear that? My ever lovin' is coming to town.

But it still takes a moment before this news penetrates his sleep-befogged mind.

The scene then dissolves to a full view of a PORTABLE DELOUSING UNIT. The delousing mechanisms are at both ends of four showers. The men feed their combat clothes in at one end, stand in line for their showers, and emerge cleansed at the other end to receive their deloused clothing. A QM Sergeant —snappily uniformed, clean shaven, wearing horn-rimmed glasses—directs the operations.

SERGEANT (*officiously*). Okay men, your three minutes are up—now move out of there—Come on, get out of there. (*He is greeted with ad libs.*) Snap it up, men! Two minutes to lather—one to rinse! We haven't got all day! (*Barking at a bather*) What do you think this is—a bubble-bath?

Mew and another GI, both bearded, dirty, exhausted, stop before the Sergeant and stare at his "fruit salad," his ribbons.

MEW (*innocently*). Hey, Sarge, what's all that?

SERGEANT. This?

MEW. Yeah, yeah.

SERGEANT (*Proudly; pedantically*). Well, the yellow one is for National Defense; the red and white is for very good conduct; and the real pretty one with all the colors, is for being in this theatre of operations.

MEW (*in amazement*). No kidding!

GI (*innocently*). Yeah. Know any good war stories, Sarge?

SERGEANT. Yeah, as a matter of fact—(*Laughing*) Oh, come on, your three minutes are up.

SPENCER and LOPEZ, naked, are waiting in line to shower.

SPENCER (*looking toward the showers*). Hey, look at Murph.—He's falling to sleep on his feet.

He pushes toward Murph, whom we then see under the shower. Bearded, hollow-eyed, he desperately tries to keep his eyes open as he lathers. Spencer comes up to him and pokes him.

SPENCER (*troubled*). Hey, Murph, come on! This is your big day!

MURPH (*heroically; between globs of water*). Okay. If Red wants to go through with it, I'm game. (*He almost falls asleep there and then; Spencer shakes him as the scene dissolves out.*)

AMELIA's STREET dissolves in as Dondaro comes tearing down to DOOR NO. 29, and as he disappears through the door it slams closed.—This dissolves to ANOTHER STREET where Warnicki, holding his blanketed record, comes up to a group of Italians. Ayrab is with him.

WARNICKI. Hey! Know where I can find a phonograph? (*The group doesn't seem to understand.*) A phonograph—a victrola—a music box, see? What's the matter? Can't you understand plain English?

Heart-broken in their eagerness to be helpful, the Italians volubly canvass each other. Warnicki watches hopefully.

We get a close view of AYRAB looking up, a little ashamed of his master for even deigning to listen to this jabber. Then we see the GROUP again. No luck; none understood. Warnicki's face "neons."

WARNICKI. Look—A phonograph, a victrola, a music box.

He motions as if winding a machine. A light dawns on one of the women.

WOMAN (*in a rising scale*). Oh! Oh!! OH!!

She also makes a winding motion. Warnicki nods. The woman hurries into her ruined house.

WARNICKI (*elated*). She's got one, Ayrab! We're gonna get to hear Junior yet!

The Italians are delighted. Jabbering, they assure Warnicki she's a smart woman, a fine woman, a brilliant woman. She'll find it. And there she comes—with an old-fashioned coffee-grinder. The Italians look eagerly at Warnicki—and are crestfallen at his look of disgust.

WARNICKI. No! No! NO!! (*Another idea hits him.*) Look—(*He starts singing.*) "Oh, Marie! Oh, Marie! Did-da-da-tum   ti-da-dum   -ti-da-dum—"

Again the Italians brighten. Eager to oblige their liberator, they sing too.

ITALIANS. "Oh, Marie—Oh, Marie—"

WARNICKI (*with abysmal disgust*). Aw, nuts!

He continues down the street, Ayrab after him. The Italians helplessly twirl their fingers at their temples as the scene dissolves out.

A half blown out BUILDING dissolves in, the view moving up along the shattered building past one demolished floor, then another, and then a third, holding on Warnicki in the bomb-shattered flat, where he has finally unearthed a battered old portable victrola.

WARNICKI, with an intense, happy gleam, examines the battered phonograph, trying to make it go. He presses the lever. Nothing happens. He spins the plate with his finger. But all he can get is a grinding noise. Warnicki listens:

WARNICKI. Little rusty—(*The scene widens to include Ayrab cocking his ear.*) Ayrab, you're gonna hear Junior, or else . . . (*Hastily he searches through his pockets for a knife, as the scene dissolves.*)

The scene dissolves to a close view of MURPH soaping up his two-week beard before a mirror propped against his helmet. His eyelids still weigh a ton. As he starts a jaw-breaking yawn, the view expands, disclosing a half-ruined cottage. Mew, Spencer and Lopez are with Murph. Lopez is practicing a wedding march. Murph yawns again.

SPENCER. Hey, cut that out! You can't let Red down now.

MEW. If you do, the best man'll take over.

MURPH (*shaking his head*). I'm afraid I'll fall asleep and cut my fool head off with this Eytalian razor.

SPENCER. So what? If we can't marry you, we'll bury you. (*He signals Lopez to go on with the music.*)

LOPEZ, also yawning, starts to play the wedding march again, when suddenly there's a metallic crash.

LOPEZ. *Ay dime!* Look at that!

And we see that Murph has collapsed over the table.

SPENCER. He's folded! Gimme that razor. I done a little barbering in my time. The whole town must have shaved with this thing.

Mew hands Murph's razor to Spencer. Spencer pulls back Murph's head with a professional flourish and starts to shave him. A soldier, Jacob, comes running in while this goes on.

JACOB. Everything's fixed to the Queen's taste.

SPENCER (*as he shaves*). Get Ernie. He's gonna give the bride away.

MEW. Yeah! We'll get this wedding in the papers. (*Mew starts toward the door.*)

LOPEZ' VOICE. Get the Captain, too. He's an okay Joe.

As Mew and Trenton hurry out the scene dissolves to a view of the BATTERED PHONOGRAPH. The plate whirls about merrily.

WARNICKI'S VOICE (*elated*). It works! What did I tell you! It works!

The scene expands and we see that Warnicki's sweaty face is lit with joy. Ayrab's head follows the revolving plate suspiciously. Treasuringly, Warnicki unwraps the record, places it carefully on the plate and cranks up the motor. But as he's about to lower the arm, he discovers that it lacks a needle.

WARNICKI (*dismayed*). No needle.

Frantically, he searches around the box. No needle. He looks around the apartment, sees a broken-down dresser. He rushes to it in almost a frenzy of excitement, and searches through the drawers for a needle.

The scene dissolves to a BARN. Sleeping comfortably on a pile of hay, is Ernie. His snores come regular and sweet. Mew hurries in and tries to awaken him.

MEW. Ernie—

ERNIE (*rousing himself*). Ugh.

MEW. Wake up. We need you. Red wants you to give her away.

ERNIE (*too sleepy to know what he's talking about*). What I wanna give her away for? I like Red. (*He turns over and goes back to sleep.*)

MEW (*shaking him*). Hey, don't go back to sleep.

ERNIE (*slurring*). Oh, leave me alone. The only way you'll get me out of here is to carry me out.

MEW. We figured on that too.

He looks off and gives a sharp whistle. The angle widens as Jacob and another GI, carrying a stretcher, come up to Ernie. They roll our very sleepy and very astonished correspondent on to it, and haul him away.

This dissolves to a SHATTERED APARTMENT, where, in the fading daylight, Warnicki is breaking off the tip of a safety pin which he has found. As he bends it forward and backward, his bearded face gleams with sweat and excitement. Suddenly the pin snaps off, needle size. Feverishly, he puts the needle in place, almost fumbling it in his anxiety. He picks up the record, kisses it and breathlessly replaces it.

WARNICKI (*in a whisper of excitement*). Here goes, Ay-rab—Junior's goin' to talk to his papa.

He presses the lever. The record whirls around. Gently, perspiration tipping his nose, he places the needle on the record —and the "sweetest voice in the world" goes backwards—!

VICTROLA (*screeching*). A-*gul*-ub! A-*gul*-ub! A-*gul*-ub!

Ayrab jumps back, barking indignantly. Warnicki's face is a study in dismay and disappointment. Hastily, he shuts the phonograph off.

WARNICKI (*almost apologetically, to Ayrab*). Backwards! I'm a son-of-a—

Suddenly, there's a sharp whistle from down below.

SPENCER'S VOICE. Hey, Warnicki—!

Warnicki looks down, and from his angle we look down below, across the street: The wedding procession is nearing the ruined church. Twilight is fast falling.

SPENCER (*calling up*). Come on, Warnicki! Murph's getting married.

WARNICKI (*hastily gathering up the phonograph and record*). I'll fix it later. Come on—

He hurries over to the stairs and starts down, Ayrab with him, the scene cutting to the CHURCH. Led by Lopez and

Spencer, playing the *Wedding March,* the procession moves slowly toward the altar and the Army Chaplain. Red is on Ernie's arm. Murph, bestmanned by Mew, waits for them beside a rubble heap at the altar. Walker is in the procession. Various GI's bring up the rear. As they reach the altar, the music stops and they form before the Chaplain, who is now seen close; he is wearing a stole over his uniform.

CHAPLAIN. Dearly beloved, we are gathered here . . .

MURPH and RED are seen close. Murph has court plaster patches over his face. He valiantly tries to keep his eyes open. Red's eyes are shining.

CHAPLAIN'S VOICE. . . . in the sight of God and this company. . . . .

Now Warnicki appears at the church door. He almost stumbles over the threshold.

WARNICKI (*cautioning Ayrab*). Sh! Sh!

As he clumsily tiptoes to the outer fringe of the wedding party, we hear the Chaplain's voice continuing:

CHAPLAIN'S VOICE. . . . to join together this man and this woman in holy matrimony.

Twilight is now turning to night, as the scene cuts to the Chaplain and to some GI's with Ernie among them.

CHAPLAIN. Who giveth this woman to be married to this man?

No one moves. Several eyes turn on Ernie, who is then seen close. Ernie's eyes and thought are far away. After a pause, the Chaplain repeats:

CHAPLAIN'S VOICE. Who giveth this woman to be married to this man?

Ernie comes to himself and steps forward as the angle widens. A little sheepishly he takes Red's hand.

ERNIE. I do.

Red presses his hand and smiles at him as, embarrassed, he returns to his place..

CHAPLAIN (*to Murph*). Repeat after me—I, Robert Murphy take thee, Elizabeth . . . to be my wedded wife . . . to have and to hold from this day forward . . . (*Murph repeats each phrase after the Chaplain.*)

We get a close shot of MEW. He is beaming. Suddenly he gets an idea. He looks secretively about him, withdraws his insurance blank and with a stubby pencil writes some figures on it as the Chaplain's voice comes over, Murph repeating.

CHAPLAIN'S VOICE . . . for better, for worse . . . for richer for poorer . . . in sickness and in health . . .

We see the INSURANCE BLANK. It is marked: Beneficiary—Warnicki—$2,-000 Junior—$2,000. And now Mew's stubby pencil adds—Mrs. Murphy—$2,000.

RED and MURPH are seen close as the Chaplain continues:

CHAPLAIN'S VOICE. . . . to love and to cherish, till death us do part. . . .

It is night now outside, and German DIVE BOMBERS appear in the sky.

We see the CHAPLAIN in the foreground, in the church, as he continues with the wedding ceremony.

CHAPLAIN. Those whom God hath joined together . . . (*Rushing the ceremony as the sound of the dive bombers increases and the bombers go into action*) . . . let no man put asunder . . HIT THE DIRT!

He throws himself flat. The whole party follows suit. The shell explodes with a bang beyond the ruined walls. Warnicki, in the background, covers the phonograph and record with his body.

We see RED and MURPH on the ground.

MURPH (half-covering Red's body). Take a better man than that to put us asunder.

They kiss, and the scene dissolves to a moving view of the newlyweds as, accompanied by the musicians and their escorts, they reach the edge of a road.

MEW (suddenly yelling out). Procession—halt! Okay, kids . . . It's yours.

Grinning he points off to the right, and the view moves past a ruined wall and "holds" on a wrecked ambulance with a sign planted beside it: "Bridal Suite." Where once the doors were, blankets have been tacked and looped back with GI neckties. A horseshoe is suspended over the entrance; a battered field telephone at one side is marked: "Room Service." Red and Murph enter the scene, laughing and breathless.

RED (looking back). Boys—honestly, thanks.

And Murph sweeps up Red and carries her over the threshold.—This cuts to the WEDDING PARTY, the faces displaying varied emotions as they stare across at the married pair.

Next, in the AMBULANCE, Murph removes the neckties, and the blankets drop over the entrance. The blankets are chalked with huge letters: DO NOT DISTURB.

This cuts to the WEDDING PARTY outside. The men haven't moved; they stand and stare.

WARNICKI (finally; gruffly). Awright . . . What are you guys looking at? . . . Let's get going.

They start to leave. Lopez, however, sits down with his guitar, deliberately turning his back to the ambulance.

LOPEZ (singing as he strums). Tu eres, Lupita, divina Como los rayos del sol—

[As Lopez' singing comes over, the GI's move away, one by one, their thoughts far away. They are joined by superimposed images of their beloved ones: Warnicki holding Junior in his arms with Mollie by his side, Ernie with "That Girl," Spencer with his mother, etc. Then, as they recede down the night-shadowed road, the superimposed figures have vanished. The men are alone, forlorn.

LOPEZ' VOICE.
Tu es la flor nicaragua
En la morada de amore.

We see AYRAB near the AMBULANCE. He has remained behind. He cocks his head curiously, up toward the ambulance. Lopez' singing continues.]

Inside the AMBULANCE Murph has collapsed, and is fast asleep. Tenderly, Red bends down and kisses him as she tucks the blanket over him. Lopez' song can be heard from outside.

The view looks toward snow-capped CASSINO. Flashes of artillery burst on the horizon.

LOPEZ' VOICE.
Recibe se esta cancion
Tu eres, Lupita, divina
Como los rayos del sol. . . .

His voice fades away. And now only the low rumble of distant gunfire is heard as the scene fades out.

# PART FIVE

The ROAD LEADING from the city fades in at dawn. The GI's, led by Walker and Ernie, are slogging on again in the gray dawn. The view moves past several GI's to Warnicki and Mew, then to Murph, gloomily thinking of the brilliant figure he cut on his honeymoon; then to Dondaro tearing up the road, double quick. Beyond him lies the town of San Vittorio. Reaching the line he sneaks in furtively between Spencer and Murph.—He looks wonderfully relaxed, in sharp contrast to the others. Suddenly he is attracted to something on Murph's back, which we see from DONDARO'S VIEWPOINT: Some company wag has chalked on it, "JUST MARRIED."—Dondaro grins. Spencer leans over.

SPENCER. Hey! (*Seeing Dondaro's beaming face*) Oh, oh! (*Then ironically*) Tell me, Dondaro, what's your power over women?

DONDARO (*glibly giving his recipe*). Klk! Klk! (*Looking around, grinning*) Whatsamatter with you guys, you all look tired?

Murph's doleful face looks over at Dondaro. Their faces are a perfect study in contrast. Dondaro grins.

DONDARO (*cheerily*). Good morning, dear.

As Murph starts to curse, the scene dissolves to a moving view of a ROAD favoring WALKER and ERNIE. The GI's spirits have risen with the sun. Walker, however, has a troubled look on his face as he looks ahead.

WALKER. I don't like it—too quiet.

ERNIE. Maybe they've pulled back all the way to Rome—

WALKER (*shaking his head doubtfully*). Uh uh—

From another ANGLE we see several GI's; having met no opposition, they are feeling pretty chipper.

SPENCER. A walk-away—a walk-away—

LOPEZ. At this rate we'll be in Rome in three days.

SPENCER (*with a sly dig*). Maybe Dondaro will give us a knock-down to some of his cousins—Klk! Klk!

As they turn a bend in the road, Dondaro suddenly spots someone up ahead. This dissolves to a ROCKY HILLSIDE at dusk. Tense, cautious, wary of attack, our company spreads out to occupy the hill slope. The men watchfully work their way toward the crest on which stands an old stone farmhouse. It is a rocky defile. Somewhere beyond that gap is the enemy.

We see the crest of the HILL, the STONE HOUSE in the background. Crawling up to the crest are Walker and Ernie. Walker looks through his binoculars.

WALKER. Look at that old monastery. So peaceful—(*Handing the glasses to Ernie*) You'd never think . . .

The scene cuts to the MONASTERY and MOUNTAINS: Atop Mt. Cassino, the Monastery dominates the entire countryside—aloof, brooding, eternal.

WALKER. . . . there was a war within a thousand miles of it.

ERNIE'S VOICE. Or a thousand years.

Ernie hands the glasses back.

CHAPLAIN: Dearly beloved, we are gathered here . . .

RUBEN: You've just won the Pulitzer prize, that's all!

On the road to Rome.

"It's the Cap'n."

WALKER. Well, maybe you're right about the Krauts pulling back to Rome. I don't get it, though—(*Shaking his head*) If they want to slug it out here, they can make it plenty tough . . .

At this, the scream of several shells splits the air. Ernie and Walker "hit the dirt" and start scrambling down the slope.

As the GI's scramble behind rocks for cover, shell after shell bursts on the hillside. The stonehouse is struck.

We get a view of a SHELL CRATER as Ernie tumbles into it and cowers from repeated explosions.

We next see a shallow FOXHOLE with FIELD PHONE and ROCKS. Walker's runner ducks behind the rocks as Walker scrambles into the foxhole and grabs the phone.

WALKER (*into the phone*). Get me Artillery Fire Control. (*He ducks as debris falls.*) Pete? Walker. Y'know that building on top of the mountain?

In a close view of an AMERICAN OBSERVATION POST we see LT. PETERSON at the phone.

PETE (*looking off*). The monastery?

WALKER (*at the phone*). Call it that if you want to, but I call it, in military terms, an observation post. If you don't want to get us all killed you had better give it the works.

We get a close view of WALKER at the phone.

PETE'S VOICE. Can't. Got an order about it. Religious shrine.

WALKER (*angrily, as a shell screams over*). Does that sound like religion to you?

He reaches up and places the telephone on the parapet of the foxhole.—This cuts to a close view of PETERSON as the explosions nearly wreck his phone. He grimaces.

We again see the HILLSIDE, with the MONASTERY and MOUNTAINS in the background. A piercing cry of "Medic! Medic!" rises as more shells scream over. In the distance the monastery stands like a symbol of eternal tranquility—ostensibly beyond reach of violence.

The scene dissolves to a HILLSIDE at twilight in the rain. The men are wearily digging their foxholes deeper, making use of the terrain for added protection. In the foreground Ernie is watching a patrol, led by Warnicki, slog past the shattered stonehouse with its little shrine as the scene dissolves to a full view, shooting toward a DEFILE at NIGHT in the RAIN. Lit by flashes of distant artillery, the remnants of the patrol straggle back. They are drunk with exhaustion and foul beyond recognition. As they pass, the view moves to Ernie, watching . . .

WARNICKI. All right, men—let's go! (*To Ernie*) Lost three.

The scene dissolves to an outcrop of SHELF ROCK in a fog. Ernie and Mew are widening the entrance to a dugout under the slanting shelf of rock. Ernie straightens wearily—and bangs his head against the rocky ceiling.

ERNIE. Guess it could be deeper.

MEW. Yeah, kind of looks like we'll need a permanent home here.

ERNIE. Yeah . . .

He looks off, and from Ernie's angle we see the MONASTERY and MOUNTAINS still standing aloof and imperturbable.

Into the scene, heading toward the defile, comes a sizeable patrol, again led by Warnicki.

SPENCER (*shaking his head*). Patrol, patrol, patrol . . . one more patrol and I'll go nuts!

DONDARO. Personally, I'd feel a lot healthier if that monastery wasn't lookin' down my throat.

They head into the defile, and the scene dissolves to a view of the DEFILE as Ayrab comes romping gaily out of the defile, his tail up like a flag—his friends are back! In direct contrast to Ayrab, come the men, great leaden hunks of exhaustion. Several heads stick out of the dugouts and silently watch them returning. The men separate and head for their foxholes. Warnicki heads for Walker's dugout.

WALKER'S DUGOUT: Lit by a candle, the dugout is dank, wet, dreary, just big enough for three people. Gas cans serve as furniture. With Walker is Lieutenant Henry. Walker, haggard and grimy, looks up as Warnicki enters.

WARNICKI (*with flat weariness*). Just got back, Captain . . . Drew lot of small arms fire on Hill 457 . . . Mortar fire 793 . . . Terrific artillery fire, but couldn't locate it. (*After a slight pause*) They got Lt. Josephs, Spencer and Trenton . . . Michaelson got it in the arm, but I got him back okay.

There's a moment's pause; then Walker speaks quietly:

WALKER. Okay, Steve . . . Better get some chow.

Warnicki turns and wearily goes out. Walker turns to his papers.

WALKER. You take over Josephs' platoon . . .

HENRY (*starting to leave*). Right, sir . . .

WALKER. And, oh—

Henry half turns; Walker speaks without looking at him.

WALKER. . . . If Lieutenant Josephs had any personal stuff, send 'em over . . . will you?

Henry nods and goes. For a moment Walker stares before him; then shakes himself and concentrates on his maps. A shell whines over. Walker stiffens.

Inside WARNICKI'S DUGOUT as Warnicki enters and slumps down to a flat rock: This dugout is under a slanting rock which seems to crush down oppressively on the men's heads. They sit around huddled in their great coats, mud-caked, begrimed, exhausted. The only decoration is a picture of Murph's wife, Red. Mew is heating coffee over a fitful fire. Murph, his big knees under his chin, is huddled in a corner sipping coffee. Dondaro is lying on his back, staring up at the rock. There's the constant sound of enemy shells slugging over. Slow drops of water keep dripping on Dondaro's face.

DONDARO. Somebody ought to phone the plumber. (*But he doesn't move.*)

MURPH. You know, it sounds pretty silly when you say it, but sometimes resting like this, I get a kick out of just breathing.

MEW (*offering Warnicki a cup*). Hot java, Steve—?

WARNICKI. No.

Warnicki shakes his head, picks up his battered victrola and spins the platter. It emits some outlandish sounds. Suddenly there's a swift succession of shell bursts nearby. The entire hillside trembles. Fragments of rock fall. No one stirs.

MURPH (*exasperated*). Between the monastery and Steve's phonograph . . .

WARNICKI (*grimly*). I'll fix 'em both before I'm through!

Two more shells slug the hillside.

MURPH (*bitterly*). There goes that monastery again. Everybody knows it's an Observation Post. Why don't they bomb it!

There's an unspoken answer. The men look away, and in a view favoring LOPEZ we see him looking from one to the other.

LOPEZ (*quietly*). I'm a Catholic, and I say bomb it to hell!

DONDARO. Check, brother.

LOPEZ. I got a wife and a kid. Think I want to die for a piece of stone?

DONDARO (*sighing*). Why wasn't I born a 4-F instead of good-looking?

Which reminds him: Secretively he pulls a small phial from his pocket and passes it under his nose. His eyes melt with memories and longing. Offscene Warnicki's record emits some outlandish sound.

The scene dissolves to a HILLSIDE. Led by a Lieutenant, a squad of replacements trudge up the mule trail, coming to a halt before Walker's dugout. The Lieutenant heads toward it.—He enters and salutes.

LIEUTENANT. Lieutenant Hawkins reporting, sir—replacements.

WALKER (*after a pause*). Yeah, I'll be right with you.

Hawkins goes. Walker takes another sip of coffee, obviously stalling against a job he hates. Finally he buttons his coat and goes; Ernie follows.

ERNIE. Maid'll clean it up later.

This cuts to the HILLSIDE: Approaching the squad, Walker looks over the new men. They are all young. Some look eager, some look scared, but all look young. Warnicki comes up.

WALKER. Okay, Sarge, you line the men up.

SERGEANT. All right men, fall in.

WALKER (*his voice unnecessarily harsh*). You first four—First Platoon —Sergeant Warnicki'll show you to your hotel suites . . . (*As the four men fall out and go with Warnicki*) Next six—Second Platoon—The corporal will take care of you. The rest of you go wth Lt. Hawkins—(*Turning to Hawkins*) You'll replace Lt. Henry—Third Platoon. Turn right past the mansion, and down the hill and turn to the left. All right, take over. (*The men start off.*)

This cuts to WARNICKI and his REPLACEMENTS trudging through the mud.

WARNICKI. Any of you dogfaces know anything about a phonograph?

As the men merely exchange puzzled glances, he is disgusted.

WARNICKI. The cream of the crop, I always get.

There's the scream of shells. Everyone dives as geysers of mud and rock cascade, and we get a close view of one of the soldiers looking out bewildered from a boulder.

GI. Gee—a guy could get killed here—

The scene dissolves to the GROUP on the hillside: Tensely, three Lieutenants wait with Walker for some signal.

WALKER. All right . . . Let's synchronize our watches. (*To Hawkins*) You stick with Sergeant Warnicki,

Lieutenant. He knows the terrain. Okay, move out.

We see a flash of an AMERICAN BATTERY abruptly firing a terrific barrage of shells, then the HILLSIDE. Led by their Lieutenants, Warnicki and the GI's start through the defile. Ernie holding Ayrab in his arms, grimly watches them.

MURPHY. So long, Ayrab.

ERNIE (*murmuring*). Good luck . . .

His face is blue with cold as the raw wind rips across. The thunder and scream of shells mount. It's begun to rain. Ayrab whines softly and snuggles against Ernie. He pats the pup and continues to stare out bleakly. The rain falls as the scene fades out.

# PART SIX

WARNICKI'S DUGOUT fades in. Ernie is sitting alone. Ayrab lies disconsolately at his feet. There's a fire going, coffee bubbling. Suddenly Ayrab leaps up and dashes madly out. Ernie looks up hopefully. And now he sees the returning soldiers. As the men return and flop down in their corners—one by one—sodden masses of mud and exhaustion, Ernie silently counts them. There's Lopez! And then Mew! Pause. And that new kid, Whitey! A longer pause which seems like an eternity. And Dondaro! Again a long pause. Ernie's gaze falters, and then there's Ayrab—and Warnicki! And that's all. Ernie watches for Murphy. But that's all.

WARNICKI. My poor aching back.

ERNIE looks at the corner where Murphy always sat. Then at Red's picture. Then at Mew, who slowly takes out his tattered insurance paper and a pencil, and starts to rub something out, following which we see the INSURANCE PAPER: Crossing out Murph's name, Mew changes the sum opposite Mrs. Murphy's name to $4000. The list now reads: Warnicki $2000; Junior $2000; Mrs. Murphy $4000.

Deeply moved, Ernie, who has watched this, rises, takes Murph's wife's picture off the wall, and goes out of the dugout. We then see Ernie coming out, and Walker, standing at the entrance of the dugout, watching him disappear over the hill. ERNIE is then seen trudging along, looking down at the ground, still stunned by the news, with hunched shoulders and a frozen face.

This cuts to the CORRESPONDENTS HEADQUARTERS as Ernie nears the shack. Prominent over the entrance is a sign that reads: NEWSPAPER ROW. Directly below these words is the legend:

DON'T LOOK NOW—BUT THROUGH THESE PORTALS PASS THE WORLD'S MOST BEAUTIFUL WAR CORRESPONDENTS.

Ernie, still walking slowly, enters the scene and goes into the building.

Inside the CORRESPONDENTS HEADQUARTERS, there are three correspondents—Roberts, Landry and Ruben. Ruben is hunched over his typewriter. As Ernie enters the room, the correspondents look up—then quickly stand up and make a deep salaam to Ernie.

CORRESPONDENTS (*in unison*). Our hero! Our hero! Our hero!

ERNIE. What's the gag?

ROBERTS (*subserviently*). Your mail, Mr. Pyle—(*He throws Ernie a crumpled cablegram.*)

ERNIE. Thanks. See you already opened it.

LANDRY. Why not? It was marked "Personal."

ERNIE (*smoothing out the cablegram*). What's in it?

RUBEN. Oh, nothing much. You've just won the Pulitzer Prize, that's all.

ERNIE. Well, I'll be darned. (*Reading the cablegram with a blank expression. He is still stunned by Murphy's death*).

ROBERTS. I regret to inform you, Mr. Pyle—you are no longer a newspaperman . . . you are now a distinguished journalist—

Landry, Ruben and Roberts turn their backs on Ernie. The view moves with Ernie as he walks toward his desk. Over the scene we hear Ruben's voice.

RUBEN'S VOICE. Poor devil will probably be famous now . . .

LANDRY (*sympathetically*). Tsk-tsk-tsk . . .

Ernie makes his way toward his desk, slowly, still numb. He sits down at his typewriter. Slowly he puts the telegram down and mechanically rolls a sheet of paper into the typewriter. He stares at it for a moment, then begins to type.

Looking past ERNIE'S SHOULDER we see slowly emerging on the sheet of paper the words: "I had long ago come to think of Private Wingless Murphy as an old, old friend. He was just a plain Hoosier boy." The typewriter moves back and forth: "Now you couldn't imagine him ever killing anybody."

Ernie's eyes fill with emotion, his fingers are poised for typing, but nothing comes out. He shakes his head, reaches for a bottle of liquor in his desk, takes a swallow, blinks and then begins typing furiously as the scene fades out.

# PART SEVEN

The HILLSIDE, the MONASTERY in the background, fades in. The stone house is now only a rubble, the shrine cracked. It is raining. In the distance the monastery is dimly seen through the mist. This cuts to WARNICKI'S DUGOUT. The first thing noted is the sound of a radio in this dank, dreary hole. It's a portable and the boys, huddled in everything they own, are gathered around it. The men are listening to the radio.

ANNOUNCER'S VOICE. . . . it will be a comfort to you to know that your sons, wherever they are . . . at sea, or in the sky or in their foxholes . . . Yes, sir, your boys are celebrating too . . . with the finest turkey . . . cranberry sauce . . . and all the fixin's . . .

And then the radio starts playing "I'm

Dreaming of a White Christmas."

DONDARO (*tapping his ration can, out of which he is eating*). Tough skin on this bird.

WAYNE (*digging at some beans*). I always like to eat the stuffing first.

GROSS (*to an imaginary waiter*). Cranberry sauce . . . Mm, mm!

DONDARO. Poor folks back home. Sure got it rugged.

WARNICKI (*at his "vic," trying to play it; morosely*). Shoulda got a phonograph.

This dissolves to a battle-scarred street at dusk as Ernie, walking hunched through the snow-filled muddy street, sees something that attracts his attention. Then we see the QUARTERMASTER'S BUILDING from Ernie's viewpoint. Through the office window, Walker can be seen furiously pounding the desk of a startled QMC Lieutenant.

WALKER. You had turkey . . . The other outfits had turkey . . . The general had turkey . . . My men are going to have turkey.

LIEUTENANT (*spluttering*). But we did try to . . .

WALKER. Trying ain't good enough! (*Suddenly, very quietly*) You either get those turkeys or the Supply Corp is going to have to get themselves a new Lieutenant!

His hand slowly moves toward his holster—And by God, he means it! He is holding his gun in a menacing attitude. Ernie, unnoticed by either, has entered the scene.

LIEUTENANT (*nervously*). I—I'll scrounge around and see what I can do, s-sir . . . (*He starts.*)

ERNIE (*innocently*). How about cranberries and stuff?

LIEUTENANT (*turning back; exasperated*). Oh, now—wait a minute—

WALKER (*after a swift glance at Ernie; coldly*). Cranberries!

LIEUTENANT. Cranberries!

The Lieutenant nods and goes. Walker turns heartily to Ernie.

We next see the men on the HILLSIDE as jouncing along, laden with provisions, Ernie and Walker's jeep pulls to a stop before Walker's dugout. As the two men hop out and start to unload, Warnicki approaches.

WARNICKI. Phone for you, sir. Battalion Headquarters. (*Walker and Ernie exchange a glance.*)

WALKER (*ironically*). Probably the Rules and Regulations Committee on Uplift and Morale . . .

He starts off. Ernie continues to unload with the aid of a couple of GI's who drift up.

Inside WALKER'S DUGOUT:

WALKER (*into the phone*). Yes, sir . . . Captain Walker . . . I see . . . (*Then; mildly ironic*) Just one prisoner or two . . . Naturally, sir, as many as we can get . . . (*His face shadows.*) Replacements . . . No, they haven't gotten here yet . . . yes, sir . . .

As he hangs up, the angle widens to include Warnicki entering.

WALKER. Another patrol . . .

WARNICKI (*quietly*). I'll go.

WALKER. Like hell you will! You've been on enough.

WARNICKI (*stolidly*). Every step forward is a step closer . . . to home.

WALKER (*looking up at Warnicki; then*). Okay. Get me ten men . . .

Warnicki starts out of the dugout. Walker starts getting ready.

The scene cuts to WARNICKI'S DUGOUT. Suddenly, through the opening, a box appears, followed by Ernie, followed by a GI (Simmons). Instantly the boys come to life.

ERNIE. Believe it or not, it's turkey, on the level!

In less than a second flat, they're at work on that turkey.

DONDARO. Wine? You bring wine?

ERNIE (*holding a bottle up*). What's Christmas without wine? After that little repast one cigar apiece.

Next we get closeups of WARNICKI and WALKER, who realize it's time to go on patrol; we see them going out of the dugout, Walker looking at his watch, and the patrol disappearing in the rainy night, the scene fading out. When the DUGOUT fades in again, the boys are in a relaxed mood. Lopez tinkles softly on his by now one-stringed guitar. Wayne puffs a corn-cob. Gross chews a wad, Dondaro, near Ernie, is luxuriously smoking a cigar. Mew is half-asleep. Although the air is cold, there's a feeling of old-shoe warmth among them.

DONDARO (*stretching*). Hey, Ernie, you been to Hollywood. . . . Ever know Carol. . . .

The sound of bombardment bursts into the merriment.

ERNIE (*a little startled*). Well . . . I've met her . . .

DONDARO (*intrigued*). Is it true she's got those great big . . .

Two shells slam over, drowning out his words.

DONDARO. Is it?

ERNIE (*half-embarrassed*). That's the rumor.

DONDARO (*doubly intrigued*). Well, tell me something. Are they really on the level?

Two more shells slam over.

ERNIE. I forgot to ask. Probably.

DONDARO. Klk! Klk! (*Then very seriously*) You been around a lot—Washington, New York, Hollywood, everywhere, haven't you, Ernie? Y'know, when this shindig's over, I'm gonna look you up . . . I might ask you to get me a job.

ERNIE. Yep.

The scene cuts to the HILLSIDE then: Returning wearily down the road come Walker, Warnicki and two GI's with a sullen Nazi prisoner in tow. Nearing Walker's dugout, they are met by a lieutenant.

WALKER (*wearily indicating the Nazi*). Take him down to Headquarters . . .

LIEUTENANT (*putting the Nazi under guard*). Replacements came up, Sir . . .

He hands Walker a list. Walker takes it; his face shadows.

WALKER. Fine . . . I'll assign them . . . But we'll need five more. (*The lieutenant tows off the Nazi.*) Get him down to headquarters, and even if it hurts take good care of him.

GI. But good!

The scene cuts to WALKER'S DUGOUT as, lighting a candle, Walker sinks wearily to a seat. He almost dozes off, but the list of names catches his eye. He tries to avoid them, but can't. He lifts a bottle from under his box, pours himself a drink and starts checking off the names . . . The scene then cuts to WARNICKI'S DUGOUT where entering leadenly, Warnicki is greeted by the others.

AD LIBS. Hi, Steve!—Saved you some turkey, Sarge.

Warnicki silently slumps to his corner and concentrates on his victrola.

WARNICKI (*with a sudden growl*). Don't want any . . .

The boys, taken aback by this moroseness, exchange glances. Ernie looks at Warnicki steadily.

WAYNE (*muttering*). Sure wish he'd get to hear Junior.

Dondaro, meanwhile, has stolen across to his duffle-bag and withdrawn a small bottle of "Aphrodisiac." He sniffs the "ambrosia" ecstatically and secretively dabs some behind his ears.—Thereupon, in a fairly close view, favoring WAYNE and GROSS, we see the latter taking off his socks as the pungent "fragrance" penetrates to their corner. Gross sniffs and looks over at Wayne. Wayne also sniffing, looks over at Gross. They eye each other suspiciously, then down at the sock—but shake their heads. That's a "Chanel #5" from another bottle. Sniffing, they look around at the others.—The others have also begun sniffing and eyeing each other suspiciously. Their eyes focus toward innocent Ernie.

ERNIE (*grinning wanly*). It's not me . . .

WAYNE. Klk! Klk!

But as Dondaro swiftly slithers out, their faces light up. The candle splutters and begins to die. Ernie rises and yawns.

ERNIE. Well, I guess I better turn in. Good night, fellows.

GI's. Thanks for the merry Christmas, Ernie.

He goes amid mumbled "Good nights" and "Merry Christmases." The scene then cuts to the HILLSIDE. As Ernie comes out, hunched against the cold,

Dondaro can be seen disappearing down the road. Ernie heads toward Walker's dugout . . . The distant roll of artillery is heard.—Dondaro slithers down the village street and slips into the wine shop.

Inside WALKER's DUGOUT: Hollow-eyed with fatigue, Walker sits huddled over his papers. The candle flickers fitfully, casting strange shadows on the dank walls. There's a great loneliness about this man as he sits there in this little hollow tomb carved in this foreign hillside. Ernie is caught by it as he enters. Walker glances up. Ernie goes to him with a second joint of turkey he has saved for him.

ERNIE (*handing it to him*). Merry Christmas, Bill.

WALKER (*taking it*). Merry Christmas, Ernie.

His eyes shadow; he looks away; then, as if remembering holds up the bottle.

WALKER. Night cap?

ERNIE. Don't mind . . .

Ernie sinks to a seat. There's only the soft gurgling of the bottle in the silence. They lift their cups and drink. It's murderous stuff.

ERNIE (*coughing*). What's this—a secret weapon?

WALKER (*smiling*). Grappa. Italian moonshine. A Purple Heart with every third drink.

ERNIE (*smiling*). I'd rather have some good Albuquerque sunshine . . .

WALKER (*wistfully*). It must be pretty nice in New Mexico this time of the year . . . .

ERNIE. Sure is . . .

WALKER. Always wanted to get out West—Someday—maybe—

ERNIIE. If you do, look us up. . . .
That girl and I will show you how
it's done . . . You married?

WALKER (*filling his cup*). Well, yes
and no . . . She wanted one thing; I
wanted another . . . She walked
out . . . Chapter closed . . .

He drinks, shudders as the drink goes
down. Ernie fingers his cup. Again the
silence; only the wail of the wind and
the distant rumble of artillery.

WALKER. . . . Names . . . I've
been crossing out old names . . .
putting new names in . . . (*He
looks up and laughs.*) You're not
the only writer in this bunch . . .
I've been writing too . . .

He checks himself, Ernie glances up,
understanding the burden on Walker's
heart.

WALKER. Jones—Peterson—McCarthy
—Spidofsky—Smith . . . Dear Mrs.
Smith, your son died bravely today
on the . . .

He fills his cup again. But doesn't
drink. There is a short laugh from him
—but there's no laughter in his eyes.

WALKER. And the new kids coming
up. . . . . That's what gets you
. . . Some of them have just got
fuzz on their faces . . .

We get a close view of ERNIE listening
to him.

WALKER'S VOICE. . . . They don't
know what it's all about . . . And
they're scared to death . . .

We see them together.

WALKER. . . . I know it's not my
fault they get killed . . . but I get
so I feel like a murderer . . . (*Bitterly*) I hate to look at 'em—the new
ones . . . (*Then, almost mockingly*) Drink up, Ernie . . . Here's

to Faid Pass . . . Salerno . . .
Anzio beachhead . . . (*He drinks.*)
Geez, I'm tired . . .

ERNIE. You better try and get some
sleep.

WALKER (*laughing*). That reminds
me of W. C. Fields' sure cure for insomnia. Get lots of sleep.

Silence . . . The candle flickers. Ernie
sips at his cup.

WALKER (*fighting sleep*). . . . Names
and addresses . . . and hills to be
taken . . . You'd be simply amazed
at the number of hills still to be
taken . . . (*Suddenly looking up at
Ernie*) Tell me, Ernie, why the devil
don't you go home?

ERNIE (*looking into his cup*). I've
often asked myself.

WALKER. If only we could create
something good out of all this energy
and all these men . . . (*His voice
trails off.*) They're the best, Ernie
. . . the best . . .

The view draws closer to Ernie as he
stares into his cup.

ERNIE (*quietly*). Yip! They live in
a world the other world'll never
know . . . Even the Air Force . . .
Up there they approach death differently. When they die they're well-
fed and clean-shaven . . . (*Wryly*)
If that's any comfort . . . (*He stares
ahead deeply moved.*) But the GI
. . . he lives so miserable and dies
so miserable, you just . . .

He turns toward Walker, stops and
smiles gently. Walker is asleep in deep
exhaustion, head on the table. Ernie
rises and puts a blanket around
Walker's shoulders. He looks down at
the sleeping man—then snuffs out the
candle . . . There's the distant roar
of artillery as the scene fades out.

# PART EIGHT

The HILLSIDE fades in, as Dondaro is returning in the pitch before dawn, a happy relaxed expression on his face. He furtively steals past Walker's dugout. Walker, shivering, comes out in the bone-chilling morning.

WALKER. Dondaro!

As Dondaro shakily approaches, Walker looks him over keenly, but his tone is amiability itself. The sky's begun to gray.

WALKER (*smiling*). Have a nice time?

Expecting a lacing, Dondaro is taken aback by Walker's friendly tone. He nods, puzzled.

WALKER (*still friendly*). Always like to see one of my men get some relaxation . . . (*Almost intimately*) Y'know, Dondaro, it would give me a great deal of personal pleasure . . .

Dondaro begins to beam. After all, the Cap's human. Maybe he'd like a "telephone number" too . . . Walker's sudden cold tones knife him out of his daydreams.

WALKER (*incisively*). . . . to break every bone in your body! Goofin' off down there was one thing! Up here it's another! (*Dondaro gulps; Walker blazes.*) Now get out! Before I kick the—

Dondaro hastily starts to scoot. Heads have begun to stick out of the dugouts to listen to this lashing.

WALKER. Wait! (*Dondaro halts.*) Report to Sergeant Warnicki. Tell him you're going to dig latrines for every man in this company from here to Rome! Nice deep ones.

Dondaro scoots. The GI's' faces light with delightful anticipation. A sudden shell-burst slams over as the scene dissolves to a view of the HILLSIDE, where, wielding a pickaxe, Dondaro has dug about two feet of trench. He's tired, disgusted, grimy.

GROSS' VOICE. You're lucky, Dondaro. You're learning a trade.

The angle widens to include several GI's ribbing him.

DONDARO. When this war's over, I'm gonna write a book exposin' this Army.

WAYNE (*leaning over to Dondaro*). Hey, Dondaro, tell me confidentially, was it worth it?

DONDARO (*his eyes melting*). Klk! Klk!

He digs with renewed vigor. Suddenly there's a deep all-encompassing drone in the sky—a far-away surge of doomlike sound. They all look up, crying out:

GI's. Hey, look! Look!

In a rising crescendo, a vast armada of planes approaches, wave on wave, blacking out the sky. Hurrying out of his DUGOUT, Walker swiftly looks at his watch, looks at the sky, and starts shouting to Warnicki—

WALKER (*crisp; businesslike*). Okay, Steve! Let's go!

WARNICKI (*shouting to the men*). Okay, men. This is what you've been waiting for! Okay, men—let's go! On the double!

The GI's start running up excitedly, falling into their formations ready to start out.

ERNIE'S VOICE (*heard over the scenes*). General Eisenhower had made his decision. Bomb the monastery. If we have to choose . . . between destroying a famous building and sacrificing our men's lives . . . then our men's lives count infinitely more. And—here was one of the grim ironies of war—the very rubble of the monastery became a fortress for the Nazis and they stopped us cold. We were right back where we started from.

We see the MONASTERY. A bomb explodes on the abbey. Then three—then six—Then all hell.—The hillside seems to lift.—We see that the entire company is elated at the pasting the Monastery is getting.

AD LIBS.

On the button!

Paste 'em one for me!

That's the old haymaker!

Hit 'em on the kisser!

Tons of bombs pulverize the monastery! The bombardment is volcanic. Then in a long view directed toward the STONE HOUSE and DEFILE we see the men excitedly moving out into the defile in a general attack. A GI salutes the statue in the niche as he passes.

GI. So long, St. Chris. We won't be seein' you no more.

Next we get a series of views showing the withdrawal of the troops from the attack on Cassino. Limping back, our tanks slowly grind past several overturned, still burning, tanks.—This cuts to WARNICKI'S DUGOUT as, beaten, scarcely able to breathe, our GI's stumble in and flop down in exhaustion.

Several are missing; Wayne and Gross are gone . . . Dondaro lifts his head and looks around.

DONDARO. Warnicki—ain't he back?

This cuts to the HILLSIDE, near the DEFILE. Walker moves tensely about, hunched in his rain coat. His nerve-strained face keeps looking toward the mist-filled defile. But there is no one. Only the swirling mist. His lips tighten. . . He keeps pacing . . .

Outside the GI's DUGOUT, three GI's look up very much concerned, toward Walker.

FIRST GI. Better take him some coffee . . . and keep your eye on him, too.

One of them, Babyface Pete, starts toward Walker with a pot of steaming coffee.

SECOND GI (*to another GI*). When are we hittin' 'em again?

GI (*glancing at his watch*). Eighteen hundred.

WALKER stops as Babyface Pete approaches, silently offering him the coffee.

WALKER (*gratefully*). No, thanks. . . .

PETE. It's hot.

WALKER. No thanks, Pete.

He continues pacing, keeping his eye on the defile. Babyface moves off behind a boulder and watches Walker.— Still pacing, Walker anxiously glances at his watch and then toward the defile. Still only the swirling mist . .—Hopelessly now, Walker slowly starts back toward the dugout. But suddenly he hears something in the defile. He looks up, his eyes lighting. . . . And in a distant view of the DEFILE, slowly emerging out of the mist, we see a great leaden, mud-caked figure—a mass of fatigue and weariness—Warnicki!

Walker starts to him with a cry of joy. . . . But the cry fades as he sees the abysmal weariness in Warnicki's face.

WARNICKI (*tonelessly*). Tough time gettin' back, sir.

Walker nods, and Warnicki slogs on leadenly toward the dugouts.

We get a close shot of WALKER staring after Warnicki. His eyes are filled with pain. Then the scene cuts to WARNICKI's DUGOUT. Entering, Warnicki slumps down to his corner. He does nothing but sit there for a moment, just breathing. Ayrab slides up and licks his torn, mud-caked hands. Then, automatically, without thought, Warnicki reaches down for the one comfort that has sustained him so long. His horny blood-torn hands bring the PHONOGRAPH to his knees and habitually, as he has done so often before, his thick fingers fumble at the lever—the disc revolves—but now, instead of the usual grating sound, there emerges from it the sweetest, softest, most innocent voice in the world. Junior's childish treble . . . and . . .

WOMAN'S VOICE. Come on Junior, say hello to your Daddy.

JUNIOR'S VOICE (*on the phonograph*). Hello, daddy . . . Hello, daddy . . . Hello, daddy . . . Hello, daddy . . . Hello, daddy . . .

The calloused mud-caked hand near the phonograph trembles. The view slowly moves up to WARNICKI's FACE. And it's a horrible, terrifying thing to see. For this face of rock, this granite face, this face that has endured every torture and abomination of war, is cracking. Cracking as a child's voice innocently sings on and on—

VOICE. Hello, daddy . . . Hello, daddy . . . hello, daddy . . .

The giant frame of the man seethes with a volcanic emotion; the tears burn out of his eyes. His breath comes in short tortured gasps. And suddenly he can endure no more. He rises and breaks. And it's like a great heart breaking. Not weakly, but like a storm suddenly gone berserk.

WARNICKI (*terrifyingly; between gasps*). If it wasn't for them, I'd be home with Junior . . . I'd be home with little Junior. I'll . . . I'll kill every mother's son of them . . . I'll kill them! (*He lunges fiercely toward the opening.*)

DONDARO. Grab him!

The phonograph goes on and on . . . —Springing at him, Waters and Moss try to stop him. But he tosses them aside like chips.—Tearing out of the dugout, Warnicki bulls wildly toward the defile, tearing past Walker.

WARNICKI. If it wasn't for them . . . I'd be home with little Junior! If it wasn't for them! . . . I'll kill 'em!

WALKER (*sharply*). Warnicki! Warnicki!

But Warnicki doesn't hear. He has only one thought. To get at those Nazis who have destroyed so much of his and everyone's happiness. To rip them apart with his own bare hands! Dondaro, coming down from the road, leaps at Warnicki. But Warnicki throws him aside . . . —Walker hurls himself in a football tackle at the frenzied man . . . —The two men go down in a heap near the ruins of the stone house. But Warnicki lashes himself free. Dondaro now pounces on. And Waters and Moss! But all four can't hold Warnicki in his berserk strength . . . From the dugout, the phonograph continues on . . .

WARNICKI (*frothing fiercely*). Little Junior . . . Little Junior! Let me go! What's the matter with you? You son of a—

His wildness seizes all of them like a contagion. They battle with him frenziedly, until . . . Walker suddenly shoots over four sharp vicious jabs to the button, and Warnicki sags . . . They let him down gently . . . The phonograph winds down . . . stops . . . — Waters and Moss bend over Warnicki . . . Walker and Dondaro stand there panting . . . Finally they help Warnicki up, but as they do they hear—

> WARNICKI'S VOICE (*muttering like a gibbering idiot*). . . . hello, daddy . . . hello, daddy . . . hello . . . Go on, Junior . . . say hello to daddy . . . hello, daddy, hello, daddy, hello . . .

Deeply shaken, Walker fights to keep from turning away. The men look to him for help.

> WALKER (*his voice treacherously uneven*). Take him to the medics. . . .

But now, as they lead the still gibbering Warnicki off with Ayrab dancing playfully at his shambling feet, a lieutenant swiftly runs up to Walker. (In the background the company is forming for the attack.)

> WALKER (*grimly*). All right, men, let's do something about that.

> ERNIE'S VOICE. The machines had done their best but it wasn't enough. Now came the time, as it does in every war, for the greatest fighting machine of them all—the infantry soldier—to go in and slug it out.

The scene dissolves and is followed by a series of scenes representing the victorious attack of the infantry, concluding with a close view of a SIGNPOST at night. It reads "ROMA" with an arrow pointing up ahead. Then we see the ROAD TO ROME as a long surge of troops is heading upward toward the capital. There is a spirited victorious swing to their movement. The moonlight reflects on their helmets, their rifles, their armor. The sound of battle is faint, intermittent, far to the north . . .

In the midst of these fresh buoyant troops is Ernie. He slogs along with them, an older man, reflectively noting their swing, their excited gum chewing. Snatches of conversation drift around him.

> ERNIE. Where you from, Joe?

> GI. Louisiana.

> ERNIE. Louisiana? Good.

> GI (*looking back, smiling*). Cassino looks a lot better from this side.

> AD LIBS.

All away to Rome!

I got a good telephone number there!

As Ernie tiredly smiles, he sees someone off the road. And on the ROADSIDE, with the moonlight on the HILLS in the background we see a GI who looks as though he's been thru battle. Ernie approaches him.

> ERNIE. Hey fellows, do you know where the 18th Infantry is?

> GI. This is it.

> ERNIE. C Company—?

> GI. What's left of it.

He nods over his shoulder. Ernie starts up along a narrow trail in the direction of his nod. He then see him coming to a GLEN where lying about, mud-begrimed and weary, are several GI's of our company, among them Babyface and Moss. They are exhausted, but there is a certain sense of elation over their victory. One of the men is wearily playing a harmonica to himself. As Ernie comes up, he is greeted by one or two—

AD LIBS.

Hiya, Ernie—

Welcome to this side of Cassino—

Where you been, Ernie?

ERNIE. Hiya, boys—Finally made it. Covertly he counts heads as he looks around to see which of the GI's of his company are still there; which are gone.

GI (*smiling*). Guys moving up the road look kind of chipper, don't they, Ernie?

ERNIE. Sure do!

They look toward the troops on the main road, and next, in the background, a long line of GI's can be seen marching up the road to Rome, their helmets glinting in the moonlight.— Ernie continues down the line.

GI. Hi, Ernie.

ERNIE. Hi, boys.

FIRST GI (*not bitterly*). Yeah—we kick the door open and them guys make the grand entrance.

SECOND GI. Let 'em have their fun— they're still young.

ERNIE. Got an extra chair here? . . . Haven't you eaten that dog yet?

He suddenly stops as across their vision up the hills on the opposite side of the road, comes a slow line of mules winding their way down. The mules bear a burden slung across their pack saddles, the nature of which is indistinct.

The MULE TRAIL is now seen, and so is the burden the mules are carrying.

They are dead bodies lashed, belly down, across the saddles. The stiffened legs stick out awkwardly. The mules are slowly led toward a cowshed just off the road.

The boys silently watch the mules being led toward a cowshed in the background. The line of troops marching toward Rome has passed on. GI's unlash the bodies and lift them from the pack saddles and lay them, one after another, in the shadow of the cowshed's stone wall.

GI (*looking toward the mule trail; suddenly, quietly*). It's Dondaro. . . .

They all look up, and we see the MULE TRAIL, from their viewpoint. Slowly, carefully, a GI is leading a mule with its dead burden down the trail. As he leads the mule toward the cowshed, we see that it's Dondaro. He looks half-dead himself. Gently, he unlashes the body and slides it down the mule. For a moment the dead man is stood on his feet. In the half light he looks merely like a sick man standing there leaning against Dondaro.—Then we see the GROUP.

BABYFACE (*in a half whisper*). It's the Cap'n . . .

They watch Dondaro lay Walker's body on the ground in the shadows and sit down near him.—Then we see, from another angle, Dondaro sitting there staring at Walker. Slowly some of the men across the road in the background stir and go toward Walker's body, one by one, Ernie with them. Several remain behind.

The men trail slowly up, pausing a little distance away from Walker's body. Then one goes slowly forward and looks down at Walker's body. Ernie watches them.

[G.I. God damn it!

That's all he says and walks away. And then another GI comes up.

SECOND G.I. God damn it to hell, anyways!

He looks down for a moment and then he too turns and goes.] And now a third comes up—an officer and looks down into Walker's face and speaks to him directly, as though he were alive.

OFFICER. I'm sorry, old man.

And he turns away. Finally, Babyface files up, and we see WALKER'S BODY, the view including DONDARO and ERNIE. Dondaro remains immobile. The Babyface runner comes up and speaks, not in a whisper, but awfully tenderly.

BABYFACE. I sure am sorry, sir.

And he too goes. Ernie watches, deeply moved. And now Dondaro slowly reaches out and takes Walker's dead hand into his own and stares intently into his captain's dead face, for what seems to be a long time. And he never utters a word . . .

Finally Dondaro puts the hand down and reaches over, gently straightening the points of the captain's shirt collar. Then, tenderly, he sort of rearranges the tattered edges of the uniform around Walker's wound.—And this is the gesture that breaks Ernie completely, as we see him closely. He turns away sharply to hide his emotion, and fighting for control, he walks away from the scene, toward the moonlit trail leading to the main road . . . . leaving Dondaro and Walker in the shadowed background. . . . The scene then cuts to an OFFICER.

OFFICER (*quietly*). All right, men—let's go.

And finally against the background of white wooden crosses gleaming in the moonlight, we see the troops marching onward to Rome. Ernie turns, walks after them. They go off into the distance, becoming silhouettes in the background, and the film fades out as Ernie concludes:

ERNIE. That is our war and we will carry it with us as we go from one battleground to another until it is all over. We will win. I hope we can rejoice with victory—but humbly—and that all together we will try, try out of the memory of our anguish, to reassemble our broken world into a pattern so firm and so fair that another great war can never again be possible. (*After a pause*) For those beneath the wooden crosses there is nothing we can do except perhaps to pause and murmur "Thanks, Pal."

# THIRTY SECONDS OVER TOKYO

*(A Metro-Goldwyn-Mayer Picture)*

Screenplay by DALTON TRUMBO
Based on the book and Collier's
story by CAPTAIN TED W. LAWSON *and* ROBERT CONSIDINE
Produced by SAM ZIMBALIST
Directed by MERVYN LeROY

## The Cast

| | |
|---|---|
| JAMES H. DOOLITTLE . . | Spencer Tracy |
| TED LAWSON . . . . . | Van Johnson |
| DAVID THATCHER . . . | Robert Walker |
| DEAN DAVENPORT . . . | Tim Murdock |
| CHARLES MCCLURE . . . | Don DeFore |
| BOB CLEVER . . . . . | Gordon McDonald |
| ELLEN LAWSON . . . . | Phyllis Thaxter |
| "DOC" WHITE . . . . . | Horace McNally |
| "SHORTY" MANCH . . . | John R. Reilly |
| BOB GRAY . . . . . . | Robert Mitchum |
| DAVEY JONES . . . . . | Scott McKay |
| LIEUT. RANDALL . . . | Donald Curtis |
| LIEUT. MILLER . . . . | Louis Jean Heydt |
| DON SMITH . . . . . | Wm. "Bill" Phillips |
| "BRICK" HOLSTROM . . . | Douglas Cowan |
| CAPTAIN "SKI" YORK . . | Paul Langton |
| LIEUT. JURIKA . . . . | Leon Ames |
| BUD FELTON . . . . . | Bill Williams |
| "JIG" WHITE . . . . . | Robert Bice |
| DR. CHAN . . . . . . | Dr. Hsin Kung |
| YOUNG DR. CHAN . . . | Benson Fong |
| "GUERILLA CHARLIE" . . | Ching Wah Lee |
| MR. PARKER . . . . . | Alan Napier |
| MRS. PARKER . . . . . | Ann Shoemaker |
| JANE . . . . . . . . | Dorothy Ruth Morris |
| EMMY YORK . . . . . | Jacqueline White |
| MRS. REYNOLDS . . . . | Selena Royle |

Film Editor—FRANK SULLIVAN

# THIRTY SECONDS OVER TOKYO

[It is the feeling of the producers in approaching Captain Lawson's material that a heavy responsibility rests upon them; that the motion picture resulting from it can and must contribute constructively and dynamically to the public morale. The best propaganda, of course, is the truth; and in Captain Lawson's book the truth is presented simply, decently and dramatically. We wish to make a picture in which there are no individual heroes because all are heroes; a picture in which the leading characters are the living symbols of millions of service men and their wives who quietly and gallantly offer to the American people the greatest sacrifice within their power to give.

In dramatizing the close cooperation between the Army and the Navy without which there could have been no Tokyo raid, we seek to destroy the malingering whisper that a harmful rivalry exists between these two branches of the service. Those scenes portraying the devotion and courage of the Chinese people as they smuggled scores of American airmen to safety will, we hope, constitute a genuine contribution to relations between the American people and their courageous Chinese allies.]

A LARGE WALL MAP reveals the areas of Japan, the Chinese Coast through the Malay States and on down to Java, Sumatra, etc., the South Pacific Islands, and the upper portion of Australia. Then we see the shoulder and arm of an army officer. In the officer's hand is a long pointer. On his shoulders are the three stars of a Lieutenant-General. As the scene starts, the pointer is resting on Bataan Peninsula.

GENERAL'S VOICE. We are retreating here . . . and here . . . and here . . . and here . . .

The pointer moves to a point on the Malay Peninsula about sixty miles north of Singapore, and at this the view draws back to reveal the speaker. He is a man in the indefinite fifties, erect, grave-faced.

GENERAL. The British are falling back on Singapore under heavy Japanese pressure. (*The faintest flicker of surprise, quickly suppressed and almost imperceptible, passes over the faces of one or two of his listeners.*) When Singapore falls, Sumatra—Java— (*pointing at the map*)—Borneo—the Celebes—New Guinea—all of them become practically indefensible. (*The pointer moves to the sea-lanes to America in the Pacific northeast of Australia.*) The enemy will control our sea-lanes to Australia. From these positions he will be able to launch an attack against—(*moving the pointer again*)—Midway, Hawaii, the Aleutians, or even the mainland of North America. (*He turns from the map to face his auditors.*) That, gentlemen, is the situation which will confront us within six months. (*The General lays his pointer aside, pauses*

428

*for a moment, then continues:*) The enemy almost knocked us out at Pearl Harbor, and he has continued against all principles of military caution, to strike us again and again. We are still retreating. Either we deliver an attack which will force the enemy to revise his strategy, or we *continue* to retreat. We have decided to attack.

The view draws back to reveal no less than three, no more than five, high ranking officers of the Army and Navy. They are seated, their backs to us, their faces focussed upon the speaker who faces us.

GENERAL (*continuing*). Our objective is to divert enemy forces from the combat zone to the homeland, and cause the Japanese General Staff to proceed with more caution than heretofore. (*He pauses for a moment; then his eyes narrow, his lips grow thin as he clips the words out.*) Therefore, we have resolved to bomb the principal cities of Japan.

The view draws back still further. The General pauses, to let the full import of his information sink home.

GENERAL. The hazards of such a raid cannot be overestimated. The fullest cooperation of both the Army and Navy will be required. Strictest secrecy must prevail. We in this room —with one distinguished exception— are the only persons in the world who share knowledge of the project. The men participating in the raid will not know their destination until the last moment. Volunteer personnel are already enroute to their training center. . . .

On this last sentence the view begins rapidly to pull back, and as the words trail off with distance, the scene dissolves, and three B-25 medium bombers

are seen flying over the semi-tropical landscape of northern Florida, following which there is a view of the INTERIOR of LIEUT. TED LAWSON'S SHIP, disclosing the PILOT and the CO-PILOT. The pilot is Lieutenant Ted Lawson, twenty-five, from Los Angeles. The co-pilot is Lieutenant Dean Davenport, approximately the same age, from Portland, Oregon. Lawson is quiet, good-looking, with a finely developed sense of personal responsibility. Davenport is a little the taller of the two—a handsome, cocky young man with a glint in his eye. Both of them are looking ahead and downward.

TED (*yelling over the engine noise*). There's the field.

From their angle, looking toward the ground, we see an airfield ahead.

DAVENPORT'S VOICE (*yelling in return*). Boy, did you ever see such a wide runway!

Then a close view shows TED and DAVENPORT still staring below.

TED. She's big all right. You could almost close your eyes and get in. (*Into the interphone*) Eglin Field straight ahead.

DAVENPORT. And I'd give plenty to know where we go from here . . .

TED (*nodding thoughtfully*). Yeah . . . so would I.

The scene cuts to the NAVIGATOR'S COMPARTMENT as Lieutenant Charles McClure, the navigator, peers out the window, then makes a frantic scramble for his movie camera, which is under his navigator's table. He shouts into the pilot's compartment directly forward.

MCCLURE. Hey! Don't do anything 'til I load my camera!

In the PILOT'S COMPARTMENT: Davenport looks over his shoulder and down into the navigator's compartment, which is directly behind them and below.

DAVENPORT. Oh, we wouldn't think of it, McClure. We'll cut the engines and hang right here in mid-air.

MCCLURE'S VOICE. Thanks.

TED. Don't mention it.

The NAVIGATOR'S COMPARTMENT: Chuck finishes loading his camera and rushes to the window. He lines his camera up, squints it, and starts it.

CHUCK. Okay! I'm all set! How does she look from the nose, Clever?

The BOMBARDIER'S COMPARTMENT: Lieutenant Bob Clever is riding in the windowed nose of the ship, the whole countryside spread out before him. Davenport, McClure and Ted, being very close together in the ship, can talk to each other by raising their voices. But Clever, in the nose, is completely removed (as is the rear gunner in the tail), and hence must speak by interphone.

CLEVER (with enthusiasm). Great! Florida. Palm trees. Alligators. Bathing beauties! Hey, Thatcher—have a look at some real country!

At this the REAR GUNNER'S COMPARTMENT comes into view and we see DAVID THATCHER, nineteen, young and very serious, looking out the window. He is the gunner-mechanic, and only a corporal. He takes care always to be respectful of his superiors (all others in the crew are second lieutenants), even though they would prefer him to be more at ease. He looks a little pale and wan, for he is subject to airsickness—an unfortunate weakness, since his position in the plane is the roughest.

THATCHER (into the interphone). It's not as pretty as Billings, sir.

CLEVER'S VOICE (over the interphone). Greatest country on earth.

THATCHER (into the interphone). I guess it is, sir . . . if you've never seen Montana . . .

We see the PILOT'S COMPARTMENT as Ted and Davenport exchange chuckles.

TED (into the interphone). Did you keep your cookies this trip, Thatcher?

THATCHER'S VOICE. Yes, sir. Had a little trouble over the mountains, but I hung on.

Suddenly Ted and Davenport become alert, as Lieutenant Davey Jones' voice comes over the radio. Jones is the leader of the group of three planes.

TED. Hey—wait a minute!

The scene then cuts to the PILOT'S COMPARTMENT of LT. JONES' PLANE, where Jones and his co-pilot are listening for directions from Eglin Tower.

JONES (into the radio). Army zero-two-two-four-one to Eglin Tower. Go ahead.

EGLIN TOWER (heard over the radio). Eglin Tower to Army zero-two-two-four-one. Go ahead.

JONES (into the radio). Army zero-two-two-four-one to Eglin Tower. Three B-25s request traffic and landing instructions. Go ahead.

EGLIN TOWER (heard over the radio). Army four-one. The left-hand pattern. Wind direction north by northeast. Land on runway number three.

JONES (into the radio, to his men). You fellows hear that? We're landing on runway number three.

And this cuts to the PILOT'S COMPARTMENT of TED'S PLANE as Jones' directions are heard over the radio by Ted and his co-pilot.

JONES' VOICE (*over the radio, continuing*). We'll go around and make an echelon right, do a fifteen second break-away and land at thirty-second intervals. Come over the field once, and then break away. Let's make it pretty!

Ted starts manipulating instruments to carry out the orders. As he does so, he executes a small piece of business with his white silk scarf, as if he were shining the back of his neck. This business is Ted's particular good luck charm.

TED. Here's for luck. . . . .

We get a full view of the SKY as the three bombers fall into echelon right, and carry out the order, Davey Jones' plane going first, Lawson's second, Lieutenant Brick Holstrom's third; and this cuts to EGLIN FIELD as Davey Jones' plane lands, taxis up to the ramp, and parks itself beside another B-25, wing to wing. There is a double row of B-25's already on the ramp, numbering fourteen to twenty. Next Ted's plane comes in for the landing, and we follow it as it likewise taxis up to the ramp, and moves into the wing-to-wing position beside Jones'. The rear-gunner on Jones' plane is just climbing out of the rear hatch as Ted's plane taxis up. With quiet efficiency, a gasoline and oil truck, manned by ground crew personnel, moves up to gas and oil Jones' plane. The rear hatch of Ted's plane drops open, and Thatcher emerges. He begins to carry the bags of the crew members off a little distance from the plane, sets them down, and returns for more. As the only enlisted man on the ship, this is his duty.

This cuts to Ted's PILOT'S COMPARTMENT, where Ted is busy with the various instruments, bringing the ship's two motors to silence. Davenport reaches for the form, looks at his wrist-watch, carefully notes the time of their arrival.

DAVENPORT. Five-twenty-eight. Not bad time.

TED (*still occupied with the instruments*). We moved. Better write that left engine up. She sounded a little rough.

DAVENPORT (*nodding and writing*). Yeah . . . there's a bug in her somewhere . . .

We then see the exterior of TED's PLANE as Clever and McClure come out. The gas truck, in the background, is just starting to service their ship. Also, the roaring motors off-scene indicate that Holstrom's ship is moving up to the ramp. McClure winds his camera, then surveys the landscape for a likely shot. Thatcher passes through the scene, headed for the gas crew. As mechanic, he likes to supervise the gassing of the ship, which is always done the moment of landing. Finally, Lawson and Davenport emerge from the ship.

TED (*with a jerk of his head toward the very busy ground crew hovering around the ship*). They really give you service around here. (*Davenport nods.*)

MCCLURE (*coming up*). I got some swell shots, Lawson. You really made a nice break-away—gave me kind of an artistic angle.

LAWSON (*grinning*). Some day I'll do a crash landing so you can get a real movie.

MCCLURE (*also grinning*). Great, if I could take it from the ground. Ed Kelsey up at March got a shot from his trainer just as she was sloughin' off a wing, and some photography magazine, it gave him forty bucks.

(*As he puts the camera to his eye*) Only trouble was—his widow got the dough.

The view expands to include Lawson, Davenport, and Clever, who are busying themselves checking over the ship. Thatcher is in the background superintending the gassing operation. McClure is still shooting.

CLEVER (*loudly*). Thatcher says Florida can't compare to Billings.

DAVENPORT. Trouble with Thatcher is he thinks any place with more than three hundred people is overcrowded.

THATCHER (*turning briefly from his work, with considerable solemnity*). According to the last census, sir, Billings has a population of 16,380.

CLEVER (*with pretended astonishment*). Sixteen *thousand!* Oh, no, Thatcher—you must be thinking of *Greater* Billings.

DAVENPORT. No, he's right, Clever. They count the cows up in that country.

Thatcher, shaking his head in pity for their ignorance, addresses himself to his work. At this moment an M.P. arrives in the scene and goes up to McClure, who is still shooting.

M.P. I'm sorry, sir, no cameras are allowed on the field.

MCCLURE (*slowly lowering the camera, looking at the M.P. in outraged astonishment*). *What?*

M.P. That's right, sir. A lot of secret work goes on here. They're very strict about it.

MCCLURE (*trying to shrug it off*). I can't see anything secret from here.

M.P. Then I'll have to report you to the Commanding Officer, sir. Those are my orders.

The others are grinning, taking pleasure in McClure's predicament. McClure looks at the M.P.; the M.P. sternly returns his gaze; and McClure realizes he is licked.

MCCLURE (*lowering the camera*). Okay. Go tell the C.O. five German spies just landed in a B-25 and please would like to know the way to some first-class airplane factories.

M.P. (*saluting gravely and being saluted in return*). Thank you, sir.

A wider view next includes Holstrom's plane on the ramp, with Holstrom just coming out of the forward hatch. Ted shouts at him.

TED. Why look, men! Brick Holstrom's still with us! (*To Brick*) We were afraid you wouldn't get that turkey in till tomorrow.

BRICK (*shouting back*). This baby flies so pretty we floated the last two hundred miles.

CLEVER (*with a deprecating gesture*). Yeah, you guys generate enough hot air on that tub to float a B-17.

BRICK (*starting toward Ted's gang*). Where might I find accommodations for myself and party, gentlemen? You people look like natives here.

MCCLURE (*with an affected drawl*). That we are, suh, that we are. (*Pointing to Holstrom's feet with a surprised look*) Hey, lookie—he's wearing *shoes!*

At this moment Davey Jones comes up from the plane on the other side of Ted's.

DAVEY (*to Ted and Holstrom*). You guys ready?

TED (*nodding*). Sure. (*To Thatcher*) I'll be right back, Thatcher, and tell you where your quarters are.

THATCHER. Yes, sir.

At this, Jones and Holstrom and Lawson start walking across the field.

HOLSTROM. Ski York going to be in charge down here?

JONES (*with a shrug*). Search me.

TED. Come on, Davey—you've got an idea. What's the dope? Where do we go from here?

JONES. I already told you. All they said was that it'd take us out of the country, and that we'd be gone about three months, and that it would be dangerous.

HOLSTROM. Look, I got the real dope from Joe Randall. He says they're forming patrol squadrons to guard the Canal.

TED. What's dangerous about Canal patrol?

JONES (*as they shake their heads perplexedly*). What are we worrying about? Ski'll give us all the dope when we check in, anyhow.

Then we see the interior of SKI YORK'S OFFICE, a small, sparsely furnished room. Captain Ski York rises as our three characters walk in.

JONES (*saluting, as do Ted and Holstrom; the salute being returned by York*). Three ships in, sir. Holstrom, Lawson and myself. (*Once the salutes and the formal reports are over, all formality instantly vanishes.*)

YORK. Good. Your ships okay?

JONES. Yes, sir. (*All three of them nod.*)

HOLSTROM. Where we staying, Ski?

YORK. The Government's leased a hotel near here. They call it the Officers' Club. The men whose wives are coming can stay there. The other officers' quarters are in barracks five.

JONES. Emmy coming down?

YORK. She'll be here in a couple of days.

TED. Where'll I put Thatcher, Ski?

YORK. The enlisted men are assigned to barracks twelve.

TED. Okay.

JONES. Anything else?

YORK. Nope. At least not until tomorrow morning.

JONES (*reluctantly starting toward the door, the others with him*). Well . . . we'll see you. . . .

HOLSTROM (*turning suddenly*). Say, Ski, the guys are all crazy to know what's up.

YORK. You know as much about it as I do. We may be given more information in the morning.

As the three absorb this information, and start out of the office, the scene dissolves to the interior of BARRACKS FIVE at dusk. This is a large wooden barracks, accommodating perhaps a hundred men on beds which line the walls. The place is filled with varied activity. Some are lying on their beds, reading. Some are playing poker. Some are listening to an electric phonograph which plays jive music blaringly. Some are gathered in little groups. There is a constant movement at the exits, men coming and going, and there is the occasional sound of airplane motors from outside.

We get a close view of SHORTY MANCH: He is a lieutenant, tall as Abraham Lincoln, and a lover of jive. The electric pick-up is his, and he is now sitting in front of it, tapping softly on the floor in the rhythm of "Chattanooga Choochoo." With him are Bob Gray and Don Smith.

SHORTY (*speaking with a thick Southern accent as he bobs his head up and down with the music*). Now wait for the clarinet again—it really sends you. (*He looks off, his eyes widening with surprise.*) Well, beat me Daddy—look who's comin'!

He and his companions rise and start off toward the entrance as Ted, Davenport, Holstrom, Jones, McClure, Clever, and five or six others enter, carrying their bags. They are immediately surrounded by those who have already arrived. Shorty Manch, fist out-thrust, rushes up to him.

SHORTY. Plant me now and dig me later, if it isn't the pride of Randolph Field! How are you, boys!

TED (*as they shake hands heartily*). Great, Shorty! The minute we heard that razz-ma-tazz——(*gesturing toward the music machine*)——we knew you must be somewhere around. You volunteer for this deal, too?

SHORTY. Sure enough. They had me stationed up in Minneapolis. Coldest country I ever did see. I'd have volunteered for anything to get back into the sunshine. Where you been?

TED. Columbia, South Carolina.

And now Bob Gray rushes up to them and grabs Ted's hand.

TED (*startled*). Bob!

SHORTY. You guys know each other?

BOB. We went through Kelly together, that's all.

TED. Sure. Bob was bridesmaid at my wedding.

SHORTY. *Wedding!* Nobody tells me anything any more! How long you been balled up an' chained down!

TED (*proudly*). Six months in—ah—(*thinking rapidly*)——in five more days.

SHORTY. Well, blow my foot off! Skin me again, boy! (*Since "skin me" in jive parlance means "shake hands," they shake.*)

BOB (*starting away*). Hey, Davey! What *you* doing down here? (*And he moves off toward the newly arrived Davey Jones.*)

We get a close view of HOLSTROM as Don Smith comes up to him and grabs his hand.

DON. Brick! I thought you were hunting subs!

HOLSTROM. Was. Got me one, too.

DON. You in on this deal?

HOLSTROM. Sure. I've got a swell crew —and it looked like it might be *something*—so why not?

DON. Any ideas what we might be up to?

HOLSTROM (*wisely*). Just a hunch.

DON (*eagerly*). Yeah? Give!

HOLSTROM (*lowering his voice*). South Seas. Knock ourselves off a few meat-balls.

DON. Yeah?

Evidently Holstrom has changed his theory about the Canal, for he gives this information with the air of a man who is completely in the know.

The scene dissolves to the picture of a RECORD PLAYER, then the view draws back to the OFFICERS' BARRACKS, the same night, an hour or two later. Shorty Manch, Hoss Wyler, and three or four others are around the electrical pick-up, which now is blaring out with "Deep in the Heart of Texas," with half the hall automatically coming in on the claps. The activity is still animated inside the barracks, but now of a different sort. Reunions have been completed, and the men are relaxing. Several have already undressed and clambered into their beds where they read, or watch, or talk between beds, or fruitlessly try to sleep. In a fairly close view we see FOUR MEN playing poker. They are: Lawson, Davenport, Holstrum and Gray. Bob Gray is dealing.

HOLSTROM. Three.

GRAY (*dealing three*). Honest man. Dealer takes two. (*He deals himself two.*)

TED (*thoughtfully, paying little attention to his cards*). You know, I just got an idea . . .

DAVENPORT (*glancing up from his hand*). About what?

TED. About where we might be going. The way it looks to me—(*But he breaks off, frowns, shakes his head.*) —No, that's not right. Forget it. (*He returns his attention to his hand, dismissing the subject, as Bob Gray looks at him keenly.*)

DAVENPORT (*shoving two white chips in*). Says two.

BOB GRAY (*to Ted, seriously*). You know I've got an idea, too.

TED (*as all of them look at Bob*). Yeah?

BOB GRAY. I've got an idea you're pretty much of a dope to have come in on this deal in the first place.

TED (*surprised*). What kind of a crack is that?

BOB GRAY. I don't know . . . you're married—got a swell gal—I'd never have stuck my neck out if I were in your boots.

TED (*a little surprised, then grinning, giving him a gesture with his hand*). Ah, go 'way. (*To Davenport*) You say two? (*As Davenport nods*) And up two. (*He puts four chips in.*)

Holstrom looks off suddenly. The tune has changed from "Deep in the Heart of Texas" to "Eyes of Texas."

HOLSTROM. Oh-oh! Those Texas guys are off again!

The view moves to Shorty Manch, Hoss Wyler and two or three others of hefty build and determined mien, who are raucously singing "Eyes of Texas," and lifting various of their sitting comrades to their feet. (*We see this from a considerable distance.*) Then the scene cuts to DON SMITH and BILL FARROW, who are lying in adjoining beds, both of them in shorts. Don Smith is staring quietly toward the ceiling. Suddenly he turns his head toward Bill Farrow.

SMITH. Have you ever carried a navigator in your ship before, Bill?

FARROW. Huh-uh.

SMITH (*thoughtfully*). Neither have I until I volunteered for this job.

FARROW. Oh, we're going to see some fancy stuff all right. I've kind of got a feeling—

They are interrupted by the entrance of Shorty Manch, Hoss Wyler, and the others, lustily bellowing "Eyes of Texas."

SHORTY (*addressing them in outraged tones*). Shoot me for a polecat! Do I see two red-blooded citizens lying on their backsides while the Texas anthem is being rendered?

HOSS WYLER. On your feet, men!

SMITH (*to Shorty*). What're *you* beefing about, Shorty? You're from Virginia.

SHORTY. That's right, sharp cat, but my pal here—(*indicating Hoss*)—he's from Texas, an' he takes offense easy! Do you come to attention, outlander, or do you require assistance?

SMITH (*turning wearily to Farrow*). Should we kill these guys, Bill?

FARROW. There's too many Texans in the room. (*He rolls out of his bed in disgusted fashion.*) This'll save time and trouble.

Both Smith and Farrow stand briefly at attention, while the chorus around them sings touchingly. But a young Lieutenant excitedly enters at this point, tries to say something to Shorty and the crowd around him, who pay no attention to him as they continue singing. The young Lieutenant obviously has something to tell, and since he can't get an audience in this little group, he moves off.

SHORTY (*spotting somebody off-scene*). Well, fry me in an open skillet—do I see Chuck McClure *sittin' down* at a time like this?

Still singing, the gang starts toward the off-scene McClure, leaving Smith and Farrow alone. The two quickly clamber back into their beds, while off-scene shouts are heard: "Hey you guys, shut up! . . . Lay off! . . . Can the corn! . . ."

And at this Shorty and his chorus

reluctantly subside, and look toward the newcomer.

Looking toward the door we see the newcomer, surrounded by three or four of the men, signaling for attention.

VOICES. Go ahead, spill it, Joe! Yeah? Go on! Give!

JOE. Jimmy Doolittle's down here. (*After a blank silence*) He's a Lieutenant Colonel now.

There is a surprised buzz over the room, following which we see SHORTY MANCH and his gang. They have joined Joe.

SHORTY. Jimmy Doolittle! A Southern boy from Southern California! (*To Hoss Wyler*) Hoss—let's have "Eyes of Texas" for Lieutenant-Colonel Jimmy Doolittle!

There are protests, shouts, yells: but Hoss, Shorty and the gang once more start bellowing their state anthem, until the scene dissolves to the EXECUTIVE OFFICE DOOR of the OPERATIONS OFFICE of Elgin Field as Lieutenant-Colonel James Doolittle enters briskly from it toward the desk, following which the scene cuts to a full view of the interior of the OPERATIONS ROOM. One hundred and forty men, among them all the characters introduced in our previous sequence, are gathered in a room intended to accommodate perhaps half that many. The officers are seated on benches, which are arranged in a double row with an aisle between, clear to the back of the room. The enlisted men stand behind the benches in the rear. At the extreme end of the room are packing boxes, dismantled machine guns, etc. In front of the room is a plain desk. Behind the desk are two offices, one of them the executive office, the other the operations office. Facing the desk, the executive office is on the right. The room is filled with the conversation of the waiting officers and enlisted men. The first man to see Doolittle immediately leaps to his feet. As he does so, he cries out: " 'Ten-shun!" and every man in the room instantly rises to his feet.

SKI YORK (*quietly*). Gentlemen— Lieutenant-Colonel Doolittle.

DOOLITTLE comes to a standing position behind the desk, and then waives the formalities aside with an "At ease" and "Rest," as if he were almost too busy for them. He carries no command papers, no notes. He immediately begins to speak.

DOOLITTLE (*quietly, with emphasis, but not dramatically*). You men are here because you've volunteered. You've been told it's a dangerous mission. That is all I can tell you now—but I want to emphasize the danger. The most important thing at the moment is secrecy. I don't want you even to tell your wives what you see down here. If you think you've guessed where we're going, you're probably wrong. But don't even talk about your guess.

We get a fairly close view of TED and BOB GRAY sitting together, listening intently. Bob shoots a sidewise glance at Ted, then looks back to Doolittle.

DOOLITTLE (*continuing*). If the slightest word of this mission gets around, you will endanger not only your own lives, but the lives of thousands of other men. Now I want to ask a question. Has anybody tried to talk to you about this?

DOOLITTLE is seen closely as he scans the room, waiting for an answer to his query, and the view moves around the room, showing the serious, respectful attention he is receiving. These men

may have behaved like overgrown kids in their barracks last night, but here they are on combat duty, and are all business.—Then we again see DOO-LITTLE as, his inspection completed, he nods briefly.

DOOLITTLE. Good. If anybody on the field or off the field tries to engage you in conversation about why you're here, no matter how innocently—get his name and I'll turn him over to the F.B.I. (*He glances off, and stops abruptly; he seems to be waiting.*)

Next Doolittle is seen looking toward the front of the office at two officers— a captain and a colonel—who have inadvertently entered the office. They pause at the sudden silence, look embarrassed, and hastily leave. This is followed by a fairly close view of SHORTY MANCH and DON SMITH as they exchange meaningful looks at this. Obviously Doolittle trusts absolutely nobody with the details of their mission, and they are impressed.

DOOLITTLE'S VOICE (*heard over the scene*). This is going to be the toughest training any of you have ever had. You're going to have the same crew all the way through, and the same ship. The man or ship that fails will be dropped. You're going to do things with a B-25 you'll think are impossible.

At this, the scene cuts to TED and BOB GRAY listening, as Bob looks at Ted.

DOOLITTLE'S VOICE. If any of you have any doubts, I'd like you to pull out right now. I promise you no one will think any the worse of you. If you have wives or children—(*Again Bob looks sidewise at Ted. Ted, conscious of the gaze and the meaning of it, casts an irritated look at Bob and turns back to the colonel.*)—or any other considerations that might get on your nerves in a crisis—it's perfectly all right—as a matter of fact, it's your *duty* to drop out now.

We get a close view of DOOLITTLE as he pauses and waits for this to sink in. Then he continues:

DOOLITTLE. Very well. We'll have these talks as often as possible. That's all.

He turns abruptly, walks rapidly to the door of the executive office, enters it, and closes the door behind him quietly. Ski York, who has been sitting on a bench in front of Doolittle, now rises, goes to a large map which hangs in back of the desk, and picks up a pointer.

YORK. We're going up this morning for an orientation flight. There are four auxiliary fields. (*Pointing them out on the map*) Line them up and locate them all. We don't know which we're going to use for our confidential experiments, so familiarize yourselves with all of them. Look over the countryside, and we'll meet here again at 3:30 this afternoon. Any questions?

SMITH (*rising*). Sir, the plugs are being changed in my engines. To save time may I go along in Jones' ship?

YORK (*nodding*). Right, Smith. (*He looks around.*) Anything else? (*But there are no questions.*) All right. You can go to your ships now.

The men rise from their benches, and start streaming toward the two exits.

BOB CLEVER, DAVE THATCHER, and MC-CLURE are seen moving toward the door.

MCCLURE (*to Dave*). Looks to me like it's gonna be a long time before you swing down Main Street in Billings again, Thatcher.

THATCHER (*with dignity*). In Billings, sir, the Main Street is Minnesota Avenue.

McClure and Clever exchange amused glances; but Thatcher, serenely confident in the worth of Billings, Montana, is untouched by the remarks.

Outside the OPERATIONS OFFICE as Ted, Bob Gray and Davenport emerge:

BOB GRAY (*quietly*). You know, that guy means business. He had me sweating a little.

TED (*soberly*). Yeah. Me, too.

At this a sergeant approaches, and salutes.

SERGEANT (*to Ted*). Lieutenant Lawson?

TED. Yes.

SERGEANT. There's someone to see you in front of the P.X. on J. Street, sir.

TED. Thanks.

The sergeant salutes and leaves. Ted turns to Davenport.

TED. I wonder who—I'll be right back. You go on to the ship and line up the fields on the map so we won't waste too much time.

DAVENPORT. Okay.

TED (*starting off*). And see if they've checked that left engine.

Davenport nods. Ted walks out of sight, and Davenport and Bob Gray continue toward the hangars until the scene dissolves to J. STREET, and we see Ted coming up to the Post Exchange, looking around. The Post Exchange is thronged with flyers and airfield attachés. It has a rough verandah in front and on the far side of it, with tables, etc. The inevitable bottled drink dispensing machine is on the verandah outside the front door of the exchange. Ted carefully looks over the men on the verandah, searching for whoever wanted to see him. Suddenly we hear the sound of an automobile horn, and Ted, attracted by the noise, looks off to: ELLEN LAWSON, his twenty-two-year-old wife, who is waving and just climbing out of a 1940 Buick roadster. Ted runs up to her, and takes her a little awkwardly in his arms. After all, they have been married less than six months, and can scarcely be considered old married folk. Moreover, the crowd in front of the canteen is staring curiously.

TED. Ellen!

He brings her to him, pecks her chastely on the cheek, then holds her a little stiffly away from him. She is smiling rapturously, enjoying his half-shy discomfiture.

TED. Where did *you* come from?

ELLEN. I drove to Carolina to surprise you, and then they told me you were down here.

TED (*with a nervous little laugh*). Well—how—how *are* you?

ELLEN (*with some inner amusement*). I'm—just fine, thank you. And how are you bearing up?

TED. Great. You—(*looking down at her admiringly*)—you *look* just the same.

ELLEN (*with a gay laugh*). Of course I do! You can't expect any change *this* soon.

TED (*blankly*). Huh? (*As she laughs again, a full laugh of deep amusement and pleasure*) Well, what's the joke?

ELLEN (*choking her laughter off*). Nothing. Except you're so funny. Tell me, honey—were you surprised?

TED (*with an affectionate grin*). I couldn't believe my eyes. (*He takes her arm.*) Here—let me buy you a drink.

He takes her arm, and they walk across the road, up the steps of the canteen, and onto the verandah. Ted disengages himself from Ellen, goes to the soft drink dispenser, places coins in it, and brings two bottles from the compartment. The uniformed men on the verandah stare with good-natured interest at Ellen. Ted opens the bottles and comes back to her. She stands, watching him with a pleased happy smile, as if every move he made amused her. He takes her arm.

TED (*starting with her toward . the side of the verandah*). Let's go around here.

We then see TED and ELLEN as they go to that portion of the crude verandah which runs along the side of the Post Exchange rather than in front of it. It is quite deserted. He escorts her to the far end of it, sets the two drink bottles down on the floor (there are no tables here), and takes her in his arms. Here he has the privacy he requires. He kisses her on the lips. They break the kiss, but continue to cling to each other.

TED (*grinning down at her*). Tell me —how come you're so cute?

ELLEN (*smiling up at him, making a little face*). I had to be if I was going to get such a good-looking fella!

Ted chuckles and lifts her up to the balustrade that surrounds the verandah.

TED (*as he lifts her up*). There. (*He picks up the two bottles and hands one to her.*) Here.

She accepts the bottle. He leans against the balustrade, looking up at her. She swings her legs gently back and forth and smiles pertly down at him.

TED (*clearing his throat solemnly*). You know I—I've got a lot of things to talk over with you.

ELLEN (*nodding vigorously*). Go ahead. Were you—*really* surprised?

TED (*thoughtfully*). Well, not exactly. You go into something like this with your eyes open. Naturally you've got to take your chances.

ELLEN (*a cloud coming over her face*). I see. (*She looks at him searchingly.*) Isn't that kind of a—a cold-blooded way to look at it?

TED. You've got to be cold-blooded. You see, it's the most important thing that's ever happened to me.

ELLEN (*in a small, startled voice*). What about *me?*

TED (*with a smile, patting her hand*). Of course you're in on it too. That's why I want to talk it over.

ELLEN (*slowly, her eyes filled with a hurt bewilderment*). That's—very generous. Go on, Ted.

TED (*so immersed in the Doolittle talk that he fails to note her changed attitude*). Well, in the first place, we've got to keep it a secret. I don't want you to tell a soul.

ELLEN (*anxiously*). You're not—I mean—you don't wish it hadn't happened, do you?

TED. No, of course not. But it's a military secret, and I've got my orders.

ELLEN (*astounded*). A military *sec*—! (*Breaking off, looking at him in exasperation*) Say, what are you talking about?

TED (*innocently*). This job I volunteered for. Didn't you get my letter?

ELLEN. No. Didn't you get *mine?*

TED (*shaking his head*). No.

Suddenly Ellen bursts out into relieved peals of laughter. Ted looks at her in bewilderment, and shakes his head.

TED. I suppose it's very funny, but— I don't—

At this point, Bob Gray's voice from the front of the canteen, comes over the scene.

BOB'S VOICE. Lawson! Ted Lawson!

TED (*calling out*). Around here!

And now Bob Gray rounds the corner, and moves rapidly toward them.

BOB (*talking as he comes*). What are you hiding out—(*As he sees Ellen*) Ellen! (*Coming up to them and grasping Ellen's hand warmly*). When did *you* get in?

ELLEN. Five minutes ago. How's my bridesmaid?

BOB. Great, only I'm going to have to break this up. (*To Ted*) Doolittle came out to watch us take off.

TED. Okay. (*He lifts Ellen down, and kisses her.*) See you for dinner.— Hotel's a mile and a half down the road—(*He gestures.*)—I haven't seen it, but they tell me you can't miss it.

ELLEN. I'll find it.

TED (*kissing her again*). Sorry to have to rush off like this. (*As he follows Bob*) Remember—dinner!

ELLEN (*nodding*). Goodbye.

Both men give her little salutes, then round the corner of the verandah almost at a run. For a moment Ellen stands there, watching the spot at which they disappeared. Then she chuckles to herself, makes a little face, and starts briskly toward the front of the verandah.

The scene dissolves to a full view of the FIELD as the B-25s, one after another, roar down the wide field and take to the air; and this dissolves to a full view of the SKY, with LAWSON's SHIP close enough for us to identify Ted and Davenport, with Clever in the glassed-in nose. Then the scene cuts to a close view of the PILOT's COMPARTMENT. Ted is flying the ship, Davenport beside him. Both are watching the landscape below. Ted points. Davenport nods.

DAVENPORT. That's number three.

Ted nods. They drone on. Then Ted, with the attitude of a man who has just thought of something, snaps on the interphone, and speaks into it.

TED. Say, did anybody pick up a letter for me?

We get a close view of the GUNNER's COMPARTMENT where Thatcher listens, starts guiltily, then feels in his pocket.

THATCHER (*into the interphone*). Yes, sir. I did this morning. I forgot all about it.

He starts to crawl through the passageway above the bomb-bay, which leads to the navigator's compartment, and through it to the pilot's compartment. This involves crawling on his stomach. This crawl takes us along a passage over the bomb-bay, through the navigator's compartment, and then forward and a step upward into the pilot's compartment. Thus we get a clear idea of the plane's interior and of the relative positions of all of our crew, save Clever in the bombardier's compartment in the nose. Thatcher makes his way forward, and hands a letter to Ted.

THATCHER. I'm sorry, sir.

TED. That's okay.

Thatcher moves back to his position in the ship. Ted glances at the letter.

TED (*to Davenport*). Take over for a minute?

DAVENPORT. Sure. (*He does so.*)

We get a close view of TED as he casually opens the letter, leans back in his seat, and begins to read. An expression of bewilderment comes to his face, quickly followed by one of complete stupefaction—and then delighted surprise. He looks at Davenport wide-eyed and astounded.

TED (*with a shout*). Hey!

This cuts to a front-to-rear view of the plane, disclosing the entire crew, as Ted turns, shouting, and gestures toward the letter.

TED. I'm gonna have a *baby!* (*He points foolishly to the letter.*) It's from Ellen! She's gonna be—I mean, I'm gonna be a *father!*

The B-25 deserts her serene course, does a dip, then begins to climb rapidly in a ponderous take to the news it has just received.

The scene dissolves to a close view of ELLEN, who is sleeping peacefully, her breath coming in a deep, regular rhythm. The hint of a smile plays about her lips. Then we see the HOTEL ROOM as Ted enters. Carefully he removes his flying jacket, and silently throws it over a chair. The scene moves with him as he tip-toes to the figure of Ellen which lies on one of the twin beds. He stands for a moment, looking down at her. A quiet, tender smile passes over his face. He reaches out as if to touch her brow, then thinks better of it, and withdraws his hand.

We get a close view of ELLEN and TED as Ted turns from the bed. A floorboard creaks loudly. Ted hunches over quickly, as if this involuntary gesture would stay the sound. He looks at Ellen. Slowly her eyes open. It seems that she requires no adjustment to come from deep slumber to complete wakefulness. She smiles up at him. Ted doesn't know exactly how to treat her. The last time he saw her, she was his bride. Now she is a pregnant woman. He has a feeling of reticence, of shyness—a feeling that she might break if he touched her.

ELLEN (*her voice almost a whisper*). Hello . . . flyer . . .

TED (*contritely*). I'm sorry I woke you up. I—

ELLEN. I wasn't sleeping, really. I was just dozing . . . and thinking.

TED (*gently*). I'm sorry I didn't get back for dinner. We had a lot of checking to do. (*As Ellen smiles, Ted continues awkwardly:*) You must have thought I was an awful dope this morning. But you see, I—I didn't get your letter until later, so I didn't—

ELLEN. I know.—Sit down.

TED (*sitting down on the edge of her bed, taking one of her hands in his*). I think it's—swell—about the baby.

ELLEN (*smiling, bringing his hand under her chin to caress it*). I knew you would. I wasn't a bit worried.

TED (*quietly*). It's going to seem funny . . . I don't care whether it's a boy or a girl. Not that much. (*He snaps his fingers to show her how much.*) I—I just want you to be okay. It's—it's pretty serious. (*A little moment of silence—She giggles.*) What's funny?

ELLEN. I was just thinking. Here you're getting ready to go off on something really tough—and you're worrying about me!

TED. Huh! If I were in your spot I'd be scared to death. I guess I am anyhow.

ELLEN. Purely routine stuff, flyer. The kind of job every girl takes on once or twice in her life. Why don't you lie down?

He stretches out on the bed beside her. He is outside the covers and fully clothed. She is under them, and attired in night clothes. Her hand seeks his again. They lie in silence for a moment. Finally Ted speaks.

TED (*thoughtfully, softly*). You know, Ellen—I'm kind of glad I got you.

ELLEN (*nodding*). Um-hmm. I guess that's what I was thinking about in my sleep. It—it almost frightened me. It seemed that I was thinking—(*Her voice sinks to a whisper.*)—"What if I'd never met him?"

TED (*chuckling, squeezing her hand again*). Well, for one thing you wouldn't be traipsing around the country from one airfield to another trying to catch up with me. And for another—you wouldn't be having a baby right in the middle of a war.

ELLEN (*quickly*). Oh no, it wasn't that. I was thinking that if I hadn't met you—I'd never have felt really close to anybody—never in my whole life . . .

TED (*with gruff tenderness*). Married six months and together less than two weeks. That's not being as close as I'd figured on.

ELLEN. But don't you see, Ted, that's just it. If people can be close when they're far away from each other—well, that's what it should be.

TED (*quietly*). Yes. I guess so.

ELLEN. Cuddle me.

PHYLLIS: People can be close when they're far away from each other —

DOOLITTLE: We're going to bomb Tokyo . . .

DAVENPORT: Your whole face is pushed in!

They are carried through the village —

He grins, puts one arm under her head for a pillow. She wriggles closer to him, heaves a contented little sigh.

ELLEN. I was thinking about last Christmas. The tree we set up in that Portland auto court—wasn't it an awful little room?—And the Christmas dinner we were planning on. And then you ran out of gas—and landed in the mud up at Ilwaco—and Christmas Eve and Christmas were all over before I saw you again.

TED (*nodding*). That was tough. But I got a scarf out of it, anyhow.

ELLEN. Well . . . it *wasn't* exactly as we'd planned it. But it was our first Christmas, and somewhere way off—it didn't matter where—I knew I had you. And oh, Ted, it was the nicest Christmas of my life!

TED (*squeezing her head closer to him in the crook of his arm*). You were born to marry a flyer, Ellen. I knew it the minute I saw you. Matter of fact—(*grinning at her*)—that's why I married you.

ELLEN (*tantalizingly*). You know—I've got a confession to make.

TED. Yeah?

ELLEN. Um-hmmm. The truth is, you *didn't* marry me. I married *you*.

TED (*with mock resentment*). Oh, you did, eh?

ELLEN (*nodding*). The first time I saw you in the library at L.A.C.C. I said to myself, "Oh-oh! That's for me!" (*She steals a mischievous glance at him.*) And from then on, clear up to the night we got the judge out of bed in that little Idaho town, nothing was an accident, Ted. I—I planned it that way.

TED (*pleased, but feigning disillusion-ment*). Think you're pretty smart, don't you?

ELLEN (*with a giggle*). I'm not sure whether I do or not. You see—you didn't put up much of a fight.

TED (*with a chuckle*). I suppose you figured on the baby, too.

ELLEN (*with a mischievous smile*). That's something you'll never know, flyer—you'll never know . . .

Ted smiles and holds her closer. From the open window comes the sound of airplane motors being tuned and tested at Eglin Field a mile and a half distant. It is the voice of the heavy, the rival, the enemy. For a moment they both listen to it, their faces solemn, their eyes deep with speculation.

TED (*clearing his throat*). Boys are working late these nights.

ELLEN (*faintly*). Yes. (*After a moment*) Do you have any idea how long you'll be gone?

TED (*trying to change the mood*). Huh-uh. But after this job's over, I'm going to ask for a leave. Two, maybe three weeks. We'll have that honeymoon you're always talking about.

ELLEN (*smiling*). Yes—just the three of us.

Ted chuckles. He kisses her; then, as they break, instead of releasing him, she clings to him, and we see the back of his head, and all of her face, with her arms twined tightly around his neck. Her eyes are wide.

ELLEN. Ted . . .

TED (*turning his face*). Um-hmmm?

ELLEN. I do hope I don't get big and fat—like that lady in Chicago . . .

As Ted grins and holds her closer and kisses her, the scene dissolves to a full view of the OPERATIONS ROOM at EGLIN FIELD, where the men are assembled in approximately the same fashion as previously. (We have come in on the scene toward the end of Doolittle's speech.)

DOOLITTLE. Another important job will be to check your life rafts. Inflate them and learn exactly what to do in an emergency. We have a marked course over the Gulf, with life buoys every three miles. Check your airspeed indicators against this course for absolute accuracy.

We get a fairly close view of BOB GRAY and SHORTY MANCH with others in the background.

DOOLITTLE'S VOICE. I want a fuel report from each pilot. We already know the approximate throttle setting for minimum gas consumption, but I want you to prove it for yourselves. An extra quart of gas at the right time may save your lives.

As Gray and Manch exchange glances, the scene cuts to DOOLITTLE.

DOOLITTLE. I want everyone of you to know at least something about the others' jobs. Pilots will practice every job on the plane. Navigators will learn the work of bombardiers, and so on. (After a significant little pause) That's just in case any of you are shot up.

This cuts to a view of the room as DOOLITTLE continues.

DOOLITTLE. One more thing. Inevitably, some of your ships will fall into the hands of the enemy. Because of this, I've ordered your Norden bombsights removed. Captain Greening has designed a sight that will be perfect for this job. (He gives them a little smile.) If there are no questions, Captain York will take over.

He pauses a moment, nods to York who is near him, and exits into his office in the rear. York rises.

YORK (looking at a piece of paper). Gray, Hoover, Smith—

HALLMARK, HOLSTROM and FARROW are seen together as the crews move toward the hangars.

HOLSTROM (wisely). Just like I said —we patrol off Brazil.

HALLMARK. Yeah—but what about taking the Norden bombsight out? There's no chance of falling into the hands of the enemy if you're hunting subs.

HOLSTROM (scratching his head, nodding reluctantly). I hadn't thought of that . . .

Next TED and DAVENPORT are seen moving along, with the rest of their crew.

TED (with a wry grin). That Doolittle's a cheerful cuss, isn't he?

DAVENPORT (with a nod, quoting Doolittle). "Just in case any of us are shot up"—-A bundle of sunshine!

This dissolves to a MEADOW at night. There are FIVE FIRES on the ground in the form of the five design on a dice. Then, silhouetted low against the sky, a B-25 roars in like a gray ghost, releases a missile from 500 feet, bounces from the concussion, recovers, and roars out again, having scored a hit.— Following this, three other bombers are seen approaching the target, one behind the other. The first of them drops its bomb, scores a near miss, wavers, flies out of scene.

We now get a close view of the B-25 in the air at night. Clever is in the bombardier's nose; Thatcher is beside him. The bomb-bay doors of the plane slowly swing open. Then inside the BOMBARDIER'S COMPARTMENT, Clever is seen instructing Thatcher in the intricacies of the bombsight.

CLEVER (*into the interphone*). Bombbay doors open. (*To Thatcher*) It's very simple—just like aiming a .22. Just hold her here until the target lines itself up with the sights.

This cuts to the PILOT'S COMPARTMENT. Davenport is flying, and there is no one else with him.

CLEVER'S VOICE (*over the interphone*). Bomb away!

Davenport looks at the instrument panel, and notes the red light which signifies that the bomb is away, following which the scene cuts to the NAVIGATOR'S COMPARTMENT where McClure is teaching Ted the intricacies of celestial navigation. They are peering into a sextant.

MCCLURE. See it?

TED. Yeah.

MCCLURE. Well, that makes the third point of your triangle, so now you've got—

There is a heavy sound of explosion below, the plane scutters upward, and McClure and Ted roll over each other. Thereupon the scene dissolves and we get a full view of the BEACH close to the hotel. A number of girls are there: Ellen, Emmy York, and a girl we shall call Jane. They are on the beach close to the hotel. Jane is in a bathing suit; Ellen is in shorts; Emmy York is in a sports outfit.

JANE (*trying to be casual, as if to pry a secret*). Well, Ski's the executive officer. He must have told you where they're going.

EMMY (*with an indulgent little chuckle*). He doesn't have any more idea than I do, because, if he did, he wouldn't go around trying to look so mysterious all the time. (*Then smugly*) You know how they are.

The girls respond as only women do when they are explaining how well they understand their husbands, but their attention is distracted by the sound of a plane overhead, and we follow the girls' eyes to the sky as Ted's plane zooms down toward them and buzzes the beach.—ELLEN waves gaily, and turns to her friends.

ELLEN. That's Ted buzzing us.

JANE. George used to buzz me when we were first married. (*She chuckles.*) I was driving to Columbia one day and he came down and buzzed me and chased everybody off the road.—He doesn't do it any more. I wonder if he still loves me.

EMMY (*with a laugh*). I wouldn't worry about that. Every time Ski gets a new ship he has a terrible love affair with it, but he always comes back to me, especially when he's hungry.

ELLEN (*with a sigh*). Just think—they'll be gone three months.

JANE. I think I'll go into a defense factory. I couldn't stand just sitting around some little apartment and waiting.

EMMY. What are you going to do, Ellen?

ELLEN (*with a smile*). I'm just going to sit around and have a baby.

JANE (*crying out*). A *baby*—!

EMMY (*delighted*). You *are*! Why Ellen—why didn't you tell us?

ELLEN. I don't know. I guess—I just never thought of a way till now. (*She smiles.*) As it turns out, it wasn't hard to tell at all.

EMMY (*taking a deep breath*). Well —I'm going to have one, too!

ELLEN (*astounded*). *Really?*

JANE. I think it's wonderful! George and I have talked about it, but, with him away and all—I—I guess I'm just too scared.

ELLEN. I thought I would be too. But Ted and I figure that everything since Pearl Harbor has been just so much velvet. Then I guess—that if anything *should* happen to him— only I *know* nothing will—I'd have the baby—and that would be a little bit of Ted still living.

EMMY. I sometimes wonder how we'll feel when it's all over. Just think— being able to settle down in a house somewhere—raise your children— and never be in doubt about anything.

JANE (*with a little laugh*). We'll have a lot of the same doubts then that we have now. For example— will he, or will he not be home to dinner?

ELLEN (*jumping up from the bench*). Goodness! I'd better change clothes and get some makeup on—just in case they *do* show up! (*Offering a hand to Emmy*) Get up, Mother York. You can stand a little going over, too.

The scene dissolves to AUXILIARY FIELD Number 4, where all of the men are grouped around Doolittle in an informal circle. With Doolittle is Lieutenant Miller of the Navy.

DOOLITTLE. We're about to enter the most secret part of our training. This field is patrolled on all sides so that nobody can disturb you in your work. I have with me here Lieutenant Miller of the Navy. He is going to

instruct you in take-offs. Instead of the normal B-25 take-off of fifteen hundred feet at ninety miles an hour, Lieutenant Miller is going to show you how to do it with a full load of bombs and gas in five hundred feet at fifty miles an hour. (*Manch, and various others in the background, react with surprise.*) You're not to attempt any short take-offs from Eglin, where people can see you. Lieutenant Miller will also give you a series of short talks on Naval etiquette. If this gives you any hints as to your destination or the kind of work you're going to do—don't even discuss them among yourselves. I'm going to ask Lieutenant Miller to take over now.

In a view favoring TED with several others, we see them as they react to this astonishing news. They look at each other, blank-faced. Holstrom winks and nods wisely to Lawson as if this confirmed all of his previous prognostications. The scene then cuts to LT. MILLER, surrounded by Shorty Manch, Bob Gray, Dick Joyce and Ted Lawson, together with their crews.

MILLER. Those flags out there—

He points, and as the men follow his direction the FIELD comes into view. It has three flags set up in a line. Down the center of the runway is a white mark which runs its full length.

MILLER'S VOICE.—at two hundred, three hundred and five hundred feet from the starting line. The line down the center of the field is to guide you in your take-off. The kind of work you're going to do won't permit any deviations.

The scene then cuts back to the group as the officers listen, their crews in the background.

MILLER. The whole idea is to get full power up before you release your brakes, and then start at maximum r.p.m. and manifold pressure. You'll have to rev your motors till you think they're going to burn up, with your wing flaps all the way down. When they reach the right pitch—and that's a matter of sound and feel more than instruments—then release your brakes and hunt for heaven. I don't expect any of you to do it the first time. Gray—

GRAY. Yes, sir.

MILLER'S VOICE. Supposing you and Manch try it first. The rest of us will stay on the ground, mark your take-off point and check the wind.

GRAY. Yes, sir. (*He starts off, followed by his crew.*)

MILLER (*to the others*). I think at first we can learn as much by watching trial runs as by actually flying the ships. Let's go over here and see how he does.

As they start walking off the scene dissolves to a view of AUXILIARY FIELD Number 4, with GRAY'S PLANE at the starting line. Our various crews are scattered up and down the field so that they can mark the point of take-off. Captain York, beside Lieutenant Miller, holds the anemometer. Manch's plane is warming up its motors. Lawson and Joyce are near Miller, to get the benefit of any advice he may offer.

In a close moving view we see GRAY'S PLANE as the flaps come down. The motors "rev" and start off. He flashes by all three flags and takes off a good six hundred feet beyond the five hundred feet marker. A man runs out to mark the place where he took off.— Then the scene cuts back to the GROUP.

MILLER (*to York*). What kind of surface wind, Ski?

YORK. Eight miles an hour.

MILLER (*to Ted and Joyce*). He didn't have his engines revved up enough. (*To Ted*) Lawson, you go next. Now remember, for our purposes if you get your wheels a foot off the ground, that's good enough. You don't need height—but you've *got* to get your wheels off before you hit the last flag. A little later we'll try retracing the wheels at around four hundred fifty feet and rely on your motors to float the ship. (*He smiles.*) Don't try that just yet, though.

TED. Right, sir.

MILLER. Grab the column and pull her until you can feel the inside of your backbone.

TED (*starting out for his ship*). Yes, sir.

The scene dissolves to LAWSON'S PLANE as we watch the flaps coming down slowly, and this cuts to the PILOT'S COMPARTMENT, where TED is pushing the throttles more and more forward. He finally gets them full throttle. He waits. He and Davenport look at each other and shake their heads seriously. They don't like the idea of harming their engines.

This cuts to the group on the field which has been rejoined by Manch and Gray.

MANCH (*with a sheepish grin*). Did you ever take off a B-25 in five-hundred feet, sir?

MILLER (*smiling*). No. But you men will. Don't worry about it. Watch Lawson there—you'll have to rev your motors at least that high—and maybe higher.

As they all stare off at Lawson's plane, the scene cuts to TED and DAVENPORT in their PILOT'S COMPARTMENT as the motors reach what seems to be their crescendo. They exchange glances. Ted grabs the column with his left hand, pulls it toward him. The whole ship is shaking. Ted releases his brakes. The ship starts out.

We get a full view of Ted's ship as it leaps forward. For a moment it appears that he is going to make it. About the one-hundred mark the nose wheel comes off the ground—at about the six-hundred mark the other two wheels leave the ground. But the tail drags. For another three-hundred feet the plane seems like a crippled bird, its tail on the ground and its nose in the air. Suddenly it takes to the air. Men start to mark off the point at which the plane took to the air.

The GROUP is seen watching.

MILLER. Not bad—about nine hundred feet. He burned his tail skid off, didn't pull his wheels up soon enough. Joyce, you try it as soon as Lawson comes in.

This dissolves to another view of the FIELD as Lawson's plane is just taxiing back after landing. It comes to a stop. Ted cuts his motors. Shorty Manch and possibly one or two others of his crew come up. Shorty looks at the burned tail skid.

SHORTY (chuckling, to Ted). Brother, that take-off was strictly on the cob! That airplane of yours looked exactly like a ruptured duck!

TED (turning disgustedly to his crew). How do you like this guy? He takes off like an old lady in a high wind— and then he's got the guts to talk about a real ship!

SHORTY (pointing to the tail skid). It's lucky you didn't have a muddy field or you'd still be there!

TED (quietly). If I were you I'd worry about that turkey you and Gray are pushing around the sky. The Ruptured Duck will get along okay. . . .

This dissolves to TED and ELLEN'S BEDROOM at night. ELLEN is cuddled up on one of the beds in a dressing gown, scribbling with a pencil on a piece of paper. As she finishes writing, she surveys the list critically, frowning. Then her eyes rise, and she gazes at Ted. A troubled look comes over her face.— Then a longer view of the room includes TED at a desk in the foreground, and over his shoulders we see the two books he is studying. One is entitled: Principles of Navigation, and the other: U. S. Navy—Courtesy and Etiquette— A Glossary of Nautical Terms. Ted is frowning abstractedly as he writes. Suddenly we hear the sound of a phonograph pick-up from downstairs, fairly shrieking a jive rendition of "Chattanooga Choo-Choo." Both Ted and Ellen look up.

TED (banging the book on the desk). Shorty again!

At this cries are heard from other parts of the hotel: "Hey, cut that out! I'm trying to sleep! Kill him!"

TED. Let's get some air.

Abruptly the music is choked off, making the silence in the room seem even more profound than before. Ted looks across at Ellen, rises, stretches, and grins at her. He moves over to her and extends his hand. She accepts his hand, permitting him to pull her to her feet. They pass through a pair of French windows which lead to a tiny balcony.

The BALCONY comes into view as Ted

and Ellen come out on it. Palms and foliage can be seen in the background, with the Gulf shimmering in the distance. Ted and Ellen stand for a moment, looking at the moonlit grounds. Then Ted looks down at her.

TED (*with a gesture of his head toward the moonlit background*). Nice. . . .

ELLEN. Um-hmmm.

TED (*huskily*). I—I'm sorry we haven't had more time together, Ellen.

ELLEN (*smiling*). We can spare a little. We've got all the rest of our lives.

TED. That's right. (*Sniffing the air*) Smells good, doesn't it? (*As she nods*) Something blooming.

ELLEN (*looking up at him*). Ted. . . .

TED. Um-hmm?

ELLEN. You—you look tired.

TED. Nah! Not a bit!

ELLEN. Are you sure nothing's worrying you?

TED. Why of *course* not! What makes you think that!

ELLEN. I just wondered.

TED (*with sudden suspicion*). Look here—(*his hands on both her shoulders*)—what was Bob Gray talking to you about downstairs?

ELLEN (*with a vague little gesture*). Oh . . . nothing.

TED. He wasn't trying to scare you, was he?

ELLEN. Of course not!

TED (*with a little too much emphasis*). Okay. Because there's nothing to worry about. *Nothing.*

ELLEN (*softly*). Silly! As if I didn't know that.

TED. Besides, if anything did happen —which it won't—you've got all that government insurance. That'll take care of you and the baby for a good long spell.

Ellen looks up at him for a moment. He avoids looking at her. Suddenly she smiles.

ELLEN. Ted . . .

TED (*without looking at her*). Yeah?

ELLEN. Look at me. (*He turns, a little puzzled, looking down at her.*) That baby and I—we won't ever need anything but you. We mustn't either of us be scared about it, Ted. Because the baby—(*her voice breaking slightly*)—the baby's why I *know* you're coming back to us . . .

Suddenly he smiles, as if a great load had been taken from his shoulders.

TED (*gently, huskily, with genuine relief in his voice*). You're right, Ellen. I—I'm such a dope. (*Grinning comically*) Now why couldn't I have figured that out for myself?

He kisses her. Then his arms go around her, and he holds her close to him, as the scene dissolves out.

A close view of AUXILIARY FIELD Number 6 then dissolves in. Three planes are on the field, two of them warming up. The third, in the foreground, which has the symbol of a turkey on it (Gray's and Manch's insignia), is just about to take off.—GRAY'S PLANE is seen at close view, with Manch and Gray at the controls waiting for the take-off signal. We see MILLER closely as he gives a signal, and from his angle see GRAY'S PLANE as its brakes are released, and it races toward the five-hundred foot marker. The nose lifts, and then, just as the five-hundred foot flag comes parallel with the ship, the *Turkey* takes to the air.

The GROUP on the field is very excited, as this is the first plane to make the grade in the take-off tests. The men, excepting Miller, Doolittle, and York, frankly cheer. The three senior officers smile, very pleased with the exhibition. —Miller gives a signal for the next plane to have a try.

We get a close view of another B-25. Its nose has been painted a replica of a Ruptured Duck with crossed crutches underneath. And as the view draws back Lawson, Davenport and the others are seen in their places. *The Ruptured Duck* is taxiing to its take-off position. It begins to "rev" its motors.—Then the scene cuts to the PILOT's COMPART-MENT.

TED (*shouting*). We'd better make this one, or Shorty'll never let us hear the last of it.

Davenport nods. The motors "rev" to their peak, Ted's hand pressing steadily forward on the throttle. Ted makes a downward motion. Davenport nods, begins to operate the wing flaps to lower them. Clever seems fairly urging the plane forward with his body. His face is tense, expectant. The motors reach a higher pitch.

The NAVIGATOR's COMPARTMENT: McClure is standing, tense and watchful, trying to help the ship. He looks down the passage over the bomb-bay compartment, sees Thatcher looking tensely at him. The two of them exchange silent signs of prayer. The motors "rev" even higher.

The PILOT's COMPARTMENT: Ted grabs the column, wraps his left arm around it, pulls it into his stomach so hard

that his face is contorted with the effort. Ted quickly executes his charac-teristic luck gesture with his scarf. Then he gives a quick nod to Davenport, and suddenly releases his brakes.

A full view of the FIELD appears as the *Ruptured Duck* leaps forward with a rush, hurtles toward the five-hundred foot flag, takes off almost forty feet short of the mark, hangs for a moment churning the air, then levels off and starts a slow, triumphant circle of the field.

Inside the PILOT's COMPARTMENT, Ted and Davenport, their faces wreathed in grins, look at each other triumphantly.

DAVENPORT (*yelling*). Hear those engines?

TED (*nodding enthusiastically, grinning*). Like music!

This dissolves to a view of an ORCHES-TRA. Shorty Manch is presiding at the piano. Beside him is a corporal handling the banjo, a captain playing the ukelele, and Hoss Wilder who has no drum, but has carved a set of sticks and is beating out perfect time on the upraised portion of the top of the grand piano. Another lieutenant is singing the lyrics . . . . "I love you, I love you . . ." A number of couples are dancing, as we get a full view of the LOUNGE of the OFFICERS' CLUB HOTEL at night. The room is filled with dancing couples.

Ted and Davenport have just entered. They look around the place in astonishment. Music and dancing continue. Brick Holstrom passes through the scene.

TED (*calling out to Brick*). What gives?

BRICK. Shorty's throwing a party.

TED. Why a party?

BRICK. I don't know. Somebody said he's celebrating Texas Constitution day! (*He passes on.*)

TED (*shaking his head in bewilderment, surveying the scene*). For a guy who never *saw* Texas, that Manch is really sold!

DAVENPORT (*shoving ahead into the crowd*). I'm going to sample this.

Ted stands for a moment; Davenport disappears among the dancers. Ted seems to be searching the crowd for someone.—We get a full view of the LOBBY, from TED's point of view. With one or two exceptions, every woman in the room is dancing. The music is slow, the song nostalgic, and they seem fairly intent on the dance and upon their partners. One or two men hold empty or half-empty glasses in their right hands around their partners' waists. Into the "camera" dance a young lieutenant and his wife. They are very close. The girl has her head snuggled against his shoulder. Suddenly the girl lifts her head and whispers directly into his ear.

GIRL (*as a self-appointed singer by the piano bursts into the chorus: "I love you, I love you"*). And I love you, Tom. I love you . . . I love you . . . I love you . . .

Her escort responds by sweeping her even closer, whirling .her out of the scene. Ted grins as they pass.

We get a close view of TED still looking through the crowd. Suddenly his eyes light up, and the scene moves with him as he weaves his way through the dancers, toward the wall, toward Ellen.

ELLEN is sitting, surveying the scene with shining eyes. Ted comes up to her.

TED (*with a grin*). Hello.

ELLEN (*so pleased he has come*). Hello . . . flyer . . .

TED. My dance?

ELLEN (*rising*). All of them, my boy. (*They go into each other's arms, Ellen whispering tenderly into his ear.*) Every dance from now on out . . . including the last one.

TED (*as they dance, his face tender and earnest, looking down at her*). You know, Ellen, there's something I mean to tell you more often and never seem to get a chance to.

ELLEN. What is it?

TED. Just . . . that I love you. (*They whirl away into the crowd.*)

BOB GRAY and BOB CLEVER are seen looking admiringly at the Lawsons.

GRAY. It's a funny thing. Lawson used to be about as graceful as a Texas steer. Now look at him.

CLEVER. Maybe the girl's got something to do with it.

GRAY (*quietly, but with real conviction*). You said it, Clever. You really said it. . . .

TED and ELLEN, dancing, are seen as they pass Bob Gray.

TED. Hey, Bob! (*As Bob turns and grins.*) What's Manch throwing the party for?

BOB (*pretending shock*). Nobody knows. But Hoss Wyler says it's Sam Houston's birthday.

Ted and Ellen look at each other, laugh and dance away, the scene cutting to a BOY and GIRL dancing.

GIRL (*into his ear*). You know what I'm going to do when you come back?

BOY. What?

GIRL. Spoil you. I'm going to spoil you rotten. I'm going to be the best little wife in the United Nations. They—they'll put my picture in *Vogue*.

He chuckles, but she puts her cheek next to his, her face suddenly grave, suddenly fearful. Then we see TED and ELLEN again. As they come up to the orchestra, Ted leans over and taps Manch on the shoulder. Manch looks over his shoulder.

TED (*shouting above the music*). What's the idea of the party?

MANCH. It's Texas Admission Day!

ELLEN. Bob Gray said it was Sam Houston's birthday!

TED. And Brick said it was Constitution Day!

HOSS WYLER. What's the difference—they all come in March!

He turns, and thumps the piano strenuously as Ted and Ellen pass out of the scene, giggling.

As the waltz comes to a flourishing conclusion, Shorty turns briefly around, shouting at the room.

SHORTY. Hey—this party needs a little jittersauce! (*He turns and "knocks out" the first bars of "Deep in the Heart of Texas."*) Everybody sing!

The orchestra really swings into it now, and we get a full view of the FLOOR as the dancers break their lazy waltz tempo and burst into the frenzied strains of jive. A number of couples quit dancing and cluster around two pair who are really cutting rugs in the center of the room. Practically everyone in the room sings at the top of his lungs. Over at the service table, Bob Gray takes a bottle, knocks out the "clap-clap-clap-clap" against an empty ice bucket. Stomping feet, clapping hands join him. There is an atmosphere close to hysteria in the room. BOB CLEVER, and OTHERS are singing loudly, clapping enthusiastically; Ted and Ellen, singing, clapping, laughing, keeping time with the rug cutters; the "RUG CUTTERS" enthusiastically go through their complicated gyrations, their audience joining almost frenziedly in their fun.

We see the ORCHESTRA. Beads of perspiration stand out on the players' foreheads. This is real exertion. As they come to the end of the second chorus, Shorty's fingers ripple over the keys, and the tune changes to "There's a Long Long Trail A-Winding."

SHORTY. Sing, everybody—*sing!*

The entire room begins to sing this remembered song of another war. The jive stops. Only three or four couples are dancing now. The singing seems to form an emotional release. They sing fully, as if from the heart. As they finish the first chorus, Shorty at the piano again goes into a transposition, and sweeps into "Auld Lang Syne." The song is taken up—as if this were really farewell, as if this were really the end of their stay—almost as reverently as a hymn. Now the dancing stops altogether, and the last stragglers join the thronged semi-circle around the improvised orchestra.—Tears suddenly well up. Silent toasts are made. Arms steal around waists. Couples move closer together.—Suddenly the girl who was going to spoil her husband chokes, breaks off, and runs out of the scene with her hands over her face. Her boy follows her anxiously. Courteously, none of their neighbors pays any attention to the little emotional outburst, but continue singing the song with deep and tender sincerity.

We then see TED and ELLEN. They are standing arm in arm, both of them singing. They might be in church, so enthralled are they by the massed chorus of their friends and companions. Suddenly Ellen chokes up and stops singing. Ted looks down at her, then he too stops singing. He bends his head close to hers.

TED (*chucking her tenderly under the chin*). Here, here . . . (*He kisses her cheek.*) Smile, now . . . and sing . . .

Ellen looks full into his face. For one tense moment it. seems that she will not regain control of her muscles. Then she makes it. A radiant smile returns. They both begin to sing, looking at each other. A single tear comes from Ellen's eye, splashes down on her cheek.

TED AND ELLEN. "And the days of auld lang syne. . . ."

And now the scene dissolves to TED and ELLEN's BEDROOM at night. They are sound asleep. Both of them seem to be smiling in their sleep. Ellen has her arms around her pillow, as if she were embracing it. The telephone on the night stand between their beds rings, and Ellen awakens sleepily.

ELLEN. Ted.

TED (*moving in his bed, hugging his pillow tighter*). Huh?

ELLEN. The telephone's ringing.

TED. Huh? (*He burrows deeper under the covers.*)

ELLEN (*very sleepily*). The telephone, Ted.

TED (*in his sleep*). Oh. Sure.

He turns over away from the telephone, adjusts himself as if to sleep more soundly than before. Then he does a double take, and sits straight up in bed.

—TED jumps, and rubs his eyes. The phone rings again. With a muffled groan, he reaches out savagely for the instrument.

TED (*into the phone*). Yeah? Right now? Okay, okay, okay . . .

Mumbling under his breath he hangs up the receiver and rubs his forehead for a moment. He looks over at Ellen.

ELLEN's VOICE. What was it?

In a view including both we see Ellen sitting up in bed, not particularly alarmed.

TED (*grumbling, yawning, scratching his head, swinging his feet to the floor*). Ah, just another night call. But *what* a night!

ELLEN. I'm sorry.

TED. What time is it?

ELLEN (*peering at the clock*). Three-ten.

TED (*rising, muttering softly*). Oh. . . .

ELLEN (*sympathetically*). Hung over . . . maybe a little?

TED (*reaching out blindly for his clothes which are draped over a chair back*). Just a headache. I'm not used to party life.

ELLEN. Poor baby . . .

TED (*finding a sock, sitting on the edge of the bed, and starting to pull it on*). You go to sleep. I'll be back by breakfast time.

ELLEN (*with a delicious sigh*). And I'm *so* sleepy . . . (*Sinking back against her pillow, she nestles for a moment.*) . . . Good night, darling. Or rather . . . good morning . . .

TED (*smiling at her*). Dream of me.

As he reaches for the other sock, and Ellen turns over in the bed to a more comfortable position the scene dissolves to EGLIN FIELD as BOB GRAY and TED trudge through the murk toward the entrance to the operations office. The dark accentuates the ghostliness of the thin stream of men who move toward the dimly lighted entrance of the building. The fog is in from the Gulf. The atmosphere is quiet, strangely muted, almost eerie. A jeep slips by, its motor making a discordant noise. Then it disappears, its noise fading suddenly.

BOB. If I ever get a leave, I'm going to sleep for six days solid.

TED (dully). Umm. (Thrusting his hands into his pockets) Chilly . . .

As they enter the building, the scene dissolves to a full view of the interior of the OPERATIONS OFFICE, where Doolittle waits for the assembled men to settle down. There is a strange air of tenseness about the room.

DOOLITTLE (quietly). Well, men . . . (He pauses, looking around the room.) Your planes are serviced, gassed, ready to go. You'll take off in shifts, first shift leaving in forty-five minutes.

TED and BOB are seen closely. This news hits Ted hard. He whispers out of the corner of his mouth to Bob.

TED (whispering). I hope I get a chance to tell Ellen goodbye.

Both snap their eyes back to the speaker, as Doolittle continues.

DOOLITTLE'S VOICE. Captain York will give you your clearances. One thing must be thoroughly understood. After you take off this morning, you're to see no one, speak to no one, telephone no one. Not even your wife. There are no exceptions.

We see DOOLITTLE and others around him as he continues.

DOOLITTLE. Continue gas consumption tests to your destination. The work you're going to do requires low altitude flying, so hedge-hopping on this trip is okay. (Smiling) Only remember, cowboys wear pretty tall hats. So be careful, men. That's all. I think you're well prepared for what you have volunteered to do. Thanks for a lot of hard work. I'll see you in a few days. Good luck.

YORK. Your destination is Alameda Field. Take the Southern Route. Refuel at San Antonio and March. Take no more than twenty pounds of luggage in your B-4 bags. If any of you have cameras, bring them along. Take all the pictures you want of the mission. The government will pay you for them, and return the negatives in good shape after the war.

McClure almost gurgles with triumph and jostles Davenport violently with his elbow. Davenport grins.

YORK. If any of you have goodbyes to make—make them as soon as you get your clearances. And don't mention your destination. As your names are called, you can start. (Consulting a paper) First flight—Holstrom, Jones, Lawson . . .

Ted rises from his seat, squeezes Bob's shoulder and starts out of the scene. In the background we see a dozen men rising and moving toward the entrance.

YORK'S VOICE. . . . Second flight, Hallmark, Farrow, Gray . . .

And the scene dissolves to the HOTEL BEDROOM.—Ellen is asleep. Suddenly there is the sound of a starting airplane engine, and Ellen's eyes open. She stares at the ceiling; then, with an expression of sudden alarm, she sits up in bed.

ELLEN (*hearing the door open*). Ted!

TED snaps on a small light which is on a table near the door.

TED (*huskily*). Well—this is it, honey. We're off.

ELLEN (*clambering out of bed, throwing a robe around herself*). How soon?

TED. Just got time to pack. Where's my B-4 bag?

ELLEN. In the closet! I'll get it!

She rushes off to the closet, opens the door and begins to fumble for the bag.

TED (*going to the bureau, hastily running through the contents of a drawer, tossing what he doesn't need on the top of the bureau*). Let's see . . . socks . . . underwear . . . shirts . . . My ties in the closet?

ELLEN (*who has the bag on the bed and has opened it*). Yes. I'll find them.

Ted moves quickly from the bureau, throws the clothing on the bed beside the bag, moves into the bathroom. Ellen brings his ties over to the bag, and begins hastily to pack his things. The bathroom medicine cabinet being opened is heard. Bottles jingle and there is a sound of glass falling to the tile floor, breaking.

TED'S VOICE (*muffled*). Wow! (*Emerging from the bathroom he comes over to the bed and puts his shaving materials on it.*) Don't go in there in your bare feet. I broke a glass.

ELLEN. All right! (*She begins to check over the things he brought from the bathroom; she giggles nervously.*) You forgot your toothbrush!

TED. Doggone it!

He dashes off to the bathroom again. Ellen finishes putting his things in the bag. We hear the sound of a shoe stepping on broken glass, crunching it. Ted comes back from the bathroom, tosses the toothbrush into the bag, and goes over to the closet. He takes his service coat from it. He has not taken his cap off during the entire scene. Now he comes over to Ellen.

TED. We got everything?

ELLEN (*looking down at the bag, biting her lower lip*). I—I think so.

TED (*huskily*). Swell.

He bends over and snaps the bag shut. He picks it up with his left hand. Over his left arm he has thrown his service coat. Suddenly the two look at each other. The hurry of packing, the excitement of little things has kept their emotions under control thus far.—TED and ELLEN are then seen closely as they stand, looking blank-faced at each other. The moment has come.

TED. Well . . . be a good girl. (*Ellen nods.*) And—take good care of that baby.

ELLEN (*nodding*). I—I will, Ted.

TED (*tenderly*). Yourself, too. (*Awkwardly, almost shyly, he puts his free right arm around her.*) Goodbye, Ellen.

ELLEN (*in a rush of words*). Oh, Ted, I—I'm going to write you a letter every day you're gone! I know they won't deliver them! I won't even mail them! But I'll write them just the same. (*Tears come into her eyes, her voice chokes up.*) That way— we'll kind of be in touch. That way —we'll feel close . . .

TED. Sure. (*They kiss, then break.*) 'Bye.

ELLEN (*very softly*). 'Bye, flier.

He turns abruptly, goes over to the door and opens it. Ellen, her eyes filled with tears which do not fall, stands where he left her, watching him.—At the door he turns, looks at her, and suddenly smiles.

TED. Tell me, honey—how come you're so cute? ·

ELLEN (*swallowing hard, smiling*). I had to be—if I was going to get such a g-g-good-looking fella!

TED (*softly*). I'll be back. (*He turns, closing the door behind him.*)

We get a close view of ELLEN as she stands motionless, looking at the closed door. Then she turns and walks slowly toward the window. Before she reaches the window, the scene dissolves to ELLEN'S HOTEL ROOM WINDOW, as seen from the outside. Ellen comes up to the window and looks toward Eglin Field in the distance. The first rays of the morning sun break over the countryside. We see this light, reflected in the window pane. We hear the sound of airplane motors from Eglin Field. Then, rising suddenly above the flat landscape—seen by us as a reflection in the window pane—there rises the silhouette of three B-25's taking off. Ellen's hands press against the window as she watches. We do not hear her voice, since we are separated from her by a glass, but we see her lips as they form the words:

ELLEN. Good luck . . . (*Her right fist suddenly clenches against the window.*) God be with you . . .

The scene dissolves to a view, from the AIRPLANE, of SAGEBRUSH on a DESERT. A coyote is streaking through the sagebrush in terror-stricken flight. Then we see THREE AIRPLANES among which we identify the *Ruptured Duck*, fifteen to twenty feet off the ground, pursuing the coyote. A telephone line looms up. They go under it, one, two, three, in breathless fashion. Gay music is heard—the planes actually seem joyous.

This dissolves to a full view of a COUNTRY TOWN-ROAD with several automobiles. Suddenly three planes from the heavens dive down close enough to graze the paint. The automobiles precipitately scramble off the road. The planes continue serenely on their way. The gay music continues.

This dissolves to a view of the *Ruptured Duck* in flight. The view favors that portion of the nose which bears the painted symbol of the Ruptured Duck. Through the glass nose, we see that, pencil in hand, CLEVER is concentrating intently upon a piece of paper, which he has backed up with a magazine. He pauses, stares at it thoughtfully for a moment, then places his pencil to the paper. For all we know he might be figuring out some problem which has to do with the trajectory of bombs or the flight of the ship itself. Finally he holds the paper out at arm's length to inspect it more carefully.— We then see that he is looking at a sketch. It is a picture of a farm mother, middle-aged and pleasant-faced, setting pies out to cool on the sill of an open window. We see indications of a farm background. Obviously Clever is thinking of his youth and his mother. And even more obviously, he is a young man of considerable talent.

CLEVER, as he squints, makes a little grimace of satisfaction, and allows his eyes to wander from the picture. For a moment they are glazed over with day-dreams. Then suddenly they focus in startled surprise, and he yells out, pointing downward involuntarily, "Hey!" He grabs his interphone, and snaps it on.

CLEVER (*into the interphone*). The Bay Bridge off to our right! (*He waits for an answer, gets none, looks impatient, then starts to speak into the interphone again.*)

This cuts to the PILOT'S COMPARTMENT as Dean Davenport is piloting the ship. Ted is quietly dozing. McClure's head and shoulders come into the scene from the rear. He shakes Ted's arm. Ted starts, looks around questioningly.

MCCLURE (*pointing down, yelling*). The Bay Bridge! How about flying under it?

TED (*with a disgusted chuckle*). For why?

MCCLURE. So I can get some pictures. You know, shooting up at the super-structure. C'mon, Lawson.

TED (*to Davenport*). Do you want to?
DAVENPORT. Sure, go ahead if it'll make him happy.

McClure goes to his compartment. Davenport thrusts the column forward and the nose slides down. As they move swiftly toward the objective, Ted leans over to Davenport.

TED. I hope there are no cables hang-ing under that span!

This cuts to the NAVIGATOR'S COMPART-MENT as the *Ruptured Duck* goes under the bridge and comes up on the other side. McClure triumphantly completes taking his movies. His face is aglow. He takes the camera from his eye, looks at the film indicator. A look of terrible disappointment comes over his face. He scrambles forward frantically.—Then

we again see the PILOT'S COMPARTMENT as McClure enters with a yell.

MCCLURE. Let's take a turn and go it again. I forgot to put film in!

TED. We're due at the field. Forget it.

MCCLURE (*shaking his camera as if it were responsible, suppressed rage in his voice*). I may never get another crack at—!

DAVENPORT (*pointing*). Hey, look!

Viewed through the WINDSHIELD, down below, tied up to a wharf, is an aircraft carrier with three B-25's on its deck; then the scene cuts again to the PILOT'S COMPARTMENT.

TED (*shouting out*). McClure! Take a look down there!

MCCLURE (*staring down, an awed look on his face*). It's a carrier!

DAVENPORT. Yeah—and look at her deck!

TED (*with a nod and a wink*). B-25's. Three of them.

MCCLURE. Holy smoke—then this is it! (*He stares down at the carrier. There's a pause as the reaction to the carrier hits them.*) Kind of small, isn't she?

While McClure and Davenport stare at the carrier, Ted snaps on the inter-phone.

TED (*into the interphone*). Pilot to bombardier. (*He pauses, listens, and frowns at getting no reply.*) Pilot to gunner. Pilot to gunner. Thatcher! (*He waits again, receives no answer, and snaps the interphone off with a look of impatience.*) Dead again!

DAVENPORT. We'd better report it to Doolittle when we get in.

TED (*sourly*). Yeah, and that left

engine along with it. Still seem a little rough to you?

DAVENPORT (*tapping his ear*). I can't tell any more.

We get a full view of the SKY as the *Ruptured Duck* banks for a landing on the airfield just adjacent to the wharf, and this scene dissolves to ALAMEDA FIELD as the *Ruptured Duck* is just landing. In the foreground Doolittle and York are beckoning to it. The *Ruptured Duck* taxies up beside Doolittle and York. Ted rolls back the window.

DOOLITTLE. Is everything on your ship okay?

TED. Why—(*A hunch comes over him.*) Yes, sir! *Yes, sir!*

Davenport gives Ted a look.

DOOLITTLE (*pointing*). Taxi over to the edge of the carrier's wharf. They'll take care of you there.

TED. Yes, sir.

The *Ruptured Duck* taxies on past the Colonel and Captain York, and we see her next arriving at the edge of the wharf. The hatch opens and the first of the crew comes out. Instantly a group of Navy men swarm about them. The crew piles out of the ship.

TED (*disapprovingly*). They don't even wait till a fellow gets out.

MCCLURE (*flatly*). All navy guys are cocky.

DAVENPORT. Miller is a navy guy.

MCCLURE. Well—Miller isn't exactly Navy. He's a pilot.

We hear a putt-putt-putt sound. Our "gang" watches nervously. Then we see that an army donkey has hooked the *Ruptured Duck's* main gear and is towing it down the pier, following

which we see the *Ruptured Duck's* crew as they walk along behind, like five lost spirits. They encounter a solitary figure, standing staring forlornly toward the carrier. It is Lieutenant Spike Henderson.

CLEVER (*calling out*). Hey, Spike! Is your plane on yet?

By this time they have come up to him. Spike turns an anguished face to them, shakes his head and says nothing.

TED. Spike—what's the matter?

SPIKE (*with heart-broken self-disgust*). I put in a beef about my fuel pump and Doolittle told me to take her to the hangar.

DAVENPORT (*incredulously*). Then you're not going?

SPIKE (*shaking his head*). No. And there's nothing really wrong with that plane. Best ship in the squad.

TED (*sympathetically*). Boy, that's rough. (*"He does a take."*) I—and I almost told him about our interphone!

They all look at each other, stunned at the possibility of what might have happened.

SPIKE. You'd have been a cooked goose.

THATCHER (*nervously*). I—I think, sir, I'll go on and watch these Navy guys. They might bang her up or something.

TED (*with equal nervousness*). I—that's a good idea. We'll go—

He looks off and stops as he sees the claws of a big crane descending upon the *Ruptured Duck*. Then we again see the GROUP as the men stare at the spectacle, slack-jawed and panic-stricken.

DAVENPORT (*tensely*). They're going to break the *Duck's* back sure.

TED. How did we get in the clutches of these Navy guys?

Looking back, we see the crane settling down over the *Ruptured Duck*. It adjusts itself so delicately to the contours of the big ship that there is not even a jar as it fastens its claws and gently 'ifts the plane upward.

The GROUP traces the upward course of the *Ruptured Duck* by the tense upward course of their heads and eyes as they follow it. Nobody says a word.

In a full view, looking toward the SHIP we see the *Ruptured Duck* as she is swung slowly up onto the flight deck. It is set down without a jar, and immediately another swarm of Navy men climbs over it.

The men in the GROUP relax, sighing.

MCCLURE (*looking up at the carrier*). Boy—that's an awful big ship.

TED. Yeah, let's take a look at her.

As our group moves toward the ship ladder we see another B-25 being towed down the wharf behind them, and the scene dissolves to a fairly close view of the DECK of the CARRIER. The Officer of the Deck has about twenty sailors lined up on the deck at the head of the ladder.

Ted comes onto the deck first. Carefully remembering the etiquette taught him by Miller, he faces the rear of the ship and salutes the national ensign. Then he turns and smartly salutes the Officer of the Deck, who returns his salute.

TED. Lieutenant Lawson, sir.

OFFICER OF DECK (*to the first sailor*). Take the Lieutenant to 21A.

SAILOR. This way, sir.

TED (*preceded by the sailor as they go through a door*). I'll see you guys later.

Ted and the sailor are next seen descending a steep set of iron stairs, then going down through a hatch, while Ted is beginning to look puzzled at the many passages.

This dissolves to the. INTERIOR COMPANIONWAY as the sailor leads Ted up to a door. He knocks on the door. There is no answer. The sailor throws it open.

SAILOR. These are your quarters, sir. Mr. White and Mr. Felton are on shore leave.

TED (*entering*). Thank you.

SAILOR (*hesitating for a moment*). Do you think you can find your way back to the deck, sir?

TED (*loftily*). Oh, sure. Thanks. (*The sailor smiles and leaves.*)

The INTERIOR COMPARTMENT: It is a small room featuring two built-in bunks and an army cot. The walls are plastered with near nudes and pin-up girls. There are two small desks and a couple of chairs. The room is immaculately neat. Ted puts his hands in his pockets, as he walks slowly around the room, whistling softly to himself. He tries the cot, then he turns, opens the door and peers out into the companionway to see if all is clear. It is. He leaves the room.

This dissolves to a STAIRWAY as Ted climbs up. At the top there is a hatch. He tries to open it but it is bolted down. Ted is puzzled; he turns and goes down the stairs. He has three possible companionways to take now. He stands for a moment in thought. The look of frustration on his face grows. A sailor passes and looks at him curiously.

SAILOR. Lost, sir?

TED (*casually*). Oh, no. Just looking around. (*And he starts determinedly down the companionway.*)

This dissolves to another COMPANION-WAY. Ted is walking very rapidly now. He hears footsteps coming from behind him. He stops and turns around.

DAVENPORT. What are *you* doing down here?

TED. Oh . . . just looking around. What are *you* doing?

DAVENPORT. Oh . . . looking around. (*They start down the companionway.*)

TED (*grinning*). You lost, too?

DAVENPORT. Am I lost! I'm trapped like a rat. I've been walking for miles. (*They both burst into laughter at their predicament.*) This is the biggest cock-eyed ship I've ever seen.

TED. Yeah. And I wish the deck were *twice* as big!

LOUDSPEAKER. The smoking lamp is out. The smoking lamp is out.

Ted and Davenport are walking along, Ted smoking. At the loudspeaker's voice, they look at each other in puzzlement. A sailor, passing, notices Ted smoking, and approaches respectfully.

SAILOR. Smoking lamp is out means no smoking anywhere on the ship, sir.

TED (*dousing his cigarette*). Okay.

DAVENPORT. Why is that?

SAILOR. They're refueling. They'll let us know when they're through.

They nod their thanks, and the sailor continues. As they stride down the companionway, they run into Don Smith.

DON. You guys finally got on, eh?

TED. Sure. Just been looking the tub over.

DON. How are your quarters?

TED. Perfect. Nice room with two bunks and a cot . . .

DON (*with a contemptuous gesture*). A cot! Follow me, brothers—I'm gonna show you real quarters. And I mean *quarters!* (*They follow him.*)

This dissolves to a COMPANIONWAY as DON, DAVENPORT and TED come to a door.

DON (*stopping*). Your shoes clean?

DAVENPORT. C'mon—what's the gik?

DON (*with a bow*). Just this—

He opens the door; then the scene cuts to the ADMIRAL'S CABIN as our trio enters. Ted and Davenport stand stupefied. It is a large room, probably thirty-five by twenty feet with heavy tables, beautiful over-stuffed leather furniture and a floor that is carpeted from wall to wall. The carpeting is thick and luxurious. The only touch that is not in keeping with the room is the fact that there are perhaps a dozen Army cots around the wall to accommodate the flyers who have been assigned to these quarters. There are perhaps a dozen men in the room. Some of them are lounging elegantly, while others have opened a door which is flush with the side of the ship and are looking at the sea in the slanting rays of the afternoon sun.

We get a close view of DAVENPORT, TED and the GROUP staring.

JUNGLE JIM HALLMARK (*calling out*). What's the idea of bringing people up here from the tenement districts?

.BOB GRAY. This joint's strictly for the better boys. You guys can't come in unless you're disinfected first.

DON (*in superior tones*). This is jocularly known as the Admiral's cabin.

DAVENPORT (*staring around the room; shaking his head*). Looks like you guys'll have to start bathing.

DON (*confidentially*). There's something else. Follow me.

He leads them toward a doorway at the far side of the room, the view moving with them.

DON (*as they go across*). Careful of the rugs, please. (*As they reach the door*) Now just inside, gentlemen, is something to really feast your peepers on. (*He drops his voice.*)The first guy turns in after dinner gets this bed for the trip. You know who *that'll* be. (*He throws the door open.*) Enter.

Bob Gray, grinning with anticipation, follows them, and the scene cuts to the ADMIRAL'S BEDROOM.

This room even excels its predecessor, if not in size, at least in appointments. It is richly carpeted and it is amply supplied with beautifully upholstered furniture. But the principal feature of the room is a bed at least six feet wide. The center of the bed is strangely rumpled. Don's face clouds over as he looks at the bed.

TED (*with a grin*). It looks like somebody's beat you to it.

DON (*gritting his teeth*). What dirty, low-lived—!?

He starts for the bed, Ted and Davenport following him. They come up to it. Whoever is occupying its luxurious

center has covered his head. Don silently reaches over for the top of the cover and gives it a sudden jerk.

DON. Come out of there, you bollweevil!

Like a jack-in-the-box, Shorty Manch pops up into a sitting position. He is in pajamas.

SHORTY (*wide-awake, with a broad grin*). Well, feed me corn and watch me grow! (*To Don, scowling*) How did all this scum get in?

TED (*disgusted*).—And me in an army cot!

DON (*turning, frustrated, to go*). That's where he'll end up, before the night's over. Let's get out of here.

As they turn and start for the door, Manch calls out sweetly to them.

MANCH. Oh, Lieutenant . . . (*Don barely pauses to throw a glum look over his shoulder.*) When you guys go down to dinner, would you mind bringing back a roast beef sandwich, rare, on white bread, and a couple of bottles of milk? (*The men react with complete disgust as they go out, and Don calls after them:*) . . . and a piece of blueberry pie!

This dissolves to the FLIGHT DECK at night, as BOB GRAY and TED pass the lashed-down B-25. Fog is billowing in over the deck. Shore lights show, but indistinctly. They are walking along slowly, hands in their pockets. The *Hornet* is still at anchor. Someone is playing a harmonica—"Carry Me Back to Old Virginia."

BOB (*quietly*). Still glad you came along?

TED. Sure. Aren't you?

BOB. I got a funny feeling about this job.

TED. Yeah?

BOB. Uh-huh. I think maybe it isn't going to be as much of a cinch as we figured on.

TED. I've been thinking the same thing.

BOB (*pausing and peering into the gloom*). There's my ship. Think I'll take a look at it.

TED. The *Duck's* up ahead. See you in the morning.

BOB. Goodnight.

As Bob turns off to his own plane and Ted continues toward his, the scene cuts to another view of the *Ruptured Duck*, identified by the symbol on her nose, as Ted comes up to her. He gives her a little pat on her metal skin. Then a voice challenges him.

VOICE. Who's that?

Ted peers into the gloom, and finally looks down beside one of the wheels.

TED. That you, Thatcher?

Thatcher is sitting down, his back against one of the wheels, his arms clasped around his knees.

THATCHER (*starting to rise*). Yes, sir.

TED. Forget it, Thatcher.

He looks at the large blocks under the *Ruptured Duck's* wheels. He sees the ropes which keep her in place.

TED. They've got her pretty well lashed down, haven't they?

THATCHER. Yes, sir. They did a good job. I was kind of worried about her, so I—I thought I'd have a look.

Ted leans against the body of the plane, crosses one foot over the other, and stares off.

TED. Lonesome?

THATCHER (*after a pause*). I guess everybody is—a little, sir.

TED. Don't bother with the sirs, Dave. Your quarters all right?

THATCHER. Yes. Fine.

TED. Grub's good, too, isn't it?

THATCHER. Best I've had in a long while, sir.

TED (*smiling a little*). What are you going to do when we get back home, Thatcher?

THATCHER. I have a girl in Billings, sir. I'm going to marry her . . . if we get back.

TED (*confidently*). We'll get back all right.

A figure looms up in the fog. Ted and Thatcher both look up. It is McClure. He is carrying a bubble sextant.

MCCLURE (*surprised*). Oh! Hello. I— I thought I'd come up and shoot the stars for a little while. (*Looking up*) —But I guess it's too foggy.

TED (*looking up, pretending to notice fog for the first time; then smiling*). Pretty foggy, all right.

Footsteps sound from the other side of the plane. All three are silent as they listen to the approaching footsteps. Then, around the end of the wing, come Davenport and Clever.

DAVENPORT (*in surprise*). What are you guys doing here?

TED. Just getting a little air.

DAVENPORT (*with a shrug*). Yeh . . . pretty stuffy down below.

A grin breaks over Ted's face. He is very pleased with this crew of his.

TED (*affectionately*). You guys worry over the *Ruptured Duck* like a bunch of old maids. Me—I'm going to bed. (*As he turns*) Goodnight.

GROUP (*ad libbing*). Goodnight.

Ted starts away. As he goes, he calls back over his shoulder.

TED (*smiling to himself*). Wonderful air, isn't it?

LOUDSPEAKER (*looming out weirdly through the foggy night*). The smoking lamp is lit .... the smoking lamp is lit ...

Ted is then seen walking away in the foreground, with airplanes and men, dim, fog-bound figures, in the background. Matches begin to flare—little pinpoints of light in the fog—all over the deck.

This dissolves to TED'S COMPARTMENT at gray dawn as TED is still asleep on his army cot. There is the sound of a bugle call through loudspeaker.

LOUDSPEAKER. General Quarters! Man your battle stations! General Quarters! Man your battle stations! Army personnel man your planes!

Ted awakens with a great start, stares blankly, tries to turn over, falls on the floor, and finally scrambles frantically to his feet.

This cuts to the COMPARTMENT as Ensigns Jig White and Bud Felton, immaculately attired in their uniforms, are standing looking down at Ted with superior smiles. Ted gets excitedly to his feet.

TED (*in a startled voice*). What's wrong—What happened?

JIG (*grinning*). Just battle stations. Around sun-up and sun-down the pig

boats give us a little trouble, so we always lay for 'em.

BUD. This is Jig White and I'm Bud Felton. (*They start for the door.*) See you later.

TED (*as they go*). Are we under way?

JIG (*as he closes the door behind him*). For the last five hours.

This dissolves to a series of shots of: Men in gun galleries, on the alert; deck crews, on the alert; bridge personnel scanning the skies.

This dissolves to JIG WHITE and BUD FELTON walking across the deck toward the *Ruptured Duck*. As they come up to the ship, Ted is coming out of the forward hatch.

BUD (*looking at the* Duck). Boy, the only way you're going to get that off of here is with a crane.

TED (*quietly*). Maybe so. But we kind of think we can take off under our own power.

DAVENPORT (*from the pilot's compartment, suddenly interrupting and pointing*). Hey—where'd they come from?

As they all stare out to sea, we see several war ships in the distance which are accompanying the *Hornet*. They are cruisers and destroyers.

BUD'S VOICE. That's what's known as an escort.

Next we see TED, BUD and JIG.

JIG (*smiling with quiet pride*). They just slipped up on us during the night. The Navy likes to do things quietly.

TED (*thoughtfully*). Looks like it's really gonna be a show, doesn't it? (*Shorty Manch comes up to them.*)

SHORTY (*grinning widely*). Boy did I hate to part skin from sheet this morning! What a bed!

TED. This is Shorty Manch—Jig White and Bud Felton. (*They shake hands and exchange greetings.*) This lucky stiff's sleeping in the bedroom off the admiral's cabin.

MANCH (*slyly*). Wonderful accommodations—but nothing much to do. (*With a side glance at Ted*) I thought there'd be at *least* a poker game or something going on. (*But neither of the Navy men fall for this.*)

BUD (*winking at Jig*). I guess they have 'em once in a while.

JIG. Mind if I go in and look at the controls?

TED. Go ahead. (*Jig goes into the ship. Ted remains with the others.*) I'd like to go below and take a look at your planes.

SHORTY (*apropos of nothing at all*). What kind of poker do you play on this ship?

BUD (*shrugging*). You know—just poker. Not too hot.

Manch looks more and more pleased. Jig sticks his head out of the *Ruptured Duck*.

JIG. You've really got a mess of clocks in there.

BUD (*standing off, looking at the plane admiringly, and nodding his head approvingly*). Yeah, that's a lot of airplane.

MANCH. How about Seven-Toed Pete? Ever play much of that around here?

JIG (*blankly, to Bud*). What's Seven-Toed Pete?

Bud and Jig shake their heads solemnly.

MANCH (*his face positively beaming*).

Well, it's a kind of seven-card poker. I—I'd be glad to teach it to you sometime.

BUD (*winking at Jig*). Never heard of it. (*Manch's face lights up.*)

LOUDSPEAKER. Attention Army personnel. Attention Army personnel. Assemble in Ward Room. Assemble in Ward Room.

MANCH (*ingratiatingly, as he goes*). Well, it's been a great pleasure, fellows. We'll certainly have to get together soon. Maybe—heh—heh—get up a little game or something.

BUD AND JIG. Goodbye. So long.

The Army personnel exits from the scene. Bud and Jig stand, staring off thoughtfully at them.

JIG (*rubbing his chin thoughtfully, speculatively*). You know, I believe that boy wants to play poker.

BUD (*very seriously*). I wonder if they got their pay before they came aboard.

This dissolves to the WARD ROOM, first disclosing a corner of the room near the ceiling. Here we see the only insignia which identifies the ship. It is a real hornet's nest, attached to the limb of a tree and mounted in a corner of the officers' wardroom. The scene pulls back to a full shot of the WARDROOM. The room is large and—considering the fact that it is on a war ship—very swank. The metal walls are painted and glistening. No pipes are visible. The tables are forty feet long; chairs are overstuffed leather. The men are filing in, and the wardroom is rapidly filling.

This cuts toward the FOREPART of the WARDROOM as Doolittle enters, accompanied by York and Davey Jones, Miller and half a dozen Navy officers.

MAN IN FRONT. 'Ten*shun!*

Immediately Army men are on their feet. Doolittle, as usual, puts them at ease and wastes no time in getting directly to the subject.

DOOLITTLE (*clearing his throat*). For the benefit of those of you who haven't already guessed, we're going straight to Japan. The Navy will take us within four hundred miles of the Japanese mainland. We're going to bomb Tokyo, Yokohama, Kobe, Osaki, and Nagoya. It'll be a night job, and you will have the opportunity of choosing the city you prefer.

We see the ROOM from his angle. It seems as if every man in the room exhales a sigh of relieved suspense at the information.—DOOLITTLE, seen close, gives a grim little smile.

DOOLITTLE. It's going to be a tight squeeze. The Chinese have prepared small fields just outside Japanese occupied territory for us to land on after the raid. They'll tank us up, and we'll take off for Chungking.

The view moves across, revealing TED, DAVENPORT, SHORTY MANCH, BOB GRAY, MCCLURE, THATCHER, CLEVER and DON SMITH. They are all listening tensely; then DOOLITTLE is seen again, speaking.

DOOLITTLE. From now on we're in constant danger of enemy action. In case of a surface attack, stand by your planes with fire extinguishers, and let the Navy handle it. If we're attacked by air, take off immediately and try to make the nearest land. The Navy will give all navigators their bearings twice a day. Now once more, I want to emphasize that if any of you feel you're not going to be up to the job, you're perfectly free to drop out. We have a few spare men, and I'm sure

we can fill your place. Get together with Captain York, find out what to do with your planes and we'll meet here tomorrow at 2:30. Are there any questions?

There's a long pause, followed by a close view of a LIEUTENANT in the back of the room whom we have not previously identified. He rises.

YOUNG LIEUTENANT (*in a thick voice*). Colonel—do you mind if we smoke during these assemblies?

A chuckle goes over the room. They've just been told they are to bomb Japan and the only question asked is can they smoke. Even Doolittle smiles.

DOOLITTLE (*pleasantly*). I see no objection to that. Anything else? (*Receiving no response*) Dismissed!

He waits a moment, then turns and goes out, following which we see LAWSON and HIS CREW looking at each other, then breaking out with grins.

This dissolves to the FLIGHT DECK AS TED is pacing off the deck.

TED (*as he steps it off; whispering under his breath*). Sixteen, seventeen, eighteen, nineteen . . . (*He has a worried look on his face.*)

Coming straight toward Ted is Manch. Shorty also has a worried look and is also stepping off the deck, although moving in the opposite direction from Ted.

MANCH (*to himself*). . . . eighty-seven, eighty-eight, eighty-nine . . .

At this moment, Ted enters the scene and they bump into each other. They both look up, surprised.

TED (*quickly, abashed*). Oh, I'm—sorry, Manch. I was . . getting a little exercise.

MANCH. Yeah? Well *I* wasn't. I'm measuring off this cockeyed deck! (*He determinedly continues stepping it off with a worried look on his face.*) Ninety . . . Ninety-one . . .

Ted looks after him and grins, then continues his own pacing. They are brought up short by the ship's loud speaker. They stop and listen. Navy men in background, among them Felton and White, react as they all listen. During the following speech some of the *Duck's* crew join Ted and listen with him.

LOUD SPEAKER. Attention all personnel: You have been wondering about the mission we are on. I think you might like to know that the Army personnel on the *Hornet* are going to bomb Japan. We of the Navy are going to take them in as close to the enemy as possible. This is a chance for all of us to give the Japs a dose of their own medicine. It's an Army-Navy show. Let's extend every courtesy to the Army men on the *Hornet* who are going to do the job. Good luck—good hunting—and may God speed us on our mission!

The RUPTURED DUCK: Our crew look at each other with quiet smiles. A sailor, who has been standing in the background close to Thatcher, comes up to him.

SAILOR (*respectfully, offering a package of chocolate*). Have some?

Thatcher looks surprised for a moment. Then he grins, and takes the chocolate.

THATCHER. Thanks, Buddy. (*The sailor does not resent the nickname.*)

The scene dissolves to TED'S COMPARTMENT at night. Ted, Shorty, Jig and Bud are gathered around, playing poker. There are big stacks of chips

in front of Jig and Bud. We see that Manch holds a small straight.

JIG (*smugly*). They tell me Virginia's a great hunting country, too.

Bud is just dealing the last card to Shorty. He puts the deck aside.

SHORTY (*picking up his card, trying to concentrate*). What's that? Oh, yeah. (*Eager for the show-down*) Let's play, fellows. What's the bet? (*They are playing Seven-Toed Pete.*)

BUD (*looking at Shorty*). It's up to you, Manch. Don't they call Virginia the mother of presidents?

SHORTY. Er . . . yes. I mean—bet five. (*He puts five chips in.*)

JIG (*carelessly*). Up ten. Thomas Jefferson lived there, too, didn't he?

TED (*enjoying Shorty's discomfort*). I drop.

From this point on Ted watches the scene with amusement at Shorty's predicament.

SHORTY (*a little irritably*). A lot of guys lived there! Are you *sure* you never played Seven-Toed Pete before?

BUD (*putting in more chips*). Makes it ten to you, Manch. Have they finally got the hook worm situation under control down there?

MANCH (*throwing out the chips, burning*). There's *never* been a case of hook worm in Virginia! I've got a small straight.

JIG. Mine's seven to the jack.

BUD. All pink. (*He puts his cards out.*)

SHORTY (*without even showing his*). That beats. (*He rises.*) I think I'll turn in. (*He stares down at the table.*) Somebody's won a lot of dough.

JIG. A little. (*The chips are stacked up until he can scarcely see over them.*) You had a run of bad cards, Manch.

SHORTY (*curtly*). Yeah.

BUD. What say we get together again, pretty soon?

SHORTY (*opening the door*). Oh, *sure!* See you later.

JIG (*as he goes*). Say, you haven't got any books on Virginia, have you, Manch?

As Manch slams the door, Bud, Jig, and Ted burst into roars of laughter.

JIG (*still laughing, sitting down on Ted's army cot*). You army guys are real pigeons! I wish you were in the Navy. (*He begins to untie his shoes, and glances up very casually at Ted.*) You take the bunk, Lawson. I'll sleep here, if you don't mind.

TED (*who is taking his necktie off, a little puzzled*). What's the idea?

JIG (*his voice rising defensively, with a contemptuous gesture toward the bunk*). A-a—that thing's soft as a featherbed. I never could sleep in it.

TED, seen sitting on the bunk, grins understandingly.

TED (*feeling the bunk, appreciatively*). Yeah. Not bad . . .

This cuts to the WARDROOM. Doolittle, with Army and Navy officers clustered near him, is at the head of the room. The men are gathered around tables, listening carefully. Some of them are smoking. There is an air of ease, of workmanlike informality about the place. Doolittle is speaking. We have come in on the latter part of his talk.

DOOLITTLE. You'll have ten five-gallon cans of extra gas, so beginning right now you'd better start to time your pumping. After the take-off, you'll have to get the gas out of your inflammable tanks and into the self-sealing wing tanks before you run into enemy fire. (*He indicates men as he mentions them.*) Lieutenant Randall is going to tell you something about a carrier take-off. Take over, Mr. Randall.

We see TED and HIS CREW, with other crews in the background. Randall comes to the point at once.

RANDALL. From the minute you're in your planes, I'm the man to watch. Have your engines turning over as soon as the man ahead of you starts taxiing. When I want you to rev up, I'll give you this. (*He makes a whirling motion with a checkered flag.*) If your engines don't sound right to me, I may have to keep you revved up for longer than you think necessary. I can hear your engines and tell when they're missing better than you can. Now when I want you to taxi up, I'll give you this . . . (*He gives a come-on motion with both hands toward the chest.*) One hand up—(*holding the hand up in come-on gesture*)—means to come on on that side, and brake the other wheel. When I make this motion—(*squeezing tightly with both hands, palms forward*)—that means apply brakes. Idle engines is this. (*Both hands cross in front of his face with palms forward.*) Now you're in position. I give you a final rev—(*whirling the flag*)—and when I drop it—(*dropping the flag*)—you're off. We'll aim you straight for Japan. One more thing. Once we line up for the take-off, there can be no delays. If your plane stalls, if it doesn't start immediately, if you have trouble of any kind—we won't have time to do anything about it. The navy crew has orders to push the ship overboard to make way for the next one. (*He sits down.*)

DOOLITTLE (*rising*). Commander Jarika has detailed maps and pictures of cities and specific targets. He spent a good many years in Japan. I think it's a good idea for him to tell you of the kind of people you're going up against in case you're forced down. (*With a gesture toward Jarika*) Commander Jarika.

JARIKA (*rising*). I was assistant naval attaché at our embassy in Japan long enough to learn a few things about the Orient. In the first place, get the word "yellow" out of your minds.

We see TED, GRAY, DAVENPORT and MC-CLURE with others. They are listening.

JARIKA'S VOICE. To say that this is a war of the white races against the yellow is an insult to our 400,000,000 Chinese allies.

We then see JARIKA again.

JARIKA. You'll find a great many differences between the Chinese and the Japs. The Chinese are one of the most tolerant and civilized peoples on earth. You'll like 'em.

We see, in a slow-moving "shot," TED, GRAY, DAVENPORT, MCCLURE, CLEVER, MANCH, SMITH, HOLSTROM, HALLMARK, FARROW, and others.

The view passes over their faces not only to see their reactions to what Jarika is to say, but also to remind our audience that not all of these men came back; that some of them suffered the treatment implied by Jarika in the following.

JARIKA'S VOICE (*continuing*). The Japanese, on the other hand, is the

Nazi of Asia. He is fanatically devoted to the divine right of his leaders to conquer the world. He has become a rapist, a looter and a murderer. He will abide by no rule of civilized peoples. He will stop at no cruelty.

This cuts to a GROUP OF MEN, favoring BOB GRAY, who rises.

BOB. Just what should we do, Mr. Jarika—how should we conduct ourselves—in case we *are* forced down over Japan?

JARIKA is seen considering this question. Then his face grows grim.

JARIKA (*with deadly emphasis*). My advice is—see that you're *not* forced down over Japan.

This dissolves to a close view of a RADIO SPEAKER in the RADIO ROOM. During the following speech, the view pulls back and expands to reveal Navy operators and half a dozen Army flyers, including Ted, McClure, Bob Gray, Manch, and others. They are all silently listening to the following Japanese propaganda broadcast:

VOICE OVER RADIO (*in a cultivated English voice*). . . . Thirty thousand prisoners were taken in the final capitulation of the American and Philippine forces in Bataan, the Imperial Staff announced this morning. The Americans fought desperately, but were overcome by the heroic onslaughts of our glorious Japanese army. The Americans wept for joy when they were given food and tobacco by their chivalrous conquerors. While your American cities, thanks to the war-mongering of your President Roosevelt, are blacked out and your people herded into air-raid shelters, we in beautiful Japan celebrate our cherry festival. Picnics and dances and pilgrimages are enjoyed by happy Japanese workers with their immaculate wives and their neat children. There are no restrictions of liberties in Japan, and our cities gleam at night with lights. All this is because the mighty Imperial Navy, the invincible Japanese armies, and the heroic Japanese air forces guarantee this island empire forever from attack. This is Radio Tokyo addressing all lovers of peace in the Americas. We now play for you your favorite American melody, rendered by the Shin-Kyota Military Band.

The record follows, a miserable interpretation by the band of "Home, Home on the Range." The Navy operator quietly switches the radio off.

SHORTY MANCH (*grimly*). Well grind me up for a meatball . . .

Ted looks quietly at McClure.

MCCLURE (*grimly*). You know, I—I'd kind of like to drop an egg on that guy.

TED. Doolittle *said* we get our pick of targets. Tokyo suits me.

This dissolves to a closeup of a PAIR OF DICE in the ADMIRAL'S QUARTERS, as the dice roll across the carpet and come up on a seven. It is early evening.

SHORTY MANCH'S VOICE. Solid-sendin' babies, travel home!

As they seven, Shorty's hand scoops them up again, and the scene cuts to the GROUP shooting crap in the corner of the CABIN at night.

In the background we see men sitting and reading; men talking in little groups; men lying on their cots trying to get some sleep. Clever is quietly working on a drawing. But the triumphant exhortations of Manch divert

most attention to the crap game. Among the participants are Gray, Lawson, Davey Jones, and Holstrom. Manch has just scooped up the dice. He leaves his winnings on the carpet.

MANCH. Bless my soul! Get on, boys, make your bets and say your prayers!

There is a general grumble of dissatisfaction from the losers. They hesitate to cover.

HOLSTROM (*teeth gritted*). If those weren't my own dice . . . oh well, I got five. (*He places his bets.*)

MANCH. Come on, you truck drivers, you wanta die rich? Lay out a little of that green stuff. You heard what the big guy said—only half of you guys'll come through anyhow.

AD LIBS. Okay, you're covered. All right, now, snake eyes!

MANCH (*fondling the dice passionately*). All set to go? Okay! (*As he throws them*) Come on, you little sharp-cats, kill the croaker with a *seven!*

Shorty kisses the dice, begins an elaborate wind-up, finally lifting his left leg and throwing them backhand. They roll out seven.

MANCH (*exultantly, to the dice*). Oh you little lovers! (*He leaves some money out.*) Manch shoots the works! All or any part! Step right up, boys, and bet your money on the spotted tuskers!

TED (*laying out some money*). I'll cover this.

MANCH. A sportsman! Lawson knows you can't take it with you! C'mon, Holstrom! You've got Yokohama, haven't you?

HOLSTROM (*sourly*). So what?

MANCH. So what good's a pocketful of dough gonna do you when you've got sixty thousand meatballs on your tail? Believe Daddy Manch, you'll wish you'd gotten a little fun outa your dough!

HOLSTROM (*throwing money in*). Try you once more. *Once.*

MANCH. A man with courage! C'me on, hep-cats, the sugar loaves are gettin' cold! (*As the others cover*) That's better! All in? And all *covered!* (*He goes through another elaborate routine with the dice.*) Oh you jitter-saucin' love birds, hit the groove for Pappy Manch! (*Another breathless silence, then a triumphant whoop and swoop*) Seven! Hep-jills, come to Daddy! And Daddy shoots the works!

HOLSTROM (*rising*). Not me.

MANCH (*appalled*). What's the matter here, what's the matter? Short of courage?

HOLSTROM (*showing his empty pocket*). Just short of dough.

MANCH (*with cold comfort*). Oh well, you might not've lived to spend it anyhow. Always look on the bright side. Get in here, boys—put in a little—take out a little—

TED (*rising*). Count me out.

MANCH (*with pretended astonishment*). What kind of an air force is this? Look fellas—(*He begins almost to plead.*) Let's not think about money at a time like this! Let's not be vulgar! When it's dunked in sea water, you can't tell a five from a ten anyhow!

JONES. Not for me.

GRAY. I've had enough.

MANCH (*holding a fistful of money up*). You can't bribe the laws of gravitation. I'm just trying to get rid of the stuff. (*The men look at each other.*)

HOLSTROM (*moving toward Manch*). Let's *help* him get rid of it, eh, fellows? (*They begin to crowd in on Manch.*)

MANCH (*in alarm*). Hey, what's the idea?

TED. Kind of a loan.

MANCH (*emphatically*). Nope! Nope! A man gambles, he's got to stand the loss. If I gave you guys any dough, it'd—it'd weaken your characters. (*They close in further, and he is a little frantic now.*) But honest, boys, I haven't got enough even for myself!

GRAY. You've won close to fifteen hundred bucks, Manch. How come you're so short?

MANCH (*as they lay a hand or two on him; now talking very fast*). Wait a minute! No roughness, boys! No physical contact! All I got is what I won tonight—about a hundred and twelve bucks! Bleed me for a stuck pig if that isn't the truth!

JONES. Where'd the rest go?

MANCH (*frantically*). I lost it to the Navy! Now look—

HOLSTROM (*with a roar*). The *Navy!*

We see the rest of the room as Holstrom turns and addresses them.

HOLSTROM. Hey, you guys! Know where all our dough's gone? Manch has siphoned it all out to the Navy!

He starts menacingly toward Manch. Hallmark rises from a poker table.

AD LIBS. Making fools of us in front of the Navy! No wonder those guys are lookin' so smug!

MANCH (*almost hysterically*). Don't make a move, fellows! You'll regret it as long as you live! You'll begin to brood—!

HOLSTROM. At him, men!

Just as they close in to seize the scrambling Manch, the ship's loudspeaker system booms out:

LOUDSPEAKER. General Quarters! Man your battle stations! General Quarters, man your battle stations!

They break, hesitate, and realize they must give up their project.

MANCH (*triumphantly*). Duty calls, fellows! Duty calls! I gotta keep a lookout for the pig boats! (*And as they all break and start for their ships, the scene dissolves out.*)

A LARGE AIR PHOTOGRAPH MARKED "TOKYO" dissolves in, and we see Commander Jarika standing in front of it. He is the only one in the scene. He is pointing out certain buildings to the off-scene characters.

JARIKA (*indicating on the map*). These pins here—(*pointing to them*) —are balloons, as of our last report on them. You'll find Tokyo Bay just as it is here, lined with wharves. Most of the stuff we want to hit is located close to the bay.

Then the view expands to reveal Ted, McClure, Clever, Davenport and Thatcher. They are studying the photograph intently, listening to Jarika. Doolittle and Davey Jones are to one side, likewise absorbed in the photograph. There are others in the room studying other maps.

JARIKA (*pointing*). The run I've got figured out for you starts here. The smokestack is bright red brick, and you can't miss it. One of the largest

smelters in Japan. Then, following the line of the bay, and allowing for ten seconds between bombs, you could take out this . . . and this. Both of them are machine shops. Owned by brothers. I forget their names, but I remember I didn't like 'em. (*There are chuckles, and Jarika grins.*) And then on out here to drop your incendiary. (*To Ted and his crew*) How does that line up for you?

TED (*turning to Clever*). You're going to drop 'em, Clever. The run seems all right with me if it's okay for you.

CLEVER (*quietly*). We can take 'em out.

JARIKA. Fine. (*To Davey*) Jones, have you got the course laid out for this run?

DAVEY (*picking up a map*). Yes. (*To Ted and the crew*) Over here, fellows.

They move over to a table, gather around it and begin to inspect the map.

We get a close view of the MAP of Japan and China and the South Pacific as Jones' finger comes in over the map, pointing out the route. The map has a course marked out.

JONES. You'll take off about here . . . and go due west to Tokyo at minimum cruising speed, flying at about fifty feet. When you hit the bay, get up to fifteen hundred, complete your bombing run, then down again and out to sea. South by southeast to Yaku Shima. I'll give you plenty of identification on that. From there on just follow the 29th parallel across the east China Sea and pray yourselves in at Choo Chow Lishui. Got any more questions about the party?

MCCLURE (*as the group is seen again*). Can we take the maps with us?

DOOLITTLE (*quickly*). All you need, but they mustn't have any marks on them which might let the Japs know where you came from if you're captured. By the way, I'm taking off first with four incendiaries. That ought to light Tokyo up pretty well for you.

TED. Suppose by the time we get to China the Japs have taken over the landing fields?

DOOLITTLE. The Chinese have arranged a signal which will warn you at the field if it's Jap occupied. If the field is captured, you'll have to go on till you run out of gas, then bail out and destroy your planes.

Jarika steps forward, says something inaudible to Doolittle. Doolittle nods. Jarika turns to the room.

JARIKA. There's just been a change in the disposition of the barrage balloons over Tokyo. (*He goes to the map.*) This balloon, and this one— (*pulling two pins from the map and consulting a paper in his hand*)— were changed this morning to here— (*sticking a pin in the new place*)— and here. (*He puts the other pin in.*)

We see the ASSEMBLED MEN as they exchange astounded glances at the perfection of our intelligence service. A low murmur of approbation rises from them as the scene dissolves out.

A close view of a FIVE-HUNDRED POUND DEMOLITION BOMB dissolves in. Vice-Admiral Halsey's hand is in the scene, pinning a medal to the bomb. There are two others already attached to it. In a full view we then see that HALSEY is facing and addressing all of the Army flyers, and a good portion of the Navy

men. Doolittle, and all the Army and Navy executive officers are on hand. Two newsreel cameras are grinding.

HALSEY (*as he finishes putting medals on the bomb*). These medals were conferred upon members of our navy by the Japanese government for services rendered to the people of Japan during the great earthquake of 1923. You are going to return these medals in the form of another earthquake. (*He dismisses the subject of the medals.*) This is the only time I'll have a chance to get together with you. I hope you don't think we on the *Hornet* are strictly Navy. Over half of our men are flyers, and we know your problems. We'll do everything for you we can. We'll get you in as close as possible before we turn back. From there on, it will be your show. They've got it coming. Good luck— and good hunting!

There is a big yell from the men as Halsey finishes, then the scene dissolves to the DECK at night, showing TED and BOB GRAY seated on the deck, their backs against the *Ruptured Duck's* wheel. Both of them are staring out at the calm south sea through which the *Hornet* is moving.

TED (*shaking his head solemnly, as if unable to comprehend fully the thing about which he is speaking*). You know . . . the changes in those balloons threw me. Just think—a bunch of guys sweating all day in a sub down under Tokyo Bay—you know, guys just like us—sneaking up at night to radio balloon positions. . . . (*He pauses, and shakes his head again.*) Just let me hear anybody talk about the Navy again! Boy, they're—they're *good!*

BOB (*quietly*). Plenty. (*With a slow grin*) Not bad at poker, either.

TED (*a wry expression crossing his features*). You're not kidding.—I kind of figured on getting Ellen a present in Chungking—you know, maybe a kimono or something. But these Navy guys—they've cleaned me. Believe it or not, I've only got fourteen bucks!

BOB. I—I got eight or ten dollars I could lend you.

TED. No. I've been thinking. Cigarettes sell for sixty cents a cartoon on the boat here . . . . but in Chungking I hear the boys'll pay seven bucks.

BOB (*instantly interested*). Yeah?

TED (*nodding*). So I figure I may load the *Duck* with coffin nails.

BOB (*nodding with approval*). That's a swell idea. (*Softly*) Good night for subs.

We see the SEA, calm and beautiful.

TED's VOICE (*thoughtfully*). Yes.

We see TED and BOB GRAY again. There is a moment's silence, then Bob suddenly chuckles quietly to himself.

BOB. Funny thing. You know when I was a kid, I used to dream of going somewhere on a ship. Well—(*with a shrug*)—here I am.

TED (*staring out to sea*). And out there is Japan.

BOB. Celebrating the Cherry Festival.

TED. My mother had a Jap gardener once. He seemed like a nice little guy . . .

BOB (*turning to Ted*). You know—I don't hate Japs yet. Funny, isn't it? I don't like 'em—but I don't hate 'em.

TED. I guess I don't either. You get kind of mixed up.

BOB. Yeah.

TED. It's hard to figure—yet here we are. All I ever wanted to be was an aeronautical engineer. I joined the army in '40 because I figured it was the best way to learn. I wasn't sore at anybody. But—here—you suddenly realize you're going to drop a ton of high explosives on one of the biggest cities in the world.

BOB (*shooting Ted a curious glance*). Not getting squeamish, are you?

TED. Of course not. I don't pretend to like the idea of killing a bunch of people—but it's a case of drop a bomb on them or pretty soon they'll be dropping one on Ellen.

There is a moment's silence, while both of them consider this. Then Ted glances covertly at Bob.

BOB. That's right . . .

TED. I wonder how many of us will pull through?

BOB (*with a shrug*). They figure about half.

TED (*with a slight chuckle*). And everybody thinks he'll be in that half.

BOB. Yeah. Only in a thing like this, it's not always the *best* pilots that come out alive—just the luckiest.

TED. If anything should happen—I know it won't, but if it *did*—I'd kind of like you to have a visit with Ellen. You know—just give her a pat on the back. That is if you're in the lucky half.

BOB (*quietly*). Okay. (*A little pause —then Ted turns to Bob.*)

TED (*suddenly*). When are you going to get married, Bob?

BOB (*with a grin*). When I find somebody like Ellen.

TED. It'd be swell, you know—the four of us . . .

BOB (*dreamily*). After this is over, I'd like to get me a small ranch. Something that'd run forty or fifty head of cattle. Good well and a house. Be wonderful for kids.

TED. I've always been kind of nuts about ranches myself.

BOB. I've been thinking . . . if you and I would both save just a part of what we make—we could probably come out with enough to *buy* us a ranch.

TED. I suppose we could. Ellen and I could come down for vacations.

BOB. Besides, the place would make a little money—and you'd *have* something. In a decent year you can make real dough off forty head of cattle, if you've got feed.

TED. Why don't we do something like that?

BOB. I'm game if you are.

TED (*with sudden decision*). Okay, it's a deal. Shake.

BOB (*as they shake hands*). Swell! (*After a little pause*) Of course if we had *eighty* head of cattle—we'd *really* have ourselves a layout.

TED. Yeah. And our own meat, too.

BOB. Sure, and milk and butter and eggs—the works. A guy who's got himself a place—he doesn't have to worry about anything.

TED. With a little hunting near. . . .

BOB. Oh, sure. That's easy.

There is a moment of silence while they contemplate the magnificence of the dream that has come to them.

TED (*suddenly*). Gosh, I'll be glad when this war ends. . . .

The scene dissolves to the WARDROOM as Doolittle and his staff are assembled about the table in the fore-part of the room. Doc White is addressing the men.

WHITE. We've got your emergency rations all worked out. They'll keep you going for a limited period. We've been inoculated for everything under the sun, but food poisoning, and we can't do anything about that. Therefore, don't drink water unless it's been boiled, or food unless it's been cooked.

We see TED, BOB, HOLSTROM and others, listening.

WHITE. You'll be equipped with a canteen, morphine and sterilized bandages. When one of your crew gets shot up, and his condition is such that you can still use him, give him one-fourth of a tube of morphine and let him carry on. If he's badly hurt, give him the whole tube. That'll knock him out for about twenty hours. (*He nods at Doolittle, indicating he's all through.*)

We get a close view of TED and BOB as Ted smiles, and turns to Bob.

TED (*whispering*). Notice he didn't say *if* a man gets shot up. He said *when*. (*Bob nods, and winks.*)

And now Doolittle rises, looks gravely about the room for a moment, then speaks.

DOOLITTLE. Barring any sudden switch in plans, we take off tomorrow night. But in case of an emergency there'll be no assembly, no last minute instructions. We'll just take off. If you develop motor trouble within a half hour after leaving the *Hornet,* fly back and land in the water, and the Navy will try to fish you out. But if trouble develops *after* the first half hour, keep right on going. By that time the fleet will have to fire on any craft overhead.—I don't want you to throw out your extra gas cans as they're used. If you do, they will leave a perfect trail for the Japanese to follow back to the *Hornet.* Save the cans and dump them all at one time.

The view moves around the room and we get the reactions, the serious expressions of all our characters, as Doolittle continues on a more ominous note.

DOOLITTLE'S VOICE. Let me repeat what I have previously said: *You are to bomb the military targets assigned to you, and nothing else.* Of course, in an operation of this nature, you can't avoid killing civilians, because war plants are manned by civilians. If any of you have moral feelings about this necessary killing of civilians—if you feel you might think of yourself afterward as a murderer—drop out, and we can substitute someone else in your place. No one will blame you for your feelings.

The scene cuts to the FRONT of the ROOM as Doolittle continues. We notice Commander Jarika coming quietly into the room with a piece of paper. He goes over to the large wall map, and waits for Doolittle to finish.

DOOLITTLE. We won't have any more meetings, so if there are questions, now is the time to ask them.

We see DOOLITTLE looking over the room, and suddenly a warm smile crinkles his face.

DOOLITTLE (*grinning*). One more thing—when we meet in Chungking, I'm going to throw you a party you can tell your grandchildren about! Good luck!

The tension breaks. The men laugh with relief, and start milling for the

exits as the scene dissolves to the COUNTER of the SHIP'S STORE. Behind the counter is the ship's store clerk, as Ted enters.

TED. Twelve cartons of cigarettes.

SHIP'S CLERK (*looking harassed*). Twelve cartons! Say, what gives with the Army! I've never sold so many cigarettes in my life!

TED (*grinning*). We're chain smokers.

SHIP'S CLERK. You must *eat* 'em. What kind do you want?

TED (*airily*). Any kind.

SHIP'S CLERK (*giving him a strange look*). You just want lots of cigarettes.

TED (*grinning*). You hit it on the head.

SHIP'S CLERK (*with a shrug, as if to dismiss the whole puzzling affair from his mind*). All right. . . .

He reaches under the counter, begins to bring out the cartons, and stacks them on the counter.

SHIP'S CLERK. That'll be seven-twenty.

Ted reaches into his pocket, and puts bills on the counter. And then, suddenly, both of them freeze. From above, we hear the sound of the muffled, vibrating roar of gunfire. It is instantly followed by the loudspeaker:

LOUDSPEAKER (*not quite so impersonal as usual*). Battle stations! Man your battle stations! All Army personnel, man your planes!

For a moment Ted and the clerk stare at each other in stupefied surprise. On the counter between are the cigarettes and the money. For one agonizing moment both of them look at the counter, then, the call of duty being so ingrained, Ted runs out of the scene in one direction, while the clerk dashes off in the other. The cigarettes and the money still remain on the counter. Over the scene we get the continued sound of the roaring of guns. The loudspeaker blares out monotonously.

LOUDSPEAKER. Battle stations! Man your battle stations! Army personnel, man your planes!

There is a sound of running feet through the companionway and excited shouts; then the scene dissolves to the COMPANIONWAY as Ted dashes along it, and scrambles up a flight of steps at its far end. The companionway is filled with other personnel of the ship, rushing to their posts, some of which are above, some below. The rumble of gunfire from above continues. We get the idea here of great speed and efficiency. Thus, although the companionway fairly boils with men, the confusion is an ordered one.

The scene dissolves to the FLIGHT DECK. The Navy deck crew, in the characteristic sweaters we previously saw on Lieutenant Randall, are already swarming over the deck, starting to work on the Army planes—the first job being to unfasten the cables and remove the blocks which hold them in their scattered positions on the deck. We also see Army men rushing to their ships. As Ted emerges in the foreground of the scene, he pauses for one brief inspection of the sea whence comes the sound of continued firing. Jig White, hurrying by, spots him; stops and points.

JIG. There goes a Jap! Just three minutes after we sighted her!

This cuts to the SEA. One of the ships, a cruiser, fires a broadside. In the distance, rising up from the horizon, is a column of black smoke which marks the grave of the enemy vessel which started the uproar. The wind is up, a heavy sea is running, and the ships of the task force roll and pitch heavily.

We see TED and JIG as they turn their eyes from the burning ship to each other.

TED (*starting off toward his plane*). Yeah, that means she had two minutes to tell Tokyo what she saw!

Ted starts off in a run, and encounters Ski York, who is hurrying in the opposite direction.

TED (*hailing York*). Is this it, Ski?

SKI (*nodding*). Yeah. Get your things! It'll take 'em a little time to line the planes up!

TED. Okay.

He turns, starts off at a run in the direction whence he came. He runs into Thatcher, who carries his B-4 bag; he stops briefly.

TED. You all packed?

THATCHER. Have been for five days, sir.

TED. Swell! Better watch how those guys handle the *Duck!*

THATCHER. I will, sir.

TED. Don't tell anybody about that bum turret!

THATCHER (*with a grin*). I won't, sir.

Ted starts to his quarters; Thatcher continues on toward the *Ruptured Duck*. Then the scene dissolves to the COMPANIONWAY as Ted dashes down toward his compartment. Manch is coming from the opposite direction, so that they meet briefly. There are others passing rapidly through the scene.

MANCH (*anxiously*). We're off, aren't we?

TED. Yeah.

An expression of almost rhapsodic delight comes over Manch's face. He grins widely, and extends both hands to heaven as if in thanks.

MANCH (*exultantly*). Bomb me, daddy, eight to the block!

He sets off down the companionway at a dead run, while Ted moves ahead a few feet, and enters his room.—This cuts to the COMPARTMENT as Ted enters. Bud Felton is there, hastily packing Ted's things in the B-4 bag. He looks up as Ted enters.

BUD. I think I've got everything here.

TED (*grabbing the bag*). Swell. Thanks! (*He looks around the room for anything that Bud might have overlooked.*)

BUD (*grinning*). I—I'm sorry we couldn't have picked out a little better weather for you.

TED. We'll make it. (*He extends his hand.*) So long, Felton.

FELTON (*shaking hands*). Give 'em a pasting they'll never forget.

TED. We will. Look, I—thanks for everything. You guys in the Navy are —well, you're okay. Seeing you!

He turns abruptly, and goes out at a fast clip. Bud Felton grins, and follows him at a slightly slower pace. Suddenly Ted re-enters the compartment, looks around, and spots the white scarf Ellen gave him. He gives a soft whistle which seems to say: "Boy, what if I'd forgotten that!" Then he carefully, although hastily, puts it on under his jacket, and goes out once more.

This cuts to the COMPANIONWAY, by the ship's store, as Ted hurries along with his bag. He comes up to where his cigarettes still remain on the counter. The clerk is not there. Hastily he scoops them under his arm. The money he placed on the counter in payment is still there.

TED (*yelling*). Hey, how about my change!

As the clerk does not appear, Ted scoops up some bars of candy and dashes off, following which the scene dissolves to a full view of the HORNET's FLIGHT DECK as Ted comes onto it in the foreground. There has been great progress in moving the big bombers. The deck swarms with be-sweatered Navy men, and the whole bow of the carrier is now clear. The Navy men are criss-crossing the planes on the after-deck. The pitching movement of the ship seems to have increased. The wind is blowing a forty mile gale. The men lean into it as they work. And now Ted dashes toward the after-deck, to the *Ruptured Duck*. The Navy crew is gassing it, pushing the wings up and down to prevent air bubbles and thus give her the last possible drop of fuel. A navy dolly with the five-gallon cans of gas is just pulling up. Thatcher is supervising the gassing, and now rushes up to the dolly. McClure is just getting ready to enter the plane. Davenport is already in the pilot's compartment. Ted and Clever enter the scene. At this point Ted comes up to within speaking distance.

THATCHER (*to Ted*). We're getting fifteen extra cans instead of ten, sir.

TED. Good. (*To McClure*) How far do you figure we are from the mainland?

MCCLURE. At least seven hundred miles. Maybe more. We'll need that extra gas.

TED (*a little grimly*). You can say that again!

CLEVER. At least getting off now will bring us over Tokyo in daylight.

MCCLURE. And we can forget about the barrage balloons in daylight.

TED (*with a slight grin*). Next you'll be telling me it's swell because you can get better pictures in the daytime.

MCCLURE. Now you're not kiddin' about *that*, either!

Ted, with a chuckling, tolerant snort, starts toward the *Ruptured Duck's* forward hatch.

TED. Let's give her a final look-see.

As they start into the plane, Thatcher is swinging the five-gallon cans of gas into the rear hatch; and this cuts to a close view of DOOLITTLE'S PLANE. We can see Doolittle in the pilot's compartment. Two men are steering his front wheel. He is taxiing slowly into position. Other men follow the wheels, placing blocks behind them so that the plane won't get away. The wind from the storm, plus that of the propellers, almost flattens those in the rear of the wheels. The *Hornet* is plunging ahead at thirty-two knots into the swelling sea.

We then see LIEUTENANT RANDALL giving Doolittle the signal to continue taxiing. Then he gives him the braking signal. Then DOOLITTLE'S PLANE is seen as it comes to a halt.

We get a full view of the HORNET. Admiral Halsey is there, standing against the wind, grimly watching preparations. He turns to a subordinate, and says something. Immediately the men whose job it is on the island, break out with cards giving compass readings and wind speed.

This cuts to DOOLITTLE'S PLANE. Her bomb bays are open, and the Navy crew is loading her four incendiaries. Doolittle is watching the operation, Lieutenant Miller and Commander Jarika beside him. They are talking, but the uproar of wind, motors and surging sea, drowns their conversation out.

We see a NAVY PHOTOGRAPHER taking pictures of the planes. He has great difficulty standing erect in the wind. Then we see what the newsreel man is shooting. Doolittle's plane has its wheel on the white line which is to guide him off. Behind him are four other ships, all of them idling their motors. The bomb bays of Doolittle's plane slowly swing upward. Doolittle shakes hands with Jarika and Miller, then moves toward his plane. As he enters it, Lieutenant Randall in the foreground, his back to us, begins to give the signal to taxi forward once more.

We get a full view of the HORNET. We can see the height of the waves, the fashion in which the *Hornet* is tossed up and down upon them. From her stern the wings of the assembled B-25's protrude over the water, so close packed are the decks. And the Doolittle plane, like a fly on the back of a turtle, is beginning to edge into final take-off position, guided by an ant with a tiny flag in its feelers.

This cuts to the RUPTURED DUCK. The Navy crew has just finished loading her bomb bays. The doors are slowly swinging shut, and the Navy crew is just moving out of the scene. All our crew are in their ship. Bob Gray, running by, passes the *Duck*. Ted rolls back the window, and yells at him. His voice is barely audible amid the general uproar. Bob turns and moves closer to the window.

TED (*shouting*). You up ahead?

BOB (*nodding, yelling*). Fourth spot!

TED. See you in Chungking! (*Bob waves, and hurries on.*)

This cuts to SHORTY MANCH as he is making his perilous way among the planes, dodging the Navy crew, his face intent. Under his arm he is carrying a package.—

We get a close view of LIEUTENANT RANDALL as he stops giving the taxi forward sign, and signals for a stop, then see DOOLITTLE'S SHIP as it comes to a halt, the navy crew expertly blocking its wheels, while two ships behind it now start their motors.

We then observe the NAVY PERSONNEL at close range, working with one of the planes whose motor has just started. The danger, with the wind from the storm and the propeller noise and the motion of the ship, is so great that these men crawl like snakes on their bellies under the big ships, lest, if standing, they be thrown into the propellers. A line is tangled around one of the wheels of the plane. A man quickly rises and goes forward to clear the wheel. The wind throws him forward, his arm catching in the whirling propeller. He gives a surprised, hurt yell which is drowned out by the noise, and instantly sinks to the deck. Three men crawl toward him, and begin to pull him along the deck to safety.

This cuts to the RUPTURED DUCK as Shorty Manch, carrying the bundle, comes up and gestures frantically.

SHORTY (*shouting*). Put these under your seat?

TED (*shouting*). What are they?

SHORTY. Sizzle-platters! I've got the player in my ship, but I haven't got

room for the records! We'll meet in Chungking and cut a Chinese rug!

TED (*reaching out for them*). Okay, Shorty!

Ted accepts the records, and puts them inside the plane. Shorty gestures his thanks, and starts down the line toward his ship. Then we see the PILOT's COMPARTMENT as Ted stows the records away. He and Davenport grin briefly, before they return their anxious looks to the deck straight ahead. Suddenly Ted snaps on the interphone.

TED (*on the interphone*). Pilot to gunner.

THATCHER'S VOICE (*from the interphone*). Gunner to pilot. Go ahead, sir.

TED. Have you got those cans lashed down so they won't brain you?

THATCHER'S VOICE. They won't come loose, sir.

TED. Fine. Try the turret if you get a chance.

THATCHER'S VOICE. I've been working on it, sir. She's still jammed.

TED. We'll use the auxiliary power if we have to.

THATCHER'S VOICE. Right, sir.

Ted snaps off the interphone.

DAVENPORT (*thoughtfully*). We've got ourselves in a fine jam, haven't we, Lawson?

TED (*flaring*). Well, this is a swell time to think of *that!*

DAVENPORT (*hastily*). Oh no—I meant having to take off ahead of schedule.

TED (*instantly contrite*). Oh. I'm sorry, Davenport. Guess maybe I'm a little on edge.

DAVENPORT (*with a grin*). Yeah. Me, too.

McClure moves into the compartment from his navigator's compartment, and thrusts his head in between the seats.

MCCLURE (*tensely*). How are they doing?

TED (*straining to see ahead*). Doolittle'll be off any second. Then Hoover—Holstrom—Gray—Davey Jones—and Hallmark. We're seventh.

MCCLURE. Seven's a lucky number.

Davenport and Ted stare anxiously ahead. The *Ruptured Duck's* motors are not yet started.

TED (*yelling*). I think Doolittle's starting!

This cuts to a view of DOOLITTLE'S PLANE, with Randall in the foreground with his flag. He has "revved" the motors up until it seems impossible they can endure the strain without burning up. Then Randall gives a signal. The Navy men release the blocks from under Doolittle's plane.—A close view of RANDALL shows him looking grimly away from Doolittle's plane to the bow of the ship, and we next see what he sees: The *Hornet* has her nose deep in the trough of a wave. As she begins to come up, we again get a close view of RANDALL, now turning to Doolittle's ship and dropping his flag for the go signal.

DOOLITTLE'S PLANE is seen with full flaps, motors at full throttle, as Doolittle releases his brakes. The plane waddles along the white line for a moment, then fairly lunges into the wind. And another view of the plane shows that Doolittle's left wheel follows the white line as if it were a trolley. The right wing barely clears the wall of the island.

The left wing extends over the ship's side.

A close view shows LAWSON, DAVENPORT, CLEVER, and MCCLURE. They are tense as they watch breathlessly to see if Doolittle will take off.

As Doolittle's plane rushes toward the bow, the *Hornet's* nose reaches the apex of its upward movement. The ship is off.—At the very moment its wheels leave the deck, a tremendous cheer rises from the *Hornet*. It is so loud that it drowns the sound of the propellers, the thunder of the waves, the howls of the wind.

The scene cuts to the CREW of the RUPTURED DUCK. Their pent-up emotions are released and they break into grins.

CLEVER (*shouting*). He made it!

We then see, in succession, Army and Navy men yelling wildly, watching the skies; GUN CREWS in position shouting as if this were their own personal accomplishment; NAVY PERSONNEL on the HANGAR DECK leaning over the rail, to see the sky beyond the line of the flight deck above, cheering wildly.

Outside the RUPTURED DUCK, two of the Navy crew, in their sweaters, execute a little dance of triumph, while the *Ruptured Duck's* crew in the pilot's compartment are watching the sky.

Doolittle's plane executes a tight circle around the *Hornet,* then shoots low over the deck straight down the line painted there.

We then see HOOVER'S PLANE as Randall gives it the taxi signal, and it moves slowly into the starting position, surrounded by its Navy crew.

And now Lieutenant Miller comes up

to the RUPTURED DUCK, and enters it through the forward hatch. And this cuts to the PILOT'S COMPARTMENT as Lieutenant Miller comes into it. Ted and Dean turn.

MILLER (*offering his hand*). Good luck, fellows. Hand 'em a couple for the navy! (*He shakes hands with the crew.*)

DAVENPORT. We sure will, Miller.

TED. And thanks to you!

MILLER (*turning to go*). I—I wish I were going with you. S'long!

We see the HORNET'S DECK as Randall drops the flag as a signal for Hoover's plane to go. It starts down the deck, slowly at first, then with a final lunge. Hoover's plane leaves the deck. We note here once again the careful timing, which places his plane at the take-off point at the exact moment the *Hornet's* prow lifts up on the crest of a wave.

Inside the PILOT'S COMPARTMENT, Ted and Davenport watch tensely. McClure and Clever are there too.

MCCLURE. They're doing great.—So far.

TED. There's our signal.

DAVENPORT (*nervously*). Let's go!

TED. Clear? (*And Ted reaches for the switches.*)

Outside the RUPTURED DUCK we see a MAN with a fire extinguisher:

DAVENPORT (*after rolling back the window*). Clear on right?

FIRE EXTINGUISHER MAN. Clear on right.

We get a closeup of the RIGHT PROPELLER as it is turned over two or three times by a Navy man. Then, as he steps

aside, there is the sound of the starter, and the motor hums into action. Then we again see the PILOT'S COMPARTMENT as Ted and Davenport exchange looks of relief. Ted rolls back his left window.

TED (*calling out*). Clear on left?

NAVY MAN (*outside*). Clear on left!

Ted reaches forward, turns the switch, and the starter gets into action. Then we see the LEFT MOTOR. It gives a chug, turns over and stops. Then two more chugs. It stops again. The Navy crew in the background look serious, and move forward, prepared for the emergency of pushing the plane overboard if she doesn't function. The motor gives another helpless snort, and chokes out.

This cuts to the PILOT'S COMPARTMENT as Ted and Davenport exchange frantic looks. They work the starting button once more. There is another helpless little snort from the engine.

DAVENPORT. Those navy guys are moving up to push us over!

TED (*viciously*). They're not gonna toss *this* ship overboard! C'me on, baby—give—give . . *give* . . !

Another try at the starter, and this time there are four chugs.—This cuts to the LEFT MOTOR as she takes hold weakly, gives a dozen snorts, and suddenly grabs on; and to the NAVY CREW as they move back from the plane with looks of relief. Over the scene we hear the smooth sound of the motors now. —In the PILOT'S COMPARTMENT Ted and Davenport go almost limp from relief.

DAVENPORT (*reverently*). Boy-y-y——! (*He reaches for the check sheet, and starts in a trembling voice to call out its details.*) Check prop pitch.

TED (*checking*). Okay . . .

DAVENPORT. Check mixture control.

TED (*checking*). Okay.

DAVENPORT. Check gasoline . . .

CLEVER. There goes Holstrom!

We see the HORNET'S DECK as Brick Holstrom's plane roars down the deck to a take-off, then the PILOT'S COMPARTMENT of the RUPTURED DUCK as Ted and Davenport continue their checking in tense, subdued voices.

DAVENPORT. Check fuel valve.

MCCLURE'S VOICE (*from the interphone*). Okay fuel valve.

DAVENPORT. Check hydraulic pressure.

TED. Hydraulic pressure okay.

DAVENPORT. Check brake pressure.

We see the HORNET'S DECK as Bob Gray's plane responds to the signal, and leaps ahead for a take-off, then the PILOT'S COMPARTMENT of the RUPTURED DUCK where Ted is looking up and out of the window.

TED. There goes Bob!

DAVENPORT. Two more ahead of us. Check fuel booster.

TED. Okay.

DAVENPORT. Check controls!

TED. Okay.

We get a close view of JIG WHITE as he runs toward the *Ruptured Duck*. Davey Jones' plane, in the background, is just moving up to the starting position. Jig White comes up outside Ted's window, and howls for attention. Ted sees him, and opens the window.

JIG (*yelling*). Give 'em hell, Army!

TED (*shouting back*). When we get to Chungking, we'll tell 'em it was a Navy show, too!

JIG (*yelling*). They'll know that when they see how broke you are!

(*Ted waves, and Jig responds.*)

We see the DECK as Davey Jones' plane rushes forward to a take-off, then the PILOT'S COMPARTMENT of the RUPTURED DUCK as Ted and Davenport stare tensely ahead, following which we see what they are observing: HALLMARK'S PLANE, just ahead of them, begins to taxi up to the starting position.

TED (*to Clever*). Bomb bay doors closed?

CLEVER (*over the interphone*). All closed.

TED (*over the interphone*). Pilot to gunner. All set, Thatcher?

THATCHER'S VOICE. Everything okay, sir.

TED (*to Davenport*). Wing flaps down.

DAVENPORT (*working the lever until we hear the whine of the mechanism*). Wing flaps coming down.

We see the RUPTURED DUCK, with the Navy crew around her now, in a position to help her forward. Men with blocks—two men with each wheel—bending very low, working cautiously against the gale. The wing flaps slowly come down.—On the HORNET'S DECK, next, we see Hallmark's plane rush down the deck, take off and start its circle.—And now RANDALL as he turns toward the *Ruptured Duck*, and gives her the taxi ahead signal.

In the PILOT'S COMPARTMENT, Ted adjusts his scarf, and snaps on the interphone.

TED. We're taking off, fellows. Happy landings. (*He begins slowly to taxi forward.*)

The RUPTURED DUCK moves forward onto the white line, her crew working busily to hold her.—THATCHER, seen close, is pale and tense. He tightens his belt.—RANDALL gives the signal for "revving."—In the PILOT'S COMPARTMENT Ted gives her the forward throttle. The motors rise higher and higher and higher. Ted and Davenport both look tense.—RANDALL listens to the motors, finally seems satisfied, and drops his flag.—In the PILOT'S COMPARTMENT, Ted releases the brakes, and grabs onto the column, sucking it tightly into his belly.—There is a full view of the HORNET'S DECK as the *Duck* starts out slowly, then gathers speed; she takes off in beautiful shape.—There is a full view of the sky as the *Ruptured Duck* levels out, does a tight circle around the *Hornet,* and comes in low over the straight line. As she comes over, we can see the plane behind Ted's taxiing up to the starting position. The *Duck* starts out for sea, headed for Tokyo. She puts distance between her and the carrier. Then, as she recedes, the scene cuts to the PILOT'S COMPARTMENT. Ted and Davenport sit tensely in their seats as the ship bites into the air and levels off. Between them we can see McClure's white face from the navigator's compartment; Clever is beside him. McClure and Clever unstrap themselves. McClure slowly turns, and addresses himself to his work.

DAVENPORT (*with a motion as if wiping sweat from his brow*). Whew!

TED (*tensely*). Yeah.

This cuts to the GUNNER'S COMPARTMENT, with Thatcher by the window, looking pale and tense. He suddenly puts his hand to his mouth, holds it there for a moment, then removes it and takes a deep breath, stopping his incipient air sickness. He turns to test the lashings on his gasoline cans.— Then we again see the PILOT'S COMPARTMENT.

TED. Milk the flaps up.

Davenport reaches down for the lever controlling the flaps, and suddenly looks astounded. Ted looks at him questioningly.

DAVENPORT (*in a stunned voice*). We didn't even have 'em down!

TED (*after a brief "take"*). How do you like that! I wonder what else we forgot?

CLEVER (*who has come up from the navigation compartment*). Coffee, sandwiches, water. Plenty.

He starts down into the bombers compartment. Ted nods. He snaps the interphone on.

TED. Pilot to gunner.

THATCHER'S VOICE (*over the interphone*). Gunner to pilot. Go ahead, sir.

TED (*on the interphone*). Are you all right, Thatcher?

THATCHER'S VOICE. Yes, sir.

TED (*over the interphone*). You'd better get started on those cans. We've burned over forty gallons already.

GUNNER'S COMPARTMENT:

THATCHER (*on the interphone*). Yes, sir. (*He turns, unlashes one of the cans, and screws a spigot on it.*) I'm ready, sir.

In the PILOT'S COMPARTMENT, Ted throws in a switch. We see the INSTRUMENT BOARD as Ted's hand twists a knob to "Rear Turret Tank," then throws a switch to "Left Wing." Instantly we get the sound of the pump going into action.—Then Ted speaks into the interphone.

TED. Okay, Thatcher. You can empty about eight of them now.

In the GUNNER'S COMPARTMENT, Thatcher turns the can up into the bullet-proof tank.

PILOT'S COMPARTMENT:

TED. How's our course, McClure?

MCCLURE (*singing out from behind*). We're right on it.

TED. You'd better check that rear gun turret as soon as you're through with the gas, Thatcher.

THATCHER'S VOICE (*on the interphone*). Yes, sir.

There is a little moment of silence. Ted and Davenport seem to be straining ahead, helping the ship on its flight. Then:

TED. Well, we're on our way. If anybody's carrying a rabbit's foot—hang on to it tight.

Unconsciously he adjusts the white scarf—Ellen's gift to him—a little higher against the left side of his throat —his personal gesture toward his personal rabbit's foot as the scene dissolves out.

The SKY: The *Ruptured Duck* drones eastward, flying at forty feet, with the crest of the heavy waves almost touching her belly.—The PILOT'S COMPARTMENT:

TED (*turning his head slightly*). What's our position, McClure?

MCCLURE (*his head coming into view*). I figure an hour and fifty-eight minutes from the Coast.

TED (*into the interphone*). Get that, Thatcher? We can expect their fighters any time now. Keep your eyes open.

GUNNER'S COMPARTMENT:    Thatcher turns his head from his post.

THATCHER (*into the interphone*). Watching, sir. Nothing in sight. Could we try out this turret again?

TED'S VOICE (*over the interphone*). Okay, relay switch on.

Thatcher turns to the turret and manipulates it. He fires once or twice.

THATCHER (*into the interphone*). It works all right, sir, but that emergency power's not going to hold out long if we run into trouble.

PILOT'S COMPARTMENT:

TED (*into the interphone*). Turning it off now. (*He reaches down, and turns the emergency power off.*)

DAVENPORT (*to Ted*). How far are we behind our first gang?

TED. About an hour.

DAVENPORT (*mentally calculating, nodding to himself*). Then we can really get set for trouble.

TED (*nodding*). Yeah, but nothing like what the guys behind us will run into.

DAVENPORT (*shaking his head as he considers the project*). I'd feel a lot better on a night job.

TED (*grinning, trying to lighten the conversation*). I worked nights two years at North American. It's not so hot.

Davenport gives Ted a blank look. Ted, who has tried to lighten the mood, loses it very quickly himself. He assumes a listening attitude. He stiffens. Davenport throws him an inquiring glance.

TED (*to Davenport*). Did you hear that left engine miss?

DAVENPORT (*shaking his head*). No. Singing like a lark.

TED (*with a grin*). Must be hearing things.

We see the RUPTURED DUCK as she flies steadily along, fifty feet above the water, and this dissolves to the NAVIGATOR'S COMPARTMENT where McClure is working on the navigator's table, concentrating intensely. He reaches for the interphone, checks once more with his watch, then speaks into the interphone.

MCCLURE (*into the interphone*). Navigator to pilot. We ought to hit the Japanese Coast any minute.

We then see the PILOT'S COMPARTMENT as Ted and Davenport stiffen and look instinctively ahead.

DAVENPORT (*pointing, then yelling*). Look!

And, at this, through their window we see the SEA dotted with FISHING BOATS which fly the Japanese flag. The Japanese fishermen line their decks, and wave eagerly to the plane.

The PILOT'S COMPARTMENT: Ted and Davenport look at each other.

TED (*tensely*). See that flag?

DAVENPORT (*a look of shock and revulsion on his face*). Yes!

The BOMBARDIER'S COMPARTMENT: Clever is looking down in astonishment.

CLEVER (*on the interphone*). Those guys must be nuts! (*He turns from the interphone, bends over, and peers at the waving fishermen. Then, with a beatific smile, he waves back at them, grinning, hissing, waving.*) Saving bombs today.

The PILOT'S COMPARTMENT: Ted suddenly tenses, and points silently ahead. Davenport's eyes follow his pointing arm.

TED (*on the interphone*). Japanese Coast straight ahead!

We get a close view of THATCHER in the GUNNER'S COMPARTMENT. .He moves to a window, briefly, and stares at the sight below. His face is tense, somber. —This cuts to the BOMBARDIER'S COMPARTMENT where Clever isn't smiling now. He is looking at the Japanese mainland with a fascinated stare, as if it were something he hadn't ever expected to see.—This cuts to the NAVIGATOR'S COMPARTMENT where McClure, his camera out at the window, is tensely grinding away.

The smooth beach of Japan is rushing toward the plane. The sea below is dotted with fishing boats and small commercial craft. Many of those on the boats still wave their hands.

The *Ruptured Duck* comes in at under fifty feet, barely over the masts of the small craft beneath, and then sweeps in over the land.

The PILOT'S COMPARTMENT: Ted and Davenport are tense as statues, their eyes drinking in the countryside below them.

TED (*on the interphone, sharply*). We'll be catching buckshot any second now!

Through the window can be seen a rushing panorama of soft rolling fields, little farms cultivated with mathematical precision, blooming fruit trees, farmers working in their fields with their women, stopping at their labor to wave. Although they are still traveling at their cruising minimum, the fixity of the landscape below as it tears by seems to accentuate their speed.

In the PILOT'S COMPARTMENT, Davenport points at something, and we next

see, through the glass, a large flat building, with Japanese school children rushing out from all exits. And in the center
of the play-yard a flag—The Rising Sun
of Japan against a white field.

In the PILOT'S COMPARTMENT, Ted and
Davenport now exchange queer looks,
and we next see, through the window
that two tight echelons of Zeros, three
in each, are coming straight for the
*Ruptured Duck*. They are about a
thousand feet higher than our bomber.
—Then, as Ted's and Davenport's
heads are following their flight, both
pass over the ship and out of vision.
But as the second passes from vision,
it peels off as if to dive for the bomber.

TED (*clicking on the interphone*).
Pilot to——

THATCHER'S VOICE (*over the interphone*). I saw him.

TED (*on the interphone*). Shall I turn
the power on for the turret?

This cuts to the GUNNER'S COMPART-
MENT as Thatcher, at his gun turret, is
watching the sky.

THATCHER (*on the interphone*). No,
wait a minute. . . . (*He stares up at
the sky.*)

From his position through the glass, we
see that the sky is innocent of all aircraft.

THATCHER (*on the interphone*). I
don't know what happened to him.
Must have gone back into formation.
(*He searches the sky.*)

The scene dissolves to the PILOT'S COM-
PARTMENT, and we look through the
pilot's windows toward the earth below,
with the heads and shoulders of Ted
and Davenport in the immediate foreground. The plane is traveling at about
twenty feet altitude. A hill looms up

ahead. On top of the hill is a temple.
The plane rises, skims the hill, almost
touches the temple with its underparts,
and then, spread out before them,
sparkling in the warm, spring sunlight,
we see Tokyo Bay—a huge crescent
lined with docks and a dense mass of
buildings extending as far as the eye
can see in all directions.—TED and
DAVENPORT gaze silently at the city
ahead of them; then Ted speaks into
his interphone.

TED (*quietly*). There she is, fellows.
Take a good gander; when we get
back home, the folks will want to
know what Tokyo used to look like.

We get a view of the city of Tokyo
with the heads and shoulders of Ted
and Davenport in the foreground. We
see the four balloon barrages. There are
several clouds of smoke visible from
the bombs of previous planes. In the
distance, an airplane can be discerned,
with little black puffs of smoke exploding around it.

DAVENPORT. That must be Davey
Jones giving them the works!

Ted nods. He pulls back on the column. As he does so, he speaks into the
interphone.

TED (*into the interphone*). Pilot to
bombardier. Bomb bay doors open.

In the distance we see Davey Jones'
plane making its bombing run and disappearing.—And now the *Ruptured
Duck* goes into a steep climb, changing
its altitude from fifty feet to 1500 feet.
We see the bomb bay doors swing open
from her belly.—THATCHER is tense at
his gun.—In the PILOT'S COMPARTMENT
Davenport takes out his stop watch,
holds it in position with his thumb
above the stem.

DAVENPORT. There we are—the big,
red smoke stack.

TED (*into the interphone*). Pilot to bombardier. Approaching smelter.

CLEVER'S VOICE (*over the interphone*). I'm on it.

Through the window, looking downward, we then recognize the huge brick smelter with an enormous smoke stack.

In the BOMBARDIER'S COMPARTMENT, Clever is now over the twenty-cent bomb sight, holding it with both hands. —Through the bomb sight, the scene comes into view as the smelter lines up with the sight.—Then we get a close view of CLEVER as he presses the bomb release.

CLEVER (*into the interphone*). One away!

PILOT'S COMPARTMENT: Both pilots look at the red light on the dash indicating that the bomb has been released. Davenport clicks the stop watch.—We get a close view of the STOP WATCH as the second hand begins to move in its rightward circle.

We see the bomb exploding in the smelter, and a vast billow of smoke arises; LAWSON and DAVENPORT as they feel the explosion; CLEVER in the BOMBARDIER'S COMPARTMENT releasing another bomb; a second bomb falling from the bomb bay.

This cuts to the PILOT'S COMPARTMENT.

CLEVER'S VOICE (*over the interphone*). Two away!

The red light flickers, and Davenport looks at his watch.—We get a close view of the STOP WATCH, showing that ten seconds have elapsed.—The second bomb hits the target; and, through the pilot's window, a black puff appears about a hundred yards or so in front of them, they race past it at great

speed. More puffs appear! The pompoms are working.

TED. They've got our altitude.

CLEVER'S VOICE (*over the interphone*). Three away!

Again the red light flickers. Again Davenport looks at his watch, and the STOP WATCH shows that twenty seconds have elapsed.—A third puff of smoke in a direct line indicates the explosion of our third bomb.

In the BOMBARDIER'S COMPARTMENT, Clever presses the bomb release button.

CLEVER (*into the interphone*). Four away!

The red light flashes on in the PILOT'S COMPARTMENT, and Davenport clicks his watch.—The second hand on the STOP WATCH stops exactly on the thirtysecond mark. Ted pushes the column forward.—Then we see from the plane that the fourth bomb—which was the incendiary—divides into dozens of small fire bombs as it hurtles earthward.— And now, through the pilot's window, we see the city rushing toward them. The plane goes into a steep dive. Ted pulls back on the column, and the plane begins to level out.

In the distance we see fires over Tokyo. Our plane is now twenty feet above the ground again, snaking back and forth to present as elusive a target as possible to the enemy.—In the PILOT'S COMPARTMENT, Ted and Davenport are tense, quiet, alertly on the lookout for any enemy craft ahead of them.—In the NAVIGATOR'S COMPARTMENT, McClure has his camera up to the window and is taking pictures.

And now we get a closeup of MCCLURE, with his eye close to the lens. A look of startled surprise comes into his face. He squints into his camera with a kind of incredulous concentration. — Then, through the camera lens, we see a flight of six Japanese bi-plane pursuits exactly in the center of the frame.

MCCLURE is still squinting through the camera, but suddenly, he realizes what impedes his vision. He moves the camera aside, looks out of the window and shouts into the interphone.

MCCLURE. Six fighters just above and to the left!

In the PILOT'S COMPARTMENT, Ted and Davenport look upward, and spot the planes.

TED (*into the interphone*). Have you got 'em, Thatcher?

In the GUNNER'S COMPARTMENT, Thatcher, his guns ready, is waiting for the planes to dive.

THATCHER (*into the interphone*). Ready for them, sir.

In the PILOT'S COMPARTMENT, Ted and Davenport watch the planes.

TED (*nervously*). Why don't they dive!

And through the window, we see the planes wheel and move off in another direction.

The PILOT'S COMPARTMENT:

DAVENPORT (*incredulously*). They're going away.

Ted and Davenport stare at each other for a moment of blank surprise. Then Ted jams the throttle forward.

TED. I'm not going to wait for 'em to come back! We're getting out of here!

The needle of the SPEED INDICATOR begins to climb.

We see MCCLURE staring out of his window tensely.—THATCHER is seen almost frozen to his weapon, waiting for an atack.—CLEVER, with his gun ready, is peering in all directions.—Davenport, in the PILOT'S COMPARTMENT, points to the sea which lies ahead of them. Ted nods.

DAVENPORT. I guess maybe we're in that lucky half.

TED (*without relaxing*). Not yet. Not 'til we get to China.

This dissolves to a long view of the RUPTURED DUCK flying over water; there is no land in sight, indicating that they are some distance out of Tokyo. And this cuts to the PILOT'S COMPARTMENT where Davenport has the controls. He is tense in his seat. His eyes constantly scan the skies for enemy planes. Ted is rubbing his eyes with his hands, as if nervously exhausted. When he has finished this, he shakes his head to clear it, and begins to search the sky for signs.

Next we see the NAVIGATOR'S COMPARTMENT, where McClure, looking disheveled and sweaty, concentrating intensely, is working at his maps and navigation charts. He is biting his lower lip in concentration. Looking quietly over his shoulder is Clever. Clever, too, shows the strain of the mission. He pulls out a cigarette and lights it. His hands tremble as he tries to apply the fire to the tobacco. He notices the trembling, even looks at it for a moment, then blows the match out, throws it down, and looks once more over McClure's shoulder. Suddenly he looks up to something, and we see THATCHER. He is just crawling along the passageway leading to the pilot's compartment from the rear gunner's compartment. He looks pale. He comes into the navigator's compartment. He and Clever look at each other. Suddenly Thatcher retches, turns his face, gains control of himself, and looks apologetically at Clever.

This cuts to the PILOT'S COMPARTMENT where the same air of tenseness still prevails. Suddenly Ted puts both hands to his temples, and presses them.

TED. Wow! What a headache! (*And at this, Davenport looks at him in surprise. Then comprehension comes over his face.*)

DAVENPORT (*in a startled voice*). Why —(*shaking his head*)—so have I!

This cuts to the NAVIGATOR'S COMPARTMENT as McClure puts his pencil down, relaxes for a moment, and looks up at Thatcher and Clever.

THATCHER. Were you scared? (*McClure and Clever nod their heads slowly.*)

CLEVER. I'm still scared!

In the PILOT'S COMPARTMENT, Ted turns around, attracts Clever's attention by nudging him, and points to McClure. Clever indicates to McClure that Ted wants him. McClure rises and goes over.

TED (*shouting*). On our course?

McClure makes a sign indicating that they are exactly on the course.—Ted taps Davenport's arm. He indicates that he will take over. He does so. Davenport points to the gas gauge.—The GAS GAUGE, seen close, indicates 160 gallons. —Ted nods after looking at the gauge. Davenport moves over and shouts at him.

DAVENPORT (*shouting, after a look at his watch*). I hope it gets us to Choo Chow Lishui!

TED (*nodding gravely*). And I hope the Japs don't get there first!

In the NAVIGATOR'S COMPARTMENT, the three men, listening, react with grave looks, which show they comprehend their dangers, following which we get a close view of the WINDSHIELD of the Pilot's Compartment as the first drops of rain are flattening against its outer surface. Ted and Davenport look at the raindrops, then gravely at each other, as the scene dissolves to a view of the sky: there is practically no visibility. Claps of thunder come over the scene. Jagged rents of lightning punctuate the heavy storm clouds. The plane is flying low enough so that we can discern the turbulent sea beneath her. And this cuts to the PILOT'S COMPARTMENT where Ted and Davenport, taut and thin-lipped, are peering into the storm.

TED (*into the interphone*). What's the dope, McClure?

The NAVIGATOR'S COMPARTMENT:

MCCLURE (*consulting his maps*). About two hundred miles to Choo Chow Lishui.

The PILOT'S COMPARTMENT:

TED (*after a moment's thought*). We'll never find it in the dark. (*Davenport shakes his head in agreement. For a moment Ted concentrates. Then he speaks into the interphone.*) Pilot to crew. We're going up and fly in on instruments. When the gas is gone, we'll bail out.

In the GUNNER'S COMPARTMENT, we see THATCHER, stunned by the information, reaching for his parachute.—In the BOMBARDIER'S COMPARTMENT, we see Clever adjusting his parachute.—In the NAVIGATOR'S COMPARTMENT, McClure also starts putting on his parachute. Then we get a view of the sky in deep dusk as the *Ruptured Duck* puts her nose into the clouds and flies up to perhaps five hundred feet.

In the PILOT'S COMPARTMENT, Ted and Davenport are looking around watching. Suddenly Davenport nudges Ted, and points down. Through the windshield, we see what they see: below them a sudden rift in the clouds reveals a clean, concave beach, wide enough and long enough for a landing.

In the PILOT'S COMPARTMENT, Ted squints thoughtfully at the sight below, and nods his head.

TED (*into the interphone*). We'll buzz it. Maybe we can land. Keep a lookout for rocks or logs.

As he pushes the column forward, we get a view of the SKY and SEA with the *Ruptured Duck* sweeping in low over the beach, which seems fairly solid in spite of the rain which pounds it. It seems free of obstacles. The *Ruptured Duck* swings out to sea in a circle designed to bring it back for a landing. Then, in the PILOT'S COMPARTMENT, Ted adjusts his scarf.

TED (*into the interphone*). All set for landing! (*Calling back to McClure*) McClure!

MCCLURE (*his head appearing*). Yeah?

TED. Get our guns out. (*McClure turns back into his own compartment, and Ted speaks into the interphone.*) Take off chutes and be sure you've got your life jackets on. Carry your guns. (*To Davenport*) Wheels down. (*Davenport complies.*) Flaps down. (*Again Davenport complies.*)

McClure comes from the navigator's compartment and places forty-fives in their holsters behind Ted's and Davenport's seats.

DAVENPORT. Air speed one thirty-five . . . one thirty . . .

We see the *Ruptured Duck* sliding on at a slight curve toward the beach in the heavy rain; then the scene cuts back to the PILOT'S COMPARTMENT where Ted is tense at the wheel, peering ahead. McClure is kneeling behind the pilot seats, sticking his head between them and bracing his shoulders against their back rests.

DAVENPORT. . . . one hundred and ten . . .

Suddenly both motors cough and lose their power. We get a frozen tableau of Ted, Davenport and McClure, reacting with shock at the disaster. Ted's hands work rapidly, automatically. He hits the throttles and prop pitch controls with the same hand, and thrusts them forward.

This cuts to the BOMBARDIER'S COMPARTMENT, where Clever is staring straight ahead, horrified at the coughing motors; to the GUNNER'S COMPARTMENT, where Thatcher is rigid, unbelieving; to the PILOT'S COMPARTMENT, where Ted's left arm wraps around the column in a desperate effort to lift the ship's nose into the air, the motors still coughing feebly.

The *Ruptured Duck,* still over water, is losing altitude rapidly. She comes so low that her landing wheels strike the top of a wave. With a tremendous roar she plunges into the angry sea, and next we see the pilots, navigator and bombardier being shot through the smashed nose of the ship like bullets from a gun, then being lost from view in the overpowering blackness and confusion of the stormy sea.

THE SEA: It is almost night now, and one of the plane's wings, the motor torn off from it, is floating.

We see the comical insignia of the *Rup-*

*tured Duck* slowly sinking from view, a white silk scarf drifting by it. Suddenly a figure, supported by a life belt, breaks surface, smashes against the wreckage, and is swept ahead. The figure is carried by the waves past the hull of the stricken plane. Then we see the figure as it reaches the point where the waves are breaking. It is carried under, lost from sight, then spewed up again. The rain is beating savagely against the surface of the water. The waves fill the air with their angry thunderings.

This cuts to the rain-pelted BEACH as the figure is washed up. It struggles desperately for a hand hold in the slippery sand, then is caught in the backwash of a wave and swept out again. In a moment it is caught on the crest of a second and larger wave, and this time deposited on the beach. Now we see the figure crawling on all fours away from the water line. Then, slowly, painfully, it rises to its feet. We see that it is TED. His clothes are ripped to shreds. He begins to walk dazedly in short little circles, obviously without purpose or intent. He turns, looks toward the sea, and this cuts to what he is looking at.

The SEA, with the two rudders of the *Ruptured Duck* sticking up above the waves like two solitary tombstones, then we see TED on the BEACH as he starts to shout.

TED (*hoarsely*). I lost my ship! I lost my—

Suddenly the shout is choked off. This is the first time we really have a chance to see his face, which is a bloody pulp out of which stare two dazed, stupefied eyes. His lower lip is slashed clean through to the bone. Half of it hangs down, loose as a slice of liver.

Slowly Ted puts his right forefinger into his mouth, trying to straighten his teeth. Then he grasps his front teeth with thumb and forefinger to adjust them. A surprised look comes over his face. For the teeth have come out, together with chunks of bone and gum. He stares at the handful of teeth and flesh and bone dazedly for a moment. Then, almost absent-mindedly, he turns his hand palm downward and the teeth fall to the sand. He starts slowly to stagger up the beach. His torn pants reveal a long gash from thigh to ankle of his left leg.

The scene widens as Ted, hearing someone behind him, turns. Davenport is stumbling up to him. For a moment neither of them speaks. Then Davenport reaches out with both hands, takes Ted's face between his palms, and stares at Ted with horror-stricken eyes.

DAVENPORT (*his forehead covered with running blood.*) Your whole face is pushed in!

TED (*with difficulty*). You hurt bad?

DAVENPORT. I think so. I don't know.

For a moment they stand there in the rain, breathing in short, animal-like grunts, broken occasionally by a moan. Then Davenport staggers unsteadily off.

DAVENPORT (*in a stupefied, expressionless voice*). Hey . . . Hey . . . Hey . . .

Ted remains where he is, looking shakily toward the water. Then he starts forward as he sees something. It is McClure coming out of the water. He holds his arms limply in front of him. He slips and falls several times. Then he falls flat, but gets himself up without using his arms. Several times he only falls to his knees. His inability to use his arms gives his struggles the effect of comic horror. Ted comes up to him. They begin to inspect each other's head wounds, groaning and muttering. Then they turn at the sound of something behind them. They look off to: CLEVER, who is in the sand on his hands and knees, with his head hanging down limply between his arms. The waves flow over him and recede. He makes no movement, no sound. The blood flowing from horrible head wounds makes a gurgling sound as it trickles down upon the wet beach. With each wave that sweeps over him his knees and hands sink down a little in the slipping sand. Ted comes over to him and begins weakly to tug at him. Finally, stumbling and leaning on each other, they start up from the beach. Ted is moaning, but Clever is quite silent. His head wobbles from side to side.— The scene then moves with Davenport, who is wandering aimlessly.

DAVENPORT. Hey . . . Hey . . .

Thatcher is seen walking out of the water, and up on the beach, following which the scene cuts to TED and CLEVER as Ted, exhausted, permits Clever to sink from his arms. Again Clever lands on his hands and knees, in which position he remains. Thatcher comes up. From another direction, McClure enters the scene, walking awkwardly on his knees.

TED (calling to Davenport). Over here, Davenport!

CLEVER, seen close, is aroused by the sound of Ted's voice, but he looks blankly around, failing to recognize his comrades. Then he suddenly gets to his feet, takes two faltering steps, and falls down again on all fours.

We see the GROUP on the BEACH, including Clever, McClure and Ted. Thatcher, supporting Davenport, comes up to them. Slowly Clever sinks to the sand. McClure lies down. Davenport slumps from Thatcher's arms. All five of them lie, huddled together for warmth against the cold rain. Their clothes are literally torn to shreds with white flesh and dark wounds showing through the rents. The only sounds, aside from the heavy surf, are the harsh grunts, the shivering moans of the shocked and wounded men.

There follows a closeup of TED'S FACE. His eyes are closed. Then they open, stare fixedly for a moment, and begin to roll backward under his upper eyelids. As they roll, the screen blurs over and the scene dissolves to a close view of ELLEN looking up at him for a moment as she did in the balcony scene. He avoids looking at her.

ELLEN (suddenly smiling). Ted . . .

TED. Yeah?

ELLEN. Look at me. (He turns, a little puzzled, and looks down at her.) That baby and I—we won't ever need anything but you. We mustn't either of us be scared about it, Ted. Because the baby—(her voice breaking slightly)—the baby's why I know you're coming back to us . . .

Suddenly he smiles, as if a great load had been taken from his shoulders. The scene blurs as it dissolves to a closeup of TED'S FACE. He opens his eyes and looks around in surprise at his surroundings. The rain beats down on his face.

We see the GROUP as Ted raises his head, and looks around in a bewildered fashion. Then, as if he had important business to transact somewhere else, he rises and staggers several steps down the beach.

DAVENPORT (sharply). Lawson!

Ted turns.

TED (*vacantly*). Huh? (*Then the horrible comprehension dawns and he moans.*) Oh . . .

He staggers back and sinks in a heap beside the others. Thatcher's forehead has stopped bleeding. He is in far the best condition of the bunch, aside from shock which quite naturally has rendered him pale and weak.

MCCLURE (*to nobody in particular*). Camera. Lost camera . . . (*Then there is silence, broken only by their almost continual groans.*)

But now THATCHER, seen close, suddenly looks off, quietly takes his .45 pistol from its holster, and aims the gun.

THATCHER (*to Ted, quietly*). Shall I shoot them, Lieutenant?

All of them except Clever, who is too far gone, look in the direction in which Thatcher's gun is pointed, and we see what they are looking at. The beach ends abruptly in a small cliff, four or five feet high. On the cliff, staring down at them, are two squat-looking men, bundled up in some sort of coats that shine almost like raincoats. They wear flat, woven hats.—Then the scene cuts back to the GROUP while Thatcher still has his pistol trained on the intruders, awaiting orders.

TED. No. Hold it.

THATCHER. They might be Japs, sir.

TED (*in a muffled voice*). Don't shoot, Thatcher.

DAVENPORT (*suddenly*). Hey! Hey!

At this the MEN on the CLIFF come into view as they step down cautiously, and walk over to the group. Our men stare up in the darkness at the two strangers,

whose faces are almost indistinguishable. The two men bend over, and go from man to man, peering at their wounds.

MEN (*as they stare at the wounds*). Hmmmmmm. Hmmmmmm.

It is a sound half mournful, half incredulous. Our crew has no reaction. They are too badly wounded to care. Six more men come into the scene, repeat the examination, and hum as their predecessors did. Finally one of the intruders comes up to Ted, while his comrades chatter excitedly amongst themselves in Chinese.

A close view shows the MAN touching his chest very simply.

MAN. Chinga.

Our men exchange glances.

TED. He says he's Chinese. What's that word for American.

THATCHER (*after a moment of intense thought*). Lishua Megwa.

ALL THE MEN (*babbling and nodding their heads*). Lishua Megwa! Lishua Megwa!

The Chinese stare impassively, then proceed to help the wounded men to their feet. Two of them place Clever on their backs. Two of them brace Ted. The others arrange themselves about Davenport, McClure and Thatcher, and, pointing off, indicate the direction in which they are to go.—Then the scene moves with the GROUP as the men start out very slowly. The grunts of agony increase with the unwelcome exertion.

DAVENPORT (*despairingly*). How do we know these guys are really Chinese!

This dissolves to a THATCHED ROOFED HOUSE at night, with the rain pouring down outside. The house is rectangular, made of mud bricks. It is divided into two rooms. Illumination is provided by a smoking lamp. The floor is packed earth. In the far right-hand corner of the room is a low bed made of rawhide strips, stretched over a kind of cot structure.—As we come in on this scene, we see two Chinese women, three little Chinese girls, and two or three of the men who helped in the rescue of our previous sequence. They are staring helplessly, their eyes wide with a mixture of sympathy and incredulity. Then we see what the Chinese are looking at. Davenport and Lawson are on the cot, their backs to the wall. McClure is sitting on the floor, his broken shoulders grotesque against the wall. Clever, completely out, is stretched out on the side floor, his head resting on a heap of rags and refuse. All of them have a blank, stunned expression. They are soaking wet, and no attempt has been made to repair their clothes. Thatcher is kneeling in front of Ted, examining his leg. His face tells us clearly how horrible the wound is. He turns and looks off toward the Chinese.

THATCHER (to Ted). That leg's got to be sewn up! (He turns to the Chinese, and pantomimes sewing.) Hasn't anybody got a needle and thread?

The scene next includes the Chinese. They shrug helplessly and look at each other as if seeking interpretation of all Thatcher has said, then return to their staring. The attention of everyone in the room is suddenly distracted by a commotion outside which can be heard even over the beating rain. Several people are talking, with the strange lyrical intonation of the Chinese. A little start of alarm runs through our wounded men, as they look apprehensively toward the door. Guerilla Charlie enters.

We get a close view of CHARLIE as he enters the room, accompanied by several comrades. He pauses and stares around the place. His face is strong, immobile, utterly devoid of sympathy. He gives the impression of enormous strength, although he is not a large man. His eyes are black, set in a muscular dead pan. They dart around the room alertly, suspiciously. Then he briskly starts over to the cot. Swiftly, silently he inspects their wounds, their buttons, their insignia, and all other identifying marks on their torn clothing. Charlie himself is dressed in an old pair of American-looking pants, heavy shoes, a thick hunting shirt, open at the neck. He wears no hat. All the Chinese in the room show him quiet deference. McClure, walking very carefully with his dead arms limp in front of him, moves over to the couch, and sits down.

We get a close view of CHARLIE and his AIDES. When he completes his inspection of the Americans, he straightens up and engages in a short, pithy conversation with the tallest of his aides. They shift their eyes from each other to the men on the cot, thus indicating the nature of their conversation. Charlie's principal aide, a villainous-looking man, approaches Ted. He peers at him intently. Ted almost flinches before his gaze, not knowing whether the man's intentions are good or evil. Suddenly the Chinese bends down deliberately and thrusts a lighted cigarette into Ted's mouth. A little tremor of relief passes over Ted's face. He tries to smile his thanks. The Chinese passes on to Davenport, puts a cigarette into his mouth also. Ted's eyes, which have been following the Chinese, now shift to Charlie who approaches deliberately.

CHARLIE (*pointing to himself*). Me, Charlie. (*At this the group reacts to the fact that Charlie speaks English.*)

MCCLURE AND LAWSON. Americans . . . . we're Americans! Lishua Megwa! (*They point at each other, and try to smile ingratiatingly.*)

CHARLIE. Melican.

TED (*breathlessly*). We need a doctor and some help to get to Choo-Chow Lishui.

Charlie stares at them uncomprehendingly, and shakes his head, indicating he doesn't understand.

TED (*frantically*). Chiang Kai-shek! We're his friends. In Chungking.

The last word arouses some faint recognition on Charlie's dark countenance.

CHARLIE (*nodding*). Chungking.

DAVENPORT. That's right! We go—Chungking.

CHARLIE (*shaking his head*). Chungkin—many—many days. Many.

Ted holds up a badly cut hand, and begins to count off on his fingers.

TED. How many?

CHARLIE (*shaking his head*). Many day.

MCCLURE. Doc-tor. Doc-tor.

DAVENPORT (*imploringly*). Charlie go doc-tor. Charlie bring doctor here.

TED (*starting to point out all their wounds*). Charlie bring doctor or we die!

CHARLIE (*after a moment's thought*). Doc-tor— (*holding up his finger*)— one li—

DAVENPORT. One li! That's a Chinese mile.

TED (*eager*). One li. Go. Bring doctor!

CHARLIE (*shaking his head regretfully*). Doc-tor Japanese man—Japanese doc-tor.

McClure, Davenport, and Ted exchange glances. Then Ted voices their common fear.

TED (*anxiously*). Maybe Japanee men —Japanee soldier—come here.

Charlie comprehends. For the first time during the whole meeting a trace of a smile touches the corners of his hard mouth.

CHARLIE (*a hard glint in his eye*). Japanee men no come at night. (*His expression indicates what kind of welcome they might expect if they did come.*)

The scene dissolves to a beautiful MOUNTAIN PATH. The rain has stopped, the sun is shining. Our procession moves along, as the coolies, with incredibly perfect balance, seem actually to dig their toes into the rocks as they bear their burdens. Charlie is some distance ahead of the procession, maintaining an alert watch. Occasionally he runs back, addresses the lead coolies, and they increase their speed to match his.

This dissolves to a VALLEY, with our procession moving along a dike-like path between level rice paddies which extend on all sides. One of the coolies, exhausted, pauses for an instant. Charlie runs up to him, and exhorts him angrily. The coolie is clearly in a bad way, but he uncomplainingly takes up his burden and continues faster.

This dissolves to a silhouette view from the top of the low cliff. Our procession is passing along the top. In the background below the cliff is the sea. Then we get a closer view of the GROUP, revealing that below them and a little distance ahead is a small cove.

TED (*to Thatcher*). We must be on an island.

CHARLIE (*suddenly letting out a little exclamation, and pointing toward the sea*). Boat!

Ted and our other characters look in the direction pointed out by Charlie, and we next see that a small Chinese sampan is just moving into the cove. Then TED and CHARLIE are seen close in the group.

CHARLIE (*pointing to the boat*). Boat. (*Pointing to Ted*) You. (*Pointing to the boat again*) Boat.

Suddenly there is an off-scene cry, and a Watcher is heard calling "Hi-hi! Hi-hi!"

Instantly the little caravan freezes. Suddenly the stretchers are dropped to the earth. The wounded men cry out with pain. The bearers and guerillas fall flat on their faces, motioning to the crew for silence. We see what they see. The sampan has just reached the beach, when a small, fast Japanese patrol boat, its rising sun ensign flapping smartly in the wind, sweeps into the cove, and hails the sampan. In a moment the patrol boat has drawn up to the sampan.

A close view shows TED watching the scene tensely. His face is full of pain, as he tries to adjust his wounded leg to a more comfortable position. We see what he sees.

Japanese sailors are swarming over the decks. The sampan crew are standing with their arms thrust over their heads.

A close view shows CHARLIE watching, his face full of hatred. He growls to himself. This cuts to a full view of the GROUP, all prone. The six armed men of the escort, including Charlie, have their rifles yearningly trained on the

scene below. We see what they see. The Japanese begin to stream back to their patrol boat. The Chinese on the sampan wave at them as the patrol boat's motors roar, and she starts in a clean, fast swerve out of the cove. In a moment she has passed beyond the far cliff, and the sampan is alone in the cove.

Thereupon the men in the GROUP on the cliff rise, lift their burdens, and start down a steep incline leading to the cove; and this cuts to the COVE BEACH where the sampan's crew is standing ready. Our cortege comes into view, the bearers and soldiers splashing through the water to the sampan. As the sun breaks through a cloud, she breaks out the Japanese flag at her stern, the flyers reacting with glances of surprise.

The men on the sampan quickly reach over the side, and assist the wounded men off the stretchers. We notice that Charlie clambers over the side of the sampan with them.

On the SAMPAN, our characters quickly collapse, groaning, in the gummy mixture of bilge water and sawdust which covers the floor of the junk. As McClure is assisted into position, they grab his arms, and he cries out in anguish. One of the boatmen rolls down a latticework blind to conceal the men in the bottom of the boat.

Now Charlie appears in the bottom with them. He is grinning and smiling. He moves to Thatcher, reaches out, and tries to take Thatcher's .45. Thatcher quickly puts his hand protectively over the weapon.

THATCHER. Hey—cut that out!

For a moment Charlie has the look of a hurt child. Then he points to his own rifle. Next he points to a fine automatic he carries. Then he shakes his head, trying to indicate that he does not wish to steal Thatcher's revolver. Thatcher watches this pantomime with a puzzled expression. Then Charlie takes out his automatic and ejects a cartridge from it; this he hands to Thatcher with a smile. Thatcher accepts it doubtfully. Charlie smiles and waits. A look of growing disappointment comes over his face.

TED (*who has been watching*). I think he wants to trade bullets with you, Thatcher.

Thatcher takes his .45 from its holster and ejects a cartridge. Charlie begins to nod happily. Thatcher extends the cartridge to him. Charlie accepts it with a grateful nod of his head.

CHARLIE (*holding the cartridge up*). Friend. (*Then he rises, bows to everyone, smiling, and exits. At the point of exit, he turns smilingly once more.*) Charlie—friend. (*They all nod in reply.*)

AD-LIBS. Goodbye. Goodbye—Charlie. Sure—friend.

Charlie leaves them. There is a little moment of silence, broken only as Clever groans and turns over in his sleep. Then they hear a splash from outside indicating that Charlie has left the boat. There are sharp, staccato commands from above—then a creaking and rolling. The sampan is under way. The movement of the boat rolls the wounded men from side to side. Involuntarily they groan with each movement. They are in great pain, and speak haltingly. Thatcher moves to McClure and helps adjust him against the side of the boat.

MCCLURE (*faintly*). Thanks. (*With great effort, bitterly*) The Japs must be all around us.

DAVENPORT (*quietly*). I wonder where the rest of the gang is . . .

MCCLURE. Scattered all over the China Coast . . . if they're alive . . .

DAVENPORT. I wonder if they—if they've heard back home what's happened to us . . .

TED (*painfully*). I hope they haven't heard too much. It's our only chance to get out.

MCCLURE (*with disgust*). You can't keep a thing like this secret. We'll—we'll *never* get out.

Suddenly the boat lurches. Ted lets out a grunt of pain as his leg hits the side of the boat.

TED. I—(*An expression of agony comes over his face; his voice sinks.*) —I guess I'm going to pass out . . . (*His eyes close.*)

We get a closeup of TED's FACE as he begins to sink into unconsciousness. The closeup blurs over as his eyes dim and it dissolves through the blurred screen to: A COURTROOM at night, where TED and ELLEN, seen close, their backs turned, are looking up at a kindly-faced Judge, who is speaking to them from the bench. We get the feeling that this particular spot in the room is the only point which has any illumination—a small lamp on the Judge's desk so that the darkness outside of its rays is accentuated.

JUDGE. I, Ted, take you, Ellen. . . . We see the two faces looking up at him. Ted and Ellen's faces have that rare and wonderful look which occurs only at high emotional points in a person's life.

TED (*repeating*). . . . I, Ted, take you, Ellen. . . .

JUDGE'S VOICE (*over the scene*). . . . to be my lawfully wedded wife. . . .

TED. . . . to be my lawfully wedded wife . . .

JUDGE'S VOICE. . . . to have and to cherish. . . .

TED. . . . to have and to cherish. . . .

We see the Judge's face looking toward them; we see only the backs of their heads.

JUDGE. . . . until death us do part. . . .

Ted and Ellen turn and look at each other. This reveals their faces to us. For just a moment they look at each other, as if realizing the significance of this phrase. Then Ted repeats:

TED. . . . until death us do part.

The scene immediately begins to move down the middle aisle of the courtroom. Dialogue of the marriage ceremony continues but becomes a mumble. As the view reaches the rear of the courtroom we see, as if from a great distance, four figures (Ted, Ellen, Bob Gray and Frank Grub) facing the Judge under the little pinpoint of illumination. This shot emphasizes the vastness of the room and the smallness of our principals. It also tells us that the marriage ceremony is a sudden thing, that they have awakened the Judge and that the courthouse has been opened in the middle of the night for the ceremony. The scene blurs over and dissolves to a big closeup of TED. He is perspiring—his face is dirty—his mouth is dry—and he is rolling to and fro as if in the grip of some terrible dream.

TED (in delirium). Don't let them cut my leg off! Please don't let 'em cut my leg off!

DAVENPORT begins to shake Ted. We see they are still on the boat, that it is night; and over this and the preceding scene we get the movement of the small boat, the slap of waves against her hull,

the sound of a drizzling rain. As Davenport shakes Ted, Ted opens his eyes and slowly becomes rational.

TED (in a startled voice). Wh-wh-what's the matter?

DAVENPORT. You were yelling.

TED. I—Oh—(He reaches out and takes hold of Davenport's arm and speaks intensely, pleadingly:) Look, Davenport—you've got to promise me something. I might pass out again and—don't let anybody cut my leg off. Promise?

DAVENPORT. Sure. You'll be all right. Don't worry, Lawson.

TED. Thanks—

Temporarily reassured, Ted nods a little dazedly as the scene dissolves to a dilapidated PIER at dawn. The boat crew and new coolies, with the help of Thatcher, are just finishing the job of transferring our men to sedan chairs. The operation, as indicated by the faces and the groans of our characters, is extremely painful. The Chinese in charge of the boat moves gravely over to Thatcher. He is carrying a small, paper umbrella. With a princely gesture, he gives the umbrella to Thatcher who accepts it, doubtfully. The Chinese bows. Thatcher smiles.

THATCHER. Thank you.

The Chinese says something to him in Chinese, and moves off toward his boat, very pleased. The coolies pick up the chairs. They start toward a clump of trees. Overhead there is the sound of a plane. The coolies instantly freeze.—A Japanese scouting plane is seen, flying very low and at a slow speed.—The men look skyward. They are motionless.

THATCHER. A Jap!

The group watches the plane breathlessly. The sound of the airplane diminishes in the distance. The coolies burst into animated conversation, obviously in relief that the Jap failed to discover them. Then they start out at an even pace. This dissolves to a CHINESE STREET in the afternoon, as our cortege of stretchers and coolies approaches a clean-looking little building and enters through a gateway. In the scene are a dozen or so interested Chinese who walk along beside the procession, chattering to themselves and pointing at the chairs, and who hang back reluctantly as our group enters the gateway. In front, above the gate, is a China Relief poster, indicating that this is a China Relief Station.

The PATIO: The coolies enter with their burden of four men, Thatcher walking. Moving toward them is a young Chinese man wearing glasses, followed by three or four Chinese nurses, immaculate in their white uniforms. The Chinese come up to Ted and Davenport.

CHINESE MAN (*in perfect English with a Chinese accent*). My name is Foo Ling. Everything we have is yours. We know what you have done and we honor you for it.

He speaks to the coolies in Chinese. The group are carried toward the interior of the relief station. Foo Ling is walking beside Ted.

TED. Our navigator has both his shoulders broken. (*He indicates McClure.*) Is there anybody—who could set them for him?

FOO LING (*shaking his head*). No one. We hope that help will soon arrive for you.

Ted and Davenport exchange despairing looks, as if sickened by the information . . The coolies continue carrying them toward the inside of the relief station.

This dissolves to the CENTRAL ROOM of the CHINA RELIEF STATION, where the men are disposed on cots. Clever is unconscious. One of the nurses and Foo Ling are just finishing washing and bandaging Ted. Thatcher is moving from cot to cot, taking care of his wounded comrades, giving them water and whatever else they may need. All of the men are so knocked out by their journey and by the misery of their injuries that they simply lie back against their pillows, content for the moment to resign their fates to others.—We then see TED'S COT.

TED (*to Foo Ling, with a vague gesture of his hand*). How are they?

FOO LING. We have washed them. They are bandaged. But we have no medicines—not even aspirin.

Ted looks across the room, and we see the CHINA RELIEF POSTER, then the scene cuts back to TED, on the cot, looking at the poster. Foo Ling and the nurse are just finishing the bandages on his face.

TED (*turning from the poster to Foo Ling*). Mr. Ling, I—(*his words coming with difficulty*)—back home I saw—posters like that. (*He points at the China Relief poster.*) Sometimes —maybe I'd put in a dime or a quarter. (*He closes his eyes briefly, frowns, then continues:*) I used to feel pretty—generous. All I want to say now is—(*A paroxysm of pain shakes him and he pauses briefly.*)—I wish I'd put in more.

FOO LING (*smiling*). A dime often saves a life in China. You must sleep.

There is the sound of a sudden commotion from the courtyard. Ted's eyes shake off their pain-drugged expression, and become alert.

TED (*with a note of alarmed anxiety*). What's that?

Foo Ling also has an expression of alarm on his face. He straightens and looks off toward the door. Then we see it open to admit a young Chinese, dressed in American clothes. From his appearance he has obviously traveled a long way. He moves directly over to Foo Ling, and they exchange brief remarks in Chinese. Then Foo Ling turns to Ted.

FOO LING. This is Doctor Chan.

DR. CHAN (*with a polite little bow*). How do you do.

From this point on Dr. Chan continues the conversation while examining Ted's wounds.

TED (*wandering a little*). We've come a long way . . . and we're going home now . . . and we've been hunting a doctor everywhere.

DR. CHAN. I understand.

THATCHER (*entering the scene; addressing himself to Dr. Chan*). Have you got anything that will knock 'em out, Doctor? They're in awful pain.

DR. CHAN (*shaking his head*). We hope to have some medical supplies by the time we get to my father's hospital.

TED (*focusing on this point of information*). Hospital? Where's that?

DR. CHAN. Lin Hai. About sixty li from here. I have come to take you there.

TED. It's a funny thing, Doctor. There were a lot of planes . . . and we had to take off early. You see how it was?

DR. CHAN (*recognizing this as approaching delirium*). Of course.

THATCHER. They're not in any shape to make much of a trip, Doctor.

DR. CHAN. We'll *have* to move them at once. The Japanese captured one of your crews yesterday, not very far from here.

TED (*rubbing his head as if it were difficult for him to remember so far back*). So many planes . . . and we don't know what happened to the others.

DR. CHAN (*putting a hand on Ted's forehead to soothe him*). All up and down the Chinese Coast my countrymen are seeking your countrymen. We will bring them through.

Dr. Chan and Foo Ling exchange a few brief words, then Foo Ling makes a signal to the coolies. They advance with stretchers and start to lift the wounded men onto them, Thatcher assisting. Ted motions weakly to Foo Ling. Foo Ling comes over to him.

TED (*searching for his wallet*). I have some money—I want to give it to you—

FOO LING (*quickly putting a restraining hand on Ted*). Please, Lieutenant . . . you have given us enough already.

TED (*dazed, shaking . his head*). Huh—

FOO LING (*gently*). The bombs you dropped on Japan . . . Please now . . . try to rest.

As Ted sinks back against the support of his stretcher, the coolies pick the chair up and they start out of the room.

The scene dissolves to a CHINESE VILLAGE STREET. Our procession is moving slowly. All five of our men are riding in the sedan chairs now. Doctor Chan moves swiftly, easily, from chair to chair, adjusting a leg here, a bandage there. The men are stunned from their injuries and quite silent. They are passing through massed rows of the villagers, who have come to see them off. As they pass along through the crowd-lined street, a murmur rises with their arrival and diminishes with their departure. Women are pressing in to see the strangers on the stretchers. Their faces are full of sympathy, and their principal expression is "Hmmmmm. Hmmmmmm!" It is almost melodically soft, and its implication is one of the utmost sympathy and compassion. Some of them run along beside the stretcher, clucking with concern and pity. We begin to hear the sound of children's voices singing "The Star Spangled Banner" in Chinese.

We see a COMPANY OF CHINESE SOLDIERS standing smartly at attention. Their uniforms are shabby, but their guns are excellent, and their morale, as they come to attention, is something splendid to see.—

This cuts to the FIVE SEDAN CHAIRS as Davenport and Ted try weakly to salute. Thatcher salutes very smartly. McClure tries to salute, winces with pain, and simply nods. Clever's head rolls from side to side against the back of his sedan chair.

The men next pass the company of soldiers and now come upon a company of Chinese Boy Scouts—they are dressed as American Scouts are. Their faces are freshly scrubbed; they look very manly as they salute. Again, our characters try to return the salute.

This cuts to a COMPANY OF GIRL SCOUTS lined up beside the street. They are looking, indicating that our procession is approaching them. They continue their Chinese rendition of "The Star Spangled Banner," as our procession comes into view. The anthem sounds more Chinese than American as their shrill, high voices cope with its range. We then get close views of THATCHER saluting the Girl Scouts; MCCLURE swallowing hard and nodding; DAVENPORT managing a salute, looking very serious, very soldierly; TED also saluting. He beckons to one of the Chinese children—a ragged, dirty little girl. She comes forward, smiling, bobbing her head. Ted takes his wings off and hands them to her. She shyly giggles and backs away. Before the refrain of the Girl Scouts' song has died away, our procession passes beyond them.

This dissolves to a MOUNTAIN PATH at night. Up the path comes our group of sedan chairs, and Doctor Chan is moving from chair to chair, ministering to the needs of his wounded charges. And as the procession goes on we see Doctor Chan pouring water from his canteen onto a cloth, wiping Clever's face; Clever rousing himself long enough to smile, then closing his eyes again; Doctor Chan passing on to Ted and adjusting the covers and bandages on Ted's injured left side. At this point, there is the distant sound of explosions.

TED (*in sudden alarm*). What's that?

DR. CHAN (*looking briefly backward*). The Japanese. They are in the village we just left.

Ted looks backward in the direction of the explosions, and in the direction in which Doctor Chan looked, following which we see what they see: the earth and sky, at a distant point in the lowland, lit up by a sullen, red glow.—Ted turns away in distress. Doctor Chan hands Ted the water container. Ted lifts the canteen to his lips. He is so weak that Doctor Chan has to assist him.

This dissolves to a VILLAGE STREET at

night as the procession, moving silently through the deserted street, comes to the entrance of a building. Doctor Chan trots ahead of the procession. Then we see him inside the COURTYARD of the building as he meets Mr. and Mrs. Parker, a middle-aged English couple who are missionaries to the town of Lin Hai. They apparently have been waiting for the arrival of our characters.

MRS. PARKER. Are they all right?

DR. CHAN. They are very, very sick. I'll need your help.

The sedan chairs, borne by coolies, enter the courtyard. Mr. and Mrs. Parker and Doctor Chan walk along with them.—Doctor Chan calls out an order and the coolies move toward an entrance door of the hospital proper.

PARKER. How close are the Japanese?

DR. CHAN. They took Chee-foo three hours after our departure. One of the American crews has already fallen into their hands.

MRS. PARKER (*anxiously, indicating the direction in which the sedan chairs are entering the building*). Hadn't they better be taken straight through to Hop-sai?

DR. CHAN (*shaking his head*). They couldn't stand the trip.

They enter the building, and the scene dissolves to a LARGE HOSPITAL ROOM. There are six or seven cots in the room and a few chairs. The coolies are placing their charges onto the cots. Three Chinese nurses minister to the comfort of the men as soon as they are placed on cots. Thatcher also is assisting, together with Mr. and Mrs. Parker and young Dr. Chan.

An elderly, white-bearded Chinese, fastidiously dressed in a silken robe, en-

ters the room from another door, and comes up to young Doctor Chan. They converse for a moment in Chinese. They look off in the direction of Ted, and the elderly man nods gravely. They move over to Ted's cot. The older man removes the covers from Ted, bends over and begins to take the bandages from his leg.

YOUNG CHAN. This is my father, Dr. Chan.

TED (*wincing as the older doctor works on his wounds*). The others— please help them—they're—

YOUNG CHAN. Please don't worry, Lieutenant. We'll take care of everybody.

TED (*his eyes wandering to Old Chan*). How does the leg look, Doc?

YOUNG CHAN (*quickly*). My father only speaks Chinese.

Young Chan addresses old Chan in Chinese. Old Chan, with a look of profound sympathy at Ted, makes reply. Young Chan nods.

TED (*with quick anxiety*). You won't have to take it off, will you?

YOUNG CHAN (*evasively*). We hope not . . . one cannot tell.

We then see THATCHER and MR. PARKER, two nurses with Clever in the background.

MR. PARKER. All we have is a little antiseptic fluid and bandages. But we've sent runners out for supplies.

THATCHER. Is there any way I could get a message out? I'd like my mother to know I'm okay.

MR. PARKER (*shaking his head*). The whole region is swarming with Japanese.

THATCHER. Well—do you think

they've heard back in the States what happened to us?

MR. PARKER (*nodding*). We've been listening in on the short wave. They know about the raid, but apparently they're keeping the details secret until the rest of your men have been saved.

THATCHER (*nodding*). Have they found *any* of the others?

MR. PARKER. We have word that one crew will be coming through very soon now. We understand there's a doctor among them.

THATCHER (*his face lighting up*). That must be Lieutenant Smith's crew. Excuse me, please.

Thatcher walks over to Ted's cot, where the older Dr. Chan and a nurse are working on Ted's leg. Ted's eyes are glazed over with pain. He is slightly delirious.

THATCHER. Lieutenant Smith's crew has been rescued, sir.

TED (*vaguely*). Smith's?

THATCHER. They've found Lieutenant Smith and Doc White and they're coming here.

TED (*his mind beginning to wander*). Don Smith's crew. The Doc was flying with Don Smith . . . (*He frowns, seems to forget.*) There was that school house, just like American kids, only the flag was different . . . they'll be here any minute now . . . (*He manages a smile, his eyes becoming increasingly vague.*) It's pretty funny, isn't it? I mean—Clever's head just rocks back and forth . . . somebody ought to . . (*his voice sinking*) . . . . help Clever.

As his eyes flutter vaguely about the room, the scene dissolves to the HOS-PITAL ROOM by day. Just outside the window, peering in, are Chinese children, massed closely, their noses and faces flattened against the pane. Some of them stare in silent wonder at what they behold within the room. Others point and giggle.—Then we see that the children are staring at our crew members. We get some evidence of passage of time by the fact that Bob Clever is now sitting up in bed. His head is bandaged. A phonograph is situated between the beds of McClure and Clever. McClure's arms are propped up with a brace.

MCCLURE. I think the Chinese are a swell bunch of people, but I can't say I go for their music.

CLEVER (*with a grin*). Shorty Manch would go all to pieces if he heard a little of this.

MCCLURE (*grinning*). Yeah. (*After a little moment of silence*) I wonder if Shorty got through.

CLEVER. If he didn't, I bet he's giving the Japs an awful line of jive.

The door opens and Thatcher enters. Immediately McClure and Clever look up at him.

MCCLURE. How's Lawson?

THATCHER. His leg's pretty bad, sir. Davenport's with him now.

Suddenly they become silent, and we hear an airplane flying low. At this Thatcher walks over to the window and looks out and up.

THATCHER. Looks like one of their zeros.

The men exchange tense glances.—The children's heads follow the passage of the plane, indicating its direction. Some of them smile.—In LAWSON's ROOM, Davenport is sitting beside Lawson's bed, his cane beside him. Davenport is listening to the drone of the plane. Ted's face is covered with perspiration. He is gritting his teeth. He speaks with a great deal of difficulty. He is still delirious, and so weak that he can scarcely move.

TED. You guys ought to go on and leave me. They think I'm passed out half the time, and—I—I hear what they say. The Japs are coming closer all the time. Why don't you guys go?

DAVENPORT. We're not sticking around because of you, Lawson. Nobody here's able to travel yet.

TED (*paying no attention to the reply*). I've just been thinking—I guess Ellen and I aren't going to ski any more. That's too bad. I was going to teach her some—some fancy stuff. (*His voice fades away and he pants with the exertion of his conversation.*)

DAVENPORT. Now don't start talking like that. You're going to pull through all right.

TED. What do you think a girl would do? I mean—say Ellen and I liked to ski. Be kind of funny if they cut my leg off, wouldn't it?

DAVENPORT. Why don't you try to go to sleep, Lawson?

TED. Yeah, it'd be kind of funny— marry a guy—he's got two arms and two legs and all of his teeth—then he comes back—and—(*He stops.*)

This cuts to the COURTYARD by day. Don Smith, Sergeant Williams, Doc White, and three other members of the crew of Don Smith's plane have just arrived. These men, surrounded by an admiring crowd of Chinese and their guides, are walking toward the hospital entrance. Some of the Chinese in the crowd are so full of admiration for them that they come close to them just to try to touch their garments. The children who have been looking through the window, burst into excited conversation and laughter. They enter the hospital, the scene cutting to the HOSPITAL BEDROOM where McClure and Clever are in bed, Thatcher in the scene, as the men enter the bedroom. The new arrivals are dirty, and heavily bearded, and although weary from their long journey, excited and happy to meet the crew members of the *Ruptured Duck*. The newcomers practically mob Clever, McClure and Thatcher. There are big ad lib greetings from all sides. Smith and the others try to be light-hearted over the injuries of Clever and McClure.

SMITH. Holy Joe! What happened to you guys?

MCCLURE (*grinning*). Nothing serious. The *Duck* just took to water.

CLEVER (*imitating with his arms the propped-up position of McClure's arms*). And McClure's been trying to do his own flying ever since.

DOC WHITE (*staring at them, shaking his head*). This really looks like something left over from a massacre! (*He begins to prod around Clever and McClure.*)

CLEVER. You don't look so good yourselves.

MCCLURE. And you don't *smell* so good, either.

DOC WHITE. Nothing wrong with us that a good bath won't fix. (*He shakes his head at McClure.*) I wish I could say as much for you.

WILLIAMS. How's the grub around here? I think I'd like a good, thick steak—(*gesturing*) french fried onions and a baked potato with plenty of butter, and about three bottles of beer and—

THATCHER. You'll take bean sprouts and like 'em.

DOC WHITE (*looking around the room*). Where's Lawson and Davenport?

MCCLURE. They're upstairs. Lawson is in pretty bad shape.

CLEVER. You better go up and see him. He needs you pretty bad, Doc.

As Doc White starts to go, led by Thatcher, the scene dissolves to TED'S ROOM. Don Smith is lying on a cot beside Ted's bed. Their veins are connected by a rubber tube. Ted is receiving a blood transfusion from Don. The transfusion apparatus is a weird combination of bladder and rubbery arms, that have to be shaken so that the blood won't coagulate. Doc White superintends this. Ted and Don are discussing their crack-ups and experiences since the raid.

DON.—Yeah, and when Shorty jumped he had two forty-fives, a forty-four rifle, a twenty-two automatic, that Luger of his, a hunting knife, a bowie knife and an ax.

TED (*grinning*). What a guy!

DON. He stuffed his shirt full of chocolate bars, but he forgot to button his collar. So when he pulled the rip cord, he just naturally molted candy all over north China.

TED. What happened to his record player?

DON. Went down with the ship. Next morning Manch scared the natives right out of their wits. They didn't know anything human grew that tall.

TED. What about Bob Gray?

DON. He's okay. I think they moved on to Chungking.—Oh, yeah, and that guy, "Me, Charlie," said to tell you "hello."

TED. If it hadn't been for Charlie the Japs would have had us that first day.

DON. Yeah. Us, too.

TED. I hope I can come back someday and fight alongside that guy.

DON. Me, too.

DOC WHITE (*cheerfully*). All over. (*He pulls the tube out of Don's arm, and quickly sterilizes the wound there.*) And let's save some of this talk for tomorrow. (*He pulls the tube out of Ted's arm.*) A pint and a half. That's not bad. (*To Don, quietly*) You better get to bed now.

DON. You're an old grandma, Doc. (*He rises, wobbles a little, and grins foolishly.*) But I'll take it slow just as a favor to you. (*To Ted*) Be seeing you, Lawson.

TED (*nodding as Don goes out*). Thanks (*To the doctor*) How's the leg, Doc?

DOC WHITE (*after a moment of silence*). It's not good, Lawson. The next forty-eight hours will tell the story.

TED. Do everything you can, Doc. (*He smiles.*) I've had that leg for a long time and I'm kind of used to it.

This dissolves to a HOSPITAL COURTYARD where six sedan chairs with their coolie bearers are now lined up. There are other Chinese in the scene watching curiously. Out of the hospital come Don Smith and four members of his crew, followed by the Drs. Chan, Mr. and Mrs. Parker, and Doc White. There are also two or three nurses who have come out to witness the departure. The five crew members go over to the sedan chairs and start to climb into them. Their attention is distracted by Davenport's voice.

DAVENPORT'S VOICE (*shouting out*). Hey, Don.

And we see McClure, Clever and Davenport hanging as far out of the open window as their condition permits.

DAVENPORT. Tell Doolittle to hold off that party till we get there.

DON SMITH (*yelling back*). Okay, Davenport, we'll wait for you!

MCCLURE. If you see Shorty, tell him we're sorry we lost his records.

SERGEANT WILLIAMS. Don't be sorry! His crew'll give you a medal for that.

DON SMITH. Is Thatcher with you guys?

DAVENPORT. He's in with Lawson. He'll be right out.

This cuts to TED'S HOSPITAL ROOM where Thatcher is standing by Ted's bed. They are saying goodbye.

THATCHER. I wish you'd let me stay on till you're ready to go, sir.

TED (*shaking his head*). These people will take care of us and—there's no reason for you fellows to hang around and maybe get caught.

THATCHER (*smiling*). I might come in handy if the Japs show up, sir.

TED (*shaking his head*). When you get back to the States—if you should run into my wife—just tell her I'm okay. Don't let her know about—anything being wrong.

THATCHER. I understand, sir. (*Ted extends his hand. Thatcher grips it.*)

TED. And say hello for me to that girl in Billings.

THATCHER. That I will, sir. Goodbye.

TED. Goodbye.

Thatcher turns at this and goes out, and the scene dissolves to the HOSPITAL WARDROOM. MCCLURE, DAVENPORT and CLEVER wistfully watch the procession, through the window, as it leaves the courtyard. Someone in the procession starts the refrain of "Deep in the Heart of Texas," and in a moment the rest of them are singing. The three characters grin at each other, then grow sober. Throughout the remainder of the scene the diminishing sounds of the chorus of the song, sung lustily by Don Smith's crew come over to us. And this dissolves to TED'S HOSPITAL ROOM where Ted is lying on his cot, half-asleep, as Doc White and the two Drs. Chan enter the room. Ted turns his head weakly as they enter and watches them as they come over to his cot. Their faces seem unusually grave. They go directly to the leg, pausing only for the briefest greetings to Ted.

DOC WHITE (*a little loudly, a little gruffly*). 'Morning, Lawson!

TED (*suspiciously*). Hi, Doc.

Both Drs. Chan nod politely.

DOC WHITE (*as he begins to unbandage the leg*). I'll try not to hurt you, Lawson. We'll have a look at this.

TED stiffens and winces with pain as the process of unwinding the bandages progresses. Fine droplets of perspiration bead his forehead. Young Dr. Chan appears, wipes Ted's face with a damp cloth, and smiles encouragingly.

TED. Thanks.

Ted raises his head obliquely, to get

a look at Doc White and the elder Chan.

We then see (from Ted's position) Doc White and the elder Chan, but we do not see what they are looking at. They both seem very grave. Finally, they lift their glances from the injured leg, and exchange a brief, significant look.— We then get a close view of the group as Ted sinks back to the pillow, then speaks.

TED (*in an attempt to be casual*). Going to take the leg, Doc?

There is a pause, while Doc White considers his answer.

DOC WHITE (*finally*). Yeah . . . I think so. (*With a gesture toward the two Chans*) We talked it over, and—there's nothing else to do.

TED (*after another pause*). Oh.

Doc White looks at him for a moment, then moves toward the head of the bed. Doc White finds speaking somewhat difficult, but he speaks nevertheless.

DOC WHITE (*gruffly*). It's pretty rough to have to cut a man's leg off.

TED (*after a moment's thought, attempting a grin*). I guess it'll be all right. After all, a—a wooden leg is just kind of like wearing a shoe with a high instep. (*There is a long pause.*) When are you going to do it?

DOC WHITE (*going to his medical case*). Might as well give you a shot right now.

TED. You mean we—we've got something to knock me out?

YOUNG CHAN (*nodding*). Our runners arrived with anesthetic this morning.

DOC WHITE (*taking the hypodermic needle from its case*). It'll only be a spinal, Lawson. You won't feel anything from the waist down, but you'll be conscious. That's the best we can do.

TED (*still attempting humor*). Swell. I can watch you and make sure you don't take off too much.

Doc White starts to say something, then thinks better of it.

DOC WHITE. All right, Lawson. We'll have to roll you over.

The three doctors help Ted to roll onto his stomach. Ted groans once as this maneuver is completed. Then Doc White goes quickly, efficiently, silently to the work of administering the anesthesia. The elder Dr. Chan goes to the door and signals. Two Chinese enter, bearing a stretcher. They move over beside Ted's cot.

DOC WHITE. It'll take it a little time to work. We'll get you over to the operation room.

TED (*tensely*). Okay.

With a gesture to the Drs. Chan, Doc White begins the delicate job of transferring his patient from the cot to the stretcher. Ted pants heavily during this operation, but restrains his groans. The elder Chan issues directions to the stretcher bearers in Chinese, and they raise or lower the stretcher as the occasion may require in response to his instructions. Finally, Ted is carried out.

This dissolves to the OPERATING ROOM. Present in the room are Doc White, the Drs. Chan, and three Chinese nurses. Ted is on the operating table. They are preparing him for the amputation. The surgical instruments for the operation are neatly laid out on a table beside the patient.

TED. Doc. . . .

DOC WHITE. Yes?

TED (*bluntly*). How high are you going to cut?

DOC WHITE (*hating to say it*). Not too high.

TED (*in a strange voice*). Will I have a knee, Doc?

DOC WHITE. I'm afraid not, Lawson. (*He reaches down, touches the leg, and changes the subject.*) Any feeling there?

TED. No. Look, Doc . . .

DOC (*hastening to avoid the disagreeable subject*). We can't waste any time, Lawson. When that anesthetic wears off—we haven't got any more.

TED (*a little frantically*). Okay, but just one more thing, Doc.

DOC WHITE (*impatiently, to cover his real emotions*). Yes?

TED. If anything happens—don't let Ellen know about the operation. She might just as well think I died with —all in one piece.

DOC WHITE (*hurriedly*). All right, Lawson. (*He signals to the nurses, who advance.*) You're not going to feel this but—well, you might get nervous and jump, or something. So the nurses are going to hold you.

TED (*his lips pinched tightly together*). Okay, Doc. Fire away.

The nurses move up and take hold of Ted's wrists. Doc White, the Drs. Chan, and the third nurse go to the lower end of the table. Doc White takes a scalpel and begins to cut; following which there is a close view of TED and the NURSES as Ted is straining, his head slightly raised to see what is being done, then sinks back to the pillow.

TED (*weakly*). When you said "no knee," you weren't kidding——

Next, Doc White is seen working rapidly.

DOC WHITE (*without looking up*). If I cut any lower, we might have to do it again, and your system couldn't take it.

Doc White straightens briefly, and nods to the Drs. Chan, who move closer to the operating table. Then the Drs. Chan lift Ted's leg, bending it at the knee, while Doc White deftly cuts the underneath portions. Again we see that Ted has raised his head and is watching. Slowly the leg is lowered. Doc White lays his scalpel aside and picks up something else. Ted's head sinks back to the pillow.—We then have a close view of TED and the NURSES as one of them wipes the perspiration from his face.

TED (*irritably*). What're you stalling for, Doc?

DOC WHITE'S VOICE. We're doing the best we can, Lawson. Take it easy.

TED (*panting a little*). Okay. Only hurry. It seems like I'm beginning to feel my other leg.

We see the LOWER END of the OPERATING TABLE as Doc White and young Chan exchange worried glances. Young Chan speaks to his father. The older man nods and moves toward the head of the table. Doc White nods to young Chan. The young Chinese hands him a silver saw.—Then the scene cuts to the HEAD of the BED as the elder Chan places a hand on Ted's shoulder. The touch is gentle, but it is obvious that the old Doctor is there to assist the nurses in restraining Ted should the anesthetic wear off.

TED (*his voice vibrant with alarm*). It seems like I can move my toes, Doc!

From the lower end of the table comes the sound of the saw, biting with rhythmic strokes into the bone. Ted's face grows taut.

TED. Hurry, Doc! I think I can move my ankle now! I'm *sure* I can!

Doc White is heard increasing the tempo of his sawing and Ted suddenly stiffens, winces, and calls out frantically.

TED. Hurry, Doc! Hurry—!

A shudder passes through his body. He makes a convulsive effort to pull himself into a sitting position. For a moment it seems that the pain has given him such strength that the two nurses and the elder Chan will be unable to restrain him.—A closeup shows Ted's head slumping back against his pillow. A long sigh issues from his lips. His eyes begin to roll vacantly from side to side. The sound of the saw continues persistently, mercilessly over the scene. Then the screen blurs out, and the scene dissolves to a view through a window.

Hanging from a ring in the window blind is a wreath of holly. Through the window we see that our locale is a lumber camp. The building in which we play our scene is at the summit of a slope, and shooting down we see the stumps of pine trees that have been cut. In the middle background two men are sawing a tree. The ground is covered with snow. There is a stack of logs in the background. What we see of the interior of the room is of rough pine boards. The SOUND of the men sawing continues over the scene, replacing the sound of Doc White sawing in the previous scene. As we come in, the screen is blurred over. As it clears, the view expands to reveal Ted standing beside the window, at a wall telephone. Suddenly his eyes light up.

ELLEN'S VOICE (*over the phone*). Hello?

TED (*into the phone*). Hello, Ellen!

ELLEN'S VOICE (*over the phone*). Ted! Where are you?

TED. I'm in a lumber camp. Had to make a forced landing in a mud-puddle.

ELLEN'S VOICE. You aren't hurt, are you?

TED. Not a scratch. Only I've got to stay here for a day or two 'til a repair crew shows up. Have you got the tree all fixed?

This cuts to a close view of a TINY CHRISTMAS TREE and ELLEN. The tree has been placed on a table in front of a window. Through the window we can see the opposite side of the Motor Court, which is our locale. The tree has been lovingly decorated with plenty of tinsel, tiny electric lights, and a heap of cotton snow at its base. There are two packages underneath it. Over the scene we get the continued sound of the doctor's saw.

ELLEN (*into the phone*). Oh, yes, Ted, you should just see it. It's *so* beautiful!

TED'S VOICE. Anything under it?

ELLEN (*nodding and smiling*). Oh, yes!

TED'S VOICE. Well, let's open 'em up!

ELLEN. Oh, we can't do that!

TED. Sure we can. Go ahead!

ELLEN'S VOICE (*doubtfully*). Well . . . . . if you say so. . . . .

Ted is seen now.

TED. I'm not going to be cheated out of my Christmas by a cracked-up airplane.

ELLEN'S VOICE. *Ted!* It's the most beautiful box of candy I've ever seen in my life!

TED. Swell. Isn't there maybe—something else lying around?

ELLEN'S VOICE. Let me see . . . . . yes, there *is!*

TED. Well open *it!*

This cuts to the MOTOR COURT amid the continuing sound of sawing. Ellen opens Ted's box and withdraws a white silk scarf, fringed at both ends.

ELLEN. It's a silk scarf. And it looks like it's hand-made, too.

TED'S VOICE. I'll bet it's got my initial on it.

ELLEN *(laughing)*. That's not fair! You peeked while I was making it!

TED. Huh-uh. I just know my wife.

ELLEN'S VOICE *(small and regretful)*. Oh Ted, I—I wish you were here.

TED *(suddenly sober)*. So do I, honey.

ELLEN'S VOICE. I'll be thinking of you tonight. I'll sit in front of the tree and turn the radio on to Christmas carols and—just think of you.

The sound of the sawing suddenly stops. We hear the crack as the giant tree begins to topple. This attracts Ted's attention to it. The scene blurs over and dissolves out .

TED'S FACE dissolves in, and as his eyes flicker open, the still blurred scene clears. Ted stares vacantly about him for a moment, then focuses on some moving object off scene, whereupon we see the two Chinese nurses who were holding Ted's wrists carrying the amputated leg out of the room. (The leg is covered.)

As they pass through the door the scene dissolves to a LETTER beginning: "Liangcheh District Directorate of Salt Administration, Taichow Salt Collectorate, Linghai, 23rd April, R.C. 31st." Then the view draws back to reveal DAVENPORT reading the letter.

DAVENPORT *(reading)*. To our dearest American Friends. Gentlemen: Having heard that you have bombed Japan, we are very glad and obliged. Now we prepare the following goods for complementing to you, and hope you are victory forever. With best wish, Your sincerely Chinese Friends, Staff members of Taichow Salt Collectorate.

We then see TED'S HOSPITAL ROOM as Davenport finishes reading. The room is jammed with people and gifts. Present are Mr. and Mrs. Parker, Doc White, the two Drs. Chan, the three nurses we previously established, perhaps a dozen Chinese men and women, varying from dignitaries to peasants, and the members of our crew. Ted, looking much better, is sitting up in a chair, a bathrobe draped over his legs, a brand new pair of crutches beside him. Davenport is standing, supported by a cane. McClure has both shoulders in a cast, with his arms therefore sticking straight out from the elbows in front of him. Clever, with the exception of head bandages, seems to be on the road to rapid improvement. The place is a litter of gifts. There are bottles of wine; live chickens tied by their feet and squawking futilely; pieces of silk; embroidered shirts and other articles of clothing; dried vegetables; sacks of rice; canned butter; salt; and packages the contents of which are still wrapped. Through the window can be seen the faces of Chinese youngsters, watching the presentation ceremonies, giggling and pointing among themselves.

As Davenport finishes reading the letter, we get a series of close shots of our crew members, all of them deeply touched by the letter, and by the gifts which have accompanied it. Davenport, who has had to read it, swallows hard at its conclusion. The people in the room look expectantly toward Ted who, as commander of the *Ruptured Duck*, should make response to the gift.

TED looks around, a little appalled at his responsibility, then wets his lips and begins hesitantly but sincerely to speak.

TED. I—I mean all the fellows here—want to say that we—that we thank you very much. For—for everything.

The YOUNG DOCTOR CHAN nods to Ted, turns to the group of Chinese and repeats the thanks in Chinese.

We get a full view of the ROOM. The Chinese seem very pleased with what Ted has said. They nod to each other and bow silently to the crew members. Then without any ceremony or words, they move sedately from crew member to crew member, shaking hands and bowing. The elder Doctor Chan, who has been watching the scene like a benignant patriarch, moves over to his son. He speaks quietly to his son in Chinese and presses something into young Chan's hand. Young Chan nods. Then as the last of the Chinese leaves, he walks over to Ted. Then we see YOUNG CHAN and TED together.

YOUNG CHAN. My father has asked me to present this to you. It has been in our family since the fifteenth century. My father begs me to tell you that beauty belongs to beauty—and asks that you honor him by presenting it to your wife.

He presents Ted with an exquisite jade bracelet. Ted accepts it with considerable confusion.

TED. I—I didn't know that—that you knew about Ellen. I—I mean, my wife.

YOUNG CHAN (*nodding and smiling*). You spoke of her a number of times. . . . .

TED (*realizing young Chan must be referring to delirious moments*). Oh. . . .

He stares speechlessly at the magnificent gift. Young Chan, too gracious to wait for Ted to formulate his thanks, bows and retires. Ted, stunned by the gift, simply shakes his head and looks up at Mr. Parker, who smiles and nods in return.

We see MCCLURE, DAVENPORT and MRS. PARKER as Davenport is holding up a gift shirt. On the pocket of the shirt are embroidered some Chinese characters. Mrs. Parker is translating the inscription into English for McClure and Davenport.

MRS. PARKER. It says—"This is an American hero who has bombed Japan. Whenever he goes among the people of China, let him be accorded respect and honor."

There is a moment's silence while both Davenport and McClure ponder these words. Davenport frowns as if he were trying to frame a thought which he found difficult to express.

DAVENPORT (*finally*). You know—there were a few times—maybe when we were stumbling around there on the beach—when the whole thing didn't seem worthwhile. But after having seen the Chinese people—you know it *was* worthwhile . . . all of it.

The door opens to admit an incredibly ancient Chinese peasant, ill-clad, travel-stained, bearded, and apparently excited. Under his arm he carries four parcels wrapped in brown paper. His anxious eyes seek out young Chan, and he moves quickly over to the young doctor. He addresses young Chan in a voluble burst of Chinese. Young Chan's face grows grave. He nods occasionally throughout the Old Man's discourse and when the newcomer has finished, young Chan turns to Doc White.

YOUNG CHAN (*to Doc White*). He has just come from Kow-Chei. Another one of your crews has been captured, and the Japanese are moving in this direction.

DOC WHITE (*gravely*). I see. I think Lawson will be ready to travel in a couple of days.

TED (*interrupting*). There's nothing wrong with me, Doc. I can travel right now!

YOUNG CHAN. I'm afraid a couple of days will—will be too long.

The newcomer during this conversation has been anxiously plucking at young Chan's coat sleeve and looking off toward the members of our crew. Now young Chan pays attention to the Old Man's anxiety and nods. Young Chan turns toward the members of our crew.

YOUNG CHAN. This is Wang-tsung. He has walked all the way from his native village of Kow-Chei and he begs the honor of presenting gifts to his American allies.

Wang-tsung bows quickly, eagerly, four times—once for each crew member —then, with astonishing agility darts forward to McClure. He thrusts a package into McClure's hands, and stands back.

MCCLURE. Thank you.

Wang-tsung bows quickly again, as McClure opens the package and holds up a pair of silk bedroom slippers, beau-

tifully embroidered. Wang-tsung goes over to Davenport who accepts the gift; repeating the previous ritual Wang-tsung then bestows a package upon Clever. While Clever is unwrapping his package, Wang-tsung goes over to Ted and thrusts a package upon him. Ted smiles and begins to unwrap the package. He opens the package and sees the two slippers. He stares at them for a moment. Then we get a close view of WANG-TSUNG as he notices that Ted has only one leg.

WANG-TSUNG and TED: A look of horror comes over Wang-tsung's face, the horror of a man who has committed an unforgivable social crime. He bows once; then, to indicate his abject embarrassment, he covers his face with both his hands. Ted realizes that his own reaction to the gift has embarrassed poor Wang-tsung. He turns to the old man, who is standing very close to him and puts his hand on his shoulder. The Old Man withdraws his hands from his face. Ted smiles.

TED (*extending a hand*). Thank you. Thank you very much.

The Old Man's face suddenly assumes an expression of genuine delight that he has been forgiven. He smiles, takes Ted's hand and bows. Then, still wreathed with smiles, he exits hurriedly from the room. Ted looks around the room and gives a little laugh.

TED. He felt a lot worse than I did. (*He reaches down and puts one of the slippers on his right foot. Then he takes his crutches and hoists himself up on them. He stands for a moment in the middle of the room, swaying slightly from the exhaustion of the effort. But he does not break from his mood of determined gaiety. He painfully takes a step.*) You see? I can get along pretty well already.

PARKER (*kindly*). Very well, I should say, for your first day out of bed.

Ted suddenly totters and reels backward. Parker leaps forward to his assistance, catches him and helps him to his chair. Ted leans back, panting heavily, closes his eyes for a moment, then opens them.

TED (*his voice strained with emotion*). I guess I'll have to be a little more careful! I don't ever want anybody to see me do that! (*His voice rising*) I don't want anybody to see me until I get a new leg!

His voice grows fainter as he nears the end of the sentence, and the scene dissolves to the HOSPITAL COURTYARD at night. A fine drizzle of rain is falling. The courtyard is the scene of great confusion. Coolies, carrying lighted torches, are running back and forth, shouting excitedly to each other in Chinese. Old Dr. Chan runs across the courtyard. Mr. and Mrs. Parker enter the courtyard hurriedly. The mingling of white and yellow faces, the flickering of torches and the movement of the scene give us a feeling of great urgency. Ted, McClure, Clever and Davenport are being loaded into sedan chairs. Doc White is superintending the loading. Young Dr. Chan enters the scene, accompanied by a Chinese runner who is travel-stained and exhausted. He addresses the group.

YOUNG CHAN. He just brought word that the American plane will pick you up in Choo Chow Lishui tomorrow afternoon at five.

DOC WHITE. That's wonderful!

The runner speaks once more to young Chan. Young Chan turns to the group.

YOUNG CHAN. He says if we don't hurry, the Japanese may get there first.

Mr. and Mrs. Parker are next seen shaking hands with the departing men.

TED (*to Mrs. Parker*). When are *you* leaving?

MRS. PARKER. We're going to stay here. We're quite used to it, you know. (*She hands him a basket.*) This is all I could find, but it may come in handy.

TED. Thank you. You and Mr. Parker have done so much for us and—and we'll never forget it.

MRS. PARKER (*moving on to another sedan chair*). Goodbye, and God bless you!

Mr. Parker, we notice, is shaking hands with Davenport. In the background old Dr. Chan comes up to Ted, accompanied by his son. He bows solemnly and says something to his son.

YOUNG CHAN. My father says that you have honored us with your visit and that he will offer prayers for your safe return to America.

TED. Isn't he coming along with us?

YOUNG CHAN. My father feels that he must stay with his people. They will need him here.

Old Chan and Ted shake hands. Even as they are shaking, the sedan chairs begin to move. There are confused farewells in Chinese and English as the cortege starts out of the courtyard.

We then see the PROCESSION as it gets under way and begins to spill out of the narrow street beyond. We see young Dr. Chan moving from sedan chair to sedan chair, adjusting covers for the men, trying to repair leaks in the oilskin paper tops of their conveyances. The coolies are carrying paper umbrellas. They wave farewell and the Chinese in the courtyard brandish their torches, cheer, and call out blessings upon them in Chinese.

The scene dissolves to the COUNTRYSIDE. The men, Dr. Chan accompanying them on foot, are passing along a dike, on either side of which are rice paddies. We see harvesters, workers, in the distance—mostly women and children, for the men are all at war. Two or three children are working on the dusty roadway of the dike as our group passes by. They are carefully sifting the dust for any grains of rice that may have carelessly been dropped by the harvesters in transporting it. This, then, cuts to DOC WHITE and DR. CHAN walking in the foreground.

DOC WHITE. How much further have we got to go, Dr. Chan?

DR. CHAN. About eighteen li—six miles.

CLEVER (*exultantly*). Hey, guys, how will it seem to be up in the air again?

The reactions on the faces of our characters indicate that it will seem pretty swell.

This dissolves to an AIRPORT, in the background, as our group arrives on the field. In the distance we see a small hut, and approaching the new arrivals are a pair of Chinese officers. They are running. We notice that there are a dozen or so Chinese soldiers out on the field, apparently digging in the earth at various points. One of them suddenly runs toward the boundary of the field. He reaches safety barely in time to escape being caught in a tremendous explosion in the center of the air field.

We see the GROUP startled by the explosion. Instinctively they look toward the sky. Two officers who have arrived during the previous scene are talking in sharp, imperative tones to young Dr. Chan. While they talk, another explosion further increases the confusion among our crew, who are too astonished to say anything yet. Dr. Chan and the two officers complete their conversation. Young Chan turns quickly to the group.

YOUNG CHAN. They're dynamiting the field. Jap planes have been overhead all day.

There is a moment of stunned disappointment. One of the Chinese officers addresses young Chan again. Young Chan turns apologetically to the crew.

YOUNG CHAN. We must go on to Chow-Kai, thirty miles to the North. A plane will meet us there.

But before we have an opportunity to get any reaction from our characters, aside from surprise and keen disappointment, the scene dissolves to a view of a PLANE bearing an American insignia, just dropping down, and this cuts to the LANDING FIELD as the American plane makes a landing. In the foreground are our five characters, still in their sedan chairs. Young Chan is beside them. As the plane taxis to a stop, the coolies lift the chairs and trot toward it.—And after this dissolves we see the men all grouped around the plane saying goodbyes. The motors are slowly turning over.

DR. CHAN (*to McClure*). Goodbye, sir.

MCCLURE (*huskily*). Goodbye, Doctor, and—thank you.

DR. CHAN (*moving on to Davenport, shaking hands*). I hope, sir, that we may meet again.

DAVENPORT (*grinning self-consciously*). That goes double.

CLEVER (*with genuine feeling*). If you ever come to the States, Doctor, look me up, will you? I'll be in the Portland telephone directory.

DR. CHAN (*smiling*). With pleasure.

He comes up to Ted and offers his hand. Ted grips it warmly. He leans on his crutches and is supported on either side by a coolie.

DR. CHAN. I have one sorrow, Lieutenant—that we did not have the medicine to ease your pain.

TED (*a little gruffly, to conceal his emotion*). You saved my life, Doc.

DR. CHAN. I hope someday you can come back to us.

TED (*with genuine emotion and eloquence*). We'll be back, Doc. Maybe not us—ourselves—but a lot of guys like us. And I'd like to be with them. Because you—(*pausing, smiling awkwardly*)—you're our kind of people.

Ted turns abruptly toward the plane, unable to conceal his emotion. Dr. Chan smiles. Two coolies and Doc White help Ted into the ship, the sergeant standing beside them and assisting the others who are less seriously injured. Doctor Chan stands a little apart from the coolies who remain by their sedan chairs. Gravely he watches as the last man enters the plane. The hatch closes.

DOCTOR CHAN stands very erect, watching the plane with sober, unsmiling eyes.—The heads of the flyers appear at the plane's windows, nodding, saluting, or waving to Doctor Chan. The motors of the plane start to "rev" up.—As the plane starts down the field on its run, Doctor Chan, although in civilian clothes, salutes stiffly. As the plane takes to the air, Doctor Chan shades his eyes against the slanting rays of the afternoon sun and watches the plane grow smaller and smaller in the western sky.

The TRANSPORT PLANE is next seen flying over a moonlit sea, its running lights out and its windows darkened, following which we see Ted, McClure, Clever, Davenport and Doc White and a few other men leaning back in their seats, dozing or sleeping.—But TED is not asleep. He is staring soberly out of the window. He looks around restlessly at his companions. Then suddenly he rises, painfully gets to his crutches, and starts uncertainly toward the front of the ship, and we next see him entering the PILOT'S COMPARTMENT. The pilot looks up at him, a little surprised. The co-pilot's seat is empty. The pilot is a happy-go-lucky, gusty, sentimental Irishman.

TED. Hello.

PILOT (*looking up*). Hello.

For a moment Ted stands, staring at the instruments, glorying in the feel of once more being in a pilot's compartment. The pilot notices this.

PILOT. Go ahead—sit down.

Ted smiles gratefully and sits down in the co-pilot's seat with a great deal of effort.—He sighs blissfully at being this near the controls of a plane once more. His eyes dart eagerly over the instrument panel. Automatically he finds himself scanning the sky, as any good pilot does. He glances longingly at the wheel. Out of the corner of his eye, the pilot is watching Ted. After a moment of this observation, he grins slightly to himself.

PILOT (*suddenly*). I know how you feel. Take it for a while.

Ted looks over at the pilot, too startled for a moment to make reply. Then a smile breaks over his face. The pilot takes his hands off the wheel.

TED (*with a grin*). Thanks.

TED reaches eagerly for the wheel, and an expression close to actual love for the ship comes over his face. He looks happy—content. He is flying again.—There is a little moment of silence while Ted feels the plane and savors the joy of flight. The pilot rolls back the window. A gust of air enters the compartment, ruffling their hair, fluttering about their lapels. The pilot inhales a deep breath of air.

PILOT. Smell that? (*Ted likewise inhales, exhales reluctantly, and nods.*) That's America. That's the U.S.A. (*Sniffing again*) Every time I make a trip back, she smells better and better.

TED. Yeah. I think I know what you mean.

PILOT. I'm from Pittsburgh. I know it may seem screwy to you—but— (*taking another sniff*)—it seems to me like I can smell some of that coal smoke right off the old Monongahela River. That sound crazy?

TED (*shaking his head*). No. I'm from California—(*sniffing*)—and I can smell orange blossoms. (*At this the pilot makes a little face and shakes his head.*)

PILOT (*flatly*). Couldn't be. That's *too* far. Must come from Florida.

TED (*with a grin*). Oh, if you want flavor, you've got to have a California orange, but for smelling—(*He sniffs again.*)—Florida's just as good.

The pilot chuckles. They continue flying in silence.

The scene dissolves to the JONES' LIVING ROOM at night. The telephone which rests on the desk, rings harshly the moment we come in on the scene. There are quick footsteps, and a pleasant-faced woman picks up the receiver and answers the phone. Her name is Mrs. Jones.

MRS. JONES (*into the phone*). Hello? . . . Yes! What's that—? Oh, just a minute! (*She is very agitated by now; she turns from the phone and calls out:*) Ellen, *Ellen.* Washington on the phone!

The door bursts open and Ellen runs toward the telephone, the view moving with her. The living room through which she passes is that of a typical, middle-class, Los Angeles home, clean, neatly furnished.

Ellen is dressed in a simple maternity frock. She is entering her seventh month of pregnancy, and her condition is apparent. Ellen takes the receiver, and speaks into the instrument, as we get a close view of her.

ELLEN. Hello! Yes, this is Mrs. Lawson . . . Oh—hello, Colonel—I mean General Doolittle. (*Her voice is tense, expectant.*) Yes . . . I'm fine, thank you . . . No, I'm not a *bit* excited, General . . . *Oh!* (*To her mother, her voice broken, tears in eyes*) He's back, Mother! Ted's back! He's *back!* (*Into the phone again*) Yes, General . . . How is he? (*Her eyes widen with pain.*) Oh . . Oh . . Yes, I—I understand . . Of *course* I do! Yes, yes! I'll be ready! I know! I know! Oh, that's *so* nice of you, General. Thank you! . . . Yes, yes. Thank you, General! (*Her voice comes in sobs of relief.*) Yes. Th-thank you! Oh th-thank you . . .

Slowly she hangs up the telephone, and remains seated at the desk, her face a battleground of emotions upon which tearful relief finally wins the day.

Mrs. Jones comes over and places an arm around her daughter's shoulders.

MRS. JONES (*tenderly, understand-*

*ingly*). Just cry, darling . . . cry it out . . .

Ellen turns a tear-stained face to her mother.

ELLEN (*speaking rapidly, her voice choked with sobs of happiness*). H-he got in this morning, Mother! General Doolittle just saw him, so it's *true!* General Doolittle is sending a plane ticket for me. Ted doesn't want to see me! He doesn't want to see me because he lost his leg, and he—he doesn't even want me to know it happened until—until he gets a new leg and—and learns how to use it! As if it would make any difference—as if *anything* would make any difference to me so long as he's alive! (*Suddenly she embraces her mother.*) I'm going to *see* him—I'm going to *see* him!

MRS. JONES (*who knows that practical considerations can ease such stormy moods*). That means we'll have to get your clothes ready in a hurry.

Ellen, completely distracted and excited by the news, breaks her embrace with her mother, moves rapidly toward a door, and opens it to reveal a closet beyond. She begins taking things from it, throwing them over the back of a chair.

ELLEN (*talking rapidly as she throws things around*). Have my things come from the cleaner's yet? Here—I'll take this suit—and my blue coat—(*throwing the coat over the chair*)—he always liked it best—and my—(*She stops suddenly, looking tragically across to her mother.*)—I can't take these things! I can't take *any* of my *pretty* clothes! They—they don't *fit* me any more!

MRS. JONES (*smiling very gently*). Do you think Ted's going to pay any attention to the kind of clothes you wear, or how you look?

ELLEN (*in a strained voice*). He always *did!*

A frightened look comes over her face. Suddenly the excitement drains from her. Like a girl in a trance she walks slowly across the room, and sits down in a chair, staring across pathetically at her mother.

ELLEN. Oh, Mother, I—I'm scared. . . . Mrs. Jones moves across to her daughter, and embraces her.

MRS. JONES (*smiling*). There's nothing to be frightened about, Ellen. Lots of people lose a leg or an arm, and continue living perfectly normal lives.

ELLEN (*quickly*). Oh, I'm not scared about Ted. I'm scared about *me!*

MRS. JONES. About *you?*

ELLEN (*pathetically, almost comically*). Because, you see, most husbands and wives are together while —(*searching for a word*)—while things are changing. Husbands get used to things like that because they're *around!* (*Beginning to sniffle*) B-but Ted's been *gone* all the time! When he left, I was so slim! And all the time he's been away, he's been thinking of me like that!

MRS. JONES (*still smiling, but understanding completely*). Ted loves you, Ellen—and you love him. (*With slow, gentle emphasis*) And that's why neither of you is going to notice any change when you meet.

ELLEN (*hopefully, her face still streaked with tears*). You—you think so, Mother?

MRS. JONES (*nodding*). I know so.

Ellen smiles, then quickly walks over

to the chair upon which a moment ago she hurled the clothes she can no longer wear. She picks up the blue coat, folds it carefully over her left forearm, then holds her arm in such a position that it drapes across the front from the waist down.

ELLEN. All the same . . . If I held my coat like *this*—when I walk into the room—don't you think it would hide me—just a little?

As she looks off hopefully, her attitude almost that of a beautiful child seeking encouragement, the scene dissolves to a WALTER REED HOSPITAL ROOM where Ted, attired in a bathrobe and pajamas, is sitting in a chair beside the window, at a point farthest from the door. His crutches are leaning against the chair. He is staring out the window. There is a sudden sound of someone knocking on the door—two brisk, authoritative raps and then it opens to admit General Doolittle. The General walks briskly across the room. Ted involuntarily starts to rise in the presence of his superior officer, grins apologetically; Doolittle notices the gesture, and smiles warmly.

DOOLITTLE (*extending his hand*). Hello, Lawson. How you feeling?

TED. Pretty good, sir.

Doolittle looks at Ted closely and smiles. He is about to say something, then changes his mind, moves over to the window sill and leans against it, trying to appear as casual as possible.

DOOLITTLE. Got any plans?

TED (*puzzled*). About what, sir?

DOOLITTLE. About the future. Have you decided what you're going to do?

TED. Not particularly. I always wanted to be an aeronautical engineer. I suppose I'll start studying

again—(*with a glance at his leg*)—after they muster me out.

DOOLITTLE (*fiercely*). Who *said* they'd muster you out?

TED (*confused*). Why, I—I'll not be much good to anybody with—

DOOLITTLE. No, we can't let a man with your experience get away from us!

For a moment Ted stares at his superior, as if he were unable to believe this good news. Then a wide, relieved grin appears on his face.

TED. Well, that's *fine*, sir! Thank you.

DOOLITTLE (*a little gruffly*). Don't thank me! (*The General pauses and shoots a keen look at Ted; Doolittle decides to bring up the real reason for his visit.*) I just happened to think of something, Lawson.

TED (*questioningly*). Yes, sir?

DOOLITTLE (*shifting his position, firing his questions rapidly to cover his embarrassment*). What about your wife? She know you're back?

TED. No, sir.

DOOLITTLE (*sharply*). Why not?

TED. I—I thought I'd wait till I get my new leg and—and my face fixed up. It won't be so much of a shock to her that way.

DOOLITTLE. Shock! (*He takes refuge in gruffness.*) What kind of a girl did you marry, anyhow?

TED (*defensively, not knowing whether to be angry*). She—she's okay, sir. She's a fine girl.

Doolittle moves toward Ted, smiles suddenly and puts a hand on his shoulder.

DOOLITTLE. Then she *deserves* to know. She deserves to see you, too. And I—

TED (*a little panicky and very sincerely*). Oh no, sir. If you don't mind, I—I'd rather wait. When I see Ellen again I'm going to be all dressed up and—have a new leg—and I'm going to take her out to the best place in town—(*his voice dropping*)—and I'm going to dance with her. . . . .

DOOLITTLE (*wavering*). But that'll be a long while, Lawson.

TED (*still panicky*). Oh no, sir—you see I—I'm getting along fine and—in a month or two—

DOOLITTLE (*breaking it up, gruffly again*). In a month or two you'll be back at work. *Hard work!* (*He hesitates a moment, then slaps Ted gently on the shoulder.*) I'll try to drop around to see you again, Lawson. (*He walks across to the door.*)

TED (*smiling*). I hope you can, sir.

At the door, Doolittle's mood suddenly shifts. Up to this point he has been gruff and a little brusque out of embarrassment. Now, suddenly, he softens.

DOOLITTLE (*quietly*). Your wife's going to have a baby, isn't she?

TED. Yes, sir.

DOOLITTLE (*fumbling for words throughout the speech; not wanting to preach, and yet feeling that he really has some comfort to offer Ted*). I've got a couple of kids myself. Both of 'em in the service. (*He pauses, thinks.*) It's a hard thing to put your finger on and—and I guess there's never been a war but what people said it was going to be the last one— but I think this time we've got a chance. Oh, I know—people say you've got to have one every twenty or twenty-five years—always have had so you always will have— (*Thoughtfully, quietly*) But this time I'm not so sure—this time I think maybe we can all get together. This time I think we've got an inside chance of—of winning what we're fighting for. And if—if we *did* —why that means your kid would have—he'd have quite a break, wouldn't he?

TED. He sure would, sir.

DOOLITTLE (*with a warm smile*). You know, Lawson . . . . I think you're going to be okay . . . (*He delivers the last line with a friendly wink and goes through the door.*)

We get a close view of TED as he considers the information which the General has given him. The prospect of seeing Ellen is more than he can consider. An expression of pain comes over his face. There is the sound of a doorknob slowly being turned, Taut, tense, Ted looks toward the door.—It slowly opens to reveal Ellen standing there timidly, hesitantly, a coat carefully draped over her front, as she had decided upon in the previous scene. She smiles, tears start in her eyes, but they do not fall, and her face is not contorted. She simply stands, looking off with an expression of utter happiness toward TED, still seated in his chair. He says nothing, for there are no words to express the stunned, unbelieving adoration upon his face. Then we see them both. Ellen moves slowly inside, and closes the door quietly behind her. She still carefully holds the coat before her to conceal her pregnancy. Then, as if feeling the necessity for some kind of words, she swallows hard, and speaks.

ELLEN (*weakly*). I—I—

The sound of her voice seems suddenly to galvanize Ted into action, to convince him of her reality. Forgetting his crutches—forgetting that he has only one leg, he bounds from his chair and starts to her, as if he had both legs. He falls, face downward, at her feet as she moves toward him. With a low cry, Ellen instantly falls to her knees.

ELLEN (*her tears flowing fast*). T-Ted! (*She begins to tug at his shoulders to help him up.*) L-l-let me help you!

Instantly Ted turns to her and tries to take her hands from his shoulders. His face is contorted with the effort not to weep.

TED (*frantically*). Don't, Ellen! You'll hurt the baby!

She sinks to a sitting position. Then she tenderly pulls him to her, and cradles his head in her arms. Then we see TED and ELLEN on the floor. Both of them are panting a little, from suppressed sobs, and their exertions. Both of them are crying. Ted, his head still in her arms, simply looks up at her, as if he were afraid she might vanish in an instant, and he would have to remember her forever from this moment's sight of her. Ellen looks down at him ten-derly, then bends and kisses his forehead. The lower part of his face is still swathed in bandages. As she finishes her caress, he looks up at her. He shakes his head slowly, unbelievingly. His eyes are misted with tears, and that part of his face which is uncovered is smiling.

TED (*almost a whisper*). When things were worst—when there didn't seem to be any chance at all—I could see your face——

Ellen is looking down at him, smiling, caressing him with her eyes, loving him.

ELLEN (*softly, beautifully*). I knew you were coming home, Ted.

Tears are now falling from Ellen's eyes onto his face. But she is smiling. Ted reaches up and chucks her gently under the chin with a curved forefinger.

TED (*huskily*). Tell me, honey—how come you're so cute?

ELLEN (*a happy break in her voice*). I—I *had* to be if—if I was going to get such a—such a good-looking fella —!

And as she puts her arm around him and holds him close to her the scene fades out.

# OVER TWENTY-ONE

*( A Columbia Picture—A Sidney Buchman Production )*

*Screenplay by* SIDNEY BUCHMAN

*Adapted from the Play by* RUTH GORDON *as produced on the stage by* MAX GORDON

*Directed by* CHARLES VIDOR

## The Cast

| | |
|---|---|
| PAULA WHARTON . . . | Irene Dunne |
| MAX WHARTON . . . . | Alexander Knox |
| ROBERT GOW . . . . . | Charles Coburn |
| JAN LUPTON . . . . . . | Jeff Donnell |
| ROY LUPTON . . . . . . | Loren Tindall |
| MRS. FOLEY . . . . . . | Lee Patrick |
| FRANK MACDOUGAL . . | Phil Brown |
| MRS. GATES . . . . . . | Cora Witherspoon |
| COLONEL FOLEY . . . . | Charles Evans |
| JOEL I. NIXON . . . . . | Pierre Watkin |
| MRS. DUMBROWSKI . . . | Anne Loose |
| MRS. CLARK . . . . . . | Nanette Parks |
| MRS. COLLINS . . . . . | Adelle Roberts |
| MRS. GREENBERG . . . . | Jean Stevens |

NOTE: *The characters and incidents portrayed and the names used herein are fictitious, and any similarity to the name, character or history of any person is entirely accidental and unintentional.*

*Film Editor*—OTTO MEYER

# OVER TWENTY-ONE

## PART ONE

A TELETYPE MACHINE fades in, dramatically pounding out:

> Max Wharton—editor of New York newspaper
> *Bulletin*—resigns to enlist in Army.—

The teletype drops down a space and continues:

> *Bulletin* started five years ago—backed by Robert
> Drexel Gow, owner and publisher.—

As the words "owner and publisher" come over, the teletype paper is ripped from the machine, and this dissolves to GOW'S OFFICE, with GOW at his desk. He is a well-fed, blustering fellow nearing sixty. He has just risen as though shot from behind—the teletype paper aquiver in his hand—while a male secretary stands alarmed.

GOW (*as the teletype ticker continues to be heard*). My paper—*my* editor— (*brandishing the paper*) —and this is how he tells me!

We then see the TELETYPE continuing with facts on Wharton: "—age 39— married to Paula Wharton—famous novelist—now in Hollywood adapting her book *Fellow Americans—*"

On the last four words the teletype recedes gradually—then dissolves into PAULA WHARTON'S HOLLYWOOD APARTMENT: PAULA—known to her friends as Polly—a smart, alert-appearing gal —is on the phone. (We have caught her at her writing desk, in a mountain of work.)

POLLY (*into the phone*). Look, *Los Angeles Post*—there couldn't be any *doubt* about this? (*She listens an instant.*) No—no comment—*except* if that's what Max Wharton did, that was the right thing to do! Thanks.

She hangs up quickly, thinks an instant, then lifts the receiver again.

POLLY (*into the phone; eagerly*). Honey—look—put a call in to New York—the fastest you ever did it— to Max Wharton—newspaper *Bulletin*—that's right, dear—

We again see GOW'S OFFICE, this time with the editorial board of the *Bulletin* present. The board consists of four men besides Gow. One is Ed Kennedy, assistant editor, a man of fifty, nervous, intimidated by Gow. Then there is Hinkle, managing editor; Howell, circulation manager; and a fellow named Meredith. Kennedy and Meredith are seated. Hinkle and Howell are on their feet. All eyes are on Gow, who is steaming up and down behind his desk, the teletype papers in his hands.

GOW (*bellowing*). From the teletype! That's how we find out. Like he owed nothing to this paper—or to me! Like he never heard of us! The man's out of his mind—!

Gow breaks off, looking toward the door. Max Wharton enters in business suit and hat. He is composed, smiling, assured.

MAX. Hello, boys. Hello, Robert.

They say "hello" softly—all except Gow. Max comes forward.

MAX. It seems you've heard—

KENNEDY. You might have told someone, Max.

MAX. I thought I did. For the past two months. It was just a question of—what day.

GOW (*explosively*). It was the wrong thing to do on *any* day—without consulting me and this board. We decided that your war job was here on this paper!

MAX (*quickly*). No—that was *your* decision, Robert. I told you a hundred times that *my* job was to get as close to this war as they'd let me—

GOW (*angrily*). A schoolboy urge—to go off with flags flying—and come back a sort of tin hero—!

MAX (*flaring*). At my age?

GOW. *Schoolboy* stuff!

MAX. Don't be a stubborn idiot! You know my reasons—and you know they concern the future of the paper more than they do "medals for Maxie."

GOW. *If* there's a paper left when you come home!

MAX. We're on that again!

GOW. You heard me! Since the days of Horace Greeley and William Allen White—a paper is built around one man. When you leave, this paper

doesn't exist—because this paper is you!

MAX. It's all the men in this room who've worked together for five years—on a policy that's never changed. With Ed Kennedy in my place, it'll go right on—

GOW. And that's what I'll never believe! (*To the men*) I respect Ed—and all of you— (*then to Max*) —but no policy is worth a hoot without the brains and courage of the right man to put it into words. And in this case, I gambled two million bucks on the spirit of a man named Wharton—

MAX. Is that what you're concerned about—your two million bucks?

GOW. To a degree—yes! Is that vulgar?

The dictograph buzzer has sounded during Gow's last words. He rushes to it and snaps up the key.

GOW. What is it?

SECRETARY'S VOICE. Mrs. Wharton calling Mr. Wharton—long distance.

Max leaps for the phone, exclaiming "Polly."

MAX (*into the phone*). Hello!—Yes, I'm on.

GOW. Does Polly know you did this?

MAX. No. (*Then*) Hello—Polly—! Yes, it's true, darling. First time I ever held anything out on you—

PAULA WHARTON'S HOLLYWOOD APARTMENT comes into view disclosing POLLY at the phone.

POLLY. Well, good for you, darling! What are they going to do with you? Max, where are you going?

GOW'S OFFICE appears in full view. The

men look at each other as Max talks into the phone.

MAX. I don't know. Somewhere first for Basic Training. I report in five hours.

GOW. Going—in five hours!

MAX (*to Gow*). Quiet! (*Then to Polly*) That's Robert Drexel Gow—having kittens. After that—maybe Officer Candidate School—*if* I can make it.

A close view of POLLY at the phone.

POLLY. Sure you'll make it, Max! And that's when I join up with you.

MAX (*seen at close view*). When you —*what?*

POLLY (*again seen at close view*). You heard me, sweetheart. I need seven or eight weeks to finish this script for Joel I. Nixon. And when you go off to Officer's School—that's where I go.—Don't argue, Max. I couldn't hold out any longer than that. I miss you like the dickens. And you took me for better or worse—peace or war! Now listen, I'll be sitting here waiting to know where I go. For weeks I'll be sitting on this hard little chair—

GOW'S OFFICE again appears in full view, Max still speaking on the phone.

MAX. Okay, darling—you win. You're a fool, but hang onto your seat—Yes, Angel, I'll write every day. Goodbye, Polly—Goodbye.

Max hangs up. Gow just stands glumly through the following.

HINKLE. Max—you aren't leaving right away!

KENNEDY. I need some time with you.

MAX. Boys—what you don't know about this sheet now you won't learn

in another hour. Same policy. Call a foul motive, no matter who owns it. Go after the fellas dreaming up the next war. Show this country how to keep the victory—after they win it—for fifty generations to come. (*Taking Kennedy's hand*) Good luck, Ed.

Then he shakes hands with the others, calling them by their first names—Bob, Horace, Mark. Finally he extends his hand to Gow.

MAX. Goodbye, Robert—

GOW. Now, look—I've got to know where you are. There's going to be a thousand problems come up around here!

MAX. That's out, Robert.

GOW. *What's* out?

MAX. This is going to be a tough grind for me. When I leave here to-day—I *leave.*

GOW. You think you're going to walk out *cold* on this whole shebang?

MAX. You heard me. No inter-office communications from Robert Drexel Gow. *Nothing.*

Gow just stares an instant.

MAX. That's the way it's got to be.

GOW (*suddenly quite sweet*). Oh, well —in that case, goodbye, Max, old son.

MAX (*suspiciously*). I mean it, Robert.

GOW. Naturally. That's why I say—don't give us a thought.

Max looks into Gow's eyes a second—then moves quickly toward the door. He is gone. The men look from the door to Gow, who smiles, and this dissolves to an insert of a TELEGRAM as an operator spreads the telegraph ribbon.

PAULA WHARTON
BÉVERLY HOTEL
LOS ANGELES, CALIFORNIA
I MADE IT, ANGEL. ASSIGNED OFFICER
CANDIDATE SCHOOL, TETLEY FIELD,
FLORIDA. COME AHEAD, DARLING. PAL-
METTO COURT. BUNGALOW 26-D. WAIT-
ING WITH LOVE.

MAX.

This dissolves to PAULA WHARTON'S
HOLLYWOOD APARTMENT. The scene is
one of activity with last minute packing, just before Polly leaves. In the
room besides Polly are Joel I. Nixon,
motion picture producer; Elsie, Polly's
secretary; a young studio publicity man;
a couple of hotel porters with hand
trucks, ready to take the two trunks
which are spattered with foreign labels.
The trunks are being locked by Elsie.
Polly is supervising the trunks in a very
business-like, though hurried, manner.

POLLY (*to the trunk men*). All right
—they can go.

The men tip the trunks onto their hand
trucks.

NIXON. Look at those labels—Savoy,
London—the Normandie—Paris—
Ritz. Next stop—Bungalow 26-D.

POLLY. Joel Nixon, you're just a great
big snob. Why, this looks like a
chance to get in with the furnished-
room crowd. (*To the studio man;
rapidly*) You can have the car
brought around, Norman. I'll be
ready in a minute.

She hurries to her desk and piles her
writing materials into a small case—
pencils, carbon, etc. Meanwhile, Elsie is
closing the two traveling bags, which a
couple of bellboys come in to get.
(Norman is phoning down asking "to
have Mr. Nixon's car pulled up front
and waiting.")

POLLY. Joel—that script is super. It
won't need a line changed. If it does,
get somebody else to do it.

NIXON. Now who can pick up where
Paula Wharton left off?

POLLY. Aw, that's how you get me
to work cheap. Another week away
from Max and I'd bust.

NIXON. Polly—that Bungalow Court!
They live like canned sardines in
those places. You won't be able to
take it.

POLLY. What woman has taken,
woman can take.

NIXON. You'll go crazy down there—
unless you intend to do some writing.

POLLY. Not a line. My typewriter goes
everywhere. And without a dozen
pencils, I'm lonely. I took pencils on
my honeymoon.

She snaps the case closed—rushes for
her hat and starts to put it on before
the mirror.

POLLY. No—not a line, Joel. This is
a full time job.

NIXON. *What* job, Polly?

POLLY. Max Wharton. The most important man I know. What the world
will be like is entirely up to him.
And when he decides on a different
way to fight—right in the middle of
the war—I've got to know why—and
then I've got to see that he gets it
done.

She whirls about, very smart in her
expensive outfit, her hat at a jaunty
angle.

POLLY. Well—we're off, fellas! (*She
kisses Elsie.*) Write me when you
get to New York, Elsie.—Grab that
case, Norman. Come on, Joel. (*She
sails toward the door.*) Bungalow
26-D—I am here!

As she goes through the door, Joel and Norman following, the scene dissolves to PALMETTO COURT at dusk.

A fairly close view shows POLLY staring ahead. Her smart hat is a little askew; she looks travel-worn. Behind her, in the background, we see the entrance to Tetley Field. Immediately behind her is a jalopy which has brought her. Polly is handing the driver a bill. Her eyes are still front. We then get a full view of PALMETTO COURT, which consists of a group of thirty or forty identical bungalows—crowded, run-down in appearance, weed-grown. They are filled with officers' wives and families. Now, in the dusk, the lights are on and all kinds of sounds emerge from the community—talk, radio, music. Then POLLY and the DRIVER are seen closer as the driver is pocketing the money Polly handed him.

DRIVER. Much obliged.

He hops into the jalopy and starts off. Polly's two rather heavy traveling bags are at her feet. She lifts the two—first determining where, in that mass of bungalows, she's apt to find 26-D. The bags are heavy. She picks up the lighter one—and pushes the other one along with her foot. Suddenly, a bugle blast from behind her, issuing from the camp across the way, is heard. Polly is startled. Then the bungalow colony ahead of her becomes suddenly alive. Doors burst open and candidates come tearing out, heading for camp. Some are fastening parts of their wearing apparel. Polly is a little island around which rushes this school of dashing men. When she recovers sufficiently, she tries to stop one or two of them to ask:

POLLY. Uh—26-D? 26-D, please.

But they dash on. Finally, a cute little fellow cannot help but pause. His eyes bug out a little. He swallows.

POLLY (smiling sweetly). 26-D?

The cute little fellow points to the aisle running left.

CUTE LITTLE FELLOW. S-s-second row.

POLLY. Thanks.

CUTE LITTLE FELLOW (pointing to the camp). I'll—I'll get ten demerits for being late—but—it was worth it!

And he roars past as Polly smiles. The bungalow court is normal again. She pushes the heavy bag along with her foot and carries the lighter one.

In a moving view we see POLLY as she heads for the second row of bungalows. At the first one, she peers through the dusk for the number, and finally spots BUNGALOW 26-D, which is then seen close. The number is on the post. The light is on in the living room but no one can be seen moving inside. The door is open.

POLLY, happy that she has found it "first crack," takes up the weary business of pushing and carrying her bags, heading up the short walk to the steps of 26-D. Next, Polly, at the BUNGALOW DOOR, lifts the case she has been pushing into the room and sets the other one down. She peers in.

The LIVING ROOM as Polly looks it over quickly: No one is there, though there are signs of habitation such as an open cosmetic box, an Army barracks bag filled to the top, an officer's khaki, duck folding bag, and a lady's suitcase. As Polly takes another step inside, Jan Lupton, a very young and pretty thing, emerges from the bedroom with a box of Kleenex. Each woman is startled on seeing the other.

POLLY. Oh, I beg your pardon.

Jan stares at this stunningly dressed woman. Polly is about to push one of the suitcases out with her foot.

POLLY. I thought this was 26-D.

JAN. This *is* 26-D.

POLLY (*remembering the number*). Oh, of coùrse it is.—And—you're leaving, aren't you?

She stops, because Jan's face opens in amazement.

POLLY. Something the matter?

Without answering, Jan rushes to the suitcase, rummages in it quickly and brings out a book, turning it to look at the back of the dust jacket which is taken up by a large picture of Polly. Jan glances from the book jacket to Polly.

JAN. Why—why you're Paula Wharton!

POLLY. Uh-huh.

JAN (*indicating the book excitedly*). "Fellow Americans!" Talk about coincidence! I just finished it. I think it's my favorite of all your books.

POLLY. Well, thank you.

JAN. I certainly never thought I'd meet *you*. Of course, I should have connected—when your husband came over this afternoon to leave some of his things—he said his name was Wharton and that his wife was coming from California—but I just never connected!

Polly smiles to be friendly and at the same time starts to pull her suitcases into the room.

POLLY. Did Max say when he would be back? My husband?

JAN (*running to help Polly*). Oh, let me! Max Wharton? Haven't I heard that name—?

POLLY. Well, before he enlisted he used to be editor of—

JAN. Of course! That newspaper Roy's so crazy about. Roy's my husband. He's terrific—I mean, *your* husband is!

POLLY. Well, thank you.

JAN. He must be awfully unusual. You hardly ever hear of anyone like an editor getting to be only a private!

POLLY. And what's more, he didn't use any pull. (*Jan laughs. The suitcases have been pulled into the room.*)

JAN. Do sit down. (*In a stream, as Polly throws herself wearily into a chair*) We'll be leaving any minute. I'm just waiting for Roy to get back. He graduated today. I thought I was going to faint when Colonel Foley handed him his commission. Roy went over to get his orders—that is, where they're going to send him. I just can't wait to find out. If it's Crocker Field, Arkansas—I'll just die! Don't ever let them send your husband there!

POLLY. Why? Isn't it on our side?

JAN. Yes—but it's awful. Simply awful. Wives *never* go along to Crocker. From camp to the only hotel is twenty miles through a swamp—and that hotel is packed full of wives that are permanent.

POLLY. Permanent *wives*?

JAN. I mean—that live there permanently. Honest—I'd just die! After the way Roy has worked down here, too. I hardly ever got to see him.

POLLY. Really?

JAN. Oh, they just work all the time. It's awfully hard. Of course, if you're young, it isn't so bad. But it was terrible for Roy. He's *twenty-five*.

POLLY. Oh.

JAN. A friend of Roy's in the Surgeon General's Department said that over twenty-one you don't absorb any more. You simply don't absorb a thing.

POLLY. Well, mercy. What about Max then? He's going on forty.

JAN. He is? Oh, well, he's special. Would you like a drink?

POLLY. Well, this'll surprise you. *Yes.*

Jan fishes into her traveling case and brings out a small peculiarly shaped medicinal bottle.

JAN. Here we are.

Polly, curious about the bottle, comes closer and looks at it. The label reads: PEROXIDE.

POLLY. Oh, I hadn't thought of peroxide.

JAN. Oh, no. I just put what we had left in the bottle to travel with. It's really Scotch. (*The phone rings. Jan goes for it.*) Excuse me. (*She picks up the phone.*) Hello? . . . Yes . . . Oh, just a moment . . . (*To Polly*) It's for you. It's New York.

Jan hands Polly the phone and then goes to the kitchenette concealed in the back wall, opening the doors to reveal it.

POLLY (*taking the phone; to Jan*). Thank you. (*Into the phone*) Yes? . . . No, Mr. Wharton isn't here now. This is *Mrs.* Wharton. Who is calling please? . . . Oh, well, would you ask Mr. Gow if he would like to speak to Mrs. Wharton . . . Yes, I'll hold on.

During the above, as Polly stares at the kitchenette, Jan has gotten four lily cups, nested two and two—also an empty milk bottle. She brings the lily cups to the end table near the phone.

JAN. I guess we haven't got anything to go with this. Just only water.

POLLY. Oh, that'll be fine. (*A little bewildered, as Jan starts for the bedroom*) I said—water'll be fine.

JAN. That's what I'm going to get. It's out here in the bathroom. None of the bungalows have sinks in the kitchens.

Jan goes toward the bathroom, via the bedroom. Polly stares at this extraordinary kitchenette.

JAN'S VOICE (*from the bedroom*). Isn't it crazy? A kitchen without a sink?

POLLY (*mumbling*). What'll they think of next? (*Then, into the phone*) Yes, operator—No, I'm not calling anyone. They're calling *me*, you said . . . All right, I'll be right here.

She hangs up. Jan emerges from the bedroom with the milk bottle.

JAN. Here we are. Help yourself.

During the following, Polly pours two drinks into the lily cups, giving one to Jan.

JAN. I remember the first book of yours I ever read—*The Whispering Town*. Your own life, wasn't it?

POLLY. Sort of.

JAN. Both those men?

POLLY. Uh—no, not that part.

JAN. But you did work on a newspaper.

POLLY. Oh, yes.

JAN. Mr. Wharton's?

POLLY. That's right. Some feature writing. On politics and things. I stayed just long enough to marry the editor.

Jan laughs. Polly raises her cup.

POLLY. Well—to 26-D—sink or no sink.

They drink. Polly falls back onto the sofa. She is tired and bewildered.

JAN. I hope you're going to like it here. It's the best bungalow in the Court. Of course, if you aren't just terribly careful, there *are* moths. And, oh, yes—there's no shower.

The refrigerator starts to whine and cough and clatter.

POLLY. No shower? Oh, well—

JAN (*pointing; raising her voice*). The roof *used* to leak something awful, but Roy fixed it—

POLLY. Good for him— (*Then, indicating the refrigerator*) What's that?

JAN. Refrigerator. It used to be worse, but Roy fixed that, too.

POLLY. Noisy, isn't it?

JAN. Yes, but at least when it does that— (*the noise stops; Jan goes on shouting*) —you know it's working. (*Dead silence, then both laugh.*) Did I tell you about the lights? They're sort of peculiar.

She goes toward the bedroom door.

JAN. The one in the bedroom doesn't work from the bedroom. You have to turn it off and on out here. (*She flips the switch to demonstrate.*) And the lights in here are peculiar, too. (*She crosses now to the front door, which is still ajar.*) You have to step *outside* to turn them on and off.

Jan, out on the porch, demonstrates with the light switch outside next to the door frame. Then, entering the living room, she heads for the double window.

POLLY. Very interesting.

JAN. And then there's this window— the only way you can open it is—

She stamps her foot on the floor near the window in several places, searching for the right spot. On her third attempt the window flies open. She indicates it with a gesture of triumph.

POLLY. Does it close the same way?

JAN. No, you just— (*She reaches out and closes the window.*)

POLLY. Well! And where is the place your skirts blow up?

JAN. Your skirts? (*Then she "gets it."*) Oh—!

A voice breaks in on them:

ROY'S VOICE. Honey!

Roy Lupton comes bounding in. He is a one-day-old Second Lieutenant— young, handsome, energetic. He is waving a large envelope as he comes in.

JAN. Roy! (*She points at Polly.*) Darling! Look! It's Paula Wharton!

ROY. Oh, my gosh! How do you do. Your husband's in the next bunch.

POLLY. I believe so.

JAN. Roy—where do we go?

ROY (*indicating the envelope*). I don't know. We have to open it together. (*He pushes the envelope at her.*) Go ahead, honey. Hurry up.

JAN. No, honey—*you* do it.

ROY. No, you.

POLLY. Please—*some*body!

Jan tears the envelope open and reads.
She groans.

JAN. Oh—Roy—no! (*At this, Roy grabs the paper and reads.*)

ROY. Crocker Field, Arkansas! Oh, my gosh!

JAN. Roy—go and talk to them. Tell them you're married. Tell them I just couldn't live there.

ROY. Sweetheart—in the Army you *can't* talk to them. You just have to do it.

JAN. Even a Second Lieutenant?

ROY. Honey—this is one place you just can't go. You've got to go back to Kansas City.

JAN (*clinging to him fiercely*). You'll be going overseas right after. I won't see you again.

ROY. Now, sweetheart—that's silly. Listen—you can go on the same train with me as far as Arkansas. It's on the way. And Jake loaned me his car to get us down to the station. Train leaves eight o'clock! (*He looks at his watch.*) Oh, my gosh—we've got to get started! Come on, honey—get everything together.

Jan flies to the open bags and starts to put away the last small articles. At the same instant the phone rings, and Polly goes for it.

POLLY. That's probably for me. You go right ahead.

JAN. Oh, Roy—get the war over quick, huh?

ROY. You're telling me!

POLLY (*into the phone*). Yes, operator. . . . Well, if you find Mr. Gow, you call me. And if *I* find him, I'll call *you.*

As she hangs up, Max appears in the doorway—wearing the summer uniform of the Officers' Candidate School and overseas cap.

MAX. Polly!

Polly whirls, her eyes open wide—and she makes a rush for his outspread arms.

POLLY. Max—darling!

MAX (*kissing her violently*). I didn't know you were here!

POLLY (*excitedly looking him over*). Baby—I—I wouldn't know you—you —you look wonderful—!

MAX (*grabbing her again*). Polly—

POLLY (*holding him off*). Max—I can't get over it—that *tan*— (*pressing his arms*) —and *muscles!*

MAX (*laughing*). That basic training, honey—you know, that's done outdoors! (*He grabs her again.*) When did you get here?

POLLY. Right now—

MAX (*holding her tight*). Polly—am I glad to see you—!

POLLY (*remembering the Luptons*). Oh, Max—

JAN. Mr. Wharton! I should have known who you were this afternoon —but I just didn't realize— (*Then indicating Roy*) My husband—*Lieutenant* Lupton.

Roy takes a step toward Max—and Max comes eagerly to Roy. They shake hands.

ROY. It's sure great to meet you and your wife.

MAX. Thank you, sir.

JAN. Oh!

ROY (*as they all turn in alarm to Jan*). What's the matter, honey?

JAN. Excuse me—but that's the first time I ever heard anyone call Roy "sir."

POLLY. Shouldn't he have saluted?

ROY (*very seriously*). Oh, no. Only when we meet outdoors. Indoors he isn't required to.

POLLY. Well, we can step outside and then he can. (*Roy and Jan laugh. Then Roy jumps.*)

ROY. I'm sorry, but we've got to push off! We'll miss that train!

MAX. Can I give you a hand with your bags, sir?

ROY. Thanks.

He pushes the heavier suitcase and khaki folding bag down to Max, who picks them up.

ROY. That's very nice of you.

Max is staggering under his load. The khaki folding bag is very heavy. Roy picks up the little cosmetic bag. He follows Max. Max stops at the door to let the lieutenant go out ahead of him. A closeup of POLLY shows her, with lifted eyebrows, watching Max with his load.

JAN'S VOICE. Well, I guess I've got everything.

Jan is next seen rushing back to the kitchenette.

JAN. I left a few things in the kitchenette. They weren't enough to pack— and too good to throw away. (*Pointing out the items*) Just some crackers and cereal biscuits, and some dried-up fruit cake, and ketchup and—

POLLY. Oh, thank you.

Roy and Max come charging back in, deep in conversation.

ROY. —a darn sight worse than techniques of zone reconnaissance.

MAX. They are, sir?

Roy picks up the loaded and very heavy duffle bag and swings it onto Max's shoulder. Max's knees buckle a bit.

ROY. Sure. There's lots of things you can bog down on, all right.

Max is staggering toward the door under the load, Roy following with his fingertips under the bag, ready to catch it if it should fall. Polly follows Max's progress, in imagination carrying the load with him, swaying when he sways.

JAN. Oh, I didn't tell you about ants. There isn't a single ant in this bungalow. People say there must be, but there aren't because I always keep a little pinch of salt in that cup up there— (*pointing to the refrigerator*) —and it keeps them away.

POLLY. Do you think it's that? I think they're scared of the moths.

Jan is putting on her hat before the hanging mirror. Roy and Max are in again. Roy is saying:

ROY. —to identify a hundred and thirty-seven enemy aircraft in less than one tenth of a second each.

MAX. Wow!

Roy takes off his hat and mops his brow as if he had been working.

ROY. Well, that's it. (*To Jan*) Are you ready, darling?

JAN. I guess so.

She grabs her purse. Roy shakes Polly's hand—then Max's.

ROY. Goodbye.

POLLY. Goodbye.

MAX. Goodbye, Lieutenant. Nice trip.

ROY (*as he shakes hands*). So long. And don't let it get you. Wade right into it.

MAX. Thank you, sir.

JAN (*to Polly*). Well, goodbye. It's been just wonderful.

POLLY. Good luck. And thanks for letting me in before the doors opened.

JAN. Goodbye, Mr. Wharton.

Roy and Jan go out and Max and Polly follow them to the front door, watching as they run down the walk to the jalopy that waits at the curb, and pile in. In the back of the car is the luggage that Max had hauled. Roy starts the car up. It snorts and roars. Jan waves toward the bungalow.

JAN. Bye-e-e!

We see Max and Polly still standing on the tiny front porch of the bungalow, waving back.

POLLY. Bye!

MAX. Good trip!

We get a full view of the STREET as the jalopy starts off—bucking and snorting —and Jan, who is still waving, nearly loses her arm as the car jerks off. Then MAX and POLLY are again seen as they wave the car out of sight, the car noise receding. They turn to each other and Max takes her in his arms.

MAX. Polly—where have you been?

POLLY. Oh, angel, am I really here? Or are we writing all this in a letter? In a moving view we see TWO OFFICER CANDIDATES on the SIDEWALK. They walk along, look off, and pause. Suddenly, they whistle, the regulation U.S. Army sex whistle, following which, from the

candidates' point of view, we see the bungalow. Max and Polly are silhouetted against the open, lighted doorway —in each other's arms, as the whistling continues.

MAX and POLLY, in a fairly close view, separate, realizing they are on exhibition. Max looks back into the room.

MAX. Fine thing—right here in a lighted doorway.

Without Max's noticing, Polly reaches up to the electric switch which we know to be out on the porch.

MAX. Hey!

POLLY (*as she snuggles up to him*). Well, that's good, isn't it?

MAX. The fuse blew!

Polly now switches the lights on and off as Max watches amazed.

POLLY. Uh-uh. They work from out here.

MAX. What's the idea?

POLLY. Maybe it's to help make conversation—or if you don't like the guests, you can always blow a fuse.

Max, smiling, is about to take her in his arms, then remembering the street, grabs her and pulls her inside.

We see the LIVING ROOM as they enter and Max closes the door. The minute they are inside, he pulls her into his arms.

MAX. Polly—you were crazy to come down here—

POLLY (*snuggling*). Sure—sure—

MAX. No kidding, angel—look at this place. It's the only thing I could get for you anywhere near the field.

POLLY. I think it's lovely.

MAX (*dryly*). It's the big rooms I like.

POLLY. I'm mad about it.

MAX. You're going to be all alone in it, sweetheart. I've got to live in the dormitory—strict schedules. I thought the *other* camp routine was strict—but this is terrific. We'll be lucky to have an hour a week together. And Florida in summer. Polly—why do you want to do this?

POLLY. Well, dames are funny—holding on to what they have just as long as they can.

MAX. You're no dame. You're different.

POLLY. I don't want to be different. I want to be like those other girls—with *their* fellas.

Suddenly, from the Field, comes the bugle sounding "Tattoo." Max jumps.

MAX. I've got to go back pretty quick.

POLLY. Was that for you?

MAX. No. But you see, honey—my feet were killing me—I got permission to run over here and change my socks—

POLLY. Isn't it good my train was on time? I wouldn't want to miss *that*.

MAX (*with a quick laugh*). Yeah—(*Then rapidly*) You see, darling—I thought I'd leave a few things over here—a few shirts and socks—so at least you'd know I was around—

POLLY (*lightly*). Having your socks around—how sweet!

Max pushes out of her arms and starts for the bedroom.

MAX. I've got to be back in *reasonable* time, honey. I'd better get busy—

POLLY. And I'd like to get out of these clothes, Max. I'm steaming. Take the big bag in for me, will you?

Max goes for the big bag. Polly enters the bedroom, already taking off her jacket. Max, bending over the bag, is conscious that his blouse pocket button is not fastened. In fastening the button, he is next conscious of the manual in that pocket. He grabs it out suddenly and turns to a page. He begins to mumble.

MAX. "Airplane chemical bombs are used to disperse agents of varying persistency—and require protective measures—"

He reads the next page quickly to himself, then covers the page and tries to repeat it, his face screwed up.

MAX. "White phosphorus is used as standard filling in the seventy-five millimeter, one hundred-five millimeter and one hundred—uh—" (*taking a peek*) "—and one hundred forty-five millimeter—"

POLLY'S VOICE. Ma-ax!

Max jumps, grabs up the bag and starts for the bedroom. He tries again as he goes.

MAX. "—is used as standard filling in the seventy-five millimeter, one hundred—uh—"

We see the BEDROOM as Max comes in and dumps the bag on the bed.

MAX. Dog-gone! Stick in the same place every time!

POLLY. *What* sticks, darling?

MAX (*indicating the book*). This—this. Just one of *thirty-three* subjects you have to know cold. And no time to learn 'em.

During the following, Polly gets pajamas and negligee and mules out of the valise.

POLLY. Not worse than that basic training!

MAX. Sweetheart—against this, basic training was a lark. You got used to that. That was just forcing yourself into new physical habits. It can be done—even at my age—if you just hang on. But, darling—this is the works.

POLLY (*entering the bathroom with her things*). Thirty-three subjects! That sounds like a short history of the world.

MAX (*sitting on the bed heavily*). And all the cleaning, scrubbing, polishing, drilling—that goes right on. Boy—this was a day! (*He falls back on the bed.*)

POLLY'S VOICE. Tell me about it, Max.

MAX. At the crack of dawn—inspection. Spot on my shirt—didn't even see it. Five demerits. Then we had a quiz. You have to get eighty-nine to pass. Know what I got?

POLLY'S VOICE. What?

MAX. Eighty-nine.

POLLY'S VOICE. Well, that's good, isn't it?

MAX. And regimental review this afternoon. Stood at attention for an hour. You can wiggle your toes and move your eyeballs—and that's all. Saw the neck of the fellow ahead of me turn brick red in the sun. Then it started to go white—his neck, I mean—and bam!—he falls flat on his face. Along comes the meat wagon and picks him up—

POLLY (*emerging from the bathroom in negligee*). Meat wagon?

MAX (*mumbling*). Ambulance—

Then he sees her, and his eyes fasten on her. She comes toward the bed to him.

POLLY. What a thing to call it!

MAX (*reaching his arms up for her; then, softly*). Polly—holy smoke—I —I forgot what you were like. (*A pause; then*) You didn't get here a minute too soon, sweetheart. Don't leave me 'til you have to.

POLLY (*in his arms*). When's that?

MAX. Depends on where I go for advanced training.

POLLY. Any place but Crocker Field, Max. Wives can't go. I just won't *have* Crocker Field.

MAX (*suddenly holding her tight, and speaking rather dramatically*). Polly—

POLLY (*softly*). Yes, Max—?

MAX. I wouldn't have done it unless I thought I was right.

POLLY. Done what?

MAX. Leave the paper.

POLLY. Is that worrying you, Max?

MAX. No and yes. What do you think?

POLLY. That can wait, can't it, dear?

MAX. No—let me tell you, Polly—

He is on his feet suddenly, under the drive of his thoughts on the subject. Polly can only sit and watch him.

MAX. —I began to think of the ten million men in the Army—and their families. That's a big part of this country's population. What about those people when the war is over? You don't think they're going to settle back into their old ruts? They'll have new ideas about how this country should be run—and the world too. There's a big change coming up, Polly. Any decent newspaperman worth his salt should keep up with it. What would I know sitting at a desk getting my information second-hand? I belong in the middle of it —with the people it's happening *to*. Not for any personal glory. You know that. But to give the paper some authority in the future—when we come to talk about reorganizing the world—and what kind of peace we want—and how to make it stick. If I've been in it, I'll have earned the right to talk my head off—and what's more—I'll know what I'm talking about. (*He stops.*) You see what I mean?

POLLY (*thoughtfully*). Uh-huh.

MAX. Well, what do you think?

POLLY. Nothing.

MAX. I never caught you without an opinion yet. Come on, Polly—I've got to know what you think.

POLLY (*carefully*). Well—you were right, Max—except—there's a home front. They're fighting this war too —and they're going to help make the future. It's important they know what it's all about. You put in five years making the *Bulletin* a paper they listen to. If your leaving it now means that an influence like that might fold up and disappear—

MAX. That's right, darling—and the paper *can't* fold. If I didn't think Kennedy could do the job, I would never have walked out. (*Then suddenly*) Or are you trying to say you don't think Kennedy can?

POLLY. If *you* think he can—then that's all there is to it.

MAX (*eagerly*). In fact, Polly—

POLLY (*rather sharply*). Max!

MAX. What?

POLLY (*smiling*). Max—that's *all* we're going to say about the paper.

MAX (*smiling and going to her again; taking her in his arms*). I'm sorry, baby. (*He kisses her; then, softly in her ear*) I—I've got to change my socks, sweetheart.

POLLY (*softly*). I know.

MAX (*very softly*). A man can get a lot of demerits for being late—

POLLY (*softly*). That'd be dreadful, wouldn't it?

Suddenly there is a sharp rapping on the bedroom window outside, and a woman's voice.

WOMAN'S VOICE. Yoo-hoo!

Max and Polly are startled out of their skins. Polly half jumps up.

POLLY (*yelling*). Yes, yes—what is it?

WOMAN'S VOICE. Movies! Are you coming, Jan?

POLLY (*answering in a high shrill voice, in imitation of Jan*). Not to-night, honey. Thanks just the same.

WOMAN'S VOICE. Okey-doke!

Polly smiles at Max; the imitation evidently succeeded.

MAX. Chummy little community, isn't it?

POLLY. Kitchen window, bedroom window—it's just wonderful. (*Then she turns back to the business of Max.*) Are demerits very serious, baby?

MAX (*very seriously*). Well—yes and no. (*Then suddenly*) What's *wrong* with Kennedy?

POLLY. Darling, I didn't say—

MAX. You as good as said it. Come on, tell me.

POLLY. For heaven's sake, darling— I was only thinking—you have a genius for making people indignant —you call skullduggery as you see it. You don't pull punches. Kennedy is on the careful side. And there's a touch of Pollyanna in him that makes him a little naïve about people's motives—

MAX. But Gow'll be there—and the rest of the boys.

POLLY. Well, sure. And things have been going along well for weeks and weeks. You've seen the paper?

MAX. At first. Then I just couldn't keep up with the paper and march ten miles a day. So the paper was out. (*Then suddenly*) You mean about Kennedy—if some big issue comes up—

POLLY. Max—if that happens, Gow and the boys are *still* there.

MAX. Yeah—exactly—Then why question Kennedy?

POLLY. *Who* questioned Ken—? (*Then softly*) Max—darling—who is Kennedy?

MAX (*smiling*). Never heard of him. (*As Max reaches to take her in his arms, he again suspends himself.*) If Gow has any notion he's going to yell for me when something happens—

POLLY. He hasn't so far, Max—

MAX. I know. But I could tell from that sweet farewell. He will. He's a mule, you know—a maniac.

POLLY. I know he is.

MAX (*in sudden reversal*). But a pretty wonderful guy. •

POLLY. All right. We'll build a monument to him.

MAX. If I had no time for the paper before—*now* it's out of the question.

I don't want to hear about it. I don't want to *see* it!

POLLY (*seizing Max with force*). Max, we won't have it in the house. And if Gow comes near the place, I'll shoot him dead!

She kisses him hard. As Max is about to succumb, for the third or fourth time, there is a knocking from the next room. They separate, looking at each other. Polly rises grimly and starts for the living room.

POLLY. I'll get rid of *that*.

As she walks out, Max suddenly starts to unlace his shoes. Then the LIVING ROOM is seen as Polly crosses to the front door. The lights have been left on. A few more bangs on the door are heard as Polly enters and opens it. There stand the Luptons. A wind has whipped up outdoors.

POLLY. Well! How was Arkansas?

JAN. Oh, isn't this awful.

POLLY (*as her negligee is being blown about*). Come in.

Jan enters, carrying the small, blue cosmetic bag. Roy follows. Polly slams the door shut against the wind.

JAN. That train! Eight hours late!

ROY. Won't be here 'til five o'clock in the morning.

Max is seen standing in the bedroom door in stocking feet.

MAX. Hello—

JAN (*looking down at Max's stockinged feet*). Oh, my goodness—!

POLLY. Quite all right. (*Pointedly; for Max*) We were discussing the *Bulletin*. He always does that in his socks. (*Then; also to Max*) Their train—eight hours late.

ROY. We came back to the Court—we thought they'd maybe let us use a bungalow just for the night.

JAN. And there isn't a thing—not a thing.

There is a long pause. Max looks at Polly, but she turns away and looks out through the window at the storm. Finally Max gives a low whistle and Polly turns to him. He pantomimes to her that something's got to be done, but Polly turns to see what the Luptons are going to do about it. Jan has been watching the pantomiming out of the corner of her eye, and Polly gets caught in her gesturing and assumes a pose of nonchalance. Jan edges over to Roy and, moving her lips without sound, pantomimes that they leave. But Roy spreads his hands as if to say "where can we go?" Max and Polly are very eagerly watching the pantomime. Suddenly Jan is aware of this and motions to Roy that Polly and Max are watching them. The two women laugh nervously at their embarrassment. Finally Max, who tries one more low whistle at Polly, is getting desperate. Now on inspiration, he looks at his watch and realizes a very obvious fact.

MAX. Hey, look! I've got to go right back to the field anyway—

JAN. Oh, no!

MAX. Why, sure—!

POLLY (*with a glance at Max*). Of course—he just had a *reasonable* time off, you see.

Max goes to the sofa, lifting the slip cover and revealing a sheet and khaki blanket.

MAX. This makes up into a bed, doesn't it? And there's a bedroom in there—

JAN. You don't mean Mrs. Wharton on the sofa?

POLLY. I'll just love it.

JAN. No, honest. We couldn't.

POLLY. Now where are you going to find a place like this? It's away from it all and at the same time in touch with everything—

MAX. There you are! (*To Roy*) Let's get the bags in. Are they outside?

Max heads for outdoors in his stocking feet, Roy following.

ROY. This sure doesn't seem right.

POLLY. Your shoes, Max!

But Max is gone. Polly flies into the bedroom, evidently to get the shoes. Jan follows a few steps.

JAN. Gee, Mrs. Wharton, are you sure—?

POLLY (*coming out of the bedroom with Max's shoes*). I'll love it! . . .

JAN. But it seems an awful imposition at a time like this.

Polly's eyes bug out as she sees Max staggering in with the duffle bag over his shoulder and carrying the khaki folding bag in his other hand. Roy follows him, carrying nothing.

ROY. Yeah, but if you take Aircraft Structures, Terminology and Theory of Flight—you don't have to take Elementary Aero-Dynamics.

MAX (*dropping the load with a grunt*). You mean Aircraft Structures, Terminology and Theory of Flight make up for it.

ROY. Certainly.

Polly comes forward, pressing the shoes into Max's hand. Max takes them somewhat absently, at the same time saying:

MAX (*to Roy*). But what about chartings and findings?

Max starts for the door with his shoes in his hands, Roy following him.

ROY. Chartings, findings and soundings. (*Both men are now out.*)

POLLY. Are they speaking English?

JAN. It's Army. They have to or else they'd never learn it.

POLLY. You know, when this war is over, won't we know a pack of useless stuff?

Now Max enters again, carrying the last bag in one hand and his shoes in the other. Roy follows, his hands empty.

ROY. —but when you get through the Rollitts Interceptor, that's nothing, because then you're into interceptor alignments and interceptor variants in reverse. (*Indicating a bag to Jan*) Well, there it all is, darling.

MAX. Sounds like a tough course, all right. (*He looks at Polly, who points to his shoes and then to his feet.*) Oh, I think I'll put my shoes on.

POLLY. That's up to you, dear. We're very informal here.

Max starts to put on his shoes. (From this point on, the two conversations—between Jan and Polly, and between Roy and Max—are spoken together.)

JAN (*to Polly*). Oh, I forgot to tell you about shopping. There're only two stores—Dale's and Hutchinson's. At Hutchinson's you can get anything—meat, vegetables—anything. Only it's awfully crowded and you have to wait for hours.

POLLY. Uh-huh.

JAN. You have to carry everything home yourself. They don't deliver.

POLLY. Well, what about the other store? What's it like?

JAN. Oh, they're lovely. And they deliver.

POLLY. Fine!

JAN. Only they haven't got anything.

During the above, Max and Roy are heard conversing.

ROY. The course is not really so tough. The bare technical side of it isn't as important as realizing how it all hooks up. (*At this point, Roy has seen the manual on the table.*) Say, this manual's no good.

MAX. What!

ROY. There's a new directive washes all this stuff out.

MAX. Holy smoke—and I'm breakin' my head over it!

ROY. Oh, well, most of it's the same.

Max has just finished lacing his shoes. He stands up.

MAX. Well—I'd better start back, Polly—

POLLY. Oh, Max.

Polly goes to him. Max puts the manual in his pocket and picks up his cap.

POLLY. When'll I see you?

MAX. I don't know, darling. I'll try.

He puts his arm around Polly and starts walking toward the door, calling back:

MAX. So long, folks.

ROY. Goodnight—and thanks.

JAN. Thanks ever so much.

At the door Max embraces and kisses Polly and is gone quickly. Polly closes the door, and turns.

POLLY. He's nice. Let's have him over again.

JAN. Gosh, he's wonderful. Is he really almost forty?

POLLY. Yes, he really is. We've been everywhere about it but there's nothing they can do.

ROY. We ought to let you get to bed. You must be awfully tired after traveling all the way from California.

POLLY. I suppose I am.

ROY. Our train's at five. We'll leave very quietly. You won't hear a thing.

POLLY. Oh, don't mind me at all. If you'll just get my bag out of the bedroom, Lieutenant—

JAN (*as Roy heads for the bedroom*). You take the bedroom. Please do. It's yours.

POLLY (*sitting quickly on the sofa, holding it tightly*). Oh, no. No, really —this is mine. One, two, three—for me.

JAN. Honestly, Mrs. Wharton—I just hate to do this.

POLLY. Why, for goodness sake, you have that stuffy, little room. And look at the big, airy room I've got.

Roy comes lumbering in under the weight of Polly's big suitcase. As Polly sees him come in, she says somewhat under her breath:

POLLY. Too bad Max isn't here to help. (*Then quickly*) That's just fine. Thanks ever so much.

JAN (*to Roy*). Bring the blue bag, darling. (*To Polly*) Goodnight, Mrs. Wharton—and thank you very much.

ROY (*following Jan to the bedroom, carrying the blue suitcase*). Goodnight.

POLLY. Goodnight. (*They have entered the bedroom and closed the door.*)

Polly, alone, sits thinking for a moment. Then she lifts the end of the slip cover and takes it off the sofa, rolling it up and putting it on the arm of a chair. Now she comes back and examines the patched army khaki blanket. Between thumb and forefinger, she lifts the blanket off gingerly and drops it over another chair. Then she opens her suitcase and takes out a pale, blue Aspery shawl and a lacy, round pillow. She spreads out the shawl to make a blanket, puts the little lacy pillow in place. Now she takes out several articles needed for the night— her black eyeshade, her box of pink cotton. These she deposits on the shelf of the lamp stand, at the head of her sofa bed. Then she takes out a toothbrush in a glass holder and toothpaste. With the toothbrush and paste in her hands, she takes an involuntary step toward the bedroom. She is about to take hold of the doorknob but thinks better of it. Instead, she goes back to the kitchenette, takes out her toothbrush and spreads toothpaste on it. She begins to brush her teeth vigorously. (*The wind has increased in velocity and is howling outside.*)

Having brushed her teeth awhile, she pauses suddenly. There is no water! How will she rinse her mouth!? She spies the pint milk bottle in which Jan had brought some water from the bathroom. Slightly frantic, she finds that it is empty. All this time her mouth is bulging with toothpaste foam. In this growing desperation, her eyes light on the peroxide bottle containing the Scotch. What else can she do? She takes the bottle up, goes toward the kitchenette and pours it into a Lily Cup. With sudden determination, she takes a mouthful of the "peroxide." The next crisis hits her suddenly. Where is she going to get rid of this mouthful? She rushes to the big window and tries the handle. It won't open! Then she remembers how Jan did it. She begins to rush about in a small area, stamping once—twice—three times—with one foot. It won't open. Really frantic now, she jumps hard with both feet—and the window flies open! She leaps for the window. The wind howls and the curtains blow up. With difficulty she closes the window.

Well, that's that! She's ready for bed. She comes down to the sofa and starts to unbutton her negligee. As she reaches the third button, we hear "Taps" from the Field.

POLLY (*to the unseen bugler*). All right, all right—don't rush me!

She removes her negligee disclosing a dainty pair of pajamas. She takes off her mules. Now, with great care, she pulls back the sheet and shawl, smoothing the undersheet. She climbs into bed and arranges herself. She has just begun to relax in this bed which she distrusts when suddenly the refrigerator sets up a terrific clatter. She takes pink cotton out of the box and stuffs it in her ears. Just then the noise stops. She listens hard at this point to see if she can hear the refrigerator—but no! the cotton seems to work. She is quite pleased about this. We are the only ones who know the refrigerator has stopped. She reaches up and pulls the cord on the lamp stand. This light goes out—but the main lights are still on. The switch for this room is outside. Damnation! Now she must get up, put on her mules, and go to the door.

In a moving view of POLLY we see her reaching the door, then pulling it open.

The wind whips at her as she reaches around, trying to find the switch while still remaining for the most part inside the room. This doesn't work. So, very boldly, she rushes out through the door onto the porch, feeling quickly for the switch. At this moment a big gust of wind slams the door shut.

Next we see Polly out on the PORCH. The door is locked. Polly begins to knock at the door, groaning against the cold wind which lashes her. She knocks and knocks and turns the lights on, off, on, off, hoping foolishly that this will be a signal for someone. At this instant, from a slight distance away, we hear male voices:

MALE VOICES (*singing*). "Off we go, into the wide, blue yonder—Climbing high, into the sun—"

And we see THE WALK. There are three officer candidates singing as they walk. Suddenly they spot Polly.

Then from the CANDIDATES' point of view we see Polly being whipped by the wind, a lovely figure in her pajamas. The THREE CANDIDATES are next seen closely.

CANDIDATES. Hi ya, kid! Yoo hoo!

POLLY is seen closer as the male calls come over. Her predicament is horrible.

The OFFICER CANDIDATES continue yelling—but suddenly, looking off, their yells freeze. Several steps from them, having paused in his walk, is Colonel Foley—elderly, erect, very military. His glance travels from them to the extraordinary spectacle of Polly in negligee. The candidates gulp, salute, and slink off. Colonel Foley now turns his puzzled attention to the lady in distress.

Back in the BEDROOM the young Luptons, getting ready for bed, are astonished by the racket beyond the living room. Jan is in negligee. Roy's tunic is off and his shirt-tails are out.

Outside the BUNGALOW we get a close view of COLONEL FOLEY. He starts for Polly—his face expressing honest concern mixed with a slight question as to the lady's moral status.

POLLY, seen closely, is pounding and yelling; switching the lights on and off.

POLLY. Hey! Jan! Roy! (*She sees the Colonel coming toward her—and is terrified.*)

Inside the BUNGALOW: Jan and Roy burst out of the bedroom, looking around excitedly.

JAN. Mrs. Wharton?! Are you all right?!

They are aware that the knocking comes from outside. Shirt-tails flying, Roy dashes for the door.

The PORCH: The Colonel has approached Polly. They get a good look at each other. The Colonel, embarrassed, starts to speak:

COLONEL. Is there something I can—?

He breaks off as the bungalow door is opened from the inside by Roy. Polly dashes in, bumping Roy harshly, and slams the door shut. The Colonel shrugs and moves off. The bungalow lights, on Polly's last switch, are off.

In the LIVING ROOM: Polly, a little breathless, is indicating the outside.

POLLY. And—off I went, into the wide blue yonder!

Roy is staring at her sleeping outfit. He gulps with embarrassment—tries to tuck up his loose shirt-tails—and

dashes for the bedroom. Polly goes to her bed and takes off her mules.

POLLY. They ought to have a couch out there, just in case. Oh—and the wolves in this neighborhood—all ages! How their eyes shine in the dark!

JAN. Yes—well, goodnight—again.

POLLY (*who has crept into bed and tucked herself in*). Goodnight.

Jan goes out, closing the bedroom door. Polly plugs her ears again with cotton.

POLLY (*testing for audibility*). Hello —hello—hello—

The bedroom door opens. Roy sticks his head in fast, meanwhile getting another good look at Polly.

ROY. Did you say something, Mrs. Wharton? (*Polly smiles and shakes her head.*)

JAN'S VOICE. Roy!

Roy ducks his head back in and closes the door fast. Polly, all snug now, reaches for the lamp stand and puts out the light.

POLLY (*softly; with a sigh*). Bless Mommy and Daddy—

Instantly the phone rings, two short rings. Polly, annoyed, pulls the light on again and reaches for the phone.

POLLY (*into the phone*). Hello?— What?—Well, speak up!

Then she realizes she has cotton in her ears. She removes it.

POLLY. Yes?—Oh—uh—well—is Mr. Gow *really* on the line?—Robert? It's me—Polly.

GOW, in a close view, is seen in his office at night. He is at his desk.—A desk lamp illuminates the scene. His coat is off, his collar open. He has been hard at work.

GOW. Hello, Polly! When did *you* get there?—Uh-huh—Oh, I'm great —just great. Is Max around?

POLLY is seen at the phone.

GOW at the phone:

POLLY. No, lamby. He had to go back to the field. Why?

GOW (*in faint irritation*). I've *got* to *talk* to him. I've held off for months —while the paper's been losing a little ground every day. The time's come when I've got to discuss it with Max. When'll he be back?

POLLY at the phone: Her voice becomes a little hard.

POLLY. There's no telling, Robert. He's in and out of here like a morning glory. You better make up your mind—he isn't going to be a bit of use to you from now on. . . . You heard me, lamby. In fact, as far as the paper is concerned, he doesn't want to hear about it—he doesn't even want to see it!

We get a closeup of GOW at the phone getting steamed up, his voice turning acid.

GOW. How quaint of Max! Walks out on this whole responsibility—and now, if you please, he wouldn't care to be annoyed!

POLLY is seen in a closeup at the phone, her temper gradually rising.

POLLY. Don't be stupid! Deep inside, he's yearning over that paper like an anguished mother. But he's got a terrible headache on his hands down here. . . . Well, who *hasn't* got headaches. It's war. *I've* got a kitchen where the water is in the bathroom. If you had the proper respect for what Max is trying to do. . . . Listen, will you stop trading on my lovable disposition and be sensible!

GOW appears in another closeup, uncorking explosively.

GOW. When I've got to talk to Max, I've got to talk to him! And when it happens I really need Max, I'm going to have him!

We again see the BUNGALOW LIVING ROOM with POLLY at the phone.

POLLY. Listen, Robert—if you butt in down here, I'll kill you. Next to Max I love you more than anything in the world—but I swear I'll tear you apart with my two bare hands— you bull-headed old—

The refrigerator sets up a sudden, terrific clatter, drowning out the last word, which is undoubtedly censorable. She hangs up with a bang—stuffs the cotton in her ears, and puts out the lamp with a violent pull.

POLLY (*with a forced, sweet smile*). Bless Mommy and Daddy, and make me a good girl!

She falls back, cuddles up in her bed, as the scene fades out.

# PART TWO

A montage fades in contrasting the events and duties in the lives of Polly and Max during the succeeding weeks.

POLLY, the housewife, wearing a dust cap made of a colorful scarf, is tackling the double bed in the bedroom, dusting, scouring the washbasin, washing clothes in the bathtub, sewing material for a new sofa cover and new curtains, and scrubbing the floor on her hands and knees.

MAX, in contrast, is making his dormitory bed, washing out socks in his washbasin, polishing the metal bathroom fixtures, polishing his buckles, polishing his shoes, sewing on a button. (Always, he is reading his books. We see him scrubbing the floor, pushing the book ahead of him.)

POLLY is trying to cook.—She is bathed in steam.—She is burning her fingers on hot handles.

MAX is working like a fiend in classes. He is being hazed as he walks on the field's sidewalks. A sergeant or lieutenant brings him to attention: "Suck your gut!" and "Rack your back!"— "You're a poor excuse for a soldier! What makes you think you're fit for anything?"—They put rapid questions to him on Infantry Drill Regulation.— We see him exercising, drilling, marching. At the end of this workout we see Max walking across the field, dragging himself along. A young candidate comes up to him.

CANDIDATE. Wharton? (*At this, poor Max comes to smart attention and "sucks his gut."*) Relax. I'm a student—like you. (*He puts his hand out.*) Johnson's my name.

Max collapses with relief and puts out a limp hand.

MAX (*weakly*). Oh. Glad to know you.

CANDIDATE. I'm a reporter on the camp paper. We want to run a story on you. Just who you are and all about you. We do that on all the important students and you're about the top celebrity in camp.

MAX (*awfully weary*). You don't say.

CANDIDATE. We want you to write it yourself.

MAX. My friend, I—I'm not sure I could lift a pencil.

CANDIDATE (*urging*). Make it as short as you like.

MAX. No—you go right ahead. Must be a few facts around in "Who's Who" or someplace. Thanks just the same. (*Max starts to move off wearily.*)

CANDIDATE (*calling after him*). Think it over.

As Max keeps going, waving back with an aimless arm, the scene dissolves to the BUNGALOW COURT. POLLY is seen coming home from market. She is dressed to the hilt. It is certainly incongruous to find her pulling a huge market basket behind her. It is one of those rolling affairs with a handle at one end and two small wheels on the other. The basket is loaded with grocery packages. Polly is entering the short walk that leads to her bungalow. As she approaches, she calls out:

POLLY. Yoo-hoo! Mrs. Collins! Mrs. Dumbrowski! Mrs. Greenberg! Mrs. Clark! Come and get it!

From four bungalows, in a full view, we see four women as they come bustling out. They are four contrasting types, very young to middle-aged. One carries an infant in her arms. A third is followed out by a toddler. They come flying to Polly.

Next, the GROUP is seen fairly close, as Polly begins to fish out packages. The women are saying: "Oh—it's so nice of you, Mrs. Wharton!" "Was anything left?" "I haven't got a drop of milk in the house!"

POLLY. No butter. Not a smidge. Got the milk though—

MRS. GREENBERG. Oh—good!

POLLY. —after I threatened to call out the militia. No meat—

CHORUS. No meat? *Nothing?*

POLLY. Stew—that's all. Beef stew.

CHORUS. What's the matter with that? That's wonderful! Stew will taste like breast of peacock!

POLLY. Well, we're all having it—every darn one of us.

During the above, Polly has been handing out the packages.

POLLY. Mrs. Dumbrowski—carrots—no tomato juice—got vegetable juice instead—

MRS. DUMBROWSKI. That's swell!

POLLY. —celery— (*Then*) Cornflakes, Mrs. Collins—fruit—it's apples—only fruit I couldn't put my thumb through—peas— (*To Mrs. Collins*) Got you beets, too, Mrs. Collins—you said anything that looked healthy—and your soap— (*In triumph*) Oh —cigarettes! (*A yell goes up.*) Boy, what a fight! He says, "Sister, how do I *know* you're getting them for four other dames besides yourself?" I said, "Brother, I'm *telling* you—and one more word out of you, I'll bring all four of 'em over here—and they're all like me!" That did it!

MRS. CLARK. You're wonderful!

MRS. COLLINS. How did you remember everything?

POLLY. Easy. A string on every finger. (*She chucks one of the kids.*) Hi'ya, Mac.

MRS. DUMBROWSKI. Come in and eat with us tonight, Mrs. Wharton.

POLLY. Oh, no! (*Pointing at her basket*) Look at the mess I bought for myself. Girls, I'm cooking again tonight!

CHORUS. No! Really!

POLLY. Honest. I'm getting so I can *eat* it now. (*With a laugh*) To tell you the truth—I've got my husband for dinner tonight.

CHORUS. Good for you! Aw—that's nice.

POLLY. And that isn't all. A *guest.* (*In a confidential whisper*) The most important catch in the camp. I know you'll think I'm boasting.

MRS. GREENBERG. Who? Colonel Foley?

POLLY. No. Max's bunkmate—Frank MacDougal—the man with the highest marks in the whole class.

CHORUS. No! Well, what'd'ya know!

POLLY. Well, I've got to get started. Bye, girls.

She starts for her bungalow. As the others start for theirs, they call back, "Thanks a lot, Mrs. Wharton!" "You're an angel to get my stuff for me!" "Thanks, Mrs. Wharton. I'll do as much for you!"

POLLY. Don't mention it. The Wharton Delivery service makes two trips daily.

POLLY is now seen on her doorstep where she turns and calls out:

POLLY. Oh, girls! If you could spare a minute later on to help me with my stew—

CHORUS. Sure! Just yell!

POLLY. I don't mind poisoning Mac-Dougal—but I love Max!

As Polly pulls her basket up on the

porch, tugging at it, the scene dissolves to the BUNGALOW LIVING ROOM at night. It is full of activity. Two of the women of the previous scene are crowded around the kitchenette with Polly—stirring, tasting, seasoning. A third is putting the finishing touches to the dining table which is really a small side table which has been pulled out into the room.

A close view of the WOMEN AT THE STOVE: Mrs. Dumbrowski is dipping up a spoon of stew gravy and is giving Mrs. Clark a taste. Mrs. Clark nods. Mrs. Greenberg has finished mashing the potatoes and puts them into a serving dish.

MRS. CLARK (*to Polly*). The stew is perfect.

MRS. GREENBERG. Your potatoes are all mashed. Don't forget—put the rolls in to heat just when you sit down.

POLLY. You're the cleverest women I ever met in my life!

MRS. CLARK. Oh, sure—and we write books, too, Mrs. Wharton.

As the others laugh, Mrs. Collins comes bounding in, carrying something under a paper cover.

POLLY. Mrs. Collins! What *have* you done?

MRS. COLLINS (*displaying a pie*). Apple pie.

POLLY. Not a dear little apple pie for me!

MRS. COLLINS. Only it's a miracle if it tastes that way. It's all substitutes—except the apples. (*Mrs. Collins walks back with it to the kitchenette.*)

POLLY. I—don't know what to say. You're all just too wonderful.

She breaks off as the door opens and there, on the threshold, stands Max with a youngish man—Frank Mac-Dougal. The four women drop everything. Max looks around, puzzled. MacDougal is a rather smart, cocky little fellow. Polly rushes into Max's arms.

POLLY. Max!

MAX. Hello, honey.

POLLY (*eyeing MacDougal with big eyes*). And *this*, of course, is—

MAX. Frank—Frank MacDougal.

MAC DOUGAL (*seizing Polly's hand*). Glad to meet you, Mrs. Wharton.

POLLY. Oh, Mr. MacDougal. How nice. Do come in. (*Turning quickly*). Oh, my husband, ladies. Mr. Wharton, Max—Mrs. Collins, Mrs. Greenberg, Mrs. Clark, Mrs. Dumbrowski. Oh—Mr. Frank MacDougal, ladies. Mr. MacDougal—Mrs. Collins, Mrs. Clark, Mrs. Dumbrowski, Mrs. Greenberg.

The men nod and the ladies nod awkwardly, with barely uttered "How-do-you-do's."

POLLY. Our neighbors, Max. (*To MacDougal*) You are the brightest man in the class, aren't you, Mr. Mac-Dougal?

MAC DOUGAL (*cockily, but with humor*). I don't know how I do it, but—there y'are.

POLLY (*to the women; triumphantly*). See?

MRS. DUMBROWSKI. Well, I'll have to be getting back.

OTHER WOMEN. So will I. Me, too. Gee, I've got to get back, too!

The women head for the door, saying: "Nice to have met you, Mr. Wharton."

"Nice to have met you, Mr. Mac-Dougal."

POLLY. Goodbye, girls. Drop in anytime and look at our guests!

The "girls" go out. Max grabs Polly tightly.

MAX. Polly! This is still you, isn't it?

POLLY. Oh, darling—and you're still holding together— (*Then she breaks out of his arms.*) For goodness sake, Max. Come in, Mr. MacDougal. Here—let me have your cap.

Polly is the perfect, if rather fluttery, hostess. She seizes MacDougal's cap. Max has gone toward the kitchenette.

MAC DOUGAL. Thank you. I've certainly heard a lot about you, Mrs. Wharton.

POLLY. And Max certainly talks a lot about you. He hopes whatever makes you bright—is catching.

MAX (*breaking in; from the direction of the stove*). Hey—you mean *you* cooked this stew?

POLLY (*to MacDougal*). Well, now, just listen to him—like he was surprised or something. Just because I never had occasion to cook in our married life.

MAX (*coming over to Polly and throwing his arms around her*). Honey—you're sensational! (*To MacDougal*) You should smell that, Mac—

MAC DOUGAL (*sniffing*). I am.

POLLY (*modestly*). Oh, shucks, boys —just a little thing I whipped up—

MAX. Darling, Mac's got just one hour.

POLLY. Oh—why didn't you say so. —You, too?

MAX. I've got a *couple* of hours.

POLLY (*rushing back toward the stove*). Goody! Well, go on—sit down —I'll have it on in just two minutes. Pull up, fellas.

Max heads for the table. Meanwhile, Polly is at the stove, her hands fluttering, looking perfectly helpless. Not only didn't she cook the meal, but at this moment she doesn't even know how to go about serving it. She goes for the stew, starting to ladle it into a serving dish. Max is now at the table, ready to pull up but MacDougal has stood off from the table some little distance, smiling.

POLLY (*at the stove*). We start with stew, boys. No trimmings. You plow right into it. Don't wait for me.

She now comes toward the table with the dish of stew. Offhandedly, she says to the standing MacDougal:

POLLY. Sit down, Mr. MacDougal.

MAC DOUGAL (*with a smile; lightly*). I'm afraid I can't.

Polly deposits the stew on the table and looks up at Mac. Max also stares up at MacDougal.

MAX. What's wrong, Mac? What'd'ya mean?

POLLY. Honest, Mr. MacDougal— Mrs. Dumbrowski tasted it and said it was delicious.

MAC DOUGAL (*smiling*). No, it isn't that. I haven't the right to sit down at the Wharton table.

POLLY. Why not?

MAC DOUGAL. Because I'm a dirty ingrate. I've lived in New York all my life and never read your paper, the *Bulletin*. (*He adds:*) I ask you, is that right?

Polly and Max guffaw. Max goes to

MacDougal and pulls him toward the table.

MAX. Don't be funny, Mac. (*MacDougal, smiling, sits down at the table.*)

POLLY. Would you believe it, Mr. MacDougal? We don't read the *Bulletin* ourselves. It isn't allowed in this house.

MAC DOUGAL (*laughing*). Why I hear it's a pretty good paper!

MAX. You're darn right it is—but this is Army, Mac. What paper you read —and politics—are out.

Max begins to dish up the stew for MacDougal and himself. Polly has gone back to get the mashed potatoes.

POLLY. Never read the *Bulletin!* Why, do you know something, Mr. MacDougal—that makes you distinguished!

MAC DOUGAL. You mean I'm the *only* person in the United States who never reads it?

MAX (*laughing*). Well, there may be one or two others.

Polly has brought up the mashed potatoes. MacDougal has his stew and so has Max and both have begun to take the first mouthful.

POLLY. In fact, I'm going to touch him. (*Which she does; then impatiently*) Well, well, well—how is it?

MAC DOUGAL. Terrific!

MAX. Uhmmmmmm—terrific!

Polly stands a second and watches them attack.

POLLY. That's what Mrs. Dumbrowski said. In fact, if you want to know, those women were *really* in here to see what I had for dinner. *Always* poking into my dinners. How do I

make this—how do I make that? They just don't see how I do it.

MAX, seen in a closeup, is eating without lifting his eyes from his plate.

MAX. I don't either.

A closeup of POLLY shows her eyes snapping to Max. Was that a wisecrack?—Thereupon the scene dissolves to the BUNGALOW LIVING ROOM at night, affording a fairly close view of MAX, POLLY, and MAC DOUGAL still at dinner —about forty-five minutes later. They are at the apple-pie and coffee stage. MacDougal and Max have had about two bites of the pie. Polly is testing it.

MAC DOUGAL. Mrs. Wharton—this is *pie!*

POLLY (*surprised herself*). Hmmm— *is* good, isn't it?

MAX. Polly—when did you learn to bake a pie like this? Not since *I've* known you!

POLLY. Oh, shucks—it was way back when I was a little girl—at my mother's knee. You never forget those things—once you learn.

MAC DOUGAL. How do you go about it, Mrs. Wharton. Always wondered.

POLLY. You mean—uh—?

MACDOUGAL. Making a pie.

POLLY. Oh, now—I don't want to bore you two nice people.

MAX. Always wanted to know myself.

MAC DOUGAL. What do you do first?

POLLY. Well, first—since it's an *apple* pie—naturally, first you—you take your apples—

MAX. Yeah?

POLLY (*in pantomime*). Well—you just cut 'em up—in—in ever so many little pieces. And then—well—then you have your apples.

MAC DOUGAL. Then comes the crust. My mother says that's the real test of pie—the crust.

POLLY. Your mother never spoke a truer word, Mr. MacDougal. A nice, flaky crust is at the bottom of the whole thing— (*With gestures*) That's a joke. Crust—at the bottom—

MAC DOUGAL. Yeah—how do you *make* the crust?

POLLY. Well, now—that's very interesting. First you take a little pot—not very big—about so high—*or* a little bigger—

MAX. What's the size of the pot got to do with it?

POLLY. That's an ignorant question.

MAX. All right—so you've got your pot.

POLLY (*gesturing; rapidly*). Very *well*. You set your pot right here. *Now*—you put the things into it—and just mix it. Keep mixing—until you're sure it'll turn out nice and flaky. Then roll it out. Into the pan it goes. In go your apples. Then more crust on top. Then into the oven with the whole thing. And before you know it, you're eating apple pie! (*Polly ends on a note of triumph.*)

MAX. Yeah, but—those things you mixed in the pot—

POLLY (*quickly*). Ah—no two women will ever mix *exactly* the same things. That's every woman's secret. You don't expect me to tell mine!

MAX. No, but—

POLLY. I should think not! (*Then, quickly*) What do you hear from home, Mr. MacDougal?

MacDougal and Max, left high and dry by the sudden switch of the subject, try to grope their way back to normal.

POLLY (*following up fast*). Folks writing regularly?

MAC DOUGAL. Yes, oh, yes—they are.

POLLY. That's nice. You miss New York, too, I bet.

MAC DOUGAL. Certainly do.

POLLY. It's just killing us. We've *never* been so completely out of touch.

MAC DOUGAL. Yeah—I know. Every time I come across a home paper laying around the social room, I make a grab for it—like a long, lost brother.

MAX. Don't tell me you ever find time to read a paper, Mac?

MAC DOUGAL. Well—just the headlines.

POLLY. Tell us one bit of news you've read about New York—or anything.

MAX (*looking at his watch*). Mac's got to be back in ten minutes—

MAC DOUGAL (*looking at his watch*). Yeah—

POLLY (*to MacDougal; persistently*). Just *one* crumb of news. I'm starving.

MAC DOUGAL. Well—Brooklyn's back in the cellar.

POLLY. Why, that's thrilling. (*Pleading*) Anything else, Mr. MacDougal?

MAC DOUGAL. Well—the last paper *I* saw was full of the big meeting—Roosevelt, Churchill, Stalin—

POLLY. Yes. Wonderful!

MAX (*to Polly*). You manage to keep up, don't you?

POLLY. Over Mrs. Clark's radio, darling—about once a week.

MAX. How was the conference going, Mac? How are the boys getting along?

MAC DOUGAL. Well, now—that's politics. And you said politics was out.

MAX (*with a quick smile at Polly*). That's not politics, Mac. Politics suggests something to scrap about—a difference of opinion. There's no argument about the kind of world we all want—when this is over.

MAC DOUGAL. No—except we don't stand much chance of getting it.

MAX (*spiritedly*). Well, I don't say it'll be easy. But the same allied team that won a war as tough as this one ought to be able to win the right peace—if they tackle it with the same teamwork. (*After a slight pause*) You don't doubt it, do you, Mac?

MAC DOUGAL. Well, you *have* to have teamwork to win a war—but comes the peace, and the boys start to relax —then it starts all over—

MAX. What does?

MAC DOUGAL. The same old business. Every country out for itself—out to grab—getting ready for the next war—grinding the same old axes.

POLLY. Suppose—for once, Mr. MacDougal—everybody says, let's lay our axes on the table. That goes for ours too. And now here are the rules. Grind a little, if it'll make you happy —but *no* grinding in the dark—and no grinding that'll cost anybody their freedom—or make poverty for anybody—or ever lead to another war. Don't you think that might work?

MAC DOUGAL (*slowly*). Yeah—if they lay 'em *all* on the table—and don't keep a couple of aces up their sleeves—

MAX (*after a quick look at Polly*). Let me ask you, Mac—what do you figure you're *in* this war for? I mean —what makes you want to fight it at all?

MAC DOUGAL. Well, I always take one thing at a time. A couple of bad boys started this thing—and *we're* gonna finish it. And the sooner the quicker.

MAX. That's right—but what worries me is the bad boys of the *next* generation. The way they build machines to kill nowadays, the world won't survive the next war. That's what *I* want to stop, Mac. And you know—to finally lick those bad boys of today, it took about fifteen years to get the decent countries into an unbeatable team. They were too busy grinding their axes. Keeping that team together now is about the only hope there is for the future. It's a partnership that's got to work. And the point is, Mac—we won't get very far with our partners calling them crooks before we even sit down. We ought to be *rooting* for them. See what I mean?

MAC DOUGAL (*his attention going to his watch*). Holy smoke—I'm late!

MAX. Gee, I'm sorry, Mac! (*Now Polly is up and MacDougal is rushing for his cap.*)

MAC DOUGAL. You don't mind if I run—

POLLY. No, of course not—

MAC DOUGAL (*backing quickly toward the door*). Thanks a lot, Mrs. Wharton. It was swell of you to have me over.

POLLY (*following him*). I enjoyed it. You've got to come again.

MAC DOUGAL (*at the open door*). I sure will. Thanks. The pie was sensational.

And MacDougal is gone. We hear his footsteps down the walk. Max is at the table, deep in thought.

POLLY. Nice boy.

MAX. Yeah.

POLLY (*coming to Max slowly*). Hard to believe anybody can still be thinking like that, isn't it?

MAX. Or *writing* such stuff for fellows like Mac to read. That subtle dose of poison. Look out for your allies. A better world, yes. But don't cooperate too far. Can't trust those fellows, you know.

MAX (*starting to walk around, blowing off steam*). And we *must* join the big, decent human family—oh, sure. Only let's not be *too* Christian about it. Let's sit tight behind our boundaries at the same time and count our material blessings.

POLLY. Now take it easy, Max.

MAX. Great Jehoshaphat! This hanging back, this suspicion of your allies —that's the road to death and destruction!

POLLY. Tell me—do many boys in camp think like Mac does?

MAX. No. As a matter of fact—the morale is terrific. The lectures on our allies and why we're fighting, are great. We're getting an army that can think as well as fight.

POLLY. Then why the alarm, Max?

MAX. Because just a whiff of that poison, when I come across it, drives me nutty. (*Then*) Kennedy should be going to town on this Big Three meeting—plugging cooperation for all he's worth! I wish I could see what he's doing.

POLLY. I can send for the last issues of the paper, darling.

MAX (*throwing his hands in the air*). No! No! If I stop to take one look at that paper—I'm sunk! We said— *no* paper!

POLLY. I know, dear. It's only because you just said you'd—

MAX. Well, I'm crazy. It's none of my business. I've got business of my own— (*He flings himself down on the sofa, stretching out as if he were dead.*) And it's positively murder!

POLLY (*coming to him quickly, and sitting beside him*). What's the matter, darling?

MAX. Polly—this conversation we had with Mac tonight—about the world —we never had it, see?

POLLY. Yes, dear.

MAX. It was three other fellas.

POLLY. Yes, dear. Now what's the murder?

MAX. This course is tougher than I ever believed.

POLLY. Another quiz today?

MAX (*nodding*). What do you think I got?

POLLY (*in a small voice*). Eighty-nine?

MAX. Never more. Never less. It's nerve-wracking. I'd almost rather flunk once in a while.

POLLY. Never!

MAX. My best doesn't seem to do it. Lately I've been asking myself questions. What is this? Are you ever going to be any good to the Army? Shouldn't you have stayed home? Didn't you go running off to war like a boy scout? (*A pause, then*) Polly—I haven't said this to anyone, not even myself—but there's a chance I—I'll never graduate.

POLLY. I don't believe it. I still say you're the smartest, handsomest, blue-eyedist, sexiest sol— in this whole Army.

MAX (*pulling her down to him*). You're blind as a bat.

POLLY. The whole world should be blind like me. (*Max releases her suddenly and falls back groaning.*) Max —what?

MAX. I can just see it in every paper in the country: "Max Wharton— *bright* young editor of the *Bulletin* —was heaved out of the Army on his whatzis—an incompetent moron!" Oh—that'll be just fine for the *Bulletin!* (*He starts to sit up.*)

POLLY (*pushing him back down*). Max—stop seeing headlines. Why don't you relax for fifteen minutes? —Here now— (*starting to unlace his shoes*) —you just pass out—and I'll clean up the dinner things—quiet as a mouse.

MAX (*mumbling*). And I haven't seen you for five days—fine thing.

POLLY. Oh, I require very little—like just looking at you and adoring you— (*She pulls off his shoes and gets up. He grabs her hand.*)

MAX. Angel—would you still love me if I didn't graduate?

POLLY. Oh, no. I've got my heart set on a second lieutenant and you'd better see he turns out to be you. Be quiet.

She snatches her hand away and goes toward the table. Max's eyes are closed. After a moment—

MAX. Polly—

POLLY. Yes?

MAX. You might drop Kennedy a line and tell him how extra important this allied meeting is.

POLLY. Yes, Max—yes—lie still—

MAX. Say we were talking it over. No, not "we"—I don't want to have anything to do with it. Say "you" were thinking about it.

POLLY. Okay. Now shut up.

Max relaxes again. Polly very carefully and quietly picks up some dishes and starts to the kitchenette with them. Suddenly Max swings his legs off the sofa with a roar.

MAX. One drop of that poison is murder!

POLLY (*startled, dropping a dish*). Look what you made me do! (*She starts to pick up the pieces.*)

MAX. Doesn't matter how little of it there is—if you have a chance to fight it, you ought to fight it. Right?

POLLY. Naturally—

MAX (*excitedly*). Well, listen—a fellow stopped me yesterday—on the camp paper—wanted to run something on me—said I could write it myself. I turned him down. But isn't that passing up a chance? If I write about myself, I write about what I believe in. My autobiography up to the minute!

POLLY. If you feel like doing it— that's wonderful.

Max is up on his feet excitedly.

MAX (*looking at his watch*). It would take me a half hour. Just one half hour.

POLLY. Fine—go ahead—

Then Max whirls on Polly, attacking her as if she had started the whole thing.

MAX. Yeah—but wait—I write this blast for the camp paper—and some smart guy—just *one* smart guy— picks on a word or a phrase. He writes an answer—or a question about it. They print *that*. Then where am I? I've got to reply. It's endless. And meanwhile, when am I studying? (*Angrily*) Haven't I got troubles enough? Isn't that just what I swore I wouldn't do? No! No! It's out! (*He flings himself down again on the sofa.*)

POLLY. Darling—I'm not sure—but I *think* it was your idea.

MAX. Well, it was no good. (*Holding out his arms*) Come here, baby.

Polly comes to the sofa. But before she can reach it, Max swings his feet off again, almost hitting her.

MAX. But that's up to me, isn't it? Whether I get dragged into a controversy or not—is up to me! Suppose I write it—and forget it—*absolutely* forget it!

POLLY. If you can, darling, that's—

MAX (*jumping up*). *Sure* I can! Why *can't* I?

POLLY. Max—I'm on your side!

MAX. Where's the typewriter, darling?

POLLY (*flying for the typewriter*). Hurray! We've decided!

She brings the typewriter to the dinner table and pushes the dishes aside. As Max opens the case, she flies for paper. As she comes back to the table, Max grabs her.

MAX. Polly—you won't let me get into trouble—you'll help me see that it's this one half hour—and no more. Won't you?

POLLY. If I have to chloroform you, angel.

She pushes him away. Max sits down and feverishly puts the paper into the typewriter.

POLLY. I'll leave everything as it is— and go into the bedroom—

She picks up a magazine and a book. Max begins to type. As Polly takes a step toward the bedroom, the phone rings! Max pauses, looks at Polly who looks from the phone to Max with forebodings. As she hesitates—

MAX (*a touch impatiently*). Well— get it, will you, honey?

POLLY (*stepping to the phone and picking it up gingerly*). Hello—Yes, this is Mrs. Wharton—Who's call— (*Evidently the operator has clicked off for a second.*)

MAX. Who is it?

POLLY. Uh—long distance.

MAX. Gow!

POLLY. Oh, no!

MAX. That's all I need—to go stark, staring mad!

POLLY. I'm sure it isn't. Go ahead, darling. (*Then; into the phone*) Yes . . . . Hello . . . . Oh, *hello!*

We get a closeup of GOW in his office at night. He is a disturbed and anxious man, but full of energy.

GOW. Hello, Polly. This is Robert. Listen, I've got to get in touch with Max.

POLLY, in a closeup, at the phone, swallows hard as she throws a quick glance back at Max.

POLLY (*into the phone*). Oh, I'm fine, Joel. How are you? (*Covering the mouthpiece; to Max*) Joel Nixon. Hollywood.

MAX, seen in a closeup, is relieved. He tackles the typewriter again.

POLLY's VOICE. Yes, Joel?

A closeup of GOW at the phone:

GOW. Hello! Polly! This is Robert—*Gow!*—Well, where do you get that *Joel* stuff? Listen—I said it's very important I get in touch with Max!

POLLY at the PHONE:

POLLY. Oh, no. We'll have none of that. I made my position quite clear the last time we talked, Joel.

GOW at the PHONE:

GOW. And you'll remember I told you—! (*Breaking off sharply*) Joel? (*Then*) Max is *there!*—Don't lie to me, Polly! I'm desperate! Let me talk to him.

POLLY at the PHONE:

POLLY. What a fantastic notion, Joel. Exactly *what* are you desperate about?

GOW at the PHONE:

GOW (*yelling*). Read the paper—that's all—*read* it! Read what's coming out of Kennedy's half-pint brain on this Big Three meeting! I want Max to pitch in and decide what to do! This is *still* his responsibility as much as mine! Put him on!

POLLY is seen in another closeup, as we hear Max pounding away behind her.

POLLY (*into the phone*). I'm sorry, Joel—we went over the reasons once—well, I *do!* And the reasons are more important now than they were a month ago. So you'll have to take care of it the best way you know—by yourself. (*Firmly; angrily*) *You*

heard me! Goodbye, *Joel!* (*She hangs up.*)

Max pauses to look at her. She smiles weakly.

POLLY. Imagine. Go back and do some silly rewrite on the script—and —and sit around while they're shooting it. The man must be mad!

MAX. Is he really in trouble?

POLLY. Naw! You know him. That's how he is when things are going well. You have to be firm with Joel. (*She goes to Max, and pats his shoulder.*) I'm sorry, dear. I'll keep quiet now.

MAX (*kissing her hand*). You're nice —and incidentally, you bake a whale of an apple pie.

POLLY. Oh—that! (*She kisses the top of his head.*) Go ahead. And make it good, darling.

Max hits the keys again, but before Polly has taken more than a step the front doorbell rings. A glance passes between Polly and Max. Polly rushes to the door.

POLLY. Darn!

At the DOOR, as Polly opens it, stands Mrs. Clark.

MRS. CLARK. Sorry, Mrs. Wharton—could I have the tin I brought the pie in?

Polly closes her eyes, swallows, turns slowly to look at Max, and then we see MAX looking at Polly with eyebrows faintly raised as the scene fades out.

# PART THREE

A TRAINING FIELD comes into view, showing men at drill and exercise. This is used as the background for a superimposed insert which comes toward the camera. It is a part of the Tetley Field camp paper—a column with the box at top reading:

AMONG

OUR

STUDENTS

—and under this box, in bold type, stands:

AUTOBIOGRAPHY

BY

MAX WHARTON

This dissolves to quick flashes of men on the field, reading the paper, and presumably reading the Autobiography by Max. This in turn dissolves to a CORNER OF A GROCERY STORE: In a closeup we see the ARMS OF TWO WOMEN reaching up for the only box of Brillo on a high shelf. Both hands clutch it. As the box comes down off the shelf with the two hands still holding it the view moves down to reveal Polly and Mrs. Gates facing each other belligerently. Mrs. Gates is a bluff woman of sixty, ample-bosomed, bull-faced.

POLLY. I had that. Sorry.

MRS. GATES. Sorry yourself.

POLLY. Now look here—you should see my pots and pans!

MRS. GATES (*a smile of recognition crossing her face*). Why, you're Paula Wharton!

POLLY (*deflated*). Uh—yes.

MRS. GATES. Of course! Everyone knows you're down here. Your husband's in camp.

POLLY. Yes.

MRS. GATES. Well, so is my son-in-law —Colonel Foley.

POLLY. Colonel *Foley?* The Commanding Officer? Your son-in—! Why, how *do* you do?!

Polly pumps her hand. Mrs. Gates beams.

POLLY. *He* doesn't have to worry about graduating, does he?

MRS. GATES. No! My daughter's just crazy to meet you.

POLLY. Well!—I'm just crazy to meet *her.* Why not call on us some time!

MRS. GATES. Could we?

POLLY. *Could* you? (*Then; indicating the Brillo*) Here—I know—we'll split this!

And she proceeds to do so, ripping open the package.

MRS. GATES. Oh, no!

POLLY. Of course we will! This is war. One for you—one for me—one for you—

As Polly doles out the pieces, the scene dissolves to COLONEL FOLEY'S OFFICE where Colonel Foley (whom we should recognize as the man who *nearly* rescued Polly the night she was locked out) is behind his desk, saying to Max, who is just entering:

COLONEL. Come in, Wharton. Come in. (*Max advances stiffly toward the desk. He swallows nervously.*) How are you getting along?

MAX. Oh, fine, sir.

FOLEY. Good. Wharton—I—uh—understand your wife is down here with you.

MAX. Yes, sir.

COLONEL. Well—*Mrs.* Foley—and her mother—happen to be great admirers of your wife. They're calling for me in a little while and we thought we might drop around and pay you both a call.

MAX. Oh—that would be fine, sir!

This dissolves to the BUNGALOW COURT where we see a group consisting of POLLY, MRS. DUMBROWSKI, MRS. CLARK and MRS. GREENBERG. The women have a few grocery articles in their hands which Polly has given them. Polly is talking excitedly.

POLLY. "Maybe we could call *today*," she says. And I says, "Any time at all—the sooner the better!"

MRS. DUMBROWSKI. The Colonel too?

POLLY. No—I guess not. That would be *too* much. But *Mrs.* Foley! And I thought MacDougal was a catch! Now—if you hear footsteps—peek out and you'll see the Foleys! No charge—no addition to your rent. Goodbye, girls.

As she starts off, Mrs. Greenberg waves a copy of the camp paper.

MRS. GREENBERG. Did you see Mr. Wharton's article in the camp paper?

POLLY (*coming back and grabbing the paper excitedly*). Oh, gee—no! How is it?

THE WOMEN. Wonderful!

POLLY. Could I please have it to read?

MRS. GREENBERG. Sure.

POLLY. Thanks. Thanks ever so much!

She heads quickly for the bungalow with the paper and the market basket clutched firmly in her hands.

A close view of POLLY as she barges into the LIVING ROOM: She stops dead, staring as she sees GOW lying on the sofa, gazing back at Polly grimly.

POLLY. Robert Gow!

Gow shakes his head and whispers confidentially:

GOW. No. Nixon. Joel Nixon.

POLLY. You bull-head! I *told* you not to come down here.

GOW (*swinging his feet off the sofa*). It's nice to see you, Polly. When do you expect Max?

POLLY. He may not get over here for days! Robert—you're going to gain *nothing* by coming here. I've warned you—

The phone rings. There is a shocked pause—then Polly runs for it.

POLLY (*into the phone*). Hello—Oh —yes, Max.

We get a close view of Max in a phone booth somewhere in camp.

MAX (*very excited*). Polly—who do you think's calling on us?

Back in the LIVING ROOM we see GOW and POLLY. Gow is standing behind Polly, who is extremely nervous and doesn't realize what she's saying when she answers absently:

POLLY (*into the phone*). The Foleys.

A closeup of MAX at the phone:

MAX. How did you know? Who told you?

POLLY, seen in a closeup as she catches herself:

POLLY. Uh—I—I didn't. Imagine making a guess like that! The Foleys! Angel—how did you ever get them?

MAX (*at the phone*). I'll tell you later. Listen, the Colonel, too!—Yes, the *Colonel*. They'll be there right away. I'm coming right home. Get ready, baby—get all spruced up. Shoot the works!

POLLY (*at the phone, with forced humor*). Formal, informal, or costume ball?—Okay, darling. (*Polly glances back at Gow, then adds quickly into the phone:*) Oh, Max—stop off someplace for—for soda and gingerale—and gin—and Scotch and Bourbon.—Yes, all of them. They may be awfully thirsty.—Thank you, darling.—Goodbye.

GOW and POLLY are again seen together.

GOW. That won't delay him long.

POLLY (*low and savage*). Robert—if Max comes through that door and sees your ugly face—that'll be the end. I want you to get out of here, I'll see you later—tonight—and we'll talk it over. Now—go on! (*She rushes to the window, leans out and yells:*)

POLLY. Yoo-hoo! Mrs. Clark—Mrs. Greenberg—Mrs. Dumbrowski! Yoo-hoo! (*A pause; then*) The Colonel too! The Colonel too!

She ducks back in. Gow has pulled a

dozen copies of the *Bulletin* from his briefcase and holds them up.

POLLY. What's that?

GOW. Recent issues of a little paper called the *Bulletin*.

POLLY. That paper isn't allowed in this house!

GOW. That's what I thought. High time it was. I want you to read Mr. Ed Kennedy on recent world events.

POLLY. I'll do nothing of the kind. I've got to get dressed. Now will you please go, Robert—and take those papers with you.

GOW. Not 'til you've read this latest editorial. It'll take you two minutes. *Read* it!

He presses it into her hands. In spite of herself, Polly starts to read, while Gow rants:

GOW. Read Mr. Kennedy on the greatest issue of the day—on the bright, new world! Read a lot of words—without a spark of courage or heart. And why? Because Kennedy has no true convictions in himself. He isn't a living man—feeling history in his bones. He's a mechanical, writing hack. And that's what Max left me instead of a brain! (*Suddenly there is a loud and rapid bugle call from the Field.*) What's that?

POLLY (*absently*). Oh—that's the one that doesn't mean anything. (*She resumes her reading.*)

GOW (*resuming his rampage*). Well, does that sound like the *Bulletin*—or like every other paper on the street? Go ahead, tell me! But I'll tell you first. The old *Bulletin* doesn't exist!

POLLY (*dropping the paper slowly*

*from her eyes*). And what do you expect Max to do?

GOW. I expect Max to look at that and tell me *now* what's more important—playing soldier or keeping that paper alive!

POLLY (*rather quietly*). Robert—why do you suppose he won't even have the paper around? Because he doesn't care? Obviously, it's because this job here is killing him. He's worried stiff. He knows that *one* second for any outside interest—and he's sunk!

GOW. Of course *I'm* in great shape!

POLLY (*rushing for the Army Manual which is on the trunk*). Here—I'll give you an idea of what he has to go through. (*Reading*) *Theory of Flight*. Yes. This will do. "Resultant. The resultant of two vectors is defined as the single vector which will produce the same effect upon a body as is produced by the joint action of the two vectors."

GOW. What's a vector?

POLLY. How would I know? And that's simply nothing. He has to learn everything in this whole book.

Gow rushes for the manual with wide, incredulous eyes.

GOW (*glancing through it*).That's a terrible thing to put a man through. Does Stimson know about this?

POLLY. That's the Army Manual. What do you think they're training on—*McGuffey's Reader?*—And I'll tell you something else. This is scientific. Did you know that after twenty-one years old you simply don't absorb a thing?

GOW. What *do* you do with it?

POLLY. With what?

GOW. With your brain or your nerve

—or whatever it is that makes *you* earn a fortune a picture—and makes Max a great editor. Nobody ever did that *before* they were twenty-one!

POLLY (*impatiently*). All right—maybe it's no good to absorb. I don't know. I'm just trying to tell you. Max is down here competing with twenty-year olds. He's thirty-nine. He's hanging on by his eyebrows.

GOW. Then his chances of passing this thing are slight. Is that right?

POLLY. So what?

GOW. So let him stop this nonsense right now. Let him get a discharge and go back to work.

POLLY (*glaring at him scornfully*). For a millionaire, you're not very bright. (*Before Gow can answer*) What do you think's terrifying Max? Just *passing?* It's what they will say now—in headlines—if he doesn't. The only thing worse would be to throw in the sponge and quit in the middle. You ought to know Max. He wouldn't even consider it.

GOW. What am I supposed to do? Wait for him to flunk out?

POLLY. If he does. And I hope he doesn't.

GOW (*sarcastically*). And he may not besides! That's fine. But I'm just to *wait*—on that chance. How long?

POLLY. I don't know—a month—six weeks—

GOW. I'm telling you right now that's *too* long!

POLLY. And I'll tell you something, Robert—if Max ever feels that he flunked out because you interfered—he'll never forgive you as long as he lives! That's the end of you and him and the paper—forever! So go ahead

—don't be intelligent about it—don't deal with the situation as it exists—just go ahead—wreck everything!

GOW (*after a pause; quietly*). Well—then there's just one intelligent thing I *can* do.

POLLY. Yes?

GOW. I've got a good offer for the paper—effective any minute I care to pick up the phone.

POLLY. You wouldn't *sell* it!

GOW. I'm just as sentimental as you are. But not stupid. That paper's going down hill a mile a minute. What would *you* do—with a couple of million bucks of *your* money tied up in it? Sit back on the chance Max will be back? Or would you exercise good business judgment and get out while the getting's good?

POLLY. Max'll die. I *guarantee*, if he hears anything about it, he'll—

The screech of car brakes outside causes Polly to freeze. She rushes to the window and sticks her head out.

We get a FULL view of the STREET from POLLY's angle at the window. Max is taking a large amount of stuff in two large paper bags from out of the back of a jalopy driven by a soldier.

Back in the LIVING ROOM Polly ducks back in from the window with a gasp.

POLLY. It's Max! Now listen, Robert —(*spotting the* Bulletins) Oh, my gosh!

She rushes for the copies of the *Bulletin,* and shoves them under one of the sofa cushions.

POLLY (*rapidly*). Robert—not a word —about *anything!* If there's a hope in all this—*some*where—it's in keeping your mouth shut! You just

dropped in. The paper's fine. You're very happy.

Max's hurried footsteps are on the walk. He is whistling. Polly flies to the door. Max enters, his arms full.

POLLY. Darling!

Then Max sees Gow across the room. His jaws clamp tight.

POLLY (*airily*). Look who dropped in, dear. Out of the blue! Just five minutes ago!

GOW. Hello, Max.

POLLY. Uh—that's *Gow*, dear. Look at him—happy as can be. Not a care in the world.

MAX (*loudly, to Polly; his eyes always on Gow*). What does he want? What's he *doing* down here?

POLLY. Oh, he came down with Sorenson to look at some property—

MAX. Some property named Max?

GOW. My dear boy—

MAX. What's in that briefcase?

Gow picks up the open briefcase which now has in it just a few odd bits of correspondence.

GOW. Well, for heaven's sake—a few private letters—a—a contract for the property—

POLLY. Darling—you know there's never *anything* in his briefcase. But he's Robert Drexel Gow. People expect him to carry one.—Sweetheart —honestly—he hasn't a thing on his mind. He just dropped in to say hello.

MAX (*relaxing a little*). Hello.

GOW. Well! He said hello! Right *at* me!

MAX. If he has to hurry away, we don't want to keep him.

POLLY. Darling—it's great! Us having a high-class character like Robert Drexel Gow just sitting around. It'll knock the Foleys for a loop.

MAX. Yeah—not bad. (*Max heads for the kitchenette with his packages.*) Hello, Robert! How are you?

GOW. Gee whiz—I'm overwhelmed!

Then Max dashes back toward the kitchenette with his bundles.

POLLY. Did you get everything, angel?

MAX. Yeah. Some cigars too—

POLLY. Great. Oh—I'm not dressed yet.

MAX. They'll be here any minute. Go on!

POLLY (*rushing for the bedroom*). Sit down, Robert. And *relax*.

GOW (*dryly*). Thanks.

Polly disappears. Max is pulling things out of the bags. Gow takes a seat on the sofa, always watching Max.

MAX. Robert, I never thought I'd live to see the day you'd be any use to me. But you work in just great. (*Then calling*) Polly! I didn't tell you about the Foleys!

POLLY'S VOICE. How did it happen? I'm dying to know!

GOW. Will somebody tell me—who the dickens is Foley?

MAX. The Commanding Officer of the whole Field, that's all! *Colonel Foley.*

GOW. Never heard of him.

Max, in the meanwhile, has been rummaging in a drawer and now brings out a shoe brush and polish.

MAX (*to Polly*). All of a sudden they say, "Colonel Foley wants to see you." So I go up there and he says, very cordially, "Why, come in, Wharton. How are you getting along?" he says. And I says, "Oh, fine, sir," and he says—"Mrs. Foley happens to be a great admirer of you and your wife—" I don't remember whether he included me or not. Well, anyway, he says, "We thought we might drop around and pay you a call!" What do you think of that?

GOW. Why, that's the greatest thing since Spearmint!

POLLY'S VOICE. Shut up, Robert. And you do everything right. Just the way Max tells you to.

Max glares at Gow, who is now aware of Max's polishing.

GOW. You mean you polish your own shoes?

MAX. And press my pants and sew on my buttons! Anything wrong?

POLLY'S VOICE. Max loves it.

MAX. I love it!

GOW (*looking for an opening*). Well, love makes the world go round. That's how I feel about the newspaper business. And speaking of the newspaper business—

POLLY'S VOICE. Which nobody *was*, Robert!

GOW. Kennedy sends his regards.

POLLY'S VOICE. Kennedy's getting along beautifully, Max!

MAX. I told you he would if you'd give him a chance. You never liked him, that's all.

GOW. I still don't. He eats too loud.

MAX. Don't eat with him.

The sound of an automobile is heard,

and Max dashes to the window. We then see the STREET in full view as seen by MAX from the window. A car is coming to a stop—a four-door sedan, driven by a soldier. In the back are the Colonel and two women.

We again see the LIVING ROOM as Max jerks his head back in.

MAX. Polly—they're here! Hurry up, baby!

Max rushes back to put the shoe brush away. Polly comes out of the bedroom, done up to the nines in the greatest housecoat ever seen in Florida, doing some last minute fastening. Gow's eyes bug out at the sight of the bedazzling Polly.

GOW. Wow! What is this—a night at the opera?

Max charges back to the window again for a peek.

MAX (to Gow). Now, you sit there and don't forget to act the way they write about you in the papers!

POLLY (closing the kitchenette doors). And not just the way they write about you in your own paper. They don't want a big, natural, homespun millionaire. They want a millionaire that's got class.

Gow takes all the instructions with an expression alternately annoyed and dazed by the great flurry about him.

MAX (reporting from the window). He's leaning on the car, talking to the driver.

GOW. Well get 'em in here. I'm sick of relaxing.

MAX. I can't order a Colonel in here if he isn't ready to come in!

Out on the STREET we get a fairly close view of the COLONEL, MRS. FOLEY and MRS. GATES as they start from the sidewalk toward the bungalow, looking at the numbers. Mrs. Gates we remember from the grocery store. Mrs. Foley is in her late thirties—a bleached, vivacious blonde. Both women carry copies of Polly's book.—This is followed by quick flashes of MRS. DUMBROWSKI, MRS. GREENBERG, MRS. COLLINS and MRS. CLARK—their heads out of the windows, fascinated by the Foley parade.—The FOLEY PARTY notes the heads of the women in surprise. The Colonel bobs his head at them and smiles weakly. Mrs. Gates points off.

MRS. GATES. There. 26-D.

In the LIVING ROOM, Max ducks his head back in like a shot.

MAX. Get ready, darling!

GOW. How did I get curved into this?

MAX. Shut up, Gow. (He swallows.) Well, here goes.

He sticks out his chest—for courage— and steps out onto the porch.

At the BUNGALOW PORCH as Max appears before the Foley party:

MAX. How do you do, Colonel?

COLONEL. How do you do, Wharton.

MAX (to Mrs. Gates). How do you do, Mrs. Foley.

MRS. GATES (correcting him). Mrs. Gates. How do you do.

COLONEL. Mrs. Foley's mother. (Indicating) This is Mrs. Foley.

MAX. Oh, of course. How do you do, Mrs. Foley. I—I'm very glad you could come. Shall—shall we go in? Please.

He steps aside to let the party through. Mrs. Gates goes first, then Mrs. Foley, then the Colonel.

Back in the LIVING ROOM, Gow has risen. Polly is at the door, extending her hand to Mrs. Gates. They meet like old friends.

POLLY. Well! Mrs. Gates!

MRS. GATES. Here we are, Mrs. Wharton—good as my word.

MAX (*Mrs. Foley, the Colonel, and Max, having piled in too*). Polly—Mrs. Gates.

MRS. GATES. Oh, we know each other.

POLLY. Yes, indeed. Old pot-cleaning acquaintances!

The women laugh. Max is amazed. He just stares and Mrs. Gates takes the introducing play out of his hands.

MRS. GATES. My daughter—Mrs. Foley.

POLLY (*extending her hand*). I'm *so* pleased to meet you, Mrs. Foley.

MRS. FOLEY. Oh, Mrs. Wharton. This is wonderful!

MAX. Darling—Colonel Foley!

POLLY (*extending her hand*). Oh, Colonel, how nice of you—

She breaks off. His face is familiar, now that she looks at him fully. The Colonel too, vaguely recalls her.

COLONEL. Somehow, I seem to have—

POLLY. Yes, I'm sure I've— (*Then remembering*) Oh!

COLONEL (*remembering too*). Of course! (*They shake hands warmly and laugh. Max is dumbfounded.*)

MAX. Polly—I didn't know you—

POLLY (*winking at Colonel*). Oh, *yes!*

COLONEL (*winking back*). Yes, indeed!

MRS. FOLEY. Pet, you never told me that—

COLONEL. One doesn't tell his wife everything, pet.

GOW (*loudly, distinctly, startling everyone*). I am Robert Drexel Gow!

MAX. Oh—Mrs. Gates—our friend Mr. Gow.

GOW. How do you do.

MRS. GATES. Well, I never thought I was going to meet *you*.

MAX. Mrs. Foley—Mr. Gow.

GOW. Robert Drexel Gow.

MRS. FOLEY. Oh—yes!

MAX (*rattled*). Colonel Gates—I mean, *Foley*. I must be mad!

GOW (*coming forward and seizing the Colonel's hand*). Glad to know you, my friend.

MAX (*under his breath*). Colonel Foley.

GOW (*loudly*). I know he's a Colonel. (*Then*) Well, I don't know about you folks—but I'm tired of standing.

POLLY. Oh yes,—please. Do sit down. (*She indicates an odd chair.*) Mrs. Foley? (*She indicates the sofa.*) Mrs. Gates?

MAX (*hauling a large chair toward the sofa*). Let me give you this chair, Colonel.

Mrs. Gates sits on the sofa seat under which Polly has put the *Bulletin* copies. Mrs. Gates jumps up.

MRS. GATES. Oops! Something under here.

POLLY (*with an alarmed glance at Max*). Oh, yes—my knitting!

MRS. GATES (*starting to take it out*). I'm sorry—

POLLY. No, please—I hoped *somebody'd* sit on it. It's curling at the edges. Do *please* flatten it out. (*She urges the amazed Mrs. Gates back onto the sofa.*)

MRS. GATES. Well, if you say so. I'm quite a flattener.

POLLY (*irritated by Gow's expression*). Well—sit *down*, Robert.

GOW (*moving to the place on the sofa next to Mrs. Gates*). Any other *flattening* you want done?

POLLY. No—just sit down.

GOW (*to the Colonel*). You don't mind if I sit next to your wife?

COLONEL (*nodding at his wife*). Mrs. Foley is my wife.

MRS. GATES. She's my daughter.

GOW. Why, I thought you two were sisters.

POLLY (*quickly*). Will you have a cigarette, Mrs. Foley?

MRS. FOLEY. Why, yes—thank you.

MAX. Oh, Colonel—will you have a cigar, sir?

COLONEL. Thank you, Wharton.

Max rushes for the cigars and brings one to him. Gow extends his cigarette case to Mrs. Gates.

MRS. GATES. No thanks.

Max has snapped his lighter out and begins to light the Colonel's cigar. Mrs. Foley holds her unlit cigarette.

POLLY. Max, darling—er—light Mrs. Foley's cigarette.

Max turns to Mrs. Foley's cigarette, leaving the Colonel's cigar half lit. He half finishes lighting that, turns back to finish lighting the Colonel's cigar. On a signal from Polly, he turns back to Mrs. Foley and this time she gets her light. Now Gow gives the same signal as Polly, with respect to the Colonel's unlit cigar. Frantically Max turns back to the Colonel's cigar.

GOW. There! We got *that* done.

POLLY. What would you like to drink? (*To Gow*) Robert, you get the ice and gingerale.

GOW. Me?

MAX. Yes, Robert.

Gow rises in perplexity. Polly indicates the kitchenette doors.

POLLY. Right up there, dear. (*Gow starts for the kitchenette.*) What will you have to drink, Mrs. Foley? Bourbon and gingerale—Scotch and soda—

MRS. FOLEY. Well—

Gow has seized the kitchenette doors and now pulls them open with a great clatter.

POLLY. Robert!

Gow begins to fidget around, getting the lay of the kitchenette.

MRS. FOLEY. Oh, Mrs. Wharton. I just think I will have to pinch myself.

POLLY. Well, you go right ahead.

MRS. FOLEY. I told the Colonel driving over here—I said, pet, let's drive the carefulest we've ever driven because I could not positively stand it if anything should happen now when I am just about to meet Paula Wharton. (*Suddenly; to the Colonel*) And all that time you didn't tell me that you and— (*She looks at Polly.*)

MAX. Yes, by the way, Polly, how—?

COLONEL. Stop prying, Wharton.

We get a closeup of GOW. He has the ice-box open and is tugging at the tray. He braces himself by putting his foot on the bottom shelf. Then he digs a small frying pan out of a lower compartment.

MRS. FOLEY's VOICE. I don't think there's anyone at the Field that hasn't written home to someone that Paula Wharton is down here.

It is at this point that Robert Drexel Gow starts hitting the ice-tray with the frying pan. At this Polly and Max rise in surprise.

POLLY. Robert!

GOW (*angrily*). It's stuck!

MAX. Here. I'll help. (*He goes up and starts to tug.*)

MRS. FOLEY. Ours is like that.

GOW. You ought to have a hammer and chisel. Got a hammer and chisel?

MRS. GATES. Why don't we have the drinks warm, is what I say.

POLLY (*starting for the kitchenette*). It's really simple, if you just—

Gow slams the ice-tray twice more with the frying pan. By now the Colonel is up and starts for the kitchenette, too.

COLONEL. I can usually manage these things. (*He takes the frying pan from Gow.*) Pardon me— (*Motioning to make room*) Now, if you'll all just—

They clear for him and he whams the ice-tray. The contents of the two middle shelves come tumbling into the room.

MRS. FOLEY. Why, pet!

COLONEL. Oh! I'm sorry.

MAX (*as everybody starts picking up the spilled fruit and vegetables*). That's all right, Colonel!

GOW, seen in a closeup, is triumphant. Very calmly he moves over and leans on Polly's trunk, watching the others scurry around.

GOW. All you needed in the old days was an ice pick and a chunk of ice. Now you have to be a bloomin' safe cracker.

The contents of the refrigerator are put back in their places or on the kitchenette table.

MAX. It's just that we don't use it often enough.

Colonel Foley opens the right lower door of the kitchenette and hauls out a *large* saucepan.

COLONEL. I can do it with this, all right. (*He raises his arm and is about to swing.*)

POLLY. Oh! If you'll just wait a minute. I think I'd better take all these things out first.

With that she first takes out a large platter on which there is a raw mackerel. She hands it to the Colonel who passes it on to Max, who, in turn, hands it on to Mrs. Gates. Then Mrs. Gates to Mrs. Foley. It winds up with Gow! In the same way come heads of cauliflower and iceberg lettuce—and a box of strawberries, etc. The stuff passes along like the old bucket brigade—all the while there is conversation like "Would you just hold this?"—"Do you mind—for a moment?" (Mrs. Gates, incidentally, winds up with the strawberries and samples a few.) When Polly has taken everything out, the Colonel again raises the saucepan to strike.

COLONEL. Hold on—let me try something.

He goes to the tray, tries it with thumb and forefinger. It comes out easily.

COLONEL (*to Gow*). All you need is —just a little common sense.

POLLY. Everything back, please. (*Now comes the bucket brigade in reverse.*)

Robert, we'll all have Bourbon and gingerale. That'll make it easier for you.

GOW. Oh. Thank you.

POLLY (*as the last of the stuff is put back in the refrigerator*). There! Now let's get nice and settled again.

MAX. Hurry it up, will you, Robert?

Everyone goes back to his place. Robert sets about busily fixing the drinks. A new conversation strikes up.

MRS. FOLEY. You've just come back from Hollywood, haven't you, Mrs. Wharton? (*As Polly nods*) You've been adapting your new book for the screen, I read.

POLLY. Yes.

MAX (*just to be pleasant*). They can't get along without her there. Her producer keeps phoning here all the time.

There is a closeup of GOW on that last "crack." He jerks his head to Polly. He has a row of glasses in front of him and a plate full of ice cubes in one hand. Then we see the entire GROUP as Polly casts a quick glance back to Gow. We hear the ice cubes rattling into the glasses as if Gow were playing a harp.

MRS. GATES. What's that Charles Boyer like?

POLLY. Oh, he's terribly nice.

MRS. GATES. Really? I'm glad to hear that.

POLLY. Why, did you hear anything different?

MRS. GATES. Oh, heavens no! I like him so much—I just want to be sure I'm not wasting my time on the wrong man. (*General laughter—including Mrs. Gates, who has a bit of wit.*)

MRS. FOLEY. Oh, mother! (*Then to Polly*) Tell me—when a star like Rita Hayworth gets married, doesn't that upset a lot of people?

POLLY. It didn't upset *me*.

MRS. GATES. Let's see—is it Hayworth who sleeps in her—?

MRS. FOLEY. And what *I'd* like to know is—do the actresses have their babies in between the *pictures* or do they make the pictures in between the *babies?*

Gow is approaching with the drinks— six glasses pressed together in both hands like an old-fashioned waiter in a beer parlor. He intends to make only one trip.

GOW. Heads up!

MAX. For goodness' sake, Robert.

GOW. Saves a couple of trips.

They all grab for the glasses to get them out of Gow's grip before he has an accident. They ad lib "thank you's."

POLLY. Robert—the ice cubes.

GOW. I have. Everybody's got 'em.

POLLY. You have to fill the tray up for next time.

GOW. Oh. I thought I was only catering for this party. You mean to say I can begin to look ahead? (*All eyes are on Gow as he heads back to the kitchenette.*) Where's the water? I don't see any water?

POLLY. You have to get the water out of the— (*To the guests*) Excuse me— (*Then; loudly to Gow*) —The bathroom.

GOW. Pardon me, I have to powder my ice cubes.

Gow walks toward the bedroom and there is a general sigh of relief.

POLLY. Now, I have something I want to ask the Colonel. Do all men when they're graduated from here get sent to Crocker Field, Arkansas?

MAX. Darling, you shouldn't ask the Colonel that.

MRS. FOLEY. Why, they get sent all over, don't they, pet?

COLONEL. That's right, they—

MRS. FOLEY. Of course, there's no way of knowing until they get their orders the day they graduate. (*At this, Gow re-enters with the filled tray and puts it back into the icebox.*)

MAX. Polly was just curious.

GOW (*suddenly and loudly*). How's he doing, Colonel?

COLONEL. Pardon?

GOW. Max. Is he going to pass? I hear old dogs like him don't learn a thing in school here. In fact, after twenty-one, you just don't absorb.

MRS. FOLEY (*to the Colonel*). Is that true, pet?

COLONEL. Nonsense.

MAX. Where did you get a fantastic notion like that, Robert?

GOW. Why, it's scientific. Polly was telling me.

POLLY (*as all eyes click to Polly, who could just die*). Oh—that young couple that was here, Max—the young girl—that's what *she* said—I was telling Robert about it—silliest thing I ever heard!

MRS. FOLEY. I should think so. Because, really—in Mr. Wharton's case —being so awfully clever—

MRS. GATES. The whole camp's talking about the thing he wrote.

GOW. Max *wrote* something?

POLLY. Nothing, Robert, nothing. A little sketch about himself in the camp paper.

MRS. GATES. You're too modest, Mrs. Wharton. It was wonderful—in fact, about the best thing on the war I ever read.

GOW. Oh? A little something on the war?

MAX (*sharply*). Robert—don't get any silly notions! We don't go in for politics down here.

MRS. FOLEY (*to the Colonel*). Didn't you think it was wonderful, pet?

All eyes are on the Colonel who hesitates a second.

COLONEL. Yes—uh—pretty strong.

GOW. Oh, *strong?*

COLONEL. In fact, I'd make it a point to tell you, Wharton—that little piece of yours went on to Washington.

MAX. Washington! (*This is a bombshell.*)

MRS. FOLEY. Now isn't that nice?

POLLY. You mean—*you* sent it on, Colonel?

COLONEL. No. They asked for it.

MAX (*anxiously as Polly and he again exchange alarmed glances*). Yes— but how would they hear about it, ·sir?

COLONEL. Oh, they hear about everything.

MAX. You—you don't think that— that they could object to it?

GOW. Well, after all, if it was *strong.*

COLONEL. I don't try to outguess Washington, Wharton.

MRS. FOLEY. Pet—you can say *more* without saying anything!

GOW (*while Max is in a lather of nervousness*). Yes, sir—when Max goes strong—there isn't a better man in the country. 'Course, he *will* sound off every now and then and cause a little embarrassment. I recall the time he wrote a series for the *Bulletin*—

MAX. Robert, I don't think the Colonel will be interested!

Just then a bugle call sounds from the Field. The Colonel looks at his watch, reaches for his hat and is up.

COLONEL. Well, dear. That's us. (*The two women get up immediately. So do Polly and Max.*)

MRS. GATES. I'm not going to budge a step until I hear Mrs. Wharton make one of her famous remarks.

POLLY. Oh, good. Which one would you like to hear?

There is general laughter at this retort. Mrs. Foley extends Polly's book which she has carried—fountain pen all ready.

MRS. FOLEY. What I wonder is, Mrs. Wharton—would you autograph this book?

MRS. GATES (*proffering hers too*). Mercy, yes!

POLLY. Oh, of course.

Gow has moved near the Colonel. Max is standing nervously near the table behind the sofa. Polly autographs the books.

A closeup of MAX shows him to be worried. He happens to glance down and sees the copy of the camp paper. He reacts as though he'd been stuck with a pin.

GOW'S VOICE. Secretary Stimson been around lately, Colonel?

COLONEL'S VOICE. No, he hasn't.

We again see the entire GROUP. The Colonel is very stiff and cautious.

GOW. How many men have you down here, Colonel?

COLONEL. Quite a few.

GOW (*getting the point*). Ahem. That's good.

Now the two visiting women have their books signed.

MRS. FOLEY. Thank you, Mrs. Wharton. This has been wonderful.

MRS. GATES. Just wonderful. Goodbye.

COLONEL. Goodbye, Mrs. Wharton.

POLLY. Goodbye. Now that you've found us, I hope you'll come often.

There is a further chorus of "goodbyes" to Gow and from Gow to everyone. The Foleys are at the door now.

COLONEL. Your hour's about up, Wharton.

MAX. *Yes*, sir! I'll start back to the Field in one minute, sir.

We see the BUNGALOW COURT as the Foley group starts up the walk to the car.

MRS. FOLEY. Pet—what *I'd* like to know is—where did you and Mrs. Wharton—?

That's as much as we stay to hear. Back in the LIVING ROOM, we get a full view of MAX, POLLY, and GOW. Max is lashing at Gow, who is somewhat back on his heels.

MAX. You meddlesome baboon! What are you trying to do—get me thrown out of here?

GOW. What did *I* do?

MAX. Trying to find out what my report card is going to read—waiting around like some dirty ambulance chaser to pick me up if I don't pass —making me out a doddering idiot —then steaming the Colonel on that Washington business!— (*Breaking off his attack on Gow suddenly, and turning on Polly*) Polly—what— what do you think that means? *Why* Washington? I've got a horrible feeling—

POLLY. Now, Max—

MAX. I shouldn't have done it! They sent me here to study—not to run the world. You heard what he called it— strong! They're going to heave me out of here! I know it!

GOW (*lightly*). Well—what's so tragic about that?

MAX (*angrily*). Sure! Anything that gets me thrown out of here is fine with you. That's what you were just meddling about!

GOW. I don't have to meddle! The Army's telling you right now "Sorry, but you're forty and it's showing—"

POLLY. Now stop this!

GOW. You haven't any more chance of getting to be a second lieutenant than I have!

MAX. That's what you're praying for, isn't it?

GOW. I'll lay you two to one on it!

POLLY. You take that bet, Max!

GOW. You're just down here engaged in a wilful piece of self-indulgence ·at the expense of—!

POLLY (*loudly*). Max—you're five minutes late!

MAX. Ow!

POLLY (*shaking a finger under Gow's nose*). He'll get ten demerits for that!

Max, without a goodbye or even a "go-to-hell" to Gow, rushes to the door. He grinds to a halt on the threshold.

MAX. Polly! *Where* did you know Colonel Foley?

POLLY. Oh, for heaven's sake—he caught me with my negligee on! You're *late!*

Max's eyes bulge. He dashes out. Polly turns and glares at Gow, who is puzzling that negligee business.

GOW. *You*—and the *Colonel?*

POLLY (*ignoring that*). You were going to blab about the paper, weren't you? (*Gow is guiltily silent.*) After what I told you. After what you saw in this room. After this *Washington* bombshell—

GOW. How come he's up to his neck but finds time to write documents for some one-horse paper?

POLLY. Never mind that! I told you —if Max can ever say—"It was Gow's fault I didn't get through—it was that threat to sell the paper—" if Max can ever say that, you and he are through!

GOW (*evenly; firmly*). What I want to know is—how come he found time to—

POLLY. For heaven's sake—he *didn't!*

GOW. *Did* he write it—or didn't he!?

POLLY. Yes! I mean—a situation came up—he grabbed a frantic half hour to do it in— (*Then*) Robert—either this Washington thing gets him thrown out—or it comes to the same thing—he'll worry about it—and flunk out hopelessly. Isn't that enough for you? You're practically certain of having him back in six weeks!

GOW. I want him before that.

POLLY. Didn't you hear anything I said? How can you have him before that?

GOW. By getting an editorial from Max—one every week—until he gets out of here.

POLLY. You want—?

GOW. A "frantic" half hour of Max's time—once a week. If he can do it for some *local* situation—

POLLY. And you call Max wilful!

GOW. When it comes to having stuff like that— (*pointing to the sofa*) —hit the streets day after day for the next two months—Yes—I'm *plenty* wilful! And you ought to be too. (*Gow snatches up his briefcase and digs a document out of it.*) So somebody's got to tell Max something. Either *you* do—to get that weekly editorial out of him— (*holding up the paper*) —or *I* do—to get his signature on this deed. He's an officer of the corporation and he's got to sign this if the paper's going to be sold.

POLLY walks over and takes the paper from Gow, and we see her staring rather vacantly at it and thinking while Gow is heard arguing.

GOW'S VOICE. Great heavens, Polly— he's no child! This is a lot bigger situation than he found time to write about down here. I don't mean you have to get him alarmed. But you can hint about Kennedy. You can tell him just enough—

The TWO are seen fairly close as mechanically, Polly starts to tear the document into many pieces.

POLLY. Well—if you've got to have your editorials, Robert—you've got to have them.

GOW. You mean you'll *tell* him? (*Polly stares vacantly.*) Oh, boy— now we're getting somewhere! Polly, I need the stuff quick!

POLLY. And I need a little time, Robert. After all, I may not see him for a few days.

GOW. A few days. But that's all I've got to have it.

POLLY (*becoming impatient; irascibly*). The quicker you get out of here, the quicker I can start thinking.

GOW (*alive and energetic now; looking at his watch*). I can catch a northbound plane at six o'clock.

He runs for his briefcase and his hat. Suddenly he straightens up.

GOW. Polly! At the end of six weeks —he *doesn't* flunk out of here—and they send him ten thousand miles away! *Then* where am I? Might as well sell the paper now.

POLLY. Everything in the world is *against* his getting through. What do you want—my personal guarantee?

GOW (*going to Polly hurriedly and embracing her*). All right, just get the stuff to me, baby. Goodbye, Polly.

POLLY. Goodbye, Robert. And one thing—I'll handle this—*you* keep strictly out.

GOW. Sure. Sure. I'll be waiting. (*He heads for the door.*) Give my love to Max!

He is gone. After a long pause, Polly moves to the sofa. From under the sofa cushions she lifts the copies of the *Bulletin*. She thumbs through them idly. Then her eyes seek something. She walks over and picks up the typewriter which rests on the trunk. She brings it to the table. And as she opens the case the scene dissolves to MAX'S DORMITORY at night. MAX is seated at a small desk —in terrible concentration at work on his studies. This is followed by a view of the BUNGALOW LIVING ROOM, where POLLY is in dreadful concentration too —pounding the typewriter. Around her are spread the copies of the *Bulletin*. Suddenly she stops typing. She picks up one of the papers, studies it awhile, lays it down, thinks, rereads what she has written. Then she gets up from the chair and walks around it. She eyes the typewriter like something she is going to pounce on—and pounces! Again, as she tackles the typewriter, the scene dissolves to the exterior of the WHARTON BUNGALOW, and now it is day. MRS. DUMBROWSKI, her arms full of groceries, is approaching the door of 26-D. She raps. From the inside we hear the typewriter. She knocks again. The typewriter stops. A pause—the door is flung open. A tousled, bleary Polly appears.

POLLY. Oh! Thank you, Mrs. Dumbrowski! This is terribly sweet of you! (*Polly starts taking the packages from Mrs. Dumbrowski.*) I'd ask you in, only—

MRS. DUMBROWSKI. No, you go ahead and work. You're having a hard time.

POLLY. The toughest job of writing I ever did in my life! Right now I'm on the forty-third version of it— (*Startled*) How did you know?

MRS. DUMBROWSKI (*smiling*). We've heard the typewriter for two nights.

POLLY. Oh—I'm sorry.

MRS. DUMBROWSKI. We don't mind. Go right ahead. Only you ought to get some sleep.

POLLY (*as Mrs. Dumbrowski is start-*

*ing away*). I'll make a note of that! You're an angel!

Polly ducks inside, closing the door, and the scene cuts to the LIVING ROOM as Polly hurries in with her groceries and rushes back to the kitchenette with them. The kitchenette is crowded with dishes. She sets the groceries down wherever there happens to be room and rushes back to her writing table. Moving in toward her we see the mess her work-table is in. Many papers are strewn over it, though the copies of the *Bulletin* are folded up in a pile.

As Polly hammers the machine the scene dissolves to the exterior of the BUNGALOW at night. The light is on in the window—and the typewriter can be heard. Coming quickly along the walk is—Max!

We get a full view of the LIVING ROOM as Polly works at her table in furious concentration under the light of the lamp. She is startled out of her skin at the sudden appearance of Max.

POLLY. Max!

In the next frantic second, she glares down at her work, shoves a few papers together—then runs for Max.—Then POLLY and MAX are seen together as she comes rushing into his arms.

POLLY. Darling! What a surprise! How long can you stay?

MAX. Just long enough to press my pants. (*Indicating the table*) What are you doing?

POLLY (*nervously*). Oh. Well, Joel Nixon finally caught up with me. I mean—the script. I've got to make some changes. He's been phoning from Hollywood like a maniac.

MAX (*leaving her; taking a few steps toward the table*). My gosh—you've really been working! Look at the place.

POLLY (*getting around in front of him*). Well, I'm doing it against time, Max. The picture's shooting *now.*—Your pants, sweetheart. Take 'em off. I—I'll get the board ready. (*She pushes him in the direction of the bedroom.*)

MAX. You don't look as if you've slept.

POLLY. Yes, I have—as much as I need. Go on. Go on.

MAX. Gee, honey—that's too bad.

Max enters the bedroom. Polly leaps to the work table, gathering everything in a heap, *carefully covering* the *Bulletins.*

POLLY (*calling to him*). I like work. I thrive on it.

She carries her stack of papers to the kitchenette. There's no room there. Finally she deposits the pile on the sofa. She runs back to the table and takes the typewriter off it. Then she gets the ironing board from somewhere in the kitchenette and spreads it from the work table to the trunk. It's a bit on a slant, but that's the way it works. Then she scrambles under the sofa for the iron—and plugs it into one of the sockets in the stand lamp. During the above they are both conversing.

POLLY. Take your shoes off too, darling. I'll brush 'em up for you.

MAX'S VOICE. You're going to get awfully sick of me if all I do around here is shine shoes and press pants.

POLLY. Sure. Don't forget your tooth, angel.

MAX'S VOICE. What?

POLLY. Your tooth, lovey. Is it in your mouth or your pocket? If it's in your pocket, I just don't want you to keep on ironing it—like you did last time.

Max appears from the bedroom in bathrobe and slippers. Under one arm he has his shoes—and from the pocket of his pants he is taking certain articles, among them a couple of quiz papers. Max puts these various articles into the pockets of his bathrobe.

MAX. Gosh, the way you talk about my false tooth. People get awfully careless, married. You just say any old thing.

POLLY. Well, what the dickens, sweetheart. One false tooth isn't a disgrace. And I don't tell people. (*Going to him, smiling at his moroseness*) What's the matter, darling? Are you worried about anything?

Polly has pulled the belt out of his pants, and now takes the shoes from him.

MAX. No, not a thing. (*Suddenly*) Nice and restful around here without Gow, isn't it? The darn nerve-tester! I'd like to see his face if I finished top of the class!

POLLY. Max—you're not taking anything Robert said seriously?

MAX. No.

POLLY. Then what? Your little eyes look so sad.

MAX. It's the quiz we have coming up tomorrow. I was just running it over in my mind. (*He moves away from her restlessly, up toward the ironing board.*)

POLLY. What quiz is it, darling? Couldn't I help?

MAX (*testily*). No. It's reviewing a lot of stuff. A paper they gave me. (*He pulls one of the papers out of his bathrobe pocket.*) Ten questions.

JAN and ROY: That train . . . won't be here 'til five o'clock
in the morning!

POLLY: And — off I went into the wide blue yonder!

MAX: Don't forget to act the way they write about you in the papers!

POLLY: Don't stand there and tell me you don't know a simple thing like question two —

They pick out five at random and spiel it out.

POLLY. Well—why don't you study and let me iron?

Max hurriedly puts his pants on the board. He sets the questions down at the end of the board.

MAX. No—I'm faster at this, baby—

POLLY. Or I can be asking you the questions while you're ironing.

MAX (*with quiet vehemence*). Polly —*please! Hang* the questions.

There is a second's silence. This is Max in a new mood.

POLLY. All right, dear.

Polly gets the shoe brush and a rag and paste to polish Max's belt buckle. She comes back near the sofa to perform these operations. Max prepares to iron. After a pause—

MAX. Well, I'm still here. Nothing from Washington yet.

POLLY. That's the main worry, isn't it, Max?

MAX (*very quietly*). That. And everything else. (*After a pause*) Gow's probably right. I don't think I'm going to make it, Polly.

Max walks back a step and drops into a chair, covering his face with one hand. Polly rises quickly, dropping the shoe she's been polishing. She walks toward him.

POLLY. Max—you need a little sleep yourself.

He shakes his head. His face is still covered.

MAX. It's no good, darling. What they say—over twenty-one—makes a lot of sense. I'm outclassed.

POLLY. You sound as if you want to quit, Max.

MAX. What should it be?—Another month of useless punishment—or that same month back in my old line, where I'm good? There'll be music to face—if I flunk. Why not face it now?

The phone rings. Polly jumps and runs for it.

POLLY (*into the phone*). Yes—

She looks nervously back at Max, who isn't thinking about the call.

POLLY (*into the phone; nervously*). Uh—all right. (*She waits a second.*) Hello!—Tomorrow, Joel! It goes off tomorrow! (*She hangs up.*)

We get a view of GOW'S OFFICE as GOW is seen holding the receiver in amazement. He has just been party to the shortest long distance conversation in history.

GOW. Tomorrow, Joel.

We again see the BUNGALOW LIVING ROOM as Polly turns from the phone and goes back to Max.

MAX. There's a lot to say for quitting now, Polly. *One* thing—Gow would meet me with a band.

Polly, wringing her fingers, looks from the phone to Max. The temptation is great.

POLLY. But *you* wouldn't be feeling so chipper, would you? (*As he is silent*) In fact, you'd be taking a pretty bad licking—inside. Wouldn't you, Max? (*Max looks at her an instant, then gets up from his seat.*) And that's your genius, angel—never *knowing* when you're licked. Certainly never *saying* you were. What would this one do to you? Would you ever be quite the same again?

Would you fight *exactly* as you used to?

Then Polly looks from the telephone to the pile of stuff on the sofa, to Max. She makes a decision.

POLLY. No. Flunking out—after giving the best you have—there's some self-respect in that. Quitting in the middle—that's a licking. (*She hurries to the ironing board.*) Where's that paper?

She finds the piece of quiz paper and lays it out on the ironing board. Her manner is now positive and alert.

POLLY (*reading*). Lovey—define me "polyconic projection."

At the same time she lays out the pants for ironing.

MAX. It's no good, darling. I told myself all that. But I *know*—I'm too old!

POLLY. Old! Max—that "over twenty-one" business is a lie. Like the one about you can't teach old dogs new tricks. *Both* of them are *frauds* that progressive men should fight! Why, that means experience counts for nothing—that nothing ever changes. The fellas who spout those lies don't think the *world* ought to change either—it's too old a dog. Well, you *show* them, Max!—Define me polyconic projection—and holler it so loud that even Gow can hear it. (*As Max groans*) Come on.

MAX. Polyconic projection is the projection of the earth's surface on a series of right circular cones tangent to the earth at prescribed standard parallels and with their apices on an extension of the earth's polar axis.

POLLY. Angel! That's it! You got it!

MAX. But that's only the first one. I don't know the others.

POLLY (*ironing*). Oh, Max—don't stand there and tell me you don't know a simple thing like question two— (*Leaning over to read*) What is meant by polar stereographic projection? (*As Max is silent*) Darling, please—you got this first one just absolutely perfect. Won't you just *try* this one?

MAX (*putting his hand over his eyes; screwing up his face*). Polar stereographic projection is a perspective conformal projection upon a plane tangent at the pole with the point of projection located at the opposite pole.

He sits down hard. Polly is staring with her mouth open. She rushes over and falls on her knees before Max.

POLLY. Angel! You're wonderful! It was just absolutely perfect. (*She scrambles up and rushes back to the ironing board.*) Question number three. Define azimuth and cite the standard example.

MAX (*up and walking*). Azimuth is the measurement of direction in degrees by the clock method. Example: using twelve o'clock as either True or Magnetic North, the direction of three o'clock reading clockwise is—the direction of three o'clock reading clockwise is—uh—uh—

POLLY. What street did we used to live on?

MAX. East Ninetieth—oh—*ninety!* The direction of three o'clock reading clockwise is ninety degrees—of nine o'clock is two hundred seventy degrees—of ten o'clock is three hundred degrees.

POLLY. Wonderful! All right, here we go. Question number four. What is resection?

MAX. Resection is the method of determining an unknown location by sighting from the unknown location —sighting from the unknown location—

POLLY. Max—remember that lady you told me about that used to give you piano lessons?

MAX. Who—Mrs. Poynter? (*Then*) Oh, yeah—on two known *points* and after making proper corrections, plotting the reciprocal of the azimuths obtained.

POLLY. See, stubborn. You knew it. You just couldn't think—

MAX. What's the use of kidding, Polly? You either know it or you don't. That's what you get graded on, not on how you play twenty questions with your wife.

POLLY. But with reminders, this way, you'd learn it, Max.

MAX. I'm more likely to say "so that each point on her reciprocal piano corresponds to Mrs. Poynter teaching me 'The Pixie Drill.' "

POLLY. Haven't heard you play that in years. (*Getting down to business*) Come on, now—question number five. What's a rhumb line?

MAX. A rhumb line is— (*Then; tensely*) Wait a minute. What's the date on the paper?

POLLY. July fifth.

MAX. That's last week's paper!

POLLY. No!

MAX. Last week's paper and I don't even know it—and I've already *passed* it! (*He walks an agonized circle.*) See what I mean?

POLLY (*going over to him*). Max—where is *this* week's paper?

He fishes in his pocket viciously and brings out the other paper. She takes it from him and walks back to the ironing board.

POLLY. All right—let's go.

MAX. No—no! It's no use, Polly.

POLLY. Max, we've gotten this far. *Please*—let's graduate.

MAX. You're indestructible!

POLLY. Aw—you say that 'cause you know my people've got money. (*She picks up the iron again—the paper laid out on the board where she can follow it.*) Question number one. What is a spinner? (*As Max is silent*) Well—anybody knows *that*, I should think. Come on now, let's hear it. What is a spinner?

MAX. I don't know.

POLLY. Yes, you do know. What is a spinner?

MAX. Polly, I know when I'm licked. I can't do it!

POLLY (*doggedly, putting down her iron and picking up the paper*). Max —what is—?

MAX. Give it up, will you, Polly?

POLLY. Did Mrs. Marshall and Mrs. Eisenhower give it up? What is a spinner?

MAX (*flinging himself into the chair again*). Polly—leave me alone!

POLLY (*going over to him, holding the paper, kneeling beside him*). Come on—a spinner is a fairing—

MAX. —is a fairing—

POLLY. —of approximately conical—

MAX. —of approximately conical—

POLLY. —or parabaloidal shape—

MAX. —or parabaloidal shape—

POLLY. —which is fitted coaxially—

MAX. —which is fitted coaxially—

POLLY. —with the propeller hub—

MAX. —with the propeller hub—

POLLY. —and revolves with the propeller!

MAX. —and revolves with the propeller!

Polly, her voice choked and tears in her eyes, pats Max.

POLLY. *That's right!* (*Then doggedly*) Question number two: What is the difference between the—

On her last line—as Max slumps in terror of what is to come and as Polly perseveres doggedly, reading through her tears—the scene fades out.

# PART FOUR

GOW'S OFFICE fades in. GOW, seen close, is turning the next to the last page of a sheaf of typewritten pages. The sheets tremble in his excited hands. His head moves rapidly sideways from line to line—until about midway down the page. He drops the paper and reaches for the dictograph, slapping a key down violently.

GOW. Kennedy! Get in here and read an editorial by a man who can write one! Get *in* here!

This dissolves to an insert of the front page of the *BULLETIN* as it comes "riding up to the camera." In bold type we see:

*SPECIAL EDITORIAL*
from
*MAX WHARTON*

This dissolves to: the BUNGALOW LIVING ROOM, where we see a "head closeup" of POLLY who is talking on the phone. She is so nervous she can hardly talk.

POLLY. It—it's really all right, Robert?

This cuts to a closeup of GOW who is talking on the phone.

GOW. It's the Max of old! Kiss him for me! And keep the stuff coming, honey . . . . Hello! Did you hear me, Polly?

POLLY is frightened and dry-mouthed. She speaks in a low voice.

POLLY. Sure—keep 'em coming.—Goodbye, Robert.

She sets the phone down. She is weak in the knees.—Then the closeup of Polly dissolves to a quick montage of Polly back at her typewriter, harassed and desperate. Intermixed with these "shots" of her are the following editorial titles, under the heading of dispatches from Max Wharton at camp: A WORLD COMING AWAKE—CROSSROADS—BIG AS LIFE—PEACE KNOCKS AGAIN—IT'S A SMALL WORLD—VICTORY IS WHAT YOU MAKE IT—CITIZENS OF THE WORLD—This in turn dissolves to a section of an OFFICER CANDIDATE CLASSROOM, where MAX is seen at a SCHOOL DESK taking his examinations, working from a sheet of printed questions. Around him are other men at similar desks. (MacDougal, the bugler, is prominent.) This dissolves to the BUNGALOW LIVING ROOM, where POLLY is again speaking on the phone. She is a haggard, bleary-eyed creature.

POLLY. He's still taking his final

exams, Robert. We won't know 'til tomorrow— (*She swallows.*) Tomorrow's the day, yes— (*Impatiently*) You know his chances as well as I do! Why do you ask me that every time you call? We *know* he hasn't got a prayer! (*Then; wearily*) Yes, Robert—I will—the minute I know.

As she hangs up, the scene dissolves to MAX'S DORMITORY ROOM at night. Max is in bed. The view moves in toward him as he lies awake in the dark, his eyes directed at the ceiling. (Across from him, MacDougal is asleep.) Max directs a prayer to heaven.

MAX. Second Lieutenant Max Wharton. (*Fervently*) Please—let it come to pass.

This dissolves to the BUNGALOW BEDROOM at night.

POLLY is in bed, and like Max, she lies awake in the dark, her eyes fixed upward.

POLLY. —and please—let Max graduate— (*A troubled pause*) No— maybe You'd better flunk him out— that is, if You can do it without breaking his heart— (*Then*) Or, look—if You could pass Max and at the same time not let Robert sell the— (*In a choked voice*) Or, I don't know, really! You'll just have to work it out Yourself! I really don't know!

The scene dissolves to an insert of a poster with the dramatic heading:

GRADUATES

The word comes forward on the screen! And now the scene starts moving rapidly down the list of names—one to one hundred, one hundred to two hundred; finally we are traveling down the "two hundred" column—and there is a sudden stop. The line reads:

### 271. MAX WHARTON

A closeup of MAX shows him staring open-mouthed, eyes wide. Other graduates mill around him as the scene dissolves to the BUNGALOW COURT, and Max is seen in full view, dashing for the bungalow from the Field across the way. He leaps onto the porch and bursts inside.

MAX. Polly!

The scene cuts to the LIVING ROOM as Max bursts in. Polly is not in evidence. Max rushes to the bedroom, calling in:

MAX. Polly!

No answer. Evidently Polly isn't home. He rushes outside.

Max emerges on the PORCH. Obviously believing she might be with one of the neighbors, Max yells to the bungalow court.

MAX. Polly! Polly!

From their respective bungalows emerge Mrs. Collins, Mrs. Dumbrowski and Mrs. Greenberg.

MRS. COLLINS. Mrs. Wharton went out an hour ago!

MAX. Where?

MRS. DUMBROWSKI. She said—for a walk—anyplace—where she wouldn't hear any news!

MAX. Why—the silly—! I *graduated!*

MRS. COLLINS. Oh, that's wonderful!

MRS. GREENBERG. You mean the names are posted?

MAX. Number two seventy-one! That's me!

Mrs. Dumbrowski starts toward the Field, the others with her.

MRS. DUMBROWSKI. Well, then— where's Fred?

MRS. COLLINS. Hurray! I don't care whether Harry graduated or not—we're out of *here!*

Max watches them go—he is still laughing. Then, suddenly he notices a man who is coming up the walk. A cab which had pulled up during the above is standing at·the curb.

We get a fairly close view of the MAN (Joel I. Nixon) with a briefcase—standing a moment to figure out where 26-D might be. Then his eyes fasten on Max.

MAX's VOICE. Joel Nixon!

Nixon hurries forward, and then the two men reach each other with outstretched hands.

NIXON. Well, well, Max! How are you?

MAX. How *am* I? I'm a second lieutenant! I graduated five minutes ago!

NIXON. That's simply marvelous, Max. Congratulations! (*Another warm handshake. Max pulls Nixon inside.*)

MAX. Thanks! Come on in, Joel—come in.

NIXON. What a time finding this place! I was all over camp.

A full view of the LIVING ROOM as they sweep in: Max is deliriously happy.

MAX (*sweeping his hand*). A humble dwelling—but a scene of triumph! It was here, my friend, that a plain little woman cooked and scrubbed, skimped and deprived herself of the simple necessities—actually worked her fingers to the bone, to give her boy an education!

NIXON. Who would that be?

MAX. Polly! Polly! No one will ever know the miracle that woman's performed for one Max Wharton!

NIXON. Uh—where is she, Max?

MAX. She'll be back any minute. (*Then; racing on*) —And did it all under heroic circumstances—plagued by that telephone day after day—poring over that typewriter night after night—to save the scalp of Joel I. Nixon!

As he talks, Max points dramatically to both the phone and typewriter on the work table.

NIXON. To save—what?

MAX (*laughing*). All right—all right —it was her scalp, too. But, brother, how she worked. You should get down on your knees! And if her stuff wasn't up to par, Joe—remember what the poor girl was going through!

NIXON. *What* stuff?

MAX. The copy—the work—the scenes!

NIXON. Max—take it easy. *What* scenes?

MAX. The picture, silly. The one Polly wrote. The one you're producing, for heaven's sake! The one shooting right now!

NIXON. You mean—Polly's picture?

MAX. Joel—what's the matter with you? How many other pictures would I know about?

NIXON. That picture has been postponed for two months.

MAX. But—the script's in trouble—a *lot* of trouble.

NIXON. Who said so? It's perfect. Always was.

MAX. Then why drive Polly crazy with desperate phone calls? Is that your idea of a joke?

NIXON. I haven't spoken to Polly since she left Hollywood!

MAX. Now cut it out, Joel.

NIXON. Not *once!*

MAX (*after a short pause, slowly, pointing to the typewriter*). And—that script—you never *asked* for it—or *saw* any of it?

NIXON. I don't know what you're talking about. Max, this graduation has gone to your head.

MAX (*shaking his head as if to get his brains sorted out*). Wait a minute. Let me start over. Joel—you *did* come all the way from Hollywood to see Polly?

NIXON (*tapping his briefcase*). I brought an idea she might be interested in working on. I knew she wouldn't come back to Hollywood to talk about it—and it couldn't be discussed over the phone—

MAX. Joel—and you swear—you never called her *once!*

NIXON. Are we back to that? (*Max starts walking circles.*) You say she was working?

MAX. Like a dog! Never even slept! (*He comes to the typewriter, his brain churning.*)

NIXON. It's simple! She's got a new book in her head. She *always* works hard when she writes.

MAX. Not like that. And besides, there was—that phone. (*Then*) Wait. Wait a minute— (*His eyes grow big.*) It's hard to believe but—I know how to prove it.

Max suddenly snaps to action. Nixon is utterly bewildered. Max grabs his cap.

MAX. I've got to run into town, Joel. You don't mind if I use your cab?

NIXON. What about Polly? Aren't you going to wait?

MAX (*half way to the door, stopping*). Oh, I just remembered—she—she won't be back until late tonight, Joel.

NIXON. But you said—

MAX. I recall now—she told me when I last saw her—that was three days ago—she'd have to go over to St. Petersburg. Her mother's there—been ill. But she wouldn't miss tomorrow—graduation exercises. (*He comes over and takes Nixon's arm.*) You're staying in town, I assume, Joel. Let's ride in together. I'll drop you off. (*He starts leading a puzzled Nixon toward the door.*) Why not come out for the graduation in the morning, Joel? Then you and Polly can have all the talk you want—

This dissolves to the FACADE of a BUILDING. We see just that part of the pediment which tells us this is the MIAMI PUBLIC LIBRARY and this quickly dissolves through to the interior of the PUBLIC LIBRARY.

In a small corner section of the newspaper morgue, Max is just sitting down with a large section of papers, snapped together and labelled on the stick *New York Bulletin.*—He opens the large pile of hung-together papers. Looking at the date lines and thinking an instant, he turns the papers rapidly. He turns midway through. Suddenly, what hits his eye rocks him!—We see an insert: the first announcement in the *Bulletin* of "EDITORIAL by MAX WHARTON."

When MAX recovers from this shock, he frantically flips the page and starts to read, the scene dissolving to the BUNGALOW COURT: POLLY and NEIGHBORS are near the porch of 26-D. Polly is surrounded by Mrs. Collins, Mrs. Dumbrowski, and Mrs. Greenberg.

MRS. GREENBERG. Yes! *He graduated!*

MRS. COLLINS. Two hundred and seventy-something!

MRS. DUMBROWSKI. Isn't that wonderful!

POLLY (*weakly sitting down on the porch step*). It—it certainly is.

MRS. GREENBERG (*as the phone is heard ringing from inside 26-D*).

Your phone's ringing, Mrs. Wharton. Polly knows what that means. She casts a nervous glance toward the door, but gives no indication of budging.

POLLY (*weakly*). I—I think I'll just let it ring.

This dissolves to a closeup of GOW at his desk. He is listening to his secretary's voice over the dictograph.

SECRETARY'S VOICE. Nobody answers on the Wharton call, Mister Gow.

GOW. Keep trying! Ring every fifteen minutes! Keep trying!

This in turn dissolves to the interior of the MIAMI PUBLIC LIBRARY, where MAX is reading, as before, with the same absorption. We notice that the bundle of papers is now turned to almost the last one of the pile. As Max finishes, he leans back. As he mechanically turns the last paper to flatten out the pile of papers in front of him the scene dissolves to the BUNGALOW LIVING ROOM at dusk. Polly is seated several feet from the phone. It is getting somewhat dark. The phone rings. Polly is startled. She makes no move toward it. The phone continues to ring.—And this dissolves to the interior of a CAB

where MAX is seen slumped in a corner, thinking, puzzling. Suddenly the cab stops. Max shakes himself out of his stupor, and moves to the door.

The FIELD and BUNGALOW COURT entrance come into view, showing that the cab has pulled up at the bungalow court. As Max gets out and prepares to pay the driver the scene cuts to the LIVING ROOM, where POLLY is still watching the phone. She looks at her watch. It is time for it to ring again. It does. Now, with a sigh, she gets up. She advances on the instrument. Taking a deep breath, she picks it up.

POLLY (*without preliminaries*). Put Mister Gow on. (*A pause; then forthrightly*) Max graduated, Robert—That's what I said. He's Second Lieutenant Max Wharton. (*She listens; then angrily*) Must you do that right away? . . . I'll tell you what I expect—

Out on the porch MAX is seen coming to a pause, arrested by Polly's voice from inside, the more startling since the windows are dark.

POLLY'S VOICE (*passionately*). I expect you to act like a man with some feeling! I expect you to let Max *enjoy* a triumph like this—not come rushing down here with tragic news, waving a paper that says his child was sold out from under him—

MAX is seen in a closeup. He understands everything.

POLLY'S VOICE (*continuing*). —saying "that's what you get for serving your country—and for going through tortures to do it"—I don't know! But if you could just wait a little while. I don't mean long—

Max has moved several feet from the porch. Now he walks quickly again toward the door, yelling:

MAX. Polly!

He rushes up onto the porch and bursts into the bungalow, following which we see the LIVING ROOM as Max bursts in. The room is quite dark. Polly has evidently hung up with great suddenness.

POLLY. Max—Max, darling!

The two are seen together as Polly rushes into Max's arms. She is crying and laughing—and hanging onto him hard.

POLLY. My wonder boy! (*Brushing a tear*) I'm so darned happy I—! (*Then; rapidly*) Dark in here, isn't it? Well, you see, I was lying down and the phone— (*A touch hysterically*) Of all people—*Gow!* He was curious—and I *told* him—*yes*, sir— (*proudly*) —two hundred and seventy—in a class of three hundred! *My* Max—brighter than thirty other fellas—

MAX (*quietly*). Two hundred seventy-one, dear.

POLLY. All right—twenty-nine fellas! Robert was—was very happy. He—he may come down for graduation, dear—

MAX. Polly . . .

POLLY. It wouldn't matter—seeing that old stinkweed *now*, would it, darling?

MAX. Polly—listen—

But before he can get any further, the phone rings. Max makes a move for it.

POLLY. No, no—let me, Max. That—that's Joel Nixon again, I'm sure. (*She grabs the phone.*) Hello . . . Yes, he is, Mac . . .

At mention of "Mac," Max grabs the phone from Polly.

MAX. Mac—what is it?

The interior of a PHONE BOOTH at camp comes into view. MAC DOUGAL is seen phoning. He is pretty excited and worried.

MAC DOUGAL. They've been looking all over camp for you—to report to Colonel Foley!

In the LIVING ROOM, POLLY and MAX are seen together. Max is in an immediate dither.

MAX. Okay. Thanks. (*He hangs up.*) Holy smoke! Colonel Foley!

He grabs Polly and kisses her fast, then rushes for the door. With the door open, he turns.

MAX. I love you, baby! I will 'til I die!

He is gone; and on Polly's tearful, miserable attitude the scene dissolves to GOW'S OFFICE at night as Gow at his desk, with his chin on his chest, grimly reaches over and flips the dictograph key.

SECRETARY'S VOICE. Yes, Mister Gow.

GOW. Miss Gilbert—you remember the deed of sale requiring Mr. Wharton's signature—the one I took down there six weeks ago?

SECRETARY'S VOICE. Yes.

GOW. I want another copy.—And get me a reservation on a plane to Florida—*tonight!*

As Gow flips the key back up, and sits back grimly the scene dissolves to COLONEL FOLEY'S OFFICE at night. Max is standing stiffly before Colonel Foley.

COLONEL FOLEY. —about that piece you wrote for the camp paper, Wharton—Washington has made up its mind about that— (*A pause; then smiling*) They like it.

MAX (*in a very small voice*). They do?

COLONEL FOLEY. We'd like you to make the graduating speech to the class tomorrow, Wharton.

We get a CLOSEUP of MAX.

COLONEL FOLEY'S VOICE. Could you prepare one tonight?

Max simply stares, his eyebrows flung up in surprise as the scene dissolves to the PARADE GROUNDS of TETLEY FIELD. Bands are playing. (In the foreground is the speaker's platform and flanking audience, their backs to the camera.) The point of focus is on the other side of the Field where the marching companies are appearing out of the camp streets.

In a fairly close view we then see the AUDIENCE in the RIGHT WING BLEACHER. Polly is sitting with Mrs. Foley and Mrs. Gates. They are looking off to the companies advancing. Polly's face is alight.

The SPEAKERS' PLATFORM now comes into view and we see Colonel Foley among other Army dignitaries; and finally the marching COMPANIES.— There is a closeup of MAX marching in the company of graduates.

Farther out on the field the companies are making their formations and approaching the bleachers.—And now they advance toward the graduating platform.—We then see the graduating class and around it the seven thousand men in the school—an imposing spectacle.

POLLY, seen at close range, is thrilled by the spectacle. All she can say to Mrs. Foley and Mrs. Gates is: "Here comes Max."

Mrs. Gates and Mrs. Foley "register" this remark. Polly is unconscious of having said anything funny.

We again see the marching companies as they approach the bleachers, then POLLY, as she looks off a little to her right; her breath catches as in a wider view she sees Gow pushing through the row ahead to take a seat directly in front of her.

POLLY (*with an involuntary gasp*). Robert!

The two women with Polly smile at Gow. Gow doffs his hat and smiles back, keeping a very grim expression for Polly. Without a word he sits down, his briefcase in his lap, eyes front, back straight. He is there on business and nothing will swerve him. Polly looks from the back of Gow's head to Max out on the field. She is an agonized woman.

MRS. FOLEY (*to Polly*). Isn't it nice of Mr. Gow to come all this way for the graduation?

POLLY (*grimly*). Yes, isn't it?

The companies are now coming to their positions in front of the speakers' stand. The graduating class of three hundred men forms front and center. Behind it are formed the six or seven thousand men. All remain standing.

We get a close view of MAX fairly down front among the men who have come to a halt. He is stiff and proud and smiling. Then we see GOW and POLLY as we hear the commands which bring the various companies to their positions. In this "shot" we face directly on Gow in the foreground, and behind him, a little higher in the next row, Polly. Polly ·bends forward and hisses into Gow's ear.

POLLY (*almost blubbering*). You couldn't wait, could you? You couldn't let Max have his little day of triumph—You had to come flying down here like an old crow!

Gow doesn't move a muscle. He just sits clutching his briefcase, his jaws snapped closed. His eyes look front.

GOW (*without expression*). Very impressive.

Next there is a close view of MAX as his eyes turn and locate Polly in the stands; it is followed by a close view of POLLY spotting Max, putting on a brave little smile for him; and this dissolves into a full view of the MASSED COMPANIES indicating a part of the graduation ceremony. We see MAX, his arm raised, in the course of taking the oath; POLLY looking off at Max; and then GOW and POLLY. Gow is still looking front, like the executioner· himself. Polly has reached a pitch now that causes her to lean forward again, in heart-breaking pleading.

POLLY. Robert—that Bill of Sale you want Max to sign—*I'll* get it done for you.

GOW. I'll do it.

POLLY. I don't want you to see him or talk to him!

GOW. Why not?

POLLY. Because—he'll hate you—after breaking his back to write those editorials. Why rake all that up again?

GOW. I don't mind.

Polly is about to say something more when suddenly her head jerks off to the far right. Next, we see what she sees: JOEL NIXON is approaching a seat a little way down in the bleachers. And another close view of POLLY makes it plain that Joel Nixon is disastrous news to her at this point. Polly is frozen, as the oath is being delivered at the graduation ceremony.

NIXON is seen sitting down. He glances in Polly's direction, and suddenly spots her. His face lights up. He waves his hand cheerfully at · her, mouthing "Hello, Polly." POLLY, with a very sickly smile, waves a feeble hand back and mouths "Hello, Joel." And on her completely sick expression, the scene dissolves to a full view of the graduation ceremony, revealing the speakers' platform and the audience bleachers. Colonel Foley, at the microphone, is just finishing saying:

COLONEL FOLEY. —Second Lieutenant Max Wharton.

There is applause from the bleachers; and from out of the massed men, in perhaps the second or third row, Max Wharton emerges and starts toward the speakers' platform.

MAX gains the speakers' platform and starts to move toward the center.

COLONEL FOLEY is seen speaking again.

COLONEL FOLEY. Lieutenant Wharton will now respond for the graduating class.

There is a close view of GOW and POLLY as before—Gow grimly looking toward the speakers' platform, without expression, and Polly, desperate beyond words, leaning forward from behind him.

POLLY (*whispering in Gow's ear*). Robert, please! Go back home. I'll have the paper in New York tomorrow—signed. (*But Gow acts as if he hadn't heard.*)

MAX, seen close, approaches the speaker's stand. His first glance is to his right, toward Polly. He smiles a little in that direction.—And POLLY, seen close, smiles back in Max's direction. Then her frantic attention is again on Gow's back.

MAX takes from his pocket a single sheet of paper, unfolds it, and lays it before him. He speaks his introductory words *ad lib,* looking out at his audience.

MAX. To be asked to address this class is a great honor. There are many things I've wanted to say since coming here—important things, about the job we're doing and the bigger job yet to do.

POLLY and GOW are leaning forward.

POLLY. Robert, please!

Then the scene cuts back to MAX:

MAX. I've looked for ways to say all that. And then, just yesterday, I came across something written that said it more simply and far better than I could ever hope to. And I decided instead of a speech of my own, I would read this to you. It has a rather curious title—*The World and Apple Pie.*

GOW and POLLY: Gow's eyebrows jump at Max's last statement. The title rings a bell. Polly does not seem to have heard. Her entire attention is on Gow. Mrs. Foley and Mrs. Gates smile.— This cuts to a closeup of MACDOUGAL standing among the graduating class. In his mind too the "apple-pie" phrase remotely touches a chord. And this is followed by a close view of MAX beginning to read from the paper.

MAX. "What has apple pie got to do with the world? Simply this: You go about making them in exactly the

same way. For instance, apple pie. You just put a lot of things in a little pot and mix. That's where the secret is—the right ingredients in the little pot, down to the last pinch of flour and the last grain of salt. Because what comes out of the oven can never be any better than the things that went into the making. That's the rule to remember. It's very simple."

POLLY: Her head jerks toward Max.

POLLY (*half under her breath*). The editorial!

A closeup of MACDOUGAL shows that he recalls the pie incident now and smiles as Max's voice is heard.

MAX'S VOICE. "And the world—that's in the making right now, isn't it? Well, if you want it to turn out right, just remember the rule. Whatever goes into the making, no matter how small, will show up in the end."

A closeup of POLLY shows her listening in amazement as Max continues.

MAX'S VOICE. "Joe Adams found that out—a young reporter I knew. Joe's world looked perfect. My dish, he said. But some pretty foul things were cooking in it—like the murder of a far-off country called Manchuria, and of another called Ethiopia—and the victory at Munich of a certain maniac. Just little things happening thousands of miles away."

A closeup shows MAX reading earnestly.

MAX. "What did they have to do with Joe's world? Why everything! Because Manchuria, Ethiopia and Munich were his world, too—whether he knew it or not. And those little crimes were cooking in it. And I'll tell you what they had to do with Joe—they caught up with him and they killed him. And Joe is buried now on an island in the Pacific."

A closeup of POLLY: Her eyes and head are directed steadily at Max—as if she were carved in stone. Tears began to form slowly. Then we see MAX again.

MAX. "You see, Joe died to tell us you can't beat the rules. The right things have to go into the making. Remember, if the smallest ingredient is wrong, you will find it in the final result. Or, no—it will find you."

We see MACDOUGAL serious-faced—as Max's words come over.

MAX'S VOICE. "So, what is it you're dreaming of for the future? Is it happiness you want? Then start by making certain of happiness for the two billion other souls on this planet." (*As we see him again*) "And prosperity? Then, mix in prosperity for every other human being alive. Don't overlook the farthest corner of the earth, and the humblest man living in it."

MAX, seen closer, is now delivering the piece strongly, warming to the conclusion.

MAX. "Lasting peace? And a life of spirit for yourself and your children —is that what you want? Then, add those same things for two billion others, of every kind and creed. And finally, add this, too—add the Sermon on the Mount as the rule of life. And add your voice and your means and your strength until there is mercy and justice for the humblest man on earth. For otherwise, when the final story of your life is told, like Joe's— you will have had none of these things yourself."

He looks up and folds the paper. Applause—and cheers from the men— breaks over him. Then this cuts to MRS.

GATES and POLLY as Mrs. Gates is applauding her head off. She turns to Polly.

MRS. GATES. He's just wonderful! (*Then*) Why, Mrs. Wharton—where are you going?

But Polly, tears in her eyes, has already fled her seat and stumbles out quickly.

MRS. GATES (*calling after Polly*). Mrs. Wharton—

The scene dissolves to the BUNGALOW LIVING ROOM. Nixon is sprawled on the sofa, fanning himself. Gow is on his feet, annoyed, perspired, and anxious. The trunks are packed and prominently placed—and so are Polly's suitcases. She had obviously packed the night before. Gow tries to open the window by stamping about.

GOW. Well, what's holding them up? I haven't got all day!

NIXON. Why didn't you go down on the field?

GOW. In that wild crush? What I've got to do couldn't be done on the field.

Suddenly running steps are heard outside and Max comes bounding in.

MAX (*calling*). Polly!

GOW. Well! Here we are!

MAX (*going right for the bedroom*). Polly!

NIXON. She's not here, Max.

MAX. Where is she?

GOW. How should I know?

MAX. You were sitting right with her!

NIXON. Didn't she come down on the field?

MAX. No! (*To Gow*) What happened to her?

GOW. All I know is—she looked for a minute like she'd passed out—then all of a sudden she was all right—except she was blubbering her head off—and away she went!

MAX. *Where?*

GOW. I haven't the faintest idea! But she can't be lost! (*Gow is quickly reaching into his briefcase.*) Now, if you'll settle down for a minute, *Lieutenant Wharton,* I've got something to take up with you—

MAX. Whatever it is—and I can imagine—first I intend to find Polly!

GOW. Now, wait—!

MAX (*starting for the door*). You heard me, you old bullhead—!

Max is at the door when he stops abruptly. The door is opening and a rather dreary-looking Polly is entering the room.

GOW. Hurray! She's found.

NIXON (*getting up*). Hello, Polly!

Polly is looking at no one but Max. He smiles at her.

MAX. Hello, darling. Where were you?

POLLY (*quietly*). Taking a long walk.

NIXON. A walk?

GOW. This is the nuttiest family I ever saw—!

POLLY (*suddenly rushing into Max's arms, blubbering*). Oh, Max! There's nobody like you—nobody in this whole entire gorgeous stinking world!

MAX (*softly; as he holds her*). I agree, darling.

GOW. He agrees!

POLLY (*lifting her face*). Max, how —how did you find out—?

MAX. Well, now—who do you think I bumped into around here yesterday? Your old friend, Joel Nixon.

POLLY. Oh.

NIXON. How are you, Polly?

MAX (*with a wink at Polly*). Wasn't satisfied with phoning every other day—he had to trail you down here besides.

NIXON. Who? Me?

GOW (*who has whipped the paper out of his briefcase, suddenly*). Now, look, Max—there's something here you've got to sign. I'm selling the paper.

MAX (*casually*). You don't say?

POLLY (*tearfully*). Yes, Max. You see, that was why—

MAX (*breaking in lightly*). Great speech I made today, wasn't it, Polly?

GOW (*explosively*). His own editorial was great, he says. "Beautifully expressed," he announces to ten thousand people. Why don't you let somebody else say so?

MAX (*turning to Gow*). Well, go ahead. *You* say so.

GOW (*angrily*). All right—*I* say so! And I also say—*sign* this thing!

MAX. Then why sign it? Why not keep the fellow who wrote a thing like that?

POLLY. Max!

GOW. Wait a minute. You mean you'll quit—?

MAX. No, I mean Polly. She wrote it.

GOW. You're crazy.

MAX. It's true, Robert. The first time I ever saw it was yesterday—at the public library. She did all of them right here—with her own little brains—and Nixon interrupting twenty times a day—

NIXON (*bewildered up to now, reacts in shock*). Hey—look—

MAX (*laughing*). Oh, hello, Joel— (*Then to Gow*) Right under your nose, you chowder head—the greatest hunk of editorial brains in the country! Make her an offer before I wire the truth to every paper in New York!

GOW (*approaching meekly*). Polly—my dear Mrs. Wharton—

POLLY (*to Gow*). You mean go back to New York? No, I'm going to stay with Max until he's shipped out of the country. So just forget it, boys.

Polly walks away from them. The two men follow her.

MAX (*following*). Darling, there's a home front job to do—and you were born to do this one.

GOW (*also following*). Polly—you darn fool—this answer came straight from heaven!

POLLY (*who keeps on walking*). Policeman—these men are following me.

NIXON (*as she passes him*). Hello, Polly—remember me?

She ignores him, walking right by him. The men keep following her.

MAX. Polly, listen—

POLLY. Ho-hum— (*But now Mrs. Foley's voice breaks in on them.*)

MRS. FOLEY'S VOICE. Yoo-hoo—may we come in?

All the people circulating pause as Mrs. Foley, followed by Mrs. Gates and Colonel Foley, comes traipsing in.

MRS. GATES. It's us, again.

MAX. Hello, there! Hello, Colonel.

(*There is an exchange of hellos between Gow and the Foley party.*)

NIXON. Ahem—I'm glad I came.

MRS. FOLEY (*to Polly*). Where on earth did you rush off to, Mrs. Wharton?

MAX (*laughing*). It was just something she'd written.

POLLY. Well, sit down, everybody.

COLONEL FOLEY. We can only stay a second—and Lieutenant Wharton will have to be at the station in a half hour.

POLLY. A half hour? Where's Max going?

MRS. FOLEY. Ah! Now wouldn't you like to know?

Colonel Foley has taken Max's orders out of his pocket.

MRS. GATES (*to Max*). The Colonel picked up your orders.

The Colonel hands Max the envelope. Polly takes it from Max and rips open the envelope as the Colonel says:

COLONEL FOLEY. You thought I wasn't paying any attention that day when you talked to me about it here. Well, I guess I can take a hint. (*Then; to Max*) You want to go to Crocker Field, Arkansas—and that's where you're going!

Polly, by this time, is reading the same information from the orders, her expression frozen.

POLLY. Crocker!

MRS. FOLEY. And it wasn't the easiest thing in the world to fix.

MRS. GATES. No, it wasn't.

MRS. FOLEY. But Daddy just put his foot down and you got it.

MAX (*as Polly and he exchange glances*). Well, I don't know what to say, sir. Thank you very much.

POLLY. Yes—it was just wonderful of you—

COLONEL FOLEY. Not at all. Well, we're on our way. (*He shakes hands with Polly.*) And someday when the war is over, we must all get together.

MRS. FOLEY. Goodbye, Mrs. Wharton. It was wonderful knowing you—and write lots of books, won't you?

MRS. GATES. And we'll certainly try hard to read them.

There are goodbyes all around as the Foleys move to the door and exit.

POLLY. Crocker!

MAX. That's awful!

GOW. What is? What happened?

POLLY (*exclaiming again to herself*). Crocker!

GOW (*to Nixon*). What's going on? What's this Crocker all about?

NIXON. Don't ask me. I'm not even here.

GOW (*loudly*). Will somebody tell me what's going on?

MAX. Crocker Field, Robert, is for men only. The wives never go.

GOW (*beginning to understand this*). The wives never go! You don't say!

POLLY (*blurting*). Max, you got graduated today—not divorced.

GOW. You mean not even Paula Wharton could go to Crocker!

POLLY (*angrily*). That's what the *Army* thinks!

MAX. Polly, listen—there's no hotel —you'd have to find a room and you couldn't—

POLLY. I'll pitch a tent!

MAX. Darling, the field is twenty miles away. I could never get to see you. You're not going! I won't let you!

GOW. That means Polly goes back to New York with me—is that right?

Polly doesn't answer him. She goes into Max's arms.

POLLY. Oh, Max!

MAX. Darling. Be a brave kid, will you? I've got just one half hour to make the station.

POLLY (*pushing out of his arms*). Yes, that's right. Well, I can be ready in a minute. (*She takes a few steps toward the bedroom.*)

MAX. Ready for *what*?

POLLY. Why, I'm going to ride with you all the way to Crocker.

MAX. You can't!

POLLY. Sure I can! Everything's packed— (*She starts again for the bedroom.*)

GOW. Polly—I want an answer!

MAX (*to Polly*). Darling—wait—how do we know you can get a ticket?

POLLY. You mean one of those silly little pieces of paper? Hah! (*Then*) All right, boys. Don't stand around. There's baggage. Who's got a car?

MAX (*protesting mildly*). Sweetheart—

POLLY. There was a taxi waiting out there. Speak up. Whose is it?

GOW (*explosively*). Mine!

POLLY. That's more like it. Well, come on—get this stuff moving.

NIXON. Polly—can I have *one word*—?

POLLY (*casually*). Oh, hello, Joel. Glad you came. You take those two there.

She indicates the baggage, sort of pushing Joel at it.

POLLY (*adding*). That's a boy.

GOW. One second!

POLLY. *Move*, Robert. Grab a couple of those and stop yammering! (*Gow moves to grab some of the pieces.*)

MAX (*laughing*). Come on—my wife and I are taking a trip. Let's not waste time.

Bewildered, Nixon and Gow take up bags and so does Max. In this operation Polly helps load them up, heaving a duffle bag on Gow's shoulders. During all this, she is full of words of encouragement—

POLLY. Easy does it! That's the spirit!

As the three men start for the door, they are arrested by a suitcase which is pushed in by a young girl who follows it. All look in surprise at the girl.

GIRL (*mildly*). Is this bungalow 26-D?

POLLY (*quickly*). Yes, yes, it is! (*Waving the girl away from the door*) Would you mind, dear?— Thank you, very much. (*Then*) Everything clear, boys.

GOW (*protesting as he goes through the door*). Polly—

That's as far as Gow gets because either Nixon or Max following him gooses

him with the baggage. The young girl is totally bewildered, looking from the exiting men to Polly. Polly immediately heads for the bedroom, saying as she goes:

POLLY. The new tenant! Well, well —come right in. Make yourself comfortable. (*Charmingly*) You'll have to excuse me—I'm in a bit of a hurry.

Polly has disappeared into the bedroom.

GIRL (*amazed, calling after Polly*). You're Paula Wharton!

Polly comes out of the bedroom with hat, purse and gloves and during the following is putting on both hat and gloves with great speed and excitement.

POLLY. Yes, I am. You're absolutely right. Oh, you'll love it here. Nicest bungalow in the whole court. 'Course the roof leaks a little—and there's no shower. (*She adds with a laugh:*) But there *are* moths. And if you just put a few ants in the cupboard it keeps the salt—I mean, it's the other way around! And there's no water in the kitchen sink, but you'll get to like it that way. And—let's see—oh, yes, this window here is a little tricky—you don't open it—you just—

MAX'S VOICE. Polly!

POLLY (*yelling back*). Coming! (*Starting to stamp*). You just—

On the third attempt, the window drops, but Polly also goes through the floor.

POLLY. Oh my goodness—!

At this point Gow and Nixon come bustling in and see Polly extricating herself from the floor.

NIXON. For heaven's sake!

GOW. What—?

POLLY (*to the girl*). That's the general idea, but you're not supposed to go through the floor. (*Then to the men*) Well, goodbye! Thanks a lot, fellas! (*She moves for the door.*)

NIXON. Polly, could I just—?

MAX'S VOICE (*from outside*). Polly!

POLLY (*smiling at Joel*). It was nice seeing you again, Joel. (*She continues to head for the door.*)

GOW (*pursuing her*). Wait a second!

POLLY (*stopping in the doorway*). Robert, have those trunks sent to New York.

GOW. You mean you'll be there? You're taking the job?

POLLY (*now through the door, sticking her head back in, smiling at him*). What do *you* think? You big, friendly stinkweed! (*She dashes out, and Gow rushes to the door.*)

Next we see Max waiting at the curb near the taxi, waving to Polly, and Polly going toward Max. Gow's voice is heard, calling "Polly!" She pulls up for a second.—This cuts to GOW in the doorway.

GOW (*with a broad smile*). How shall I address you in the future—sir or madam?

POLLY (*seen close, calling back to Gow*). Robert—you bring out the sentimental in me. Just call me boss.

She starts out, and we then see her rushing toward Max as the scene fades out.

# A MEDAL FOR BENNY

## (A Paramount Picture)

Screenplay by FRANK BUTLER

Additional Dialogue by JACK WAGNER

Story by JOHN STEINBECK and JACK WAGNER

Produced by PAUL JONES

Directed by IRVING PICHEL

## The Cast

| | |
|---|---|
| LOLITA SIERRA . . . . . | Dorothy Lamour |
| JOE MORALES . . . . . | Arturo de Cordova |
| CHARLEY MARTIN . . . . | J. Carrol Naish |
| RAPHAEL CATALINA . . | Mikhail Rasumny |
| CHITO SIERRA . . . . . | Fernando Alvarado |
| ZACK MIBBS . . . . . . | Charles Dingle |
| EDGAR LOVEKIN . . . . | Frank McHugh |
| TOODLES CASTRO . . . | Rosita Moreno |
| MAYOR OF PANTERA . . | Grant Mitchell |
| THE GENERAL . . . . . | Douglass Dumbrille |

and others

Film Editor—ARTHUR SCHMIDT

# A MEDAL FOR BENNY

## PART ONE

The following words fade in: "Pantera, in the spring of 1942—a small California town which pretends for its own pride that it is a city." This sentence dissolves into: "In the old part of town are the Paisanos—Americans of mixed Indian and Spanish blood. A simple, friendly people, they have been here for more than a hundred years, and are the original California settlers." This dissolves into: "This is a story of these people, but in particular the story of—"

And this dissolves into a long view of the PANTERA MISSION in the morning. It is a typical early California Mission. A young paisano in his twenties, bareheaded and wearing a white shirt and faded blue-jean pants, is walking briskly toward the entrance.

This dissolves to a little old PRIEST, with a kindly face and wearing a threadbare cassock, on his knees setting out spring flowers with a trowel. He is perspiring a little, and his hands are stained with the good earth. This is FATHER BLY. The shadow of a man falls athwart the scene.

MAN'S VOICE. Good morning, Father.

As Father Bly turns and looks up the scene draws back to show the young paisano. His hair is curly, black and tousled, his skin the color of old copper. This is JOE MORALES. For a moment the old priest stares up at him, then smiles with dawning recognition.

FATHER BLY. Why, *Joe Morales!*

JOE. Sure. That's me. (*Grinning*) By golly, Father, you've got a good memory. (*Joe squats on his heels cowboy fashion; then speaks urgently:*) Look, Father, I got a big problem. I want your advice. (*The old man gives him a little smile.*)

It is very necessary that I pray to the right Saint. Tell me, Father, who has the most importance with the fishes? Rafael Catalina says Saint Andrew. Pamfilo Chavez says Saint Peter.

FATHER BLY (*solemnly*). Is it with fish or with the fishermen?

JOE. It is with both.

FATHER BLY (*smiling*). Then, my son, I would advise you to pray to Saint Peter, although Saint Andrew is very efficacious.

JOE (*briskly, getting up*). I will talk to Saint Peter. Thank you very much, Father. (*He starts out quickly toward the Mission.*)

FATHER BLY (*calling after him*). Don't be such a stranger around here, Joe Morales.

This scene dissolves to the MISSION.— Subdued music is heard as the view follows JOE to an ancient shrine of Saint Peter. He drops a nickel in the offertory box, takes a candle, sets it in one of the candlesticks, lights it, drops on his knees, then crosses himself. He looks shyly up at Saint Peter.

JOE (*with great reverence*). Blessed Saint Peter, I am Joe Morales . . .

A fellow who has not been to church, maybe, as much as he should, but who has always had very nice thoughts about you. Blessed Little Saint, I have taken upon myself a great responsibility . . . I have bought a boat. I have put all my eggs into one box, and with my friend Charlie Martin, I am about to go into the fish business.

The IMAGE of SAINT PETER is seen in a semi-closeup as Joe prays. The Face is ageless, serene.

JOE'S VOICE. So, Blessed Saint, as a great favor, I am asking you to let me have a good share of the fish and for you not to give them all to the Portagees and Italians.

JOE and the statue are seen together as he continues.

JOE. And that will hurt nobody because in Santa Cruz Bay there is plenty of fish for everybody.

He pauses, smiles wistfully up at Saint Peter, and continues:

JOE. Blessed Saint—Little Santito— it is of great importance that I catch lots of fish. Because then I can make plenty of money and marry a girl that I love very much. This girl you know, because she comes here every Sunday. (*With growing passion*) Little Santito, if you will only look into my heart you will see here how good she is—how beautiful. And you will understand why it is that I cannot sleep, or eat, or even live at all unless I am with her forever. So, Beloved Little Saint, make it so that my nets are heavy with big fishes, and that in the storms at sea I may travel safely back to this girl who is all my life. This is my sole desire. (*There is a little pause. Then he concludes softly:*) Amen.

He crosses himself and rises, his face serene, full of confidence. As he starts out the scene dissolves to a STREET in SLOUGH TOWN, a picturésque grouping of small frame houses. Front yards are separated from the road by tired-looking picket fences. The ancient buildings are sun blistered, streaked with old whitewash; but climbing roses of Castille and masses of bougainvillea lend a certain dignity, a nostalgic loveliness. There are women gossiping, sweeping off their front porches; children in the yards, on the roads. There are no men visible. The men are working in the fields.

The view moves toward three dwellings. The first, a one-room shack inhabited by JOE MORALES; the center one houses CHARLIE MARTIN and the last one is the home of LOLITA SIERRA.

A continuous camera movement picks up JOE MORALES striding urgently towards Lolita's house. The camera passes him, moves onto the porch and, like an inquiring eye, peers through a neatly curtained window, and sees within a lovely young paisano girl up to her shoulders in a wooden tub filled with steaming, sudsy water. This is LOLITA SIERRA. The interior—spotless, feminine and typically Mexican—is a combination living room and kitchen, with a stove and a sink recessed in an alcove. There is a door leading into a bedroom, one to the back porch. As though aware of the camera, Lolita turns, reaches out and jerks down the shade.

The camera pulls back quickly and picks up Joe again. He jumps up the steps and knocks on the door.

LOLITA'S VOICE. Go away!

JOE. This is Joe. I got to come in!

LOLITA'S VOICE (*angrily*). I tell you— *Go away!!*

Inside the room we see Lolita up to her shoulders in suds, lathering one leg. She freezes as the door handle rattles. The door, however, is locked.

JOE'S VOICE (*urgently*). For just a minute, please, let me put my head in? It is something of great importance!

LOLITA. I am in the bathtub!

JOE'S VOICE. Then put on your clothes!

LOLITA (*furiously*). No!

JOE'S VOICE. Then I will kick the door down a little.

LOLITA (*as a violent bang is heard on the door*). All right. All right! Wait a minute! (*She reaches for a large towel.*)

We now see the PORCH where, sprawled on the flat roof directly above Joe, is a tousle-headed, barefooted, ten-year-old boy. This is CHITO, Lolita's brother. He uncorks a shrill whistle. Joe startled, backs off the porch, looks around and then up. He grins, and waves a friendly hand.

JOE. Hello, Chito!

CHITO (*eyeing him dispassionately*). What are you doing here?

JOE. Waiting to see your sister.

Looking down at Joe from the roof, Chito shakes his head slowly, implying "You poor, stupid sonofabitch!"

The PORCH door opens a little, revealing Lolita in a silk kimono. She is definitely annoyed.

LOLITA. Well, what do you want?

But even as she speaks Joe jumps up the steps. She tries to slam the door in his face but he crowds in. He "shoulders" it, and we see the ROOM as Joe crashes in, gets Lolita in his arms, overwhelms her struggles, and kisses her hard on the mouth. She breaks away, hauls off and lets him have a full-arm slap in the face, hard enough to fell an ox. It doesn't even faze him—doesn't even wipe the smile off his face. He starts right in talking:

JOE (*urgently*). Look, kiddo, quick like a mouse, throw on your clothes and come with me!

LOLITA (*starting away from the door*). Stupid! I have to work at Mrs. Kelly's house!

Joe follows her into the center of the room.

JOE. Aw, you come with me and for the rest of your life at Mrs. Kelly you can throw tomatoes—big, squashy ones! (*Pleading—with great sincerity.*) Look, Lolita, I have a scheme. The greatest scheme—(*He taps his forehead.*)

LOLITA AND JOE (*speaking together— Lolita tapping her forehead, too*).— These brains have ever manufactured!

JOE. Yes! And this time it cannot fail me, because I have the support of a very important Character!

LOLITA (*picking up her brush and starting to brush her hair*). Well, what is it?

Joe's excitement and his urgency are bubbling out of him. He strides up and down, and waves his arms in extravagant gestures.

JOE. Oh, it is so big, so good, that it cannot be said in words! With your own beautiful eyes you've got to see it!

LOLITA (*skeptically*). Ah! There you go . . . always you're making fine pictures. Always you're asking me to look at them. Then when I do—*where are* they? (*Snapping her fingers*) Not there!

Joe pleads. His words, his manner, his gestures are honey-sweet.

JOE. But Lolita, this is not a vision. This is something with a beauty you can see. With a strength you can feel. With a—with a . . . (*Then, at a loss for words, he shouts ecstatically:*) By golly I tell you *this is money in the bank!*

We get a fuller view of the ROOM as Lolita studies him a moment, then resigns herself.

LOLITA. All right, Joe Morales—but if I go, you keep your hands to yourself. I want no part of you.

JOE (*delighted*). Then you'll go?

LOLITA. Yes.

JOE (*striking his hands together*). Zas!

LOLITA. Now get out of here while I put on my clothes!

Joe starts out. En route, and from sheer exuberance, he makes a tentative pass at Lolita, backs away though, and goes hurriedly as she threatens him with the palm of her hand.

Next, Joe comes out onto the porch where Chito is leaning against the wall. Again he encounters that pitying shake of Chito's head.

JOE (*sizzling*). Go on. Shake your head. Then maybe one day it will come off. (*At this Chito sidles up to him, is very confidential.*)

CHITO. Look, as a friend, would you like some advice?

JOE (*Flatly*). No! (*Joe starts to roll a cigarette, and leans against the wall.*)

CHITO (*nodding towards the house*). It's about *her.*

JOE (*looking up, interested*). Oh . . . well—what is it?

JOE and CHITO are seen together closely, as Chito rubs his thumb and finger together significantly.

CHITO. It will cost you money.

JOE (*licking the cigarette paper*). How much?

CHITO. For advice about my sister, Benny Martin always paid me five cents . . . (*As Joe reaches into his pocket*) For you it will be ten. (*Joe is furious, but he hands over the dime.*)

JOE. All right here is the ten cents. Now the advice.

CHITO (*pocketing the dime*). Simple . . . Give up trying with my sister and get yourself another girl.

JOE. You little devil! Give me back my dime!

CHITO (*calmly*). You will get your money's worth . . . (*Tapping Joe's arm*) Look—ever since Benny Martin went away you have tried to steal his girl—

JOE (*indignantly*). Now wait a minute! She was my—

CHITO (*silencing him*). Please! . . . And what have you got with her? Nothing but a bunch of slaps. And all you will ever get is more slaps. Believe me—because I know women.

JOE (*scathingly*). Ah, what do you know about women?

CHITO. Plenty! Look, Joe—I have lived with my sister for nine years.

The door back of them opens and Lolita comes out briskly. She is now dressed.

LOLITA (*curtly, to Joe*). All right—where do we go?

JOE. To the ocean.

She starts out hurriedly, Joe falling into step beside her. Joe looks back, sees Chito following. Whereupon, as one would scare a dog, Joe pretends to pick up a rock.

LOLITA. Ah, let him come!

The scene dissolves to a wharf, which is crumbling into picturesque decay. There are a few fishing boats, some of them old and water-logged. In the foreground there is a twenty-two-foot power boat. Beyond the wharf we see a small harbor and the open sea. Joe, Lolita and Chito are walking swiftly toward the power boat in the foreground.

This dissolves to the POWER BOAT: The boat's age and dilapidation is partially concealed by a coat of fresh paint. On the deck of the boat Joe, bursting with enthusiasm, is showing Lolita his "scheme." Sitting on the edge of the wharf, slightly above them, Chito is watching Joe skeptically. Eagerly, enthusiastically, talking fast, Joe raps his knuckles on the rail of the boat, on the wall of the deck house, on the deck, Lolita watching him dubiously but obviously beginning to be impressed.

JOE. Look! Look! Here you have it! A beautiful boat—solid—strong! Come on, let me show you. (*He rings the ship's bell.*) Look—a bell! (*Flipping back a length of fish net*) A net! (*Pointing*) A fine engine of great power!

Joe jumps to a locker, whips out a foghorn and gives it a terrific blast. Lolita starts convulsively.

JOE. For the fog! (*He slaps his thigh ecstatically.*) By golly, I tell you this is money in the bank!

Lolita looks the boat over—appraises it. She is now definitely impressed. Looking up, Joe sees—

Young CHITO as he shakes his head pityingly—the shake conveying his complete lack of faith in Joe's venture.

Then we see the DECK of the POWER BOAT, with Chito above on the wharf.

LOLITA. How much did you pay?

JOE (*proudly*). Sixty dollars.

LOLITA (*startled*). Sixty dollars! Where did *you* ever get money like that?

JOE (*evasively*). Listen, my Light—my Love—wait until you have seen the full performance of the investment, the boat up to my knees—(*pantomiming knee-high*)—in big fishes. [And then I will tell you. (*grandiloquently*) I can only say that in the buying of this boat I was exceptional. I tell you up here—(*tapping his forehead*) I got brains. (*He chuckles reminiscently.*) You should have heard that Pantera Jack cry when I squeezed the price on him.

LOLITA (*looking around, dubiously*). It is a lot of boat for sixty dollars.

JOE (*very superior*). Look, my little chicken, what do *you* know about boats?

LOLITA. Nothing. But I know Pantera Jack.]

CHITO (*from the wharf*). Lolita . . . wait till he tries to start the engine.

JOE (*to Chito*). You think you're smarter than a Santa Rita lawyer, don't you? All right—I'll show you. (*He jumps down into the engine cockpit.*)

This cuts to the ENGINE COCKPIT, with Chito on the wharf directly above. Joe turns over the motor. As he does so, Chito raises his hands and crosses his fingers derisively. The motor starts up.

CHITO (*crossing himself*). Truly a miracle has happened.

The DECK of the BOAT is seen fairly closely as Joe jumps out of the cockpit and busies himself with the mooring rope.

JOE (*as he does so*). Now I'll show you the demonstration.

LOLITA. Hey, Chito—come on. Get in.

CHITO (*nastily*). No. I do not swim that good.

Ignoring this crack, Joe casts off, kicks in the clutch, jumps to the steering wheel, puts it half over, and the boat, towing a diminutive dinghy, puts out smartly from the wharf. As it does so, Joe turns and shouts back at Chito.

JOE. Goodbye, Mr. Santa Rita lawyer!

We get a close view of young Chito, who says nothing. He only shakes his head as the scene dissolves to the COCKPIT of the BOAT. The boat is now out in the bay. Joe is at the wheel, Lolita sitting on the edge of the cockpit. The loveliness of the day, the cool wind whipping her hair, is softening Lolita's mood. She looks at Joe. Joe turns and catches her eye. He is completely self-assured, completely happy. He flashes Lolita one of his devastating grins.

JOE. A good boat, eh? (*Lolita nods.*) You know with you here—all the fish in Santa Cruz Bay will want to climb aboard just for the ride. (*He laughs at his own little joke.*) You want to steer a little?

Lolita takes the wheel. Joe steps directly in back of her, his arms go around her and he, too, takes the wheel—his hands over hers. After a moment he draws his right hand caressingly down the side of her face and neck, along her shoulder, and down her arm.

JOE. This side is called the starboard. (*Joe repeats the process, but this time with his left hand.*) This side—the port.

LOLITA (*smiling in spite of herself*). You do that again, Joe Morales, and I will show you how to abandon ship.

Joe laughs. His hands drop off the steering wheel, out of sight. There is a brief silence. The spell of the sea, of the boat, is on Lolita; she smiles vaguely, serenely. Joe, directly back of her, smiles too. A moment and the girl snaps out of her reverie. A slow frown washes out her smile.

LOLITA (*sharply*). Joe—take your arms from around my waist!

Lolita relaxes, her frown fades. Joe's grin, however, broadens.

LOLITA (*ominously*). I tell you to stop doing that! (*After a pause, the Joe!*

Joe rubs his nose against her hair. His voice is a caress.

JOE. Ah, come on . . . you like it.

We now see that Joe's arms are locked firmly around the girl's waist. She twists around, faces him, beats furiously on his chest with her clenched fists.

LOLITA. Joe! . . . Joe!

And then he overwhelms her, forces her back in the crook of his left arm, kisses her on the lips, and holds the kiss.

LOLITA and JOE are seen in a closeup as she fights against him furiously, then slowly relaxes. Her eyes close—she yields to his kiss. Finally Joe releases her. The girl is breathless, gasping a little.

JOE (*triumphantly*). You like that, eh?

LOLITA (*breathing hard*). Sure I like it . . . but not with you.

JOE (*not that he doesn't know*). With who, then?

LOLITA. You know well enough.

Joe flares angrily, bangs his fist savagely on the roof of the deckhouse.

JOE. A-ah, that Benny! That no-account! That crook! [A fellow the police ran out of town! Every time I move to do any little thing—(*Striking his hands together*) Zas! I fall over that *Benny!* I tell you I am sick of him!

LOLITA. That's a fine way to talk. I thought Benny was your friend.

JOE. Sure he is my friend—when I am watching him! (*He calms down.*) Look—my Life—if he were any part of a man at all, I would say to you—(*gesturing*) take him. But for you Benny is no part of anything.

LOLITA. No? (*She. laughs into an imaginary sleeve.*) I laugh.

JOE. All right! Laugh! Have a good one! Because I am going to tell you something. (*Right· at her*) Listen, Lolita Sierra—in your heart you know that you love *me*.]

LOLITA (*through her teeth*). Joe Morales—that's a lie! I am promised to Benny! You know it, everybody knows it! And when Benny comes back I'm going to marry him!

JOE (*sardonically*). Yes—*when* he comes back!

LOLITA. He'll be back—he'll be back in two weeks.

JOE. How do you know? You never hear from him.

LOLITA. I got a postcard!

JOE. Sure. Nine months ago. One cheap little postal card with not even a picture on it. And Benny's father, that nice old Charlie—does Benny ever send him so much as a dollar? No! He sends him nothing!

With a furious movement, Lolita flings away from the wheel, and plumps down on the edge of the cockpit. Joe grabs the wheel as it spins.

LOLITA (*bitterly*). So *that's* what you brought me out here for—to take me away from Benny! It's like all your dirty schemes!

JOE (*an odd sort of fury seizing him; blazing*). Sure! Dirty schemes—anything! For you I would steal, I would lie, I would kill . . . for you!

LOLITA (*quietly*)., Sure you would—like all the rest of them—for me. But for what? For a house, for trust, for honor, for kids and a pay check on Saturday nights? For some broad shoulders that I can hang onto that are mine? *No!!!*

[JOE (*the words pouring out*). Yes! All my thinking and planning to get money quick—(*slapping the wheel*) this boat—all the crazy ideas that bubble in my head like beans on a hot stove, are to give you those things! Yes, *por santos*—and with honor!

LOLITA (*with abysmal disgust*). Ah, potatoes! I have heard all that before!]

JOE, seen in a semi-closeup, speaks with quiet and emotional sincerity.

JOE. All right. Marry Benny. Marry anybody. It makes no difference, because even if I am on the other side of the world—like the ghost of the old Portagee who fell into the slough, I shall always be around.

LOLITA, seen in a semi-closeup, is now seated by the rail.

JOE'S VOICE. When you are caressing your husband, he'll say: "Look, Lolita—over there in that corner there is that fellow again!" (*The girl's eyes are wide, she is absolutely rigid.*) When you are having your first kid in the hospital, your husband will say: "Lolita, who, for the love of heaven, is that fellow waiting outside?"

We next see JOE and LOLITA in a closeup.

JOE. "In the name of all the saints, Lolita, who is that fellow?" And you will not be able to stop from crying out: "That is Joe Morales—the man I should have married."

There is a silence. The two of them stare at each other—the girl wide-eyed, stunned. In the silence the "putt—putt —putt" of the motor ceases abruptly.

JOE (*startled*). The engine!

We see the ENGINE HATCH closely as Joe jumps down to it. He takes one look, and lets out a yell.

JOE (*anguished*). The engine! Oh, the beautiful engine!

LOLITA. What's the matter with it?

JOE (*pointing*). Where it was there is now a big hole!

Lolita also jumps down, staring down into the hatch. Then from JOE and

LOLITA's angle, through the hatch, we see that the engine has dropped through the ancient bottom of the boat. A geyser of water gurgles and bubbles up through the hole.

This dissolves and we see the power boat's DINGHY: Lolita is rowing. The dinghy is so absurdly small that Joe and Lolita are crowded knee-to-knee. Lolita rests her oars. She and Joe stare off at—

The POWER BOAT as water gushes over the sides and overwhelms it. There is a pathetic gurgle, an explosion of air bubbles, and then—nothing. Thereupon the scene cuts back to the DINGHY.

LOLITA (*bitterly*). There goes the fish-business . . .

Joe has nothing to say, the catastrophe having crushed and flattened him. As Lolita starts to row furiously the scene dissolves to LOLITA and CHITO on the WHARF, as she walks briskly away from the wharf. In the background Joe is tying off the dinghy to the wharf.

CHITO (*calling out to Joe*). You are lucky you got Lolita to bring you back. (*Suddenly*) Hey, Lolita—do you love that Joe?

The abruptness of the question catches Lolita off balance. She has to search for the answer in her mind.

LOLITA. Thanks to Heaven—No!

CHITO. Then what are you always going around with him for?

LOLITA (*angrily*). You be quiet and mind your business!!

This dissolves to SLOUGH TOWN featuring CHARLIE MARTIN'S HOUSE. In the immediate foreground there is a flashy Buick roadster. Crescendo, diminuendo, fortissimo, pizzicato and con spirato, the voices of two men raised in anger bubble and squeak from the interior of Charlie Martin's house. One does not hear the words, only the sound of them —and it is appalling. Dogs are barking: Poultry gobbling. Attracted by the uproar, half a dozen or so neighbors, all women but two, are moving up the garden path toward Charlie's house. Among them are MR. and MRS. PAMFILO CHAVEZ, and MR. and MRS. RAFAEL CATALINA.

As the camera comes to a medium close shot of CHARLIE MARTIN'S PORCH, a prosperously dressed, middle-aged Mexican in a derby hat emerges violently. He is tremulous with anger. This is MR. FRANK ALVISO. Following him comes CHARLIE MARTIN—a stocky little paisano in his late fifties—in need of a shave and wearing faded blue jeans. Charlie is angry, too—but his is the quiet anger of a righteous man. Alviso backs halfway down the steps, Charlie remains on the porch. The neighbors are in the scene.

ALVISO. I tell you again—I have no faith in your fish-business, and I especially have no faith in that person, Joe Morales. All I want is the six months rent for my house!

CHARLIE (*more in sorrow than anger —turning to his friends*). This man is crazy. I find it not possible to argue with a man who is crazy.

We now see the PORCH from another angle, with JOE'S SHACK in the background. Alviso addresses the neighbors.

ALVISO. Is it crazy to ask for sixty dollars back rent, which I need to pay my taxes?

Charlie's friends give him no encouragement. Charlie comes down to Alviso. He speaks with terrible restraint.

CHARLIE. Mister Alviso, for the last time—in a *week* now you will have your sixty dollars. I gonna be so rich from my fish-business that I'll buy this house to keep my goats in. (*With great dignity*) So please, as a favor, no more arguments!

ALVISO (*with equal restraint*). Mister Martin—to all those fancy words I have only one answer. (*He jabs at Charlie with a quivering finger.*) By the first of the month I want my money or I want my house!

Alviso turns and strides toward his car —the neighbors opening up to let him pass. During the last lines of the above, Lolita and Joe have come into view— Joe easing off toward his shack.

LOLITA. What's the matter, Charlie? Didn't you pay the rent? You had it.

But Charlie has spotted Joe sneaking toward his shack. He bellows at him, waving his arm.

CHARLIE. Joe! Joe! Come here! Here is that wonderful fellow. Come here, Joe. (*To Lolita*) Sure I had my rent! And but for that Joe Morales my money would now be in the pockets of that blood-squeezer, Alviso.

We see the GROUP closely as Joe enters reluctantly. He's on the spot and knows it. Charlie throws an arm affectionately around Joe's shoulder.

CHARLIE (*expansively*). Tell her, Joe. Tell her about our boat.

JOE (*unhappily*). She already knows about the boat.

CHARLIE (*to Lolita*). By golly, she's something, eh? By golly, I bet she's the best boat in Santa Cruz Bay!

Lolita has gotten on to it. Eyes narrowed she turns on the wretched Joe.

LOLITA. Joe! In buying the boat—was that Charlie's money?

CHARLIE (*happy, full of confidence, cutting in boisterously*). You bet your life it was! (*Giving Joe a little hug*) Eh, Joe? (*To his friends*) I tell you—next to my Benny for being a-smart there is nobody like this good Joe Morales, huh?

JOE (*feebly; withering under Lolita's blistering stare*). Look, Charlie, I—I have a little something to tell you . . . I—

CHARLIE (*cutting him short with a gusty laugh*). Sure! Fine! But first let us go into the house for a little drink! (*Waving his arms*) Everybody! Please to come in! At a time like this a man needs his friends to share his good fortune! (*Charlie's friends crowd up the steps. He brushes them inside.*) Lolita! Joe—everybody—please!

Charlie herds his friends into the house, and follows them in. Joe hangs back. Lolita nudges him with her elbow.

LOLITA (*ominously*). All right! In you go!

JOE. Maybe later. Right now I don't feel so good . . .

LOLITA. You got to tell him.

Charlie's laughter comes from within the house. Joe winces.

JOE. There is a happy old man—*I can't* tell him *now*.

LOLITA (*through her teeth*). Either you do or I will! (*Shoving him forward*) Go on!

As Joe enters miserably and Lolita follows, the scene cuts to CHARLIE'S LIVING ROOM, Mexican in feeling, spit-and-polish clean, on the wall a large chrome of Charlie's dead wife. There is a woodburning stove and a shrine containing an Image of the Virgin of Guadalupe.

The women are sitting stiffly in chairs around the room. Pamfilo Chavez is perched on the edge of the table. Rafael Catalina, squatting on his heels against the wall, is rolling a cigarette. Charlie has dug up a gallon jug of Dago Red, filled glasses for his friends, has now just filled three more on the table as Joe, prodded on by Lolita, enters dejectedly.—Picking up two glasses of wine, Charlie scuttles over and hands them to Lolita and Joe.

CHARLIE (*on a pink cloud*). Here! Lolita, Joe—(*He scuttles back to the table, picks up a glass for himself, and raises it.*) My friends—everybody! We will drink to the good health of those two rich millionaires . . . Joe Morales and *me*—Charlie Martin!

Everybody drinks. Murmurs of: "Salud! . . . To your good healths! . . . To Joe and Charlie!" Neither Lolita nor Joe drink theirs. Charlie is refilling his friends' glasses. Lolita jabs Joe with her elbow.

LOLITA (*sotto voce*). *Tell him!*

JOE (*after clearing his throat, bracing himself to spill the news*). Look, Charlie, I—I got a little something to tell you . . .

Charlie is filling Mrs. Chavez's glass. He uncorks a great, gusty laugh.

[CHARLIE. Everybody listen to that Joe . . . (*Chuckling delightedly*) "A *little* something," he says. Ah, what a modest one! I bet, by golly, he is going to tell me that tomorrow we start a fish-cannery! (*He slaps Joe on the back.*) Eh, Joe?

LOLITA. No, Charlie—you will have no need of a fish-cannery. (*She nudges Joe again with her elbow.*)]

JOE (*unhappily*). You see, Charlie—

it is like this . . . You and I have encountered an Act of God—

CHARLIE (*at this, Charlie really bub-
·bles*). An Act of God—oh, that is
fine! (*To his friends*) You see—what
did I tell you? Already we are
started to be blessed with the good
luck! (*He fairly hugs Joe.*) Eh, Joe?

JOE (*shaking his head*). No, Charlie
. . . (*He makes another stab at it.*)
Listen, Charlie, you remember the
engine—

CHARLIE (*bubbling, to his friends*).
Do I remember that engine? (*to
Lolita*) You saw it—eh, Lolita?

LOLITA (*nodding*). Yes, I saw it.'

JOE (*sadly*). Well—the bottom of the
boat fell out a little and the engine
sank into the ocean.

We see the GROUP from another angle,
the view favoring CHARLIE. His friends
are in the background. Charlie is staggered. Little murmurs of distress come
from his friends.

CHARLIE (*feebly*). O-o-oh . . .

He sinks heavily into a chair, and looks
around at his friends. In his expression
there is almost an apology.

CHARLIE (*shaking his head*). That is
not good . . . (*As he looks up at Joe*)
You mean . . . ? (*He makes a
"power-dive" with his hand. Joe
nods.*) No—that is bad.

There is a hushed silence. Everybody
is watching Charlie. Suddenly he jumps
up.

CHARLIE (*hopefully*). Maybe in the
boat we can put a new engine—eh,
Joe? (*Joe looks sick.*)

LOLITA (*shaking her head*). Not in
this boat, Charlie. It is at the bottom
of Santa Cruz Bay.

Flattened, crushed, Charlie flops back
into the chair. His friends are filled with
sympathy. Mrs. Catalina, a pleasant-
faced, 250-pound dumpling, leans forward and pats Charlie's hand consolingly.

MRS. CATALINA. Ah, Charlie, don't
worry. Soon Benny will be home and
all your troubles will be over.

Charlie sighs unhappily, then nods his
head.

CHARLIE. Yes. And if my son had
been here—(*looking up at Joe*) he
would not have permitted me to
make such an unlucky investment.

Lolita looks at Joe—bangs it right in his
teeth.

LOLITA. By golly—I bet you my life
*he wouldn't!*

And having said this, she sits down.
Joe sizzles. Like the fluttering of leaves
in the wind, we hear a gentle chorus
of voices:

VOICES.
Ah, that Benny—what a son.
So lively.
Loved by everybody.
How we have missed him. Always
things were happening.
He is so handsome. So strong.

(Every once in a while during the following eulogy of Benny, Lolita looks
up at Joe, who is leaning against the
wall, and nods her head gloatingly—
punctuating each tribute. This is slowly
burning Joe up.)

CHARLIE (*nodding unhappily*). When
my Benny was home my stomach
never went empty. Under my bed
there was always a gallon of wine—
in the oven there was always a
chicken.

MRS. CATALINA (*fondly reminiscent*).

Ai, yes. The little animals—how they loved Benny. The little chickens, the little ducks—how they used to follow him home.

CHAVEZ. And dogs, too—all the way from town.

CHARLIE. Expensive dogs. Never less than ten dollar reward—never!

MRS. CATALINA. There are some people who say that Benny was too wild.

RAPHAEL. Sure—like the time of his big trouble. You remember?

CHAVEZ. Benny had so many big troubles. Which one?

RAFAEL. Last Fourth of July. At the Fiesta. His big fight.

CHAVEZ (*his eyes lighting up*). Aw—that one. Sure—who can ever forget it?

We see the GROUP in an extreme close shot, the view favoring RAFAEL who jumps up, his eyes shining. Against the wall, back of him, Joe is getting bored by this tribute to Benny.

RAFAEL (*with broad gestures*). My friends, *mis amigos!* I have traveled —I have been from San Diego to the Oregon border. I have seen fights— many fights! But I swear to you by the eleven thousand saints that never, never have I seen a fight like that one!

The GROUP is seen closely as Rafael continues.

RAFAEL. There he was—(*spreading his arms wide*) like Daniel in the lions' den! Policemen and sheriffs on all sides!

Rafael warms up. Gesturing, posturing, he plays all the roles in "Benny's Last Stand." He has moved across the room and directly back of him, in the scene, are Lolita and Joe. Lolita, proud of Benny's exploits, looks up gloating, at Joe. Joe's look at her says: "Ah, baloney!"

RAFAEL (*striking his hands together*). Zas! Like tigers they sprang at him! Zas! Benny hits them! He swings! He crunches! He tears! The air is filled with pieces of policemen!

Rafael has got a great audience. They are living every moment of the great fight, particularly' Lolita, and Joe is sizzling.

RAFAEL (*with "terrific" tempo*). Through the streets the battle rages! The whistles are blowing! (*A shrill whistle through his teeth*) More policemen from the left! (*Whistling again*) More policemen from the right! Then they got him. But like a madman Benny is still fighting even to the jail doors! Now he is inside— (*Rafael is "inside"*) with his noble blood running down his face. Ka-lang go the doors behind him! The Chief of Police pulls a gun! But Benny takes the gun away and—

JOE (*suddenly and disgustedly*).— with his beautiful, strong teeth he bites off the barrel and swallows the whole works like a handful of peanuts!

At this Rafael gives Joe a disgusted look, sinks exhausted into a chair, and mops his face and neck.

MRS. CATALINA. And that Judge—that cruel man. For him to throw Benny out of town for a whole year . . . Ah, that was inhuman.

CHARLIE (*wistfully*). Yes. That Judge should not have driven my son from his family and the friends who loved him. No. They should have put him in jail a little, like the other fellows. (*The others nod solemnly, and sigh gently.*)

MRS. CATALINA. When Benny comes home, I think maybe we will have a big celebration. (*She leans over and pats Lolita's hand.*) To have such a man as Benny, you should be very proud.

CHARLIE (*as Joe starts towards the door*). Hey, Joe—where you going?

JOE. I am going back to church to pray to St. Benny!

CHARLIE. He is a very religious fellow.

And as Joe goes through the door the scene fades out.

# PART TWO

The MISSION GROUNDS fade in as JOE walks dejectedly past the Mission. His face is sombre, thoughtful. After a little while he spots somebody off scene, and uncorks a shrill whistle.—A moment and young Chito dashes into view.

JOE. Look, kiddo—is your sister still mad at me?

CHITO (*emphatically*). Plenty!

JOE. Did you tell her that maybe I would give myself to the Army? (*Chito nods.*) What did she say?

CHITO. She said: "Good!"

JOE (*crushed*). Oh . . . Did you tell her that maybe in the Army I would be killed?

CHITO. Sure.

JOE. What did she say to *that*?

CHITO. She said with her that would be fine.

JOE (*wretchedly*). What else did she say?

CHITO. On holy ground like this I cannot repeat it.

JOE continues his walk, Chito falling into step beside him. Joe appears to arrive at a conclusion. He reaches in his pocket, produces a coin, stops and hands it to Chito.

JOE. Hey, here is a nickel. I want to ask you something serious . . . With

Lolita, what did Benny have that I haven't got?

CHITO (*with an expressive paisano gesture*). Money . . . Always he was doing things for her—buying her fine presents. Once even a beautiful red dress to take her to the circus.

JOE (*as he grunts and continues to walk, Chito with him*). Yes. But such things are expensive.

CHITO. And with a girl like my sister —plenty for your money.

JOE. Yes, sure. But where do I encounter the money? Under a chicken like an egg?

CHITO (*significantly*). Benny would find it.

JOE (*bitterly*). Benny would steal it.

CHITO (*spreading his hands*). Well . . . This brazen implication gets Joe mad. He stops, and shakes his finger indignantly at Chito.

JOE. Hey! Why aren't you in school?

CHITO. The teacher sent me out to clap the erasers.

JOE. When?

CHARLIE: Tell her, Joe. Tell her about our boat.

JOE: Give *me* your money . . . *I* will be your bank.

JOE: You two girls ought to have plenty to talk about.

MAYOR: The medal was — awarded posthumously.

CHITO. The day before yesterday.

JOE (*violently*). You little devil you —you run off to school.

Chito hesitates, whereupon, as one would scare a dog, Joe pretends to reach for a rock. As the boy runs off Joe continues on his walk, and the scene dissolves to JAKE'S PLACE, a saloon in the old part of town, a ramshackle wooden building with a false two-story front. Joe slouches dejectedly toward the entrance and enters, the scene dissolving to the rear of JAKE'S PLACE. The interior is dark and cool. There is sawdust on the floor, a pool table, an old-fashioned mahogany bar and a chromo of "Custer's Last Stand."—Joe, with a schooner of vino in his hand, is leaning over a juke box against the rear wall. He runs his finger down the list of attractions, finds what he wants— "The Abandoned Lover"—and feeds it a nickel. As the plaintive refrain drips from the juke box like melted butter, Joe heaves a melancholy sigh, takes a long drink, then slumps wretchedly into a chair at a nearby table. Suddenly his eye catches a hand-lettered poster on the wall. It reads:

*BRING YOUR GIRL*

to

THE BIG SATURDAY NIGHT DANCE

at

THE OCEAN BEACH PAVILION

June 24, 1942

\* \* \*

Music—Dancing—Eats!

Admission $2.00 per Couple

No Cover Charges

\* \* \*

As he stares at it moodily, we see the ENTRANCE—the door opens and CHARLIE floats in on a small pink cloud of alcohol. Under one arm he's got an empty gallon-bottle, under the other a plucked chicken. Beaming happily, he floats over to the bar where JAKE, the proprietor—a tough-looking Westerner with gold-plated teeth—is reading a newspaper. As Jake looks up, Charlie grins owlishly, and holds up the naked chicken by the neck.

CHARLIE. For you, Jake my very old friend, a little present.

Jake takes the chicken by the legs and the neck, stretches it out, and gives it a quick once-over.

JAKE (*suspiciously*). What did it die of?

CHARLIE. Me.

As Jake puts the chicken away, Charlie sets the empty gallon-bottle significantly on the bar. Jake eyes the empty bottle, gets the implication, and eyes Charlie. Charlie smiles ingratiatingly, giving a faint hiccough. Jake picks up the bottle, and looks at Charlie keenly.

JAKE. You're a little high, aincha, Charlie?

CHARLIE (*with a flutter of his hand*). Oh . . . so-so.

Jake sets the bottle under the vino keg and turns the spigot.

JAKE. When you expectin' Benny home?

CHARLIE. Pretty quick now. (*Then, as an afterthought*) I hope.

JAKE (*snapping his fingers*). By golly, Charlie—I almost forgot. There's a letter here for ya!

Leaving the spigot, Jake takes a letter out of the cash register and hands it to Charlie. We then see CHARLIE in a semi-closeup as he takes the letter gingerly and stares at it—*upside down*. He examines it from all angles, feels it, smells it, and finally looks at it—right side up. It is obvious that he cannot read.—Charlie catches Jake's eye—his unspoken "Why don't you open it?"

CHARLIE (*sheepishly*). I forgot my eye-glasses . . .

He pockets the letter. Jake slides the gallon-bottle across the bar. As Charlie takes it, his face melts into a wonderful smile as he sees—JOE. The juke box "klunks" into silence. Joe drains his glass in one long swallow, gets up and feeds his last nickel into the machine for an encore. At this moment Charlie intrudes with his gallon of vino and a clean glass.

CHARLIE (*eyeing the juke box*). Uummmmmm . . . that is sad music you are playing.

JOE (*gloomily*). Somebody shoved a knife in my heart. It makes me feel good to turn it in the wound.

CHARLIE. A woman?

JOE. Yeah.

He sits down wearily. Charlie "clucks" sympathetically.

CHARLIE. Aw! Tch, tch, tch! Poor, poor boy. (*He sits down opposite Joe.*) With your permission, I will suffer with you.

Charlie uncorks the bottle and fills the glasses. They both drink sadly. Charlie takes the letter out of his pocket, and hands it to Joe.

CHARLIE (*diffidently*). As a favor . . . please read it to me. (*As Joe takes it*) I am a man of not much education.

Apathetically, Joe opens the letter, extracts a note and shakes the envelope violently—five new, crisp five-dollar bills fall out onto the table. Joe's melancholy vanishes like snow on a hot shovel.

JOE AND CHARLIE (*in an awed whisper*). It's money!

They both grab for it, Charlie beating Joe to the punch. He fans out the bills incredulously.

CHARLIE. *Twenty-five dollars* . . . I bet, by golly, it's from Benny!

JOE (*who has picked up the letter*). No. Listen . . . (*He reads aloud.*) "Dear Charlie—I take pen in hand to say 'Hello'—

CHARLIE. Hello.

Joe gives him a funny look, and goes on reading:

JOE. "—and to tell you I was sorry to leave town without paying you for the fine riata you made me. Anyway here is the money which I hope finds you as it leaves me. Your old friend, Henry Espinosa, El Paso, Texas."

CHARLIE. *Texas!* Imagine to yourself —out of the State and he still pays me. With your permission—(*He reaches for the bottle, then raises it.*) To Henry Espinosa—an honest man.

He drinks. Joe takes the bottle from him, and also raises it.

JOE. To the twenty-five dollars. (*He drinks—then asks too casually:*) What are you going to do with it?

CHARLIE. Give it to Mister Alviso for some of his rent.

[Without a word, Joe gets up.

JOE (*coldly*). Goodbye.

CHARLIE. Hey—what's eating you?

JOE (*starting away*). It's too disgusting to talk about.

CHARLIE. Disgusting to pay a man what I owe him?

JOE. A bloodsucker like Mister Alviso—*yes*. Even an animal wouldn't do that. (*He comes back to the table.*) Look, let me ask you something . . .

Joe sits down again. He points a finger across the table.

JOE. When you're an old man, crippled from hard work—hungry, with no friends, no money, no home . . . Will this Mister Alviso take care of you?

CHARLIE. N-no . . . But Benny will.

JOE. By that time they will have hung Benny. No. You must look out for yourself. Save your money.

CHARLIE. I have saved my money.

JOE (*too impulsively*). Where is it?

CHARLIE. I gave it to you for the fish business.

JOE (*wishing he hadn't brought this up*). Oh . . . that? (*Then, hurriedly*) Yes, and now but for an Act of God you'd be a rich man—so let that be a lesson to you. This time put your money in a Bank. Collect the interest.

CHARLIE (*blankly*). What is interest?

JOE. Interest? Well, it's—well, it's the thing . . . It's what your money earns.]

Joe hitches his chair closer. His voice gets soft, persuasive.

JOE (*emotionally*). Look, Charlie— you are the best friend I've ever had. Often at night I lay awake and think of all the fine things you've done for me . . . and I say to myself, "Joe," I say, "be patient. The time will come when you can do something really fine for poor Charlie . . ."

Charlie is very much touched; he is also touched by better than a quart of vino. With deep emotion he pats Joe's hand affectionately.

JOE. Well, that time has come. I can now repay you . . .

He pauses. His eyes bore into Charlie hypnotically.

JOE (*very gently*). Charlie, old friend, give *me* your money . . (*extending his hand*) *I* will be your bank.

Charlie draws back, the money clutched tightly against his breast. Joe leans toward him, and gets his fingers on the bills. Charlie shakes his head: an owlish but stubborn "No!" Joe tries to ease the currency out of Charlie's fingers.

CHARLIE (*brushing Joe's hand away*). No. As a favor, no!

JOE. All right. One day you will be sorry. (*He stares fixedly at Charlie.*) I can see you now—a starving old man sitting like poor blind Lazarus on the steps of Mister Alviso's beautiful home—begging for crumbs . . .

CHARLIE (*horrified, fascinated*). Does he give me any?

JOE. No. He kicks you into the street like a bundle of old rags.

CHARLIE (*whistling*). What a barbarian!

JOE. And passing by, people are saying: "What is that pile of bones that the buzzards are picking on in the fields?" (*Charlie is shaken. He licks his dry lips.*) And others will say: "That is poor, dead Charlie who wouldn't let his good friend Joe Morales be his bank and pay him good interest on his money."

The pathos and horror of his demise is too much for Charlie. Great tears of self-pity splash down his cheeks, "plop" onto the table.

Very gently Joe disengages the money from Charlie's pudgy, unresisting hand. He gets up and pats his stricken friend on the shoulder.

JOE. There . . now your troubles are all over. (*He hands him a five-dollar bill.*) See, Charlie—your interest. Not one dollar like the Pantero Bank, but *five*. And in advance.

Charlie stares at the "five" incredulously, and brightens up.

CHARLIE. *Five dollars!* By Golly—do I get *that* already?

JOE (*putting the balance in his pocket*). Sure Mike! I told you I was a good bank.

Charlie jumps up, and hugs Joe affectionately.

CHARLIE. By Golly, Joe, that's the best and the most generous bank in California! (*Rising and raising his glass*) To the interest.

JOE. In advance!

And as they drink the scene dissolves to LOLITA'S HOUSE, from an angle facing the window overlooking the front yard. Lolita is setting the supper table. Through the window she spots Joe coming briskly toward her front door. He is carrying a large, flat pasteboard box. A moment later there is a sharp knock on the door.—Lolita goes to the front door and opens it. There is nobody there. Astonished, Lolita peers out onto the porch. Nobody there either. Lolita closes the door, turns and frowns and we see from Lolita's angle, Joe standing in front of the open back door —with a really good-looking print dress of outstanding design draped full-length over an outstretched arm.

The dress box is on the floor beside him. On his face there is an unctuous, ingratiating grin.

JOE (*pointing to the dress*). Here you have it, kiddo.

Lolita comes toward him, her annoyance at Joe's intrusion over-ridden by her interest in the dress.

LOLITA (*fingering the material*). Oh, Joe—that's beautiful.

JOE. You bet you my life it is . . .

From behind, he holds it up against her body, turns her so that she faces a wall-mirror.

JOE. And it is yours to surround the most beautiful body in California.

Joe steps away, leaving Lolita holding the dress.

JOE (*holding out two dance-tickets*). Look—for you and me. For the dance tomorrow night.

Lolita looks up from the dress to the tickets. One senses her reluctance to refuse them.

LOLITA (*shaking her head*). It's nice of you, Joe, but I—

CHITO (*coming in boisterously*). Hey, Joe!

LOLITA (*cutting him short*). *Callate!* Can't you see I'm talking to Joe. Go eat your supper.

Chito subsides at the table, and reaches for a pot of beans.

JOE. Tomorrow night if you go with me—it will be like going with Juan D. Rockefeller. Such luxury.

Lolita lays the dress over a chair, fingers the material just once more, then looks up at Joe.

LOLITA (*shaking her head*). No . . . I'm sorry, Joe.

JOE. Somebody else will be sorry too. (*Solemnly*) Your sainted mother who is in heaven.

LOLITA (*startled*). My mother! What has she got to do with it?

JOE. Plenty! (*Emotionally*) Only last night I had a dream about her. She came to kneel by my bed: "Joe Morales," she said, "I am unhappy in heaven because my little girl, Lolita, is sad and lonely. Joe Morales," she said, "why don't you buy her a nice new dress and take her to the dance?"

LOLITA (*laughing outright*). Ah, that is a lot of potatoes! Joe, such lies!

We see all three in a wider angle as Chito tries to say something to Joe.

CHITO. Hey, Joe!

LOLITA. Quiet! Didn't I tell you not to interrupt your elders! (*Chito subsides.*)

JOE (*coming to Lolita, pleading*). Look, my Life—please, why don't you come? (*He holds up the dress again.*) Figure to yourself how pretty you are going to look in this dress.

LOLITA (*with finality*). No, Joe. I'm sorry—but I can't go with you.

JOE. You show me one good reason and I'll eat it—(*indicating the dress*) fried, without chili.

LOLITA. I'll tell you a reason—and a good one, *Benny!* . . . You know I'm promised to Benny—everybody knows I'm promised to Benny. And here's something maybe *you* don't understand. When two people are promised to each other, they are true to each other.

JOE (*sardonically*). And you think Benny is true to you?

Lolita faces him—straight, with dignity, with poise. She is very beautiful at the moment.

LOLITA. Look at me, Joe Morales— and look plenty . . . (*Right in his teeth*) If *you* were Benny Martin would *you* be true to me?

JOE (*eyeing her a moment; then, reluctantly*). Yes.

LOLITA (*with a gesture of finality*). All right then!

JOE (*sore*). Oh—you think pretty good of yourself, don't you?

CHITO. Hey, Joe! Charlie says for me to tell you he wants his twenty dollars back!

This is a bombshell. Joe winces. Lolita stiffens like a bird-dog. She looks at Joe, sees his guilt. This last perfidy puts her beyond anger into a sort of helpless resignation.

LOLITA (*almost a wail*). Oh no—not again! Don't tell me you've robbed poor old Charlie again!

JOE (*indignantly*). Is it robbery to borrow a man's money and pay him good interest?

LOLITA (*snatching the dress from him and stuffing it into the box*). Joe Morales—I want no more of your slippery words! (*She shoves the box at him.*) Here! You take this dress back and get the money! (*She starts toward the door. Catching Joe's eye, Chito gives him the old critical shake of the head.*)

LOLITA (*flinging open the door*). And give Charlie back his twenty-dollars!

Joe, with the box under his arm goes out wretchedly. Lolita slams the door.

[Joe's voice drifts through, wheedling, coaxing—

JOE's VOICE. Light of My Life—If I take it back will you go to the dance with me?

LOLITA. No! I'm going with somebody else!

JOE's VOICE (*very unhappily*). Who with?

LOLITA. Mind your business!

We hear Joe's footsteps "cluk" down the steps. Lolita moves to the window. Over her shoulder we see Joe slouch dejectedly toward town.

> LOLITA (*to nobody in particular*). That's a pretty good dress he picked out. (*After a pause*) I bet you I would've looked good in it.]

And the scene dissolves to the REAR of JAKE'S PLACE,—where Joe, with an almost empty schooner of vino in his hand, is feeding a nickel into the juke box. He is very unhappy. On a chair near a table is the dress box. As the melancholy strains of the number drip out of the juke box, Joe leans dejectedly against the machine and drains his schooner.—As he does so a girl drifts in behind him. She is definitely "a package," and gaudy is the word for it. She is pretty all right, but her make-up, her beaded eyelashes and her hair-do are all a bit overboard. Her figure, however, would knock the hat off a Marine. This is MISS TOODLES CASTRO.

> TOODLES (*in a voice like hot molasses*). Hello, Joe. (*As Joe turns, and stares at her blankly*) Don't you remember me?

JOE (*without enthusiasm*). A little.

TOODLES. I'm Toodles Castro from Santa Marta. (*She laughs significantly*).

JOE (*apathetically*). Oh, sure. I remember now.

TOODLES (*wiggling her body to the rhythm of the music*). Don't you ever play anything lively?

JOE (*gloomily*). Do I look like one who would want to jitterbug?

TOODLES (*all sympathy*). Ah, poor little one—A Woman? (*As he nods wretchedly, Toodles slips her hand through his arm.*) Look, kiddo—maybe if you buy me a drink you'll feel better.

JOE (*disengaging his arm from her predatory hand*). No. My heart is so heavy there isn't enough dago-red in California to float it. (*He turns toward the dress-box*) Besides, I have a thing to do.

JOE is coming directly toward us now.

TOODLES (*petulantly*). Ah, you're no fun! I just wish Benny Martin was in town!

At the word "Benny" Joe stops dead. Over a split-second he stands there—thinking. Then he turns back, and we then see JOE and TOODLES close together.

JOE (*casually*). Benny Martin . . . what do you know about Benny?

TOODLES (*coming close, and looking up at Joe*). Are you kidding? (*Laughing*) Look—after his big trouble here, Benny came to Santa Marta. Why, I was seeing him all the time.

JOE (*perking up at this, suddenly interested*). You were, eh?

TOODLES. Sure. And he still would have been around except for a little trouble he had with a couple of fellows I was going with.

JOE. Oh.

She extends her hand under Joe's nose. On the second finger of her right hand there is a heavy, ornate gold ring.

TOODLES. Look. He gave me *this*.

(*She laughs significantly.*) Do I know Benny?

Joe stares at the ring. His gloom vanishes in a slow grin. He hooks his hand through her arm.

JOE. Come on, kiddo—maybe after all I better buy you a drink.

As they move toward THE BAR—Jake comes towards them.

JAKE. What'll it be, Joe?

JOE. A couple of extra-specials.

Jake turns to fill two schooners from a spigot. Joe flashes a quick look at Toodles, produces the two dance tickets, and "fans" them under her nose.

JOE. Hey, good-looking—how about the dance tomorrow night?

TOODLES. Tomorrow night I got a date in Santa Marta. Besides, I haven't got my party-dress here.

JOE (*giving her the works*). Look—you go with me and I'll *buy* you a dress. What do you say to that?

TOODLES. Well . . . That's different. (*She laughs. Then:*) Sure I'll go.

Jake sets the two schooners down on the bar, and goes out of sight. Toodles and Joe pick them up.

TOODLES (*coyly*). If I wasn't so afraid of you—I'd say a toast.

JOE (*quite happy now*). Ah, don't be afraid. What is it?

TOODLES (*raising her schooner*). Uh —to Benny!

Joe hesitates, then suddenly laughs all to himself.

JOE (*holding up his schooner*). Sure. To Benny!

And as they drink the scene fades out.

# PART THREE

The OCEAN BEACH PAVILION fades in at night disclosing a large, unpainted wooden building with a low-pitched roof. There is a deep, railed veranda facing the sea with wide, glass doors opening into the pavilion. There are lights and the strains of marimbas, accordions and fiddles. Paisano couples in their Saturday-night-best are drifting in and out, back and forth to the parked cars. The view moves onto the veranda, showing through the open doors the dancers within skimming the floor like swallows to the strains of a waltz. Charlie and Lolita waltz out of the crowd, through the doors, and onto the veranda. Breathing hard, Charlie mops his face. He's as pleased as punch. As though looking for somebody, Lolita glances quickly around. The scene then moves with them along the veranda—past four young mothers bottle-feeding four infants.

CHARLIE (*panting*). By golly, I was good in there.

LOLITA. By golly, you were nearly as good as Joe.

CHARLIE. That jitterbug! By golly, I was better!

Lolita grabs his arm as one tired leg

does a "Leon Errol," and the moving scene brings them into a group of friends—among them the Chavezes, the Catalinas, and a pretty young matron with a ten-month-old baby. There's a table with beer-bottles, hot-dogs, a deep copper pot of chili, and soft-drinks.

MRS. CHAVEZ. You better look out, Charlie, or they'll put you in the movies.

CHARLIE. Ah, that is nothing. At my wedding when I dance with that blessed saint, my wife . . . (*Softly, as an afterthought*) God rest her soul—then you should have seen me.

MRS. CATALINA. I did. (*Chuckling, to the others*) With buckets of cold water they had to stop ʌim.

Charlie has grabbed a hot-dog, and dropped heavily into a chair.—The young mother with the baby is taking a "feeding-bottle" out of a bag. Lolita comes in, and sits down beside her.

LOLITA. Rosita—let me take little Franklin while you go and dance with your husband . . . (*smiling*) before you lose him.

ROSITA (*eagerly, handing over little Franklin and the bottle*). If he don't like his milk give him a hot-dog.

Rosita hurries out. Lolita, shaking a few drops of milk out of the bottle onto her wrist, sticks the rubber nipple into little Franklin's mouth—but little Franklin's not having any.

LOLITA (*trying again*). Come on, Franklin—come on, take your nice milk . . .

But as little Franklin yelps a "to-hell-with-it!" Lolita sets down the bottle, takes a hot-dog off the table, and tries that. Again she has no success, whereupon Charlie leans into sight.

CHARLIE. Try it with a little chili.

Lolita dips the hot-dog into a bowl of chili, and this apparently is it. As little Franklin "gums" it voraciously the clatter and rattle of an approaching jalopy is heard crescendo. Looking off, Lolita stiffens as she sees—

Outside the PAVILION an ancient jalopy without a top, is leaping and bouncing along ʌa dirt road paralleling the sea. Toodles Castro, in a sports coat, is driving and Joe is beside her. Its radiator boiling, it stops with a convulsive shudder at the wooden steps leading up to the veranda. Joe hops out, and helps Toodles out of the car.

Thereupon the scene cuts to LOLITA and HER FRIENDS. Seven pairs of eyes appraise Joe's girl-friend. Lolita cranes her neck to get a better look at her, then frowns.

LOLITA. Who is she?

MRS. CHAVEZ. I never see her before in my life.

CHARLIE (*leaning forward*). With such pretty legs she ought to walk on her hands.

We now see JOE and TOODLES a little closer. Joe is all slicked up, and has his arm around Toodles' waist as they go up the steps and onto the veranda. As they move toward the entrance to the pavilion Joe spots Charlie, Lolita and the others. He stops. There is a gleam in his eye.

JOE (*sotto voce*). Come on, Toodles,

I want you to meet Benny's father. His arm still around her, Joe leads Toodles over to the group near the table. Lolita's eyes never leave the girl with Joe.

JOE. Miss Castro—this is Benny's father, Charlie Martin. (*Charlie beams and mumbles a "pleased-to-meet-you!"*)

Still holding her around the waist, Joe turns Toodles to face Lolita.

JOE. Miss Sierra—this is Miss Toodles Castro from Santa Marta. (*Significantly*) Miss Castro is a great friend of Benny's. (*With equal significance to Toodles*) So is Miss Sierra . . . you two girls ought to have plenty to talk about.

The two girls exchange curt little bows —but their eyes are appraising each other like strange roosters. Then we see the GROUP from another angle as Charlie jumps up.

CHARLIE. A friend of my Benny's! (*He puts his hand on Toodles' shoulder.*) That is good. Any friend of Benny is a friend of us all. (*And he pulls up a chair.*) Please . . .

Toodles and Charlie sit down on either side of Lolita. Joe leans over the back of Toodles' chair, his face and hers not a foot apart. Mrs. Chavez has been staring hard at Toodles.

MRS. CHAVEZ (*without enthusiasm*). Some place I have seen your face before?

JOE. Sure. Her picture was in the papers. (*He and Toodles exchange an intimate little smile.*)

LOLITA. Oh, yes, I remember now. She was Miss Santa Marta of 1941. (*With unpleasant emphasis*) The Vegetable Queen.

MRS. CHAVEZ. By golly, that's right! Sure—the Vegetable Queen! (*To the others, with pantomime*) Sure! Here she had a little skirt made from celery. Up here, a few parsnips. And on here an artichoke.

The Five Matrons nod, and sit back; then we see the GROUP closer as Joe, leaning complacently over the back of Toodles' chair, makes an intimate little picture. Lolita watches them—one almost feels her hackles rising.

CHARLIE. Miss Castro, when is the last time you have seen my Benny?

TOODLES. When he was in Santa Marta—after his trouble here.

JOE (*practically in her ear*). But, My Soul, you heard from him since he left?

TOODLES. Oh, sure. His last letter was from San Francisco, but that was quite a while ago.

LOLITA. Miss Castro, how long have you known Benny?

TOODLES (*laughing significantly*). Ah, to know that man for five minutes is to know him forever.

Charlie and Joe laugh. Lolita doesn't. She hands little Franklin to Mrs. Chavez.

CHARLIE (*chuckling*). Oh, that Benny —he's a lively one.

TOODLES. Are you telling *me*? He boarded at our house. (*She laughs again, aware of Lolita's reaction.*)

We see LOLITA in a semi-closeup as she sits bolt upright in her chair, skewering Toodles with a baleful, hostile stare. This cuts to the GROUP as still laughing, Toodles takes out a compact and starts working over her make-up. Lolita has spotted—and is staring at the ornate gold ring on TOODLES' finger.

LOLITA (*leaning forward*). That's a pretty ring you have. Can I look at it?

Toodles "fans" out her jungle-red tipped fingers. Lolita takes her hand, and examines the ring closely. She looks up at Toodles.

LOLITA (*sharply*). That was Benny's.

TOODLES. Sure. He—(*Then she abruptly snatches her hand away. Her eyes narrow.*) Say—how do you know it was Benny's?

LOLITA. Because I gave it to him.

TOODLES. It could have been one like it.

LOLITA. No. That was my father's wedding-ring.

TOODLES (*examining the ring with renewed interest*). Wedding-ring, huh ... (*A little chuckle*) Then maybe I ought to wear it on the other hand. (*She looks up at Joe.*) Or maybe leave it where it is—eh Joe?

She laughs and Joe joins in. Abruptly Toodles is aware of—CHARLIE, who is mad, and LOLITA, whose eyes are dangerous. Then we see the Group again; Toodles is confused, then angry.

TOODLES (*angrily, to Joe*). Say—what goes on here, anyway?

She gets up. So do Lolita and Charlie. Lolita starts to say something, but Charlie beats her to it. He wags a stubby, angry finger under Toodles' nose—

CHARLIE. Now, you look here, Miss 1941 with all your celery and parsnips, why don't you take your dirty businesses back to Santa Marta! (*He nods towards Lolita.*) This fine young woman here is the one that is promised to Benny and when he comes home he will marry her!

TOODLES (*contemptuously*). Baloney! Don't kid yourself! (*Right at Lolita*) When Benny's ready to come home, *I'll* be the one to know about it.

As she says this, she takes off her sports coat: She is wearing the dress Joe bought for Lolita.

TOODLES (*handing Joe her coat*). Joe, honey—let's go inside and dance.

And with an insolent little wiggle she turns with Joe and starts toward the pavilion.—We then see Lolita grabbing Joe, spinning him around. Toodles, surprised, also turns.

LOLITA (*blazing*). What is the idea— (*pointing at Toodles*) giving her *my* dress?

JOE (*staggered*). *Your* dress?

LOLITA. Sure! The one you bought for *me!*

TOODLES (*to Joe*). What's she talking about? Come on, let's go and dance.

LOLITA (*to Joe*). Tell her she's got on my dress—that's what I'm talking about!

TOODLES (*getting mad, to Joe*). And you tell her I got on *my own dress*— the one you bought for *me!*

The two girls are eyeing each other like a couple of strange dogs—Joe is sweating.

JOE (*soothing Toodles*). But my soul, *please*, as a favor. (*Soothing Lolita*) Look, my life, you said you didn't want the dress.

LOLITA. Well—I've changed my mind. Make her take it off! (*Toodles laughs ominously. Joe is "dying."*)

JOE (*his voice high*). You mean— take it off—now?

LOLITA. Right now. And if you don't —*I will!* (*As Joe hesitates she moves ominously towards Toodles.*)

TOODLES (*to Lolita, contemptuously*). Ah, go clean a fish!

And with a violent shove she sends Lolita staggering back against the table, turns, and again starts towards the pavilion. But Lolita lunges after her, grabs the dress from behind and rips it half off her body.

What happens now happens fast: Toodles, boiling now, rushes Lolita back against the table, grabs up a beer bottle, and swings it savagely at Lolita's head. Lolita ducks, Toodles makes another swing at her, but Joe, stepping in, wrenches the bottle from her hand, turns and tosses it over the veranda rail. Simultaneously, and with a berserk yelp of fury, Toodles snatches up a large earthen-ware pot of chili-and-beans, raises it high and inverts it neatly over Joe's head, jams it well down over his ears, then straight arms him clear over the rail of the veranda. —But even as Joe's heels vanish, Lolita pins a terrific haymaker on Toodles' jaw and knocks her spinning through one of the doors into the pavilion— glass, frame and all.

Six feet below the veranda rail, the pot wedged firmly over his head, Joe rises into a sitting position. The faces of Lolita, Charlie and the others, appear over the rail staring down. They get one look at the "potted" Joe and burst into a roar of laughter.

Joe tries to get the pot off, but fails. Panic seizes him. He gets up, lunges forward—smack into one of the veranda pillars. The impact shatters the jar, and bangs him down again into a sitting position—his head and face a solid, indistinguishable mass of chili and beans.—There is another roar of laughter from the veranda. But Lolita is running down the steps toward the hapless Joe.

We get a close view of Joe as Lolita runs into view. This chili-and-beans gargoyle is even too much for her, and she laughs outright. Joe scoops the mess out of his eyes, gives her a reproachful look, then starts to get up.

LOLITA (*laughing and holding out a handkerchief*). Oh, please, stay still, Let me wipe it off, Joe.

With an imperious gesture, Joe waves her away. Words come through a hole in the chili-and-bean mask.

JOE. Please, as a favor, no!

This causes another burst of laughter from the veranda. Joe gets slowly to his feet and then—with the laughter of his friends ringing in his ears, and gathering the rags of his dignity about him like a cloak, he stalks majestically away into the night . . .

The scene dissolves to the ROCKS and SEA BELOW the PAVILION. Under a full moon the breakers spout jets of silver over the rocks. We hear the lonely cries of the gulls and curlews. Lolita appears, in search of Joe. The breeze fans out her hair, whips her dress against the curves of her body. She rounds an enormous bastion of rock, almost stumbling over a pair of shoes and socks. They are a man's. She eyes them a moment, moves on, comes to a white shirt and a pair of pants. They have been washed out in salt water and spread on a rock. Lolita smiles, and looks around. There is no sign of Joe.

LOLITA (*shouting*). Joe! . . . JOE!

She starts convulsively as almost from beneath her feet she hears Joe's voice.

JOE'S VOICE (*unhappily*). Please go away.

A yard away she sees a ragged lip of rock. Six feet or so below it is a natural, rock-bound pool, filling and emptying with the tide.

LOLITA (*calling*). Come on up, Joe! I got things to say to you.

This cuts to the LIP of a ROCK: From where she stands Lolita cannot see Joe below.

JOE'S VOICE. No! All you want to do

is to laugh at me—like all the rest of them. Gimme my pants!

LOLITA (*dropping his pants over the edge*). They are still wet. You will catch your death of cold.

JOE' VOICE. That is of no importance . . . Gimme my shirt!

Lolita drops the shirt over. A moment later Joe's head and shoulders appear over the edge of the rock. His hair is wet and tousled. His face is so lugubrious, so wretched that Lolita laughs outright but instantly stifles it. Joe stares up reproachfully from the rock-ledge.

JOE. There you have it. Like all the rest of them you laugh. (*With a helpless gesture*) My dignity, my self-respect—all is lost. By golly I tell you it is more than a man can bear. By golly, I bet you my life, when I am an old man all the little kids will yell at me on the streets. "Old Joe Morales," they'll say "take off your hat, we want to see the beans!" (*Almost in tears*) What a future!

Trying to hold back her laughter, Lolita drops down on the rock, Joe's head level with her knees.

LOLITA. Who knows? Maybe the beans are lucky.

JOE. How can a horrible thing like that be lucky?

LOLITA. Look, Joe—when you bring that Miss Parsnips to the dance, and stood there with your arm around her—I was mad. And then when she poured the beans over you, I felt sad and silly like a woman in love . . . so I hit her.

JOE (*beaming—his voice high*). You —you did?

LOLITA. Sure.

JOE. Oh!

Abruptly she takes Joe's face between her hands, and turns it to the moonlight.

LOLITA. Look at me, Joe. (*Their eyes meet. She looks at him searchingly. Then, simply:*) Joe—do you love me?

Joe is so astonished that he almost falls backwards into the pool.

[JOE (*voice high in amazement*). Hey! You crazy or something? *This* is Joe Morales!

LOLITA (*nodding*). And I'm asking you—do you love me?

This makes Joe mad. He heaves himself up over the lip of the rock, yanks Lolita to her feet, and shoves her off at arm's length.—Then LOLITA and JOE are seen in a semi-closeup as Joe struggles to hold in his exasperation; he clenches his fists, tosses them heavenward.

JOE (*breathing hard*). Oh, what a question! What a thing to ask! (*Then, in a sort of repressed fury*) Lolita Sierra—in the name of all the Saints—what have you got for ears? ] Do I love you? (*Holding himself in*) Look—My Life, My Light, you think all this time I have been talking deaf and dumb? No! I have been telling it to you—shouting it—singing it— crying it! I am like an old, busted phonograph record saying—(*pivoting his head ludicrously back and forth*) I love you—I love you—I love . . . (*Grabbing her suddenly in his arms*) Ah, come here!

He folds her in his arms, holds her close, tilts back her head and kisses her long and hard on the lips.

JOE (*breathless*). There! Do you know *now*?

LOLITA (*her eyes like stars, breathless,*

*too*). Yes. (*She smiles up at him.*) Now, I think, even my grandmother who has been dead forty years knows.

As he kisses her again—her hair, her eyes, her ears . . . the scene cuts to the BEACH, and we see young CHITO on the run. Like a bird-dog he is tracking Joe's and Lolita's footprints in occasional patches of sand. He comes around a huge bastion of rock. Something he sees pops his eyes wide open and he whistles shrilly through his teeth!—We see LOLITA and JOE from Chito's angle as they are standing on

the flat rock, Joe's arm around her. They look back, see Chito, and Joe whistles in return—a whistle which says, "Come here!" Joe makes no effort to remove his arm from around Lolita, who is radiant. Chito comes in.

LOLITA (*putting her arm around her brother's shoulder*). Chito—how would you like it if Joe came to live with us?

CHITO (*without enthusiasm*). Okay . . . But he cannot sleep with me. (*And on this the scene fades out.*)

# PART FOUR

MR. FRANK ALVISO fades in. He is hammering a sign on Charlie Martin's picket-fence. It reads:

*HOUSE FOR RENT*
Do Not Disturb Tenant
*Phone Pantera 521*

A backward movement of the camera shows Charlie running down the garden path toward the sound of hammering. He comes through the sagging gate, and stares at the sign. Mr. Alviso ignores him.

CHARLIE. What does that sign say?

ALVISO (*driving in the last tack*). It says: "House for Rent."

CHARLIE (*angrily*). You are insane! How can the house be for rent when I am living in it?

ALVISO. But you won't be—tomorrow you will be o-u-t, spells out!

And with one swipe of a black grease-pencil he blocks out the "Do Not Disturb Tenant," and stalks majestically away toward his beautiful car. Charlie is suddenly and pitifully frightened. He scuttles up the path toward JOE's SHACK. [He grabs up a rock, hurls it against the clapboard siding. The crash

produces Joe, who is shaving, his face a mask of soap-lather.

CHARLIE (*frantically*). Hey, Joe! This time I got to have my money! I got to withdraw it!]

The scene dissolves to a view ("a panoramic shot") of the DIRT ROAD THROUGH SLOUGH-TOWN. In single file, Charlie and Chito trudge past the picket-fences and the shacks back of them. Charlie is leading a reluctant goat, Chito, another one. In addition, and by some miracle of adjustment, they have distributed about their persons and on a small push-cart the following items: two geese, six chickens, one rooster (its head protruding from Charlie's pocket), four ducks, two rabbits, a small pair of silver candlesticks, a large wooden clock, and Charlie's Sunday suit. From the livestock comes a subdued but incessant "farmyard obbligato."—And now they go past the house of Pamfilo Chavez, as Pamfilo, on his knees, is weeding his tomato patch. He sees Charlie and comes a-running.

PAMFILO (*shouting*). Hey—Charlie!

Charlie and the youngster stop under their load. Pamfilo leans over the fence. He is very agitated.

PAMFILO. Charlie, what's the matter? You are not moving away?

Charlie stiffens convulsively; the mere thought frightens him.

CHARLIE (*with great emotion*). Moving away from here—from all my friends that I love—from the place where I was born? (*Shaking his head emphatically*) No, Pamfilo—to leave here I think I would die. No, I am not going!

So relieved, so happy is Pamfilo that he laughs outright, and slaps Charlie affectionately on the back.

PAMFILO. Ah, now you are talking . . .

Charlie laughs with him, and without knowing quite why, Chito laughs, too. This starts off the ducks, the geese and the hens—for a moment there is quite a racket.

We next see CHARLIE and PAMFILO close together. Pamfilo is leaning over the fence to fondle the goat's ear.

PAMFILO. Then where do you take the little animals?

CHARLIE. To the bank . . . This is—uh—Chito?

CHITO. Collaterals.

CHARLIE (*importantly*). Collaterals.

PAMFILO. What is "collaterals?"

CHARLIE. Willie Zabala, who was once a janitor in a bank, and has had much experience, told me collaterals are properties you must leave with the bank to borrow money with. (*Indicating their burdens*) For example—such as these little animals.

PAMFILO. But Charlie—you told me you already had money in the bank drawing fine interest!

CHARLIE. Yes. But that was a private bank.

PAMFILO. Ah—you should know that private banks are no good!

CHARLIE (*sadly*). That I have just found out. That bank is busted.

This scene dissolves to the FARMERS and MERCHANTS BANK. The big clock over the entrance says 12:20. Folks are at lunch, the sidewalk is deserted. Hot, tired, dusty, Charlie and Chito cross diagonally across the street and come, with the "collaterals," to the bank entrance. Somewhat awed, Charlie hesitates, then leads the way in—the goats' hooves "tap-tapping" on the imitation marble steps.

This dissolves to the REAR of the TELLER'S WINDOW. The bank is empty, drowsily silent. Back of the ground-glass screen, facing the closed Teller's Window, EDDY KRINCH, the relief teller, is deeply absorbed in a sandwich, a thermos of coffee, and a "Funny" sheet. In an eye-shade and black sleeve-guards, he looks vaguely like Andy Gump. Hearing a diffident tap on the closed window, Eddy opens it, revealing the perspiring face of Charlie Martin. Chito and the "collaterals" are not visible. Charlie takes off his hat and ducks his head in a nervous little bow. Eddy swallows a hunk of sandwich, his

Adam's Apple jumping like a rabbit in a snake's belly.

EDDY. What is it?

CHARLIE. Please, with your permission, I would like to borrow sixty dollars?

EDDY. Brother—you'll have to see the president.

CHARLIE (*dismayed*). To borrow sixty dollars do I have to ask Mister Roosevelt?

EDDY. Naw! Mister Mibbs. The President of the bank.

CHARLIE. Where is this Mister Mibbs?

EDDY. You'll have to wait, brother. Mister Mibbs has gone to lunch.

Eddy closes the window, goes back to his "Funnies" and his sandwich. There is a muffled squawk of a hen—instantly cut off. Eddy looks up—decides he didn't hear it, and continues reading as the scene dissolves to a LABEL BUTTON—the size of a saucer and labelled:

ZACK (Mibbs)
BANKER

The legend "Pantera Pepsters Club of California" encircles it. A man's voice is orating as the camera zooms swiftly back to show the lapel-button on the breast of a lantern-jawed dyspeptic— the President of the Club, of the Bank, and of the Chamber of Commerce. MR. MIBBS is on his feet, punctuating a pep-talk with whacks of his gavel.

The camera movement has also disclosed the gaudy decor of the El Pantera Hotel Blossom Room, the town's "classiest" hostelry. From the debris of their weekly luncheon a score or so of local Pepsters (all fastened to saucer-like lapel-buttons) are listening attentively to Mr. Mibbs.

MIBBS. Every once in a while, it seems, some folks have got to be reminded that we're in a war! (*With a whack of the gavel*) A Total War! A war we've got to win—or else! (*Whack!*) So, men—let's put our shoulders to the wheel! Let's strain every sinew, bend every effort—let's make every sacrifice to *slap the Jap and stun the Hun!* (*Whack!*)

There is tremendous applause, [the loudest coming from—EDGAR LOVEKIN, seen close at the head of the table. EDGAR, whose lapel button reads: EDGAR (Lovekin)—PUBLICITY, is an unctuous, pudgy little gent with an oily, gurgling chuckle. He is also a notable sucker-upper. He is applauding vigorously, his hands practically under Mibbs' nose.

EDGAR (*the apple-polisher*). Zowie! Did you get that one, fellas? Wow!

Mibbs eyes Edgar coldly, raises his hand for silence, and gets it.

MIBBS. A while back I said I had a beef coming. (*He points a finger at Edgar.*) Well, here it is! (*Scornfully*) Look at him, boys—our Publicity man—ain't he a lulu?

We see the LUNCHEON TABLE in a wider angle as Edgar's brother Pepsters "look at him" and murmur ominously.

EDGAR (*unhappily*). Aw now, fellas . . .

MIBBS. Why, I'll bet back in Washington they never even heard of this town—I bet they think Pantera's the name of a patent medicine! (*This is followed by another ominous murmur.*)

EDGAR (*sweating*). Aw come on now, Zack . . .

MIBBS (*turning on Edgar*). Listen, Useless—two years ago we hired you to put this town on the map! And you sure did—on the map of oblivion! (*He prods Edgar's "button."*) I ought to cram that button smack down your gizzard! You a *Pepster!* Why, you haven't got enough pep to lift the skin off a rice pudding!

There is vigorous applause. Edgar is scared stiff, and looks pitifully around, hoping for one friendly face, but sees none.

MIBBS (*pouring it on*). Either you're an *is-er* or an *ain't-er* and there's sure no place around here for any *ain't-ers!* And another thing—]

And at this moment the door flies open to frame the vast bulk of MR. SAM SMILEY, MAYOR OF PANTERA. Sam wears good clothes, has a square jaw and kindly eyes. He's an honest, forthright guy, and a good American. He is under some tremendous emotional stress. Mibbs and the others, astonished to see him, nevertheless greet him effusively.

A PEPSTER. Hyah, Mister Mayor!

MIBBS. Hello, Sam!

EDGAR. Come on in, Mister Mayor, and grab some eats!

There are ad lib greetings as, like a man who has been running (and he has), the Mayor fights for air. Fumbling in his pockets he lumbers towards the table, as Edgar, the publicity man, tries to make a place for him. The Mayor brushes him aside. He is still fumbling distractedly in his pockets.

MAYOR (*trembling with excitement*). Look, fellas, I—(*Fumbling in his pockets*) Darn it, where's that telegram . . . (*He finds it.*) Ah, here it is! What I want to know, fellas, and it's mighty, mighty important—anybody here ever heard of a guy named Benny Martin?

The Pepsters exchange glances, and shake their heads.

EDGAR. Benny Martin? . . . Can't say that I have. Not offhand.

MIBBS. Me either, Sam. Why?

MAYOR (*emotionally*). Because, fellas—because right now this Benny Martin, this kid from our own home town, is *America's Number One Hero.*

There is a momentary silence as this news sinks in. There follow flashes of the Pepsters, mouths agape, cigars poised, stricken dumb by this bombshell; Edgar's chin is hanging on his vest. This, then, cuts to a close view at the table.

MIBBS (*incredulously*). Aw, come on, Sam—come on now . . . A *Pantera* boy?

EDGAR (*tremulously*). You mean a—a local boy?

MAYOR. That's what it says here. (*Indicating the wire*) Right here that's what it says. It's from the Associated Press and they ought to know. It says President Roosevelt's just awarded this Martin kid the Congressional Medal of Honor. (*Impressively*) And, boys, that isn't just *a* medal—that's *the* medal . . . I guess it's just about the biggest thing an American fighting man can get. So what we got to do is find Benny's family and—

But Edgar doesn't let him finish. He grabs the Mayor's hand, and pumps it ecstatically.

EDGAR (*with an oily chuckle*). Oh boy, oh boy, oh boy! (*Flopping the Mayor's hand up and down like a dead fish*) That's the break I been waiting for! All I been waiting for is a break like this! I—

But the Pepsters surrounding the Mayor sweep Edgar aside, and we see the GROUP very closely as Mibbs gets hold of the Mayor by the arm.

MIBBS. What's this Benny done?

A PEPSTER. Yeah—what did he get the medal for?

Edgar pushes back into the scene. He pulls at the Mayor by his coat lapels.

EDGAR. Yeah, give us the dope!

MAYOR. For killin' Japs! He was in the Philippines and this—this Benny, single-handed, killed pretty near a hundred Japs! Mowed 'em down! (*He mops his brow.*) Can you beat it? A fellow from our own home town—born right here in Pantera.

Edgar bubbles like an Alka-Seltzer, slapping the Mayor on the back.

EDGAR. You get it, Mister Mayor? (*He slaps Mibbs on the back.*) You get it, Mr. Mibbs? A local boy!! That's the angle . . . Gosh a'mighty, what a tie-up! (*With wide gestures*) Can't you see it? Pantera! The Home of America's Number One Hero! I'll plaster it all over the country— papers, radios, news-reels! Boy, oh boy, what a break! (*He grabs the Mayor again.*) Say, Mister Mayor— when's this hero coming home?

The Mayor hesitates, and clears his throat.

MAYOR (*quietly*). Benny Martin isn't coming home. He—he died of wounds. The Medal of Honor is to be awarded posthumously to his family. (*He pauses. You can hear a pin drop in the silence.*) Now what we've got to do is to find his family . . . The President will be sending somebody to give them the medal.

MIBBS. Then we better start looking.

As they all make a bee line to the door the scene dissolves to a moving view of the FARMERS & MERCHANTS BANK. The lobby splits the main floor lengthwise. One section is devoted to banking, the other given over to the Chamber of Commerce. This is separated from the bank proper by a low mahogany rail, and half of it is partitioned off into a Chamber of Commerce Committee Room.—Mibbs, trailed by half a dozen Pepsters and with Edgar dog-trotting beside him, crashes violently into the bank. (The Mayor is not with them.) They head straight for the C of C Committee Room.

VOICES (*overlapping—urgent*). Not in the telephone book—huh? Nope! Anybody checking the tax records? Sure—George's down to the Court House now!

They are moving past Charlie who, with Chito, knee-deep in the "collaterals," is still waiting on the bench.

MIBBS. What's worryin' me—supposin' this family's left town!

EDGAR. Naw, Mr. Mibbs—hasn't been a family left town in two years.

MIBBS (*savagely*). Yeah—nor a family moved in in twenty.

As they sweep by, the view stays on CHARLIE. He has reacted to the word "Mibbs." He jumps up.

CHARLIE (*to Chito, triumphantly*). Mister Mibbs . . .

And he scuttles across the lobby to where the Pepsters are crowding through the door into the Committee Room. He plucks Mibbs by the sleeve.

CHARLIE (*beaming diffidently*). Mister Mibbs, please?

The telephone jangles urgently within the room.

MIBBS (*impatiently*). Yes, yes, what is it?

CHARLIE. With your permission, I want to borrow sixty dollars from the bank.

MIBBS (*explosively*). Go away! Go away! Can't you see I'm busy!

CHARLIE (*as the door is slammed in his face*). But I have this collaterals.

We now see the COMMITTEE ROOM featuring a long conference table, two telephones, and the president's leather upholstered chair at the head. The walls are plastered with real estate development maps, "Buy War Bonds" slogans, etc. There are two doors—one into the lobby, one into the C of C section. As Mibbs comes from the door, Edgar, surrounded by his brother Pepsters, is at one of the two telephones. His eyes are rolling in his head like marbles.

EDGAR (*awed, into the phone*). Gosh a'mighty, Clem—you don't say! . . . You *don't* say . . . You don't *say.* . . . . . Okay, Clem! Bye-bye!

He hangs up, rises. He is trembling with excitement.

EDGAR. That was the Telegraph Office! Clem says he's goin' crazy! Says they're burnin' up the lines! Clem says—

MIBBS. All right—all right! But what? Who?

EDGAR. Newspapers—news agencies—from gosh darn near every town in the good old U.S.A.! Clem says—

MIBBS (*violently*). Yeah—but what do they want?

EDGAR. The dope on this Martin guy's next of kin.

The telephone jangles at the far end of the long table. Edgar races the whole length and grabs up the phone. The others follow him like sheep.

EDGAR (*speaking into the phone*). Yeah? . . . . . . Okay, George. Okay. (*He hangs up, then turns to Mibbs.*) That was George down to the Records Office! No soap—not a smell!

MIBBS (*bitterly*). That's a heck of a note! Suddenly we got a hero—and in a town the size of a gopher hole nobody's ever heard of him! (*To the Pepsters*) If anybody finds this out a fine bunch of rummies we're goin' to look.

A Pepster, LES PALMTAG, has been rumbling in Edgar's ear.

EDGAR (*excitedly*). Hey! Les here says there's some Martins over to Bakersville!

MIBBS (*leaping at Edgar, shaking him*). Bakersville!! Why, you poor cookie—if Bakersville claims this Martin boy, that's the finish! We might just as well pick up this blasted town and move it over there!

The telephone jangles at the far end of the table. Edgar makes a dash down the full length of it, the others following. Simultaneously with this there is a knock on the door.

MIBBS. Come in!!

The door opens a foot, and Charlie peeks in, beaming.

CHARLIE. Mister Mibbs, please, if you—

MIBBS. Get out!!

As Charlie closes the door hurriedly we see the BANK in a wider angle, and the camera in the entrance shows Chito with the "collaterals" in the foreground and Charlie moving unhappily toward them from the Committee Room door.

A sleek, fortyish dowager with two "tailored" poodles on a single leash comes into the scene and moves toward the Teller's Window. By this time there are quite a few people doing business.

We next see in quick succession—the TWO POODLES: they get one whiff of Charlie's goats and stiffen like coiled springs. They bare their teeth, rumble ominously as they see—the TWO GOATS: tethered to the wire over the chicken crate they stare at the dogs, their ears wobbling nervously.—Snarling hideously the poodles hurl themselves at the goats jerking the Dowager flat on her face, and breaking her grip on the leash. The goats plunge backwards and rip the wire off the chicken-crate, filling the air with feathers and squawking terrified hens.

Charging in to the rescue, Charlie trips over the box of geese, falls onto the crate of ducks, splits them wide open, and scatters ducks and geese across the lobby. Chito yells bloody murder. Like four bullets, the goats and the poodles have "whammed" out of the scene.

The two poodles—still yoked together and discarding the goats in favor of assorted chickens—cut a swath through the bank, the Dowager, Charlie, Chito in hot pursuit. Women scream; men shout; ducks, chickens and dogs add to the bedlam.

The COMMITTEE ROOM now becomes the scene of confusion. Mouths agape, Mibbs and his henchmen are frozen in their tracks. Squawking chickens power-dive over the partition—one of them crash-landing square in Mibbs' face. Spitting feathers, Mibbs dashes to the door and yanks it open. A goat charges between his legs, carries him

back six feet, spills him on the floor, circles the room, charges out—Pepsters scattering right and left. Mibbs makes another dive for the door . . . and as he comes out ducks, geese, goats flash by with the poodles, men and women in pursuit. Mibbs grabs the Bank Guard as he hurtles by. The din is appalling.

MIBBS (*shouting to be heard*). Hey—what *is* this?

GUARD (*gasping*). Collaterals . . . 's little guy—wants to borrow money.

And on that, a goose under each arm, Charlie comes in.

CHARLIE (*gasping, too*). Mister Mibbs, please I—

MIBBS (*screaming*). You!! (*To the Guard*) Get him out of here! Get him out! (*He turns to the Pepsters back of him.*) For Pete A'mighty's sake, will somebody do something—will somebody *try and find that family!*

Meanwhile the Guard, powerful and big-bellied, has grabbed Charlie. He starts to give him the bum's rush and the view moves with them through the chaos half across the lobby, Charlie losing the geese. Chito charges the Guard, wraps himself around his leg, and sinks his teeth in ferociously. With a scream of anguish, the Guard drops Charlie.—

In the BANK LOBBY, next, we see MR. KRINCH in hot pursuit of a goat. He grabs the goat by the horns and "bulldogs" it. Lying across it, he pries open the goat's mouth, pulls out a handful of ten-dollar bills, checks them hurriedly, reaches into the goat's mouth, pulls out one more "ten," and gets up triumphantly.

A DUCK seen at a low angle has now lit on a desk and overturned a bottle of ink. As it waddles out of the black messy pool,—we see a BOOKKEEPER, undisturbed by the uproar (he wears an ear-phone plugged into one ear); the little man broods myopically over an enormous bank ledger. Then, at eye-level, the duck, on inky feet, waddles across the virgin whiteness of the ledger. As the little man reacts to this the burglar alarm cuts loose outside the bank.

The burglar alarm is raising hell, the pedestrians are racing in from all directions. With screaming siren, a police car bangs to the curb. Three policemen with drawn guns, race for the entrance where they are met by chickens zooming right into their faces. These are followed violently by the "tossed out" Charlie, Chito and what's left of the "collaterals."

The uproar has subsided in the COMMITTEE ROOM. Breathless, disheveled, Mibbs, his henchmen and Edgar come in, and close the door.—We see the PRESIDENT'S CHAIR as a large white hen jumps out leaving an egg behind her.—EDGAR is seen grabbing the hen, and tossing it over the partition.—Mibbs is backing toward the chair; and is just about to sit down on the egg when the door bursts open and in comes George, one of the Pepsters. Mibbs straightens up.

GEORGE (breathing hard). Hey, this Martin kid—I just got a line on him.

MIBBS. Good work, George. Where? (He starts to sit on the egg.)

GEORGE. At the Police Station! They got his record!

MIBBS (straightening up convulsively). Police Station!

GEORGE. Sure! He's the guy they ran out of town!

MIBBS (this is the last straw; wailing). That's fine. That's great. (He sits down on the egg.) We get a hero and he turns out to be a guy we ran out of town! We get a million dollar break and—

Abruptly he breaks off, and stiffens in his chair. His eyes open wide then, and a most extraordinary expression comes over his face as the scene dissolves out . . .

CHARLIE MARTIN'S HOUSE dissolves in. With broom, mop and bucket, LOLITA has been giving Charlie's place its bi-weekly spit-and-polish. Right now she is dusting. Joe comes in through the open door. The knuckles of his right hand are tied up in a clean handkerchief.

LOLITA. Hello, Joe!

JOE (putting a gardenia in her hair). With the salutations of the rich millionaire, Don Jose Maria de la Vega Morales!

LOLITA (laughing). Rich millionaire?

JOE. Lookee, kiddo—I am so rich I am sick to my stomach. Where's Charlie? I want to give him back his sixty dollars. (He spreads six ten-dollar bills on the table.)

LOLITA. I don't know. I am just returned from working at Mrs. Kelly's (Eyes wide) Joe, you didn't . . . ? (She makes the paisano gesture of stealing.)

JOE. No. You remember Pantera Jack—the one I bought that boat from? (She nods.) Well, I sold it back to him.

LOLITA (aghast). But the boat is at the bottom of Santa Cruz Bay!

JOE (calmly). Sure. I know it.

LOLITA. But does Pantera Jack?

JOE. Sure. He felt so bad about it— (*He blows on his bandaged knuckles.*) He is now in the hospital a little.

Lolita very gently takes Joe's bandaged hand and examines it.

LOLITA (*reproachfully*). Oh, your poor hand! You've broken it. Now you cannot use it.

JOE (*laughing*). You bet your life I can.

And he grabs her around the waist, swings her off her feet, plunks her down on the table-edge, puts one hand behind her head and kisses her on the mouth. She caresses his face, his hair— looks into his eyes in an ecstasy of adoration.

LOLITA (*low-voiced*). Joe—you got to believe me when I tell you something . . .

JOE (*smiling down at her*). Sure. What is it?

LOLITA (*with deep emotion*). That for me you are the only one—because like this there has never been anybody else.

JOE. Not even Benny?

LOLITA. Not even Benny.

And pulling his head down, she kisses him. For a moment he holds her possessively, then releases her. Then Joe steps to the sideboard, picks up Lolita's hat, and "plops" it all askew on her head.

JOE. Okay, kiddo—let's go.

LOLITA (*startled*). Go where?

JOE. To the City Hall. With three dollars we can buy a piece of paper that says we can get married.

LOLITA (*skeptically*). Have you got the three dollars?

JOE. Sure . . . I tell you I got lots of money. (*Very pleased with himself*) Today I got a good job with Mister Tomas Zonzales—the big constructor.

LOLITA (*frowning as she taps her forehead*). For more schemes?

JOE. No. (*With a broad grin as he clenches his hands*) Working with these . . .

LOLITA. Oh, Joe . . .

She runs to him and hugs him ecstatically. She turns to a mirror, adjusts her hat, and turns as a thought strikes her. She is a bit worried.

LOLITA. We have got to tell Charlie about us.

JOE (*without enthusiasm*). Sure.

LOLITA. It will be bad news for him because he's always been crazy for me to marry Benny.

JOE. Oh, yeah. (*Brightening with an idea*) But maybe when we give him back the money he won't feel so bad about it, huh?

LOLITA (*dubiously*). I don't know . . .

Lolita picks up the sixty dollars, runs to the mantelpiece, stuffs it into a china ornament and follows Joe briskly towards the door.

LOLITA (*stopping dead*). By Golly— and *Benny!* (*Joe turns convulsively.*) I just thought—this is going to be a big surprise for him, too.

JOE (*grimly*). It will be a big surprise to everybody.

LOLITA. But mostly for Benny.

JOE. Ah, do not worry. When he comes home I will be very diplomatic.

"Benny," I will say—(*with a gesture toward Lolita*) "I want you to meet an old friend of yours—Mrs. Joe Morales."

At that moment they hear footsteps on the porch. They turn as Charlie comes in wretchedly. He is carrying the silver candlesticks, the clock, and his Sunday suit. He is a beaten man.

LOLITA (*spotting the "collaterals"*). Where have you been with those?

CHARLIE. To a failure. (*He sets down the "collaterals."*) Tomorrow night I will not even have a roof to put my head under. (*He sighs wearily.*) Oh, I wish Benny was here.

He starts convulsively as the crescendo scream of police sirens shatter the stillness of the afternoon. Our three, exchanging glances of alarm, dash to the open door.

JOE. Look, Charlie, don't worry—

From their point of view we see the SLOUGH TOWN ROAD as, piloted by two motorcycle cops with their sirens wide open, a funereal procession of big, black, shining cars is heading at fifty miles an hour toward Charlie's house. Alarmed by this intrusion, paisanos are running out onto their porches, down to their picket fences. The procession stops outside Charlie's gate. This cuts to LOLITA, CHARLIE and JOE, seen speechless with amazement, staring, and then to CHARLIE'S GARDEN GATE.

Headed by the two motorcycle cops, and a tubby little gent in the uniform of Chief of Police (Don Paxton), Mayor Smiley, Mibbs and Edgar are coming through the gate. Other cars disgorge "Pepsters," a couple of local newshawks and a cameraman. Neighbors are closing in from all angles.

The scene cuts back to LOLITA, CHARLIE and JOE.

CHARLIE (*in a frightened whisper*). Police.

JOE. Yes. With the Chief.

LOLITA. What troubles have you been making now?

CHARLIE. No, too many cops. It must be Benny!

The door closes on the sound of a key turning in the lock, and the GARDEN PATH comes into view, along with the Pantera cohort. In a solid phalanx they march swiftly and in silence toward Charlie's house. The scene moves back to pick up Edgar as the cameraman, jerking open his Graflex, catches up with him.

CAMERAMAN (*sotto voce*). Criminy, what a dump.

EDGAR (*bitterly*). Yeah—and he had to go an' be born here.

We see CHARLIE'S FRONT PORCH as the two cops and the Police Chief spring up the steps; Mayor Smiley, Mibbs, Edgar and the cameraman crowding after them. The Chief knocks diffidently on the door. There is no reply. Instead, the window-blind is jerked down from within.

Inside the LIVING ROOM CHARLIE steps back from the window and joins Lolita and Joe in the center of the now darkened room. As they stare at the door the knock is repeated—gentle, persistent. Nobody moves. The back door opens cautiously and admits Pamfilo, Raphael, their wives, and Chito.

PAMFILO (*low-voiced*). In big troubles, Charlie, a man has need of his friends.

There is another knock on the door.

Feet shuffle on the porch, voices murmur. The door-handle turns and rattles.

CHARLIE (*staring at the door*). Those are not angry men—with Benny they always kicked down the door a little.

The PORCH, seen closely, is jammed now. The Mayor leans toward the door.

MAYOR. Mr. Martin! This is Mayor Smiley . . . I want to talk to you!

The key turns, the door opens a crack and frames Charlie's frightened face.

MAYOR (*just as the door opens*). It's about your son—

CHARLIE (*convulsively*). Benny didn't do it!!

He tries to slam the door, but a cop gets his foot in it.—As Charlie tries to close the door, Lolita intervenes.

LOLITA. It's no use, Charlie . . .

She throws the door open, revealing the jam-packed porch and the crowd of paisano neighbors in the garden.

LOLITA (*right at the Mayor*). Well, what is it? What do you want? (*At this, the Mayor takes off his hat. His smile inspires confidence.*)

MAYOR (*indicating Charlie*). If that's Mister Martin, we'd like a few words with him.

With a jerk of her head, Lolita gets over a curt "Come in!"—Lolita snaps up the blind. The Mayor, the Chief of Police, Mibbs, Edgar and the cameraman enter. A mad scramble of "Pepsters" jams the doorway—a few manage to get in.

MAYOR (*angrily, to the cops*). Hey! Boys! Keep 'em out of here! Close that door!

The cops brush them out of the door, exit, closing it.

CAMERAMAN. We've gotta have some pictures.

This cuts to a close view of CHARLIE, LOLITA and JOE, with Charlie's friends in the background. The Mayor comes in.

MAYOR. Mr. Martin? (*Overwhelmed, Charlie nods.*) I'm Mayor Smiley. Speaking for all of us I'd say it was a great privilege to know you. (*He extends his hand.*)

Charlie goggles, but at a nudge from Lolita he wipes his hand on his pantsleg, and takes the Mayor's.

MAYOR (*clasping Charlie's hand*). We've just heard about your son, Mr. Martin, and we're here to tell you that the citizens of this community are mighty proud of him.

Charlie rolls his eyes helplessly to Joe and Lolita, but they can't get it, either. Mibbs and Edgar enter, but Charlie is too dazed to recognize them.

CHARLIE. Proud of my Benny? . . . But please, what has he done?

The MAYOR and MIBBS are seen in a semi-closeup as, stunned by Charlie's unawareness of Benny's heroism and death, they look at each other uncomfortably.

MIBBS (*aghast*). You mean you haven't heard? You don't know?

Charlie shakes his head, and looks appealingly from Mibbs to the Mayor.

MAYOR. You haven't heard from the *War Department*?

CHARLIE. Please, Mister Mayor, I am a humble man.—What for the—the War Department want to talk to me?

MIBBS (*explosively*). But, Mr. Martin —your son's a hero!

EDGAR (*bursting it out*). I'll say he is!

Killed more'n a hundred Japs! All by himself!

LOLITA (*in amazement*). Benny a soldier?

EDGAR. He sure wasn't picking spinach!

CHIEF OF POLICE. Yes, Benny was a soldier.

CHARLIE (*proud as hell*). By—by golly, I bet he is a good one—huh, Joe?

MAYOR. They don't come any better than Benny, Mr. Martin . . . (*Quietly*) The President has awarded him the Nation's highest tribute to her fighting men, the—(*after a split second pause*) the Congressional Medal of Honor.

The Mayor's words hang in a deep silence. Outside, we hear the shuffle of feet, the murmur of voices as we see flashes of: CHARLIE . . proud of Benny, proud of his share in him—the old man's face melts into a beautiful smile. —LOLITA and JOE . . they look at each other quickly. Joe shakes his head and the shake says: "Well, I'll be a sonofabitch!"—CHARLIE'S PAISANO FRIENDS . . they beam with happiness for Charlie. Little murmurs of "Ah, that Benny! . . What a fellow! . . By golly, what a man!"—CHITO, bug-eyed.—And now the DOOR opens and more paisanos seep in.

CHARLIE (*rushing in to meet them*). Come in! All of you! (*Grabbing one of them*) Hey—what you think? My Benny is a hero! From the President of the United States of America he has got a big, gold medal! (*Gleefully*) By golly, I think we all got to have a drink on that!

And Charlie plunges through his friends to the stove, kicks open the oven

door, and whips out a gallon of wine. He holds up the bottle.

CHARLIE. Excuse please, Mister Mayor, I only got the red wine. (*He rushes back to the table.*) Lolita! Glasses please, for the Mayor and all his friends.

Lolita hurries to a shelf. The Mayor— even Mibbs—is shrinking uneasily from the blow that they must deal Charlie. They watch him wrench the cork out with his teeth—see him bursting with pride and ecstasy.

EDGAR. Mr. Martin, you got any pictures of Benny?

CHARLIE. Pictures? No. (*Thinking a minute, then*) Wait! (*Grabbing Edgar's arm*) Come here—come here.

He hustles Edgar toward the WALL. On it hangs an enlargement of a beautiful paisano girl in her middle twenties— Charlie's dead wife.

CHARLIE (*with pride and happiness*). See! That saint, my wife! There is my Benny for you! The eyes—the nose—the mouth . . . I tell you, Mister Mayor, that Benny has the looks to warm your heart! Even his laugh —I swear it is like hearing my Maria laughing out of Heaven!

The camera whisks him—pushing through his friends—back to the table where Lolita is setting up the glasses. He grabs up the wine-bottle and starts to fill the glasses. Words bubble out of him, tumble over each other. The Mayor is "dying."

CHARLIE. Ah, that Benny—what a one!

This cuts to a semi-closeup of CHARLIE and the MAYOR.

CHARLIE. Just to look at him is to feel

good all day! (*The scene moves as he leans toward Mibbs.*) And how that boy likes to eat—to drink a little good red wine! Hah!

We see the GROUP close, as Charlie takes Lolita's arm, and draws her up to the Mayor and the others.

CHARLIE. Oh, Mister Mayor—this is Lolita Sierra, the one Benny is going to marry. (*He pinches her cheek.*) By golly, Lolita, you better marry the soldier boy quick! With this medal now, all the girls in town is going to be after him.

The paisanos laugh. Not Lolita, though—the irony is like a fist in her face. Charlie turns to the Mayor, and puts his hand on his arm.

CHARLIE. Mister Mayor—when is my Benny going to bring this medal home?

PAISANO VOICES. Yes, 'yes, Mister Mayor, when?

We see the GROUP very close now. The Mayor's face is whiter than his collar. He looks appealingly at Mibbs, but gets no help at all.

MAYOR (*emotionally*). Mr. Martin—Charlie, I . . well, we all sort of figured that you'd have heard about it, but in this case the medal was—was awarded posthumously.

Lolita is stunned. Charlie—even though he senses something is dreadfully wrong—doesn't get it.

CHARLIE (*with a little smile*). Yes, all right. I don't care how he got it—but when is my Benny coming home?

This is all the Mayor can take; he looks helplessly at Lolita. Then we see her with CHARLIE in a semi-closeup, as with infinite tenderness she turns Charlie toward her.

LOLITA. Charlie—Benny isn't coming home . . Benny is dead.

Tears glaze her eyes and spill down her cheeks. Slowly, like ice congealing on a pond, Charlie's face goes dead, his shoulders droop, his fingers pick aimlessly at a button on his shirt. It is so quiet in the room that one hears the clucking of the hens in the yard outside.

And now we get a series of flashes: JOE . . his face is blank, wooden.—The PAISANOS . . they are rigid, bleak. Their grief, turning inwards, leaves their faces almost hard.—Quietly, like men filing out of church, the Mayor and his henchmen go out, closing the door behind them. Charlie hasn't moved, he is staring vaguely at the floor. Then he sighs, gropes among his "collaterals," rescues the silver candlestick, walks to his wife's picture, looks at it, and crosses heavily toward the Image of the Virgin of Guadalupe in the niche in the wall, his friends watching him bleakly.

We next see the NICHE in the WALL as Charlie comes in and sets the candle in front of the Virgin. Fumbling a little, he strikes a match, lights the candle, and stands there staring at the little flame with eyes that look beyond it to Benny.

Then the scene cuts to the PORCH, at the door, the late afternoon sun coming through the foliage. Joe comes out and leans against the pillar of the porch. He stares out, his face bleak and hard. A moment later Lolita comes out and stands beside him. Her eyes are dry now, tired. Joe says nothing, doesn't even look at her. Lolita, as the view draws closer, studies Joe's face briefly, senses that he is emotionally disturbed.

LOLITA (*low-voiced*). Joe—what's the matter?

JOE (*turning, looking at her*). I am scared.

LOLITA. Scared? What of?

JOE (*almost in a whisper*). Benny.

LOLITA. Benny?

JOE. Yes. Even from the grave he comes between us . . .

The view draws closer to LOLITA as children's voices drift in from the yards. "Benny is a hero! . . . Benny Martin is a hero!" As it begins to dawn on Lolita what Joe is driving at . . . the scene fades out.

# PART FIVE

The PANTERA TELEPHONE EXCHANGE fades in at night. Swamped with trunk calls, SIX GIRLS are going crazy at the switchboard. Over the clicking of the plugs comes the hysterical monotony of:

GIRLS' VOICES. Pantera! This is Pantera! [Line is busy! Will call you back! Line is busy! Will call you back! Gimme Chicago Operator 238! Operator 238! San Francisco—here's your party! All lines are busy! Will call you back!

The camera has been moving up on an over-manicured blonde with a "permanent" set in concrete. She wears a wedding ring.

BLONDE (*with hysterical repression*). Look. Mama, I told you before—I can't talk to you now . . . (*Blowing her top*) All right—put a hot water bottle on it! . . . Okay—then try an ice pack! (*Jerking out the plug, replugging*) Okay, New York, here's your party! Here's your party!

This dissolves to the COMMITTEE ROOM at night. The hysteria of the Telephone Exchange spills over into what has become the headquarters of L'Affaire Martin. FOUR STENOGRAPHERS are working furiously at their machines on the long conference table, now littered with files, telegrams, box lunches, milk bottles, potato chips and dill pickles, the debris of a dinner eaten on the job. Cigar-ed, shirt-sleeved "Pepsters,"

GEORGE among them, are helping to stem an avalanche of national curiosity. TWO TELEPHONE-MEN are installing extra telephones. ZACK MIBBS, shirt-sleeved, tousle-headed, his vest unbuttoned, is talking with hysterical calm into one PHONE, EDGAR into another. All through the scene phones jangle, typewriters clatter, people bang violently in and out of doors.

The camera zooms through this bedlam to the door into the bank lobby. Here, an American and two paisano helpers are fighting an enormous, brand-new desk through the door and into the Committee Room. One of the paisanos is RAFAEL, Charlie's pal. They are making a lot of noise.—Then the camera moves on and picks up MIBBS at the phone.

MIBBS (*into the phone*). No, Mibbs—"M" as in marbles—*Zack* Mibbs, President of the Chamber of Commerce! *Sure* we got pictures. They're being finished up right now . . . You bet you! We'll airmail 'em tonight! Sure—and of the girl, too!

The view moves quickly to EDGAR—coat off, vest unbuttoned, talking feverishly into the phone.

EDGAR. Sure—that's right—Lolita Sierra! You bet she's a good-looker! In town here she's making the front page—(*Very excited*) Sweetheart of America's Number One Hero! How d'you like that? Dynamite, huh? . . . Yeah—we're getting pictures of her run off right now. I'll airmail 'em tonight along with the others! Okay! G'bye. (*He hangs up as Mibbs hurries in.*) That was the Kansas City Globe! Boy, oh boy, this hero's sweetheart stuff sure is getting everybody steamed up!]

The view moves swiftly to GEORGE. Shirt-sleeved, chewing a cigar, he is talking into another phone.

GEORGE. Hold on—wait a minute! You better talk to Mr. Mibbs! (*Shouting off*) Hey, Zack—Zack!! (*A minute and Mibbs scurries in. George hands him the receiver.*) 'S Noo Orleens! (*Gleefully*) Oh boy, and are they burning up their britches!

At the PHONE, as Rafael is backing into the scene, lowering his end of the new desk into place:

MIBBS (*into the phone*). Yeah—yeah? You mean the "Marteens"! (*Laughing ironically*) Say—are you kidding? (*Laughing again*) Do I know the *Martins*? Why, the Martins are some of the best people we got.

Rafael, just back of him, practically does a double-take. Saucer-eyed, mouth open, he stands and listens.

MIBBS (*continuing*). Fine old California family. Spanish grants and all that kind of stuff. Why, only this noon Benny's father was doing business right here in my Bank—

The camera is moving up on the flabbergasted Rafael.

MIBBS' VOICE. —been doing business

here for years. Yeah—Charlie certainly is a fine old fellow. A good citizen and a pillar of the community . . .

[As Rafael absorbs this and other telephones jangle frantically, the scene cuts to the COMMITTEE ROOM. The camera is on the door as it bursts open to admit RED, the photographer. He is carrying a large stack of 8x10 stills. The camera precedes him through the room toward the conference table.

RED (*as he crosses to the table with the stills*). Well, fellas—here they are!

Mibbs, Edgar, George and other Pepsters, some of them with milk bottles and sandwiches, get up and follow him to the table. There are stenographers there and piles of cardboard folders for mailing pictures, on which the girls are pasting addressed labels. Red dumps the stills on the table.

RED. Here they are, girls!

He grabs up a milk bottle, punches in the top and takes a long drink. As he does so Mibbs and Edgar, munching a sandwich, grab up the stills and examine them—they are all head and shoulder portraits of Lolita. Other Pepsters have also picked up copies. Red picks up a copy, too—looks at his own handiwork admiringly.—And we get a closeup of the "STILL" in Red's hand. It is an extremely good portrait of Lolita, but her face is sad and wistful.

RED'S VOICE. Pretty good job I did, huh? Considering the rush.

Next the GROUP is seen looking at the pictures of Lolita. A telephone jangles off scene.

MIBBS. Where's the one of Charlie?

EDGAR. Yeah—and the one of Charlie's home?

RED. They'll be over as soon as they're dried off.

GIRL (*dashing into the scene*). Mr. Mibbs! The Mayor wants you on the phone! (*Mibbs and the girl go out hurriedly.*)

A PEPSTER (*admiring the picture of Lolita*). She certainly is an eyeful, all right.

GEORGE (*critically*). Kind of sad looking though.

EDGAR. Sure she is. With the guy she was going to marry dead—why shouldn't she be?]

The scene cuts to the ROOM, including the door, which bursts open. Two men charge in, separate, and spread an ENORMOUS BANNER between them, which reads:

YOU ARE NOW ENTERING
PANTERA!

Home of

BENNY MARTIN

AMERICA'S NUMBER 1 HERO!

MAN (*proudly*). How's this, fellas? Edgar rushes at the banner. He stabs at it angrily.

EDGAR. Aw, what's the matter with you guys? That "Pantera!" Blow it up! Blow it up! That Pantera's got to be a mile high!

Mibbs comes pushing past the men with the banner. He is bug-eyed with excitement.

MIBBS. Listen, the Mayor just phoned! He says the Governor just called from Sacramento! (*They crowd in.*) He says the Governor and some Army General are comin' here to Pantera—

EDGAR AND OTHERS (*explosively*). *The Governor?* Here? To Pantera? Aw,

quit your kidding! Oh boy! Oh boy!

Edgar bursts in and grabs Mibbs by the lapels of his coat, almost shaking him.

EDGAR. Oh boy, what a break, what a break! When are they coming, Zack? When are they coming?

MIBBS. Day after tomorrow! They're comin' to present the medal to Benny's family! Sam says they've been deputized to do it by the President of the United States!

The Pepsters "whoop" lustily. There is an ecstasy of handshaking and back-slapping. Mibbs calms them down.

MIBBS. And that's only the half of it —there's goin' to be soldiers, tanks, a military band—the whole business! Right here in little old Pantera! (*He laughs a little crazily.*) Just you wait 'til Bakersville hears about this!

Again the door bursts open and in dashes RED's assistant with a pile of 8x10 stills. He slaps them down on the table.

ASSISTANT. Here y'are, fellas!

Mibbs and the others crowd around. They examine the stills, and we next see one of them close, showing Charlie Martin's shack—its poverty, its decay. Charlie and Lolita are in the foreground —lonely and forlorn. A couple of goats lend them no dignity.

MIBBS' VOICE. That's a heck of a place to take the Governor!

Next we see the GROUP.

MIBBS (*staring at the photo*). That's awful! (*To the others*) The family of the greatest man we ever had living in a place like *that*. It's a disgrace to the community—makes us look like a bunch of heels!

EDGAR (*bitterly*). Yeah—in thirty thousand newspapers.

Consternation has enveloped the Pepsters.

MIBBS. Well, don't stand there with your mouths open! What're we goin' to do about it?

GEORGE (*feebly*). While the Governor's here we could let him stay in another house.

EDGAR (*snapping his fingers*). George—you got something there! (*To another Pepster*) Say, Rod—how about that house of yours? The one on San Ramon Street?

ROD (*staggered*). Yeah—but it ain't furnished.

MIBBS. Oh, George'll take care of that!

LES. Swell.

GEORGE (*voice high*). Me . . . *Furnish* it?

MIBBS. Sure. What the heck are you in the furniture business for?

GEORGE (*unhappily*). Yeah, but—I—

LES. Awww!

MIBBS (*snapping him off*). No buts! You get the place fixed up and get the old man into it, and get him in there quick!

EDGAR. And move the girl in with him! (*To Red, the photographer*) And, Red—soon as they're in you grab your camera and knock off some pictures of them and the new house.

RED. Right.

EDGAR dashes to the conference table where the girls are addressing the last few folders.

EDGAR. Hey—no use holding up the pictures of the girl! Get 'em off! We'll airmail the others tomorrow!

And now the scene dissolves to the HOUSE on SAN RAMON STREET. The camera is moving swiftly toward a house of California-Spanish design. The camera passes cars parked at the curb, then comes to rest on the entrance to the house. Here is Red, several out-of-town photographers and newshawks, local and otherwise; all under the supervision of the ubiquitous Edgar. On the sidelines is a motion picture newsreel camera; at the moment they are taking publicity stills of Charlie and Lolita. Charlie is done up in a brand-new, tight-fitting black suit, black nobby-toed shoes, and his crowning glory, a black derby hat. Lolita is wearing her simple "best." Sitting on a camera case and watching the proceedings with a disapproving eye is young Chito. Hanging over the fences of the adjoining houses are curious neighbors, all Americans.—Red, with his old-fashioned view-camera, is all set to squeeze the bulb on a solo of LOLITA—Charlie lingering dejectedly on the sidelines. Other cameramen, with Speed Graflexes and flash-bulbs, are taking candid pot-shots.

[RED. All right, Miss Sierra—hold it! (*He squeezes the bulb as Edgar "bumbles" up to Lolita.*)

EDGAR. You were swell, Lolita—now take it easy. I think we got about enough of you.

CHITO (*disgusted*). Fifty-three. I counted! (*Edgar gives him a dirty look.*)

As Lolita exits gratefully, Edgar hooks Charlie, self-conscious and poker-stiff, in front of the battery of lenses.

EDGAR. Hey, Red—now let's get one of Charlie alone!

As Red starts to change his film-carrier on his camera, the scene cuts to a close view of EDGAR and CHARLIE, including RED and his camera. Charlie is wilting wretchedly.

EDGAR (*unctuously*). Now, Charlie, let's make this a good one, huh? I want you to try and relax—sort of look nonchalant.

CHARLIE. What is that, please?

EDGAR. Well—instead of being all froze up, act like you owned the place. See what I mean? (*Charlie nods.*) Okay. Let's try it.

Edgar steps back beside the camera. Charlie "tries" it, and freezes stiff as a board.

EDGAR. No. No. No. (*Coming to him again*) I tell you what, look out over all that country—(*with a sweeping gesture*) as far as your eye can see. Now imagine your ancestors owned it.

CHARLIE (*simply*). They did.

EDGAR (*with a double take*). Huh? . . . Oh! . . . Well, give it to me then—(*Indicating Charlie's face*) Here. All right, we'll try it. Now look off.

Charlie "looks off," but he's still just a little paisano, bewildered and uncomfortable. Edgar shakes his head in despair.

We then see the GROUP from another angle as a newshawk comes in with a couple of "props"—a serape and an enormous Mexican sombrero, the sort bankers wear at the Santa Barbara Fiesta. It has a high crown and silly little pompons all around the brim.

NEWSHAWK. Hey, Edgar—maybe this'll do it.

EDGAR. Oh, swell. That's sure-fire!

Edgar drapes the serape over Charlie's shoulder, removes Charlie's derby, substituting the sombrero, which is a trifle too small. Charlie's eyes dwell longingly on the derby.

EDGAR (*stepping back admiringly*). There—that's got it!

Under the horror of the sombrero, Charlie's misery increases. As he looks around, his eye lights on—LOLITA and CHITO, who are sitting side by side on the wooden camera case. Chito shakes his head and the "shake" speaks volumes. Lolita gets up quickly, comes toward Charlie, and takes the sombrero off Charlie's head.

LOLITA (*to Edgar*). Please, as a favor —no.

EDGAR. What's the matter? That looks fine!

LOLITA. Maybe so to you. But if Charlie's friends saw him in that they would laugh.

CHARLIE. Laugh! They would throw rocks at me, big ones! (*He hands back the serape to Edgar and puts his derby back on.*) Please, no.

EDGAR (*shrugging, stepping away, nodding to Red*). Okay, Red! Shoot! (*Red squeezes the bulb and Charlie relaxes.*) All right, Charlie. That's all. And thanks a lot.

Charlie and Lolita start toward the house. Chito runs in and joins them.

EDGAR. Hey, Chito! C'mere a minute!

Chito comes back reluctantly. Charlie and Lolita go on into the house.

EDGAR (*as Chito comes in*). Stand here, will you? We'd like to get a picture. (*Turning*) Okay, Red.

CHITO. To get a picture of me will cost you ten cents.

Edgar reacts with a prop laugh, fumbles out a dime and hands it over to Chito.

EDGAR. All set, Red?

Red nods. Chito instantly freezes his face into a gloomy mask.

EDGAR. Hey! How about a nice smile?

CHITO. For a smile it is fifteen cents extra.

EDGAR. Fifteen cents?'

CHITO (*nodding*). But you will get plenty for your money.

With another prop laugh, Edgar fumbles out the money and hands it over.

EDGAR (*sarcastically*). Quite the little businessman, huh?

CHITO. You bet you my life—I buy War Stamps.

CHITO, in a closeup, is still gloomy and forbidding.

EDGAR'S VOICE. Okay—now let's have it!

Chito's face melts into a wonderful, dazzling smile.] The scene dissolves to the LIVING ROOM of the NEW HOUSE. It is filled with overstuffed furniture. Charlie, Lolita and Chito are sitting there. Lolita is sewing; the other two are doing nothing and bored to death with it. For a moment nothing is said, then Charlie heaves a long sigh.

LOLITA. Charlie, you are not going to be lonely up here, are you? In this beautiful, big house? (*At this, Charlie gets up and wanders toward the fireplace.*)

CHARLIE (*too cheerfully*). Oh, I guess not. I got so many rooms. Pretty soon, Lolita, for the little animals and the goats I gotta fix a place. (*A distant sound strikes his ear and he listens intently.*) Listen!

CHARLIE (*as they both listen*). Do you hear that?

Now we too hear the sound of automobiles, very old and noisy ones.

LOLITA. Automobiles.

CHARLIE. I know those automobiles! By golly, Lolita, it's our friends coming to visit us.

He starts for the door, remembers his coat, and runs back for it; then, putting it on follows Lolita and Chito out to the door.

We see the HALL as Charlie comes in and opens the door wide. Over Charlie's shoulder we see parked jalopies and a score or so of Charlie's friends coming toward the house. Jake is here, too, with four stooges carrying gallon jugs of wine; he also is carrying two. The women are carrying large baskets of food, bowls of beans and platters of pies.

PAMFILO (*sympathetically*). Charlie— we have come to cheer you up a little.

We hear murmurs of "Sure, Charlie! . . . To cheer you! . . . A man gets lonely."

CHARLIE (*his melancholy lifting*). It is so good. Please to go inside.

They surge toward the door. We get a glimpse of JOE striding determinedly toward the entrance from a car parked on the sideline. He is not dressed up, but wears his everyday clothes. Then we see the HALL with our attention focussed on Pamfilo and his wife, who are the first to go through the door, the others pouring in after them. Everybody is talking at once—

MRS. CHAVEZ (*holding out a bowl to Charlie*). To put in your fine electric icebox. I bet you my life you got one.

LOLITA. The kitchen is right through there.

CHARLIE (*as Mrs. Chavez walks toward the kitchen*). Over there, yes.

His friends are eyeing the place, awed, glad that it is Charlie's. They express their appreciation in the hope of taking Charlie's mind off his grief.

[VOICES OVER THE ABOVE. By golly, Charlie—what a place! What luxury! Such fine, expensive furniture! And look—a separate room to eat in! For them to give you a place like this, Charlie, you are a lucky man! Look—a big mirror! Ai! And that chair!

While the above remarks are made, Pamfilo puts his arm around Charlie and squeezes him.

PAMFILO (*with deep emotion*). Old Charlie! By golly, it is a good thing to be with you again.

PAMFILO'S WIFE. Ai! (*With great sympathy*) When a man is lonely he has need of his friends.]

CHARLIE. Everybody, please come in. Oh, Pamfilo, how are you? There's a beautiful piano—everything. Come here—look. (*As he walks out with Pamfilo*) Here—see what I got over here.

And at this moment, with a curt "Hello, Charlie!" Joe shoves through the crowd, past Charlie and right on into the living room.

The LIVING ROOM: Voices from the hall are heard. Lolita is in the act of setting a tray of glasses on the long table when Joe, driven by a terrific, sweating urgency, comes to her from the hall.

JOE (*low-voiced, tense*). Lolita, come out of this house. I have to talk to you. (*He takes her by the elbow.*)

LOLITA. But, Joe, I can't. Not now. All Charlie's friends are here.

JOE (*desperately*). Please—my life

. . . If I never ask you to do another thing—this one thing you got to do!

LOLITA. But Joe, I tell you—I *can't* leave now. Maybe a little later when—

She breaks off as JAKE comes in from the hall, fumbling a telegram out of his pocket. The hall is filling up behind him. The voices are louder now.

JAKE (*with a friendly grin*). Hyah, Joe. (*Joe nods impatiently.*) Lolita, this came for Charlie. (*He gives her the wire.*) Been layin' around my joint now for a couple of days. Thought I'd better give it to you.

Lolita opens the wire, and stares at it bleakly. She looks up at Jake. Her eyes are blank.

LOLITA. It's from the Army . . . telling about Benny. There's no use to give it to Charlie—he knows. (*She folds the wire carefully.*)

Jake puts a friendly, comforting hand on Lolita's shoulder.

JAKE. I know how you feel, kid . . . It sure is tough.

Charlie and his friends come into the scene. Noisily they plant baskets of food, gallon jugs of wine, great bowls of beans, platters of salads and pies on the table.

At the TABLE: RAFAEL—the last to arrive—comes plunging through the crowd toward Charlie, his ponderous wife a few feet behind lugging an enormous basket of food. Rafael has the superficial calm of a volcano three minutes before it erupts.

RAFAEL (*putting his hand on Charlie's shoulder—with great restraint*). Charlie! (*He turns to the others.*) Everybody!

The chatter subsides; they pause in

whatever they are doing and look at Rafael expectantly.

RAFAEL. I want everybody, as a favor, to tell me truthfully—(*A light pause, then*) Do I look like a man *who is an imbecile?*

CHARLIE (*with sincerity*). To me, Rafael, you look the same as always. (*The others murmur, and nod their complete agreement.*)

RAFAEL (*solemnly*). Then please do not ask me to tell you the things I have seen and heard with Mister Mibbs and his people. Please do not ask or you will say that my brains are scrambled like a dish of old eggs.

There are murmurs of "Come on, Rafael—tell us, please!" Rafael suddenly plops down into a chair.

RAFAEL (*with a little gesture*). No— as a favor.

CHARLIE (*urgently*). Please, Rafael— what are these things?

CHITO (*sitting on the arm of Rafael's chair*). Tell us quick. You're going to tell us anyway!

Looking past Rafael and Charlie in the foreground we see Lolita and Joe on the side. Some of the women sit down, some of the men, too, waiting for Rafael to unburden himself.

RAFAEL (*getting up*). What are they? (*He emits a crazy little laugh.*) First I must tell you . . for two days now, like Jonah in the belly of the whale, I have been enclosed in the Chamber of Commerce . . . Imagine to yourselves—(*flings his arms wide*) one room—and all these people so squeezed up together that they have to take turns to draw in their breath.

He pauses and beams on his audience. They nod and murmur among themselves.

RAFAEL. My dear, distinguished peoples, I am a man of the world and lots of things have I seen, but nothing—*nothing to the comparison of this!* (*Warming up*) There is much sweat and emotion! Typewriters making noises like a million woodpeckers! The telephones are ringing *t'ling —ka-lang!*

Abruptly Rafael becomes Mibbs, becomes Edgar, becomes George. He leaps clear across to the table and snatches up an imaginary telephone.

RAFAEL (*into the "phone"*). 'Ello, New York, 'ello!! Mister Zack Mibbs talking!! *T'ling—ka-lang!!* (*He leaps across to another "phone."*) 'ello, 'ello! . . . 'Ello, Sacramento! This is Mister Mibbs! 'Ello, Mister Governor of the State of California, pleased to meet you! *T'ling—ka-lang!!* (*He across to another "phone."*) 'Ello, Chicago! Sure! *T'ling—ka-lang!*

Rafael spins back and forth across the room. Sweat bursts out on his forehead. His tempo speeds up to a dizzy crescendo. The others are watching him, fascinated.

RAFAEL (*into the imaginary phones*). Mister Mibbs! Mister Martin! *T'ling —ka-lang!* Minneapolis! *T'ling—ka-lang!* Buffalo! 'Ello, 'ello! Mister Mibbs! Mister Martin! *T'ling—ka-lang!!*

RAFAEL is seen in a WIDER ANGLE, as he jumps to a "phone" near Lolita and Joe.

RAFAEL (*into the "phone"*). 'Ello, 'ello! This is Mister Lovekin! (*Very excited*) 'Ello, Mister General of all the Army of the United States!! Sure—with all your soldiers and your guns, with all your bullets and your tanks, we will be pleased to meet you! *Sure*—and with all your bands!!

And with a series of tuneful "instrumental noises," Rafael gives a brief but fantastic imitation of a Military Band in the throes of a "march number." He cuts it off short, then flops exhausted into a chair. Charlie's friends buzz their appreciation, nod their approval of Rafael's efforts. Rafael makes a feeble gesture toward Charlie.

RAFAEL. And all for you, Charlie . . .

Charlie, seated now, shakes his head dubiously.—Abruptly, Rafael pops up again, and goes to Lolita where she stands between Joe and Mrs. Chavez.

RAFAEL. And, by golly, for *you*, too, Lolita. (*He shakes her limp hand, then turns to the others.*) Joe—everybody—you all better shake hands with Lolita, because now she is the sweetheart of America's big hero. (*Joe and Lolita stare at him helplessly.*)

MRS. CHAVEZ. What do you mean—now? Lolita was always promised to Benny.

RAFAEL. Sure. But now Mister Lovekin has promised her to Benny in all .he newspapers in America.

We see JOE and LOLITA in a semi-closeup as they get the impact of this. With a curious gesture, Joe draws his hand downwards across his face.

CHARLIE's VOICE. That is good. That is as it should be.

The voices of Charlie's friends drift into the scene like the whispering of dry leaves: "Ai—that is how it should be! . . . Sure—that is good! That is right!" Joe moves slowly out of the scene, Lolita staring after him helplessly.—This cuts back to the GROUP.

RAFAEL (*going to Charlie*). Charlie, will you please to get up? (*As Charlie rises, he solemnly shakes his hand.*) *Chocala!* . . . I am honored to shake

hands with a fine old California family and a pillar of the community! (*As Charlie thinks he's gone nuts*) It is a great privilege to know a man with so many fine Spanish Grants!

CHARLIE. Who said I had?

RAFAEL. Mister Mibbs.

CHARLIE. What is Spanish Grants?

RAFAEL (*shaking his head*). That I do not know.

The scene moves a little, showing Jake, with a couple of young paisanos helping him, filling up a score or so of glasses from gallon jugs of wine.

JAKE (*with a friendly shout*). Hey, folks—come and get it!

There is a noisy and concerted rush of customers toward Jake, following which we get a close view of CHITO at the table while the voices of CHARLIE's FRIENDS are heard. Young Chito is seizing the opportunity to filch an enormous slab of cherry pie. Lolita enters, grabs his wrist, and forcibly rescues the pie.

LOLITA. Pig! Wait for your elders!

CHITO (*sotto voce*). That Joe is out back. Says he has got to see you. (*Significantly*) I think you better go.

As Lolita goes in the direction of the French windows, Chito calmly recovers the slab of pie, eyes it gloatingly, takes an enormous mouthful and commences to munch contentedly. Then we see the REAR of the HOUSE: a full moon is shining through the foliage of a pepper tree. Beyond that are the brown, rolling California hills. LOLITA comes running from the house, toward JOE. He grabs her in his arms, and crushes her to him.

LOLITA. Joe—Joe! You're hurting me! (*Then, gasping.*) What are you doing out here?

Joe's arms are still around her—tight. His urgency is almost a frenzy.

JOE (*words pouring out*). Look, I'm scared! I'm crazy like! All day I've walked—in the roads, in the fields, on the beach! But everywhere it is the same thing—the grass, the trees, the sea, even the rocks, they say to me, "Joe Morales, you're going to lose your woman!"

She is leaning away from him, his arms around her shoulders. His frenzy alarms her.

LOLITA. What is the matter with you, Joe?

JOE (*savagely*). *Callate!* (*He tightens his grip.*)

LOLITA. Joe! I tell you you are hurting me!

JOE. Then listen! (*His words come fast and low.*) We got to get away from here. Far away—where nobody knows us. Now—before it is too late.

Through a window in the background we see Charlie and his friends around the table, eating, drinking a little wine.

LOLITA. Joe—you don't know what you're doing! (*She points to the window.*) Look in there—at that old man! Do you want to break his heart?

JOE. What do you want to do? Break *ours?*

LOLITA. But, Joe, this will not last forever. It will be forgotten, and in a short time we will be together for always.

JOE (*desperately*). A little while— even tomorrow—will be too late. I feel it—(*banging his fist over his heart*) *here!* I tell you the world— the outside—is taking you away from

me! [Lolita—you better come now! Before it is too late!

She puts her hands on his arms, looks up at him, and smiles wistfully, reassuringly.

LOLITA. With me—for '*you* . . . a hundred years won't be too late. (*She kisses him gently.*) Now come back into the house. And, Joe—have patience and wait like I tell you . . (*She leaves him and starts toward the house.*) Come on.

Lolita is almost at the door when Joe overtakes her. He grabs her by the shoulders, and spins her around and into his arms. His words and his actions are like the blast of a hot, strong wind.

JOE. All right! But first, I'm going to wrap you up in Joe Morales! (*His arms crush her. He kisses her ears.*) That is so you will not hear the world! (*He kisses her eyes.*) Nor see the world! (*He kisses her on the mouth.*)And that is so you will not talk to the world!

He releases her, almost hurling her against the door. In a sort of a fury she throws her arms around his neck, and pulls his head down savagely.

LOLITA (*through her teeth*). And this is to shut your big, ugly mouth!

She kisses him hard on the lips, then turns and goes into the house through the French windows. And next, as Joe follows, we see the LIVING ROOM through the French windows. Charlie's guests are eating, talking, drinking a little wine. Lolita comes in from the garden, Joe back of her. She presses a white handkerchief to her lips as though they hurt. She lowers the handkerchief and glances at it.]

At this moment MRS. CATALINA bounces into view, waving her arms excitedly.

MRS. CATALINA (*shouting to be heard*). Everybody! Please! Everybody please to be quiet! (*The voices begin to fade.*) Listen! On the radio they are talking about Benny and Lolita!

Lolita and Joe, who are coming forward, stop dead in their tracks.—As the voices fade into a complete silence we see the big CAPEHART RADIO, with Lolita, Joe, Charlie and his friends standing in attitudes of frozen activity, staring at the Capehart. The VOICE of the announcer, lush and throaty, drips into the room like hot molasses.

THE VOICE. . . . and in that sun-drenched little town of Pantera, California, they said goodbye—Benny the soldier and Lolita the girl.

We see, in a moving view, the faces of Charlie's friends—absorbed, completely expressionless as they listen to—

THE VOICE. Lolita, pledging the for-ever-ness of her love, promising to wait for Benny, promising to marry him when he came home. (*The camera rests briefly on* CHARLIE; *his eyes are filled with sadness.*) But Benny Martin, Private First Class, United States Army, isn't coming home. He was killed in the Philippines, giving his life in the service of his country. [And today, the people of America are acclaiming him as one of their great heroes—mourning him as a gallant son. (*The camera comes to* LOLITA *and* JOE. *They are rigid, their faces bleak, expressionless.*) The memory of Benny and his heroic deeds will, I am sure, linger in our hearts.] But in the heart of Lolita—the girl who loved him—the memory of Benny will be enshrined forever!

Mrs. Chavez leans toward Lolita, and squeezes her hand gently.

MRS. CHAVEZ (*whispering emotion-ally*). Ah, poor little one—how we suffer for you.

Nobody has moved in the room. They are all staring at the Capehart.

THE VOICE. And now, with your permission, I shall pause for a few words from my sponsors, the makers of—

Somebody leans forward and snaps off the program. And at that moment, Edgar Lovekin, like a slightly soggy tennis-ball, bounces through the archway and into the room. Edgar is a bit "high"; not in any sense of the word drunk, he's just had a few quick ones.

EDGAR (*with a friendly yelp*). Hi, folks! Hi, everybody! (*He comes bouncing toward Charlie.*)

Everybody has turned. They watch him politely. He comes to Charlie, grasps his hand, and shakes it vigorously.

EDGAR (*pump-handling Charlie*). Charlie, old boy, old boy, old boy!

CHARLIE (*pleased*). Mister Lovekin, this is a great honor! (*To the others*) Everybody please to meet ·Mister Lovekin . . . Mister Lovekin, these are all my good friends! (*There are polite murmurs of acknowledgment.*)

EDGAR (*waving a hand*). Hyah, folks! Well, as you people say—(*In awful Spanish.*) Me alegro de conocer a Usted!

Edgar swoops down upon Lolita where she stands beside Joe. He grasps her hand, pump-handles it vigorously, and bubbles—

EDGAR. Well, well, well—if it isn't the lil' lady! How are you? I'm glad to see you. (*As Lolita murmurs a polite "I am very well, thank you"—To Charlie*) Just dropped in to check up on tomorrow's jamboree—you know, sorta get you all set! (*He laughs*)

CHARLIE (*coming in with a glass of wine*). Please . . . (*Handing it to Edgar*) How about a little one?

EDGAR (*raising the glass*). Lolita—Charlie—folks . . . as you people say: "*Salud y pesetas!*"

Charlie and the others murmur politely: "*Y tiempo para gastar las! . . . Salud! . . . Your good health!*" They all drink —Edgar taking a terrific slug. He coughs and his eyes pop a little.

EDGAR (*blowing*). Wow! *Wow!* That stuff's sure got a hook in it! (*He taps Charlie on the chest.*) Now here's the schedule, Charlie—the big doings where they give you the medal is at the Ball Park . . eleven-thirty sharp. Means me bein' here with a car for you at ten-thirty. You'll be ready, won't you, Charlie? (*He sugar-coats the following with a little chuckle.*) You know—all shined, shaved, and slicked up. Lolita—you won't let him get away without a tie, will you?

At this—Edgar's audience freezes a little, and we see the GROUP looking toward the archway leading into the hall. Joe moves in to Edgar.

JOE (*quietly*). Don't worry, Mister Lovekin, tomorrow you will not have to be ashamed of Charlie.

LOLITA. No—or of his friends.

Edgar's few drinks have dulled his sensibilities. He pats Lolita on the shoulder.

EDGAR. 'Atta girl. (*To Charlie*) Then, after the ceremony—

MRS. CATALINA (*bustling in*). Good night, Charlie—I'm glad we came but we gotta go now. (*As they shake hands*) And thank you for such a fine chair.

CHARLIE. Ah, that is nothing . . .

And just then, Rafael, with an enormous over-stuffed armchair inverted over his head and shoulders and looking like a gigantic crab, comes into view. Edgar spots him, and reacts in astonishment.

RAFAEL (*muffled, from beneath the chair*). On this one I shall not have to put new legs every time my old woman sits down. (*To his wife*) Come on! This thing is heavy!

And Rafael, under the chair and with only his legs visible, starts toward the hall, his wife following.

EDGAR (*convulsively*). Good gosh a'mighty, Charlie—you can't give him *that!*

He makes a start to go after Rafael, but Joe grabs him by the elbow.

JOE. Why can't he?

LOLITA. Yes. Why not? It belongs to Charlie, doesn't it?

Edgar stares at them stupidly. He begins to sweat.

CHARLIE (*a bit puzzled now*). Sure it does. What is the matter with giving a friend one little chair when I have so many now?

EDGAR. Well, you see, Charlie.

JOE (*grabbing Edgar's arm and turning him around*). Sure. What is wrong with that?

Lolita has been watching Edgar—his reactions have aroused her suspicions. She comes close to him.

LOLITA. The house—all these things —they are Charlie's, *aren't they?*

Charlie's friends are all staring at Edgar, their faces beginning to lose all expression. Charlie is dumbfounded. Edgar hesitates, staring helplessly at Lolita and Joe.

JOE (*almost a threat*). Aren't they?

EDGAR (*with a sickly smile*). Well it's like I told Charlie—uh—we—uh—well—(*To Charlie*) The Reception Committee, we—(*Abruptly giving up under Joe's searching stare*) No. I—I guess not.

LOLITA (*quietly*). Then why did you bring. Charlie up here?

We see the GROUP fairly closely, as Edgar is getting more and more confused.

EDGAR (*almost double-talk*). Well—uh—take where you folks live . . . I mean pictures of it—plastered all over the country . . . it might look kinda funny, you know, the father of a hero—People might get the wrong impression . . .

Sweating and confused, Edgar is dying under the peculiar, wooden stares of his audience. Charlie's own dignity forces him to Edgar's rescue.

CHARLIE. Please! Please, Mister Lovekin—give it no importance . . (*With a laugh that is a little too loud*) Lolita—Joe—think a little. Where I ever encounter the money to pay the taxes for this place? Where would I? Mr. Lovekin, . . .

Charlie turns quickly to Edgar, and gives him a chance to get out.

CHARLIE. I know you are a busy man, Mister Lovekin, and we will understand if you got to leave. Please give Mister Mibbs my remembrance and tell him from our hearts we thank him for the honor he has done us and—for my son.

Edgar is vastly relieved. He takes a drink. He beams, and rushes headlong to his destruction. His voice is a little thick now.

EDGAR. Aw, that's nothing, Charlie—

that's nothing at all. It works both ways. Tomorrow—there's going to be five thousand outsiders in Pantera, every one of 'em good for three bucks. Add that up. It comes to a lot.

LOLITA (*quietly*). A lot of nickels for hamburgers and hot-dogs?

EDGAR (*as this goes right over his head*). Yeah, that's right, that's right. You said it!

We see the faces of Charlie and his friends—Lolita, Joe. Their faces are expressionless—their eyes unwinking.

EDGAR'S VOICE (*thick and loud*). But that's chicken-feed! This medal is going to do for Pantera just what the Quintuplets did for Canada!

We get a very close view of EDGAR and CHARLIE as Edgar lays his hand on Charlie's shoulder and Charlie stiffens under his hand.

EDGAR. No, sir,—you don't owe us a *thing*. You get the honor. We get the gravy.

There is a ghastly silence in the Group. Edgar drains his glass and sets it on the table.

CHARLIE (*quietly, almost sadly*). Mister Lovekin—Benny was a wild boy, but even *Benny* would not do a thing like this. (*He sighs, then goes on:*) Never he would use the bravery and a beautiful medal to sell a lot of hot dogs and real estate. (*Shaking his head*) No—even Benny would not do that!

Edgar, his eyes glazed, is staring stupidly. Charlie's voice fades into another silence. He sighs, and suddenly looks old and tired. He takes his wife's picture down from the wall, and picks up the clock from the mantel.

CHARLIE. Come, Lolita—everybody—we will go home now.

The tension snaps. There is movement, a scuffling of feet, a sighing murmur of voices, and a movement toward the hall. Edgar's jaw drops.

LOLITA. Come on, Chito.

As they move out, Edgar grabs Charlie by his co : lapels.

EDGAR (*frantic*). Charlie, you can't leave!

CHARLIE (*with great dignity, breaking Edgar's grip on his coat*). Please, as a favor . . .

EDGAR (*grabbing him again*). But there'll be five thousand people there!

JOE. Go away!

And with the palm of his hand against Edgar's chest, Joe sends him spinning as the scene fades out.

# PART SIX

A BANNER strung across Main Street at the entrance to Pantera fades in. It reads:

## YOU ARE NOW ENTERING PANTERA
### Home of
#### BENNY MARTIN
##### AMERICA'S NUMBER 1 HERO

(Lively orchestration is heard throughout the scene.) Superimposed over the banner we see an escort of motorcycle officers followed by three large black limousines, which zoom toward and past the camera.—A moment later, a staff car comes up with a Lieutenant General sitting beside the driver—his aides in the back seat. Following it are Jeeps, truck-loads of Troops, Tanks, Guns, and Army Mobile Equipment. As the staff car passes, we get a glimpse of GENERAL H. TAGGART, of the Western Division and a fine type of American General. As the rumble of a convoy blends with the orchestration . . . the scene dissolves to the CITY HALL. The General's staff car and limousines are at the curb; townspeople crowd around the cars. In the foreground we see a small group of impatient men, the General, and his aides, the Governor of the State, Mayor Smiley, and other local businessmen. They are looking at their watches, glancing down the street. Mayor Smiley is sweating a little.

GENERAL (*looking at his watch*). Well, what's holding us up?

GOVERNOR. We're waiting for Mr. Martin, General—the boy's father. (*To the Mayor*) What d'you suppose is delaying him?

MAYOR (*nervously*). I don't know, Governor. Couple of the boys went after him half hour ago.

This dissolves to CHARLIE'S PORCH.

[Sweating with anxiety, Mibbs is knocking loudly on the door.

MIBBS. Mister Martin . . *Charlie!* It's me—Zack Mibbs! At least let me talk to you!

No reply from within. Not a sound. Mibbs glances at his watch—at the drawn shades, and begins to get panicky. His eyes take in—a quick panoramic view of the HOUSES. There is not a soul in sight. Blinds are drawn. The place is like a graveyard. One face withdraws furtively from a window.] Mibbs stoops down, and tries to peer under a window-blind. Edgar, hot and dishevelled, comes running around the side of the house, up onto the porch. Mibbs straightens up. They talk in hissing whispers.

MIBBS. Raise anybody?

EDGAR. Uh-uh. But somebody's home. I heard 'em.

MIBBS. Hearin' 'em is no good. We got to get 'em out. (*Venomously*) Oh, brother—if you've jimmied this thing up I'm sure goin' to nail your ears on the Courthouse doors!

Mibbs knocks again—louder, more insistently. He calls through the door.

MIBBS. Mr. Martin! Won't you please come out! (*Rattling the door handle*) The car's all ready. We're all set to go!

Still no sound from within. And again Mibbs looks at his watch.

EDGAR (*whispering*). Lemme talk to him?

MIBBS. You keep out of it! You chicken-headed, blabber-mouth—shooting your face off last night is what's done this! (*He knocks frantically on the door.*) Charlie, won't you—won't you please open the door? Listen if your feelings've been hurt, why—

Quite suddenly the door opens, revealing Charlie in his dungarees, standing on the threshold. Back of him is Lolita. Their faces are cold, devoid of expression.

Mibbs rushes at Charlie, and tries to clasp his hand.

MIBBS (*gushing with relief*). That a boy, Charlie! I knew you'd—

CHARLIE (*quietly, politely*). As a favor —go away and leave us alone.

MIBBS (*aghast*). Oh, Charlie—you don't get it. You got to come with us. The Governor of the State himself—(*clutching Charlie's arm*) the General—the one who's going to give you the medal—

CHARLIE (*very gently disengaging Mibbs' grasping hand—softly*). Please go away.

[EDGAR (*appealing frantically to Lolita, voice high, sweating*). Miss Sierra—my goodness—talk to him— I tell you he's crazy! He doesn't know what he's doing! The whole town—people from all over're down at the ball park waiting for him—

LOLITA (*interrupting him*). Please, why don't you go.

MIBBS (*passionately*). Charlie, you can't do *this*! If you know what's good for you, you'll cut out all this nonsense and come with *us*!]

Brushing Charlie gently aside, Lolita steps out onto the porch. Her face is as hard as a rock—dangerous.

LOLITA (*with finality*). Charlie has had *enough* of people like you. He isn't going with you or anybody! He is staying here in his home where he belongs. Go—go away!

The hope drains out of Mibbs and Edgar as they see—

LOLITA in a semi-closeup. She is full of cold determination, as the scene dissolves to the exterior of the CITY HALL, where the Governor, the Mayor, Mibbs and Edgar are in a huddle, the Mayor and his two henchmen squirming wretchedly.

GOVERNOR (*testily*). What do you mean—*he won't come?*

MAYOR (*red to the ears*). Well—(*Glaring at Edgar*) It seems—

GENERAL (*entering briskly*). What's all the trouble?

GOVERNOR. Seems there's been a misunderstanding, General. The Mayor here tells me Mr. Martin has refused to show up.

GENERAL (*staring at Mibbs and Edgar*). Has, eh?

MIBBS (*eagerly*). I begged and pleaded with him. Even had a special car to take him to the ball park.

GENERAL. Ball park, my eye! Where does he live? (*There is an anguished silence from Smiley, Mibbs and Edgar.*) Well—(*sharply*) where does he live?

MAYOR (*wretchedly*). Slough Town . . .

GENERAL (*to the Governor*). All right . . . (*As he starts for his car*) We'll go to Slough Town.

Edgar's voice shoots up two octaves. He grabs the General's arm.

EDGAR. You can't go over there, General!

GENERAL (*looking him up and down, not liking him*). I can't, eh? (*Dangerously*) And why can't I?

EDGAR (*desperately, squirming under the General's piercing eye*). Well, it's just nothing but a lot of shacks.

GENERAL. A lot of mighty fine Americans have come out of shacks.

[GOVERNOR (*to Edgar, with disgust*). You wouldn't know—but there was a fellow named Abraham Lincoln—

(*To the General*) All right, General —let's go.

The General and the Governor leave the scene toward their cars. Mibbs and Edgar are about to follow when the Mayor grabs them and yanks them violently backwards.

MAYOR (*through his teeth*). Oh, no you don't! Where we're going there's decent people! What Charlie should have done is rode you outta town on a rail! (*As Mibbs starts to protest*) Go on—beat it!]

Leaving the shattered Edgar and Mibbs on the sidewalk, the Mayor goes toward the cars. As the rumble of starting cars and trucks comes into the scene, it dissolves to CHARLIE'S LIVING ROOM, where, utterly bewildered, Charlie is staring through the window. The crescendo roar of approaching trucks comes over the scene as Charlie turns and calls out excitedly.

CHARLIE. Lolita! Come here! (*As she enters, he points outside.*) Look!

She stares over his shoulder through the window. And we see from her point of view the ARMY CONVOY, headed by the Governor's black car, snaking down the hill toward Slough Town. And this cuts to another view of Charlie and Lolita watching at the window.

CHARLIE. Soldiers! Hundreds and hundreds.

LOLITA. Look, Charlie—the Army! (*Incredulously*) Charlie, they are coming to you!

This dissolves to SLOUGH TOWN. It has the appearance of a natural amphitheatre, the core of which is the group of paisano shacks. The porches, the balconies and the open spaces are crowded with spectators—paisanos and Pantera citizens. The troops and the convoy are on the dirt road. There is subdued musical underscoring.—(The camera is now moving swiftly down toward a medium close shot of Charlie and the General.) In the background we see the Governor, the Mayor and the General's aides. We also see Lolita, Joe and some of Charlie's immediate friends. There is also a suggestion of a body of troops in parade formation. It is solemn and impressive, but the beauty of it, the heart of it, lies in the simple dignity of Charlie Martin standing there in his dungarees, his face radiating a sort of inner ecstasy. THE GENERAL, in a crisp, clear voice, is reading the citation.

GENERAL. The President of the United States has directed me to present to you, Mr. Charles Martin of this city, in the name of the Congress of the United States, the Congressional Medal of Honor—

As the GENERAL proceeds, CHARLIE, in an odd sort of way, seems to grow in stature, to dominate the ceremony.

GENERAL (continuing).—awarded to your son, Private Benjamin Martin, for services rendered in battle above and beyond the call of duty.

Next, in a silence so deep that one can almost feel it, the GENERAL hangs the MEDAL around Charlie's neck. Charlie is full of pride, straight and erect. Lolita's eyes are fixed on Charlie—her expression inscrutable.—Finally, the General steps back from Charlie.

[GENERAL. Mr. Martin, I and the Officers of my Command, representing the Army of the United States, desire to convey to you not only our great sympathy for the loss of your son, but also our great admiration and esteem in the fact that you have been privileged to give to your country so worthy a son—a soldier whose memory we will presently salute.]

In a brief silence, a sigh like the rustle of leaves stirs in the crowd.

CHARLIE (his voice a little choked). Is it now, sir, that I can say something?

GENERAL. Yes, Mr. Martin.

Charlie steps forward a pace. He is deeply moved, a little uncertain. He looks around—and we get a swift panoramic view of the hills, the balconies, the porches, the front yards, the people, the soldiers. Not a sound. Not a movement.

We get a close view of CHARLIE as his voice gathers strength and authority . . .

CHARLIE. I—don't talk too good. When honor came to Benny and his family it was good. [But then there were people—(glancing at the Mayor, but without bitterness) who did not think that honor can live in a humble place like this . . .

The view has been drawing back, and now shows Lolita in the background, her expression unchanged.

CHARLIE (continuing). I didn't know about that. So they moved us to a new house—(looking toward his people) away from our friends—away from our people. That made me angry. (With a little smile) I even thought that I would not be here for the medal.

The view moves past Charlie to show Lolita, Joe and Charlie's friends.

CHARLIE. But all those things are of so little importance compared to this —(He looks down at the medal and touches it reverently.)] Benny came from that house—(*pointing to his home*) and Benny is a hero.

We get flashes of CHARLIE'S FRIENDS—JOE—LOLITA—the GENERAL—a couple of simple G.I. JOES—and Pantera citizens.

CHARLIE'S VOICE (*over the flash of citizens*). I know there can be heroes from other kinds of houses, too, because a man is only what he grows out of—his family, his friends and his home. (*Over a flash of the Mayor*) Maybe it was kind of people to want to change us, but Benny came from us and we will not change. Maybe that is a good thing for the whole country. (*Over a flash of G.I. Joes*) Maybe it is good for the country that she must depend for her life on all kinds of people—

We next get a close view of CHARLIE facing the General and the Adjutant.

CHARLIE. On men like my son—(*pausing as he searches the faces in the crowd*) and on such women as their mothers, their wives—

LOLITA is seen in a semi-closeup. Her self-control begins to break as CHARLIE'S VOICE comes over the scene.

CHARLIE'S VOICE.—and their sweethearts, like this girl here who, for her country, gave the man she loved. To do that, I think, is very brave.

Under the impact of this Lolita goes to pieces. Her eyes close briefly, open wide in a sort of horror, then suddenly tears come, filling her eyes, pouring down her cheeks.

CHARLIE'S VOICE (*continuing*). I know if she could speak, she would tell you Benny's not dead; he is alive in her heart—mine, too—for always.

Lolita's eyes are blinded with tears. A sob almost shakes her apart.

We see the GROUP in a wider angle, as in a deep silence, Charlie turns to the General.

CHARLIE (*simply*). Thank you, sir.

The General signals for Charlie to stand beside him. Charlie does so, and shakes hands with the General.

GENERAL (*crisply*). Have the Command pass in review.

We get a full view of SLOUGH TOWN, as we hear a shrill blast of a whistle—the hoarse shouts of command. The crowd of onlookers stiffen. Infantry columns snap to attention with a crash of heels and rifles. The engines of mobile units roar. The march past starts. The Military Band crashes into a "March."—A close view shows the GENERAL and CHARLIE—the General at attention, saluting as the colors pass him in the foreground, Charlie standing erect, his shoulders squared.—Then, in rapid succession, we see: LOLITA, her face wet with tears; RAFAEL, with his WIFE, Rafael bursting with pride for Charlie, tears splashing down Mrs. Catalina's plump face; and JOE, curiously abstracted. His mind, one feels, is a million miles away.

This is followed by flashes of:—the GOVERNOR and the MAYOR, their hats in their hands, deeply moved; CHITO—his eyes bulging, tears running down his cheeks; a full view of SLOUGH TOWN as the crashing strains of the band and the rhythm of marching infantry are heard.

This is followed by a moving view of CHARLIE and the GENERAL, with the heads, shoulders and bayonets of the marching infantry flashing past them. The General is at attention; Charlie is very erect beside him. As the military band swells over the scene, the view focusses on CHARLIE. Two great tears fill his eyes, spill over, and trickle down his cheeks as the scene fades out.

JOE'S SHACK fades in. Except for a moonlit window it is pitch dark. We see only the door, and at the rear the window. There is a light tap at the door, then it opens quietly and Lolita looks into the darkness of the room.

LOLITA (*in a tense whisper*). Joe!

JOE'S VOICE. Lolita!

Lolita crosses up to the window and pulls down the shade, then comes down to the couch on which Joe lies, fully dressed. His presence is indicated by the glow of his cigarette. She sits on the edge of the couch.

[LOLITA. Turn on the light.

JOE (*as he reaches up and pulls the cord of the light on the wall*). What are you doing here?

LOLITA. I have to talk to you.

JOE. What is there for us to say?]

LOLITA. Joe, what are we going to do?

JOE. Ah, don't worry.

LOLITA. [Half the night I haven't slept. I tell you, I think I am losing my mind. Over and over I keep hearing Charlie—what he said when they gave him the medal. You heard what he said, Joe—he married me to Benny's ghost.] But in front of all those people, those soldiers—he married me to a dead man.

[JOE (*snuffing out his cigarette*). Sure. I know.

LOLITA. If only I had done like you asked me—last night, when you wanted me to go away! I was wrong, Joe. Then we'd be far away now.

JOE (*slowly*). No, my Life, you were right.

LOLITA. Joe! What is the matter with you? Don't you love me? Don't you want me?

JOE (*pulling her down to him*). That is like asking me if I want to breathe—to live—to get up in the morning and see the sun. I love you more than anything in the world.

LOLITA. All right! Then like you said —take me away from here!

JOE. It would be no good.

LOLITA (*pulling away from his grasp*). Why not? Away from our friends—some place where people wouldn't know us.

Joe draws her back into his arms. His voice is tender, compassionate.

JOE. Don't you understand, my sweet, there is no such place? It isn't just our friends, it's everybody in America. Now they all know. Everywhere your picture, in every newspaper, in every magazine, all about you and Benny. And people would point at us. They would say, "She has forgotten already." And you would want to hide from the world. No, my love. They have given you to Benny. He has won you for a little while.]

He suddenly sits erect and holds her close.

JOE. But only a little while, by golly! Maybe the world gives you to him for a little bit, but I will be too much for him. I got a scheme—(*with the old familiar gesture, tapping his forehead*) the greatest scheme these brains have ever manufactured. (*He tilts her tear-wet face toward his.*)

This scene dissolves to a moving view of the AMERICAN LEGION BAND—at the railroad station. They are banging out "OVER THERE!" The view moves to the side of an old-fashioned day-coach.

There is crude lettering in chalk: "TOKYO OR BUST!"

The view moves swiftly along the open windows—recruits and draftees, still in civilian clothes, are hanging out, kidding, laughing, with mothers, wives, sweethearts.

The moving view picks up JOE on the vestibule steps. He is wearing a white shirt and clean dungarees. Lolita and Chito are at his elbow. Charlie and his friends are grouped a few feet away, Charlie prosperous-looking in a derby hat and well-fitting new clothes. An Army Sergeant is herding two more draftees with bundles past Joe and into the train.

LOLITA and CHITO are seen close as Joe leans down from the vestibule.

JOE (*sotto voce, to Lolita*). Look, my Life—I was always twice as good as that Benny. I will come back with two medals.

LOLITA. Sure you will.

At that moment Chito catches Joe's eye. Chito shakes his head and the shake says "The hell you will!" Joe's reaction of dismay is so ludicrous that it seems to touch Chito's heart, for the kid changes his mind and nods vigorously, and the nod says "You bet you my life!" As Joe beams, the scene cuts to the VESTIBULE, showing Charlie and his friends crowding in.

PAMFILO. Hey, Joe, you old coyote— why did you join the Army so quick?

RAFAEL. Yes—even before you were drafted?

CHARLIE and LOLITA are seen together.

CHARLIE. To get revenge for Benny and the other fellows—what do you think? Eh, Joe?

Lolita "gets this." She smiles wistfully at JOE, who "gets it," too and smiles tenderly at Lolita. Then we see Joe leaning down, putting his arm around Charlie's shoulder, and giving him a big hug.

JOE (*to Lolita*). Look, kiddo—all that money old Charlie will get from Benny's insurance—put it in a good bank for him. (*With a wide grin*) It is too bad that *my* bank is now busted.

There are shouts off scene of "All aboard! All aboard!" And the band swells crescendo.—We see the VESTIBULE in a wider angle as Mrs. Catalina, the women, Charlie and the others crowd in.

MRS. CATALINA. Go on, Lolita—(*Nodding at Joe*) Give the soldier a kiss. (*At this, Lolita is startled and frightened. She looks at Charlie.*)

CHARLIE (*grinning, shoving her forward*). Sure. Kiss him for good luck!

Joe leans down toward her. She hesitates—then kisses him—A closeup of JOE and LOLITA shows their lips are barely touching. But all their love seems to flow between them. Lolita's eyes close. So do Joe's, as shouts of "ALL ABROAD! ALL ABOARD!" come over the scene.—Then we see the GROUP, and as Lolita and Joe still hold the kiss, Charlie taps Lolita on the shoulder.

CHARLIE. Hey—too much luck is plenty!

Everybody laughs as Lolita steps back. The COACH begins to move out of sight. Hands wave, handkerchiefs flutter. There are shouts of "Goodbye, Joe! Good luck!"

JOE, in a closeup, neither waves nor moves. His face is serene and confident; he is staring at—LOLITA: Also seen in a closeup, she is smiling wistfully through a gleam of tears. She is staring at the TRAIN as it pulls away and out of the station. There is a final blast from the band.

LOLITA, CHARLIE and CHITO are seen in a very close view as they watch the receding train. Suddenly young Chito uncorks a shrill whistle through his teeth, and the scene cuts to the receding TRAIN as a faint answering whistle drifts back from the distant, white-shirted figure on the vestibule steps.

And finally, we see Lolita, Charlie and all our paisanos watching the train recede. The view moves up to LOLITA and CHITO, framing them in a closeup. Her lips tremble in a wistful smile, but her eyes are wet and shining. She neither moves nor waves as the scene fades out.